Lecture Notes of the Institute for Computer Sciences, Social Informatics and Telecommunications Engineering 131

Ivan Stojmenovic · Zixue Cheng
Song Guo (Eds.)

Mobile and Ubiquitous Systems: Computing, Networking, and Services

10th International Conference,
MOBIQUITOUS 2013
Tokyo, Japan, December 2–4, 2013
Revised Selected Papers

 Springer

Editors
Ivan Stojmenovic
University of Ottawa
Ottawa, ON
Canada

Zixue Cheng
Song Guo
School of Computer Science
   and Engineering
The University of Aizu Tsuruga
Fukushima
Japan

ISSN 1867-8211
ISBN 978-3-319-11568-9
DOI 10.1007/978-3-319-11569-6

ISSN 1867-822X (electronic)
ISBN 978-3-319-11569-6 (eBook)

Library of Congress Control Number: 2014949557

Springer Cham Heidelberg New York Dordrecht London

Printed on acid-free paper

Springer is part of Springer Science+Business Media (www.springer.com)

Preface

MobiQuitous 2013 has provided a successful forum for practitioners and researchers from diverse backgrounds to interact and exchange experiences about the design and implementation of mobile and ubiquitous systems.

We received 141 technical papers from all around the world. All submissions received high-quality reviews from Technical Program Committee (TPC) members or selected external reviewers. According to the review results, we have accepted 52 regular papers and 13 short papers for inclusion in the technical program of the main conference.

In the main technical program, we had two inspiring keynote speeches by Prof. Xuemin (Sherman) Shen from University of Waterloo, Canada and Prof. Nei Kato from Tohoku University, Japan, and 12 technical sessions, including 10 regular-paper sessions and two short-paper sessions. Besides the main conference, we also had a joint International Workshop on Emerging Wireless Technologies for Future Mobile Networks (WEWFMN 2013). The conference successfully inspired many innovative directions in the fields of mobile applications, social networks, networking, and data management and services, all with a special focus on mobile and ubiquitous computing.

It is our distinct honor to present the best paper, Focus and Shoot: Efficient Identification over RFID Tags in the Specified Area, and the best-student paper, Protecting Movement Trajectories Through Fragmentation, for MobiQuitous 2013. The two papers were voted out based on the reviewers' recommendations and on the papers' significance, originality, and potential impact.

The technical program is the result of the hard work of many individuals. We would like to thank all the authors for submitting their outstanding work to MobiQuitous 2013. We offer our sincere gratitude to the technical committee members and external reviewers, who worked hard to provide thorough, insightful, and constructive reviews in a timely manner. We are grateful to the Steering Committee and Organizing Committee of MobiQuitous 2013, and especially to the TPC Chairs, Prof. Guojun Wang from Central South University, China, Prof. Kun Yang from University of Essex, UK, Prof. Amiya Nayak from University of Ottawa, Canada, Prof. Francesco De Pellegrini from Create-Net, Italy, and Prof. Takahiro Hara from Osaka University, Japan for their invaluable support and insightful guidance. Finally, we are grateful to all the participants in MobiQuitous 2013.

Zixue Cheng
Ivan Stojmenovic
Song Guo

Organization

Steering Committee

Imrich Chlamtac	Create-Net, Italy
Fausto Giunchiglia	University of Trento, Italy
Tao Gu	University of Southern Denmark, Denmark
Tom La Porta	Pennsylvania State University, USA
Francesco De Pellegrini	Create-Net, Italy
Chiara Petrioli	Universita di Roma "La Sapienza", Italy
Krishna Sivalingam	University of Maryland at Baltimore, USA
Thanos Vasilakos	University of Western Macedonia, Greece

Organizing Committee

General Chairs

Zixue Cheng	University of Aizu, Japan
Ivan Stojmenovic	University of Ottawa, Canada

General Co-chair

Song Guo	University of Aizu, Japan

TPC Chairs

Guojun Wang	Central South University, China
Kun Yang	University of Essex, UK
Amiya Nayak	University of Ottawa, Canada
Francesco De Pellegrini	Create-Net, Italy
Takahiro Hara	Osaka University, Japan

Local Chair

Naohito Nakasato	University of Aizu, Japan

Workshop Chairs

Chonggang Wang   InterDigital Communications, USA
Baoliu Ye   Nanjing University, China
Shanzhi Chen   Datang Telecom Technology & Industry Group,
                              China

Publicity Chair

Shui Yu   Deakin University, Australia
Susumu Ishihara   Shizuoka University, Japan
Hirozumi Yamaguchi   Osaka University, Japan

Publication Chair

Lei Shu   Guangdong University of Petrochemical
                              Technology, China

Web Chair

Deze Zeng   University of Aizu, Japan

Conference Manager

Ruzanna Najaryan   EAI, Italy

Technical Program Committee

Jemal Abawajy   Deakin University, Australia
Muhammad Bashir Abdullahi   Federal University of Technology, Minna, Nigeria
Christian Becker   University of Mannheim, Germany
Roy Campbell   University of Illinois at Urbana-Champaign, USA
Jiannong Cao   Hong Kong Polytechnic University, Hong Kong
Iacopo Carreras   Create-Net, Italy
Liming Chen   University of Ulster, UK
Marcus Handte   University of Duisburg-Essen, Germany
Min Chen   Huazhong University of Science and Technology,
                                   China
Franco Chiaraluce   Polytechnical University of Marche, Italy
Michel Diaz   LAAS-CNRS, France
Pasquale Donadio   Alcatel-Lucent, Italy
Wan Du   Nanyang Technological University, Singapore
Andrzej Duda   Grenoble Institute of Technology, France

Kary Framling	Aalto University, Finland
Chris Gniady	University of Arizona, USA
Teofilo Gonzalez	University of California at Santa Barbara, USA
Sergei Gorlatch	University of Münster, Germany
Yu Gu	Singapore University of Technology and Design, Singapore
Deke Guo	National University of Defense Technology, China
Clemens Holzmann	University of Applied Sciences Upper Austria, Austria
Henry Holtzman	MIT Media Lab, USA
Susumu Ishihara	Shizuoka University, Japan
Yoshiharu Ishikawa	Nagoya University, Japan
Xiaolong Jin	Institute of Computing Technology, Chinese Academy of Sciences, China
Jussi Kangasharju	University of Helsinki, Finland
Stephan Karpischek	Swisscom (Switzerland) AG, Switzerland
Fahim Kawsar	Bell Labs, USA
Yutaka Kidawara	NICT, Japan
Matthias Kranz	Universität Passau, Germany
Mo Li	Nanyang Technological University, Singapore
Xu Li	Huawei Technologies, Canada
Zhenjiang Li	Nanyang Technological University, Singapore
Xiaodong Lin	University of Ontario Institute of Technology, Canada
Hai Liu	HongKong Baptist University, Hong Kong
Yunhuai Liu	TRIMPS, China
Tomas Sanchez Lopez	EADS Innovation Works, UK
Rongxing Lu	University of Waterloo, Canada
Xiaofeng Lu	Xidian University, China
Oscar Mayora	Create-Net, Italy
Iqbal Mohomed	IBM T.J. Watson Research Center, USA
Felix Musau	Kenyatta University, Kenya
Mirco Musolesi	University of Birmingham, UK
Sushmita Ruj	Indian Institute of Technology, India
Hedda R. Schmidtke	Carnegie Mellon University, USA
Joan Serrat	Universitat Politècnica de Catalunya, Spain
Zhenning Shi	Orange Labs Beijing, China
Hiroshi Shigeno	Keio University, Japan
Stephan Sigg	National Institute of Informatics, Japan
Philipp Sommer	CSIRO, Australia
Danny Soroker	IBM T.J. Watson Research Center, USA
Mineo Takai	UCLA, USA and Osaka University, Japan
Ning Wang	University of Surrey, UK
Song Wu	Huazhong University of Science and Technology, China
Xiaofei Xing	Guangzhou University, China

Ke Xu   Tsinghua University, China
Hirozumi Yamaguchi   Osaka University, Japan
Zhiwen Yu   Northwestern Polytechnical University, China
Haibo Zeng   McGill University, Canada
Jianming Zhang   Changsha University of Science & Technology,
                                 China
Yanmin Zhu   Shanghai Jiao Tong University, China
Ali Ismail   Awad Al Azhar University, Egypt

Contents

Short-Paper Session

Workshop

Main Conference Session

OPSitu: A Semantic-Web Based Situation Inference Tool Under Opportunistic Sensing Paradigm

Jiangtao Wang[1,2], Yasha Wang[1,3(✉)], and Yuanduo He[1,2]

[1] Key Laboratory of High Confidence Software Technologies,
Ministry of Education, Beijing 100871, China
wangys@sei.pku.edu.cn
[2] School of Electronics Engineering and Computer Science,
Peking University, Beijing, China
[3] National Engineering Research Center of Software Engineering,
Peking University, Beijing, China

Abstract. Opportunistic sensing becomes a competitive sensing paradigm nowadays. Instead of pre-deploying application-specific sensors, it makes use of sensors that just happen to be available to accomplish its sensing goal. In the opportunistic sensing paradigm, the sensors that can be utilized by a given application in a given time are unpredictable. This brings the Semantic-Web based situation inference approach, which is widely adopted in situation-aware applications, a major challenge, i.e., how to handle uncertainty of the availability and confidence of the sensing data. Although extending standard semantic-web languages may enable the situation inference to be compatible with the uncertainty, it also brings extra complexity to the languages and makes them hard to be learned. Unlike the existing works, this paper developed a situation inference tool, named *OPSitu*, which enables the situation inference rules to be written in the well accepted standard languages such as OWL and SWRL even under opportunistic sensing paradigm. An experiment is also described to demonstrate the validity of *OPSitu*.

Keywords: Semantic web · Situation inference · Opportunistic sensing

1 Introduction

In the research of situation-aware systems, situation inference is considered to be an important technique, which focuses on how to infer the situation of an entity (i.e. a person, a thing or a place) based on sensing data collected from the physical space or the cyberspace [1]. Among multiple approaches for situation inference, the Semantic-Web based approach is widely adopted [2–6]. In this approach, standard Semantic Web languages, such as OWL (Web Ontology Language) and SWRL (Semantic Web Rule Language), are used to model the related concepts and inference rules at design time. After obtaining the sensing data, situation inference process is conducted by a semantic inference engine

© Institute for Computer Sciences, Social Informatics and Telecommunications Engineering 2014
I. Stojmenovic et al. (Eds.): MOBIQUITOUS 2013, LNICST 131, pp. 3–16, 2014.
DOI: 10.1007/978-3-319-11569-6_1

at runtime. In these works, there is a common assumption that the sensing data are certain and complete during the inference process [1].

In recent years, with the technological advance and popularity of IOT (Internet of Things) and mobile computing, sensing infrastructures have been established in our daily surroundings. The massively existing sensing devices include static sensors spreading across buildings, streets, public parks and rivers, and mobilizable sensors carried by people and vehicles, such as built-in sensors in smartphones, tablets, wearable devices, vehicles borne radars, GPS, cameras, etc. Together with the sensors, wireless communication infrastructures, such as WSN, Wi-Fi and 3G/4G mobile network, are also available almost everywhere to deliver sensing data. With these abundant sensors and sensing data delivery infrastructures, a new sensing paradigm emerges, which is referred to as *Opportunistic Sensing* [7–11]. Instead of pre-deploying application-specific sensors, opportunistic sensing applications make use of sensors that just happen to be available to accomplish its sensing goal [11].

Due to the sensor sharing mechanism, the opportunistic sensing paradigm is less costly and more environmental friendly. However, it leads to new technical challenges to those applications that adopt the Semantic-Web based situation inference approach. Firstly, opportunistic sensing attempts to discover and utilize sensors available by chance. Therefore, when there are no sensors to acquire sensing data that is necessary during situation inference process, the situation of an entity cannot be deduced. Secondly, even if all needed sensors are available, the confidence of sensing data is unpredictable. There are two reasons for the unpredictability. On the one hand, the sensors to fulfill a sensing goal are by products of other sensing systems rather than application-dedicated, and the accuracy of the same type of sensors vary dramatically from one sensing system to another. On the other hand, it is hard to predict what sensor will be selected to accomplish a sensing goal at runtime.

The above stated problems may be abstracted as how to do semantic reasoning with uncertainty. To solve this problem, various extensions of OWL and SWRL have been proposed with different mathematical theories [12]. These works have proved their validity to varying degrees, but they also have a common deficiency, i.e., the extended languages are often very complicated and hard to be learned, even for those people who are familiar with standard Semantic Web languages.

Therefore, this paper developed a situation inference tool, named *OPSitu*. Instead of extending languages, *OPSitu* provides the developers of situation-aware applications with standard OWL and SWRL to write the situation inference rules, no matter the application will run under opportunistic sensing paradigm or not. The uncertainty of sensing data in opportunistic sensing is handled at runtime by the situation inference engine of *OPSitu* with the help of a pre-built knowledge base.

The rest of this paper is divided into 5 sections. Section 2 presents an example for opportunistic sensing. Section 3 gives a system overview of the *OPSitu*; Sect. 4 introduces the implementation of the situation inference engine in detail.

Section 5 describes the experiment. Section 6 reviews related works. Finally, directions of future works are concluded in Sect. 7.

2   Running Example

A situation-aware application, named *MyClassroom*, is to provide different services for students in classrooms according to their different situations. Thus *MyClassroom* has to identify current situation of a student in the classroom out of a set of possible situations. There are only five possible situations for a student user in the classroom that *MyClassroom* focuses, and they are class attendance, open lecture, student meeting, class exam and self-study. To infer the users situation, there are also five contexts to be exploited and the relevant sensing modules to acquire these contexts are described in Table 1. *MyClassroom* is running under opportunistic sensing paradigm, because there are two contexts whose availability is uncertain, i.e., status of the projector and existence of human voice.

Moreover, to infer the student's situation in classrooms, five rules are given in Table 2, and one row for each possible situation. For example, if a student is in a large classroom, the projector in that room is on, human voice exists in that room, and the acquaintance proportion of Tom in that room is low, then Tom

Table 1. Context and Relevant Sensing Modules

Context	Relevant Sensing Module	Availability
Classroom Capacity	Observed by human and stored in the database	Available
Projector Status	Based on the light sensor on the screen of projector	Uncertain
People Speaks	Based on the microphone on the rostrum	Uncertain
Location	Based on Wi-Fi fingerprint	Available
Acquaintance proportion	Based on the Bluetooth in persons smartphone	Available

Table 2. Situation Inference Rules

Context / Situation	Location	Classroom Capacity	Projector Status	Human Voice Existence	Acquaintance Proportion
Class Attendance	In Classroom	Small/Mid/Large	On	Yes	High
Open Lecture	In Classroom	Large	On	Yes	Low
Student Meeting	In Classroom	Small/Mid	Off	Yes	High
Class Exam	In Classroom	Mid/Large	Off	No	High
Self-Study	In Classroom	Small/Mid/Large	Off	No	Low

is attending an open lecture. By adopting the Semantic-Web based approach, these inference rules are written in OWL and SWRL. In Fig. 1, the inference rule for specifying "Open Lecture" is written in SWRL in (a), and related concepts appearing in the rule are defined in the ontology model in (b).

3   System Overview

3.1   Key Concepts

For the convenience of description, some concepts are interpreted in the follow.

Situation & Context. In this paper, a situation is the semantic abstraction about the status of an entity and the adaptions of the situation-aware application are triggered with the change of situations. A context is the information for characterizing the situation of an entity, and a situation is specified by multiple contexts based on human knowledge. For the example in Sect. 2, the situation of a student in a classroom is specified by five contexts based on the inference rules in Table 2.

Situation Candidate Set (SCS). Generally speaking, although the possible situations of some entities (for example, a person) are infinite, the situations that an application focuses are limited. Therefore, situation inference can be considered as a classification problem. The candidate situations of an entity form a set, which is referred to as an *SCS (Situation Candidate Set)* in this paper. For the example in Sect. 2, the SCS for *MyClassroom* is S = {Attending Class, Attending Open Lecture, Having Meeting, Taking Exam, Self-Studying}.

Context Assertion (CA). In this paper, *Context Assertion (CA)* is defined as a logic expression describing the condition that a context should be satisfied. For the example in Fig. 1 there are five contexts. Correspondingly, there are five *Context Assertions (CAs)* denoted as $A(C_i)(i = 1, 2, \ldots, 5)$, and they are listed in Fig. 2.

Situation Inference Rule (SIR). The *Situation Inference Rule (SIR)* is a first-order logic expression defining the relationship between contexts and a situation. More specifically, an *SIR* consists of two parts, the antecedent and the consequent. The antecedent part is a set of *Context Assertions (CAs)* connected with each other using logic AND. Thus the antecedent part of an *SIR* for a candidate situation S_i can be represented as $R(S_i) = A(C_1) \wedge A(C_2) \wedge \ldots \wedge A(C_m)$, where $A(C_i)$ is the *ith CA* and the *SIR* is related to m contexts. The consequent part is the logic expressions for a candidate situation. The semantic inference rule in Fig. 1(a) is an example of an *SIR*. Its antecedent part is $A(C_1) \wedge A(C_2) \wedge A(C_3) \wedge A(C_4) \wedge A(C_5)$, where $A(C_i)$ are expressed in Fig. 2 respectively, and its consequent part is $Situate(?p, ?stu) \wedge OpenLecture(?stu)$, which means the person $?p$ is attending an open lecture.

Person(?p) ∧ ClassRoom(?r) ∧ LocatedIn(?p,?r) ∧ RoomCapacity(?r,?cap) ∧
equalTo(?cap,'Large') ∧ Projector(?pro) ∧ EquippedWith(?r,?pro) ∧ HasStatus
(?pro,?s) ∧ equalTo(?s,'on') ∧ ExistHumanVoice(?r,?x) ∧ equalTo(?x,'yes') ∧
AcquaintanceProportion(?p, ?y) ∧ equalTo(?y,'Low') → Situate(?p,?stu) ∧
OPenLecture(?stu)

(a) Situation inference Rule Written in SWRL: an Example

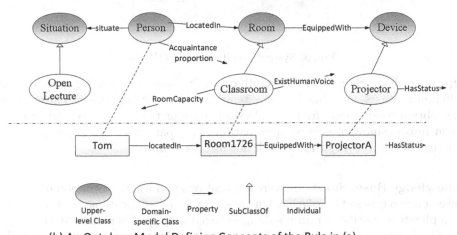

(b) An Ontology Model Defining Concepts of the Rule in (a)

Fig. 1. Situation Inference Rule: An Example

$A(C_1) = LocatedIn(?p,?r) \wedge ClassRoom(?r) \wedge Person(?p)$ // the person is in a classroom

$A(C_2) = RoomCapacity(?r,?cap) \wedge ClassRoom(?r) \wedge equalTo(?cap,'Large')$ // the room is large

$A(C_3) = HasStatus(?pro,?s) \wedge Projector(?pro) \wedge EquippedWith(?r,?pro) \wedge$

$ClassRoom(?r) \wedge equalTo(?s,'on')$ // the status of projector is on

$A(C_4) = ExistHumanVoice(?r,?x) \wedge Classroom(?r) \wedge equalTo(?x,'yes')$ // human voice exists

$A(C_5) = AcquaintanceProportion(?p,?y) \wedge Person(?p) \wedge equalTo(?y,'Low')$

// acquaintance proportion of the person in the room is low

Fig. 2. Example of context assertions

3.2 Architecture

Figure 3 demonstrates the architecture of *OPSitu* system and some other components that cooperate closely with *OPSitu*, and they are described in the follow.

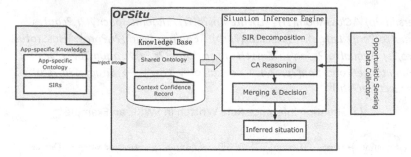

Fig. 3. System architecture of *OPSitu*

Opportunistic Sensing Data Collector. It consists of sensing modules for different contexts, including location, temperature, light, sound, etc. Those modules obtain sensing data from the physical space or the cyberspace and process them into meaningful context information. This part has been done by many existing works [7–9,11], thus we will not discuss it in detail.

Knowledge Base. Situation-aware applications perform the situation inference based on two types of knowledge. One is shared by all applications, and the other is application-specific. *OPSitu* is designed according to this classification.

The knowledge shared by applications is stored and managed in a pre-built *Knowledge Base*. It consists of the *Shared Ontology* and the *Context Confidence Record*. The *Shared Ontology* defines commonly used concepts for all applications as *Class* and *Property* in OWL (Web Ontology Language). To address the unpredictability of sensing data's confidence pointed out in Sect. 1 the *Context Confidence Record* pre-stores the confidence of contexts, which is measured by the accuracy of the sensing data collector. At runtime, the situation inference engine can query the *Context Confidence Record* and utilize them in the inference process.

Application-specific knowledge is injected into the *Knowledge Base* by application developers. It is comprised of the *App-specific Ontology* and the *SIRs*. The *App-specific Ontology* is derived from the *Shared Ontology*. Therefore, it not only contains all concepts in the *Shared Ontology* but includes some additional concepts just for a specific application. *SIRs* are logic expressions defining the relationships between contexts and situations, and they are also application-specific.

Since the management of knowledge base is a mature technology and there are many existing tools [13], *OPSitu* directly adopts Protégé [14], a free open-source Java tool, to support the creation and management of knowledge in OWL and SWRL.

Situation Inference Engine. The *Situation Inference Engine* is to conduct situation inference with uncertainty at runtime, and it is on the basis of the knowledge and opportunistic sensing data. It consists of three modules, *SIR*

Decomposition, *CA Reasoning* and *Merging & Decision*. Compared with the sensing data collector and knowledge base, the design and implementation of *Situation Inference Engine* is more challenging due to its complexity. Thus it is the main contribution of this paper, and we will describe it in detail in Sect. 4.

4   Situation Inference Engine Implementation

For a semantic reasoner that only supports the certain reasoning, two conditions must be satisfied in order to infer the situation of an entity. Firstly, an inference rule is considered as a whole. Secondly, before the inference process is activated, some variables in the rule must be assigned with specific value. However, this is not compatible with opportunistic sensing, because the value of some variable may not be determined when corresponding sensors are not available. To address this problem, the *Situation Inference Engine* adopts an inference process including the following three steps. Firstly, it decomposes the *SIR* into several *CAs* at first. Secondly, it performs the reasoning for the *CAs* whose context can be determined at runtime. Thirdly, it merges the reasoning results of all *CAs* and makes a decision about which candidate situation is the most possible.

4.1   Semi-automatic SIR Decomposition

Although it is easy for human to recognize what is a *CA* in an *SIR*, it is difficult to make *OPSitu* smart enough to decompose an *SIR* into *CAs* in a fully-automatic way. Thus, we come up with a semi-automatic strategy, and it consists of following two steps.

Step 1: Sensible Atomic Formula Selection. After finish writing an *SIR* at design time, the developer is required by the system to select the atomic formula that are directly related to sensing data (either from physical sensor or cyberspace), which are referred to as *Sensible Atomic Formula* in this paper. For the *SIR* in Fig. 1 (a), five atomic formulas, $LocatedIn(?p, ?r)$, $RoomCapacity(?r, ?cap)$, $HasStatus(?pro, ?s)$, $ExistHuman\ Voice(?r, ?x)$, and $Acquaintance\text{-}Proportion(?p, ?y)$ should be selected by the developer as *Sensible Atomic Formula* in this step.

Step 2: Runtime Decomposition. At runtime, the *SIR Decomposition* module will decompose an *SIR* into several *CAs* based on the *Sensible Atomic Formula* that developer has selected. For each Sensible Atomic Formula, its related atomic formulas including itself are combined together with logic AND as a CA. Take $LocatedIn(?p, ?r)$ as an example. $?p$ relates to $Person(?p)$, and $?r$ relates to $ClassRoom(?r)$. Therefore, three atomic formulas, $LocatedIn(?p, ?r)$, $Person(?p)$ and $ClassRoom(?r)$, are connected together with logic AND as a CA $A(C_1)$. Similarly, $A(C_2)$, $A(C_3)$, $A(C_4)$ and $A(C_5)$ becomes another four *CAs* after the decomposition phase, and they are listed in Fig. 2.

4.2   Topological-Ordering Based CA Reasoning

After the decomposition, *OPSitu* directly exploits Pellet to conduct the reasoning for each *CA* whose context can be acquired. However, the reasoning of each *CA* is not independent, and this gives *OPSitu* an opportunity to improve its reasoning performance. Let us take $A(C_1)$, $A(C_3)$ and $A(C_4)$ in Fig. 2 as an example to illustrate the dependency issue.

Before runtime reasoning, some variables in a *CA* have to be assigned with a specific value. For instance, the value of variable $?r$ must be assigned before the reasoning of $A(C_3)$ and $A(C_4)$. This is because only when the room is specified, whether human voice exists and the projector's status in that room can be determined. Moreover, if one wants to determine where Tom is located in, a query must be issued by using the OWL API [15] *getObjectPropertyValues(Tom, LocatedIn)*. Therefore, the reasoning of $A(C_3)$ and $A(C_4)$ depends on *LocatedIn($?p, ?r$)*. Here we define the dependency between *CAs* in Definition 1. According to this definition, $A(C_3)$ and $A(C_4)$ depends on $A(C_1)$.

Definition 1. *If the reasoning of $A(C_i)$ depends on the Sensible Atomic Formula of $A(C_j)$, then $A(C_i)$ depends on $A(C_j)$.*

In fact, after the reasoning of $A(C_1)$, the value of $?r$ (a specific room) has already been determined. Consequently, if the following two conditions are satisfied, the *OPSitu* does not need to query the value of $?r$ when reasoning $A(C_3)$ and $A(C_4)$, thus improving its reasoning performance.

Condition 1: OPSitu performs the reasoning of $A(C_1)$ before $A(C_3)$ and $A(C_4)$.

Condition 2: OPSitu records the value of $?r$ as an intermediate result after the reasoning of $A(C_1)$.

Based on the analysis above, we propose a method for arranging a reasonable reasoning order so as to enhance the reasoning performance. It consists of two steps, the dependency analysis and the Topological-Ordering based reasoning.

Step 1: Dependency Analysis. In this step, OPSitu will analyze the dependency among all *CAs* of an *SIR*. In this process, the dependency analysis is designed as the generation of a directed graph, in which a *CA* is a vertex, and the dependency between two *CAs* is a directed edge linking two vertexes.

Step 2: Topological-Ordering Based Reasoning. After the dependency analysis, all *CAs* of an *SIR* are to be arranged in a topological order based on the Topological Ordering algorithm. Then the *CAs*, whose context can be acquired, will be reasoned one by one according to the topological order. Since the Topological Ordering is a well-known algorithm and the reasoning of *CAs* is based on the open-source semantic reasoner (the Pellet), we will not describe the ordering and reasoning in detail.

4.3 Similarity-Based Merging and Decision

After the reasoning of all *CAs*, the reasoning results would be merged together to compute the possibility of each candidate situation based on a similarity function, and to make a decision about which situation is the most possible one.

To describe the merging and decision phase, some concepts should be defined at first.

Firstly, the truth-value of a CA is extended from the conventional $0/1$(*false/true*) to the interval $[-1, 1]$. The absolute value of the truth-value indicates the confidence of the context, and the positive/negative symbol represents the assertions tendency of being true or false. The semantic interpretation of this extension is represented in Formula 1, in which $k \in (0, 1]$ is the confidence of context C_i obtained from the *Context Confidence Record* in the knowledge base.

$$
TruthValue((A(C_i))) = \begin{cases} k & \text{if } acquired\ C_i \text{ indicates that}(A(C_i)) \text{ is true} \\ 0 & \text{if the } C_i \text{ can not be acquired} \\ -k & \text{if } acquired\ C_i \text{ indicates that}(A(C_i)) \text{ is false} \end{cases}
$$
(1)

Secondly, *CTV (Contexts Truth Vector)* and *BV (Benchmark Vector)* are defined in Definition. In this paper, we assume that all situations in an *SCS* are based on a common set of *CAs*.

Definition 2. *An* SCS *is denoted as* $S = S_1, S_2, \ldots, S_n$ *the objective of situation inference is to find the situation that most likely to be from S. At a given time t, the antecedent of an* SIR *for* $S_i \in S$ *is denoted as* $R(S_i) = A(C_1) \wedge A(C_2) \wedge \cdots \wedge A(C_m)$, *where* $A(C_i)$ *is a* CA *and the* $R(S_i)$ *is related to m contexts.* CTV (Contexts Truth Vector) *and* BV (Benchmark Vector) *are defined in (a) and (b)*

(a) Denote $TV_t(S_i) = (T_1, T_2, \ldots, T_m)$ *as* CTV (Contexts Truth Vector) *of* $R(S_i)$, *where* $T_i = TruethValue(A(C_i))$, *and m is the number of contexts.*

(b) Denote $bV = (1, 1, \ldots, 1)$, *a m-dimension vector, as the* BV (Benchmark Vector).

Thirdly, we define a similarity $function Sim(S(t), S_i)$ to represent the similarity between S_i and $S(t)$ in Formula 2, where $S_i \in S$ and $S(t)$is the actual situation at time t. It is measured by the cosine similarity between *Contexts Truth Vector* TV_t and *Benchmark Vector* bV.

$$
Sim(S(t), S_i) = \cos(TV_t(S_i), bV) = \frac{TV_t(S_i) \cdot bV}{|TV_t(S_i)||bV|}
$$
(2)

Finally, our merging and decision phase is described in Fig. 4. The main idea of this process is to compute the degree of possibility of each candidate situation, and the possibility is measured by the a similarity function $Sim(S(t), S_i)$. Then the candidate situation with maximum possibility is considered to be the inferred situation.

Denote a *SCS* as $S = \{S_1, S_2, ..., S_n\}$, for a specific *SIR*'s antecedent $R(S_i) = A(C_1) \wedge A(C_2) \wedge ... \wedge A(C_m)$, where $A(C_i)$ is a *CA* and the *SIR*'s antecedent $R(S_i)$ is related to m contexts $C_1, C_2, ..., C_m$.

Step 1: For $i = 1, 2, ..., n$, computes the value of $Sim(S(t), S_i)$ using formula (2).

Step 2: Make a decision about which situation is most likely to be at time t(denoted as $S_{inferred}(t)$). $S_{inferred}(t) = S_k$, if S_k let $Sim(S(t), S_i)$ to be maximum. $i = 1, 2, ..., n$.

Step 3: If there is more than one S_i whose $Sim(S(t), S_i)$ reach to the maximum value, randomly choose one of them as the inference result.

Fig. 4. The merging and decision phase description

5   Experimental Evaluation

5.1   Experimental Methodology

To evaluate the validity of *OPSitu*, an experiment has been conducted based on the example in Sect. 2. Firstly, we construct and store *SIRs* in Table 2 into SWRL format in the *Knowledge Base*. Secondly, the sensing modules in Table 1 serve as the *Opportunistic Sensing Data Collectors*.

After establishing the *SIRs* and sensing data collectors, our experiment comprises two steps:

Step 1: Context Confidence Generation. We generate the confidence of contexts in two ways. One way is through experiment. For example, the confidence of projector status is generated by experiment. As the length of the paper is limited, we put the details of four experiments on the website [16]. The other way is set by experience. For example, as the classroom capacity is observed by human and stored in a database, its confidence is set to be a constant 100 % without experiment. The generated confidence of each context is listed in Table 3, and we store them in the Context Confidence Record of *OPSitu's Knowledge Base*.

Table 3. Context Confidence

Context	Confidence	Generation Method
Classroom Capacity	100 %	Experience
Projector Status	100 %	Experiment
People Speaks	82.5 %	Experiment
Location	93.2 %	Experiment
Acquaintance Proportion	94 %	Experiment

Step 2: Simulative Situation Inference. The parameters of this simulative inference are the confidence of each context, which are generated by the real-world experiment above. The process of the simulative situation inference is described in Fig. 5. In Step A and B, we simulate an opportunistic sensing environment by programming, and then adopt the *Situation Inference Engine* of *OPSitu* to infer the situation in Step C. For the simulation of the opportunistic sensing environment, there are two points need to be explained.

(1) Based on a survey in university P, in the step B (2) 90 % of all virtual classrooms are randomly selected to be equipped with light sensors, and 95 % to be equipped with microphone.

(2) In the Step B (3) we assign the value of contexts based on the corresponding *SIR*. This is because the objective of this experiment is to evaluate the validity of *Situation Inference Engine of OPSitu* rather than the reliability of *SIR*, thus we assume that all *SIRs* are reliable in this simulative inference.

Step A: Create N virtual Classrooms: $R_1, R_2, ..., R_N$.

Step B: for (i = 1 to N) {

    (1) Randomly assign a situation for R_i;

    (2) Assign the availability of sensors opportunistically for R_i;

    (3) Assign value to context based on *SIRs*. }

Step C: for (i = 1 to N) {

    (1) Adopt the *OPSitu*'s *Situation Inference Engine* to infer situation;

    (2) Compare the inferred situation with the assigned one. }

Fig. 5. Situation inference in a simulative opportunistic sensing environment

5.2 Experimental Result

We set the number of virtual classroom N to be 10000. The experimental result is demonstrated as the confusion matrix in Table 4. By analyzing the confusion matrix in Table 4, the overall situation inference accuracy by *OPSitu* reaches to 94.9 % in such a simulative opportunistic sensing environment.

The misclassification is caused when the key sensing data to classify similar situations is missing. For example, when the light sensor is not available, class attendance and student meeting are easy to be misclassified. Therefore, the limitation of *OPSitu* is that the fewer contexts are determined, the lower inference accuracy would be. However, the opportunistic sensing paradigm has a basic assumption that the sensors are abundant enough in the environment where the application is expected to be used [9]. Thus under this assumption, *OPSitu* can conduct Semantic-Web based situation inference with a satisfactory accuracy.

Table 4. Situation Inference Confusion Matrix

Context / Situation	Class Attendance	Open Lecture	Student Meeting	Class Exam	Self-Study
Class Attendance	1830	0	162	0	0
Open Lecture	0	1990	0	0	10
Student Meeting	155	0	1762	83	0
Class Exam	0	0	89	1911	0
Self-Study	0	9	0	0	1991

6   Related Work

To deal with uncertainty in the Semantic Web and its applications, many researchers have proposed extension of Semantic Web language with special mathematical theories. [17,18] extended OWL based on the probability theory. Reference [19] proposed an extension for terminological logics with the possibility theory. Reference [20–23] extended either OWL or SWRL based on fuzzy logic, etc. In addition to language extension, some of these work developed corresponding semantic inference engines. In terms of the expressiveness, those extensions for semantic web languages are capable of dealing with the uncertainty brought by opportunistic sensing. However, these extended languages are often complicated and hard to learn, even for those who are familiar with the standard semantic web languages. Besides, there are already many situation inference rules written in OWL and SWRL on the Semantic Web. If we want to share and reuse this existing knowledge in opportunistic sensing applications, they have to be transformed into the format of those extended languages. However, since the extended languages are quite complex, the transformation process is very time-consuming.

To avoid the shortcomings of the language extension approaches above, [24] provided a guidance to use OWL and SWRL to express fuzzy semantic rules. This approach models the binary predicate with uncertainty as a 3-ary predicate. Since SWRL is a rule language only supporting unary and binary predicates, this paper adopts a procedure called the reification to express a 3-ary relation via unary and binary relations. Therefore, under this guidance, developers can express fuzzy rules without the modification of OWL and SWRL. However, the reification process is very complicated and it is conducted by developers. Besides, the rules after the reification process, although expressed by SWRL, are too complex to be understood.

7   Conclusion

In order to solve the problem of uncertainty during situation inference brought by the opportunistic sensing paradigm, this paper proposed *OPSitu*, a Semantic-Web based situation inference tool. *OPSitu* enables the developers of opportunistic sensing applications to write the situation inference rules with standard OWL and SWRL, and utilizes a pre-built knowledge base to handle the uncertainty at runtime.

The future work about *OPSitu* include two parts. Firstly, taking the weights of contexts into consideration. In some cases, different contexts contribute to the inference of a situation to different degrees. However, the current version of *OPSitu* does not consider this aspect. Hence we plan to take the weight of context into consideration in the next version of *OPSitu*. Secondly, this paper assumes that all candidate situations in an *SCS* are based on the same set of contexts. However, in some circumstances, this may not be true. Thus we plan to revise the inference engine of *OPSitu* to make it able to handle more complex conditions.

Acknowledgments. This work is funded by the National High Technology Research and Development Program of China (863) under Grant No. 2013AA01A605, the National Basic Research Program of China (973) under Grant No. 2011CB302604 and the National Natural Science Foundation of China under Grant No.61121063.

References

1. Ye, J., Dobson, S., McKeever, S.: Situation identification techniques in pervasive computing: a review. Pervasive Mob. Comput. **8**(1), 36–66 (2012)
2. Goix, L.-W., Valla, M., Cerami, L., Falcarin, P.: Situation inference for mobile users: a rule based approach. In: 2007 International Conference on Mobile Data Management, pp. 299–303. IEEE (2007)
3. Matheus, C.J., Baclawski, K., Kokar, M.M., Letkowski, J.J.: Using SWRL and OWL to capture domain knowledge for a situation awareness application applied to a supply logistics scenario. In: Adi, A., Stoutenburg, S., Tabet, S. (eds.) RuleML 2005. LNCS, vol. 3791, pp. 130–144. Springer, Heidelberg (2005)
4. Oberhauser, R.: Leveraging semantic web computing for context-aware software engineering environments. In: Wu, G. (ed.) Semantic Web. In-Tech, Vienna (2010)
5. Wang, X.H., Zhang, D.Q., Gu, T., Pung, H.Q.: Ontology based context modeling and reasoning using owl. In: Proceedings of the Second IEEE Annual Conference on Pervasive Computing and Communications Workshops, 2004, pp. 18–22. IEEE (2004)
6. Yau, S.S., Wang, Y., Karim, F.: Development of situation-aware application software for ubiquitous computing environments. In: Proceedings of 26th Annual International Computer Software and Applications Conference, COMPSAC 2002, pp. 233–238. IEEE (2002)
7. Hoseini-Tabatabaei, S.A., Gluhak, A., Tafazolli, R.: A survey on smartphone-based systems for opportunistic user context recognition. ACM Comput. Surv. (CSUR) **45**(3), 1–27 (2013)
8. Roggen, D., Lukowicz, P., Ferscha, L., del Mill, R., Tröster, G., Chavarriaga, R., et al.: Opportunistic human activity and context recognition. Computer **46**, 36–45 (2013)
9. Conti, M., Kumar, M.: Opportunities in opportunistic computing. Computer **43**(1), 42–50 (2010)
10. Ferscha, A.: 20 years past weiser: what's next? IEEE Pervasive Comput. **11**(1), 52–61 (2012)

11. Kurz, M., Hölzl, G., Ferscha, A., Calatroni, A., Roggen, D., Tröster, D., Sagha, H., Chavarriaga, R., Millán, J.D.R., Bannach, D., et al.: The opportunity framework and data processing ecosystem for opportunistic activity and context recognition. Int. J. Sens. Wireless Commun. Control, Special Issue on Autonomic and Opportunistic Communications **1**, 102–125 (2011)

12. Stoilos, G., Simou, N., Stamou, G., Kollias, S.: Uncertainty and the semantic web. IEEE Intell. Syst. **21**(5), 84–87 (2006)

13. Schmidt, J.W., Thanos, C.: Foundations of knowledge base management: Contributions from logic, databases, and artificial intelligence applications (2012)

14. Gennari, J.H., Musen, M.A., Fergerson, R.W., Grosso, W.E., Crubézy, M., Eriksson, H., Noy, N.F., Tu, S.W.: The evolution of protégé: an environment for knowledge-based systems development. Int. J. Hum Comput Stud. **58**(1), 89–123 (2003)

15. Bechhofer, S., Volz, R., Lord, P.: Cooking the semantic web with the OWL API. In: Fensel, D., Sycara, K., Mylopoulos, J. (eds.) ISWC 2003. LNCS, vol. 2870, pp. 659–675. Springer, Heidelberg (2003)

16. http://219.143.213.95/experiments/

17. Ding, Z., Peng, Y.: A probabilistic extension to ontology language owl. In: Proceedings of the 37th Annual Hawaii International Conference on System Sciences, 2004, pp. 1–10. IEEE (2004)

18. Ding, Z., Peng, Y., Pan, R.: A Bayesian approach to uncertainty modelling in owl ontology. Technical report, DTIC Document (2006)

19. Hollunder, B.: An alternative proof method for possibilistic logic and its application to terminological logics. Int. J. Approximate Reasoning **12**(2), 85–109 (1995)

20. Pan, J.Z., Stoilos, G., Stamou, G., Tzouvaras, V., Horrocks, I.: f-SWRL: A Fuzzy Extension of SWRL. In: Spaccapietra, S., Aberer, K., Cudré-Mauroux, P. (eds.) Journal on Data Semantics VI. LNCS, vol. 4090, pp. 28–46. Springer, Heidelberg (2006)

21. Stoilos, G., Stamou, G.B., Tzouvaras, V., Pan, J.Z., Horrocks, I.: Uncertainty and the semantic web. In: OWLED, Fuzzy owl (2005)

22. Wang, X., Ma, Z.M., Yan, L., Meng, X.: Vague-SWRL: a fuzzy extension of SWRL. In: Calvanese, D., Lausen, G. (eds.) RR 2008. LNCS, vol. 5341, pp. 232–233. Springer, Heidelberg (2008)

23. Wlodarczyk, T.W., Rong, C., O'Connor, M., Musen M.: Swrl-f: a fuzzy logic extension of the semantic web rule language. In: Proceedings of the International Conference on Web Intelligence, Mining and Semantics, pp. 1–39. ACM (2011)

24. Ciaramella, A., Cimino, M.G.C.A., Marcelloni, F., Straccia, U.: Combining fuzzy logic and semantic web to enable situation-awareness in service recommendation. In: Bringas, P.G., Hameurlain, A., Quirchmayr, G. (eds.) DEXA 2010, Part I. LNCS, vol. 6261, pp. 31–45. Springer, Heidelberg (2010)

Model-Driven Public Sensing in Sparse Networks

Damian Philipp$^{(\boxtimes)}$, Jarosław Stachowiak, Frank Dürr, and Kurt Rothermel

Institute of Parallel and Distributed Systems,
University of Stuttgart, Stuttgart, Germany
{damian.philipp,jaroslaw.stachowiak,
frank.duerr,kurt.rothermel}@ipvs.uni-stuttgart.de

Abstract. Public Sensing (PS) is a recent trend for building large-scale sensor data acquisition systems using commodity smartphones. Limiting the energy drain on participating devices is a major challenge for PS, as otherwise people will stop sharing their resources with the PS system. Existing solutions for limiting the energy drain through model-driven optimizations are limited to dense networks where there is a high probability for every point of interest to be covered by a smartphone. In this work, we present an adaptive model-driven PS system that deals with *both* dense and sparse networks. Our evaluations show that this approach improves data quality by up to 41 percentage points while enabling the system to run with a greatly reduced number of participating smartphones. Furthermore, we can save up to 81 % of energy for communication and sensing while providing data matching an error bound of 1 °C up to 96 % of the time.

1 Introduction

Public Sensing (PS) is a recent trend for building flexible and large-scale sensor data acquisition systems, facilitated by the proliferation of commodity smartphones [3]. Modern smartphones feature various sensors such as camera, light intensity, and positioning sensors like GPS. In addition, they offer capabilities for processing and communicating sensor data. Thus, sensor data can be obtained without having to support a fixed sensor network.

In building such PS systems, we face several challenges. On the device side, the main issue is a limited energy supply. While smartphone batteries are frequently recharged, keeping the energy consumption for PS minimal, i.e., ensuring that the battery still makes it through a whole day, is a key requirement as otherwise participants may be unwilling to support PS. On the data side, problems are to specify tasks and to deliver data with sufficient quality. Due to node mobility, it is likely that each time data is requested, a different device is best suited to take readings for the task at hand. However, if we want to minimize the energy consumption on participating devices, querying all smartphones for readings or even proactively collecting location information for all devices is prohibitive.

© Institute for Computer Sciences, Social Informatics and Telecommunications Engineering 2014
I. Stojmenovic et al. (Eds.): MOBIQUITOUS 2013, LNICST 131, pp. 17–29, 2014.
DOI: 10.1007/978-3-319-11569-6_2

These challenges require careful planning which smartphones should take readings where and when to ensure that useful data of sufficient quality is delivered to a client of the system while keeping the energy consumption minimal.

To address the problem of how to specify interesting data and thus enable flexible PS systems, the concept of *virtual sensors* (v-sensors for short) was introduced [12]. V-sensors provide a mobility-transparent abstraction of the PS system. They are configured to report a set of readings at a client-defined sampling rate at a given position, thus presenting a view on a static sensor network. The PS system then selects nearby smartphones to provide readings for a v-sensor.

However, due to node mobility, some v-sensors may not have any smartphone nearby and may thus be unable to report data readings. Model-driven approaches can be used to fill these gaps with a value inferred from available data [10] and to improve the energy consumption by leaving out v-sensors where values can be inferred with sufficient accuracy [13], thus making large-scale PS viable.

However, these approaches are tailored towards dense networks where most v-sensors are well covered (and thus available), e.g., in a busy city center or a business area at lunchtime. For model-driven approaches to provide accurate inferred readings, a minimum set of input data from available v-sensors is required. Collecting this minimum set of data is a problem in (partially or completely) sparsely populated areas, e.g., business areas during off-hours or housing areas during business hours, where the density of smartphones is overall low, or when the most interesting v-sensors are unavailable while many less interesting v-sensors are available.

We address this challenge by presenting an approach for optimized model-driven PS that works in both dense and sparse networks. To this end, we extend our previous model-driven approach. The basic idea is to derive knowledge on v-sensor availability from ongoing query executions. This knowledge is then used in a multi-round approach to iteratively refine the set of v-sensors to query.

In detail, the main contributions of this paper are: (1) An approach for building knowledge on v-sensor availability without extra energy cost. (2) An adaptive query execution model that exploits this knowledge to compensate for unavailable v-sensors, thus making optimized PS viable in both dense and sparse networks. (3) Evaluations analyzing the performance of our approach and showing significant improvements compared to previous approaches.

The quality of data obtained by our system is improved by up to 41 percentage points while at the same time useful data can be provided with a greatly reduced number of participating smartphones. Furthermore, we show that we can save up to 81 % of energy for communication and sensing while providing inferred readings matching an error bound of $1\,^\circ$C up to 96 % of the time. As a by-product, our system is privacy-friendly, i.e., it provides data readings of good quality without tracking the position of individual smartphones.

The remainder of this work is structured as follows. Section 2 presents the system model and problem statement. In Sect. 3 we present the model-driven PS system before we describe the extensions for sparse networks in detail in Sect. 4.

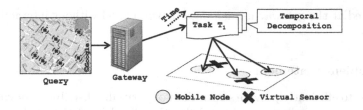

Fig. 1. Overview of sensing task execution

Evaluation results for our system are discussed in Sect. 5. Section 6 compares our approach to related work while Sect. 7 concludes this work.

2   System Model and Goals

First, we present our system model and formulate the problem to be solved by our enhanced PS system.

2.1   System Model and Architecture

Following the general design of PS systems, our system consists of two kinds of components: *mobile smartphones* and a *gateway server* (see Fig. 1). Each smartphone features a positioning sensor such as GPS, has constant Internet access, e.g., via 3G, and has access to a set of environmental sensors (sound, temperature, air pollution, etc.) that may be built-in or connected via Bluetooth. We assume that each smartphone has access to all sensors necessary to satisfy any request posted to the system. Users of mobile smartphones are assumed to be walking with no further assumptions about their mobility. The *gateway server*, located on the Internet, serves as an interface for clients to request data from the system and redistributes these requests to the smartphones. Note that for scalability the gateway may be implemented as a distributed service.

To request data, clients submit a query $Q = (V, p, QoS)$ to the gateway, consisting of a set of virtual sensors $Q.V$, a sampling period $Q.p$, and a set of quality parameters $Q.QoS$. The sampling period dictates the interval at which readings for all v-sensors should be provided. The quality parameters control the operation of our algorithm and will be explained in the corresponding sections. *Virtual Sensors* are attributed with a type of reading $v.type$ and a position $v.loc$, thus specifying where to take data readings. Furthermore, each v-sensor has a coverage area $v.area$ defined relative to its location. When a smartphone is located in $v.area$, it may take a reading for v and we say that v is *available*. Otherwise, v is *unavailable*. Coverage areas of v-sensors in a query $v \in Q.V$ must be pairwise disjoint to ensure a unique mapping of smartphones to v-sensors, but may otherwise be chosen arbitrarily.

Each v-sensor v can provide either an *effective reading* or an *inferred reading*. An effective reading is taken by a smartphone in $v.area$ whereas an inferred reading is computed at the gateway using a data-driven model without interaction with any device.

2.2 Problem Statement

Our goal is to efficiently provide sensor data on spatially distributed environmental phenomena according to a client-defined quality bound $Q.QoS$, independent of the current distribution of smartphones in the observed area. We want to minimize the number of requested effective readings while at the same time compensating for unavailable v-sensors and maximize the number of v-sensors $|V'|$ for which the quality constraints are fulfilled.

3 Optimized Query Execution in Dense Systems

In this section we first introduce the multivariate Gaussian distribution model used by our approach. We then present the basic model-driven execution for energy-efficient PS systems (DrOPS), based on [13], that will be extended with adaptive algorithms for compensating for unavailable v-sensors in later sections.

3.1 Multivariate Gaussian Distribution

Multivariate Gaussian Distributions (MGD) have been shown to be a suitable model for inferring values for spatially distributed phenomena, e.g., in [4,5,10]. Their advantage over other methods, e.g., spatial interpolation approaches such as linear interpolation, is that they capture the correlation of observed values rather than relying on indirect criteria, e.g., spatial distance. Note that other types of phenomena, e.g., discrete events, may require a different model. In our system, an MGD model is used in two ways: Inferring missing values from a set of incomplete observations and selecting the best set of v-sensors to observe.

Given a model MGD_V over a set V of v-sensors and a vector of effective readings V_{eff} at v-sensors $V_{\text{eff}} \subset V$, we can infer the most likely current values $\mu_{u|P_{V_{\text{eff}}}}$ at (currently unobserved) v-sensors $u \in V_{\text{inf}} = V \setminus V_{\text{eff}}$ as

$$\mu_{u|P_{V_{\text{eff}}}} = \mu_u + \Sigma_{u,V_{\text{eff}}} \Sigma_{V_{\text{eff}},V_{\text{eff}}}^{-1} \left(P_{V_{\text{eff}}} - \mu_{V_{\text{eff}}}\right) \tag{1}$$

$$\sigma_{u|V_{\text{eff}}}^2 = \sigma_u^2 - \Sigma_{u,V_{\text{eff}}} \Sigma_{V_{\text{eff}},V_{\text{eff}}}^{-1} \Sigma_{V_{\text{eff}},u} \tag{2}$$

where μ_V is the vector of mean values for all $v \in V$ and $\Sigma_{V,V}$ is the matrix of (co)variances between all v-sensors in the model. The output is a Gaussian distribution where $\sigma_{u|V_{\text{eff}}}^2$ indicates whether the observations V_{eff} were a good choice for inferring $\mu_{u|P_{V_{\text{eff}}}}$.

To optimize the operation of our system, we strive to minimize the size of V_{eff} while ensuring good data quality, i.e., limiting $\sigma_{u|W}^2$ to a client-defined threshold $Q.QoS.\sigma_{max}^2$. Finding the smallest V_{eff} that still achieves a given quality of inferred values is an NP hard problem, for which the near-optimal heuristic

GREEDY algorithm was proposed [8]. GREEDY iteratively selects a fixed number of v-sensors. Initially, $V_{inf} = V$. In each iteration, the v-sensor v with the maximum mutual information is moved to V_{eff}, i.e., the v-sensor that reduces the uncertainty about the values at v-sensors in $V_{inf} \setminus \{v\}$ the most. For a detailed discussion of this algorithm and the mutual information criterion, see [8].

To adapt the algorithm to selecting a set of v-sensors based on the requested result quality rather than a predetermined fixed number, we change the termination criterion: in our system, MODIFIEDGREEDY adds v-sensors to V_{eff} until $\forall u \in V_{inf} : \sigma^2_{u|V_{eff}} \leq Q.QoS.\sigma^2_{max}$.

Note that the achievable degree of optimization depends on the magnitude of the correlations found in the data. If only weak correlations exist, MODIFIED-GREEDY will select $V_{eff} = V$. Furthermore, the accuracy of the selection as well as the inference relies on the accuracy of the MGD. As we will show, our system ensures that the MGD in use always reflects current data.

3.2   Model-Driven Query Execution

Next, we look at how to apply the model-based optimization in a PS system.

The operation of DrOPS is driven by the gateway. Given a query $Q = (V, p, QoS)$, in each sampling period, the gateway creates a sensing task $T = (V_{eff}, QoS), V_{eff} \subseteq V$ as depicted in Fig. 1. T is then broadcast to all smartphones. On receiving T, each smartphone samples its position and determines whether it is located in the coverage area of any v-sensor $v \in V_{eff}$. If so, it takes a reading of the requested type and returns the reading along with the identity of the v-sensor to the gateway. Should there be more than one effective reading reported for a v-sensor v, only the reading that was taken closest to $v.loc$ is retained. All other readings for v are discarded.

To optimize data acquisition, DrOPS alternates its operation between two phases. In *Basic Operation Phases*, V_{eff} is equal to V, i.e., no optimization is performed. Data is gathered to build or update an MGD model of the phenomenon observed in this query and only effective readings for available v-sensors are reported to the client. To keep the optimized operation phase short, an online learning algorithm is used [13]. When an MGD model is available, the system switches to an *Optimized Operation Phase*. In this phase, MODIFIEDGREEDY is used to minimize the size of V_{eff} and inferred readings are provided for all v-sensors $v \in V_{inf} \cup$ *unavailable v-sensors*, i.e., where no effective reading was taken. In parallel, an online model validity check algorithm determines whether the current MGD has become inaccurate and if so, switches the system back to a basic operation phase.

4   Alternate Virtual Sensor Selection for Sparse Networks

The optimized query execution presented in the last section *assumes*, that most or all of the v-sensors are constantly available. This assumption does not hold in a

Require: V, MGD_V, V_{unav}, V_{avl}, $Q.QoS.\sigma^2_{max}$
    $V_{eff} = V_{avl}$, $V_{inf} = V \setminus V_{eff}$
    while $\exists v \in V : \sigma^2_{v|V_{eff}} > Q.QoS.\sigma^2_{max}$ and $V_{eff} \neq V \setminus V_{unav}$ **do**
        $u = argmax_{u \in V_{inf} \setminus V_{unav}}$ MUTUALINFORMATION(u, V, MGD_V, V_{eff})
        $V_{eff} = V_{eff} \cup \{u\}$, $V_{inf} = V_{inf} \setminus \{u\}$
    end while
    return V_{eff}

Fig. 2. ADAPTIVEGREEDY algorithm

sparse network setting, which is characterized by a low probability for each individual v-sensor to be available. Therefore, we begin by introducing the ADAPTIVEGREEDY algorithm that includes *knowledge* about the (un)availability of v-sensors in the selection. Finally, we present how to use ADAPTIVEGREEDY in our *Round-based Alternate V-Sensor Selection* to extend DrOPS to compensate for unavailable v-sensors.

4.1 Adaptive Greedy Algorithm

Compared to the previously described MODIFIEDGREEDY algorithm, ADAPTIVEGREEDY depicted in Fig. 2 takes two additional parameters: A set of v-sensors *known* to be unavailable $V_{unav} \subseteq V$ and a set of v-sensors *known* to be available $V_{avl} \subseteq V$, $V_{avl} \cap V_{unav} = \emptyset$. The availability of v-sensors not contained in $V_{avl} \cup V_{unav}$ is unknown. Using an optimistic strategy, ADAPTIVEGREEDY *assumes* these v-sensors to be available, although they may turn out to be unavailable during task execution. A pessimistic strategy would need to probe the availability of all v-sensors beforehand by querying all smartphones for their position. This would cause the PS system to use as much energy as an approach without any optimization just for probing v-sensor availability, thus voiding the entire optimization approach.

Given these parameters, ADAPTIVEGREEDY computes a new selection of v-sensors V_{eff} analogous to MODIFIEDGREEDY under the additional constraints that no v-sensor known to be unavailable is selected and that all v-sensors known to be available are selected, i.e., $V_{eff} \cap V_{unav} = \emptyset$ and $V_{avl} \subseteq V_{eff}$. Forcibly selecting all of V_{avl} is warranted by the fact that in our system detecting the availability of v-sensor v coincides with getting an effective reading for v (see Sect. 4.2). Thus, not selecting all of V_{avl} would be a waste of effort.

4.2 Round-Based Alternate Virtual Sensor Selection

We now introduce the *Round-based Alternate V-Sensor Selection*, depicted in Fig. 3, where the gateway subdivides each sampling period into a number of $Q.QoS.rounds$ rounds. The duration of each round is $\frac{Q.p}{Q.QoS.rounds}$. At the beginning of each round we first update our knowledge about current v-sensor availability. Based on this knowledge, we then select a new set of v-sensors for which effective readings should be acquired. Note that for long sampling periods $Q.p$,

Require: V, MGD_V, $Q.QoS$
$\quad V_{avl} = \emptyset, V_{unav} = \emptyset, E_0 = \emptyset, V_{eff,0} = \emptyset$
$\quad$**for** $i = 1..Q.QoS.rounds$ **do**
$\quad\quad V_{avl} = V_{avl} \cup E_{i-1}, V_{unav} = V_{unav} \cup (V_{eff,i-1} \setminus E_{i-1})$
$\quad\quad V_{eff,i} = \text{ADAPTIVEGREEDY}(V, MGD_V, V_{unav}, V_{avl}, Q.QoS.\sigma^2_{max})$
$\quad\quad V_{eff,i} = V_{eff,i} \setminus \bigcup_{j=1}^{i-1} V_{eff,j}$
$\quad\quad$**if** $V_{eff,i} = \emptyset$ **then**
$\quad\quad\quad$**return** $\bigcup_{j=1}^{i-1} E_j$
$\quad\quad$**end if**
$\quad\quad E_i = \text{EXECUTETASK}(V_{eff,i}, Q.QoS)$
$\quad$**end for**
$\quad$**return** $\bigcup_{j=1}^{Q.QoS.rounds} E_j$

Fig. 3. Round-based alternate v-sensor selection

round duration should be limited to, e.g., 5 s each to ensure that smartphones cannot move too much between individual rounds. Otherwise, the availability of v-sensors may significantly change during each round, thus voiding the knowledge on v-sensor availability built so far. For the same reason, we do not carry over knowledge from past sensing periods, as nodes may have moved significantly between sensing periods.

In the first round, $V_{avl} = \emptyset = V_{unav}$, thus we assume all v-sensors to be available. Therefore, the initial selection of $V_{eff,1}$ is identical to using MODIFIED-GREEDY as in the non-adaptive system. In fact, when setting $Q.QoS.rounds = 1$, the system behaves exactly as previously presented in Sect. 3. The resulting subtask T_1 is distributed to the smartphones. For all v-sensors in $V_{eff,1}$ that are actually available an effective readings will be reported to the gateway. All readings received in this round are stored in set E_1.

In subsequent rounds $i = 2 \ldots Q.QoS.rounds$, we first update our knowledge on v-sensor availability by setting $V_{avl} = V_{avl} \cup E_{i-1}$ and $V_{unav} = V_{unav} \cup (V_{eff,i-1} \setminus E_{i-1})$. Thus, all v-sensors for which a reading was requested but no effective reading was received are known to be unavailable for the remainder of the sampling period. Based on this new knowledge we then compute a new selection $V_{eff,i}$ using ADAPTIVEGREEDY. A new subtask $T_i = (V_{eff,i} \setminus \bigcup_{j=1}^{i-1} V_{eff,j})$ is then distributed to the smartphones. We repeat this process until either the maximum number of rounds has been reached or no additional v-sensors were selected. At this point, inferred readings are computed from all effective readings that have been collected.

5   Evaluation

We evaluated our approaches based on real-world environmental measurements and generated mobility traces. In the following, we will first present the setup of our evaluation before discussing the results in detail.

5.1   Simulation Setup

We evaluate our algorithms in a simulated PS system, implemented using Omnet++, driven by two real-world datasets containing temperature measurements: LAB data from 50 fixed sensors deployed in an indoor lab [5] and LUCE data from over 100 fixed sensors from an outdoor deployment [11]. Using real-world data readings is important to make the performance of the model-driven optimization comparable to that of a real deployment of our system, i.e., to observe realistic correlations of individual v-sensors. Queries are generated by replicating the fixed sensors of each data set as v-sensors in order to generate a temperature map of the observed area. For our PS system, we generated mobility traces for a varying number of smartphones, following the available paths in each deployment area. Energy cost is modeled using empirical energy models for communication [2] and sensing [14]. We do not consider energy for positioning, as it is amortized over other location-based applications frequently running on a smartphone. Each simulation runs for 6 simulated hours with a time offset between simulations increasing in steps of 3 h from the start of each data set. Quality parameters are set to $Q.QoS.\sigma^2_{max} = 0.1$ for the ADAPTIVEGREEDY algorithm and $Q.T = 1\,°C$ as an absolute acceptable error threshold for the model validity check algorithm.

We analyze the performance of our system under three metrics: *Quality, Broken Queries,* and *Relative Energy Consumption.* We compare the performance of our system to a naive algorithm without optimization, i.e., $V_{eff} = V$ always, and the original DrOPS system for dense networks.

5.2 Quality

The *Quality* metric, depicted in Fig. 4, is defined as the fraction of queries in which the QoS-constraints are met out of all queries for which at least one effective reading was received, thus characterizing the data quality a client can expect from the system. Values are averaged over all simulation runs for each number of mobile smartphones.

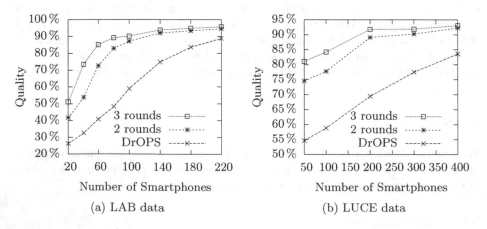

(a) LAB data   (b) LUCE data

Fig. 4. Results for quality metric. Fraction of queries in which the QoS constraints are met.

Under the DrOPS system, quality is good at just under 90 % for both datasets in a dense system, i.e., when using the maximum number of smartphones, but quickly degrades to under 60 % for 100 smartphones or less. Using our adaptive approach, the quality increases to over 90 % in a dense system. Furthermore, it is far more robust to a decreasing number of smartphones. In the LUCE data, for example, using 3 rounds we can still provide 81 % quality using 50 smartphones, whereas using DrOPS requires 400 smartphones to match this quality.

5.3   Broken Queries

Next, we analyze results for the *broken queries* metric, denoting the fraction of queries for which no effective readings were received at the gateway, i.e., characterizing how both approaches perform at finding available v-sensors.

Evaluation results are depicted in Fig. 5. Again, values are averaged over all simulation runs for each number of smartphones. Similar to the quality metric, the number of broken queries using DrOPS drastically increases for a decreasing number of smartphones, while our extended algorithm is much more robust. Under the LAB data, for a single round the fraction of broken queries increases to 5 % for 140 smartphones whereas using 3 rounds, we can provide 7 % of broken queries with only 40 smartphones. For the LUCE data, DrOPS cannot match the fraction of broken queries when using 3 rounds and at least 100 smartphones.

5.4   Relative Energy Consumption

Finally, we use the *relative energy consumption (REC)* metric to characterize the energy consumption. As the absolute energy consumption varies greatly for different time offsets, e.g., due to a varying number of sensing tasks, the REC is computed by normalizing the energy consumption for each node in a simulation

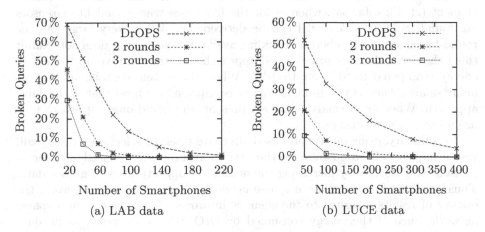

(a) LAB data   (b) LUCE data

Fig. 5. Results for broken queries metric. Fraction of queries for which no effective readings were obtained.

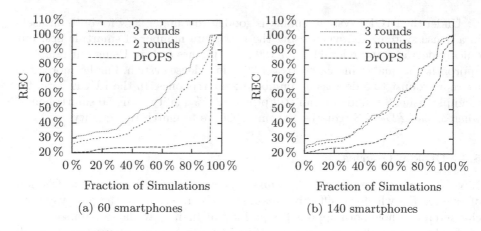

Fig. 6. Cumulated relative energy consumption, LAB data

by the average energy consumption per node using the naive algorithm for the same simulation parameters. Figure 6 shows the cumulated average REC per simulation for the LAB data. Results for the LUCE data are similar and thus not shown due to space constraints. Note that the energy drain is nearly uniformly distributed among all nodes in a simulation. The maximum difference between nodes in a simulation was 14.4 percentage points.

We see that additional communication for additional rounds increases the energy consumption. The difference is greatest in a sparse setting, where few effective readings are collected in early rounds, i.e., most work is done in later rounds. In a denser setting, the difference diminishes, as later rounds add fewer readings and thus less energy is used in later rounds. Note the sharp increase in REC for DrOPS in Fig. 6a. For about 90 % of simulations, hardly any data is collected, i.e., only few available v-sensors are found and thus little energy is spent (cf. Figs. 4a, 5a), whereas for the few cases where available v-sensors are found, only a weak model can be derived, i.e., V_{eff} is very large. As the round-based approach is better at finding available v-sensors, it does not exhibit this behavior. Using our round-based approach, we still can save up to 77 % of energy (compared to 81 % for DrOPS). When the system contains at least as many smartphones as v-sensors, energy consumption is at most that of the naive approach. When fewer smartphones are present, the round-based approach may use up to 6 % more energy.

In summary, using our round-based alternate v-sensor selection strategy will vastly improve the robustness of the system regarding a reduced number of participating devices by increasing the number of opportunities to gather data. Thus, it allows for operation in sparse networks. Even in a dense network, the quality of results returned to the client is improved. Furthermore, in a sparse network much of the energy consumed by DrOPS goes to waste, as no data is obtained for that energy. In the round-based approach, the increased energy consumption results in many more useful data readings and thus less wasted energy. Finally, robustness and result quality further increase when using additional rounds, while the energy cost for using additional rounds only increases when the additional rounds provide an actual benefit.

6   Related Work

The idea of Public Sensing (PS) has spawned a growing research interest over the last few years [3]. To address hardware and software systems challenges, several prototype architectures have been proposed, e.g., [6,7]. However, none of these systems deals with possible optimizations of the data acquisition process.

Reddy et al. analyze past mobility and participation of smartphones to recommend which devices to query in the future [15]. While this might be feasible in sparse networks, it requires long setup times and manual operator intervention.

Several works explored how to increase the efficiency of PS systems. An approach for location-centric task execution at a single v-sensor is proposed by Lu et al. [9] while in our previous work we show how to efficiently sample fixed sensors using mobile smartphones [16] and extend this idea to task execution at multiple v-sensors in parallel [12]. Furthermore, there are extensions for sampling along road segments [17] and updating road-maps [1]. Optimizations presented in these works are targeted at densely populated systems and are limited to individual v-sensors. Mendez et al. showed how a model-driven approach, a well-researched topic in fixed sensor networks [5,8], can improve result quality [10] while we presented how to use the model to optimize large-scale data acquisition in PS [13]. All of these approaches assume densely populated networks. Krause [8] presents an algorithm for selecting most informative v-sensors in the presence of unavailable v-sensors. This algorithm assumes that only a true subset of the selected v-sensors is unavailable, which does not hold in a sparse PS system.

7   Conclusion

In this work, we presented an adaptive extension for a model-driven public sensing system to enable operation in sparse networks, where most v-sensors are unavailable. Model-driven data acquisition systems can reduce the energy consumption of PS systems by requiring fewer effective readings. However, to provide sufficient result quality, a minimum number of effective readings is required. With our extended round-based v-sensor selection algorithm, we can find the required readings even when the majority of v-sensors is unavailable.

Our evaluations show that we can enable the system to work with a greatly reduced number of smartphones and that result quality is improved by up to 41 percentage points. Furthermore, we can save up to 81 % of energy for sensing and communication while providing inferred readings matching an error bound of 1 °C up to 96 % of the time.

In future work we plan to further evaluate our algorithm in a real-world deployment and to extend our approach by including a hybrid 3G/WiFi ad-hoc routing scheme to further reduce energy for communication.

Acknowledgements. This work is partially funded by the German Research Foundation under the ComNSense project (www.comnsense.de).

References

1. Baier, P., Weinschrott, H., Dürr, F., Rothermel, K.: MapCorrect: automatic correction and validation of road maps using public sensing. In: 36th Annual IEEE Conference on Local Computer Networks, Bonn, Germany, October 2011
2. Balasubramanian, N., Balasubramanian, A., Venkataramani, A.: Energy consumption in mobile phones: a measurement study and implications for network applications. In: Proceedings of the 9th ACM SIGCOMM Conference on Internet Measurement, pp. 280–293. ACM, New York (2009)
3. Campbell, A.T., Eisenman, S.B., Lane, N.D., Miluzzo, E., Peterson, R.A., Lu, H., Zheng, X., Musolesi, M., Fodor, K., Ahn, G.-S.: The rise of people-centric sensing. IEEE Internet Comput. **12**(4), 12–21 (2008)
4. Cressie, N.A.C.: Statistics for Spatial Data. Wiley-Interscience, New York (1993)
5. Deshpande, A., Guestrin, C., Madden, S.R., Hellerstein, J.M., Hong, W.: Model-driven data acquisition in sensor networks. In: Proceedings of the 30th International Conference on Very Large Databases, VLDB Endowment, pp. 588–599 (2004)
6. Hull, B., Bychkovsky, V., Zhang, Y., Chen, K., Goraczko, M., Miu, A., Shih, E., Balakrishnan, H., Madden, S.: Cartel: a distributed mobile sensor computing system. In: Proceedings of the 4th International Conference on Embedded Networked Sensor Systems, pp. 125–138. ACM, New York (2006)
7. Kanjo, E., Benford, S., Paxton, M., Chamberlain, A., Fraser, D.S., Woodgate, D., Crellin, D., Woolard, A.: MobGeoSen: facilitating personal geosensor data collection and visualization using mobile phones. Pers. Ubiquit. Comput. **12**, 599–607 (2008)
8. Krause, A.: Optimizing Sensing - Theory and Applications. Ph.D. thesis, Carnegie Mellon University (2008)
9. Lu, H., Lane, N.D., Eisenman, S.B., Campbell, A.T.: Bubble-sensing: binding sensing tasks to the physical world. Pervasive Mob. Comput. **6**(1), 58–71 (2009)
10. Mendez, D., Labrador, M., Ramachandran, K.: Data interpolation for participatory sensing systems. Pervasive Mob. Comput. **9**(1), 132–148 (2013)
11. Nadeau, D., Brutsaert, W., Parlange, M., Bou-Zeid, E., Barrenetxea, G., Couach, O., Boldi, M.-O., Selker, J., Vetterli, M.: Estimation of urban sensible heat flux using a dense wireless network of observations. Environ. Fluid Mech. **9**, 635–653 (2009)
12. Philipp, D., Dürr, F., Rothermel, K.: A sensor network abstraction for flexible public sensing systems. In: Proceedings of the 8th International IEEE Conference on Mobile Ad-hoc and Sensor Systems, pp. 460–469, October 2011
13. Philipp, D., Stachowiak, J., Alt, P., Dürr, F., Rothermel. K.: DrOPS: model-driven optimization for public sensing systems. In: IEEE International Conference on Pervasive Computing and Communications, San Diego, CA, USA, March 2013, pp. 185–192. IEEE Computer Society (2013)
14. Priyantha, B., Lymberopoulos, D., Liu, J.: Eers: Energy efficient responsive sleeping on mobile phones. In: International Workshop on Sensing for App Phones, Zurich, Switzerland (2010)
15. Reddy, S., Estrin, D., Srivastava, M.: Recruitment framework for participatory sensing data collections. In: Floréen, P., Krüger, A., Spasojevic, M. (eds.) Pervasive 2010. LNCS, vol. 6030, pp. 138–155. Springer, Heidelberg (2010)

16. Weinschrott, H., Dürr, F., Rothermel, K.: Efficient capturing of environmental data with mobile RFID readers. In: Proceedings of the 10th International Conference on Mobile Data Management, Washington, DC, USA, 2009, pp. 41–51. IEEE Computer Society (2009)

17. Weinschrott, H., Dürr, F., Rothermel, K.: StreamShaper: coordination algorithms for participatory mobile urban sensing. In: Proceedings of the 7th IEEE International Conference on Mobile Ad-hoc and Sensor Systems, San Francisco, CA, USA, November 2010. IEEE (2010)

An Integrated WSN and Mobile Robot System for Agriculture and Environment Applications

Hong Zhou[1(⊠)], Haixia Qi[2], Thomas M. Banhazi[3], and Tobias Low[1]

[1] Faculty of Engineering and Science,
University of Southern Queensland, Toowoomba, Australia
{hong.zhou, tobias.low}@usq.edu.au
[2] College of Engineering, South China Agriculture University,
Guangzhou, China
qihaixia@scau.edu.cn
[3] National Centre for Engineering in Agriculture (NCEA),
University of Southern Queensland, Toowoomba, Australia
thomas.banhazi@usq.edu.au

Abstract. Agriculture and environment issues are becoming increasingly important and are facing some new challenges. It is believed that wireless Sensor Networks (WSNs) and machine automation are among the key enabling technologies to address these challenging issues. Although extensive research has been conducted on individual technologies, their seamless integration to solve complex environmental problems has not been done before. This paper provides a design concept and some preliminary results for an integrated autonomous monitoring system. The integrated system will provide a powerful and cost-efficient tool for optimal, profitable, and sustainable management of environment and agriculture and thus bring significant social and economic benefits.

Keywords: Wireless sensor networks · Robot localization · Air quality · Environment monitoring · Animal welfare

1 Introduction

Agricultural and environmental issues, such as water shortage, food safety, air quality, climate change, and rising food prices have caused serious global economic and political concerns. Humanity depends on the environment and agriculture for survival. The optimal, profitable, and sustainable management of land, water and air quality is critical. These requirements can be better addressed through using the integrated and established technologies such as Wireless Sensor Networks (WSNs).

WSN has been regarded a disruptive technology by many technology and business analysts. The MIT Technology Review called WSNs one of the ten emerging technologies that will change the world. The Business Week Magazine labeled WSNs one of the 21 most important technologies for the 21st century. If we consider the Internet as connecting human beings through computers, the wireless sensor networks will connect human beings with the physical world. With the advances of microelectronics,

© Institute for Computer Sciences, Social Informatics and Telecommunications Engineering 2014
I. Stojmenovic et al. (Eds.): MOBIQUITOUS 2013, LNICST 131, pp. 30–36, 2014.
DOI: 10.1007/978-3-319-11569-6_3

the intelligent low-cost low-power small sensor nodes can be developed to sense almost anything of human's interest. A sensor network consists of a large of number of sensor nodes which are densely deployed and connected through wireless links in a self-configured and self-organised manner [1, 6]. Such sensor networks would enable numerous new and exciting applications and bring another technology evolutionary wave to penetrate every aspect of our lives (e.g. home, health, environment, military, agriculture, transport, manufactory, entertainment).

Environment, animal and farm monitoring and control are natural applications for WSN. Cheap, smart devices networked through wireless links and connected intimately with the physical environment can enable detailed and localised data collection at scales and resolutions that are difficult or impossible to obtain through traditional instrumentation. Many networked systems have been successful developed for such applications. For example, a ZigBee WSN was designed for the cattle localization in grazing areas [5] and WSN systems were deployed in a wheat field to monitor the soil property, such as soil water-holding capacity, moisture content, bulk density, temperature and salinity [6]. The WSNs have great potential in agriculture as their cost and improved performance compares favourably with traditional wired networks.

This study took air quality monitoring at poultry buildings as a practical example. Environmental quality within livestock buildings can potentially affect the health and welfare of the animals and also the stockmen working in these buildings [2, 3]. The main factors influencing environmental conditions inside livestock buildings include air temperature (AT), relative humidity (RH), ammonia (NH_3), carbon dioxide (CO_2) and airborne dust [11]. Dust concentrations in poultry buildings are usually quite high especially when compared to average dust concentrations measured in pig and cattle buildings [8]. High temperatures in the piggery buildings might affect the appetite and fertility of pigs that can lead to reduction in production efficiency [4]. Therefore, it is very important to control the temperature and relative humidity levels as well as minimise dust concentrations inside livestock buildings to maintain optimal environmental quality.

This paper describes the design and implementation of an integrated system with WSN to address the above environmental and agricultural problem. The system aims to achieve autonomous monitoring of livestock movement, welfare and environmental impact. The system will provide not only a solid base for the development and delivery of air quality control system at large poultry buildings but also a general solution for the domain of applications in environment and farm management. The cost-effective solution that addresses the important agriculture issue will bring significant social and commercial benefits.

2 The System Design and Implementation

A measurement system was designed to utilise a combination of WSN technology and a mobile robot. The system deployed a number of wireless sensor nodes which was evenly distributed in a laboratory building. These sensor nodes continuous collected the environmental data such as temperature and humidity at the interval suitable for the task. A mobile robot/vehicle is deployed to carry the more expensive sensors (such as NH_3 and Co_2) and a wireless gateway. The mobile robot regularly walks through the defined path in the building at a certain interval. The data at the fixed sensor nodes will be uploaded to the mobile gateway when the robot approaches to the closest point to the individual sensors. The fixed sensor nodes not only help collect certain environmental data but also assist the robot to identify its location through the signal strengths during the communications.

The time interval for the fixed sensor nodes deployed in the field can be set at an arbitrary interval (e.g. every 1 h). However, the optimal time interval can be chosen by balancing the need of adequate capture of the environment changes and the energy consumption saving of the sensors. For much less frequent interval based on the requirements (e.g. every 24 h), the mobile vehicle travels along the path around the field to collect the data. When the vehicle is near to one of the nodes, the GW communicates with the node and collects the node's data. These field nodes' data include the environmental AT & RH situation of the building within a 24 h period. The sensors on the mobile vehicle itself also collect the environmental AT & RH data and dust concentration data while the vehicle moves along the given path.

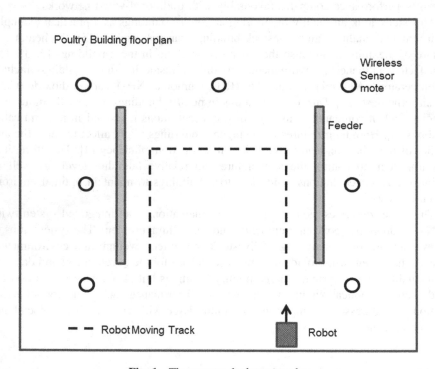

Fig. 1. The system deployment plan

One example of the system is illustrated in Fig. 1. The combined temperature and relative humidity sensors (SHT1X; Manufactured by OFROBOT) and a dust sensor (GP2Y1010AU0F COM-09689, Little Bird company Pty Ltd.) are fixed on the vehicle together with a Crossbow gateway. The fixed sensor motes (Crossbow MPR2400 Motes) included temperature and relative humidity sensors. The gateway (Crossbow,

MIB520CA) was connected to a computer via a USB interface board. The vehicle measurement system structure is shown in Fig. 2.

The system prototype was implemented and experiments were carried out at our labs at Faculty of Engineering at USQ, i.e. Z, Z2, and P12. The same system and experiment methods were used at three different experimental fields to test the instrumentation's accuracy and reliability.

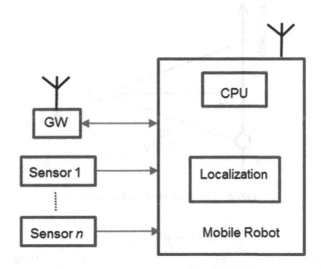

Fig. 2. Mobile robot measurement system

3 Mobile Robot Localisation

Besides the function of measuring the environmental data, the fixed sensor nodes were used in our design to track the movement of the mobile sensor nodes and accurately identify the location of automatic mobile robot. RSSI (Received Signal Strength Indicator) parameter was measured in our experiments to determine the relative distance between the mobile robot and the fixed sensor motes. The conceptual idea behind this is illustrated in Fig. 3.

In the design, it is assumed that the robot moved in a straight line and at a constant speed. The *RSSI(t)* value increased when the robot moved towards the fixed sensor nodes, and the value decreased when the robot moved away from the fixed sensor node. When the RSSI value reaches a minimum point, the environmental data was transmitted to the robot. *RSSI(t)* value is directly related to the distance between the moving robot and fixed nodes. The wireless signal and RSSI may also be affected by the building structure and hardware around the area. However, the distance can be accurately calculated based on some tests during the initial set up at a specific farm and for a specific node. The RSSI value can be recorded and analysed by the localisation function in the microprocessor embedded in the robot.

The experiments with several sensor nodes involved were carried out at level 4 of an office building Z. We collected the data over a period of time with sensors displayed at different distances from the gateway. The average data collected is presented in Table 1. From the results, we observed that the RSSI value decreased as the distance between the fixed sensor nodes and the gateway. However, the RSSI value is not simply the linear function of the distance. As the end node was further away from the gateway, the drops slowed down (Fig. 4).

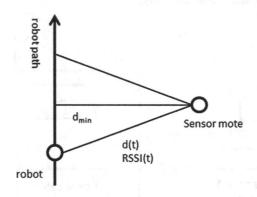

Fig. 3. Localisation of mobile robot

Table 1. Mean RSSI vs. distance

Distance (m)	1 m	5 m	10 m	15 m
RSSI (dbm)	78.6	60.1	49.3	46.6

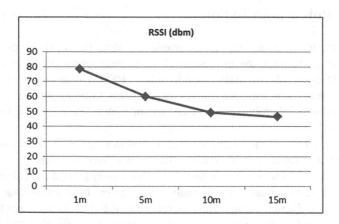

Fig. 4. RSSI value vs. distance between the end node and coordinator

4 Conclusions

In this research, we designed and developed a new environment measurement system for agriculture and environment management applications. The system uses both fixed and mobile wireless sensor motes to automatically monitor the environment. The system can automatically collect the environmental data with high accuracy, flexibility, and reliability. The number of sensors deployed to cover the building and the energy consumption by the sensors can be minimised in our design. In future research, we plan to use a wireless gateway to collect the data from the mobile vehicle to a central workstation and carry out the experiments over larger building areas. Another area of research is to enhance the mobile vehicle localisation function based on the signal from different fixed sensor motes.

Acknowledgements. We would like to acknowledge the assistance of staff at the University of Southern Queensland and the National Centre of Engineering in Agriculture (NCEA). We also would like to acknowledge the financial support from Chinese Scholarship Council (CSC).

References

1. Mainwaring, A., Polastre, J., Szewczyk, R., Culler, D., Anderson, J.: Wireless sensor networks for habitat monitoring. In: The Proceedings of the 1st ACM International Workshop on Wireless Sensor Networks and Applications (2002)
2. Banhazi, T.M., Currie, E., Quartararo, M., Aarnink, A.J.A.: Controlling the concentrations of airborne pollutants in broiler buildings. In: Aland, A., Madec, F. (eds.) Sustainable Animal Production: The Challenges and Potential Developments for Professional Farming, pp. 347–364. Wageningen Academic Publishers, Wageningen (2009)
3. Banhazi, T.M., Currie, E., Reed, S., Lee, I.-B., Aarnink, A.J.A.: Controlling the concentrations of airborne pollutants in piggery buildings. In: Aland, A., Madec, F. (eds.) Sustainable Animal Production: The Challenges and Potential Developments for Professional Farming, pp. 285–311. Wageningen Academic Publishers, Wageningen (2009)
4. Chang, C.W., Chung, H., Huang, C.F., Su, H.J.J.: Exposure of workers to airborne microorganisms in open-air swine houses. Appl. Environ. Microbiol. **67**(1), 155–161 (2001). doi:10.1128/AEM.67.1.155-161
5. Huircán, J.I., Muñoz, C., Young, H., Von Dossow, L., Bustos, J., Vivallo, G., Toneatti, M.: Zigbee-based wireless sensor network localization for cattle monitoring in grazing fields. Comput. Electron. Agric. **74**(2), 258–264 (2010). doi:10.1016/j.compag
6. Karl, H., Willing, A.: Protocols and Architectures for Wireless Sensor Networks. John Wiley and Sons Ltd., New York (2005)
7. Li, Z., Wang, N., Franzen, A., Taher, P., Godsey, C., Zhang, H., Li, X.: Practical deployment of an in-field soil property wireless sensor network. Comput. Stan. & Interfaces (2011). doi:10.1016/j.csi.2011.05.003
8. Takai, H., Pedersen, S., Johnsen, J.O., Metz, J.H.M., Groot Koerkamp, P.W.G., Uenk, G.H., Phillips, V.R., Holden, M.R., Sneath, R.W., Short, J.L., White, R.P., Hartung, J., Seedorf, J., Schro der, M., Linkert, K.H., Wathes, C.M.: Concentrations and emissions of airborne dust in livestock buildings in northern europe. J. agric. Engng Res. **70**, 59–77 (1998)

9. Tian, J., Shi, H., Guo, W., Zhou, Y.: A RSSI-based location system in coal mine. In: 2008 China-Japan Joint Microwave Conference, pp. 167–171 (2008)
10. Wang, N., Zhang, N., Wang, M.: Wireless sensors in agriculture and food industry—recent development and future perspective. Comput. Electron. Agric. **50**(1), 1–14 (2008). doi:10. 1016/j.compag.2005.09.003
11. Wathes, C.M., Phillips, V.R., Holden, M.R., Sneath, R.W., Short, J.L., White, R.P., Hartung, J., Seedorf, J., Schroder, M., Linkert, K.H., Pedersen, S., Takai, H., Johnsen, J.O., Groot Koerkamp, P.W.G., Uenk, G.H., Metz, J.H.M., Hinz, T., Caspary, V., Linke, S.: Emission of aerial pollutants in livestock buildings in northern europe: Overview of a multinational project. J. Agric. Eng. Res. **70**(1), 3–9 (1998)

Sensor Deployment in Bayesian Compressive Sensing Based Environmental Monitoring

Chao Wu$^{(\boxtimes)}$, Di Wu, Shulin Yan, and Yike Guo

Imperial College London, London SW7 2AZ, UK
{chao.wu,di.wu11,shu.yan09,y.guo}@imperial.ac.uk

Abstract. Sensor networks play crucial roles in the environmental monitoring. So far, the large amount of resource consumption in traditional sensor networks has been a huge challenge for environmental monitoring. Compressive sensing (CS) provides us a method to significantly decrease the number of sensors needed and Bayesian compressive sensing (BCS) makes it possible to deploy sensors selectively rather than randomly. By deploying sensors to the most informative places, we expect to reduce the reconstruction errors further compared with random sensor deployment. In this paper we employ multiple sensor deployment algorithms and BCS based signal recovery algorithm to build novel environmental monitoring systems, in which the environmental signals can be recovered accurately with undersampled measurements. Besides, we apply these environmental monitoring models to ozone data experiments to evaluate them and compare their performance. The results show a significant improvement in the recovery accuracy from random sensor deployment to selective sensor deployment. With 100 measurements for 16641 data points, the reconstruction error of one of the sensor deployment approaches was 40 % less than that of random sensor deployment, with 3.52 % and 6.08 % respectively.

Keywords: Environmental monitoring · Compressive sensing · Sensor networks · Sparse Bayesian learning

1 Introduction

Since the ozone depletion in Antarctic was found in 1985, environmental issues have been drawing global attentions. Environmental monitoring can be used to estimate the future environmental impacts and evaluate the performance of strategies designed to mitigate environmental damage.

As the main approaches to monitor environment signals, sensor networks play important roles in signal sampling phases. However, the enormous cost for the sensors has been hampering the development of environmental monitoring in many countries. Even a single sensor station could be very expensive for some specific environmental signals [7]. In such cases, compressive sensing, which allows sensing at rates much smaller than the Nyquist-Shannon limit and reconstructing the signal without much loss [1, 2, 15], can be applied to decrease the number of the sensors needed and recover the monitored signal accurately.

Where to deploy the sensors and how to recover the environmental signals based on the measurements are two fundamental but crucial tasks in environmental monitoring.

© Institute for Computer Sciences, Social Informatics and Telecommunications Engineering 2014
I. Stojmenovic et al. (Eds.): MOBIQUITOUS 2013, LNICST 131, pp. 37–51, 2014.
DOI: 10.1007/978-3-319-11569-6_4

In our previous work, we applied Bayesian compressive sensing (BCS) techniques to environmental monitoring and built a novel environmental monitoring system with random sensor deployments [3]. The reconstruction error was less than 5 % with the number of used sensors no more than 1 % of all possible sensor places in the ozone monitoring experiments presented in [3]. In this paper, we attempt to decrease the reconstruction errors further by deploying sensors to the most informative places. To be specific, we combine different sensor deployment algorithms with Bayesian compressive sensing based signal recovery algorithm to build the environmental monitoring systems and evaluate their performance by ozone monitoring experiments.

Both open-loop and closed-loop sensor deployment algorithms are involved in this paper. Open-loop means that the deployment of the sensors and sampling phase are separated, while closed-loop (adaptive) means that the sampling phase and the deployment of sensors are implemented simultaneously, i.e. the two processes are interrelated. The experiment results show significant improvements in reconstruction accuracy using adaptive BCS sensor deployment algorithms.

The remainder of the paper is organised as follows. In Sect. 2, we consider the environmental monitoring problem as a linear regression problem and introduce the Bayesian learning algorithm to solve it. This is also the algorithm to reconstruct environmental signals based on sensor measurements. In Sect. 3, we introduce open-loop sensor deployment algorithms with different criteria, such as entropy criterion and mutual information criterion, and how they can be used in environmental monitoring. An adaptive compressive sensing approach to deploy sensors is also presented in Sect. 3. In Sect. 4, we evaluate how well these sensor deployment algorithms perform with respect to their reconstruction errors in ozone monitoring experiments. Conclusions and future work are presented in Sect. 5.

2 Bayesian Compressive Sensing Based Environmental Monitoring

In this section we will briefly introduce the method to reconstruct environmental signals based on the sensor measurements. This signal recovery algorithm is also the one used in the environmental monitoring system presented in [3].

We consider the monitoring of ozone as an example. Given all the ozone data in a monitored region, these values can be aggregated into an n by 1 vector X_r. X_r represents the instant ozone distribution in this region. The goal in environmental monitoring is to recover X_r with the measurements of a limited number of sensors. The reconstruction of the signal X_r can be summed up as solving a linear regression problem as follow:

$$Y_{m \times 1} = \varnothing X_r + e = \Theta_{m \times n} w_{n \times 1} + e \qquad (1)$$

where $Y_{m \times 1}$ is an m by 1 vector (m $\ll$ n) stands for the sensor measurements, $\Theta = \varnothing B$ is the projection matrix, B is a fixed Basis matrix, $\varnothing$ is the sampling matrix, w is the sparse weights to be estimated, and e are the zero-mean Gaussian distributed noises in the measurements. The measurement/sampling matrix ϕ represents the sensor locations to observe the ozone signal. Each row in the sampling matrix $\emptyset$ is exactly a unit vector with only one non-zero element in it. In this way, $\emptyset X_r$ is an m by 1 vector composed of the observed values of the sensors.

Compressive sensing is a technique for estimating sparse solutions to underdetermined linear regression. Only when w is sparse (whose elements are mostly zeros) will the estimate of w be feasible and accurate [15]. It is reasonable to assume that most environmental signals are sparse under Gaussian Kernel basis B. Thus, the algorithm is executed by decomposing the original environmental signal X_r as $X_r = Bw$, and the reconstructed signal X can be recovered by multiplying the basis matrix B and w. The Gaussian basis matrix $B_{n\times n}$ is defined as follow:

$$B = [\Psi(X_{r1})\Psi(X_{r2}) \cdots \Psi(X_m)]^T \tag{2}$$

wherein $\Psi(X_{ri}) = [K(X_{ri}, X_{r1}) \cdots K(X_{ri}, X_m)]$ and $K(X_{ri}, X_{rj})$ is Gaussian Kernel function

$$K(X_{ri}, X_{rj}) = \exp\left\{-\eta_1(X_{ri1}, -X_{rj1})^2 - \eta_2(X_{ri2} - X_{rj2})^2\right\} \tag{3}$$

where η_1 and η_2 are hyper-parameters of the kernel function, and the coordinates of X_{ri} is (X_{ri1}, X_{ri2}).

Generally speaking, we have l_p minimization [5], greedy/iterative algorithms and some other algorithms, such as the model based CS [6] and Bayesian compressive sensing, to reconstruct the signal in CS. Bayesian compressive sensing is proposed by Shihao Ji in 2008 [10] to estimate the sparse vector $w_{n\times 1}$ in (1), in which Bayesian models are applied to maximise the posterior probability of $w_{n\times 1}$.

BCS recovery algorithm combines hierarchical sparseness priors for $w_{n\times 1}$ and e [10] with Relevance Vector Machine (RVM) based Bayesian CS inversion [13] to estimate $w_{n\times 1}$. Given $Y_{m\times 1}$ and $\Theta_{m\times n}$, we estimate α and σ_0^2 that are the hyper-parameters in Gaussian priors for $w_{n\times 1}$ and e [10] by maximising $P(w|y, \alpha, \sigma_0^2)$, and then the sparse vector w can be determined. Moreover, the BCS recovery algorithm used in this paper employs a fast sparse Bayesian learning algorithm to improve the computational speed. The detailed processes in this fast algorithm can be referred in [14]. Compared with other recovery algorithms in compressive sensing, BCS provides the posterior density function for $w_{n\times 1}$ instead of a point estimate of w. This property enables us to indicate the measure of confidence of the reconstructed signal with the "error bars" provided by BCS. Furthermore, the construction of the sampling matrix $\emptyset$ can be diversified in BCS, which means different sensor deployment strategies can be employed in BCS rather than deploying the sensors randomly.

3 Sensor Deployment

In this section, we will present one of the crucial tasks in environmental monitoring, i.e. how to deploy the sensors to the most informative places. The following subsections identify two open-loop sensor deployment algorithms that deploy sensors before the sampling phases and one adaptive sensor deployment algorithm that deploys sensors during the sampling phases.

3.1   Open-Loop Entropy Approach

Given some sensors that have been deployed in the monitored region, we consider the case that we want to deploy another sensor and hope to achieve the best recovery accuracy with the BCS recovery algorithm. Intuitively, we can deploy the sensor to the place with the highest uncertainty.

"Entropy" is a widely used measure of the uncertainty in the information theory and many other areas. In this open-loop entropy approach, the "entropies" of all possible sensor places are calculated and we deploy the next sensor to the place with the highest entropy. We denote y as one of all possible sensor places, A as the set of the places that have been sensed and X_y as the sensor measurement at place y. The entropy in this approach is defined as follow:

$$H(X_y|X_A) = \frac{1}{2}\log\left(2\pi e \sigma^2_{X_y|X_A}\right)$$ (4)

where $\sigma^2_{X_y|X_A} = \Sigma_{yy} - \Sigma_{yA}\Sigma_{AA}^{-1}\Sigma_{Ay}$ [11] is the variance of X_y given X_A and Σ_{ij} is a measure of the information redundancy between place i and place j.

There are many methods to define Σ_{ij} so far [11]. The most commonly used method is to define Σ_{ij} as a Gaussian function that decreases exponentially with the distance between place i and place j. As the distance between y and A increases so does the value of $H(X_y|X_A)$. Thus, far apart places tend to give high entropies. In this way, the sensor deployments can be estimated by maximising $\sigma^2_{X_y|X_A}$ repeatedly.

3.2   Open-Loop Mutual Information Approach

The entropy criterion presented in Sect. 3.1 tends to place sensors along the boundary of the monitored region [11]. Thus, a sensor on the boundary cannot detect the signals out of the region and may waste sensed information. The phenomenon was noticed by Ramakrishnan in 2005 [8].

Andreas Krause presented in [9] that the mutual information (MI) criterion can be applied to solve the problem. The mutual information of a possible sensor place y is defined as follow:

$$MI(y) = H(X_y|X_A) - H(X_y|X_{V\backslash A}) = \frac{1}{2}\log\left(\frac{\sigma^2_{X_y|X_A}}{\sigma^2_{X_y|X_{V\backslash A}}}\right)$$ (5)

where A is the set of the places that have been sensed and V is the set of all possible sensor places.

In this approach, we maximise the mutual information criterion shown in Eq. (5) to estimate the optimal sensor places. The place y with the highest MI(y) is the optimal place to deploy the next sensor based on the set of former sensor places A. This equation is sub modular style and it avoids the problem deploying sensors along the boundaries by subtracting the uncertainty of place y given V\A from the entropy $H(X_y|X_A)$. We will evaluate its performance in Sect. 4.

3.3 Adaptive BCS Approach

Bayesian compressive sensing (BCS) provides us the "error bars" to measure the uncertainty of the reconstructed signal [10]. This property enables us to adaptively estimate the optimal next projection to be added into the measurement matrix. In this way, our measurement matrix is designed based on former measurements and the recovery accuracy could be improved compared with other methods.

Selecting Projections Adaptively. The sparse weights vector w is actually a multi-variate Gaussian distribution with the mean μ and covariance matrix Σ [11]. In [10], Shihao Ji proposed to design the projection matrix Θ to minimise the differential entropy [12] $h(X) = -\int P(X) \log P(X)dX$ for the reconstructed signal $X = Bw$. To deploy a new sensor is equivalent to adding a new row on the projection matrix. If we add a new projection τ on Θ, where τ^T is a new row, and we want to minimise the $h(X)$, it has been proven in [10] that the goal is equivalent to maximising the $\tau^T\Sigma\tau$.

$$\tau^T\Sigma\tau = \tau^T\text{Covariance}(w)\tau \cong \text{Variance}(Y) \qquad (6)$$

We can conclude from (6) that the τ^T to be added into Θ represents the most informative measurement. $\tau^T\Sigma\tau$ is equivalent to a measure of the "information gain" in our case.

Given the environmental monitoring problem shown as Eq. (1), the projection matrix $\Theta = \phi B$ is actually choosing rows from basis matrix B and we aim to choose the optimal row from B one by one to build the Θ and minimise $\tau^T\Sigma\tau$.

In this case, τ^T is a row in B. The measure of how informative τ^T is can be then be described as follows:

$$\text{next}_{\text{score}}(i) = \tau^T\Sigma\tau = a^T B\Sigma Ba = B_a^T\Sigma B_a \qquad (7)$$

where a^T is a 1 by n unit vector in which the i-th element is one and B_a^T is the i-th row of the basis matrix B.

This adaptive sensor deployment algorithm uses the measurements of deployed sensors as the feedbacks to help guide the deployment of the next sensor. Thus, the information Moreover, the approach greedily takes the current estimated variances as the criterion to optimising sensor deployments. Thus, the results of this method may not be absolutely optimal.

The Computational Model. Compared with non-adaptive BCS approach, the main difference is that our adaptive BCS approach first builds a random small projection matrix to do initial measurements, and then we add measurements gradually based on the feedback of former measurements. With the same number of measurements, the adaptive method improves the recovery accuracy by designing the projection matrix selectively instead of randomly. Figure 1 shows the work flow of the adaptive BCS.

There are three phases in the adaptive BCS environmental monitoring model, which are sampling, recovery and reconstruction. The three phases are detailed as follows:

1. Sampling phase: We sample the environmental signal with the sampling/sensing matrix, in which sensor deployment information is contained. An initial sensor deployment consisted of few random sensor places is generated to start the work flow shown in Fig. 1.
2. Recovery phase: We estimate the sparse vector w and its covariance matrix with the BCS technique. Then we estimate the next sensor location with the method described in this section and revise the sampling matrix. We run the sampling-recovery loop until termination condition is met.
3. Reconstruction phase: The monitored signal can be reconstructed via a simple matrix multiplication X = Bw.

In the adaptive BCS approach, the sensor deployment phase and sampling phase are implemented simultaneously. This property of the adaptive BCS environmental monitoring model may bring difficulties to practical engineering. Thus, we propose to train the sensor locations with history data. This history data based adaptive BCS approach will be discussed in Sect. 4.3.

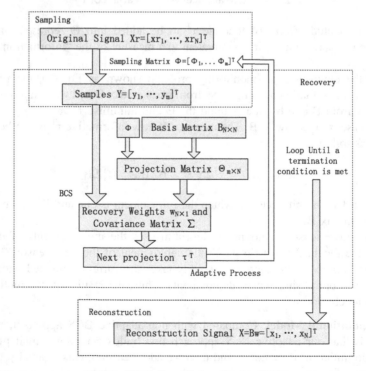

Fig. 1. Work flow of the adaptive BCS

4   Experiment and Results

With the open-loop sensor deployment algorithms and the adaptive BCS approach presented in Sect. 3, the sensors are deployed selectively rather than randomly in the monitoring systems. Thus, we expect to achieve better recovery accuracy than the environmental monitoring system proposed in [3].

To evaluate these monitoring models, we applied different sensor deployment algorithms to ozone monitoring experiments and compare their performance. We mainly introduce the environmental monitoring tests on two different sizes of ozone signals and analyse the performance of the history data based adaptive BCS approach. The ozone distribution data can be retrieved from the database of NASA and is available at ftp://toms.gsfc.nasa.gov/pub/eptoms/data/monthly_averages/ozone. The ozone data sets used in our experiments are monthly averages data sets that are merely the daily ozone values for an entire month divided by the number of days. The discussion of the experiment results is shown in Sect. 4.4.

4.1   30 by 30 Ozone Distribution Monitoring

To compare the performance of the sensor deployment algorithms presented in Sect. 3, we apply these algorithms to a 30 by 30 ozone distribution monitoring experiment in this subsection. The original ozone distribution data we need to recover is a part of the global ozone distribution map available from NASA. It is a 30 by 30 ozone distribution in Feb 2005 (Latitudes 36.5 North to 65.5 North with 1 degree step and Longitudes 179.375 West to 143.125 West with 1.25 degree steps).

The proposed adaptive Bayesian compressive sensing algorithm in the ozone data experiment is as follow:

1. Randomly choose 30 rows from B to build the projection matrix Θ and run the BCS recovery algorithm [13, 14].
2. Calculate the next_scores shown in Eq. (7) for all the rows in B that are not in Θ so far. Add the row that corresponds with the largest next_score to Θ.
3. Run the BCS recovery algorithm with the new Θ.
4. If the termination condition is met, otherwise goto 2.
5. Reconstruct the signal with Basis matrix B and the sparse weights vector w.

In Fig. 2(a) and (b) show the deployment of 60 sensors with entropy criterion and mutual information criterion respectively in this experiment.

It can be seen from Fig. 2 that the number of the boundary sensors in (b) is significantly less than that in (a). The mutual information criterion solves the problem that entropy criterion tends to deploy sensors along boundaries very well.

The reconstruction errors of different approaches can be seen in Fig. 3. The adaptive BCS approach and the open-loop entropy approach perform the best in this experiment. It can also be seen that the mutual information criterion performs no better than the entropy criterion.

Both entropy criterion and mutual information criterion are open-loop approaches. Thus, the whole sensor deployment tasks in these two approaches are completed before

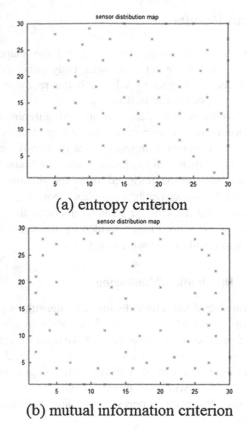

(a) entropy criterion

(b) mutual information criterion

Fig. 2. The sensor distribution map of entropy criterion and mutual information criterion (60 sensors)

measurements. Although mutual information criterion prevents deploying too many sensors on the boundary, we cannot say one criterion is dominating the other one in terms of their recovery accuracies.

4.2   129 by 129 Ozone Distribution Monitoring

In order to adequately bear out the recovery accuracies brought by the sensor deployment algorithms, we apply these algorithms to a 129 by 129 ozone distribution monitoring experiment in this subsection. Compared with the experiment in Sect. 4.1, this experiment is implemented upon an ozone dataset with much larger resolution. The performance of these environmental monitoring models when dealing with massive environmental signals can be evaluated through this experiment typically. Figure 4 shows the original ozone distribution map that we need to recover.

A comparison of the reconstructed signals with the random sensor deployment approach and the adaptive BCS approach can be seen in Fig. 5 (100 sensors).

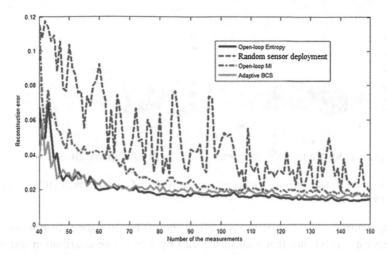

Fig. 3. Comparison of the reconstruction errors of different approaches

It can be seen from Fig. 5 that the reconstructed signal with adaptive sensor deployment is much closer to the original one compared with random sensor deployment. The adaptive BCS approach can improve the signal recovery accuracy of the environmental monitoring system significantly.

A comparison of the reconstruction errors with different approaches can be seen in Fig. 6.

It is shown in Fig. 6 that the adaptive BCS performs the best among the three approaches. Its properties are especially suitable for monitoring environmental signals with few sensors.

It is worthwhile to point out that the open-loop approaches depend heavily on the definitions of $\sigma^2_{X_y|X_A}$ shown in Eqs. (4) and (5). The hyper-parameters in $\sigma^2_{X_y|X_A}$ will greatly affect the performance of the algorithms. With same hyper-parameters, the

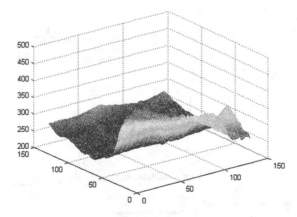

Fig. 4. A 129 by 129 ozone distribution in Feb 2005 (Latitudes 62.5 South to 65.5 North with 1 degree step and Longitudes 179.375 West to 19.375 West with 1.25 degree steps)

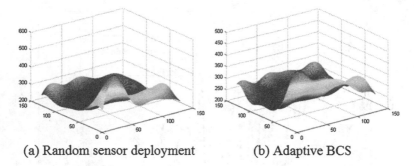

(a) Random sensor deployment   (b) Adaptive BCS

Fig. 5. The reconstructed signals with conventional BCS and adaptive BCS (100 sensors used, based on Fig. 4)

open-loop entropy approach performs well in the 30 by 30 ozone distribution monitoring experiment, but not that well in the 129 by 129 ozone distribution monitoring experiment.

Furthermore, the computational complexities for open-loop approaches are generally very high, especially when the set of all possible sensor places V is very large. This is also the reason that we do not have the reconstruction error curve for the open-loop mutual information approach in Fig. 6.

4.3   Ozone Monitoring with History Data

Adaptive BCS approach has achieved good performance in our experiments. It is a closed-loop approach that bases on real observed values. That means the sensor locations are closely related to the measurements. The sensor places will be changed if the monitored environmental signal changes. In the real phenomena monitoring industry, the environmental signals are always changing and this will bring difficulties to the adaptive BCS approach.

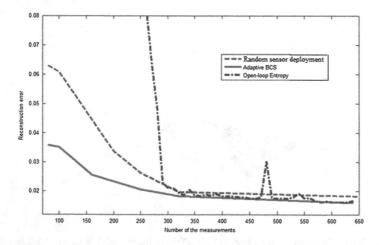

Fig. 6. Comparison of the reconstruction errors with three different approaches (Based on Fig. 4)

On the other hand, it is impossible that a fixed sensor deployment works very well for all environmental signals. If the sensor deployment cannot be changed adaptively, what we can do is to find a fixed sensor deployment that generally works well or deploy more sensors.

If the history dataset is similar to the test dataset, the sensor deployment trained by the history data would work also very well for the test data in general. In the real world, a signal usually changes little if the time does not change a lot. Thus, applying the sensor deployment trained by the latest data to the environmental monitoring tasks will work, especially for the environmental signals such as ozone signals that change slowly.

In this subsection, we train the sensor placements with the adaptive BCS approach based on an ozone data of February 2005 and test it on the ozone data of March 2005. Moreover, we will compare its performance with other approaches.

The training data and test data is shown in Fig. 7.

Figure 8(a) shows the reconstructed ozone signal with the sensor deployment trained by Fig. 7(a), and Fig. 8(b) shows the reconstructed ozone signal with the sensor deployment trained by Fig. 7 (b).

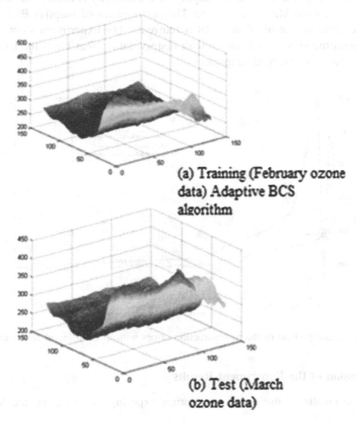

(a) Training (February ozone data) Adaptive BCS algorithm

(b) Test (March ozone data)

Fig. 7. Training ozone data and test ozone data

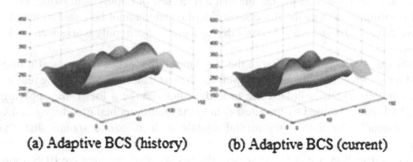

(a) Adaptive BCS (history)   (b) Adaptive BCS (current)

Fig. 8. The reconstructed ozone distributions with different approaches (150 sensors used)

It can be seen from Fig. 8 that the adaptive BCS (history) approach performs even better than adaptive BCS (current) approach in terms of the recovery accuracies.

The curves of the reconstruction errors with three different sensor deployments are illustrated in Fig. 9.

It is shown in Fig. 9 that the sensor deployment trained by February ozone data also works very well for the March ozone data. The performance of adaptive BCS (history) is nearly the same as that of adaptive BCS (current). The experiment shows that our strategy to train the sensor deployment with history data is feasible if the locations of the sensors cannot be changed adaptively.

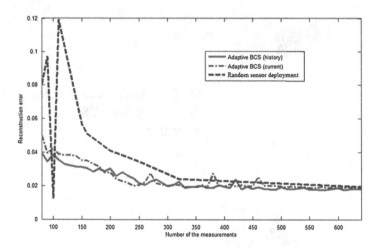

Fig. 9. A comparison of the reconstruction errors with three different approaches

4.4 Discussion of the Experiment Results

Based on the results of the ozone monitoring experiments, we have the following discussion:

Open-loop entropy and mutual information: In our experiments, open-loop approaches perform well with proper hyper-parameters. We used the same hyper-parameters in Sects. 4.1 and 4.2. Based on our experiment results, we believe that adjusting the hyper-parameters carefully in Sect. 4.2 will improve the performance of the open-loop entropy approach further. Adaptive algorithms for adjusting the parameters can be investigated in the future.

Mutual information can solve the problem that entropy criterion tends to place sensors along the boundaries and avoid the "information wasting" of the sensors in many cases. However, mutual information does not perform better than entropy criterion in terms of the reconstruction error.

The computational complexities of the open-loop approaches are generally very high. We built a truncated algorithm by ignoring the influence between far apart sensors (removing the small elements in the Σ presented in Sect. 3.1) [11] and applied it to our experiments. We also did not calculate Eqs. (4) and (5) for all possible sensor places, but for selected places. Although these approaches had been used in our experiments, the computational complexities were still very high. This problem is particularly acute in dealing with massive environmental signals.

Adaptive compressive sensing approach: Adaptive BCS environmental monitoring model generally performs the best in our experiments. With this environmental monitoring model, we do not need to worry about the hyper-parameters and computational complexities. Thus, adaptive BCS based sensor deployment algorithm is more applicable compared with other sensor deployment algorithm.

Sometimes the sensors cannot be placed adaptively for practical purposes. We proposed to use the adaptive BCS approach to train the sensor placements with the latest history data. The results of our experiments validated the feasibility of this approach.

5 Conclusions and Future Work

The environmental monitoring task can be generalised as a problem to solve the equation $Y_{m \times 1} = \Theta_{m \times n} w_{n \times 1} + e = \varnothing_{m \times n} B_{n \times n} w_{n \times 1} + e$. We applied different sensor deployment algorithms and BCS based signal recovery algorithm to environmental monitoring and compare their properties. Their performance was tested under different ozone data resolutions.

It can be seen that compression degree was even lower for larger environmental signals. Generally speaking, compressive sensing is particularly suitable for decreasing the number of the samples needed in the monitoring of massive environmental signals.

The performance of open-loop design methods can be very well with proper hyper-parameters. Thus, scholars have been trying to design better definitions for the variances in the open-loop sensor deployment algorithms to improve their performance, such as nonstationary covariance matrices proposed by Nott [4]. However, the high complexities of the open-loop approaches presented in this paper are hampering these algorithms. Truncated algorithms can be applied to reduce the complexity of open-loop design approaches to some extent, but the problem has not been resolved satisfactorily so far. How to adjust the hyper-parameters adaptively is also a research direction remained to be developed in the future.

Given the measurements of placed sensors, the mechanism of the adaptive Bayesian compressive sensing approach can be explained as deploying the next sensor to the place with the highest estimated variance. With 100 measurements for 16641 global ozone distribution data points, the reconstruction error of adaptive sensor deployment approach was 40 % less than that of random sensor deployment, with 3.52 % and 6.08 % respectively. We then presented the feasibility to train the sensor placements by the adaptive BCS approach with history data and evaluated its performance with experiments. This approach works well especially for steady environmental signals such as ozone.

The adaptive BCS approach generally performed very well in our experiments. It is a greedy algorithm to choose the next sensor location based on current measurements. Sensors are deployed one by one with this algorithm. Thus, the final sensor deployment of this approach may not be global optimal solution. Inspired by the history data based adaptive BCS approach, we may combine the history data to restrict the "score" in the Eq. (7) to improve its performance further. To be specific, we may ignore the places that have been proved to contribute less in the monitoring of history data.

We will apply our environmental monitoring system to real environmental monitoring industries in the future. A lot of unveiled problems in our experiments will appear in environmental monitoring industries. For example, there will be a lot of locations that are not physically reachable in the real world. Furthermore, the world is a multiple dimensions world rather than two dimensions in the experiments, thus where to localise the sensors in the real world becomes a problem. The accuracy of the GPS system will also affect the accuracies of sensor placements.

Acknowledgments. This work is partially supported by the Guangdong Innovation Group Project from Guangdong Government of China.

References

1. Candès, E.J., Romberg, J., Tao, T.: Stable signal recovery from incomplete and inaccurate measurements. Comm. Pure Appl. Math. **59**, 1207–1223 (2006)
2. Donoho, D.L.: Compressed sensing. IEEE Trans. Inf. Theor. **52**(4), 1289–1306 (2006)
3. Yan, S., Wu, C., Dai, W., Ghanem, M., Guo, Y.: Environmental monitoring via compressive sensing. In: Proceedings of the SensorKDD'12 Sixth International Workshop on Knowledge Discovery from Sensor Data, 12–16 August 2012, Beijing, China, pp. 61–68 (2012)
4. Nott, D.J., Dunsmuir, W.T.M.: Estimation of nonstationary spatial covariance structure. Biometrika **89**, 819–829 (2002)
5. Candès, E.J., Braun, N., Wakin, M.B.: Sparse signal and image recovery from compressive samples. ISBI **2007**, 976–979 (2007)
6. Baraniuk, R., Cevher, V., Duarte, M.F., Hegde, C.: Model-based compressive sensing. IEEE Trans. Inf. Theor. **56**(4), 1982–2001 (2010)
7. Ingelrest, F., Barrenetxea, G., Schaefer, G., Vetterli, M., Couach, O., Parlange, M.: SensorScope: application-specific sensor network for environmental monitoring. TOSN **6**(2) (2010)

8. Ramakrishnan, N., Bailey-Kellogg, C., Tadepalli, S., Pandey, V.N.: Gaussian processes for active data mining of spatial aggregates. In: SIAM Data Mining (2005)
9. Caselton, W.F., Zidek, J.V.: Optimal monitoring network designs. Stat. Probab. Lett. **2**(4), 223–227 (1984)
10. Ji, S., Xue, Y., Carin, L.: Bayesian compressive sensing. IEEE Trans. Signal Process. **56**(6), 2346–2356 (2008)
11. Krause, A., Singh, A.P., Guestrin, C.: Near-optimal sensor placements in gaussian processes: theory, efficient algorithms and empirical studies. J. Mach. Learn. Res. **9**, 235–284 (2008)
12. Cover, T.M., Thomas, J.A.: Elements of Information Theory. Wiley, New York (1991)
13. Tipping, M.E.: Sparse Bayesian learning and the relevance vector machine. J. Mach. Learn. Res. **1**, 211–244 (2001)
14. Tipping, M.E., Faul, A.C.: Fast marginal likelihood maximisation for sparse Bayesian models. In: Bishop, C.M., Frey, B.J. (eds.) Proceedings of the Ninth International Workshop on Artificial Intelligence and Statistics, Key West, FL, 3–6 January 2003
15. Davenport, M.A., Duarte, M.F., Eldar, Y.C., Kutyniok, G.: Introduction to Compressed Sensing. In: Eldar, Y., Kutyniok, G. (eds.) Compressed Sensing: Theory and Applications. Cambridge University Press, Cambridge (2011)

A Mobile Agents Control Scheme
for Multiple Sinks in Dense Mobile Wireless
Sensor Networks

Keisuke Goto, Yuya Sasaki, Takahiro Hara$^{(\boxtimes)}$, and Shojiro Nishio

Department of Multimedia Engineering,
Graduate School of Information Science and Technology,
Osaka University, Yamadaoka 1-5, Suita-shi, Osaka, Japan
{goto.keisuke,sasaki.yuya,hara,nishio}@ist.osaka-u.ac.jp

Abstract. In Mobile Wireless Sensor Networks (MWSNs) where mobile sensor nodes densely exist, it is desirable to gather sensor data from the minimum number of sensor nodes which are necessary to guarantee the sensing coverage in order to reduce communication traffic. In the past, we have proposed a data gathering method using mobile agents in dense MWSNs. However, since this method assumes that only one sink is present in a network, it cannot effectively reduce traffic in environments where multiple sinks exist. In this paper, we propose a mobile agents control scheme which guarantees multiple sinks' coverages and efficiently gathers sensor data. In the proposed method, mobile agents are communalized if their sensing points overlap, and sensor data are aggregated to transmit them to same direction.

Keywords: Mobile wireless sensor networks · Data gathering · Mobile agent

1 Introduction

Recently, *participatory sensing* by ordinary people having mobile sensor nodes such as PDA and smart phones with sensor devices has attracted much attention [3,7]. In mobile wireless sensor networks (MWSNs) for participatory sensing, the number of sensor nodes is generally very large, and thus, there are basically many sensor nodes that can sense (cover) a geographical point in the entire sensing area (i.e., dense MWSNs). From the perspective of applications, a lot of same sensor data are not useful, but just waste limited network resource of communication bandwidth. Rather, applications require a certain geographical granularity of sensing in most cases. To reduce the data traffic for data gathering, it is desirable to effectively and reliably gather sensor data so that the geographical granularity required from an application can be guaranteed with the minimum number of sensor nodes.

In [4], we have proposed a data gathering method that efficiently gathers sensor data by using *mobile agents* which control sensor nodes' transmission of

© Institute for Computer Sciences, Social Informatics and Telecommunications Engineering 2014
I. Stojmenovic et al. (Eds.): MOBIQUITOUS 2013, LNICST 131, pp. 52–65, 2014.
DOI: 10.1007/978-3-319-11569-6_5

sensor data. A mobile agent is an application software that autonomously operates on a sensor node and moves between sensor nodes. This method reduces traffic for gathering sensor data since the number of sensor nodes that transmit sensor data is minimized by mobile agents. However, this method cannot effectively reduce traffic in environments where multiple sinks gather sensor data based on different conditions (e.g., gathering cycle and geographical granularity) each other, because this method basically assumes only one sink gathering sensor data, and thus when multiple sinks are present, each sink respectively deploys mobile agents and separately gathers sensor data.

In this paper, we propose a mobile agents control scheme to guarantee the sensing coverages designated by multiple sinks and efficiently gather the sensor data. In the proposed method, mobile agents are communalized if sensing points overlap, and sensor data are aggregated to transmit to some sinks which locate in the same direction. We verify that the proposed method achieves small traffic while keeping high delivery ratio, through extensive simulation experiments.

The remainder of this paper is organized as follows. In Sect. 2, we introduce related work. In Sect. 3, we describe assumptions in this paper. In Sect. 4, we explain the details of our proposed method. In Sect. 5, we show the results of the simulation experiments. Finally, in Sect. 6, we summarize this paper.

2   Related Work

First, we introduce existing researches for data gathering in WSNs. In [9], the authors proposed a hierarchical data gathering method. In this method, sensor nodes are hierarchically arranged, where a sensor node in a lower level sends the sensor data to a node in a higher level, and then the sensor node in the highest level sends the aggregated sensor data to the sink. This method can reduce the traffic for data gathering since nodes in higher levels aggregate and compress the sensor data. In [1], the authors proposed a grid-based routing protocol for extending network lifetime. A master node is elected from sensor nodes in each grid that is predefined by the sink. Each master node monitors node density in its handling grid and share the information each other. Other sensor nodes send their sensor data to the master node in each grid, and then the master node transmits the sensor data to the sink through dense areas (grids). This helps saving non-master nodes energy and maintaining network connectivity, and thereby extending network lifetime. The existing studies presented above do not assume the movements of sensor nodes, and thus, cannot handle the change of network topology.

Next, we introduce existing researches for data routing in mobile ad hoc networks (MANETs). In [11], the author assumed location-based services, and proposed a data gathering and disseminating method in MANETs. This method uses a mobile agent that stays within a certain geographical area by moving between mobile nodes. This work assumes services to disseminate location-based information that is generated by disseminating nodes and passed to mobile nodes located near the location. This work is different from our work which assumes that sensor data generated by sensor nodes are sent to the sink located far from them. In [10], the authors proposed a group communication algorithm in MANETs. If group nodes receive a join request packet from source nodes, they reply their location and velocity. When a source node sends a data packet to its group nodes, it predicts their mobility and constructs a multicast tree based on the Euclidean Steiner tree [6]. The group communication algorithm efficiently transmits messages through the multicast trees and reduces traffic for location update by predicting mobility of group nodes. This algorithm is not efficient for data gathering because each source node constructs a multicast tree and messages to the same destination are individually transmitted.

Finally, we introduce an existing research for mobile P2P systems. In [8], the authors proposed an efficient data access method for location-based data in an environment where mobile nodes densely exist. In this method, nodes exchange their having data each other so that the data are being held by a node located within a half of the node's communication range from the geographical point corresponding to the data. Hence, it is guaranteed that any node can access data by sending a packet to the geographical point corresponding to the data. This study is different from our work that aims at gathering sensor data necessary to guarantee the geographical granularity of sensing. However, the method keeping data close to its corresponding point uses an idea similar to the method keeping mobile agents close to sensing points in this paper.

3 Assumptions

3.1 System Environment

We assume the use of dense MWSNs constructed of mobile sensor nodes that are equipped with a radio communication facility and periodically observe the physical phenomena (e.g., sound, temperature, and light). Communication infrastructures are not available in the area where the sensor nodes exist so they communicate with each other using multi-hop radio communication. There are number of sinks and they periodically monitor the sensing area while guaranteeing the geographical granularity of the sensing, according to the requirement from an application. We call the combination of a sink's position and the requirement from an application a *data gathering condition*.

The entire area is assumed to be a two-dimensional plane. Application $app_i(i = 1, 2, \cdots)$ specifies its sensing condition (Table 1). Sensing area A_i is a rectangular area whose horizontal to vertical ratio is $M_i{:}N_i$ (M_i and N_i are positive integers), and the requirement of the geographical granularity of sensing is a $k_i^2 \cdot M_i \cdot N_i$ integer. Here, multiple sinks and requirements from the applications exist in the network and the sinks receive a requirement from the applications. A sink that receives the requirement divides its sensing area into $k_i \cdot M_i \times k_i \cdot N_i$ lattice-shaped sub-areas and determines the center point of each sub-area as a sensing point, which is the data gathering target (Fig. 1). The sink gathers sensor data from sensor nodes located within distance s from each sensing point at the time of $P_i + l_i T_i (l_i = 0, \cdots, L_i - 1)$ where P_i is app_i's start time

Table 1. App_i's sensing condition

Contents	Symbols
Sensing area	A_i
Geographical granularity of sensing	k_i
Start time	P_i
Number of gathering	L_i
Gathering cycle	T_i

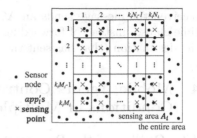

Fig. 1. Sensing area and sensing points

of data gathering and T_i is app_i's gathering cycle. The sink's location o_i is in the sensing area.

As previously mentioned, we assume the use of MWSNs constructed of mobile sensor nodes held by ordinary people. The communication range of each sensor node is a circle with a radius of r. Each sensor node is equipped with a positioning device such as GPS, and they communicate with each other using multi-hop radio communication based on their positions (i.e., geo-routing described in the next subsection). The position information is represented as a pair of longitude and latitude. Each sensor node freely moves throughout the entire area, while the sinks are stationary. We assume that sensor nodes can reliably sense location data within a radius s of their position. Since the number of mobile nodes is very large, there are multiple sensor nodes that can cover each geographical point within the entire sensing area.

3.2   Geo-routing

Sensor nodes adopt a geo-routing protocol that is based on that proposed in [5] to transmit a message to the specified destination as a location (not a node). In this protocol, the nodes perform a transmission process using the information on the positions of the transmitter and the destination, which is specified in the packet header. In particular, the transmitter writes the information on the positions of the destination and itself into the packet header of the message, and broadcasts it to its neighboring nodes. Each node that receives this message judges whether it locates within the forwarding area which is determined based on the positions of the transmitter, the destination, and the communication range. Any node in the forwarding area is closer to the destination than the transmitter and can communicate directly to all the nodes in that area. The node within the forwarding area sets the waiting time (the node closer to the destination sets a shorter waiting time), and then it forwards the message after the waiting time elapses unless it detects that the message was sent by another node during the waiting time. By repeating this procedure, the message is forwarded to the nodes that are closer to the destination. If the transmitter node exists within half of the communication range ($r/2$) from the destination, each node that

received the message sends an ACK to the transmitter node after the waiting
time elapses instead of forwarding the message. As a result, the nearest node to
the destination (that has sent the ACK) finds that the nearest one is itself.

4 Mobile Agents Control Based on Data Gathering Conditions of Multiple Sinks

4.1 Outline of the Proposed Method

In the proposed method, a sink that has initially received a request from an
application app_i deploys mobile agents into $k_i \cdot M_i \times k_i \cdot N_i$ sensing points that
are determined as described in Sect. 4.2. If a sensor node on which a mobile agent
runs moves away from the sensing point having been deployed, the mobile agent
moves from the sensor node to another node that is the closest to the point,
according to the method described in Sect. 4.3. At each sensing time, the mobile
agents send sensor data generated by sensor nodes on which they run to the sink
according to the method described in Sect. 4.4.

4.2 Deployment of Mobile Agents

The proposed method reduces the transmission traffic for sensor data and the
movement of the mobile agents by communalizing the mobile agents that handle near-by sensing points. Algorithm 1 shows the procedures to deploy mobile
agents. In this pseudo code, $Address(x)$ denotes the sensing point in a neighboring sub-area in the direction of x.

Algorithm 1. Deploying mobile agents

1: **Procedure for sink S receiving the requirement from application** app
2: $A \leftarrow$ information of sensing condition of app
3: send A to the sensing point in the sub-area where S exists

4: **Procedure for sensor node receiving A**
5: **if** the node has no agent data **then**
6:     boots the mobile agent
7: **end if**
8: $C \leftarrow C \cup A$
9: **for** $\forall \, C_i \in C$ **do**
10:     $dist_i \leftarrow$ the distance between the sensing points of C_i and A
11: **end for**
12: broadcast a message with the furthest distance $dist\_max$
13: **if** A is sent from S or upward, right, or left sensing point **then**
14:     send A to $Address$(DOWN)
15: **end if**

16: **if** A is sent from S or right sensing point **then**
17:     send A to $Address$(LEFT)
18: **end if**
19: **if** A is sent from S or downward, right, or left sensing point **then**
20:     send A to $Address$(UP)
21: **end if**
22: **if** A is sent from S or left sensing point **then**
23:     send A to $Address$(RIGHT)
24: **end if**

25: **Procedure for sensor node receiving the messages with the distance from other nodes**
26: **if** the node has not broadcast a message **then**
27:     break
28: **else if** the $dist\_max$ in the received messages is smaller than the $dist\_max$ **then**
29:     $C \leftarrow C - A$
30: **end if**

First, a sink that receives the requirement from application app creates the
agent data that is needed to boot the mobile agent (line 2). Then, the sink sends
the agent data to the sensing point in the sub-area where the sink exists by

using geo-routing (line 3). The sensor node closest to the sensing point receives the agent data and boots a mobile agent. If a mobile agent has already been running near the sensing point, it receives the agent data instead of the sensor node closest to the sensing point (lines 5 to 8). In this way, a communalized mobile agent stores several agent data, and if one of the data gathering processes completes, its role changes on the fly. More concretely, if the distances among sensing points are smaller than a threshold $\alpha(\alpha < s)$, the mobile agent charges into these sensing points.

Additionally, mobile agents in the proposed method have their territories to avoid that multiple nodes receive agent data and run the same agent. More concretely when a mobile agent receives an agent data, it broadcasts a message with the information on the furthest distance among the sensing points of its stored agent data and the received one to its neighboring nodes (lines 9 to 12). If multiple mobile agents having received the agent data exist, they receive the above messages from each other. Only the mobile agent with the minimum distance stores the new agent data and the other mobile agents discard it (lines 26 to 30).

Figure 2 shows an example where two mobile agents receive agent data. There are two mobile agents MA_1 and MA_2, two sensing points p_1 and p_2, and a destination of agent data q_1. MA_1 and MA_2 respectively handle into p_1 and p_2, and they receive the agent data whose destination is q_1 because the distance among p_1, p_2, and q_1 are smaller than α. MA_1 broadcasts a message with the information on the distance between p_1 and q_1, and, MA_2 broadcasts the distance between p_2 and q_1. They receive these messages from each other, and MA_1 stores the agent data and MA_2 discards it because the minimum distance is the distance between p_1 and q_1.

Moreover, a mobile agent that is newly booted or receives the agent data retransmits it to the sensing points in some of the sub-areas based on its existing sub-area (lines 13 to 24). The agent data transmission by the mobile agent is propagated in the crosswise direction, followed by the lengthwise direction. By repeating these procedures, the sink deploys mobile agents near all its sensing points (i.e., within the circle whose center is a sensing point and radius is the sensing range s). In this procedure, the sink and the mobile agents construct their

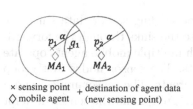

× sensing point   + destination of agent data
◇ mobile agent   (new sensing point)

Fig. 2. Example that mobile agent exchange their territories

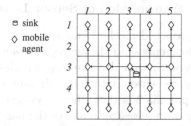

Fig. 3. Example of forwarding agent data between mobile agents

parent-child relationship with each other according to the agent data transmission (transmitter-receiver corresponds to parent-child). We call the tree structure consisting of the parent-child relationships a *forwarding tree* (e.g., Fig. 3). As a result, the number of mobile agents and thus the communication traffic for movement of the agents decrease.

4.3   Movement of Mobile Agent

If a sensor node on which a mobile agent operates moves away from the sensing point, it may not be able to cover that point. Additionally, it may not be able to receive the sensor data sent from its child nodes on the forwarding tree. Therefore, in the proposed method, a mobile agent moves from the current sensor node to another node that is closest to the sensing point to avoid such a situation.

In particular, a mobile agent starts moving when the distance between the sensing point and itself becomes longer than threshold β. β is a system parameter that is set as a constant value smaller than $r/2$ and s, which can guarantee that a sensor node on which a mobile agent operates can communicate with all the sensor nodes located near (within $r/2$) the sensing point and can sense the data at the sensing point. In order to move to the sensor node closest to the sensing point, the mobile agent broadcasts a message containing the agent data to its neighbor nodes within $r/2$ from the sensing point. The sensor node located closest to the sensing point sends an ACK and boots a mobile agent at first as in geo-routing. The other sensor nodes cancel sending own ACK and the original mobile agent stops its operation because they can detect the first ACK.

If a mobile agent handles multiple data gathering processes (i.e., it has multiple sensing points), the node must stay within less than s from any sensing points. The mobile agent start moving when the distance between any sensing point and itself becomes longer than β. The mobile agent broadcasts a message containing the all agent data which the node has. The mobile agents move to the middle point among these sensing points. However, the sensor node that receives the agent data may be more than β away from some sensing points. In such cases, the sensor node separates these agent data and individually move them to their sensing points.

4.4   Transmission of Sensor Data

Our proposed method can reduce the traffic for sending sensor data since the mobile agents send the aggregated sensor data to the sinks through the forwarding trees. Specifically, the sensor nodes on which multiple mobile agents operate aggregate sensor data for their multiple parents. The sensor nodes first group their parents based on the directions of their parents. The sensor nodes send a sensor data message to one of the parents in each group, and the sensor data for the others parents are stored as *additional data*. The additional data consists of a set of *destination groups*, each of which is composed by the destination address, and a set of sensor data that are addressed to the destination.

Algorithm 2 shows the transmission procedures. In this pseudo code, *Destination*(x) denotes a position information on destination group x. Algorithm 2 includes procedures for grouping and sending a data message (Algorithms 3 and 4, respectively). At every sensing time, sensor nodes on which mobile agents operate transmit their sensor data to the sinks of the agents. First, the sensor nodes on which mobile agents operate get sensor readings (line 2). The sensor readings are valid among communalized mobile agents because distances from their sensing points are kept smaller than the sensing range. Next, the sensor nodes on which multiple mobile agents operate group the mobile agents according to their parent directions in order to aggregate the sensor (line 3 and Algorithm 3). Then, the sensor nodes send a message including the sensor data (line 5).

Each sensor node that receives this message, stores all sensor data contained in the message and sends a message in the same way (lines 8 to 13). If the attached additional data contains a destination group whose destination address is different from any of sensing points of the agents running on the receiver node, the node composes a message consisting of sensor data for the destination group and sends it to the destination address. (lines 14 to 19). When sensor nodes on which mobile agents operate in the sub-areas where the sinks exist complete collecting all the necessary sensor data from all their child nodes, they send a message containing all the received and its own sensor data to the sink (lines 20 to 28).

Algorithm 4 shows the procedures for sending sensor data. In this pseudo code, *Position*(x) denotes a position information on sensing point of mobile agent x, and *Index*(x) denotes an index for sensor data x indicating a number as an order which x appears in a sensor data message. Before sending a sensor data message, for a certain group, a sensor node checks if it has all sensor data which should be sent from their child nodes with respect to the group (lines 1 to 3). Here, since a leaf node on a forwarding tree has no child node, it can skip this step. If this node has all sensor data to send to its parents, it creates a sensor data message, which contains the sensor data for the corresponding parent (lines 4 to 5), and sensor data for the other parents and the information of sensing points of those parents as additional data (lines 6 to 22). Then, the sensor node sends the messages to the parents by using geo-routing (lines 23 to 24).

By the above procedures, the sink can receive sensor data at all the sensing points from the sensor nodes on which mobile agents operate.

Figure 4 shows an example in which mobile agents send sensor data whose sensing times overlap. In Fig. 4, there are four mobile agents MA_1, MA_2, MA_3, and MA_4, and the parents of MA_1 are MA_2 and MA_3, and a parent of MA_2 is MA_4. MA_1 sends its sensor data SD_1 and additional data for MA_2 and MA_3 to MA_2 because both MA_2 and MA_3 exist in the right direction and MA_2 is closer to the center of MA_1's sensing points. Here, the message has additional data that is the pair of the position information of MA_3 and an index to SD_1. MA_2 receives SD_1 from MA_1, and then sends SD_1 and its sensor data SD_2 to its parent MA_4. MA_2 also independently sends SD_1 to MA_3 by referring to the additional data of the received message.

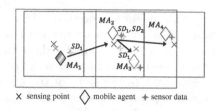

X sensing point ◇ mobile agent ✦ sensor data

Fig. 4. Example of transmission of sensor data in multiple data gathering

---

Algorithm 2. Transmitting sensor data

1: **Every time when the sensing cycle of any agent data comes,**
2: get the sensor reading
3: $G \leftarrow$ Group(all agent data: A)
4: **for** G_i ($i =$LEFT, RIGHT, UP, and DOWN) **do**
5:     SendData(G_i)
6: **end for**

7: **Procedure having received a message containing sensor data and additional data: D and L**
8: **for** $\forall E \in$ sensor data in D **do**
9:     store E
10: **end for**
11: **for** G_i ($i =$LEFT, RIGHT, UP, and DOWN) **do**
12:     SendData(G_i)
13: **end for**
14: **for** $\forall$ destination group: $T \in L$ **do**
15:     **if** *Destination*(T) is not the sensing point of any of its own agent data **then**
16:         sensor data: $D^* \leftarrow$ all sensor data containing or indexed in L
17:         send D^* to *Destination*(T)
18:     **end if**
19: **end for**
20: **if** $G_{\text{SINK}} \neq \phi$ **then**
21:     **for** $\forall A \in G_{\text{SINK}}$ **do**
22:         **if** A receives sensor data from its all child nodes **then**
23:             sensor data: $D^* \leftarrow$ sensor data received from A's all child nodes
24:             send D^* to A's sink
25:             $G_{\text{SINK}} \leftarrow G_{\text{SINK}} - A$
26:         **end if**
27:     **end for**
28: **end if**

Algorithm 3. Group(A)

1: **for** $\forall A_i \in A$ **do**
2:     $P \leftarrow A_i$'s parent direction
3:     **if** A_i's parent is its sink **then**
4:         $G_{\text{SINK}} \leftarrow G_{\text{SINK}} \cup A_i$
5:     **else if** $P =$ UP **then**
6:         $G_{\text{UP}} \leftarrow G_{\text{UP}} \cup A_i$
7:     **else if** $P =$ RIGHT **then**
8:         $G_{\text{RIGHT}} \leftarrow G_{\text{RIGHT}} \cup A_i$
9:     **else if** $P =$ DOWN **then**
10:         $G_{\text{DOWN}} \leftarrow G_{\text{DOWN}} \cup A_i$
11:     **else if** $P =$ LEFT **then**
12:         $G_{\text{LEFT}} \leftarrow G_{\text{LEFT}} \cup A_i$
13:     **end if**
14: **end for**

Algorithm 4. SendData (G)

1: **if** $G = \phi$ or $\exists A \in G$ does not receive sensor data from its child nodes **then**
2:     return
3: **end if**
4: $A_* \leftarrow$ the agent data $\in G$ whose sensing point is closest to the center of the node's sensing points
5: sensor data message: $D \leftarrow$ sensor data sensed by the node and A_*'s all descendant nodes
6: $G \leftarrow G - A_*$
7: additional data: $L \leftarrow \phi$
8: **if** $G \neq \phi$ **then**
9:     **for** $\forall A \in G$ **do**
10:         **if** If *Position*(A's parent) $\neq$ *Destination*($\forall$ destination group $\in L$) **and** *Position*(A's parent) $\neq$ *Position*(A's parent) **then**
11:             destination group: $T \leftarrow$ *Position*(A's parent)
12:             **for** $\forall E \in$ sensor data received from A's all child nodes **do**
13:                 **if** E is included in $D \cup L$ **then**
14:                     $T \leftarrow T \cup Index(E)$
15:                 **else**
16:                     $T \leftarrow T \cup E$
17:                 **end if**
18:             **end for**
19:             $L \leftarrow L \cup T$
20:         **end if**
21:     **end for**
22: **end if**
23: send D and L to *Position*(A_*'s parent)
24: $G \leftarrow \phi$

It should be noted that the traffic produced by these procedures is expected to be smaller than that produced by the procedure in which mobile agents individually sends their sensor data to their parents. This is because some parents of a mobile agent may exist in the same direction, and thus it is more efficient to send the sensor data to multiple parents with one message.

5   Simulation Experiments

In this section, we show the results of simulation experiments regarding the performance evaluation of our proposed method. For the simulation, we used the network simulator, Scenargie 1.6.[1]

5.1   Simulation Model

There are 2,000 mobile sensor nodes $(M_1, \cdots, M_{2000})$ and p sinks $(S_1, \cdots, S_p)$ in a two-dimensional field of 1000 [m]$\times$1000 [m]. $S_i(i = 1, \cdots, p)$ is fixed at the point of $(PX_i$ [m], PY_i [m]) from the left and the bottom edges of the sensing field. Each sensor node moves according to the random waypoint model with a home area [2] where it selects a random direction and a random speed from 0.5 to 1 [m/sec] at intervals of 60 [sec]. Sinks and sensor nodes communicate with IEEE 802.11a whose transmission rate is 6 [Mbps] and communication range r is about 100 [m]. Each sensor node continuously senses the field and the sensing range s is 50 [m]. Application $app_i(i = 1, \cdots, p)$ requires the sink S_i to gather sensor data. For all app_i, P_i and k_i are 4,400 [sec] and 4, respectively. For $app_{2i-1}(i = 1, \cdots, \lfloor p/2 \rfloor)$, L_i, and T_i are 240, and 30 [sec], while for $app_{2i}(i = 1, \cdots, \lceil p/2 \rceil)$, L_i, and T_i are 120, and 60 [sec], respectively. A_i is a rectangle area whose point of (left, bottom) and point of (right, top) are $(PL_i$ [m], PB_i [m]), $(PL_i+800$ [m], PB_i+800 [m]), respectively. Each sink divides its sensing field into 16 lattice-shaped sub-areas whose size is 200 [m] $\times$200 [m] and sets the center point of each sub-area as a sensing point.

Each sink deploys a mobile agent at each of its sensing points after 4380 [sec] from the start time of the simulation. The sensing operations start at 4400 [sec]. The sensing times of $S_{2i-1}(i = 1, \cdots \lfloor p/2 \rfloor)$ and that of $S_{2i}(i = 1, \cdots \lceil p/2 \rceil)$ are $4400 + \{30, 60\}m(m = 0, 1, \cdots, \{239, 119\})$ [sec]. The size of an agent data is set as 128 [B], assuming that each sensor node has the source code of mobile agent in advance. The size of a sensor data generated at each sensor node is set as 24 [B]. The size of an address of sensor data in the additional data is set as 1 [B]. Additionally, parameters of our proposed method α and β are respectively set as 48[m] and 49[m], according to the results of our preliminary experiments.

For comparison, we also evaluate the performances of the proposed method without aggregating sensor data (*nonAggregation*) and our previous method where each sink individually gathers sensor data without communalization of mobile agents (*comparative*).

---

[1] Scenargie 1.6 Base Simulator revision 10864, Space-Time Engineering, http://www.spacetime-eng.com/.

Table 2. Message size

Object	Message name	Size [B]
Deploying a mobile agent	Deployment	256
Moving a mobile agent	Movement	$128 + 128 \cdot i$
	Broadcast distance	96
Sending sensor data	Sensor data	$64 + 32 \cdot j$
	(+Additional data)	$(+\sum_{u=1}^{U}(24 + 32 \cdot k_u + 1 \cdot l_u))$
Common	ACK	96

In the above simulation model, we performed experiments in which the initial position of each mobile sensor nodes was randomly determined where there was the same number of sensor nodes in each of 200 [m] × 200 [m] rectangle areas (sub-areas). The end of sensing operations of all sinks are 8000 [sec], and we evaluated the following three criteria.

1. Traffic: The traffic is defined as the summation of the size of all packets sent by the sink and all sensor nodes during the simulation. Table 2 shows messages used in our method and the comparative method, and their sizes at the Mac layer. In this table, i denotes the number of agent data, j denotes the number of sensor data aggregated, and k_u and l_u denote the number of sensor data containing and indexed on destination group $u(u = 1, \cdots, U)$ in an additional data, respectively.
2. Delivery ratio: The delivery ratio is defined as the ratio of the number of sensor data sent to the sinks in the data gathering processes to the total number of sensor data that should be acquired during the simulation.
3. Delay: The delay is defined as the average elapsed time from the start of each sensing time to the time that the sink successfully receives all sensor data.

5.2   Effects of Number of Sinks

First, we examine the effects of the number of sinks p. Table 3 shows sinks' positions and sensing areas in this experiment. Figure 5 shows the simulation results. In these graphs, the horizontal axes indicate p, and the vertical axes indicate the traffic in Fig. 5(a), the delivery ratio in Fig. 5(b), and the delay in Fig. 5(c), respectively.

Figure 5(a) shows that the traffic in the proposed method is smaller than nonAggregation and the comparative method. This is because in the proposed method, the number of packets decreases by collectively sending aggregated sensor data to multiple sinks locating in the same direction.

Figure 5(b) shows that the delivery ratio in all methods is high. In particular, our method always achieves almost perfect delivery ratio (i.e., 1). This shows that all sensor data which all sinks received are valid, i.e., every mobile agent

Table 3. Sink's position and sensing area in Sec. 5.2

ID	PX_i [m], PY_i [m]	PL_i [m], PB_i [m]
S_1	(140, 140)	(100, 100)
S_2	(180, 140)	(110, 100)
S_3	(220, 140)	(120, 100)
S_4	(260, 140)	(130, 100)
S_5	(140, 220)	(100, 120)
S_6	(180, 220)	(110, 120)
S_7	(220, 220)	(120, 120)
S_8	(260, 220)	(130, 120)

Table 4. Sink's position and sensing field in Sec. 5.3

ID	PX_i [m], PY_i [m]	PL_i [m], PB_i [m]
S_1	(140, 140)	(0, 100)
S_2	(180, 140)	(d, 100)
S_3	(220, 140)	(2d, 100)
S_4	(260, 140)	(3d, 100)

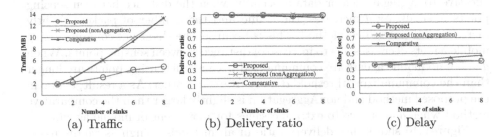

(a) Traffic   (b) Delivery ratio   (c) Delay

Fig. 5. Effects of number of sinks

always stays within its valid range of sensing. However, the delivery ratio in the comparative method slightly decreases as the number of sinks increases. This is because packet losses occur due to increase of traffic.

Figure 5(c) shows that the proposed method and nonAggregation can gather sensor data in shorter time than the comparative method when p is larger than 1. In the proposed method, the sensor data are aggregated by communalized mobile agents and are collectively sent to the multiple sinks. On the other hand, in the comparative method, the sensor data are individually sent to the multiple sinks. This increases the number of packets, resulting in congestion of network bandwidth, and thus transmission of packets delays in the MAC layer. Though nonAggregation also increases the number of packets, it suppresses the congestion by delaying the timings of sending packets in the application layer.

5.3   Effects of Distance Between Sensing Areas

Next, we examine the effects of distance between sensing areas d. Table 4 shows sinks' positions and sensing areas in this experiment, where we fix the number of sinks as 4. Figure 6 shows the simulation results. In these graphs, the horizontal axes indicate d, and the vertical axes indicate the traffic in Fig. 6(a), the delivery ratio in Fig. 6(b), and the delay in Fig. 6(c), respectively.

Figure 6(a) shows that the traffic in the proposed method is always smaller than the comparative method except that $d = 50$. This shows that because it is

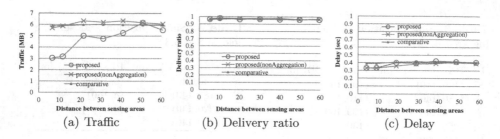

Fig. 6. Effects of distance between sensing areas

effective to aggregate sensor data especially when the distance between sensing points is small. As d increases, the traffic and the number of packets slightly increase in the proposed method. This is because, the chance of communalizing mobile agents decreases due to increase of distance between sensing points. When $d = 50$, no mobile agents are communalized because all sensing points are longer than the communalizing threshold α away from each other. As a result, traffic in the proposed method and nonAggregation is slightly larger than the comparative method when $d = 50$ due to extra messages for movement of mobile agents.

Figure 6(b) shows that delivery ratio in all methods is high as we discussed above.

Figure 6(c) shows that the proposed method can gather sensor data in shorter time than the comparative method when d is 10 because it is effective to aggregate sensor data when the distance between sensing points is small.

6 Conclusion

In this paper, we proposed an agent control method that guarantees the coverages of multiple sinks and efficiently gathers sensor data. In the proposed method, mobile agents are communalized if the sensor node on which a mobile agent operates can sense multiple sensing points.

Simulation experiments show that the proposed method decreases traffic by collectively sending aggregated sensor data to multiple sinks locating in the same direction and keep high delivery ratio even when the number of sinks is high.

Our proposed method may not work well in environments where there are obstacles such as buildings because few or no sensor nodes may exist close to some sensing points. We plan to extend our proposed method to approximate sensor readings at such sensing points.

Acknowledgment. This research is partially supported by the Grant-in-Aid for Scientific Research (S)(21220002), and (B)(24300037) of the Ministry of Education, Culture, Sports, Science and Technology, Japan.

References

1. Banimelhem, O., Khasawneh, S.: GMCAR: grid-based multipath with congestion avoidance routing protocol in wireless sensor networks. Ad Hoc Netw. **10**(7), 1346–1361 (2012)
2. Camp, T., Boleng, J., Davies, V.: A survey of mobility models for ad hoc network research. Wireless Commun. Mob. Comput. **2**(5), 483–502 (2002)
3. Cha, S., Talipov, E., Cha, H.: Data delivery scheme for intermittently connected mobile sensor networks. Comput. Commun. **36**(5), 504–519 (2013)
4. Goto, K., Sasaki, Y., Hara, T., Nishio, S.: Data gathering using mobile agents for reducing traffic in dense mobile wireless sensor networks. In: Proceedings of MoMM 2011, pp. 58–65 (2011)
5. Heissenbüttel, M., Braun, T., Bernoulli, T., Wälchli, M.: BLR: beacon-less routing algorithm for mobile ad hoc networks. Comput. Commun. **27**(11), 1076–1086 (2004)
6. Hwang, F.K., Richards, D.S., Winter, P.: The Steiner Tree Problem. North-Holland, Amsterdam (1992). ISBN: 044489098X
7. Jabeur, N., Zeadally, S., Sayed, B.: Mobile social networking applications. Commun. ACM **56**(3), 71–79 (2013)
8. Landsiedel, O., Götz, S., Wehrle, K.: Towards scalable mobility in distributed hash tables. In: Proceedings of P2P 2006, pp. 203–209 (2006)
9. Lu, K.-H., Hwang, S.-F., Su, Y.-Y., Chang, H.-N., Dow, C.-R.: Hierarchical ring-based data gathering for dense wireless sensor networks. Wireless Pers. Commun. **64**(2), 347–367 (2012)
10. Mitra, P., Poellabauer, C.: Efficient group communications in location aware mobile ad-hoc networks. Pervasive Mob. Comput. **8**(2), 229–248 (2012)
11. Yashiro, T.: A new paradigm of V2V communication services using nomadic agent. In: Proceedings of V2VCOM 2006, pp. 1–6 (2006)

Highly Distributable Associative Memory Based Computational Framework for Parallel Data Processing in Cloud

Amir Hossein Basirat[(✉)], Asad I. Khan,
and Balasubramaniam Srinivasan

Clayton School of IT, Monash University Melbourne, Melbourne, Australia
{Amir.Basirat, Asad.Khan, Bala.Srinivasan}@monash.edu

Abstract. One of the main challenges for large-scale computer clouds dealing with massive real-time data is in coping with the rate at which unprocessed data is being accumulated. In this regard, associative memory concepts open a new pathway for accessing data in a highly distributed environment that will facilitate a parallel-distributed computational model to automatically adapt to the dynamic data environment for optimized performance. With this in mind, this paper targets a new type of data processing approach that will efficiently partition and distribute data for clouds, providing a parallel data access scheme that enables data storage and retrieval by association where data records are treated as patterns; hence, finding overarching relationships among distributed data sets becomes easier for a variety of pattern recognition and data-mining applications. The ability to partition data optimally and automatically will allow elastic scaling of system resources and remove one of the main obstacles in provisioning data centric software-as-a-service in clouds.

Keywords: Associative memory · Neural networks · Big data · MapReduce · Graph Neuron

1 Introduction

While the opportunities for parallelization and distribution of data in clouds have brought some efficiency, existing relational and object-oriented data models in particular, make storage and retrieval processes very complex, especially for massively parallel real-time data. Chaiken et al. [1] observe that the challenge of processing voluminous data sets in a scalable and cost-efficient manner has rendered traditional database solutions prohibitively expensive. At the other end of the spectrum high-performance computing (HPC) has advanced rapidly but dominantly focused on computational complexity and performance improvements. Virtual HPC in the cloud has significant limitations especially when big data is involved. According to Shiers [2], "it is hard to understand how data intensive applications, such as those that exploit today's production grid infrastructures, could achieve adequate performance through the very high-level interfaces that are exposed in clouds". The efficiency of the cloud system in dealing with data intensive applications through parallel processing essentially lies in how data is partitioned and processing is divided among nodes. As a result,

© Institute for Computer Sciences, Social Informatics and Telecommunications Engineering 2014
I. Stojmenovic et al. (Eds.): MOBIQUITOUS 2013, LNICST 131, pp. 66–77, 2014.
DOI: 10.1007/978-3-319-11569-6_6

data access schemes are sought to be able to efficiently handle this partitioning auto-matically and support the collaboration of nodes in a reliable manner. Google's Ma-pReduce [3] and Microsoft Dryad [4] have achieved greater scalability than parallel databases. However this comes at a cost; time-consuming analysis and code custom-ization are required when dealing with complex data inter-dependencies. Moreover, real-time reliability guarantees remain elusive. Conceptually, the approach also suffers from certain key limitations:

In the MapReduce type of query processing, the map tasks are assumed to to be fully independent. Applied to massive relational or object-oriented data, however, large records or objects resulting after aggregation and analytics are themselves often broken into parts and distributed creating dependencies and requiring trade-offs between redundancy (for speed), coherence (for integrity under frequent updates) and com-promises to parallel schedulability, as they break assumptions of mutual independence. In practice, MapReduce functions are implemented imperatively and produce numer-ous intermediary entities - between the map and reduce stages e.g. in the form of intermediate files. In many applications, these files must be sorted and moved around before they are input to the reduce function. This system wide sort and redistribution incurs considerable processing and communication costs and is either fundamentally non-scalable or requires fine-tuned architecture-aware access mechanisms.

While assisting designers and developer s with few predefined architectural patterns [5] for many applications, the MapReduce data flow model is also rigid, limits variation and hence increases the complexities of dealing with errors, fault-tolerance, perfor-mance and other end-to-end non-functional issues. Some exploratory research imple-mentations are using key/value pairs with distributed "Spaces" (for instance Java Spaces or other derivatives of Linda tuple spaces [6]) to simplify data sharing and conceptually separate shared data from the computational tasks. However, this sim-plification comes with significant efficiency loss and exacerbates uncertainty of pre-dicting reliability and real-time behavior.

Hence, MapReduce cannot automatically scale up for many applications and data sets, in practice. Reconciling MapReduce with Associated Memory concepts, in particular for adaptive and fast data access, aggregation and movement will be a key contribution of the proposed technique in this paper. Our proposed scheme preserves the strength of the MapReduce model and eliminates/alleviates most of these constraints in a well-integrated manner where there is no outward change to the way in which MapReduce models are deployed and used. In this context, our proposal will investigate inclusion of an asso-ciative approach in the MapReduce model to support application specific pattern recog-nition and data-mining operation. For efficient analytics, Map functions need to be embedded in streams as it is unrealistic to literally preserve and record all raw data from sensor streams. On the other hand the complexity of some analytics tasks renders them inappropriate for real-time online processing (for example in transport and plant health monitoring). Hence it necessitates a combination of (1) selective stream functions that efficiently query, filter and aggregate information in adaptable ways and, (2) streaming the results into the cloud for later offline processing and analytics.

An associative memory based processing scheme that efficiently performs large-scale data processing will offer a broad spectrum of innovative cloud applications by formatting data universally within the network. It helps alleviate data imbalances by replacing rigid referential data access mechanisms with more distributable associative processing. Hierarchical structures in associative memory models are of interest as these have been shown to improve scalability whilst preserving accuracy in pattern recognition applications [7]. Our proposal is based on a special type of Associative Memory (AM) model, which has been specially designed for distributed processing [8–14] and readily implemented within distributed architectures. Thus our primary aim in this paper is to introduce an access scheme that will enable fast data retrieval across multiple records and data segments associatively, utilizing a parallel approach. Doing so will yield a new form of database-like functionality that can scale up or down over the available infrastructure without interruption or degradation, dynamically and automatically.

2   Graph Neuron for Scalable Recognition

Transforming big data into valuable information requires a fundamental re-think of the way in which future data management models will need to be developed on the Internet. Unlike the existing relational, hierarchical and object-oriented schemes, associative models can analyze data in similar ways to which our brain links information. Such interactions when implemented in voluminous data clouds can assist in searching for overarching relations in complex and highly distributed data sets with speed and accuracy. This proposal improves MapReduce-based cloud applications in a number of different ways by uniformly formatting data in a standard two-dimensional representation. It eliminates data imbalances and completes transition to cloud by replacing referential data access mechanisms with more versatile and distributable associative functions, which allow complex data relations to be easily encoded into the keys as patterns. These patterns can be applied in a variety of applications requiring content recognition e.g. image databases, search within large multimedia files, and data mining. Algorithmic strengths of the MapReduce approach are investigated for the first time in context with the effectiveness of one-shot learning based parallelism provisioned via our distributed pattern recognition approach.

The principle of associative memory based learning will be implemented through the use of hierarchically connected layers, with local feature learning at the lowest layer and upper layers combining features into higher representations. Our approach will entail a two-fold benefit. Applications based on associative computing models will efficiently utilize the underlying hardware that scales up and down the system resources dynamically and automatically, controls data distributions and allocation of the computational resources in the cloud. In order to achieve the aforementioned objectives, an initial step would be to develop a distributed data access scheme that enables record storage and retrieval by association, and thereby circumvents the partitioning issue experienced within referential data access mechanisms. In our model, data records are treated as patterns. As a result, data storage and retrieval can be performed using a distributed pattern recognition approach that is implemented through the integration of loosely-coupled computational networks, followed by a divide-and-distribute approach that facilitates distribution of these networks within the cloud dynamically. Our online-learning associative memory scheme is conceived on the principle that "moving computation is much cheaper than moving data". Hence, it will provide methods for automatic aggregation and partitioning of associated data in the cloud for widely used data sets.

The MapReduce model does not explicitly provide support for processing multiple related heterogeneous datasets. While processing data in relational models is a common requirement, this restriction limits its functionality when dealing with complex and unstructured data such as images. Relational databases use a separate, uniquely-structured table, for each different type of data for specific applications; programmers must know the precise structure of every table and the meaning of every column a priori. To overcome this, we explored possibilities to evolve a novel virtualization scheme that can efficiently partition and distribute data for clouds. For this matter, loosely-coupled associative techniques, not considered so far, can be pivotal to effectively partition and distribute data in the cloud. Our associative model will use a universal structure for all data types. Information about the logical structure of the data – metadata – and the rules that govern it may be stored alongside data. This allows programmers to work at a higher level of abstraction without having to know the structural details of every data item. Hence, our approach to cloud-based data processing is unique. It elevates the MapReduce key-value scheme to a higher level of functionality by replacing the purely quantitative key-value pairs with higher order data structures that will improve parallel processing of data with complex associations (or dependencies). By having an associative key/value framework, we can deal with data in any form and in any representation simply by using a pattern matching model (including fuzziness), which treats data records as patterns and provides a distributed data access scheme that enables balanced data storage and retrieval by association. We believe that the performance of MapReduce parallelism as a scalable scheme for data processing in clouds may be significantly improved by transforming the data processing operations into one-shot distributed pattern matching sub-tasks, which in distributed computations are performed in-network, enabling data storage and retrieval by association (instead of pre-set referential data access mechanisms).

2.1 Graph Neuron (GN)

Graph Neuron (GN) [12] is an associative memory algorithm, which implements a scalable AM device through its parallel in-network processing framework. Associative memory architecture differs from conventional memory architecture in the sense that the store and recall operations on memory contents are based on the association with input value rather than based on the address of the memory content. Hence, associative memory-based pattern recognition algorithms are able to offer high recognition accuracy as compared to other algorithms which implement recognition using conventional memory architecture. In addition to its associative memory architecture, GN also follows some characteristics of graph-based pattern recognition algorithms [8]. However, GN implements in-network processing that solves the scalability issue (computationally prohibitive against an increase in the size and database of patterns) in other graph-based pattern recognition algorithms [9].

GN recognition process involves the memorization of adjacency information obtained from the edges of the graph. Adjacency information for each GN is represented using the (left, right) formation. Each activated GN therefore records the information retrieved from its adjacent left or right nodes as illustrated in Fig. 1. In the GN terminology, this adjacency information is known as bias entry where each GN maintains an array of such entries. The entries for the entire stored pattern are collectively stored in the bias arrays. Each GN would hold a single bias array containing all the bias entries obtained in the recognition processes. In this context, GN offers low storage complexity in recognition process since each GN is only required to store a single array. Furthermore, each GN's bias array only stores the unique adjacency information derived from the input patterns.

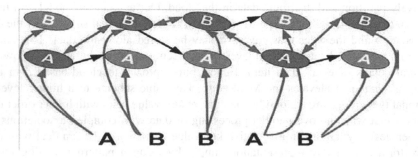

Fig. 1. GN activation from input pattern "ABBAB"

GN's limited perspective on overall pattern information would affect a significant inaccuracy in its recognition scheme. As the size of the pattern increases, it is more difficult for a GN network to obtain an overview of the pattern's composition. This produces incomplete results, where different patterns having similar sub-pattern structure leads to false recall. The limited perspective of GNs, owing to purely adjacency based computations, was widened through the Hierarchical Graph Neuron (HGN) approach [11].

2.2   Hierarchical Graph Neuron (HGN)

In order to solve the issue of the crosstalk due to the limited perspective of GNs, the capabilities of perceiving GN neighbors in each GN is expanded in Hierarchical Graph Neuron (HGN) to prevent pattern interference. The underlying principle of HGN implementation is such that the capability of "perceiving neighbors" in each GN within the network must be expanded. This is achieved by having higher layers of GN neurons that oversee the entire pattern information. Hence, it will provide a bird's eye view of the overall pattern. HGN extends the functionalities of GN algorithm for pattern recognition by providing a bird's eye view of the overall pattern structure. It thus, eliminates the possibility of false recalls in the recognition process.

3 Edge-Detecting Hierarchical Graph Neuron (EdgeHGN)

An important aspect in the development of pattern recognition scheme is its algorithmic design. A proper design will lead to high efficiency and has the ability to generate a more accurate classification strategy. Graph Neuron based algorithms have been developed based upon two different concepts known as graph-matching and associative memory. These two concepts have given an added advantage in terms of scalability for GN-based algorithm implementations. GN has the ability to perform pattern recognition processes on distributed systems due to its simple recognition procedure and lightweight algorithm. Furthermore, GN incurs low computational and communication costs when deployed in a distributed system. Previous parts of this paper have analyzed GN and HGN. In this section, the algorithmic design of a newly proposed Edge Detecting Hierarchical Graph Neuron (EdgeHGN) algorithm for distributed pattern recognition scheme for large-scale data sets is presented. The proposed approach extends the scalability of the existing Hierarchical Graph Neuron (HGN) implementation by reducing its computational requirements in terms of the number of neurons for recognition processes while providing comparable recognition accuracy as HGN implementation. EdgeHGN provides a capability for recognition process to be deployed as a composition of sub-processes that are being executed in parallel across a distributed network. Each sub-process is conducted independently from each other, making it less cohesive as compared to other pattern recognition approaches.

3.1 EdgeHGN Architecture

In our proposed novel EdgeHGN model, we reduce redundant data content for recognition by applying a Drop-Fall algorithm on the input pattern. This results in lesser number of processing neurons which in turn results in lower communication overhead within the scheme. The dividing path produced by Drop-fall algorithm depends on three aspects: a start point, movement rules, and direction. In our approach, a drop-fall scheme will be applied to the pattern which ensures producing the least number of neurons. By applying a simple drop-fall algorithm, we can reduce number of redundant processing neurons in the binary character image while maintaining all character data bits. This approach is shown in Fig. 2 where a Descending-left drop-fall algorithm is applied on the input pattern reducing number of processing nodes for each EdgeHGN subnet significantly (total number of GN nodes are decreased from 49 to 39 in this example). This reduction will not only minimize communication costs but also having an edge detection feature within the scheme can improve recognition accuracy to a high degree. Furthermore, lesser number of neurons results in lower response time which is of high interest for real-time pattern matching problems. EdgeHGN adds a clustering mechanism in pattern recognition by dividing and distributing patterns into sub-patterns. Each of the sub-patterns undergoes a one-shot recognition procedure. The results of sub-recognition will cumulatively add up to obtain the actual recognition result. Each processing node in clustered EdgeHGN configuration may perform recognition on each sub-pattern independently from other processing nodes.

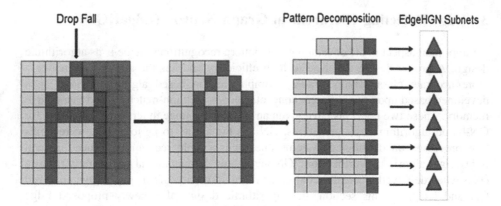

Fig. 2. EdgeHGN progressively removes unnecessary nodes from the two dimensional data representation.

This configuration is intended to be used on coarse-grained networks such as grid and cloud computing, in which additional processing and storage capacity made available to be used. An important benefit of having this EdgeHGN cluster performed on a single processing node is such that it eliminates all the communication actions involved in EdgeHGN message passing model for distributed systems. For each sub-pattern recognition process, each node only communicates back the corresponding index generated, therefore reducing the chances of recognition failures due to transmission or communication errors.

3.2 EdgeHGN Subnet Communication Scheme

In EdgeHGN implementation, after applying drop-fall scheme on the input pattern and removing redundant processing neurons, we will form EdgeHGN subnets. In Edge-HGN implementation, the core recognition process is conducted at the sub-pattern level. There are four stages involved in this process for each EdgeHGN subnet:

Stage 1. After receiving an input, each activated GN at the base layer will send a signal message to other nodes in the adjacent columns containing the row number/address of the activated node. Those activated nodes that are at an edge of the layer will only send the activation signal messages to the GNs in the penultimate columns. The activated GNs that receive the signal messages from their adjacent neighbors will respond by updating their bias array noting the activation signals. All other GNs will remain inactive.

Stage 2. All active GNs at the base layer will then update their bias arrays. If the bias entry value, received from both the activated nodes in proceeding and succeeding columns have been recorded, the index of the entry will be sent to the respective GN in the same position at the higher layer. If the value is not found within the bias array, then a new index will be created and sent to the GN node in the higher layer. Note that active nodes at the edges of the base layer will not be communicating with higher layer nodes since there is no node present at the edges of the higher layer owing to the pyramid-like structure of the EdgeHGN subnets.

Stage 3. GN nodes at a layer above the base that receive a signal message, containing the index of the bias entry that has been created or recalled from stage 2, will be activated. Similar process as in stages 1 and 2 will occur. However, the contents of the signal messages from preceding and succeeding columns would be in the form of (*left, middle, right*) for non-edge nodes and either (*left, middle*) or (*middle, right*) for the edge nodes. The values for left, middle, and right are derived from the indices retrieved from the lower layer nodes. After the message communication between adjacent nodes has completed, the active GNs will update their bias arrays and send the stored/recalled index/indices to the node at the same position in the higher layer (except for the GNs at the edges). This stage will be repeated for each layer above the base layer, until it reaches the top layer GN nodes.

Stage 4. One of the top layer GNs will receive a bias index from a GN in the layer underneath it. This top layer activated node will search its bias array for this index. If the index is found, then this node will trigger a recall flag with the recalled index. Otherwise, it will trigger a store flag and store the new index in its bias array. The signal message sent by the top layer active GN marks the completion of the recognition at sub-pattern level.

3.3   EdgeHGN Communication Complexities

Communications in the EdgeHGN recognition scheme involve a message-passing mechanism, in which a single processing node communicates with other nodes in the network for exchanging messages. It is composed of two different types, namely macro- and micro-communication. In *macro-communication*, communication costs at system level are taken into account, i.e. communications incurred between SI Module and EdgeHGN subnets. On the other hand, *micro-communication* deals with GN communications within a particular subnet for each pattern introduced into the system.

EdgeHGN Macro-Communications. Macro-communication in EdgeHGN implementations happens between SI Module node and either base layer GNs or top GNs in each subnet. It occurs at three different phases:

Network generation phase: SI module is responsible for communicating possible input values of the patterns, which will be used in the recognition process to all base layer GNs within EdgeHGN subnets.

$$n^{msg}_{SI \to sub} = n_{sub} \times S_{sub} \times v$$

Pattern input phase: SI module decomposes pattern into a number of sub-patterns according to the number of subnets available. Consequently, these sub-patterns will be sent to each subnet within the network. However, in the actual format, SI module will communicate directly with each GN at the base layer of each EdgeHGN subnet. Hence, the number of messages communicated is similar to the number of messages in network generation phase

$$n^{msg}_{SI \to sub} = n_{sub} \times S_{sub} \times v$$

Result communication phase: After recognition process in each EdgeHGN subnet is completed, the results (in terms of recall or store) will be communicated back to SI module for further analysis. In regards to the communication cost, the total number of messages communicated from subnets to SI module is equivalent to the number of subnets available:

$$n^{msg}_{sub \to SI} = n_{sub}$$

EdgeHGN Micro-Communications. In terms of micro-communications, we have communications among GNs within the base layer. For each GN in the base layer, the amount of message communications incurred could be derived from the number of messages communicated between adjacent neurons for each input sub-pattern.

Base Layer: For GNs at the edge of base layer, the number of communication exchange is equivalent to the number of different elements within the sub-pattern. For non-edge GNs, the communication is required between adjacent neurons in both the preceding and the succeeding columns as well as the communication of bias indices to the GNs at the next higher layer. In this context, the amount of message exchange is $v^2 + 1$.

$$n^{msg}_{l_{base}} = \left((v^2+1)(S_{sub} - 2) + 2v\right)$$

Middle layers: The communication costs for GNs in the middle layers are similar to that at the base layer. However, the difference would be in the number of nodes available within each layer. For each middle layer i, where $1 \le i \le top-1$, the number of message exchanges occurred for single input sub-pattern recognition could be derived as the following:

$$n^{msg}_{l_i} = \left((v^2+1)(S_{sub} - (2i+2)) + 2v\right)$$

$$n^{msg}_{l_{total}} = \sum_{i=1}^{top-1} \left((v^2+1)(S_{sub} - (2i+2)) + 2v\right)$$

Top layer: These GN nodes are only responsible for communicating the final index for each sub-pattern stored/recalled to the SI module. The costs for communicating these indices have been included in the macro-communication evaluation.

4   Simulation and Results

Hadoop can be set-up and configured in 3 different modes. Standalone or local mode is where no Hadoop daemons running and everything runs in a single JVM. In Pseudo-distributed mode, Hadoop daemons run on the local machine, thus simulating a cluster on a small scale. And in a fully distributed mode the Hadoop daemons run on a cluster of machines. For our performance benchmarks, a Pseudo-distributed mode Hadoop environment is set-up with default configuration settings but some changes are made to the settings to gain better performance, e.g. the max data chunk size is set to 256 MB instead of 64 and heap size for task executer JVM is increased to 512 MB for better memory allocation and garbage collection. In addition, the performance of Hadoop MR and newly proposed EdgeHGN based MR against is compared against one of the commonly used parallel database management systems called Vertica. The Vertica database is a parallel DBMS designed for large data warehouses. The main distinction of Vertica from other DBMSs is that all data is stored as columns, rather than rows. In Fig. 3, we can see performance of all three schemes while performing a simple task of a pattern search. In Vertica, a pattern search for a particular field is simply running a query in SQL which requires a full table scan:

SELECT * FROM Data WHERE field LIKE '%XYZ%';

On the other hand, the MR program consists of just a Map function that is given a single record already split into the appropriate *key/value* pair and then performs a sub-string match on the value. If the search pattern is found, the Map function simply outputs the input key/value pair to HDFS. Because no Reduce function is defined, the output generated by each Map instance is the final output of the program. As clearly shown here, distributed MapReduce and EdgeHGN based MapReduce perform equally well. For some data input splits EdgeHGN even responds sooner in time and average response time looks better. Vertica performs the best here as we simply run a very single query against the database.

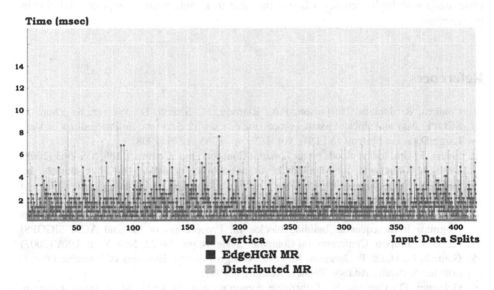

Fig. 3. Comparing Distributed MapReduce, EdgeHGN based MapReduce and Vertica, performing alphanumeric pattern search on input data splits of 256 MB in size.

One of the reasons that Hadoop performance and EdgeHGN performance are lower compared with Vertica is the fact that we are running both in a Pseudo-distributed mode and not in a fully distributed mode in a cluster where memory is allocated to the process independently. The other reason is that considering the limited number of data chunks that we process in both Pseudo distributed Hadoop and EdgeHGN based MR, Hadoop's start-up costs can become the limiting factor in its performance. In fact for small queries, Hadoop startup costs can dominate the execution time. In our observations, we found that it can take 10–20 sec before all Map tasks have been started and are running at full speed.

5 Conclusion and Remarks

Existing cloud frameworks such as Hadoop MapReduce involve isolating low-level operations within an application for data distribution and partitioning. This limits their applicability to many applications with complex data dependency considerations. This paper explored new methods of partitioning and distributing data in the cloud by fundamentally re-thinking the way in which future data management models will need to be developed on the Internet. Loosely-coupled associative computing techniques, which have so far not been considered, can provide the break through needed for a distributed data management scheme. Using a novel lightweight associative memory algorithm known as Edge Detecting Hierarchical Graph Neuron (EdgeHGN), data retrieval/processing can be modeled as a pattern recognition problem, conducted across multiple records within a single-cycle, utilizing a parallel approach. The proposed model envisions a distributed data management scheme for large-scale data processing and database updating that is capable of providing scalable real-time recognition and processing with high accuracy while being able to maintain low computational cost in its function.

References

1. Chaiken, R., Jenkins, B., Larson, P.A., Ramsey, B., Shakib, D., Weaver, S., Zhou, J.: SCOPE: easy and efficient parallel processing of massive data sets. In: Proceedings of Very Large Database Systems (VLDB), vol. 1(2), pp. 1265–1276 (2008)
2. Shiers, J.: Grid today, clouds on the horizon. Comput. Phys. Commun. **180**, 559–563 (2009)
3. Dean, J., Ghemawat, S.: MapReduce: simplified data processing on large clusters. In: OSDI'04: Proceedings of the 6th Conference on Symposium on Operating Systems Design and Implementation, Berkeley, CA, USA (2004)
4. Isard, M., Budiu, M., Yu, Y., Birrell, A., Fetterly, D.: Dryad: distributed data-parallel programs from sequential building blocks. In: Proceedings of the 2nd ACM SIGOPS/EuroSys European Conference on Computer Systems, pp. 59–72, New York, USA (2007)
5. Gamma, E., Helm, E., Johnson, R., et al.: Design Patterns: Elements of Reusable Object-oriented Software. Addison Wesley, Reading (1995)
6. Gelernter, D., Carriero, N.: Generative communication in linda. ACM Trans. Program. Lang. Syst. **7**(1), 80–112 (1985)

7. Ohkuma, K.: A hierarchical associative memory consisting of multi-layer associative modules. In: Proceedings of 1993 International Joint Conference on Neural Networks (IJCNN'93), Nagoya, Japan (1993)
8. Muhamad Amin, A.H., Khan, A.I.: Commodity-grid based distributed pattern recognition framework. In: 6th Australasian Symposium on Grid Computing and e-Research (AUSGRID 2008), Wollongong, NSW, Australia (2008)
9. Khan, A.I., Amin, A.H.M.: One shot associative memory method for distorted pattern recognition. In: Orgun, M.A., Thornton, J. (eds.) AI 2007. LNCS (LNAI), vol. 4830, pp. 705–709. Springer, Heidelberg (2007)
10. Baig, Z.A., Baqer, M., Khan, A.I.: A pattern recognition scheme for distributed denial of service (DDOS) attacks in wireless sensor networks. In: Proceedings of the 18th International Conference on Pattern Recognition (2006)
11. Nasution, B.B., Khan, A.I.: A hierarchical graph neuron scheme for real-time pattern recognition. IEEE Trans. Neural Netw. **19**, 212–229 (2008)
12. Khan, A.I.: A peer-to-peer associative memory network for intelligent information systems. In: Proceedings of the 13th Australasian Conference on Information Systems, vol. 1 (2002)
13. Baqer, M., Khan, A.I.: Energy-efficient pattern recognition for wireless sensor networks. In: Mobile Intelligence, pp. 627–659. John Wiley and Sons Inc., Hoboken (2010)
14. Khan, A.I., Muhamad Amin, A.H.: Integrating sensory data within a structural analysis grid. In: Topping, B.H.V., Iványi, P. (eds.) Parallel, Distributed and Grid Computing for Engineering. Saxe-Coburg Publications, Kippen (2009)
15. Catterall, E., Van Laerhoven, K., Strohbach, M.: Self-organization in ad hoc sensor networks: an empirical study. In: ICAL 2003: Proceedings of the Eighth International Conference on Artificial life, pp. 260–263. MIT Press, Cambridge

MobiPLACE*: A Distributed Framework for Spatio-Temporal Data Streams Processing Utilizing Mobile Clients' Processing Power

Victor Zakhary, Hicham G. Elmongui[✉], and Magdy H. Nagi

Computer and Systems Engineering, Alexandria University, Alexandria, Egypt
{victorzakhary,elmongui}@alexu.edu.eg, magdy.nagi@ieee.org

Abstract. The problem of continuous spatio-temporal queries' processing was addressed by many papers. Some papers introduced solutions using single server architecture while others using distributed server one. In this paper, we introduce MobiPLACE*, an extension to PLACE* [13] system, a distributed framework for spatio-temporal data streams processing exploiting mobile clients' processing power. We will extend the Query-Track-Participate (QTP) query processing model, introduced as a system architecture in PLACE*, by moving the Query server role to mobile clients. This will reduce memory and processing load on our regional servers in exchange for a little additional communication and memory load on mobile devices. This makes the system more scalable and enhances average query response time. Improvements in mobile devices' and communication links' capabilities encouraged us to introduce this extension. In this paper, we will focus on range and k-NN continuous queries and their evaluation on MobiPLACE*. Experimental study is made to compare between MobiPLACE* and PLACE* in terms of server response time and memory.

1 Introduction

Location detecting devices is now wide spread in wide range devices e.g. (mobile phones, cars and many moving devices). Those objects can send their location updates periodically to servers and these data can be used to solve navigation and many location aware services' problems. Such problems can be solved by a system doing continuous queries over those data streams. One of the main challenges to those systems is **scalability**. Mainly, it is about how to design the system and distribute load between system components to scale up to support larger number of moving objects and continuous queries.

Previously, system designers depended on servers to handle all query processing because mobile clients' were poor in capabilities. Nowadays, smart phones, embedded devices in cars and all mobile devices have a PC like capabilities. Designing a system to utilize those capabilities will lead to reduce server loads and allow the servers to handle more client objects, queries and respond with queries' answers shortly. We will focus on continuous range and k-NN (k Nearest Neighbor) queries on objects moving over road networks. In a range query,

© Institute for Computer Sciences, Social Informatics and Telecommunications Engineering 2014
I. Stojmenovic et al. (Eds.): MOBIQUITOUS 2013, LNICST 131, pp. 78–88, 2014.
DOI: 10.1007/978-3-319-11569-6_7

the issuer requires to find objects e.g., taxis or clients of taxis in a certain range. In a k-NN query, the issuer requires to find the nearest k objects to her location. We focused on continuous queries instead of snapshot ones. Also, we considered query's incremental evaluation instead of periodic re-evaluation solution. In incremental evaluation, the result is calculated once and saved on either client, server or both and updates to it is only calculated and sent. In periodic re-evaluation, the result is re-calculated from scratch periodically. Incremental evaluation is advantageous because it leads to less tracking and response time but requires some additional memory to save query's result. We need a real-time responses for the query so we chose to save moving objects' locations and do all our computations in memory instead of hard drive. We also assumed that our objects are restricted to move on road networks. This means that the shortest path between object will be used instead of Euclidean distance as a distance metric.

The development of devices' capabilities and mobile broadband services, either in bandwidth or in cost, over the world encouraged us to migrate a server role to mobile clients. This will reduce load on servers with a little increase on communication messages. The ICT 2013's report for mobile broadband service development mentioned that by early 2013, the price of an entry-level mobile-broadband plan represents between 1.2 and 2.2 % of monthly GNI p.c. in developed countries and between 11.3 and 24.7 % in developing countries, depending on the type of service.

In this paper, we extend the work done in [11]. In [11], Sallam applied a modified version of the Incremental Monitoring Algorithm (IMA) [9] on PLACE* [13] Query-Track-Participant (QTP) query processing model to make a **distributed** processing of continuous spatio-temporal queries over **road networks**. We applied the same algorithms by Sallam but on MobiPLACE* QTP query processing model. The difference between the 2 models is in the role distribution of query processing steps between clients' devices and servers.

The rest of this paper is organized as follows. In Sect. 2, we highlighted the related work and explained the systems that we extend in this paper. We gave an overview about MobiPLACE* architecture and communication messages in Sect. 3. We explained how could we execute continuous range and k-NN queries in our system in Sects. 3.3 and 3.4 respectively. Performance evaluation and experiments made were introduced in Sect. 4. Finally, the paper is concluded in Sect. 5.

2 Related Work

Many papers have addressed the problem of continuous queries over spatio-temporal data streams. SINA [7], sets an algorithm to evaluate concurrent continuous spatio-temporal queries. It uses three phases, the hashing phase, the invalidation phase, and the joining phase; to calculate positive and negative updates. SOLE [6], keeps track of only the significant objects in order to save the scarce memory resource. MQM [2] divided the region of study into domains and object reports its location to server whenever its movement affects any range query results (i.e., crossing any query boundaries) or it changes its current domain. MobiEyes [3] ships some part of the query processing down to the moving objects, and the server mainly acts as a mediator between moving objects. CPM [8], YPKCNN [15], and SEA-CNN [14] introduce 3 algorithms for exact k-NN continuous monitoring in Euclidean space. The above systems assumed a central server architecture for query processing and the Euclidean distance as a distance metric. Some papers considered some restriction on objects motion i.e. (objects are moving in a road network). In this case, the shortest path between objects would be considered as the distance metric. In [4], they designed a prototype system and algorithm to answer nearest neighbor queries over objects moving in road networks. Papadias, Zhang, Mamoulis and Tao integrated network and Euclidean information to efficiently prune the search space and answer range, nearest neighbor, closest pairs and e-distance join queries in the context of spatial network databases [10]. In [5], Kolahdouzan and Shahabi proposed a novel approach to efficiently and accurately evaluate KNN queries in spatial network databases using first order Voronoi diagram. This approach is based on partitioning a large network to small Voronoi regions, and then pre-computing distances both within and across the regions. Shahabi proposed an embedding technique that approximates the network distance with computationally simple functions in order to retrieve fast, but approximate, k-NN results [12]. The Incremental Monitoring Algorithm (IMA) and Group Monitoring Algorithm (GMA) algorithms [9] are introduced to calculate continuous nearest neighbor in **road networks**. IMA retrieves the initial result of a query q by expanding the network around it until k NN's are found. GMA benefits from the shared execution among queries in the same path, and the reduction of the problem from monitoring moving queries to (monitoring) static network nodes. PLACE* [13] introduces Query-Track-Participate (QTP) processing model to process continuous queries. Figure 1 shows the steps of query evaluation in PLACE*. In PLACE*, each moving object is associated with a server called its visiting server ($VS(O)$, initially it is object's home server $HS(O)$). For a query q, the querying server $QS(q)$ is the regional server of that the query issuer, i.e., $QS(q) = VS(i_q)$. A participating server for a query q, PS(q), is a regional server whose coverage region overlaps the search region of q. For a query q, the tracking server $TS(q)$ is the regional server that q's focal object, f_q, currently belongs to. Participating servers send update of the query result to the query server QS of the query. The QS forwards updates to the query issuer (i). If the focal of the query changed its position, $TS(q)$ sends the new position to $QS(q)$. $QS(q)$ calculates the new search region for q and updates the participating servers.

Sallam used an enhanced version of IMA, for query processing over road networks, and applied it on PLACE* QTP distributed architecture [11]. In our work, We applied Sallam's algorithms in [11] for continuous queries over **road networks** on our MobiPLACE* system architecture. We aim to provide more system scalability by enhancing server response time and reducing memory usage. A comparison between Sallam's algorithms performance on PLACE* and

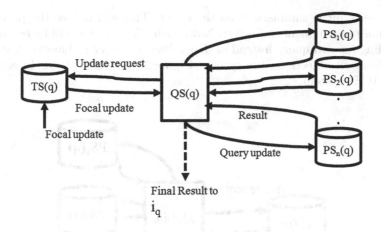

Fig. 1. Query evaluation in PLACE*

on MobiPLACE* architectures is made to illustrate the benefit of using Mobi-
PLACE* architecture.

3   MobiPLACE*: An Overview

In this section, we discuss the details of MobiPLACE* architecture and algorithms to process continuous queries. Query processing algorithms are introduced
in [11] with different roles of system components. We modified those algorithms
to work correctly with our architecture. In Sect. 3.1, we discuss the details of
system architecture and the role of system components. In Sect. 3.2, we present
the communication messages between system components in order to execute
queries, update object location and update query result.

3.1   System Architecture

MobiPLACE* system architecture is inspired from Query-Track-Participant
(QTP) communication model introduced in PLACE* [13]. We divided the area
where objects are moving into regions and each region is covered by a regional
server. In PLACE*, each regional server has 3 roles; querying, tracking and participating server roles. In MobiPLACE*, the role of querying is moved from
server to mobile client. When clients connect to our system, a mapping file is
downloaded to those clients. This mapping file determines the IP address of each
regional server paired with its coverage region boundaries. When a client needs
to initiate a query, it connects to the home server of this query focal $(HS(f_q))$ to
know its current regional server which will act as a tracking server to the query.
For simplicity, we assume that each object is the focal of its queries and in this
case the previous step could be ignored. Then the client determines the set of
regional server to participate on this query. It connects to them and gather the

result. The result is summarized on the client. This will reduce the processing and memory requirements on server. Now, each client device will be responsible on handling its own query instead of depending on server to handle all steps of queries from all objects on the system. Figure 2 illustrates the architecture of MobiPLACE* system.

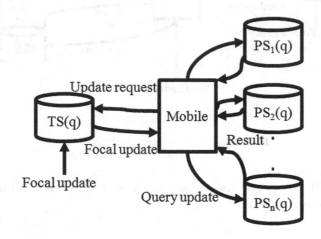

Fig. 2. MobiPLACE* system architecture

3.2 Communication Messages

The area is divided into n sub-regions that are covered with n regional servers; each is responsible on a sub-region. Information of road junctions and roads is stored at servers responsible on this region. All-pairs shortest paths, between road junctions, matrix is pre-computed. Each server stores the shortest path cost from all nodes in the network to the junctions it stores in a list sorted according to the path cost and this will be used in query evaluation. When a new object (O) connects to the system, the following steps are taken as below.

1. Object O sends a connection request to the Default Server DS (a previously known server for all objects upon installing our application on O).
2. DS searches the regional servers and locate O's Home Server (HS(O)) which covers O's location and sends its connection details to O.
3. O sends a connection message to HS(O).
4. HS(O) attaches O to the nearest road to its location and generate a unique identifier for the object O by adding a prefix of server's ID to object O ID (will be used later to locate HS(O)).
5. O sends updates to its home server until it moves outside its coverage area and in this case O migrates to another server which is called O's visiting server VS(O). HS(O) keeps track of O's current visiting server for easier locating later.

Moving objects can issue range and k-NN queries. As a difference from PLACE*, Querying Server role is now moved on mobile client. This means that mobile client and participating servers cooperate to answer the query continuously.

The steps of query execution on MobiPLACE* architecture are similar to those on PLACE* architecture except moving the querying server execution steps on mobile devices. In order to enable this, a mapping file of region/IP of regional server (which tells the mobile client the coverage area of each server and its communication information) is downloaded on new object connection to our system. When a query initiated on the mobile client, the issuer i asks the home server of query focal f (this is known from object's ID prefix) about the current visiting server of the focal VS(f) which will act as a tracking server for this query TS(q). The home server informs the issuer about the current TS(q) of its query. The issuer then contacts the TS(q) to know the exact location of the query focal f. Using the regional server mapping file, the issuer i can determine the set of participant servers PSs(q) for this query that will participate to collect the query result. TS(q) informs the issuer of any updates of focal location and based on those update, the issuer updates the plan and informs the participants the new plan. Without loss of generality, we can assume that the issuer itself is the query focal. In this case, the steps of asking about TS can be ignored.

When an object O issues a new query q (assuming that the issuer itself is the query focal), the following steps describes how to evaluate range and k-NN queries.

1. O expands the search from its position.
2. O finds the regional servers whose regions overlap the query search region PS(q).
3. O sends an evaluation request to all PS(q). This request contains O's position and query parameters (i.e. range in range queries) and waits for answers from PSs(q). O keeps track of its queries that have not been answered completely yet by keeping track which servers have responded and which have not yet.
4. When receiving the answer from all servers in PSs(q), O gather the result and display it as the final result to the user. O can display results incrementally upon receiving any answer from any server but making sure that those answers should be updated and may content some false results (i.e. in k-NN query).

3.3 Continuous Range Query Evaluation

To evaluate a new range query q, the visiting server of the focal start expanding from focal's road ends to the neighbor road junctions. It either stops when reaching nodes out of query's range or reaching some road junctions covered by another server. At the same time, each participant server start a similar process (expanding) like the visiting server of the focal but from road junctions that are within query range. Server can know which nodes are in range using all-pair shortest path matrix, which is previously calculated offline, between road junctions. Those junctions are pushed in a queue to continue the expansion process using similar algorithm in [11]. We define a leaf junction in 2 ways. Either it has only one neighbor junction and we could not expand from it anymore or it is out of range junction that is a neighbor to an in range junction. Those leaves are used in incremental evaluation of queries as described later in Sect. 3.5.

3.4   Continuous k-NN Query Evaluation

The range of k-NN query is not known in advance. By assuming uniformity of object distribution over servers, we can transform k-NN query to a range one by estimating the range to find k neighbors. As in [13], we can calculate the range of objects within object's regional server by $d * \sqrt{k/n}$ where d^2 is the area covered by objects' server and n is the number of objects in this server (Fig. 3). After calculating the range of the query, requests to PS are sent and results are gathered and sorted in a min priority queue. If the result reaches k objects or more, the algorithm is stopped and result is displayed. If not, the range is expanded by a factor and the process is repeated. Server expand the search of the query by starting from leaves junctions and start expanding to the new range. Results are updated to client until reaching k moving objects. Participant servers of the query store the leaves of the search tree in order to be used later in the incremental updates.

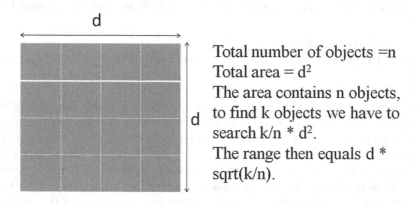

Total number of objects =n
Total area = d^2
The area contains n objects, to find k objects we have to search k/n * d^2.
The range then equals d * sqrt(k/n).

Fig. 3. Calculate k-NN query's range

3.5   Query Incremental Evaluation

Every object periodically updates its location to its current visiting server VS(O). If O moves outside its current visiting server, it sends a connection request to the new Visiting Server and a disconnection message from to the old one. It will also notify its Home Server with the new visiting server ID.

Upon receiving an update from an object O, VS(O) performs the following steps.

1. Locate the new road for O and calculate the cost from O to this road end junctions.
2. Update mobile clients whose queries are affected either by adding or removing O.
3. Send message to O itself confirming its connection to VS(O).

4   Performance Evaluation

Amazon instances with dual 1.88 GHZ processors and 1.7 GB of RAM are used in the experiments. The region under studying is divided into 4 equal sub-regions. A regional server is responsible for each region. Each regional server runs on a dedicated machine. Servers are connected on Amazon private network and TCP connections are used as a connection protocol. Two more servers are used as a default server and an event simulator server. There are many input parameters to the simulation model: road network, represented by the set of nodes and edges, moving objects number, objects' velocity and update period. We used the city of Oldenburg in Germany as the underlying network with 6105 road junctions and 7035 edges. Input parameters are summarized in Table 1.

Table 1. Summary of system input parameters

Parameter	Range values	Default value
Network edges	–	7035
Network nodes	–	6105
Update period	–	10 s
Moving objects velocity	Low, medium, high	Medium (50 Km/h)
Object update percentage	10, 50, 100 %	10 %
k of k-NN	1, 10, 100, 1000	100
R of range	2, 5, 7, 10, 30 (%)	10 %
Population size	50K, 100K	50K

We used Thomas Brinkhoff [1] generator to generate 50K moving objects over road networks. Objects update their position every 10 s and randomly generate continuous queries. We made many experiments to compare between Mobi-PLACE* and PLACE* processing models. We focused on response time and server memory usage in the comparison.

Figures 4 and 5 show the effect of varying the parameters of range and k-NN queries respectively on response time of the proposed two architectures. Figure 4 studies the effect of changing the range between 2 %, 5 %, 7 %, 10 % and 30 % of the network area when the population size is 50K moving objects, while Fig. 5 does the same with NN queries. The figures show that MobiPLACE* with client connection bandwidth equals 1 Mb/s performs better than PLACE*, on the same

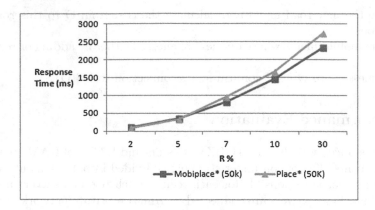

Fig. 4. Range query response time with 50K population

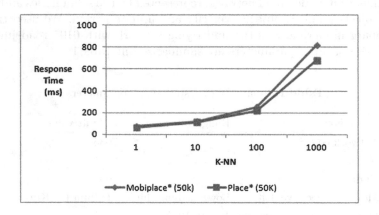

Fig. 5. k-NN response time with 50K population

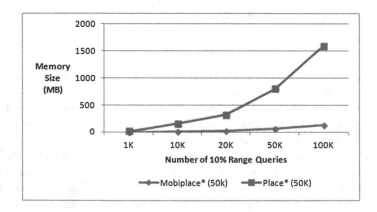

Fig. 6. Memory requirements for 10 % range queries

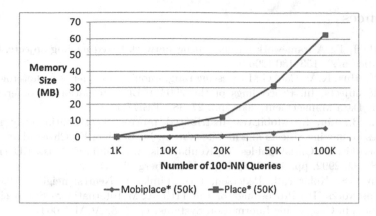

Fig. 7. Memory requirements for 100-NN queries

algorithms and conditions, when query range becomes large and show than it is a little worth in case of k-NN because the amount of data sent to client object is larger in case of MobiPLACE*.

Figure 6 shows the estimated total server memory usage of range queries on the 2 architectures and verifies that MobiPLACE* requires a significant lower amount of memory than PLACE*. Figure 7 shows the same for k-NN queries.

5   Conclusion

In this paper, we discussed MobiPLACE* a distributed framework for continuous processing of spatio-temporal queries over road network by utilizing mobile clients' processing power. It is built based on PLACE* QTP communication model. Experiments showed that moving Query Server role to mobile clients slightly enhanced query response time and significantly reduced the server memory usage. We have many future extension that we could not cover in this paper. Many papers, that solved the same problem, did not mention how to distribute regional servers over region. We need to determine a set of standard experiments to calculate the best number of servers and their distribution to achieve the best query's average response time for each application. Privacy issues should be taken into consideration. Also, we need to make a detailed study of the communication links effect on performance. We took connection bandwidth as a parameter and simulated it only using delays. More connection details like latency, network congestion and connection initiation time should be taken into consideration later in order to provide more accurate results.

References

1. Brinkhoff, T.: A framework for generating network-based moving objects. GeoInformatica **6**(2), 153–180 (2002)
2. Cai, Y., Hua, K.A., Cao, G.: Processing range-monitoring queries on heterogeneous mobile objects. In: Proceedings of the 2004 IEEE International Conference on Mobile Data Management, 2004, pp. 27–38. IEEE (2004)
3. Gedik, B., Liu, L.: MobiEyes: distributed processing of continuously moving queries on moving objects in a mobile system. In: Bertino, E., Christodoulakis, S., Plexousakis, D., Christophides, V., Koubarakis, M., Böhm, K. (eds.) EDBT 2004. LNCS, vol. 2992, pp. 67–87. Springer, Heidelberg (2004)
4. Jensen, C.S., Kolářvr, J., Pedersen, T.B., Timko, I.: Nearest neighbor queries in road networks. In: Proceedings of the 11th ACM International Symposium on Advances in Geographic Information Systems, pp. 1–8. ACM (2003)
5. Kolahdouzan, M., Shahabi, C.: Voronoi-based k nearest neighbor search for spatial network databases. In: Proceedings of the Thirtieth International Conference on Very Large Data Bases, vol. 30, pp. 840–851. VLDB Endowment (2004)
6. Mokbel, M.F., Aref, W.G.: SOLE: scalable on-line execution of continuous queries on spatio-temporal data streams. VLDB J. **17**(5), 971–995 (2008)
7. Mokbel, M.F., Xiong, X., Aref, W.G.: SINA: scalable incremental processing of continuous queries in spatio-temporal databases. In: Proceedings of the 2004 ACM SIGMOD International Conference on Management of Data, pp. 623–634. ACM (2004)
8. Mouratidis, K., Papadias, D., Hadjieleftheriou, M.: Conceptual partitioning: an efficient method for continuous nearest neighbor monitoring. In: Proceedings of the 2005 ACM SIGMOD International Conference on Management of Data, pp. 634–645. ACM (2005)
9. Mouratidis, K., Yiu, M.L., Papadias, D., Mamoulis, N.: Continuous nearest neighbor monitoring in road networks. In: Proceedings of the 32nd International Conference on Very Large Data Bases, pp. 43–54. VLDB Endowment (2006)
10. Papadias, D., Zhang, J., Mamoulis, N., Tao, Y.: Query processing in spatial network databases. In: Proceedings of the 29th International Conference on Very Large Data Bases, vol. 29, pp. 802–813. VLDB Endowment (2003)
11. Sallam, A., Nagi, K., Abougabal, M., Aref, W.G.: Distributed processing of continuous spatiotemporal queries over road networks. Alex. Eng. J. **51**(2), 69–152 (2012)
12. Shahabi, C., Kolahdouzan, M.R., Sharifzadeh, M.: A road network embedding technique for k-nearest neighbor search in moving object databases. GeoInformatica **7**(3), 255–273 (2003)
13. Xiong, X., Elmongui, H.G., Chai, X., Aref, W.G.: PLACE*: a distributed spatio-temporal data stream management system for moving objects. In: 2007 International Conference on Mobile Data Management, pp. 44–51. IEEE (2007)
14. Xiong, X., Mokbel, M.F., Aref, W.G.: SEA-CNN: scalable processing of continuous k-nearest neighbor queries in spatio-temporal databases. In: Proceedings of the 21st International Conference on Data Engineering, 2005. ICDE 2005, pp. 643–654. IEEE (2005)
15. Yu, X., Pu, K.Q., Koudas, N.: Monitoring k-nearest neighbor queries over moving objects. In: Proceedings of the 21st International Conference on Data Engineering, 2005. ICDE 2005, pp. 631–642. IEEE (2005)

Modelling Energy-Aware Task Allocation in Mobile Workflows

Bo Gao(✉) and Ligang He(✉)

Department of Computer Science, University of Warwick,
Coventry CV4 7AL, UK
{bogao,liganghe}@dcs.warwick.ac.uk

Abstract. Mobile devices are becoming the platform of choice for both business and personal computing needs. For a group of users to efficiently collaborate over the execution of a set workflow using their mobile devices, the question then arises as to which device should run which task of the workflow and when? In order to answer this question, we study two common energy requirements: in the *minimum group energy cost problem (MGECP)* we build the model as a quadratic 0–1 program and solve the optimisation problem with the objective to minimise the total energy cost of the devices as a group. In the *minimum max-utilisation problem (MMUP)* we aim to improve the fairness of the energy cost within the group of devices and present two adjustment algorithms to achieve this goal. We demonstrate the use of a Mixed Integer Quadratic Programming (MIQP) solver in both problem's solutions. Simulation result shows that both problems are solved to good standards. Data generated by different workload pattern also give us a good indication of the type of workflow that benefit the most from MMUP. The model used in this work can also be adapted for other energy critical scenarios.

Keywords: Mobile computing · Energy-aware · Collaboration · Workflow

1 Introduction

Recent years have seen significant growth in the size of the mobile computing market, and yet the rarest commodity in the world of mobile computing remains to be its battery power. Development in battery technology is slow compared to other components of a mobile smart device. Hence, despite the moderately improved battery capacity on modern smart devices, with increasingly more complex functionality required from the user, developments of mobile applications remain largely energy-constrained [17].

In less than a decade, mobile devices have enriched their functionalities from being a simple dialling device to a hub of rich media applications. It is predicted that by 2015, mobile application development projects will outnumber desktop projects by a ratio of 4:1 [10]. The unique portability of a mobile device coupled with its ever growing hardware capability brings business and ad hoc workflows

© Institute for Computer Sciences, Social Informatics and Telecommunications Engineering 2014
I. Stojmenovic et al. (Eds.): MOBIQUITOUS 2013, LNICST 131, pp. 89–101, 2014.
DOI: 10.1007/978-3-319-11569-6_8

that are traditionally supported by fixed location resources to be implemented over wireless mobile platforms.

Researches show that in a mobile environment, communication tasks are especially energy-demanding compared to local computation tasks [16]. Hence, this type of applications, namely *mobile workflows*, which has a particular emphasis on collaboration between users, is likely to be more energy-demanding than others and requires to be managed in an energy-efficient manner. Furthermore, unlike its desktop counterparts, mobile computing devices are often exposed to the open environment. Changing conditions in data connection, sudden drain of battery caused by user actions can bring disruption to a device's availability.

Our research investigate ways to model and analyse the energy efficiency of such workflows running atop a group of mobile devices. Our goal is to provide an energy efficient execution platform for mobile workflows, while utilising fair share of each mobile device's energy. Our objective is two-fold: First, in the MGECP, we aim to minimise the workflow's total energy consumption. Second, in the MMUP, our objective is to minimize the maximum device utilisation in the group while keeping the overall energy cost close to the minimum.

In this paper, we first give use cases from possible application areas of a mobile workflow and discuss related work. We then construct the system energy model in Sect. 3. The allocation problem is modelled as a quadratic 0–1 program, and its two objectives (MGECP and MMUP) are studied in Sects. 4 and 5. We conclude the paper in Sect. 6 with a simulation study the result of which verifies our formulation and compares the results of our algorithms when applied to different types of workflows.

2   Applications and Related Work

Mobile workflow can be found when a group of mobile users are to share or communicate with each other in order to accomplish a certain task. Such scenario commonly exists in a business environment. With growing adaptation of mobile devices within their business models [10], modern *enterprise applications* often include or are entirely based on mobile devices. For instance, in a supply chain business, as illustrated in Fig. 1a, the commencement of a workflow is triggered by a member of staff registering receipt/sales of goods on their mobile devices. The system database is then updated via a query module[1]. A forecast module is then evoked to produce a forecast based on the update, which is then projected onto the manager's smartphone as a live trend graph or a production plan. In order to lower the overall energy cost of the workflow, our objective in Sect. 4, the forecast module which requires complex computation for data mining purposes is more suitable to be allocated to a device that has a fast processor and low energy draw while running computation tasks. Additionally, it is preferable that modules that communicate frequently, e.g. invoice and query, are allocated to the same device to reduce communication cost.

---

[1] E.g. we can assume that the support system is similar to that of an Excel application with embedded VBA macro modules. Data is stored in the local spreadsheet.

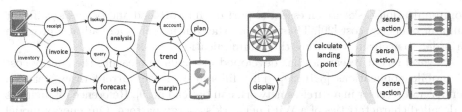

(a) Workflows in enterprise application   (b) Workflow in consumer application

Fig. 1. Examples of mobile workflow use cases. In the centre of both figures, the tasks between the pair of ") (" are not restricted to be executed on any specific device. Allocation of these tasks can affect the energy-efficiency of the workflow.

Another use case illustrated in Fig. 1b includes the use of three smartphones and a tablet, and expands on the idea of a popular *consumer application* [12] which lets its users to play darts with their mobile devices. During the game, a tablet is used to display the dartboard, participating players use their smartphones as darts. The workflow starts when a player throws a dart (by a throwing gesture from the phone towards the tablet). Sensor readings (accelerometer and gyroscope) are then taken from the phone and fed into a calculation module to work out where the dart should land on the board. Result from the calculation is then passed on to the display module on the tablet.

Like all multi-player competitions, the game can only function until its weakest player withdraws, which in this case, is the device that runs out of battery first. Although the calculation module does not require much energy at each run, repeated execution is required. As the game goes on, the battery of the device to which the calculation task is allocated drains faster than the others'. A fair task allocation, which we study in Sect. 5, is needed in such scenarios to balance the contribution made by participating members of the mobile workflow.

A workflow engine is often required to oversee the execution of mobile workflows. In [15] a detailed mobile workflow engine is implemented and tested on Nokia devices. A decentralised workflow coordination architecture designed for mobile devices is presented in [1] for use in biological studies and the supply-chain industry. Authors of [14] propose a rapid application development framework based on a dynamic workflow engine for creating mobile web services.

Several researches has been carried out in workflow management issues in Mobile *Social Content Sharing applications* [6,11,18]. A mobile P2P social content sharing framework was proposed in [6]. In [18], a Java API based mobile workflow system was proposed. A content distribution protocol was proposed in [13] for vehicular ad hoc networks (VANET). Clusters of mobile devices has been proposed in [22] to support the execution of parallel applications.

The common approach towards an allocation problems often model the problem as a linear program [7,19,21]. A linear program is suitable for modelling situations where communication time is not considered or when there are only two devices involved in the process. However, in the cases of mobile workflows, communication tasks are an essential part of the workload and occurs significant amount of energy cost [20]. Thus we construct our model as a quadratic program in order to accurately capture the communication costs.

Several recent researches has developed methods to measure the energy cost of mobile applications [8,16,20]. The difference in the current draw between sender and receiver in a wireless network can be read at [9]. Reference [3] includes a detailed characteristics of a WiFi network's energy pattern. Our energy model draws ideas from these researches.

3   System Model

3.1   Mobile Platform Model

We consider a mobile platform MP consisting of m *mobile devices*, $M_1, \cdots, M_m$, and denote a device profile as $M_i\left(s_i, e_i^{cmp}, e_i^{snd}, e_i^{rcv}\right), i \in \{1, 2, \ldots, m\}$ with parameters defined as follows:

s_i	Peak processing speed of M_i, measured in the number of clock cycles available in a millisecond;
e_i^{cmp}	Current draw from the battery when the device is executing computation tasks at peak speed;
$e_i^{snd/rcv}$	Current draw from the battery when the device is sending/ receiving data to/from the data network.

These devices are interconnected via a network, and we use b_{ij} to denote the bandwidth between devices M_i and M_j, $i, j \in \{1, 2, \ldots, m\}$. Thus, we have an m-matrix $B = (b_{ij})_{m \times m}$ which holds all of the bandwidth information of the underlying network of the MP. When two adjacent tasks are assigned to the same device, we assume that they share the same memory address space on the device. Therefore, we assign positive infinite values to the principal diagonal elements of B, that is $b_{ii} = +\infty, i \in \{1, 2, \ldots, m\}$.

3.2   Workflow Model

The workflow hosted on MP is represented by a directed acyclic graph $W = (T, R)$ whose vertex set $T = \{t_1, \ldots t_n\}$ denotes the set of *tasks* of the workflow. We assume that all tasks are defined via a service-oriented architecture and that all services are available from each device. An n-matrix $D = (d_{a,b})_{n \times n}$ denotes the weighted adjacency matrix of W, where $d_{a,b}$ is the size of the data package that is to be sent from t_a to t_b for $(t_a, t_b) \in R$. The acyclic property of W implies that D has all principle diagonal elements zero.

Each task has profile $t_a\left(d_{(.a)}, d_{(a.)}, c_a\right)$, $a \in \{1, \ldots n\}$ where $d_{(.a)}$ and $d_{(a.)}$ are the a-th column and the a-th row of D which represent the incoming and outgoing data respectively. c_a denotes the size/workload of the task.

3.3   Mobile Energy Model

Given an allocation scheme $\psi : T \rightarrow M$, we first derive the energy cost of computing $t_a, a \in \{1, \ldots n\}$ to be

$$\mathcal{E}^{cmp}_{a\psi(a)} = e^{cmp}_{\psi(a)} \times \frac{c_a}{s_{\psi(a)}} \tag{1}$$

where $\psi(a)$ is the device to which t_a is assigned. Secondly, we have the energy cost of transferring $d_{ab}, (t_a, t_b) \in R$ as

$$\mathcal{E}^{tran}_{ab\psi(a)\psi(b)} = \underbrace{e^{snd}_{\psi(a)} \times \frac{d_{ab}}{b_{\psi(a)\psi(b)}}}_{\text{sender's cost}} + \underbrace{e^{rcv}_{\psi(b)} \times \frac{d_{ab}}{b_{\psi(a)\psi(b)}}}_{\text{receiver's cost}} \tag{2}$$

4   Minimum Group Energy Cost Problem (MGECP)

In this section, we first show that the Minimum Group Energy Cost Problem can be modelled as a generalised Quadratic Assignment Problem (QAP) [5] and then we convexify the objective function in order to solve it using a MIQP solver.

To represent an allocation scheme ψ, we first construct an $n \times m$ binary matrix $X = (x_{ai})$, such that

$$x_{ai} = \begin{cases} 1 & \text{if } \psi(a) = i, \\ 0 & \text{otherwise.} \end{cases} \tag{3}$$

We call matrix X an *assignment matrix* and a valid assignment must satisfy the following constraints

$$\sum_{i=1}^{m} x_{ai} = 1, \quad a = 1, 2, \ldots, n, \tag{4}$$

$$x_{ai} \in \{0, 1\}, \quad a = 1, 2, \ldots, n, \quad i = 1, 2, \ldots, m. \tag{5}$$

(4) ensures that every task must be assigned to one and only one device. (5) states that all tasks are indivisible.

4.1   Quadratic Program Formulation

With (1) (2) and (3), we can derive the total energy cost function as

$$\sum_{b=1}^{n} \sum_{j=1}^{m} \sum_{a=1}^{n} \sum_{i=1}^{m} (e^{snd}_i + e^{rcv}_j) \frac{d_{ab}}{b_{ij}} x_{ai} x_{bj} + \sum_{a=1}^{n} \sum_{i=1}^{m} e^{cmp}_i \frac{c_a}{s_i} x_{ai} \tag{6}$$

The quadratic terms in (6) gives the total energy cost for data transmission, whereas the linear term gives the total energy cost for executing computing tasks. We introduce $(nm)^2$ coefficients q_{aibj}

$$q_{aibj} := \begin{cases} e_i^{cmp} \dfrac{c_a}{s_i} + \left(e_i^{snd} + e_j^{rcv}\right) \dfrac{d_{ab}}{b_{ij}} & \text{if } (a,i) = (b,j), \\ e_i^{snd} \dfrac{d_{ab}}{b_{ij}} & a < b \\ e_i^{rcv} \dfrac{d_{ba}}{b_{ij}} & a > b \end{cases} \tag{7}$$

and with (7) we can transform (6) to

$$\sum_{b=1}^{n} \sum_{j=1}^{m} \sum_{a=1}^{n} \sum_{i=1}^{m} q_{aibj} x_{ai} x_{bj} \tag{8}$$

Theorem 1. *Let coefficients q_{aibj} be the entries of an $mn \times mn$ matrix Q, such that q_{aibj} is on row $(i-1)\,n + a$ and column $(j-1)\,n + b$, and $x = vec(X) = (x_{11}, x_{12}, \ldots, x_{1n}, x_{21}, \ldots, x_{mn})^T$ be the vector formed from the columns of X. Equivalent formulations for the minimum workflow energy cost problem's objective function are given by (8) and*

$$vec(X)^T Q\, vec(X) \tag{9}$$

Proof. From the construction of $vec(X)$, we observe that its u-th element $vec(X)_u = x_{ai} \Leftrightarrow u = (i-1)\,n + a$. Furthermore, given $u = (i-1)\,n + a$ and $v = (j-1)\,n + b$, $u, v \in \{1, 2, \ldots, mn\}$, we also get $Q_{uv} = q_{aibj}$. Hence,

$$(8) = \sum_{v=1}^{mn} \sum_{u=1}^{mn} vec(X)_u^T Q_{uv}\, vec(X)_v$$

$$= \sum_{b=1}^{n} \sum_{j=1}^{m} \sum_{a=1}^{n} \sum_{i=1}^{m} x_{ai} q_{aibj} x_{bj} = (9)$$

□

4.2   Convexification

In order to exploit the power of modern MIQP solvers, we first need to pre-process the problem and convexify the objective function [4]. There are a number of ways of convexification. Our process is similar to that use in [2].

Theorem 2. *Let $Q^* := 1/2\left(Q + Q^T\right) + \alpha I$, where I is the $mn \times mn$ identity matrix, then Q^* is positive definite if scalar $\alpha = 1 + \parallel Q \parallel_\infty$*

Proof. Due to the length of this paper, interested reader are referred to the appendix of [2] (on a negative definite matrix) for a similar proof.   □

Addition of a constant on the main diagonal of Q only add a constant to (9) which does not change its optimal solution. Hence we can rewrite our objective function as

$$\text{min: } vec(X)^T Q^*\, vec(X) \tag{10}$$

This together with (4) and (5) completes the formulation of the optimisation problem of MGECP. The positive definite property of Q^* ensures that (10) is strictly convex and a global minimum can be found by an MIQP solver.

5 Minimum Max-Utilisation Problem (MMUP)

While MGECP ensures that a workflow consumes minimum amount of energy from the mobile devices as a group, it does not consider the stress it has on individual devices. This causes unfair energy cost distribution within the MP, and creates *over-utilised* devices. Having such workflow executed repeatedly over time without adjustment to its task allocation scheme could lead to early retirement of the over-utilised devices. In a business environment, it is common to have authorisation constrained tasks taking critical roles within workflows. In such cases, the MP's inclusion of these authorised devices is critical to the fulfilment of the workflow's functionality. This requires the workflow engine to shift its priority from reducing the total energy cost of the device group to ensuring the availability of key devices.

Hence in this section of the paper, we investigate ways to adjust the task allocation provided by the MGECP so that the availability period of a workflow can be lengthened. We refer to this class of problem as the Minimum Max-Utilisation Problem (MMUP). We first introduce the measure of utilisation:

Definition 1. *Given an allocation scheme ψ, the utilisation of M_i, denoted $\mathcal{U}_i^\psi$, equals $\mathcal{E}_i^\psi/\mathcal{E}_i^R$, for $1 \leq i \leq m$, where $\mathcal{E}_i^\psi$ is the energy cost of M_i under ψ and $\mathcal{E}_i^R$ is the size of the residual energy in M_i.*

The reciprocal of a device's utilisation, $(1/\mathcal{U}_i)$, is the number of times the workflow can run with M_i before it runs out of battery. The availability of a workflow is hence constrained by the member with the highest value of utilisation. As illustrated in Fig. 2, we introduce a *guide utilisation* value $\mathcal{U}^G$ to classify devices into two groups: *Over-Utilised (OU)* and *Under-Utilised (UU)*. The objective then is to shift workload from devices in the OU group to those in UU.

We present two adjustment methods, both utilising the quadratic program formed in MGECP and use the result it produces to apply tight constrains to both methods' variables so that the group's overall energy cost remains minimised to a good degree. Upon need, or periodically, the workflow engine executes the adjustment algorithm in order to map the workflow to an updated task allocation scheme so that no device is over stressed unnecessarily and thus improve the availability of the workflow.

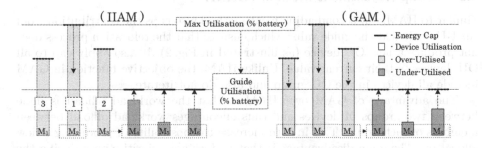

Fig. 2. MMUP adjustment algorithms

For both adjustment methods, in order to constraint each device's energy cost, we introduce a device specific cost matrix Q^i as an addition to the quadratic program formulated in MGECP.

Theorem 3. *Let*

$$Q^i_{uv} = \begin{cases} Q_{uv} & \text{if } n \times (i-1) < u \leq n \times i, \\ 0 & \text{otherwise.} \end{cases} \tag{11}$$

Then given an allocation scheme ψ and its allocation matrix X^ψ, we have the energy cost of M_i to be $\mathcal{E}^\psi_i = vec\left(X^\psi\right)^T Q^i\, vec\left(X^\psi\right)$

Proof. Proof is similarly to that of Theorem 1 and can be worked out easily. □

5.1 Iterative Individual Adjustment Method (IIAM)

In this method, we aim to reduce the energy cost of devices in OU individually (as illustrated in Fig. 2). With (11), we formulate a quadratically constrained quadratic program (QCQP) with an objective function that minimise the energy cost of the device with the highest utilisation value. As constraints in the QCQP, we cap all other OU devices' energy cost to their current value and all UU devices to the guide utilisation value. (For brevity we use the average utilisation of the current allocation scheme as our guide value. This can be replaced with tailored values to suit the requirement of certain workflows).

If the solver returns a new allocation, we then update the OU and UU group and again select the highest utilised device to the objective function. If this device is same to the one we picked at the earlier iteration, this means that we have reached the optimum solution under the constraints and exit. Otherwise, we repeat the process with the updated group classification until no new device can be picked from the OU group and provide a new allocation.

The advantage of this method is that it pin-points the highest utilised device of the MP, and support its workload offload with the entirety of UU devices. The disadvantage of this method is that all other members of the OU group is capped at their current utilisation value, this restraints the workload offload on the objective device when communication tasks exist between these devices.

5.2 Group Adjustment Method (GAM)

Similar to IIAM, our second adjustment method also caps the contribution from the UU devices at the guide value which ensures that the relocation process does not produce a new OU device (as illustrated in Fig. 2). It also apply cap to all OU devices to their current value. Unlike IIAM, the objective function in GAM include all devices in the OU group and also do not iterate.

The advantage of GAM over IIAM is that the workload offload is done between two groups of devices and thus encourages workload offload between members of each group. This in turn increase the possibility of producing a new allocation. The main disadvantage is that it does not prioritise on reducing the maximum utilisation which the workflow's availability is limited to.

6   Simulation

6.1   Environmental Settings

While it is intractable to cover all possible use cases of mobile workflows, we aim to base our simulation closely to the characteristics of an average mobile application and a modern smart device. We construct our simulation with the multiples of two essential building blocks: a *typical device* and a *unit workload*.

Definition 2. *A typical mobile device has a battery capacity of 2000 mAh, draws a current of 250–400 mA during data transmission and 100–200 mA when executing local computation tasks.*

In order to accurately emulate the correlation between modern mobile applications and the behaviour and capability of a state-of-the-art smart device, we consult the data presented in recent researches [8,16,20].

Definition 3. *A task has a* unit workload *if its execution takes 1 s to complete on a typical device.*

In our simulation, we specify each task's workload size using multiples of a unit workload. For instance, in the first plot of Fig. 3a, the tests are in 3 groups and the workflow generated in each test group has a task size that ranges in from 8 to 16, 16 to 24 and 24–32 units of a unit workload.

Apart from task size, many other factors (e.g. network bandwidth, etc.) also affects the energy cost of a workflow. Due to the length of this paper, we select to present the effect of different device to task ratios in our simulation settings to further verify our model and adjustment methods, as shown in the latter two plots of Fig. 3a. We also present the effect of different workload size distribution

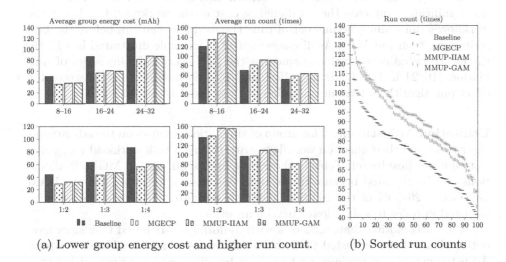

(a) Lower group energy cost and higher run count.   (b) Sorted run counts

Fig. 3. Reduction in group energy cost and increase in workflow run count

Table 1. Comparison of adjustment methods

Workloads[‡]	Tests	No.	MMUP-IIAM (MGECP)			No.	MMUP-GAM (MGECP)		
			Max.[†]	Avg.[†]	Dev.[†]		Max.[†]	Avg.[†]	Dev.[†]
Exp. 6	100	35	0.311(0.332)	0.210(0.192)	0.069(0.103)	29	0.295(0.320)	0.204(0.191)	0.062(0.098)
Uni. 4-8	100	41	0.329(0.360)	0.229(0.214)	0.068(0.105)	38	0.334(0.367)	0.230(0.214)	0.068(0.106)
Exp. 8	100	33	0.399(0.436)	0.266(0.242)	0.092(0.141)	30	0.403(0.437)	0.266(0.244)	0.093(0.141)
Uni. 4-12	100	45	0.440(0.486)	0.308(0.287)	0.087(0.140)	42	0.440(0.488)	0.306(0.289)	0.087(0.140)
Exp. 12	100	29	0.651(0.728)	0.425(0.391)	0.151(0.238)	31	0.628(0.706)	0.420(0.391)	0.137(0.225)
Uni. 4-20	100	44	0.640(0.716)	0.464(0.427)	0.124(0.221)	42	0.646(0.727)	0.452(0.424)	0.131(0.226)
Exp. 20	100	26	0.987(1.050)	0.640(0.598)	0.243(0.329)	26	1.014(1.082)	0.651(0.601)	0.250(0.349)
Uni. 4-36	100	49	1.113(1.244)	0.773(0.714)	0.234(0.378)	50	1.097(1.202)	0.754(0.701)	0.226(0.365)

† - All utility values are percentages (%) of residual battery (mAh). ‡ - Distribution and task size.

pattern in Table 1. For each simulation setting 100 instances are randomly generated and worked on. Averages are taken for comparison. We use AMPL and CPLEX 12.5's MIQP solver to solve the formulated problems.

6.2   Results and Analysis

Minimum Total Energy Cost. The first group of our simulations aims to verify the formulation of MGECP. As a comparison, we use a baseline algorithm which attempts to reduce the total energy cost by distributing the number of tasks evenly across the MP. This algorithm provides a good baseline value because although it does not seek the benefit of using an energy efficient device, its chance of being able to take that advantage is consistent.

As shown in Fig. 3a, the total energy cost of a baseline allocation is reduced by 30–35% with MGECP applied. Both adjustment algorithms are applied to allocation produced by MGECP. As shown in Fig. 3a, the adjustments does not significantly increase the total energy cost of the workflow, but boost the workflow's run count (the number of time the workflow can run before the first retirement from the MP). As discussed with the example illustrated in Fig. 1b, the fair distribution of workload amongst the MP is critical. One series of simulation (16–24 in Fig. 3a) is magnified and plotted in Fig. 3b to illustrate the effect our algorithms have in extending the run count of workflows.

Utilisation Adjustment. This group of simulations focuses on the adjustment algorithms and their effect on workflows with different task workload range and distribution. Results (cf. Table 1) show that first of all, not all MGECP allocations can be adjusted because of the tight constraints we apply in both IIAM and GAM. 26–50% of the 100 test instances generated in each setting can be adjusted in order to gain a lower maximum utility.

It is worth noting that workflows with uniformly distributed task sizes have better chance to be adjusted than those with exponential distribution pattern. Adjustments can be made when tasks can be offloaded or exchanged between

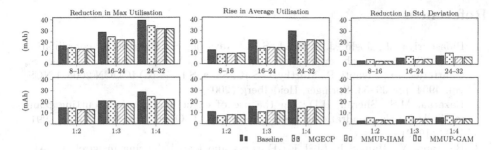

Fig. 4. Effect of adjustments within the MP.

devices without causing sizeable disturbance in each devices' energy cost. Contrary to that of exponential distribution, when workload's distribution is uniform within a set range, it is likely for a task to find another task that has similar workload size, thus a "minor" exchange of tasks is more likely to exist.

Device Energy Cost. This group of simulation focuses on the energy cost of individual devices. Figure 4 shows that in order to reduce the maximum utilisation, tasks has to be offloaded or exchanged to a device where it will cost more energy to execute which increase the average utilisation of the group. Increase in the group's standard deviation caused by MGECP shows that in order to minimise the group's energy cost, devices with better energy-efficiency are required to take on more workload than the others. On the other hand, the reductions of this value from MGECP to MMUP show that the workflow's energy cost is distributed more evenly within the MP after adjustments.

7   Conclusion

In this paper, we introduced a model that captures both computation and communication costs of a workflow with a 0–1 quadratic program. We demonstrated the use of MIQP solvers which produces exact solutions for the MGECP. We also investigated ways to adjust the allocation to lengthen the workflow's availability with minimal impact on its overall energy cost. Our simulation produces good results for both problems and gives an insight into workflows of different characteristics. Our model is also applicable to other energy critical scenarios, its extension can be tailored for workflows of specific use cases.

Acknowledgement. This work is sponsored by the Research Project Grant of the Leverhulme Trust (Grant No. RPG-101).

References

1. Balasooriya, J., Joshi, J., Prasad, S.K., Navathe, S.: Distributed coordination of workflows over web services and their handheld-based execution. In: Rao, S., Chatterjee, M., Jayanti, P., Murthy, C.S.R., Saha, S.K. (eds.) ICDCN 2008. LNCS, vol. 4904, pp. 39–53. Springer, Heidelberg (2008)
2. Bazaraa, M.S., Sherali, H.D.: On the use of exact and heuristic cutting plane methods for the quadratic assignment problem. J. Oper. Res. Soc. **33**(11), 991–1003 (1982)
3. Bejerano, Y., Han, S.J., Li, L.E.: Fairness and load balancing in wireless LANs using association control. In: MobiCom'04 Proceedings of the 10th Annual International Conference on Mobile Computing and Networking, p. 315 (2004)
4. Billionnet, A., Elloumi, S.: Using a mixed integer quadratic programming solver for the unconstrained quadratic 0-1 problem. Math. Program. **109**(1), 55–68 (2006)
5. Burkard, R.E., Pitsoulis, L.S., Linearization, J., Polytopes, Q.A.P.: The quadratic assignment problem. In: Pardalos, P.P., Resende, M.G.C. (eds.) Handbook of Combinatorial Optimization. Kluwer Academic Publishers, Dordrecht (1998)
6. Chang, C., Srirama, S.N., Ling, S.: An adaptive mediation framework for mobile P2P social content sharing. In: Liu, C., Ludwig, H., Toumani, F., Yu, Q. (eds.) ICSOC 2012. LNCS, vol. 7636, pp. 374–388. Springer, Heidelberg (2012)
7. Cuervo, E., Balasubramanian, A., Cho, D.k., Wolman, A., Saroiu, S., Chandra, R., Bahl, P.: MAUI: making smartphones last longer with code offload. In: MobiSys'10 the 8th International Conference on Mobile Systems, Applications, and Services (2010)
8. Dong, M., Zhong, L.: Self-constructive high-rate system energy modeling for battery-powered mobile systems. In: MobiSys'11 the 9th International Conference on Mobile systems, Applications, and Services (2011)
9. Feeney, L., Nilsson, M.: Investigating the energy consumption of a wireless network interface in an ad hoc networking environment. In: INFOCOM'01. Conference on Computer Communications. Twentieth Annual Joint Conference of the IEEE Computer and Communications Society (2001)
10. Gartner Research: Gartner Reveals Top Predictions for IT Organizations and Users for 2012 and Beyond (2011). http://www.gartner.com/it/page.jsp?id=1862714
11. Huang, C.M., Hsu, T.H., Hsu, M.F.: Network-aware P2P file sharing over wireless mobile networks. IEEE J. Sel. Areas Commun. **25**, 204–210 (2007)
12. Key Lime 314 LLC: KL Dartboard (2011). https://itunes.apple.com/gb/app/kl-dartboard/id376234917?mt=8
13. Lee, U., Park, J.S., Yeh, J., Pau, G., Gerla, M.: CodeTorrent: content distribution using network coding in VANET. In: MobiShare'06 1st International Workshop on Decentralized Resource Sharing in Mobile Computing and Networking (2006)
14. Mnaoue, A., Shekhar, A.: A generic framework for rapid application development of mobile web services with dynamic workflow management. In: SCC'04 IEEE International Conference on Services Computing (2004)
15. Pajunen, L., Chande, S.: Developing workflow engine for mobile devices. In: EDOC'07 11th IEEE International Enterprise Distributed Object Computing Conference (2007)
16. Pathak, A., Hu, Y.C., Zhang, M.: Where is the energy spent inside my app? fine grained energy accounting on smartphones with eprof. In: EuroSys'12 7th ACM European Conference on Computer Systems. ACM Press (2012)

17. Pentikousis, K.: In search of energy-efficient mobile networking. IEEE Commun. Mag. **48**(1), 95–103 (2010)
18. Philips, E., Carreton, A.L., Joncheere, N., De Meuter, W., Jonckers, V.: Orchestrating nomadic mashups using workflows. In: Mashups '09/'10 the 3rd and 4th International Workshop on Web APIs and Services Mashups (2010)
19. Shachnai, H., Tamir, T.: On two class-constrained versions of the multiple knapsack problem. Algorithmica **29**(3), 442–467 (2001)
20. Sharkey, J.: Coding for life - Battery Life, that is. Google IO Conference (2009)
21. Tang, C., Steinder, M., Spreitzer, M., Pacifici, G.: A scalable application placement controller for enterprise data centers. In: WWW'07 the 16th International Conference on World Wide Web (2007)
22. Zong, Z., Nijim, M., Manzanares, A., Qin, X.: Energy efficient scheduling for parallel applications on mobile clusters. Cluster Comput. **11**(1), 91–113 (2007)

Recognition of Periodic Behavioral Patterns
from Streaming Mobility Data

Mitra Baratchi[✉], Nirvana Meratnia, and Paul J.M. Havinga

Department of Computer Science,
University of Twente, Enschede, The Netherlands
{m.baratchi,n.meratnia,p.j.m.havinga}@utwente.nl

Abstract. Ubiquitous location-aware sensing devices have facilitated collection of large volumes of mobility data streams from moving entities such as people and animals, among others. Extraction of various types of periodic behavioral patterns hidden in such large volume of mobility data helps in understanding the dynamics of activities, interactions, and life style of these moving entities. The ever-increasing growth in the volume and dimensionality of such Big Data on the one hand, and the resource constraints of the sensing devices on the other hand, have made not only high pattern recognition accuracy but also low complexity, low resource consumption, and real-timeness important requirements for recognition of patterns from mobility data. In this paper, we propose a method for extracting periodic behavioral patterns from streaming mobility data which fulfills all these requirements. Our experimental results on both synthetic and real data sets confirm superiority of our method compared with existing techniques.

1 Introduction

With ever-increasing emergence of ubiquitous location-aware sensing technologies, collecting huge volumes of mobility data streams from moving entities has nowadays become much easier than before. Mining and analyzing such large mobility data can uncover information about behaviors, habits, life style of moving entities, and their interaction [1]. Periodicity is an important essence of the activities of humans and animals. Animal's yearly migration and weekly work pattern of humans are examples of periodic behavioral patterns. Knowledge of such periodicity is required in various domains. For example, ecologists are interested to know the periodic migration pattern of animals and how human activities in vicinity of their living terrain cause abnormality in this behavior [2, 3]. In humanitarian studies, it is interesting to identify interruptions in periodic routines by major life events or daily hassles, as this identification helps in understanding stress-induced changes in daily behavior of people [4]. Identification of such abnormalities in human behavior can be useful in designing solutions which alleviate the effect of such stresses (as used in various healthcare based participatory sensing systems [5]).

Apart from uncertainties associated with mobility data (such as noise and missing samples) which make mining periodic patterns challenging, online extraction of patterns from streaming mobility data is difficult due to availability of limited processing and memory resources. The problem of identification of periodic behavioral patterns has been studied previously. What distinguishes this paper from the existing research,

© Institute for Computer Sciences, Social Informatics and Telecommunications Engineering 2014
I. Stojmenovic et al. (Eds.): MOBIQUITOUS 2013, LNICST 131, pp. 102–115, 2014.
DOI: 10.1007/978-3-319-11569-6_9

however, is its focus on identification of periodic patterns from *streaming mobility data* through a *light, accurate,* and *real-time* technique. Our automatic pattern recognition method requires limited storage and processing capability and is able to detect periodic patterns upon arrival of every new mobility measurement. To this end and in the context of identification of periodic patterns from streaming mobility data, our contributions in this paper are:

- *accurate discovery* of *periods* of repetitive patterns from streaming mobility data
- *real-time* extraction of *periodic patterns* with *bounded memory requirement*
- performance evaluation using both *synthetic* and *real data sets*.

The rest of this paper is organized as follows. Related work is presented in Sect. 2. In Sect. 3, we will define the problem of finding periodic patterns from streaming mobility data. Our methodology is described in detail in Sect. 4. Sections 5 and 6 present performance evaluation, and conclusions, respectively.

2 Related Work

Existing solutions for pattern mining from mobility data can be divided into solutions addressing either *frequent* pattern mining or *periodic* pattern mining. The former techniques focus on the "number of times" a pattern is repeated, while the latter focus on the "temporal trend by which" a pattern repeats itself.

Frequent Pattern Mining: Association rule mining [6] has been popularly used for extracting frequent trajectory patterns [7–11]. The general approach taken by all these techniques is to use a support-based mechanism to find the *longest frequent trajectory pattern*. Support-based mechanisms focus on the number of occurrences of patterns. The main drawback of exiting frequent pattern mining techniques is that the longest frequent pattern cannot completely and accurately describe the normal behavior. Specifically, these techniques fail to detect behaviors that do not occur frequently but they happen more than a prior expectation at a certain period.

Periodic Pattern Mining: In the domain of time series analysis there are a number of papers considering different questions regarding periodicity [12], such as asynchronous periodic patterns [13], and partial periodic patterns [14] of time series. Recently, mining periodic patterns from mobility data has also received attention [15–17]. The authors of [15] proposed an automatic periodicity detection mechanism to find the periodic behaviors. They further extended their work for extracting periodicity from incomplete observations in [17]. Similar to [17] we are interested in detection of periodic patterns from incomplete data. However, there are two main differences between the two techniques. Firstly, detection of periodic behavior in [17] is based on reference spots. These spots are places where the moving object spends a considerable amount of time. Therefore, it is needed that the regions of interest are extracted beforehand. This requires a preprocessing phase, which is not needed by our technique, as we work with raw GPS measurements. Secondly, method of [17] is not designed for streaming data and consumes considerable amount of memory. Our method, on the other hand, has low resource consumption and complexity which makes it applicable in streaming settings.

3   Problem Definition

In this section, we clearly define the problem of finding periodic patterns from streaming mobility data. We first start by providing some definitions:

Definition 1: A trajectory $L_1, L_2, \ldots$ is composed of a sequence of points denoted by $L_i = (x_i, y_i, t_i)$ where (x_i, y_i) represents a spatial coordinate and t_i is a time-stamp.

Definition 2: A period of length T is a time frame composed of T equally-sized segments denoted by $seg^T_{1..T}$.

Definition 3: A spatial neighborhood $sn_{(x_i, y_i)}$ is a set of all points that fall within the radius r of (x_i, y_i).

Definition 4: A spatial neighborhood is visited periodically in a period T, if the probability of being in this neighborhood in a seg^T_t of period T is more than a threshold in all or a fraction of observation time.

Problem: Having memory of size $6T_{\max}$ where $T_{\max}$ is our guess about the maximum period followed in data, we are interested in the latest periodic pattern followed in data stream $L_1 \ldots L_i (i > 6T_{\max})$ in form of $< T, \left[SN^T_1, \ldots, SN^T_T \right] >$ where T is a period and SN^T_t is either empty or it is a spatial neighborhood $sn_{(x_j, y_j)}$ which is expected to be visited periodically in seg^T_t.

4   Methodology

Our method to find periodic patterns from streaming mobility data is composed of three stages (shown in Fig. 1): (i) Measuring the self-similarity of the streaming data in different lags (described in Sect. 4.1), (ii) discovery of the periods of repetition from the self-similarity graph (described in Sect. 4.2), and (iii) extracting periodic patterns (described in Sect. 4.3).

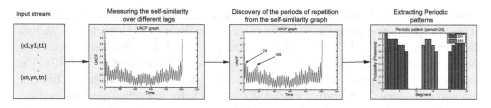

Fig. 1. Our framework for finding periodic patterns from streaming mobility data.

4.1   Measuring Self-Similarity of the Mobility Data in Different Lags

Behavioral patterns can have different periodicities (e.g. daily, weekly, monthly, and yearly). Therefore, it is important to be able to identify the period of repetition of visits to a certain spatial neighborhood. One of the most commonly used methods[1] for identifying these periods is the circular Auto-Correlation Function (ACF) [18]. ACF measures the similarity of a time-series to itself in different lags. ACF of a time series ts, of size N over lags $\tau \in \{1...N\}$ is computed as follows:

$$ACF_N(\tau) = \sum\nolimits_{i=1}^{N} ts(i).ts(i+\tau) \tag{1}$$

Due to difficulties such as cloud cover, or device malfunction, GPS data is often sparsely measured and mixed with noise while ACF requires the data to be uniformly sampled.

In order to measure the self-similarity from GPS measurements we propose the following optimization to the original ACF: Assuming that we denote missing samples with invalid and the rest with valid, we calculate the Uncertain circular Auto-Correlation Function (UACF) for a set of the mobility data $(L_1...L_N)$ using Eq. 2:

$$UACF_N(\tau) = \frac{1}{v_{1..N}^{\tau}} \sum\nolimits_{i=1}^{N} \Psi_{i,i+\tau} \tag{2}$$

Where $\Psi_{i,i+\tau}$ is equal to 1 when the Euclidean distance between a valid pair L_i and $L_{i+\tau}(dist(L_i, L_{i+\tau}))$ is less than a threshold θ, and $v_{1..N}^{\tau}$ is the number of pairs $(i, i+\tau)$ in which both $L_i, L_{i+\tau}$ are valid. Computing UACF in this way will help us to measure the self-similarity of GPS data only in an offline fashion when the entire mobility data is available. In the next section, we optimize UACF (Eq. 2) to lower down its memory requirements and enable it to measure self-similarity over different lags upon arrival of each mobility data measurement.

4.1.1 Measuring Self-Similarity in Streaming Setting (Online)

We believe that finding periodic behavioral patterns in real-time helps in reducing the data transmission and storage (as not the raw data but only the patterns or whether the entity conforms to the pattern can be transmitted or stored). Computing UACF requires the entire data to be kept in memory. Therefore, its memory requirement is $O(N)$ (N is the number of measurements). Ubiquitous location-aware sensing devices have limited resources (both memory and power). Therefore, storing the entire data set (especially in case of high frequency sampled data set) for a long period of time or transmission of this data set to a central server for further analysis is neither practical nor possible. This motivates us to lower down the memory requirements. To do so, we need to calculate the UACF in such a way that upon arrival of each new GPS measurement L_N, we can still measure self-similarity over lags $\{\tau|N \bmod \tau = 0\}$. We claim that it is possible to reduce the memory requirement from $O(N)$ to $O(T_{\max})$, by having an estimation of the maximum period being followed in data ($T_{\max} \ll N$). (Since $N \bmod \tau = 0$ in what follows instead of N we use $n\tau$).

---

[1] Fourier transfrom is also used for period detection. However, this method has a low performance in identifying large periods [15].

Theorem. Suppose that $L_1 L_2 \ldots$ represent the stream of mobility data. We can compute the $\{UACF_{n\tau}(\tau) \mid \tau < T_{max}\}$ for each $\{n > 3\}$ of this stream by having $O(T_{max})$ memory.

Proof. In order to prove the above theorem we first prove that we can re-compute Eq. 2 through an alternative way. Consequently, we prove that in its new form, the memory requirement of computing UACF is bounded by $6 * T_{max}$. Therefore, we will first prove through mathematical induction that for each $(n > 3)$, $UACF_{n\tau}(\tau)$ can be computed as follows:

$$
\begin{aligned}
UACF_{n\tau}(\tau) = \frac{1}{v_{1..n\tau}^\tau} & \left(v_{1..(n-1)\tau}^\tau \left(UACF_{(n-1)\tau}(\tau) \right) \right. \\
& \left. - \sum_{i=1}^\tau \Psi_{(n-2)\tau+i,i} + \sum_{i=1}^\tau \Psi_{(n-2)\tau+i,(n-1)\tau+i} + \sum_{i=1}^\tau \Psi_{(n-1)\tau+i,i} \right)
\end{aligned}
\tag{3}
$$

Base Step. The base step is to check the validity of the above equation for $n = 4$. For $n = 4$ computing $UACF_{4\tau}(\tau)$ by Eq. 2 results in Eq. 4 and computing this value by Eq. 3 will result in Eq. 5 (please note that due to circular shift operation $(\sum_{i=1}^\tau \Psi_{2\tau+i,3\tau+i} = \sum_{i=1}^\tau \Psi_{2\tau+i,i})$:

$$
\begin{aligned}
UACF_{4\tau}(\tau) &= \frac{1}{v_{1..4\tau}^\tau} \sum_{i=1}^{4\tau} \Psi_{i,i+\tau} \\
&= \frac{1}{v_{1..4\tau}^\tau} \left(\sum_{i=1}^\tau \Psi_{i,\tau+i} + \sum_{i=1}^\tau \Psi_{\tau+i,2\tau+i} \right. \\
&\quad \left. + \sum_{i=1}^\tau \Psi_{2\tau+i,3\tau+i} + \sum_{i=1}^\tau \Psi_{3\tau+i,i} \right)
\end{aligned}
\tag{4}
$$

$$
\begin{aligned}
UACF_{4\tau}(\tau) = \frac{1}{v_{1..4\tau}^\tau} & \left(v_{1..3\tau}^\tau \cdot (UACF_{3\tau}(\tau)) - \sum_{i=1}^\tau \Psi_{i,2\tau+i} \right. \\
& \left. + \sum_{i=1}^\tau \Psi_{2\tau+i,3\tau+i} + \sum_{i=1}^\tau \Psi_{3\tau+i,i} \right)
\end{aligned}
\tag{5}
$$

We replace $UACF_{3\tau}(\tau)$ in Eq. 5 to see if it is equal to Eq. 4. Using Eq. 2 we will have:

$$
\begin{aligned}
UACF_{3\tau}(\tau) &= \frac{1}{v_{1..3\tau}^\tau} \sum_{i=1}^{3\tau} \Psi_{i,i+\tau} \\
&= \frac{1}{v_{1..3\tau}^\tau} \left(\sum_{i=1}^\tau \Psi_{i,\tau+i} + \sum_{i=1}^\tau \Psi_{\tau+i,2\tau+i} + \sum_{i=1}^\tau \Psi_{2\tau+i,i} \right)
\end{aligned}
\tag{6}
$$

By replacing $UACF_{3\tau}(\tau)$ in Eq. 5 with Eq. 6 we get Eq. 4 as:

$$
\begin{aligned}
UACF_{4\tau}(\tau) &= \frac{1}{v_{1..4\tau}^\tau} \left(v_{1..3\tau}^\tau \cdot \left(\frac{1}{v_{1..3\tau}^\tau} \right) \left(\sum_{i=1}^\tau \Psi_{i,\tau+i} + \sum_{i=1}^\tau \Psi_{\tau+i,2\tau+i} + \sum_{i=1}^\tau \Psi_{2\tau+i,i} \right) \right) \\
&\quad - \sum_{i=1}^\tau \Psi_{2\tau+i,i} + \sum_{i=1}^\tau \Psi_{2\tau+i,3\tau+i} + \sum_{i=1}^\tau \Psi_{3\tau+i,i} \bigg) \\
&= \frac{1}{v_{1..4\tau}^\tau} \left(\sum_{i=1}^\tau \Psi_{i,\tau+i} + \sum_{i=1}^\tau \Psi_{\tau+i,2\tau+i} \right. \\
&\quad \left. + \sum_{i=1}^\tau \Psi_{2\tau+i,3\tau+i} + \sum_{i=1}^\tau \Psi_{3\tau+i,i} \right)
\end{aligned}
\tag{7}
$$

Induction Step. Let $\{k \in \mathbb{N} | k > 3\}$ be given and assume Eq. 3 is true for $n = k$. Then we can prove that the Eq. 3 is valid for $n = k + 1$ as below:

$$UACF_{(k+1)\tau}(\tau) = \frac{1}{v^{\tau}_{1..(k+1)\tau}} \Sigma_{i=1}^{(k+1)\tau} \Psi_{i,i+\tau}$$

$$= \frac{1}{v^{\tau}_{1..(k+1)\tau}} (\Sigma_{l=\left(\frac{v^{\tau}_{1..k\tau}}{v^{\tau}_{1..k\tau}}\right)_1}^{\tau} \Psi_{i,\tau+i} + \cdots + \Sigma_{i=1}^{\tau} \Psi_{((k+1)-3)\tau+i,((k+1)-2)\tau+i} + \Sigma_{i=1}^{\tau} \Psi_{((k+1)-2)\tau+i,((k+1)-1)\tau+i} +$$

$$\Sigma_{i=1}^{\tau} \Psi_{((k+1)-1)\tau+i,i})$$

$$= \frac{1}{v^{\tau}_{1..(k+1)\tau}} \left((\Sigma_{i=1}^{\tau} \Psi_{i,\tau+i} + \cdots + \Sigma_{i=1}^{\tau} \Psi_{(k-2)\tau+i,(k-1)\tau+i}) + \Sigma_{i=1}^{\tau} \Psi_{((k+1)-2)\tau,((k+1)-1)\tau+i} + \Sigma_{i=1}^{\tau} \Psi_{((k+1)-1)\tau+i,i} \right)$$

$$= \frac{1}{v^{\tau}_{1..(k+1)\tau}} \left((v^{\tau}_{1..k\tau}) \left(\frac{\lambda}{v^{\tau}_{1..k\tau}}\right) (\Sigma_{i=1}^{\tau} \Psi_{i,\tau+i} + \cdots + \Sigma_{i=1}^{\tau} \Psi_{(k-2)\tau+i,(k-1)\tau+i} + \Sigma_{i=1}^{\tau} \Psi_{(k-1)\tau+i,i}) - \right.$$

$$\left. \Sigma_{i=1}^{\tau} \Psi_{(k-1)\tau+i,i} + \Sigma_{i=1}^{\tau} \Psi_{((k+1)-2)\tau,((k+1)-1)\tau+i} + \Sigma_{i=1}^{\tau} \Psi_{((k+1)-1)\tau+i,i} \right)$$

$$= \frac{1}{v^{\tau}_{1..(k+1)\tau}} \left(v^{\tau}_{1..k\tau} \cdot (UACF_{k\tau}(\tau)) - \Sigma_{i=1}^{\tau} \Psi_{((k+1)-2)\tau+i,i} + \Sigma_{i=1}^{\tau} \Psi_{((k+1)-2)\tau,((k+1)-1)\tau+i} + \Sigma_{i=1}^{\tau} \Psi_{((k+1)-1)\tau+i,i} \right)$$

Now we prove that we can calculate Eq. 3 with bounded memory. In this equation, $\Sigma_{i=1}^{\tau} \Psi_{(n-1)\tau+i,i}$ is calculated from $L_{1...\tau}$ and $L_{(n-1)\tau+1...n\tau} \cdot \Sigma_{i=1}^{\tau} \Psi_{(n-2)\tau+i,(n-1)\tau+i}$ is calculated from $L_{(n-2)\tau+1...n\tau}$. $UACF_{(n-1)\tau}(\tau)$ and $(\Sigma_{i=1}^{\tau} \Psi_{(n-2)\tau+i,i})$ are single values computed in the previous round. It is straightforward with induction to prove that we can also compute $v^{\tau}_{1...n\tau}$ from $v^{\tau}_{1...(n-1)\tau}$ through $(v^{\tau}_{1...n\tau} = v^{\tau}_{1...(n-1)\tau} - v^{\tau}_{(n-2)\tau...\tau} + v^{\tau}_{(n-2)\tau...n\tau})$ where $v^{\tau}_{(n-2)\tau...\tau}, v^{\tau}_{(n-2)\tau...n\tau}$ are computed from $L_{1...\tau}$ and $L_{(n-1)\tau+1...n\tau}$ (The proof is omitted due to lack of space). We know that $(\tau < T_{max})$ so $(L_{1...\tau} L_{1...T_{max}})$ and $\left(L_{(n-2)\tau+1...n\tau} \cdot \in L_{(n\tau-2T_{max}+1)...n\tau}\right)$. Therefore, if we have $L_1...T_{max}, L_{(n\tau-2T_{max}+1)...n\tau}$ and $\{v^{\tau}_{1...n\tau}, UACF_{(n-1)\tau}(\tau), \Sigma_{i=1}^{\tau} \Psi_{i,(n-2)\tau+i} | \tau < T_{max}\}$ in memory we can compute $UACF_{N=n\tau}(\tau)$ for any τ. Thereby, instead of keeping N measurements in memory we only need to keep $6T_{max}(T_{max} \ll N)$ values and the rest of data can be removed. As stated before, by having an estimation of T_{max}, the correct periods can be extracted. In order to have the highest accuracy, choosing T_{max} can be performed considering the maximum memory available and changing the sampling rate.

4.2 Discovery of Periods of Repetition

If there is a single period of repetition in a time-series, the self-similarity graph (with both ACF and UACF) will show a peak in that period and all of its integer multiples. For instance, if there is a pattern repeated with period of 24 then the peaks will appear at 24, 48, 72, and so on. In order to extract periods of repetition from the self-similarity graph, normally the first highest peak is chosen. Since we cannot ignore the fact that there may exist multiple periodic patterns in mobility data, it is advantageous to be able to extract all periodic patterns and not only the one with the first highest peak. To clarify the case, in which multiple periodic patterns exist, let us consider the following example. Consider Bob, a student, who goes to school every weekday during the study year and stops going to school during summer. From one perspective, this behavior is periodic over a year (9 months going to school and 3 months holiday). From another view, we can also observe some other periods of repetition in this behavior (24 h, 7 days) as Bob goes to school every weekday and stops going to school on weekends. If we build a binary presence sequence for this activity of Bob for four years by placing 1 at each time stamp when Bob is present at school and 0 at other times, the self-similarity graph by computing *ACF* on this sequence will look like Fig. 2(a, b).

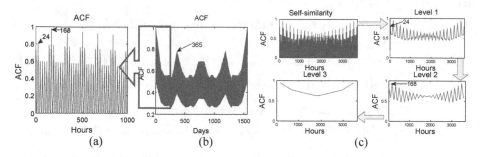

Fig. 2. (a) ACF self-similarity graph on the presence sequence of Bob on visiting school for the first 1000 h of 4 years ($\tau = 1$ h). (b)The result of performing ACF on the presence sequence data of Bob on visiting school ($\tau = 24$ h). (c) Extracting periods of repetition (Algorithm 1).

As seen in Fig. 2(a, b), in this self-similarity graph there are multiple valleys and hills, which are hierarchically ordered. The peaks with the highest ACF result are the ones which belong to the multiples of longer periods (in this example 365 days) and the lower hills belong to multiples of shorter periods (24 and 168). We can see intuitively in Fig. 2(c) that if we iteratively get peaks of self-similarity graph we can find such periods by choosing the first peak in each iteration. This will enable us to define periods of repetition as:

Definition 5: *Time lags $T_1 \dots T_n$ are the periods of repetition in a data stream if (i) the self-similarity graph has a local maxima in lags $T_1 \dots T_n$ and (ii) T_i is the first peak among peaks of level $i-1$ which is repeated in integer multiplies $(2T_i, 3T_{i,\dots})$.*

Our procedure of extracting the periods of repetition is presented in Algorithm 1.

Algorithm 1: Extraction of Periods of Repetition

INPUT: $UACF_N(1 \dots N)$(self-similarity graph)
OUTPUT: T (set of periods)
1:    Find first level peaks, $Peaklevel(1)$ among $UACF(1 \dots T)$ and set $i = 1$;
3:    **Repeat while** $Peaklevel(i)$ is not empty
4:        Find $Peaklevel(i + 1)$ among $Peaklevel(i)$ and set $i = i + 1$;
5:    **For each** $(j < i)$
6:        Set period $T(j)$ to the first peak in $Peaklevel(j)$ which is repeated in integer multiplies;

4.3 Extracting Periodic Patterns in Streaming Setting

Successful discovery and extraction of periods of repetition only tells us that some spatial neighborhoods are visited periodically. This, however, does not indicate which spatial neighborhoods and when (in which segment of the period) they have been visited. Considering that the random existence of a moving entity in a spatial neighborhood $sn_{(x_j,y_j)}$ at seg_t^T of a discovered period T follows a Bernouli distribution (being in $sn_{(x_j,y_j)}(1)$, not being in $sn_{(x_j,y_j)}(0)$), the probability that this entity appears in $sn_{(x_j,y_j)}$

at seg_t^T randomly is 1/2. If this probability is more than 1/2, it shows that the moving entity has not appeared in that $sn_{(x_j,y_j)}$ randomly and its visit conforms to a periodic pattern. Therefore, in order to find the periodic patterns we need to find spatial neighborhoods which have been visited with a probability more than ½ in each segment of the discovered period of repetition. Algorithm 2 summarizes how we can extract both temporary and permanently periodic behaviors from streaming data. The algorithm proceeds as follows. Firstly, we use UACF to extract the periods. Next, for each discovered period of repetition T_i, we update the entries of a list of size T_i (referred to as $PL^{T_i}, PL^{T_i} = \left[\left(P_1^{T_i}, V_1^{T_i}, SN_1^{T_i}\right), \ldots, \left(P_{T_i}^{T_i}, V_{T_i}^{T_i}, SN_{T_i}^{T_i}\right)\right]$). For each spatial neighborhood $SN_i^{T_i}$, $P_i^{T_i}$ denotes the number of presences in $SN_i^{T_i}$ and $V_i^{T_i}$ represents the number of valid observations $V_i^{T_i}$ in segment $seg_i^{T_i}$. In each timestamp entities of PL^{T_i} lists get updated. Each measurement $\{L_N | N \bmod T_i = t\}$ will be compared with the value of $SN_t^{T_i}$ of PL^{T_i} list. In case the measurement lies within $2r$ from $SN_t^{T_i}$, the value of $SN_t^{T_i}$ will be updated with the average of the previous $SN_t^{T_i}$ values and the new value L_N. The values of $P_t^{T_i}$ and $V_t^{T_i}$ will be also updated correspondingly. Finally, the pattern composed of the value of spatial neighborhoods with a probability over (1/2) will be returned as periodic pattern and those $SN_t^{T_i}$ with a probability less than (1/2) will be removed.

Algorithm 2: Extraction of Periodic Patterns

INPUT: L_N(data point), *Buffer*, $PL^{T=1\ldots TMax} = [P_{i.T}^T, V_{i.T}^T, SN_{i.T}^T]$, T_{max}, r(radius)

OUTPUT: *Buffer*, $PL^{T=1\ldots TMax} = [P_{i.T}^T, V_{i.T}^T, SN_{i.T}^T]$, $PPatterns_{1\ldots T_{max}}$

1:   Add L_N to the end of the *Buffer* and remove a point from the beginning of *Buffer;*

2:   Update $UACF_N(\tau)$ using the *Buffer* where $N \bmod \tau = 0$;// Equation (3)

3:   Find periods of repetition $T_{1\ldots k}$ from self-similarity graph $UACF(1 \ldots T_{max})$;// Algorithm 1

4:   **For each** period T_i in periods $T_{1\ldots k}$

5:       $t = N \bmod T_i$

6:       **If** $(dist\,(SN_t^T, L_N) {<} 2r)$, $P_t^{T_i} = P_t^{T_i} + 1, SN_t^{T_i} = (P_t^{T_i} \cdot SN_t^{T_i} + L_n)/(P_t^{T_i} + 1)$;

7:

8:       **Else if** $(\frac{P_t^{T_i}}{V_t^{T_i}} < 1/2)$, $SN_t^{T_i} = L_N$, $P_t^{T_i} = 1, V_t^{T_i} = 0$;

9:

10:      $V_t^{T_i} = V_t^{T_i} + 1$;

11:

12:      $PPattern_{T_i} = \{SN_{t \in 1..T_i}^{T_i} | P_t^{T_i} > 1 \,\&\, \frac{P_t^{T_i}}{V_t^{T_i}} > 1/2)\}$

---

5   Performance Evaluation

5.1   Complexity Analysis

In this section, we analyze the processing complexity and memory resources needed for extracting periodic patterns from streaming data of size N by Algorithm 2 assuming that the maximum repetitive period in the stream is less than T_{max}. We compare our method with the method proposed in [17] and with the original ACF. It should be mentioned that ACF and [17] only measure self-similarity. Therefore, we only have to address their memory and processing power in this task. In our method, arrival of each new point, extracting repetition periods, and updating the PL lists have processing complexity of (T_{max}), $O(T_{max} \log T_{max})$, and $O(T_{max}^2)$, respectively. As shown in Sect. 4.1.1, we reduced the memory requirements of measuring self-similarity to $O(T_{max})$ and discovery of the periods of repetition has memory complexity of $O(T_{max})$. In pattern extraction, we keep a PL list of size T for each period $(T < T_{max})$. Therefore, memory requirement of this task is $O(T_{max}^2)$. The method proposed in [17] extracts periodicities from each region of interest (rather than original data). In order to perform real-time and streaming period extraction, this method should be able to identify the regions of interest first. The regions of interest are not known beforehand. Therefore, to be able to compare our technique with [17], we simply assume that we compare each new GPS measurement with cells of a grid of size G. In this case, the processing complexity for this comparison will be $O(G)$. In order to measure the self-similarity, this method requires having all the previous points in memory and update probability of presence in each segment of each period. Then it measures the self-similarity for each possible period by $O(T_{max}N)$ processing. This task should be performed C number of times (C is a constant value) in order to normalize the data. Therefore, the processing power is $O(CNT_{max}) + O(G)$ and memory requirements will be $O(N)$. Complexity of ACF using Eq. 1 is $O(N^2)$ and it also requires the whole data in memory. Table 1 summarizes the memory and processing complexity of these three techniques. As seen, only our method is suitable for streaming settings.

Table 1. Complexity comparison

Method	Processing			Memory		
	Measuring self-similarity	Period extraction	Pattern extraction	Period extraction	Period extraction	Pattern extraction
Our method	$O(T_{max})$	$O(T_{max} \log T_{max})$	$O(T_{max}^2)$	$O(T_{max})$	$O(T_{max})$	$O(T_{max}^2)$
[17]	$O(G)$ $+O(GNT_{max})$	–	–	$O(N)$	–	–
ACF	$O(N^2)$	–	–	$O(N)$	–	–

5.2   Performance Evaluation Using Synthetic Dataset

5.2.1   Synthetic Dataset

Validation with a synthetic dataset helps us to check the sensitivity of our period detection algorithm under several parameters which cause imperfections in mobility data. We wrote a moving object sequence generator to produce a synthetic periodic sequence of a person's movement in N number of days. This periodic sequence is in form of $test_i = \{(x_i, y_i) | i \in [1, N \times 24]\}$ where each index represents a spatial neighborhood where a person is between $[(i - 1) \bmod 24, i \bmod 24]$ on the $(\frac{i}{24} + 1)$ th day. Ten spatial neighborhoods are defined, each composed of two dimensional points lying within radius r from a predefined center. We consider two of these spatial neighborhoods (representing home and office) being periodically visited (daily, and weekly) in specific intervals. For workdays, the interval 10:00-18:00 is chosen for "being at work" and 20:00-8:00 for "being at home". On weekends, the interval between 01:00-24:00 is chosen for "being at home". Each of these intervals is subject to a random event with probability of μ and is normal otherwise. In normal intervals with defined start (t_{start}) and end (t_{end}), the event of "visit" (being at home or office) starts somewhere between $(t_{start} \pm \sigma_1)$ and ends around $(t_{end} \pm \sigma_2)$. The behavior in abnormal intervals is randomly chosen from other 9 spatial neighborhoods with a random start-time and random duration. Such abnormal intervals can represent different un-periodic events such as absence at work, working overtime, or visit to places such as cinemas, shops, etc. After defining the normally and abnormally visited places (spatial neighborhoods) for each day, we add trajectories between them, each with different duration. This can represent different modes of transport (for instance, car, or bike). The effect of missing samples was tested by removing data from the random indexes with probability of α. In order to add noise, we formed a randomly permuted array of data between the maximum and minimum longitude and latitudes in selected spatial neighborhoods. Next, we randomly picked indexes with probability of β and replaced them with the values in the random array. The parameters used to form the test sequence are: radius of spatial neighborhood (r = 100 m), number of periodic repetition (N = 100), missing samples (α=0–50 %), noise (β = 0–50 %), standard deviation of start/end-time ($\sigma_1, \sigma_2 = 2$), and probability of random events (μ = 0–50 %).

5.2.2 Performance Evaluation with the Synthetic Dataset

The synthetic dataset generated by movement generator entails two periods of repetition (24, and 168 h corresponding to a day and a week). In this section, we evaluate Algorithm 1 to see how successful we are in extraction of these two periods using ACF and UACF self-similarity graphs (method of [17] is not applicable on raw data). We calculate self-similarity in different lags by ACF on latitude (lat), longitude (long) and their root mean square (RMS) $\sqrt{lat^2 + long^2}$. We test the effect of noise (β), missing samples (α), and random events (μ) on detection of correct periods by running the experiments 100 times (Fig. 3(a–f)). Figure 3(g) compares the precision computed by $\frac{P^+}{P^+ + P^-}$ where P^+ is the sum of correct prediction of two periods and P^- is the number of false alarms in all the previous experiments.

Looking at Fig. 3, we can see that UACF clearly outperforms ACF in presence of noise, missing samples and random events. Even when these parameters is near 50 %, considerably high percentage of correct periods is discoverable through using UACF by overcoming the effect of pattern-less data through taking into account the effect of points that fall into a spatial neighborhood. ACF, however, measures self-similarity by multiplying pattern-less data and those which follow a pattern. The overall precision using UACF is also higher than ACF.

5.3 Performance Evaluation Using Real Dataset

5.3.1 The Real Dataset

The real dataset we use (plotted in Figs. 4a and 5a), was collected using custom-designed GPS-enabled wireless sensor nodes carried around by two researchers. The devices were set to take one measurement per minute for a period of 31 days by first candidate and 109 days by the second one. When used inside the building, the nodes were placed near the window to obtain data. This however had made the dataset

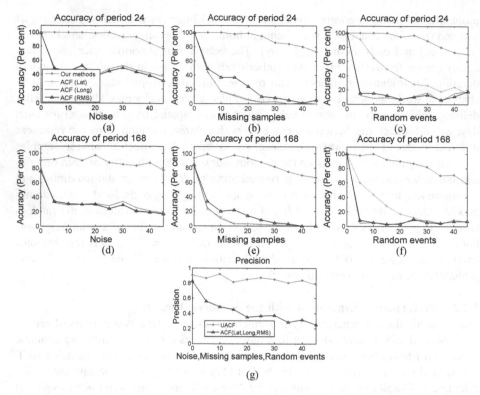

Fig. 3. (a–f) Comparison of the accuracy of Algorithm 1 in extracting periods of repetition (24,168) using UACF and ACF in presence of noise, missing samples and random events. (g) Average precision of Algorithm 1 in extracting periods of repetition.

extremely noisy. The data collected by first candidate is extremely sparse. This person, has kept the node off for all the weekends and the rest of data partly shows his regular behavior in commuting between home and work (weekdays) and very few irregular visit. The data collected by second candidate has less missing samples, while this person had a more dynamic behavior. She has gone on (i) work days to office, (ii) Saturdays to the open market in the city center, and (iii) regularly to a language class for a short period of time, and (iv) irregularly to a supermarket and a gym. Several other irregular behaviors have emerged for this person during the short period, such as traveling to another city, being absent at work or working overtime.

5.3.2   Performance Evaluation

Using the real data set, we calculated the self-similarity over different time lags with UACF and ACF (root mean square) (shown in Figs. 4b–c, 5b–c). We used Algorithm 1 to extract the periods of repetition from the self-similarity graph for both candidates. For the first candidate, we were able to extract the period of 24 h using UACF, while no period was found using ACF. We noticed that it was not possible to extract the period of 168 as no data was available for weekends. For the second candidate, UACF was able to detect both periods of 24 and 168 h, while ACF could only find the period of 24. This is because as it can be seen in Fig. 4b–c, the lag of 24 has the first highest peak in ACF graph and there is no distinguishable peak after that. The hierarchy of peaks, however, is clearly distinguishable using UACF. Therefore, both periods were easily found using Algorithm 1. After finding the spatial neighborhoods for each segment of discovered periods using Algorithm 2, we merged those ones which were closer than the diameter of the spatial neighborhood. Our approach is able to find two spatial neighborhoods for the first candidate (his home and office) (Fig. 4a) and 3 spatial neighborhoods are identified for the second candidate (her home, office, and city center) (Fig. 5a).

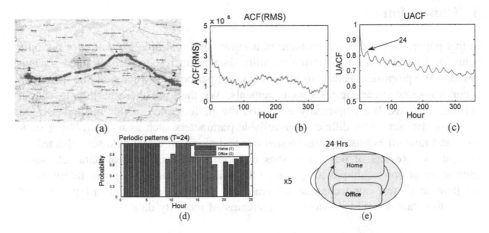

Fig. 4. (a) Mobility data stream (shown in blue) and identified periodically visited spatial neighborhood corresponding to this dataset (shown in red) of candidate 1. (b, c) Extracting periods from self-similarity graph of real dataset using ACF and UACF. (d) Periodic patterns extracted from algorithm 2, (e) state-diagram of periodic behavior.

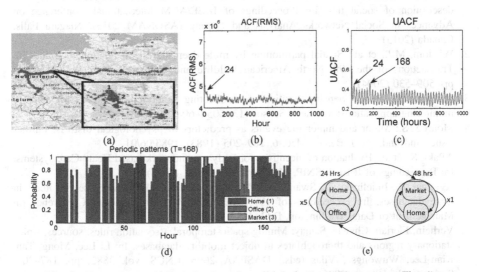

Fig. 5. Extracting periodic behavior of candidate 2. ((a–e) The same as Fig. 4)

The histograms in Figs. 4d and 5d are representing the probability of appearance in SP_i^T in segment seg_i^T of each of the larger discovered period found (from Algorithm 2). The state diagrams on right are drawn based on the histograms to represent the periodic pattern. As illustrated in the state diagrams, the periodic pattern of the first candidate is composed of a loop between home and work. For the second candidate, a periodic pattern of two loops is identified. These loops are repeated 5 times with the duration of 24 h (Weekdays). Next, a new loop of 48 h emerges which is only followed once, after which the first loop is repeated again.

6 Conclusion

In this paper, we address the problem of accurate and real-time extraction of periodic behavioral patterns from streaming mobility data using resource constrained sensing devices. We propose a method to identify correct periods, in which periodic behaviors occur from raw streaming GPS measurements. We then use these periods to extract periodic patterns. We empirically evaluated the performance of our method using a synthetic data set under different controllable parameters such as noise, missing samples, and random events. We also tested our technique on a real data set collected by two people. Results of our evaluations on both synthetic and real data sets show superiority of our technique compared to the existing techniques. In our future work, we plan to (i) test our technique for real data set of a large group of people and (ii) finding "abnormal" behaviors using streams of mobility data.

References

1. Baratchi, M., Meratnia, N., Havinga, P.J.M.: On the use of mobility data for discovery and description of social ties. In: Proceedings of IEEE/ACM International Conference on Advances in Social Networks Analysis and Mining (ASONAM 2013), Niagara Falls, Canada (2013)
2. Wisdom, M.J., et al.: Spatial partitioning by mule deer and elk in relation to traffic. In: Transactions of the 69th North American Wildlife and Natural Resources Conference, pp. 509–530 (2004)
3. Baratchi, M., et al.: Sensing solutions for collecting spatio-temporal data for wildlife monitoring applications: a review. Sensors **13**, 6054–6088 (2013)
4. Monroe, S.: Major and minor life events as predictors of psychological distress: Further issues and findings. J. Behav. Med. **6**, 189–205 (1983). 1983/06/01
5. Aflaki, S., et al.: Evaluation of incentives for body area network-based HealthCare systems. In: Proceedings of IEEE ISSNIP, Melbourne, Australia, (2013)
6. Agrawal, R., Imielinski, T., Swami, A.: Mining association rules between sets of items in large databases. In: Proceedings of 1993 ACM SIGMOD International Conference on Management of Data, Washington, D.C., USA (1993)
7. Verhein, Florian, Chawla, Sanjay: Mining spatio-temporal association rules, sources, sinks, stationary regions and thoroughfares in object mobility databases. In: Li Lee, Mong, Tan, Kian-Lee, Wuwongse, Vilas (eds.) DASFAA 2006. LNCS, vol. 3882, pp. 187–201. Springer, Heidelberg (2006)

8. Giannotti, F., et al.: Trajectory pattern mining. In: Proceedings of 13th ACM SIGKDD International Conference on Knowledge Discovery and Data Mining, San Jose, California, USA (2007)
9. Wei, L.-Y., Zheng, Y., Peng, W.-C.: Constructing popular routes from uncertain trajectories. In: Proceedings of 18th ACM SIGKDD, Beijing, China (2012)
10. Mamoulis, N., et al.: Mining, indexing, and querying historical spatiotemporal data. In: Proceedings of tenth ACM SIGKDD, Seattle, WA, USA (2004)
11. Baratchi, M., Meratnia, N., Havinga, P.J.M.: Finding frequently visited paths: dealing with the uncertainty of spatio-temporal mobility data. In: Proceedings of IEEE ISSNIP, Melbourne, Australia (2013)
12. Elfeky, M.G., Aref, W.G., Elmagarmid, A.K.: Periodicity detection in time series databases. IEEE Trans. Knowl. Data Eng. **17**, 875–887 (2005)
13. Jiong, Y., Wei, W., Yu, P.S.: Mining asynchronous periodic patterns in time series data. IEEE Trans. Knowl. Data Eng. **15**, 613–628 (2003)
14. Yang, R., Wang, W., Yu, P.S.: InfoMiner + : mining partial periodic patterns with gap penalties. In: Proceedings of ICDM 2002, pp. 725–728 (2002)
15. Li, Z., Ding, B., Han, J., Kays, R., Nye, P.: Mining periodic behaviors for moving objects. In: Proceedings of 16th ACM SIGKDD, Washington, DC, USA (2010)
16. Sadilek, A., Krumm, J.: Far Out: predicting long-term human mobility. In: Proceedings of Twenty-Sixth AAAI Conference on Artificial Intelligence, pp. 814–820 (2012)
17. Li, Z., Wang, J., Han, J.: Mining event periodicity from incomplete observations. In: Proceedings of 18th ACM SIGKDD, Beijing, China, (2012)
18. Oppenheim, A.V., Schafer, R.W., Buck, J.R.: Discrete-Time Signal Processing. Prentice Hall, Upper Saddler River, NJ (1999)

Detection of Real-Time Intentions
from Micro-blogs

Nilanjan Banerjee[1]([✉]), Dipanjan Chakraborty[1], Anupam Joshi[1],
Sumit Mittal[1], Angshu Rai[1], and B. Ravindran[2]

[1] IBM Research - India, New Delhi, India
{nilanjba,cdipanjan,anupam.joshi,sumittal}@in.ibm.com,
angshurai1@gmail.com
[2] Indian Institute of Technology, Madras, India
ravi@cse.iitm.ac.in

Abstract. Micro-blog forums, such as Twitter, constitute a powerful medium today that people use to express their thoughts and intentions on a daily, and in many cases, hourly, basis. Extracting 'Real-Time Intention' (RTI) of a user from such short text updates is a huge opportunity towards web personalization and social networking around dynamic user context. In this paper, we propose novel ensemble approaches for learning and classifying RTI expressions from micro-blogs, based on a wide spectrum of linguistic and statistical features of RTI expressions (*viz.* high dimensionality, sparseness of data, limited context, grammatical in-correctness, etc.). We demonstrate our approach achieves significant improvement in accuracy, compared to word-level features used in many social media classification tasks. Further, we conduct experiments to study the run-time performance of such classifiers for integration with a variety of applications. Finally, a prototype implementation using an Android-based user device demonstrates how user context (intention) derived from social media sites can be consumed by novel social networking applications.

Keywords: Social networks · Micro–blogs · Intention mining

1 Introduction

Social networking sites like Facebook, Twitter, Plazes and Jaiku, provide easy means for users to share their thoughts and form a portal for media–rich social exchanges. Interestingly, much of what is exchanged is 'context-indicative'- ranging from moods and opinions, to plans of a movie outing or a weekend hike. Prior work [2] report significant content (around 20 %) of messages on Twitter contain expressions of user interest and intentions. With the growing popularity of several social exchange portals, that too on the now ubiquitous mobile phones, it is inevitable that there would be a demand for applications having capabilities to exploit 'real-time' user context, like "find me buddies who are available and

© Institute for Computer Sciences, Social Informatics and Telecommunications Engineering 2014
I. Stojmenovic et al. (Eds.): MOBIQUITOUS 2013, LNICST 131, pp. 116–128, 2014.
DOI: 10.1007/978-3-319-11569-6_10

interested in seeing the Harry Potter movie tonight" or "Who all are interested in playing badminton today eve?". As such, applications like FourSquare[1] and research studies [4] centered around *ephemeral social networking* is a recent area of focus in industry and academia.

While users are rampantly providing cues about their real-time intentions via mobile social media channels, state-of-the-art in social networking systems, unfortunately, is not automated to capture these free-text "context cues". Users still need to manually organize such spontaneous events. A multitude of context-sensitive applications can benefit via automatic extraction of user's intent from inputs available ubiquitously at the user's finger tips and channelling them to relevant applications. Research along this vein has focused mainly on large-scale event extraction such as earth quakes, mass movements, and the like [15]. However, efficient and personalized extraction of real-time intention is challenging. This is the focus of our paper.

Conceptually, we define a Real-Time Intention (RTI) as *"text expression signifying an intent to perform an activity in near future"*. In particular, we focus on the two-class classification problem - is the update an RTI or a Non-Intention (NI)? Towards this, our goal is to investigate classification models that perform well with micro-blog feeds. The following challenges need to be addressed for such a task:

- *Limited Context Information:* Post size is restricted to a few characters (e.g. 140 in Twitter) – this gives a very short context window for traditional knowledge extraction algorithms [8] to be effective. Moreover, often the context is fragmented, making it difficult to mine the underlying intention, as in the tweet "Gorgeous evening. Out of work. Off to football. Life is sweet."
- *Richness of Exchange:* Postings are of several kinds: (1) daily activities (2) conversations, discussions (e.g. using hash-tags in Twitter) (3) URL mentions (4) Random thoughts (e.g. moods, feedbacks). For example, "Watching X-Men movies is fun" expresses an opinion, whereas "Can't wait to see the latest X-Men!!" suggests an activity intention. Efficiently segregating data pertaining to RTIs from other postings therefore becomes challenging.
- *High Dimensionality:* The use of language in a micro-blog is often informal and sometimes grammatically incorrect or ambiguous, contains mis-spellings, spoken acronyms and morphological variants (e.g. "me wanna play ice hokey nowwwwww!"). These factors along with inherent vastness of English vocabulary and proper nouns make the data highly dimensional in nature.

In this paper, we detect (and classify) RTIs in micro-blogs by taking into account micro-blog characteristics described above and provide a platform for efficient classification. Our feature extractors are built around the central intuition that relationships 'of several types' between word classes would yield better discriminatory power. This also reduces the dimensionality of the feature space. Ensemble classifiers are well suited for combining features that observe different aspects of the data. We propose three ensemble techniques to combine information from the feature extractors - late fusion, early fusion, and multiple kernel

---

[1] http://foursquare.com

learning (MKL) [14], based on SVM classification models. Our experiments show significant improvement in classifying RTIs and NIs over commonly used classification techniques that use word level features.

We demonstrate a prototype implementation that is connected to Twitter and is capable of funneling interesting tweets to a user's (Android) device. We believe that such selective context-cast of updates to interested users impacts a large class of current social networking applications. The R-U-In? application [4] that we developed earlier is a representative example of such emerging geo-social networking systems that can benefit from effective utilization of user context.

2   Related Work

Mining of user intention from natural language based dialogs have been a classical problem, researched extensively by computational linguists. A number of works [1] exist on the recognition of user intentions of different nature from dialogs between people and computers in co-operative task oriented environments. A natural progression of these works was to apply the techniques to mine user generated textual data obtained from either specialized application databases [13] or from the World Wide Web [6]. However, most of the work focused on the problem of document classification [11]. Work also exists towards extraction of user intentions and insights from informative one-to-one dialogs generated in a call center [5]. In comparison to dialogs and documents, micro-blog domain presents a unique platform where many of the user updates imply a *state of mind* in a few words. Furthermore, the conversations on these platforms take place in a fragmented and ad-hoc fashion.

Social networking websites, blogs and discussion forums are fundamentally different in nature from micro-blogs as they usually contain a large set of semantically interlinked statements, describing a view point. The above cited works exploit this property and reveal relatively *static* or *long-term* trends in user interests, content generation patterns, etc. Our focus, on the other hand, is on capturing real-time intentions in micro-blogs which are characterized by limited contextual information and spontaneous, incoherent expression of *short-term* to RTIs.

In [2], we show that a fractional (20 %), but quantitatively significant bulk of micro-blog content contains keywords indicative of user intentions, and reported results on keywords and n-grams commonly observed in Twitter for expressing real-time context. Inspired by these findings, we proposed [3] methods to extract linguistic and statistical features for RTI expressions, and demonstrated a heuristic-based fusion model for classifying RTIs. In this paper, we significantly enhance our initial work and focus on more effective techniques of building ensemble classifiers, and demonstrate an end-to-end system integrating such a classifier.

Hashtags are well-known to index and channel social media content to applications. However, they require user's attention and are suited for stable topics of discussions rather than spontaneous indications of real-time intentions.

Along these lines, recent works like [15] exploit free-text updates as *Social Sensor data* to rapidly detect real-time events such as earth quakes, tornadoes, etc. Basic SVM models used in prior work is sufficient here as events are of a broader nature (e.g. earthquake) and the hints are significantly stronger with a large learning corpus. Basic SVM models using word-level features led to about 60 % classification accuracy for our case, where events are more ephemeral in nature, and text expressions are much more varied, and learning corpus is relatively much lesser. Hence we focus on building better ensemble approaches.

3   Real-Time Intention (RTI) Classifier

We first provide the definitions of various concepts related to *Real-Time Intention* (RTI), followed by the description of our overall system for RTI detection and classification.

Terminology: *Content-Indicative Word (CI word):-* *"keywords that carry the central subject in an RTI."* These are typically proper or common nouns (e.g. movie, football), but not necessarily restricted to these parts of speech (POS). Each CI word belongs to a category (class). For e.g. "football" belongs to "sports".

Usage-Indicative Word (UI word):- *"Keywords that characterize the activity associated with a particular CI word"*. These can be either *Temporal* keywords : T-Words (e.g. evening, morning) or *Action* keywords: A-words (e.g. watch, go, see). We define T-words as words that describe the concept of *time* in a given statement. A-words are words that qualify the *action* associated with the CI word, normally verbs. Our definition is geared towards not imposing strong restrictions on the POS associated with these categories. Just like the CI words, each UI word also belongs to a category.

RTI:- *"A text expression containing* **one or more CI words** *providing* **class** *of intent; with* **one or more UI words** *that further qualify the intent, with no specific ordering"*.

Intuitively, our definition is generic and covers range of expressions to characterize RTIs in a single micro-blog, without grammatical constraints, while safely avoiding ambiguous expressions like *"excited about fishing"*. Note that we define all the terms using loose semantics since we do not want the definitions to be strictly grammatical or linguistically binding in nature.

Figure 1 schematically depicts our Real-Time Intention (RTI) Classification System that takes social updates of users, and classifies them into 'Intentions' or 'Non-Intentions'. As shown in the figure, the classification process is a 3-step one. In the first step, dimensionality of data is reduced in a manner that preserves the relationships amongst words and noise is filtered. In the second step, we extract features using the reduced data dimension space. In the final step, we combine these features to classify an update as intention (RTI) or non-intention (NI). This classification can be used by a plethora of social networking applications.

Let us discuss the three core steps of the classification system in more detail.

3.1 Noise Filter and Dimensionality Reduction

To bootstrap, we first create a vocabulary of CI and UI words that are indicators of presence of RTIs, following an iterative seed-set expansion process [3] from a corpus of micro-blogs and external sources like WordNet.

Keeping in mind that the solution we propose needs to deal with micro-blog data where documents of interest are very sparsely distributed, we use a *"Noise Filter"* that tests every input micro-blog for presence of at least one CI word in the vocabulary. This filter is applied to a micro-blog before allowing it to be passed through the series of feature extractors and classifiers.

We then canonicalize the occurrences of CI and UI words by reducing them to their base category representation. For example *"football"* is converted to *"sport"*, *"sushi"* to *"food"*, etc. This reduces the vocabulary size and hence the dimensionality of the data in a simple and interpretable manner, while preserving the word positions, and hence relationships in the lower dimension. For e.g., the tweet "rushing through friday...is going bowling tonite" is interpreted as "<rushing>[A Word; category $= Verb_{move}$] through <friday>[T word; category $= TypeOfDay_{weekday}$]...is <going>[A word; category $= Verb_{generic}$] <bowling>[CI Word; category$=sports$] <tonite>[T word; category $= TimeOfDay_{evening}$]. These canonicalizations are used subsequently by several feature extractors as outlined in the next step.

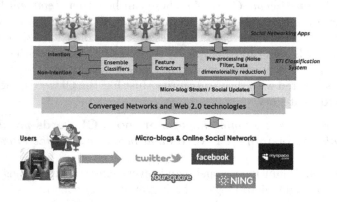

Fig. 1. Intention classification in micro-blogs

3.2 Feature Extraction

We learn a wide variety of information from each micro-blog by inspecting the linguistic relationships and statistical associations among words and phrases after representing the micro-blog in the reduced dimension of CI and UI word categories, for RTIs and NIs. Moreover, we inspect words and phrases *around* these canonicalized representations that show distinctive biases towards these classes. For these purposes, we use several 'Feature Extractors' that can inspect different aspects of information in the micro-blog, while handling issues of limited context information, use of informal language and presence of noise. The output is a feature vector representing the micro-blog. We provide a summary of the features we use for the learning. The details of how these features are extracted can be found in [3].

Co-occurrence Feature Extractor: This extractor analyses the micro-blogs based on the following intuition – if more relevant words co-occur in a micro-blog, likelihood of the micro-blog expressing an intent increases. For this, we find all the gappy bi-grams between relevant CI and UI words and compute the co-occurrences. Gappy bi-grams as features condense the data further across several words while addressing the issue of informal language, and keeps the contextual information intact and interpretable. For each micro-blog, this feature extractor produces the number of co-occurrences between CI and A-words, CI and T-words, A-words and T-words.

POS Feature Extractor: This extractor exploits the fact that although micro-blogs often lack grammatical accuracy, at a sub-sentence level, a user is likely to arrange words in correct grammatical order. For example, consider a tweet: *"me want to watch movie tonight"* and *"me hungry got to eat something"*. Though both examples lack grammatical correctness, the words are more or less in correct grammatical order around the intention. We capture these sub-sentence grammatical constructs *around* the CI words, and produce a feature vector representing the nouns, past tense verbs, and adverbs around the CI words.

Rule-Based Feature Extractor: This extractor learns a set of conjunctive rules that capture words and phrases, containing CI/UI words, commonly used to express RTIs. This produces a set of *intention favorable* rules (*RTI-Rules*) and *non-intention favorable* rules (*NI-Rules*); the rules themselves may not necessarily be grammatically correct. We use a conjunctive rule learner algorithm [9] to learn word based rules for both classes and use presence of these rules as features. This extractor produces a vector representing the number of matched RTI-rules and NI-rules.

Dependency Based Feature Extractor: This extractor identifies *relationships* shared by words in RTI and NI sets based on their grammatical roles, beyond what can be captured by simpler co-occurrence and POS extractors. The intuition is that words play *different grammatical roles* when used to express RTIs as when used for NIs. We capture these roles played by CI, A and T-words and how they relate to words around them. Each role is represented as a *relation* between the source word and a target word. We consider frequently occuring relations as candidates in the feature vector. Given a micro-blog, the output here is a feature vector indicating the number of frequently occuring relations that are present in the micro-blog. For e.g., in the tweet *"out of a head baking meeting... now some soccer!!!"* the tuple *"sport,now"* can be identified as following a dependency relationship using this technique.

Δ-TFIDF Feature Extractor: This technique captures words whose usage is heavily biased towards either one of the sets. Δ-TFIDF driven SVM models have been shown to improve performance in document classification tasks [12]. We first compute the TF-IDF values for different words separately for the RTI and NI sets for each category. Then the difference of two sets of TF-IDF values is assigned to each word as the Δ-TFIDF value. For non-discriminating words, Δ-TFIDF scores are nearer to 0. For each micro-blog, the output is: vector V=[$\Delta_1,\Delta_2..\Delta_n$], where n= no. of distinct words in the micro-blog, and Δ_i=Δ-TFIDF value for word w_i. By their very nature, TF-IDF based methods are grammar agnostic, hence Δ-TFIDF scoring efficiently handles informal usage of language while identifying discriminating utterances in micro-blogs. Also, since Δ-TFIDF are computed using canonicalized data, this approach is robust against emerging CI and UI words (and phrases) as they get accommodated in the vocabulary through regular updates to the different categories.

3.3 Multi-View Ensemble Classifiers

Each feature extractor looks at a different representation of the data. An ensemble classifier is suited for our classification task since they can combine insights from extractors that inspect different views of each micro-blog. Ensemble approaches have been found to be useful with respect to obtaining better classification performance, scale and parallelizability than single classifier approaches [7,10].

We present three support-vector machine (SVM) based ensemble approaches with the objective of exploring various design choices between computational overhead and accuracy. We choose SVM-based fusion techniques as this provides a theoretically sound approach to determining decision boundaries from complex multi-dimensional datasets, and has been found useful for two-class pattern recognition problems in text classification [15].

Late Fusion Approach: In this approach, we treat the output of each feature extractor as a vector. We learn *individual* SVM models for each of these feature vectors from training data. For each micro-blog, SVM_i outputs ρ_i= predicted probability of the micro-blog containing RTI by SVM_i. Thereafter, overall relevance value for a micro-blog is computed as the weighted sum $S = \sum_{i=1}^{5} \rho_i * w_i$, where w_i is normalized weight of the model SVM_i based on model accuracy. A micro-blog m contains an RTI if $S \geq \tau$ for m, NI otherwise.

Intuitively, this approach exploits the discriminatory power of individual feature extractors for classification, while compromising on the potential correlations present in the mixed feature space combining all feature extractors.

Early Fusion Approach: In this approach, all the feature vectors from different feature extractors are combined together to form a single, master feature vector. These feature vectors from the training data are then used to build a single SVM classification model which is used to perform classification. The prediction probabilities are used to assign class values after comparison with τ.

Intuitively, this approach exploits the true multi-dimensional feature representation, combining all features, right from the start. However, on the other hand, learning an effective model combining all features becomes more difficult as the optimization problem being solved by SVM classifier involves more features simultaneously, incurring additional computational overhead as compared to Late Fusion.

Multiple Kernel Learning (MKL) Approach: This is a theoretically stronger and intuitive approach of combining information from multiple sources by altering SVM internals [16]. We use a MKL formulation on the lines of SimpleMKL [14] for our classification task. We first build a master kernel using a linear combination of kernel values obtained from different feature extractors as follows: $\sum_{i=1}^{L} w_i k_i(\mathbf{x}_{in}, \mathbf{x}_{im})$, where $n, m = 1, ..., D$, $\sum_{i=1}^{L} w_i = 1$, $0 \leq w_i \leq 1$, L is the number of different kernels (corresponding to different feature extractors), and $\mathbf{x}_{in}$ is the feature vector obtained from feature extractor i corresponding to micro-blog n. The individual kernels used are linear kernels. So the SVM optimization problem now becomes the one of maximizing:

$$\tilde{F}(\mathbf{a}, \mathbf{w}) = \sum_{n=1}^{D} a_n - \sum_{n=1}^{D} \sum_{m=1}^{D} a_n a_m t_n t_m \sum_{i=1}^{L} w_i k_i(\mathbf{x}_{in}, \mathbf{x}_{im}) \qquad (1)$$

Where $\mathbf{a}$ $[a_1 \ldots, a_D]$ are Lagrangian coefficients and $\mathbf{t}$ $[t_1 \ldots, t_D]$ the class labels. Once the optimal weights are obtained, a test micro-blog $\mathbf{x}$ represented by multiple feature vectors $\mathbf{x}_1, \ldots \mathbf{x}_L$ is classified by the class value obtained from the reformulated function $sign(y(\mathbf{x}))$, where $y(\mathbf{x}) = \sum_{n=1}^{D} a_n t_n \sum_{i=1}^{L} w_i^* k_i(\mathbf{x}_i, \mathbf{x}_{in}))$. This may lead to a suboptimal solution due to stagnation at a local optima given the non-smooth nature of the solution space. To address this, we follow standard practise of choosing best values through multiple random initiations of $\mathbf{w}$.

4   Experiments and Evaluation

We implemented the RTI Classifier in JAVA, using APIs provided by libsvm, openNLP and Stanford's Dependency Parser[2] to build the different modules. We used the maximum entropy based POS tagger from OpenNLP[3] toolbox as the POS tagger.

Training and Test Data: For the purpose of learning the classification models and evaluating its discriminatory power, we use the data set available with [2]. This data set contains over 20 million publicly available tweets and a set of manually labelled micro-blogs containing a mixture of RTIs and NIs, totalling to 13206 tweets. The RTIs fall in five categories: *Movie, Sports, Music, Food, Dance*. For each category, a tweet that means an intention to perform an activity strictly in the near future was marked as an RTI. All other tweets, including ones that indicate activities being performed at present (e.g. watching a movie) or past activities and other irrelevant ones were marked as NI.

We used a 10-fold cross validation process for performance evaluation. Experiments were performed on a 2.83 GHz, 64 bit quad-core Intel processor system

---

[2] http://nlp.stanford.edu/software/lex-parser.shtml
[3] http://incubator.apache.org/opennlp/

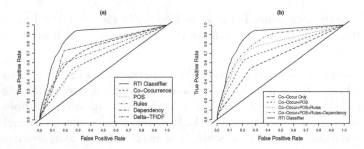

Fig. 2. ROC curves for RTI classifier using late fusion approach ($RTI_{class} = sports$) (a) SVMs built on individual feature extractors Vs RTI classifier, (b) Incremental contributions of individual feature extractors to RTI classifier performance. Results for other categories were similar.

with 4 GB RAM and 6 MB L2 cache. Different embodiments of RTI Classifier incorporate one of the three ensemble learning approaches discussed before. Along with each ensemble classifier that makes use of all feature extractors, we also study the corresponding classifiers that utilize only a single feature extractor, named as $Individual_{svm}$. This is to understand incremental contributions of different feature sets. We use the area under the Receiver Operating Characteristic (ROC)[4] curve (referred to as AUC) to compare performance. This provides useful insights into expected performance of the classifiers over the entire operating region. The plots use "RTI Classifier" as the uniform label to represent respective ensemble approaches.

4.1   Classification Results

SVM Ensemble vs. $Individual_{svm}$ **Classifiers:** Fig. 2 shows the comparative performance of Late Fusion Learning against SVMs built using individual

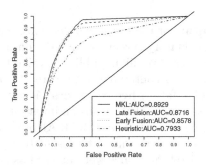

Fig. 3. Performance comparison of heuristic, late fusion, early fusion and MKL approach ($RTI_{class} = sports$). Results for other categories were similar.

---

[4] http://en.wikipedia.org/wiki/Receiver_operating_characteristic

feature extractors. We observe that the fusion approach performs better than the $Individual_{svm}$ classifiers. This shows that different features jointly contribute additional information towards building better decision boundaries for our task. Among different $Individual_{svm}$ classifiers, POS and Co-occurrence features produce similar results; Dependency and Rule based features perform better than these two; while Δ-TFIDF features due to its capability of exploiting discriminatory words performs best. Finally, from Fig. 2b, we notice that single classifiers in fact contribute to various degrees to provide an overall improvement to the ensemble.

Cross-comparison of Ensembles: Fig. 3 shows performance comparison of all three ensembles and the best prior result on this data set using a heuristic-based linear classifier [3]. In the heuristic-based approach, each feature extractor adds a bias in the classification of a given micro-blog. For each extractor, a relevance score R_{c_i} is computed, which is the confidence given by the extractor to a given micro-blog to contain an RTI for class c_i. The combined relevance value S is a weighted linear sum of the individual R_{c_i} scores. A micro-blog is classified as an RTI of class c_i if S > discrimination threshold τ; NI otherwise.

We observe from the AUC that the ensemble approaches provide substantial improvement over the known heuristic. Going into deeper analysis, Late and Early Fusion approaches work similarly, specially at lower values of τ. However, Late Fusion performs better than Early Fusion at higher values of τ. This indicates that combining features across different dimensions early is having a slight deteriorating effect for our data-set. This has also been reported for other classification tasks. We observe for MKL approach, the performance is sustained till TPR (True Positive Rate) beyond 90 %. It also largely provides the best TPR for the same FPR compared to others. Moreover, we found that time delay in MKL is comparable to the two fusion approaches. This makes it best suitable for applications requiring high precision and recall. We wish to point out that by nature of formulation of the MKL approach used here, it was not guaranteed that optimal weights would be obtained. However, our trainings with different random seeds resulted in identical performance plots.

We obtained accuracies of 52–65% from experiments conducted using bag of words as features using the standard SVM classifier (as well as J48 decision trees, naive bayes). Across all categories, we obtained ≈20–25% improvement in AUC, on use of different ensemble approaches. This provides evidence that the feature extraction techniques are generic towards deriving useful aspects of RTI. Further, the ensemble techniques provide effective integration of these features, leading to an effective classification system.

4.2   Run-Time Performance

We measure classification delay of the complete system under two conditions: (1) Without Noise Filter (2) With Noise Filter, on a stream of 50,000 tweets, containing sparsely located RTIs, emulating real-life situations. Table 1 presents the results. Heuristic approach has minimum classification delay (sec/tweet) owing

Table 1. Run-time performance of different approaches

Approach	W/O Noise Filter (sec/tweet)	W/ Noise Filter (sec/tweet)	W/O Noise Filter (tweets/month)	W/ Noise Filter (tweets/month)
Heuristic	0.237	0.0189	10×10^6	137×10^6
Late Fusion	0.677	0.0216	3.8×10^6	120×10^6
Early Fusion	0.840	0.0227	3×10^6	114×10^6
MKL	0.736	0.0219	3.51×10^6	118×10^6

to its simplicity. We observe that Late Fusion approach performs slightly better than Early Fusion and MKL approach while MKL approach, in turn, performs slightly better than Early Fusion approach. We note that the ensemble systems with Noise Filter (last column) are capable of catering to the overall tweet generation rate of $\tilde{1}00$ million tweets per month[5]. Going forward, we intend to improve the throughput further via parallel computation of features, kernels and individual classifier scores.

5   System Demonstration

In this section, we present how we leveraged the RTI Classifier and integrated Twitter with R-U-In? [4] - an activity-oriented social networking system for users to collaborate and participate in activities of mutual interest. R-U-In? essentially enables a user interested in a certain activity (e.g. movie, game of tennis, etc.) to

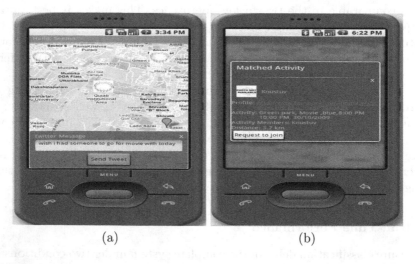

(a)   (b)

Fig. 4. Integration of Twitter with R-U-In? exploiting RTI Classification

---

[5] http://blog.twitter.com/2010/02/measuring-tweets.html

look for people who have expressed similar interests and to schedule an activity based on their availability over preferred modes of communications. However, following conventional models, R-U-In? depends on *structured* user interests that are expressed explicitly with some tools or applications (e.g., SMS, gtalk, etc.). RTI Classifier brings the power of intelligent suggestions inferred from implicit expression of user interests (e.g., somebody tweeting about an activity-related intention) and enhances the overall R-U-In? experience.

We consider the following scenario to illustrate this claim. Let us assume that Joshua has already scheduled a movie-watching activity with some of his interested and available friends following the procedure described in [4]. Now, another of his friends, Sam, gets interested in going for a movie and uses his Android based mobile phone to express his intention. Figure 4a, shows a screenshot of Sam's Android phone, where he logs into the R-U-In? portal and uses the Twitter box to post the tweet *"wish i had someone to go for movie with today"*. This tweet is automatically captured by RTI Classifier that declares this tweet as carrying real-time intention along with keywords describing the intention (e.g. category, and any temporal word describing time). This interest along with Sam's location (obtained from other offline channels such as phone's inherent location tracking mechanism or GPS) is semantically matched thereafter by R-U-In?'s match-making engine and a number of matching activities in Sam's neighborhood is shown in the Google map of R-U-In? portal. Figure 4a also shows Sam's current location and the matching activities. A click on a matching activity shows further details of the activity (e.g., time, location, owner of the activity) and an option to join it. This is shown in Fig. 4b. Sam selects an activity of interest and ends up joining his friends over the movie.

We argue that our RTI Classifier can be similarly integrated with several other social networking applications, thus progressing the state-of-art in social communication.

6 Conclusion

This paper carried out a thorough analysis of micro-blogs towards detection and classification of Real-Time Intentions (RTIs) of users. We presented feature extractors that obtain relational features in a reduced dimension of the complex micro-blog data along with the performance evaluation of ensemble learning approaches for combining these features. We believe our methodology, system demonstration and performance evaluation offer significant insights to applications aiming to exploit free-text intentions from social media.

References

1. Allen, J.: Recognizing intentions from natural language utterances. In: Brady, M., Berwick, R.C. (eds.) Computational Models of Discourse, pp. 107–166. MIT Press, Cambridge (1983)

2. Banerjee, N., et al.: User interests in social media sites: an exploration with micro-blogs. In: International Conference on Information and Knowledge Management (CIKM) (2009)
3. Banerjee, N., et al.: Towards analyzing micro-blogs for detection and classification of real-time intentions. In: ICWSM (2012)
4. Banerjee, N., et al.: R-U-In? - exploiting rich presence and converged communications for next-generation activity-oriented social networking. In: International Conference on Mobile Data Management Systems (MDM), Services and Middleware (2009)
5. Chalamalla, A.K., et al.: Identification of class specific discourse patterns. In: ACM Conference on Information and Knowledge Management (2008)
6. Chen, Z., et al.: User intention modeling inweb applications using data mining. World Wide Web: Internet and Web Inf. Syst. 5, 181–191 (2002)
7. Dietterich, T.G.: Ensemble methods in machine learning. In: Kittler, J., Roli, F. (eds.) MCS 2000. LNCS, vol. 1857, pp. 1–15. Springer, Heidelberg (2000)
8. Han, J., et al.: Mining frequent patterns without candidate generation (2000)
9. Han, J., et al.: Data Mining Concepts and Techniques, Chap. 6, 2nd edn, pp. 318–327. Morgan Kaufmann, San Francisco (2006)
10. Hastie, T., et al.: The Elements of Statistical Learning: Data Mining, Inference, and Prediction, 2nd edn. Springer, New York (2009)
11. Liu, R.-L., et al.: Incremental context mining for adaptive document classification. In: KDD, pp. 599–604 (2002)
12. Martineau, J., et al.: Delta TFIDF: an improved feature space for sentiment analysis. In: AAAI Internatonal Conference on Weblogs and Social Media (2009)
13. Nasukawa, T., et al.: Text analysis and knowledge mining system. IBM Syst. J. 40(4), 967–984 (2001)
14. Rakotomamonjy, A., et al.: SimpleMKL. J. Mach. Learn. Res. (JMLR) 9, 2491–2521 (2008)
15. Sakaki, T., et al.: Earthquake shakes twitter users: real-time event detection by social sensors. In: WWW (2010)
16. Varma, M., et al.: Morje generality in efficient multiple kernel learning. In: ICML (2009)

Fast and Accurate Wi-Fi Localization in Large-Scale Indoor Venues

Seokseong Jeon[1]([⊠]), Young-Joo Suh[1], Chansu Yu[2], and Dongsoo Han[3]

[1] ITCE, POSTECH, Pohang, Korea
{ngelquee,yjsuh}@postech.ac.kr
[2] ECE, Cleveland State University, Cleveland, OH, USA
c.yu91@csuohio.edu
[3] CS, KAIST, Daejon, Korea
ddsshhan@kaist.ac.kr

Abstract. An interest and development of indoor localization has grown along with the scope of applications. In a large and crowded indoor venue, the population density of access points (APs) is typically much higher than that in small places. This may cause a client device such as a smartphone to capture an *imperfect* Wifi fingerprints (FPs), which is essential piece of data for indoor localization. This is due to the limited access time allocated per channel and collisions of responses from APs. It results in an extended delay for localization and a massive unnecessary traffic in addition to a high estimation error. This paper proposes a fast and accurate indoor localization method for large-scale indoor venues using a small subset of APs, called *representative APs* (rAPs). According to our experimental study in a large venue with 1,734 APs, the proposed method achieves the estimation error of 1.8~2.1 m, which can be considered a very competitive performance even in small-scale places with a few hundreds of APs.

Keywords: WiFi fingerprints · Indoor localization · Probe response

1 Introduction

Location-based services (LBS) are becoming a huge market with the proliferation of mobile devices such as smartphones and tablets. To make it ubiquitous, localization and navigation indoors within urban structures is critically important. This is evident by recent news including the foundation of In-Location Alliance (Broadcom, Nokia, Sony Mobile, Samsung, Qualcomm, etc.), Qualcomm's IZat chipset, Google's Indoor Maps, and Apple's acquisition of WiFiSLAM. WLAN (IEEE 802.11)-based Positioning System (WPS) attracts a lot of attention for this purpose because GPS signal is not reachable but existing WiFi infrastructure is abundant. A set of *received signal strength* (RSS) values from reachable WiFi *access points* (APs), called *fingerprint* (FP), is used to estimate the location in WPS [2,24]. A WPS typically consists of offline and online phases.

© Institute for Computer Sciences, Social Informatics and Telecommunications Engineering 2014
I. Stojmenovic et al. (Eds.): MOBIQUITOUS 2013, LNICST 131, pp. 129–141, 2014.
DOI: 10.1007/978-3-319-11569-6_11

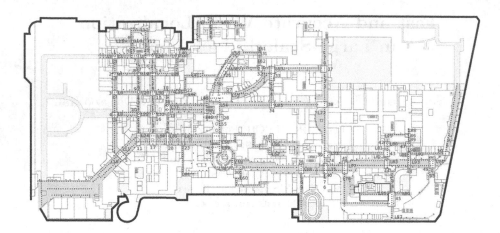

Fig. 1. A map of underground mall of Coex of $505 \times 237\,\text{m}^2$ or $119,685\,\text{m}^2$ in downtown Seoul, South Korea. (Small dots denote 2,028 locations where FPs are collected. Shaded areas and numbers represent 96 line segments and 50 intersections, respectively, which will be explained later in this paper.)

In the offline phase, FPs are collected at several locations in the venue, creating a *WiFi radiomap*, where each FP is annotated with the corresponding location information. In the online phase, the location of a client device is estimated by searching the radiomap to find the FP(s) that is(are) closest to the measured FP by the client device.

In this paper, we show that FPs are *imperfect* in large-scale indoor venues due to the *probe response explosion problem*. This has not been studied in the literature mainly because most of previous work have been tested in small places We, then, propose to use a predetermined subset of APs called *representative APs* (rAP) instead of an exhaustive set of all APs in the neighborhood, which leads to indoor localization at a higher accuracy with a fraction of time during the online phase. Note that rAP can be considered as a landmark [16] or an anchor [22] in the context of localization in sensor networks and robot navigation. According to our experiments with real-life radiomap of a large-scale indoor venue with 1,734 APs, the proposed method achieves an estimation error as small as 1.8 m while conventional Wifi FP-based method cannot make it lower than 5.2 m. To our knowledge, this can be considered one of the best performance reported in the literature. Estimation delay is an order smaller than conventional methods as it uses less APs.

The rest of this paper is organized as follows: Sect. 2 explains characteristics of a large-scale indoor venue contrasting with a typical academic building. It also overviews Wifi FP-based indoor localization methods. Section 3 presents a notable phenomenon exhibited in a large, AP-crowded place. Section 5 proposes the idea of rAP and how it can help improve the localization accuracy and reduce the estimation delay, which is followed by performance study in Sect. 5. Finally, we will conclude this paper in Sect. 6.

2   Background and Related Work

2.1   Characteristics of a Large Indoor Venue

The main subject we are dealing with in this paper is a very large indoor site. As an example venue, we surveyed underground mall of Coex, which is a building of business and shopping complex. It is about $120,000\,m^2$ of total floor space $(505 \times 237\,m^2)$ with 1,734 APs as shown in Fig. 1. It is obvious that any single AP cannot cover the entire area. FPs are collected at 2,028 locations in the venue (marked as blue crosses in the figure) but as a matter of fact, we measured FPs 20 times at every measurement location to deal with noise and signal fluctuation as discussed in [2].

Figure 2a visualizes the radiomap matrix of Coex mall, where rows and columns represent FPs (locations) and APs, respectively. In the matrix, RSS of APs at every location is marked by a white point whenever the corresponding AP is detected and its beacon message is received successfully. As shown in the figure, the radiomap is sparse, i.e., only $2.8\,\%$ of the 3,516,552 cells have meaningful values. In order to compare the scale of Coex mall with typical indoor venues studied elsewhere, an academic building at the Hong Kong University of Science and Technology (HKUST) has been used in this paper [23]. It has a dimensions of $145.5\,m \times 37.5\,m$ with 101 APs and 247 FPs measured. Figure 2b shows the radiomap matrix of HKUST with the sparsity of $8.7\,\%$. One important observation is that each FP (location) has almost an order of magnitude greater number of features (APs) in Coex than in HKUST. One can observe 52 APs at a location on the average in Coex but this number reduces to 9 APs in HKUST. For more detailed comparison between Coex and HKUST, please refer to [1].

2.2   Related Work on WPS

WLAN-based positioning system (WPS) is an attractive indoor localization technique because of the wide deployments of Wifi infrastructures. It is based on location fingerprinting, or known as scene analysis as discussed in Introduction. RADAR [2] is the first of this kind that determines user location using kNN (k-nearest neighbor) for matching. In other words, it finds 'k' closest locations (FPs) in terms of Euclidean distance in RSS space and estimates the location of a client device as the centroid of those 'k' locations. Other methods such as probabilistic methods [24] and neural network [3] can be used instead of kNN.

Due to the large amount of radiomap data, there has been an active research in reducing the computational cost for WPS localization [7,14,15,24,25]. Previous work either reduces $|FP|$ or $|AP|$ (subsetting either FPs or APs) to decrease the search space. Note that most of previous work focused on the former because small-scale environments like academic buildings, where most of previous studies experimented, have a small $|AP|$ and $|FP| \gg |AP|$. A widely used approach is to divide FPs into a number of clusters based on, for example, the commonality of strongest APs (APs with the highest RSS values). This reduces the computational time because the search space is reduced to a particular cluster rather than the entire radiomap [14,24].

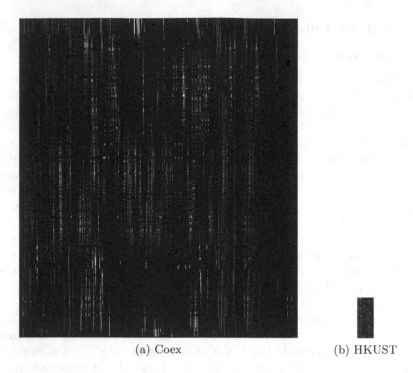

(a) Coex   (b) HKUST

Fig. 2. Radiomap matrices (The horizontal and the vertical axis represent APs and locations, respectively, and the size of the two matrices are $2,028 \times 1,734$ and 247×101. In Fig. (a), $|FP| \approx |AP|$ while, in Fig. (b), $|FP| \gg |AP|$.)

However, with a large number of APs observed at each location (or FP) in Coex mall, the difference in RSS values of two subsequent APs may be very small when they are ordered according to the RSS values. Slight variations in RSS measurement would result in a different set of the strongest APs as well as a different cluster. Some clustering algorithms group FPs based on the commonality of the existence of a few APs. However, with a large-scale dataset collected from Coex, this would produce a huge number of clusters, rendering the online phase of the localization an overwhelming process. Some other cluster FPs based on their physical locations [8], which seems not feasible due to the continuous nature of the huge indoor space such as Coex mall.

Although not very popular, it is also possible to use a subset of APs for the purpose of reducing the computational cost [7,15,25]. However, this idea of subsetting APs or choosing more "discriminative" APs may not be trivial in a large-scale environment due to the large number of APs. Moreover, it may not be effective because every AP could be important to localize a place or a store where the AP is installed. This is due to the fact that a majority of APs are observed at less than ten locations at Coex, which is in turn caused by the greater path loss in urban structures with lots of obstacles and people movement [1]. Elimination of some APs in the radiomap may need to trade a significant performance degradation in exchange of less complexity.

Alternately, there are approaches that do not rely on Wifi FPs [6,21]. Even they represent meaningful improvements, mostly they require additional hardwares including image sensors and bluetooth devices [6], or need to modify lower layer implementation [21].

3   Explosion of Probe Responses and Missing APs

3.1   WiFi FP and Scanning

A more serious problem in large-scale indoor venues is *probe response explosion problem* introduced earlier. WPS-based localization requires WiFi FPs, which is essentially the scanning of APs in the proximity. It has been an active area of research for at least two decades because it is an important part of handoff procedure [5,19,20]. *Passive scanning* depends on periodic beacon messages from APs. Although it does not incur any additional traffic in the network, it causes a non-negligible delay as the beacon interval is typically 100 ms.

On the other hand, *active scanning* uses *probe request* and *probe response* management frames. A client device sends a probe request frame with the destination of broadcast address and receives probe responses from nearby APs as well as their RSS to constitute a FP. Since there are multiple channels in 802.11, the client device switches from one channel to the next to scan all available channels. It stays at one channel during a predefined time period, called *MinChannelTime*. However, it does not stay more than another predefined time, called *MaxChannelTime*, in a channel. 802.11 standards do not specify the values but they are typically 1 and 30 ms, respectively [20].

3.2   Missing APs

The standard scanning process mentioned above does not pose a challenge in small venues, which are typically used in most of previous work on indoor localization. However, it poses a serious problem in large indoor venues. For example, in Coex mall, there are about 52 APs within the communication range at a certain random location. If a majority of them use one of three non-overlapping channels (1, 6 and 11), each channel is crowded with more than 15 APs, probe responses from which cannot be accommodated within the given *MaxChannelTime*. FPs will be *imperfect* as the client device cannot receive all probe responses. Moreover, it is possible that a stronger probe response captures weaker ones in case two or more APs send simultaneously.

Imperfect FP: Missing some APs could affect the accuracy of WPS in a significant manner because it results in incorrect Euclidean distances and thus offers a wrong set of closest FPs. However, investigation of the radiomap of Coex mall shows that a single scan misses a large number of APs. In other words, the AP population detected at a location is much less than what can be observed as

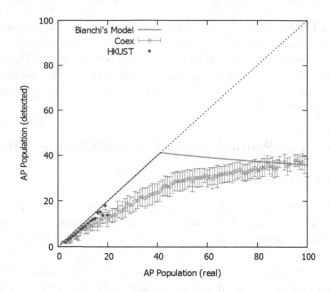

Fig. 3. AP population: real versus detected per scan. (Real and detected almost coincide at HKUST but they diverge in Coex mall when real exceeds 40. Parameters for Bianchi model are: Data rate 11 Mbps, Slot time 20 μs, SIFS 10 μs, DIFS 50 μs, MaxChannelTime 30 ms, Packet header 100 bytes, Payload 300 bytes, ACK 14 bytes.)

clearly shown in Fig. 3. Note that the real AP population is obtained because we surveyed 20 times at each of 2,028 locations in Coex mall. With a such reception ratio shown in Fig. 3, an intact FP cannot be composed. And the imperfect FP will cause miscalculation of a vector distance leading to an incorrect location estimation. In typical Wifi FP-based localization methods, missing values in a FP is replaced by the smallest possible value (i.e., −95 dBm) assuming that they are not detected because their signals are too weak. It is evident that this could cause a high estimation error in large places with many APs.

It is important to note that the phenomenon of missing APs is no surprise considering the analysis results in Fig. 3. It is based on Bianchi's model [4], in which throughput of the IEEE 802.11 DCF is analyzed according to the number of competing devices. We have simplified the problem to count the number of successful probe request and response pairs during the *MaxChannelTime* with parameters defined in the figure assuming that each of 11 channels has a similar number of devices (APs). According to the result, the AP population detected gets saturated when the real AP population goes beyond 40. The analysis shows a bit more number of APs in the figure because it does not take into consideration other packets in the network.

Another important observation is that, in a crowded place with many APs, there is a probability that probe response packets can collide with each other. A weaker response is missing but a stronger response signal is affected as well due to the phenomenon called *signal capture*. While this is not a concern in general communication, it is the case in indoor localization because signal's RSS values are as important as the signal's contents.

Estimation Delay for Localization: With a large number of AP in the area, a client device would experience an intolerable delay to estimate its location. This is because it observes APs in every channel and thus waits for MaxChannelTime at every channel, which is compounded by the high computational complexity searching for the matching FP(s) in the radiomap.

On the other hand, it is desirable to increase MaxChannelTime to collect all responses, which in fact pushes the estimation delay even further. A longer time allocated per scan means less time and a higher delay for normal data traffic. Nonetheless, it was suggested that at least 50 ms is needed per channel in the network with many APs [19]. A simple calculation is that 50 ms for each of 11 channels gives 550 ms. If it is combined with the scanning frequency, for example every 600 ms [13], network performance could be significantly degraded. In the context of localization, this could be overwhelming when fast localization is needed for quick navigation of the venue.

4 Representative Access Points (rAPs)

Conventional Wifi FP-based localization algorithms have a serious problem in terms of accuracy and delay in large-scale venues as discussed in the previous section. The main cause of the problem is the scanning process and the corresponding probe response traffic. In the context of handoff studies, [10] suggested to use passive scanning as it does not cause any additional traffic. Reference [5] suggested unicast probe request in case the destination APs are known in advance. The proposed method in this paper adopts the latter approach where a subset of APs are identified during the offline stage. They are called *representative APs* (rAPs) and help address the probe response explosion problem by directing probe requests to rAPs only during the online stage. Assuming that localization is a continuous operation, i.e., each client device has a rough idea of its whereabout in terms of line segments, the localization problem is restricted to a certain hallway with reference to a few rAPs specific to that area.

Offline Phase to Identify Line Segments and rAPs: The proposed rAP-based method divides the entire map of a venue into small areas of hallways (line segments) and corners (intersections) and identifies a few rAPs for each of those line segments and intersections. Observe 96 line segments and 50 intersections in Coex mall as shown in Fig. 1. For your reference, HKUST has 6 line segments and 3 intersections.

To choose rAPs in each line segment, the following criteria are used: (i) rAPs should be observed over the entire range of the line segment. For that matter, we divide a line segment into several if it is too long. (ii) rAPs should exhibit high RSS values because weak APs typically are prone to signal fluctuations and thus, impact the estimation accuracy. (iii) rAPs should be distinctive with each other, which can be translated as rAPs positioned as far as possible among themselves. On other hand, at about an endpoint of a line segment or an intersection, rAPs are chosen in a way to identify which line segment or direction the client is heading. Note that the process of choosing rAPs and discarding the rest represents the elimination of redundant information in the radiomap as some nearby APs would offer no additional information in terms of localization.

Online Phase to Estimate Location via Probing Representative APs: During the online phase, a few rAPs chosen for the particular line segment will be probed individually (unicast) rather than probing all nearby APs (broadcast). If a client device is at about an intersection, then rAPs along with multiple line segments connected to a corresponding intersection will be probed in a similar fashion.

The measured RSS values from rAPs can be used to find the closest matching FPs (locations) in the radiomap. Since we're using a fraction of features (APs), the computational complexity is greatly reduced. On the other hand, the estimation accuracy could be impacted because the proposed method does not utilize all observable APs. Alternatively, it is possible to utilize propagation model to improve the localization accuracy. A series of RSS values from a certain rAP along a line segment can be analyzed during the offline stage to derive the propagation parameters (path loss exponent and wall attenuation factor) for the particular rAP. This can be used during the online stage to estimate the position of a client device. For that matter, we use the propagation model developed in [2,17], which takes the path loss along the distance and across walls. Path loss at distance d is measured as

$$PL(d) = PL(d_0) + 10\,n\,\log\left(\frac{d}{d_0}\right) + p \times SAF + q \times CAF,$$

where d_0 is the reference distance, n is the path loss exponent, p and q are the number of soft walls and concrete walls, and SAF and CAF are the attenuation factor of a soft wall and a concrete wall, respectively. Please refer to [2,17] for details about the propagation model.

Example Line Segment in Coex: In the below, we show an example line segment identified along a vertical hallway in the rightmost part of the Coex mall as shown in Fig. 4a. It is 96 m long and observes 93 APs marked as small diamonds in the figure. However, a single probe detects 40 APs on the average. Note that we have estimated the locations of each of those 96 APs by averaging all of coordinates that observes a particular AP with weights based on RSS values. Based on the criteria mentioned earlier, we chose three rAPs that are positioned at the top, middle and bottom of the line segment, which are marked with arrows in the figure. The corresponding RSS values in the radiomap is drawn in Fig. 4b. During the online phase, RSS values of the three rAPs are measured and used to calculate the best closest location along the line segment. Alternatively, as mentioned earlier, the trend of RSS values in Fig. 4b is used to derive parameters (path loss exponent n, SAF and CAF) for the propagation pattern, which then is used to estimate the client device's location during the online stage. Note that

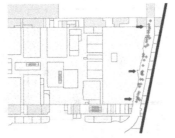

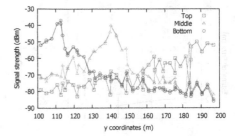

(a) Diamonds are estimated locations of APs along the line segment and arrows indicate the three rAPs.

(b) RSS patterns of the three rAPs along the line segment

Fig. 4. rAP-based localization method

choosing rAPs with different propagation patterns is important because those with similar propagation patterns offer redundant information.

5   Performance Evaluation

This section presents experimental results of rAP-based indoor localization in comparison to conventional Wifi FP-based approach. For the former, we used both propagation model-based approach as well as FP matching method with various number of rAPs (2~13). For the latter, the entire radiomap is searched to find the closet matching FPs. This is to obtain the optimal performance (least estimation error), which is hardly achieve in reality because it typically searches a subset of radiomap as discussed in Sect. 2.2. In both cases, we applied kNN (k-nearest neighbor) method for matching (see Sect. 2.2), where k varies from 3 to 9. Note that propagation model-based approach does not use kNN because it applies the analytical model mentioned earlier

The measurement was taken to test at 153 test points, which are independent from 2,028 FP collection locations, along the 96 line segments. (For brevity, we skip the test results and the corresponding discussions on the test at intersections.) The performance metric is estimation error in distance. The time taken during the online phase is estimated based on the probing time and the computation time, which are closely related to the number of channels to probe and the size of radiomap to be searched for matching.

Estimation Accuracy: Fig. 5a shows the average estimation error of those at the 153 test points. It is surprising to observe that propagation model-based approach offers the highest estimation error, which is more than 10 m. In a very crowded area like Coex mall with more than 150,000 visitors per day, there exist more obstacles and interferences in addition to complex building structures. Analytical model does not work well due to numerous uncertainties in signal propagation in large-scale venues. On the other hand, rAP-based approach achieves much higher accuracy. With just two rAPs, it achieves 7~8 m,

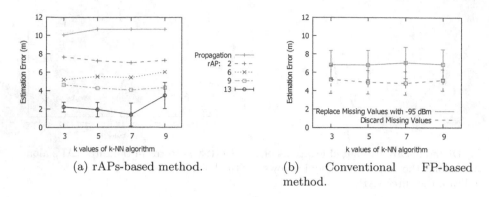

(a) rAPs-based method.   (b)   Conventional   FP-based method.

Fig. 5. Estimation error in distance (For propagation model-based approach, x-axis represents the number of rAPs. In Fig. a, ranges are shown for the case of rAP=13 only for simplicity. Ranges in other cases are usually wider than that.)

which is still on par with the conventional method in Fig. 5b. It is possible to estimate a location with only a few rAPs with a reasonable accuracy because knowing which line segment a client is in simplifies the problem into a small scale localization.

The accuracy gets much better when we uses more number of rAPs. With 13 rAPs, it achieves 1.8~2.1 m, which is considered one of the best performance reported in the literature. More importantly, the error distance range is restricted to be less than 2.3 m except $k = 9$ as shown in Fig. 5a. Average distance is important but the range is also important because this gives us a higher confidence in the estimated location in the venue. Impact of k values is minimal as observed in previous studies. Note that a large k does not necessarily improve the estimation accuracy because FPs (locations) far from the actual location can also be included in the averaging procedure [2].

Figure 5b shows the average error distance of the conventional Wifi FP-based approach. The figure shows two results that are different in dealing with missing values. To calculate the Euclidean distance, we need to either skip or replace the missing component corresponding to missing APs. As discussed in Sect. 3.2, replacing it with the smallest possible value (i.e., -95 dBm) causes a higher estimation error in large places with many APs because they are missed out not because of the weak signal but because of the probe response explosion problem mentioned above. It achieves the error distance of 6.5~6.9 m. Just discarding those missing values in calculating the Euclidean distance results in the error distance of 4.8~5.2 m, which is better than the other. However, this is not usually recommended because discarding missing components in effect reduces the Euclidean distance as discussed earlier. Therefore, it can be summarized that, comparing the former, the rAP-based approach improves the error distance 4.4~5.1 m or 69~72 %.

Estimation Delay: Estimation delay can be divided into two parts. First, the time taken to send and receive probe requests and responses. With the conventional method which probes all APs in every channel, the client should wait for *MaxChannelTime* (e.g., 30 ms) and another 9 ms for switching between channels [11]. It takes 420 ms to probe all 11 channels as it observes at least one AP at each channel and thus has very little chance to wait *MinChannelTime* instead of *MaxChannelTime*. With the rAPs method proposed in this paper, on the other hand, the client doesn't need to probe all 11 channels. Instead, only the channels in which the rAPs operate need to be probed. Moreover, it does not have to wait for long because unicast communication is employed. Since each exchange of probe request and response is relatively shorter, it can be deduced that 9 ms × |rAP| assuming that all rAPs operate in different channels. When rAP=6, it is 54 ms, which is ten-fold reduction compared to the conventional method.

Second, after probing, the client sends the measured FP to the server, which then searches the closest FPs in the radiomap. Because we have a smaller FP, the computational time becomes much smaller, too. With the PC configuration used for this experiment (Intel i7-3770, 3.4 GHz, 8 cores, 12 GB RAM, Windows 7, radiomap Database MySQL version 5, processing tool MATLAB 7), the processing time is about 200 ms and 2 ms with the conventional and the proposed method, respectively. This is a hundred-fold reduction although dimension reduction techniques discussed in Sect. 2.2 may alleviate this problem partially. In summary, the proposed rAP-based method greatly reduces the estimation delay such that it can be useful in applications that need fast localization or navigation.

6 Conclusions

In this paper, we have analyzed the characteristics of the AP-crowded large scale indoor places. In such an indoor venue, a fingerprint becomes imperfect due to the limited time allocated per channel during the scanning process. In order to address this problem, this paper proposes the *representative access points* (rAP)-based method. It probes only the chosen APs among the whole set of access points and thus reduces the estimation delay as well as estimation error.

One of our future work is to develop an AP-based solution, which is based on the selection of rAPs during the online stage. In other words, an AP ignores weak probe request messages (smaller RSS values) and does not send the corresponding probe response message, intentionally giving up its role as an rAP. A client device receives a smaller number of probe responses. Another future work is to develop further with the propagation model-based approach. It has an obvious advantage of demanding less APs for the localization purpose. With a more sophisticated algorithm and the accuracy requirements of different applications, this may offer the cheapest localization solution.

Acknowledgment. This research was supported in part by the NSF under Grant CNS-1338105, Basic Science Research Program through the NRF (Korea) funded by the Ministry of Education, Science, and Technology (2011-0029034).

References

1. Bak, S., Jeon, S., Suh, Y.-J., Yu, C., Han, D.: Characteristics of a large-scale wifi radiomap and their implications in indoor localization. In: Fourth International Conference on Network of the Future (NoF'13) (2013)
2. Bahl, P., Padmanabhan, V.N.: RADAR: an in-building RF-based user location and tracking system. In: IEEE INFOCOM (2000)
3. Battiti, R., Nhat, T.L., Villani, A.: Location-aware computing a neural network model for determining location in wireless LANs. Technical report DIT-02-0083. University of Trento (2002)
4. Bianchi, G.: Performance analysis of the IEEE 802.11 DCF. IEEE JSAC **18**(3), 535–547 (2000)
5. Chang, C.-Y., Wang, H.-J., Chao, H.-C.: Using fuzzy logic to mitigate IEEE 802.11 handoff latency. In: IEEE International Conference on Fuzzy Systems (2005)
6. Chawathe, S.S.: Low-latency indoor localization using bluetooth beacons. In: IEEE International Conference on Intelligent Transportation Systems (2009)
7. Chen, Y., et al.: Power-efficient access-point selection for indoor location estimation. IEEE TKDE **18**(7), 877–888 (2006)
8. Deasy, T.P., Scanlon, W.G.: Simulation or measurement: the effect of radio map creation on in-door WLAN-based localisation accuracy. Wirel. Pers. Commun. **42**(4), 563–573 (2007)
9. Elias, R., Elnahas, A.: Fast localization in indoor environments. In: IEEE International Conference on Computational Intelligence for Security and Defense Applications (2009)
10. Franklin, J., et al.: Passive data link layer 802.11 wireless device driver fingerprinting. In: USENIX Security (2006)
11. Harris, M., Harvey, S.: Channel swithcing overhead for 802.11b. Technical report. Southern Illinois University (2009)
12. Konstantinidis, A., et al.: Towards planet-scale localization on smartphones with a partial radiomap. In: ACM International Workshop on Hot Topics in Planet-scale Measurement (2012)
13. King, T., Kjrgaard, M.B.: ComPoScan: adaptive scanning for efficient concurrent communications and positioning with 802.11. In: ACM Mobisys (2008)
14. Kuo, S.-P., et al.: Cluster-enhanced techniques for pat-tern-matching localization systems. In: ACM Mobihoc (2007)
15. Kuo, S.-P., Tseng, Y.-C.: Discriminant minimization search for large-scale rf-based localization systems. IEEE TMC **10**(2), 291–304 (2011)
16. Loevsky, I., Shimshoni, I.: Reliable and efficient landmark-based localization for mobile robots. Robot. Auton. Syst. **58**(5), 520–528 (2010)
17. Seidel, S., Rappaport, T.: 914 mhz path loss prediction models for indoor wireless communications in multifloored buildings. IEEE TAP **40**(2), 207–217 (1992)
18. Stone-Gross, B., et al.: Malware in IEEE 802.11 wireless networks. In: International Conference on Passive and Active Network Measurement (2008)
19. Teng, J., Xu, C., Jia, W., Xuan, D.: D-Scan: enabling fast and smooth handoffs in ap-dense 802.11 wireless networks. In: IEEE INFOCOM (2009)

20. Velayos, H., Karlsson, G.: Techniques to reduce the IEEE 802.11b handoff time. In: IEEE ICC (2004)
21. Wu, K., et al.: FILA: fine-grained indoor localization. In: IEEE INFOCOM (2012)
22. Xiao, B., Chen, L., Xiao, Q., Li, M.: Reliable anchor-based sensor localization in irregular areas. IEEE TMC 9(1), 60–72 (2009)
23. Yang, Q., et al.: Estimating location using wi-fi. IEEE Intell. Syst. 23(1), 8–13 (2008)
24. Youssef, M., Agrawala, A., Shankar, A.U.: WLAN location determination via clustering and probability distribution. In: IEEE Percom (2003)
25. Youssef, M., Agrawala, A.: The Horus location determination system. Wirel. Netw. 14(3), 357–374 (2008)

Reality Mining: Digging the Impact of Friendship and Location on Crowd Behavior

Yuanfang Chen[1]([✉]), Antonio M. Ortiz[1], Noel Crespi[1], Lei Shu[2], and Lin Lv[3]

[1] Institut Mines-Télécom, Télécom SudParis, Paris, France
{yuanfang.chen,antonio.ortiz_torres,noel.crespi}@telecom-sudparis.eu
[2] Guangdong University of Petrochemical Technology, Maoming, China
lei.shu@lab.gdupt.edu.cn
[3] School of Software, Dalian University of Technology, Dalian, China
lvlin_george@mail.dlut.edu.cn

Abstract. Crowd behavior of human deserves to be studied since it is common that people are influenced and change their behavior when being in a group. In pervasive computing research, an amount of work has been directed towards discovering human movement patterns based on wireless networks, mainly focusing on movements of individuals. It is surprising that social interaction among individuals in a crowd is largely neglected. Mobile phones offer on-body tracking and they are already deployed on a large scale, allowing the characterization of user behavior through large amounts of wireless information collected by mobile phones. In this paper, we observe and analyze the impact of friendship and location attributes on crowd behavior, using location-based wireless mobility information. This is a cornerstone for predicting crowd behavior, which can be used in a large number of applications such as crowdsourcing-based technology, traffic management, crowd safety, and infrastructure deployment.

Keywords: Crowd behavior · Mobile devices · Wearable computing · Complex social networks

1 Introduction

With increasing size and frequency of mass events, such as traffic congestion on a highway, swarming in a tourist attraction, or clogging at weekend shopping sale, the study of crowd dynamics has become an important research area [27]. However, even successful modeling approaches such as those inspired by Newtonian force models are still not fully consistent with empirical observations and are sometimes difficult to be adapted for crowd prediction. With the prevalence of smart devices (such as smart cellphones and tablet PCs), on-body sensing, computing and communication have become widespread [14] (carry-on smart devices can be called "social sensors"). These developments have made it possible to obtain real-time and comprehensive empirical data required by crowd

© Institute for Computer Sciences, Social Informatics and Telecommunications Engineering 2014
I. Stojmenovic et al. (Eds.): MOBIQUITOUS 2013, LNICST 131, pp. 142–154, 2014.
DOI: 10.1007/978-3-319-11569-6_12

behavior[1] analyses [22]. This "reality mining" [16] is deemed adequate to provide objective measurements of human interaction, and it can be called "honest signals" [23]. These options open up new pathways in Computational Social Science [15], where large amounts of information obtained from wireless mobile devices can lead to new perspectives for the analysis of crowd behavior and social dynamics.

In order to develop reliable prediction models for crowdsourcing-based technology, traffic management, urban infrastructure deployment, or crowd safety, it is necessary to understand what laws determine the formation of a crowd. While a lot of studies know the "physics" of crowd behavior, it is surprising that social interaction among individuals in a crowd has been largely neglected. Indeed, the great majority of existing studies investigate a crowd as a collection of isolated individuals, and each individual has its own motion speed and direction [18]. However, it turns out that in practice, the majority of individuals do not take action alone, but in groups with social relationships [8,24].

In this paper, we first focus on recognizing human crowd behavior by analyzing the data measured by internet-accessible mobile phones from a location-aware online social network. By crowd behavior recognition, we understand that the movement of a large number of individuals has a pattern and can be attributed, depending on relevant parameters such as the friendship between individuals[2] and check-in locations (with time) of these individuals. Based on the recognition, we can realize that it is possible to predict the formation of a crowd from wireless information related to individuals. For instance, the formation of downtown pedestrian flow is related to the interaction between individuals, and the flow can be distinguished by collecting the wireless information of pedestrians.

Second, we investigate how "friendship" and "location" impact human crowd behavior. Nathan Eagle *et al.* have obtained an important result: "Data collected from mobile phones has the potential to provide insight into the relational dynamics of individuals. Furthermore, it is possible to accurately infer 95 % of friendship relations only considering the observational wireless data" [7]. This implies that there is a relationship between the friendship and the behavioral patterns of humans. Based on this result, we observe the patterns of friendship in different crowds. The contributions of this paper are listed as follows.

- We design a crowd recognition model. One of the main challenges in crowd behavior recognition is to infer the most likely crowd behavior using the data collected from a set of persons. We use check-in time and location (*Time* and *Location_id*. We convert each latitude/longitude coordinate of the earth

---

[1] Crowd behavior is a branch of human dynamics. A large number of individuals are gathered or consider to gather together as some particular groups with some special purposes such as crowdsourcing-based knowledge learning, social contact and event-based gathering.

[2] For a location-aware online social network, if B is in the friend list of A, we consider that there is friendship between A and B, and the relationship is directed.

into a unique *Location_id*) to quantify the track of each individual. Then, a clustering algorithm[3] is used to find the likely crowds.

- We investigate how friendship influences crowd behavior. In order to measure this influence, we use the friendship degree of each user, the probability distribution of various degrees, and the relationship between friendship degree and number of users for each crowd.
- We investigate how individuals' locations influence crowd behavior. For measuring the influence, we investigate these relationships for different clusters: (i) users and their locations; (ii) check-in time and users' locations.

The paper is structured as follows. Section 2 introduces the related work. Section 3 presents the data used in our study and statistic analysis. Section 4 shows how to recognize human crowd behavior from datasets. Section 5 reveals the impact of attributes (check-in time, check-in location and friendship) on crowd behavior. Finally, some conclusions are given in Sect. 6.

2   Related Work

Recently, a number of scientific communities, from computer science to physics, have been working in human dynamics. Pedestrian movement patterns have been studied using wireless-based personal location data [21]. In physics, for human crowd behavior analysis, many approaches have been proposed inspired by using fluid dynamics [11], swarms [2] and cellular automata [1]. Car-based human movement patterns have also been studied by utilizing the data from GPS-equipped vehicles [25]. Thereinto, the approaches which are based on wireless mobility information are more reliable, objective and environment-independent compared with model-based approaches, e.g., habit-based model [13]. Model-based approaches are environment-sensitive. Moreover, because the factors of environment influence each other, a simple model is not sufficient to reflect the interaction between these factors. Furthermore, the performance of a model is related to the experience of modeler.

As an important aspect of human dynamics, "crowd dynamics" is worthy to be deeply analyzed, since it helps to extract some useful conclusions about how humans behave when they are in large groups. For the crowdsourcing-based technology such as Quora, Yahoo Answers and Google Answers, mining intelligence at group and community levels [26] (a group or a community can be thought as a crowd) will be helpful to develop and improve this type of technology. Further, predicting the formation of a crowd is helpful in some emergency situations, e.g., evacuation route control; and even the prediction is also beneficial for studying and improving the performance of public infrastructures, e.g., network usage during a mass event. However, the prediction of crowd events is

---

[3] An Expectation-Maximization (EM) clustering algorithm is used in this paper. The EM assigns a probability distribution for each track record (instance), which indicates the probability of each instance belonging to each of the clusters. The EM can automatically decide how many clusters to create.

still a challenge, even if a lot of new technologies can be used, e.g., GPS-based human trace tracking technology. Moreover, GSM, bluetooth or WiFi localization technologies have been explored to be used to collect sufficient data for analyzing crowd behavior [5].

The prediction of human behavior is the main topic of a number of publications. The method proposed in [12] estimates an object's future locations, by considering the patterns of recent movements. They present the concept of a Trajectory pattern (T-pattern), a special association rule with a timestamp that is able to define a sequence of locations with a certain probability. They also propose the Trajectory Pattern Tree (TPT), a data access method that indexes trajectory patterns to efficiently answer predictive queries, and finally, they detail a Hybrid Prediction Algorithm (HPA) that provides accurate prediction for both near and distant time queries. T-patterns are also used in [17], where *WhereNext* is presented, which is a technique to predict the next location of a moving object. It uses an evaluation function that efficiently creates TPTs by considering the previous movements of all moving objects in a certain area. The model presented in [19] is based on behavioral heuristics that predict individual trajectories and collective motion patterns such as the spontaneous formation of unidirectional lanes or stop-and-go waves. These heuristics consider visual information to describe the motion of pedestrians.

Most of the previous research in crowd dynamics has ignored the internal connection between social relationships and crowd formation. While discrete observations of an individual's idiosyncratic behavior seem to be merely random, and most studies of crowd behavior only consider interaction among isolated individuals, the results presented in [20] show that up to 70 % of people in a crowd are actually moving in groups such as friends, couples, or families, concluding that the social relationships affect crowd forming. In addition, group sizes are commonly distributed according to a poisson distribution [10]. Thus, social ties between individuals impact the forming of crowd. In this work, we consider friendship and location relationships between individuals as an important parameter for crowd recognition.

3   Data Description

The dataset used for analyzing crowd behavior consists of anonymous check-in data from mobile devices collected by a location-based social networking service provider where users share their locations by check-in, and the friendship between these mobile users is collected using their public API [4]. This aggregated and anonymous mobile device information is used to correlate, model, evaluate and analyze the relationships between the check-in time, locations, friendship and crowd behavior of users in 772,966 distinct places. The dataset consists of 58,228 nodes (users) and 214,078 friend edges (friendship is directed between any two nodes).

Check-in behavior of users. Based on users' check-in behavior, we can obtain users' locations, and our recognition and observation are check-in-location-aware. Moreover, through check-in frequency, some special places can be inferred. For example, the home location of a user can be defined as the location which has maximum average number of check-ins for a period of time. Manual inspection shows that this infers home locations with 85 % accuracy [4]. We can deduce that there is a relationship between users' social relations (e.g., the kinship of users at home) and check-in locations with check-in frequency.

Friendship and mobility. Our study aims at understanding how the location of user A's friend B affects the movement of A. Intuitively we are more likely to move to a place in which we have friends (crowd behavior is a natural instinct of human). To quantify this effect we proceed as follows. User A "visits" the location of friend B, if A checks in within radius r of B's location, and we aim at computing $p(d)$, which measures the probability that A "visits" a friend (near the friend) within the range, $r = d$ (we set $r = 10$ m). In the dataset, using the "location_id", we can draw the "ranges" corresponding to different friends and obtain relevant probabilities to which range A belongs. Moreover, In Fig. 1, we show, for each user, the number of records and to which cluster belongs based on January, 2010 dataset (Fig. 1(a)) and February, 2010 dataset (Fig. 1(b)).

The original dataset provided by the service provider can not be directly used to mine the basic laws that govern human crowd behavior, or even the impact of these laws, so we apply a process to perform an association of the mobility check-in data with the friendship information. The process involves two steps: (i) perform a spatial-temporal analysis of the records to detect which users form a crowd (e.g., places in which some people have stopped for a sufficiently long time); (ii) infer in every crowd which users are friends and what kind of friendship they have $(1, 2, 3, ..., N$-hop friends, e.g., "1-hop" is for direct friends).

In order to infer "where and when crowds are forming?" from a large number of records, we first characterize the individual activity by mathematical modeling.

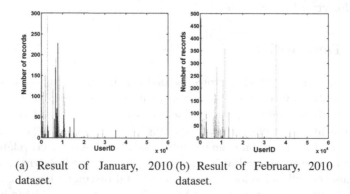

(a) Result of January, 2010 dataset. (b) Result of February, 2010 dataset.

Fig. 1. Number of records and which cluster belongs for each user in the January and February, 2010 datasets (different colours represent different clusters) (Color figure online).

Each location measurement m_i, collected for every mobile device, is characterized by a position p_i expressed in latitude and longitude, and a timestamp t_i. We also measure the interval time between different check-in activities [9]. The average interval time measured for the whole population is 30 min. So within the interval we can detect a gathering of humans from the dataset. Moreover, this time interval is comparable to the average length of real social events.

To confirm the friendship in a crowd, we merge the friendship dataset with the check-in record dataset, e.g., for a crowd, if there is a record of any two users in the friendship dataset, the two users are 1-hop friends, and then we add this information into the check-in record dataset as a value of a new attribute column (friendship). Multihop friendship will be also recognized, and we record the identity number of minimum-hop-count friend for every user as the value of the friendship attribute column.

4 Crowd Behavior Recognition

We formalize a series of processing steps which can be used to infer crowd behavior from location-based wireless information. In this section we build a mathematical model for recognizing the crowd behavior of population.

First, based on the processed dataset, we confirm whether the crowd behavior of individuals can be identified. Figure 2 shows the results of data clustering with *Friendship* and *Location_id* attributes, respectively (these two attributes are evaluation classes for clustering), using Expectation-Maximization (EM) algorithm [6]. From Fig. 2, the crowd behavior has been recognized using the processed dataset (in our study a crowd is defined in Definition 1). Moreover, we can find that different evaluation classes have different clustering accuracy levels, so the impacts of different attributes on the crowd behavior are different. Figure 3 shows the number of users for each cluster corresponding to Fig. 2 (Fig. 2 only shows the users who are "1-hop" friends, but in Fig. 3, the users who are multihop friends are also counted for each cluster). For Fig. 3, more detailed explanations are necessary: why some clusters are composed by thousands of users when we use "Friendship" attribute as the class of clustering evaluation? Because (i) we use "multihop" friends in the clustering evaluation; that is to say, if A is a friend of B within the range r and B is a friend of C within the range r, A, B and C all will belong to a same crowd; (ii) the error of clustering evaluation is existent; (iii) we use the evaluation dataset which is from one special month (e.g., some data of the dataset is from a major celebration (a lot of users are gathered together); however, the background of "special" is not important in this paper) to show the impact of "Friendship" attribute on crowd behavior of human[4].

Definition 1 (Crowd). *A group of individuals at the "same" physical location (the range radius r for every user is 10 m) at the "same" time (the time range*

---

[4] Even if the dataset is special, it still can be used to show that "the impact of Friendship is existent on crowd behavior".

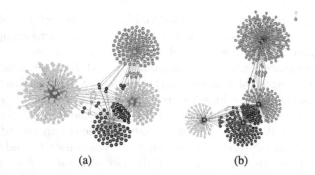

(a)   (b)

Fig. 2. For clearness, we only show one-month clustering result using *Friendship* and *Location_id* attributes as the classes of clustering evaluation, respectively. 5 clusters can be found for the two clustering processes, and we use different colours to distinguish different clusters. Note that the shape for the center node of any cluster is squared. (a) Clustering result with *Friendship* attribute. (b) Clustering result with *Location_id* attribute.

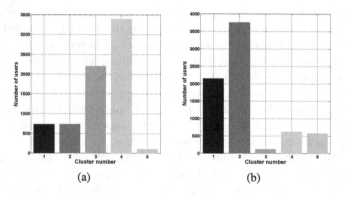

(a)   (b)

Fig. 3. Number of users for each cluster. (a) Number of users for each cluster using *Friendship* attribute as the class of clustering evaluation. (b) Number of users for each cluster using *Location_id* attribute as the class of clustering evaluation.

for a crowd is set to 15 min; namely, if the check-in time difference between two users is within 15 min, we consider that they are at the "same" time).

The characteristics of the crowd behavior of each single person can thus be inferred from his/her check-in records. We refer to this as their "individual behavior". This shows which individuals participate in a specific crowd. From the EM algorithm, a given record belongs to each cluster with certain probabilities. Moreover, the likelihood is a measurement of "how good" a clustering process is and it is increased at each iteration of the EM algorithm. It is worth mentioning that the higher the likelihood, the better the model fits the data.

Second, the clustering process (crowd behavior recognition model) is as follows. We define two parameters: (i) the user u's check-in data S^u which is a sequence of activity observations about u; (ii) a set of unknown values θ (i.e., the serial numbers of clusters). These two parameters are used along with a Maximum Likelihood Estimation (MLE): $L(\theta; S^u) = p(S^u|\theta)$. Our purpose is to seek the MLE of marginal likelihood. In other words, we need to find the most probable θ which the user u belongs. The EM algorithm iteratively applies the following two steps to achieve our purpose:

1. Expectation step (E step): calculate the expected value of the log-likelihood function under the current established clusters $(\theta^{(t)})$: $Q(\theta|\theta^{(t)}) = E_{S^u, \theta^{(t)}}[\log L(\theta; S^u)]$;
2. Maximization step (M step): find the appropriate value of parameter θ, which maximizes this quantity: $\theta^{mle} = \arg \max_{\theta} Q(\theta|\theta^{(t)})$.

MLE estimates θ by finding a value of θ that maximizes $Q(\theta|\theta^{(t)})$, and the estimation result can be flagged as: θ^{mle}.

Further, based on our recognition model, we add the spatio-temporal pattern into the crowd behavior (clustering). We use a triple $q = (\theta, p_i, t_i)$ to replace θ. Then the expectation step becomes:

1. Expectation step: $Q(q|q^{(t_i)}) = E_{S^u, q^{(t_i)}}[\log L(q; S^u)]$, where p_i is the position characteristic of location measurement m_i, and t_i is timestamp of m_i. Moreover, $q^{(t_i)}$ is a set of current established clusters with their locations and timestamps;
2. Maximization step: choose q to maximize $Q(.)$, $q^{mle} = \arg \max_{q} Q(q|q^{(t_i)})$.

Finally, in order to preserve the model integrity, the recognition accuracy must be measured. In our crowd behavior recognition model, the value of the log-likelihood can be used to measure the accuracy. For instance, using the *Friendship* attribute as the evaluation class, based on one-month data, the log likelihood of crowd identification is: -16.42186, and using the *Location_id* attribute as the evaluation class, the log likelihood is: -16.87742. Their accuracy is different, and the *Friendship* attribute is more effective for improving the recognition ability of the model.

5   Impact of Attributes on Crowd Behavior

Most previous studies of crowd behavior only consider interaction among isolated individuals, and assume that the motion of individuals is random. The work in [20] affirms that the walking behavior of pedestrians is affected by social relationships, such as friends, couples, or families walking together. The results presented in Fig. 2, show that some population attributes impact the crowd motion of humans, and these impacts are different for diverse attributes. In this section, we go deeper into the impact of these effects by analyzing how friendship and location affect crowd behavior.

5.1   Impact of Friendship on Crowd Behavior

In this section, we analyze the impact of social relationships (i.e., friendship) on the complex dynamics of crowd behavior. For this, we use the empirical data of the motion of individuals by means of check-in recordings of public areas. Observations are made under varying-density collections of population.

First of all, we analyze the friendship of a group of people. Figure 4 shows the friendship degree of each user and the probability distribution of various degrees (based on the dataset of January and February, 2010). We can find that friendship exists in almost all observed users in the datasets. It means that friendship is an influencing factor for human behavior. It is worth noting that a Poisson distribution is met for the friendship degree probability distribution of all observed users. Moreover, from Fig. 4(b), friendship degree is less than 10 for almost 90 % users. So the crowding propensity of an individual is not primarily oriented by friendship.

Secondly, several crowds exist in the observed group of people and we investigate the friendship degree probability distribution of each crowd. Figure 5 shows the friendship degree distributions of 5 clusters which are based on January, 2010 dataset. For some crowds, friendship degrees show approximative scale-free power-law distributions, e.g., crowds 0, 1, 2, and 3.

Finally, how many users have friendship between each other for each cluster? Figure 6 exposes an interesting phenomenon: even though the average friendship degree of cluster 2 is larger than that of cluster 3 (shown in Fig. 5), the number of users who have friendship in cluster 2 is less compared to cluster 3. This means that there is no relation between the number of users (who have friendship) and friendship degree in a crowd.

5.2   Impact of Location on Crowd Behavior

With the increasing ubiquity of location sensing included in mobile devices, we realize the arising opportunity for human crowd analysis through mobile

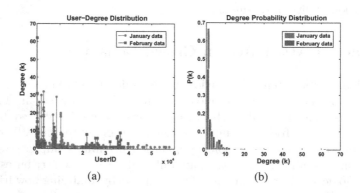

Fig. 4. (a) Friendship degree of each user and (b) probability distribution of various degrees (January and February, 2010 datasets).

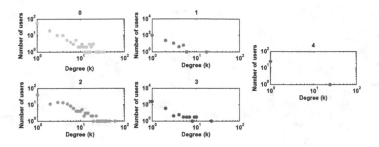

Fig. 5. Relationship between friendship degree and number of users for each crowd (January, 2010 dataset).

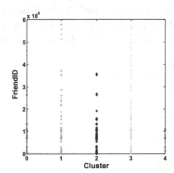

Fig. 6. IDs of users (friendship occurs among these users) for each crowd.

wireless information from the real world context. Thereby, the spatial locations of individuals become a kind of important and available information for extending the analysis and modeling of human crowd behavior to the physical world. Most prediction models of crowd events use some kind of location information. In [3], Calabrese *et al.* believe that the attendees of crowd events are related to areas: "Sport events such as baseball games attract about double the number of people which normally live in the Fenway Park area. Moreover, those events seem to be predominantly attended by people living in the surrounding of the baseball stadium, as well as the south Boston area". From our investigation, we can find the impact of location on crowd behavior. Figure 7 shows *location_id* distribution of users.

Analyzing Fig. 7, we can see that users are obviously clustered, and an approximate diagonal line divides the User-Location (see Fig. 7(a)) and Check-in time-Location (see Fig. 7(b)) space. Moreover, we can observe: the range of activity for any user is limited; and duration time is different for different crowds in different locations. We can assert that human crowd behavior is centralized; namely "hot spot" exists. We use this character of crowd behavior to do centralized population monitoring or urban public facility deployment.

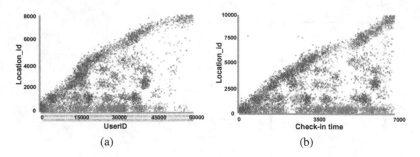

(a)   (b)

Fig. 7. Relationship among users, check-in time, clusters and locations (different colours denote different clusters; we set a unique ID for each user and the order of these user IDs is based on the order of recorded check-in times of users in a dataset). (a) Location distribution of clustered users. (b) Along with the change of check-in time, the location distribution of clustered users (Color figure online).

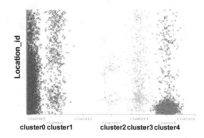

Fig. 8. Location distribution of users for each cluster.

Figure 8 shows the location distribution of users for each crowd[5]. We can find that the distances between users are different (the location distribution of users is uneven) in any crowd. For instance, in cluster 3, there are two small subclusters. We believe that the *small-world phenomenon* exists in crowd behavior.

6   Conclusion

The analysis of crowd behavior can give us an idea of how we behave when we are part of a group. Different actions can be taken by individuals when being surrounded by others. In this paper, we have focused on analyzing crowd behavior, considering check-in data from location-aware mobile social networks.

There are several parameters that affect the forming way of a crowd. Social relationships, e.g., friendship, as well as current locations, can impact the way that a crowd is formed. Understanding how these parameters determine crowd formation and evolution is the first step prior to the creation of predictive approaches. After grasping the relationship between these parameters and crowd

---

[5] The number of clusters is manually set to 6 for clustering; only 5 clusters are outputted at last.

behavior, our ongoing research focuses on the prediction model of crowd behavior. This model will be useful for preventing disasters from the pushing of crowds, facilitating efficient massive event planning, or even for traffic management.

Acknowledgment. This work was supported by the EU ITEA 2 Project 11020, "Social Internet of Things-Apps by and for the Crowd" (SITAC). Lei Shu's work is supported by the Guangdong University of Petrochemical Technology Internal Project (2012RC0106).

References

1. Bandini, S., Manzoni, S., Vizzari, G.: Crowd behaviour modeling: from cellular automata to multi-agent systems. Multi-Agent Systems: Simulation and Applications, pp. 204–230 (2009)
2. Bellomo, N.: Modeling crowds and swarms: congested and panic flows. Modeling Complex Living Systems, pp. 169–188 (2008)
3. Calabrese, F., Pereira, F.C., Di Lorenzo, G., Liu, L., Ratti, C.: The geography of taste: analyzing cell-phone mobility and social events. In: Floréen, P., Krüger, A., Spasojevic, M. (eds.) Pervasive 2010. LNCS, vol. 6030, pp. 22–37. Springer, Heidelberg (2010)
4. Cho, E., Myers, S.A., Leskovec, J.: Friendship and mobility: user movement in location-based social networks. In: Proceedings of the 17th SIGKDD International Conference on Knowledge Discovery and Data Mining, pp. 1082–1090. ACM (2011)
5. Cook, D.J., Das, S.K.: Pervasive computing at scale: transforming the state of the art. Pervasive Mob. Comput. 8(1), 22–35 (2012)
6. Do, C.B., Batzoglou, S.: What is the expectation maximization algorithm? Nat. Biotechnol. 26(8), 897–899 (2008)
7. Eagle, N., Pentland, A.S., Lazer, D.: Inferring friendship network structure by using mobile phone data. Proc. Natl. Acad. Sci. U S A 106(36), 15,274–15,278 (2009)
8. Ge, W., Collins, R.T., Ruback, R.B.: Vision-based analysis of small groups in pedestrian crowds. IEEE Trans. Pattern Anal. Mach. Intell. 34(5), 1003–1016 (2012)
9. Gonzalez, M.C., Hidalgo, C.A., Barabasi, A.L.: Understanding individual human mobility patterns. Nature 453(7196), 779–782 (2008)
10. Griesser, M., Ma, Q., Webber, S., Bowgen, K., Sumpter, D.J.: Understanding animal group-size distributions. PloS One 6(8), e23,438:1–9 (2011)
11. Helbing, D., Molnar, P.: Social force model for pedestrian dynamics. Phys. Rev. E 51(5), 4282–4286 (1995)
12. Jeung, H., Liu, Q., Shen, H.T., Zhou, X.: A hybrid prediction model for moving objects. In: Proceedings of the 24th International Conference on Data Engineering, pp. 70–79. IEEE (2008)
13. Jiao, Y., Liu, Y., Wang, J., Wang, J.: Model for human dynamics based on habit. Chin. Sci. Bull. 55(24), 2744–2749 (2010)
14. Ko, M.H., West, G., Venkatesh, S., Kumar, M.: Online context recognition in multisensor systems using dynamic time warping. In: Intelligent Sensors, Sensor Networks and Information Processing Conference, pp. 283–288. IEEE (2005)

15. Lazer, D., Pentland, A., Adamic, L., Aral, S., Barabási, A.L., Brewer, D., Christakis, N., Contractor, N., Fowler, J., Gutmann, M., Jebara, T., King, G., Macy, M., Roy, D., Van Alstyne, M.: Computational social science. Science **323**(5915), 721–723 (2009)
16. Mitchell, T.M.: Mining our reality. Science **326**(5960), 1644–1645 (2009)
17. Monreale, A., Pinelli, F., Trasarti, R., Giannotti, F.: Wherenext: a location predictor on trajectory pattern mining. In: Proceedings of the 15th ACM SIGKDD International Conference on Knowledge Discovery and Data Mining, pp. 637–646. ACM (2009)
18. Moussaïd, M., Helbing, D., Garnier, S., Johansson, A., Combe, M., Theraulaz, G.: Experimental study of the behavioural mechanisms underlying self-organization in human crowds. Proc. R. Soc. B Biol. Sci. **276**(1668), 2755–2762 (2009)
19. Moussaïd, M., Helbing, D., Theraulaz, G.: How simple rules determine pedestrian behavior and crowd disasters. Proc. Natl. Acad. Sci. U S A **108**(17), 6884–6888 (2011)
20. Moussaïd, M., Perozo, N., Garnier, S., Helbing, D., Theraulaz, G.: The walking behaviour of pedestrian social groups and its impact on crowd dynamics. PloS One **5**(4), e10,047:1–7 (2010)
21. Paul, U., Subramanian, A.P., Buddhikot, M.M., Das, S.R.: Understanding traffic dynamics in cellular data networks. In: Proceedings of the 30th International Conference on Computer Communications, pp. 882–890. IEEE (2011)
22. Pentland, A., Choudhury, T., Eagle, N., Singh, P.: Human dynamics: computation for organizations. Pattern Recogn. Lett. **26**(4), 503–511 (2005)
23. Pentland, A.S., Pentland, S.: Honest Signals: How They Shape Our World. MIT press, London (2008)
24. Tang, L., Liu, H.: Toward predicting collective behavior via social dimension extraction. Intell. Syst. **25**(4), 19–25 (2010)
25. Trasarti, R., Pinelli, F., Nanni, M., Giannotti, F.: Mining mobility user profiles for car pooling. In: Proceedings of the 17th SIGKDD International Conference on Knowledge Discovery and Data Mining, pp. 1190–1198. ACM (2011)
26. Zhang, D., Guo, B., Yu, Z.: The emergence of social and community intelligence. Computer **44**(7), 21–28 (2011)
27. Zhang, X., Weng, W., Yuan, H., Chen, J.: Empirical study on unidirectional dense crowd during a real mass event. Phys. A Stat. Mech. Appl. **392**(12), 2781–2791 (2013)

Robust Overlay Routing in Structured, Location Aware Mobile Peer-to-Peer Systems

Christian Gottron$^{(\boxtimes)}$, Sonja Bergsträßer, and Ralf Steinmetz

Multimedia Communications Lab, TU Darmstadt, Darmstadt, Germany
{cgottron,bergstr,ralf.steinmetz}@kom.tu-darmstadt.de

Abstract. Mobile Peer-to-Peer architectures provide object and service lookup functionality in absence of a preexisting communication infrastructure. Therefore, those architectures can be harnessed in several application scenarios like disaster relief scenarios where no infrastructure can be assumed and mobility is required. Yet, Mobile Peer-to-Peer architectures inherit the vulnerability to routing attacks from the underlying communication technologies. Further, even though many security mechanisms were developed for traditional Peer-to-Peer architectures, those mechanisms cannot be applied without adaptations to Mobile Peer-to-Peer architectures due to the wireless, mobile underlay network. In this paper, we analyze the vulnerability of the overlays routing algorithm of structured, location aware Mobile Peer-to-Peer architectures against a prominent routing attack. Therefore, we discuss and analyze existing security mechanisms that were developed to ensure a reliable routing process of these architectures. Moreover, we validate and adapt analytic models for the routing algorithm and those previously mentioned security mechanisms.

Keywords: Mobile Peer-to-Peer · Security · Routing

1 Introduction

Mobile Peer-to-Peer (MP2P) networks combine the benefits of Peer-to-Peer (P2P) systems and Mobile Ad hoc networks (MANET). The resulting architecture provides storage and retrieval services without a predefined infrastructure in a decentralized way. Furthermore, MP2P networks are resilient to single node failures. Due to these features, they meet the requirements of application scenarios like disaster relief, development aid, and military operations.

In MP2P networks, data objects as pictures, text, or other media files can be stored in a decentralized way. Structured P2P systems as distributed hash tables (DHTs) and, therefore, structured MP2P systems are based on unique overlay identifiers. These overlay identifiers are used by the routing mechanism of the overlay to perform lookup operations for objects and to initially map objects on nodes. In most cases, the network address of the node that stores and maintains an object, henceforth called the root node, is unknown to the sender of

© Institute for Computer Sciences, Social Informatics and Telecommunications Engineering 2014
I. Stojmenovic et al. (Eds.): MOBIQUITOUS 2013, LNICST 131, pp. 155–167, 2014.
DOI: 10.1007/978-3-319-11569-6_13

the lookup request. Therefore, the lookup message is sent to a node that is numerically closer to the root according to the overlay identifier. These intermediate nodes are used to forward the message to a node with an identifier that is numerically closer to the destination, until the lookup request is received by the root.

However, even though multiple MP2P architectures were proposed in the recent years, providing security in terms of robustness (as increasing the availability of stored objects) was mostly neglected. Due to their decentralized architecture, MP2P networks are highly vulnerable to routing attacks. Further, new challenges arose due to the combination of a P2P network with a MANET. Those challenges include a strongly limited bandwidth, an increased packet loss due to the characteristics of the wireless channel and a highly dynamic topology due to node mobility. As a result, existing security mechanisms for traditional P2P architectures that are based on the Internet as underlay cannot be directly applied without adaptations in an MP2P scenario.

In the scope of this paper, we analyze attacks performed by maliciously behaving intermediate nodes that do not forward lookup requests correctly but drop them. Thus, we survey the effects of this *Incorrect Lookup Routing Attack* on the reliability of a location aware MP2P systems lookup mechanism in the following sections. Moreover, we evaluate and compare the most promising, existing security mechanism for DHTs and the Overlay WatchDog, an approach developed for a structured, location aware MP2P architecture [1]. Based on these results we validate and optimize our analytic models for these security mechanisms, which have been proposed in [1].

The rest of the paper is structured as follows, in the next section we introduce related work that has motivated our work. In Sect. 3 we provide background information on MP2P systems. Section 4 focuses on the validation and adoption of the analytic models for the *Incorrect Lookup Routing Attack*. In Sect. 5, we discuss and evaluate security mechanisms that have been developed to increase the robustness of the overlay's lookup algorithm. Moreover, we validate the analytic models of these mechanisms in the light of MP2P systems. In the last section we conclude this paper and discuss future work.

2   Related Work

The *Incorrect Lookup Routing Attack* has initially been introduced by Sit and Morris [2] in the context of DHTs. This attack is based on maliciously behaving intermediate nodes that do not forward received lookup requests but misroute or drop them. As a result, an increased fraction of lookup requests fails. Several security mechanisms were proposed for traditional DHT architectures to increase the robustness against this attack. However, existing mechanisms for DHTs are mostly based on the following three basic concepts.

The first concept harnesses an iterative routing mechanism. During routing, feedback is provided to the source node of the lookup request on each step. Thus, misdirected or dropped lookup messages can be detected by the source node based on this feedback or whenever no feedback is received. This concept has been initially introduced by Sit and Morris [2]. However, other mechanisms as Myrmic [3] or Sechord [4] are also based on an iterative lookup algorithm.

Another mechanism to increase the network's robustness against the *Incorrect Lookup Routing Attack* is based on introducing redundancy. Here, instead of sending a single lookup message, multiple messages are sent over different routes. Thus, the probability that at least a single lookup request is received by the destination is increased. This redundant routing has been initially proposed by Castro et al. [5]. However, other approaches are also based on a redundant routing algorithm, such as Cyclone [6] or HALO [7].

The third kind of security mechanisms harnesses the reputation of the nodes in the network to detect malicious behavior. Due to these mechanisms, messages are routed via reliable nodes only. Artigas et al. [6] introduced a reputation based system that is combined with a redundant routing algorithm. The Exclusion Routing Protocol [8] or the Higher-Reputated Neighbor Selection [9] are other examples for reputation based security mechanisms.

Also MANET routing mechanisms have to rely on the benign behavior of intermediate nodes. Thus, the underlay routing can also be attacked by malicious intermediate nodes that drop messages. Marti et al. [10] proposed Watch-Dog, an intrusion detection system (IDS) for MANETs. Messages sent via the wireless channel can be overheard by all nodes within transmission range of the sender of the message. This IDS uses those overheard message to detect malicious behavior. Whenever an intermediate node has to forward a message, WatchDog analyzes overheard messages to detect whether the message was forwarded correctly. If the message has not been forwarded within a specific amount of time, a malicious behavior is assumed. In [1] we proposed an Overlay WatchDog that can also be used to monitor the overlay of an MP2P System.

3   Clustered Pastry Mobile Peer-to-Peer System

MP2P architectures, as considered in this paper, combine a MANET underlay with a P2P overlay. Thus, a completely decentralized storage and retrieval of data objects can be ensured. Yet, multiple challenges are introduced by these architectures due to the characteristics of the underlying systems. This includes a strongly limited bandwidth and an increased fraction of dropped messages due to the wireless channel. The Clustered Pastry MP2P [11] system combines a MANET underlay with a DHT overlay to meet these requirements. The DHT overlay of this MP2P system is based on the Pastry [12] DHT and is used to store and manage objects in a decentralized manner.

We differentiate between overlay lookups and underlay routing. A lookup is initiated whenever an application requests or stores an object from or in the network, respectively. In order to determine the root node of an object, a lookup request is sent. In most cases intermediate nodes are required to forward lookup requests. To deliver this lookup request to the next intermediate overlay node, an underlay route is required. An example for a lookup request is shown in Fig. 1. The black node is the sender of the lookup request. The dark gray nodes are

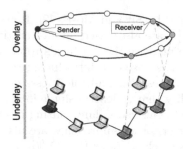

Fig. 1. Schematic representation of a lookup process in an MP2P network

intermediate overlay nodes and the root of the requested object. As shown in the figure, most overlay hops consist of multiple underlay hops. For example, the first overlay hop consists of three underlay hops. Therefore, this first overlay hop requires a complete underlay route (from the black node to the first dark gray node).

In order to combine the underlay with the overlay efficiently, both architectures, the MANET as well as the DHT have to be adapted. We harness location awareness of the mobile nodes in order to optimize the lookup mechanism. For this, the operation area, in which the MP2P network is established, is clustered. Each cluster defines the prefix of the overlay identifier of all nodes that are located in this cluster. As the lookup mechanism of Pastry is based on forwarding the lookup message to a node that is logically closer to destination with each hop, we are able to reduce not only the virtual distance but also the physical distance to the destination with each hop. This results in a reduced overhead caused by routing. Also the average number of hops required for an overlay route is affected by our location-aware architecture. In traditional DHTs, the average number of hops is a logarithmic function of the network size. In our clustered Pastry architecture, the average overlay hops is a function of the number of clusters as shown in Eq. 1 [13].

$$h_{CP} = 1 + log_{(2^b)}(C) * (1 - \frac{1}{2^b})$$ (1)

3.1   Implementation, Assumptions, and Setting

We implemented the previously introduced MP2P architecture for the OMNeT++ [14] simulator. Moreover, we integrated security mechanisms that have been discussed in Sect. 2 into this implementation of the Clustered Pastry MP2P system.

In the underlay we assume bidirectional links. Furthermore, all nodes participate in the MP2P network. The fraction of malicious nodes f is defined by $0 \le f \le 0.5$. Malicious nodes may initiate insider attacks. We assume that security mechanisms are in use to harden the underlay against MANET related attacks. Furthermore, we assume that a public key infrastructure is available and that nodes are able to sign sent messages. Using identity based cryptography [15] would be a promising approach as, otherwise, every node has to know the public keys of each node in the network. Yet, in the interest of simplification we assume pre-shared keys.

We assume a disaster relief scenario where the first responders are equipped with mobile nodes. Due to this fact, a rather low number of nodes participate in our MP2P network compared to traditional static P2P file-sharing scenarios. Therefore, we simulated our scenarios with 100 nodes. Each node was mobile using the random waypoint model. As we assume that all nodes were carried by pedestrians, the node speed was randomly chosen between 0 m/s and 1 m/s. The transmission range was according to WiFi in an open field up to 200 m. Further, all nodes were placed randomly in a field with a total size of 1100 m * 1100 m. The field size was chosen such that a connected network is typically achieved. We used 4 clusters in our scenarios as proposed by [11] for scenarios with 100 nodes.

4   Incorrect Lookup Routing Attack

DHTs and, therefore, MP2P architectures that are based on a structured overlay have to rely on the benign behavior of intermediate nodes during a lookup. Those intermediate nodes have to forward received lookup requests correctly toward the destination node. Yet, benign behavior cannot always be assumed. Malicious nodes that perform the *Incorrect Lookup Routing Attack* drop or misroute incoming lookup requests.

According to Castro et al. [5], the impact of the *Incorrect Lookup Routing Attack* on a recursive lookup request depends on the fraction of maliciously behaving nodes (f) and the overall number of hops (h). The resulting model that displays the fraction of successfully completed lookups is shown in Eq. 2.

$$\sigma = (1 - f)^{h-1} \tag{2}$$

4.1   Validation of Castro et al.'s Model in MP2P Scenarios

The analytic model proposed by Castro et al. has been developed in the light of traditional static DHTs. Thus, characteristics of MP2P systems have been neglected. Therefore, we simulated Clustered Pastry in scenarios with maliciously behaving intermediate nodes that drop incoming lookup messages. As the model proposed by Castro et al. [5] predicted a strong impact of the number of average overlay hops required for a lookup, scenarios have been simulated with 2, 4 and, 16 clusters. Thus, on average a lookup has to be forwarded 1.5, 2 and 3 times, respectively. As shown in Fig. 2, the outcome of the simulation of these scenarios with a fraction of up to 50 % of maliciously behaving nodes matches quite good with the analytic model. Yet, the analytic prediction fails in scenarios with a small fraction or high fraction of malicious nodes. On one hand, this is the result of neglecting the impact of the lossy wireless channel. Therefore, we proposed an adapted model that considers the fraction of lost messages

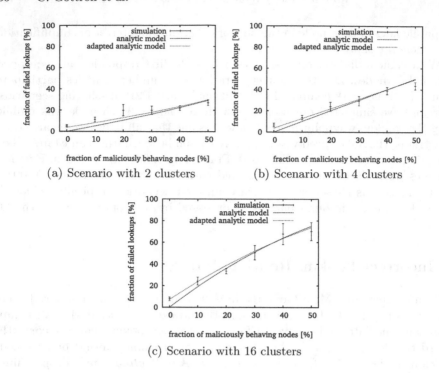

(a) Scenario with 2 clusters   (b) Scenario with 4 clusters

(c) Scenario with 16 clusters

Fig. 2. Impact of the *Incorrect Lookup Routing Attack* on a recursive, unsecured lookup algorithm

due to, e.g., the collisions of sent packets. This can be seen in settings without maliciously behaving nodes. Moreover, Clustered Pastry harnesses a basic replication mechanism in order to ensure the availability of objects even in scenarios with a churn. However, these replicas are not used during a lookup, but only to redistribute whenever a root node leaves a cluster or the network. Yet, whenever lookup is initiated, locally stored objects and replicas are used if available. As a result, we developed an optimized Equation as shown in Eq. 3. The probability p_{loss} represents the fraction of lost lookup messages per overlay hop. Moreover, the number of nodes in the Network (N) and the average number of root nodes of an object (N_{rep}) are used to cover the impact of the basic replication mechanism. As shown in Fig. 2, this adapted analytic model matches the simulation results better than the analytic model proposed by the related work.

$$\sigma_{Optimized} = \sigma * \frac{N - N_{rep}}{N} * p_{loss}^h + \frac{N_{rep}}{N} \tag{3}$$

5 Security Mechanisms

In Sect. 2, different security mechanisms were introduced that were developed for DHTs to reduce the impact of the *Incorrect Lookup Routing Attack*. In this section

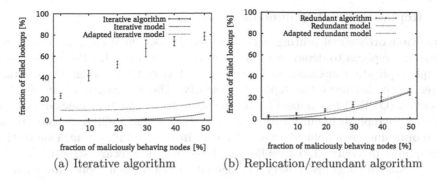

(a) Iterative algorithm   (b) Replication/redundant algorithm

Fig. 3. Comparison of the analytic models with the simulation results of a redundant and iterative routing algorithm

we evaluate the most promising approaches in the context of MP2P systems. This includes the adapted WatchDog approach, the iterative and redundant routing algorithm. Reputation based mechanisms are neglected as we assume that the lossy wireless channel would result in a high fraction of false positives. In [1], analytic models for the iterative, the redundant and the Overlay Watchdog security mechanism have been introduced. However, these models have not been validated by now and consider failed lookups due to malicious behavior only.

5.1   Iterative Routing Algorithm

The iterative routing mechanism ensures reliable lookup services due to the feedback provided to the source of the lookup as discussed in [2]. Yet, the source node is only able to respond to incorrectly routed or dropped lookup requests as long as sufficient addresses of nodes are available, that may be used as next hop intermediate nodes. Therefore, the number of routes per routing table entries (r) limits the efficiency of the iterative security mechanism regarding the fraction of successful lookups $(\sigma_{Iterative})$. Moreover the number of intermediate nodes that are required to forward the lookup request (h) also affects the probability of a successfully completed lookup as shown in Eq. 4 [1].

$$\sigma_{Iterative} = (1 - f^r)^{h-1} \qquad (4)$$

To validate this analytic model, we simulated scenarios with 4 clusters, 100 nodes, and maliciously behaving intermediate nodes. The efficiency of the iterative lookup mechanism is evaluated by measuring the fraction of the failed lookups. As shown in Fig. 3(a), the fraction of failed lookups is displayed as a function of the fraction of malicious nodes in the network. The simulation results indicate that the iterative lookup mechanism introduces a high fraction of failed lookups. This is a result of the increased traffic due to the feedback provided to the source of the request. As network congestion is neither considered by the basic nor the adapted models, analytical models can not be used to predict the fraction of failed lookups due to the iterative lookup mechanism.

5.2   Replication and Redundant Routing

As multiple orthogonal routing paths to a single root node are hard to ensure, we harness replicas to deploy a robust routing mechanism. In [13] we proposed multiple replication mechanisms for Clustered Pastry that harness the location awareness to distribute the replicas efficiently. The *Optimized Cyclic Replica Allocation* (OCRA) mechanism has been shown to be the most efficient scheme to distribute replicas in our location aware MP2P system. OCRA allocates replicas to opposing geographical areas (clusters) in the MP2P system. Due to this geographical diversity of the replicas and the location aware structure of the routing table of Clustered Pastry, orthogonal routes to each replica are ensured [13]. Thus, a redundant routing mechanism is enabled.

The resulting fraction of successfully completed lookups is described by Eq. 5 [1] and is a function of the fraction of maliciously behaving nodes (f), the number of parallel requests that have been sent (s), and the average number of required overlay hops per lookup (h). However, the number of sent requests is limited by the number of distributed replicas, in order to ensure orthogonal routing paths. Contrary to sending the requests in parallel as proposed by [5], redundant lookups are only initiated when a lookup fails. Moreover, the replica that is located geographically closest is routed first. Due to this adoptions, the traffic overhead can be reduced.

$$\sigma_{Redundant} = 1 - (1 - (1 - f)^{h-1})^s \tag{5}$$

We simulated this redundant routing algorithm in settings with 100 nodes, 4 clusters, and maliciously behaving intermediate nodes. Moreover, a replica is stored for each object that has been stored in the network using the OCRA replication mechanism. A comparison between the outcome of these simulations and the analytical model of Eq. 5 is shown in Fig. 3(b). The analytical model of the fraction of failed lookups is quite similar to the simulation results. Yet, the basic replication mechanism as well as the characteristics of the wireless transmission channel have been neglected. Therefore, we harness Eq. 3 to derive an adapted analytical model. By considering the increased amount of replicas, the adapted analytical model matches the outcomes of the simulations.

5.3   Overlay WatchDog

In [1] we introduced a theoretical approach on how to improve the robustness of the lookup mechanism while keeping the overhead on a reasonable level. This approach is based on an adapted WatchDog mechanism. In the following paragraphs, we discuss this adapted approach.

Mostly, multiple overlay hops are required for a single lookup. For each of those overlay hops an underlay route is required. The traditional WatchDog is only capable of detecting malicious behavior on the network layer and, therefore, can only detect malicious behavior on the underlay route between two overlay nodes. Thus, further information is required in order to detect malicious overlay behavior. In Fig. 4 an example for a lookup is shown. Nodes marked with

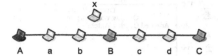

Fig. 4. An example of an MP2P lookup

uppercase letters are involved in the lookup and, therefore, are either overlay intermediate nodes (B), the source (A), or the destination of the lookup (C). All other nodes are either intermediate underlay nodes (a, b, c, d) or nodes that are not involved in the overlay or the underlay routing (x). Two overlay hops are required in order to forward the request from the source node to the destination node. Therefore, two underlay routes are required to perform the lookup. Route one from node A to B and route two from node B to C. The traditional WatchDog mechanism is capable of detecting malicious behavior within any of those underlay routes. Yet, a maliciously behaving node B that performs the *Incorrect Lookup Routing Attack* within the P2P overlay can not be detected. Therefore, the WatchDog mechanism has to be adapted in order to also detect malicious behavior in the overlay.

Whenever a lookup request is received by a node, this node has to determine whether the next hop node is part of the overlay route. Therefore, the intermediate nodes have to be aware of the overlay identifier of the physical neighbors as well as of the destination identifier of the request. Furthermore, basic information about the lookup mechanism is required. The lookup mechanism is well defined in DHTs and, therefore, malicious behavior that violates this algorithm can be detected by an adapted WatchDog with little effort. The overlay identifier of the destination node can be determined by cross-layer information. The destination identifier has to be extracted from the lookup request message. Therefore, overlay messages have to be identified and processed by the underlay. In our example, only two nodes (b and d) have an overlay node as next hop. Both nodes have to compare the node identifier of the next hop node with the destination identifier extracted from the lookup message. As a result, node b identifies node B as intermediate overlay node. Therefore, node B has to forward the message to a node that is logically closer to the destination identifier. As node b is aware of this, messages sent by node B have to be overheard in order to detect a message that includes the lookup request with a next hop overlay node that satisfies the constrains of the overlay routing algorithm. In the example, the next hop overlay node is the destination. Therefore, a benign behavior is assumed by the adapted WatchDog mechanism at node b. Node d on the other hand identifies the next hop node C as destination of the lookup request. A benign behavior is detected when a reply message is sent, to the sender of the request.

Whenever a node detects malicious behavior, the node has to respond in order to increase the network's robustness. The node, that has detected the malicious behavior has to be within transmission range of the malicious node and, therefore, has to be physically close to this node. Due to this, the probability

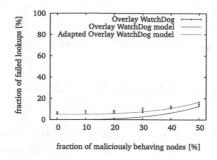

Fig. 5. Robustness provided by the *Overlay WatchDog* to the *Incorrect Lookup Routing Attack*

that the node that has detected the malicious behavior is within the same cluster as the malicious node is high. Due to this, both nodes have similar routing table entries and the node that has detected the malicious behavior is able to provide the same routing functionality as the malicious node should provide. This results in a reduced overhead as no notification message is required.

As shown in Eq. 6 [1], the fraction of successful lookups ($\sigma_{OverlayWatchdog}$) strongly depends on the number of overlay hops. Yet, also the number of physical neighbors (n) and the number of routes per routing table entries (r) affects the impact of maliciously behaving intermediate nodes.

$$\sigma_{OverlayWatchdog} = (\sum_{i=1}^{r}(\sum_{j=1}^{n} f^j * (1 - f))^i * (1 - f) + (1 - f))^{h-1} \qquad (6)$$

Again, we simulated a scenario with 100 nodes and 4 clusters. As shown in Fig. 5, these simulation results of the Overlay WatchDog mechanism match the prediction of the previously discussed analytic model, especially when considering the adaption of Eq. 3.

5.4   Comparison of the Security Mechanisms

By now we have simulated a unsecured recursive routing algorithm and three different security mechanisms in the context with the *Incorrect Lookup Routing Attack*. In Fig. 6 the fraction of failed lookups of these mechanisms is shown as a function of the fraction of malicious nodes in the network. As the recursive lookup mechanism does not provide any robustness against this attack, a high fraction of lookup messages is dropped. The Overlay WatchDog approach and the redundant routing mechanism provide better results compared to the recursive mechanism, while the iterative algorithm performs worse, even in scenarios without maliciously behaving nodes.

The WatchDog mechanism benefits from the structure of the geographically clustered architecture, as mentioned in the previous subsection, and, therefore, introduces a minimal overhead. Whenever a maliciously behaving intermediate

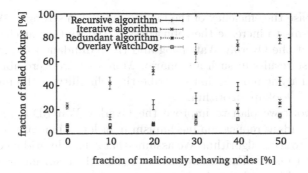

Fig. 6. A comparison between the different security mechanisms

node drops a lookup message, the Overlay Watchdog defines another node in the physical neighborhood that provides the lookup services that have been denied by the malicious node. Thus, only a minor overhead of about 5 % of the overall overlay traffic is introduced by this security mechanism.

The iterative mechanism on the other hand requires feedback at the sender side whenever a lookup message is received by an intermediate node (no matter whether this node behaves maliciously or benignly). Therefore, an increased number of control messages is required. This results in a highly increased fraction of collisions in the wireless channel and, therefore, in the highly degraded reliability of the lookup mechanism, as discussed previously.

The redundant routing mechanisms also introduces replicas. Thus, excellent results are achieved in scenarios with a small fraction of maliciously behaving intermediate nodes. This is the result of the adapted lookup mechanism that always requests the physically closest replica. Therefore, the probability of a dropped lookup message due to the lossy wireless channel is reduced. Yet, due to the distribution of the replicas, the overall traffic is increased by 10 %.

To sum it up, the redundant, replication based mechanism provides the most reliable lookup services in scenario with only a small fraction of maliciously behaving intermediate nodes. Yet, this mechanism introduces the highest traffic overhead. However, the Overlay Watchdog provides the best results in scenario with an increased fraction of malicious nodes. The iterative routing algorithm results in a congested network and, therefore, performs worse than the unsecured recursive routing algorithm.

6   Conclusions and Future Work

Multiple MP2P architectures have been proposed in the recent years. Those architectures benefit from the underlying decentralized architectures. Yet, the robustness of the lookup mechanism against maliciously behaving intermediate nodes during a lookup was neglected by now. Therefore, we discussed the impact of the *Incorrect Lookup Routing Attack* attacks on a structured, location aware MP2P architecture in this paper. As shown, the *Incorrect Lookup Routing Attack* is able to decrease the efficiency of the lookup algorithm strongly. We have evaluated mechanisms to increase the robustness of the routing mechanism. It has been shown that the Overlay WatchDog and the redundant routing mechanism provide the best results in such a scenario. Moreover, we were able to validate and optimize analytic models that describe the reliability of the unsecured and secured overlay's lookup algorithm.

In future work we plan to improve the Overlay WatchDog mechanism by including a redundant replication mechanism in order to increase the robustness of the overlay's routing algorithm. We assume that such a hybrid mechanism provides even better results. Further we have to reduce the resulting traffic overhead that is introduced by such a hybrid mechanism to avoid network congestion.

References

1. Gottron, C., et al.: A cross-layer approach towards robustness of mobile Peer-to-Peer networks. In: 7th IEEE International Workshop on Wireless and Sensor Networks Security (2011)
2. Sit, E., Morris, R.: Security considerations for Peer-to-Peer distributed hash tables. In: Druschel, P., Kaashoek, M.F., Rowstron, A. (eds.) IPTPS 2002. LNCS, vol. 2429, pp. 261–269. Springer, Heidelberg (2002)
3. Wang, P., et al.: Myrmic: secure and robust DHT routing. Technical report, University of Minnesota (2006)
4. Needels, K., Kwon, M.: Secure routing in Peer-to-Peer distributed hash tables. In: 24th ACM Symposium on Applied Computing (2009)
5. Castro, M., et al.: Secure routing for structured Peer-to-Peer overlay networks. In: Proceedings of 5th Symposium on Operating Systems Design and Implementation (2002)
6. Artigas, M.S., et al.: A novel methodology for constructing secure multipath overlays. IEEE Internet Comput. 9(6), 50–57 (2005). (IEEE Press, New York)
7. Kapadia, A., Triandopoulos, N.: Halo: high-assurance locate for distributed hash tables. In: 15th Annual Network and Distributed System Security Symposium (2008)
8. Roh, B.-S., Kwon, O.-H., Je Hong, S., Kim, J.: The exclusion of malicious routing peers in structured P2P systems. In: Joseph, S., Despotovic, Z., Moro, G., Bergamaschi, S. (eds.) AP2PC 2006. LNCS (LNAI), vol. 4461, pp. 43–50. Springer, Heidelberg (2008)
9. Sànchez-Artigas, M., García-López, P., Skarmeta, A.F.G.: Secure forwarding in DHTs - is redundancy the key to robustness? In: Luque, E., Margalef, T., Benítez, D. (eds.) Euro-Par 2008. LNCS, vol. 5168, pp. 611–621. Springer, Heidelberg (2008)
10. Marti, S., et al.: Mitigating routing misbehavior in mobile ad hoc networks. In: 6th International Conference on Mobile Computing and Networking (2000)
11. Gottron, C., et al.: A cluster-based locality-aware mobile Peer-to-Peer architecture. In: 8th International Workshop on Mobile Peer-to-Peer Computing (2012)
12. Rowstron, A.I.T., Druschel, P.: Pastry: scalable, decentralized object location and routing for large-scale peer-to-peer systems. In: IFIP/ACM International Conference on Distributed Systems Platforms (2001)
13. Gottron, C.: Security in mobile Peer-to-Peer architectures - introducing mechanisms to increase the robustness of overlay routing algorithms of Mobile-Peer-to-Peer architectures. Dissertation, Technische Universität Darmstadt (2013)

14. Varga, A.: OMNeT++. In: Wehrle, K., Günes, M.M., Gross, J. (eds.) Modeling and Tools for Network Simulation. Springer, Heidelberg (2010)
15. Boneh, D., Franklin, M.: Identity-based encryption from the Weil pairing. In: Kilian, J. (ed.) CRYPTO 2001. LNCS, vol. 2139, pp. 213–229. Springer, Heidelberg (2001)

Crossroads: A Framework for Developing Proximity-based Social Interactions

Chieh-Jan Mike Liang[1]([⊠]), Haozhun Jin[2], Yang Yang[2], Li Zhang[3], and Feng Zhao[1]

[1] Microsoft Research, Beijing, China
{liang.mike,zhao}@microsoft.com
[2] Tsinghua University, Beijing, China
{genezetta,geraint0923,zlfenyang}@gmail.com
[3] USTC, Hefei, China

Abstract. Proximity-based Social Interaction (PSI) apps are emerging on mobile platforms. While both industries and academic communities have developed frameworks to simplify the PSI app development, our framework, Crossroads, brings a set of features to balance the development overhead and developer expressiveness. We argue that APIs with application hints give developers the expressiveness, and core services (such as virtual links over the star topology) simplify network maintenance. Finally, PSI-specific primitives (such as presence beaconing with interval decaying and group dissemination) improve the energy efficiency. Evaluation results on real smartphones show the energy efficiency gain, topology robustness, and lower group dissemination load.

1 Introduction

With rich connectivities and features, smartphones today are capable of extending our presence virtually. A simple example is the increasing popularity of social apps [21]. Building on this momentum, a disruptive form of social interactions is emerging on the market: *Proximity-based Social Interactions* (PSI). With PSI, people's virtual interactions become more location-centric and tied to their current physical neighborhood (typically <150 ft). This is different from the rather static "friend lists" in typical online social interactions.

Industries and academic communities have developed several frameworks for PSI app development [13,14,18]. These frameworks recognize device resource management and network maintenance as the primary challenges. An example is the rich choice of physical radios on modern mobile devices, which have a wide range of characteristics (e.g., range, throughput, and energy). While existing frameworks represent a significant step forward, we argue that they lack a set of well-defined APIs and services that balance the development overhead and expressiveness. At one extreme, Windows 8's Proximity API [14] abstracts away many low-level intricacies, at the expense of app-specific tuning of certain parameters such as device presence beaconing frequency. On the other hand, Android exposes many low-level functionalities and controls, but the developers

© Institute for Computer Sciences, Social Informatics and Telecommunications Engineering 2014
I. Stojmenovic et al. (Eds.): MOBIQUITOUS 2013, LNICST 131, pp. 168–180, 2014.
DOI: 10.1007/978-3-319-11569-6_14

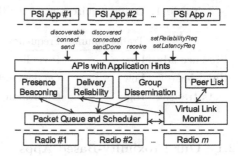

Fig. 1. Our PSI game – Big Doodle.

Fig. 2. Crossroads framework architecture.

are taxed with the burden to use them properly. While Qualcomm's popular AllJoyn [18] sits in between these two extremes, its fundamental designs do not incorporate several mobile-specific optimizations.

The contributions of our work come from defining powerful PSI programming abstractions, robust networked PSI device management, and efficient operating system services. To this end, the paper presents our PSI framework, *Crossroads*. We drive design decisions from first-hand PSI app development experience and observations from existing frameworks. Crossroads has three main differentiators. First, based on PSI-specific application hints, Crossroads aggregates and schedules pending transmissions while matching the app requirement. Second, Crossroads combines star topology and interval-decaying beacons to better achieve link robustness and device efficiency. Finally, recognizing group communication as an important PSI primitive, we designed a group dissemination protocol that addresses the problem of load hot-spots in many existing solutions.

Evaluations on real smartphones show an energy reduction up to 66 % with application hints, and a group dissemination completion time reduction by up to 50 %. Finally, Crossroads is able to fix network disconnections via physical radio link migration within 3.5 s.

Next, Sect. 2 first highlights the design patterns across PSI apps. Section 3 discusses design decisions and features of our framework, and Sect. 4 presents our current implementation. Then, Sect. 5 evaluates the performance of our framework. Finally, we present related work in Sect. 6 and conclude in Sect. 7.

2   Background

Hundreds of PSI apps [6,7,9,16,22] and games [1,20,23] are already available on the market. We first present two PSI apps we have developed, and then discuss the typical design patterns across most PSI apps to motivate our framework.

Table 1. Traffic requirement of the three types of messages in PSI apps.

	Traffic volume	Frequency	Reliability requirement	Delay tolerant
Presence adv.	Low	Periodic	Low	Yes
Handshake	Low	On-demand	Low	No
Data transfer	High	On-demand	High	Maybe

2.1   Our Proximity-Based Apps

Big Doodle. Big Doodle (c.f. Fig. 1) explores the class of collaborative gaming, where a group of people work together to accomplish a task. In our case, the goal is to collaboratively doodle an object on a large virtual canvas. During the game play, participants have limited real-time view of the canvas sections adjacent to theirs. The result from cooperation without explicit coordination can usually be unexpected and humorous.

SyncUp. Exchanging ideas forms the basis of meetings and rendezvous discussions, and conversations can lead to impromptu sharing of files and documents. In contrast to related solutions [8], SyncUp builds on-demand and ad-hoc connections among participants, rather than relying on centralized back-end application servers. This design removes both the dependency on the cloud and the overhead of data transfer over the public Internet.

2.2   Traffic Patterns of Proximity-Based Apps

Our experience suggests that PSI apps typically exhibit similar design patterns: presence advertisement, connection handshake, and data transfer. As similarities realize a framework, we now look at their network requirement (c.f. Table 1).

Presence Advertisement. PSI starts by discovering neighboring devices and services. One approach is to periodically beacon on short-range radios to infer the relative proximity. And, the reception of beacons would suggest the receiver is near to the transmitter. The beacon frequency and range are tunable to satisfy the requirement of discovery speed and neighborhood area.

Connection Handshake. Before app instances on two devices can exchange data, they need to agree and establish a logical link. A logical link specifies several parameters: the physical medium, end-point addresses, end-point roles, delivery reliability, etc. We use the notion of logical link here to abstract away many of the physical layer differences and intricacies. First, as most mobile platforms support multiple radio options, apps are free to choose the one that closely matches their requirement. Windows 8 Proximity API offers the option of connecting over Wi-Fi Direct or Bluetooth. Second, some network mediums assign different roles to each of the link end-points. For example, in the context of Wi-Fi Direct, one node acts as the soft access point (AP), and other nodes initiate the 802.11 association procedure to establish the link.

Data Transfer. Finally, bi-directional data exchange happens on the established logical link. The data object can vary in size, delivery latency and reliability, number of receivers, etc.

3 Architectural Design Overview

3.1 APIs with Application Hints

We now present the architecture of our Crossroads framework (c.f. Fig. 2). One
challenge is to match the app requirement with system resources. At the extremes,
the framework can either infer the traffic semantics with a generic model for all
apps, or expose all the low-level network functionalities to apps. However, both
do not balance between developers' burden and intention expressiveness. Crossroads adopts the approach of passing application-level hints via APIs to achieve
the sweet spot. As one contribution, we identify four key PSI hints below.

Destination(s). Knowing the destined group size allows optimizations for
application requirement, such as the delivery reliability. For point-to-point transmissions, a simple retransmission mechanism is sufficient to achieve delivery reliability. However, for group dissemination, the same mechanism can overload the
sender with retransmission requests.

Delivery Reliability. As reliable transmissions have the cost of additional control transmissions, knowing the reliability requirement helps the framework to
avoid unnecessary overhead. An example is device presence beaconing, where one
missing reception does not significantly impact the overall operation. Under certain conditions, Crossroads can exploit data objects with low delivery reliability,
e.g., artificial packet drops on senders with low remaining battery life.

Delivery Latency. Latency represents room for the framework to schedule
packet transmissions for the benefit of amortizing some costs. An example is the
tail energy of many radios [2] (e.g., 3G, GSM, and Wi-Fi). Section 5 evaluates two
approaches in achieving this goal: piggy-backing onto existing radio operations,
and batch transfers.

Delivery Frequency and Transmission Range. These two properties mostly
define the behavior and the scope of neighborhood/service discovery. A higher
delivery frequency for beacons speeds up the device discovery. While the property
of transmission range can be used to set the radio transmission power, it can
also be a hint of the physical radio to use.

3.2 Network Topology Management

Star Topology. While many existing frameworks opt the bus topology, we
argue that the star topology better fits the PSI communication pattern.

In the bus topology, all devices within a neighborhood connect to a single
virtual bus. The virtual bus can span multiple hops via intermediate relay nodes.

The star topology shifts the focus from being bus-centric to node-centric. The node-centric view implies that node a can send packets to node b only if there is a physical link between them. We note that this link is a one-hop asymmetric link, as most proximity-based interactions happen among direct neighbors. In cases where the requirement on neighborhood size is relaxed, mobile devices already support network mediums of large coverage, such as the cellular network.

We next elaborate the advantages of the star topology over the bus topology, in the context of PSI apps. First, the star topology has a lower topology maintenance overhead, as star nodes need to maintain only a list of their directly reachable neighbors. In contrast, bus nodes can address a packet to any other node on the same virtual bus, even nodes being relayed. This implies that every node require a globally consistent view of the virtual bus. While the bus topology is manageable in static and wired networks, we believe the overhead represents unnecessary costs in dynamic networks. Second, the lower topology maintenance overhead also translates into topology robustness. In other words, maintaining the neighbor list can be achieved by simply monitoring presence changes in the neighborhood [17].

Persistent Virtual Links. The abstraction below topology is link, and Crossroads exposes the notion of virtual links to apps. Each virtual link sits on top of multiple physical links, and it hides the complexities of managing multiple radio interfaces. In addition, if the current physical link deteriorates, Crossroads can switch to another radio interface without interrupting the apps. This automatic interface migration addresses the fact that mobility is inevitable on mobile platforms, where network disconnection can happen if users move out of the range of each other or some infrastructure. Although fixing on a long-range radio mitigates the disconnection problem, radios typically have the trade-offs among range, bandwidth and energy.

3.3   Group Dissemination Support

Group dissemination is a primitive, especially that many PSI apps function in a group setting. The common approach for group dissemination is originator centric, where only the originator is responsible for reliable delivery. However, this puts a significant burden on the originator in terms of transmissions, and the originator will consume energy much faster than the receivers. To this end, our group dissemination protocol is based on the concept of peer-to-peer (P2P)[1].

Packet loss is generally not uniform across a group of mobile platforms in proximity. In an experiment where four Nokia N800 smartphones were connected to the same 802.11g access point (AP), we instrumented one to stream 10,000 (unreliable) 1,500-byte multicast packets to the other three at an interval of 50 ms. While only 7.51 % of the packets were successfully received by all, 91.94 %

---

[1] While modern smartphones support a wide range of physical radios, we illustrate with 802.11 networks for ease of discussion.

were received by at least one receiver. This suggests that originator is not the only node capable of retransmissions, which motivates the P2P design.

Table 2. ProximityLink class.

Name	Arguments	Return values	Type
discoverable	{radio_types}, isDiscoverable, initAdvInterval		Method
discovered	{device_IDs}		Event
connect	device_ID, radio_types	ishandshakeStarted	Method
connected	device_ID, radio_types		Event
getConnected		{device_IDs}	Method
send	ProximityObj_ptr, device_ID		Method
sendDone	ProximityObj_ptr, isSuccessful		Event
setReliabilityReq	ProximityObj_ptr, reliability_class		Method
setLatencyReq	ProximityObj_ptr, latency_seconds		Method
receive	ProximityObj_ptr,		Event

Table 3. ProximityObj class.

Properties	Descriptions
objPtr	Pointer to the data object in memory
objSize	Size of the data object
latencyReq	Latency class of the data object
reliabilityReq	Reliability class of the data object

4 Current Implementation

4.1 Application-Hints APIs

ProximityLink and *ProximityObj* class represent the logical link and the network data object, respectively (c.f. Tables 2 and 3). Every PSI app has an unique app ID, and each app instance on a device first instantiates a copy of *ProximityLink*.

An app first calls `discoverable` to find neighboring devices of the same app ID, with constraints on radio types and the initial presence beaconing interval. The former constraint allows apps to specify the list of radio interfaces to maintain virtual links, and the latter enables an energy-efficient discovery (c.f. Sect. 4.2). The `discovered` event is signaled as neighboring devices are found.

`connect` and `connected` allow an app to start the handshake with the found app instance on another device, and be notified when a virtual link has been established.

For data transfer, we support two common reliability classes: best-effort and reliable. In addition, the latency requirement translates to maximum queuing delay on the sending device.

4.2   Network Topology Management

Presence Beaconing with Interval Decaying. Calling `discoverable` triggers beaconing all available app IDs on the device. In related work, all devices typically beacon with a fixed frequency. Our interval decaying minimizes this beaconing energy overhead. Considering the case of two devices, a discovery happens when any one device can hear the beacons from the other. In other words, it is theoretically feasible for only one of the two devices to beacon. Unfortunately, this naive solution does not perform well as devices do not know whether there is a neighbor actively beaconing.

Our basic idea is for all devices to slowly decrease their beaconing frequency. The advantage is that, as the neighborhood stabilizes, all devices would beacon rather infrequently. The design does not add latency to discovering new neighbors, as new devices would beacon at high frequency. The initial beaconing interval is passed as an applicant hint to `discoverable`. Big Doodle uses an `initAdvInterval` of one second to ensure fast multi-player discovery, and then doubles the interval every five beacons.

Topology Maintenance. `connect` establishes the virtual link with a two-way handshake between two devices, x and y. The information exchanged during the handshake sets up both end points for physical link migration. The first message from x declares the intent for virtual link establishment to y, with a list of radio interfaces to use. Upon receiving this message, y acknowledges back if it can support the requested link parameters. This acknowledgment then triggers x to update its peer list to reflect the new virtual link. During data transmissions over the virtual link, Crossroads translates destined device ID to the address of the physical radio interface currently in use.

Crossroads actively maintains live virtual links by monitoring the quality of underlying physical links. First, in the idle state, node x assumes a disconnected virtual link if presence beacons from node y have not been heard for a period of time. Second, during an active transfer, the sender assumes broken link if it does not receive acknowledgment after several tries. For receivers, the condition is a timeout since the last successful packet reception. Big Doodle sets the sender threshold to be 10 tries (once per sec), and the receiver wait timeout to be 10 s.

If the underlying physical link is no longer usable, Crossroads immediately switches to a physical radio interface with longer range, if available. Big Doodle prioritizes by the radio coverage: Cellular > Wi-Fi (infrastructure mode) > Bluetooth. The challenge lies in the interface switching timing (c.f. Sect. 5.2).

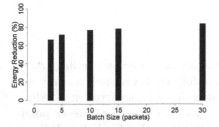

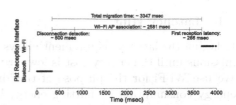

Fig. 3. The energy reduction due to batching on transmitting 600 UDP packets over Wi-Fi at 1 Hz.

Fig. 4. Virtual link switches to Wi-Fi link after the Bluetooth link becomes unavailable.

4.3 Group Dissemination

Crossroads divides the data object of size S_{obj} into fragments of size S_{pkt}. Each network packet includes the 32-bit data object ID and the 16-bit fragment sequence number to identify the packet payload. After the dissemination originator advertises the 32-bit unique data object ID, file name, and file size (S_{obj}), it multicasts all fragments of the data object to the group. Then, the network enters the recovery phase.

Reliable Packet Loss Recovery Phase. After a node stops hearing any multicast packet for some time, it scans received data for lost packets and broadcasts a request packet, *REQ*. *REQ* is sent via multicast to reach all Crossroads nodes in the group. Our current implementation sends each request three times to compensate for the lower delivery reliability of multicast.

Upon receiving the first *REQ*, node x starts a 1-s delay timer for additional *REQ*s from other nodes. Then, by aggregating all requests, nodes can estimate the network-wide reception ratio for each packet. After the delay timer fires, node x compiles a list of requested packets that it can fulfill. The challenge is to minimize the chance that multiple eligible nodes contribute to the same packet recovery. Our duplication suppression mechanism implements two techniques.

First technique is the queue randomization. Each node randomizes the ordering of requested packets that it plans to fulfill. In contrast to the naive sequential ordering, queue randomization minimizes the chance that two nodes send the same packet at the same time. Second, through overhearing, nodes can learn which data fragments have been sent on the network, and remove them from their queue. This effectively suppresses any duplicated effort.

The group may go through multiple rounds of requests and retransmissions before all nodes successfully receive the data object. After stopping receiving any multicast packet for 1 sec, nodes return to the request phase and send a new request packet with their current data reception summary.

5   Evaluations

5.1   Latency Hint

Relaxing the latency requirement allows the framework to delay pending transmissions until the energy cost is low, or when a duty-cycled radio is already up. We use Wi-Fi for the purpose of this discussion. Modern smartphones reduce energy consumption by putting energy-hungry radios to sleep whenever possible. An example is the Power Saving Mode (PSM) on Wi-Fi. When PSM is enabled, smartphones periodically wake up to check whether the associated AP has buffered packets destined to them[2]. As each wake-up incurs a fixed cost, we evaluate the usefulness of latency hints with two approaches below.

The first approach is to delay pending transmissions until Wi-Fi radio's periodic wake-ups to listen for beacons from the associated AP. The experiment consists of two Nexus S smartphones connecting to the same TP-Link 802.11g AP, and one device sent one 1,500-byte UDP packet to another device at an average interval of 30 s for an hour. We connected the sender to the Monsoon Power Monitor [15] for energy measurement. The comparison baseline is where the sender transmits according to a random timer with a mean of 30 s. Then, we instrumented the same sender to delay each transmission until the Wi-Fi radio is up. Results suggest the latter has an energy reduction of about 3 %, and this improvement is from amortizing a fixed radio wake-up cost.

The second approach is to batch a set of delay-tolerant transmissions on the device. We used the same setup as previous, and instrumented the sender to generate packets at a rate of 1 Hz. However, the actual radio transmissions do not take place until the number of pending packets reaches the predefined batch size. Figure 3 shows that the energy reduction, as compared to the case without batching transmissions. The interesting observation is that the reduction can be significant even for small batches (e.g., 66 % for a batch size of three). In addition, the energy reduction lowers as the batch size increases, which represents a diminishing return on amortizing a fixed amount of the wake-up cost.

5.2   Topology Robustness

For the star topology, the topology robustness is mainly determined by how stable the virtual link between app instances on two different devices is. In the context of mobile platforms, mobility is a major factor contributing to poor link quality and disconnections. Therefore, we evaluate the virtual link stability by looking at how Crossroads mitigates these problems.

We experimented on two Nokia N800 smartphones connected via a virtual link over both Bluetooth and office Wi-Fi network. One device transmitted a 30-MB object over Bluetooth while we varied the inter-device distance at the (adult) walking speed. The distance increased from ∼1 m until the devices were beyond the Bluetooth range. Then, after 10 s, they were brought back to the initial position.

---

[2] The Wi-Fi beacon listen interval on smartphones is typically 200 ms.

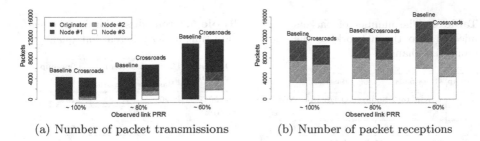

(a) Number of packet transmissions   (b) Number of packet receptions

Fig. 5. The number of packet transmissions and receptions of each smartphone under different observed link qualities.

Figure 4 shows the switch from Bluetooth to Wi-Fi. As the two devices moved out of the Bluetooth range, the sender stopped receiving packet acknowledgments, and the receiver stopped receiving packets. After a time-out of 500 ms, both devices activated the Wi-Fi radio to reestablish the virtual link (~2581 ms). We note that the IP addresses were exchanged during the connection handshake. Finally, the first Wi-Fi packet arrived at the receiver after ~266 ms.

Switching back from Wi-Fi to Bluetooth took a much shorter time, as the data transfer can continue on Wi-Fi while the sender probes for the receiver on Bluetooth. Then, after the Bluetooth link is available, the sender immediately stopped the transfer on Wi-Fi and then restarted it on Bluetooth. We observed a delay of ~300 ms before the first Bluetooth packet arrived.

5.3   Group Dissemination

The evaluation of the group dissemination is based on the energy efficiency, which is derived from two metrics: (1) The number of packet transmissions and receptions on each node. (2) The group-wide dissemination completion time.

We evaluate our group dissemination on a local Wi-Fi network, given the high bandwidth and native multicast support. All six Nokia N800 smartphones connected to a single TP-Link 802.11g access point (AP). During each experiment run, one node disseminated a 3-MB data object to the other five phones. Each experiment was repeated three times at different time of the day to capture any temporal variation.

The comparison baseline is the common originator-centric dissemination protocol. After each round of multicast flooding, all receivers report back their list of missing data packets. With this report from all receivers, the sender then starts another round of multicast flooding to retransmit only the missing packets.

Node Transmission Counts. Figs. 5(a) and (b) show the amount of network traffic generated by each node under different link quality. We controlled the link packet reception ratio (PRR) by injecting artificial packet losses following the Gilbert-Elliot model. As both packet transmission and reception consume a

Table 4. The number of packets injected into the network as the group size changes.

Group size	Crossroads		Baseline	
	Originator	Node average	Originator	Node average
4	3516	306	3798	0
5	3633	255	4255	0
6	3477	165	7471	0

Table 5. Group dissemination completion time under different link qualities.

Observed link PRR	Total time (sec)		Speedup (%)
	Baseline	Crossroads	
~100 %	20	17	15
~80 %	37	32	13
~60 %	130	53	59

significant amount of energy, smaller values are desirable. There are two interesting observations from Fig. 5. First, the Crossroads group collectively received less packets than the baseline. This difference is due to the fact that Crossroads switches to unicast if the number of intended receivers is one, which leverages the relatively higher reliability of unicast. Second, from the network point of view, Crossroads injects more packets than the baseline. In the worse case, this difference is about 20 %. However, the break down in Fig. 5(a) reveals that half of the originator's load shifts to other nodes in the network.

Building on the discussion of load shifting, Table 4 suggests that, in the case of Crossroads, the load of the originator decreases as the group size increases. This observation is related to the decreasing probability of a packet not being received by any node in the group. On the other hand, in the case of baseline, the originator's load increases with the group size.

Dissemination Completion Time. Table 5 examines the dissemination completion time under different link quality in a six-node group. When the observed link PRR is close to perfect, both the baseline and Crossroads finished very closely to each other. This is because multicast packets were rarely dropped, and the flooding can successfully deliver almost all of the data packets. As the network link quality became worse, the difference between finish times increased. In the case of 60 % PRR, the difference is more than a factor of two. A closer investigation shows that, with multiple concurrent transmitters, Crossroads is able to more closely saturate the radio medium capacity. Since Crossroads nodes can successfully receive the data objects faster than the baseline, they can turn off the radio much earlier to save energy.

6   Related Work

Proximity-based App Framework. Qualcomm's AllJoyn [18] is a cross-platform framework. Like Crossroads, AllJoyn also sits between the application layer and the physical radios, and provides APIs for data exchange among applications on devices in proximity. However, AllJoyn limits what traffic-specific properties that PSI applications can pass, and it does not have PSI-related optimizations, such as reliable group dissemination. Windows 8 ships with a Proximity API that provides an even more limited set of functionalities [14]. The problem of managing multiple radio interfaces on a node has been explored by several prior projects. However, in this problem space, our work explores PSI-specific issues and optimizations. Like Contact Networking [3], we try to provide the illusion of persistent links between applications on neighboring devices. And, we share the view of supplying hints of traffic semantics from applications to lower layers for optimization [11]. This design is absent in some related projects [24].

Reliable Group Dissemination. Previous efforts on Bluetooth mostly focus on building a multicast tree with respect to some metrics, such as energy and latency [4,5]. The lack of link-layer acknowledgment (ACK) is one source of low multicast delivery reliability on Wi-Fi. However, requiring ACKs from all receivers can cause an acknowledgment explosion in the network. Kuri et al. [12] proposed a leader-based protocol; RMAC [19] and 802.11MX [10] generate an out-of-band tone to signal positive and negative ACKs respectively. However, these work do not consider the energy constraint of smartphones, as the burden of packet retransmissions is still entirely on the sender.

7   Conclusion

Compared to solutions from the industry and the academic communities, Crossroads brings a set of expressive APIs and PSI-optimized services to balance PSI app development overhead and developers' expressiveness. Our design was driven by first-hand PSI app development experience, and supported by the evaluation results. We are working on bringing Crossroads to more mobile platforms.

References

1. Baber, C., Westmancott, O.: Social networks and mobile games: the use of blue-tooth for a multiplayer card game. In: Brewster, S., Dunlop, M.D. (eds.) Mobile HCI 2004. LNCS, vol. 3160, pp. 98–107. Springer, Heidelberg (2004)
2. Balasubramanian, N., Balasubramanian, A.,Venkataramani, A.: Energy consumption in mobile phones. In: IMC (2009)
3. Carter, C., Kravets, R., Tourrilhes, J.: Contact networking: a localized mobility system. In: MobiSys (2003)
4. Chang, C.-T., Chang, C.-Y., Chang, S.-W.: Tmcp: two-layer multicast communication protocol for bluetooth radio networks. Comput. Netw. **52**, 2764–2778 (2008)
5. Chang, C.-Y., Shih, K.-P., Chang, H.-J., Lee, S.-C., Yu, G.-J.: Pamp: a power-aware multicast protocol for bluetooth radio systems. In: ICCCAS (2004)
6. Chatter, Inc. Buzzmob- social media for real life. http://www.buzzmob.com
7. Color Labs, Inc. Color - Broadcast Live. http://color.com
8. Davis, R.C., Landay, J.A., Chen, V., Huang, J., Lee, R.B., Li, F.C., Lin, J., Morrey III, C.B., Schleimer, B., Price, M.N., Schilit, B.N.: Notepals: lightweight note sharing by the group, for the group. In: CHI (1999)

9. Foursquare Labs, Inc. Foursquare. http://www.foursquare.com
10. Gupta, S.K.S., Shankar, V., Lalwani, S.: Reliable multicast MAC protocol for wireless LANs. In: ICC (2003)
11. Higgins, B.D., Reda, A., Alperovich, T., Flinn, J., Giuli, T., Noble, B., Watson, D.: Intentional networking: opportunistic exploitation of mobile network diversity. In: MobiCom (2010)
12. Kuri, J., Kasera, S.K.: Reliable multicast in multi-access wireless lans. In: Infocom (1999)
13. Le, A., Keller, L., Fragouli, C., Markopoulou, A.: MicroPlay: a networking framework for local multiplayer games. In: MobiGames (2012)
14. Microsoft, Inc. Windows.networking.proximity namespace. http://msdn.microsoft.com/en-us/library/windows/apps/windows.networking.proximity
15. Monsoon Solutions, Inc. Power Monitor. http://www.msoon.com/LabEquipment/PowerMonitor/
16. Nearverse, Inc. LoKast - Real-time Interactive Spaces. http://www.lokast.com
17. Parsons, J.J., Oja, D.: New Perspectives on Computer Concepts 2012, 14th edn. Cengage Learning, Independence (2011)
18. Qualcomm Innovation Center, Inc. AllJoyn. https://www.alljoyn.org
19. Si, W., Li, C.: Rmac: a reliable multicast mac protocol for wireless ad hoc networks. In: ICPP (2004)
20. Spanek, R., Kovar, P., Pirkl, P.: The bluegame project: ad-hoc multilayer mobile game with social dimension. In: CoNEXT (2007)
21. TechCrunch. Nearly 40% of facebook use is from mobile apps. http://techcrunch.com/2011/12/29/nearly-40-of-facebook-use-is-from-mobile-apps/
22. Tencent, Inc. Weixin. http://weixin.qq.com
23. Zhang, Z., Chu, D., Chen, X., Moscibroda, T.: Swordfight: enabling a new class of phone-to-phone action games on commodity phones. In: MobiSys (2012)
24. Zhuang, S., Lai, K., Stoica, I., Katz, R., Shenker, S.: Host mobility using an internet indirection infrastructure. Wirel. Netw. **11**(6), 741–756 (2005)

Merging Inhomogeneous Proximity Sensor Systems for Social Network Analysis

Amir Muaremi[1]([✉]), Franz Gravenhorst[1], Julia Seiter[1], Agon Bexheti[2], Bert Arnrich[3], and Gerhard Tröster[1]

[1] Wearable Computing Lab, ETH Zurich, Gloriastrasse 35, 8092 Zurich, Switzerland
{muaremi,gravenhorst,seiter,troester}@ife.ee.ethz.ch
[2] Artificial Intelligence Laboratory, EPFL, 1015 Lausanne, Switzerland
agon.bexheti@epfl.ch
[3] Computer Engineering Department, Bogaziçi University, 34342 Istanbul, Turkey
bert.arnrich@boun.edu.tr

Abstract. Proximity information is a valuable source for social network analysis. Smartphone based sensors, like GPS, Bluetooth and ANT+, can be used to obtain proximity information between individuals within a group. However, in real-life scenarios, different people use different devices, featuring different sensor modalities. To draw the most complete picture of the spatial proximities between individuals, it is advantageous to merge data from an inhomogeneous system into one common representation. In this work we describe strategies how to merge data from Bluetooth sensors with data from ANT+ sensors. Interconnection between both systems is achieved using pre-knowledge about social rules and additional infrastructure. Proposed methods are applied to a data collection from 41 participants during an 8 day pilgrimage. Data from peer-to-peer sensors as well as GPS sensors is collected. The merging steps are evaluated by calculating state-of-the art features from social network analysis. Results indicate that the merging steps improve the completeness of the obtained network information while not altering the morphology of the network.

Keywords: Proximity · Smartphones · Bluetooth · ANT+ · Pilgrims

1 Introduction and Motivation

1.1 Social Networks Based on Proximity Data

Social networks are omnipresent and an essential part of many peoples' lives. Social scientists have introduced social network analysis (SNA) methods to better understand and interpret relationships between individuals. They are an important tool to understand individual and group behavior within communities or crowds. This kind of information is not only beneficial for intelligence services but can also be used to improve the security or well-being of individuals at crowd events as well as to improve individualized advertisement campaigns.

© Institute for Computer Sciences, Social Informatics and Telecommunications Engineering 2014
I. Stojmenovic et al. (Eds.): MOBIQUITOUS 2013, LNICST 131, pp. 181–194, 2014.
DOI: 10.1007/978-3-319-11569-6_15

A key question from a technical point of view is how data can be obtained to reconstruct these social networks. Traditional research methods are based on surveys and manual observations. More recently, however, data is collected digitally from communication hubs or online media. Online social network platforms are emerging but can only represent a fraction of the social network, which exists in our offline world. Identifying an offline social network with technical means to convert it into a digital representation is a challenging task.

One approach to identify offline social networks is to measure the proximity between individuals within a group. Individuals who are spatially close to each other are potentially also linked in a social sense. There are several technical tools to measure spatial proximity between individuals. One possibility is to measure the absolute positions of individuals and then calculate their mutual spatial distance. Another method is to use peer-to-peer transceivers, which are worn by the individuals. If one transceiver picks up the signal of another one, the two individuals are considered to be close to each other.

Smartphone based sensors, like GPS, Bluetooth and ANT+, can be used to obtain proximity information between individuals within a group. However, in real-life scenarios, different people use different devices, featuring different sensor modalities. To draw the most complete picture of the spatial proximities between individuals, it is advantageous to merge data from an inhomogeneous system into one common representation.

1.2 Data Collection During Pilgrimage

One of the biggest, global annual events is the Hajj pilgrimage of Muslims. Consequently, we identified it as a particularly useful event to collect data about social networks. During this pilgrimage millions of people from all over the world congregate for religious rituals at holy sites in the cities of Makkah and Madinah and their surrounds. The holy mosque in Makkah covers an area of approximately 350,000 square meters and the holy site in Madinah is approximately 80,000 square meters in size. Umrah, also known as the "lesser pilgrimage", is the visit to the sacred sites outside the period of Hajj (for details see, e.g., [5]).

The pilgrimage of Hajj/Umrah is useful to our study for the following reasons:

- It is a big event and features real-life conditions.
- Daily routines are very structured which simplifies the annotations.
- The fixed and synchronized schedule concerning prayer activities enables comparisons of data.
- Each individual performs five prayers each day, prayers have dynamic, semi-dynamic and static parts and involve re-groupings of the individuals. This ensures a high but still predictable variety of recorded proximity data.
- There are fixed religious rules the pilgrims have to comply with and which can be exploited to de-noise the data.

1.3 Related Work

In [13], organizational human behavior is measured and analyzed by using proximity information, for example: time spent in close proximity to other people, this is determined by special wearable electronic badges. Nowadays, the emerging technologies of smartphones have replaced the wearable sensors as sensing devices. The work in [4] uses Bluetooth (BT) links to identify friendship networks by detecting people sharing the same space. Do et al. [3] demonstrate the usage of smartphone BT as a real, i.e., face-to-face, proximity sensor to identify social networks. In the aforementioned examples the target subjects were employees working in offices or students living on university campuses.

As well as BT, the ANT+ protocol has recently been used as a proximity sensor. In [6] and [7], ANT+ is used for monitoring and assessing the performance of firefighting teams in training scenarios.

The combination of BT and ANT+ has not been an area of significant interest in the literature to date. Most of the studies are performed in controlled lab environments and settings. There are few technical challenges and the noise levels, i.e., the external influences, are highly predictable.

Apart from our work, there are only a few studies about the Hajj pilgrimage and these focus mainly on tracking pilgrims for security issues rather than understanding social networks. For example, in [9] and [10] the authors describe two frameworks that provide pilgrim tracking using smartphones, with the goal of improving transportation infrastructure and crowd management services. In [8] simulation tools are built to support pilgrims in navigating through religious sites.

1.4   Contributions

We present two ways of obtaining proximity data of peers within a crowd, firstly based on peer-to-peer sensor nodes and secondly on positional (GPS) information. Both approaches are discussed qualitatively from a technical point of view. Additionally data collection is performed which enables a quantitative comparison from a practical point of view.

The main contributions and outcomes of our work are as follows:

1. We present the implementation of two types of peer-to-peer proximity sensor nodes, which are based on mobile phones using BT and ANT+ technology respectively. We suggest a method for merging these inhomogeneous sensor sources into one common proximity matrix. Interconnection between both systems is achieved by using additional infrastructure and accessing pre-knowledge about religious and social rules in a specific community, in our example a Muslim community.
2. We present an approach to extract proximity information from position sensor (GPS) data.
3. We apply our methods to a data collection with n=41 participants during 8 days in a real-life scenario and describe practical challenges.
4. Based on this data collection we compare proximity information obtained from peer-to-peer sensors with proximity information based on position data both qualitatively and quantitatively and discuss the results.

2   Data Collection and Data Processing Schedule

In this section, we briefly describe the data collection. More information can be found in our previous work in [11].

2.1   Participants

41 pilgrims, equipped with Android smartphones participated in our study during the Umrah pilgrimage over 8 days. The youngest was a 7 year old boy and the oldest a 53 years old man ($\mu = 30, \sigma = 13$). There were 31 males and 10 females, among which there were 10 couples, 10 children and 11 single participants.

2.2   Smartphone as Sensing Device

As sensing application we extended the Android open sensing framework Funf [1]. The app collects proximity information, absolute GPS location, 3D-acceleration of the device and audio features. The smartphones were configured either as BT devices or as ANT+ devices and were only able to capture nearby devices from the same configuration type. We distributed 22 BT devices (Samsung Galaxy SII, SIII and SIII Mini) and 19 ANT+ devices (Sony Xperia Active and Neo). Participants were encouraged to wear the smartphones in their pockets, preferably for the whole day, but at least around the times of the 5 daily prayers.

We distributed the smartphones based on information gained from personal questionnaires and interviews at the beginning of the study that identified socially connected groups. Two BT devices and two ANT+ devices were given to two couples, crosswise distributed to the four participants as shown in Fig. 1.

2.3   Wearable Devices

Amongst the 41 smartphone participants, there were also 10 pilgrims wearing the chest strap Zephyr Bioharness 3[1]. These devices, designed to gather

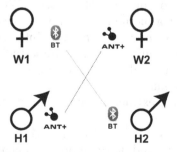

Fig. 1. Crosswise distribution of BT and ANT+ smartphones to two couples, wives (W) and husbands (H)

---

[1] http://www.zephyranywhere.com

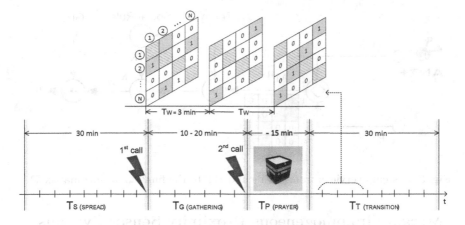

Fig. 2. Data processing schedule with 4 time intervals

bio-physiological data of the body, were used for another independent study [12]. In our work we used these auxiliary devices since they were already available.

2.4 Data Processing Schedule

Within the pilgrimage, we only concentrated on group behavior during and around the prayers, since they are the most frequent events of the day. Figure 2 schematically depicts the data processing schedule around the prayers. Two events, 1st call and 2nd call, define the following four time intervals:

- T_S **Spread Groups:** Pilgrims could be spread in and around the mosque performing rituals, shopping or resting in their hotels. The data collecting starts 30 min before the first call.
- T_G **Gathering:** The first call for prayer informs the people that in the next 10 to 20 min the prayer is going to begin. The pilgrims start to gather from wherever they are.
- T_P **Static Prayer:** The prayer starts immediately after the second call. In this period there is no change in group formations.
- T_T **Transition to T_S:** When the leader of the prayer finalizes the prayer, the people spread again until they reach the initial formations of T_S. Data collection continues for the next 30 min.

Within each section (except T_P) the time is divided into $T_W = 3$ minute windows. This window length is lower bounded by the minimum sampling frequency of all sensing devices, and upper bounded by the time within which we assume the group formation stays constant.

For each window, we create an adjacency matrix **A**, an N × N matrix with elements a_{ij} being 1 if user i was in proximity of user j during that period of time (T_W), i.e., i saw j, and 0 otherwise, with N being the number of users.

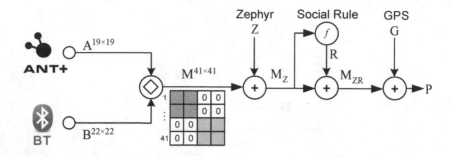

Fig. 3. System overview: from ANT+ and BT to the final adjacency matrix **P**

3   Merging Inhomogeneous Proximity Sensor Systems

3.1   System Overview

Figure 3 shows a general overview of the steps involved in processing the proximity data. Two inhomogeneous systems, ANT+ and BT, provide the initial inputs. ANT+ proximity data is represented as a binary symmetric adjacency matrix $\mathbf{A}^{19 \times 19}$ of size equal to the number of participants (19). Similarly, BT proximity data is an adjacency matrix $\mathbf{B}^{22 \times 22}$ of size 22. These two matrices are merged into one matrix $\mathbf{M}^{41 \times 41}$ of size equal to the total number of smartphones (41), using the operator "$\diamond$", as follows:

$$\mathbf{M} = \begin{pmatrix} 0 & \cdots & 0 \\ \vdots & \ddots & \vdots \\ 0 & \cdots & 0 \end{pmatrix} , \mathbf{M}_{1:19,1:19} = \mathbf{A} , \mathbf{M}_{20:41,20:41} = \mathbf{B} . \qquad (1)$$

The structure of the merged matrix $\mathbf{M}$ contains the two systems (colored blocks) and two zero blocks. All following matrices in the processing chain are of equal size (41×41). "$+$" is the matrix logical OR operator. $\mathbf{Z}$ is the adjacency matrix filled out with information gathered from the Zephyr wearable sensors. $\mathbf{M_Z} = \mathbf{M} + \mathbf{Z}$ is the merged matrix with added Zephyr knowledge. Special social rules (f) are applied to the existing proximity matrix. The additional connections extracted from these rules are stored in the adjacency matrix $\mathbf{R}$. $\mathbf{M_{ZR}} = \mathbf{M_Z} + \mathbf{R}$ is the previous matrix, with knowledge added from the social rules.

The multi-modal aspect of proximity sensing is enriched by using the GPS sensor as well. The adjacency matrix $\mathbf{G}$ is built from GPS locations, and the final matrix $\mathbf{P} = \mathbf{M_{ZR}} + \mathbf{G}$ contains all previous proximity information.

The initial merged matrix $\mathbf{M}$ is improved by updating the zero values in each step of the chain.

3.2   ANT+ and BT Proximities

ANT+ is a proprietary wireless sensor network that operates in the 2.4 GHz frequency range. It is mainly available in sport equipment devices such as bike

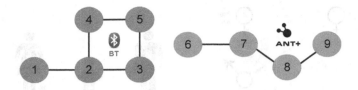

Fig. 4. Social network graphs of ANT+ and BT proximity systems

computers or heart rate monitors. ANT+ radio devices support up to eight logical channels using time division multiplexing on one physical channel.

ANT+ Search Strategy. Each device periodically transmits its ID on one of the eight logical channels. Given a list of devices to search for, the remaining seven channels are used to search in parallel for all the devices provided in the list. There is a time out approach for cases when the device being searched is not present in the proximity range.

BT scans were used as means of identifying other BT capable devices that are in the proximity range. In order for a smartphone to be "seen" by other devices, its BT adapter needs to be in discoverable mode. The smartphone devices used in this study are equipped with a Class 2 BT adapter.

BT Search Strategy. The BT search algorithm uses methods from the Android API to asynchronously initiate BT scans and retrieve scan results. The scan method performs a 12 second scan and for each newly discovered device a page scan is done to retrieve its BT name.

The scores of the adjacency matrices **A** and **B** provide information about the proximity relationship between each pair of devices, e.g., $a_{i,j} = 1$ indicates that the ANT+ devices i and j are in proximity range. Moreover, the matrices are symmetric, i.e., if i sees j, then j sees i as well. Figure 4 illustrates a social network graph constructed from ANT+ and BT adjacency matrices. The graphs are undirected and because of the inhomogeneity of the systems, there is no link between the two groups.

3.3 Wearable Sensor Proximity

Zephyr wearable sensors were provided to 10 pilgrims. The devices were equipped with a BT adapter for transmitting the logged data to a smartphone and during the study were configured to always be in discoverable mode. From the 10 devices, 6 were assigned to users that were using ANT+ smartphones for proximity sensing, and the other 4 were distributed to BT smartphones users. In this way, the 6 ANT+ smartphones participants contribute to connecting the two inhomogeneous systems, as it appears to the other participants that the 6 users carry both types of smartphones. On the other hand, the 4 BT smartphones users do not contribute directly, however, as they carry 2 discoverable BT devices, it is more likely to be seen by others when they enter the proximity region.

Fig. 5. First and second social rules

3.4   Social Rules for Proximity

From discussions with experts, and after clarification with participating pilgrims, we learnt and applied the following social rules of pilgrims while the Umrah pilgrimage:

1. If a woman (W1) sees a man (H2), then the corresponding wife (W2) of that man is also present (see Fig. 5 left).
2. One child is always together with one of the parents (see Fig. 5 right).

The first rule is particularly helpful, i.e., contributes into merging ANT+ and BT proximity systems, if the distribution of the smartphone types to socially connected pairs is done in the described crosswise manner. We assume that W2 is between W1 and H2, and therefore we apply one further collaborative step: People seen by W2 using ANT+ protocol are added to the proximity range of both W1 and H2, and the intersection of people seen by W1 and H2 are added to the proximity range of W2.

In addition to these rules, most of participants knew each other as well.

3.5   Location Based Proximity

Each GPS location record stores the longitude/latitude coordinates and the accuracy distance (in m) of the estimation position. Location errors are according to Android normally distributed with one standard deviation equal to the estimated accuracy distance. This means that, there is a 68 % chance (cumulative percentage from -1σ to $+1\sigma$) that the correct position is inside the circle with the radius equal to the location accuracy distance.

For each sliding window interval around the prayer, the weighted centroid, i.e., locations with lower accuracy distance are more important, of all GPS points of the same user is calculated. Figure 6 shows the GPS locations of some users in the mosques of Madinah and Makkah for one time interval.

The simplest way to construct the adjacency matrices **G** is for each user to calculate the physical distance to all other users and to fill in the corresponding element of **G** in case the distance is below a threshold, e.g., 10 m. This procedure is due to the run time complexity of $O(n^2)$ not feasible for a high number of users. To mitigate this problem, we propose the following approach: Firstly, the full cloud of points is divided roughly into clusters using the density based

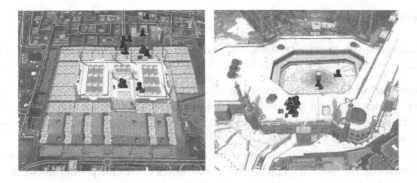

Fig. 6. Visualized GPS user locations in Madinah and Makkah

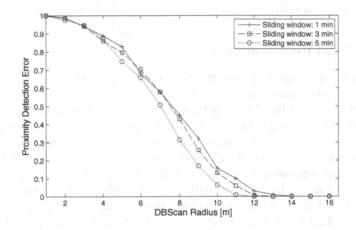

Fig. 7. DBScan parameter sweeping

scan algorithm (DBScan). Then, walking through these clusters, parts of **G** are constructed, meaning that the one big problem is divided into many smaller problems. This approach is payed off when the number of clusters is large and the fast DBScan algorithm, with runtime complexity $O(n \cdot \log n)$, is used.

The main parameter of DBScan is the radius of the circle with which the algorithm tries to find clusters in the cloud of points. The higher this parameter is, the less clusters we get and the less the algorithm is efficient. On the other side, a higher number of clusters can lead to errors in proximity detection, when, e.g., two real neighbours are not assigned to the same cluster. Figure 7 shows the normalized proximity detection error in function of the DBScan radius for three different sliding window lengths T_W. The shapes of all T_W look similar and the optimal radius is located at around 13 m.

4   Evaluation

We aggregate the proximity data, i.e., average adjacency matrices, over a time interval T and extract the following SNA state-of-the-art features [2]:

- **Average node eigenvector centrality (ANEC)**
  NEC shows how well a node is connected to the most important nodes. Centrality features are used to identify pitchers (leaders) and catchers (followers).
- **Network density (ND)**
  ND is the ratio of links over the total number of possible links in a network. It measures the network connectivity and is used for comparing networks.
- **Network clustering coefficient (NCC)**
  NCC is the density of network neighbourhoods and can be used for detecting subgroups in a network.

4.1   Graphical Representation

Figure 8 shows an example of proximity data over one interval T_S. Initial ANT+ and BT nodes and connections are plotted in (a). The systems are inhomogeneous and there is no link between them. (b) shows is the state after incorporating proximity data from Zephyr, where the number of links is doubled. The new links between the two systems occur because BT smartphones have indirectly detected the presence of ANT+ devices through the Zephyr BT radios. There is also an improvement within the BT nodes, due to the extra BT signal available from Zephyr. The contribution of applying the pilgrimage social rules is displayed in (c) where the network density increases significantly. And, (d) shows the final state of the network when GPS data are integrated.

4.2   Quantitative Evaluation

Table 1 lists the SNA features of all matrices described in Fig. 3, averaged over all prayers.

We observe that ANEC is almost constant with a value around 10 %. We can therefore say, that the centrality property of the network, i.e., the information about the importance of people (nodes) is not changed across all merging steps.

For NCC, we take the value of **G** as a baseline, because GPS proximity is a fair representation of a homogeneous equivalent network of the two inhomogeneous systems ANT+ and BT. Going through **M**, **M$_Z$**, and **M$_{ZR}$**, we can see a small decrease of NCC at each step. The value at **M$_{ZR}$** is 16 % smaller than the baseline of **G**. Thus, we conclude, that the clustering property of the network is moderately worsened compared to the GPS social network.

An increase in ND is observed at all steps. GPS contributes with only 9 % to the overall density, while the social rule with 40 % is the most effective modality for merging. The cummulative plot and the pie chart are shown in Fig. 9.

The colored bars show the ND of the individual auxiliary proximities, while the black bars represent the cumulative ND values of all the previous merging steps. The pie chart illustrates the percentage of ND increase from each proximity system.

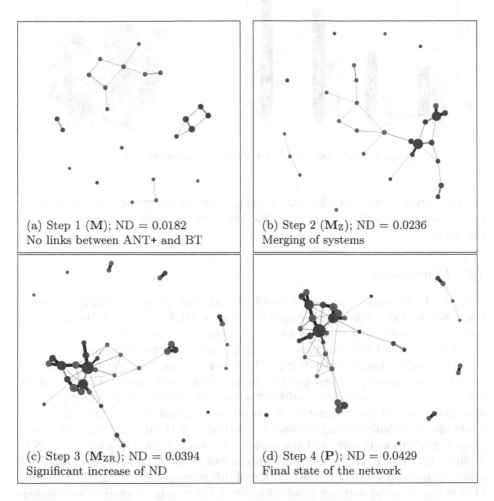

(a) Step 1 (**M**); ND = 0.0182
No links between ANT+ and BT

(b) Step 2 (**M$_Z$**); ND = 0.0236
Merging of systems

(c) Step 3 (**M$_{ZR}$**); ND = 0.0394
Significant increase of ND

(d) Step 4 (**P**); ND = 0.0429
Final state of the network

Fig. 8. Proximity data visualizations of the interval T_S for a prayer where ANT+ devices are in red and BT in blue. The size of a node is a figure of the number of total links. The line thickness represents the number of times the two connected nodes have been in proximity range.

Table 1. SNA feature comparison of system steps from Fig. 3

	M	Z	M$_Z$	R	M$_{ZR}$	G	P
ANEC	0.0994	0.0955	0.1123	0.0528	0.1263	0.1024	0.1301
ND	0.0182	0.0078	0.0236	0.0202	0.0394	0.0048	0.0429
NCC	0.5265	0.3008	0.4870	0.0661	0.4196	0.5784	0.5497

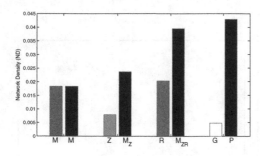 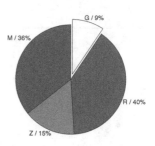

Fig. 9. Evaluation of ND for all system matrices of Fig. 3

These results indicate that the merging steps improve the completeness of the obtained network information while not altering much the morphology of the network.

4.3   Limitations

In each of the steps, there are limitations and challenges. The GPS sampling frequency and the distance threshold of 10 m for GPS locations to be declared as nearby, and the fact that BT can have a larger radius in open air, influence the evaluation and the comparison to other systems. It would be helpful to see how the results change depending on these parameters. The social rule that is valid for the pilgrimage might practically not always be followed. There are also other rules that we have not considered so far. The extracted SNA features are averaged over the whole duration of prayer and around prayer. These features could also be calculated and evaluated separately for the defined time intervals: spread, gathering, prayer, and transition. Moreover, using the extracted SNA features for evaluating the merging process can be premature if generalized to other scenarios. We evaluate the merging of different proximity systems in terms of changes in social network topologies. Since there is no numerical evaluation with absolute numbers, we cannot compare the results of the merged system with the cases where all participants would use ANT+, BT or GPS for spatial proximity.

5   Conclusion and Future Work

In this work, we have shown that it is possible to merge two inhomogeneous peer-to-peer proximity systems, namely ANT+ and BT. We have used auxiliary data derived from wearable sensors and information extracted from special social rules that are valid in the pilgrimage domain. On top of that, we have introduced an approach for computationally efficient proximity estimation from GPS locations to improve the adjacency matrix. Using a graphical representation we have shown how the merging steps influence the network graph. State-of-the-art SNA features are used to evaluate the validity of the merging. The centrality remains constant during all steps, the clustering property is moderately reduced and the overall network density is much higher compared to GPS only, which makes us believe, that GPS can be neglected for proximity estimation where fine grained information is needed. The data for this work is collected from 41 participants during an Umrah pilgrimage in Spring 2013.

As future work, we are planing to incorporate the speech and the environmental sound as an additional source for proximity detection. Moreover, using the results of our work, we are now able to answer questions related to social network analysis and to understand the grouping behaviour of pilgrims around the rituals. The upcoming Hajj pilgrimage offers the next opportunity to improve and evaluate our work.

References

1. Aharony, N., Pan, W., Ip, C., Khayal, I., Pentland, A.: Social fMRI: investigating and shaping social mechanisms in the real world. Pers. Ubiquit. Comput. (PUC) 7(6), 643–659 (2011)
2. Bounova, G., de Weck, O.: Overview of metrics and their correlation patterns for multiple-metric topology analysis on heterogeneous graph ensembles. Phys. Rev. E 85, 016117 (2012)
3. Do, T., Gatica-Perez, D.: Human interaction discovery in smartphone proximity networks. Pers. Ubiquit. Comput. (PUC) 17(3), 413–431 (2012)
4. Eagle, N., (Sandy) Pentland, A.: Reality mining: sensing complex social systems. Pers. Ubiquit. Comput. (PUC) 10(4), 255–268 (2006)
5. Peters, F.E.: The Hajj: The Muslim Pilgrimage to Mecca and the Holy Places. Princeton University Press, Princeton (1994)
6. Feese, S., Arnrich, B., Bürtscher, M., Meyer, B., Jona, K., Tröster, G.: CoenoFire: monitoring performance indicators of firefighters in real-world missions using smartphones. In: Proceedings of the ACM Ubiquitous Computing (UbiComp) (2013)
7. Feese, S., Arnrich, B., Bürtscher, M., Meyer, B., Jona, K., Tröster, G.: Sensing group proximity dynamics of firefighting teams using smartphones. In: Proceedings of the International Symposium on Wearable Computing (ISWC) (2013)
8. Hamhoum, F., Kray, C.: Supporting pilgrims in navigating densely crowded religious sites. Pers. Ubiquit. Comput. (PUC) 16(8), 1013–1023 (2012)
9. Mantoro, T., Jaafar, A., Aris, M., Ayu, M.: Hajjlocator: a hajj pilgrimage tracking framework in crowded ubiquitous environment. In: International Conference on Multimedia Computing and Systems (ICMCS) (2011)
10. Mohandes, M.: Pilgrim tracking and identification using the mobile phone. In: IEEE International Symposium on Consumer Electronics (ISCE) (2011)
11. Muaremi, A., Seiter, J., Bexheti, A., Tröster, G.: Monitor and understand pilgrims: data collection using smartphones and wearable devices. In: International Workshop on Human Activity Sensing Corpus and its Application (HASCA) (2013)

12. Muaremi, A., Seiter, J., Gravenhorst, F., Bexheti, A., Arnrich, B., Tröster, G.: Monitor pilgrims: prayer activity recognition using wearable sensors. In: Proceedings of the International Conference on Body Area Networks (Bodynets) (2013)
13. Olguin, D., Waber, B., Kim, T., Mohan, A., Ara, K., Pentland, A.: Sensible organizations: technology and methodology for automatically measuring organizational behavior. IEEE Trans. Syst. Man and Cybern. **39**(1), 43–55 (2009)

Device Analyzer: Understanding Smartphone Usage

Daniel T. Wagner[✉], Andrew Rice, and Alastair R. Beresford

Computer Laboratory, University of Cambridge, Cambridge, UK
{dtw30,acr31,arb33}@cam.ac.uk

Abstract. We describe Device Analyzer, a robust data collection tool which is able to reliably collect information on Android smartphone usage from an open community of contributors. We collected the largest, most detailed dataset of Android phone use publicly available to date. In this paper we systematically evaluate smartphones as a platform for mobile ubiquitous computing by quantifying access to critical resources in the wild. Our analysis of the dataset demonstrates considerable diversity in behaviour between users but also over time. We further demonstrate the value of handset-centric data collection by presenting case-study analyses of human mobility, interaction patterns, and energy management and identify notable differences between our results and those found by other studies.

1 Introduction

Smartphones are highly capable computing platforms containing a wide range of sensors and communications interfaces. They have been widely used in mobile and ubiquitous computing, including location systems [27], measurement [18] and context-sensing [28]. Additional efforts have focussed on understanding and optimising the platform itself, considering the measurement of energy use [23], computation offload [7], or resource sharing between devices [25]. However, understanding the importance or effectiveness of these contributions is difficult due to the lack of generally available, detailed data about how smartphones are actually used.

A large dataset of smartphone use can help direct research efforts, confirm whether local observations hold in a large and diverse population, uncover human behaviour, and show the prevalence of particular software or hardware in the wild.

Collecting usage information on smartphones is difficult: The collection mechanism itself needs to be built and deployed to a diverse group of participants running a multitude of devices in the wild; data must be collected for extended periods of time to overcome novelty effects and find long-term trends. Consequently, researchers are often forced to rely on their intuition or on the results from limited small-scale studies.

We have built and deployed Device Analyzer, which has collected 1,900 years of phone-usage information from 1277 different types of devices used by

© Institute for Computer Sciences, Social Informatics and Telecommunications Engineering 2014
I. Stojmenovic et al. (Eds.): MOBIQUITOUS 2013, LNICST 131, pp. 195–208, 2014.
DOI: 10.1007/978-3-319-11569-6_16

over 16,000 contributors in 175 countries over the course of two years. Table 1 describes the dataset in more detail. We observe extreme variation in usage not only between individuals but also for particular individuals over time. In this paper:

- We describe and make publicly available the largest dataset of smartphone use in terms of users, duration of study and granularity of collected data available to date.
- We highlight considerable diversity in behaviour not only between users but also over time, which was only possible due to the extended duration of our study. This emphasises the importance of participant selection and extended experiment durations. It also means that summative statistics (such as averages) should be considered and reported carefully to ensure that the true variation in behaviour has been captured.
- We evaluate smartphones as a platform for mobile ubiquitous computing in the wild, presenting for the first time expected device uptime and access to critical resources like power, network connectivity and location context from a large, diverse user base.
- We demonstrate the value of handset-centric data collection by presenting case-study analyses of human mobility, interaction and communication patterns, and energy management. We compare and contrast our results against previous studies.
- We show how limiting data collection to the phone's interaction with the cellular network (e.g. when using Call Data Records from network operators) can produce a notable effect on results like extracted movement patterns.
- We present our mechanism to provide researchers with access our data archive, and to run their own studies using Device Analyzer.

2   Related Work

Some studies reporting on mobile phone usage gather insights from mobile phone providers' Call Data Records (CDRs) that are generated when a phone interacts with the mobile network. By their nature, CDR-based studies have the potential to gather data from vast amounts of users, often 100,000 or more [15] or even capture data about every mobile subscriber of a country [10]. At these scales, CDRs can be used to track migration patterns between rural and urban areas, or build an entire country's social network graph. However, due to their proprietary nature, obtaining the data can be difficult. CDR-based studies lack fine-grained data, which on-device collection provides at the expense of study size. In Sect. 5 we demonstrate that a handset-centric view can come to significantly different conclusions.

Installing software directly on participants' devices allows researchers to access sensor and application data, and record actions that occur offline. Examples of such studies include the MIT Reality Mining dataset which collected data from 100 mobile phones given to undergraduates [11], a study of application usage of 250 Windows Mobile and Android smartphones [12] and a study of application usage of 4,000 Android smartphones [4]. Studies have successfully collected data from up to 20,000 users by providing useful functionality to the user [14] or by bundling the logging software as a library with other applications [20].

A third type of study uses surveys or diary studies to capture usage behaviour. Examples include a 4-week diary study with 20 participants about mobile information needs [6] and an online survey of 350 people, followed by 20 structured interviews, about mobile phone power consumption [21].

Diary studies typically have few participants due to the large amount of work involved. Device Analyzer has captured fine-grained data from several thousand participants in longitudinal collections over the course of months.

3   The Data Collection Tool

Device Analyzer is a free application for Android version 2.1 or higher. This represents more than 99 % of the devices connecting to Google Play.[1] The application collects data continuously in the background after initial setup, even when the user is not actively using the device. Device Analyzer was built with a focus on low resource use in order to impact the user experience as little as possible. We collect data asynchronously through event-driven notifications where possible and poll data only where necessary. This allows the device to spend more time in energy-saving sleep states. On most devices the battery drain from Device Analyzer is reported as less than 2–3 %. We measured the additional power draw of Device Analyzer on a Samsung Galaxy S III and found the amortized power draw over longer periods of time to be an additional 0.048 mA.

On average, the Device Analyzer mobile application collects of the order of 100,000 data points per day on a given device. Storage files are periodically compressed and later uploaded over an encrypted connection while the device is charging. Local data on the device is deleted after uploading finishes. The server uses a custom-built distributed analysis framework to extract insights from the raw data stream [26].

In contrast to other data collection tools, Device Analyzer is a stand-alone application that must be installed from the Google Play store. We have never embedded our tool as a library into third-party applications. The purpose of the application is clearly stated on the Google Play store, in the confirmation dialog when data collection is activated, and on the project website. We also remind users of on-going data collection once a month. We take care to enumerate the data collected, how sensitive data is processed, and what is transmitted to our servers. We provide a "quick feedback" feature inside the application to allow participants to send feedback without revealing their email address.

One user commented on the Google Play store "I wouldn't normally participate in such a thing, but the attention to detail in disclosure and handling of data is quite refreshing and deserves to be rewarded."

---

[1] http://developer.android.com/about/dashboards/index.html

3.1   Design Decisions and Trade-Offs

Device Analyzer was designed from the ground up to be minimally invasive, both in terms of privacy and user experience. Data collection was designed with a public release of the dataset in mind. The following design decisions result from these paradigms.

No demographic information is collected. Instead, we provide a mechanism that allows researchers to recruit, tag, and later re-identify participants (see Sect. 3.3).

The dataset is inhomogeneous in that we have so far encountered 1277 different types of devices, whereas other studies use a single type of device that facilitates comparisons between people. We see this diversity of devices in the wild as a strength as we avoid novelty effects from handing out handsets for the duration of the study.

Polling of not event-driven data occurs only every 5 min; this includes information about the 10 most recently started applications and network traffic. However, for 10 % of screen-on sessions application starts are collected with a frequency of 2 Hz, a rate we adopted from a previous study of application usage on Android [4].

Device Analyzer does not collect GPS location, but instead relies on network and WiFi location. Apart from saving energy this means that the set of requested permissions is somewhat less invasive. We also traded participant privacy for reduced utility for researchers by hashing all personally identifying information like phone numbers, network names, and SSIDs with a salted hash (see Sect. 3.2).

Lastly, we do not provide the application's source code. We believe that a multitude of slightly different, small-scale studies generating separate data silos is not in the interest of the research community. We encourage other researchers to feed data back to the community by deploying Device Analyzer for their own studies, taking advantage of a working, maintained platform where functionality can be augmented and users re-identified as described in Sect. 3.3.

3.2   Privacy

We strive to protect our participants' privacy as best we can by transferring data only over encrypted connections and removing direct personal identifiers and other sensitive information before they reach our servers. Device Analyzer was reviewed and approved by the University of Cambridge ethics committee. Our approach is compatible with an earlier set of recommendations made to researchers in ubiquitous computing [17].

We use a salted hash function derived from a hardware identifier, which allows us to correlate entries after Device Analyzer was re-installed, but prevents correlating these data between devices. Phone call records for example can only be used to compare whether two calls were made to the same number on the same device. It is not possible to determine whether two separate devices called the same number.

Device Analyzer requires user consent before any data is uploaded to our servers. Users can inspect the data before making that decision. We observe that roughly 40 % of our 26,800 installations were never activated. Data collection can be paused and users can explicitly withdraw from further collection at any point in time (4 % of users did so) and optionally also request all of their historic data to be deleted (2.5 %).

Participants can download all of their collected raw data from the project website. So far, 2100 participants have chosen to do so. Finally, participants can choose the extent to which they want to share data with other researchers. While some participants chose not to share their recorded data with third parties, we have observed that a small subset of participants elected to opt-in to share more sensitive information.

3.3   Access to the Dataset and Deployment for Custom Studies

Despite the care we have put into addressing privacy concerns, there remain ways in which the privacy of our participants could be compromised. We invite the community to request summary records from us; we will do our best to accommodate all reasonable requests. Alternatively, researchers can sign a contract that grants them access to the dataset itself as a basis for both further research and commercial work, but prohibits re-identification of individuals.

When a specific group of people should be surveyed, or additional data is required, accessing the existing dataset is not sufficient. We provide researchers with a way to deploy the Device Analyzer platform and receive raw data from re-identifiable users.

Interested parties can contact us to recruit their own users and are given unique participation codes that users enter in the stock Device Analyzer application. This code then allows re-identification of individuals as well as access to the collected raw data. In summary, researchers can leverage the expertise and engineering effort that went into building Device Analyzer without having to implement their own logging application.

4   Description of the Dataset

Device Analyzer captures a rich, highly detailed time-series log of approximately 300 different events. As much detail as possible is captured. For example, Device Analyzer not only records when a device connects to a WiFi network; it records all the details captured whenever a WiFi scan occurs, including AP MAC address, SSID, signal strength, frequency and capabilities. Table 1 shows the categories of data collected. Data is pre-processed on the device to remove direct personal identifiers (see Sect. 3.2).

While previous work has examined some of the topics present in this paper, we want to stress that we are not aware of any study that rivals this dataset in detail, duration of data collection and size. We believe it is important to optimise all three dimensions in order to derive sound insights into user behaviour.

Table 1. Overview of data collected. A complete list is available online (http://deviceanalyzer.cl.cam.ac.uk/keyValuePairs.htm).

Number of data points	75 billion
Aggregate trace duration	1,900 years
Countries covered	175
Unique phone types	1277
Unique OS versions	884
Installed copies of DA	26,800
Consented to collection	16,000
Users requested deletion	426
Participation > 1 day	12,300
Participation > 1 month	4,700
Participation > 3 months	2250
Participation > 6 months	960
Participation > 1 year	321

Category	Event types collected
Device settings	33
Installed Applications	17
System Properties	29
Bluetooth devices	21
WiFi networks	11
Disk storage	6
Energy & Charging	5
Telephony	20
Data usage	38
CPU & memory	11
Alarms	10
Media & Contacts	8
Sensors	15

We present evidence that many interesting, abrupt changes in behaviour are visible only in longitudinal datasets.

5   Analysis

To highlight the value of this dataset, we investigate some of the areas we believe are of particular interest for mobile and ubiquitous applications: communication, context, and the capacity to run long-lived applications. We also investigate interaction with the devices as well as communication behaviour.

5.1   Movement Patterns

Human mobility patterns are a valuable resource in fields like urban planning and when characterising environmental impact. Previous work looked mainly at Call Data Records (CDRs) that are generated when a phone interacts with the mobile network. Location accuracy of CDRs has been reported as $3\,km^2$ on average [15].

CDR-based movement traces will be inaccurate if users do not use their phone everywhere they travel. We set out to quantify this error. Device Analyzer collects location data every 5 min using the Google location API which fuses signal maps and WiFi fingerprints to improve accuracy. We simulate CDR-based movement traces by selecting only locations where text messages were exchanged or calls started or ended.

A previous study, using data from AT&T, reported users' *daily range*, which is the maximum distance that a phone has travelled in one day [16]. We adopt this measure for the purposes of comparison. Median/90th percentile daily ranges across our dataset were 5.8/51 km but only 0.9/28 km for simulated CDR-based movement traces. We note that a significant number of days record no movement at all for lack of calls and text messages. While CDR-based studies can choose to measure the most active users only, this inherent error is likely present in much previous work dealing with CDRs.

The AT&T data reports human mobility in Los Angeles and New York City. Their dataset partially mitigated the above effect by including locations where data transfers occurred. The authors state that they collected an average of 21 locations per day from 5 % of AT&T subscribers in each region, while Device Analyzer collects on average 208 locations per day, but included only about 140 participants in these regions with a total of 8500 phone-days of contributed data. Despite the large difference in scale both datasets show the same trends, namely shorter weekend daily ranges and overall larger numbers for LA residents: Median weekday/weekend daily ranges in our dataset are 7.0/3.3 km for NYC residents and 8.0/4.8 km for LA residents, compared with 7.2/5.6 km for NYC and 9.5/8.5 km for LA residents in the previous study.

We suspect the notably larger weekend movement distances in the AT&T dataset are due to their much larger dataset which is bound to include more variation of use than we were able to observe. At the same time, the reported median figures ignore outliers. Indeed, our 25th and 75th percentiles are much wider than the AT&T figures.

In particular, the reported 98th percentile maximum daily ranges per user are just below 4000 km, covering the continental US. However, the maximum daily ranges in our dataset are over 11500 km from LA and 16000 km from NYC, as we do have data from international travels that are missing from the AT&T dataset. González et al. note that their data does not include movement larger than 1000 km for the same reason [15].

The lack of extra-territorial data is a fundamental issue of network-centric datasets which—by virtue of their sheer volume—suggest near-perfect coverage and accuracy. User behaviour abroad can change abruptly due to unfamiliar surroundings and lack of mobile data connectivity. Journeys that exit country boundaries are more common in Europe than in the US, owing to the denser packing of countries and more frequent travel between them. Modelling human mobility from data that ignores these international journeys will result in incomplete and potentially misleading models.

Our dataset captures movement patterns in a global context (see Fig. 1). Device Analyzer contains data collected from 175 countries, rather than just a single country as in most network-centric datasets. The AT&T 50th percentile maximum daily ranges for LA and NYC residents of approximately 58/43 km are considerably larger than results from a study by González et al. that reports almost 50 % of their European participants staying within a 10 km radius over the duration of the 6 month study [15]. We observe the 50th percentile maximum daily ranges to be 89/65 km for LA/NYC residents, 188 km for the US overall, and 144 km for Europe. We also computed the radius within which all recorded locations of a given participant fall and observe the 50th percentile to be 47/40 km for LA/NYC residents, 129 km for the US overall, and 90 km

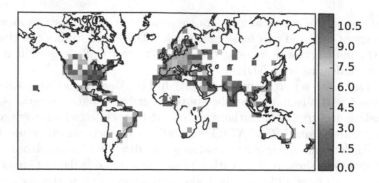

Fig. 1. Median daily ranges (km) of users living in different locations

for European participants. Indian participants travel less: The 50th percentile maximum daily range and total travel radius are 57 km and 25 km, respectively.

These figures suggest that at least in the US many city dwellers stay within a smaller area than their rural counterparts. The reported numbers also stand in direct contrast the previous findings of movement radii by González et al. Indeed, we note that for large parts of Europe the median daily range is of similar size as the previously reported gyration radius over multiple months. Device Analyzer was also able to replicate trends that the large-scale study of human mobility using AT&T data found, uncovering between-city effects in an untargeted, global dataset. We believe this showcases the suitability of on-device data collection for large-scale human movements.

5.2 Connectivity

Network communication is a central aspect of many mobile applications. As Device Analyzer collects data on the handset, we have the unique ability to measure connectivity as experienced by the user. We observe that 10 % of participants have no network connection for at least 40 % of the time, while half of our population spends less than 5 % of their time without a connection. When connectivity is available, we observe that 10 % of devices communicate over a 2G connection at least 54 % of time. However, faster connectivity is often available: 50 % (or 80 %) of our users are connected to 3G, LTE or WIFI for at least 80 % (or 45 %) of the time. The top 10 % of users spend as much as 98 % of their time on these fast connections.

Users experience large temporal changes: Fig. 2 shows individual traces for users with good, average and poor connectivity. Each column of an individual trace is a histogram of time spent using various technologies during one week. The second trace in Fig. 2 (left) suffers from low WiFi availability in the last seven weeks. The bottom trace with poor connectivity typically has 2G connectivity but in week 37 sees good HSPA connectivity followed by a week of no connectivity. We find such abrupt changes in many long traces across our dataset.

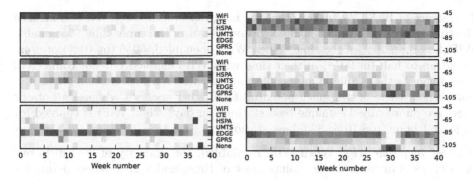

Fig. 2. Technology availability (left), GSM signal strength (right) for three devices

Energy costs per byte transmitted can be as much as six times higher for a weak connection over a strong one [24]. This can have a noticeable effect on the battery performance of a communication-heavy application [9]. The majority of devices in our dataset saw signal levels of −85 dBm or lower most of the time, with occasional spikes of good signal. Only 15 % of devices spending the majority of their time at signal levels of −75 dBm or higher. Figure 2 (right) highlights changes over time and between individuals: The top trace shows mostly signal levels around −65 dBm, which are very rare in the other two traces. The bottom trace shows no signal levels above −85 dBm and includes a period of several weeks with very poor signal.

CDMA and WiFi signal levels followed a similar pattern where less than 10 % of devices spend time predominantly in very good signal conditions whereas 80 % of devices spend the vast majority of time in medium to poor signal conditions.

Changes in mobile network connectivity present opportunities for applications to improve performance and reduce resource consumption through adaptation. Changes in connectivity manifest themselves either gradually over time or abruptly, which suggests that forecasting and planning cannot be done using signal strength alone and will require additional contextual information. Researchers should take these qualitative differences into consideration when interpreting results or planning studies.

5.3   Location

Location is a primary source of context in ubiquitous computing [1]. We investigate how well mobile ubiquitous systems can establish user location. Smartphones spend 88 % of their time in close proximity to the user, making them a good proxy for the user's location [8]. WiFi fingerprinting uses readings of WiFi signal strengths to locate a device indoors [3], producing more accurate results as the density of visible base stations increases [5]. We investigate the number of base stations that participants in our study were able to see at any given time, thereby giving an indication for the accuracy of positioning that can be expected from WiFi fingerprinting techniques.

Prevalence of WiFi: We observe that the majority of users keep WiFi off most of the time. Only 2 % of users enable WiFi over 80 % of the time while 56 % enable WiFi less than 20 % of the time. When WiFi is enabled, 50 % (or 10 %) of users spend up to half (or 90 %) of their time with WiFi enabled but not connected. This suggests that while many people disable their WiFi connection when it is not needed, there is still much potential for further energy savings. Half of our users see on average 17 unique base stations on days when WiFi is enabled for at least 1 hour (top 10 %: 82.6 base stations).

Number of visible APs: When WiFi is enabled, the majority of devices in our dataset see 3 or fewer access points most of time, and 1 or 2 access points for 29 % of time, which limits the usefulness of WiFi fingerprinting systems. For 4 % of the time, the majority of participants see no networks. On the other end of the spectrum we observe that roughly 1 in 10 devices spends most of its time in the presence of at least 8 base stations, providing ample information for WiFi location systems. Individual traces were omitted for reasons of brevity, but many users show significant deviations from their usual WiFi environment for weeks at a time.

Researchers have also considered using Bluetooth for location estimation. We find that over half of our participants activate Bluetooth at most 1 in 14 days. On those days Bluetooth is active for 52 min for a typical user, which would make parasitic location estimation highly unreliable.

5.4   Energy Management

Battery lifetime depends highly on idiosyncratic usage behaviour and can severely limit the utility of modern smartphones. Power draw varies drastically over time, with one participant draining their battery by 298 % one day (charging 3 times) and discharging only 38 % on another day. We observe that 17 % of participants fully charge their phone on at least 9 out of 10 days and 40 % fully charge their phone on at least 7 out of 10 days. Overall, we observe that while 24 % of all charges are over USB, the vast majority of these are short charges that may result from transferring data to or from the device.

Emptying the battery can be interpreted as a failure of the user or phone to adequately manage energy consumption. This happens at least every 11 days for 50 % of our participants. Some participants exhaust their device's battery nearly every day, and several participants have distinct periods where their device dies frequently. On average, depleted batteries are charged within one h, which suggests that the device is near a charger when it runs out of battery or that the user is on their way to a location with a charger. 90 % of down times due to low battery are resolved within 12 h.

Ubiquitous applications on mobile devices can expect to see a median uptime of 92.4 % (90 % of devices have an uptime of at least 63 %). Furthermore, while numbers vary a lot across our dataset, 50 (or 80 %) of devices can be expected to spend 10.3 % (or 3.1 %) of their powered-on time plugged into a charger and fully charged. Across devices, a long-running application can expect to see at least 1 h of plugged-in, fully-charged time on 50 % of days (6 h 35 min on 20 % of days). Applications could use this time to perform long-running and energy-intensive tasks.

A previous study of charging behaviour that collected data from a battery monitoring application over 4 weeks from 4,000 participants reported a large fraction of charges that lasted 14 h or longer [13]. We observe only a very small fraction of charges to last 14 h or longer. Instead, our dataset shows the majority of long charges to be between 6 and 10 h in duration, which correspond to overnight charges.

Furthermore, this previous study reports mean charging duration as 3.9 h, based on 1525 charge cycles. Our dataset shows a mean charging duration of 2 h 21 min (median: 43 min) based on 1.7 million charge cycles. 95 % of datasets with 1525 charge cycles would be expected to have a mean charge duration between 2 h 9 min and 2 h 33 min (two standard deviations). The results presented by this previous study are 16 standard deviations away from the mean found in our dataset, which indicates that a different population was sampled. We suspect that users installing a battery monitoring app may be susceptible to unusual charging behaviour.

Overnight charges: A recent study investigating of battery charges of 15 participants over 3 weeks [2] reported that charges during the day and over night vary dramatically in length, with charges between 10pm and 5am having a median duration of 7 h while other charges had a median duration of 30 min. Our dataset supports their findings, with a median AC charge duration of 5 h 10 min (4 h for AC and USB combined) for the above definition of overnight charges and a 33 min median for charges during the day, irrespective of charge type. We believe that the difference in median charge duration stems mainly from the small sample size of 15 participants.

5.5   Interactions

The frequency and duration with which a user interacts with their device, as well as the time that passes between interactions, provides a context within which ubiquitous applications need to perform their activities. Modulating energy consumption in reaction to available resources is a key aspect of mobile ubiquitous applications.

We observe that some interactions are purely status checks where the device is never unlocked, but the screen is turned on to check the time or whether any notifications are present. The mobile platform can save energy by not waking up some core-components of the device in such situations, thereby extending battery life. Half of our participants perform these status checks on average 9 times or more per day, while 10 % of participants check their device on average 52 times per day.

A 2010 study of 17,000 BlackBerry users by Oliver [19] looked at a number of metrics of interaction length and frequency. We observe mean daily device use across our dataset to be longer (2.05 h vs 1.68 h on BlackBerry), but median daily device use to be shorter (1.22 h vs 1.31 h). The presence of days with very heavy use hints at the diversity of the underlying population that we captured and highlights the variability of environments and modes of interaction that mobile ubiquitous systems must cope with. Interestingly, we find that while Android users interact less frequently with their device than their BlackBerry counterparts (on average 57 vs 87 interactions per day), the average duration of each interaction is much longer (115.8 s vs 68.4 s).

5.6   Calls and Texts

Users in our dataset place or receive on average 7.5 calls per day (median: 3) and send or receive on average 11 text messages per day (median: 2). The average length of a text message is 55 characters. Using text messages and phone calls, our participants communicate with 4.9 unique numbers per day on average (median: 3). Per week, our participants communicate on average with 21.3 unique numbers (median: 16).

Across our dataset, 36 % of calls end up unanswered. We observe that callers wait on average 21 s for the other side to pick up before cancelling the call. This is the same amount of time it takes the callee to pick up 95 % of calls.

An analysis of the Reality Mining dataset reported [22] that 71 % of calls are shorter than 1 min, and 90 % of calls are shorter than 5 min. Our dataset shows slightly longer calls, with 50.4 % of calls shorter than 1 min and 88.5 % of calls shorter than 5 min. This may be an artefact of participant selection, as participants in the Reality Mining study were all undergraduate students at MIT.

6   Conclusions

We presented a novel collection platform that enabled us to collect the largest dataset of mobile smartphone use to date. Specifically, the dataset improves on previous studies in terms of duration of data collection, amount and diversity of devices covered, and amount of detail collected. In total the dataset contains 75 billion data points covering over 1,900 phone-years of active usage data from 16,000 participants.

To illustrate both the depth and versatility of the dataset, we extracted a multitude of different aspects about human movement patterns, interaction and communication patterns, connectivity and bandwidth, WiFi network availability in the wild, battery use, and reliability of the smartphone platform itself form the broad range of data available.

We contrasted and compared our results with previous work and found important differences in our new dataset. Crucially, we highlighted the importance of long-term data collection: many users show abrupt changes in usage behaviour or resource availability over long time periods to which ubiquitous applications need to adapt. These drastic changes are an important characteristic of real-world usage data and are typically not present in datasets collected over shorter time frames by previous studies.

We provide access to the dataset as well as a mechanism for other researchers to use Device Analyzer as a proven, reliable platform to run their own experiments on. As our dataset grows further we hope to create a sustainable, rich resource that will provide the community with invaluable data for years to come.

Acknowledgements. We would like to thank Samuel Aaron for his many insightful comments and suggestions related to this work and Andy Hopper for his insight and support. This work was supported by the University of Cambridge Computer Laboratory Premium Studentship scheme, a Google focussed research award and the EPSRC Standard Research Grant EP/P505445/1.

References

1. Abowd, G.D., Dey, A.K., Brown, P.J., Davies, N., Smith, M.E., Steggles, P.: Towards a better understanding of context and context-awareness. In: CHI (2000)
2. Arslan, M.Y., Singh, I., Singh, S., Madhyastha, H.V., Sundaresan, K., Krishnamurthy, S.V.: Computing while charging: building a distributed computing infrastructure using smartphones. In: CoNEXT (2012)
3. Bahl, P., Padmanabhan, V.: RADAR: an in-building RF-based user location and tracking system. In: IEEE INFOCOM (2000)
4. Böhmer, M., Hecht, B., Schöning, J., Krüger, A., Bauer, G.: Falling asleep with angry birds, facebook and kindle-a large scale study on mobile application usage. In: MobileHCI (2011)
5. Cheng, Y.-C., Chawathe, Y., LaMarca, A., Krumm, J.: Accuracy characterization for metropolitan-scale Wi-Fi localization. In: MobiSys (2005)
6. Church, K., Smyth, B.: Understanding mobile information needs. In: MobileHCI (2008)
7. Cuervo, E., Balasubramanian, A., Cho, D.-K., Wolman, A., Saroiu, S., Chandra, R., Bahl, P.: MAUI: making smartphones last longer with code offload. In: MobiSys (2010)
8. Dey, A.K., Wac, K., Ferreira, D., Tassini, K., Hong, J.-H., Ramos, J.: Getting closer: an empirical investigation of the proximity of user to their smart phones. In: UbiComp (2011)
9. Ding, N., Wagner, D., Chen, X., Pathak, A., Hu, Y.C., Rice, A.: Characterizing and modeling the impact of wireless signal strength on smartphone battery drain. In: SIGMETRICS (2013)
10. Eagle, N., de Montjoye, Y.-A., Bettencourt, L.M.: Community computing: comparisons between rural and urban societies using mobile phone data. In: CSE (2009)
11. Eagle, N., Pentland, A.S.: Reality mining: sensing complex social systems. Pers. Ubiquit. Comput. **10**(4), 255–268 (2005)
12. Falaki, H., Mahajan, R., Kandula, S., Lymberopoulos, D., Govindan, R., Estrin, D.: Diversity in smartphone usage. In: MobiSys (2010)
13. Ferreira, D., Dey, A.K., Kostakos, V.: Understanding human-smartphone concerns: a study of battery life. In: Lyons, K., Hightower, J., Huang, E.M. (eds.) Pervasive 2011. LNCS, vol. 6696, pp. 19–33. Springer, Heidelberg (2011)
14. Girardello, A., Michahelles, F.: AppAware: which mobile applications are hot? In: MobileHCI (2010)
15. González, M.C., Hidalgo, C.A., Barabási, A.-L.: Understanding individual human mobility patterns. Nature **453**(7196), 779–782 (2008)

16. Isaacman, S., Becker, R., Cceres, R., Kobourov, S., Rowland, J., Varshavsky, A.: A tale of two cities. In: HotMobile (2010)
17. Langheinrich, M.: Privacy by design - principles of privacy-aware ubiquitous systems. In: Abowd, G.D., Brumitt, B., Shafer, S. (eds.) UbiComp 2001. LNCS, vol. 2201, pp. 273–291. Springer, Heidelberg (2001)
18. Maisonneuve, N., Stevens, M., Niessen, M.E., Steels, L.: NoiseTube: measuring and mapping noise pollution with mobile phones. In: ITEE (2009)
19. Oliver, E.: The challenges in large-scale smartphone user studies. In: HotPlanet (2010)
20. Oliver, E.A., Keshav, S.: An empirical approach to smartphone energy level prediction. In: UbiComp (2011)
21. Rahmati, A., Zhong, L.: Human-battery interaction on mobile phones. Pervasive Mob. Comput. 5(5), 465–477 (2009)
22. Ravi, N., Scott, J., Han, L., Iftode, L: Context-aware battery management for mobile phones. In: PerCom (2008)
23. Rice, A., Hay, S.: Decomposing power measurements for mobile devices. In: PerCom (2010)
24. Schulman, A., Navda, V., Ramjee, R., Spring, N., Deshpande, P., Grunewald, C., Jain, K., Padmanabhan, V.N.: Bartendr: a practical approach to energy-aware cellular data scheduling. In: MobiCom (2010)
25. Vallina-Rodriguez, N., Crowcroft, J.: ErdOS: achieving energy savings in mobile OS. In: MobiArch (2011)
26. Wagner, D.T., Rice, A., Beresford, A.R.: Device analyzer: large-scale mobile data collection. In: ACM SIGMETRICS Performance Evaluation Review, March 2014 (in press)
27. Ye, H., Gu, T., Zhu, X., Xu, J., Tao, X., Lu, J., Jin, N.: FTrack: infrastructure-free floor localization via mobile phone sensing. In: PerCom (2012)
28. Ye, J., Dobson, S., McKeever, S.: Situation identification techniques in pervasive computing: a review. Pervasive Mob. Comput. 8(1), 36–66 (2012)

Evaluation of Energy Profiles for Mobile Video Prefetching in Generalized Stochastic Access Channels

Alisa Devlic$^{(\boxtimes)}$, Pietro Lungaro, Zary Segall, and Konrad Tollmar

Mobile Service Lab, Royal Institute of Technology (KTH), Kista, Sweden
{devlic,pietro,segall,konrad}@kth.se

Abstract. This paper evaluates the energy cost reduction of Over-The-Top mobile video content prefetching in various network conditions. Energy cost reduction is achieved by reducing the time needed to download content over the radio interface by prefetching data on higher data rates, compared to the standard on demand download. To simulate various network conditions and user behavior, a stochastic access channel model was built and validated using the actual user traces. By changing the model parameters, the energy cost reduction of prefetching in different channel settings was determined, identifying regions in which prefetching is likely to deliver the largest energy gains. The results demonstrate that the largest gains (up to 70%) can be obtained for data rates with strong correlation and low noise variation. Additionally, based on statistical properties of data rates, such as peak-to-mean and average data rate, prefetching strategy can be devised enabling the highest energy cost reduction that can be obtained using the proposed prefetching scheme.

Keywords: Energy profiles · Stochastic access channel · Mobile video prefetching

1 Introduction

1.1 Motivation

We are witnessing a large increase in mobile Internet data traffic in the last years, with predictions to increase 18-fold by 2016 (i.e., reaching 10.8 exabytes per month) [2]. The following trends contributed to this phenomenon: an increasing number of powerful mobile Internet devices (such as tablets and smartphones) that can deliver superior user experience, faster Internet connections, and a large amount of video streaming content available. According to a Cisco's study [2], video accounted for 52% of the mobile data traffic at the end of 2011 and will account for two thirds (over 70%) of the world's mobile data traffic by 2016.

Video streaming in mobile environments can be a challenge, due to sharing of available capacity among large number of users and intermittent connectivity.

© Institute for Computer Sciences, Social Informatics and Telecommunications Engineering 2014
I. Stojmenovic et al. (Eds.): MOBIQUITOUS 2013, LNICST 131, pp. 209–223, 2014.
DOI: 10.1007/978-3-319-11569-6_17

Additionally, the energy consumption in mobile devices increases proportionally with the duration of data transfers, which depend on the download data rates achievable by the device. Content prefetching addresses these problems by decoupling the time when the content is prepositioned on a user's terminal from the time when this content is accessed and consumed by the user. By exploiting the times and locations with high data rates to prefetch content, the time needed to transfer data over a radio interface is reduced, resulting in energy consumption reduction when compared to the standard on demand access to content [1].

Content prefetching and its impact on energy savings have been investigated in many related works. In [7,8] prefetching is scheduled based on predictions of WiFi availability and cellular signal strength, respectively, achieving up to 60 % energy savings. In another work [6] prefetching is based on predicting what data is needed and when it will be used, by observing a user behavior and availability of WiFi connectivity, power & signal strength at different locations, thus achieving up to 70 % savings. N. Gautam and his colleagues [5] showed that energy savings of 84 % can be achieved by video prefetching over WiFi when compared to streaming over 3G, due to the high download data rates. However, while WiFi availability can be used as indicator of high data rates, its use is limited to the user's stay duration under the coverage of WiFi AP. Signal strength, on the other hand, *cannot indicate variations in a user bandwidth* that occur due to sharing of aggregated cell capacity with others. Even if signal strength is strong, the available bandwidth might be low, resulting in potentially increased energy consumption, if prefetching is performed under this condition.

1.2   Contribution

This paper evaluates the energy cost reduction of content prefetching in various network conditions. It generalizes results from our previous paper [3], where an opportunistic OTT context-aware mobile video pre-fetching scheme has been proposed and evaluated on a single user data rates log. Prefetching was scheduled based on *downlink data rates*, while the potential energy savings were investigated based on frequency of probing a channel quality and setting a target pre-fetching data rate, which to our knowledge has not previously been studied.

Note that obtaining a mobile user data rate traces on a large scale in per-second granularity is economically very costly. Therefore, in order to derive some conclusions about the prefetching performances, we synthetically generated data rates. A simple model, an autoregressive process of order 1, was used to simulate different network conditions and user behavior. Ten of actual user traces that were collected in Stockholm city area were fitted to this model with an error of up to 10 %. Due to having only three parameters, it was easy to generate data rates simulating different access channel states. Note that we do not claim that this model can accurately describe all channel conditions nor do we compare it with other models. Hence, it enabled us to evaluate prefetching performances of the data rates that can be fitted to this model, identifying regions with potentially largest energy reduction gains.

Finally, we found a dependency of a target prefetching data rate at which the maximum energy cost reduction is obtained to statistical data rate properties, such as mean and peak-to-mean data rate ratio. By combining these parameters, we created optimization guidelines for reducing energy cost that a mobile device can employ when prefetching video.

2   OTT Prefetching Scheme

This section briefly describes the over-the-top context-aware content prefetching (OTT PRE) scheme adopted from our previous paper [3]. The prefetching is envisaged to run on mobile devices, *without* any prior knowledge of connectivity or data rates. It is based on periodically probing the channel quality to estimate the achievable data rates, combining this probing phase with the transfer of the remaining content bits at data rates that are equal to or higher than the target prefetching data rate $(\hat{R})$. Whenever probing reveals low achievable data rates (i.e., lower than $\hat{R}$), the data retrieval operation is paused in order to limit a potential increase in energy consumption associated with a file download.

On demand download downloads content *independently* of the data rates. The difference between prefetching and download is shown in Fig. 1, using the following metrics: *prefetching SLA*, *prefetching cost*, and *downloading time*.

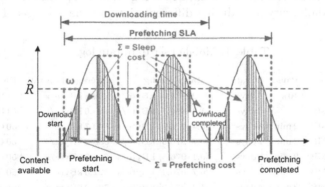

Fig. 1. Evaluation metrics for content downloading and prefetching

The *prefetching SLA* represents the duration from the start until the end of content prefetching, which is initiated by a specific condition (e.g., data rate threshold or periodic time interval) and which needs to be completed before the content is offered to the user for download/viewing. The *prefetching cost* refers to the time spent actively prefetching the content, while the *downloading time* denotes the time that is needed to download the content on demand.

Besides $\hat{R}$, the OTT PRE uses two additional parameters to implement periodic probing: the wake up time (ω) and the sleep time (τ). During ω, the method prefetches bits, computes the data rate during this period, and checks if the obtained data rate is equal to or above $\hat{R}$. If this is the case, it continues prefetching bits until the end of file transfer round; otherwise it goes to sleep for τ seconds, stopping the prefetching of the content until this time expires, after which prefetching is resumed. The total sleep time during which the prefetching was stopped is referred to as the *sleep cost*.

The benefit of periodic channel probing is estimating the achievable data rates without involvement of a mobile operator and using the estimated data rates as context information to drive the prefetching. However, periodic probing of data rates has the associated energy cost of prefetching some of the content bits at data rates that are *lower* than $\hat{R}$. This cost can potentially be reduced by reducing the probing frequency, hence with a potential risk of missing the prefetching opportunity if the device is not frequently exposed to the target data rates. The number of prefetching opportunities can potentially increase if $\hat{R}$ is carefully chosen to reflect the frequency of the device experiencing the same data rates throughout a day. Therefore, it is important to: (1) evaluate if a device can estimate the data rates and achieve energy cost reduction while prefetching content, (2) determine under which channel conditions is the potential energy cost reduction the highest, and (3) estimate the corresponding prefetching SLA.

3   Actual User Data Rates

This section briefly examines the data rate logs that were collected by different users in Stockholm city area during different times of the year (see Table 1).

Table 1. Mobile user data rate logs

User ID	File size	Pause	Duration	Data rate range	Average data rate	Data plan
1	13 MB	10 s	3 days	[0.02–974.8] kByte/s	280.8 kByte/s	5 GB
2	5 MB	2 s	3 days	[1.4–350.7] kByte/s	163.6 kByte/s	5 GB, EDGE
3	50 MB	2 min	3 days	[0.4–976.5] kByte/s	540.7 kByte/s	50 GB
4	100 MB	2 min	2 days	[0.7–976.3] kByte/s	388.2 kByte/s	50 GB
5	200 MB	2 min	5 days	[0.1–976.5] kByte/s	646.3 kByte/s	50 GB
6	50 MB	2 min	3 days	[0.7–976.4] kByte/s	522.6 kByte/s	50 GB
7	50 MB	2 min	4 days	[1.4–974.9] kByte/s	707.2 kByte/s	no limit
8	50 MB	5 s	2 days	[1.0–970.8] kByte/s	628.7 kByte/s	no limit
9	50 MB	2 min	3 days	[0.6-976.5] kByte/s	550.9 kByte/s	50 GB
10	13 MB	5 s	8 days	[0.02–976.5] kByte/s	464.5 kByte/s	5 GB

The logs were collected by mobile devices periodically downloading a video file of a predefined size from a server for a couple of days and pausing for a predetermined time after completing each downloading round. During the experiment phones were connected to Internet through the mobile access networks only. The users that performed the logging were researchers from our University, a research centre in Kista, and one working professional, whose routes and stay durations at particular locations are shown in Fig. 2.

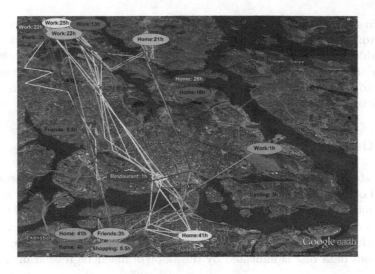

Fig. 2. Users mobility routes

Figure 3 shows a data rate log of user 1, from which pause times have been removed. Data rates were recorded every second, representing a sequence of data points at equally spaced time intervals. This motivated us to examine the time series models as a candidate for generating synthetic data rates.

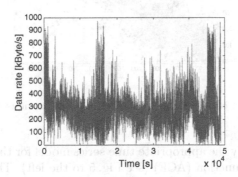

Fig. 3. Data rate vs. time log used in the experiment

Time series analysis consists of methods for extracting meaningful statistical properties and other characteristics of this data. It assumes that there is some internal structure, such as autocorrelation, trend, or seasonal variation that should be considered when analyzing or modeling such data. Our work has been driven by similar assumptions – that data rates exhibit certain statistical properties that can be used to identify a generative process from which our experimental data are drawn, representing one out of many realizations of this process.

Our **first goal** was to identify the underlying process and its parameters, in order to: (1) generate synthetic data rates whose prefetching results will be compareable to the results obtained with actual user data rates and (2) estimate the maximum energy cost reduction for different parameter values. The **second goal** was to relate the target prefetching data rate at which the maximum energy cost reduction can be achieved to statistical properties of data rates.

4   Method

As a first step in determining if there is some underlying stationary process that generated our experimental data, we checked if the data rate values arranged in time exhibit some serial correlation. To answer this question, we plotted the user data rates at time t against the data rates in previous period t-1, as shown in Fig. 4 on the example of user 1. A strong serial correlation between the current and previous data rate is indicated by the slope of linear regression line.

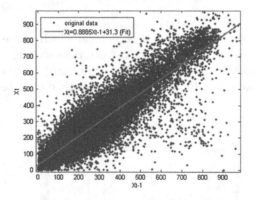

Fig. 4. Serial correlation between current and previous data rate

In order to identify the appropriate time series model for the data, we plotted the autocorrelation function (ACF) (see Fig. 5 to the left). The ACF plot illustrates exponential decay, indicating that our data can potentially be described by autoregressive (AR) process. In AR model future values depend on past time series values, while its order indicates how many lags in past they depend on.

The partial autocorrelation function (PACF), illustrated in Fig. 5 to the right, is used to determine the order of AR model, p. PACF removes the effects of the shorter lag autocorrelation from the correlation estimate at longer lags, cutting off abruptly to zero after lag p. By looking at the lag where PACF falls (close to) zero, we can conclude that the order of AR process should be 1.

AR(1) process is defined by a first order linear difference equation:

$$X_t = c + \phi_1 X_{t-1} + \epsilon_t \tag{1}$$

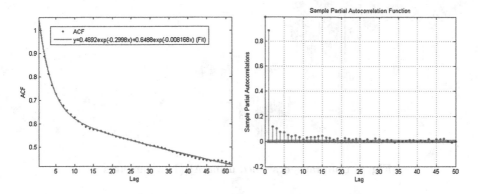

Fig. 5. Autocorrelation and partial autocorrelation function of actual data rates

where t is a point in time, c is constant, ϕ_1 is the autoregressive coefficient, and ϵ_t are Gaussian distributed error terms or innovations with zero mean and variance σ_ϵ^2 that introduce variability into the process.

Since X_t is a stationary process, its expected value does not change over time. Inserting $E[X_t] = E[X_{t-1}]$ into (1), we obtain:

$$E[X_t] = \mu = \frac{c}{1 - \phi_1} \tag{2}$$

The autocovariance of X_t at lag s for $s \neq 0$ indicates how much a random variable changes with the time-shifted version of itself:

$$\gamma(s) = \phi_1 \gamma(s - 1) \tag{3}$$

Raising (3) on the power of two gives the autocovariance of X_t at lag 0, which is the variance of AR(1) process:

$$\gamma(0) = Var(X_t) = \phi_1^2 Var(X_{t-1}) + \sigma_\epsilon^2 \tag{4}$$

Since $Var(X_t) = Var(X_{t-1})$, variance becomes:

$$Var(X_t) = \sigma_{AR}^2 = \frac{\sigma_\epsilon^2}{1 - \phi_1^2} \tag{5}$$

We can now derive the equation for ϕ_1:

$$\phi_1 = \sqrt{1 - \frac{\sigma_\epsilon^2}{\sigma_{AR}^2}} \tag{6}$$

From (2) and (5) follows that AR(1) process can be described with the process mean μ, process variance σ_{AR}^2, and noise variance σ_ϵ^2. This approach has been adopted for modeling our data rates signal, as illustrated in Fig. 6.

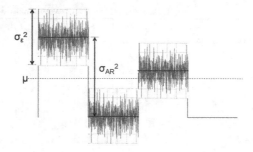

Fig. 6. Data rates described using AR(1) parameters

Data rates are fitted to AR(1) using Burg method, minimizing sum of squares of the error between original and estimated values [9]. $\hat{\epsilon}_t$ were estimated using:

$$\hat{\epsilon}_t = X_t - \hat{\phi}_1 X_{t-1} - \hat{c} \tag{7}$$

and fitted to Gaussian probability distribution in order to obtain the noise mean ($\hat{\nu}$) and variance ($\hat{\sigma}_\epsilon^2$), checking if these innovations are uncorrelated.

The fitting results for all users data rates are shown in Table 2, showing that innovations mean values are close to zero, thus can be approximated by the white noise. Normalized Root Mean Square Error represents the fitting error (err).

Table 2. Fitting AR(1) parameters and residuals for mobile user data rate logs

User	1	2	3	4	5	6	7	8	9	10
$\hat{\phi}_1$	0.8885	0.5407	0.8899	0.8344	0.8228	0.8410	0.6276	0.6545	0.8966	0.7878
$\hat{c}$	31.3	75.1	59.5	64.3	114.5	83.1	263.4	217.2	56.9	98.6
$\hat{\sigma}_\epsilon^2$	4032.4	1318.7	11764.1	11040	10644.6	14558.7	18755.8	22313.6	9602.3	23041.3
$\hat{\nu}$	−4.6e-4	4.7e-3	−2.9e-3	−0.019	−3.2e-12	−1.9e-3	−1.2e-12	−4.8e-3	2.5e-3	2.9e-3
err	4.56 %	9.27 %	5.92 %	7.06 %	5.82 %	7.10 %	10.13 %	10.84 %	5.78 %	8.75 %

5   Prefetching Results

100 realizations of synthetic data rates were generated using AR(1) model with $\hat{\phi}_1$, $\hat{c}$, and $\hat{\sigma}_\epsilon$ parameters obtained from fitting the actual user data rates. 10000 iterations of content prefetching and on demand download were performed over each synthetic data rate realization with different starting indices. The target prefetching data rate was set to range from 100 kByte/s up to 800 kByte/s with a step of 50 kByte/s, while the sleeping time was 1 s up to 31 s with a step of 5 s at the end of each prefetching round (the same as in [3]). From each iteration we extracted the prefetching costs, downloading time, and prefetching SLAs obtained for different target prefetching data rates and sleep times (as defined in Sect. 2). Using these values the maximum energy cost reduction (E_{max}) was

computed in each iteration by finding the lowest prefetching cost that can be achieved by reduction in the duration of the content download time:

$$E_{max} = \frac{download\_time - min(prefetching\_cost)}{download\_time} \tag{8}$$

Next, the minimum and maximum of 10000 E_{max} values were computed in order to obtain the E_{max} range for the fitted set of AR(1) parameters. The obtained E_{max} range is compared with the E_{max} obtained using the actual user data rates, resulting in 25.3–27.7 % and 30 %, respectively.

Table 3 shows the E_{max} obtained from prefetching over actual and fitted data rates of ten mobile users, demonstrating that the results are comparable.

Table 3. E_{max} obtained from prefetching over actual and fitted users data rates

User	1	2	3	4	5	6	7	8	9	10
E_{max} actual	30 %	7.2 %	23.6 %	29.6 %	15 %	23.7 %	6.6 %	11.9 %	29.8 %	32.1 %
E_{max} synthetic min	25.3 %	6.5 %	20.6 %	21.5 %	12.2 %	18.3 %	6.2 %	8.8 %	19.8 %	18.2 %
E_{max} synthetic max	27.7 %	8.8 %	22.4 %	26.8 %	13.3 %	20 %	7 %	10.6 %	22 %	19.6 %

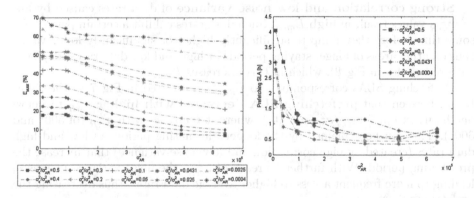

Fig. 7. E_{max} and prefetching SLA as a function of σ^2_{AR}

In order to simulate different access channel states and user behavior, we scanned the entire parameter space of the identified AR model (μ, σ^2_{AR}, and σ^2_ϵ), generating synthetic data rates[1]. The prefetching and on demand download simulations were performed over these data rates to determine their E_{max}.

Figure 7 to the left illustrates E_{max} as a function of σ^2_{AR}, for different $\sigma^2_\epsilon/\sigma^2_{AR}$. The $\sigma^2_\epsilon/\sigma^2_{AR}$ ratio determines a shape of data rates signal, representing the amount of serial correlation in time series data. Serial correlation determines how much information about the current data rate is contained in the previous

---

[1] c has been excluded from the parameter space, since it can be derived from (2). Hence, its impact on E_{max} is discussed with other model parameters in the text.

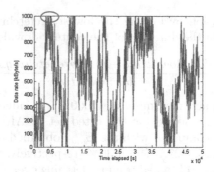

Fig. 8. Data rates generated with high correlation coefficient and little noise variance

value, which is repeated over various time periods. To preserve the same process, $\sigma_\epsilon^2/\sigma_{AR}^2$ was fixed in all experiments, while changing other parameter values.

It can be observed that E_{max} **decreases with an increase of** σ_{AR}^2 and σ_ϵ^2, given the fixed $\sigma_\epsilon^2/\sigma_{AR}^2$. This can be explained by the higher σ_{AR}^2 and σ_ϵ^2 values causing more frequent access to higher data rates, which leads to less difference in duration of on demand download and content prefetching.

Strong correlation and low noise variance of data rates caused by low $\sigma_\epsilon^2/\sigma_{AR}^2$ values result in **high E_{max}**. Such data rates exhibit a certain pattern for some time before they jump to significantly higher or significantly lower value, thus creating areas of longer staying periods at high and low data rates (depicted with red circles in Fig. 8), which in turn increases E_{max}.

Prefetching SLAs corresponding to E_{max} are plotted in Fig. 7 to the right. It can be seen that **prefetching SLA decreases with higher** σ_{AR}^2 to below one hour, except for $\sigma_\epsilon^2/\sigma_{AR}^2=0.0004$, where it *increases* with σ_{AR}^2 (of 500^2 and 600^2). This can be explained by the longer alternating periods of low and high data rates (created by high correlation and low noise variance) that increase the prefetching period. With further increase of σ_{AR}^2, the noise variance increases, leading to more frequent access to higher average data rates, thus decreasing the prefetching SLA.

Table 4 illustrates the impact of different constant (c) values on the average data rate ($\bar{R}$) and data rate range: the larger the c, the higher the $\bar{R}$. The data rate range also increases with higher c until the maximum data rate is reached, after which point the range starts decreasing if further increasing c.

Table 4. Range and average data rate for increasing c and $\phi_1=0.8885$

μ	0	280.8	561.6	842.5
c	0	31.3	62.6	92.9
$\bar{R}$	123.3	290.7	561.5	802.7
range	0.5–587	0.5–840	25.3–998.7	268.2–999.9

As defined in (4), c can be derived from μ and ϕ_1. In Table 4, μ values are selected to yield different $\bar{R}$ in the 0.5–1000 kByte/s range, while ϕ_1 of 0.8885 was obtained by fitting a user data rates to AR(1) model with constant.

Figure 9 to the left illustrates that the **higher c results in lower** E_{max}. Prefetching SLAs corresponding to E_{max} are illustrated on the right side.

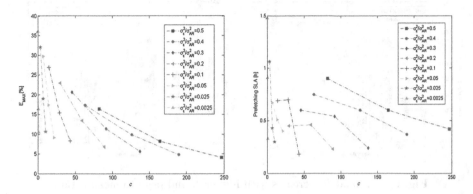

Fig. 9. E_{max} and prefetching SLA as a function of c for different $\sigma_\epsilon^2/\sigma_{AR}^2$, $\sigma_{AR}^2 = 100^2$

6   Prefetching Recommendations

Figure 10 depicts $\hat{R}$ as a function of $\bar{R}$ and peak-to-mean ratio. This $\hat{R}$ is said to be *optimal*, since it was extracted from prefetching results with E_{max}. Observe that the **higher peak-to-mean** and **lower** $\bar{R}$ require **lower optimal** $\hat{R}$.

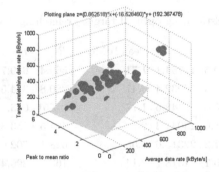

Fig. 10. Optimal $\hat{R}$ for $\bar{R}$ and peak-to-mean ratio

Fitting the optimal $\hat{R}$ to a plane with $\bar{R}$ and *peakToMean* variables yields:

$$\hat{R} = 0.853 * \bar{R} - 16.528 * peakToMean + 192.367 \tag{9}$$

with goodness-of-fit (R^2) being 0.8372 and root-mean-square error = 75.9483.

Figure 11 plots the original and estimated $\hat{R}$ as a function of $\bar{R}$ and *peak-ToMean*, computed from the entire model parameter space. Setting $\hat{R}$ to an optimal value can potentially maximize the energy cost reduction of a mobile device while prefetching video content using the proposed method.

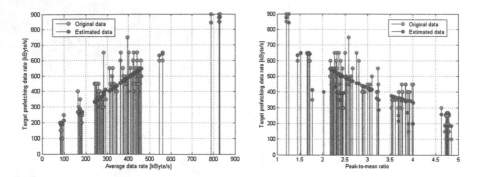

Fig. 11. Optimal $\hat{R}$ increases with higher $\bar{R}$ and peak-to-mean ratio

Table 5 predicts the optimal $\hat{R}$ for six different channel states ($\hat{R}_{est}$) that are extracted from users traces. Observe that $\hat{R}_{est}$ values of channels with strong correlation are similar to $\hat{R}$, while differing more for moderate correlation, due to a larger noise variance. Note that moderate correlation was observed in shorter data rate logs and where a mobile user behavior deviated from a daily routine (by visiting new locations with different data rate characteristics). However, the more precise (and longer) the log is, the closer $\hat{R}_{est}$ to optimal $\hat{R}$ are expected.

Table 5. Estimating optimal target prefetching data rates

ϕ_1	c	σ_ϵ^2	PeakToMean	$\bar{R}$	$\hat{R}$	$\hat{R}_{est}$
0.8899	59.5	11764.1	1.71	569.4	649.7	650
0.8885	31.3	4032.4	3.47	280.8	374.5	300
0.8704	15.6	2348.6	1.77	551	633.1	650
0.7878	98.6	23041.3	2.1	464.5	553.8	550
0.6545	217.2	22313.6	1.55	628.1	702.6	600
0.5407	75.1	1318.7	2.14	163.5	296.4	150

7   Discussion

The obtained results in this paper can be used in a real system, by monitoring a mobile user data rates and deriving the AR(1) model parameter values. The derived parameter values could be used by content providers to estimate the user's potential energy savings along with the time when the content will be available to the user for viewing. Additionally, using the fitted model parameter values, content providers can set the optimal prefetching parameters for the particular user in order to maximize their energy cost reduction or reduce the time to complete content prefetching. This flexibility of estimating the prefetching parameters to satify user preferences enables a content provider to define a new type of Service Level Agreement (SLA) that can guarantee a strict upper bound on content delivery delay to users, while allowing them to optimize their energy budget needed to complete mobile video content download.

A real system for mobile video prefetching has been implemented in our lab [4], which we plan to enhance with user preferences, model parameters learning, and estimation of the prefetching parameters that can produce the desired energy savings and delivery delay constraints. Such an enhanced system will be tested with real users and mobile devices.

8   Conclusion

This paper investigates the energy consumption reduction of content prefetching in different network conditions. A mobile device estimates the available downlink data rates by periodically probing the channel quality, prefetching the rest of content bits if the estimated data rate is equal to or higher than the set threshold.

The downlink data rates from actual user traces recorded in the mobile network were fitted to **autoregressive model of order one**. However, since AR coefficient was difficult to physically interpret, the following parameters were analytically derived: *process mean*, *process variance*, and *noise variance*. In order to generalize results concerning the potential maximum energy cost reduction (E_{max}) and the time needed to complete the prefetching (i.e., prefetching

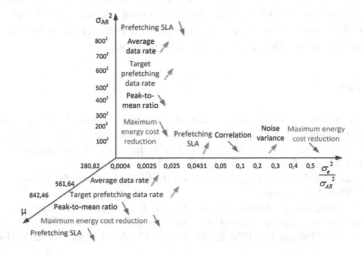

Fig. 12. Dependencies of prefetching results on model parameters

SLA), the entire model parameter space was used to generate synthetic data rates. Figure 12 illustrates conclusions of this evaluation, depicting how different prefetching metrics perform with the increasing parameter values.

The OTT prefetching provides high energy savings in the areas of alternating high and low data rates (indicated by **strong correlation between subsequent data rates and low noise variance**), since it stops downloading content as soon as it encounters the low available bandwidth, which would otherwise be performed on demand. Moreover, the **lower the average data rate and the higher the peak-to-mean ratio** (which can be achieved **by decreasing the process mean or process variance for the same** $\sigma_\epsilon^2/\sigma_{AR}^2$), the higher the energy savings. The $\sigma_\epsilon^2/\sigma_{AR}^2$ ratio determines the *shape* of data rates signal, representing a particular AR process type.

A **short prefetching SLA** is a result of frequent and long access to **high data rates**, which can be generated by **high process mean, high process variance, and/or low noise variance**.

Finally, based on identified dependencies of a target prefetching data rate on statistical properties of data rates (such as mean and peak-to-mean ratio), we proposed **recommendations on how to set** $\hat{R}$ in order to achieve E_{max}.

A deficiency of the OTT prefetching method is in periodic channel probing that estimates the available data rates, since the method prefetches some of the content bits at lower data rates, which decreases the potential energy savings. By employing longer sleep times, the method can faster avoid the areas with poor network conditions, thus increasing the likelihood of prefetching at high data rates. An additional knowledge about channel quality is, therefore, desired (such as signal strength, connectivity type, and cell IDs with the time when high data rates are usually available), either from historical user data or a mobile operator, in order to signal the method when there are good opportunities for prefetching.

Future work includes enhancing our method with this information and comparing the obtained energy savings with the results from this paper. Additionally, we plan to experiment with setting the prefetching parameters in the real system, optimizing the potential energy savings and prefetching delays according to user preferences and the fitted model parameters.

References

1. Balasubramanian, N., Balasubramanian, A., Venkataramani, A.: Energy consumption in mobile phones: A measurement study and implications for network applications. In: Proceedings of the ACM SIGCOMM Internet Measurement Conference (IMC'09), Chicago, Illinois, USA, pp. 280–293, Nov 2009
2. Cisco. Cisco Visual Networking Index: Global Mobile Data Traffic Forecast Update, pp. 2011–2016. White paper
3. Devlic, A., Lungaro, P., Kamaraju, P., Segall, Z., Tollmar, K.: Energy consumption reduction via context-aware mobile video pre-fetching. In: IEEE International Symposium on Multimedia (ISM 2012), Irvine, California, pp. 261–265, Dec 2012

4. Kamaraju, P., Lungaro, P., Segall, Z.: A novel paradigm for context-aware content pre-fetching in mobile networks. In: Proceedings of the IEEE Wireless Communications and Networking Conference (WCNC 2013), Shangai, China, pp. 4534–4539, Apr 2013
5. Gautam, N., Petander, H., Noel, J.: A comparison of the cost and energy efficiency of prefetching and streaming of mobile video. In: Proceedings of the 5th ACM Workshop on Mobile Video (MoVid 2013), Oslo, Norway, Feb 2013
6. Walfield, N.H., Burns, R.: Smart phones need smarter applications. In: Workshop on Hot Topics in Operating Systems (HotOS 2011), Napa Valley, CA, pp. 1–5, May 2001
7. Rahmati, A., Zhong, L.: Context-based network estimation for energy-efficient ubiquitous wireless connectivity. IEEE Trans. Mobile Comput. $10(1)$, 54–66 (2011)
8. Schulman, A., Navda, V., Ramjee, R., Spring, N., Deshpande, P., Grunewald, C., Jain, K., Padmanabhan, V.N.: Bartendr: A practical approach to energy-aware cellular data scheduling. In: ACM International Conference on Mobile Computing and Networking (MobiCom 2010), Chicago, Illinois, USA, pp. 85–96, Sept 2010
9. Stoica, P., Moses, R.: Spectral Analysis of Signals. Prentice Hall, Upper Saddle River, NJ (2005)

MITATE: Mobile Internet Testbed for Application Traffic Experimentation

Utkarsh Goel, Ajay Miyyapuram, Mike P. Wittie$^{(\boxtimes)}$, and Qing Yang

Department of Computer Science,
Montana State University, Bozeman, MT 59717, USA
mwittie@cs.montana.edu

Abstract. This paper introduces a Mobile Internet Testbed for Application Traffic Experimentation (MITATE). MITATE is the first programmable testbed to support the prototyping of application communications between mobiles and cloud datacenters. We describe novel solutions to device security and resource sharing behind MITATE. Finally, we show how MITATE can answer network performance questions crucial to mobile application design.

Keywords: Mobile networks · Testbed · Application · Performance

1 Introduction

Innovative mobile applications, such as multiplayer games and augmented reality, will require low message delay to provide a high quality of user experience (QoE) [1,2]. Low message delay, in turn, depends on low network latency and high available bandwidth between mobile devices and cloud datacenters, on which application back-end logic is deployed. Unfortunately, mobile network performance can change rapidly [3]. Worse, traffic shaping mechanisms in cellular networks, such as as cap-and-throttle, traffic redundancy elimination, and deep packet inspection (DPI), can delay application messages without being reflected in standard metrics of network performance [4–6].

If innovation in the mobile space is to achieve broad adoption, new applications must deliver a high QoE across a range of network conditions. In other words, application communication protocols must be smart enough to adapt to changing network performance to keep message delay low. Such adaptations might include changing packet size, or moving between server endpoints to deliver best traffic performance for a given client [3,7].

To design and validate adaptive communication protocols developers need to prototype their implementations in production networks. The research community has produced several testbeds capable of application prototyping in the wired Internet [8–20]. To date, however, cellular network measurement platforms are not *programmable* in that they do not provide an foreign code execution environment [21–26]. Instead applications are evaluated in network simulators

© Institute for Computer Sciences, Social Informatics and Telecommunications Engineering 2014
I. Stojmenovic et al. (Eds.): MOBIQUITOUS 2013, LNICST 131, pp. 224–236, 2014.
DOI: 10.1007/978-3-319-11569-6_18

configured to reflect measurements of network performance [3]. While measurement-based simulation allows repeatable experiments, it misses the dynamic effects of competing traffic in cellular schedulers and of traffic shaping mechanisms.

The technical problem we address in this paper is a lack of a programmable testbed for mobile application prototyping in production cellular networks. We have identified two challenges to building such a testbed. First, the personal nature of mobile devices creates user concerns over privacy, accountability for actions of foreign code being prototyped, and abuse of limited data plan and battery resources. Striking a balance between a flexible application prototyping environment and the safe execution of foreign code has been a difficult problem even in the more permissive wired environment [10,18]. Second, because mobile battery and data plan resources are limited, testbed participants need adequate incentives to share them. Difficulty in enlisting mobile users has limited measurement studies to small samples [26], high cost of testbeds based on dedicated hardware [27], and collection of only high level network performance metrics [24].

In this paper we describe MITATE – a Mobile Internet Testbed for Application Traffic Experimentation made possible by novel solutions to the problems of security and mobile resource sharing. MITATE is unique in that it allows programmable application traffic experiments between mobile hosts and backend server infrastructure. MITATE provides strong client security by separating application code execution from traffic generation. MITATE also provides incentives and protections for mobile resource sharing through tit-for-tat mechanisms. MITATE's specialized traffic experiments can help developers answer questions crucial to mobile application design such as: "What is the largest game state update message that can be reliably delivered under 100 ms?," "Does my application traffic need to contend with traffic shaping mechanisms?," or "Which CDN provides fastest downloads through a particular mobile service provider's network peering points?"

The remainder of this paper is organized as follows. Section 2 covers related research. In Sect. 3 we describe MITATE's architecture. Section 4 shows MITATE application prototyping capabilities. Finally, we conclude and present directions for future work in Sect. 5.

2   Related Work

The research community has produced several testbeds capable of application prototyping in the wired Internet [8–20]. To date, however, cellular network measurement platforms are not *programmable* in that they do not provide a foreign code execution environment [21–26]. The result is a functionality gap: new applications are either evaluated on a small number of mobile devices, or in network simulators [3,28]. While small scale studies capture real application performance, they miss variation across geographic areas, carriers, and devices. On the other hand, simulation studies configured to reflect aggregate measures of network performance miss the dynamic effects of traffic shaping and cellular schedulers [3–6].

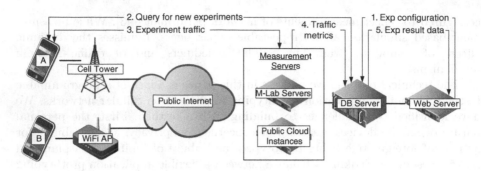

Fig. 1. MITATE architecture and steps of a network traffic experiment.

Existing testbeds share some features with MITATE, such as criteria-based filtering of testbed devices [26], (limited) evaluation of application layer mechanisms such as HTTP and DNS [23], and an M-Lab[1] back-end [24]. Closest to our approach is Dasu, which provides a custom execution environment within an extension to a PC BitTorrent client [18]. SatelliteLab is also similar to MITATE in that prototyped application logic is not executed on edge devices [13].

One mobile testbed with programmable features is PhoneLab, which provides 200 participants with mobile phones and discounted data plans [27]. In exchange, participants agree to network experiments executed on their phones. However, PhoneLab relies on a custom OS, which limits its deployment to dedicated hardware, since installing an OS is a significant barrier to entry for most users [13].

3   MITATE

MITATE goes beyond current work and allows application prototyping on mobile devices in production cellular networks. MITATE offers the flexibility of Dasu and SatelliteLab, but without the security vulnerabilities of mobile code [13,18]. To achieve wider adoption and easier access than the dedicated hardware model of PhoneLab, we adapt proven resource sharing incentives [27,29]. In this section, we describe MITATE's architecture, application prototyping capabilities, and address the challenges of security and resource sharing on mobile devices.

3.1   Architecture and Traffic Experiments

To register a device with MITATE, a user downloads our mobile application and starts it as a background service with her login credentials, obtained by creating a MITATE account. Once her device is registered, a user can conduct traffic experiments, referring to Fig. 1, as follows: In Step 1, a user creates an experiment by uploading a configuration file, described in Sect. 3.2, via the Web

---

[1] http://measurementlab.org

```
<experiment>
 <transfer>
  <id>t1</id>
  <src>client</src>
  <dst>54.243.176.74</dst>
  <prot>UDP</prot>
  <dstport>5060</dstport>
  <bytes>32</bytes>
 </transfer>
 <transfer>
  <id>t2</id>
  <src>54.243.176.74</src>
  <dst>client</dst>
  <prot>UDP</prot>
  <srcport>5060</srcport>
  <bytes>512</bytes>
 </transfer>
```

```
<criteria>
 <id>c1</id>
 <latlong>"45.666 -111.046"<\latlong>
 <radius>5000<radius>
 <networktype>cellular</networktype>
 <starttime>12:00</starttime>
 <endtime>13:30</endtime>
</criteria>
<transaction count="10">
 <criteria>
  <criteriaid>c1</criteriaid>
 </criteria>
 <transfers>
  <transferid>t1</transferid>
  <transferid delay="40">t2</transferid>
  <transferid>t1</transferid>
 </transfers>
</transaction>
</experiment>
```

Fig. 2. MITATE XML configuration file.

interface. In Step 2, MITATE devices query the database for new experiments, whose criteria they meet. To reduce resource contention, as in SatelliteLab, we allow only one experiment at a time on a device [13]. If device A, for example, meets the geographic location and network type criteria of an experiment, A will begin, in Step 3, to transfer data defined by the experiment to the measurement servers. Experiment transfer traffic is timed at each endpoint (mobiles and measurement servers) and network performance metrics, together with metadata, are reported back to the database in Step 4. Finally in Step 5, a user may access the Web interface again to visualize, or download the experiment data collected by multiple devices. Based on the collected data, the user may refine her experiment and restart the process from Step 1.

3.2 Programmable Network Traffic Experiment Configuration

MITATE offers a flexible programming environment that supports evaluation and optimization of existing application traffic traces, as well as prototyping of adaptive application communication protocols. Existing network testbeds support such flexibility through mobile code, whose potential security vulnerabilities result in designs based on dedicated testbed hardware [8,27], or execution environments constrained by custom APIs [10,18]. Neither solution is satisfactory. While the dedicated hardware limits adoption, custom APIs require application reimplementation in restricted, or non-standard programming environments.

We propose a secure and flexible network testbed design that eliminates the drawbacks of mobile code. MITATE experiments use multiple rounds of statically defined traffic transmissions. Processing between the rounds, i.e. mobile application logic, is implemented offline. Offline processing allows for the execution of unmodified application code inside an emulator[2] with message transmissions

---

[2] http://developer.android.com/tools/help/emulator.html

delegated to MITATE. Offline processing can also optimize communication protocol parameters, such as packet size, through binary parameter search, or a more powerful approach, such as CPLEX.[3] Finally, static experiment definitions allow static verification, which simplifies resource management (Sect. 3.3) and testbed security design (Sect. 3.4) and leads to a more accessible testbed.

Application Traffic Trace Experiments can help answer questions such as "What is the largest game state update message that can be reliably delivered under 100 ms?" An abbreviated MITATE experiment configuration XML file in Fig. 2 specifies two transfers, `t1` and `t2`. The transfers transmit the specified number of `bytes` between a MITATE mobile `client` and a datacenter server IP with MITATE backend logic.

The configuration file also specifies criteria definitions that `client` endpoints must meet before executing an experiment. In the Fig. 2 example, criteria `c1`, requires that a mobile be within 5000 m of geographic coordinates 45.666 -111.046 (Bozeman, MT), be connected to a cellular network, and that device time be between noon and 1:30PM. MITATE will allow experimenters to specify a wide set of criteria, for example radio signal strength, location (eg. radius, bounding box, or set of ZIP codes), availability of GPS (indoor/outdoor), or device travel speed (for example over 55mph).

Finally, configuration files specify one, or more transactions that group criteria and transfers. In the Fig. 2 example, there is one transaction, which conceptually reflects a user request (transfer `t1`), game state update (transfer `t2`) after 40 ms of server processing `delay`, and an acknowledgement (transfer `t1`). This transaction will be executed by a mobile device if the device satisfies transaction criteria when polling MITATE servers, fewer than `count` devices have completed the transaction, and the user issuing the experiment has sufficient test data credit (see Sect. 3.3) to execute the entire transaction.

To find the largest game state update that can be delivered under 100 ms, multiple experiment rounds can perform binary parameter search, with MITATE reporting individual transfer and overall transaction delays. MITATE can also be used with sophisticated optimization tools, such as CPLEX, where performance of intermediate solutions are the reported metrics in each experiment round. Because MITATE traffic experiments use production networks they are not necessarily repeatable, and so decision metrics should be averaged over multiple trials. Finally, a `repeat` attribute can indicate that a transfer, or a transaction, should be executed multiple times. These `repeat` and `delay` attributes can be combined to configure periodic traffic, for example polling every 10 min for 24 h.

Programmable Application Traffic Experiments can help answer questions such as "Which CDN provides fastest downloads through a particular mobile service provider's peering points?" To measure download times an experiment needs to issue a DNS lookup, followed by a download from the resolved

---

[3] www.ibm.com/software/commerce/optimization/cplex-optimizer/

```
<transfer>
 <id>dns_req</id>
 <src>client</src>
 <dst>DNS</dst>
 <dstport>53</dstport>
 <prot>UDP</prot>
 <bytes><![CDATA[0x0100be07de55...]]></bytes>
 <response>1</response>
</transfer>
```

Fig. 3. DNS query in MITATE.

server addresses. MITATE supports such experiments with two mechanism: explicit packet content and device-specific scheduling.

Figure 3 shows a configuration of transfer dns_req that represents a DNS lookup for a CDN server. The bytes tag contains the explicitly specified bytes of a well-formed DNS lookup request. When the response tag is set to 1, the DNS reply packet will be included in the result data set, from which a user can parse out the resolved IP addresses.

To measure the download time of an image hosted on a particular CDN network, the user would configure a second experiment with a well-formed HTTP GET request to each resolved server IP. To make sure that each mobile device contacts only the IP addresses it resolved, each MITATE measurement contains the unique ID of the device that collected the result. That ID can be subsequently used as an endpoint address instead of the "client" keyword.

One downside of our approach is a potential for delay between each round of transmissions as experiments wait to be scheduled on mobile devices. We are working on integrating MITATE with the Android emulator to make the process of experiment configuration as easy as writing to a socket. Our integration will carefully modify emulator clocks, so that they advance only by measured transmission delay, excluding experiment scheduling delay. This mechanism will allow studies of adaptive communication mechanisms, such as server-host switching in online games, implemented in native application code running inside the emulation with only traffic transmissions being delegated to MITATE.

3.3 Deployment Incentives

One of the challenges faced by mobile network measurement platforms is how to assure sufficient resource capacity for scheduled experiments. The limiting resource is mobile data, subject to monthly caps.[4] To assure a supply of mobile bandwidth that matches the demand, a mobile testbed must, first, entice users to contribute resources and, second, protect contributed resources from abuse. MITATE jointly addresses both problems using a data *credit* exchange system inspired by BitTorrent tit-for-tat mechanisms [29].

The insight behind BitTorrent's tit-for-tat mechanisms is that they reward users for contributing bandwidth, as well as for merely being willing to do so.

---

[4] While battery power is also limited, it can be more easily replenished by charging.

While in BitTorrent users make this assessment vis-a-vis each other, MITATE accounts for contribution and willingness to contribute with respect to the system as a whole. A MITATE user earns bandwidth credit for her experiments by allowing others' experiments to run on her device. A user is considered willing to contribute when her devices reliably ping MITATE servers for new experiments. The credit earned by the user, x_{earned}, is computed daily as:

$$x_{earned} = \alpha \times x_{max} \times \min\left(\frac{x_{contributed}}{x_{max}} + \frac{p_{actual}}{p_{expected}}, 1\right),$$

where x_{max} is the remaining amount of mobile data a user is willing to contribute during a monthly billing cycle divided by remaining number of days, $x_{contributed}$ is the volume of mobile data used by MITATE experiments on the user's data plan, p_{actual} is the number of pings reaching MITATE servers within 24 hours, and $p_{expected}$ is the expected number of pings based on a system wide ping frequency setting. The parameter $\alpha < 1$ creates a mismatch between contributed resources and earned credit intended to ensure high experiment completion rates in areas with fewer participating devices, such as rural states. We recalculate user credit every 24 hours to prevent users from accumulating credit that, if used all at once, could deplete system resources on any given day. We expect that some participants will use MITATE sporadically and others on ongoing basis. Similar user participation takes place in BitTorrent, yet the system as a whole is able to maintain a sustained capacity [29].

Thus, MITATE credits users for contributed bandwidth, which allows them to use the bandwidth of others, keeping the two in a state of equilibrium. A final element of the mechanism to prevent resource abuse is that daily experiment bandwidth requirements are computed at submission time, a process facilitated by the static XML experiment definition, and checked against submitting user's credit before being admitted to the system. We believe this approach is more predictable than resource caps enforced at run time that can lead to low experiment completion rates [10]. We also believe MITATE's credit based approach is simpler and more democratic than the delegated trust approach proposed in NIMI [30].

3.4   Security and Privacy

MITATE's goal of open-access necessitates a well thought out security design. With the contributed data plan resources protected by the incentive mechanisms, the security goals focus on protection of user privacy, the volunteered devices, and non-MITATE Internet resources.

Protecting User Privacy. MITATE runs on personal mobile devices, which has the potential for violations of privacy if a device owner's activity and personally identifiable information were to become public. For example, user network and calling activity is not only private, but may itself contain personally identifiable information. Similarly GPS data becoming public can lead to legal challenges if traffic laws (speeding), or property laws (trespassing) were violated.

We have designed multiple levels of protection to preclude violations of user privacy. First, MITATE can only be used for active traffic experiments and cannot monitor non-MITATE traffic on a device. Second, while MITATE does collect GPS and accelerometer readings as metadata to accompany network performance metrics, users are asked to opt-in before starting the MITATE mobile app. Finally, third, we separate all data collected on devices from personally identifiable user account information. Each device registered with MITATE receives two random IDs: one to label traffic metrics collected on the device, the other to keep track of credit data earned by the device for its owner. The dual ID system means that collected experiment data are never linked to a device owner's identifiable information.

Protecting User Devices. Users who volunteer their devices for MITATE agree to cede some control over them. It is imperative that MITATE limit other user's actions on volunteered devices to within the bounds of that agreement. MITATE protects user devices with three mechanisms.

First, a user can set usage limits for mobile data, WiFi data, and battery level on their devices. These limits are consulted during experiment scheduling to disallow experiments that exceed remaining device resource allowance. Second, users never directly interact with others' devices. To submit an experiment, or download data, users authenticate and communicate with MITATE servers over encrypted connections. Mobile devices download experiments and upload collected metrics to MITATE servers also using encryption. Finally, third, our XML experiment configuration is static in that it does not allow conditional, nor jump statements. Such static definitions enforce the separation between the on-device functionality of data transmission and off-device processing. This separation allows for static checking of XML configurations using mature schema verification tools, which is simpler than dynamic code analysis and more lightweight than mobile code sandboxing. Static experiment definition also allows for the volume of each transfer in the XML file to be added up and compared against user credit and device resource limits.

Protecting Non-MITATE Resources. Our final goal is to protect non-MITATE resources, for example from DDoS attacks configured as MITATE experiments. ScriptRoute, designed from the ground up as a secure Internet measurement system, considers two types of malicious experiments: *magic* packets and traffic amplification [10]. *Magic* packets can disrupt legitimate traffic, for example, when a spoofed FIN packet closes a TCP connection. Because MITATE allows experiments with explicitly defined packet content, we will make sure that these packets do not pose threats to other systems by matching them against signatures of known exploits using intrusion detection mechanisms.

Traffic amplification takes place when a malicious user leverages testbed nodes to monopolize the resources of a legitimate service, for example through

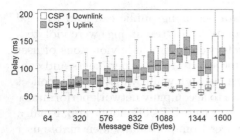

Fig. 4. Message delay vs. message size at 10 AM on CSP 1 to a CA datacenter.

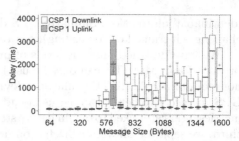

Fig. 5. Message delay vs. message size at 2 PM on CSP 1 to a CA datacenter.

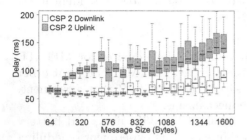

Fig. 6. Message delay vs. message size at 10 AM on CSP 2 to a CA datacenter.

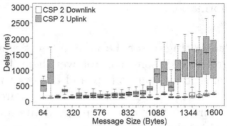

Fig. 7. Message delay vs. message size at 10 AM on CSP 2 to a VA datacenter.

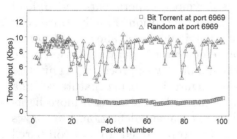

Fig. 8. Per packet throughput of BitTorrent and random payloads on CSP 1.

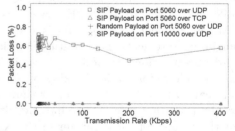

Fig. 9. Packet loss of SIP and random payloads vs. flow data rate on CSP 1.

a Smurf attack. Existing testbeds limit traffic amplification by placing a rate limit on the volume of data that can be generated by an experiment, which also constrains legitimate load testing. Instead, MITATE limits the total volume of experiment data to a user's earned credit. Although a MITATE user may request that multiple devices send data simultaneously, the user's credit will be rapidly depleted, and so even if the transmissions are malicious, they will be short-lived.

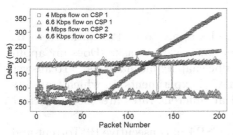
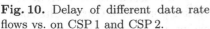
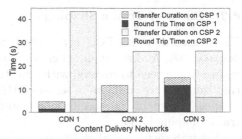

Fig. 10. Delay of different data rate flows vs. on CSP 1 and CSP 2.

Fig. 11. Round trip time and transfer time of 3 MB image from three CDNs.

4   MITATE Application Traffic Prototyping Capability

To demonstrate MITATE's traffic emulation capabilities we present a set of network experiments and collected data. We show that MITATE can elicit various network performance phenomena useful to developers in answering a wide range questions about application traffic performance. The collected data includes traffic performance metrics and associated metadata. Prior to sending experiment traffic, MITATE calculates the clock offset between the mobile and measurement servers, which allows us to time unidirectional (unacknowledged) UDP transfers [31]. Experiments were performed on several Android phones and two different cellular service providers (CSP) networks in Bozeman, MT, and over connections to two different cloud datacenters. We anonymize the identities of CSPs and CDNs.

4.1   Effect of Packet Size on Message Delay

In gaming applications game state updates need to be delivered while their content is relevant. And so, game developers may want to know: "What is the largest game state update message that can be reliably delivered under 100 ms?" To answer that question we configure a MITATE experiment with transfers of increasing size (`bytes`). We plot the results in Figs. 4, 5, 6, 7, which show message delay as a function of message size during different times of day.

Our results show that message delay increases with message size and does so more rapidly on the uplink, likely due to asymmetric network provisioning. We also observe in Fig. 5 a high delay for larger messages on the downlink, likely due to mid-day network congestion. Figure 6 shows a higher sensitivity of message delay to size on CSP 2. That effect is especially pronounced on connections to a datacenter located in Virginia, shown in Fig. 7.

From these experiments a developer might conclude that a message of 320 B can be delivered under 100 ms with high confidence to customers in Bozeman, MT on CSP 1, but a smaller message might be needed on CSP 2. Also, to keep message delay low, requests from Bozeman should not be directed to the Virginia datacenter.

4.2   Effect of Traffic Shaping

The degree to which FCC net neutrality rules apply to CSPs continues to be debated [32]. And so, application developers may want to ask: "Does my application traffic need to contend with CSP traffic shaping mechanisms?" To answer that question we configure a series of MITATE experiments, in which transfers of specific content, on specific ports, and at different rates are used to detect traffic shaping [5, 33].

Figure 8 shows downlink throughput on CSP 1 of consecutive BitTorrent and random payloads transmitted over UDP on tracker port 6969. Our results show a drop in throughput for well-formed BitTorrent packets relative to random content, which likely indicates the presence of DPI mechanisms. We did not detect similar throughput drops on CSP 2. These results show that embedding of explicit packet payloads allows MITATE to detect content based traffic shaping.

Figure 9 shows downlink percent packet loss on CSP 1 of 1000 SIP packets transmitted on port 5060 over UDP and TCP versus transmission rate. Our results show that while SIP packets over TCP are undisturbed, same packets over UDP experience close to 60 % loss rate. Because loss remains nearly constant across transmission rates, we believe that SIP packet loss over UDP is due to traffic policing, rather than traffic shaping.

Figure 10 shows per packet delay of uplink UDP flows transmitted at 4 Mbps and 6.6 Kbps on CSP 1 and CSP 2 versus packet number. The 4 Mbps flows experience an increase in delay, likely from queueing that results from the mismatch between sending and token bucket service rate limits [5]. The 6.6 Kbps flows, on the other hand, are sent below the service rate and avoid self-induced congestion. Testing different transmission rates allows developers to determine the maximum sending rate that will fall below token generation rate and avoid queuing delays. The experiments are useful for configuration of adaptive video stream encoding.

4.3   Measurement Based CDN Selection

Finally, dynamic content applications customize content for each user and have the opportunity to adapt to user's network conditions, for example, by embedding links to static content in different CDNs. And so, application developers may want to ask: "Which CDN provides fastest downloads through a particular mobile service provider's network peering points?" To answer that question we configure a MITATE experiment that sends a well-formed HTTP GET requests, configured in the bytes tag, for an image hosted in three different CDNs.

Figure 11 shows the CDN response time for the first bit, or round trip time (RTT), and last bit, or transfer duration, of a 3 MB image delivered over the two CSP networks. Our results show a lower last bit delay for requests in CSP 1, but a higher RTT variation between CDNs, likely due to different CSP peering points that lead to CDN servers. From these experiments a developer might conclude that for users in Bozeman, MT CDN 2 provides the best combination of performance across the two CSP networks.

5 Discussion and Future Work

In this paper we described MITATE, the first public testbed that supports prototyping of application communications between mobiles and cloud datacenters. MITATE separates application logic from traffic generation, which simplifies security and resource sharing mechanisms. We have presented data collected with MITATE experiments that demonstrates the system's capability in eliciting effects of cellular network performance on mobile application message delay.

Future work on the project involves deploying the current implementation onto M-Lab servers. In the meantime, we invite the community to use publicly available MITATE code[5] in private deployments. We also welcome community participation in evolving MITATE functionality in the areas of resource sharing models, GPS and accelerometer data anonymization, data visualization, and tools based on the MITATE platform.

References

1. Chen, K.-T., Huang, P., Lei, C.-L.: Effect of network quality on player departure behavior in online games. Parallel Distrib. Syst. **20**, 593–606 (2009)
2. Geerts, D., Vaishnavi, I., Mekuria, R., van Deventer, O., Cesar, P.: Are we in sync?: synchronization requirements for watching online video together. In: SIGCHI Conference on Human Factors in Computing Systems, May 2011
3. Winstein, K., Sivaraman, A., Balakrishnan, H.: Stochastic forecasts achieve high throughput and low delay over cellular networks. In: USENIX NSDI, Apr 2013
4. Zohar, E., Cidon, I., Mokryn, O.O.: Celleration: loss-resilient traffic redundancy elimination for cellular data. In: Workshop on Mobile Computing Systems (HotMobile), Feb 2012
5. Kanuparthy, P., Dovrolis, C.: ShaperProbe: end-to-end detection of ISP traffic shaping using active methods. In: ACM IMC, Nov 2011
6. Lu, X., Cao, W., Huang, X., Huang, F., He, L., Yang, W., Wang, S., Zhang, X., Chen, H.: A real implementation of DPI in 3G network. In: Global Telecommunications Conference (GLOBECOM), Dec 2010
7. Wittie, M.P., Pejovic, V., Deek, L., Almeroth, K.C., Zhao, B.Y.: Exploiting locality of interest in online social networks. In: ACM CoNEXT, Nov 2010
8. Chun, B., Culler, D., Roscoe, T., Bavier, A., Peterson, L., Wawrzoniak, M., Bowman, M.: PlanetLab: an overlay testbed for broad-coverage services. SIGCOMM Comput. Commun. Rev. **33**, 3–12 (2003)
9. Andersen, D.G., Balakrishnan, H., Kaashoek, M.F., Morris, R.: Experience with an evolving overlay network testbed. SIGCOMM CCR **33**, 13–19 (2003)
10. Spring, N., Wetherall, D., Anderson, T.: Scriptroute: a public Internet measurement facility. In: USENIX Symposium on Internet Technologies and Systems (USITS), Mar 2003
11. Simpson Jr., C.R., Riley, G.F.: NETI@home: a distributed approach to collecting end-to-end network performance measurements. In: Barakat, C., Pratt, I. (eds.) PAM 2004. LNCS, vol. 3015, pp. 168–174. Springer, Heidelberg (2004)

---

[5] http://github.com/msu-netlab/MITATE

12. Bavier, A., Feamster, N., Huang, M., Peterson, L., Rexford, J.: In VINI veritas: realistic and controlled network experimentation. In: ACM SIGCOMM, Aug 2006
13. Dischinger, M., Haeberlen, A., Beschastnikh, I., Gummadi, K.P., Saroiu, S.: SatelliteLab: adding heterogeneity to planetary-scale network testbeds. In: ACM SIGCOMM, Aug 2008
14. Choffnes, D.R., Bustamante, F.E., Ge, Z.: Crowdsourcing service-level network event monitoring. In: ACM SIGCOMM, Aug 2010
15. Manweiler, J., Agarwal, S., Zhang, M., Roy Choudhury, R., Bahl, P.: Switchboard: a matchmaking system for multiplayer mobile games. In: ACM MobiSys, June 2011
16. Geni, Oct 2012. http://www.geni.net/
17. FIRE: Future Internet Research and Experimentation, July 2013. http://www.ict-fire.eu/
18. Sánchez, M.A., Otto, J.S., Bischof, Z.S., Choffnes, D.R., Bustamante, F.E., Krishnamurthy, B., Willinger, W.: Dasu: pushing experiments to the Internet's edge. In: USENIX NSDI, Apr 2013
19. Archipelago measurement infrastructure, June 2013. http://www.caida.org/projects/ark/
20. Ripe atlas, July 2013. http://atlas.ripe.net/
21. Wittie, M.P., Stone-Gross, B., Almeroth, K.C., Belding, E.M.: MIST: cellular data network measurement for mobile applications. In: Conference on Broadband Communications, Networks and Systems (BROADNETS), Sept 2007
22. Austin, M., Wish, M.: The official story on AT&T Mark the Spot, Oct 2010. http://www.research.att.com/articles/featured_stories/2010_09/201009_MTS.html
23. Huang, J., Xu, Q., Tiwana, B., Mao, Z.M., Zhang, M., Bahl, P.: Anatomizing application performance differences on smartphones. In: ACM MobiSys, June 2010
24. MobiPerf, Welcome to MobiPerf. http://www.mobiperf.com/home, Feb 2012
25. ROOT Metrics. http://www.rootmetrics.com/, July 2013
26. Gember, A., Akella, A., Pang, J., Varshavsky, A., Caceres, R.: Obtaining in-context measurements of cellular network performance. In: ACM IMC, Nov 2012
27. Baldawa, R., et al.: PhoneLab: A large-scale participatory smartphone testbed. In: USENIX NSDI poster session, Apr 2012
28. Gao, J., Sivaraman, A., Agarwal, N., Li, H., Peh, L.: DIPLOMA: Consistent and coherent shared memory over mobile phones. In: International Conference on Computer Design (ICCD), Sept 2012
29. Cohen, B.: Incentives build robustness in BitTorrent. In: International Workshop on Peer-To-Peer Systems (IPTPS), Feb 2003
30. Paxson, V., Mahdavi, J., Adams, A., Mathis, M.: An architecture for large scale Internet measurement. IEEE Commun. 36, 48–54 (1998)
31. Mills, D.L.: Network Time Protocol (version 2) specification and implementation. Network Working Group Request for Comments: 1119, Sept 1989
32. Ammori, M.: The next big battle in Internet policy. http://www.slate.com/articles/technology/future_tense/2012/10/network_neutrality_the_fcc_and_the_internet_of_things_.html, Oct 2012
33. Dischinger, M., Marcon, M., Guha, S., Gummadi, K.P., Mahajan, R., Saroiu, S.: Glasnost: enabling end users to detect traffic differentiation. In: USENIX NSDI, Apr 2010

Declarative Programming for Mobile Crowdsourcing: Energy Considerations and Applications

Jurairat Phuttharak[✉] and Seng W. Loke

Department of Computer Science and Computer Engineering,
La Trobe University, Melbourne, VIC 3086, Australia
jphuttharak@students.latrobe.edu.au,
s.loke@latrobe.edu.au

Abstract. This paper introduces *LogicCrowd*, a declarative programming platform for mobile crowdsourcing applications (using social media networks and peer-to-peer networks), developed as an extension of Prolog. We present a study of energy consumption characteristics for our *LogicCrowd* prototype. Based on the measurements, we develop an energy-crowdsourcing consumption model for *LogicCrowd* on the Android platform and also extend the *Logic-Crowd* meta-interpreter for computing with an energy budget corresponding to a certain battery lifetime.

Keywords: Declarative programming language · Mobile application · Mobile crowdsourcing · Peer-to-peer · Mobile energy consumption model

1 Introduction

Crowdsourcing is simply known as the power of the crowd [1]. There are successful crowdsourcing services in the marketplace today, including Amazon's Mechanical Turk,[1] MicroWorker[2] and MicroTask[3] that has become more interesting. Those products offer a framework to access the crowd which enables the employers to submit individually designed tasks. To take advantage of the widespread mobile's opportunities for crowdsourcing, we attempt to engage social media networks and bring the crowdsourcing model into mobile environments. The contribution of this paper is an innovative approach to highlight the significance and advantages of using declarative programming language for leveraging the knowledge of people through mobile crowdsourcing contexts, and to study the energy implications of this.

We designed *LogicCrowd* (first briefly introduced in [2], and will be extended here), a declarative crowdsourcing platform for mobile applications, which combines conventional machine computation and the power of the crowd in social media networks and peer-to-peer networks. With the advantages of expressive power (ease of programming and compact code) and declarative semantics (ease of program transformation and

---

[1] https://www.mturk.com/
[2] http://microworkers.com/
[3] http://www.microtask.com/

© Institute for Computer Sciences, Social Informatics and Telecommunications Engineering 2014
I. Stojmenovic et al. (Eds.): MOBIQUITOUS 2013, LNICST 131, pp. 237–249, 2014.
DOI: 10.1007/978-3-319-11569-6_19

transparent parallelism), logic programming has benefits for our framework. We integrate logic programming into a crowdsourcing mobile middleware in order to provide a declarative programming platform for mobile apps that can use crowdsourcing. In addition, given that energy is a crucial resource on mobiles, energy consumed when using Wi-Fi and Bluetooth communication technologies in Android phones for crowdsourcing is experimentally measured. In this paper, we investigate relationships among energy consumption, two different types of crowd execution (Synchronous and Asynchronous) and different kinds of aforementioned network connections. We also explore the relationships between energy consumption and the waiting period of crowdsourced queries; based on those measurements, we develop an energy-crowdsourcing consumption model for the Android platform and also implement the notion of *computing with an energy budget* via an extension of the *LogicCrowd* meta-interpreter.

In the following, Sect. 2 introduces the concept of the *LogicCrowd* platform, its architecture and several example *LogicCrowd* applications. Section 3 evaluates the prototype and proposes an energy consumption model for mobile crowdsourcing. Section 4 reviews related work and Sect. 5 concludes with future work.

2 *LogicCrowd* and Its Applications

LogicCrowd, at this stage, is designed for users or mobile developers who have a basic background on Prolog, though syntactic sugar and UI forms can also be used.

Crowd Predicates. Queries to underlying crowds are abstracted as predicates. We term crowd predicates of the form: `<crowd_KW>? (<crowd_answer>)` `# [crowd_conditions]`. The request for a task for crowd computing is identified by a crowd keyword (`crowd_KW`). The `crowd_answer` is an output from the crowd for each task represented by a variable and `crowd_conditions` are the inputs or conditions when asking the crowd represented by parameters. The crowd predicate has its own operators "?" and "#" referring to crowd identity and crowd conditions, respectively. An operational semantics for the language of pure Prolog is augmented by crowdsourcing. We have clauses of the form: A :- G, where G is defined by G ::= A | D | (G, G), A is an atomic goal and D is a crowd predicate; e.g., this crowd predicate represents a person/user's query about a place, sent to the crowd:

`place? (Answer) # [asktype('photo'),question('Where is it?'),picture('a.jpg')]`

The question and picture predicates are in the crowd's conditions acting as parameters for queries to the open crowd. In our work, we define the relevant crowd's conditions based on common question templates: what to ask, whom to answer, what the location is (i.e., providing spatial scope), and when to receive the response.

Extending Meta-interpreter in *LogicCrowd*. The *LogicCrowd* meta-interpreter is presented in a simplified form as an extension of pure Prolog (in practice, we used tuProlog[4] which could be easily extended to accommodate calls to tuProlog via built-in libraries. The *LogicCrowd* meta-interpreter is given as follows.

---

[4] http://apice.unibo.it/xwiki/bin/view/Tuprolog/

```
solve(true):-!.    solve(not(P)):- !,\+solve(P).    solve((P)):- builtin(P),!, P.
solve((P,Body)) :- !,solve(P), solve(Body).    solve((P)):- clause(P,Body),solve(Body).
solve(Askcrowd?Result#Condition):- !,solvecond(Condition),
    (asyn,!,asynproc(Askcrowd,Result); synproc(Askcrowd,Result)),doretraction.
synproc(Askcrowd,Result):-
    checkcond(TypeQuestion,Question,Picture,Options,Askto,Group,Locatedin,Expiry),
    askcrowd(Askcrowd,TypeQuestion,Question,Options,Picture,Askto,Group,Locatedin,Expiry,QuestionID),
    registercallbacksyn(QuestionID,Question,Askto,TypeQuestion,Expiry,Result).
asynproc(Askcrowd,Result):-
    checkcond(TypeQuestion,Question,Picture,Options,Askto,Group,Locatedin,Expiry),
    askcrowd(Askcrowd,TypeQuestion,Question,Options,Picture,Askto,Group,Locatedin,Expiry,QuestionID),
    registercallbackasyn(Askcrowd,QuestionID,Question,Askto,TypeQuestion,Expiry,Result).
doretraction :-(asyn,!,retract(asyn);retract(syn)).
solvecond([]):-!. solvecond(Condition):- Condition =..[_H|[Head,Body]],asserta(Head),solvecond(Body).
checkcond(TypeQuestion,Question,Picture,Options,Askto,Group,Locatedin,Expiry) :-
    (asktype(A),!, TypeQuestion = A; set(TypeQuestion)), (question(B),!, Question = B; set(Question)),
    (picture(F),!, Picture = F; set(Picture)),(options(G),!, Options =G; set(Options)),
    (askto(H),!,Askto = H; set(Askto)),(group(I),!,Group = I; set(Group)),
    (locatedin(J),!,Locatedin = J; set(Locatedin)),(expiry(K),!,Expiry = K; set(Expiry)).
set(X):- X = 'null'.
```

From the above rules, the `solve/1` predicate is a meta-interpreter for pure Prolog
extended to evaluate goals with the crowd operators (? and #). This rule delegates
evaluation of such goals to `solvecond/1`, `asynproc/2`, `synproc/2`, `dore-
traction/0` predicates. The `solvecond/1` predicate represents a meta-interpreter
for the crowd conditions. It will assert the new fact (the crowd conditions) inserted into
the knowledge base. The `synproc/2` and `asynproc/2` predicates distinguish
between synchronous and asynchronous executions (these will be explained further in
the next sub-section). Both rules contain calls to the `checkcond/8` predicate and
`askcrowd/10` predicate. The first is to bind the values of the crowd conditions to
actual variables and set "null" to variables in case that the fact is not in the knowledge
base and the latter is to connect to the crowd by passing the crowd conditions to a
process outside of the main tuProlog thread. The goal `registercallbacksyn/6`
is called when the execution is synchronous and its function is to register tasks (which
have been sent to the crowd) and to manage returned results. It should be noted that in
terms of the general concepts, `registercallbackasyn/7` is rather similar to
`registercallbacksyn/6`, but it can solely operate in the asynchronous mode.

Synchronous vs Asynchronous Execution. One of the most important issues about
crowdsourcing is how to manage the answer(s) returned by the crowd. Since a delay for
the crowd to provide answers via social media networks and peer-to-peer networks is
expected. *LogicCrowd* has been designed to tackle this issue. We developed two
different methods to evaluate the rules: synchronous and asynchronous execution. In
the synchronous operation, we implement *LogicCrowd* according to the standard
Prolog program execution model. The model is running sequentially without any
parallel extensions when *LogicCrowd* is executing a crowd predicate, the evaluation
will be suspended until the system receives the answers from the crowd. We support
this mechanism via a small extension to the crowd predicate as shown in the following
form: **<crowd_KW> ? (<crowd_answer>) # [syn, crowd_conditions]**.
The query is issued in the synchronous mode when we have the atom "syn" in the
crowd conditions. In the asynchronous operation, the multi-threading capability
available is exploited since *LogicCrowd* is built on top of tuProlog which integrates
seamlessly with Java/Android. As such, a new thread is created for each such asynchronous crowd predicate evaluation, to run independently. We have a crowd predicate

of the form: `<crowd_KW> ? (<crowd_answer>) # [asyn,crowd_condi-tions]`. The asynchronous execution takes place when we specify the atom "asyn" in the crowd conditions. In contrast to synchronous processing, asynchronous operation would permit other goals to continue before answers from the crowd return; when the asynchronous method occurs, the evaluation of the crowd predicate will be in a newly created background thread, and the next sub-goal can be executed without blocking the crowd predicate.

Design and Implementation. We have built a prototype implementation of *Logic-Crowd* integrating tuProlog with Android via our own custom-built Java program called a Mediator. The execution process of *LogicCrowd* is as follows: the mobile user sets up goals (in rules, or a *LogicCrowd* program) which can query either the local facts database (i.e., conventional machine query) or the crowd. If the execution starts on the conventional machine query, it interacts synchronously with the knowledge base and returns the solutions to the main goal and/or continues to the next sub-goal(s); other-wise, the crowd is queried. The architecture of *LogicCrowd* is detailed in [2].

LogicCrowd's **Example Applications.** We illustrate how *LogicCrowd* can be applied for the purpose of conveniences. The first scenario is the application of *LogicCrowd* to ask for the meanings or clarifications of pictures. That is, one takes pictures of the unknown things (i.e., any symbols or events) and then sends them to the crowd via *LogicCrowd* (i.e., your friends or people of the area) to find out what they exactly mean. The rule for this help can be written as below:

```
askcrowd:- picture?(_)#[asyn, asktype("photo"),question("Please translate to English?"),
          picture("instruction.jpg")askto([bluetooth]), expiry("0,30,0")].
handle_crowd_answer(picture,Instruction):- show_instruction(Instruction).
```

The `asktocrowd/1` aims to ask the question by sending the photo to peers via Bluetooth connections and the crowd predicate identified using the crowd keyword "`picture`" is called as the open predicate to peers. The crowd query is in asyn-chronous mode with expiry in 30 min. With asynchronous operation, if there are goals after the crowd predicate, these goals can execute without waiting for the results from the crowd. After executing the crowd sub-goal, the question with the above conditions then appears on peer mobiles as illustrated in Figs. 1(a) and (b). After a while, peers are supposed to answer the request by translating the instruction to English. On expiry, the result is returned to the query originator in *LogicCrowd*, where the han-dle_crowd_answer/2 predicate would be automatically executed, which, in this scenario, is programmed to display the results, as shown in Fig. 1(c). Instead of only Bluetooth, Facebook could also be used.

In the second scenario, a *LogicCrowd* program can be applied to implement a recommendation system for a couple shopping in a big mall. In the rule below, there are two crowd predicates, the first one with crowd keyword "clothesShop" asks the crowd to recommend woman's clothes shops and the second with crowd keyword "shoeShop" asking about shoe shops, both in the Westfield Doncaster shopping center, by sending the query to friends via Facebook and Bluetooth and waiting up to 10 min.

Fig. 1. Sending the requests to Facebook and Bluetooth and showing the results: (left screen) execute goal, (middle screen) ask friends via Bluetooth, (right screen) display result.

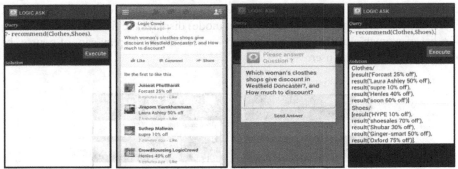

(a) Execute Goal   (b) Ask Question viaFacebook (c) Ask Question viaBluetooth (d) Display Results

Fig. 2. Sending the requests to Facebook and to devices via Bluetooth and showing the results.

```
recommend(Clothes,Shoes):- clothesShop?(Clothes)#[syn,asktype("message"),
     question("Which woman's clothes shops give discount in Westfield Doncaster?,
          and How much to discount?"),askto([facebook,bluetooth]), expiry("0,10,0")],
     shoeShop?(Shoes)#[syn, asktype("message"),
     question("Which shoes shops give discount in Westfield Doncaster?,
          and How much to discount?"),askto([facebook,bluetooth]), expiry("0,10,0")].
```

After executing the crowd sub-goal shown in Fig. 2(a), the question then appears on both Facebook over the Internet, and friends' devices connected via Bluetooth, as illustrated in Figs. 2(b) and (c). A while later, several friends' answer the question by mentioning shop(s) which offer discount. Within 10 min, i.e. the expiry time, the result is returned back to *LogicCrowd* in the originating device. The system then returns the results to the main goal. Figure 2(d) displays the result consisting of a list of the woman's clothes shops and a list of the shoes shops with discount details. We can extend the first scenario to be more flexible by using the asynchronous operation mode in one program, as shown below. The `recommend/1` rule is a goal to ask the crowd for recommendations on the shops in a particular shopping mall.

```
recommend(Clothes,Shoes):-
    clothesShop?(_)#[asyn,asktype("message"),
    question("Which woman's closthes shops give discount in Westfield Doncaster?,
             and How much to discount?"),askto([facebook,bluetooth]), expiry("0,10,0")],
    shoeShop?(ShoeList,Sdiscount)#[syn, asktype("message"),
    question("Which shoes shops give discount in Westfield Doncaster?,
             and How much to discount?"),askto([facebook,bluetooth]), expiry("0,10,0")],
    select_shop(Shoes,ShoeList,Sdiscount),  Sdiscount > 50%.
handle_crowd_answer(clothesShop,ClothesList,Cdiscount,Clothes):-
    select_shop(List,ClothesList,Cdisconunt),Cdiscount > 30%,quicksort(Clothes,'@>',List).
```

After a while, several friends might answer the request by suggesting shop(s) that offer discount. Within 10 min, the result is returned to *LogicCrowd*. Then, the handle_crowd_answer/4 predicate would be automatically executed in the first sub-goal and is programmed to first select woman's clothes shops with offers of more than 15 % discount and then to sort the list of these shops in order from the highest to lowest discount. The result from the second sub-goal was passed to the next sub-goal (select_shop/3) that chooses the shoes shops with offers of more than 30 %. Figure 3 (left – asyn. mode) and (right – syn. mode) displays the final results consisting of a list of woman's clothes and shoes shop – note that the display can, of course, be pretty-formatted for the user.

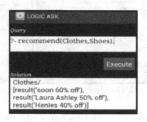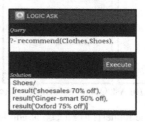

Fig. 3. The complex scenario - sending the requests to crowd and showing the results.

3   Energy Considerations in *LogicCrowd*

In this section, we present a study of the energy consumption characteristics of our *LogicCrowd* prototype and provide a model for managing energy consumption in *LogicCrowd* program execution. Our approach can be divided into four phases.

The First Phase: Setup. We first designed experiments to obtain two sets of measurements. In the first experiment, the aim was to compare the total power consumption for asking crowd in different network connections: WI-FI, Bluetooth and Mix (use both Bluetooth and Wi-Fi in the same crowd goal) and execution modes (synchronous and asynchronous). We created simple programs using the crowd predicate to send a query to the crowd as shown below. These rules show six main kinds of crowd predicates used in the measurements: Synchronous–Bluetooth, Synchronous–WIFI, Synchronous–Mix, Asynchronous–Bluetooth, Asynchronous–WIFI, and Asynchronous–Mix. In each rule, the expiry time in the crowd condition is set at 60 s. In this experiment, we increased the number of rules (and hence, the number of crowd goals) by 5 each time, going up to 30 rules in order to study the hypothesis that *if the number of rules* *increase, the power consumption will constantly increase in a simple linear form under the different connections and executions.*

```
syn_bt:- findall(B,(thai(B),melbourne(B)),A),nice?(Ans)#[syn,asktype('choice'),question
      ('Which restaurant do you recommend?'),options(A),askto([bluetooth]),expiry('0,0,60')].
syn_wf:- findall(B,(thai(B),melbourne(B)),A),nice?(Ans)#[syn,asktype('choice'),question
      ('Which restaurant do you recommend?'),options(A),askto([facebook]),expiry('0,0,60')].
syn_mix:- findall(B,(thai(B),melbourne(B)),A),nice?(Ans)#[syn,asktype('choice'),question
      ('Which restaurant do you recommend?'),options(A),askto([facebook,bluetooth]),expiry('0,0,60')].
asyn_bt:- findall(B,(thai(B),melbourne(B)),A),nice?(_)#[asyn,asktype('choice'),question
      ('Which restaurant do you recommend?'),options(A),askto([bluetooth]),expiry('0,0,60')].
asyn_wf:- findall(B,(thai(B),melbourne(B)),A),nice?(_)#[asyn,asktype('choice'),question
      ('Which restaurant do you recommend?'),options(A),askto([facebook]),expiry('0,0,60')].
asyn_mix:- findall(B,(thai(B),melbourne(B)),A),nice?(_)#[asyn,asktype('choice'),question
      ('Which restaurant do you recommend?'),options(A),askto([facebook,bluetooth]),expiry('0,0,60')].
```

The second experiment was conducted to determine whether *if there is an increase in waiting period (expiry time) for answers to a query sent to the crowd, the energy consumption will increase steadily in a simple linear curve.* The rules from the first experiment had been applied in this case. The expiry times in the crowd predicate had been changed by increasing in 5 min intervals up to 20 min. This experiment leads up to the follow-up third phase of the study where we could estimate the power consumption per query of *LogicCrowd* programs, under different communication connections and execution methods. All tests in these two experiments were performed on Nexus S running Android operating system version 4.1.2, Jelly Bean. A Power tool called Little Eye[5] was utilized for capturing the battery level and also for monitoring the power consumption of the *LogicCrowd* program.

The Second Phase: Measurements. Figure 4(a)–(e) shows total energy consumption (for display, CPU and networking) as the number of rules (i.e., correspondingly the number of crowd predicate calls) varies, when using different network connections (Bluetooth, Wi-Fi and Mix) and different execution modes (Synchronous and Asynchronous), compared with the baseline "no-communication" run of similar rules but without crowd predicates, i.e., the baseline. According to the results, the hypothesis of the first experiment has been shown in a way that all graphs display similar trends - a linear increase, which is more scalable than an exponential increase.

As shown in Fig. 4(a), asking the crowd by using Mix connection with Synchronous mode consumes the most energy, accounting for 1.11 times of the total power consumed for Wi-Fi, 1.27 times for Bluetooth, 15 times that of "no-communication". For each rule using a crowd predicate call with Mix connection, the average power consumption is spent differently: 4.872 mAh (milliamps per hour) on display (keeping the *LogicCrowd* front screen up), 0.378 mAh on CPU, and 0.018 mAh on Wi-Fi – display clearly dominates but if the application runs in the background CPU and connectivity will be important. Crowd asking using the Wi-Fi connection with the Synchronous method consumes around 1.14 times marginally more power than crowd asking using the Bluetooth connection with the same method, and spends about 13.46 times significantly more energy than using the rules. In each rule with this Wi-Fi mode, the average power consumed for display, CPU, and Wi-Fi varies: 4.674 mAh, 0.265 mAh, and 0.018 mAh respectively. Also, crowd asking using Bluetooth with synchronous execution consumes

---

[5] http://www.littleeye.co/

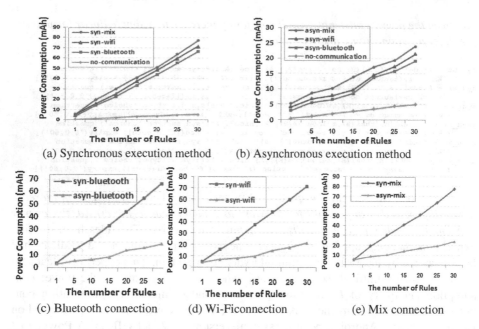

Fig. 4. The relationship between energy consumption and the number of rules/queries in different types of execution methods and communication technologies, x-axis is the number of rules/queries; y-axis is power consumption (milliamps per hour).

around 11.93 times of the total energy compared to rules without communication with the crowd - with no crowd goals, 3.396 mAh of average power per rule is used for display and 0.281 mAh for CPU. In compassion with no-communication mode, we can see that Wi-Fi, Bluetooth, and Mix all consume much higher energy. This is because with the use of the crowd predicate in crowd-communicative modes, it takes time to wait for crowd's responses. The more rules used, the longer the waiting period takes, and the higher the energy consumed. Most energy has been found to be mostly used for display, accounted for 70–90 % of the total spent on the foreground when asking the crowd (an optimization this suggests is to wait for the crowd answers in the background). Figure 4 (b) shows the differences in power consumption when using Wi-Fi, Bluetooth and Mix connections with Asynchronous mode, where the overall result is found similar to that of Synchronous operation. That is, the total power consumed when using Mix connection is around 1.245 times, and 1.463 times, slightly higher than the power consumed when using Wi-Fi and Bluetooth connection with the same method. Its energy spent 6.360 times more than the amount spent using the no crowd communication rules. Here, for each rule with Mix connection, 4.676 mAh of the mean power is spent on display, 0.489 mAh on CPU, and 0.018 mAh on Wi-Fi. While, the total power consumed when using Wi-Fi connection is around 1.17 times higher than the power consumed when using Bluetooth connection under the same method. Still, the amount of energy Wi-Fi spent is about 5.09 times higher than the energy for no crowd communication rules. The mean energy spent per rule on display, CPU, and Wi-Fi is 3.740 mAh, 0.336 mAh, and 0.015 mAh respectively. In addition, using Bluetooth with Asynchronous execution consumes around 4.26 times more energy than "no-communication" with the crowd. Figure 4(c)–(e) presents the energy consumption of different operation modes (Synchronous and Asynchronous) when the rules have been increased with equivalent interval (every 5 rules). The result shows that Synchronous execution remarkably consumes more energy than execution with Asynchronous mode. Also, 20 executed rules with Synchronous-Bluetooth mode consume 44.1 mAh whereas the Asynchronous-Bluetooth mode with the same size of rules spends only 13.8 mAh. In this regard, we can say that the average of energy consumed in Synchronous execution with Bluetooth, Wi-Fi, and Mix connection is three times higher than the average of the energy used in the Asynchronous mode. The findings of the above energy analysis cases is expected to contribute to the strategic guidance for selecting the most appropriate energy-related conditions to support the intelligent use of asking crowd in the *Logic-Crowd* program. Figure 5 shows the relationship between the energy consumption and the approximate waiting period of returned feedback from the crowd. According to the results, the hypothesis of the second experiment has been shown in that all graphs display similar trends, the regression line slopes upwards. The longer the waiting period, the more energy consumed. In Fig. 5(a), the comparison of energy consumption among Wi-Fi, Bluetooth and Mix connection in Synchronous mode is demonstrated. The graph shows that the energy of a rule using Mix connection consumes slightly more energy than that using Wi-Fi and Bluetooth connections; the energy consumption of a rule using Wi-Fi is approximately 1.11 times slightly higher than that using Bluetooth connection. The similar trend is shown in Fig. 5(b) in which the average power is 1.14 times more likely to be consumed by Wi-Fi than by Bluetooth connection' with Asynchronous operation. From the experiments, we can see that whether the method is synchronous or asynchronous, the total rate of approximate power spent is not much different. Compared with Wi-Fi and Bluetooth, Mix connection spends the most energy, whereas Bluetooth consumes the least. It should also be noted that lots of power is spent on display, accounting for around 60–90 % of the total energy. Further, the rate of energy consumption is congruent with the total amount of waiting time. Simply said, the longer we wait for crowd responses, the more power is consumed. However, Fig. 5 (c), (d) and (e) shows the energy consumption between Synchronous and Asynchronous execution. With increasing waiting period in every 5 min, the energy consumption per rule of Synchronous version grows reasonably around 1.32, 1.36 and 1.29 times more than the energy consumption per rule of Asynchronous operation among Wi-Fi, Bluetooth and Mix communication connections respectively. According to the second experiment, we designed simple linear energy consumption models for each type of execution modes and communication technologies. Those models will be explained next.

The Third Phase: Energy Consumption Models. Based on the measurements above, we constructed a simple (linear) energy consumption model. Table 1 shows energy consumption functions per rule with respect to the waiting period when using Bluetooth, Wi-Fi and Mix communication with different execution methods. Regarding the second experiment, these formulas have been designed in order to predict the power usage of a *LogicCrowd* program given the waiting period/expiry conditions in its crowd predicates. It means that these functions can estimate the power (denoted by y),

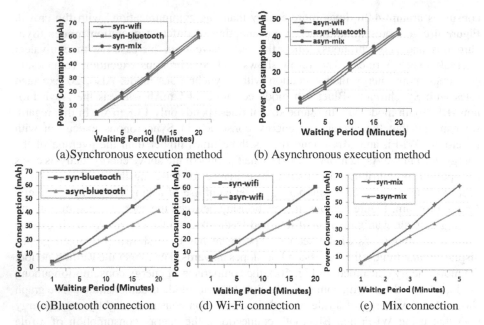

Fig. 5. The relationship between energy consumption and waiting period/expiry in different types of execution methods and communication technologies, x-axis is waiting period (minutes); y-axis is power consumption (milliamps per hour).

Table 1. Energy consumption functions per rule with respect to the waiting period when using Bluetooth, Wi-Fi and Mix communication in different execution methods.

Connections	Synchronous execution	Asynchronous execution
Wi-Fi	$y = 2.905\ T + 2.150$	$y = 2.038\ T + 2.321$
Bluetooth	$y = 2.922\ T + 0.483$	$y = 2.040\ T + 0.855$
Mix	$y = 2.991\ T + 2.748$	$y = 2.047\ T + 3.652$

which is consumed when using a particular communication technology with a particular execution method for a waiting period of T minutes.

Functions, as mentioned above, can predict the energy usage for a rule with one crowd predicate. The functions can be obtained for any Android device via a set of benchmark measurements as we have done above on our test device. To predict the energy usage for a group of crowd predicates, we created the applicable formulas as shown in Table 2. Synchronous functions from Table 1 can only be applied to these formulas. Because they are working sequentially without any parallel extensions, the energy usage of rules could be then estimated one by one. On the other hand, Asynchronous execution method is running in parallel without being blocked by incomplete processing of a crowd predicate. Hence, a function for Asynchronous method has been developed as shown in Table 2. This function can be used to calculate the power of battery (i.e. y) which is consumed when using N_{WF} rules of Wi-Fi, N_{BT} rules of

Table 2. Energy consumption functions with respect to a group of crowd predicates

Execution modes	Connections	Functions
Synchronous	Wi-Fi	$y = \sum_{i=1}^{N}(2.905T_i + 2.150)$
	Bluetooth	$y = \sum_{i=1}^{N}(2.922T_i + 0.483)$
	Mix	$y = \sum_{i=1}^{N}(2.991T_i + 2.748)$
Asynchronous		$y = 0.537\ N_{BT} + 0.562\ N_{WF} + 0.754\ N_{MIX} + 2.01\ T_{MAX} - 0.446$

Bluetooth and N_{MIX} rules of Mix connections for a waiting period of T_{MAX} minutes. In order to possibly verify our energy consumption model, we made additional measurements and compared the obtained results with the results calculated with the energy consumption functions from Tables 1 and 2. For instance, if we execute the rule which the expiry crowd condition is 30 min by using Wi-Fi with Synchronous mode, according to Table 1 and the following function $y = 2.905\ T + 2.150$, for T = 30, we spend 89.3 mAh of the battery. Measurements in a real world environment showed that the rule consumed around 88.821 mAh of energy, which is similar to the energy consumption calculated by using the functions from Table 1.

Another verification example is that if we execute the rules which have 1 rule for Wi-Fi, 2 rules for Bluetooth and 4 rules for Mix connection with Asynchronous method and 5 min of maximum waiting period, according to Table 2 and the following function $y = 0.537\ N_{BT} + 0.562\ N_{WF} + 0.754\ N_{MIX} + 2.01\ T_{MAX} - 0.446$, for $N_{BT} = 1$, $N_{WF} = 2$, $N_{MIX} = 4$, $T_{MAX} = 5$, the power consumed is 14.256 mAh. Real measurements showed the rule consumed around 14.375 mAh; which is not much different from the energy consumption estimated from the functions in Table 2.

The Fourth Phase: Extensions to the _LogicCrowd_ Metainterpreter. The proposed models in the 3rd phase have been deployed here to manage energy consumption of _LogicCrowd_ programs. In this phase, we present the algorithm implemented in _LogicCrowd_ by computing the energy budget corresponding to a certain battery lifetime. We modify the _LogicCrowd_'s meta-interpreter to use the energy estimations during run-time to monitor application workload and adapt its behavior dynamically to save energy. The estimated power per crowd goal/rule for each network connection with a particular execution method is estimated via Table 1. Managing the energy usage of _LogicCrowd_ program can be defined as follows. $E_{crowd(i)}(t_i)$ denotes the energy consumption of a crowd predicate with waiting period of time t_i, where i is six different aspects of querying the crowd (as mentioned in Table 1), where $i \in \{syn - bt, syn - wf, syn - mix, asyn - bt, asyn - wf, asyn - mix\}$. $E_{current}$ denotes the current energy level based on the current battery power remaining. Suppose that the _energy budget β_ (%) is a user's policy of energy usage allowed for the _LogicCrowd_ programs, i.e., a percentage of $E_{current}$. To manage energy consumption of _LogicCrowd_ applications and enhance battery performance, we use the condition given as follows: $E_{crowd(i)}(t_i) \leq \beta(\%) \times E_{current}$. Then, the crowd predicate goal is allowed to proceed only when the energy estimated for that crowd predicate, i.e. $E_{crowd(i)}$ at t_i minutes, is less than or equal to the amount of energy budgeted, i.e., $\beta E_{current}$. For example, assume that the mobile user specified an energy budget of 25 % of the current phone's battery level and the current battery power $E_{current}$ is 1200 mAh. When evaluating a rule with a crowd predicate under Synchronous execution using Mix network connection with a one hour waiting time, the energy consumed is estimated to be 182.2 mAh, which is less than the energy budget (300 mAh). As a result the system then continues to process this rule, and the crowd goal is allowed to proceed. In contrast, if the estimated energy of this **rule** is greater than the energy budget, the rule will be skipped and the system will stop the process in order to maintain the battery energy, **thereby** managing the energy spent on the application. This algorithm and the modified rules in the meta-interpreter are as shown below.

Define $G :- g_1, g_2, g_b ..., g_n$ where g_i is sub-goal in Prolog.
    β where the energy budget (%)
for each g_i **do**
    if g_i is a crowd predicate **then**
        check for crowd's conditions
        $j \leftarrow$ (execution mode and connection type)
        where $j \in$ {syn-bt,syn-wf,syn-mx,asyn-bt,
            asyn-wf,asyn-mx}
        $t_j \leftarrow$ expiry
        compute energy consumption = $E_{crowd(j)}(t_j)$
        get current energy level = $E_{current}$
        if $E_{crowd(j)}(t_j) \leq (\beta \times E_{current})$ **then** evaluate g_i
        else message "Not enough energy."
            break

```
    .
    .
    .
synproc(Askcrowd,Result):-
    checkcond(TypeQuestion,…,Expiry),
    enough_energy(syn,Askto,Expiry),
    askcrowd(Askcrowd,…,QuestionID),
    egistercallbacksyn(QuestionID,…, Result).

asynproc(Askcrowd,Result):-
    checkcond(TypeQuestion,…,Expiry),
    enough_energy(asyn,Askto,Expiry),
    askcrowd(Askcrowd,…,QuestionID),
    registercallbacksyn(Askcrowd,…,Result).
    .
    .
    .
```

---

4 Related Work

CrowdDB [3] and Deco [4] proposed extensions, in different aspects, to established query language and processing techniques in order to integrate human input for processing queries that a normal database system cannot answer. A common approach in such studies is to design small extensions to SQL so that the crowd can participate in the process of SQL queries. Crowd4U [5] leveraged a declarative platform for database abstraction by extending CyLog to issue open queries to the crowd. In *LogicCrowd*, we, however, propose an alternative declarative style of programming for crowd-sourcing which leverages on Prolog and is more expressive than simple crowd SQL queries and interfaces with social media and peer-to-peer networks in order to use crowdsourced data within logic programs. Balasubramanian et al. [6] measured energy consumption when using GSM, 3G, and Wi-Fi, showing that 3G and WiFi have high tail energy use at the end of data transfer. Xiao et al. [7] investigated energy consumed in mobile applications for video streaming, reporting that Wi-Fi used energy more efficiently than 3G. The work on VoIP applications over Wi-Fi based mobile phones [8] showed that using a power saving mode in Wi-Fi accompanied with intelligent scanning techniques for networks can reduce consumed energy. Our focus is, however, on the development of novel energy-efficient algorithms for managing energy consumption in *LogicCrowd* applications that use Wi-Fi and Bluetooth.

5   Conclusion

We have presented *LogicCrowd*, a logic-programming language for declarative mobile crowdsourcing, providing a practical and principled approach for query evaluation to involve the crowd. We also conducted an energy analysis of *LogicCrowd* programs, using the findings for strategically selecting the most appropriate energy-related conditions for execution, and to design a simple energy consumption model for *Logic-Crowd* on Android phones. We showed how to manage the energy consumption of *LogicCrowd* programs by implementing the notion of computing with an energy budget via an extension of the *LogicCrowd* meta-interpreter.

References

1. Howe, J.: The rise of crowdsourcing. Wired Mag. **14**, 1–4 (2006)
2. Phuttharak, J., Loke, S.W.: LogicCrowd: a declarative programming platform for mobile crowdsourcing. In: Proceedings of the 12th IEEE International Conference on Ubiquitous Computing and Communications (IUCC-2013), Melbourne, Australia. IEEE (2013)
3. Franklin, M.J., Kossmann, D., Kraska, T., Ramesh, S., Xin, R.: CrowdDB: answering queries with crowdsourcing. In: SIGMOD Conference, pp. 61–72 (2011)
4. Parameswaran, A.G., Park, H., Garcia-Molina, H., Polyzotis, N., Widom, J.: Deco: declarative crowdsourcing. In: Proceedings of the 21st ACM International Conference on Information and Knowledge Management, Hawaii, USA, pp. 1203–1212. ACM (2012)
5. Morishima, A., Shinagawa, N., Mitsuishi, T., Aoki, H., Fukusumi, S.: CyLog/Crowd4U: a declarative platform for complex data-centric crowdsourcing. Proc. VLDB Endow. **5**, 1918–1921 (2012)
6. Balasubramanian, N., Balasubramanian, A., Venkataramani, A.: Energy consumption in mobile phones: a measurement study and implications for network applications. In: Proceedings of the 9th ACM SIGCOMM Conference on Internet Measurement, pp. 280–293 (2009)
7. Yu, X., Kalyanaraman, R.S., Yla-Jaaski, A.: Energy consumption of mobile YouTube: quantitative measurement and analysis. In: Proceedings of the 2nd International Conference on Next Generation Mobile Applications, Services and Technologies, pp. 61–69 (2008)
8. Gupta, A., Mohapatra, P.: Energy consumption and conservation in WiFi based phones: a measurement-based study. In: Proceedings of the 4th Annual IEEE Communications Society Conference on Sensor, Mesh and Ad Hoc Communications and Networks, pp. 122–131 (2007)

Types in Their Prime: Sub-typing of Data in Resource Constrained Environments

Klaas Thoelen[✉], Davy Preuveneers, Sam Michiels, Wouter Joosen, and Danny Hughes

iMinds-DistriNet, KU Leuven, 3001 Leuven, Belgium
klaas.thoelen@cs.kuleuven.be

Abstract. Sub-typing of data improves reuse and allows for reasoning at different levels of abstraction; however, it is seldom applied in resource constrained environments. The key reason behind this is the increase in overhead that is caused by including hierarchical information in data types as compared to a flat list. Where hierarchical data typing is used, it is often represented using verbose textual identifiers or numerical encodings that are suboptimal with regards to space. In this paper, we present an encoding function for hierarchically typed information, based on the properties of prime numbers. It provides a compact representation of types, fast subsumption testing even on resource constrained platforms and support for the evolution of the data type hierarchy. We demonstrate the feasibility of our approach on two representative communication models in constrained environments; a publish/subscribe event bus and a RESTful application protocol. We evaluate the performance of our encoding function and show that it has limited overhead compared to a flat list of data types and that this overhead is outweighed by reduced memory and communication overhead once applied.

Keywords: Sub-typing · Constrained environments · Prime numbers

1 Introduction

Resource constrained networked systems that operate in dynamic environments often require frequent discovery and updating of information flows. Consider an environmental comfort level app on a smart phone that integrates with a smart office environment. For every change of room, the app needs to discover and connect to locally available sensor data sources. In current systems, these data sources are typically typed using a *flat-list* ordering (e.g. temperature, humidity, CO_2), which requires the individual discovery and use of each data source. An alternative practice is to arrange these types into a *hierarchy* that specifies *is-a* relationships (i.e. subsumption) between its constituent elements. This allows for reasoning over groups of elements, called *sub-types*, which are collectively represented by a more abstract element, called a *super-type*. Discovery and data retrieval can consequentially be simplified; e.g. by specifying the more abstract

© Institute for Computer Sciences, Social Informatics and Telecommunications Engineering 2014
I. Stojmenovic et al. (Eds.): MOBIQUITOUS 2013, LNICST 131, pp. 250–261, 2014.
DOI: 10.1007/978-3-319-11569-6_20

sensor data type during discovery instead of the aforementioned specific data types. As such, this results in a reduction of required configuration actions as they can be grouped on a more abstract level. Additionally, it relieves the developer from the full details of the often complex data flows and more clearly reveals the general principles and goals of the application.

The nature of resource constrained environments however poses some requirements as to how sub-typing is provided. First, resource constraints require a compact and efficient solution: (i) storage of sub-typing information should be limited to only locally relevant information, (ii) exchange of that information should occur in a compact manner, and (iii) sub-type testing should require limited computation. Secondly, in order to accomodate changes to applications running on a long-term infrastructure, it is necessary that changes to the hierarchy can be made with as little overhead and disruption as possible. Specifically, adding new types should not cause changes to the encoding of existing types already in use as this requires that type system updates be sent to all nodes in the network, an expensive and highly disruptive process.

The current state-of-the-art in typing of messages in constrained environments either provides no support for sub-typing [1–4] or sub-optimal support for sub-typing based upon textual identifiers [5,6] or simple numerical encoding techniques [7–9]. The verbosity of current approaches holds little advantage in constrained machine-to-machine environments.

Inspired by the encoding proposed in [8], we present an hierarchical type encoding function that is optimized for Class 1 [10] constrained devices ($\sim$10 kB RAM, $\sim$100 kB Flash). The encoding function exploits the properties of prime numbers and has been specifically re-designed to work within the mentioned constraints. Specifically, we (i) increase the compactness of type encodings, (ii) simplify subsumption testing and (iii) reduce the amount of in-network information needed to perform those tests. We demonstrate the general applicability of sub-typing in both a distributed publish/subscribe based event bus and on top of a RESTful application protocol. Evaluation of the encoding function and both applications show that the encoding has limited overhead compared to a flat list of data types and that this overhead is outweighed by reduced memory and communication overhead once applied.

The remainder of this paper is structured as follows. We describe the encoding function in Sect. 2 and evaluate it in Sect. 3. Two exemplary applications are described and evaluated in Sect. 4. Section 5 discusses related work and we conclude in Sect. 6.

2   Arranging Data in a Hierarchy

The structure of data hierarchies and the encoding function need to be well adapted to the dynamics and constraints of the environments under scope. E.g. in smart offices, the deployed infrastructure often hosts multiple concurrent applications which are subject to changing requirements. This drives evolution of the data hierarchy which therefore needs to provide meaningful abstraction levels with future extensions of the data set in mind. Driven by both our experience in building sensor network applications [11,12] and restrictions imposed by underlying systems [5], we restrict the data hierarchies we support to *single-inheritance* structures only. As in practice this has shown to be sufficiently expressive, we trade-off its support and expressiveness with increased compaction.

Once a hierarchy is in place, an encoding function is used to represent the hierarchical information to allow efficient subsumption testing. With resource constraints in mind, we highlight the following requirements for such a function:

– **Compact representation.** A compact representation means that a data identifier must contain all necessary sub-typing information in an encoding that uses the least amount of bytes possible.
– **Efficient subsumption testing.** Subsumption testing should require (i) minimal computation and (ii) minimal storage of hierarchical information.
– **Conflict-free incremental encoding.** Incremental encoding allows the addition of new data into the hierarchy at any time without requiring the recomputation of existing data identifiers.

To meet these requirements, we adapt our previous encoding function presented in [8]. By restricting the hierarchies to *single-inheritance* structures, we drastically increase the compaction. This results in reduced memory and communication overhead and simplifies subsumption testing; as our encodings fit standard supported integer types, we can use standard operations and no longer require additional logic for subsumption testing as in our prior work.

2.1   Prime Number Assignment and Encoding

Our encoding function is based on the multiplication of prime numbers. As shown in Fig. 1, a prime number is assigned to each data item or vertex in the tree. Once this is done, the vertex's identifier is set to the multiplication of its own prime with the primes of its ancestors; or consequentially, the multiplication of its own prime with the identifier of its parent. Following from the definition of prime numbers, this causes the identifiers to be divisible (i.e. without remainder) only by the identifiers of their ancestors. The subsumption test that we apply to test whether vertex A subsumes vertex B ($B <: A$) is thus to check whether the modulo operation of their two identifiers is equal to zero. More formally:

$$B <: A \Leftrightarrow id_B \bmod id_A = 0$$

By restricting the hierarchy to a single-inheritance tree, we can introduce a number of optimizations to the original prime number assignment in [8]. Primarily, we reuse prime numbers in the various sub-trees of the hierarchy. This means that more often identifiers are factorizations of the lower-value prime numbers and consequentially have a lower value themselves. Secondly, as there is only a single root, we can assign its *prime* the value of *1*. Although not a prime number by definition, for our purposes this is of no concern whilst again increasing the compactness of the encoding.

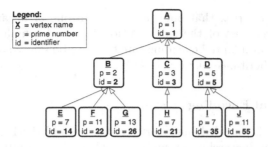

Fig. 1. Hierarchy encoding with reuse of prime numbers.

The prime number assignment algorithm works as follows. Starting at the root of the tree, we assign each vertex a prime number in a top-down and breadth-first manner. The children of each vertex are assigned prime numbers that follow the largest prime number used by that vertex or its siblings. In general, primes are thus reused across disjunct sub-trees, like the ones rooted by B, C and D in Fig. 1. As a result will each subtree contain the only identifiers which are divisible by its root's identifier. In Fig. 1 for instance, only the descendants of node B have identifiers which yield zero for modulo two.

We can prove that our prime number assignment algorithm conserves the subsumption relationships as follows. Assume a set of vertices in a hierarchy $\chi = \{C_1, C_2, ..., C_n\}$. We define $\Gamma(C_i)$ as the union of C_i's assigned prime and the set of primes it inherits from its ancestors. The encoding function that determines a vertex' identifier can then be written as:

$$\gamma(C_i) = \prod_j p_j \text{ with } p_j \in \Gamma(C_i) \tag{1}$$

As proven in [8], the subsumption relation between two vertices C_1 and C_2 can then be defined as:

$$C_1 \text{ subsumes } C_2 \Leftrightarrow \gamma(C_2) \bmod \gamma(C_1) = 0 \tag{2}$$

Now, by definition of subsumption; C_1 can only subsume C_2 if there is a subtree rooted at C_1 which contains C_2 (possibly as root). Given our prime number assignment algorithm, this means that:

$$\Gamma(C_1) \subset \Gamma(C_2) \tag{3}$$

By definition of the encoding function (1), each vertex's identifier is a multiple of each element in the set of primes it inherits. Under single inheritance, reusing primes thus does not influence the correctness of the subsumption test, as it will succeed only in case the set of primes of the more abstract vertex C_1 is a subset of the set of primes of the other vertex C_2, as stated in (3). However, under multiple inheritance and reuse of prime numbers, this equation would not hold. In that case the set of primes of a multiple inheriting vertex can also be a superset of a vertex that only inherits from one of its ancestors, hereby breaking the correctness of the subsumption test under multiple inheritance. Consequentially, our adapted encoding function can be safely applied, yet to the intended single inheritance hierarchies only.

2.2 Incremental Encoding

Once a hierarchy is encoded, new vertices can be added without the need to fully re-encode the hierarchy. To support evolution, we apply an *append-only* strategy in which new leafs can always be added to the hierarchy, yet existing vertices are never removed from it. The primary reason for this strategy, is that removing deprecated vertices also releases their primes. Reusing those primes for new vertices could lead to false positives during subsumption testing when running applications still refer to the deprecated vertices. Therefore, we abandon the deprecated vertices by no longer using them, but retain them as a placeholder for previously used primes. By exception, a hierarchy can be fully re-encoded to eliminate deprecated vertices. This should however not be done frequently as it requires an expensive update of all software referring to the hierarchy.

When adding a new leaf, some guidelines as to prime number assignment have to be respected to guarantee the subsumption relations. Two cases can be distinguished:

1. **As a sibling to siblings without offspring.** This is the easiest case as we only need to take the siblings into account. The prime to be assigned is the prime that follows the largest prime of the siblings. E.g. in Fig. 1, adding a new leaf K as a child of D will be assigned *13* as prime.
2. **As a sibling to siblings with offspring.** In this case, we need to take the offspring of the siblings into account. E.g. in Fig. 1, a new vertex K as a child of A, and thus a sibling to B, C and D, will be assigned *17* as prime.

Such an addition might thus involve a tree-traversal phase to determine the set of primes used in a certain subtree. However, as this is performed outside of the resource constrained environment, it is of a lesser concern. Adding a leave thus does not require a recomputation of other identifiers and the new hierarchy is fully backwards compatible with the old one.

2.3 Knowledge Distribution of the Hierarchical Structure

During operational use, the full hierarchy and its encoding remain off-line representations that are created, maintained and referenced to in the more resource-rich back-end. Inside the constrained network, each node only requires hierarchical information about the data that it uses and thus does not require full knowledge of the hierarchy.

We furthermore reduced the information required for subsumption testing to only the identifiers. The original encoding function still results in large identifiers

(> 8 bytes), requiring custom support for efficient modulo calculation. Therefore, it uses a more elaborate subsumption test, which uses both the identifiers
and primes to first rule out subsumption based on a number of theorems before
actually performing the modulo operation. The increased compaction however
does allow the use of the standard modulo operation on most platforms and
thus eliminates the primes from subsumption testing. Besides reducing processing overhead, this also reduces memory and communication overhead as only
identifiers and not primes need to be stored and exchanged.

3   Evaluation of the Encoding Function

We evaluate our encoding function by (i) showing its improved compaction, and
(ii) the limited processing overhead of the subsumption test.

We evaluate the compaction of our encoding function by comparing the number of bytes it requires to encode identifiers with those required by the original
encoding function. We generated artificial hierarchies of 0 up to 8 levels, with
each vertex having 0 up to 8 children. Figure 2 shows the number of bytes that
were needed to encode each tree's largest identifier. The lower inclination of the
graphs in Fig. 2b clearly show that by reusing prime numbers, identifiers can be
encoded more compact. While the original encoding requires up to 14 bytes, our
version only needs 6 bytes at the most. On average, the identifiers of all tested
hierarchies require 5 bytes for the original encoding and only 3 bytes in the
adapted version; a substantial benefit in constrained environments with small
payload sizes and limited memory.

The increased compaction is confirmed by the encoding of the more realistic
hierarchy used in the *smart-office* scenario discussed in Sect. 4.1. Table 1 shows
the reduction in primes used, compared to the original encoding. This ultimately
results in more compact encoded identifiers. Also the density, i.e. the percentage
of integers used as identifiers up to the largest identifier, is higher.

We evaluated the performance of subsumption testing on a Zigduino-r1
sensor node (16 MHz, 128 kB Flash, 16 kB RAM) [13]. Pair-wise subsumption

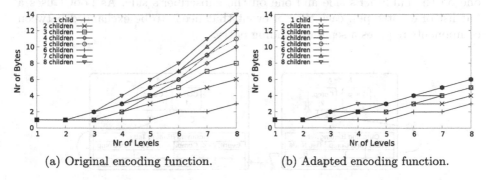

(a) Original encoding function.   (b) Adapted encoding function.

Fig. 2. The adapted encoding function substantially reduces the number of bytes
required to encode identifiers.

Table 1. Comparison of the encoding functions for the smart office hierarchy.

	Nr of vertices	Nr of primes	Largest id	Avg nr of bytes per id	Density
Original	112	112	4481481	3	0,002 %
Adapted	112	24	30914	2	0,36 %

testing among all identifiers in the smart-office hierarchy resulted in an average of 22,3 µs per test. This included deserialization from a variable-length byte-array representation. Pair-wise equality testing, as would be performed using a flat-list ordering, resulted in an average of 4,1 µs per test. This increase in processing time is considered acceptable as it is less than an order of magnitude and is accompanied with the benefits of sub-typing as discussed in the following section.

4   Sub-typing in Exemplary Applications

We applied the proposed encoding function on two representative communication models used in constrained environments. The benefits are distinct in each case. On top of a publish/subscribe event bus, sub-typing results in decreased configuration overhead; while a RESTful application protocol primarily benefits from the compact representation achieved by encoding.

4.1   Sub-typing in a Publish/Subscribe Event Bus

In the *Loosely-coupled Component Infrastructure* (LooCI) [4] sub-typing can be applied to identify events exchanged over a publish/subscribe event bus. LooCI's runtime reconfigurable event bus allows to establish bindings between the interfaces of components. Those bindings are persisted as entries in binding tables which guide the dispatching of published events as shown in Fig. 3. Distributed bindings between components on different nodes consist of two sub-bindings; one on the publisher's side and one on the subscriber's side. As LooCI uses a flat list of event types, each type of event that needs to be exchanged between components requires a separate binding entry.

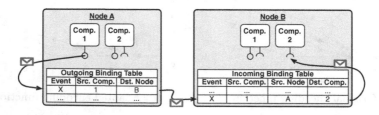

Fig. 3. Conceptual drawing of LooCI's event dispatching based on distributed binding tables.

The benefit of applying event sub-typing in LooCI is in the reduction of binding actions. Using sub-typing, bindings can be created on a more abstract level, allowing groups of similar events to be dispatched based on a single binding. This is important as every binding action results in messages that are disseminated in the network to update the binding tables of the respective nodes; one message for a local binding, two messages in case of a distributed binding.

Evaluation. Specifically, we applied sub-typing to a *smart-office* application. This features an office in which desks, doors and windows are equipped with sensor nodes that monitor the environment and presence of people. Data is collected and pre-processed on sensor nodes and forwarded to a back-end for further processing. PC and smartphone clients subscribe to the back-end for updates about the working comfort and security conditions (air quality, unauthorized access, etc.) in the office. Due to space limitations we refer to [14] for more details about the application's composition and event type hierarchy.

As shown in Table 1, the smart-office event type hierarchy includes 112 event types, with the largest identifier being 30914. On average this requires 2 bytes for encoding, which we precede by a one byte length indicator to support variable-length encoding. The resulting average of 3 bytes per identifier is close to the fixed 2 bytes LooCI uses by default to represent flat-listed even types. This small increase is more than outweighed by the resulting decrease in binding actions that are needed to compose the smart-office application. Using default LooCI, 55 binding commands were needed, which by applying sub-typing is reduced to only 35. This is a 36 % reduction in messages disseminated into the network to configure event dispatching. This reduction is substantial and subject to a multiplication effect due to frequent reconfiguration in dynamic networks.

The described results are of course application specific and bigger applications might lead to larger event hierarchies and thus larger identifiers. On the other hand, we expect larger applications to benefit more from sub-typing. In Sect. 3 we already showed that the accompanying overhead of large hierarchies remains practical. While the reduction of binding commands depends on the hierarchy's structure, overall, sub-typing will never increase the number of binding commands required and when applied sensibly can reduce the amount of commands extensively.

4.2   Sub-typing on Top of a RESTful Application Protocol

In RESTful protocols, the proposed encoding function can be used to more compactly identify hierarchically organized sources of information, called *resources*. Resources are typically identified using a Uniform Resource Identifier (URI) that contains a hierarchically structured node-local path to the resource, formatted as a human-readable string. We propose to more compactly encode these resource paths using our prime-based encoding.

Designed for constrained environments, the Constrained Application Protocol (CoAP) [5] aims at realizing a REST architecture for the most constrained

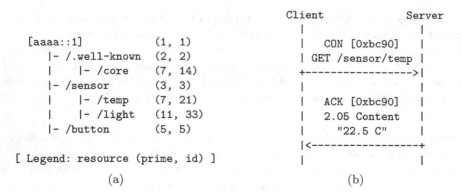

Fig. 4. A hierarchy of resources on a CoAP server with address `aaaa::1` (a), and a GET request for the `/sensor/temp` resource with matching response (b).

devices in machine-to-machine (M2M) applications. Figure 4a presents an example set of resources deployed on a sensor node. To interact with these, COAP supports the four traditional REST methods: GET, POST, PUT, DELETE. E.g. a GET method with URI `coap://[aaaa::1]/sensor/temp` can be issued to request temperature data from a CoAP server (see Fig. 4b).

We can make two important observations with regards to resource paths:

1. The string representations of resource paths form excessive identifiers that cause considerable memory and communication overhead. While practically beneficial, human-readable strings are not vitally important in a M2M environment where direct human interaction is not a primary concern.
2. Hierarchically organizing CoAP resources brings structure and thus allows *super*-resources to delegate requests to their *sub*-resources. The hierarchical information contained in the resource path is thus of practical importance.

Both observations motivate the application of our encoding function on CoAP resource paths. While retaining hierarchical information, resource paths can be represented much more compactly. This reduces memory overhead since each resource no longer involves storage of a lengthy human-readable resource path. Communication overhead is primarily reduced during intensive interactions such as CoAP resource discovery. This is executed using block-wise transfer of the description of all primary resources on a node. In case the description does not fit in a single block, subsequent blocks are requested individually. By reducing the representation of resource paths, the number of blocks can be reduced, thus eliminating not only their transmission, but also those of their respective requests.

Once resource paths are encoded, as in Fig. 4a, the numerical identifiers can be used in two ways. In the first one, a *string*-formatted representation of the identifier replaces the original human-readable path. E.g. the URI `coap://[aaaa::1]/sensor/temp` becomes `coap://[aaaa::1]/21`. The benefit of this variant is that no adaptations to CoAP are required. In the second variant,

Table 2. Comparison of the original and encoded representation sizes of the CoAP resource paths defined in the IPSO Application Framework.

Path representation	Total nr of bytes	Avg nr of bytes per path
Original	499	9,24
Encoded (string)	158	2,93
Encoded (uint)	84	1,53

more compact *uint*-formatted identifiers are used. As this is not compatible with string-formatted URI Paths, a new Option is needed in the CoAP specification that indicates the use of uint-formatted resource path identifiers.

Evaluation. We encoded the set of resource paths specified by the IPSO Application Framework [6], which defines the interfaces of 47 REST resources. Table 2 compares the original human-readable resource paths with our two encoded variants. We evaluate the total number of bytes required to represent all resources and the average number of bytes per resource this results in. While the resource paths in [6] are already fairly compact and only partially human-readable, encoding them still results in an extensive reduction in representation size; 68 % for the string-formatted representation and 83 % for the uint variant.

The added benefit of this reduction becomes apparent during CoAP resource discovery. E.g. human-readable versions of all resource paths consume 49 bytes in a discovery reply by the server in Fig. 4a. In contrast, using the averages in Table 2, only 16 bytes and 12 bytes are needed when using string- and uint-formatted encodings, respectively. This optimization can lead to considerable reduction in communication in dynamic resource constrained environments.

5   Related Work

We discuss related work in terms of alternative encoding functions and the application of sub-typing in publish/subscribe systems and RESTful protocols for constrained environments.

Sub-typing and related encoding functions have been studied in many areas like programming languages, database management, knowledge representation, policy enforcement, etc. For a detailed discussion, we refer to a survey of existing techniques in our prior work [15]. The solutions presented there support multi-inheritance hierarchies and often lack (efficient) support for incremental encoding. Based on our experience, we traded-off multi-inheritance support for increased compactness, as discussed in Sect. 2.

The publish/subscribe messaging pattern is often used in distributed computing in both constrained and traditional environments. While in traditional environments sub-typing of messages is a regular feature [16–18], it is typically implemented by reuse of language-provided inheritance (e.g. Java), ill-suited for constrained environments. Most related work concerning constrained environments does not discuss message typing [2,3,19]; suggesting a flat list ordering.

DSWare [20] does apply the notion of event hierarchies, but in a different manner; higher-level compound events (e.g. explosion event) are inferred from the detections of a set of lower-level atomic events (e.g. sensor observations). The event hierarchy is thus purely functional and does not represent typing of events. In our prior work [21], we used sub-typing to reduce the energy consumption of event routing based on semantic event information. This solution uses our original encoding function, which is significantly optimized in this paper.

Like the IPSO Alliance [6], the Open Mobile Alliance (OMA) [9] has specified templates of CoAP resources and their organization in a hierarchy. While IPSO uses compact human-readable resource paths, OMA makes use of numerical resource paths that identify resources registered with the OMA Naming Authority (OMNA). While the latter shares our application of non-human-readable resource identifiers, both solutions use less compact resource identifiers than can be realized with our encoding function.

6 Conclusion

As resource constrained environments continue to integrate with the Web and become first-class citizens in mobile and ubiquitous applications, they will be subject to higher degrees of interaction. To facilitate discovery and use of their data sources, sub-typing can be applied to allow reasoning on higher levels of abstraction. Yet, in contrast to the resource constraints at hand, sub-typing implies overhead to represent the hierarchical relations between types of data.

In this paper, we presented an encoding function for hierarchically typed data that is designed with resource constraints in mind. This encoding function features low overhead both in representation of hierarchical information and subsumption testing. However, this overhead is outweighed by the benefits that are achieved once sub-typing is applied. While on the one hand sub-typing results in reduced reconfiguration overhead in LooCI's publish/subscribe event bus. On the other hand, our encoding allows for more compact representations than the human-readable resource identifiers commonly used in CoAP's RESTful interactions. We can thus conclude that when realized efficiently, the added benefits of sub-typing can be extremely useful in more resource constrained environments.

Acknowledgement. This research is partially supported by the Research Fund, KU Leuven and iMinds (a research institute founded by the Flemish government). The research is conducted in the context of the COMACOD and ADDIS projects.

References

1. Buonadonna, P., Hill, J., Culler, D.: Active message communication for tiny networked sensors. In: Proceedings of the IEEE Conference Infocom 2001 (2001)
2. Souto, E., Guimarães, G., Vasconcelos, G., Vieira, M., Rosa, N., Ferraz, C., Kelner, J.: Mires: a publish/subscribe middleware for sensor networks. Pers. Ubiquitous Comput. **10**(1), 37–44 (2005)

3. Hauer, J.-H., Handziski, V., Köpke, A., Willig, A., Wolisz, A.: A component framework for content-based publish/subscribe in sensor networks. In: Verdone, R. (ed.) EWSN 2008. LNCS, vol. 4913, pp. 369–385. Springer, Heidelberg (2008)
4. Hughes, D., Thoelen, K., Maerien, J., Matthys, N., del Cid Garcia, P.J., Horré, W., Huygens, C., Michiels, S., Joosen, W.: Looci: the loosely-coupled component infrastructure. In: 11th IEEE International Symposium on Network Computing and Applications (NCA), pp. 236–243, August 2012
5. Shelby, Z., Hartke, K., Bormann, C.: Constrained Application Protocol (CoAP). http://tools.ietf.org/html/draft-ietf-core-coap-18
6. Shelby, Z., Chauvenet, C.: The IPSO Application Framework. http://www.ipso-alliance.org/wp-content/media/draft-ipso-app-framework-04.pdf
7. Kovacevic, A., Ansari, J., Mähönen, P.: Nanosd: a flexible service discovery protocol for dynamic and heterogeneous wireless sensor networks, pp. 14–19. IEEE Computer Society, Los Alamitos (2010)
8. Preuveneers, D., Berbers, Y.: Encoding semantic awareness in resource-constrained devices. IEEE Intell. Syst. 23(2), 26–33 (2008)
9. OMA LWM2M. http://technical.openmobilealliance.org/Technical/ release_program/lightweightM2M_v1_0.aspx
10. Bormann, C., Ersue, M., Keranen, A.: Terminology for Constrained Node Networks. http://tools.ietf.org/html/draft-ietf-lwig-terminology-05
11. Hughes, D., Thoelen, K., Horré, W., Matthys, N., del Cid Garcia, P.J., Michiels, S., Huygens, C., Joosen, W., Ueyama, J.: Building wireless sensor network applications with looci. Int. J. Mobile Comput. Multimedia Commun. 2(4), 38–64 (2010)
12. Thoelen, K., Hughes, D., Matthys, N., Fang, L., Dobson, S., Qiang, Y., Bai, W., Man, K.L., Guan, S.-U., Preuveneers, D., Michiels, S., Huygens, C., Joosen, W.: A reconfigurable component model with semantic type system for dynamic wsn applications. J. Internet Serv. Appl. 3(3), 277–290 (2012)
13. Zigduino-r1. http://logos-electro.com/zigduino-r1/
14. http://people.cs.kuleuven.be/~klaas.thoelen/mob2013
15. Preuveneers, D., Berbers, Y.: Prime numbers considered useful: ontology encoding for efficient subsumption testing, Department of Computer Science, K.U.Leuven, Leuven, Belgium, CW Reports CW464, October 2006
16. Esper. http://esper.codehaus.org/index.html
17. Java Messaging Service. http://www.oracle.com/technetwork/java/index-jsp-142945.html
18. Corba Notification Service. http://www.omg.org/spec/
19. Russello, G., Mostarda, L., Dulay, N.: A policy-based publish/subscribe middleware for sense-and-react applications. J. Syst. Softw. 84(4), 638–654 (2011)
20. Li, S., Son, S.H., Stankovic, J.A.: Event detection services using data service middleware in distributed sensor networks. In: Zhao, F., Guibas, L.J. (eds.) IPSN 2003. LNCS, vol. 2634, pp. 502–517. Springer, Heidelberg (2003)
21. Preuveneers, D., Berbers, Y.: μc-semps: energy-efficient semantic publish/ subscribe for battery-powered systems. In: Proceedings of the 7th International ICST Conference on Mobile and Ubiquitous Systems: Computing, Networking and Services, pp. 1–12, December 2010

Privacy-Aware Trust-Based Recruitment in Social Participatory Sensing

Haleh Amintoosi$^{(\boxtimes)}$ and Salil S. Kanhere

The University of New South Wales, Sydney, Australia
{haleha,salilk}@cse.unsw.edu.au

Abstract. The main idea behind social participatory sensing is to leverage social networks as the underlying infrastructure for recruiting social friends to participate in a sensing campaign. Such recruitment requires the transmission of messages (i.e., tasks and contributions) between the requester and participants via routes consisting of social links. When selecting the routes, the recruitment scheme should consider two fundamental factors. The first factor is the level of trustworthiness of a route, which evaluates its reliability to ensure that the integrity of the message is preserved. The second factor is the privacy level of the route, which measures information leakage in the form of disclosure of private information contained in the message by intermediate nodes. The best route will be the route with maximum credibility, i.e., highest trust score and lowest likelihood of privacy breach. In this paper, we propose a privacy-preserving trust-based recruitment framework which is aimed at finding the best route from the requester to the selected participants. We propose to quantify the privacy score of a route by utilising the concept of entropy to measure the level of privacy breach in each intermediate node along the route. The trust score of the route is obtained by multiplying the mutual trust rates of all links along the route. Simulation results demonstrate the efficacy of our framework in terms of recruiting suitable participants through the most secure and trustable routes.

Keywords: Privacy · Trust · Social networks · Participatory sensing

1 Introduction

The widespread prevalence of sensor-rich smartphones has propelled the emergence of a novel sensing paradigm, known as *participatory sensing* [1]. In participatory sensing, a sensing task is defined by the *requester*, and ordinary citizens, called *participants*, volunteer to contribute by using their mobile phones. A plethora of applications have been proposed, ranging from personal health [2,3] and sharing prices of costumer goods [4] to air pollution monitoring [5].

The success of a typical participatory sensing application depends on overcoming several challenges: (i) evaluating the *trustworthiness* of contributions in an effort to weed out low fidelity/quality data (ii) recruiting sufficient number of

© Institute for Computer Sciences, Social Informatics and Telecommunications Engineering 2014
I. Stojmenovic et al. (Eds.): MOBIQUITOUS 2013, LNICST 131, pp. 262–275, 2014.
DOI: 10.1007/978-3-319-11569-6_21

well-suited participants and (iii) providing a secure and *privacy-aware* environment to contribute. To address the issue of participant sufficiency, one proposed idea is to leverage online social networks as the underlying infrastructure for participatory sensing applications [6]. The resulting paradigm, known as *social participatory sensing*, enables the usage of friendship relations for the identification and recruitment of participants.

In order to address the challenge of assessing contribution trustworthiness, we proposed a trust framework for social participatory sensing system [7], which attempts to recruit social friends as participants. The trust server separately evaluates the quality of contribution and the trustworthiness of participant, which are then combined via a fuzzy inference engine to arrive at a trustworthiness score for the contribution. To allow for better selection of well-suited participants, we extended this framework in [8] such that a reputation score is calculated for each participant by using the PageRank algorithm. In our most recent work [9], we proposed a trust-based recruitment framework to address the challenge of recruiting sufficient well-suited participants by leveraging multi-hop friendship relations.

The central focus of above discussed research is on addressing the first two aforementioned challenges, which are related to the fundamental question of trust without much regard to the other equally important issue of privacy. In other words, we assumed that all participants are trustworthy and do not attempt to infer others' private information. This assumption, however, is not realistic. There are always people who are curious about others' private information and may try to access sensitive information such as a person's whereabouts, by eavesdropping the private conversations. Without sufficient assurance about safeguarding their private information, it is likely that participants may be dissuaded from contributing in participatory sensing tasks. It is thus logical that we address these privacy issues, which is precisely the focus of this paper.

In order to preserve the privacy of participant's information which is embedded in exchanged messages, it is desirable to consider potential privacy breaches in selecting the route between the requester and participant. In other words, when multiple routes exist, a reasonable approach is to select the most secure and trustable route in a way that the likelihood of a privacy breach in intermediate nodes is minimal. The information may itself be a sensitive attribute such as participant's address or his telephone number, or it may be a combination of quasi-identifying attributes which would readily allow a malicious intermediary to infer the corresponding sensitive information. For example, according to a famous study [10] of the 1990 census data, 87 % of the US population can be uniquely identified by gender, ZIP code and full date of birth. Access to such private information thus naturally results in leakage of user privacy. So, the need for protecting such personal information is eminent.

A trivial solution to preserve privacy is encryption (e.g., HTTPS) which can be used to secure communication channels and protect against eavesdropping. However, this facility is not widely used by most online social networks. Only 3 of the top 5 online social networking services currently use HTTPS. Moreover, they only make use of this security measure to protect login credentials. The rest of the communication happens unencrypted and is visible to everyone along the communication path [11]. The primary reason for not using HTTPS for all communication is to minimize the hardware and connectivity costs. Moreover, public key cryptography needs additional computations and components for key management, which makes it computationally expensive for multi-hop social networks with extremely large number of nodes. To sum up, encryption-based methods are most likely too complicated or expensive for general adoption.

In this paper, we address the challenge of privacy in social participatory sensing systems by proposing a privacy-preserving recruitment framework. In fact, we aim at removing the barriers against active participation by assuring the users about the privacy preservation of their sensitive information along the communication routes. In particular, as an integration with our previous work [9], for each potential route between the requester and participant, we quantify the *credibility* of the route by quantifying and combining the trust and privacy scores of the route. The route with maximum credibility is selected for message exchange. To quantify the privacy score, we use *entropy* to quantify the privacy leak of sensitive information at each intermediate node. To quantify the trust score, we assume that the friendship links are weighted by mutual trust ratings, which is a dynamic value and is continuously updated by parameters such as the trustworthiness of the provided contributions. The trust score of the route is obtained by multiplying the mutual trust rates of all links along the route. A credibility score is then computed by combining the trust and privacy scores, which is then used to select the best routes between the requester and participant. We investigate two different methods for combining these scores to arrive at a final credibility score: the first one is *geometric mean* which simply is the root square of the multiplication of these two parameters, and the second one is *fuzzy combination*, which leverages fuzzy inference engine to address different states of such combination.

The rest of the paper is organised as follows. Related work is discussed in Sect. 2. We present the details of our architecture in Sect. 3. The routing algorithm is described in Sect. 4. Simulation results are discussed in Sect. 5. Finally, Sect. 6 concludes the paper.

2   Related Work

To the best of our knowledge, the issue of privacy in social participatory sensing has not been addressed in prior work. Moreover, prior work on privacy in participatory sensing such as [12,13] address orthogonal issues which do not cover the social aspects and relations that are inherent in social participatory sensing. As such, we discuss related research focusing on social based routing in literature and then specifically look at the privacy-preserving routing algorithms.

Social-Based Routing. Recent studies have focused on mobile social networks and analyzed the social network properties of these networks to assist the design of efficient routing algorithms. In [14], the social similarity (to detect nodes

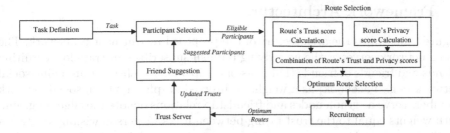

Fig. 1. Framework architecture

that are part of the same community) and ego-centric betweenness (to identify bridging nodes between different communities) has been used as two metrics to increase the performance of routing. When two nodes encounter each other, they calculate the joint utility function comprised of these two metrics for each of their destinations. The message is given to the node having higher utility for the message's destination. In [15], each node is assumed to have a global ranking which denotes the popularity of the node in the entire society, and a local ranking which denotes its popularity within its own community. Messages are forwarded to nodes having higher global ranking until a node in the destination's community is found. Then, messages are forwarded to nodes having higher local ranking within destination's community. Mashhadi et al. [16] combines social network and location information to build an information-dissemination system for mobile devices. In [17], instead of determining social network information from encounter patterns, they use pre-existing social ties.

Privacy-Preserving Routing. In [18], the authors propose a method that leverages a key management system, where users are divided into communities and public-key cryptography is used to secure communication within a community. A major drawback is that community members can observe the routing tables of all other members, resulting in eavesdropping attacks. In the context of opportunistic networks, Shikfa et al. [19] proposed an approach that uses group-based cryptography, using multiple levels of cryptography to prevent data from being accessed by different groups. They concentrate on protecting the application-layer data payload, rather than the routing information. In [20], the authors present methods to improve anonymity within an ad hoc network by compressing and obscuring a packet's routing list. Another popular mechanism is onion routing [21], where packets are routed through a group of collaborating nodes, thus making it difficult to determine the source of a communication. Onion routing, however, does not prevent eavesdropping attacks from intermediate nodes. Moreover, it requires a Public Key Infrastructure (PKI).

In this paper, we aim to propose a privacy-preserving routing algorithm that does not require encryption or PKI. As mentioned in Sect. 1, encryption is not widely supported in online social networks, and is computationally expensive for multi-hop social networks with a large number of members. So it is reasonable and also cost effective to preserve the privacy without relying on encryption.

3   Framework Architecture

Figure 1 illustrates the architecture of the proposed recruitment framework. The social network serves as the underlying publish-subscribe substrate for recruiting friends and friends of friends (FoFs) as participants. We abstract an online social network (e.g., Facebook) as a weighted directed graph, in which, social network members serve as graph nodes and friendship relations denote the edges of graph, with weights equal to the trust rating between users. A person wishing to start a participatory sensing campaign acts as a requester and defines the task, including the specification of task's main requirements such as needed expertise or location. Then, participant selection component crawls the social graph up to L levels (friends and FoFs) to determine eligible participants who can fulfil the task's requirements. The selection is performed by comparing the participants' profile information with the task's requirements.

Next, route selection component traverses the social graph to find the best route from requester to each of eligible participants. We claim that the best route will be the route with highest trustworthiness and highest privacy preservation. To do so, a credibility score, which is the combination of the trust score and privacy score of the route, is calculated (we investigate two different methods, geometric mean and fuzzy, for such combination). In case of multiple routes between the requester and an eligible participant, the route with the highest credibility is chosen. Those eligible participants for whom, the credibility of the route is greater than a predefined threshold are considered as *selected* participants. Once selected, the task is routed along the specified routes and delivered to the selected participants. The same path in reverse is used to transmit contributions back. The trust server then evaluates an objective trust rating for each contribution (which we call it the Trustworthiness of Contribution (ToC)). Based on ToC, mutual trusts between members along the route are updated (more details about the trust server functionality can be found in [7,8]).

Periodically (where a period typically spans a certain number of campaigns), the suggestion component builds a recommended participant group for each requester, containing a list well behaved participants, which is further used for recruitment or friendship establishment. It should be noted that all the computations including the evaluation of the trust and privacy scores is done inside the trust server.

4   Privacy-Preserving Trust-Based Route Selection

Once eligible participants are selected, route selection component finds the best routes to them. To do so, the trust and privacy scores of the route are considered. In the following, we elaborate how these scores are computed.

4.1   Trust Score of the Route

As mentioned in Sect. 3, we assume that the social links are labelled with weights equal to the trust ratings between two parties. If intermediate nodes exist, the trust score of the route is a combination of trust ratings of each pair nodes along the route. We leverage multiplication for the combination since it has been shown in [22] to be an effective strategy for trust propagation. In other words, we assume the set R is the set of all possible routes between the requester and a specific participant. The route R_i ($R_i \in R$) has been defined with (N_{R_i}, E_{R_i}) in which, N_{R_i} is the set of nodes within this route and E_{R_i} is the set of edges of R_i. In that case, the trust score of R_i, denoted by $Trust(R_i)$ is calculated as:

$$Trust(R_i) = \prod_{k=1}^{l} w(e_k), e_k \in E_{R_i} \tag{1}$$

where l is the length of the R_i and $w(e_k)$ is the weight of the edge e_k. $Trust(R_i)$ is in the range of $[0, 1]$.

4.2 Privacy Score of the Route

When discussing about privacy in social networks, it is important to specify what defines failure to preserve privacy. A privacy breach occurs when a piece of sensitive information about an individual is disclosed to an adversary. Traditionally, two types of privacy breaches have been studied: *identity disclosure* and *attribute disclosure*. Identity disclosure occurs when an adversary is able to map a profile in the social network to a specific real-world entity. Attribute disclosure, on the other hand, occurs when an adversary is able to determine the value of a sensitive user attribute, one that the user intended to stay private. There are three sets of personal attributes [23]:

1- Identifying attributes: attributes such as social security number (SSN) which uniquely identify a person. To avoid identity disclosure, identifying attributes should be removed from profiles.

2- Quasi-identifying attributes: a combination of attributes which can identify a person uniquely. It has been observed that 87 % of individuals in the U.S. can be uniquely identified based on their date of birth, gender and zip code [10].

3- Sensitive attributes: those that users tend to keep hidden from the public, such as politic view, location, and sexual orientation.

The messages exchanged between the requester and participant (including task or contribution) may contain private information such as sensitive attributes and quasi-identifiers, which may leak in intermediate nodes. To prevent such privacy leakage, it is reasonable to select the routes which contain intermediate nodes that are least likely to cause privacy breaches.

In order to quantify the privacy leak, we leverage the concept of entropy. Entropy is a measure of the uncertainty in a random variable [24]. In fact, our model aims to maximize the entropy which means the maximization of the unpredictability of information for an adversary node. Higher entropy means better privacy for the information contained inside a message. Since identifying attributes such as SSN are not normally kept in profiles, we assume that privacy leakage may happen if two types of information are leaked: sensitive attributes and quasi-identifiers. With this assumption, we aim at calculating the amount of uncertainty of a node about private information inside a message.

For the intermediate node $m \in N_{R_i}$, we have the following definitions:

Let $S = \{s_1, s_2, s_3, ..., s_k\}$ is the set of sensitive attributes and $Q = \{q_1, q_2, q_3, ..., q_t\}$ is the set of quasi-identifying attributes that may exist in a user's message. We aim at quantifying the privacy leakage of message in the intermediate node m who wishes to know Q in order to uniquely identify the user. So, we first measure the "initial uncertainty" of m about Q. The initial uncertainty, denoted by $H(Q)$ is generally defined using Shannon entropy [24]:

$$H(Q) = -\sum_{i=1}^{t} p(q_i) log(p(q_i)) \tag{2}$$

where $p(q_i)$ is the probability mass function.

Next, we assume the situation where m knows the value of some sensitive values of S from the user. In this case, the uncertainty of m about Q after knowing some information from S, denoted by the "remaining uncertainty" is measured using conditional Shannon entropy:

$$H(Q \mid S) = \sum_{i=1}^{t} p(q_i) H(Q \mid q_i \in S) \tag{3}$$

It is natural to measure the *privacy leakage* ($\mathcal{L}$) of a message by comparing the m's uncertainty about Q, before and after knowing the value from S. So, we use the concept of *mutual information* as: leakage = initial uncertainty − remaining uncertainty [25]. In other words, the privacy leakage ($\mathcal{L}$) of a message is:

$$\mathcal{L} = H(Q) - H(Q \mid S) \tag{4}$$

In general, if n messages have passed through node m, then the amount of privacy leakage in node m, denoted by $\mathcal{L}_m$, is calculated as: $\mathcal{L}_m = \frac{1}{n} \sum_{j=1}^{n} \mathcal{L}_{m,j}$ in which, $\mathcal{L}_{m,j}$ is the privacy leakage of message j in intermediate node m. As this equation shows, $\mathcal{L}_m$ keeps a history of privacy leakage upon each message originator. It is obvious that the privacy score of node m, ($Privacy(m)$), is inversely related to the privacy leakage ($\mathcal{L}_m$) in this node. However, in order to have the privacy score value in the range of $[0, 1]$, we divide the value of $\mathcal{L}_m$ by $log(n)$. The reason is that $H(Q)$ has a value less than $log(n)$. So, the maximum value for $\mathcal{L}_{m,n}$ and $\mathcal{L}_m$ will also be $log(n)$, which results in $\mathcal{L}_m/log(n)$ in the range of $[0, 1]$. To summarize:

$$Privacy(m) = 1 - \frac{\mathcal{L}_m}{log(n)} \tag{5}$$

in which, n are number of messages that have passed through intermediate node m. So, for each route R_i consisting of a set of nodes, the privacy of the route is:

$$Privacy(R_i) = min(Privacy(m)) \text{ where } m \in N_{R_i} \tag{6}$$

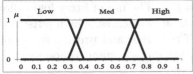

(a) Membership function for trust

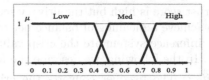

(b) Membership function for privacy

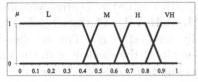

(c) Membership function for credibility

Rule no.	trust score	privacy score	credibility
1	Low	Low	L
2	Low	Med	L
3	Low	High	L
4	Med	Low	M
5	Med	Med	H
6	Med	High	H
7	High	Low	M
8	High	Med	VH
9	High	High	VH

(d) Fuzzy rule base

Fig. 2. Rule base and Membership functions of input and output linguistic variables

4.3 Credibility Score of the Route

In order to select the best route (R_{best}) among the set of routes, we combine the privacy score of each route with its trust score via a combination function F to reach to a single value for the credibility score of the route. In other words,

$$Credibility(R_{best}) = max\Big(F(Trust(R_i), Privacy(R_i))\Big) \text{ where } R_i \in R \quad (7)$$

The selection of a proper combination function F is important. F should be efficient enough to handle possible conflicts between the trust score and the privacy score in a reasonable manner. The decision on how to combine these factors affects the performance of the route selection module. In this paper, we have considered two combination functions:

Geometric Mean. The geometric mean is defined as the n_{th} root (n:count of numbers) of the product of the numbers. It is often used for comparing different items and finding a single "figure of merit" for these items, when each item has multiple properties. A geometric mean, unlike an arithmetic mean, tends to dampen the effect of very high or low values, which might bias the mean if a straight average (arithmetic mean) were calculated. This property makes geometric mean suitable for our situation since there may be situations where the trust score is high but privacy score is low (or vice versa). The combination of trust and privacy scores of the route via the geometric mean is:

$$Credibility(R_i) = \sqrt{Trust(R_i) * Privacy(R_i)} \quad (8)$$

Fuzzy Combination. Another possible option is to employ fuzzy logic to calculate a comprehensive credibility score for the route. Consider a situation where the trust score is high but the privacy score is low. The use of fuzzy logic allows us to achieve a meaningful balance between these two scores. The inputs to the fuzzy inference system are the crisp values of the trust and privacy scores of a route. In the following, we describe the fuzzy inference system components.

Fuzzifier: The fuzzifier converts the crisp values of input parameters into a linguistic variable according to membership functions. The fuzzy sets for the input and output variables are defined as: T(trust score) = T(privacy score) = {Low, Med, High}, T(route's credibility) = {L, M, H, VH}. The membership function which represents a fuzzy set A is usually denoted by μ_A. The membership degree $\mu_A(x)$ quantifies the grade of membership of the element x to the fuzzy set A. Figure 2(a)–(c) represents the membership functions of parameters.

Inference Engine: The role of inference engine is to convert fuzzy inputs to the fuzzy output (route's credibility) by leveraging If-Then type fuzzy rules. The combination of the above mentioned fuzzy sets create 3*3 = 9 different states, addressed by 9 rules as shown in Fig. 2(d). The rule based design is based on the experience on how the system should work by leveraging *max-min* composition method. The result is the credibility score which is a linguistic fuzzy value.

Defuzzifier: A defuzzifier converts the credibility fuzzy value to a crisp value in the range of [0, 1]. We employed the Centre of Gravity (COG) method.

In Sect. 5, the effect of each combination function on the performance of route selection module will be investigated.

5   Experimental Evaluation

This section presents simulation-based evaluation of the proposed system. The simulation setup is outlined in Sect. 5.1 and the results are in Sect. 5.2.

5.1   Simulation Setup

To undertake the preliminary evaluations outlined herein, we chose to conduct simulations, since real experiments in social participatory sensing are difficult to organise. We developed a custom Java simulator for this purpose.

The data set that we use for our experiment is the real web of trust of Advogato.org [26]. Advogato.org is a web-based community of open source software developers in which, site members rate each other in terms of their trustworthiness. Trust values are one of the three choices master, journeyer and apprentice, with master being the highest level in that order. The result of these ratings is a rich web of trust, which comprises of 14,019 users and 47,347 trust ratings. In order to conform it to our framework, we map the textual ratings to the range of [0, 1] as master = 0.8, journeyer = 0.6, and apprentice = 0.4.

Whenever a task is launched, one of the Advogato users is selected to be the requester. The participant selection component traverses the Advogato graph beginning from the requester until level L ($L = 3$) to find suitable participants (i.e., those whose profile information such as their expertise match the task's requirements). Next, the route selection component finds the best routes (details in Sect. 4.3). Tasks and contributions are then exchanged and trust server calculates the Trustworthiness of Contribution (ToC) for each receiving contribution. Trust ratings along the routes are then updated based on the ToC achieved. If above a threshold, all mutual trusts along the route are increased; otherwise, if less than a threshold, mutual trust is decreased (details have been presented in [8]). We run the simulation for 20 periods, each consisting of launching 30 tasks.

The amount of private information contained in the exchanged messages (tasks and contributions) may vary. Some messages may contain more sensitive information than others. To simulate these differences, we assume that the total number of attributes contained in a message are 6 and a message may belong to one of three privacy classes: (i) *Class* 0: messages in this class contain 4 sensitive attributes; (ii) *Class* 1: messages in this class contain 2 sensitive attributes; (iii) *Class* 2: messages in this class contain 1 sensitive attribute. Greater number of sensitive attributes implies more private information. Whenever a message is created, a set of sensitive attributes, defined by numbers in the range of [1, 6], is randomly assigned to it. The credibility of the route is then computed via Eq. 7. The route with highest credibility score is chosen for message exchange.

In order to observe the performance of the system in the presence of noise, we artificially create situations in which, the privacy score of a specific node reduces for a period of time. This may happen in reality when a participant starts to reveal private information about another user. Our goal is to observe whether the system is able to rapidly detect such behavioural change and demonstrate a reasonable reaction accordingly. The duration of behavioural change has been set to be between the 5th and 10th periods. We investigate the average credibility score of all routes passing through this malicious node. We expect to see that the proposed method is able to rapidly reduce the credibility score of these specific routes and thus, eliminate them from being selected for message exchange.

As mentioned in Sect. 2, since there is no related work in the area of social participatory sensing, we compare the performance of our method against the one described in our previous work [9]. To be more specific, we compare the following: (1) trust based recruitment, in which, the route selection is based only on the trust score of the route (the method in [9]). (2) privacy-trust recruitment, our proposed method in which, the best route is selected based on both privacy score and trust score.

As mentioned in Sect. 3, a ToC rating is calculated for each contribution in the trust server. We consider the overall trust as the evaluation metric. The overall trust of a campaign is defined as $OverallTrust = \frac{\sum_{i=1}^{n} ToC}{n}$ in which, n is the number of non-revoked contributions. Greater overall trust demonstrates better ability to achieve highly trustable contributions and revoke untrusted ones. Overall trust has a value in the range of [0, 1]. The overall trust values obtained for all tasks will be averaged to make a single value as the *average overall trust* for the entire simulation.

As explained in Sect. 4, the participant selection component determines a set of eligible participants. A subset of eligible participants, known as selected participants, are those for whom, the credibility score of the route is greater than a predefined credibility threshold (set to 0.6). Relevant to this selection process, we define the notion of *participation score* as the ratio of selected

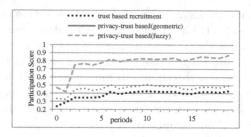

Fig. 3. Evolution of participation score

participants to eligible participants. A higher value of participation score implies better ability to recruit suitable participants via optimum routes. Participation score has a value in the range of $[0, 1]$.

5.2 Simulation Results

Figure 3 demonstrates the evolution of participation score for trust based and privacy-trust based recruitment methods with both geometric and fuzzy combination (details about combination functions can be found in Sect. 4.3). As this figure shows, our proposed recruitment framework achieves a higher score in comparison with the trust based method, thus implying better performance in terms of recruiting more participants. Note that participant selection process in both methods is limited to L levels (L = 3). Since our proposed method takes participant's privacy into account, it results in the selection of a diverse set of routes which in turn, allows selecting well-suited participants from a broader group. In other words, our proposed scheme achieves greater diversity than the scheme that purely relies on trust.

Figure 4 illustrates the average privacy score of the routes selected for message exchange between a specific requester and a set of selected participants, calculated separately for different privacy classes. As this chart demonstrates, our proposed method achieves higher privacy score for all types of messages originated from a specific requester. For instance, the average privacy score obtained in our proposed method for class 0 messages is 12 % higher than the one obtained in the trust-based method. This is because our scheme considers the privacy score of the route as an effective issue in evaluating the route's credibility. Note that this improved performance is consistent for all privacy classes (and more explicit for class 0), since the route selection method is identical for all types of messages. This implies that our proposed method is able to achieve higher privacy scores for all types of exchanged messages containing different levels of private information. The importance of this outperformance is better understood when obtained average overall trust is also considered in conjunction (details in Sect. 5.1). The average overall trust is 0.89 for trust-based recruitment method. Our scheme achieves a score of 0.89 with geometric mean and 0.84 with the fuzzy combination. This comparison shows that although our proposed method does not consider the trust score as the only determinant factor for the route

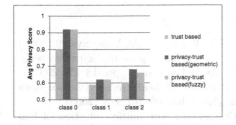

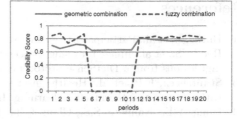

Fig. 4. Average privacy score of the selected routes for different privacy classes

Fig. 5. Evolution of average route's credibility score passing from a malicious node

selection, the achieved overall trust is still similar to trust based recruitment method, while better preserving the privacy of sensitive information.

As mentioned in Sect. 5.1, we also consider a scenario where the privacy score of an intermediate node decreases for a certain time interval (between 5th and 10th periods). The aim is to investigate the sensitivity of our recruitment method in promptly detecting and reacting to such fluctuation. Figure 5 shows the evolution of average credibility score for all routes passing through this malicious node. Observe that the credibility score for both combination methods decreases in the transition period. However, fuzzy method demonstrates better performance in early detection and severe punishment by a sudden decrease (to zero) in the credibility score. This is due to the adjustment of fuzzy rules such as rule no.1, 2 in Fig. 2(d). In other words, according to Eq. 6, low privacy score for a malicious node results in the low privacy score for all routes passing through it. We set the fuzzy rules in a way that when the privacy score of the route is low, the resulting credibility score will be L (Low). This will result in the exclusion of this route from the set of candidate routes. This is not always true for geometric mean. There may be cases in geometric mean combination (as observed in Fig. 5) where the privacy score is low, but its credibility score is above the threshold, resulting in inclusion of this route for message exchange.

6 Conclusions

In this paper, we proposed a privacy-preserving trust-based recruitment framework for social participatory sensing system. Our system leverages friendship relations to recruit participants via the optimum routes with highest level of trustworthiness and privacy preservation. Simulations demonstrated that our scheme preserves better privacy for participants while achieving acceptable overall trust as compared to the trust-based method, and provides the system with better recruitment of participants.

References

1. Burke, J., et al.: Participatory sensing. In: WSW Workshop, ACM SenSys'06 (2006)
2. Reddy, S., et al.: Image browsing, processing, and clustering for participatory sensing: lessons from a DietSense prototype. In: ACM EmNets'07, pp. 13–17 (2007)
3. Stuntebeck, E.P., et al.: HealthSense: classification of health-related sensor data through user-assisted machine learning. In: HotMobile'08, pp. 1–5 (2008)
4. Dong, Y.F., Kanhere, S.S., Chou, C.T., Bulusu, N.: Automatic collection of fuel prices from a network of mobile cameras. In: Nikoletseas, S.E., Chlebus, B.S., Johnson, D.B., Krishnamachari, B. (eds.) DCOSS 2008. LNCS, vol. 5067, pp. 140–156. Springer, Heidelberg (2008)
5. Rana, R.K., Chou, C.T., Kanhere, S.S., Bulusu, N., Hu, W.: Ear-phone: an end-to-end participatory urban noise mapping. In: ACM/IEEE IPSN'10 (2010)
6. Krontiris, I., Freiling, F.: Urban sensing through social networks: the tension between participation and privacy. In: ITWDC'10 (2010)
7. Amintoosi, H., Kanhere, S.S.: A trust framework for social participatory sensing systems. In: Zheng, K., Li, M., Jiang, H. (eds.) MobiQuitous 2012. LNICST, vol. 120, pp. 237–249. Springer, Heidelberg (2013)
8. Amintoosi, H., Kanhere, S.S.: A reputation framework for social participatory sensing systems. J. Mobile Netw. Appl. **19**(1), 88–100 (2014)
9. Amintoosi, H., Kanhere, S.S.: A trust based recruitment framework for social participatory sensing. In: IEEE DCOSS'13 (2013)
10. Sweeney, L.: Achieving k-anonymity privacy protection using generalization and suppression. Int. J. Uncertain. Fuzz. Knowl.-Based Syst. **10**(05), 571–588 (2002)
11. Huber, M., Mulazzani, M., Weippl, E.: Who on earth is "Mr. Cypher": automated friend injection attacks on social networking sites. In: Rannenberg, K., Varadharajan, V., Weber, C. (eds.) SEC 2010. IFIP AICT, vol. 330, pp. 80–89. Springer, Heidelberg (2010)
12. Huang, K.L., Kanhere, S.S., Hu, W.: A privacy-preserving reputation system for participatory sensing. In: IEEE LCN'12 (2012)
13. Christin, D., Reinhardt, A., Kanhere, S.S., Hollick, M.: A survey on privacy in mobile participatory sensing applications. J. Syst. Softw. **84**, 1928–1946 (2011)
14. Daly, E., Haahr, M.: Social network analysis for routing in disconnected delay-tolerant MANETs. In: ACM MobiHoc' 07 (2007)
15. Hui, P., Crowcroft, J., Yoneki, E.: BUBBLE Rap: social based forwarding in delay tolerant networks. In: ACM MobiHoc'08 (2008)
16. Mashhadi, A.J., et al.: Habit: leveraging human mobility and social network for efficient content dissemination in delay tolerant networks. In: WoWMoM'09 (2009)
17. Mtibaa, A., et al.: PeopleRank, social opportunistic forwarding. In: INFOCOM'10 (2010)
18. Boldrini, C., et al.: Exploiting users' social relations to forward data in opportunistic networks: the HiBOp solution. Perv. Mobile Comput. **4**(5), 633–657 (2008)
19. Shikfa, A., Önen, M., Molva, R.: Privacy and confidentiality in context-based and epidemic forwarding. Comput. Commun. **33**(13), 1493–1504 (2010)
20. Aad, I., et al.: Packet coding for strong anonymity in ad hoc networks. In: IEEE SecureComm'06 (2006)
21. Goldschlag, D., et al.: Onion routing. Commun. ACM **42**, 39–41 (1999)
22. Hasan, O., et al.: Evaluation of the iterative multiplication strategy for trust propagation in pervasive environments. In: ACM ICPS'09 (2009)

23. Zheleva, E., Getoor, L.: Privacy in social networks: a survey. In: Aggarwal, C.C. (ed.) Social Network Data Analytics, pp. 277–306. Springer, New York (2011)
24. Shannon, C.E.: A mathematical theory of communication. Bell Syst. Tech. J. **27**(3), 379–423 (1948)
25. Smith, G.: Quantifying information flow using min-entropy. In: IEEE QEST'11 (2011)
26. Levien, R., Aiken, A.: Attack-resistant trust metrics for public key certification. In: 7th USENIX Security Symposium (1998)

Privacy-Preserving Calibration
for Participatory Sensing

Kevin Wiesner$^{(\boxtimes)}$, Florian Dorfmeister, and Claudia Linnhoff-Popien

Mobile and Distributed Systems, Ludwig-Maximilians-Universität
München (LMU Munich), Oettingenstr. 67, 80538 Munich, Germany
{kevin.wiesner,florian.dorfmeister,linnhoff}@ifi.lmu.de

Abstract. By leveraging sensors embedded in mobile devices, participatory sensing tries to create cost-effective, large-scale sensing systems.
As these sensors are heterogeneous and low-cost, regular calibration is
needed in order to obtain meaningful data. Due to the large scale, on-
the-fly calibration utilizing stationary reference stations is preferred. As
calibration can only be performed in proximity of such stations, uncalibrated measurements might be uploaded at any point in time. From the
data quality perspective, it is desirable to apply backward calibration for
already uploaded values as soon as the device gets calibrated. To protect
the user's privacy, the server should not be able to link all user measurements. In this paper, we therefore present a privacy-preserving calibration mechanism that enables both forward and backward calibration.
The latter is achieved by transferring calibration parameters to already
uploaded measurements without revealing the connection between the
individual measurements. We demonstrate the feasibility of our approach
by means of simulation.

Keywords: Participatory sensing · Mobile sensing · On-the-fly
calibration

1 Introduction

Today, mobile phones already include an increasing set of embedded sensors.
Currently available phones come with built-in accelerometers and gyros, as well
as location, audio, and image sensors. With this development, mobile phones
evolve from standard phones, intended for personal communication only to ubiquitous sensing devices that are globally distributed. These devices can be utilized
to form a new kind of sensor network, so-called participatory sensing networks
(PSN) (also referred to as *mobile phone sensing* [1] or *people-centric sensing networks* [2]), where people serve as carriers for mobile phone-based sensing devices.
PSNs allow for large-scale, global data collection and real-time information display. In future, they could be used, e.g., to monitor environmental pollution,
temperature or the noise intensity of urban areas. The main advantage of PSNs
is that data can be collected on a large-scale with automatically deployed and
virtually always-on, consumer-paid and continuously recharged sensor nodes.

© Institute for Computer Sciences, Social Informatics and Telecommunications Engineering 2014
I. Stojmenovic et al. (Eds.): MOBIQUITOUS 2013, LNICST 131, pp. 276–288, 2014.
DOI: 10.1007/978-3-319-11569-6_22

Leveraging the sensors built into mobile phones as information source typically entails two main problems: On the one hand, those sensors are heterogeneous, due to the great number of different manufacturers and device models. On the other hand, sensors embedded in mobile phones Consequently, calibration is necessary in order to obtain meaningful data and poses a crucial aspect for the success of PSNs. In general, there a two types of calibration: manual and on-the-fly. The former is typically performed by field experts and is used for high precision instruments, especially if manageable amounts of sensors have to be calibrated. On-the-fly calibration describes an online process, in which sensors are automatically calibrated while being deployed and running. It is done by utilizing stationary reference stations, whose measurements are used as ground-truth. For large-scale PSNs, manual calibration is too elaborate and time-consuming, and thus on-the-fly calibration is preferred.

A calibration process can only be performed if a mobile phone user comes sufficiently close to one of those reference stations. As the mobility of users cannot be controlled, this can lead to the upload of uncalibrated measurements, especially in case of long intervals without a user's encounter with a reference station. Hence, in order to improve the system's overall quality of information, it is desirable that the server can apply backward calibration for already uploaded values, as soon as the calibration process is carried out for a client, i.e., the server adjusts previously uploaded measurement values with the newly determined calibration parameters. In order to protect the user's privacy, though, the server should not be able to link all conducted measurements of a client, as this could reveal the user's entire mobility trace. In other scenarios, this could be achieved by using changing pseudonyms in combination with MIX networks [3] to avoid the traceability of users and their measurements. But the quasi uniqueness of the calibration parameters would allow to link calibrated measurements of a user.

In this paper, we present a privacy-preserving calibration mechanism that enables both forward and backward calibration, while protecting a participating user's privacy. The latter is achieved by transferring calibration parameters to already uploaded measurements in a way that completely blurs the connection between the individual measurements.

The remainder of this paper is organized as follows. Section 2 discusses related work. In Sect. 3, we introduce the calibration model, followed by the description of our privacy-preserving calibration system in Sect. 4. Then, we evaluate our approach in Sect. 5 and finally conclude in Sect. 6.

2   Related Work

There is a lot of research work related to participatory sensing. Most work focuses on approaches and techniques that enable data collection with mobiles phones [1,2,4], but neglect calibration issues. In addition, there is also a wide range of work dealing with sensor calibration in general. Those approaches often cannot be applied to participatory sensing, as dense networks of static and resource-constrained nodes are assumed [5].

Miluzzo et al. proposed CaliBree [6], a distributed self-calibration system for mobile wireless sensor networks. Mobile sensors compare their data with those of ground-truth nodes when they experience the same environment, i.e., upon reception of locally broadcasted ground-truth information. As their nodes do not possess any positioning capabilities, they are dependent on the broadcasted information. In our approach, we assume that mobile phones are able to determine their position (e.g., using GPS), which allows for a more precise determination of whether nodes should experience the same environment. Furthermore, no direct wireless communication link between ground-truth stations and sensors is necessary, thereby facilitating the integration of already existing measurement stations and avoiding investments in new hardware. In contrast to the distributed CaliBree calibration, Honicky [7] presented an centralized approach, where the automatic calibration of sensors embedded into mobile phones is achieved by using Gaussian process regression. Through the cloud-based approach, global information about all of the sensors in the system can be integrated into the calibration process. Hasenfratz et al. [8] introduced new calibration algorithms, i.e., backward and instant calibration for on-the-fly calibration of low-cost gas sensors. The focus of the paper lies on applying the algorithms on actual data and no mechanisms for the exchange of data between the entities is described.

These approaches either neglect the privacy aspect as a central instance knows about all measurements of the nodes [7] or do not take into account that nodes pass by reference stations infrequently. The latter leads to the upload of possibly uncalibrated measurements. To the best of our knowledge, our approach is the first that preserves the users' privacy and allows for backward and forward calibration.

3   Calibration Model

We assume mobile phones to be equipped with low-cost gas sensors, which we aim to calibrate with our system. In this section, we therefore introduce the underlying calibration model.

PSNs can be seen as a special type of sensor network. Sensor networks usually aim to monitor one or multiple phenomena of interest. In order to be able to detect a phenomenon P, there needs to be a measurable signal $p : T \to D$ that arises from P, with $T \subseteq \mathbb{R}^+$ being the time and $D \subseteq \mathbb{R}$ being the value domain. Let $m_s(t_i)$ be the measurement of a sensor s at time $t_i \in T$, and $p(t_i)$ the actual value of the phenomenon at that time. If sensor s is a *perfect sensor*, $m_s(t_i) = p(t_i)$ is true for any point in time and no calibration is necessary.

However, sensors are typically not behaving perfectly, and especially for low-cost gas sensors there is a significant precision loss due to sensor aging [9] and influencing contextual settings (e.g., humidity) [10]. Calibration of sensors can hence be described as the process of minimizing the deviation of the measured values $m_s(t_i)$ from the actual values $p(t_i)$, which is achieved by applying a *calibration curve* ϕ to the measured values. We use a polynomial of order k as a representation of $\phi : \mathbb{R}^{k+1} \times D \to D$ with a vector of *calibration parameters* $c = (c_0, c_1, ..., c_k) \in \mathbb{R}^{k+1}$ and x as the measurement input:

$$\phi(c, x) = \sum_{n=0}^{k} c_n * x^n. \tag{1}$$

As a sensor can be calibrated several times, we denote $\omega : T \rightarrow \mathbb{R}^{k+1}$ as the function returning the effective calibration parameters at a certain point of time. As a result, the calibrated value $\tilde{m}_s(t_i)$ of a sensor s at time t_i is

$$\tilde{m}_s(t_i) = \phi(\omega(t_i), m_s(t_i)) = \sum_{n=0}^{k} \omega(t_i)_n * m_s(t_i)^n. \tag{2}$$

For a *perfect sensor* s that needs no calibration, it is $\forall t_i \in T : \omega(t_i) = (0, 1, 0, 0, ..., 0) \in \mathbb{R}^{k+1}$ and $m_s(t_i) = p(t_i)$. By means of calibration we aim for *perfectly calibrated* sensors that behave like *perfect sensors* from a point t_c in time onwards, so that $\forall t_i \geq t_c, t \in T : \omega(t_{i+1}) = \omega(t_i)$ and $\tilde{m}_s(t_i) = p(t_i)$. This ideal state is typically not reached, as sensors continuously degrade and thus do not remain perfectly calibrated. However, by continuously repeating the calibration process an approximation of the ideal state can be reached.

In order to determine the above introduced *calibration curve* ϕ, a set C (with $|C| \geq (k + 1)$) of calibration tuples $(m_s(t_i), p(t_i))$ is needed, i.e., for a certain number of measurements we need to know the actual value of the phenomenon of interest. For this purpose, we utilize stationary reference stations, as we assume those sensors to be perfectly calibrated at any point. For each measurement $m_s(t_i)$ and actual value $p(t_i)$, we store the time t_i and the location l_i of the mobile phone, respectively of the reference station, so that we have a set of measurements M, consisting of tuples of the form $(t, m_s(t), l(t))$, and a set of actual values S, consisting of tuples of the form $(t, p(t), l(t))$. To access the different parts of these tuples, we use the dot notation, e.g., $m.l$ for the location of a tuple $m \in M$. Hence, the set of calibration tuples C can be written as:

$$s \in S, m \in M : C = \{(s.p, m.m_s) | |s.t - m.t| \leq \delta_t \wedge |s.l - m.l| \leq \delta_l\}. \tag{3}$$

δ_t and δ_l are parameters describing the temporal and spatial distance between ground-truth and mobile measurements, which have to be adapted according to the phenomenon of interest.

4   Privacy-Preserving Calibration System

In this section, we will describe our Privacy-Preserving Calibration System (PPCS). Overall, we assume that users conduct measurements using their mobile phones and upload their data to a server, which is responsible for storing all measurements. The upload is done via MIX networks with users utilizing self-generated pseudonyms for communicating their measurements and change those on a regular basis. Users can even use a new pseudonym for each measurement. These pseudonyms are necessary in order to be able to reference specific measurements within the backward calibration process. PPCS is an on-the-fly

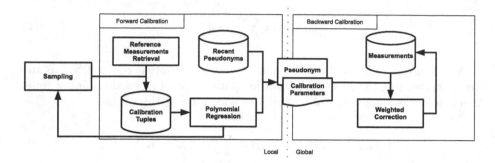

Fig. 1. Calibration pipeline showing the two calibration phases

calibration system, i.e., it calibrates sensors while they are in use by utilizing stationary reference stations providing ground-truth data. Many cities already deployed stationary sensor stations measuring the air quality in use. For instance, Zurich has four stations[1], and in Munich there are even 10 stations deployed[2]. We assume such reference stations to be available and that their measurements are accessible through well-defined web service interfaces.

Figure 1 illustrates the calibration pipeline of our system. By comparing reference measurements to the user's measurement data, instant *forward calibration* can be performed. Forward calibration refers to the process of determining a calibration curve on a user's mobile device that is applied to future measurements before uploading those. In contrast, *backward calibration* refers to the process of adjusting previous measurements by applying a newly determined calibration curve to already uploaded data. In order to instruct the server to perform backward calibration for concerned measurements, users have to transfer the freshly acquired calibration parameters in combination with the previously used pseudonym to the server. In the following, the two calibration phases are described in more detail.

4.1   Forward Calibration

In the forward calibration process, a calibration curve is determined based on the comparison of recent measurements of both the mobile phone and a reference station. First, the user's device (hereafter referred to as the *client*) needs to be aware of any reference stations within its area. Therefore, the server provides a list of reference stations together with their locations and the accessible data interface for the reference measurement retrieval. This list is requested as soon as the client enters an unknown area, and is refreshed by periodical updates. Knowing the locations of nearby reference stations, the client checks for each measurement, whether it is in proximity of one of those. If so, the reference measurements are retrieved. As mentioned in the previous section, the temporal

---

[1] http://www.ostluft.ch/
[2] http://maps.muenchen.de/rgu/luftmessstationen

and spatial ranges stating what is to be considered as "proximity" depend on the phenomena of interest and have to be specified by adapting the parameters δ_l and δ_t in Eq. 3.

The locally recorded measurements and the reference measurements are then combined and the calibration tuples are formed through a temporal and spatial filtering process (cf. Sect. 3). Basically, this step combines measurements that were taken at approximately the same time and location. These calibration tuples are then used to determine a calibration curve that is specific to the current state of a mobile user's sensing equipment. In order to avoid distorted or premature calibrations, PPCS takes the following countermeasures: First, forward calibration is only performed if a predefined minimal number of calibration tuples ($C_{MinCount}$) exist in order to reduce the impact of possible outliers within the calibration tuples. Second, calibration is only started if a certain value range within the calibration tuples is covered ($C_{MinRange}$), to avoid a calibration optimized for a limited value range. Third, in order to avoid unnecessary calibrations, the calibration process is only started if a certain timeout has been exceeded since the last calibration ($C_{Timeout}$). The actual determination of the calibration curve parameters is done by polynomial regression. The model is fitted using the method of least squares, which minimizes the sum of the squares of the deviations between reference and mobile sensor measurements. The determined calibration tuples are then used to correct future measurements before uploading them (see Fig. 2b). In a discretized form, they are also used during backward calibration to correct already uploaded measurements.

4.2   Backward Calibration

In the backward calibration process, already uploaded measurements should be adjusted with a newly determined calibration curve. As already mentioned, users change their pseudonyms on a regular basis in order to protect their privacy. As a result, only the users themselves know which pseudonyms the calibration curve should be applied to. Thus, a client that has locally determined a new calibration curve has to inform the server about the pseudonyms and the calibration parameters. A naive approach would be to send tuples consisting of the pseudonym to be adjusted and the calibration vector c. However, this would naturally lead to a breach of the user's privacy: as the exact calibration parameter vector typically differs from phone to phone, sending c could reveal the link between the different pseudonyms of a user (see Fig. 2a).

In PPCS, this is counteracted by incorporating the concept of k-anonymity [11]. To obfuscate the exact calibration parameter, the client discretizes the calibration parameters before uploading them to the server. By this, the probability of having the same calibration vector c as other clients and achieving k-anonymity is increased. For this process, a discretization function $\psi : \mathbb{R}^{k+1} \times \mathbb{R}^{k+1} \to \mathbb{R}^{k+1}$ is used, which returns a discretized (and thereby generalized) calibration vector $\tilde{c}$:

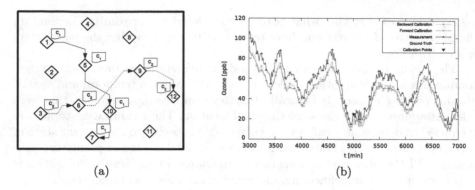

Fig. 2. (a) Applying exact backward calibration parameters (here: c_1 and c_2), can reveal the link between uploaded measurements (indicated with diamonds). (b) Example excerpt of simulated and calibrated measurements of a node over time.

$$\tilde{c} = \psi(c, d) = \begin{pmatrix} \lceil \frac{c_0}{d_0 * \theta(c)} \rfloor * (d_0 * \theta(c)) \\ \vdots \\ \lceil \frac{c_k}{d_k * \theta(c)} \rfloor * (d_k * \theta(c)) \end{pmatrix}, \tag{4}$$

where $d \in \mathbb{R}^{k+1}$ is the discretization vector that is known system-wide (i.e., all clients use the same d) and $\lceil x \rfloor$ denotes the rounding function to the nearest integer. θ describes a factor for adjusting the discretization granularity to the extent of the deviation δ of c from the perfect sensor s: $\theta(c) = 2^{max(\lceil \lg \delta(c) - \varphi \rceil, 0)}$, with δ being the degree of deviation $\delta(c) = ||c - s||_2 = (\sum_{n=0}^{k} (\frac{c_n - s_n}{d_n})^2)^{\frac{1}{2}}$, and φ being a constant for determining the steps of adjustment. To clarify this step, we illustrate the discretization with an example: We assume a calibration vector $c = (9.3292, 0.8567)$ and a discretization vector $d = (2.0, 0.1)$ with $\varphi = 2$. This leads to $\delta(c) = 4.8798$ and $\theta(c) = 2$, and finally to the discretized calibration vector $\tilde{c} = (8.0, 0.8)$.

Naturally, as c is distorted, the discretization process leads to a loss of precision, with the amount of distortion depending on d. However, the error introduced should be relatively small compared to the gain of precision achieved by calibrating and adjusting $m_s(t_i)$ to $\tilde{m}_s(t_i)$, even with deliberately distorting the calibration parameters. Furthermore, as $\tilde{c}$ is only used within the backward calibration process, the error does not propagate to future measurements.

To avoid privacy attacks based on the upload time, backward calibration parameters are only uploaded at certain specified times, resulting in so-called "calibration bursts". By this, all users that want to apply backward calibration to their measurements, upload their parameters for the total interval since the last calibration burst. As done before, the upload of $\tilde{c}$ to the server is carried out via a MIX network, so that the updates cannot be linked to the physical device.

The last step is the weighted correction of former measurements by the server. This is done by applying the received calibration parameters and calculating a new measurement value. Ideally, this new value and the former value should be combined to a corrected measurement value by using weights that depend on the point of time within the last calibration period of the corresponding node. Measurements closer to the calibration point at which the backward calibration parameters have been determined should be stronger affected by the correction than measurements closer to the previous calibration point. The idea behind this is that it is typically not reasonable to alter measurements that have just been (forward) calibrated by applying a much later determined backward calibration. However, as the server does not know the actual calibration times of a node, only an approximation can be calculated. Instead of using the actual calibration times, the server uses weights that depend on the point of time within the calibration burst. The corrected value $\tilde{m}_s(t_i)$ is calculated with the following formula

$$\tilde{m}_s(t_i) = \frac{(t_i - cb_{n-1}) * \phi(\omega(cb_n), m_s(t_i))}{cb_n - cb_{n-1}} + \frac{(cb_n - t_i) * \phi(\omega(cb_{n-1}), m_s(t_i))}{cb_n - cb_{n-1}},$$

(5)

where cb_n and cb_{n-1} denote the times of the current calibration burst and the previous calibration burst respectively. As this might heavily deviate from the ideal weighted correction, the client calculates the ideal weighted correction $\hat{m}_s(t_i)$ itself before uploading the backward calibration parameters

$$\hat{m}_s(t_i) = \frac{(t_i - ct_{n-1}) * \phi(\omega(ct_n), m_s(t_i))}{ct_n - ct_{n-1}} + \frac{(ct_n - t_i) * \phi(\omega(ct_{n-1}), m_s(t_i))}{ct_n - ct_{n-1}}, \quad (6)$$

with ct_n and ct_{n-1} denoting the actual calibration times of that node. Only if a backward calibrated value is closer to the ideally corrected value, i.e., if $|\hat{m}_s(t_i) - m_s(t_i)| > |\hat{m}_s(t_i) - \tilde{m}_s(t_i)|$, the client uploads the calibration parameters and initiates the backward calibration process.

5   Evaluation

We evaluated our concept by means of simulation. As ground truth data for our simulated measurements, we used real ozone measurements of 14 days collected at stationary stations in Munich (cf. Footnote 2). We interpolated this data in the time domain to increase the resolution from 1/hour to 1/minute, as well as in the spatial domain, in order to have a ground truth value for each position within the simulation area. For the latter, we employed Shepard's method for Inverse Distance Weighting [12] with the power parameter $p = 2$.

To simulate the deviation of mobile sensors, we used the model for ozone measurements presented in [8]: the authors deployed sensors with *MiCS-OZ-47* ozone sensing heads, and found that the measurement errors are normally distributed, if they are only initially calibrated. They observed a normal distribution $\mathcal{N}(\mu, \sigma^2)$ with $\mu \sim \mathcal{U}(-9, 9)$ ppb and $\sigma \sim \mathcal{N}(3, 1)$ ppb over the period of a day. For our simulations, we applied this model to generate artificial data, i.e., based on this model we determined an error curve for each sensor node. The error curve was set to an order of 1, i.e., a polynomial of the form $a * x + b$, where a was set to a random value ranging from $[-8.0, 8.0]$ and b to a value ranging

Table 1. Simulation setup

No. of nodes	1000, 1500, 2000	Simulation time	14 days
Mobility model	Random Walk	Max. speed	$8.33\,\frac{m}{s}$
Measurement frequency	4x per hour	No. of reference stations	5
δ_l	250 m	$C_{MinCount}$	5
$C_{MinRange}$	30 ppm	$C_{Timeout}$	5 days

from $[-0.2, 0.2]$, as those values closely modeled the mentioned behavior. We also integrated an aging factor of 0.2 ppm/day (as in [8]) to account for the loss of precision over time. As a result, a measurement was simulated by applying the error curve on the ground truth value, adding the deviation arising from sensor aging, and finally adding some noise from the aforementioned distribution.

We then conducted simulations with the setup stated in Table 1. The backward calibration was performed once per week. The calibration curve ϕ was set to an order of 1, thus c, $\tilde{c}$, and $d \in \mathbb{R}^2$. In our evaluations we used the following discretization parameters: $d_0 = \{1.0, 1.5, 2.0\}$, $d_1 = \{0.05, 0.1, 0.15, 0.2\}$, and $\varphi = \{2, 3, 4\}$, resulting in 36 different discretization combinations. In the following, discretization parameter combinations are written in the form $d_0, d_1; \varphi$.

5.1 K-Anonymity

In a first step, we analyzed our approach regarding the level of k-Anonymity. We therefore run simulations with each of the above mentioned discretization combination and analyzed how often k-Anonymity was reached for $k = \{2, 3, ..., 10\}$.

Figure 3a–c show the achieved k-Anonymity for 1000 nodes. It is obvious that more fine-grained discretization vectors, i.e., vectors with small discretization steps (such as $1.0, 0.05; 4.0$) perform worse than more coarse-grained vectors (such as $2.0, 0.2; 2.0$). It can be seen that especially the discretization parameter d_1 is decisive, and that discretizations with $d_1 = 0.15$ or $d_1 = 0.2$ reached the desired k-Anonymity level significantly more often. The results also show that smaller values for φ have a more positive impact on the anonymity level than larger values, as the discretization parameters are adapted more rapidly and thus become more coarse-grained. For $k = 5$, the k-Anonymity level was reached in more than 80 % of the time with 28 out of the 36 discretization combinations. For $k = 10$, 23 discretization combinations reached the specified level in more than 60 % of the time. We then selected the worst and the best performing discretization from the former results and simulated it with varying node numbers, i.e., $\#nodes = \{1000, 1500, 2000\}$. The results are shown in Fig. 3d. It can be seen that especially in the worst case, the increase of participating nodes significantly increases the percentage of achieved k-Anonymity.

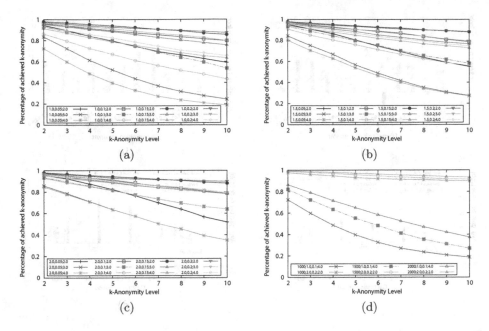

Fig. 3. Achieved average k-Anonymity level for varying discretization parameters over the simulated 14-day period.

5.2 Discretization Error

In a next step, we analyzed the error introduced by discretizing the calibration parameters in the backward calibration process. In this step, we only considered discretization parameters that achieved a k-Anonymity level of 10 at least 60 % of the time. Figure 4a, b show the average discretization error in relation to the average calibration gain (the average was calculated only over the amount of nodes that performed a calibration). For the former, we compared the results using the discretized calibration vector $\tilde{c}$ with those using the exact calibration parameters c (in relation to the ground truth value). The calibration gain is the average gain in precision when applying the discretized calibration curve $\tilde{c}$, compared to results without calibration. Here, the results are obviously orthogonal to the aforementioned results: the most fine-grained discretization results in the lowest error and the highest gain. It can be seen again that especially the choice of d_1 and φ are decisive for the result. Even though a few exceptions resulted in a negative backward calibration gain, i.e., the discretization of the calibration lead to a worse result than without the calibration, with most parameters a positive result was achieved.

We further examined the calibration gain for each calibration period, which is the time interval between two calibration points, e.g., the first calibration period (C_1) is the time interval from the simulation start until the first calibration. More precisely, we define the set of calibration periods as follows: $\{i \in 1, ..., n+1 : C_i = [t_{c_{i-1}}; t_{c_i}]\}$, with $\{t_{c_1}, t_{c_2}, ... t_{c_n}\}$ being the set of calibration times. As we

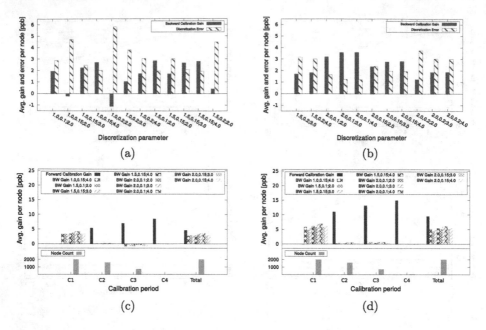

Fig. 4. (a, b) Average backward calibration gain and discretization error for varying discretization parameters over the simulated 14-day period. (c, d) Comparison of forward and backward calibration gain per calibration period with varying aging factors.

set $C_{Timeout} = 5$ for our simulations, a maximum of three calibration points was possible and consequently a maximum of four calibration periods (C_1 to C_4).

The upper parts of Fig. 4c, d show the average calibration gain for the individual calibration periods and the overall gain, whereas the lower parts show the number of nodes that were calibrated in the individual round. In each figure, the forward calibration gain was only plotted once, since forward calibration does not depend on discretization parameters. We illustrated the results for 2000 nodes and chose those discretization parameters, whose backward calibration gain was higher than the discretization error (see Fig. 4a, b). In Fig. 4c, the results with the aforementioned aging factor of 0.2 ppb/day are illustrated. In period C_1 no forward calibration gain is achieved, as forward calibration adapts only future measurements, i.e., from t_{c_1} onwards. But for the following rounds, an increasing forward calibration gain can be observed, however, with a strongly decreasing number of nodes. The backward calibration has the highest impact in C_1, as uploaded values in this period are completely uncalibrated. In the following rounds, the backward calibration is comparatively small and in the third round even negative. This stems from the relatively short time interval between the calibration points. In C_3, the sensors have already been calibrated twice and the aging factor does not distort the measurements strongly enough within this calibration interval, so that the discretized backward calibration is not reasonable in this case. In Fig. 4d, we increased the aging factor to 1.2 ppb/day. This simulates a stronger aging of the sensors, but can also be interpreted as longer periods between the calibration points with a constant aging factor (i.e., 6 times longer calibration intervals with an aging factor of 0.2 ppb/day). It can be seen that both the forward and the backward calibration gain increased; the latter now results in a positive gain in each round. As could be expected, this shows that backward calibration is reasonable if the calibration interval is long enough for the sensors to significantly deviate from their former calibration.

6   Conclusion

We presented a privacy-preserving calibration system that enables forward as well as backward calibration, while simultaneously protecting the users' privacy. We proposed a pseudonym-based system that allows for transferring calibration parameters to other pseudonyms without revealing the connection between those. Our analysis shows that we can achieve a high degree of anonymity, but only at the price of sacrificing precision. More precisely, the anonymity level and the backward calibration gain are negatively correlated, i.e., an increase of the one leads to a decrease of the other. Our results show that there are several discretization parameters that lead to promising results for both, however, the "optimal" setting depends on the application scenario and the subsequent weighting of anonymity in relation to precision. As the loss of precision is small in relation to the overall gain, we believe that PPCS represents a valid concept for privacy-preserving calibration in PSNs. In future work, we want to evaluate our concept with more extensive simulations using a realistic urban simulation environment and implement a prototype to evaluate the concept in real-life settings.

References

1. Lane, N.D., Miluzzo, E., Lu, H., Peebles, D., Choudhury, T., Campbell, A.T.: A survey of mobile phone sensing. IEEE Commun. **48**(9), 140–150 (2010)
2. Campbell, A.T., Eisenman, S.B., Lane, N.D., Miluzzo, E., Peterson, R.A., Lu, H., Zheng, X., Musolesi, M., Fodor, K., Ahn, G.-S.: The rise of people-centric sensing. Internet Comput. **12**(4), 12–21 (2008). (IEEE)
3. Chaum, D.L.: Untraceable electronic mail, return addresses, and digital pseudonyms. Commun. ACM **24**(2), 84–90 (1981)
4. Burke, J., Estrin, D., Hansen, M., Parker, A., Ramanathan, N., Reddy, S., Srivastava, M.B.: Participatory sensing. In: Proceedings of WSW'06 at SenSys '06 (2006)
5. Bychkovskiy, V., Megerian, S., Estrin, D., Potkonjak, M.: A collaborative approach to in-place sensor calibration. In: Zhao, F., Guibas, L.J. (eds.) IPSN 2003. LNCS, vol. 2634, pp. 301–316. Springer, Heidelberg (2003)
6. Miluzzo, E., Lane, N.D., Campbell, A.T., Olfati-Saber, R.: CaliBree: a self-calibration system for mobile sensor networks. In: Nikoletseas, S.E., Chlebus, B.S., Johnson, D.B., Krishnamachari, B. (eds.) DCOSS 2008. LNCS, vol. 5067, pp. 314–331. Springer, Heidelberg (2008)

7. Honicky, R.E.: Automatic calibration of sensor-phones using gaussian processes. Technical report UCB/EECS-2007-34, EECS, UC Berkeley, March 2007
8. Hasenfratz, D., Saukh, O., Thiele, L.: On-the-fly calibration of low-cost gas sensors. In: Picco, G.P., Heinzelman, W. (eds.) EWSN 2012. LNCS, vol. 7158, pp. 228–244. Springer, Heidelberg (2012)
9. Huan, C., Zhiyu, L., Gang, F.: Analysis of the aging characteristics of SnO2 gas sensors. Sens. Actuators 156(2), 912–917 (2011)
10. Kamionka, M., Breuil, P., Pijolat, C.: Calibration of a multivariate gas sensing device for atmospheric pollution measurement. Sens. Actuators B 118(12), 323–327 (2006)
11. Sweeney, L.: k-anonymity: a model for protecting privacy. Int. J. Uncertain. Fuzziness Knowl.-Based Syst. 10(5), 557–570 (2002)
12. Shepard, D.: A two-dimensional interpolation function for irregularly-spaced data. In: Proceedings of the ACM '68, New York, NY, USA, pp. 517–524. ACM (1968)

Complexity of Distance Fraud Attacks in Graph-Based Distance Bounding

Rolando Trujillo-Rasua[✉]

University of Luxembourg, SnT, Luxembourg, Luxembourg
rolando.trujillo@uni.lu

Abstract. *Distance bounding* (DB) emerged as a countermeasure to the so-called *relay attack*, which affects several technologies such as RFID, NFC, Bluetooth, and Ad-hoc networks. A prominent family of DB protocols are those based on graphs, which were introduced in 2010 to resist both mafia and distance frauds. The security analysis in terms of distance fraud is performed by considering an adversary that, given a vertex labeled graph $G = (V, E)$ and a vertex $v \in V$, is able to find the most frequent n-long sequence in G starting from v (MFS problem). However, to the best of our knowledge, it is still an open question whether the distance fraud security can be computed considering the aforementioned adversarial model. Our first contribution is a proof that the MFS problem is NP-Hard even when the graph is constrained to meet the requirements of a graph-based DB protocol. Although this result does not invalidate the model, it does suggest that a *too-strong* adversary is perhaps being considered (*i.e.*, in practice, graph-based DB protocols might resist distance fraud better than the security model suggests.) Our second contribution is an algorithm addressing the distance fraud security of the tree-based approach due to Avoine and Tchamkerten. The novel algorithm improves the computational complexity $O(2^{2^n + n})$ of the naive approach to $O(2^{2n} n)$ where n is the number of rounds.

Keywords: Security · Relay attack · Distance bounding · Most frequent sequence · Graph · NP-complete · NP-hard

1 Introduction

Let us consider a little girl willing to compete with two chess grandmasters, say Fischer and Spassky. She agrees with both on playing by post and manages to use opposite-colored pieces in the games. Once the little girl receives Fisher's move she simply forwards it to Spassky and vice versa. As a result, she wins one game or draws both even though she might know nothing about chess. This problem, known as the *chess grandmaster problem*, was introduced by Conway in 1976 [7] and informally describes how relay attacks work.

In a relay attack, an adversary acts as a *passive* man-in-the-middle attacker relaying messages between the prover and the verifier during an authentication protocol. In case the adversary is *active*, the attack is known as *mafia fraud* [8]

© Institute for Computer Sciences, Social Informatics and Telecommunications Engineering 2014
I. Stojmenovic et al. (Eds.): MOBIQUITOUS 2013, LNICST 131, pp. 289–302, 2014.
DOI: 10.1007/978-3-319-11569-6_23

and succeeds if the prover and the verifier complete the authentication protocol without noticing the presence of the adversary.

With the widespread deployment of contactless technologies in recent years, mafia fraud has re-emerged as a serious security threat for authentication schemes. Radio Frequency IDentification (RFID), Near Field Communication (NFC), and Passive Keyless Entry and Start Systems in Modern Cars, have been proven to be vulnerable to mafia fraud [10,13]. Other contactless technologies such as smart-cards and e-voting are also threatened by this attack [9,16].

The most promising countermeasure to thwart mafia fraud is *distance bounding* (DB) [4], that is, an authentication protocol where time-critical sessions allow to compute an upper bound of the distance between the prover and the verifier. However, this type of protocols is vulnerable to another type of fraud, the *distance fraud* [4]. Contrary to mafia fraud, distance fraud is performed by a legitimate prover, who aims to authenticate beyond the expected and allowed distance.

In 2010, graph-based DB protocols aimed at being resistant to both mafia and distance frauds were introduced [19]. This type of protocols is flexible in the sense that different graph structures can be used so as to balance memory requirements and security properties. However, neither the graph-based approach in [3] nor the one in [19] have computed their actual distance fraud security. Indeed, this analysis was left as an open problem in [19].

Contributions. In this article we address the open problem of computing the distance fraud resistance of graph-based DB protocols. We first reformulate the security model provided in [19] and define it in terms of, to the best of our knowledge, two new problems in Graph Theory. *The Most Frequent Sequence problem* (MFS problem) and its simplified version *the Binary Most Frequent Sequence problem* (Binary MFS problem).

We then provide a polynomial-time reduction of the Satisfiability problem (SAT) to the Binary MFS problem, proving that both the Binary MFS and the MFS problems are NP-Hard. This result suggests that a *too-strong* adversary is perhaps being considered by the security model, unless $P = NP$. However, the implications of our reduction goes beyond that. It also provides a clue of how to design graph-based DB protocols resistant to distance fraud.

Our next contribution is a novel algorithm to compute the distance fraud resistance of the tree-based DB protocol proposed by Avoine and Tchamkerten [3]. Our algorithm significantly reduces the time complexity of the naive approach from $O(2^{2^n+n})$ to $O(2^{2n}n)$ where n is the number of rounds. This paves the way for a fair comparison of graph-based proposals with other state-of-the-art DB protocols.

Organization. The rest of this article is organized as follows. Section 2 introduces graph-based DB protocols and the new problems Binary MFS and MFS. Related works close to the MFS problem are reviewed in Sect. 2 as well. Section 3 contains proofs on the hardness of the Binary MFS problem. The algorithm for computing the distance fraud resistance of the tree-based DB protocol is described and analyzed in Sect. 4. The discussion and conclusions are drawn in Sect. 5.

2 Preliminaries

2.1 Graph-Based Distance Bounding Protocols

Graph-based DB protocols were introduced in [19] aimed at resisting both mafia and distance frauds, yet requiring low memory to be implemented. The idea is to define a digraph $G = (V, E)$ and a starting vertex $v \in V$. Then, a challenge-response protocol (see Fig. 1) is executed where the challenges define a walk in G according to an edge labeling function $\ell_E : E \to \{0, 1\}$ and the responses are stored on the vertices according to a vertex labeling function $\ell_V : V \to \{0, 1\}$.

Algorithm 1. Graph-based distance bounding protocol

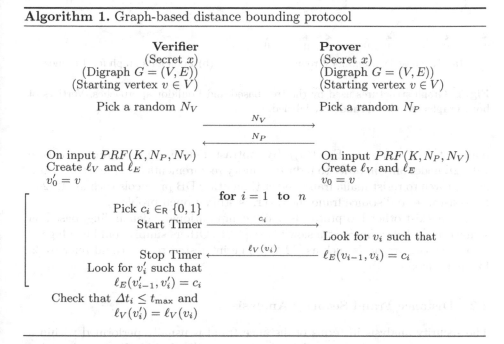

As shown by Fig. 1, prover and verifier exchange two nonces and use a pseudo-random function ($PRF(.)$) with a shared private key to compute two labeling functions $\ell_V : V \to \sum$ and $\ell_E : E \to \sum$ where $\sum = \{0, 1\}$. For ℓ_E it must hold that $\ell_E(u, v) \neq \ell_E(u, w)$ for every pair of different edges (u, v) and (u, w) in E. By contrast, ℓ_V is chosen randomly. After labeling the graph, n rounds of time-critical sessions are executed. At the ith round, the verifier sends the binary challenge c_i. Then, the prover answers with $\ell_V(v_i)$ where v_i holds that $(v_{i-1}, v_i) \in E$ and $\ell_E(v_{i-1}, v_i) = c_i$. Note that v_0 is the starting vertex v. At the end of the n time-critical sessions, the verifier checks all prover's responses ($\ell_V(v_i)$) and the round-trip-times (Δt_i), which should be below some threshold $t_{\max}$. Intuitively, the lower $t_{\max}$ the closer the prover to the verifier is expected to be.

Two graph-based DB protocols exist; the tree-based approach [3] and the Poulidor protocol [19]. As suggested by its name, the former uses a tree of depth

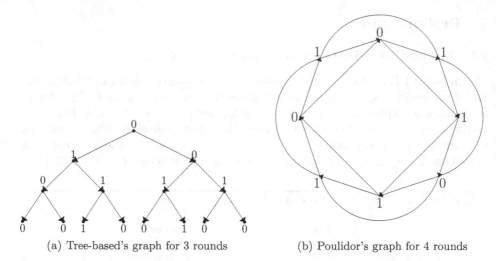

(a) Tree-based's graph for 3 rounds   (b) Poulidor's graph for 4 rounds

Fig. 1. Graph structures used by the tree-based and Poulidor approaches. Vertices of both graphs have been randomly labeled.

n and $2^{n+1}-1$ nodes (see Fig. 1(a)). By contrast, Poulidor uses a graph structure with $2n$ nodes only in order to reduce memory requirements (see Fig. 1(b)). Both have proven to resist mafia fraud better than other DB protocols such as [12,20]. Its resistance to distance fraud, however, is still an open problem.

There exist other DB protocols, more computationally demanding, based on signatures and/or a final extra slow phase [4,21]. Others simply could be plugged into most DB protocols such as [22,23]. The interested reader could refer to [2] for more details.

2.2   Distance Fraud Security Analysis

The security analysis in terms of distance fraud is usually performed within a well-known framework proposed by Avoine et al. [2]. In this framework, a distance fraud adversary uses the *early-reply strategy* to defeat the DB protocol. This strategy consists on sending the bits answer in advance (*i.e.,* before receiving the challenges.) Doing so, the adversary simulates to be closer than really is, and its success probability is lower-bounded by $1/2^n$.

In [19], the best early-reply strategy against what they called a *family* of DB protocols is defined. This *family* includes graph-based DB protocols. However, their definition is too generic to be used for simply analyzing graph-based DB protocols. Therefore, we reformulate it here in terms of a new problem in Graph Theory. The problem is named Binary MFS problem (see Definition 2) and is based on its more general version MFS problem (see Definition 1).

Definition 1 (The most frequent sequence problem (MFS problem)). *Let $G = (V, E)$ be a vertex-labeled digraph where Σ and $\ell : V \to \Sigma$ are the set*

of vertex labels and the labeling function respectively. For a label sequence $t = t_1 t_2 ... t_k$, $occ_v^G(t)$ *denotes the number of walks* $v_1 v_2 ... v_k$ *in* G *such that* $v_1 = v$ *and* $\forall i \in \{1, ..., k\}$ $(\ell(v_i) = t_i)$. *The MFS problem consists on finding, given the triple* (G, v, k), *the* most frequent sequence *of size* k *defined as* $\arg\max_{t \in \Sigma^k}(occ_v^G(t))$.

Definition 2 (Binary MFS problem). *The Binary MFS problem is an MFS problem where* G *is constrained to use a binary vertex set* $(\sum = \{0, 1\})$ *and the out-degree of every vertex should be at most 2.*

Example. Either the graph in Fig. 1(a) or the one in Fig. 1(b) can be the input of the Binary MFS problem. Assuming $k = 4$ and the starting vertex as the top one, the most frequent sequences for the tree in Fig. 1(a) is 0010 (occurs 3 times), and for the graph in Fig. 1(b) is 0101 (occurs 4 times).

To successfully apply a distance fraud attack against a graph-based DB protocol with n time-critical sessions, the best adversary's strategy consists of: (i) solving the Binary MFS problem defined by the triple $(G, v, n + 1)$ and finding the most frequent sequence $t_0 t_1 ... t_n$, (ii) sending $t_1 ... t_n$ in advance to the verifier as the responses to the n verifier's challenges. By this strategy, the adversary's success probability is maximized to $\frac{occ_v^G(t)}{2^n}$ [19]. Coming back to the previous example, the adversary success probability of the tree-based approach defined by Fig. 1(a) is 3/8, which is higher than the expected lower bound 1/8.

Definition 3 (Distance fraud success probability). *Let* $\prod$ *be a graph-based DB protocol with* n *time-critical sessions that uses the vertex-labeled digraph* $G = (V, E)$ *and* $v \in V$ *as the starting vertex. Let* $M_{G,v,n}$ *be a random variable on the sample space of all labeling functions* $\ell : V \mapsto \Sigma$ *that outputs the maximum value* $\max(occ_v^G(t))$ *where* $t \in \{0, 1\}^{n+1}$. *The distance fraud success probability of an adversary against* $\prod$ *is defined as* $\frac{E(M_{G,v,n})}{2^n}$ *where* $E(M_{G,v,n})$ *represents the expectation of the random variable* $M_{G,v,n}$.

Note that, following the design of graph-based DB protocols, Definition 3 considers that G is randomly labeled at each execution of the protocol.

To the best of our knowledge, computing distance fraud security according to Definition 3 has been only addressed in its seminal work [19]. Apparently, the problem is one of those problems that remain intractable even if $P = NP$ because all, or almost all, the labeling functions should be considered. For this reason, an upper bound was proposed in [19] and the exact distance fraud security was left as an open problem. We have shown that this problem depends on a problem named the MFS problem and, in particular, on the Binary MFS problem. Below, we review some work related to them.

2.3 Review on Frequent Sequences Problems

Sequential Pattern Mining is a well-studied field introduced by Agrawal and Srikant [1] in 1995. Given a databases of transactions (*e.g.*, customer transactions, medical records, web sessions, etc.) the problem consists on discovering all the sequential patterns with some minimum support. The support of a pattern is defined as the number of data-sequence within the database that are contained in the pattern.

The sequential pattern mining problem is $\#P$-complete [24] and several variants of it exist. For instance, Mannila et al. say that two events are connected if they are close enough in terms of time [15]. They define an *episode* as a collection of connected events and the problem is to find frequently occurring episodes in a sequence. A simpler variant, known as the *most common subsequent problem*, was introduced by Campagna and Pagh [5]. The most common subsequent problem does not consider time-stamped events. Instead, it aims to find all the label sequences in a vertex-labeled acyclic graph that appear more often. Other variants have arisen from complex applications namely, telecommunication, market analysis, and DNA research. We refer the reader to [6] for an extensive survey on this subject.

Frequent paths on a graph have also been used to define Kernel functions [17, 18]. Kernel functions has applicability in chemoinformatics and bioinformatics where objects are mapped to a feature space. In this case, the feature space representation is the number of occurrences of vertex-labeled paths and the problem is to infer the graph from such a feature vector. This problem has been proven to be NP-Hard even for trees of bounded degree [18].

It can be seen that the MFS problem is different to the sequential pattern mining problems and its nature is obviously different to the one of Kernel methods. On one hand, sequential pattern mining is an enumeration problem while MFS is just a search problem. On the other hand, the MFS problem requires all walks to begin from a given vertex and the size of the sequences should be equal. As in [5], the time dimension is not considered.

3   On the Hardness of the Binary MFS Problem

Binary MFS is a search problem that looks for the most frequent sequence of length k in a vertex-labeled digraph G starting from a given vertex v (see Definition 2). Intuitively, all or almost all the walks in G starting from v should be analyzed in order to find such a sequence, which means that Binary MFS might not be in the complexity class P. However, we cannot even state that Binary MFS is in $NP - P$ since it is not trivial how to *check* a solution in polynomial time. Nevertheless, we prove in this Section (see Theorem 1) that the general Boolean Satisfiability problem (SAT) reduces to Binary MFS. Therefore, Binary MFS can be considered NP-Hard even thought it may not even be in NP [11].

Definition 4 (SAT). *Let $x = (x_1, x_2, ..., x_n)$ be a set of boolean variables and $c_1(x), c_2(x), ..., c_m(x)$ be a set of clauses where $c_i(x)$ is a disjunction of literals. The Boolean satisfiability problem (SAT) consists on deciding whether there exists an assignment for the boolean variables x such that the function $f_{SAT} = c_1(x) \wedge c_2(x) \wedge ... \wedge c_m(x) = 1$.*

Algorithm 2 shows our reduction from SAT to an instance of the Binary MFS problem. First, it creates a binary tree T of depth $\lceil \log m \rceil$ with m leafs

$c_1, c_2, ..., c_m$[1], and a graph $G' = (V', E')$ where $V' = \{u_0^2, v_0^2, ..., u_0^n, v_0^n\}$ and $E' = \{(x,y)|\exists k \in \{2, ..., n-1\}(x \in \{u_0^k, v_0^k\} \land y \in \{u_0^{k+1}, v_0^{k+1}\})\}$. The graph $G = (V, E)$ is initialized with the two connected components T and G'. In addition, V is increased with the vertices u_i^j and v_i^j where $i \in \{1, ..., m\}$ and $j \in \{1, ..., n\}$. Then, for each clause c_i and each variable x_j $(j < n)$, the vertex u_i^j is connected with u_0^{j+1} and v_0^{j+1} if $x_j \in c_i(x)$, with u_i^{j+1} and v_i^{j+1} otherwise. Similarly, the vertex v_i^j is connected with u_0^{j+1} and v_0^{j+1} if $\neg x_j \in c_i(x)$, with u_i^{j+1} and v_i^{j+1} otherwise. Finally, for every $i \in \{1, ..., m\}$: (i) the vertices u_i^n and v_i^n are removed together with their incident edges, (ii) the edges (u_i^{n-1}, u_0^n) and (v_i^{n-1}, u_0^n) are added if $x_n \in c_i(x)$, (iii) if $\neg x_n \in c_i(x)$ the added edges are (u_i^{n-1}, v_0^n) and (v_i^{n-1}, v_0^n). The vertex-label function is simply defined as a function that outputs 0 on input v_i^j for every $i \in \{0, 1, ..., m\}$ and $j \in \{1, ..., n\}$, outputs 1 otherwise.

To better illustrate Algorithm 2, Fig. 2 shows an example of its output for a given SAT instance. Note that, Algorithm 2 does not consider tautologies such as the empty clause or one containing $x \lor \neg x$.

Algorithm 2. Reduction from the SAT problem

Require: A SAT instance where $x = (x_1, x_2, ..., x_n)$ are the boolean variables and $c_1(x), c_2(x), ..., c_m(x)$ are the set of clauses

1: Let $G = (V, E)$ be a digraph with just one vertex named *root*
2: From the root, a directed binary tree with m leafs is created such that all the leafs are at the same depth. The leaf vertices are denoted as $c_1, c_2, ..., c_m$
3: Let $G' = (V', E')$ be a digraph where $V' = \{u_0^2, v_0^2, ..., u_0^n, v_0^n\}$ and $E' = \{(x,y)|\exists k \in \{2, ..., n-1\}(x \in \{u_0^k, v_0^k\} \land y \in \{u_0^{k+1}, v_0^{k+1}\})\}$
4: Set $G = G \cup G'$
5: **for all** vertex c_i **do**
6:     Set $V = V \cup \{u_i^1, v_i^1, u_i^2, v_i^2, ..., u_i^n, v_i^n\}$
7:     Set $E = E \cup \{(c_i, u_i^1), (c_i, v_i^1)\}$
8:     **for all** $j \in \{1, 2, ..., n-1\}$ **do**
9:         **if** $x_j \in c_i(x)$ **then**
10:            Set $E = E \cup \{(u_i^j, u_0^{j+1}), (u_i^j, v_0^{j+1})\}$ and $E = E \cup \{(v_i^j, u_i^{j+1}), (v_i^j, v_i^{j+1})\}$
11:         **else if** $\neg x_j \in c_i(x)$ **then**
12:            Set $E = E \cup \{(u_i^j, u_i^{j+1}), (u_i^j, v_i^{j+1})\}$ and $E = E \cup \{(v_i^j, u_0^{j+1}), (v_i^j, v_0^{j+1})\}$
13:         **else**
14:            Set $E = E \cup \{(u_i^j, u_i^{j+1}), (u_i^j, v_i^{j+1})\}$ and $E = E \cup \{(v_i^j, u_i^{j+1}), (v_i^j, v_i^{j+1})\}$
15:     Remove u_i^n and v_i^n from G
16:     **if** $x_n \in c_i(x)$ **then** Set $E = E \cup \{(u_i^{n-1}, u_0^n), (v_i^{n-1}, u_0^n)\}$
17:     **if** $\neg x_n \in c_i(x)$ **then** Set $E = E \cup \{(u_i^{n-1}, v_0^n), (v_i^{n-1}, v_0^n)\}$
18: Create vertex-label function $\ell_V(.)$ such that $\forall i \in \{0, 1, ..., m\}, j \in \{1, ..., n\}(\ell_V(v_i^j) = 0)$, $\ell_V(.)$ outputs 1 otherwise.
19: **Return** G and ℓ_V as result.

---

[1] The leafs are intentionally labeled by using the same clause names.

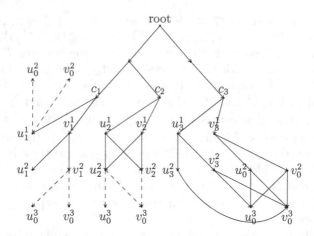

Fig. 2. The resulting graph when applying Algorithm 2 on input the boolean formula $(x_1 \lor \neg x_2) \land (x_2 \lor \neg x_3) \land (\neg x_1 \lor \neg x_2 \lor \neg x_3)$. For the sake of a good visualization some nodes have been "cloned", however, they actually represent a single node in the graph. Such "cloned" nodes can be easily identified as the ones with dashed incident edges.

Lemma 1. *The longest walk in G starting from the* root *vertex has length $n + \lceil \log m \rceil$ and ends either at u_0^n or v_0^n.*

Proof. Let $w = w_0...w_k$ be a walk in $G = (V, E)$ starting from the *root* vertex. Let us assume that w is maximal in the sense that w_k does not have outgoing edges. According to Algorithm 2, w_k does not have out-going edges only if $w_k \in \{u_0^n, v_0^n\}$ or $w_k \in \{u_1^{n-1}, v_1^{n-1}, u_2^{n-1}, v_2^{n-1}, ..., u_m^{n-1}, v_m^{n-1}\}$ (see Step 15 of Algorithm 2). Therefore, either the longest walk ends at u_0^n or v_0^n and its length is $n + \lceil \log m \rceil$ or its length is $n - 1 + \lceil \log m \rceil$. The proof concludes by remarking that there must exist at least one walk ending at u_0^n or v_0^n unless all the clauses are empty, which is a tautology not-considered in SAT. $\square$

Lemma 2. *Let $s = s_0 s_1 ... s_{n+\lceil \log m \rceil}$ and $t = t_0 t_1 ... t_{n+\lceil \log m \rceil}$ two different maximal length walks in G that start from the* root *vertex. Then, $\forall k \in \{0, ..., n + \lceil \log m \rceil\}(\ell_V(s_k) = \ell_V(t_k)) \Rightarrow \exists i \neq j(c_i \in s \land c_j \in t)$.*

Proof. According to Algorithm 2, there exist $i, j \in \{1, ..., m\}$ such that $c_i = s_{\lceil \log m \rceil}$ and $c_j = t_{\lceil \log m \rceil}$. In addition, every vertex s_k (resp. t_k) where $\lceil \log m \rceil < k < n + \lceil \log m \rceil$ is either $u_i^{k-\lceil \log m \rceil}$ (resp. $u_j^{k-\lceil \log m \rceil}$) or $v_i^{k-\lceil \log m \rceil}$ (resp. $v_j^{k-\lceil \log m \rceil}$).

Now, according to the vertex-label function ℓ_V, if $\forall k \in \{0, ..., n-1+\lceil \log m \rceil\}$ $(\ell_V(s_k) = \ell_V(t_k))$, then $\forall k \in \{\lceil \log m \rceil + 1, ..., n-1+\lceil \log m \rceil\}(s_k = v_i^{k-\lceil \log m \rceil} \Leftrightarrow t_k = v_j^{k-\lceil \log m \rceil})$. Similarly, if $\ell_V(s_{n+\lceil \log m \rceil}) = \ell_V(t_{n+\lceil \log m \rceil})$ then $s_{n+\lceil \log m \rceil} = v_0^n \Leftrightarrow t_{n+\lceil \log m \rceil} = v_0^n$ (see Lemma 1). Therefore, $i = j \Rightarrow s = t$, which is a contradiction. $\square$

Theorem 1. *The Binary MFS problem is NP-Hard.*

Proof. Let $\prod$ be an instance of the SAT problem and let G be the graph obtained by applying Algorithm 2 on input $\prod$. Let $\prod'$ be the problem of finding the most frequent sequence of length $n + 1 + \lceil \log m \rceil$ in G starting from the vertex root. Given a solution s for $\prod'$, our aim is to prove that a true assignment for $\prod$ exists (and can be found) in polynomial time if and only if s appears m times in G. Doing so, $\prod$ is proven to be polynomially reducible to $\prod'$, which is a Binary MFS problem.

First, let us assume that the most frequent sequence $s = s_0 s_1 ... s_{n + \lceil \log m \rceil}$ in G occurs exactly m times. Let $w_0 w_1 ... w_{n + \lceil \log m \rceil}$ be a walk such that $\forall i \in \{0, ..., n + \lceil \log m \rceil\}(\ell_V(w_i) = s_i)$. By Algorithm 2, there must exist $i \in \{1, ..., m\}$ such that $w_{\lceil \log m \rceil} = c_i$. Let $w_{k + \lceil \log m \rceil}$ be the vertex such that $w_{k + \lceil \log m \rceil} \notin \{u_0^k, v_0^k\}$ and $w_{k + 1 + \lceil \log m \rceil} \in \{u_0^{k+1}, v_0^{k+1}\}$. Note that, such a vertex exists due to Lemma 1 and Algorithm 2. According to such an algorithm, either $w_{k + \lceil \log m \rceil} = u_i^k$ and $c_i(x)$ contains the literal x_k or $w_{k + \lceil \log m \rceil} = v_i^k$ and $c_i(x)$ contains the literal $\neg x_k$. Therefore, if $w_{k + \lceil \log m \rceil} = u_i^k$ then $x_k = s_{k + \lceil \log m \rceil} = \ell_V(u_i^k) = 1$ satisfies the clause $c_i(x)$, otherwise $x_k = s_{k + \lceil \log m \rceil} = \ell_V(v_i^k) = 0$ does. Consequently, the assignment $x_j = s_{j + \lceil \log m \rceil} \ \forall j \in \{1, ..., n\}$ satisfies $c_i(x)$.

Considering that s appears m times, then by Lemma 2 we can conclude that all the clauses are satisfied by such assignment, whereupon we finish the first part of this proof.

Now, let $x = (y_1, ..., y_n)$ be a true assignment for $\prod$. Let us consider the induced sub-graph G_i formed by the vertex c_i and all the other vertices reachable from c_i. By design of Algorithm 2, there exists a walk $w = w_0 w_1 ... w_{n-1}$ in G_i such that $\forall k \in \{1, ..., n - 1\}(y_k = \ell_V(w_k))$ and $w_0 = c_i$. In addition, if y_j satisfies clause $c_i(x)$ (*i.e.*, $y_j = 1 \wedge x_j \in c_i(x)$ or $y_j = 0 \wedge \neg x_j \in c_i(x)$), then according to Algorithm 2 either $(x_j \in c_i(x) \wedge \{(u_i^j, u_0^{j+1}), (u_i^j, v_0^{j+1})\} \in E)$ or $(\neg x_j \in c_i(x) \wedge \{(v_i^j, u_0^{j+1}), (v_i^j, v_0^{j+1})\} \in E)$. Consequently, it must hold that $w_{n-1} \in \{u_0^{n-1}, v_0^{n-1}\}$ if and only if $(x_1, ..., x_{n-1}) = (y_1, ..., y_{n-1})$ satisfies $c_i(x)$. If $(y_1, ..., y_{n-1})$ does satisfies $c_i(x)$, the walk $w = w_0 w_1 ... w_{n-1} w_n$ where $w_n = u_0^n$ if $y_n = 1$ and $w_n = v_0^n$ if $y_n = 0$ holds that $\forall k \in \{1, ..., n\}(y_k = \ell_V(w_k))$. On the other hand, if $(y_1, ..., y_{n-1})$ does not satisfies $c_i(x)$, then $y_n = 1 \Rightarrow x_n \in c_i(x)$ and $y_n = 0 \Rightarrow \neg x_n \in c_i(x)$. According to Steps 18 and 20 of Algorithm 2, $w = w_0 w_1 ... w_{n-1} w_n$ where $w_n = u_0^n$ if $y_n = 1$ and $w_n = v_0^n$ if $y_n = 0$ is a walk holding that $\forall k \in \{1, ..., n\}(y_k = \ell_V(w_k))$. As a conclusion, for every $i \in \{1, ..., m\}$ there exists a walk passing through c_i that generates the sequence $\underbrace{11...11}_{\lceil \log m \rceil + 1} y_1 ... y_n$. This result together with Lemma 2 conclude that such a sequence repeats exactly m times. □

Corollary 1. *The MFS problem is NP-Hard.*

4   Distance Fraud Analysis for the Tree-Based Approach

In this section, the problem of computing the distance fraud resistance of the tree-based DB protocol [3] is addressed. A naive algorithm to solve this problem consists on analyzing all the labeling functions for a full binary tree of depth n and then computing the most frequent sequence for each labeling function (see Definition 3). This results in a time-complexity of $O(2^{2^n+n})$, which is unfeasible even for small values of n. We propose an algorithm that reduces this time-complexity to $O(2^{2n}n)$. Although still exponential, it might be used up to reasonable values of n (e.g., $n = 32$).

For the sake of clarity, we first adapt Definition 3 to the context of the tree-based proposal.

Problem 1. [Tree-based distance fraud problem] Let $\prod$ be a tree-based DB protocol with n time-critical sessions that uses the full binary tree $T = (V, E)$ and $root \in V$ as the starting vertex. Let M_n be a random variable on the sample space of all labeling functions $\ell : V \rightarrow \{0, 1\}$ that outputs the maximum value $\max(occ_{root}^T(t))$ where $t \in \{0, 1\}^{n+1}$. The tree-based distance fraud problem consists on finding the expectation of the random variable M_n.

Theorem 2. Let m and n be two positive integers. Let T_n^m be a tree such that: (i) the root has $2m$ children and (ii) each root's children is the root of a full binary tree of depth $n - 1$. Let M_n^m be the random variable on the sample space of all binary vertex-labeling functions over T_n^m that outputs the maximum value $\max(occ_{root}^{T_n^m}(t))$. The expectation of the random variable M_n can be computed as follows:

$$E(M_n) = E(M_n^1) = \sum_{i=1}^{2^n} \left(\Pr(M_n^1 < i + 1) - \Pr(M_n^1 < i) \right) i.$$

where

$$\Pr(M_n^m < x) = \sum_{i=0}^{2m} \frac{\binom{2m}{i}}{2^{2m}} \left(\Pr(M_{n-1}^i < x) \Pr(M_{n-1}^{2m-i} < x) \right).$$

and

$$\Pr(M_n^m < x) = \begin{cases} 0 & if \quad x = 1 \\ 0 & if \quad n = 1 \wedge m > x \\ \frac{1}{2^{2m}} \left(\binom{2m}{m} + 2 \sum_{i=m+1}^{x-1} \binom{2m}{i} \right) & if \quad n = 1 \wedge m \leq x \leq 2m \\ 1 & if \quad n = 1 \wedge 2m < x \\ 1 & if \quad m = 0 \end{cases}$$

Proof. A full binary tree of depth n can be denoted as T_n^1 and the random variable M_n is equivalent to M_n^1. Therefore, in what follows, we focus on computing the expectation of the random variable M_n^m.

Let us consider now a labeling function ℓ over T_n^m. Let V_0 and V_1 be the set of children of the T_n^m's root labeled with 0 and 1 respectively. Let $C_1^0, C_2^0, ..., C_{2|V_0|}^0$ and $C_1^1, C_2^1, ..., C_{2|V_1|}^1$ be the subtrees rooted in the children of the vertices in V_0 and V_1 respectively. Let X be a labeled tree whose root is labeled with 0 and the root's children are the full binary trees $C_1^0, C_2^0, ..., C_{2|V_0|}^0$. In the same vein, Y is defined as a labeled tree whose root is labeled with 1 and the root's children are the full binary trees $C_1^1, C_2^1, ..., C_{2|V_1|}^1$. It can be noted that, if a sequence $t = t_1...t_n$ occurs exactly k times either in X or Y, then the sequence $t = t_0 t_1...t_n$ where t_0 is the label of T_n^m's root also appears exactly k times in T_n^m. Therefore, taking into account that $X = T_{n-1}^{|V_0|}$ and $Y = T_{n-1}^{|V_1|}$, the following recurrent result can be obtained:

$$\Pr(M_n^m < x) = \sum_{i=0}^{2m} \Pr(|V_0| = i)\left(\Pr(M_{n-1}^i < x)\Pr(M_{n-1}^{2m-i} < x)\right)$$

$$= \sum_{i=0}^{2m} \frac{\binom{2m}{i}}{2^{2m}} \left(\Pr(M_{n-1}^i < x)\Pr(M_{n-1}^{2m-i} < x)\right). \tag{1}$$

Equation 1 shows that $\Pr(M_n^m < x)$ could be computed recursively. To do so, stop conditions must be found as follows:

$$\Pr(M_n^m < x) = \begin{cases} 0 & \text{if } x = 1 \\ 0 & \text{if } n = 1 \wedge m > x \\ \frac{1}{2^{2m}}\left(\binom{2m}{m} + 2\sum_{i=m+1}^{x-1}\binom{2m}{i}\right) & \text{if } n = 1 \wedge m \le x \le 2m \\ 1 & \text{if } n = 1 \wedge 2m < x \\ 1 & \text{if } m = 0 \end{cases} \tag{2}$$

Let us analyze $\Pr(M_1^m < x)$, which is the less trivial stop condition in Eq. 2. Since T_1^m has depth 1 and $2m$ children, T_1^m generates $2m$ sequences, p of them ending with 0 and q with 1. Consequently, $M_1^m = \max(p, q) \ge m$ and thus, $\Pr(M_1^m < x) = 0$ if $x < m$. Similarly $M_1^m \le 2m$, which implies that $\Pr(M_1^m < x) = 1$ if $x > 2m$. Finally, let us assume that $m \ge x \ge 2m$. In this case, $M_1^m < x$ holds if $M_1^m \in \{m, m+1, ..., x-1\}$, therefore, $\Pr(M_1^m < x) = \sum_{i=m}^{x-1}\Pr(M_1^m = i)$ where $\Pr(M_1^m = i) = \frac{\binom{2m}{m}}{2^{2m}}$ if $i = m$, otherwise $\Pr(M_1^m = i) = 2\frac{\binom{2m}{i}}{2^{2m}}$. This yields to $\Pr(M_1^m < x) = \frac{1}{2^{2m}}\left(\binom{2m}{m} + 2\sum_{i=m+1}^{x-1}\binom{2m}{i}\right)$ if $m \ge x \ge 2m$.

The proof concludes by using the definition of expectation for a discrete variable together with Eqs. 1 and 2.   □

Time-complexity analysis. The result provided by Theorem 2 can be implemented by a dynamic algorithm, meaning that a three-dimensional matrix will dynamically store the values of $\Pr(M_n^m < x)$ and will use them when needed.

In the worst case, the algorithm requires to fill the whole matrix, which results in a time-complexity of $O(2^n \times n \times 2^n) = O(2^{2n}n)$.

5 Discussion and Conclusions

Before the introduction of graph-based DB protocols, computing resistance to distance fraud was not a big issue (*e.g.*, Hancke and Kuhn [12] and Kim and Avoine [14] proposals.) Actually, the well-known early-reply strategy used to analyze distance fraud security implicitly assumes that the adversary is able to compute the *best* answer without knowing the challenges and within a "reasonable" time frame. In this article, however, we have shown that this assumption might not hold for graph-based DB protocols by proving that the Binary MFS problem is NP-Hard. This opens two interesting research questions: (i) What instances of the Binary MFS problem are actually hard to solve? (ii) In a practical setting, does the adversary have enough time to solve a probably exponential problem between the end of the slow phase and the beginning of the fast phase? (iii) What kinds of heuristics can be used and what would the implications be?

Even though we do not give answers to those questions, we provide a clue of how to build graph-based DB protocols resistant to distance fraud. As indicate our reduction from the SAT problem, a good strategy is to label the vertices of G as follows: if the vertices u and v have incident edges from the same vertex, then $\forall b \in \{0, 1\}(\ell_V(u) = b \Leftrightarrow \ell_V(v) = b \oplus 1)$. Doing so, G is likely to generate all the sequences $\{0, 1\}^n$ just once, in which case its resistance to distance fraud achieves the lower bound $1/2^n$. As a consequence, we conjecture that the best graph DB protocol in terms of mafia fraud constrained to have no more than certain number of nodes, is also the best in terms of distance fraud. Note that, this conjecture becomes trivial if no limit on the size of the graph is considered.

This article has also addressed the problem of computing the distance fraud security of the tree-based DB proposal [3]. This is an inherent exponential problem since a graph with N nodes can be labeled in 2^N different ways. The tree-based proposal uses a tree with 2^n nodes and thus 2^{2^n} labelling functions exists. However, we provide an algorithm that avoids considering all the labelling functions and has a time complexity of $O(2^{2n}n)$, which is significantly better than the naive approach with $O(2^{2^n+n})$. This result makes realistic the challenge of computing the distance fraud security of the two graph-based DB protocols proposed up-to-date; the tree-based approach [3] by using the proposed algorithm ($O(2^{2n}n)$), and the Poulidor protocol [19] by simply using a brute-force algorithm ($O(2^{3n})$). Doing so, both can be fairly compared with other state-of-the-art DB protocols. Such a challenge is out of the scope of this article and is left as future work, though.

Acknowledgments. The author thanks to Gildas Avoine, Sjouke Mauw, Juan Alberto Rodriguez-Velazquez, and Alejandro Estrada-Moreno for their invaluable comments and feedback.

References

1. Agrawal, R., Srikant, R.: Mining sequential patterns. In: ICDE, pp. 3–14 (1995)
2. Avoine, G., Bingöl, M.A., Kardaş, S., Lauradoux, C., Martin, B.: A framework for analyzing RFID distance bounding protocols. J. Comput. Secur. **19**(2), 289–317 (2011)
3. Avoine, G., Tchamkerten, A.: An efficient distance bounding RFID authentication protocol: balancing false-acceptance rate and memory requirement. In: Samarati, P., Yung, M., Martinelli, F., Ardagna, C.A. (eds.) ISC 2009. LNCS, vol. 5735, pp. 250–261. Springer, Heidelberg (2009)
4. Brands, S., Chaum, D.: Distance bounding protocols. In: Helleseth, T. (ed.) EUROCRYPT 1993. LNCS, vol. 765, pp. 344–359. Springer, Heidelberg (1994)
5. Campagna, A., Pagh, R.: On finding frequent patterns in event sequences. In: ICDM '10, pp. 755–760 (2010)
6. Chand, C., Thakkar, A., Amit, G.: Sequential pattern mining: Survey and current research challenges. Int. J. Soft Comput. Eng. **2**(1) (2012)
7. Conway, J.H.: On Numbers and Games, 2nd edn. AK Peters Ltd., Natick (2000)
8. Desmedt, Y.G., Goutier, C., Bengio, S.: Special uses and abuses of the Fiat Shamir passport protocol. In: Pomerance, C. (ed.) CRYPTO 1987. LNCS, vol. 293, pp. 21–39. Springer, Heidelberg (1988)
9. Drimer, S., Murdoch, S.J.: Keep your enemies close: distance bounding against smartcard relay attacks. In: USINEX, pp. 1–16 (2007)
10. Francis, L., Hancke, G., Mayes, K., Markantonakis, K.: Practical NFC peer-to-peer relay attack using mobile phones. In: Ors Yalcin, S.B. (ed.) RFIDSec 2010. LNCS, vol. 6370, pp. 35–49. Springer, Heidelberg (2010)
11. Garey, M.R., Johnson, D.S.: Computers and Intractability: A Guide to the Theory of NP-Completeness. W. H. Freeman, NY (1979)
12. Hancke, G.P., Kuhn, M.G.: An RFID distance bounding protocol. In: SECURECOMM, pp. 67–73 (2005)
13. Hancke, G.P., Kuhn, M.G.: Attacks on time-of-flight distance bounding channels. In: WiSec '08, pp. 194–202 (2008)
14. Kim, C.H., Avoine, G.: RFID distance bounding protocols with mixed challenges. IEEE Trans. Wireless Commun. **10**(5), 1618–1626 (2011)
15. Mannila, H., Toivonen, H., Verkamo, A.I.: Discovery of frequent episodes in event sequences. Data Min. Knowl. Discov. **1**(3), 259–289 (1997)
16. Oren, Y., Wool, A.: Relay attacks on RFID-based electronic voting systems. Cryptology ePrint Archive, Report 2009/422 (2009)
17. Shimizu, M., Nagamochi, H., Akutsu, T.: Enumerating tree-like chemical graphs with given upper and lower bounds on path frequencies. BMC Bioinform. **12**, 1–9 (2011)
18. Akutsu, T., Tatsuya, D., Fukagawa, D., Jansson, J., Sadakane, K.: Inferring a graph from path frequency. Discrete Appl. Math. **160**(10–11), 1416–1428 (2012)
19. Trujillo-Rasua, R., Martin, B., Avoine, G.: The poulidor distance-bounding protocol. In: Ors Yalcin, S.B. (ed.) RFIDSec 2010. LNCS, vol. 6370, pp. 239–257. Springer, Heidelberg (2010)
20. Kim, C.H., Avoine, G.: RFID distance bounding protocol with mixed challenges to prevent relay attacks. In: Garay, J.A., Miyaji, A., Otsuka, A. (eds.) CANS 2009. LNCS, vol. 5888, pp. 119–133. Springer, Heidelberg (2009)
21. Singelée, D., Preneel, B.: Distance bounding in noisy environments. In: Stajano, F., Meadows, C., Capkun, S., Moore, T. (eds.) ESAS 2007. LNCS, vol. 4572, pp. 101–115. Springer, Heidelberg (2007)

22. Xin, W., Yang, T., Tang, C., Hu, J., Chen, Z.: A distance bounding protocol using error state and punishment. In: IMCCC, pp. 436–440 (2011)
23. Munilla, J., Peinado, A.: Distance bounding protocols for RFID enhanced by using void-challenges and analysis in noisy channels. Wirel. Commun. Mob. Comput. 8(9), 1227–1232 (2008)
24. Yang, G.: The complexity of mining maximal frequent itemsets and maximal frequent patterns. In: KDD '04, pp. 344–353 (2004)

Protecting Movement Trajectories Through Fragmentation

Marius Wernke(✉), Frank Dürr, and Kurt Rothermel

Institute of Parallel and Distributed Systems (IPVS), University of Stuttgart,
Universitätsstraße 38, 70569 Stuttgart, Germany
{marius.wernke,frank.duerr,kurt.rothermel}@ipvs.uni-stuttgart.de

Abstract. Location-based applications (LBAs) like geo-social networks, points of interest finders, and real-time traffic monitoring applications have entered people's daily life. Advanced LBAs rely on location services (LSs) managing movement trajectories of multiple users in a scalable fashion. However, exposing trajectory information raises user privacy concerns, in particular if LSs are non-trusted. For instance, an attacker compromising an LS can use the retrieved user trajectory for stalking, mugging, or to trace user movement. To limit the misuse of trajectory data, we present a new approach for the secure management of trajectories on non-trusted servers. Instead of providing the complete trajectory of a user to a single LS, we split up the trajectory into a set of fragments and distribute the fragments among LSs of *different* providers. By distributing fragments, we avoid a single point of failure in case of compromised LSs, while different LBAs can still reconstruct the trajectory based on user-defined access rights.

In our evaluation, we show the effectiveness of our approach by using real world trajectories and realistic attackers using map knowledge and statistical information to predict and reconstruct the user's movement.

Keywords: Location management · Fragmentation · Trajectories · Privacy

1 Introduction

Nowadays, most people carry a mobile device with an integrated positioning system such as GPS. In combination with cheap and fast mobile communication technologies, location-based applications (LBAs) like geo-social networks and points of interest finders have entered people's daily life.

LBAs can be classified into two categories: LBAs using single user positions, and LBAs using movement trajectories. The first category considers individual positions, for instance, provided when a user is "checking-in" to a restaurant, to show friends his current position. The second category considers LBAs relying on movement traces of mobile objects. Examples are applications for sharing jogging paths, community-based mapping, and real-time traffic monitoring.

© Institute for Computer Sciences, Social Informatics and Telecommunications Engineering 2014
I. Stojmenovic et al. (Eds.): MOBIQUITOUS 2013, LNICST 131, pp. 303–315, 2014.
DOI: 10.1007/978-3-319-11569-6_24

Advanced LBAs rely on location services (LSs), which manage a huge number of mobile object positions and allow for sharing positions between multiple applications. LSs provide functionalities for spatial queries and relieve mobile objects from sending their position individually to multiple LBAs.

While the position of a mobile object is essential for many applications, sharing position information may raise serious privacy concerns. As shown in [13], 55 % of the 1.500 survey participants using LBAs were worried about loss of privacy. For instance, an attacker can determine habits, interests, or other sensitive information by analyzing movement trajectories. Furthermore, an attacker can misuse position information for stalking, mugging, or to trace user movement.

Existing privacy approaches protecting trajectories usually rely on a trusted third party (TTP). For instance, k-anonymity approaches [8] protecting the user identity rely on a *location anonymizer* to collect positions of different users to generate areas fulfilling the user-defined k-anonymity level. Mix zones [2] use a trusted middleware to change user pseudonyms within a predefined spatial region. Advanced obfuscation approaches [3] protecting the user trajectory use a TTP to calculate cloaked spatial regions. However, as shown by many incidents [5], even service providers that were deemed to be trusted could be compromised. Therefore, no service provider can guarantee to perfectly protect its stored information. Consequently, we have to consider that LSs are non-trusted.

To protect movement trajectories of mobile users without using a trusted third party, we present our novel Trajectory Fragmentation Algorithm (*TFA*). The general idea of our approach is to split up a user's trajectory into a set of smaller fragments that are distributed to different LSs of different providers. Thus, each LS stores only a part of the trajectory and no LS knows the complete movement trace of the user. Therefore, an attacker compromising an LS has only limited knowledge about the user's movement. To prevent an attacker compromising multiple LSs from correlating the retrieved fragments, *TFA* uses different pseudonyms for the fragments. Different clients of the LSs, for instance, different LBAs can access the trajectory of the user by querying fragments from multiple LSs based on the known pseudonym used for the corresponding LS.

In this paper, we make the following contributions: (1) A concept for distributing trajectory fragments among a set of LSs to avoid that a single LS can reveal the complete user trajectory. (2) An optimized algorithm that calculates a minimum number of fragments under the constraint of fulfilling a given level of privacy. (3) A privacy evaluation with attackers of different strength showing the effectiveness of our approach.

The rest of the paper is structured as follows: In Sect. 2, we present related work. In Sect. 3, we introduce our system model. Then, we formalize our problem statement and present *TFA* in Sects. 4 and 5. In Sect. 6, we present our privacy and performance evaluation. Finally, we conclude the paper in Sect. 7.

2   Related Work

Existing location privacy approaches can be classified based on their protection goal and whether they focus on single positions or movement trajectories. For an overview of existing location privacy attacks and approaches we refer to [15]. For single positions, k-anonymity [6] can be used to protect the identity of the user by making the user indistinguishable from $k-1$ other users. Spatial obfuscation [4] protects the position of the user by decreasing the precision of the position provided to an LS. Position sharing [14] allows for providing different precision levels to different LBAs while LSs only manage positions of limited precision. However, all these approaches focus on singular positions instead of trajectories.

Trajectory k-anonymity [8] protects the identity of a user by making the user indistinguishable from $k-1$ other users for the complete trajectory. Mix zones [2] protect the identity of a user by changing pseudonyms within an area where no user provides position information to an LBA. Trajectory obfuscation [3] uses a group-based approach to collect positions of multiple users to calculate obfuscated areas for the complete trajectory. However, all of these approaches require a TTP, while we do not rely on a TTP.

Dummy approaches [12] provide false trajectories to the LS in addition to the real user trajectory such that the LS cannot distinguish the received trajectories. However, since identifying dummy trajectories is possible [10], user privacy can be decreased. The approach presented in [1] protects the start and the destination of a trajectory without assuming a TTP. With our approach, we focus on protecting the complete trajectory rather than only its start or destination.

3   System Model

The components of our system are depicted in Fig. 1. The **mobile object** (MO) has an integrated positioning system such as GPS that is used to determine the MO's current position π. The MO executes a local software component that provides π to a set of different **location servers** (LSs), which store and manage trajectories of several MOs. LSs provide an access control mechanism to manage access to the stored positions. Different clients, for instance, different LBAs get access to the positions on different LSs based on their access rights.

The MO's position π is defined by its longitude and latitude values. Since MOs usually travel on streets, we map π to a graph representing the road network by using existing map-matching approaches. As shown in Fig. 2, the road

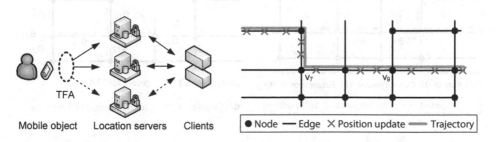

Fig. 1. System components   **Fig. 2.** Graph and trajectory example

network can be modeled as graph $G = (V, E)$ consisting of a set of nodes V and a set of edges E. Each node $v_i \in V$ represents a junction or an intermediate node that models the shape of the road. Each edge $e_j \in E$ represents a road segment between two nodes. The MO's movement trajectory $T = \{(\pi_{start}, t_{start}), \ldots, (\pi_{end}, t_{end})\}$ represents a set of consecutive position fixes π_i where the MO is located at time t_i. An example for T is shown in Fig. 2. We assume that the destination π_{end} of T is already known at time t_{start} because the MO typically knows its movement destination.

4   Problem Statement

Since we have to consider that LSs are non-trusted, an attacker can compromise an LS with a certain probability greater than zero. In this case, the part of the trajectory provided to the LS is revealed. Thus, our goal is to protect the MO's trajectory by minimizing the revealed information of an attack on an LS.

We use a distributed approach to store and manage the MO's trajectory T. Our trajectory fragmentation algorithm splits up T into a set $F = \{f_1, \ldots, f_n\}$ of n trajectory fragments (or *fragments* for short). The number n of generated fragments corresponds to the number of used LSs to store the fragments and is either predefined by the MO or calculated by the fragmentation algorithm. While traveling, the MO uses the fragmentation algorithm to update its position over time on different LSs. Each position is provided to exactly one LS and each LS receives only the positions of a single fragment.

To measure the information exposed to an LS, we use weight function $\Phi(f_j)$ assigning each fragment f_j the value of its exposed information. More precisely, we measure the length of the trajectory that is revealed to an attacker, called the *revealed trace length* $\Phi(f_j)$.

The revealed trace length $\Phi(f_j)$ is defined as the distance an attacker compromising fragment f_j can trace the MO. The value of $\Phi(f_j) = \Phi^C(f_j) + \Phi^F(f_j) + \Phi^P(f_j)$ is calculated as the sum of the following three parts (cf. Fig. 3): The first part of $\Phi(f_j)$ is the length of the current fragment $\Phi^C(f_j)$, i.e., the length of

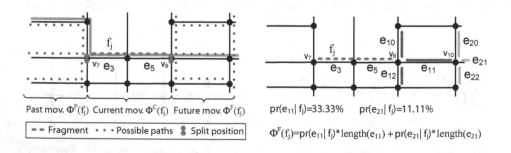

Past mov. $\Phi^P(f_j)$ Current mov. $\Phi^C(f_j)$ Future mov. $\Phi^F(f_j)$ $pr(e_{11}|f_j)=33.33\%$ $pr(e_{21}|f_j)=11.11\%$

- - Fragment   · · · Possible paths   ⚡ Split position $\Phi^F(f_j)=pr(e_{11}|f_j)*length(e_{11})+pr(e_{21}|f_j)*length(e_{21})$

Fig. 3. Different information parts   **Fig. 4.** Calculation of $\Phi^F(f_j)$

all edges $e_i \in f_j$. The second part of $\Phi(f_j)$ is the length of the predicted future movement $\Phi^F(f_j)$. This length is a probability measure, since multiple possible future paths exists. The probability that the MO travels along edge e_i after traveling on f_j is $pr(e_i|f_j)$. Then, $\Phi^F(f_j)$ is calculated as the length of all edges e_i of the predicted future trajectory T weighted by the probability $pr(e_i|f_j)$. We assume that the probability $pr(e_i|f_j)$ is given for each edge e_i, for instance, by a statistical movement analysis, or by using map knowledge assuming a uniform distribution for all edges. An example to calculate $\Phi^F(f_j)$ based on map knowledge is shown in Fig. 4. The probability $pr(e_{11}|f_j)$ is 33.33 %, since three alternatives exists to continue traveling after f_j. The probability $pr(e_{21}|f_j)$ is 11.11 % taking also $pr(e_{11}|f_j)$ into account. The third part of $\Phi(f_j)$ is the length of the reconstructed past movement $\Phi^P(f_j)$. Here, $\Phi^P(f_j)$ is calculated as presented for $\Phi^F(f_j)$ by considering the past instead of the future movement.

In order to find a fragmentation of trajectory T such that each fragment has a minimum revealed trace length $\Phi(f_j)$, we have to minimize the maximum value of $\Phi(f_j)$. This means, no matter which LS is compromised, only the maximum trace length $\Phi(f_j)$ can be revealed. Formally, we have to solve the following optimization problem:

$$\text{minimize} \qquad \max_{j \in [1;n]} (\Phi(f_j))$$

$$\text{subject to} \qquad \bigcup_{j \in [1;n]} f_j = T$$

Additionally, we want to answer the question of how many LSs are required to protect trajectory T from revealing a larger trace length than specified by a MO-defined maximum trace length Φ_{max}^{MO}. This means, we consider the problem of minimizing the number n of required LSs for Φ_{max}^{MO}. Formally, this optimization problem is defined as

$$\text{minimize} \qquad n$$

$$\text{subject to} \qquad \max_{j \in [1;n]} (\Phi(f_j)) \leq \Phi_{max}^{MO}$$

$$\bigcup_{j \in [1;n]} f_j = T$$

5 Trajectory Fragmentation Algorithm

In this section, we present our trajectory fragmentation algorithm *TFA*. We start with an overview of *TFA* and present the individual steps of *TFA* afterwards.

5.1 Process Overview

The concept of *TFA* consists of two parts: The *trajectory fragmentation* performed by the MO and the *trajectory reconstruction* performed by clients.

The trajectory fragmentation first calculates the MO's predicted trajectory T based on the given destination. Secondly, it splits up T into a set of fragments. Thirdly, each fragment is assigned to an LS. While traveling, the MO updates its position on the LSs based on the calculated fragmentation. If the predicted trajectory deviates from the real trajectory, a new fragmentation is initiated using a new set of LSs.

The process of *TFA* is shown in Algorithm 1. Since MOs normally travel on fastest paths to reach their destination as fast as possible, we predict the MO's trajectory T at time t_{start} as the fastest path from the current position π_{start} to the known destination π_{end}. Then, we split up T into set $F = \{f_1, \ldots, f_n\}$ of n fragments, one for each LS, by using function $fragment(T, n) = \{f_1, \ldots, f_n\}$, introduced below. For each fragment $f_j \in F$, we calculate a new pseudonym of the MO and select an LS to store f_j. The LS storing the positions of fragment f_j is denoted as LS_j. We use the notation $\pi_i \in f_j$ to denote that position π_i is part of f_j. As formalized in Sect. 4, the goal of function $fragment(T, n)$ is to minimize the maximum revealed trace length $\Phi(f_j)$. To solve the presented optimization problem, we use a dynamic programming approach presented below.

After calculating fragmentation F, the MO updates its position $\pi_i \in f_j$ to LS_j while traveling on f_j. As soon as a new position π_i is part of f_{j+1}, the MO changes the LS storing π_i from LS_j to LS_{j+1}. Furthermore, the used pseudonym is changed from id_j to id_{j+1}. In case the MO leaves the predicted trajectory T at position $\pi_k \notin T$, a new calculation of *TFA* is initiated for the new initial position $\pi_{start} = \pi_k$ and the destination π_{end} using a new set of LSs.

The trajectory reconstruction allows different clients to access the MO's real trajectory T by querying the LSs using the provided pseudonyms of the MO.

Algorithm 1. TFA: Process overview	**Algorithm 2.** TFA: fragmentation
Function: $TFA(n, \pi_{end})$	**Function:** $fragment(T, n)$
1: $\pi_{start} \leftarrow getPosition()$	1: $G_F \leftarrow getGraph(T)$
2: $T \leftarrow FP(\pi_{start}, \pi_{end})$	2: $M \leftarrow getAdjacencyMatrix(G_F)$
3: $F[1, \ldots, n] \leftarrow fragment(T, n)$	3: $L \leftarrow n$
4: $ID[1, \ldots, n] \leftarrow getIDs(F)$	4: $M^L \leftarrow maxMatrixMult(M, L)$
5: $\pi_i \leftarrow \pi_{start}$	5: $\Phi_{max} \leftarrow M^L[0, m]$
6: **while** $\pi_i \in T$ **do**	6: $M_{max} \leftarrow trimEdges(M, \Phi_{max})$
7: $\quad f_j \leftarrow getFragment(\pi_i)$	7: $M_{max}^L \leftarrow maxMatrixMult(M_{max}, L)$
8: $\quad LS_j \leftarrow getLS(f_j)$	8: $P \leftarrow calculateAllPaths(M_{max}^L, L)$
9: $\quad id_j \leftarrow getID(f_j)$	9: $S \leftarrow getRandomPath(P)$
10: $\quad update(\pi_i, LS_j, id_j)$	10: $F[1, \ldots, n] \leftarrow getFragments(S)$
11: $\quad \pi_i \leftarrow getPosition()$	11: **return** $F[1, \ldots, n]$
12: **end while**	

5.2 Trajectory Fragmentation

Next, we present function $fragment(T, n)$ calculating set $F = \{f_1, \ldots, f_n\}$ of fragments in Algorithm 2. As introduced, each fragment $f_j \in F$ defines to which

LS_j position $\pi_i \in f_j$ should be sent. The part of T belonging to fragment f_j is the part of T between two *split positions*. For example, fragment f_j in Fig. 3 is defined by the split positions of junction v_7 and v_9. We split up the MO's predicted trajectory T at nodes representing junctions instead of splitting up T within an edge or at an intermediate node. This approach has the advantage that all positions belonging to the same edge e_i are assigned to the same fragment which is stored by only one LS.

The problem is now how to find set $S = \{s_0, \ldots, s_n\}$ of split positions for T such that the corresponding set of fragments F is optimal considering the maximum revealed trace length $\Phi(f_j)$. To solve the proposed optimization problem, we first calculate the *fragmentation graph* $G_F = (V_F, E_F)$ as defined next: The set of nodes $V_F = \{v_i \in T\}$ consists of all possible split positions of T, i.e., the set of nodes representing a junction on T. The set of edges E_F is generated by calculating for each node $v_i \in V_F$ an edge to each node $v_j \in V_F$ if the MO will visit the junction of v_i before visiting the junction of v_j. The generated edge from v_i to v_j is denoted as $e_{ij} \in E_F$. The weight of e_{ij} is $\Phi(f(v_i, v_j))$ representing the revealed trace length of the fragment that is defined by the split position v_i and v_j. Then, we calculate the adjacency matrix M of G_F, which is of size $m \times m$ with $m = |V_F|$. Each value $M[i; j] = \Phi(f(v_i, v_j))$ defines the weight of edge e_{ij}. Since we aim for an optimal fragmentation using n LSs, we have to find a path in G_F consisting of n edges from the first split position s_0 to the last split position s_n minimizing the maximum edge weight. The L-th power of the adjacency matrix M is denoted as M^L and calculated using matrix multiplication. For each possible node v_k, we calculate the maximum value of $M^{L-1}[i; k]$ and $M^1[k; j]$. Then, we select the minimum value from all possible nodes v_k and store the determined maximum value in $M^L[i; j]$. Thus, $M^L[i; j]$ is the minimized maximum revealed trace length of a single fragment on the path of length L that leads from v_i to v_j. The maximum value for a path of length n from split position s_0 to s_n is the value of $M^n[0, m]$. This value is then stored in Φ_{max} and used to remove all edges in M with a higher value than Φ_{max}. The resulting adjacency matrix is M_{max}. To calculate all possible paths of length $L = n$ with a maximum single edge value below Φ_{max}, we incrementally calculate M_{max}^L using the introduced matrix multiplication. The nodes of the calculated paths represent the possible split positions for an optimal fragmentation. We randomly select one of all possible paths that were calculated and store the corresponding split positions in set S. Finally, we determine set F of fragments using the calculated split positions.

5.3   Minimizing the Number of Required LSs

After solving the problem of how to find an optimal fragmentation for trajectory T, we consider now the problem of minimizing the number n of required LSs to achieve a MO-defined maximum revealed trace length Φ_{max}^{MO}. To solve this problem, we adapt Algorithm 2 as follows. Instead of using a fixed value of $L = n$ to calculate Φ_{max}, we stepwise increment L. As soon as $M^L[0, m] \leq \Phi_{max}^{MO}$, the minimum path length L and thus the minimum number of required LSs is found that can provide a maximum value of Φ_{max}^{MO}. After setting Φ_{max} to Φ_{max}^{MO} we can further use Algorithm 2 without modification. If L reaches a value above L_{max}, which represents the maximum number of available LSs, no solution could be found for T and Φ^{MO}_{max}. Then, the MO has either to adjust Φ^{MO}_{max} or to use Algorithm 2 to find an optimal fragmentation using $n = L_{max}$ LSs.

6   Privacy and Performance Evaluation

In this section, we evaluate the provided privacy of *TFA* and present our performance evaluation. Next, we introduce our attacker model and privacy metric.

6.1   Attacker Model

Nowadays, map knowledge is widely available, for instance, provided by the OpenStreetMap project [9]. Therefore, we assume that an attacker has map knowledge and knows the used fragmentation algorithm. In case an attacker compromises a client, all positions provided to the client are revealed. To limit the revealed information of a client, the MO can individually specify which part of the trajectory should be accessible for each client by defining access rights on the LSs. Because the access control mechanisms do not prevent that the stored information of an LS is revealed to an attacker compromising the LS, we further consider that an attacker compromises a single or multiple LSs. If an attacker compromises an LS, all positions assigned to the stored fragment are revealed.

The goal of an attacker is to derive as much information as possible from its known positions. Therefore, we consider attackers using state of the art movement prediction methods to predict and reconstruct the MO's trajectory. More precisely, we use the first order Markov model presented in [7] to simulate attackers using different turn probability estimations. First, we consider attacker A^{NC} that cannot correlate fragments that were provided to different LSs using different pseudonyms. Secondly, we consider attacker A^{AC} that can correlate adjacent fragments based on their spatiotemporal properties. That is, A^{AC} analyses the positions of two fragments and merges both fragments if the positions belong to two adjacent edges.

In addition to the ability of correlating fragments, we distinguish two attackers which are of different strength based on their known information. The first attacker A_{MAP} uses map knowledge to determine the MO's trajectory from his known positions. To this end, A_{MAP} estimates at each junction a uniform probability distribution where the MO probably came from or where the MO is probably going to. For instance, if three alternatives exist at a junction where the MO can continue traveling, A_{MAP} assigns each edge the probability of 33.33 %. Then, A_{MAP} predicts and reconstructs the trajectory by selecting step by step adjoining edges to his known fragments based on the calculated probability distribution. The second attacker A_{SMI} uses statistical movement information gained from a road network traffic analysis from trajectories of other MOs. The goal of A_{SMI} is to improve its prediction by using more accurate turn probabilities.

6.2 Privacy Metric

To measure the provided privacy of fragmentation F, we analyze the maximum revealed trace length Φ_{max}^A an attacker can derive from its compromised positions. For an attacker who is able to correlate adjacent fragments even if different pseudonyms are used, the maximum revealed trace length Φ_{max}^A is in the worst case equal to the length of the complete trajectory. Therefore, we analyze also the probability $Pr(\Phi_{max}^A \leq \tau)$ that the maximum revealed trace length Φ_{max}^A is below or equal to a threshold value τ. The probability that attacker A successfully compromises the k LSs storing the k fragments of set $F_C \in F$ is $\alpha(F_C) = p^k * (1 - p)^{n-k}$, where $p \in (0, 1]$ is the probability that A can compromise a single LS and F_C is the set of compromised fragments. Then, we calculate for a given value τ the cumulated probability $Pr(\Phi_{max}^A \leq \tau)$ as the sum of the probability values $\alpha(F_C)$ for all sets $F_C \in F$ fulfilling $\Phi_{max}^A \leq \tau$.

6.3 Privacy Evaluation

We analyze the success of different attackers in predicting and reconstructing the MO's movement trajectory based on the compromised fragments by using current state of the art movement prediction methods. In our evaluation, we use the real-world dataset provided by [11], which consists of the traces of about 500 taxis collected for 30 days in the San Francisco Bay Area. The used map information is derived from the OpenStreetMap project [9]. The turn probabilities of attacker A_{MAP} consider a uniform distribution for all possible paths at each junction. For attacker A_{SMI}, we performed a road network traffic analysis where we analyzed the movement behavior of all taxis for a complete day (2008/06/01) and derived for each junction the corresponding turn probability distribution. For our evaluation, we selected from the next day (2008/06/02) a short trajectory of 4.49 km length within the city (denoted as *city*) and a long trajectory of 17.04 km length mainly using highways (denoted as *highway*). We assume a probability of $p = 10\%$ that a single LS is compromised and calculate the probability that multiple LSs are compromised as presented above. Next, we evaluate attacker A^{NC} and continue afterwards with attacker A^{AC}.

Attacker A^{NC}: Since attacker A^{NC} does not use fragment correlation, the cases that A^{NC} compromises multiple LSs is identical to the case that A^{NC} compromises a single LS. To show the success of protecting trajectories against A^{NC} when using fragmentation, we measure the maximum revealed trace length Φ_{max}^A that is revealed to attacker A_{MAP}^{NC} and A_{SMI}^{NC} for the introduced trajectories. The results are shown in Figs. 5 and 6. For the *city* trajectory, Φ_{max}^A of A_{MAP}^{NC} decreases to 498 m (11.07 %) when using 15 LSs. By considering statistical movement information in addition to the map knowledge, Φ_{max}^A of A_{SMI}^{NC} decreases to 1148 m (25.55 %). For the *highway* trajectory, Φ_{max}^A decreases to 5601 m (32.86 %) respectively 9283 m (54.64 %). As we can see, each trajectory has a limiting value of Φ_{max}^A such that even when increasing n, the maximum revealed trace length known to the attacker does not decrease any more. This is based on the fact that Φ^A_{max} cannot decrease below the maximum revealed trace length of a single road segment on the considered trajectory.

By comparing the relative values of Φ^A_{max} from the *highway* trajectory with the *city* trajectory, A^{NC}_{SMI} receives a higher value of Φ^A_{max} for the *highway* trajectory. This is based on the fact that the prediction of A^{NC}_{SMI} works well on the highway due to a high statistical probability that the MO stays on the highway for longer times. For the *city* trajectory, many junctions exists with approximately equal turn probabilities for alternative roads such that the attacker cannot precisely predict the MO's movement.

Next, we analyze the minimum number of LSs that is required to reveal at most a trace length of Φ^{MO}_{max} to a single LS. Figure 7 shows which values of Φ^{MO}_{max} can be provided using the map based and the statistical movement based fragmentation. By decreasing Φ^{MO}_{max} from the maximum length of the considered trajectory, the minimum number n of required LSs to provide Φ^{MO}_{max} increases. Again, each trajectory has a limiting minimum value of Φ^{MO}_{max} such that smaller values of Φ^{MO}_{max} cannot be provided even when increasing n as presented before.

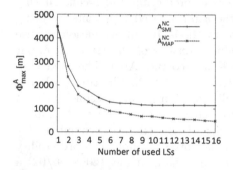

Fig. 5. City trajectory evaluation

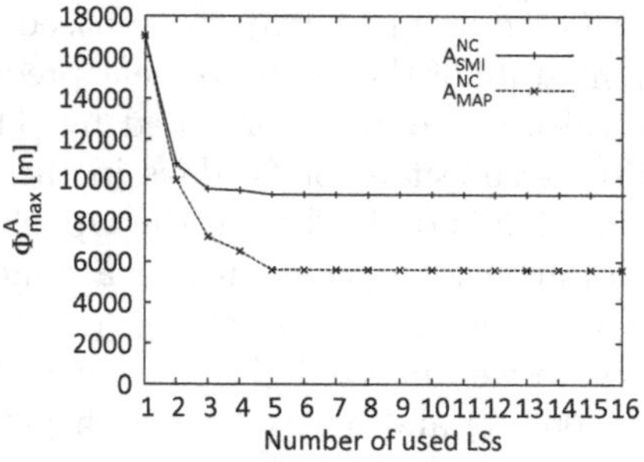

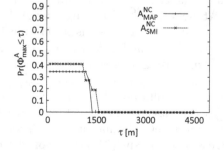

Fig. 6. Highway trajectory evaluation

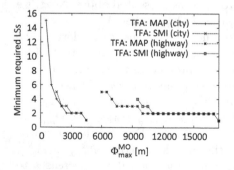

Fig. 7. Minimum n for trajectories

Fig. 8. Cumulated probability distribution for attacker A^{NC}

To show that attacker A^{NC} cannot derive a higher revealed trace length than specified by the MO in Φ_{max}^{MO}, we analyze for the *city* trajectory the cumulated probability distribution $Pr(\Phi_{max}^{A}(F_C) \leq \tau)$ using the fragmentation generated by optimizing n. We select a value of $\Phi_{max}^{MO} = 1.5$ km, which leads to $n = 4$ LSs for the map based fragmentation and $n = 5$ for the statistical movement based fragmentation. As shown in Fig. 8, the probability that A_{MAP}^{NC} and A_{SMI}^{NC} can derive a maximum revealed trace length above Φ_{max}^{MO} is zero such that the defined privacy requirement is fulfilled and *TFA* prevents that an attacker can derive a higher revealed trace length than Φ_{max}^{MO}. Altogether, we can state that *TFA* effectively prevents that attacker A^{NC} can trace the MO over longer distances.

Attacker $\mathbf{A^{AC}}$: The powerful attacker A^{AC} can correlate adjacent fragments based on the spatio-temporal properties of the compromised positions as presented in Sect. 6.1. If A^{AC} can compromise all used LSs, the complete trajectory of the MO is revealed. This results in a maximum revealed trace length of Φ_{max}^{A} equal to the length of the trajectory. To better understand this kind of strong attacker, we show the success of A^{AC} to trace the MO over a certain distance τ by analyzing the cumulated probability that A^{AC} receives a maximum revealed trace length of τ by compromising a certain set of LSs. Figure 9 shows for the city trajectory the cumulated probability that attacker A_{MAP}^{AC} can derive a maximum value Φ_{max}^{A} of τ for different values of n. As we can see, increasing the number of generated fragments increases the probability that a small part of the trajectory is revealed, whereas the probability that longer parts are revealed decreases. For instance, A_{MAP}^{AC} can trace the MO for a value of $\tau = 1$ km, which represents 22.27% of the trajectory, only with a probability of 1.08% when using 15 LS. Therefore, we can state that *TFA* can be used to prevent attacker A^{AC} from tracing the MO over longer distances with a high probability.

6.4   Performance Evaluation

Next, we evaluate the performance of *TFA* by measuring its runtime on a state of the art mobile device (HTC Desire HD). We measure the required time to

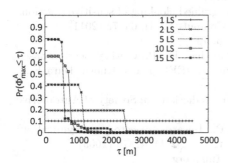

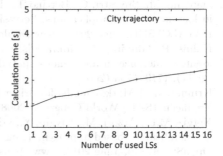

Fig. 9. Cumulated probability distribution for attacker A_{MAP}^{AC}

Fig. 10. Runtime performance

calculate for the *city* trajectory the corresponding fragmentation using n LSs. As shown in Fig. 10, the calculation time stays below 3 s even for a larger number of fragments. The runtime of *TFA* for optimizing the number of required LSs for the introduced value of $\Phi_{max}^{MO} = 1.5$ km also stays below 1.4 s. Recall that the fragmentation is only calculated initially at the start of the MO's movement or if the MO leaves the predicted trajectory. While traveling, *TFA* only performs a simple lookup of the current position against the corresponding fragment before sending the position to the LS. Therefore, we can state that *TFA* supports real-time position updates and that the fragmentation time is reasonable.

7   Conclusion and Future Work

In this paper, we presented a novel approach to protect the user's movement trajectory in a non-trusted system environment. The basic idea of our approach is to split up the user's trajectory into a set of trajectory fragments that are distributed among LSs of different providers. In case an LS gets compromised, only the positions of the stored fragment are revealed instead of the complete trajectory. In our evaluation, we used real world trajectories to show the effectiveness of our approach to protect trajectories against attackers using map knowledge and statistical movement information. In future work, we will analyze how we can improve our approach by considering LSs of different trust levels.

References

1. Ardagna, C., Livraga, G., Samarati, P.: Protecting privacy of user information in continuous location-based services. In: IEEE 15th International Conference on Computational Science and Engineering, pp. 162–169 (2012)
2. Beresford, A.R., Stajano, F.: Location privacy in pervasive computing. IEEE Pervasive Comput. **2**(1), 46–55 (2003)
3. Chow, C.-Y., Mokbel, M.F.: Enabling private continuous queries for revealed user locations. In: Papadias, D., Zhang, D., Kollios, G. (eds.) SSTD 2007. LNCS, vol. 4605, pp. 258–275. Springer, Heidelberg (2007)
4. Damiani, M., Silvestri, C., Bertino, E.: Fine-grained cloaking of sensitive positions in location-sharing applications. Pervasive Comput. **10**(4), 64–72 (2011)
5. DATALOSSDB, June 2013. www.datalossdb.org
6. Kalnis, P., Ghinita, G., Mouratidis, K., Papadias, D.: Preventing location-based identity inference in anonymous spatial queries. IEEE Trans. Knowl. Data Eng. **19**(12), 1719–1733 (2007)
7. Krumm, J.: A Markov model for driver turn prediction. In: Society of Automotive Engineers (SAE) World Congress (2008)
8. Nergiz, M.E., Atzori, M., Saygin, Y., Güç, B.: Towards trajectory anonymization: a generalization-based approach. Trans. Data Priv. **2**(1), 47–75 (2009)
9. OpenStreetMap, June 2013. www.openstreetmap.org
10. Peddinti, S.T., Saxena, N.: On the limitations of query obfuscation techniques for location privacy. In: Proceedings of the 13th International Conference on Ubiquitous Computing (2011)

11. Piorkowski, M., Sarafijanovoc-Djukic, N., Grossglauser, M.: A parsimonious model of mobile partitioned networks with clustering. In: The First International Conference on COMmunication Systems and NETworkS, pp. 1–10 (2009)
12. Shankar, P., Ganapathy, V., Iftode, L.: Privately querying location-based services with sybilquery. In: Proceedings of the 11th International Conference on Ubiquitous Computing (2009)
13. Webroot, June 2013. http://www.webroot.com/us/en/company/press-room/releases/social-networks-mobile-security
14. Wernke, M., Dürr, F., Rothermel, K.: PShare: ensuring location privacy in non-trusted systems through multi-secret sharing. Pervasive Mob. Comput. **9**, 339–352 (2013)
15. Wernke, M., Skvortsov, P., Dürr, F., Rothermel, K.: A classification of location privacy attacks and approaches. Pers. Ubiquit. Comput. **16**, 1–13 (2012)

Trust-Based, Privacy-Preserving Context Aggregation and Sharing in Mobile Ubiquitous Computing

Michael Xing and Christine Julien[✉]

The Center for Advanced Research in Software Engineering,
The University of Texas, Austin, TX, USA
c.julien@mail.utexas.edu

Abstract. In ubiquitous computing environments, we are surrounded by significant amounts of context information about our individual situations and the situations we share with others around us. Along with the widespread emergence of ubiquitous computing and the availability of context information comes threats to personal privacy that result from sharing information about ourselves with others in the vicinity. We define an individual's context to be a potentially private piece of information. Given the individual context of multiple participants, one can compute an *aggregate* context that represents a shared state while at the same time preserves individual participants' privacy. In this paper, we describe three approaches to computing an aggregate measure of a group's context while maintaining a balance between the desire to share information and the desire to retain control over private information. Our approaches allow dynamic tuning of information release according to *trust levels* of the participants within communication range. By evaluating our approaches through simulation, we show that sharing aggregate context can significantly increase the rate at which a group of co-located users learns an aggregate measure of their shared context. Further, our approaches can accomplish high quality context sharing even in situations with low levels of trust, assuming the availability of a small number of highly trustworthy partners.

1 Introduction

Ubiquitous computing allows users to share information about their personal situations directly with one another, enabling users to collaboratively construct aggregate views of their shared local situations, or *context*. Constructing these aggregate views requires sharing potentially highly sensitive and personal information, which in turn relies on users' trust in one another. Imagine a mobile app that can communicate with other nearby mobile devices and retrieve the names of the apps that other mobile devices' users are using. This could be useful from a social connectivity perspective; we could learn what other apps that other people in a similar social situation are using at a given time. For example, at a sporting event, we could determine what other apps nearby spectators are using

© Institute for Computer Sciences, Social Informatics and Telecommunications Engineering 2014
I. Stojmenovic et al. (Eds.): MOBIQUITOUS 2013, LNICST 131, pp. 316–329, 2014.
DOI: 10.1007/978-3-319-11569-6_25

to augment their experiences, for example to check scores or view replays. However, the app poses a significant threat to the privacy of the mobile device users. Our approach strives to address the tension between this privacy constraint and the incentives for exchanging context information among nearby mobile devices.

This paper explores practical mechanisms to enable ubiquitous computing users to construct aggregate views of their shared context while retaining control over the dissemination of their private data. In our target environment, participants with smart mobile devices (e.g., smart phones) collect and share information with one another directly (i.e., across peer-to-peer links) without the support of an infrastructure. Such an environment is becoming increasingly commonplace as smaller, wearable devices are becoming mainstream: mobile phones record users' locations using GPS and other localization technologies; Google Glass can take pictures, record videos, recognize a user's voice, and capture myriad context information about a user[1]; Nuubo, a wireless cardiac monitoring platform, can transmit physiological parameters to a user's doctors[2]; Sony's smart watch can connect to Android phones and display received texts, emails, and notifications[3]. These devices possess considerable computing power and can communicate through direct wireless channels. Direct interaction among nearby users enables new forms of data sharing but also presents a challenge in enabling users to control the release of their potentially private information. Only by sharing information, however, do participants reap many of the benefits of the information-rich environment.

We assume an established "trust network" in the ubiquitous computing environment. Specifically, for a given participant, this provides a trust value for every other participant in the network. Work exists in establishing flexible trust networks in mobile ad hoc environments [6,10,14,17,20]. Our context aggregation and sharing mechanisms utilize trust values computed by such a trust network to determine the amount of private information to release to other nearby users. Returning to our previous example, at a sporting event, a spectator is likely to be seated nearby a group of friends or family with whom he has a high degree of trust. The spectator is perfectly willing to share private information with these trusted friends; aggregating together the context of a group of trusted friends can *obfuscate* each individual's private information, enabling the aggregate to be shared with acquaintances with a somewhat lower level of trust. Using this novel combination of trust and aggregation, our privacy preserving context distribution mechanism reduces the risk of privacy leakage. Our approaches allow users to gradually reveal their information in aggregate, to both protect the individuals privacy and to converge to a collective (correct) aggregate of context information.

Our motivation stems from users' needs to be able to feel safe to collect and share context information in settings that lack centralized trusted authorities. Limited work exists on privacy in ubiquitous computing, but most approaches

---

[1] http://www.google.com/glass/start

[2] http://www.nuubo.com

[3] http://sonymobile.com/us/products/accessories/smartwatch/specifications

require elaborate, centralized infrastructure; we review these methods in Sect. 2. Our approaches target completely infrastructure-less environments and rely on direct, peer-to-peer wireless interactions among users' devices. We make the following concrete contributions: (*i*) we define three aggregation schemes that explicitly trade individual privacy for the degree of data sharing in mobile ubiquitous computing environments; (*ii*) we tune the amount or nature of sharing to established measures of trust; and (*iii*) we evaluate our aggregation approaches under different deployment scenarios and trust networks. We measure our approaches' abilities to converge to a correct assessment of the shared context in a short amount of time. Our approaches can significantly speed up the rate at which the entire group learns an aggregate measure of their shared context. Further, our approaches achieve a high quality of context aggregation, even with low levels of trust among participants, as long as there are a small number of highly trusted collaborators.

2   Related Work

Our basic goal is similar to that of *differential privacy* in statistical databases: it should be possible to accurately query a database while maintaining the privacy of individuals whose data is represented in that database [5]. Specifically, queries should release information about the *population* represented in the database without releasing information about any individual that is not generally publicly available. Techniques from differential privacy motivate our goals, but they assume that information about the population is collected in a single (secured) central database.

One of an individual's most sensitive pieces of data is the individual's location; many techniques exist to protect the privacy of individuals' locations. Most approaches somehow augment the location data, for example protecting sensitive location trajectories in a centralized database by inserting realistic fake trajectories [19], by perturbing location trajectories by "crossing paths" of multiple users [9], or by adding uncertainty to objects' locations in moving object databases [1]. These solutions are specific to location data, and the focus is often on attempting to maintain a high fidelity (correctness) of responses to queries about locations while preserving privacy.

Significant recent efforts have focused on privacy and on its interplay with crowd-sensing specifically and with mobile distributed sensing more generally. In the former scenarios, a query issuer requests information that is sensed by mobile participants, potentially aggregated, and returned to the querier. Ensuring participation requires ensuring privacy, most often with respect to the location of the user whose device does the sensing [4,15,16]. Other approaches take advantage of the additive properties of desired aggregates and use *data slicing* [25] or cryptographic techniques [13] to compute complete aggregates for independent sets of data providers. These approaches either assume resilient communication (e.g., no slices of data can be lost) or an ultimate back-end (centralized) server. In contrast, we aim for a purely distributed approach in which all of the users desire the aggregate of context information shared among themselves and not mediated by a service provider that sits between the querier and the tasked mobile sensing devices. We also explore the novel use of *trust* in influencing the release of private information in mobile and ubiquitous computing environments.

Other approaches have attempted to preserve privacy for data types beyond location by introducing noisy data in participatory sensing [7]; this work's motivation is quite close to our own, where individual users compute aggregates (fusions) over locally available data, but this related work does not incorporate trust (instead relying on random perturbations). The approach circumvents the fundamental limitations of perturbation for privacy by taking advantage of properties of the targeted time series data.

Our motivation (and approach) is also similar to secure multi-party computation [26], in which participants share information to jointly compute some function (e.g., an aggregate) over their individual data without explicitly releasing their (potentially private) individual information. This technique has been applied to distributed data mining [3], to computing a sum of private data while relying on data slicing [24], and even to collaborative filtering in peer-to-peer networks [2]. While the approach is decentralized, it requires a high degree of controlled coordination among participants that is not possible in purely ad hoc environments. Further, because it is based on cryptographic primitives, the computational complexity is not reasonable for mobile devices or common tasks [18]. We take advantage of the fact that coordinating parties in mobile and ubiquitous computing situations may not be *completely* distrustful of each other, and we leverage this trust to reduce the cost of achieving acceptable levels of privacy.

Existing work that combines trust and privacy generally focuses on *trading* privacy for trust, i.e., revealing private information to others to earn a more substantial level of trust [23], and on incentivizing this tradeoff [22]. We look at trust and privacy from a different perspective, presupposing a framework for establishing trust in other individuals that allows graduated release of private information based on established trust levels. Establishing trust among collaborating parties has been well studied in both completely distributed mobile ad hoc networks and in pervasive computing, and several approaches exist that we can rely on to establish trust values between individuals [6, 11, 20, 21]. For the remainder of this paper, we assume such a mechanism is in place and that, in using such a mechanism, we can rely on a *trust table* that is available to each individual on the local device. The trust table maps an another individual's identifier to a *trust level*, which our algorithms will use in determining how to share data.

3   Trust-Based Sharing of Context

Our operational model is one in which a group of participants make independent decisions about sharing context, without the aid of any infrastructure. The goal of the participants, in general, is to learn some aggregate measure of the entire group's context (e.g., the apps in use by other nearby spectators at a sporting event, the average grade of a group of students on an exam, an average of a health indicator for a group at a fitness club, or the bounding box of the locations of contributors to a participatory sensing application). When a participant i encounters a participant j, i must decide what information to share, where the options range from sharing i's individual context data (which results in the largest loss of privacy) to sharing an aggregate that combines i's data with some other participants' context values. This *partial aggregate* that each participant computes is that participant's working estimate of the target global aggregate. We assume that the only way for participants to exchange information is to encounter each other and make that exchange directly, i.e., through a peer-to-peer connection. Our approach assumes the aggregate functions can be computed incrementally (e.g., a sum, average, minimum, maximum, union, bounding box of locations, etc.) and that individuals' context values do not change. Along with each aggregate, we maintain a list of contributors to the aggregate to prevent including a participant multiple times.

The novelty of our approach lies in the following key observations. First, we do not commonly find ourselves in situations in which we have absolutely no trust in any other participants. Second, mutually trusting participants can work together to aggregate their information to obfuscate their individual context, increasing their individual levels of privacy. Third, sharing aggregate measures of context contributes positively to an entire group learning a (near) correct value for the aggregate of the entire group. While Alice may be willing to reveal her individual exam grade to her best friend, Bob, (and Bob may be willing to do the same), she may feel more self-conscious about releasing it to Cindy, who she does not know (or trust) as well. However, once she and Bob have exchanged their individual context information, they can aggregate (e.g., average) their scores and give the average to Cindy, sacrificing less of their individual privacy. Of course, an average of two grades provides only a small degree of added privacy; an average of 50 grades provide much more. Therefore, sharing aggregate context values depends not only on the trust values associated with the recipients, but also, at least indirectly, on the size of the aggregate (i.e., the number of values aggregated).

We assume that each participant (e.g., device, application, or user, depending on the application) maintains its own *trust table*, that holds a *trust value* for every other participant. It is not required that trust values are mutual (i.e., participants i and j need not have the same level of trust in each other). Trust values can be based on reputations, can be learned, can change over time, and can even be context-dependent [21]; these concerns are outside the scope of this paper. Instead, we rely on the availability of this trust information to determine when to share potentially private context information. Concretely, we assume that, when a participant is about to share private context information, the participant can query its local trust table to determine the level of trust associated with the potential recipient of the data. Based on the level of trust, the participant can determine whether to share information and what specifically to share (e.g., individual context data or an aggregate of multiple individuals' context data).

We assume trust values are on an unbounded continuous scale; a value of 0 indicates complete trust, and larger values indicate lower trust. For convenience, we assume that the trust table values correspond to aggregate sizes; if participant i has a trust value of x for participant j, then i is willing to share its information with j as long as it is contained in an aggregate with size greater than x. Practically, this representation of trust values requires a processing step to convert

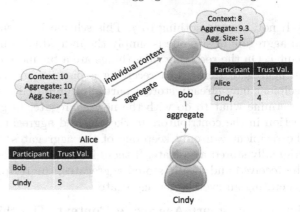

Fig. 1. An Example of Trust-Influenced Context Sharing; "Aggregate" in this case is the average value; "Agg. Size" designates the number of participants represented in the aggregate

trust values computed from a scheme such as [21]. Figure 1 shows a small example that demonstrates some of these concepts; in the figure, Alice is willing to share her individual context information with Bob, who can then combine it and share it with Cindy, who is less trusted by both Alice and Bob. We next describe four schemes that determine how to share context information, given the available trust information.

Scheme 1: Individual Context Only. The first scheme is a baseline; in the first scheme, participants only ever share individual context, and they only share that context with other participants that they trust completely (i.e., for which the trust value is 0). When participant i encounters participant j, i determines whether j is completely trusted. If not, i does nothing. If j is completely trusted, participant i sends participant j its individual context information. Upon receiving this information, j incorporates i's information into an incrementally computed aggregate (that includes j's own context information as well as any other pieces of information that j has received from other participants). In this scheme, as average trust decreases, context information moves more slowly, and the aggregate that any participant can feasibly compute is just the average of context values from other participants that completely trust the participant.

Scheme 2: Aggregate Context Only. In the second scheme, participants incrementally compute aggregates and share only those aggregates with other participants they encounter. Aggregates can be computed incrementally by adding in additional participants' context if they are not already represented in the aggregate or by merging two aggregates if their contributor lists are disjoint. When participant i encounters participant j, to determine whether to share the computed aggregate, i retrieves j's trust value from the trust table. If the *size* of the aggregate is larger than the trust value, then i sends the aggregate to

j. If not, i sends nothing to j. This scheme is a generalization of Scheme 1, as an aggregate of size one is simply the individual context information of participant i. On the receiving side, things are a bit more complicated when receiving an aggregate than when receiving a piece of individual context. Because the recipient may already store a partially computed aggregate, the recipient must determine what to do with the new aggregate. In general, if there is an intersection in the contributors to the received aggregate and the stored aggregate, the recipient can only keep one of the aggregates[4]. In Scheme 2, we keep the originally stored aggregate. If there is not an intersection in the contributors to the received and locally stored aggregates, the recipient merges the aggregates, generating an even larger aggregate.

Scheme 3: Smart Aggregate Context. This third scheme differs from the second only in that instead of the recipient keeping the original aggregate, it keeps the larger of the two aggregates (i.e., the larger of the received aggregate and the previously stored one). Intuitively, this scheme should perform better with respect to the computation of the correct aggregate value; as we will see in Sect. 4, this is not always the case.

Scheme 4: Mixed Information. The fourth scheme mixes aspects of the above approaches. When participant i encounters j, i still uses its trust value for j to determine what to send. However, in addition to sending the aggregate if the aggregate size is larger than j's trust value, if j's trust value is 0 (i.e., i completely trusts j), i also sends its individual context. Upon reception, j behaves like the second scheme unless there is an intersection between i's transmitted aggregate and j's stored aggregate. If there is no intersection, j just merges the two. If there *is* an intersection, j instead simply merges i's information into j's stored aggregate. At first glance, these seems to be an obvious addition, but this fourth scheme does come with the disadvantage of exchanging extra information, which comes at an increased cost of communication; in Sect. 4, we investigate whether this effective doubling of the overhead achieves better results.

4   Experimental Results

To compare and contrast our schemes for context sharing subject to privacy constraints, we implemented the schemes in our Grapevine context framework [8]. Grapevine piggybacks context information (whether individual context or aggregate information) on data packets transmitted in the course of other network (application) traffic.

We implemented our approaches in the ONE network simulator [12]. Each node was assigned a context value and given the task of attempting to find the average of all of the context values in the network. We assume context values are static; we discuss handling dynamic context values in Sect. 5. We measure the

---

[4] Some aggregation functions are *duplicate insensitive*, and any aggregates can be merged. We assume this is not the case, and address the issue of duplicate sensitive aggregates instead.

percent error of each node's estimate of the global aggregate. The overheads of our approaches are low (see [8] for a presentation of the overhead of piggybacking context information in Grapevine). The approaches all generate the same amount of extra data except for the Mixed Information scheme, which generates twice the number of piggybacked bits.

We first look at simple networks in which a participant can have just one of two levels of trust in another participant: high (complete trust) or low (complete distrust). Our second set of experiments extends the complexity of the trust distributions in the simple network. Our final experiments explore more realistic deploy-

Table 1. Simulation settings

Setting	Value
Transmit speed	250 KB/second
Transmit range	30 meters
Movement	Random waypoint
Speed	$U(3,4)$
World size	300m × 300m

ments. We plot the average error in the computed aggregate over time; we stopped the simulations when the aggregate had stabilized. Table 1 gives the evaluation settings.

Binary Trust. In the first stage of our experiments, we used a small network and highly control trust values to benchmark the behavior of our four schemes. These networks consisted of 10 mobile participants. Grapevine does not generate its own traffic; instead it piggybacks context (either the individual context value or a computed aggregate) on top of these application-level packets. Each participant generated a new packet for some other randomly selected participant, on average, every five seconds. In general, this relatively high traffic load is beneficial to context sharing since context information can spread more quickly. We provide results for situations when each participant trusted 100 %, 70 %, 50 %, 30 %, or just 10 % of the other participants.

Starting from the bottom of Fig. 2, we see that when the levels of trust are high, nothing significantly outperforms just sharing individual data. Because participants are able to directly collect the data that goes into the aggregate, the aggregate's error is very low. As we move to the mid-range of trust values, the quality of the four schemes comes together. At 30 % trustworthy participants, we start to see that when the trustworthiness of the participants falls, the aggregate schemes show the potential to outperform the individual scheme. Finally, for the situation with very low trust, the quality of the aggregate falls off precipitously, indicating that, when a participant trusts very few others, it is difficult to share aggregate information with any quality.

Mixed Trust. In our second experiments, we explored these last two points in more depth, attempting to identify trust distributions in which the aggregate schemes excel (and thereby push the envelope of protecting privacy in the face of untrustworthiness) and attempting to identify just how low we can push the trustworthiness of participants and still achieve a reasonably low error rate in the aggregate. We stay with our simple 10 participant network, but we explore the trust distributions shown in Fig. 3, assigning a fraction of the participants to be highly trustworthy (with whom a participant will share individual data), a fraction to be of medium trustworthiness (with whom a partici-

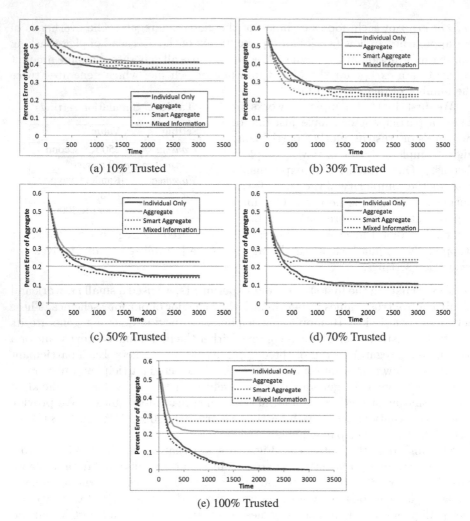

(a) 10% Trusted

(b) 30% Trusted

(c) 50% Trusted

(d) 70% Trusted

(e) 100% Trusted

Fig. 2. Average quality of computed aggregate with two trust values: high and low

pant will share a medium sized aggregate; in this example, an aggregate of size 5 or larger), and a fraction to be completely untrustworthy.

When there is a very low level of trust among the participants (Distribution 5 in Fig. 3 and the corresponding results in Fig. 4(d)), the quality of the aggregate remains quite low. Further, when the trust levels are relatively high (Distribution 2 in Fig. 3 and the corresponding results in Fig. 4(a)), directly sharing individual information remains the best option. Where the trust levels are more mixed (Fig. 4(b) and (c)):, we see potential for aggregation to improve information quality while adhering to participants' privacy requirements.

Random Trust. For our last experiments, we evaluate how our schemes would perform "in the wild." We increase the size of the network to 50 mobile participants. We assign a participant's trust value for another according to three different trust distributions, shown in Fig. 5: *Random*, in which the trust is chosen equiprobably from 10 possible trust values ranging from completely untrustworthy to completely trustworthy, *More Trusted*, in which the choice is weighted toward the more trustworthy values, and *Less Trusted*, in which the choice is weighted toward the less trustworthy values.

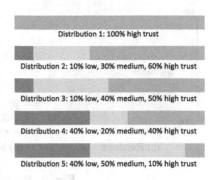

Fig. 3. Trust distributions

We highlight two key findings that demonstrate the benefits of using trust to control the release of private information in dynamic networks. Figure 6 shows that *sharing aggregate information can significantly help distribute context information, especially in situations of relatively low trust, assuming a handful of highly trusted participants in the network*. In the *More Trusted* case (Fig. 6(a)), the benefits of sharing aggregates is marginal compared to sharing individual context. Even in this scenario, however, sharing

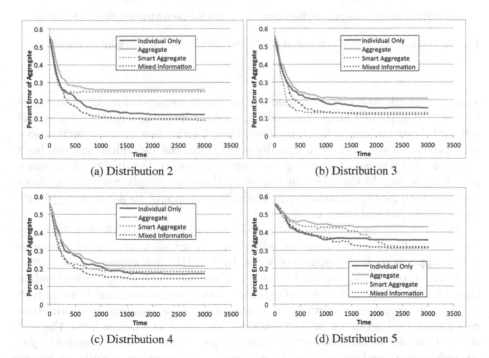

Fig. 4. Average quality of computed aggregate with three trust values in distributions from Fig. 3

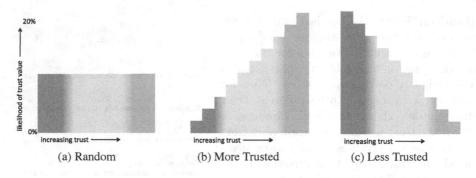

(a) Random   (b) More Trusted   (c) Less Trusted

Fig. 5. Random trust distributions

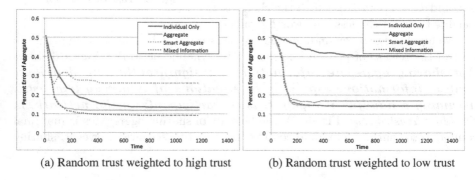

(a) Random trust weighted to high trust   (b) Random trust weighted to low trust

Fig. 6. Average quality of computed aggregate with weighted randomly assigned trust values

aggregates leads to a quicker assessment of the aggregate value (i.e., the curves for the Aggregate and Mixed Information schemes lie to the left of the Individual scheme). More strikingly, Fig. 6(b) shows that, for the *Less Trusted* distribution, all three aggregate schemes drastically outperform the Individual scheme, both in terms of the speed of assessing the aggregate and in the quality of the computed aggregate. In the Individual scheme, there are simply not enough direct contacts with highly trustworthy individuals to compute an accurate aggregate from only individual information.

In Fig. 7, we use the *Random* trust distribution from Fig. 5; Fig. 7(a) uses the same traffic generation rate as before: on average, each participant generates a new application-level packet every 5 s. In Fig. 7(b), on average, each participant generates a new application-level packet only every 50 s. Understanding the behavior of our schemes under these lower traffic conditions is important since reducing network overhead is essential in these dynamic networks that rely almost exclusively on battery operated devices and wireless links. Figure 7 shows that, *in situations when fewer opportunities are available for piggybacking context, sharing aggregate information results in much more rapid and higher quality computation of the global aggregate*.

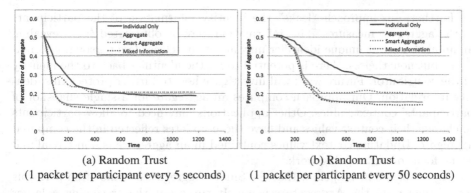

(a) Random Trust
(1 packet per participant every 5 seconds)

(b) Random Trust
(1 packet per participant every 50 seconds)

Fig. 7. Average quality of computed aggregate with randomly assigned trust for different traffic

Figures 6(b) and 7(b) highlight another key benefit of Grapevine. In many ubiquitous computing scenarios, users find themselves in situations where they will choose not to share any of their context information because of the potential sacrifice of their privacy. By enabling users to share their context information within aggregates instead of only individually, Grapevine enables a much higher degree of context sharing and learning, improving the experiences of all participants in the ubiquitous computing application.

5   Conclusions and Future Work

We explored using trust to influence how private context is shared in dynamic mobile, ubiquitous computing applications. By incrementally computing aggregate measures of context and basing how aggregates are shared on their size relative to the trustworthiness of the recipient, our context sharing schemes control the release of private information. Both the degree of trustworthiness and the desired quality of aggregate information are application-dependent; the results in this paper give a foundational understanding that application designers could use in making tradeoffs for their implementations.

For convenience, we used a linear correlation between trust values and aggregate sizes to demonstrate the relationships between decreasing trust and increasing aggregate sizes. While this gives important insights, the relationship between trust and the size of the shared aggregate may not be linear. Studying alternative (i.e., non-linear) relationships and the ability of application developers to tune them is future work. Further, when a participant shares individual context, the recipient has complete control of that information and could potentially share the individual data directly. This must be accounted for by conservatively assigning trust; this is why the results in Fig. 6(b) are so important: even in scenarios weighted towards lower trust, having a small number of highly trustworthy partners is sufficient for bootstrapping context sharing.

Further, our approach "leaks" the identity information of the participants in the aggregate measures. This information may be obfuscated (i.e., revealing an anonymous but unique identifier may arguably release less personal information), but nonetheless, there is potential to tie the identifier back to the identity of the contributor. Future work will investigate how to further protect this identity information. Our approach computes an aggregate for a single snapshot of participants' context values. Other applications may need to allow participants to change their context values and have those updates reflected in the computed aggregate. Updating context values contained in an aggregate is non-trivial and is the focus of our ongoing work.

Figures 6(a) and 7(a) show that the Smart Aggregate scheme often performs *worse* than even the Aggregate scheme. It turns out that receiving a larger number of smaller aggregates results in a higher *information diversity*, making it more likely that the recipient can merge aggregates. This points to another possible scheme, one in which a participant keeps and shares multiple smaller aggregates, sending a recipient aggregates only as large as required by the trust values. This also has potential benefits for updating context values, as updating within a smaller aggregate is likely to be easier.

In summary, this work is the first of its kind to use trust to obfuscate private context in mobile ubiquitous computing environments. This is feasible for applications that compute aggregates of shared local context and can tolerate a small error in that computation. Our schemes are particularly suited to cases where the application traffic is low and there is generally low trust mixed with a handful of highly trustworthy partners.

Acknowledgements. This work was supported in part by the NSF under grant CNS-1218232. Any findings, conclusions, or recommendations are those of the authors.

References

1. Abul, O., Bonchi, F., Nanni, M.: Never walk alone: uncertainty for anonymity in moving objects databases. In: Proceedings of ICDE, pp. 376–385 (2008)
2. Bickson, D., Dolev, D., Besman, G., Pinkas, B.: Peer-to-peer secure multi-party numerical computation. In: Proceedings of P2P, pp. 257–266 (2008)
3. Clifton, C., Kantarcioglu, M., Vaidya, J., Lin, X., Zhu, M.: Tools for privacy preserving distributed data mining. ACM SIGKDD Explor. Newslett. 4(2), 28–34 (2002)
4. Cornelius, C., Kapadia, A., Kotz, D., Peebles, D., Shin, M., Triandopoulos, N.: Anonysense: privacy-aware people-centric sensing. In: Proceedings of MobiSys, pp. 211–224 (2008)
5. Dwork, C.: Differential privacy. In: Bugliesi, M., Preneel, B., Sassone, V., Wegener, I. (eds.) ICALP 2006, Part II. LNCS, vol. 4052, pp. 1–12. Springer, Heidelberg (2006)
6. Eschenauer, L., Gligor, V.D., Baras, J.S.: On trust establishment in mobile *Ad-Hoc* networks. In: Christianson, B., Crispo, B., Malcolm, J.A., Roe, M. (eds.) Security Protocols 2002. LNCS, vol. 2845, pp. 47–66. Springer, Heidelberg (2004)

7. Ganti, R., Pham, N., Tsai, Y.-E., Abdelzaher, T.: PoolView: stream privacy for grassroots participatory sensing. In: Proceedings of SenSys, pp. 281–294 (2008)
8. Grim, E., Fok, C.-L., Julien, C.: Grapevine: efficient situational awareness in pervasive computing environments. In: Proceedings of PerCom WiP, pp. 475–478 (2012)
9. Hoh, B., Gruteser, M.: Protecting location privacy through path confusion. In: Proceedings of SECURECOMM, pp. 194–205 (2005)
10. Jiang, T., Baras, J.: Ant-based adaptive trust evidence distribution in MANET. In: Proceedings of ICDCS Workshops, pp. 588–593 (2004)
11. Kagal, L., Finin, T., Joshi, A.: Trust-based security in pervasive computing environments. IEEE Comput. 34(12), 154–157 (2001)
12. Keränen, A., Ott, J., Kärkkäinen, T.: The ONE simulator for DTN protocol evaluation. In: Proceedings of SIMUTools (2009)
13. Kursawe, K., Danezis, G., Kohlweiss, M.: Privacy-friendly aggregation for the smart-grid. In: Fischer-Hübner, S., Hopper, N. (eds.) PETS 2011. LNCS, vol. 6794, pp. 175–191. Springer, Heidelberg (2011)
14. Li, J., Li, R., Kato, J.: Future trust management framework for mobile ad hoc networks. IEEE Commun. 46(4), 108–114 (2008)
15. Li, Q., Cao, G.: Efficient and privacy-preserving data aggregation in mobile sensing. In: Proceedings of ICNP, pp. 1–10 (2012)
16. Li, Q., Cao, G.: Providing privacy-aware incentives for mobile sensing. In: Proceedings of PerCom, pp. 76–84 (2013)
17. Liu, Z., Joy, A., Thompson, R.: A dynamic trust model for mobile ad hoc networks. In: Proceedings of FTDCS, pp. 80–85 (2004)
18. Orlandi, C.: Is multiparty computation any good in practice? In: Proceedings of ICASSP, pp. 5848–5851 (2011)
19. Pelekis, N., Gkoulalas-Divanis, A., Vodas, M., Kopanaki, D., Theodoridis, Y.: Privacy-aware querying over sensitive trajectory data. In: Proceedings of CIKM, pp. 895–904 (2011)
20. Pirzada, A., McDonald, C.: Establishing trust in pure ad-hoc networks. In: Proceedings of ACSW, pp. 47–54 (2004)
21. Quercia, D., Hailes, S., Capra, L.: B-Trust: bayesian trust framework for pervasive computing. In: Stølen, K., Winsborough, W.H., Martinelli, F., Massacci, F. (eds.) iTrust 2006. LNCS, vol. 3986, pp. 298–312. Springer, Heidelberg (2006)
22. Raya, M., Shokri, R., Hubaux, J.-P.: On the tradeoff between trust and privacy in wireless ad hoc networks. In: Proceedings of WiSec, pp. 75–80 (2010)
23. Seigneur, J.-M., Jensen, C.D.: Trading privacy for trust. In: Jensen, C., Poslad, S., Dimitrakos, T. (eds.) iTrust 2004. LNCS, vol. 2995, pp. 93–107. Springer, Heidelberg (2004)
24. Sheikh, R., Kumar, B., Mishra, D.: Privacy-preserving k-secure sum protocol. Int. J. Comput. Sci. Inf. Secur. 6(2), 184–188 (2009)
25. Shi, J., Zhang, R., Liu, Y., Zhang, Y.: PriSense: privacy-preserving data aggregation in people-centric urban sensing systems. In: Proceedings of INFOCOM (2010)
26. Yao, A.: Protocols for secure computations. In: Proceedings of FOCS, pp. 160–164 (1982)

A Novel Approach for Addressing Wandering Off Elderly Using Low Cost Passive RFID Tags

Mingyue Zhou and Damith C. Ranasinghe[(⊠)]

Auto-ID Lab, School of Computer Science,
University of Adelaide, Adelaide, SA 5005, Australia
mingyue.zhou@student.adelaide.edu.au,
damith.ranasinghe@adelaide.edu.au

Abstract. Wandering (e.g. elopement) by elderly persons at acute hospitals and nursing homes poses a significant problem to providing patient care as such incidents can lead to injury and even accidental morbidity. These problems are particularly serious given aging populations around the world. While various technologies exit (such as door alarms), they are expensive and the reliability of such systems have not been evaluated in the past. In this article we propose two novel methods for a very low cost solution to address the problem of wandering off patients using body worn low cost passive Radio Frequency Identification (RFID) tags using phase based measurements. Our approach requires no modification to the air interface protocols, firmware or hardware. Results from extensive experiments show that: (i) the proposed algorithms can accurately identify whether a person is moving into or out of, for example, a room; and (ii) it can be implemented in real-time to develop a low cost wandering off alarm.

Keywords: Passive RFID · Wandering off · Walking direction detection

1 Introduction

Acute hospital patients as well as residents at nursing homes, especially those with Alzheimer's disease, dementia and cognitive impairments, may be injured as a result of wandering off [1] (e.g. elopement) around facilities or leaving cared areas [2]. There are serious consequences arising from wandering to elderly, care givers and care providers such as mortality (colliding with a vehicle from wandering outside care facilities), complete disappearances and litigations [3]. As a consequence of an ageing world population, the cohort of elderly with wandering behavior is expected to increase, for example, it is estimated that by 2050 the incidence of Alzheimer's disease will approach 11 to 16 million people in the U.S. alone [4]. Monitoring elderly and recognizing when they are leaving facilities (hospital rooms, nursing homes) in real time provide an opportunity to intervene and prevent occurrences of wandering off.

Although boundary alarms ('buzzers') based on battery powered wrist worn bracelets[1] are employed to prevent or deter elderly from wandering off, these devices are simple proximity based sensors. A recent study has used a battery powered Wifi tag

---

[1] Example: http://alert.com.au/index_files/W101TX.htm

© Institute for Computer Sciences, Social Informatics and Telecommunications Engineering 2014
I. Stojmenovic et al. (Eds.): MOBIQUITOUS 2013, LNICST 131, pp. 330–343, 2014.
DOI: 10.1007/978-3-319-11569-6_26

[5] on a wheel chair and localization methods while in [6] researchers have proposed a method of localizing individuals by highly instrumenting the subject with multiple battery powered devices (e.g. an audio recorder, wireless sensor node, an RFID wristband reader). Other researchers, for example in [7], have proposed using mobile phone devices to address wandering off. These devices cost in the range of hundreds of dollars and are battery powered and therefore require maintenance and care. Furthermore the solution to instrument wheel chairs does not address the need to monitor elderly that do not require such an aid. The other central drawback with battery powered devices is that either carers or elderly uses must remember to replace batteries and to carry a bulky device. This is a significant issue for dementia sufferers or cognitively impaired patients.

The ability by modern RFID (Radio Frequency Identification) readers to obtain phase information from passive (batteryless) tag responses is creating new possibilities to detect the direction of motion of tags in an unsupervised manner. In this paper we evaluate the performance of two methods based on estimating the direction of travel of batteryless, lost cost, lightweight RFID tags to detect wandering off patients in hospital and nursing home settings. In particular we make the following contributions:

- We propose a novel approach, for the first time (to the best of our knowledge), for determining elderly wandering off supervised areas such as hospital rooms and nursing care facilities based on them wearing a low cost passive RFID tag over their attire.
- We develop two algorithms using tag phase information to identify the direction of traversal of a person wearing an RFID tag to accurately determine persons attempting to travel beyond a threshold.
- We evaluate the performance of our proposed algorithms by conducting extensive experiments.

The following sections of the paper are organised as follows: in Sect. 2 we discuss related works in tag direction estimation; Sect. 3 describes our approach, tag phase and theoretical aspects of the proposed methodologies; Sect. 4 outlines the two unsupervised algorithms for estimating direction of tag traversal; and Sect. 5 presents results of our experiments. Finally discussion, limitations and conclusions are in Sect. 6.

2 Related Works

Although we have not found literature on the use of passive RFID tags to determine the direction of traversal of a person, a limited number of published methodologies for determining tag direction exist [8–11]. However, experimental evidence to support such methods are limited [8, 9] while performance evaluation of proposed methods are non-existent.

Nevertheless, a number of existing localization methods for spatial identification of active transmitters have been applied for tracking the direction of objects tagged with active tags. Active tags employ an active transmitter with extended tag logic and therefore can generate a strong signal back to a reader over a long distance. By contrast, the performance of passive RFID tags is affected by additional noise sources, which makes accurate spatial identification of a tagged object difficult in real-world situations. Sources of noise can be as a result of the limited working range of modulated back-scatter Ultra High Frequency (UHF) RFID, noise in the received signal, multi-path effects, tag incident power, fading and scattering [12, 13]. Existing RFID based spatial identification methods can be categorized into the following two approaches [13, 14]:

- **Scene analysis** with extra reference nodes. This approach uses statistical algorithms such as k-nearest neighbour (kNN) and probabilistic methods for spatial identification, according to the measured RSS (Received Signal Strength) of a tag response.
- **Continuous measurement of connectivity information**, i.e. distance can be estimated by using RSS, time of arrival (ToA), angle of arrival (AoA), time difference of arrival (TDoA), and phase difference of arrival (PDoA).

Typical scene analysis, such as LANDMARC [15], determines the spatial position of a tag by comparing the signal strength between reference nodes deployed in the environment, and then uses statistical algorithms to improve localization accuracy. In [16] Kalman filtering is used improve the accuracy of localization based on RSS measurements from two antennas. Overall, RSS based spatial identification methods are feasible for motion tracking, however, due to the limited working range and the noise in backscattered UHF RFID systems, these RFID localization techniques have only been successfully used to track active tags. Meanwhile, deployment of proposed infrastructure can be rather expensive due to the requirement of multiple readers and reference tags. Moreover, such approaches have only been evaluated in the determination of static tags as opposed to determining the direction of traversal (DoT) of tags, for example in or out of a hospital room.

Connectivity information based schemes have been applied for tag direction of arrival (DoA) estimation. Oikawa [8] proposed a method using time difference of signal arrival, which is measured by the strength of the received signal at two antennas, to estimate the tag DoA. Consequently, the accuracy of DoT information is deteriorated due to multipath affects [12]. Other researchers have also focused on using DoA estimation for tag localization [10, 11]. However, the accuracy of their methods decreases as a result of tag readings in overlapping reader antenna zones and the work in [10] is only theoretical and experiments to evaluate the performance of proposed approaches are absent.

Passive RFID tags have greater advantages than active tags or current battery powered proximity sensors used for determining wandering off patients because of significantly lower cost, compact form, lightweight and batteryless nature requiring no maintenance while providing disposability for reasons such as infection control. Consequently, our research focuses on estimating the direction of traversal of passive RFID tags through door thresholds (e.g. patient rooms in acute hospitals, nursing homes) to determine whether a patient wearing an RFID tag is moving *in* or *out* of a room. Furthermore, developments in wearable RFID tags [17] and commercial washable RFID tags [18] have made it possible to develop extremely lightweight tags suitable for patient monitoring. In this paper we develop and evaluate two methods to determine the direction of movement of patients out of clinical areas (such as exit doors, doors leading out of hospital rooms).

3   Systems Overview and Models

We propose a wandering off alarm system based on using four components: (i) RFID reader; (ii) two RFID reader antennas connected to a reader; (iii) wearable RFID tag; and (iv) a patient traversing direction identification algorithm as illustrated in Fig. 1.

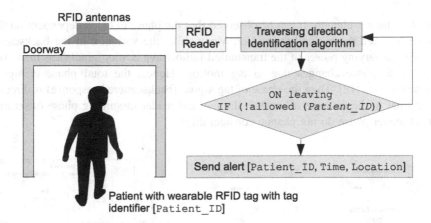

Fig. 1. Systems overview of the proposed patient wandering off alarm system where an alert can be sent to a caregiver using, for example a nurse call system, to alert them of an elderly leaving a care facility

RFID readers interrogate tags to obtain electronically stored information such as a unique identification code, for example, an EPC (electronic product code). The two RFID antennas both provide power to the passive tags and also collect tag responses (i.e. passive tags rely on the carrier wave received from the reader antenna to power the tag and backscatter a response as oppose to actively transmitting a signal). Passive RFID tags are low cost mostly due to their batteryless nature. Therefore our focus is on using such low cost passive tags to develop a wandering off alarm. The patient traversing direction identification algorithm considers an input sequence of observations as a time series of tuples [*time of read, antenna identifier, tag radial velocity*] to determine if the patient is walking out of a doorway or threshold. Although *time of read* and *antenna identifier* are directly reported by RFID readers, *tag radial velocity* must be estimated first using tag phase reported by the reader.

3.1   Tag Phase

Figure 2(a) provides an overview of radio wave propagation between a reader antenna and a passive RFID tag. It can be seen from Fig. 2(a) that a signal to a tag travels across two links: (i) forward reader-tag link; and (ii) return tag-reader link. Therefore, the total distance travelled by a radio wave is $2d$ m. Then the total phase reported by RFID readers for each tag read in any prorogation environment is $\varphi = \varphi_r + \varphi_o + \varphi_{BS}$ where φ_r is the phase rotation over distance $2d$, φ_o is the phase offset due to the reader's transmit circuits and tag's reflection characteristics, φ_{BS} is the backscatter phase of the tag [12]. In free space, the phase rotation of the radio wave over a distance $2d$ can be expressed as:

$$\phi_r = -2\pi\left(\frac{2d}{\lambda}\right) \tag{1}$$

where λ is the wavelength. It can be observed that the phase in (1) is dependent on the distance between the tag and the reader. Meanwhile, the variation of tag backscatter phase due to varying power of the transmitted radio wave is very small (less than 10°) compared to phase changes due to tag motion. Hence, the total phase is highly dependent on φ_r [12]. Then the phase of tag signal (backscattered response) is directly proportional to the distance d between the tag and reader (assuming phase offset and tag backscatter phase do not change considerably).

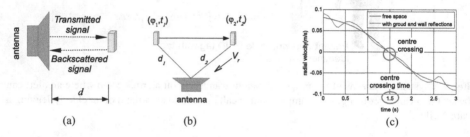

(a)   (b)   (c)

Fig. 2. (a) Illustration of radio wave propagation between a tag and antenna; (b) an iillustration of radial velocity estimation; and (c) simulation obtained using the model in [9] for the tag traversal illustrated in (b)

3.2   Tag Radial Velocity

The projection of the tag velocity vector on to the line of sight between the tag and the reader, as shown in Fig. 2(b), can be estimated by measuring the phase difference $\varphi_2 - \varphi_1$ of a tag at two different time instances t_1 and t_2 at a fixed frequency. Then by attributing the phase difference $\varphi_2 - \varphi_1$ to the path difference $d_2 - d_1$ resulting from the motion of a tag, the difference in distance between d_1 and d_2 can be obtained as:

$$d_2 - d_1 = \frac{1}{2}\left(\frac{\phi_2 - \phi_1}{2\pi}\lambda\right).$$

The radial velocity of the tag can then be expressed as $V_r = -\frac{d_2 - d_1}{t_2 - t_1}$ and substituting $\lambda = c/f$ gives,

$$V_r = -\frac{\frac{1}{2}\left(\frac{\varphi_2 - \varphi_1}{2\pi}\lambda\right)}{t_2 - t_1} = -\frac{c}{4\pi f}\frac{\Delta\varphi}{\Delta t}. \tag{2}$$

Consider a tag traversing on a path in front of an antenna (Fig. 2(b)). Then the difference in distances d between the tag and the antenna is decreasing when the tag is moving towards the antenna from the left while the difference is increasing as the tag moves away to the right of the antenna. Therefore, a positive radial velocity implies that the tag is moving towards to the antenna and a negative velocity implies that the tag is moving away from antenna as illustrated in Fig. 2(c). Theoretically, we call the time-space coordinate of when a tag's velocity changes direction (e.g. from positive to negative) the *centre crossing* and the time coordinate as the *centre crossing time* (as shown in Fig. 2(c)).

4   Traversing Direction Identification Methods

In this section we propose two tag traversing direction identification (TDI) methods: (i) center crossing time estimation method; and (ii) radial velocity distribution estimation method. Both of these methods are based on analyzing the radial velocity of a passive RFID tag worn by a person, to enable us to determine if a person wearing the tag is entering (*moving in*) or leaving (*moving out*) a doorway (Fig. 1).

Our proposed reader antenna arrangement for both methods is shown in Fig. 3. The reader antennas are arranged at a 45° angle to the vertical axis (maximize the velocity based information available, read zones and minimize read zone overlap). Here both antennas are installed opposite to each other and at the same height.

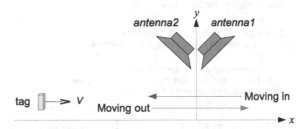

Fig. 3. Antenna configuration for the TDI methods

Algorithm: *cct_detect*

Input: Tag reads (time, radial velocity) in time $\in [t_{start}, t_{end}]$ for a given antenna
Output: Estimated center crossing time vector CCT.

---

1. $t \leftarrow t_{start}$ and $CCT \leftarrow 0$ //center crossing time vector.
2. **do**
3. $m \leftarrow 0$ //count of positive velocity estimates
4. $n \leftarrow 0$ // count of negative velocity estimates
5.   update m and n in time $\in [t, t+1]$
6.   **if** $m < n$ and $n \geq 2$, **then** //filtering noisy velocity estimations
7. $CCT \leftarrow t$.
8.   **else** $t \leftarrow t+1$
9. **while** $t < t_{end}$
10. **return** CCT.

Fig. 4. Algorithm for detecting centre crossing time

4.1   Center Crossing Time Estimation Method

Considering the arrangement in Fig. 3, if the tag *moves out* (traverses from left to right), it will pass through *antenna2* and *antenna1* in succession. Therefore, the center crossing time of radial velocity at *antenna2* can be expected to be earlier than at *antenna1*. Similarity, when tag *moves in*, the center crossing time at *antenna1* can be expected be earlier than that at *antenna2*. Hence, the tag traversing direction can be identified by comparing center crossing times at the two antennas. Assuming CCT_1 and CCT_2 are centre crossing times at *antenna1* and *antenna2*, the first TDI method can be illustrated as:

- If $CCT_1 - CCT_2 < 0$ then tag is moving from *antenna1* to *antenna2* (*move in*)
- If $CCT_1 - CCT_2 > 0$ then tag moving from *antenna2* to *antenna1* (*move out*).

However, for real-time application, we should consider an algorithm to detect the centre crossing time automatically and estimate whether a person is moving in or moving out. Shown in Fig. 4 is the algorithm developed for estimating centre crossing times, while the proposed algorithm for detecting the direction of travel is in Fig. 5.

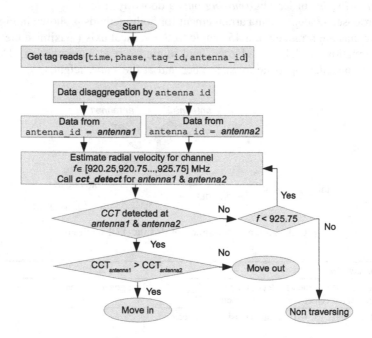

Fig. 5. TDI method using CCT

4.2   Radial Velocity Distribution Estimation Method

The second TDI method proposed is based on using the information from changing read zones of the tag in addition to its radial velocity. When a tag is moving in (see Fig. 3), because of the different coverage of the two antennas, it will mainly be detected

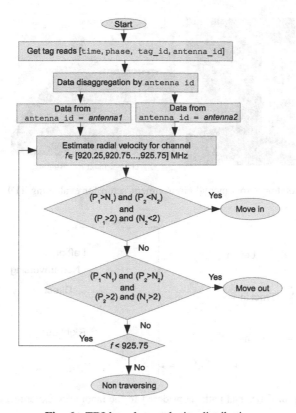

Fig. 6. TDI based on velocity distribution

by *antenna1* as approaching, and then by *antenna2* as departing. As a result, the distribution of radial velocity estimates is skewed towards positive velocities rather than negative velocities at *antenna1* and negative velocities at *antenna2*. Similarity, when a tag is moving out, distribution of velocities will be mostly positive at *antenna2* and negative for *antenna1*. Based on this theory, an alternative approach to detecting tag direction can be derived by observing the distribution of radial velocities at the two antennas. Then, using P_1 and N_1 to represent the quantity of positive and negative radial velocities at *antenna1*, P_2 and N_2 represents the positive and negative velocity quantities at *antenna2*, the second method can be illustrated as:

- If $P_1 > N_1$ & $P_2 < N_2$ then tag is moving from *antenna1* to *antenna2* (moving in).
- If $P_1 < N_1$ & $P_2 > N_2$ then tag is moving from *antenna2* to *antenna1* (moving out).

The algorithm based on the distribution of positive and negative velocities as a result of differing coverage of a moving tag at the two antennas is outlined in Fig. 6. Here we do not rely on evaluating the CCT for any of the antennas and has the ability to overcome errors in CCT detection that may results as a consequence of measurement error (for example in phase estimated by the reader).

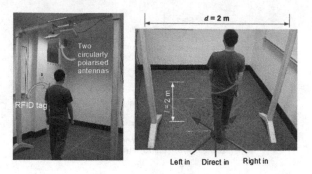

Fig. 7. Laboratory experimental environment setup for evaluating TDI algorithms

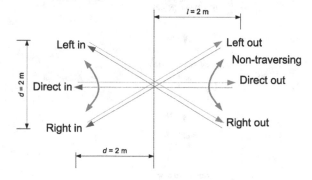

Fig. 8. Traversal paths considered in the laboratory experiments

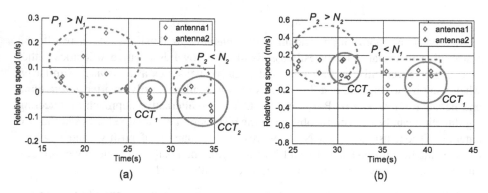

Fig. 9. Radial velocity at the two antennas depicting the center crossing times and the distribution of velocities: (a) when a person is *moving in*; and (b) when a person is *moving out*

5 Experiments

In order to evaluate the performance of the two proposed algorithms, we conducted detailed and extensive experiments in a laboratory environment under real world conditions. We evaluated the ability of the algorithms to identify the traversing direction of a person through a threshold at, for example, a critical exit at a nursing home or an acute hospital.

Although modern RFID readers can perform fully coherent detection and report the phase of the backscattered signal, as a result of phase estimation techniques used [12], π radians of ambiguity is introduced to phase measurements such that the reported phase can be the estimated phase (θ) or the estimated phase combined with a multiplicity of π radians ($\theta + k\pi$) [19]. The readers used in our experiments (Sect. 5.1) were observed to randomly flip the phase π radians. Consequently, the measured backscatter signal phase cannot be directly used for phase based measures of spatial and temporal dimensions of tags (such as radial velocity). Therefore we limited the range of phase measurements to $[0, \pi]$ by taking modulo π radians of phase measurements prior to estimating velocity.

5.1 Settings

The experiment scenario is shown in Fig. 7. The reader antennas were located 2.6 m above ground level and in order to obtain accurate measurements, the cables connected with two antennas had the same length and the two antennas employed are also of the same model (two circularly polarised antennas, model no: Impinj IPJ-A1000-USA). We used an Impinj Speedway Revolution UHF (Ultra High Frequency) RFID reader (R420) and 'Squiggle' passive tags (using an Alien Higgs 3 Integrated Circuit manufactured by Alien Technology) encased in a rubber packaging that is 3 mm thick. The equipment operated under Australian Electromagnetic Compatibility Regulations (4 W Equivalent Isotropic Radiated Power, frequency range from 920 MHz to 926 MHz, 12 channels).

5.2 Statistical Analysis

In this study, we evaluated: (i) Sensitivity = *True Positives / (True Positives + False Negatives)* and (ii) Specificity = *True Negatives / (True Negatives + False Positives)*; and (iii) Accuracy = *True Positives + True Negatives /(True Negatives + True Positives + False Positives + False Negatives)*. Here true positives (TP) were correctly identified movements (e.g. moving in). True negatives (TN) were movements of no-interest that were correctly identified (e.g. non-traversing). False negatives (FN) were movements (e.g. moving in) that were not identified (i.e. misses). False positives (FP) are other movements that were identified as a moving direction of interest.

5.3 Results

Two healthy, young adults (one female and one male) participated in the study. The RFID tag (Fig. 7) was attached over clothing using double sided tape onto the shoulder of the person (Fig. 7). The two persons were not instructed to walk at a certain speed but asked to walk at their normal walking speed. We considered eight paths with an approximate length of 4 m as shown in Fig. 8 for the study where Right In, Direct In,

Left In were considered as *moving in* paths (as depicted in Fig. 3) while Right Out, Direct Out and Left Out were considered as *moving out* paths.

In particular, we included two non-traversing paths to consider situations where elderly simply walked parallel to or walk towards and then away from a threshold of a doorway. The study participants performed a scripted routine of 45 moving in path trials (the script consisted of a list of 45 moving paths randomly selected from direct in, left in and right in paths), a scripted routine of 45 moving out path (45 randomly selected from direct out, left out, right out paths) and 90 trials for non-traversing paths.

Center Crossing Time Estimation Method (CCT-TDI): Fig. 9 shows an example of the radial velocity estimated at the two antennas for a trial where a participant moved along the direct in path and direct out path (shown in Fig. 8). We can observe the change in radial velocity from positive to negative at both antennas and the center crossing times successfully detected by the algorithms. In Fig. 9(a) we can see that the centre crossing time at *antenna1* (CCT_1) identified is smaller than centre crossing time at *antenna2* (CCT_2) when the person is moving along the direct in path, while CCT_1 is greater than CCT_2 when the person is moving along the direct out path (Fig. 9(b)).

Radial Velocity Distribution Estimation Method (RV-TDI): Fig. 9 also illustrates the distribution of positive and negative velocities at both antennas for direct in path (*moving in*) and direct out (*moving out*) path traversals. When the participant is moving in, we can reach a consensus that the distribution of positive radial velocities is larger than the negative velocities at *antenna1* while at *antenna2* the distribution of positive radial velocities is smaller than the negative velocities. Similarly, when the participant is *moving out*, we can observe more positive estimations at *antenna2* and less positive velocity estimates at *antenna1*.

Table 1. Performance of the two proposed algorithms

Algorithm	Path	TP	FN	FP	TN	Sensitivity	Specificity	Accuracy
CCT-TDI	*Move In*	38	7	8	37	84.4 %	82.2 %	84.4 %
	Move Out	39	6	9	36	86.7 %	80.0 %	83.3 %
RV-TDI	*Move In*	41	4	5	40	91.1 %	88.9 %	90.0 %
	Move Out	40	5	6	39	88.9 %	86.7 %	87.8 %

Table 1 outlines the results of our laboratory trials. Although both algorithms provide good accuracy, sensitivity and specificity, RV-TDI algorithm performs better on all three metrics. Sensitivity results (≥88 %) for RV-TDI is noticeably higher than CCT-TDI indicating a very low (≤12 %) miss rate (missing that a person moved through a monitored threshold). Similarly specificity results (≥86 %) for RV-TDI is also higher than for CCT-TDI indicating relatively lower (≤14 %) false alarm rates (detecting that a person has traversed through when they have not). The low error rates of our proposed algorithms are likely to be translated to higher levels of acceptance of the system by caregivers as they are less likely to be frustrated by false alarms and more likely to observe the benefits of the system to provide safe care.

The reason for lower performance is of CCT-TDI algorithm is because of its reliance on estimating the center crossing time. Due to the noise in phase measurements and the speed at which a participant walks across the threshold, the center crossing algorithm (*cct_detect* in Fig. 4) can fail to detect a *CCT*.

6 Conclusions and Future Work

The main finding of our study was that a single RFID tag placed over the shoulder accurately identified *moving in* and *moving out* of a threshold to address eloping in elderly in an ageing population context. The small, battery free and low cost nature of RFID tags are an advantage, especially in settings where there is significant risk of infection such as hospitals where the device offers both disposability and user-friendliness. Comparing our approach to existing wandering off alarms, the use of simple passive device as opposed to presently used expensive battery powered devices is a key advantage. Although our approach does required RFID readers, current solutions also require a powered transceiver and associated antennae at each threshold. The RV-TDI method performed better with few false negatives and false positives. These low error rates can lead to higher levels of acceptance of the system by care givers.

Although both algorithms performed well, there are a number of limitations. Firstly, we have not investigated the effect of antenna orientations other than 45° (Fig. 3) on the performance of the algorithms. Clearly reducing the angle will diminish the difference between the center crossing time at the two antennas and we can expect the CCT-TDI algorithm performance to reduce.

Secondly, the traversing speed of the tag presents an upper bound on walking speed beyond which it is not possible to distinguish center crossings. In particular, reader frequency randomly hops between 12 channels (under Australian regulations) during interrogations and maximally 2 s are required to hop back to the same channel. If a person travels at high speed, inadequate readings can be obtained from the reader at a fixed frequency to evaluate radial velocity V_r. Hence, the accuracy of our algorithms decreases as the walking speed of a person increases due to the absence of enough radial velocity information.

However, we can evaluate an upper bound for walking speed. For each antenna, at least four phase measurements are needed for the proposed CCT-TDI (Sect. 4.1). In the worst case, 8 s are required to obtain four phase measurements. Then algorithm performance can be expected to deteriorate if walking speed exceeds $d_{path}/8$ (m/s) where d_{path} is the distance over which each antenna can successfully read a tag. Taking a nominal reading rage of 5 m from an antenna, the upper bound on velocity is approximately 4.5 (km/h) which, according to mean gait speeds reported in [20] is adequate for monitoring elderly over the age of 70 years, the target population for our algorithms.

Since RV-TDI method (Sect. 4.2) relies on reaching consensus on positive and negative samples, algorithm performance can be expected to deteriorate if walking speed of a tag wearer exceeds 9 (km/h) where we assume only two phase measurements are needed within 2 s but over a d_{path} of 5 m. It is also important to note that the ability to detect walking direction at significantly higher walking speeds also relates to the better performance observed with this approach (Table 1).

Furthermore, we hope our results will serve as a benchmark for wandering off detection methods in the future as well as TDI estimation methods. We are currently looking at applying filters and pattern recognition algorithms on phase measurements, velocity and return signal strength to improve the estimation of traversal direction as well as using multiple frequencies as opposed to a single frequency and using mean radial speeds to estimate TDI to overcome the limitation posed by walking speed. Finally, we plan to evaluate our approaches on a larger cohort of older volunteers.

References

1. Thomas, D.W.: Wandering: a proposed definition. J. Gerontol. Nurs. **21**(9), 35–41 (1995)
2. Myra, A.: Dangerous wandering: Elopements of older adults with dementia from long-term care facilities. Am. J. Alzheimer's Disord. Other Dement. **19**(6), 361–368 (2004)
3. Levin, S.M., Mulligan, J.F.: Litigation nursing home wandering cases. Marquette Elder's Advis. **2**(2), 4 (2000)
4. Thies, W., Bleiler, L.: Alzheimer's disease facts and figures. Alzheimers Dement. **8**(2), 131–168 (2012)
5. Doshi-Velez, F., et al.: Improving safety and operational efficiency in residential care settings with WiFi-based localization. J. Am. Med. Dir. Assoc. **13**(6), 558–563 (2012)
6. Wan, J., O'Grady, M.J., O'Hare, G.M.P.: Towards holistic activity modeling and behavioral analyses. In: 6th International Workshop on Ubiquitous Health and Wellness, Newcastle, UK (2012)
7. Sposaro, F.: A geriatric suite of medical applications for Android powered devices. Electronic Theses, Treatises and Dissertations. Paper 5199 (2012)
8. Oikawa, Y.: Evaluation of tag moving direction detection in a UHF RFID gate system. In: IEEE Conference on Circuits and Systems, pp. 41–45 (2011)
9. Ranasinghe, D.C., Shinmoto Torres, R.L., Hill, K., Sample, A.P., Visvanathan, R.: Towards falls prevention: a wearable wireless and battery-less sensing and automatic identification tag for real time monitoring of human movements. In: 34th International IEEE EMBS Conference, pp. 6402–6405 (2012)
10. Zhang, Y., Amin, M., Kaushik, S.: Localization and tracking of passive RFID tags based on direction estimation. Int. J. Antennas Propag. (2012). doi:10.1155/2007/17426
11. Jian, Y., Wei Y., Zhang, Y.: Estimating the direction of motion based on active RFID. In: 5th International Conference on Information Science and Service, pp. 286–290 (2011)
12. Nikitin, P.V., et al.: Phase based spatial identification of UHF RFID tags. In: IEEE International Conference on RFID, pp. 102–109 (2010)
13. Williams, C.H., Grant, B., Liu, X., Zhang, Z., Kumar, P.: Accurate localization of RFID tags using phase difference. In: IEEE International Conference on RFID, pp. 89–96 (2010)
14. Bouet, M., dos Santos, A.: RFID tags: positioning principles and localization techniques. In: Wireless Days, pp. 1–5 (2008)
15. Ni, L.M., Liu, Y., Lau, Y.C., Patil, A.P.: Landmarc: indoor location sensing using active RFID. Wirel. Netw. **10**(6), 701–710 (2004)

16. Mittra, R., Pujare, U.: Real time estimation of motion and range of RFID tags. In: Proceedings of the 5th European Conference on Antennas and Propagation, pp. 3804–3808 (2011)
17. Kaufmann, T., Ranasinghe, D.C., Zhou, M., Fumeaux, C.: Wearable quarter-wave folded microstrip antenna for passive UHF RFID applications. Int. J. Antennas Propag. Article ID 129839, pp. 11 (2013)
18. Fujitsu: Washable UHF RFID Tag (2013). http://www.frontech.fujitsu.com/en/services/rfid/
19. Impinj Inc.: Low Level User Data Support. Impinnj Inc (2011)
20. Bohannon, R.W.: Comfortable and maximum walking speed of adults aged 20-79 years: reference values and determinants. Age Ageing 26(1), 15–19 (1997)

Focus and Shoot: Efficient Identification Over RFID Tags in the Specified Area

Yafeng Yin[1], Lei Xie[1(✉)], Jie Wu[2], Athanasios V. Vasilakos[3], and Sanglu Lu[1]

[1] State Key Laboratory for Novel Software Technology,
Nanjing University, Nanjing, China
yyf@dislab.nju.edu.cn, {lxie,sanglu}@nju.edu.cn
[2] Department of Computer and Information Sciences,
Temple University, Philadelphia, USA
jiewu@temple.edu
[3] University of Western Macedonia, Kozani, Greece
vasilako@ath.forthnet.gr

Abstract. In RFID systems, the reader usually identifies all the RFID tags in the interrogation region with the maximum power. However, some applications may only need to identify the tags in a specified area, which is usually smaller than the reader's default interrogation region. In this paper, we respectively present two solutions to identify the tags in the specified area. The principle of the solutions can be compared to the picture-taking process of a camera. It first focuses on the specified area and then shoots the tags. The design of the two solutions is based on the extensive empirical study on RFID tags. Realistic experiment results show that our solutions can reduce the execution time by 46 % compared to the baseline solution.

Keywords: RFID · Tag identification · Experimental study · Algorithm design

1 Introduction

RFID systems have been widely used in various applications, such as inventory control, sampling inspection, and supply chain management. Conventionally, an RFID system consists of one or multiple readers, and a larger number of tags. Each tag is attached to a physical item and has a unique ID describing the item. The reader recognizes the object by identifying its attached tag.

In recent years, many existing research works have concentrated on RFID tag identification, aiming to identify a large number of tags efficiently [1–4]. Instead of identifying all the tags, detecting the missing tags [5,6] and searching a particular subset of tags [7] only concern the part of tags. Rather than tag identification, cardinality estimation protocols count the number of tags [8–10]. However, all the literature do not research the problem of tag identification in a specified area, which is rather important in many applications. Taking the

© Institute for Computer Sciences, Social Informatics and Telecommunications Engineering 2014
I. Stojmenovic et al. (Eds.): MOBIQUITOUS 2013, LNICST 131, pp. 344–357, 2014.
DOI: 10.1007/978-3-319-11569-6_27

inventory for example, we may only need to identify the tags in some specified boxes while ignoring the others. Sometimes, it is difficult to move the objects out for tag identification, especially for the objects obstructed by obstacles. A traditional solution is to identify the tags with the maximum power. It may identify the tags out of the area, which is rather time-consuming. Due to the large number of tags, the time-efficiency is very important. Therefore, it is essential to identify the tags in the specified area efficiently without moving the tags.

Fortunately, we note that tag identification in the specified area can be compared to the picture-taking process in a camera. The camera needs to focus on the object before shooting, aiming to lock the target object while ignoring the others. In this paper, we propose the photography based identification method, which works in a similar way. It first focuses on the specified area by adjusting the antenna's angle and the reader's power, and then identifies the tags in the area. However, efficiently identifying the tags in the realistic environments is difficult. The reading performance in the realistic experiments is still unknown, especially for a large number of tags. There are a few research works concentrating on this problem and they mainly work in a situation close to free space [11–13]. Hence, we conduct a series of measurements over RFID tags in realistic settings. Based on the extensive experimental study, we respectively propose two solutions, aiming to identify the tags in the specified area efficiently. The solutions work in the realistic environments and conform to the EPC-C1G2 standards.

We make the following contributions in this paper. (1) We conducted extensive experiments on the commodity RFID system in the realistic environments and investigated the factors affecting the reading performance. (2) To the best of our knowledge, this is the first work investigating the efficient tag identification in the specified area, which is essential for many applications. We propose the photography based identification method, which works in a similar way as in a camera. Besides, we respectively propose two solutions to solve the problem, which can reduce the execution time by 46 % compared to the baseline solution. (3) Our solutions work in the realistic environments with the commercial RFID system, which conforms to the EPC-C1G2 standards.

2   Problem Formulation

2.1   System Model

Each object is attached with an RFID tag, which has a unique ID. In this paper, we use the terms 'object', 'tag' interchangeably. The number of tags and the distribution of tag IDs are unknown. The reader is statically deployed and configured with an antenna. The antenna is associated with an interrogation region, within which the reader can identify the tags. The antenna is deployed in a fixed position. It cannot change its distance to the objects, but it is rotatable. The reader can control the interrogation region by adjusting the power.

The objects are packaged in boxes. The boxes out of the specified area S has reasonable distances between the boxes in S, which means that the area S has a clear boundary. As shown in Fig. 1, the tags in S are called as *target tags*, while

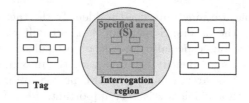

Fig. 1. Identify the tags in the specified area

the tags outside S are called as *interference tags*. The objective of this paper is to identify as many *target tags* as possible while minimizing the execution time.

2.2 Performance Metrics

We consider the three performance metrics for evaluating the solution's efficiency.

(1) *Coverage ratio ρ constraint*: Let S be the set of tags in S (target tags), $s = |S|$. Let M be the set of the tags that are identified in S, $m = |M|$. Obviously, $M \subseteq S$ and $m \leq s$. Then, $\rho = \frac{m}{s}$, $0 \leq \rho \leq 1$. The larger the value of ρ, the better the coverage ratio. Given a constant α, ρ should satisfy $\rho \geq \alpha$. α is related to the specific scenario, when the environment and the deployment of the RFID system are fixed, the value of α can be determined.

(2) *Execution time T*: It represents the duration of the whole process. It shows the time efficiency, which is rather important, especially for the identification of a large number of tags. The smaller the time T, the better the time efficiency.

(3) *Misreading ratio λ*: Let U be the set of tags out of S (interference tags) that are identified, $u = |U|$, $U \cap S = \emptyset$. Then, $\lambda = \frac{u}{u+m}$. The smaller the value of λ, the lower the misreading ratio.

The objective of this paper is to minimize the execution time T, while the coverage ratio satisfies $\rho \geq \alpha$. When $\rho \geq \alpha$, minimizing T means avoiding identifying the *interference tags*, in order to reduce the identification time. There is no constraint on λ, which is related to T. However, for the same execution time, the lower the misreading ratio, the better the performance of a solution.

3 Observations From the Realistic Experiments

In order to know the factors affecting the reading performance in the realistic environments, we conduct the following experiments. We use the Alien-9900+ reader and Alien-9611 antenna. The reader's maximum power $maxP_w$ is 30.7 dBm and its minimum power $minP_w$ is 15.7 dBm. The RFID tag is Alien 9640 tag. Each tag is attached into a distinct book. The antenna and the books are placed on the tablet chairs with a height of 0.5 m. Unless otherwise specified, we make the antenna face towards the center of the objects, set the reader's power $P_w = 30.7$ dBm, the distance between the tags and the antenna $d = 1$ m by default. For each experiment, the reader scans the tags for 50 cycles.

3.1   Identify the Tag at Different Angles

As the angle between the radiation direction and the surface of the antenna deceases, the reading performance deceases. However, when a tag is located in the center of the interrogation region, it can be identified efficiently. We observe the minimum power $P_{w_{min}}$ needed to activate one tag. We use θ_r to represent the angle between the antenna's radiation direction and the antenna's surface, $\theta_r \in [0°, 90°]$. In the first experiment, we rotate the antenna to change θ_r while keeping the tag unchanged. Figure 2(a) shows that as θ_r decreases, $P_{w_{min}}$ becomes larger. In the second experiment, we rotate the tag while keeping the antenna unchanged. We use θ_t to represent the angle between the radiation direction and the tag's surface. Figure 2(a) shows that the tag is easily identified, whatever θ_t is. Therefore, making the antenna face towards the tags ($\theta_r = 90°$) is essential for improving the reading performance.

3.2   Adjust the Reader's Power

The larger the reader's power, the larger the interrogation region, but the new identified tags may not be located in the interrogation region's boundary. However, if a tag can be identified with a low power, it must be identified with a larger power. We uniformly deploy 72 tags on the wall and the distance between two adjacent tags is 20 cm, as shown in Fig. 2(b).The new identified tags may not be

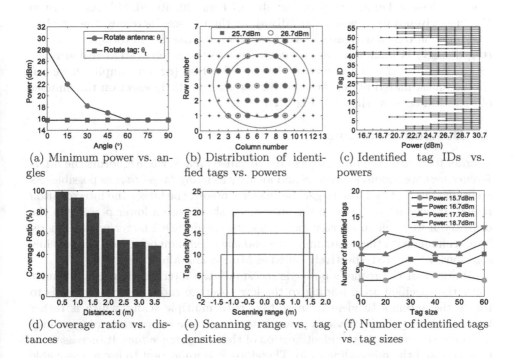

(a) Minimum power vs. angles

(b) Distribution of identified tags vs. powers

(c) Identified tag IDs vs. powers

(d) Coverage ratio vs. distances

(e) Scanning range vs. tag densities

(f) Number of identified tags vs. tag sizes

Fig. 2. Observations from the realistic experiments

in the interrogation region's boundary. We cannot distinguish a tag's position only by adjusting the power. In regard to a tag, Fig. 2(c) shows that if a tag can be identified with a low power, then it definitely can be identified by a larger power. Usually, the large power can increase the number of identified tags.

3.3   Vary the Distance Between the Tags and the Antenna

As the distance between the tags and the antenna increases, the reading performance decreases. Besides, when the distance is fixed, the maximum coverage ratio has an upper bound, whatever the reader's power is. We vary the distance d from 0.5 m to 3.5 m. Figure 2(d) shows as d becomes larger, the number of identified tags decreases. When the distance is small (eg. $d \leq 1.5$ m), the reading performance is relatively good. However, when the distance and the number of tags are fixed, the coverage ratio has an upper bound. For example, when $d = 1.5$ m and $n = 55$, the maximum coverage ratio is 78 %. Fortunately, some applications (eg. sampling inspection) just needs the coverage ratios meet the constraint instead of achieving 100 %. However, when considering the high coverage ratio, the antenna should not be placed far away from the tags.

3.4   Effect of the Tag Size

The tag size can affect the effective interrogation region. However, it has little effect on the number of identified tags. We uniformly deploy the tags in a row with length 4 m and vary the number of tags (20, 40, 60, 80). As shown in Fig. 2(e), given a fixed power (30.7 dBm), as the tag size increases, the effective interrogation region decreases. Therefore, when the tag size in the specified area (tag density) is unknown, we can not calculate the interrogation region accurately. However, if we only want to identify a few tags (eg. for sampling), we can choose an estimated power, because the tag size has little effect on the number of identified tags, as shown in Fig. 2(f).

4   Baseline Solutions

In order to identify the *target tags* in the specified area S, while ignoring the *interference tags*, we should focus on S and identify as many *target tags* as possible. As mentioned in Sect. 3.2, the larger the reader's power, the larger the interrogation region. If we want to focus on the area S, we should use a lower power. On the contrary, if we want to identify more tags, we should use a larger power. Therefore, scanning with the minimum power and the maximum power are two baseline solutions, which are respectively called as MinPw and MaxPw.

However, if the reader's power is too small, the interrogation region cannot cover the specified area, leading to the low coverage ratio. Besides, it needs to rotate the antenna to identify more tags with multiple scans, which is rather time-consuming. If the reader's power is too large, the interrogation region may be too large, leading to the identification of the *interference tags*. It increases the time cost and the misreading ratio. Therefore, it is important to use a reasonable power to identify the tags in the specified area.

5 Photography Based Identification with Distance Measurement

In this section, we propose a solution called Photography based tag Identification with Distance measurement (PID), which works with a 3D camera (eg. a Kinect). The process of PID can be compared to the picture-taking process in a camera. It focuses on the area and shoot the objects, as shown in Fig. 3. The application appoints the specified area S and the middleware collects the tag IDs in S by the RFID systems. It consists of focus module and shoot module. The focus module adjusts the reader's power and rotates the antenna to make the interrogation region focus on S. The shoot module collects tag IDs. The two corresponding process are respectively called as *Focusing Process* and *Shooting Process*.

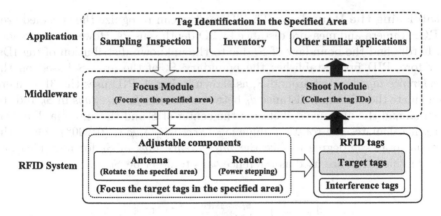

Fig. 3. The Framework of PID

5.1 Focusing Process

The focusing process aims to adjust the interrogation region to be focused on the specified area S by adjusting θ_r, P_w, while ignoring the tags outside S. It contains three phases, selecting the initial power, establishing the boundary and power stepping. The process aims to get the optimal power P_w^*, whose corresponding interrogation region is just enough to cover the area S.

Selecting the Initial Power. Before the reader identifies the tags, it selects the initial power instead of the default (maximum) one to control the interrogation region. In RFID systems, the reader's interrogation region of an antenna is like an ellipsoid. The larger the angle θ_r between the radiation direction and the antenna's surface, the longer the reader's scanning range. However, in the realistic environment, the tag size, the reader's power P_w, the radiation angle θ_r, and the distance d all affect the effective interrogation region, as mentioned in Sect. 3. Therefore, in the realistic environments, we measure the minimum power $P_{w_{min}}$

based on θ_r and d, and use them to calculate the initial power. In this paper, we measure $P_{w_{min}}(\theta_r, d)$ with the distances $d_j = 0.5\,\mathrm{m} \times j, j \in [1, 7]$ and the angles $\theta_i = 90° - 15° \times i, i \in [0, 6]$. For example, we get $P_{w_{min}}(90°, 1.0) = 15.7\,\mathrm{dBm}$, $P_{w_{min}}(75°, 1.5) = 18.8\,\mathrm{dBm}$, $P_{w_{min}}(60°, 2.0) = 23.4\,\mathrm{dBm}$. The reader first selects the reference angle θ_i closest to θ_r, $|\theta_r - \theta_i| \leq |\theta_r - \theta_k|$ ($k \in [0, 6]$ and $k \neq i$). Then, it uses d to calculate the initial power $P_{w_{min}}(\theta_r, d)$

$$\begin{cases} P_{w_{min}}(\theta_i, d_j) & if \ \ d = d_j \\ \frac{P_{w_{min}}(\theta_i, d_j) + P_{w_{min}}(\theta_i, d_{j+1})}{2} & if \ \ d \in [d_j, d_{j+1}]. \end{cases} \quad (1)$$

However, the power is only used as the initial power. In order to identify more tags, the reader can repeatedly increase the power by ΔP_w. We set $\Delta P_w = 1\,\mathrm{dBm}$, which is achievable by most of the commercial readers [14].

Establishing the Boundary. The 3D camera can recognize the specified area by RGB camera and measure distance by 3D depth sensors. However, the reader can hardly find the boundary of S, due to the unknown distribution of tag IDs. Therefore, PID first establishes the boundary S_b of the area S based on the *interference tags* located around S, as shown in Fig. 4. PID uses the 3D camera to calculate the minimum distance d_b between the *interference tags* in S_b and the antenna, and the distance d_s between the center of S and the antenna. Furthermore, it calculates the rotation angle $\varphi = arccos(\frac{d_s}{d_b})$, $\varphi \in (0°, 90°)$. Then, the antenna rotates φ degree to face the *interference tags* in S_b for identification. The identified tags are used as reference tags to describe S_b.

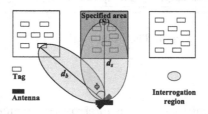

Fig. 4. Identify the tags in the specified area with a 3D camera

In PID, the antenna always faces towards the center of the objects, $\theta_r = 90°$. Then, the reader selects the initial power P_{wb} according to the distance d, $P_{wb} = P_{w_{min}}(90°, d)$. If the power P_{wb} is not large enough, the reader increases the power by ΔP_w and identifies n_b tags, as shown in Algorithm 1. It repeats the above process until $n_b \geq n_\varepsilon$, which means that it has collected enough tag IDs $N_b = \{ID_1, ID_2, \ldots, ID_{n_b}\}$ from the boundary. However, if the reader's power has achieved to the maximum value $maxP_w$, n_b is still less than n_ε, which indicates most of the *interference tags* are far away from S. Then, the reader stops the process and gets the optimal power $P_w^* = maxP_w$. After that, the antenna rotates towards the center of S for *power stepping* and tag identification.

Algorithm 1. PID: Establishing the boundary

Input: The specified area S

Determine the boundary S_b of S by the 3D camera, and calculate d_b and d_s.

The antenna rotates to S_b with $\varphi = arccos(\frac{d_s}{d_b})$.

$P_{wb} = P_{w_{min}}(90°, d_b)$, $P_w = P_{wb}$, $n_b = 0$.

while $n_b < n_\varepsilon$ and $P_w < maxP_w$ **do**

    Collect tag IDs with P_w and get n_b responses.

    if $P_w = maxP_w$ and $n_b < n_\varepsilon$ **then** $P_w^* = maxP_w$, Return.

    $P_w = min(P_w + \Delta P_w, maxP_w)$.

Get the tag IDs $N_b = \{ID_1, ID_2, \dots, ID_{n_b}\}$.

Output: Tag IDs in the boundary: N_b

Power Stepping. If P_w^* has not been determined, the reader will adjust the power through power stepping. Firstly, the reader chooses an initial power $P_{ws} = P_{w_{min}}(\theta_r, d)$ according to φ and d_b, where $\theta_r = 90° - \varphi$ and $d = d_b$. It is a critical value in theory, whose interrogation region just achieves the boundary of S. However, as shown in Fig. 2(e), the tag size can affect the effective interrogation region, P_{ws} may not be the most reasonable power. Thus we properly adjust the power by checking the tag IDs in N_b, as shown in Algorithm 2.

Algorithm 2. PID: Power Stepping

Input: Tag IDs in N_b

$P_{ws} = P_{w_{min}}(\theta_r, d) = P_{w_{min}}(90° - \varphi, d_b)$, $P_w = P_{ws}$.

Check the tag IDs in N_b and get n_c responses N_c.

if $\frac{n_c}{n_b} = \delta$ **then** $P_w^* = P_{ws}$.

if $\frac{n_c}{n_b} > \delta$ **then**

    while $P_w > minP_w$ **do**

        $P_w = max(P_w - \Delta P_w, minP_w)$.

        Check IDs in N_c, get Δn_c responses, $n_c = \Delta n_c$.

        if $\frac{n_c}{n_b} \le \delta$ **then** $P_w^* = P_w$, Break.

if $\frac{n_c}{n_b} < \delta$ **then**

    while $P_w < maxP_w$ **do**

        $P_w = min(P_w + \Delta P_w, maxP_w)$.

        Check IDs in $N_b - N_c$, get Δn_c responses, $n_c = n_c + \Delta n_c$.

        if $\frac{n_c}{n_b} \ge \delta$ **then** $P_w^* = P_w$, Break.

Output: The optimal power P_w^*

In the commercial RFID systems, the reader (eg. Alien-9900+) selects a specified tag by setting the mask equal to the tag ID. If the tag gives response, the reader gets a nonempty slot. Otherwise, it gets an empty slot. The reader checks all the IDs in N_b and gets n_c responses N_c. Obviously, $n_c \le n_b$. When $\frac{n_c}{n_b} = \delta$, the interrogation region just achieves the boundary of S. The corresponding power is the optimal power P_w^*. However, if $\frac{n_c}{n_b} > \delta$, the reader reduces the power by ΔP_w and checks the verified tag IDs in N_c. If a tag does not give response, the reader removes it from N_c. It repeats the above process until $\frac{n_c}{n_b} \leq \delta$ and gets the optimal power P_w^*. On the contrary, if $\frac{n_c}{n_b} < \delta$, the reader increases P_w by ΔP_w and checks the unverified tag IDs in $N_b - N_c = \{ID_i \mid ID_i \in N_b \text{ and } ID_i \notin N_c\}$. If the tag gives response, the reader adds the ID into N_c. It repeats the process until $\frac{n_c}{n_b} \geq \delta$ and gets the optimal power P_w^*. In the following process, the reader uses P_w^* to identify the *target tags*.

5.2   Shooting Process

In this process, the reader collects the tag IDs in S. The reader's power is equal to P_w^* and we use frame slotted ALOHA (FSA) protocol to identify the tags. FSA is a popular anti-collision protocol. In FSA, the reader first broadcasts a number f, which specifies the following frame size. After receiving f, each tag selects $h(ID)$ mod f as its slot number, h is a hash function. If none of the tags respond in a slot, the reader closes the slot immediately. If only one tag responds in a slot, the reader successfully receives the tag ID. If multiple tags respond simultaneously, a collision occurs, and the involved tags will be acknowledged to restart in the next frame. The similar process repeats until no tags respond in the frame. The collected IDs are considered as the *target tag IDs*.

5.3   Performance Analysis

In order to definitely describe the boundary S_b, PID needs to steadily get at least n_ε interference tag IDs, n_b satisfies $n_b \geq n_\varepsilon$. We measure the value of n_ε with different tag size $|N|$. When $|N| = 20, 60, 100, 140, 180, 220$, we respectively get $n_\varepsilon = 2, 4, 7, 9, 11, 12$. The tag size $|N|$ has a little effect on n_ε, which is usually very small. In order to definitely get enough tag IDs in S_b, we set $n_\varepsilon = 15$ by default, while considering the stability and time efficiency. In regard to δ, the smaller the value of δ, the lower the *misreading ratio*, the smaller the execution time. The larger the value of δ, the larger the value of *coverage ratio* ρ. Considering the constraint of ρ and time efficiency, we set $\delta = \alpha$. When $\frac{n_c}{n_b} = \delta = \alpha$, the interrogation region just achieves the boundary, while satisfying $\rho \geq \alpha$. Besides, the antenna rotates to the target direction immediately, the time for rotating the antenna can be neglected compared to the tag identification time.

6   Photography Based Identification with Angle Rotation

In PID, a 3D camera is used in the focusing process. However, in some environments, the 3D camera cannot work well (eg. in a dark space). Besides, considering the cost savings, it will not be used. Therefore, identifying the *target tags* efficiently without the auxiliary equipment is important. For this problem, we propose a solution called Photography based tag Identification with Angle rotation (PIA). It also consists of *Focusing Process* and *Shooting Process*.

The only difference between PID and PIA is how to determine the boundary of S. We only describe how to find the boundary in PIA, while ignoring the others.

Without the 3D camera, PIA cannot calculate any distance, it explores the boundary by rotating the antenna, as shown in Fig. 5. Firstly, the application appoints S and the antenna rotates towards S. Then the reader sets its initial power equal to the minimum power $minP_w$ and identifies n_s tags in S. If $n_s < n_\varepsilon$, the reader repeatedly increases the power by ΔP_w and identifies the tags until $n_s \geq n_\varepsilon$, the identified *target tags* are $N_s = \{ID_1, ID_2, \ldots, ID_{n_s}\}$. If $P_w = maxP_w$, PIA gets $P_w^* = maxP_w$. Otherwise, the antenna rotates away from S to get the interference tag IDs in the boundary, as shown in Algorithm 3.

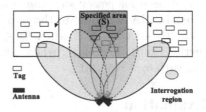

Fig. 5. Identify the tags in the specified area without any auxiliary equipment

---

Algorithm 3. PIA: Exploring the boundary

Input: The specified area S

$P_w = minP_w$, $n_s = 0$, $n_l = 0$, $\Delta\theta_{r_l} = 0°$.

while $n_s < n_\varepsilon$ and $P_w < maxP_w$ **do**
  $\lfloor$ Get n_s tag IDs, $P_w = min(P_w + \Delta P_w, maxP_w)$.

if $P_w = maxP_w$ **then** $P_w^* = maxP_w$, Return.

Get tag IDs $N_s = \{ID_1, ID_2 \ldots, ID_{n_s}\}$.

while $n_l < n_\varepsilon$ and $\theta_r \in [0°, 90°]$ **do**
  The antenna rotates to the left by $\Delta\theta_r$, $\Delta\theta_{r_l} = \Delta\theta_{r_l} + \Delta\theta_r$.
  while $P_w < maxP_w$ **do**
    Δn_s tag IDs in N_s disappear, $n_s = n_s - \Delta n_s$.
    Get Δn_l new tag IDs, $n_l = n_l + \Delta n_l$, update the set of new tags N_l.
    if $n_l \geq n_\varepsilon$ **then** Break.
    if $\Delta n_s > 0$ **then** $P_w = min(P_w + \Delta P_w, maxP_w)$. **else** Break.

$N_b = N_l$.

The antenna rotates to the right in $[0°, \Delta\theta_{r_l}]$, gets N_r, it rotates $\Delta\theta_{r_r}$ degree.

if $\Delta\theta_{r_l} = \Delta\theta_{r_r}$ **then** $N_b = N_l \cup N_r$. **else if** $\Delta\theta_{r_l} > \Delta\theta_{r_r}$ **then** $N_b = N_r$.

Output: Tag IDs in the boundary :N_b

When the antenna rotates to another direction (called as *left*), n_s decreases. As shown in Algorithm 3, when the radiation angle decreases by $\Delta\theta_r$, Δn_s tags in N_s disappear. The reader gets n_l new tag IDs, which are considered as the tag IDs from the boundary. If $n_l \geq n_\varepsilon$, the reader collects enough tag IDs

$N_l = \{ID'_1, ID'_2, \ldots, ID'_{n_l}\}$ from the boundary. Otherwise, it increases the power by ΔP_w and gets Δn_l new tag IDs. Everytime, it should make sure that $\Delta n_s > 0$, which indicates the new tag IDs are not from the area S. If $\Delta n_s = 0$, the antenna keeps rotating away from S. PIA repeats the above process until $n_l \geq n_\varepsilon$. Then, the antenna has rotated $\Delta\theta_{r_l}$ degree. After that, the antenna rotates to the opposite direction (*right*) and works in the same way. It rotates $\Delta\theta_{r_r}$ degree to the right side. If $\Delta\theta_{r_r} > \Delta\theta_{r_l}$, it indicates the boundary in the right side is farther than the left one, then the reader terminates the process. Otherwise, it obtains $N_r = \{ID''_1, ID''_2, \ldots, ID''_{n_r}\}$. The reader compares $\Delta\theta_{r_l}$ and $\Delta\theta_{r_r}$ to find the nearer boundary with the smaller angle, and gets the new set N_b of interference tags. If $\Delta\theta_{r_l} = \Delta\theta_{r_r}$, $N_b = N_l \cup N_r$. If $\Delta\theta_{r_l} < \Delta\theta_{r_r}$, $N_b = N_l$. If $\Delta\theta_{r_l} > \Delta\theta_{r_r}$, $N_b = N_r$. N_b is used for *power stepping*.

The values of parameters in PIA are equal to those in PID. In regard to $\Delta\theta_r$ in PIA, we set $\Delta\theta_r = 30°$. Based on Fig. 2, when $\theta_r \in [75°, 90°]$, the reader undoubtedly has good performance. Therefore, when $\Delta\theta_r = 30°$, each tag can be requested in the region with $\theta_r \in [75°, 90°]$.

7   Performance Evaluation

We evaluate the performance of each solution in the realistic environments. The experimental facilities are the same as those used in the observations. The *execution time*, *coverage ratio*, and *misreading ratio* are used for performance metrics.

In the experiments, each book is attached with an RFID tag, and the tag ID is 96 bits. The books are randomly deployed in three boxes and the distribution of the tag IDs are unknown. Each box is placed on a tablet chair with a height of 0.5 m, as shown in Fig. 6. PID uses a 3D camera, while PIA does not. The antenna is deployed on the smart car, which is controlled by the program and can rotate with the antenna flexibly. The antenna faces towards the tags to be identified. The specified area here is the center box, which is the *target box*, while the other two boxes are *interference boxes*. The distance between the target box and the antenna is d. The minimum distance between the interference box and the target box is l. s and u respectively represent the number of target tags (in target box) and the number of interference tags (in interference boxes). We verify the values of the parameters d, l, s, u to evaluate the performance of each solution. We set $d = 1$ m, $l = 1$ m, $s = 80$, $u = 70$ by default.

7.1   Upper Bound of α

As mentioned in Sect. 2.2, when the distance d, the number of tags n are fixed, we can determine the value of α. In Table 1, we give the upper bound of α under different conditions. We set $\alpha = 60\%$ for the following experiments by default.

7.2   Coverage Ratio ρ Constraint

We first investigate the coverage ratio ρ of each solution, as shown in Fig. 7. We can observe that scanning with the minimum power (MinPw) can not achieve

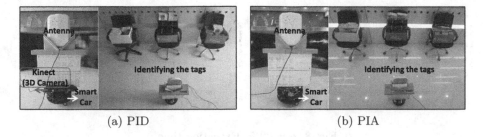

(a) PID   (b) PIA

Fig. 6. System prototypes work in the realistic environments

Table 1. Upper bound of α

d (m) $\diagdown$ n	0.5	1.0	1.5
40	100%	100%	90%
80	95%	85%	65%
120	89%	81%	63%

the requirement of coverage ratio ($\alpha = 60\%$). Because the power is too small to activate the majority of the tags. When we identify the tags with the maximum power (MaxPw) or our proposed solutions (PID and PIA), the coverage ratios are all larger than 60% ($\rho \geq \alpha$), which satisfy the requirement. As mentioned in Sect. 2.2, the coverage ratio must be satisfied. Therefore, the solution MinPw is invalid and we ignore it in the following comparisons.

7.3 Execution Time T

Figure 8 shows the execution time of each solution. Our solutions PID and PIA have better performances than MaxPw. Because PID and PIA only focus on the *target tags* in S. MaxPw identifies all the tags in the interrogation region, including a lot of *interference tags*. Usually, PID has a better performance than PIA, due to the use of a 3D camera. In Fig. 8(a), (b), the difference in execution time between PID, PIA and MaxPw is small. This is because the tag size is relatively small. When the tag size becomes large, our proposed solutions become

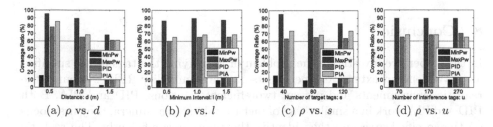

(a) ρ vs. d (b) ρ vs. l (c) ρ vs. s (d) ρ vs. u

Fig. 7. $\alpha = 60\%$, Coverage ratio

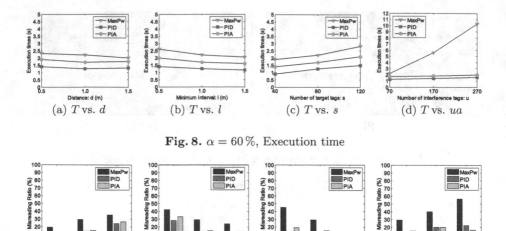

Fig. 8. $\alpha = 60\%$, Execution time

Fig. 9. $\alpha = 60\%$, Misreading ratio

more efficient. When $s = 120$, PID reduces the execution time by 46% compared to MaxPw, as shown in Fig. 8(c). When $u = 270$, PID even can reduce the execution time by 84.5% compared to MaxPw, as shown in Fig. 8(d).

7.4   Misreading Ratio λ

In Sect. 2.2, we analyze that the execution time is related to the misreading ratio. Figure 9 shows the misreading ratio of each solution. Our solutions PID and PIA have lower misreading ratios than MaxPw. This is because PID and PIA use the optimal powers instead of the maximum one (30.7 dBm). PID and PIA mainly focus on the *target tags*, while avoiding identifying the *interference tags*.

When we change the value of α, our solutions can also work well. For example, when $d = 1$ m, $l = 1$ m, $s = 80$, $u = 70$, we set $\alpha = 80\%$. The coverage ratio of MaxPw, PID, PIA is respectively equal to 89%, 82.5%, 86%, which satisfy the constraint of ρ. The execution time of MaxPw, PID, PIA is respectively equal to 2.2 s, 1.45 s, 2.0 s. Our solutions outperform the baseline solutions.

8   Conclusion

In this paper, we investigate the problem of identifying the tags in the specified area. We conduct extensive experiments on the commodity RFID system in the realistic environments and present two efficient solutions, PID and PIA. Both PID and PIA work in a similar way of picture-taking in a camera, they first focus on the specified area and then identify the *target tags* efficiently. The realistic experiments show that our solutions outperform the baseline solutions.

Acknowledgement. This work is partially supported by the National Natural Science Foundation of China under Grant No. 61100196, 61073028, 61021062; the JiangSu Natural Science Foundation under Grant No. BK2011559; and NSF grants ECCS 1231461, ECCS 1128209, CNS 1138963, CNS 1065444, and CCF 1028167.

References

1. Vogt, H.: Efficient object identification with passive RFID tags. In: Mattern, F., Naghshineh, M. (eds.) PERVASIVE 2002. LNCS, vol. 2414, p. 98. Springer, Heidelberg (2002)
2. Maguire, Y., Pappu, R.: An optimal q-algorithm for the ISO 18000-6C RFID protocol. IEEE Trans. Autom. Sci. Eng. **6**(1), 16–24 (2009)
3. Zhen, B., Kobayashi, M., Shimuzu, M.: Framed aloha for multiple RFID objects identification. IEICE Trans. Commun. **E80–B**(3), 991–999 (2005)
4. Lee, S., Joo, S., Lee, C.: An enhanced dynamic framed slotted ALOHA algorithm for RFID tag identification. In: Proceedings of MobiQuitous, pp. 166–172. IEEE (2005)
5. Tan, C.C., Sheng, B., Li, Q.: How to monitor for missing RFID tags. In: IEEE ICDCS, pp. 295–302. IEEE (2008)
6. Li, T., Chen, S., Ling, Y.: Identifying the missing tags in a large RFID system. In: ACM MobiHoc, pp. 1–10. ACM (2010)
7. Zheng, Y., Li, M.: Fast tag searching protocol for large-scale RFID systems. In: IEEE ICNP, pp. 363–372. IEEE (2011)
8. Kodialam, M., Nandagopal, T.: Fast and reliable estimation schemes in RFID systems. In: ACM MobiCom, pp. 322–333. ACM (2006)
9. Qian, C., Ngan, H., Liu, Y., Ni, L.M.: Cardinality estimation for large-scale RFID systems. IEEE Trans. Parallel Distrib. Syst. **22**(9), 1441–1454 (2011)
10. Zheng, Y., Li, M., Qian, C.: PET: probabilistic estimating tree for large-scale RFID estimation. In: IEEE ICDCS, pp. 37–46. IEEE (2011)
11. Buettner, M., Wetherall, D.: An emprical study of UHF RFID performance. In: Proceedings of MobiCom, pp. 223–234. ACM (2008)
12. Arror, S.R., Deavours, D.D.: Evaluation of the state of passive UHF RFID: an experimental approach. IEEE Syst. J. **1**(2), 168–176 (2007)
13. Jeffery, S.R., Garofalakis, M., Franklin, M.J.: Adaptive cleaning for RFID data streams. In: Proceedings of VLDB, pp. 163–174. ACM (2006)
14. Xu, X., Gu, L., Wang, J., Xing, G.: Negotiate power and performance in the reality of RFID systems. In: IEEE PerCom, pp. 88–97. IEEE (2010)

Middleware – Software Support in Items Identification by Using the UHF RFID Technology

Peter Kolarovszki[✉] and Juraj Vaculík

University of Žilina, Univerzitná 1, 010 06 Žilina, Slovakia
{peter.kolarovszki, juvac}@fpedas.uniza.sk

Abstract. This article deals with RFID technology, which is a part of automatic identification and data capture. Nowadays, the identification of items in logistic sector is carried through barcodes. In this article we would like to specify, how items can be located in metal container, identified in the transmission process of logistics chain by UHF RFID technology. All results are verified by measurement in our AIDC laboratory, which is located at the University of Žilina. Our research contains of 12 different types of orientation tags and antennas and more than 1000 tests. Our identification performance was close to 100 %. All tested items have been located in metal container. The results of our research bring the new point of view and indicate the ways of using UHF RFID technology in logistic applications. The utilization of the RFID technology in logistics chain is characterized at the end of this article.

Keywords: RFID technology · Logistics chain · Items · Identification · Middleware

1 Introduction

Automatic identification technology currently plays an important role in all areas of the national economy. In terms of optimization of logistic processes, barcode technology is used. However, radio frequency identification technology brings lot of advantages to the table, therefore it is expected that its involvement will significantly expand into all areas of the national economy. The article focuses on research of RFID technology in the process of items - placed in metal containers - identification. It also talks about software support for RFID technology, mainly about creation and configuration of RFID middleware – specialized software tool allowing mutual communication between two or several applications; also known as connector between various application components. The article talks about RFID technology as well as about the completed study of readability of RFID identifiers placed on the items that are put in metal containers. Among the results of the readability, the dependency of tags on the metal parts of the container has been studied. Based on the results of the research, a recommendation for tags positioning on items was published.

© Institute for Computer Sciences, Social Informatics and Telecommunications Engineering 2014
I. Stojmenovic et al. (Eds.): MOBIQUITOUS 2013, LNICST 131, pp. 358–369, 2014.
DOI: 10.1007/978-3-319-11569-6_28

2   Objective and Methodology

Objects of the research are the items transported in metal containers within logistics chain consisting of particular components. These items contained UHD RFID identifier that was read by 2 or 4 antennas of particular scanning device. In order to achieve the relevant results of the research, more than 1.500 measurements have been performed in different testing environments. For testing purposes, we used cubicle metal container that is actually utilized during transport of items. Within the methodology or series of steps, we have chosen a diagram of partial goals that is depicted in detail in Fig. 1.

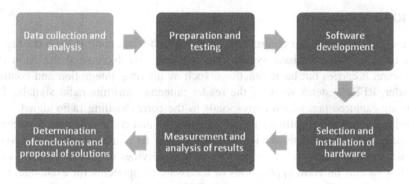

Fig. 1. Diagram of partial goals

3   Theoretically Background

Radio frequency identification is a wireless data collection technology that uses electronic tags which store data and tag readers which remotely retrieve data. It is a method of identifying objects and transferring information about the object's status via radio frequency waves to a host database. An RFID system is a set of components that work together to capture, integrate, and utilize data and information. This section describes some of them [2].

3.1   RFID Tags

An RFID tag is a small device that can be attached to an item, case, container, or pallet, so it can be identified and tracked. It is also called a transponder. The tag is composed of microchip and antenna. These elements are attached to a material called a substrate in order to create an inlay.

Tags are categorized into three types based on the power source for communication and other functionality:

- Active.
- Passive.
- Semi – passive.
- Semi – active.

3.2 RFID Reader

The second component in a basic RFID system is the interrogator or reader. The antenna can be an integral part of the reader, or it can be a separate device. Handheld units are a combination reader/antenna, while larger systems usually separate the antennas from the readers. The reader retrieves the information from the RFID tag. The reader may be self-contained and record the information internally; however, it may also be part of a localized system such as a POS cash register, a large Local Area Network (LAN), or a Wide Area Network (WAN) [1].

3.3 RFID Middleware

Middleware is software that controls the reader and the data coming from the tags and moves them to other database systems. In our cases we have used the Aton AMP middleware. It carries out basic functions, such as filtering, integration and control of the reader. RFID systems work, if the reader antenna transmits radio signals. These signals are captured tag, which corresponds to the corresponding radio signal.

This is a very special software device enabling mutual communication between two and more applications. This device is marked also as a mediator between various application components. The core activity of such devices covers the linking of and switching various different applications or hardware components for exchange, record and data modification purposes. There is a RFID middleware located between reader and server/database or other software device. This can have various functions depending on complexity of the system [5].

We can say that middleware fulfils following functions:

- Masks the communication distribution of many cooperating parts of the system located in various physical places,
- Masks the heterogeneity of various hardware components, their different operational systems and communication protocols,
- Provides unified interface enabling easier system extension and its easier communication with world.

4 Description of Measurements and AMP Model Configuration

In order to achieve relevant outcomes, it was inevitable at first to design functional system enabling realization of single measurements under laboratory conditions. In order to comprehend single measurements, we have to define the principle they operated under and what is being detected by them.

4.1 Description of Measurements

At first, we have to find out the readability of RFID tags of items placed in metal container at the moment of its passing through RFID gate with antennas. At second, we have to realize that we perform several types of measurements. These types differ in RFID tags orientation on items as well as by number of antennas; used for scanning the tags. In order to ensure the credibility of measured results, each type of measurement is repeated 100 times and therefore each single of them is called partial measurement. We do have the type of measurement and 100 partial measurements within, from which we have made statistical results. The relation between type of measurement and partial measurements:

- Type: Placing of identifiers on the top of the item: four antennas:

    - Partial measurement No. 1.
    - Partial measurement No. 2.
    - Partial measurement No. 3.

By accomplishment of single measurements, we obtained required data for deduction of results and recommendations. The accomplishment of measurements according to our requests needed certain preparation indeed. As for the preparation process, it was inevitable to select pasteboard boxes representing the items placed in container. In order to fill up the entire loading capacity, we needed 40 boxes of different size.

As each single item had to contain one RFID tag, we needed 40 passive RFID tags. The identification number (tagID) of each tag was reprogrammed by the use of hand RFID reader in order to get the other activities simplified. The structure of these IDs would be 3008 0000 0000 0000 0000 00xx. As we used 40 items overall, the last two digits would be 00–40, where the first value 00 would be assigned to launching RFID tag placed on container. At the same time, we were detecting the readability quality of particular RFID tags during the process of reprogramming. Thanks to that, we noticed that one tag had much lower level of readability in comparison to other tags. The value 01 of last two digits was assigned to this tag.

Following reprogramming process, we placed the tags to items. In order to prevent any damage of tags and at the same time, to ensure their fully functionality after realization of our measurements, we attached them by an adhesive tape. We put down the last two digits of tags ID during the sticking of tag due to later identification and analyze. All the items were placed into container, whereby the item with lower readable tag (01) was placed on the very bottom of the container. Afterwards, ID's of tags were filed into MySQL database and configurations White lists, by which we set the RFID reader exclusively for scanning of 40 + 1 tags.

The very last step was the involvement of antennas. The upper two antennas were placed onto metal construction and sides' antennas were attached to telescopic stands, by which we ensured RFID gate simulation.

4.1.1   Hardware Part

Hardware part consists of server, connecting cables, RFID gate (reader with antennas) and obviously with RFID tags placed on items and on plastic container. RFID reader Motorola was inevitable component of our hardware set. The reader consisted of – maximally - four active antennas in our configuration.

This RFID reader is characterized by its compact processing, easy installation, high performance and besides, is able to be directly hooked up by use of data network cable (Power over Ethernet). Its use is applicable also in case of limited areas.

Very important part was to choose efficient and affordably priced RFID identifier applicable for such a laboratory tests. Their structure consists of antenna and integrated circuit. These components are vapoured on elastic sticky plastic paper, so the tags can be easily attached directly to the object needed.

Each UHF RFID inlay is basically a dipole, which is located on an underlay substrate of a specified permittivity. Logically, all inlays are designed so they their range is as long as possible. In agreement with the radiolocation equation it is essential that the UHF RFID inlay antenna should be as large as possible and able to intercept the largest possible amount of EM energy and, conversely, be able to transmit energy as great as possible back to the transmitters.

$$l = \sqrt[4]{\frac{Ptx * C * K * A^2}{160\pi^2 * \mathrm{Pr}x * \lambda^2}} \tag{1}$$

I is the distance of the antenna from the target, Ptx is the transmitting power, C is a constant given by the nature of the target (design of the tag), A is the area of the receiving antenna, k – a constant given by the type of the antenna (3–10), Prx is the received power.

As it is clear from the formula, a radical increase of the range can be achieved by a change of the antenna's area or a wave length rather than a change of the transmitting power. Since the wave length and the maximum power in RFID are determined, we can work with only one variable, which is the antenna's area.

Figure 2 illustrates simulation of UHF RFID tag used in measurements.

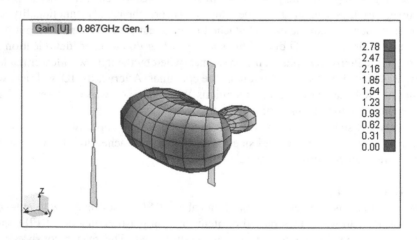

Fig. 2. UHF RFID inlays, apart 15 cm

4.1.2   Software Part

As for the software parts, we used operation system MySQL database, middleware and web application. The mutual relations of particular components (items) are depicted in the most proper way on Fig. 5. What needs to be said is that this is only a very simplified model and not every item can be marked as elementary, because each of them consists of other parts (Fig. 3).

Operation system ensures the flow of overall model, particular software items run under the system. As can be seen, web application does not communicate with middleware directly, but data are exchanged between them through MySQL database. In order to get overall view, we will explain shortly the basic functions of particular items and system operation principle.

Middleware ensures communication between hardware and software part of our model. At the same time, it enables to set up the configuration itself, so by its use we define practically what, how and when should the particular hardware and software components operate. All the data obtained from RFID gate are stored into database as well as all the data sent by user through web application. These data are accumulated

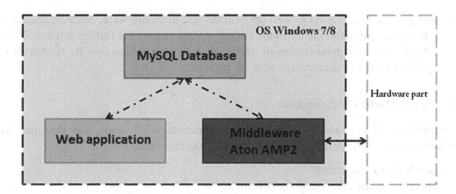

Fig. 3. Software part of measurements

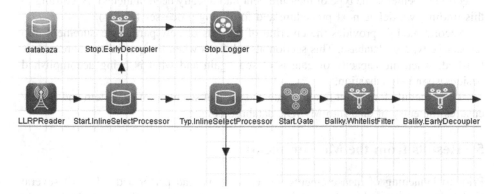

Fig. 4. Launch of measurements

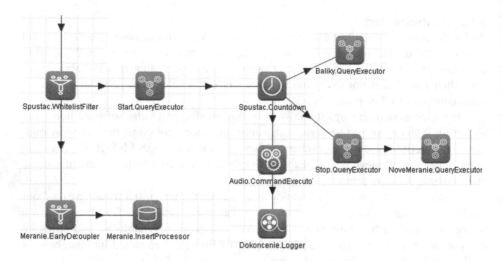

Fig. 5. Capacity control and sound signalization

here and provided by request to web application and to middleware. MySQL database serves as a place for gathering of all the collected data waiting for further demand. Web application serves for presentation of all the data from database and its further processing due to need to accomplish analyze by user.

4.2 AMP Model Configuration

Configuration of the model for readability measurement of items was designed in environment of AMP middleware. It was split into three parts:

1. Launch of measurements,
2. Capacity control and sound signalization,
3. Time formatting and recording into database.

First module serves for initialization of MySQL database, RFID reader as well as for detection, whether some type of measurement had already been launched. According to this finding, we define next procedure and following processes (Fig. 4).

Second module provides the entering of records of new partial measurement into respective type of database. This section also defines when this partial measurement is finished, when the capacity of gate is closed again and what is being accomplished besides sound signalization.

Third module formats at first the date and time of scanning of each item and mainly ensures the entry of data into MySQL database (Fig. 6).

5   Results from the Measurements

Prior to launching of measurements themselves, we had performed a line of several testing measurements in order to detect the functionality of overall system. At the same

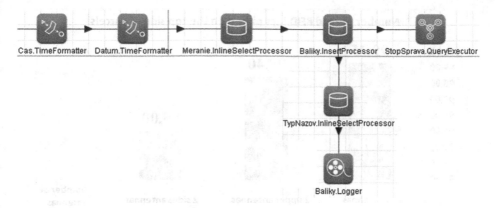

Fig. 6. Time formatting and recording into database

time, we found out by use of these tests that intensity of reader's scanning set in configuration has a minimal effect on scanning of particular tags in container. Therefore we set this intensity at each measurement for 100 % level.

Concerning the readability research of items placed in container, we performed the measurement for dependency of RFID identifiers placement on items as well as their orientation in regard to position of reading antennas. We performed following types of measurements:

1. Tags placed on the top side of items,
2. Tags placed on the bottom side of items with regard to bottom of the container,
3. Tags placed with edges towards all antennas,
4. Tags placed at the walls of container.

5.1 Tags Placed on the Top Side of Items

The choice of the first type was the one with RFID tags placed on the top side of items. We assumed that the results should be theoretically the best of all the types as the position of antennas was most favorable, considering radio frequency waviness and its impact to RFID tags (Fig. 7).

As we can see, the results of this type of measurement are indeed very positive. We measured the readability efficiency of 99.25 % by scanning the container with all four antennas. The only tag with weaker level readability was the one with tagID 01. This was successfully read only 76 times out of 100. Signal was not strong enough so that the antennas could successfully detect at each measurement the item with weaker readable tag placed on the very bottom of the container. If we ignored this one particular tag, we would have achieved overall average readability attacking level of almost straight 100 %.

5.2 Tags Placed on the Bottom Side of Items with Regard to Bottom of the Container

At this case, we assumed moderate fall of readability. This assumption was not much fulfilled at the very end (Fig. 8).

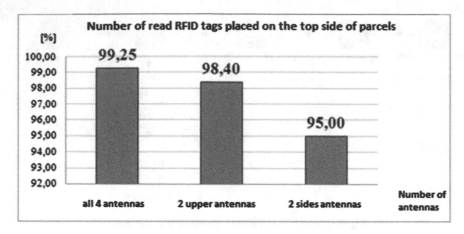

Fig. 7. Results of measurements 1

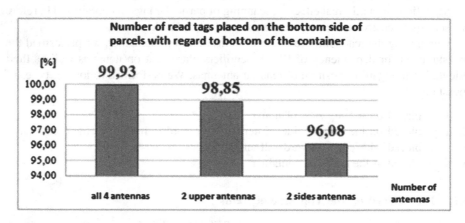

Fig. 8. Results of measurements 2

We can see that the readability was not only reduced but even increased by scanning with all the antennas up to level 99.93 %. The most relevant influence on this outcome has indeed the problematic tag 01 that was placed again at the very bottom of the container, but this time the tag was directly touching the bottom of container. The presence of the tag closer to floor and reflection of signals either from metal construction of container or from the ground very likely caused its 100 % readability by scanning with all four antennas.

5.3   Tags Placed with Edges Towards All Antennas

At this variant, we made our decision to make the reading of the tags more difficult with their placement - vertically to all the antennas. The tags were replaced on sides of items relating to back side of the container. Besides, the previous type of measurements proved that the activation of side antennas had only a moderate influence on

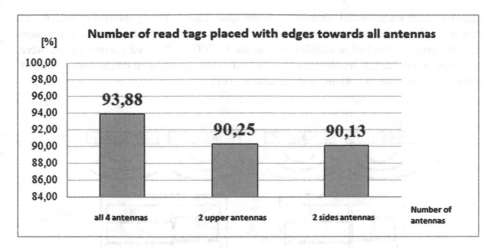

Fig. 9. Results of measurements 3

readability, unrelated to tag orientation. Therefore we placed the tags also into horizontal position (Fig. 9).

5.4   Tags Placed at the Walls of Container

We detected from previous types of measurements, that the barred metal wall of container from which the signal was reflecting has had the major influence on scanning of items. Therefore we decided that in the last variant, the majority of RFID tags on items would be placed on the walls of container. We assumed that this setting of items would have the most significant influence with regard to readability. The readability of tags did not drop significantly by scanning with all four antennas; it just dropped to still very satisfying level of 93.35 %. Despite a quite good average outcome of readability, we have to state that the tags placed at metal parts behave unpredictable from readability point of view.

5.5   Proposed Placing of Tags on Items and Lay-Out of Antennas of RFID Gate

Based on results of previous measurements, we could perform a measurement dealing with most convenient placement of RFID tags on items in container along with a placement on antennas. Tags were placed upon top side of items. As the results of measurements were not deformed by any weaker readable tag (01), we made a decision upon recommended configuration to change this tag for the other one. At first, we scanned exclusively by use of two top antennas only. After 100 repetitions, we recorded average detection of items at level 99.8 %. Then, we placed another two antennas upon second end of top construction of RFID gate, by which we ensured vertical scanning by all four antennas at once. Two antennas were placed as input and two as output of RFID gate, by which we achieved approximately the same long scanning interval of each tag in container. We performed the measurements 100 times. We achieved such configuration that the average level of readability was equal to 100 %. The very same results were achieved also in case, when the tags were turned - they were placed on the bottom side of items – in direction to bottom of the container (Fig. 10).

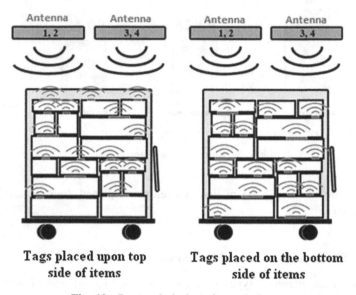

Tags placed upon top   Tags placed on the bottom
side of items   side of items

Fig. 10. Proposed placing of tags on items

6 Conclusion

We can state that introduction of passive radio frequency identification of items in logistic operation is technically feasible as a very high level of readability was achieved by scanning of particular items under laboratory conditions, reaching equal to 100 %. The results are very depending on specific placement of RFID tags on items in container and at the same time on placement of antennas of RFID reader. Another significant gained knowledge is that optimal solution is with utilization of four RFID antennas placed on top side of RFID gate enabling scanning of tags in vertical direction. Two antennas were placed at input and two at output of RFID gate. Thereby we ensured equally long scanning interval of each item in container resulting in a very high overall level of readability. Such solution would not be technically demanding under real conditions in operation. Besides, we found out that metal parts of container construction represent the prime problem of items' scanning in container. Significant signal means the potential scanning /not scanning of items would be very tough to predict. On the contrary, the highest percentage efficiency of scanning was recorded in case of RFID tags placed on top and bottom side of items. Under these conditions, the signal is not interfered by metal parts of container construction and the items are scanned without any serious problems even in case of only two top antennas utilization.

Acknowledgments. *This article was created to support project named as:*
• **Centre of Excellence for Systems and Services of Intelligent Transport II**
TMS 26220120050 supported by the Research & Development Operational Programme funded by the ERDF.

 E!7592 AUTOEPCIS - RFID Technology in Logistic Networks of Automotive Industry.

References

1. Hunt, V., Puglia, A., Puglia, M.: RFID: A Guide to Radio Frequency Identification, 201 p. Wiley, New Jersey (2007)
2. Thornton, F., Lanthem, Ch.: RFID Security, 229 p. Syngres Publishing Inc., Rockland (2006)
3. Kolarovszká, Z., Fabuš, J.: IT service management in conjunction with the universal postal service in Europe. In: Postpoint 2011, 9th International Scientific Conference: International Meeting of Postal Administration Representatives, University Educators and Researches, Žilina, Slovakia, 19–20 September 2011, pp. 114–122. University of Žilina, Žilina (2011)
4. Vaculík, J., Tengler, J.: Potential of new technologies in logistics services. In: CLC 2012 - Carpatian Logistics Congress, 7–9 November 2012, Jesenik, Czech Republic, EU: Congress Proceedings, Ostrava, Tanger (2012). ISBN 978-80-87294-33-8
5. Kebo, V., Staša, P., Beneš, F., Švub, J.: RFID technology in logistics processes. In: Proceedings of the 13th International Multidisciplinary Scientific GeoConference SGEM 2013, Albena, Bulgaria (2013). ISBN: 978-954-91818-9-0, ISSN: 1314-2704
6. Koškár, L.: Application of identifying parcels through RFID technology and their appropriate placement in the mail container in terms of readability, Žilina (2013)
7. Beneš, F., Kubáĉ, L., Staša, P., Kebo, V., Kodym, O.: The potential of RFID and augmented reality. In: Proceedings of the 13th International Multidisciplinary Scientific GeoConference SGEM 2013, Albena, Bulgaria (2013). ISBN: 978-954-91818-9-0, ISSN: 1314-2704

A Wearable RFID System for Real-Time Activity Recognition Using Radio Patterns

Liang Wang[1]([⊠]), Tao Gu[2], Hongwei Xie[1], Xianping Tao[1], Jian Lu[1], and Yu Huang[1]

[1] State Key Laboratory for Novel Software Technology,
Nanjing University, Nanjing, People's Republic of China
{wl,xhw}@smail.nju.edu.cn, {txp,lj,yuhuang}@nju.edu.cn
[2] School of Computer Science and Information Technology,
RMIT University, Melbourne, Australia
tao.gu@rmit.edu.au

Abstract. Much work have been done in activity recognition using wearable sensors organized in a body sensor network. The quality and communication reliability of the sensor data much affects the system performance. Recent studies show the potential of using RFID radio information instead of sensor data for activity recognition. This approach has the advantages of low cost and high reliability. Radio-based recognition method is also amiable to packet loss and has the advantages including MAC layer simplicity and low transmission power level. In this paper, we present a novel wearable Radio Frequency Identification (RFID) system using passive tags which are smaller and more cost-effective to recognize human activities in real-time. We exploit RFID radio patterns and extract both spatial and temporal features to characterize various activities. We also address two issues - the false negative issue of tag readings and tag/antenna calibration, and design a fast online recognition system. We develop a prototype system which consists of a wearable RFID system and a smartphone to demonstrate the working principles, and conduct experimental studies with four subjects over two weeks. The results show that our system achieves a high recognition accuracy of 93.6 % with a latency of 5 s.

Keywords: Activity recognition · Wearable RFID · Real-time

1 Introduction

With the rapid advances of wireless networking and sensing technologies in recent years, recognizing human activity based on wearable sensors has drawn much research interest. In this paradigm, wearable sensors with sensing and wireless communication capabilities are organized in a body sensor network (BSN) to capture different motion patterns of a user. Continuous sensor readings are collected and processed at a centralized server for extracting useful features, training an appropriate activity model, and recognizing a variety of activities.

© Institute for Computer Sciences, Social Informatics and Telecommunications Engineering 2014
I. Stojmenovic et al. (Eds.): MOBIQUITOUS 2013, LNICST 131, pp. 370–383, 2014.
DOI: 10.1007/978-3-319-11569-6_29

Recognizing people's activities continuously in real-time enables a wide range of applications, particularly in health monitoring, assistive living, rehabilitation, and entertainment.

While BSNs have shown the effectiveness, they do have several limitations. First, the human body affects the quality of the wireless links between sensor nodes causing packet loss [1]. This will result in incomplete sensor data received at the server, undermining the accuracy and the real-time performance of the recognition system. To improve packet delivery performance, the system can either use re-transmission mechanisms or increase the transmission power level [2]. However, this solution complicates the underlying MAC protocol, increases sensor power consumption, and degrades the real-time performance of the system. Moreover, in order to capture the user's activities, BSN nodes are equipped with sensing, computing, storage, and communication devices, making the sensor nodes large in size and high in cost. Finally, batteries are required to keep the sensor nodes alive, making energy consumption a challenging issue in BSN. The daily maintenance of the system (e.g., monitoring the remaining power and changing the batteries for multiple sensor nodes) is labor-intensive.

Recent studies show that Radio Frequency Identification (RFID) technologies have the potential to build low-cost, reliable systems to detect certain activities such as moving trajectories or gestures based on radio information [3–5]. Motivated by these work, we explore the possibility of using ultra-high frequency (UHF) RFID system for complex human activity recognition. Our system is based on two observations: (1) there exists heavy attenuation of the human body to radio communication band in which the UHF RFID operates, and (2) RFID radio communication is highly affected by the tag-antenna distance and orientation. Based on these observations, if we deploy an RFID system on a human body, user motions may result in different radio patterns which can differentiate activities. In our system, packet loss and fading provide useful information for activity recognition. Thus, simple MAC protocols and low transmission power levels are preferred. Further, we use passive tags instead of sensor nodes which are smaller and lighter that can be embedded into the clothes and daily objects. The passive tags are more cost-effective and, due to their simple structure and protective encapsulation, more robust than the sensor nodes. Finally, the passive tags operate without batteries. Once deployed, no further maintenance is required. The only device that requires battery power in our sensing system is the RFID reader. According to our previous experience in BSN-based recognition system [6] in which careful battery management is required for every sensor node to keep the system operate, we argue in this paper that using only one battery for the entire system significantly reduces the human-effort and increases its reliability. Moreover, recent technical trends show that low-cost, low-power RFID readers are becoming commonly available by integrating into the smartphones [7], making our work potentially beneficial to the mobile users in the future.

The system consists of a wearable RFID system for capturing radio patterns, and a smartphone device for collecting and processing such patterns. To make use of the radio patterns, we extract temporal and spatial features to characterize the radio patterns. These features are carefully selected to tolerate large variances in tag performance, avoiding labor intensive calibration which is typically required in many RFID and RSS-based systems [3]. We design an effective algorithm to address the false negative issue of tag readings in RFID systems. To achieve real-time recognition, we use a fixed-length sliding window to control latency bound, and develop a fast, lightweight, online algorithm based on Support Vector Machine (SVM) to be executed on smartphones. We conduct comprehensive experiments involving multiple human subjects. The results show that our system achieves a high recognition accuracy with a low delay.

The rest of the paper is organized as follows. Section 2 introduces related work. Hardware setup and preliminary experiment results are presented in Sect. 3. We present the details of our system design in Sect. 4. Section 5 reports results of empirical studies and Sect. 6 concludes the paper.

2   Related Work

Much work have been done based on sensor readings for activity recognition. These sensing based solutions [6,8] usually deploy accelerometer sensors on a human body to capture body movement. The sensor nodes are self-organized into a BSN where appropriate MAC and routing protocols are operated to ensure the quality of sensor data. Different from these work, we exploit RFID radio information for activity recognition.

RFID has been used in indoor localization and activity recognition. For example, fixed RFID readers and reference tags are deployed in the environment with known locations to track the mobile tags or persons using RSS values [3,4]. In [5], the authors use RFID for tracking hand movements in a table-size scale. The tags are placed in a grid-like structure on a table with readers located at three corners. They use tag counting information received at different readers to keep track of hand movements. Different from the above work relying on fixed RFID readers or tags for tracking locations or detecting simple moving patterns, we design a wearable RFID system to recognize human activities involving complex movements of different body parts continuously. In [6], wrist-worn HF RFID readers are used to capture the object usage information by reporting the passive tags attached to objects within its reading range (less than 7 cm in reading distance). Different from this work, we use a UHF RFID system with a larger reading range covering a user's entire body, and exploit the RFID radio patterns to recognize body movements.

Recent work have explored 2.4G RF radio information for activity recognition. In [2], the authors use the radio communication patterns extracted from a BSN to recognize activities. Their BSN consists of two on-body sensor nodes, which send simple fake packets to the sink at a low power level. The communication patterns (i.e., such as packet delivery ratio and the mean of RSSI values) from arrival packets within a time window are extracted and used as a signature to recognize the corresponding activity. Similar RSSI information of the radio communication have also used been in [9] for activity recognition. Different from these work, we design a novel RFID system with passive tags which can be potentially unobtrusive to user experience since tags can be easily embedded into clothes. Unlike the sensor nodes, the passive tags do not rely on battery power to operate. We discover rich RFID radio patterns and extract complex features, and demonstrate how they are used in a real-time activity recognition system.

3 Preliminary Experimental Studies

In this section, we introduce our system hardware setup and conduct preliminary experiments to show the tag reading performance under different conditions and the potential of using radio patterns for activity recognition.

3.1 Hardware Setup

The hardware used in this work is shown in Fig. 1. We use Impinj R2000 RFID reader module powered by a Li battery with 9000 mAh capacity. The size of the reader is $15 \times 9 \times 2.5$ cm. We use UHF RFID tags with a credit card size. We have four antennas, and each has a size of $7.8 \times 7.8 \times 0.5$ cm. The transmission power level of each antenna is adjustable from 0 dbm to 30 dbm with a minimum level of 0.1 dbm. The RFID reader module operates at 840–960 MHz and supports UHF RFID standards such as ETSI EN 302 208-1. The agility of the module is −95 dbm. When set to the tag inventory mode, the reader can read as many tags as possible (maybe multiple readings per tag) using an anti-collision protocol. For the reader we used, over 50 tag readings can be obtained in one second. Each tag reading contains the tag ID[1] and the RSS value. Tag readings obtained from the reader are sent wirelessly through a Serial-to-WiFi adapter. The readings are then received by a smartphone for processing. We use Samsung Nexus 3 smartphone with a dual-core 2.4G processor, running Android 4.0.

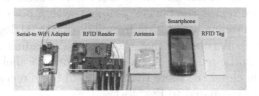

Fig. 1. Hardware setup.

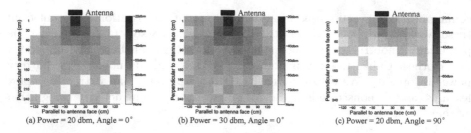

(a) Power = 20 dbm, Angle = 0°   (b) Power = 30 dbm, Angle = 0°   (c) Power = 20 dbm, Angle = 90°

Fig. 2. Average RSS values of tags at different positions with different transmission power levels and tag-antenna orientations.

3.2   Reading RFID Tags

We first study the tag reading performance of the reader under different settings in transmission power level, tag-antenna distance, and orientation.

First, Fig. 2(a) shows the RSS values obtained at different positions in the detection area of an antenna. The antenna is placed on the top of the area facing downward with the transmission power level set to 20 dbm. The tag under test is placed in an area 0 cm to 240 cm perpendicular to, and −120 cm to 120 cm parallel to the antenna face (negative values for positions on the right side of the antenna). The tag-antenna angle is 0 degree, i.e., the tag face is parallel to the antenna face. As shown in Fig. 2(a), the RSS gets stronger when the tag is placed closer to the antenna. Specifically, in the direction perpendicular to the antenna face, the tag can be stably read when placed within the distance of 60 cm to 90 cm. For a distance less than 60 cm or larger than 90 cm, the tag is not detected in some locations. In the direction parallel to the antenna face, the tag can be stably read when placed in the distance of −60 cm to 60 cm. For locations out of this range, the tag is not detected sometimes.

Next, we change the antenna's transmission power level to 30 dbm and repeat the previous experiment. The results are shown in Fig. 2(b). It is clear that all the RSS values get increased as compared to the 20 dbm results in Fig. 2(a), and the antenna's reading range covers the entire 240 cm × 240 cm area with no miss detection. Finally, we repeat the first experiment with a power level of 20 dbm, but we turn the tag-antenna orientation from 0 degree to 90 degrees. The results are shown in Fig. 2(c). We observe that the antenna's reading area has changed significantly. Tags can be read farther in the positions parallel to the antenna's face but significantly closer (no more than 60 cm) in the direction perpendicular to the antenna's face compared to Fig. 2(a).

In summary, the tag RSS values are affected by factors including tag-antenna distance, orientation, and transmission power. Moreover, human body is known to affect RFID communication [4], which is also observed in our experiments (detailed experiment results are omitted due to page limits). If the tags and antennas are worn on the user's body, the above factors will change by the move-

---

[1] We use the Electronic Product Code (EPC) stored on a tag as its ID.

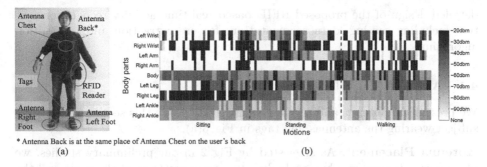

Fig. 3. (a) Wearable RFID system, (b) average RSS readings with different motions over time.

ments of different body parts when performing activities, and can be potentially used for activity recognition.

3.3   Potential of Activity Recognition

In this section, we demonstrate the potential of using RFID radio patterns extracted from RSS values for activity recognition. The experiment is carried out by one male subject performing three basic motions including standing, sitting, and walking. Four antennas and 36 tags are attached to the user as shown in Fig. 3(a) and introduced later in Sect. 4.1. During this experiment, we use the all antenna inventory mode of the reader which automatically activates the antennas for tag reading. Under this mode, the readings from the four antennas are mixed together. Also the four tags attached around the same body part share the same tag ID.

The average RSS values of tags attached to different body parts are shown in Fig. 3(b). From this figure, it is clear that different motions result in different RSS patterns. For the sitting activity, the RSS values of tags attached to the body, right leg, and left/right ankles are clearly stronger and more stable than other activities. For the standing activity, the RSS readings of the above mentioned body parts are also relatively more stable than the walking activity but the RSS values are lower than the sitting activity. Additionally, it can be seen from Fig. 3(b) that the RSS values of tags attached to the left wrist and left arm are stronger and more stable than other activities. For the walking activity, rhythmic variances in RSS values can be observed for tags attached to nearly every part of the human body, and they seem matched with arms and legs waving during the walking activity.

4   System Design

The above preliminary studies have shown the feasibility and potential of using RFID radio patterns for activity recognition. In this section, we present the detailed design of the proposed RFID-based real-time activity recognition system including sensing, data segmentation, feature extraction and recognition algorithm.

4.1 Antenna/Tag Placement

We present the antenna and tag placement strategies in this section and show a subject wearing the antennas and tags in Fig. 3(a).

Antenna Placement. As suggested by Fig. 2 in our preliminary studies, we place four antennas on a human body – two antennas (one on the chest and the other on the back) for detecting hand/arm movements, and one antenna on each of the feet for detecting lower body movements (as shown in Fig. 3(a)). Such placement ensures a total coverage of different body parts, and also meet user's comfort need.

Tag Placement. To capture the movement of different body parts, RFID tags are attached to nine body parts including both wrists, arms, ankles, legs, and the body. To increase the reliability of tag readings, we attach four tags at each body part. For example, for the right wrist, we attach four tag located at the front, left, right, and back of the wrist. This redundant tag placement strategy ensures that no matter how the user moves his/her wrist, at least one tag will face the antenna and can be read by the reader with high probability. A total number of 36 tags are attached on the user's body with each tag having an unique ID.

Inventory Mode. Instead of using the all antenna inventory mode used for our preliminary experiment, we use single antenna inventory mode to discriminate the readings of one antenna from others. The four antennas connected to the RFID reader are activated sequentially to detect tags within their reading ranges. The dwell time of each antenna is set to the default value of 2 s and the time to complete an inventory cycle is 8 s. The tag readings obtained during the activation time of an antenna is a series of tag IDs and their RSS values.

The transmission power level of the RFID reader is a key parameter in our system, and it influences the system's performance on both recognition accuracy and battery consumption. We find the optimal transmission power level by experiments in Sect. 5.3. We also evaluate the effect of different antenna and tag placement strategies in Sect. 5.2.

4.2 Data Segmentation and Completion

Given the continuous flow of tag readings, we first apply a sliding window to segment the data. In this paper, we focus on real-time activity recognition with a restricted recognition latency defined by the application. We use a fixed window size specified by L combined with the real-time activity recognition algorithm introduced later to achieve stable time performance. L is a key parameter in our system for it affects both the recognition accuracy and latency.

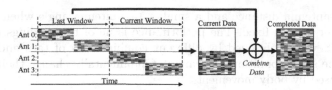

Fig. 4. Data completion method.

As mentioned in the introduction, one of the challenges in existing RFID systems is false negative readings [4,5], caused by miss detection – a tag is in the antenna's reading range, but not detected. In addition, in our system if the sliding window size is too short for the reader to complete readings for all four antennas, it may also cause false negative readings. To address this issue, we use recent historical data to complete the current readings. The intuition behind this approach is *temporal locality* – tags recently detected are likely to be detected again with similar RSS values. We illustrate the method in Fig. 4, assuming the false negative reading is caused by a short window size of 4s. While the data from antenna 0 and 1 are missing in the current data because the current window is only long enough to complete two antennas' readings, we use the last window's data to complete the current data. The same strategy is applied to the case of miss detection, technical details are omitted in this paper due to page limits.

4.3 Temporal and Spatial Features

For each data segment, we extract both temporal and spatial features to characterize the radio patterns. An known performance issue of tag readings commonly exists in RFID-based systems is that readings from different combinations of tags and antennas may be different even with the same condition [4]. One possible solution is through calibration. However, data calibration [4] is infeasible in our system because the complexity of our feature set. As a result, we carefully design our feature set that can tolerate the tag performance issue.

Temporal Features. The data in each segment are composed of series of RSS values arranged by receiving time with each series representing the RSS values of a specific tag read by a specific antenna. Seven features are extracted from each RSS series including the mean, variance, max, min, mean crossing rate, frequency domain energy and entropy of the RSS values to characterize its radio patterns temporally. The temporal features are extracted for each RSS series independently from the others. As a result, data calibration is not required for there is no cross-reference between readings from different tags and antennas.

Spatial Features. To characterize the radio patterns spatially, we extract the correlation coefficients of RSS series for different tags read by different antennas. The correlation coefficient quantifies the degree of dependency between a pair of RSS reading series by observing the similarity in their changing patterns. As shown by our preliminary experiment results, the RSS values are stronger with a closer tag-antenna distance and a smaller tag-antenna angle when the transmission power level is fixed. The performance issue of tag readings may cause different RSS values obtained by different combinations of tags and antennas even with the same condition but cannot fundamentally change their changing patterns caused by body movements.

4.4   Real-Time Recognition Algorithm

The design goal of our system is to achieve real-time activity recognition. We identify two key requirements described as follows.

1. **Online.** An recognition algorithm is offline if it requires the complete instance of an activity to be presented for recognition [6]. Offline systems cannot perform real-time recognition for they need to wait for the current activity to finish before recognition and the waiting time is uncertain. To achieve real-time recognition, the algorithm must be online that can recognize the current activity without being presented with the complete activity instance, i.e., only using data already obtained.
2. **Continuous.** To achieve real-time, the recognition result must be generated before the delay bound. Considering that the recognition system works iteratively to generate recognition results, we adapt the real-time concept from the signal processing field [10] to activity recognition systems. The acceptable recognition latency is specified by the sliding window size L which determines the data collection time. The processing time must be less than the data collection time [10] so that the recognition results can be obtained before the next data segment arrives, providing continuous recognition results without extra delays.

While the online property of our recognition system is guaranteed in our system for activity instances are generated only using the data already obtained, the continuous property is determined by the execution time of the recognition algorithm. We design a fast recognition algorithm based on a multi-class support vector machine (SVM) with radial basis function kernel. SVM is widely used in activity recognition [2]. The advantage of using SVM for activity recognition includes: (1) designed on a sound theoretical basis, SVM is promising to have accurate and robust classification results; (2) SVM scales well to the number of features; (3) the model training can be performed on very few training cases; and (4) the recognition can be executed fast at runtime [2]. The performance of our recognition algorithm is determined not only by its time complexity but also the hardware platform. We have implemented the recognition algorithm on Android smartphone, and will evaluate its real-time performance in the next section.

5   Empirical Studies

In this section, we present empirical studies to evaluate the performance of our system. The experiments are conducted in an area of our office building, including two rooms and a corridor, as well as outdoors. Our data collection involves

Table 1. Four subjects involved.

Subject	Gender	Height (cm)	Weight (kg)	Body Type
1	Male	177	70	Normal
2	Female	159	45	Slim
3	Male	180	75	Normal
4	Male	193	110	Strong

Table 2. Eight activities studied.

No.	Activity	No.	Activity
1	Sitting	5	Cleaning Table
2	Standing	6	Vacuuming
3	Walking	7	Riding Bike
4	Cleaning Window	8	Going Up/Down Stairs

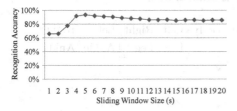

Fig. 5. Sliding window size vs. recognition accuracy.

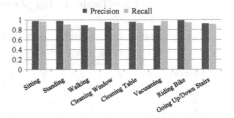

Fig. 6. Breakdown of precision and recall.

four subjects (three males and one female). The subjects are carefully selected to represent different heights and body types as summarized in Table 1. Each subject is required to perform eight activities as summarized in Table 2. Each activity is performed for at least five minutes. The data collection is carried out over a period of two weeks and a total number of over 200 activity instances are collected.

5.1 Recognition Accuracy and Real-Time Performance

In the first experiment, we evaluate the recognition accuracy which is defined by the number of correctly classified instances over the number of the total instances, and the latency which is determined by the sliding window size.

The recognition accuracies with different sliding window sizes are illustrated in Fig. 5. As we can see from the figure, when the sliding window size is small (i.e. from 1s to 4s), the recognition accuracy rapidly grows from 65.8 % to 91.8 %. The recognition accuracy reaches its peak at 93.6 % when sliding window size is 5s. It is interesting to see that the recognition accuracy drops slowly afterwards and stabilizes at around 86 % when the sliding window size increases further. This result suggests that a larger sliding window does not always result in a higher recognition accuracy. We breakdown the precision and recall of different activities with a window size of 5s and show the results in Fig. 6. Figure 6 shows that the precision and recall for most of the activities are above 0.9. By analyzing the results, we find that some of the *walking* activity are recognized as *going up/down stairs*, a few instances of the *walking, cleaning table*, and *cleaning*

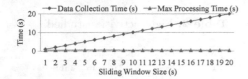

Fig. 7. Data collection time vs. maximum processing time.

Table 3. Antenna placement configurations.

Configuration	Back	Chest	Left Foot	Right Foot
Upper Antennas	✓	✓		
Lower Antennas			✓	✓
Mixed Antennas			✓	✓

Table 4. Tag placement configurations.

Configuration	Left Wrist	Right Wrist	Left Arm	Right Arm	Body	Left Leg	Right Leg	Left Ankle	Right Ankle
Upper Tags	✓	✓	✓	✓	✓				
Lower Tags					✓	✓	✓	✓	✓
Mixed Tags		✓		✓	✓	✓		✓	

window activities are recognized as *vacuuming*. Overall, our system achieves the best recognition accuracy of 93.6 % when the sliding window size is set to 5s.

Next, we evaluate the real-time performance of the system. The online property is guaranteed by using only the current and historical data for recognition. The continuous property is determined by the execution time of the recognition algorithm. Figure 7 compares the data collection time and the maximum processing time on our smartphone (data completion + feature extraction + recognition) under different sliding window sizes. As shown in the figure, our system performs real-time recognition even when the delay bound is down to 1s (by fixing the sliding window size to 1s). The maximum processing time is always less than the data collection time and remains low (around 450 ms) when the sliding window size grows.

5.2   Antenna and Tag Placement

We evaluate the performance of different antenna and tag placement strategies in this experiment. We designed three placement configurations for both the antennas and the tags as shown in Tables 3 and 4, respectively. Note that we assume the user wears all the tags when choosing different antenna configurations and wears all the antennas when choosing different tag configurations.

The recognition accuracies under different antenna configurations are illustrated in Fig. 8. To compute the accuracy of each activity, we use the same metric as in [2] defined as follows.

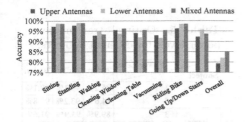

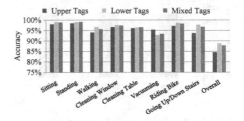

Fig. 8. Recognition accuracy under different antenna configurations.

Fig. 9. Recognition accuracy under different tag configurations.

$$activity\_accuracy = \frac{TruePositive + TrueNegative}{TruePositive + TrueNegative + FalsePositive + FalseNegative}$$

The metric for the overall accuracy is the same as we used in our first experiment. Figure 8 shows that the lower antennas are effective to activities involving more lower body movements (e.g., *sitting*, *standing*, and *walking*), and the upper antennas are more effective to activities (e.g., *cleaning window*, *cleaning table*, and *vacuuming*) with more upper body movements. The *Mixed Antennas* configuration achieves the highest overall accuracy of 85.1 %. For different tag configurations, the results are illustrated in Fig. 9. We have similar observations as in the antenna configuration experiment. The *Lower Tag* and the *Mixed Tag* configurations achieve similar overall accuracy of 88.8 % and 87.8 %, respectively.

In summary, the antennas and tags attached to the lower and upper body are effective in recognizing activities involving different lower and upper body movements, respectively. A good choice is to use the mixed configuration that places the tags and antennas on one side of the upper body and the other side of the lower body.

5.3 Antenna Transmission Power Level and Battery Consumption

In this experiment, we evaluate the system's performance with different antenna transmission power levels (i.e., 20 dbm, 25 dbm, and 30 dbm). Figure 10 illustrates the overall recognition accuracies of different power levels. The recognition accuracy is above 90 % for all transmission power levels and the highest accuracy of 94.0 % is achieved at power level of 25 dbm. We further study the optimal power levels for different subjects. As shown in Table 5, we discover that for all three male subjects, the optimal recognition accuracy is achieved at the power level of 25 dbm, followed by 30 dbm and 20 dbm. This result explains the reason for the overall optimal power level of 25 dbm shown in Fig. 10. For the female subject, the optimal power level is 20 dbm. It is possibility because the female subject is smaller in size and the fading effect is stronger with a lower transmission power level. This result suggests that the optimal power level is not the highest level but the one most sensitive to RSS radio patterns resulted from different activities.

To evaluate battery consumption, for the RFID reader, we measure the output current for the battery. The battery output current is 180 mA, 223 mA, and

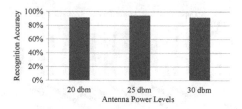

Fig. 10. Recognition accuracy of different antenna transmission power levels.

Table 5. Optimal transmission power levels for different subjects.

Subject	Power Level 20dbm	25dbm	30dbm
1	85.2%	**90.2%**	89.1%
2	**94.6%**	93.2%	92.8%
3	89.9%	**93.9%**	91.6%
4	84.2%	**91.0%**	87.0%

253 mA, for the transmission power level of 20 dbm, 25 dbm, and 30 dbm, respectively. For the smartphone, we use a battery monitoring software built on top of the Android OS's battery consumption APIs to record the battery consumption data. The results show our recognition software introduces an additional consumption of about 38 mA. Though the reader consumes a larger amount of battery power compared to BSN-based systems [2,6], according to our previous experience in data collection using a BSN [6], we find that managing only one battery for the reader is much easier than managing batteries for multiple nodes in a BSN.

6   Conclusion

In this paper, we present a novel wearable RFID systems for real-time activity recognition. We implemented the prototype system, and the experiment results show our system achieves high accuracy and low delay. As our first prototype, there are some limitations. For example: (1) the current devices are a little cumbersome; (2) a large number of tags and antennas are used. In our future work, we plan to improve our system design by: (1) using smaller RFID readers, or smartphone integrated RFID readers; (2) studying more antenna and tag placement strategies and exploring the minimum number of tags and antennas necessary to achieve better system performance.

Acknowledgement. This work was supported by the National 863 project under Grant 2013AA01A213 and the NSFC under Grants 91318301, 61373011, 61073031, the program B for Outstanding PhD candidate of NJU under Grant 201301B016.

References

1. Natarajan, A., de Silva, B., Yap, K.-K., Motani, M.: Link layer behavior of body area networks at 2.4 GHz. In: Proceedings of ACM Annual International Conference Mobile on Computing and Networking (MobiCom), pp. 241–252 (2009)
2. Qi, X., Zhou, G., Li, Y., Peng, G.: Radiosense: exploiting wireless communication patterns for body sensor network activity recognition. In: Proceedings of IEEE Real-Time Systems Symposium (RTSS), pp. 95–104 (2012)

3. Wagner, S., Handte, M., Zuniga, M., Marrón, P.J.: Enhancing the performance of indoor localization using multiple steady tags. Pervasive Mob. Comput. **9**(3), 392–405 (2013)
4. Zhang, D., Zhou, J., Guo, M., Cao, J., Li, T.: TASA: tag-free activity sensing using RFID tag arrays. IEEE Trans. Parallel Distrib. Syst. (TPDS) **22**(4), 558–570 (2011)
5. Asadzadeh, P., Kulik, L., Tanin, E.: Gesture recognition using RFID technology. Pers. Ubiquit. Comput. **16**(3), 225–234 (2012)
6. Gu, T., Wang, L., Wu, Z., Tao, X., Lu, J.: A pattern mining approach to sensor-based human activity recognition. IEEE Trans. Knowl. Data Eng. (TKDE) **23**(9), 1359–1372 (2010)
7. Peng, Q., Zhang, C., Song, Y., Wang, Z., Wang, Z.: A low-cost, low-power UHF RFID reader transceiver for mobile applications. In: Radio Frequency Integrated Circuits Symposium (RFIC), pp. 243–246 (2012)
8. Bao, L., Intille, S.S.: Activity recognition from user-annotated acceleration data. In: Ferscha, A., Mattern, F. (eds.) PERVASIVE 2004. LNCS, vol. 3001, pp. 1–17. Springer, Heidelberg (2004)
9. Quwaider, M., Biswas, S.: Body posture identification using hidden Markov model with a wearable sensor network. In: Proceedings of International Conference on Body Area Networks, p. 19 (2008)
10. Kuo, S.M., Lee, B.H., Tian, W.: Real-Time Digital Signal Processing: Implementations and Applications. Wiley, Chichester (2006)

Evaluation of Wearable Sensor Tag Data Segmentation Approaches for Real Time Activity Classification in Elderly

Roberto Luis Shinmoto Torres$^{(\boxtimes)}$, Damith C. Ranasinghe, and Qinfeng Shi

Auto-ID Lab, School of Computer Science,
The University of Adelaide South Australia, Adelaide 5005, Australia
{roberto.shinmototorres,damith.ranasinghe,javen.shi}@adelaide.edu.au

Abstract. The development of human activity monitoring has allowed the creation of multiple applications, among them is the recognition of high falls risk activities of older people for the mitigation of falls occurrences. In this study, we apply a graphical model based classification technique (conditional random field) to evaluate various sliding window based techniques for the real time prediction of activities in older subjects wearing a passive (batteryless) sensor enabled RFID tag. The system achieved maximum overall real time activity prediction accuracy of 95 % using a time weighted windowing technique to aggregate contextual information to input sensor data.

Keywords: Conditional random fields · RFID · Feature extraction

1 Introduction

The development of accurate human activity recognition methods is a growing field of study as many applications can be derived from this base. One application is the mitigation of high falls risk activities of older people in hospitals or age care facilities, as falls events occur especially in the bedroom [1]. A correct recognition of such high risk events can lead to an intervention to mitigate an event that can potentially cause further physical injury and mental distress [12]. For high falls risk mitigation the accurate recognition of real time activities is paramount as most falls occur during transfer activities, which are changes of static activities or locations (e.g. sit to stand, stand to sit or ambulating) [1,14]. In this article we consider activity recognition in the context of identifying high falls risk related activities.

Recent work on real time recognition of events have succeeded using body sensors [2,4,8,9,13,17], using tri-axial accelerometers, magnetometers and gyroscopes. These studies along with research using video images [11,18] or environment sensors [7,10] required the use of different time or data (number of

This research was supported by a grant from the Hospital Research Foundation (THRF) and the Australian Research Council (DP130104614).

samples, pixels) based segmentation approaches to extract relevant information for data classification.

The difficulty for real time recognition of activities using sensors is that individual sensor readings are limited in time-space and by themselves provide little additional information about the related activity for the classifier to predict an activity correctly. In order to provide further contextual information to data collected [6], incoming sensor data stream is segmented for feature extraction prior to evaluation.

Using data segments is not precise as there is no pre-defined window size and sizes may differ depending on the application [4,8] or sensor platform used [2,8]. In addition, a passive sensor's data stream is not continuous and data collected can be incomplete or noise distorted. These factors can influence the information quality of the individual data segment. Moreover, the occurrence and information value of future readings are uncertain and the classifier relies exclusively on current and past information to emit a result. The classifier performance is also affected by the presence of data from unrelated activities (e.g. distant past activities' data or sensor readings from unrelated areas or activities) and data from unrelated activities may outweigh current activity information in a given data segment [7].

This paper describes several sliding window segmentation methods for a real time per sensor datum prediction of human activities from a sensor and ID data stream from a battery-less wearable radio frequency identification (RFID) platform, called W^2ISP [5]. Our main focus is the implementation and evaluation of the effectiveness of segmentation methods using a multi-class classifier to identify incoming activity data in real time. We used a conditional random field (CRF) classifier because of its desirable sequence dependency modelling capabilities. The main contributions of this study are: (i) development of a real time CRF based classifier for activity recognition of passive sensor and ID data streams; (ii) implementation and testing of multiple fixed and dynamic sized windowing methods for contextual information extraction based on data characteristics; and (iii) experimental demonstration of the accuracy of these methods using data gathered from a trial with older subjects (66–86 years old) in a clinical environment.

The rest of the paper is described as follows: Sect. 2 gives a brief overview of related work, Sect. 3 discusses the methodology for our windowing approaches. Section 4 shows the evaluation results from the various methods in the previous Section and finally conclusions are given in Sect. 5.

2   Related Work

There are several studies with as many approaches for the real time recognition of human activities using threshold and machine learning classification systems. Some real time results [4,8,13] imply the timely recognition of body positions or postures, however, these methods required a data buffer from which the classifier makes a prediction. Hence, results are available periodically rather than having an output per individual sensor reading; some studies considered overlapping of data to provide faster output while having larger data buffers [8]. A study by Wang et al. [17] used a 1 s sliding window and a smartphone processing platform producing a recognition delay (time elapsed from ground truth to prediction of the ground truth) of ∼ 5.7 s. Other real time smartphone based studies relied on the sensors embedded in the device [9] or were used as a hub for other worn sensors [2]. Current smartphones are not imperceptible devices and their usage with older populations needs to be studied.

All these methods used different approaches to segmenting and windowing data. Most tried empirically different segment sizes to find that which maximized the resulting accuracy using the same set of features [8,17] or the window selection was arbitrary [9]; while others were limited by the underlying technology itself [4]. In addition, most of these studies produced periodical results only and used battery operated sensors which are bulky and not appropriate for older or frail subjects. Furthermore, none has been evaluated on an older population.

In the work of Krishnan et al. [7], several methods were applied to evaluate the best sliding window method for smart home data sets. Each method provided extra features for added information about the last received sample. The nature of irregular and incomplete data from environment sensors in the smart home is similar to that of passive worn sensors in an RFID platform, as is our case. This research study implements methods adapted from [3,7] to the ID and sensor data stream from sensor enabled passive RFID devices to evaluate time series data segmentation approaches for real time classification of scripted activities from older people.

3   Methodology

In this section, we present the developed windowing methods for feature extraction and describe the datasets and classification system used. These methods are based on the passive sensor platform (W^2ISP) constraints where signal collection is irregular, noisy and incomplete. Our RFID deployments used antennae location to obtain readings from targeted areas of high falls risk activities (in and around a bed and a chair) in two clinical rooms (Sect. 3.7).

Using a tri-axial acceleration (ADXL330) data stream from a W^2ISP we predicted the activity label (Sect. 3.7) that best represented every datum received. Our feature vector included: $V = [a_f, a_v, a_l, sin(\theta), RSSI, A_{ID}, \triangle T]$ for the recognition of bed exits, where a_f, a_v and a_l are frontal, vertical and lateral components of the tri-axial accelerometer sensor, $sin(\theta)$ refers to the body tilt angle, $RSSI$ is the strength (power) of the signal received from the W^2ISP by an RFID reader, $A_{ID} = \{aID_1, .., aID_A\}$ (where A is the number of antennae) is the identifier of the antenna that collected the datum and $\triangle T$ is the time difference between current and previous reading [15]. In [15] we obtained high accuracy for label detection using batch processing of activities sequences segmented by trial and by patient with a CRF classifier. In this study, we use CRF for real time activity recognition and apply different windowing techniques for feature extraction and predict the activity label of the last received sensor reading.

3.1 Activity Windowing (AW)

This approach considers that the system knows in advance the activity that is being performed and segments the data per each activity for both training and testing stages. Although knowing the activities performed beforehand in a real environment is implausible given that the separation of activities is unambiguous, maximum accuracy is expected from the predicted labels. Given this condition, we consider this technique our golden standard. However, this approach does not perform predictions in real-time but predicts samples in different sized pre-segmented batches where each batch represents a single activity. We use the generic set of features V for each observed sensor reading (Sect. 3) as input to the classifier.

3.2 Fixed Sample Windowing (FSW)

This approach considers a sliding window with fixed number of samples. The windowed sample sequence provides contextual information about the last sample in the window to enable the classifier to emit a more accurate prediction [7]. Different window sizes can better fit the duration of different activities (labels) as was the case in Sect. 3.1 when the activities are already known. To illustrate this case, consider resting positions such as lying or sitting on bed or the chair that usually last several minutes or hours when compared to dynamic activities such as walking. The lengths of such events are disproportionate and difficult to segment in real data; whereas a fixed sample segmentation is simple to produce.

The selection of window size is an empirical process, where the best result corresponds to the segment length that best fits all activities. For this analysis additional features are extracted and added to our generic feature vector V as contextual information. In contrast to [7] the set of extra features corresponds to the count of events reported by each antenna in the window, as we can differentiate sensor reading origin by the antenna used. Hence, the number of extra features is equal to the number of antennae present. Moreover, these summed amounts are further normalized to four levels of importance (0: unused, 1: low, 2: medium and 3: high importance) computed as follows:

$$ F(i, k) = \left\lceil \frac{3 * c_{i,k}}{\sum_{j=1}^{A} c_{j,k}} \right\rceil \tag{1} $$

where A is the number of antennae and $c_{i,k}$ corresponds to the count of antenna i events in the window for the last reading k.

Two issues are present in this method. First, the window duration can span a long time and readings from distant past activities can affect the classifier decision. Second, a large volume of readings from previous activities unrelated to the current activity or spurious readings from distant antennae covering a distinct area present in the window can also alter the classifier decision. In order to meet these issues, weighted features are considered to balance the influence of unrelated data [7] and are described in Sects. 3.3 and 3.4.

3.3   Time Weighted Windowing (TWW)

This method is based on FSW in Sect. 3.2, as it uses a fixed sample window. However, more importance is given to events closer to the last sample to reduce the effect of historical events on the classifier. This technique gives each sample i in a window a distinct weight $T(i, k)$ which is a function of the time difference $\triangle_{i,k}$ between the last received sample k and sample i in the fixed time window. The evaluation of the weights is defined by an exponential function:

$$T(i,k) = \begin{cases} 0 & \text{if } \triangle_{i,k} >= \frac{1}{D} \\ \exp(-D * \triangle_{i,k}) & \text{else} \end{cases} \tag{2}$$

where D is the rate of decay, if $D > 1$ elements very close ($\triangle_{i,k} <1$ s) are given priority as the exponential function decays quickly; smaller values of D allows the function to consider a wider time range of sensor readings. The method also considers a limited amount of time, bounded by $\triangle_{i,k} = \frac{1}{D}$, as larger values of $\triangle_{i,k}$ provide less weight. The extra features now consist of the sum of the weights for the readings corresponding to each antenna in the window and replaces the extra features from FSW method. Hence, the extra features are defined by the vector: $W = [\sum T(i,k)\delta(a_i, aID_1), \ldots, \sum T(i,k)\delta(a_i, aID_A)]$, where $a_i \in A_{ID}$ is the antenna corresponding to the ith sample and the function $\delta(a_m, a_n)$ is defined as:

$$\delta(a_m, a_n) = \begin{cases} 0 & \text{if } a_m \neq a_n \\ 1 & \text{if } a_m = a_n \end{cases} \tag{3}$$

In addition, we normalize vector W to levels of importance using (1).

3.4   Mutual Information Windowing (MI)

Similarly to TWW (see Sect. 3.3), this method uses a fixed sample window (see Sect. 3.2). However, this approach intends to reduce the influence of readings from antennae focused on areas unrelated to the current activity. In general, samples of different activities are collected from antennae depending on the activity location. Nevertheless, readings from distant antennae occur in real data with low received energy ($RSSI$), although these readings are rare. We consider two types of mutual information between the ith sample and the last sample k in a segmented window: (i) MI1: mutual information (MI) of two consecutive readings occurring from any pair of antennae as defined in [7] and given in (4); and (ii) MI2: the MI of two consecutive readings occurring from a given pair of antennae at any time (i.e. disregards the order of antenna occurrence while focusing only on antenna relationships), defined in (5), where N is the number of elements in the training sequence, $a_i \in A_{ID}$ and function $\delta(.)$ is as defined in (3).

$$MI1(m,n) = \frac{1}{N} \sum_{j=1}^{N-1} \delta(a_j, a_m)\delta(a_{j+1}, a_n) \tag{4}$$

$$MI2(m,n) = \frac{1}{N} \sum_{j=1}^{N-1} (\delta(a_j, a_m)\delta(a_{j+1}, a_n) + \delta(a_j, a_n)\delta(a_{j+1}, a_m)) \tag{5}$$

The mutual information is built from the entire training data set prior to testing where a square matrix $(A \times A)$ with all possible antennae pairs and a triangular matrix is obtained for MI1 and MI2 respectively. These MI weights are used to build the extra features, where all sensor readings in a window are weighted in relation to the last reading and summed in relation to their corresponding antenna, obtaining the vector $W = [\sum MIr(i,k)\delta(a_i, aID_1), \ldots, \sum MIr(i,k) \delta(a_i, aID_A)]$ where $r = \{1, 2\}$. Vector W is normalized to levels of importance using (1).

3.5 Dynamic Windowing (DW)

This method considers a time based window of varying size using statistical properties of the data to continually adapt the window size. This method, first devised by Jeffery et al. [3] for cleaning of RFID data streams, was applied because the algorithm balances the need to provide contextual information by increasing the window size and reducing the window size when sensor readings become more sporadic. This method considers a stepped window size increments (0.5 s per sample) but reduction is rapid (halving the window size) when required [3]. We assume a standard epoch[1] duration of 0.25 s and sensor observation probability of 90 % [3]. For this method we use the extra features of the FSW method (see Sect. 3.2).

3.6 Fixed Time Windowing (FTW)

This method considers a sliding window of fixed time duration T^*, as opposed to a dynamic changing time window size as in DW. All readings within the time interval T^* from the last received reading k are considered in a window. Given the irregular collection of data (due to the nature of the passive device), the number of samples per segment will differ. For this method we use the extra features of the FSW method (see Sect. 3.2).

3.7 Datasets

We used data from two clinical room deployments as described in [15]; where both datasets (*RoomSet1* and *RoomSet2*) used four and three antennae respectively. In *RoomSet1* one antenna is placed on top of the bed (ceiling) and three on the walls focusing on the chair and around the bed providing a wide area of coverage. In *RoomSet2* two antennae were placed on top of the bed (ceiling) and one antenna focused on the chair. Fourteen older subjects were trialled (age:74.6 ± 4.9), wearing the W^2ISP on top of their garments. They performed a series of scripted activities which included: (i) lying (in bed); (ii) sitting in bed; (iii) sitting in chair; and (iv) ambulating. The CRF classifier was used to predict these four activity labels. In order to collect the ground truth, activities were annotated in real time by an observer. The same basic features were extracted

---

[1] Epoch refers to a group of RFID interrogation cycles.

for each dataset; however, the total number of features differed for both datasets as the aggregated extra features are based on their antennae deployment.

3.8 Classifier

In this research, we used a linear chain CRF, a model for structured classification (prediction) [16], as in a previous study [15]. We have preferred this method as it models the dependencies of activities in a sequence. Due to this advantage the system is trained using the complete sequence of activities of each training trial for parameter estimation with the exception of the first method (AW) as it assumes activities are previously known and independent from each other. In CRF, training and testing stages require the probabilistic inference of the target labels (hidden variables). In general, the inference process allows us to obtain: (i) marginal probabilities of the labels (using sum-product algorithm); and (ii) the most probable global state of all our hidden variables i.e. maximum a posteriori (MAP) assignment (using max-product algorithm). Our application requires real time response, thus we use the sum product algorithm (which only propagates the messages forwards) to find the marginal probability of the current hidden variable given the past and current observation efficiently. The prediction is done by maximizing the marginal probability.

The sum product algorithm propagates messages for every edge (i,j) connecting nodes i and j in a graph. In Fig. 1, circles represent the state variables $Y = \{y_1, \ldots, y_k\}$ and squares represent factors (node and edge potentials). The message updating and marginal probability are computed as follows:

$$m_{i,k}(s_k) = \sum_{s_i} (\psi(s_i)\psi(s_i, s_k) \prod_{t \in N_i \backslash \{k\}} m_{t,i}(s_i)) \tag{6}$$

$$p(s_k) = \frac{1}{Z}\psi(s_k) \prod_{i \in N_k} m_{i,k}(s_k) \tag{7}$$

where $\psi(s_i)$ and $\psi(s_i, s_k)$ are node and edge potential respectively, s_i represents node i, $N_i \backslash \{k\}$ represents the set of neighbours of node i with the exception of node k, p is the marginal probability and Z is a normalization factor. In the case of our real time application, we are only interested in the marginal probability of the last variable (y_k) given the input observation as shown in Fig. 1, where the marginal probability of variable y_k reduces to:

$$p(y_k \mid x_{1:k}, \lambda) = \frac{1}{Z(\lambda, x_{1:k})} \psi(y_k; x_{1:k}, \lambda)m_{k-1,k}(y_k; x_{1:k}, \lambda) \tag{8}$$

where messages $m_{i,j}$ are calculated using (6) and $\lambda = \{\lambda_t\}$ represents the parameters estimated in training. Moreover, the message $m_{k-1,k}(y_k; x_{1:k}, \lambda)$ is recursive as it depends on previous messages as in the expression $m_{k-1,k}(y_k; x_{1:k}, \lambda) = \sum_{y_{k-1}} \psi(y_{k-1}; x_{1:k}, \lambda)\psi(y_{k-1}, y_k; x_{1:k}, \lambda)m_{k-2,k-1}(y_{k-1}; x_{1:k-1}, \lambda)$.

This derivation for the sum product is appropriate for real time streaming data as the sequence of information is always increasing and an activity label prediction is required for each datum. Therefore, we apply the expression in (8) for inference during testing.

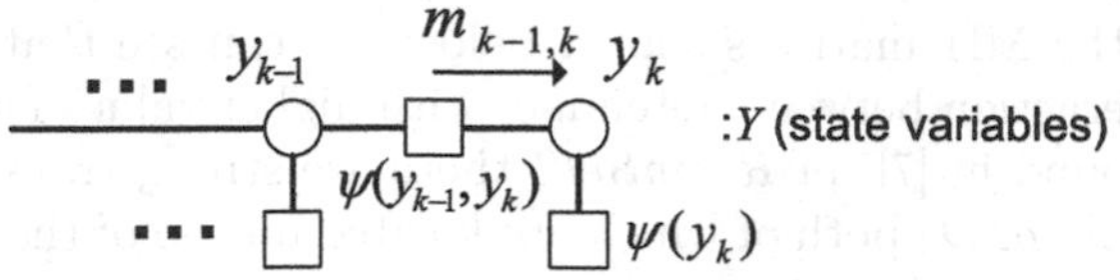

Fig. 1. Message propagation for the probability distribution of y_k

3.9 Statistical Analysis

The analysis of results was obtained using a 10-fold cross validation where general performance was measured using overall accuracy (referred as accuracy and given in (9)), and individual label performance using geometric mean (GM) and $Fscore$ as defined in (9), where N is the number of readings, TP is true positives and recall, specificity and precision are determined as per standard definitions. Results are shown as mean $\pm$ standard deviation (SD). Statistical significance is measured using a two-tailed two-sample t-test at 5 % significance level.

$$Accu = \frac{TP}{N} \quad GM = \sqrt{recall.specificity} \quad Fscore = \frac{2.recall.precision}{recall + precision} \quad (9)$$

4 Evaluation

The first evaluation corresponds to labelling a pre-segmented sequence in the AW method. High accuracies ($> 97.7\%$) and high $Fscore$ and GM values ($> 87\%$ and $> 92\%$) are obtained for $RoomSet1$ and $RoomSet2$ datasets (see Table 2). In $RoomSet2$, metrics for sitting-in-chair are affected by one test fold where only 17 samples were present for that activity which was missed (false negative), affecting all metrics. Accuracies for the FSW method are shown in Table 1(a), which tested sliding windows of 5 to 60 samples. Highest accuracy for $RoomSet1$ is achieved between $N = 10$ and 20; the largest source of error is caused by false negatives (FN) of sitting-in-bed and false positives (FP) in ambulating labels. These errors are minimal in AW approach. $RoomSet2$ is affected by one fold where samples collected during lying and sitting-in-bed caused mutual errors, which also affected the rest of the methods. Given that $RoomSet2$ metrics do not vary in this set of window sizes, we consider the window sample size of 15 as the best parameter for this method.

The TWW method was tested using a fixed window size of 15 samples as found in FSW method. For this study we tested decay rate values of $D = 2^{-7}$ to 2^0 as shown in Table 1(b). Highest accuracy for $RoomSet1$ occurs for $D = 2^{-2}$ and then drops slightly. In contrast, best performance for $RoomSet2$ occurs between $D = 2^{-1}$ to 2^{-3} with some folds affected by mutual error between lying and sitting-in-bed as in FSW method. However, accuracy is not significantly different across $RoomSet2$ ($p > 0.34$). Hence, we consider a decay rate of $D = 2^{-2}$ as the best parameter for this windowing case.

Results for MI windowing indicates that both MI1 and MI2 approaches (see Sect. 3.4) obtained similar results as shown in Table 2, where results are almost identical. From the MI1 matrices shown below, we can see that for $RoomSet1$ there is little interaction between antennae, with higher values for self transition of antennae as found in [7]; in $RoomSet2$ there are strong transition values for antennae aID_2 and aID_3 both of which are located on top of the bed and report most in-bed and around-bed sensor readings.

MI1 $RoomSet1$ (%)

	aID_1	aID_2	aID_3	aID_4
aID_1	35.12	0.25	2.18	3.28
aID_2	0.22	8.77	0.04	0.06
aID_3	2.23	0.03	16.48	4.33
aID_4	3.24	0.04	4.36	19.26

MI1 $RoomSet2$ (%)

	aID_1	aID_2	aID_3
aID_1	3.19	0.16	0.31
aID_2	0.17	21.92	18.15
aID_3	0.4	18.14	37.42

The DW method produced high accuracy (94.6%) results for $RoomSet2$ but for $RoomSet1$ results are comparable to those of previous windowing methods as shown in Table 2. However, $Fscore$ and GM are significantly different compared to MI ($p < 0.01$). Partial results for FTW are shown in Table 1(c), where time durations of 1 to 128 s were tested. The highest accuracies were achieved with a 4 s time window for both datasets. In $RoomSet2$, there is little variation among different time windows. In contrast, for $RoomSet1$ this method achieves the highest accuracy for all tested methods as seen in Table 2 but this result is still significantly different from that of the golden standard ($p \sim 10^{-7}$).

Finally, we combined time and space based segment contextual information extraction with expected performance improvement. Combination of FTW and MI1, introduced mutual information rather than counting events in FTW. The results for $RoomSet1$ lie between the amalgamated methods; however, the overall performance for $RoomSet2$ is lower than FTW and MI1. The combination case of TWW and MI1 introduced extra features from both methods, achieving the highest accuracy for $RoomSet2$ which is comparable with our golden standard ($p = 0.14$). Results for $RoomSet1$ are slightly lower than the best performance with FTW method (see Table 2). This is because TWW+MI1 had a rich extended information. However, in FTW+MI1 the fixed time window did not bring enough mutual information as the number of samples in a segment can be as low as one, performing lower than counting per antenna samples.

Further analysis of Table 2 indicates low $Fscore$ and GM values for $RoomSet1$ created mostly by FNs and FPs (false positives) for sitting-in-bed and ambulating respectively. These errors were reduced in the FTW case but not greatly. Metrics for $RoomSet2$ were affected by two main causes, one fold in particular produced large FN and FP for lying and sitting-in-bed respectively and few readings for sitting-in-chair label which in some folds are ignored produced recall, Fscore and GM values of zero and affected these averages. In both datasets, the low composition of ambulating activity data (not shown) compared to the other states affected individual and average metrics as only a couple of seconds of data are retrieved as a subject walked away from the reading range of antennae near the bed or chair.

These results indicate the real time inference algorithm (marginal inference) found most difficulty predicting ambulating and sitting-in-bed samples for *RoomSet*1. In general, no method was able to produce maximum results for both datasets, although results for FTW and TWW+MI1 methods are comparable ($p > 0.48$) in both datasets. *RoomSet*2 disposition using two antennae focusing on the bed was able to avoid classification error in *RoomSet*1, however there were relatively smaller number of sensor readings for sitting-in-chair as only one antenna powers the tag in *RoomSet*2. In terms of real time analysis, test inference calculation time for both datasets is of 5.12 µs and 7.31 µs per sample respectively and this time is minimal compared with the observed minimum inter-sample duration time of 25 ms. These results were obtained using algorithms implemented in MATLAB scripts and mex code but these algorithms will run faster if developed in a low level language as C/C++ and therefore our results also demonstrate that the classifier is capable of real time sample prediction.

Table 1. Partial accuracies for FSW, TWW and FTW methods

(a) Accuracy for Fixed Sample Window method						
Datasets	N = 5	N = 10	N = 15	N = 20	N = 30	N = 60
RoomSet1	70.6±6.0 %	71.2±6.1 %	72.5±5.9 %	72.2±6.2 %	70.6±6.2 %	70.7±5.9 %
RoomSet2	94.9±4.3 %	91.9±11.5 %	91.8±11.2 %	91.7±11.3 %	91.2±11.6 %	93.5±6.9 %
(b) Accuracy for Time Weighted Window method						
Datasets	$D = 2^0$	$D = 2^{-1}$	$D = 2^{-2}$	$D = 2^{-3}$	$D = 2^{-4}$	$D = 2^{-7}$
RoomSet1	70.3±6.1 %	71.6±6.1 %	73.1±7.5 %	71.8±6.2 %	71.7±6.0 %	71.8±6.1 %
RoomSet2	91.3±11.2 %	94.3±5.0 %	91.7±11.2 %	93.5±4.6 %	92.1±11.1 %	90.2±10.8 %
(c) Accuracy for Fixed Time Window method						
Datasets	$T = 1$	$T = 2$	$T = 4$	$T = 8$	$T = 16$	$T = 128$
RoomSet1	70.5±6.2 %	73.9±7.1 %	78.2±7.3 %	73.6±6.8 %	71.9±6.7 %	70.2±5.7 %
RoomSet2	91.5±11.3 %	91.6±11.4 %	92.3±11.2 %	92.2±11.1 %	92.2±11.0 %	91.2±11.0 %

Table 2. Classification accuracy for all tested methods for both datasets, including average Fscore and GM for all activities.

Method	*RoomSet1 (%)*			*RoomSet2 (%)*		
	Accuracy	*Fscore*	*GM*	*Accuracy*	*Fscore*	*GM*
AW	98.1±1.8	93.5±5.5	96.1±3.7	97.7±3.6	87.0±21.0	92.8±16.6
FSW	72.5±6.0	57.9±6.5	76.6±5.5	91.8±11.2	67.5±23.2	82.5±17.7
TWW	73.1±7.5	59.0±9.2	77.1±8.0	91.7±11.2	69.3±21.4	84.4±18.0
MI1	70.8±6.0	55.2±5.0	74.0±4.3	94.4±5.2	68.6±20.5	84.3±17.2
MI2	70.8±6.1	55.3±5.4	74.1±4.9	93.8±5.2	67.5±20.4	83.3±16.8
DW	74.7±8.1	61.2±10.2	79.2±8.4	94.6±4.7	68.4±22.7	83.4±18.6
FTW	**78.2 ± 7.3**	**65.1 ± 11.5**	**82.1 ± 9.2**	92.3±11.2	68.5±23.9	82.8±18.7
FTW+MI1	71.5±6.0	56.6±5.6	75.2±4.8	91.7±11.1	67.1±22.9	82.9±17.8
TWW+MI1	77.1±7.8	63.8±11.5	81.0±9.1	**95.0 ± 4.2**	**71.6 ± 20.2**	**85.8 ± 16.8**

5   Conclusions

In this study we have developed a number of sliding window based data segmentation techniques for real time prediction of human activities where contextual information was introduced as extra features to the input observation to improve classification accuracy. Although no segmentation method exceeded the golden standard for both datasets, methods TWW+MI1 and FTW achieved high performance metrics in both datasets and had comparable results with the golden standard with *RoomSet2* dataset. In general *RoomSet2* achieved better results than *RoomSet1*, due to its more focused antennae disposition which caused less prediction errors as opposed to a wider area coverage as in *RoomSet1*. Moreover, the system can process real time streaming data using fixed or variable windowing approaches on a sample by sample basis with high accuracy as in the case of *RoomSet2*; and using a CRF classifier which learned the model using complete sequences of activities and applied into real time label prediction.

A limitation comes from the scripted nature of the activity datasets. Nonetheless, all related sensor worn research (see Sect. 2) were based on scripted set of activities, where execution order was random or sequential. Further analysis is required to determine whether these segmentation techniques based on scripted models can perform well with unscripted and undirected activities.

Finally, this work sets the foundation for high level applications such as high falls risk activities (bed and chair ingress or exit, room exiting and bathroom access) recognition in real time.

References

1. Becker, C., Rapp, K.: Fall prevention in nursing homes. Clin. Geriatr. Med. **26**(4), 693–704 (2010)
2. Györbíró, N., Fábián, A., Hományi, G.: An activity recognition system for mobile phones. Mob. Netw. Appl. **14**(1), 82–91 (2009)
3. Jeffery, S., Franklin, M., Garofalakis, M.: An adaptive rfid middleware for supporting metaphysical data independence. VLDB J. **17**(2), 265–289 (2008)
4. Karantonis, D., Narayanan, M., Mathie, M., Lovell, N., Celler, B.: Implementation of a real-time human movement classifier using a triaxial accelerometer for ambulatory monitoring. IEEE Trans. Inf. Technol. Biomed. **10**(1), 156–167 (2006)
5. Kaufmann, T., Ranasinghe, D.C., Zhou, M., Fumeaux, C.: Wearable quarter-wave microstrip antenna for passive UHF RFID applications. Int. J. Antennas Propag. (2013)
6. Kern, N., Schiele, B., Schmidt, A.: Recognizing context for annotating a live life recording. Pers. Ubiquit. Comput. **11**(4), 251–263 (2007)
7. Krishnan, N.C., et al.: Activity recognition on streaming sensor data. Pervasive Mob. Comput. **10**, 138–154 (2014)
8. Lee, M.W., Khan, A., Kim, J.H., Cho, Y.S., Kim, T.S.: A single tri-axial accelerometer-based real-time personal life log system capable of activity classification and exercise information generation. In: 32nd Annual International Conference IEEE Engineering in Medicine and Biology Society, pp. 1390–1393 (2010)

9. Lee, Y.-S., Cho, S.-B.: Activity recognition using hierarchical hidden markov models on a smartphone with 3D accelerometer. In: Corchado, E., Kurzyński, M., Woźniak, M. (eds.) HAIS 2011, Part I. LNCS, vol. 6678, pp. 460–467. Springer, Heidelberg (2011)
10. Lu, C.H., Fu, L.C.: Robust location-aware activity recognition using wireless sensor network in an attentive home. IEEE Trans. Autom. Sci. Eng. **6**(4), 598–609 (2009)
11. Messing, R., Pal, C., Kautz, H.: Activity recognition using the velocity histories of tracked keypoints. In: IEEE 12th International Conference on Computer Vision, pp. 104–111 (2009)
12. Oliver, D.: Prevention of falls in hospital inpatients. agendas for research and practice. Age Ageing **33**(4), 328–330 (2004)
13. Ranasinghe, D.C., Shinmoto Torres, R.L., Hill, K.D., Visvanathan, R.: Low cost and batteryless sensor-enabled radio frequency identification tag based approaches to identify patient bed entry and exit posture transitions. Gait & Posture (2013)
14. Robinovitch, S.N., Feldman, F., Yang, Y., Schonnop, R., Lueng, P.M., Sarraf, T., Sims-Gould, J., Loughin, M.: Video capture of the circumstances of falls in elderly people residing in long-term care: an observational study. The Lancet **381**(9860), 47–54 (2012)
15. Shinmoto Torres, R.L., Ranasinghe, D.C., Shi, Q., Sample, A.P.: Sensor enabled wearable rfid technology for mitigating the risk of falls near beds. In: 2013 IEEE International Conference on RFID, pp. 191–198 (2013)
16. Sutton, C., McCallum, A.: An introduction to conditional random fields. Found. Trends Mach. Learn. **4**(4), 267–373 (2012)
17. Wang, L., Gu, T., Tao, X., Lu, J.: A hierarchical approach to real-time activity recognition in body sensor networks. Pervasive Mob. Comput. **8**(1), 115–130 (2012)
18. Xia, L., Chen, C.C., Aggarwal, J.: Human detection using depth information by kinect. In: 2011 IEEE Computer Society Conference on Computer Vision and Pattern Recognition Workshops, pp. 15–22 (2011)

MobiSLIC: Content-Aware Energy Saving for Educational Videos on Mobile Devices

Qiyam Tung, Maximiliano Korp, Chris Gniady$^{(\boxtimes)}$,
Alon Efrat, and Kobus Barnard

University of Arizona, Tucson, Arizona
{qtung,mkorp,gniady,alon,kobus}@cs.arizona.edu

Abstract. We present a context-aware system that simultaneously increases energy-efficiency and readability for educational videos on smartphones with OLED displays. Our system analyzes the content of each frame of the video and intelligently modifies the colors and presentations of specific regions of the frame to drastically reduce display energy consumption while retaining relevant content of the lecture video. We achieve this by leveraging the mapping between frames and electronic versions of slides used in the lecture. This enables separate manipulation of the slide area and the background. Further, since the slides can themselves be analyzed for content (e.g. text and images within) this approach provides substantive control over energy use and user experience. We evaluate the system using extensive energy measurements performed on phones using two different display technologies. Our method was able to reduce energy usage up to 59.2 % of the energy used by the display which amounts to 27 % of the total energy used by the device.

Keywords: Energy-efficiency · OLED · Smartphones · Lecture videos

1 Introduction

We are becoming more dependent on smartphones and expect long battery life, despite steady increases in features and performance. As more smartphone users are spending their time on multimedia applications [1], such as watching movies, the demand for brighter displays that can be visible even in bright light is growing. Among the videos that are watched on the mobile devices are educational videos available on-line [2–7]. Large and high resolution displays of modern smartphones have made it easier to access and watch educational videos lectures in situations where using a regular desktop or laptop is inconvenient, such as commuting. However, being able to watch long videos depends on a reasonable battery life.

Displays in smartphones often account for a significant amount of the total energy consumption, making them one of the primary targets for energy optimizations. In particular, organic light-emitting diodes (*OLED*) displays, whose

© Institute for Computer Sciences, Social Informatics and Telecommunications Engineering 2014
I. Stojmenovic et al. (Eds.): MOBIQUITOUS 2013, LNICST 131, pp. 396–408, 2014.
DOI: 10.1007/978-3-319-11569-6_31

energy consumption is directly related to the color and brightness of the pixels [8], present opportunities for energy savings, such as modifying the colors and intensity of pixels in regions that are less important to the viewer.

This paper develops a system for modifying educational videos with consideration of the *content* appearing in each frame. Our techniques enable us to make selective adjustments that minimize the impact on the viewing experience while at the same time significantly reducing energy consumption. In addition, our technique has the ability to improve the readability of the slides in the video. We present two main approaches for reducing energy consumption for lecture videos. First, we utilize *backprojection* to replace portions of each frame occupied by the slide by the original slide used in the presentation. The slide color scheme is also revised to reduce energy consumption and increases readability. Second, we alter background regions of the video frame to improve energy efficiency, while only impacting the visibility of the region that is less important to the context of the video.

Hints to automatically understanding the content are obtained from analyzing slides used in the lecture and cross correlate them with the video itself. Our techniques work for recorded videos and hence are applicable to any of the discussions, lectures, colloquiums, etc., recorded already, as long as one can access the electronic slides being used in the lecture.

2   Related Work

Energy conservation has been a challenging focus of mobile research due to the ever-growing demand for more features. In an extensive study, Mahesri and Vardhan identified that the CPU and display consume the most amount of power in a laptop in [9]. The LCD screen dominates during idle times, using up to 29 % of the total power draw from the backlight alone. For mobile phones, even finding the optimal schedule for switching an active display to an inactive display can decrease total energy usage by 60 % [10]. For this reason, much research has been focused on minimizing the energy consumed by displays.

Flinn and Satyanarayanan propose a method of reducing the amount of energy consumed without dimming the backlight [11]. Specifically, they use different compression settings, such as reducing the frame rate and decreasing the dimensions of the video. Similarly, Park *et al.* [12] show that by degrading video quality by 13 %, they were able to get achieve savings of 42 %, measured on an ARM/Linux-based platform. While those techniques can offer energy savings, they degrade video quality. Degrading video quality is not desirable in our scenario as lecture videos often need to be large and sharp enough for text to be legible.

OLED displays can have a significant range of power demand from 0.25 W to 2 W as compared to the CPU's range of 50 mW to 600 mW [13]. Although the maximum luminance of OLED displays rarely occur in the usage of a phone, the phone usually supplies enough voltage to do so. Chen *et al.* [14] show that by dynamically adjusting the voltage after analyzing the display contents can save from 19.1 % to 49.1 % of the OLED power. Considering that video playback on a Samsung Galaxy S2 uses 35.6 % of the phone's total power [15], finding ways to optimize display energy usage is an important task.

In fact, substantial savings can be achieved by dimming parts of the display alone. Iyer *et al.* [16] found that reducing the intensity for the background and inactive windows in a desktop environment resulted in energy savings of up to 20 %. Similar optimizations have been applied to reduce the intensity of non-active portions of an iPAQ display [17]. A user study showed that these changes unobtrusive and sometimes even preferable. A similar technique of dimming regions that are not the locus of attention in video games can also achieve savings of 11 % of the display energy [18].

In addition, Dong *et al.* show that significant energy savings can also be obtained by modifying the color scheme of the graphical user interface [19]. In the same manner, for visualization of data, such as weather data or grouping voxels by color, Chuang *et al.* [20] show that one can optimize energy by selecting energy-aware but perceptually distinguishable colors. These techniques are not applicable for lecture videos as the color selection was not designed for natural scenes. Nevertheless, selectively dimming colors is the basis of reducing energy for our system.

3   OLED Displays

While dimming the backlight was the main method of decreasing energy consumption for liquid crystal displays (LCD), OLED displays offer greater potential for energy savings as the diodes are emissive and do not depend on a global backlight. The energy in an OLED display is directly correlated to how many pixels are on and what intensity level and color they are displaying. However, different display technologies may alter the energy consumption behavior of the display. In particular, phone displays may have different subpixel arrangement of the three primary colors, as is the case with the devices we used (Fig. 1). The Samsung Galaxy S Vibrant uses the PenTile matrix array (PMA) technology [21] and the red, blue, and green OLEDs have different dimensions. Furthermore, the pixels are laid out so that each one contains only two OLEDs. In order to generate the full range of colors, PMA displays utilize subpixel sharing. For example, in order for a pixel that does not contain a blue OLED to display blue, its adjacent pixel's blue OLED would need to be activated.

Samsung Galaxy S2, on the other hand, uses a standard RGB stripe pixel array. The layout is simpler and the three OLEDs are arranged in vertical stripes of red, green, and blue and hence do not require subpixel sharing. The specifications of the two phones used in our experiments are shown in Table 1. Despite the differences, the blue channel consistently consumes the most energy in both devices, as seen in Fig. 2. Therefore, in terms of color manipulation, our methods either dim all colors equally or dim out the blue channel. The choice depends on the viewer's preference and content of the lecture.

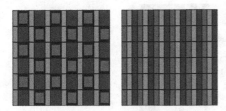

Fig. 1. Layout of pixels of different channels for the (left) Pentile matrix and (right) RGB stripe matrix.

Table 1. Smartphone specifications

Phone	Galaxy S	Galaxy S2
OS	Android 2.2	Android 2.3.5
Color depth	24 bit	24 bit
Display size	4 inches	4.5 inches
Display type	PenTile	RGB Stripe
Resolution	480×800	480×800
CPU	1 GHZ	2×1.5 GHZ
Memory	512 MB	1 GB

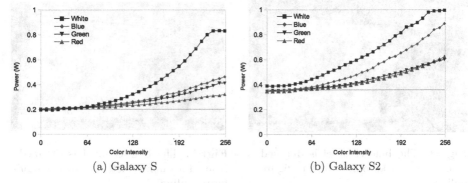

(a) Galaxy S

(b) Galaxy S2

Fig. 2. Measurements of the power draw of the three primary colors for all sRGB values

4 Improving Energy Efficiency

Energy optimizations we are proposing are tightly related to the layout of a video frame. A typical frame consists of several regions (see Fig. 3):

1. The *non-slide background* consists of the audience, walls around the screen, and any other regions outside of the projector screen.
2. The *slide region* contains elements that carry vital information, such as text, figures, pie charts, graphs, etc.
3. The region of the slide not containing the text or images is the *slide background*.

The challenge are in identifying these regions in a deck of electronic slides, as well as in the video containing these slides. The energy optimizations can be vary from recoloring of the whole frame to recoloring the individual regions as identified above.

4.1 Altering the Non-Slide Background

The slide background may contain speaker's gestures, audience reactions or interactions, etc. While a speaker's gestures may be important, the absence of a color

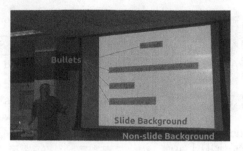

Fig. 3. The three kinds of regions in a video frame.

Fig. 4. The blue channel is dimmed from the background (color figure online).

Fig. 5. The blue channel is dimmed from the non-bullets regions (color figure online).

or background all together is unlikely to prevent a user from understanding the lecture content. However, the desirability of the background depends on the person, and is orthogonal to the rest of the discussion.

To detect the background and slide regions, we first identify the slide used in each frame, along with the geometric mapping between slide and frames. We use the automatic slide detection already developed in the SLIC project [22], which gives us both the geometric transformation, the *homography*, as well the *temporal* information, which tells us which slide in the slide deck is shown in each video frame. Once the video frame layout is identified, we can dim or alter color by removing the most power hungry color, which is blue, from the background frame, as seen in Fig. 4. Surprisingly, this approach is rather ineffective for saving energy, as the non-slide background area is often small and much dimmer than the slide portion of the frame. Subsequently, the slide portion of the frame is the most power hungry portion and critical for successful energy optimizations.

4.2 Altering the Slide Background

To further take advantage of dimming nonessential regions we need to consider slide area that is not covered by text or images as shown in Fig. 5. Slide text and images tend to occupy a relatively small portion of the slide and the video

Fig. 6. Finding the bounding box by diffing two images.

frame under consideration. Subsequently, by dimming or removing color from such regions not occupied by text or images, we can get significant savings.

To identify text, embedded equations, and figure regions in the slide, we again rely on techniques developed as a part of the SLIC project [23]. Each presentation, which could be in the Keynote or the PowerPoint format, is converted to the latest PowerPoint format for processing. The latest PowerPoint format is XML based and allows simple alteration of text color. We use such color manipulations to identify the bounding boxes of the text region. We set a particular text region to different color in the slide. Subsequently, both slides, the original and the altered text color one, are exported as images. Since the only difference between the two slides is the color of the modified text, the difference reveals every pixel of the text. This process is illustrated in Fig. 6. We repeat this sequence for each text region and identify the entire text layout on the slides in the video frame.

We use an analogous method to find the bounding boxes of images in slides. The PowerPoint format stores all of a slide's images as individual image files. We extract these images and we replace them with uniquely colored monochromatic images, and export the slides to images. We proceed by taking the pixel-difference between the images to find the maximum x and y coordinates that bound the differing pixels. This method requires minimal knowledge about the format of the presentation, and can potentially extend to other presentation formats such as Google presentations, Adobe PDFs, etc.

Once we find the text and image locations in the slide we can frame them as shown in Fig. 5 and remove the power hungry colors from or dim the regions that not text or image areas. While this seems a rather straightforward process once we know image location on the slides, in reality, it can be complicated as slides may have different sizes or angles in the video frames and the text location needs to be translated to such layout.

In order to modify the color of the video frames, we need to know the temporal information (which slide is shown in each frame) and the location of the slide, which is given by the homography. To find them, we follow Fan *et al.*'s algorithm for finding slides in a video [24]. Finding the correct pixels to color can be computed with the aforementioned homography H, a 3×3 matrix. A homography describes how to map points on a plane from one camera's view to another, which makes it ideal for describing where the slide is in the frame (see Fig. 7). The mapping is only valid, however, if the points are described in homogeneous coordinates.

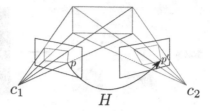

Fig. 7. A homography H describes how to map planes from one camera's viewpoint to another.

The homogeneous coordinates of a pixel in the slide, P_s, is related to its corresponding pixel coordinate in the frame P_f by the following equivalence: $HP_f = P_s$. H was derived by matching slide pixels in the frame to the slide, so to find the coordinates P_f given P_s, we take the inverse, giving us $P_f = H^{-1}P_s$. With this, dimming the color channel of the pixel is finally straightforward. We scan every pixel in the slide and reduce the color value of the channel if its corresponding frame pixel is outside the bounding box.

4.3   Altering and Replacing Slides

To achieve slide background modification we went through color alteration of text and images to detect text and image regions as well as slide mapping to the video frame. We can combine those techniques and replace the entire slide in the video frame with the slide optimized for energy efficiency. To generate energy efficient slides we can either do them by hand or utilize previously described techniques to automatically change text and slide background while keeping images unaltered.

To maximize energy efficiency and readability, each slide has its background modified to black and the text to white. Figures, pie charts, etc., appear in their original colors and intensities since automatic processing is not able to recolor images and guarantee that they contain original information content. Once modified, the slide is backprojected into each frame it was used [25], after making the geometric manipulations necessary to account for size and geometry of the slide in the video frame. The comparison of before and after optimization is in Fig. 8.

While backprojection can significantly improve energy efficiency as well as readability by improving image quality, it can hide events that happen on the projector screen, such as the lecturer pointing (with hands or laser pointer), slide animations, and videos embedded in the slides. This is due to the backprojected slide overlaying the original slide in its proper location in the video frame. For example, if the speaker walks into the region of the slide, he or she would be hidden by the slide due to the fact that it is drawn on top of the video frame.

Fig. 8. A comparison of the original (right) with the backprojected slide (left).

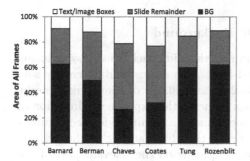

Fig. 9. Average area distributed among a slide, slide text and images, and the background areas.

Table 2. Video statistics

Video	Length [min]	Average intensity of		
		Red	Green	Blue
Barnard	4:00	86	101	105
Berman	3:15	111	139	132
Chaves	4:00	24	119	105
Coates	4:00	89	93	145
Tung	5:27	50	80	94
Rozenblit	3:15	120	114	114

5   Results

We evaluated the energy consumption of the proposed mechanisms using a National Instruments PCI-6230 Data Acquisition card (NI PCI-6230) and measuring software. The phone was connected directly to the power supply, instead of battery, for current measurements. To make the measurements reproducible, we turn off all wireless signals as well as automatic brightness adjustment. We evaluated our proposed mechanisms on the two phones, Samsung Galaxy S and Samsung Galaxy S2, over six lecture videos. We selected videos with varying lighting conditions, camera angles, and the amount of screen space that the lecture slide occupies versus background, as well as color mixes and Table 2 shows a basic statistics such selected video length and the average color composition in the video.

5.1   Efficiency of Altering the Non-Slide Background

Figure 9 shows the frame distribution between non-slide background (BG), background of the slide (Slide Remainder), and the text or image areas of the slide (Text/Image Boxes). The slide covers roughly 50 % of the total area in the video, which is not surprising as the slide has to occupy a significant portion of the screen so that the text is large enough to be legible. The figure also shows that the text and images only take up 15 % of the screen real estate on average, which means that only a fraction of the energy needed to play the original video is necessary to display the text and images.

Blacking out the non-slide background corresponds to removing the energy consumption from 50 % of the video frame, on average. However, the resulting energy savings are only 23.4 % and 19.9 % on the Galaxy S and S2, respectively. The modest savings can be accounted from the fact that the non-slide background is typically much darker that the slide area since the slides are displayed with a high power projector on a white screen and the room is dimmed to provide better slide readability.

5.2   Efficiency of Altering the Slide Background

Figure 11 shows progressive stages of dimming the slide background by reducing the RGB values by 20 %, 40 %, 60 %, and 80 %. The corresponding energy savings on Galaxy S2 are 20.0 %, 36.2 %, 44.2 %, and 50.1 % of the display energy usage. We observe that the energy savings come at the expense of alteration of the original image. While removing colors can make a lecture video seem unnatural, this particular transformation preserves the chromaticity of the original background but reduces the intensity, putting focus on the relevant part of the lecture, similar to [16–18].

Figures 10(a) and 10(b) show the average power demand of the entire phone for the combination of the display dimming techniques: video with all frames completely black (*All Black*); the video where only text and image regions are displayed (*Non-Text Black*); the video where we only remove blue, the most power hungry color, from the entire frame except the text and image regions (*Non-Text Red-Green*); and the original video without any alterations (*Full Color*). The upper bound on energy savings is attained by setting the color of the entire screen to black for the duration of the video. Playing such a video with all frames being black on the Galaxy S and S2 show the average upper bound on savings of 43.4 % and 46.4 % of the total energy needed to play the

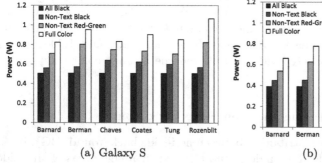
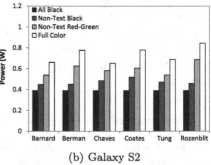

(a) Galaxy S   (b) Galaxy S2

Fig. 10. Energy consumption after dimming less relevant regions.

Fig. 11. Images whose slide background is dimmed by 20%, 40%, 60%, and 80% from left to right.

original video, respectively. For the remaining results, we will cite the savings in terms of the display energy, which is calculated by subtracting the energy to display a black video from the original video.

Non-Text Red-Green saves 37.1% to 39.8% for the Galaxy S and S2, respectively. The savings are significant, especially when considering the diversity of the color distribution in the videos. Table 2 shows the average RGB values of the 6 videos. In cases where the slide background is white, such as in *Rozenblit*, savings can increase to 19% on the Galaxy S and 22% on the Galaxy S2. The other factor in such significant savings is also due to the fact that some videos, such as *Rozenblit* and *Berman*, have long periods where no slide was shown.

While the blue channel requires the most power, red and green combined still constitute a significant portion of energy. The only exception to this is the *Coates* talk due to the fact that the slides shown have a blue background (Table 2). Dimming out all colors (*Non-Text Black*) from the slide and non-slide background can reduce energy consumption to levels close to an entirely black video (*All Black*). In general, dimming out colors from non-bounding boxes tends to save a lot of energy as bounding boxes take up only a small percentage of the screen real estate.

5.3 Efficiency of Altering and Replacing Slides

Figure 12 shows the average power demand for the Galaxy S2 and the combination of the video alteration techniques: the video with all frames completely black (*All Black*); the video where the slide region was replaced by the entirely black side and the non-slide background was unaltered (*Black Slide*); the video where the slide region was replaced by the energy optimized side and the non-slide background was unaltered (*Backprojected*); and the original video without any alterations (*Full Color*).

The *Black Slide* is the upper bounds on what can be saved by recoloring only the slide, leaving the non-slide background unaltered, and can offer 80.9% on average of screen power demand reduction. Backprojection is very efficient offering 59.2% reduction in average display power which translates to 27.4% reduction in power demand of the entire phone. Further power reduction may be possible at the expense of lower color intensity of the text and images in the slide.

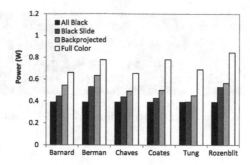

Fig. 12. Energy consumption of videos after slide backprojection on the Galaxy S2.

The efficiency of backprojecting white-on-black slides can be seen in the backprojected *Tung* video; which, despite the fact that the slide takes up only 41 % of the screen, uses only 9 % more energy than a totally black video. The savings are significant because the total area of the screen taken up by bullets is less than the 15 % that is taken up by the bounding boxes. Since the text was recolored rather than just keeping the original color of the whole region containing the text, the total area taken up by the text will have decreased as well. In other words, more pixels are blacked out and which increases the savings.

6   Conclusion

We have described a system that intelligently reduces energy consumption by replacing colors from less important regions of a lecture video. A key contribution is using slide-to-frame matching and slide semantic extraction to provide fine-grained understanding of content that can be exploited to enhance viewing and save energy. Subsequently, we have shown that removing colors from lecture videos of multiple lighting conditions is a viable method for saving a significant amount of energy consumed in mobile devices during playback. In addition, we have presented several methods to selectively remove varying degrees of different colors from portions of video frames. The resulting optimizations provided significant power reduction of displaying educational videos while minimizing the disruption of video quality by utilizing information about which areas of a video frame are the most informationally important.

Acknowledgments. This research was funded by the National Science Foundation under Grant No. 0844569 and the Microsoft Research Faculty grant.

References

1. Smith, A.: Mobile access 2010. Pew Internet & American Life Project, Washington, DC (2010)
2. MIT OpenCourseWare (2013). https://ocw.mit.edu/index.htm

3. UC Berkeley Extension Online (2013) https://learn.berkeley.edu
4. Open Yale Courses (2013). https://oyc.yale.edu
5. Coursera (2013). http://www.coursera.org
6. Udacity (2013). http://www.udacity.com
7. edX (2013). http://www.edx.org
8. Dong, M., Choi, Y., Zhong, L.: Power modeling of graphical user interfaces on oled displays. In: 46th ACM/IEEE Design Automation Conference, DAC'09, pp. 652–657 (2009)
9. Mahesri, A., Vardhan, V.: Power consumption breakdown on a modern laptop. In: Falsafi, B., VijayKumar, T.N. (eds.) PACS 2004. LNCS, vol. 3471, pp. 165–180. Springer, Heidelberg (2005)
10. Falaki, H., Govindan, R., Estrin, D.: Smart screen management on mobile phones (2009)
11. Flinn, J., Satyanarayanan, M.: Managing battery lifetime with energy-aware adaptation. ACM Trans. Comput. Syst. **22**(2), 137–179 (2004)
12. Park, S., Lee, Y., Lee, J., Shin, H.: Quality-adaptive requantization for low-energy mpeg-4 video decoding in mobile devices. IEEE Trans. Consum. Electron. **51**(3), 999–1005 (2005)
13. Kennedy, M., Venkataraman, H., Muntean, G.-M.: Energy consumption analysis and adaptive energy saving solutions for mobile device applications. In: Kim, J.H., Lee, M.J. (eds.) Green IT: Technologies and Applications, pp. 173–189. Springer, Heidelberg (2011)
14. Chen, X., Zheng, J., Chen, Y., Zhao, M., Xue, C.J.: Quality-retaining oled dynamic voltage scaling for video streaming applications on mobile devices. In: 2012 49th ACM/EDAC/IEEE Design Automation Conference, pp. 1000–1005. IEEE (2012)
15. Duan, L.-T., Guo, B., Shen, Y., Wang, Y., Zhang, W.L.: Energy analysis and prediction for applications on smartphones. J. Syst. Archit. **59**(10), 1375–1382 (2013)
16. Iyer, S., Luo, L., Mayo, R., Ranganathan, P.: Energy-adaptive display system designs for future mobile environments. In: MobiSys, pp. 245–258 (2003)
17. Harter, T., Vroegindeweij, S., Geelhoed, E., Manahan, M., Ranganathan, P.: Energy-aware user interfaces: an evaluation of user acceptance. In: Proceedings of the SIGCHI Conference on Human Factors in Computing Systems, pp. 199–206 (2004)
18. Wee, T.K., Balan, R.K.: Adaptive display power management for oled displays. In: Proceedings of the First ACM International Workshop on Mobile Gaming, pp. 25–30. ACM (2012)
19. Dong, M., Choi, Y., Zhong, L.: Power-saving color transformation of mobile graphical user interfaces on oled-based displays. In: Proceedings of the 14th ACM/IEEE International Symposium on Low Power Electronics and Design, pp. 339–342 (2009)
20. Chuang, J., Weiskopf, D., Möller, T.: Energy aware color sets. Comput. Graph. Forum **28**(2), 203–211 (2009). (Wiley Online Library)
21. Oled info (2011). www.oled-info.com/pentile
22. The SLIC browsing system (2013), http://slic.arizona.edu
23. Tung, Q., Swaminathan, R., Efrat, A., Barnard, K.: Expanding the point–automatic enlargement of presentation video elements. In: Assocation of Computing Machinery Multimedia, ACM MM (2011)

24. Fan, Q., Amir, A., Barnard, K., Swaminathan, R., Efrat, A.: Temporal modeling of slide change in presentation videos. In: IEEE International Conference on Acoustics, Speech and Signal Processing, ICASSP 2007, vol. 1, pp. I-989–I-992 (2007)
25. Winslow, A., Tung, Q., Fan, Q., Torkkola, J., Swaminathan, R., Barnard, K., Amir, A., Efrat, A., Gniady, C.: Studying on the move: enriched presentation video for mobile devices. In: 2nd IEEE Workshop on Mobile Video Delivery (2009)

An Un-tethered Mobile Shopping Experience

Venkatraman Ramakrishna[1]([✉]), Saurabh Srivastava[1], Jerome White[1],
Nitendra Rajput[1], Kundan Shrivastava[1], Sourav Bhattacharya[1],
and Yetesh Chaudhary[2]

[1] IBM India Research Laboratory, New Delhi 110070, India
{vramakr2, saurabhsrivastava, jerome.white, rnitendra,
kushriva, sav.accharya}@in.ibm.com
[2] Indian Institute of Technology, Kharagpur 721302, West Bengal, India
yetesh.ch@cse.iitkgp.ernet.in

Abstract. Smart phones with access to apps from online stores are ideal candidates to replace expensive hardware like PoS terminals for retail. A standard set of shopper and retailer apps can replace the conventional retailer IT setup in settings ranging from rural areas with low connectivity to dense urban areas. We describe how we built such a set of apps for mobile shoppers and retailers equipped only with smart phones and tablets, and who require little to no training to use them. These apps are flexible enough to be used by small shops with small inventories as well as large grocery chains. Our apps enable retailers to manage their inventories and finances, and shoppers to discover retailers, match shopping lists, and make purchases. We describe a user study of retailers in North India to understand the ecosystem in emerging markets, and ascertain their needs, helping us build a useful platform for mobile shopping.

Keywords: Mobile shopping · Mobile payment · Emerging market · User study

1 Introduction

"There's an app for that" was Apple's marketing slogan back in 2009, which tried to convey the impression that Apple devices and the apps running on them could support virtually any function desired by users. Though this slogan was the subject of jokes at the time, it was prescient in many ways. With other devices and operating systems (Samsung, Android, Microsoft, Windows, etc.) replicating Apple's smart mobile device success in the marketplace, we may indeed be heading towards a future where one can build an app for literally anything, and have it run on a combination of mobile devices, be they phones, tablets, or even spectacles (e.g., Google Glass) and watches.

Our focus is on the retail industry, which is still growing at a fast clip in emerging markets where the consumer base continues to expand and increase its purchasing power. Yet, retailing is a very competitive business with high barrier to entry because of the relatively large capital investment necessary at the outset. Economies of scale provide such capital in the developed markets. In emerging markets, research and data on the retail ecosystem, the needs of retailers, and the mechanisms to promote growth, is lacking. We conducted a user study in North India, an emerging market, to obtain

© Institute for Computer Sciences, Social Informatics and Telecommunications Engineering 2014
I. Stojmenovic et al. (Eds.): MOBIQUITOUS 2013, LNICST 131, pp. 409–421, 2014.
DOI: 10.1007/978-3-319-11569-6_32

exactly such data, and found that retail is predominantly carried out in small stores that almost exclusively use cash; inventory management and transactions are ad hoc, inefficient, and unreliable. Technology, i.e., hardware (e.g., PoS terminals) and software, is expensive and also requires reliable electricity and network connectivity; small corner shops and rural shops cannot afford this. Allowing retailers to run their shops using their personal mobile phones (which are ubiquitous, even in poor countries) or tablets will remove the primary entry barrier and provide a huge boost to the retail industry [9]. Even in the mature developed markets, enabling store management through mobile devices would allow the large shopping chains to expand at lower cost into smaller towns and rural areas through franchising.

Not only will mobile devices help retailers run and expand their business, they will also provide customers with a more seamless and richer shopping experience. Traditional online payment systems using credit and debit cards have been augmented by *mobile money* systems [1, 4–6, 8], which enable customers to make purchases using a handful of clicks. Yet such systems are not going to be popular, even in developed countries, unless compatible systems are used by retailers. Though such systems do exist, like Google Wallet [4], their adoption rate is low as they require the retailer to possess special hardware. If retailers were to run their stores out of their mobile devices, more customers would use mobile money mechanisms without being tied to a service provider. In emerging markets, where the banked population is a small subset of the cell phone-using population, telecom operator-provided money accounts help shoppers make reliable purchases easily [8]. Introducing computers into the shopping experience enables long-lived customer-retailer relationships, with loyalty points; such features are currently available only in high-end retail.

In this paper, we describe how we designed and implemented a suite of universal retailer management and shopping apps that requires no infrastructure other than mobile devices with the capability to run applications and to communicate with other devices. We show that the set of functions enabled by this suite is both minimal and complete for retail shopping scenarios. These apps can be used by shopkeepers and customers in a variety of settings (urban, semi-urban, rural, etc.) with intermittent to no connectivity. We also show how they can be operated easily by customers, shopkeepers and retail store clerks with no training. Scenarios are described in Sect. 2, and a related work survey in Sect. 3. The results of our user study to ascertain the needs of retailers in emerging markets are presented in Sect. 4. The design of our platform and application suite to realize such scenarios is described in Sect. 5, with implementation details in Sect. 6. We evaluate our platform in Sect. 7, and make concluding remarks in Sect. 8.

2 Motivating Retail Shopping Scenarios

We present below two representative retail scenarios, and discuss other examples.

2.1 At the Corner Shop

Peter needs to purchase grocery items that include milk, cereal, and spices. He walks toward the small grocery store in the neighborhood run by a retailer, John. At the store,

Peter picks some of the items he can find. Other items are currently unavailable, and John is too busy tending to his accounting and managing other customers to suggest alternative stores. In his hurry, Peter forgot to bring adequate money, and so has to leave behind some non-essential items. While returning home, Peter suddenly remembers that he forgot to purchase milk, one of the essential items on his list.

What we see above is a mildly complex shopping scenario, the result of which is far from optimal or satisfactory to shopper or retailer. Maintaining a list of essential items that Peter will not forget, matching those items with John's inventory, getting suggestions for alternative stores, paying John, and store inventory management for John, are tasks that can be easily done using computers and networks. John can enhance his relationships with faithful customers by maintaining persistent accounts for them and giving rewards and discounts. Automating these tasks will reduce the cognitive burden on users, and this does not require either party to spend much money as such tasks can easily be performed on the cheap smart phones they already possess.

2.2 At the Supermarket

John bikes toward the supermarket to do his groceries. The store is crowded, and it takes John some time to discover where many of the items he needs are kept. He then waits patiently in line at a PoS-enabled checkout counter. Just when his turn arrives, he remembers that he needed biscuits. The clerk tells him that biscuits are indeed in stock, but John does not have the patience to go through the whole process again. After he pays cash, the clerk hands him a discount coupon valid for a week. On the way to his bike, John loses the coupon, and with it, the discount he is entitled to.

As in the previous scenario, we see various tasks that can be automated but aren't. If the store possessed mobile devices capable of communication, John's phone could automatically communicate with them to determine what items are available and in what room and rack; a small store map could be exchanged as well. The store could also alert John about the presence and location of biscuits, an item he forgot. To safeguard John's discount offers, persistent customer records could be kept in-store and on John's phone; this would make transactions easier, more pleasant, and reliable.

2.3 Other Example Scenarios

The above examples roughly cover the range of retail businesses and customer shopping habits, especially in emerging markets, though one could think of enhancements. Other businesses could also benefit by automating provider-consumer interactions. The restaurant business is an example, where customers would love to be aware of all available choices in an ad hoc manner, and where restaurants would love to establish long-lived relationships with their patrons. Book stores are another example, where one often has to visit multiple stores to purchase all the required books. A store that proactively orders books, or places back-orders, for their faithful customers will see its business flourish. In the following sections, we show exactly what storeowners and shoppers need through field surveys, and design a universal set of shopper and retailer apps to realize the scenarios described in this section.

3   Related Work

Retail technology has been mostly driven by commerce, with little academic research.

3.1   Commercial Services

Square Register [5] is a specialized card-reader that allows merchants to accept card transactions via their mobile devices. Requiring such specialized hardware, though, makes this solution less likely to be adopted in small shops, especially in emerging economies. There are also several wallet services that allow users to pay for goods via their mobile phone; e.g., Google Wallet [4], Square Wallet [5], and Mobile Pay USA [6]. The merchant and the customer both have accounts with the respective service. When a transaction is made, the underlying service handles monetary exchange using pre-existing and verified traditional-bank details. Airtel Money [8] allows customers to pay bills, make purchases, and transfer money via their mobile device using USSD. Users setup an account with Airtel that is debited each time they make a transaction through their Airtel SIM card. Like Airtel Money, M-PESA [1] is another SMS- and USSD-based popular mobile money solution. Being a branchless banking service—users register and transact physical funds through a network of agents—M-PESA is deployed widely in the developing world. These mobile money solutions managed by telecom providers help ease the purchase process, but do not provide complete end-to-end shopping solutions like we do. We provide an extensible suite of mechanisms for shoppers and customers, of which seamless payment methods are but one aspect.

3.2   User Studies

A study by Medhi, Gautama, and Toyama compared mobile money user interfaces amongst low-literate users [2]. The authors studied usability, with respect to interface, of popular commercial mobile money services in several developing countries. Based on their initial ethnography, they developed and tested three interfaces across the target population and concluded that speech- and picture-based interfaces, as opposed to text-based UIs, were a more viable option for low-literate subscribers. A study of money practices in rural Ethiopia [7] revealed that existing mobile money research is biased toward technical contributions; ideally it should also consider users' monetary practices. Our ethnography-based implementation work is in line with this approach.

3.3   System Design

M-Cash is a mobile money transfer service proposed for low-resource environments [3]. Transactions are made via an SMS interface and handled, at the SMS gateway, by a web-service middleware. The authors give very little detail as to how the service is unique, and base their results on simulation rather than deployment. Hassinen et al. present a mechanism for mobile payment with real or virtual PoS systems [10]. While it does not focus on the PoS being on the mobile itself, it provides rich communication options, ranging from SMS to Bluetooth to IP based data transfer. Other solutions exist that utilize NFC and Bluetooth for money transfer [11, 12], but these are limited to the payment mechanism and do not support the entire shopping experience that has inventory, cash register, loyalty points, etc. Zdravkovic discusses a wireless PoS terminal [15] that does not incorporate inventory and billing features. Massoth and Paulus outline an inventory management system where the Blackberry platform is used to communicate latest sales information to a centralized server, but they do not support interaction with a customer's device for billing [13]. The usability aspects of mFerio [14], which facilitates mobile payments through NFC and physical touch, were studied in a controlled lab environment using Singapore undergraduates. It is hard to say if their solution would be suitable for a low literate population.

4 User Study

To understand the current ecosystem of small, medium and larger enterprises, we conducted a field study with 28 small- to medium-scale businessmen in two cities in North India: Delhi, a large city, and Lucknow, a smaller one. Five were college graduates, 9 were educated until Class 12 (K-12 system of Education), and the remaining 14 were illiterate. All of them possessed mobile phones. Their businesses ranged from mid size grocery stores, betel shops, street-side food shops to medium size grocery stores. We were interested in the following: (i) *how* these businesses worked, (ii) *what types of transactions* they performed, (iii) *context* of individual businesses, and (iv) *challenges* faced in business? To help understand these questions we carried out a Contextual Enquiry: we interviewed each participant separately for an hour; data from the studies was collected and analyzed.

4.1 Study Findings

We found that *money management* is a prime concern for all businesses, irrespective of size. Our investigation revealed that tracking sales records and management of funds in spending, borrowing, repaying, investing, and savings was a routine task for most of the participants. Also, it was common for suppliers and retailers, especially in small-scale businesses, to sell certain items on credit. Though numerical literacy was good, most of the low literate retailers were dependent on the suppliers to maintain their inventories (Fig. 1a). Credit and borrowed amounts were communicated verbally and memorized instead of maintaining persistent records. Some businesses, like ice cream or roasted peanut sales, were seasonal. Family grocery stores were common. These were small to medium stores offering daily commodities such as milk, mineral water, flours, spices etc. Most of these retailers were socially connected to their customers and had high levels of trust in each other. The larger stores typically kept central servers, associated with the point of sales kiosks, to maintain sales records.

Most of the participants emphasized the importance of *expiry management* of the commodities they sold. We found that a supplier often lent commodities to a retailer on trial basis, and the retailer had an option either to pay the supplier or to return the

Fig. 1. (a) Supplier giving inventory list to low-literate shopkeepers. (b) The grocery stores

commodity if he could not sell it. Some study participants also reported that they maintained notebooks to keep a record of products that were close to expiration. We also observed that small and medium stores commonly maintained inventories that were lower than their estimated sales, especially of perishable goods; large stores with good supply chains maintained larger inventories. Other challenges faced by our study participants included a lack of information pertaining to new offers on products and workforce management. Some also desired to have multiple alternate vendors as fallback options and not depend on a single vendor to supply goods.

We categorized businesses based on their inventory volumes. Through an affinity mapping, we identified factors that influenced these categories of businesses. Our study results are summarized in Table 1. In the future, we intend to augment our knowledge of the Indian retail industry by surveying large chain stores. The results of our surveys give us insights into the features that are both useful and necessary in the apps we want to build, regardless of the size of the stores. In no particular order, these include: payment protocols, inventory management, and enabling many-to-many searches and associations between customers and stores.

Table 1. Factors influencing the retail business, categorized by inventory volume

	Perishable Inventory	Low Inventory	High Inventory
High Priority	Money management	Money management	Money management
	Expiry date management	Stock & estimation management	Expiry date management
	Stock & estimation management	Over-expected sales	Stock & estimation management
	Over-expected sales	Alternate vendors	New offers
Low Priority	Workforce management	New offers	Over-expected sales
	Alternate vendors	Expiry date management	Workforce management
	New offers	Workforce management	Alternate vendors

5   Platform Architecture and Protocol

The bare minimum hardware requirement is a device that can run application code, communicate, and have the ability to be discovered. Any smart mobile phone or tablet, from low-end devices to sophisticated ones, will satisfy these requirements. Our software is designed to provide a seamless and uniform user experience regardless of the OS, be it Android, Windows, iOS, Blackberry OS, etc. We use *app stores*, which virtually all smart phone system service providers support, to deploy and update our platform apps. For communication, we use application-layer protocols that are independent of the underlying communication technology, which can range from IR, Bluetooth, and Wi-Fi to the broader Internet.

Our retail shopping scenario platform enables: (i) discovery of, and association to, stores by customers, (ii) exchange of product information, and (iii) financial transactions. A minimal instance of the platform software can be logically split into three parts: (i) a *shopper app*, (ii) a *retailer app*, and (iii) a *shopper-retailer protocol*. In addition, these applications may choose to link with remote databases for reliable data backup and synchronization. For larger commercial manifestations of our platform, separate financial services gateways can be used to manage money accounts and mediate shopper-retailer financial transactions. This architecture supports a minimal and complete set of functions required by a retailer and a shopper to transact with, and maintain a long-term relationship with, each other.

5.1   Shopper Application

The shopper's device runs an all-purpose application designed to serve all the transaction functions its user requires (Fig. 2). In effect, the device acts as a location engine, a search engine, and a mobile wallet all rolled into one.

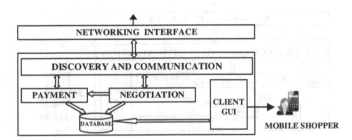

Fig. 2. Shopper application architecture

The *discovery and communication* module locates retail stores that are reachable from the shopper's device, identifying stores that it has a prior relationship with, and associating with a store as desired by the shopper or using a pre-configured policy. This module abstracts the low-level networking details from the core shopper app and offers a *send/receive* API for communication with the retailer app. Two of the abstracted details are: (i) fault tolerance: once associated, it tries to automatically reconnect if the original connection was broken or if the network adapter was reset, and (ii) protocol type: the devices may connect using Bluetooth, IR, WiFi, or even through the Internet, but the application logic does not change.

The *database* stores transaction and retailer information. This includes lists of products created by the shopper, known retailers, purchase history, and reward points. For additional reliability, this database may also sync with a remote database or cloud.

The *negotiation* module contains the core shopping app logic for querying retailers and directing transactions. Once an association is made with a store, it sends a shopping list to the store to determine what items are available and at what price. It also determines how payments are to be made (i.e., applying reward points and discount offers in addition to money transfer) before triggering a payment.

The *client interface* is an interactive GUI allowing a shopper to create, update, and remove shopping lists, select stores to associate with, and to approve payments. The interface can be tailored to suit specific devices and operating systems, without changing core application logic; if based on HTML, it will be platform independent.

Lastly, the *payment* module is responsible for completing a reliable financial transaction when triggered by the negotiation module. It is configured to conduct tri-party protocols with the retailer and a remote financial entity (e.g., bank) for payments through bank accounts or credit cards. For ease of use, it may store the user's account or credit card information (accessed securely using appropriate authentication) as well. Optionally, it may maintain a *mobile wallet* for the user if both shopper and retailer are configured to use a *mobile money* protocol [8].

5.2   Retailer Application

The retailer's device runs an all-purpose application designed to manage the store as well as conduct transactions with shoppers, as illustrated in Fig. 3 below.

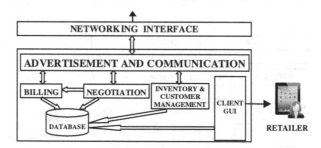

Fig. 3. Retailer application architecture

The *advertising and communication* module is the counterpart to the shopper's discovery module. It ensures that the app is discoverable on a wireless channel (IR, Bluetooth, WiFi, etc.) or through a public REST API on the web. It is responsible for receiving incoming connection requests, and hides the low-level details of the channel by exporting a *send/receive* API to the core application, whose logic is independent of the communication details. This module ensures that the store continuously advertises its presence, or decides when to advertise based on a pre-configured policy.

The *database* stores information about products sold by the retailer, and whether they are available or on back-order. Transaction records are maintained for every identifiable customer who has conducted mobile transactions with the store. For additional reliability, this database may periodically sync with a remote database or cloud. Alternatively, a large retail store with multiple checkout clerks (each with a mobile device) may have a database running on an in-store server, which is used to sync with the clerks' devices, using a standard 2-phase commit protocol for integrity.

The *management* module performs two functions. Through *inventory management*, the retailer can manage the products currently being sold, and set the positions (e.g., room, rack) they are placed in. It also allows the retailer to query distributors for information on products not currently at the store, and to place orders. *Customer management* allows the retailer to manage his customers' accounts, view customers' purchase history, and add or remove reward points and discount offers.

The *negotiation* module is the counterpart to the shopper's negotiation module. Upon receiving a shopping list, it matches the items with the products in its inventory, determines what items are available, and returns this to the shopper with associated pricing and reward points information. For a first time association, it automatically adds an account for the shopper based on his device ID. For products currently unavailable, a notification may be raised for the retailer to eventually act on, or an order automatically placed with a distributor if a suitable API is configured.

The *client interface* is an interactive GUI that enables a retailer or store clerk to view inventory, customer, billing, and purchase information. It also allows users to change inventory contents, update customer records, and process bill payments.

Lastly, the *billing* module, when triggered by the user, sends a shopper's app a payment request for billed items. Subsequently it takes part in a secure financial transaction with the shopper, the money being transferred to a pre-configured financial account. An invoice is sent to the shopper's app.

5.3   Shopping Protocol

The transaction protocol between the shopper and retailer proceeds as follows:

1. *Shopper*: discover a retailer's device and associate with it.
2. *Shopper*: create or edit a shopping list of product items.
3. *Shopper*: send list to retailer, requesting a match with its product inventory.
4. *Retailer*: perform match and return list of available items with prices to shopper.
5. *Shopper*: select items to purchase from the available products; if no items are selected, terminate the protocol; otherwise, send selections to retailer.
6. *Retailer*: look up shopper's selections, generate bill, and send it to shopper; simultaneously initiate payment request with financial back-end.
7. *Shopper*: examine bill and authorize/deny payment with financial back-end.
8. *Shopper* and *Retailer*: receive notification of successful payment, or failure.
9. *Retailer*: if payment was successful, send invoice to shopper with explicit mention of reward points or discount offers.

This is designed to be a minimal and generic protocol for transactions in our target scenarios. While augmentations could be made—more security features, for example—such discussion at this level of detail is beyond the scope of this paper.

We also do not allow the billing process to be completely automated, as we see the retailer's app waiting for a user in Step 6 above. This is because, in the most general case, stores must physically inspect items at checkout. Few stores currently have the technology to automate this process without being susceptible to shoplifting.

Information Representation: We currently encode the communicated information as JSON strings, though we plan to use XML in the future. Our shopper and retailer apps were developed together with a common vocabulary, which enabled each to understand the other's message semantics. This solution may not work when both sets of apps are developed independently. In the future, we plan to avoid this problem by publishing our data structure schemas in RDF and XML for public use and extension.

6 Application Suite Implementation

We implemented prototype Android applications for the shopper and the retailer. To run and test the apps, we used four phones running Android Linux v2.3 and communicating through Bluetooth: (i) Samsung Galaxy Ace S5830, (ii) Samsung Galaxy Y S5360, (iii) Samsung Galaxy Ace Plus S7500, and (iv) HTC Desire HD. The apps were developed on Eclipse using Java and HTML5. Though our current set of apps run only on Android, we developed the shopper application mostly in HTML5 using the IBM Worklight Studio 5.0.5; this will enable us to port the app easily to other mobile platforms (e.g., iOS). The SQLiteDatabase API was used for persistent local storage and MySQL Server 5.6 hosted on Apache Tomcat Server 7 for remote storage and sync; a REST API was exported for data lookup and manipulation. To process payments, we emulated a financial entity with the Cyclos 3.7 payment platform (http://www.cyclos.org/), running on IBM WebSphere Process Server 7.0.

6.1 Shopping Scenario Implementation

We walk through an instance of the shopping protocol (Sect. 5.3) involving retail '*Kamal Grocery*', showing selected screenshots. The shopper and retailer apps were installed as *.apk* files on two of the Android phones. The retailer app is started, and the product inventory loaded from the local database. Now the shopper app is started, and it displays the list of shopping lists created beforehand. The user walks towards the retailer's device. When he is within Bluetooth range, a notification appears asking the

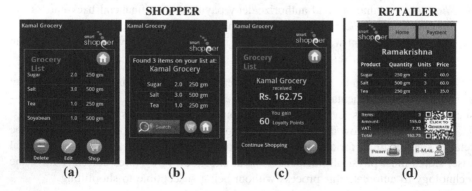

Fig. 4. Mobile shopping: querying and transaction protocol

shopper if he wishes to associate with the retailer. The shopper opts to do so and selects a list, whose contents appear on the screen (Fig. 4a). He then requests a match with the retailer's inventory, and sees the result on the screen following a silent protocol (Fig. 4b). He subsequently triggers a purchase and waits for the retailer's device to respond. The retailer loads the shopper's list and requests a payment (Fig. 4d). The payment is processed transparently through the Cyclos server, with an optional step where the shopper scans a retailer-generated QR-code of the bill, and an invoice appears on the shopper's device indicating a successful transaction (Fig. 4c). The retailer's inventory, purchase, and customer records are suitably updated.

6.2   Variations

A generic retail store was represented in the above scenario, to which we can add variations and extra features. If a shopper cannot find all the items he needs in a store, a search could be triggered for another that does contain those items, and a map of stores in the vicinity displayed. The only extra implementation this would involve is launching the maps app resident on the phone. Alternatively, the store itself may suggest other options to maintain customer loyalty; the only extra implementation this will involve is exposing new web service APIs for retailers to communicate with each other. As an extension, the shopper-retailer protocol could be augmented so that retailers may suggest alternative products or advertise new products to shoppers.

7   Evaluation and Discussion

Ease of use and low interaction time are critical factors from an end user's perspective for the shopper and the retailer app. Table 2 shows the number of clicks and average time that it takes a typical user to perform certain tasks. As seen in the table, most tasks can be performed in less than a minute, with very few clicks.

The combination of ease of use and low transaction times ensure that a low-skilled retailer can manage his store's PoS terminal, thereby reducing the customer waiting time and improve the customer experience. If PoS can be implemented on a mobile device, a large store can afford to have more checkout terminals. At the same time, low-end stores such as the one shown in Fig. 1 can feasibly use the app. In addition, large consumer products companies have informally indicated to us that they would be

Table 2. Number of clicks and average time taken for each task.

Task	# Clicks	Average time (s)
Shopper completes a transaction, given the list	5	10
Retailer creates bill from the shopper's list	2	4
Retailer creates fresh bill (5 items)	22	30
Retailer checks inventory	1	2
Retailer and shopper apps connect to each other	2	5
Retailer looks at shopping summary for a specific day	2	10

interested in using the sales data recorded at such stores to improve their sales and delivery by performing analytics that result in understanding the effect on sales for particular offers better or to understand gaps and rectify them faster.

From a larger perspective, our application suite provides the minimal functionality one needs to run a store. A shopper too has the minimal support and information he needs to purchase items without forgetting some or being unable to pay for lack of funds. Devices can use whatever communication technology is available. If WiFi or cell networks are not present, Bluetooth could be used; in our test runs, we discovered that shopper's devices reliably discovered retailers' devices close by. These apps can be ported to non-retail business scenarios easily in a short development cycle; only the information semantics and the application logic to process it must change.

8 Conclusion

The high cost of technology is a barrier to entry in retail, especially in emerging markets. As a result, most of the small scale businesses suffer from inefficiency and unreliability, as was evident from a user study we conducted in 2 cities in North India. In this paper, we demonstrated how we could eliminate the entry barrier, and make shopping easier and more reliable, by building universal shopper and retailer apps that perform a minimal set of required functions. The only hardware requirement is a smart phone or tablet, which is ubiquitous even in non-prosperous societies. Our apps can be adapted for other businesses with little investment of a developer's time. We plan to launch our apps in a variety of settings in India, both in small stores with the assistance of telecom operators, and in larger outlets with the help of commercial retailers. Data collected from these deployments will give us new insights into usage patterns. We will also conduct research in universal information representation mechanisms. This will enable new shopper apps to work with legacy store inventory systems, and new retailer apps to work with existing payment apps like Square.

References

1. Hughes, N., Lonie, S.: M-PESA: mobile money for the "Unbanked" turning cellphones into 24-hour tellers in Kenya. Innov. Technol. Gov. Globalization **2**(1–2), 63–81 (2007). MIT Press
2. Medhi, I., Gautama, S.N., Toyama, K.: A comparison of mobile money-transfer UIs for non-literate and semi-literate users. In: CHI 2009, Boston, MA, pp. 1741–1750 (2009)
3. Mirembe, D.P., Kizito, J., Tuheirwe, D., Muyingi, H.N.: A model for electronic money transfer for low resourced environments: M-cash. In: BROADCOM 2008, Pretoria, South Africa, pp. 389–393 (2008)
4. Google Wallet. http://www.google.com/wallet
5. Square Inc. (US). https://squareup.com
6. Mobile Pay USA. http://www.mobilepayusa.com
7. Mesfin, W.F.: Mobile information systems architecture for everyday money practice. In: MEDES 2012, Addis Ababa, Ethiopia, pp. 205–212 (2012)

8. Airtel Money. http://airtelmoney.in
9. Wagner, M.: Keys, money and mobile phone. In: Aroyo, L., Traverso, P., Ciravegna, F., Cimiano, P., Heath, T., Hyvönen, E., Mizoguchi, R., Oren, E., Sabou, M., Simperl, E. (eds.) ESWC 2009. LNCS, vol. 5554, p. 4. Springer, Heidelberg (2009)
10. Hassinen, M., Hyppönen, K., Haataja, K.: An open, PKI-based mobile payment system. In: Müller, G. (ed.) ETRICS 2006. LNCS, vol. 3995, pp. 86–100. Springer, Heidelberg (2006)
11. Monteiro, D.M., Rodrigues, J.J.P.C., Lloret, J.: A secure NFC application for credit transfer among mobile phones. In: CITS 2012, Amman, Jordan, pp. 1–5 (2012)
12. Pradhan, S., Lawrence, E., Zmijewska, A.: Bluetooth as an enabling technology in mobile transactions. In: ITCC 2005, Las Vegas, NV, USA, vol. 2, pp. 53–58 (2005)
13. Massoth, M., Paulus, D.: Mobile acquisition of sales operations based on a blackberry infrastructure with connection to an inventory and ERP management system. In: UBICOMM 2008, Valencia, Spain, pp. 413–418 (2008)
14. Balan, R.K., Ramasubbu, N., Prakobphol, K., Christin, N., Hong, J.: mFerio: the design and evaluation of a peer-to-peer mobile payment system. In: MobiSys 2009, Krakow, Poland, pp. 291–304 (2009)
15. Zdravkovic, A.: Wireless point of sale terminal for credit and debit payment systems. In: IEEE Canadian Conference on Electrical and Computer Engineering 1998, Waterloo, CA, pp. 890–893 (1998)

Gestyboard BackTouch 1.0: Two-Handed Backside Blind-Typing on Mobile Touch-Sensitive Surfaces

Tayfur Coskun[✉], Christoph Bruns, Amal Benzina, Manuel Huber,
Patrick Maier, Marcus Tönnis, and Gudrun Klinker

Technische Universität München, Boltzmannstr. 3, 85748 Munich, Germany
coskun@in.tum.de
http://ar.in.tum.de/Main/TayfurCoskun

Abstract. This paper presents a new and innovative gesture-based text-input concept designed for high-performance blind-typing on mobile devices with a touch-sensitive surface on their back-side. This concept is based on the Gestyboard concept which has been developed by the Technische Universität München for stationary use on larger multi-touch devices like tabletop surfaces. Our new mobile concept enables the user to type text on a tablet device while holding it in both hands, such as the thumbs are in the front of the tablet and the other eight fingers are in the back. The user can hence type text using these fingers on the back of the device. Although, the gesture-based finger movements are quite unfamiliar and the participants need to mentally rotate the QWERTY layout by −90 and 90 degrees respectively, our multi-session evaluation shows that despite the fact that their fingers are occluded by the tablet, our concept enables the users to blind-type and that they improve their performance in each session. Consequently, the user can use all ten fingers simultaneously to type text on a mobile touchscreen device while holding it comfortably in both hands. This implies that our concept has a high potential to yield to an high-performance text-input concept for mobile devices in the near future.

Keywords: User interfaces · Mobile blind typing · 10-finger-system · Touch-typing · Gesture · Touchscreen

1 Introduction

The fast and the wide spreading of tablet PCs in the recent years increased the need for high performance touchscreen-based text-input techniques. While a comfortable and ergonomic way to interact with a tablet is to hold the tablet PC in both hands while interacting with it, the user however is restricted to the usage of the thumbs which reduces the efficiency. Even if the keyboard is split in a way that all keys can be reached with the thumbs (e.g. a virtual split keyboard), the user's typing performance suffers from the latter restriction.

© Institute for Computer Sciences, Social Informatics and Telecommunications Engineering 2014
I. Stojmenovic et al. (Eds.): MOBIQUITOUS 2013, LNICST 131, pp. 422–434, 2014.
DOI: 10.1007/978-3-319-11569-6_33

The contribution of this work is to enable text-input for the eight free fingers on the back of a mobile device by positioning virtual invisible keys in an user-adaptive ergonomic manner on the backside of the tablet, rather than optimizing virtual keyboards with dictionaries (e.g. Swype [14]) or optimized layouts (e.g. 1Line keyboard [8]). Of course, using dictionaries for text-input improves the performance a lot. But our goal is to eliminate the real source for the lower text-input performance on touchscreens when compared to the classical hardware keyboard. The source for the lower text-input performance on touchscreens is the missing tactile feedback and hence the missing possibility to blind-type. Additionally, when holding the tablet in both hands, the user is restricted to the two thumbs to type text. Since, like the original Gestyboard concept, our new mobile concept is based on unique finger-based gestures for each group of keys defined by the 10-Finger-System, there is simply no need to observe the own fingers while typing, once the gestures are learned by heart or even better by the muscle-memory of the hands of the user. In the latter case, the user stops thinking about the movements and the hands are just performing what the user wants to type like it is the case for expert users on the classical hardware keyboard. The Gestyboard concept is described in more detail in Sect. 3. Our new concept for mobile use is described in Sect. 4.

2   Related Work

Providing a high performance touch-screen based mobile text-input system is a special challenge since the first smartphones started spreading out some years ago. Since then, the quality of the touchscreen itself (sensitivity, accuracy) as well as the developed text-input concepts improved a lot. But still, compared to the classical hardware keyboard, the user is very limited in the case of touchscreen based text-input concepts. One reason behind is that usually tactile feedback is missing on touchscreen. Hence, the user has to put more mental focus on the keyboard to be able to hit the correct keys with a naive button-based implementation of the touchscreen keyboard. Another reason is the limitation to one or two thumbs when the tablet is hold in one or two hands respectively or the limitation to a few fingers on one hand, while the tablet is hold in the other hand. This limitation of course has an negative impact on both, the speed and the accuracy of typing text. While the user can use all 10 fingers on the classical keyboard, it is very difficult and most of the time impossible to use all ten fingers to type. Some keyboard concepts focus on eliminating the first mentioned limitation, the missing tactile feedback by providing a hardware solution for providing some kind of haptic feedback in general. Since the accuracy of hitting the right button is naturally worse when compared to the classical keyboard, the currently best working solution is, instead of expecting the user to hit the correct key, to enhance the keyboard concept with a dictionary. Thus, the most successful keyboards on nowadays smartphones and/or tablets guess what the user wanted to type instead of what actually was typed. One example is called SwiftKey [13] and started to be developed in 2008. Swiftkey analyses personnel text of the user (E-Mails, SMS,...) to learn the style of typing of the specific user. This way, SwiftKey does not only guess what the user wanted to type it also predicts the next word the user intends to type by using the knowledge it learned from the user's text messages. Although it is very difficult to find some information about the average WPM of commercial keyboard concepts like the SwiftKey, we know from personnel reports that the users feel quite fast and successful when using it. Another famous example, also using a dictionary developed in 2011 is called Swype [14]. Instead of hitting buttons representing the keys the user performs a sliding gesture on the keyboard including all letters of the word the user wants to type. Swype then searches for all possible word combinations and suggests the correct word with a high probability. Both concepts even has been imported from some smartphone manufactures like Samsung or HTC and provide similar techniques on their own soft-keyboards. Although, the performance and the user acceptance of the mentioned keyboards is good and they also make sense for the use with smartphones, they are still not replacing the classical hardware keyboard. One reason for that is, that the users are used to the classical hardware keyboard for decades. Another reason is that the classical keyboard allows the user to type anything, even a sequence of letters which doesn't seem to make any sense and therefore does not exist in and dictionary. This is for example the case for typing passwords, writing code or just to chat in the user's own personalized way of writing like chatting or writing an E-Mail to a close friend or changing the language frequently.

For those reasons, we decided to additionally solve the second mentioned limitation of touchscreen-based text-input concept in the case of tablets, which is the limitation to one or both thumbs when holding a tablet in both hands (or to a few fingers when hold in one hand) and to enable the user to blind-type. It is well-known that a comfortable way of interacting with a tablet is to hold it in both hands and use the two thumbs to interact with the device. Microsoft provides for example a split keyboard on Windows 8 which can be reached with the thumbs. They use a previous study, to determine the positions of the keys of the splitted keyboard which was conducted in 2012 [11]. Swiftkey also provides on option to split the keyboard in two parts. While this way of interacting with the tablet is very comfortable, 8 fingers are wasted by just holding the tablet and the least precise fingers, the thumbs, are used to interact with the tablet. This of course makes sense, since first nowadays tablets usually does not provide a touch sensitive surface on the back side of the device and second the tablet occludes the fingers of the user, hence making it difficult to use them to interact with the tablet. However, devices with touch sensitive surfaces on their back indeed exists already (e.g. Playstation Vita [12]) and we expect, that this technology will be more distributed in future. Another example for enabling touch on the back of very small devices has been published in 2009 from Baudisch et al. [2]. For this, small prototype devices were built and a cursor is used to visualize the position of the users finger, hence enabling the user to interact with UI elements on the front side of the device. This way, Baudisch et al. also provides a technique solving the second problem, the occlusion of the fingers.

Wigdor et al. [16] investigated backside interaction features with a pseudo transparent display which is a similar approach but for tablets visualizing the whole fingers of the users, not only it's position with a cursor. The fingers on the back of a tablet device were shown as half-transparent shadows to ease input mapping. In their studies, besides other touch controls, Wigdor et al. implemented a simple button based keyboard. The keyboard was either split like conventional keyboards, or split and reoriented to better fit to the orientation of the hands. The participants were able to hit the buttons behind the see-through tablet. In our Back-Type solution, we also use cursors to visualize the finger's position on an external screen and also reorient the rotation of the keyboard. However, well trained users should be able to interact with our text-input concept, even without any visualization in future. For this, the Blind-Typing text-input concept for large touchscreens like tabletop called Gestyboard [4] can be adapted. Kim et al. [6] installed a physical keyboard on the back side of a smartphone with small buttons representing the QWERTY keyboard and conducted an evaluation. An average speed of 15.3 WPM were with an error rate of 12.2 %. Also in 2012 Wolf et al. [17] conducted a study in which the effect of gestures on the back of a tablet device were examined. For this, they attached two IPads to each other for evaluation purporses.

Since our mobile concept uses the original Gestyboard concept to provide unique finger gestures, it is described in further detail in Sect. 3. Afterwards, in Sect. 4, our mobile and adapted version of the Gestyboard concept and the difference to the original Gestyboard are explained.

3   The Original Gestyboard Concept for Stationary Use

This work adapts the Gestyboard concept which has been developed and evaluated by the Technische Universität München [4] in 2011. The 10-finger-system[1] and the QWERTY layout are used to define individual gestures for each finger. This way, each finger is only able to type the set of letters defined by the 10-finger-system. For convenience, especially for the people not mastering the 10-finger-system, a visual representation of the set of letters was displayed during the evaluation below each associated finger. Figure 1 shows the original representation of the Gestyboard. It is important to note that the visual representation of the keys actually is not the keyboard itself. All the keys are activated through unique finger gestures instead of hitting a button. In fact, for the final usage of the Gestyboard it is planned to hide the keyboard completely. It is automatically activated by touching the screen with 10 fingers and the user can just start typing on the interface of any application.

Key activation. The finger gestures can be either a tap or a sliding. To activate the home row key letters ('a', 's', 'd', 'f', and 'j', 'k', 'l', ';'), the user performs a tap gesture with the associated finger. This means, even though if the user

---

[1] This is also called "touch typing" in literature. However, to avoid confusion due to the association with the touchscreen, we use the wording "10-finger-system" instead.

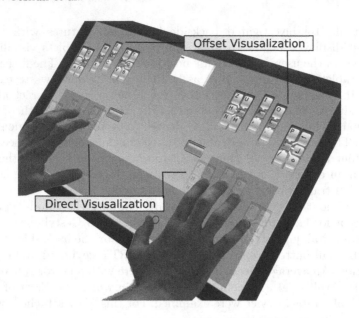

Fig. 1. The Gestyboard's visualisation

accidentally hits, for example, the visual representation of the letter 's' tapping the left pinky finger, the system will still correctly type the expected letter 'a'. In fact, tapping with the left pinky finger is a unique gesture associated to the letter 'a'. Consequently, the user can close the eyes and type an 'a' easily without worrying about the exact position of its visual representation. To activate the remaining neighboring letters, a sliding gesture has to be performed with the associated finger into the associated direction. Finally, to type a "space", all fingers have to simultaneously perform a tap gesture. This is actually the only difference to the 10-finger-system. Hence leading to an automatic reset of all fingers positions between the words. Figure 2 gives an overview about all gestures in the 2.0 version of the original Gestyboard concept. The space activation gesture has been changed to perform a tap gesture with all ten fingers. The initial reason behind was the low tracking precision of the touchscreen when the thumbs were touching the screen. The touch point detected by the system was alternating between two different positions below the thumbs which leaded to multiple touch-up and touch-down events. Our system interpretes this as a tap with the thumb which leads to wrong a space keystroke. The hand gesture were accepted by the users very well, because of that we kept this gesture for the backtouch version of the Gestyboard. As a positive side effect, the thumbs are free for any interaction with the active interface of the tablet device.

The scope of the original concept. The original Gestyboard concept is designed to be used on a large multi-touch device to replace the classical hardware keyboard. This goal could not be reached yet according to the authors, but it could be shown that the idea of building a touch-based text-input concept based on the

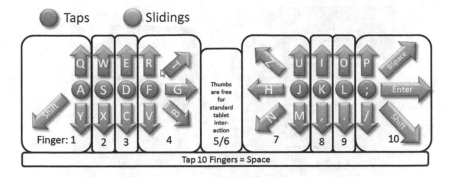

Fig. 2. The Gestyboard's gestures overview in version 2.0. Fx = Finger x.

10-finger-system works [5] and enables experienced users to blind-type. Since this concept benefits from the experience with the 10-finger-system, people lacking this experience are quite slow and error prone when using it the first time. However, most of the 42 participants of the first evaluation of the Gestyboard concept liked it and were motivated to learn it. Due to this fact, a second study followed consisting of 6 sessions with 1000 characters each. The results showed that people could reach more than 20 wpm (words per minute) with less than 2 % error rate. Encouraged by those promising results of the second iteration of the Gestyboard, our adapted concept for mobile use tackle the main challenge of allowing the user to blind type on the back-side touch surface while the fingers are not visible. As mentioned earlier, the goal of this paper is to investigate, if the Gestyboard concept can be adapted in a way people can use it on the back side of the device and to find out how they perform in multiple test sessions.

4   Gestyboard BackTouch: Transferring the Gestyboard Concept to the Back of a Mobile Device

As stated earlier, the Gestyboard concept enables the user to blind-type on a touchscreen. This concept can therefore be transformed and adapted to blind-type with the free 8 fingers on the back-side of a tablet device while holding it in both hands. The direct effect of this transfer on the users is the need to mentally rotate by $-90°$ the left half side of the keyboard and by $90°$ the right half side. Additionally, both sides of the keyboard have to be vertically mirrored (see Fig. 3). This means, that the keyboard is transformed the same way as the hands of the user. Consequently, the keyboard layout remains aligned to the fingers' orientation.

5   First Gestyboard BackTouch Prototype

Compared to the original Gestyboard, the finger movements of our adapted version are apparently more challenging. This emerges from the modification of

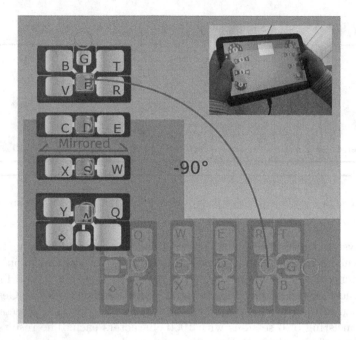

Fig. 3. The visual and mental adaptation of the Gestyboard concept and the resulting concept.

the QWERTY layout as shown in Fig. 3. Our first goal then is to see whether people are able to accommodate to the adapted concept. To be able to answer this question, an Android application has been developed for the Asus Transformer pad [1]. For evaluation purpose, the tablet is hold in a way that the front side of the device, i.e. the display, is on the back and hence is not anymore facing the holder. This way, the touchscreen of the device can be used to track the fingers' movements. For the final usage of course, a tablet with a touch sensitive surface on the back should be used. The gesture parameters are sent to the original Gestyboard application. Instead of reacting on the input of a directly attached touchscreen, our adapted version reacts on the data received from the network. This way, the Android tablet becomes a remote controller for the Gestyboard. For the final usage, the Gestyboard logic should be transferred to the tablet of course to have real mobile flexibility. Additionally, we added the capability to rotate and mirror the visualization of the key groups like described in Sect. 4. This way, the users see the visualization of their fingers' movements and the activated letters on an external monitor with the server running on it. This setup is also used during our evaluation and can be seen in Fig. 4.

This setup is a testing prototype. The future vision is to use a tablet with a touchscreen on the front side and a touch input system (e.g. a multitouch touchpad) on the back side. Additionally, it is planned to provide an option to

Fig. 4. Using an Android tablet as a remote controller for the original Gestyboard Prototype. The tablet is rotated to be able to test the concept.

disable the visualization of the finger movements and the gestures completely for expert users.

6   Evaluation

In this section we first describe the evaluation procedure and the participants in Sect. 6.1. The results are then presented in Sect. 6.2.

6.1   Procedure and Participants

It was planned to perform three evaluation sessions with ten computer scientist students for this initial test. After performing those three sessions with ten students, four among those ten asked us if they may continue with the evaluation to further improve their performance. Consequently, we decided to add another three sessions for those four participants.

The task of each session was to type 1.000 letters chosen from MacKenzie's phrase sets for text input evaluation purposes [10]. Those sentences all represent the letter frequency of real English sentences. Tipp10 software tool [15] was used to present and analyze the input data. This tool automatically collects useful data representing the user's performance in general and for each finger specifically and stores them in a database for further analysis. Finally, we asked

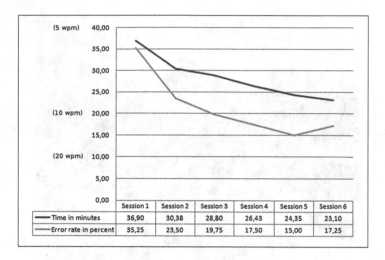

		Session 1	Session 2	Session 3	Session 4	Session 5	Session 6
Time in minutes		36,90	30,38	28,80	26,43	24,35	23,10
Error rate in percent		35,25	23,50	19,75	17,50	15,00	17,25

Fig. 5. Average time per session (minutes), error rate (percent), and the average speed (WPM)

the participants to fill out the System Usability Scale (SUS) [3] questionnaire and conducted a short interview.

6.2 Results

This section presents the quantitative evaluation results. The results are then discussed and interpreted in Sect. 7.

Performance. We obtained from Tipp10 tool the following quality measures: Typing speed, overall error rate, and the error rate per Finger. Figure 5 shows the average time needed to type 1000 letters per session in minutes (dark color curve) and the percentage of the error rate (light color curve). The Words per Minute (WPM) represents the average speed. The average speed in the first session among our 10 participants is 5.4 WPM while the error rate is 35.26 %. However, the speed is gradually increasing and the error rate is decreasing throughout the sessions. In the last session, the 4 remaining participants reached an increased average speed of 8.6 WPM and a reduced error rate of 17.52 %. Thus, despite the fact, that the tablet is occluding the fingers of the user and although there is no haptic feedback at all, our test users were able to blind-type with the 8 Fingers behind the tablet.

Error Rate per Finger. Figure 6 is showing the error rate in percentage per finger. The lowest error rates were reached with the home row keys (tap gesture) and the keys which are directly above or below them (up and down sliding gestures). The highest error rates were made with the keys placed diagonally to the home row keys (diagonal sliding gestures).

System Usability Scale. In this section we introduce the SUS values gathered from the SUS questionnaires for each participant which were filled out after

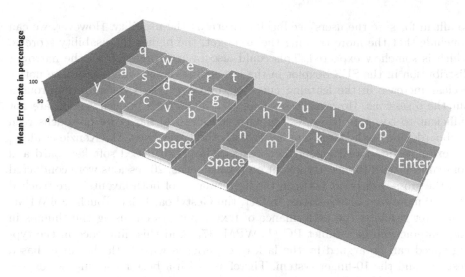

Fig. 6. Error rate per finger in percent.

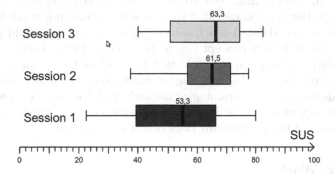

Fig. 7. System Usability Scale for each participant.

each of the three sessions to learn about the subjective initial usability rating of the users. SUS score is represented by a value ranging from 0 to 100, where 100 is the best score. Figure 7 shows the SUS scores for the first three sessions. We can clearly observe an overall increase in the SUS mean score throughout the sessions. Indeed, SUS score increased from a mean score of 53.5 in the first session to a mean score of 61.5 in the second one to reach finally a score of 63.3 in the third session. We also notice in the SUS boxplot that the distribution of SUS scores among users is getting narrower throughout the sessions and the maximum SUS score exceeded a value of 80 in the third session.

7   Discussion

From Sect. 6.2 we can observe two main conclusions. First, we notice that despite the observed increase, SUS score is still quite average, which makes it difficult to affirm for sure the users' feedback concerning the usability. However, we can conclude that the more training the users get, the higher the usability score is, which is somehow expected. This could also be interpreted from the narrower distribution in the SUS boxplot in the last two sessions. And second, we notice a clear increase in the learning curve of the Gestyboard BackTouch throughout the 6 sessions. However, 6 sessions with 255 letters in each session are not sufficient to compare these results with the classical hardware or touchscreen keyboards due to the large familiarity with the latter ones. MacKenzie et al. [9] for example developed an soft keyboard with an optimized soft keyboard and compared it with the qwerty layout on touchscreens. 20 sessions were conducted and the cross-over point between the performance of both layouts were reached after 10 more intensive sessions. In fact, the Gestyboard BackTouch (8.6 WPM) is not yet reaching the performance of text input system using the thumbs in edge interaction on a tablet PC (11 WPM) [7]. And this difference in the typing speed can be argued by the lack of experience with both the finger based gestures and the 10-finger-system. Therefore, with a better training, we expect the performance of the text input system using the thumbs to be surpassed by our solution, and the limitation to the thumbs interaction to be eliminated. Thus, although the performance in 6 quick sessions could not reach the performance of the well-established touch screen keyboards yet, we could prove that the Gestyboard stationary concept can be transferred to the back of the tablet device and that the user are able to adapt themselves to the innovative 10(or 08)-Finger-Based gestures. To reach the maximum speed possible, we expect our users need approximately a training of around 10.000 letters. This way, whole word gesture-sequences can be learned by muscle-memory, which will increase the performance of the Gestyboard BackTouch substantially.

8   Future Work

We will also correct some shortcomings of the implementation observed during the evaluation, like decreasing the load of exchanged finger gestures' events, to enhance our solution. Additionally, a long term and blind type evaluation will be performed in future. The next step is to provide a very simple kind of haptic feedback to the back of the tablet. For this, the tablet will be enhanced with a protection foil for touchscreens and the "'path"' of the finger gestures will be cut-out from this foil, hence providing haptic feedback. Haptic feedback showed to be very useful and efficient in improving the typing speed performance. If this simple kind of haptic feedback works, an ergonomically optimized hardware solution for touch-input on the back side of a tablet device would make sense and has the potential to become a high-performance and comfortable way of typing text on a tablet device without the need to occlude half of the limited tablet screen with a virtual keyboard. Additionally, it is planned to compare the performance of the Gestyboard BackTouch on different Android devices. The reason behind is that there was a noticeable difference in terms of accuracy when we tried to switch from the first ASUS Transformer to its next version, the

ASUS Transformer Prime. Unexpectedly, it was more difficult to use our concept on the newer device then it has been on the previous one, which has been used in our evaluation. It seems like that the new device was too thin and too light to provide the same grip as the previous one.

References

1. Asus. Asus transformer pad tf300t, 02 August 2012. http://www.asus.de/Tablet/TransformerPad/
2. Baudisch, P., Chu, G.: Back-of-device interaction allows creating very small touch devices. In: Proceedings of International Conference on Human Factors in Computing Systems, pp. 1923–1932. ACM (2009)
3. Brooke, J.: SUS: a 'quick and dirty' usability scale. Usability evaluation in industry (1996)
4. Coskun, T., Artinger, E., Pirritano, L., Korhammer, D., Benzina, A., Grill, C., Dippon, A., Klinker, G.: Gestyboard: a 10-finger-system and gesture based text input system for multi-touchscreens with no need for tactile. Techreport, Technische Universitaet Muenchen (2011)
5. Coskun, T., Artinger, E., Pirritano, L., Korhammer, D., Benzina, A., Grill, C., Klinker, G.: Gestyboard: a 10-finger-system and gesture based text input system for multi-touchscreens with no need for tactile feedback (poster). In: SIGCHI - APCHI 2012 (2012)
6. Kim, H., Row, Y.-K., Lee, G.: Back keyboard: a physical keyboard on backside of mobile phone using qwerty. In: CHI '12 Extended Abstracts on Human Factors in Computing Systems, CHI EA '12, pp. 1583–1588. ACM, New York (2012)
7. Korhammer, D.: Development of a single touch user interface for the efficient and intuitive completion of forms in the area of emergency rescue services. Master's thesis, Technische Universitt Mnchen, Munich, Germany, GE, October 2010
8. Li, F., Guy, R., Yatani, K., Truong, K.: The 1line keyboard: a qwerty layout in a single line. In: Proceedings of the 24th Annual ACM Symposium on User Interface Software and Technology, pp. 461–470. ACM (2011)
9. MacKenzie, I., Zhang, S.: The design and evaluation of a high-performance soft keyboard. In: Proceedings of the SIGCHI Conference on Human Factors in Computing Systems: the CHI is the Limit, pp. 25–31. ACM (1999)
10. MacKenzie, I.S., Soukoreff, R.W.: Phrase sets for evaluating text entry techniques. In: CHI '03 Extended Abstracts on Human Factors in Computing Systems, CHI EA '03, pp. 754–755. ACM New York (2003)
11. Odell, D., Chandrasekaran, V.: Enabling comfortable thumb interaction in tablet computers: a windows 8 case study. In: Proceedings of the Human Factors and Ergonomics Society Annual Meeting, vol. 56, pp. 1907–1911. SAGE Publications (2012)
12. Playstation. Playstation Vita, 02 May 2012. http://de.playstation.com/psvita/
13. Swiftkey. Swiftkey, 11 June 2013. http://www.swiftkey.net/en/
14. Swype. Swype, 02 April 2012. http://www.swypeinc.com
15. Tipp 10. Tipp 10, 02 April 2012. http://www.tipp10.com/de/

16. Wigdor, D., Forlines, C., Baudisch, P., Barnwell, J., Shen, C.: Lucid touch: a see-through mobile device. In: Proceedings of the 20th Annual ACM Symposium on User Interface Software and Technology, pp. 269–278. ACM (2007)
17. Wolf, K., Müller-Tomfelde, C., Cheng, K., Wechsung, I.: Pinchpad: performance of touch-based gestures while grasping devices. In: Proceedings of the Sixth International Conference on Tangible, Embedded and Embodied Interaction, TEI '12, pp. 103–110. ACM, New York (2012)

Passive, Device-Free Recognition on Your Mobile Phone: Tools, Features and a Case Study

Stephan Sigg[1]([⊠]), Mario Hock[2], Markus Scholz[3], Gerhard Tröster[4],
Lars Wolf[1], Yusheng Ji[5], and Michael Beigl[3]

[1] TU Braunschweig, Braunschweig, Germany
{sigg,wolf}@ibr.cs.tu-bs.de
[2] Karlsruhe Institute of Technology, Karlsruhe, Germany
mario.hock@student.kit.edu
[3] Chair for Pervasive Computing Systems (TecO), KIT, Karlsruhe, Germany
{scholz,michael}@teco.edu
[4] Electronics Laboratory, ETH Zurich, Zurich, Switzerland
troester@ife.ee.ethz.ch
[5] National Institute of Informatics, Tokyo, Japan
kei@nii.ac.jp

Abstract. We investigate the detection of activities and presence in the proximity of a mobile phone via the WiFi-RSSI at the phone. This is the first study to utilise RSSI in received packets at a mobile phone for the classification of activities. We discuss challenges that hinder the utilisation of WiFi PHY-layer information, recapitulate lessons learned and describe the hardware and software employed. Also, we discuss features for activity recognition (AR) based on RSSI and present two case studies. We make available our implemented tools for AR based on RSSI.

Keywords: Activity recognition · Passive device-free recognition

1 Introduction

In urban areas, a mobile device is constantly exposed to (possibly encrypted) communication. In contrast to traditional communication, where such data is considered as noise or congestion, we exploit implicit information on environmental situations carried by the signal strength fluctuation of overheard packets.

Fluctuation on WiFi RSSI might indicate presence, the number of people around or even activities conducted in proximity (cf. Fig. 1).

Localisation of objects and individuals [11] as well as the classification of activities [13] or crowd counting [15] has been considered recently. We distinguish between systems utilising software-defined-radio (SDR) devices to sample the fluctuation in a received signal and systems leveraging information available from received data packets. In the former case, due to the higher sampling frequency and additional information available, the recognition accuracy is generally higher. However, these systems require specialised SDR devices.

© Institute for Computer Sciences, Social Informatics and Telecommunications Engineering 2014
I. Stojmenovic et al. (Eds.): MOBIQUITOUS 2013, LNICST 131, pp. 435–446, 2014.
DOI: 10.1007/978-3-319-11569-6_34

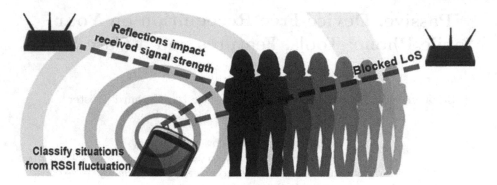

Fig. 1. Illustration of the recognition of activities via RSSI fluctuation

We recognise activities on a single device (a mobile phone) from packets broadcast by a transmitter not under our control (a WiFi access point (AP)). In particular, we investigate the frequency of received packets and the distance between the receiver and the passive subject monitored performing activities as well as the impact of utilising RSSI from multiple APs. The contributions are

(1) the presentation and discussion of Python-tools to visualise and process captured RSSI data for the recognition of environmental situations
(2) a discussion of accuracy achieved from RSSI sampled on a mobile phone
(3) an implemented toolchain for RSSI-based device-free passive recognition

This is the first study to demonstrate the recognition of activities in a passive, device-free, RSSI-based system and the first to leverage an off-the-shelf phone.

2   RF-based Device-Free Recognition

The recognition of movement, activities and gestures from RF-channel features induced by individuals in proximity not equipped with a transmit or receive device is generally referred to as device-free-radio-based recognition [10,11,13].

For instance, Sigg et. al recognise activities from the fluctuation of a continuous signal in [12]. The authors utilise the distance between signal peaks, the RMS, the third central moment and the entropy of a received signal as distinguishing features. With multiple receive antennas, also multiple activities conducted simultaneously can be distinguished [13]. Although Adith et al. demonstrated that time diversity can compensate for missing spatial diversity in a single antenna system [1], multiple antennas generally enable advanced recognition techniques. For instance, Hong et. al distinguish a moving individual at four different locations by applying random matrix theory on the received signal vectors from multiple antennas [2]. Pu and others demonstrated the accurate distinction of gestures via micro-Doppler variations from narrow-band signals [4,7].

These studies use highly accurate information on the wireless channel obtained by SDRs. Such hardware is typically missing in consumer mobile devices.

Focusing instead on RSSI fluctuation which is commonly available at contemporary wireless devices, Patwari and others estimated the breathing frequency of an individual from the RSSI of packets exchanged by surrounding nodes [6]. Each node in a token-passing protocol transmitted packets at about 4 Hz (resulting in packet transmission at 80 Hz when considering all nodes). Authors have predicted the count of up to 10 stationary or moving individuals [15] from RSSI within a field of sensor nodes. Other studies consider the detection of activities (*standing, sitting, lying, walking* and *empty*) from RSSI in a sensor network [8]. These systems utilise dedicated transmit and receive nodes and therefore have full control on the size, payload and frequency of packets transmitted [9].

In a passive, mobile phone-based system, channel access is restricted to the RSSI or other link quality indicators. These values are computed in the wireless interface at the receiver with every incoming packet. Clearly, this means that the sampling rate and the accuracy of the available data is severely reduced.

Another challenge is the access to the WiFi hardware since firmware with access to WiFi parameters is sparse. Also, standard mobile phone operating systems prevent root access to the phone's hardware, which is required to run the interface in monitor mode. More severe even, most handsets utilise the same chipset family (e.g. Broadcom bcm4329, bcm4330(B1/B2), bcm4334, bcm4335) for which the default firmware does not provide access to the desired information.

The use of an external antenna would mitigate these problems[1]. However, since this solution considerably extends the dimensions and complexity of the hardware utilised, we instead used a modified firmware for the above mentioned Broadcom chipset family that allows to run a WiFi interface in monitor mode [3].

We installed this firmware on a Nexus One running Cyanogen mod 7.2 and used tcpdump on the interface in monitor mode to capture RSSI of received packets. In monitor mode, no data can be transmitted so that no impact can be taken on the frequency of received packets. We can, however, adjust the channel monitored and utilise multiple APs on the same channel.

To-date, there is no study on passive device-free RF-based AR that leverages RSSI from environmental sources not under the control of the system. Moreover, there is no such system running on a mobile phone. We report our experiences in designing such a system and discuss challenges encountered.

With RF-based recognition on mobile phones, RF-based sensing can be broadly applied for the recognition on hardware we all carry around constantly.

3   Tools for RSSI-based Activity Recognition

We developed tools to process RSSI data. All tools are written in Python and are available for download[2]. They consist of multiple loose coupled components which are glued together by importing them into an encasing python script, that defines the workflow (cf. Fig. 2). The tools cover the following tasks:

---

[1] https://github.com/brycethomas/liber80211/blob/master/README.md
[2] All tools are available at http://www.stephansigg.de/Mobiquitous2013.tar.gz

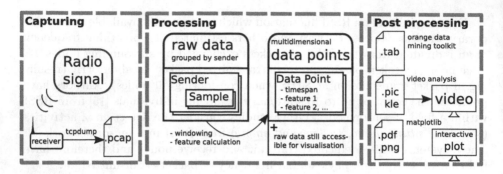

Fig. 2. Schematic overview on the functionality and workflow of our tools

- Obtain RSSI data and other meta-data from *pcap files*
- Classification, filtering and grouping of packet-data (from the pcap files)
- Feature calculation
- Feature export for the *orange* data mining toolkit[3]
- Graphical analysis of features and raw data
- Video analysis of features and raw data

Now we describe how these tasks are achieved and how to reuse components.

3.1   The Pcap Parser

An external capturing tool should be used to record traces of the radio data. It is important to use a WiFi adapter in *monitor mode* since otherwise it performs Ethernet emulation; radio specific information, like RSSI values, are not accessible then. We assume that captured traces are stored in the *.pcap* format.

The pcap files are read by the component *Pcap_Parser.py*. The function *Pcap_Parser.parse* takes a pcap-filename and optionally the number of packets to read, as input. It returns a dictionary[4] indexed by the sender mac address and storing objects of type *Storage_Classes.Sender*, defined in *Storage_Classes.py*. Such object holds metadata[5] about senders and the samples gained from them: *Storage_Classes.Sample* stores RSSI, timestamp, packet type and data rate.

The parsing itself is done by the external library *pcapy*[6] which interfaces *libpcap*[7]. It is also capable of live packet capturing.

---

[3] http://orange.biolab.si/

[4] A *dictionary* (or *associative array* is a python data type holding key-value pairs.

[5] Sender metadata: Type [station, access point, unknown]; Mac Address; SSID

[6] http://corelabs.coresecurity.com/index.php?action=view&type=tool&name=Pcapy

[7] http://www.tcpdump.org/

3.2   Data Grouping and Feature Calculation

Since the pcap parser clusters the data by sender and determines the types of these senders, APs with the highest packet count can be picked easily.

Based on the timestamps, samples can be grouped to *units*. Units are non-overlapping and contain all samples received in a fixed timespan. This can be used to normalize non-uniform sample rates; units that contain too few samples can also be dropped. Timestamp-based annotation data can be assigned to the respective units, too. These steps are implemented in the *Data_Grouping.py* component within the function *Data_Grouping.build_units*.

Further grouping can be done with the function *Data_Grouping.windowing*. This function takes a list of units, the desired window size and a boolean value determining possible overlap. Overlapping windows have an offset of one unit. Feature calculation is based on these windows. Several *features* are already implemented in the *Features.py* component, including: *mean, variance, sign*. Multiple features can be combined to one (multidimensional) data point by the function *Features.calculate_features*. It returns a list of *Data_Classes.Data_Point*.

Finally, units, windows and data points can be stored using Python's *pickle* module[8]. The later described video analysis tool takes this as input.

3.3   Visualization and Export

The calculated features, as well as the raw RSSI data can be plotted by the component *Visualization.py*. For this, the external library *matplotlib*[9] is used. It comes with an interactive plotting mode and various export modules.

Figure 3 displays the interactive plotting mode; in Fig. 3a the whole recording (5 min) is displayed, Fig. 3b shows a zoomed-in part (13 s). PDF-exports of features and raw data is supported. The module *Orange_Export.py* exports the features for post-processing in the *orange* data mining toolkit.

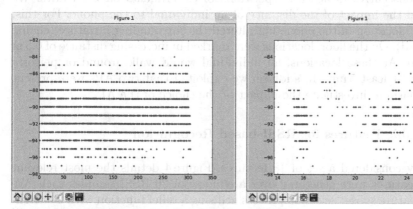

(a) Recorded RSSI data of a complete file   (b) Subset of the same file zoomed in

Fig. 3. Visualisation of RSSI raw data in the interactive plot

[8] http://docs.python.org/2/library/pickle.html
[9] http://matplotlib.org/

3.4   Video Analysis Tool

Even recognition algorithms based on machine learning depend on human expert knowledge. A set of meaningful features is chosen manually and calculated over the raw data in advance. To choose such features a human expert has to gain knowledge on how the information about the different states (e.g. performed activities) are contained in the data. The video analysis tool is supposed to help with this task.

By observing the evolution of raw data as a video stream, a human can develop an intuitive comprehension about similarities and differences of the data points during different states/activities. Also, the video analysis tool can show preprocessed data to provide insight in different aspects of the data (for instance, histograms). This can be used to investigate possible interim stages and eventually to develop a new meaningful feature for the problem. If data is tagged, tags can be associated with colors.

4   Case Study: Device-Free Passive Recognition on Phones

We conducted case studies in indoor environments at ETH Zurich and TU Braunschweig. For the recognition we utilised a Nexus One with Cyanogen mod 7.2 and the WiFi driver of [3]. For our case study at ETH Zurich (Sect. 4.2), we were interested in the sample rate required for RSSI-based recognition. The study was conducted over four days with repetitions of each experiment on the consecutive days. The phone was placed on a table but exact position and orientation of the phone and surrounding objects was intentionally altered.

The case studies described in Sect. 4.3 were conducted at TU-Braunschweig over two consecutive days with repetitions of experiments on both days. We investigated the impact of the distance of an individual to the phone. For this, we fixed the location of the phone but altered the surrounding furniture (chairs, tables, board). On the floor, locations were marked in increasing distance of 0.5 m up to 4.0 m. At these locations, an individual would walk around or perform gestures for at least 5 min. In addition we exploited that two APs were present in this scenario to investigate the impact of the choice of the AP.

4.1   Suitable Features for RSSI-based Recognition

We initially considered a set of 18 features. Figure 4 details the most relevant of those. Features were generated over a window of 20 RSSI samples each. We applied a feature subset selection process utilising a relief function with 20 neighbours and 50 reference examples. By this, the feature set has been reduced to a set of 12 features (cf. Table 1). Additionally, we manually exploited combinations of the resulting features to identify those which are most expressive.

Several combinations of the features *mean, median, variance, maximum* and the *difference between minimum and maximum* achieved best classification results.

Assume that $|\mathcal{W}_t|$ samples s_i are taken on the signal strenth of an incoming signal for a window $\mathcal{W}_t = s_1^t, \ldots, s_{|\mathcal{W}_t|}^t$

Mean signal strength

The mean signal strength over a window of measurements represents static characteristic changes in the received signal strength.

It provides means to distinguish a standing person as well as her approximate location.

$$\mathrm{Mean}(\mathcal{W}_t) = \frac{\sum_{s_i \in \mathcal{W}_t} s_i}{|\mathcal{W}_t|}$$

Variance of the signal's strength

The variance of the signal strength represents the volatility of the received signal.

It can provide some estimation on changes in a receiver's proximity such as movement of individuals

$$\mathrm{Var}(\mathcal{W}_t) = \sqrt{\frac{\sum_{s_i \in \mathcal{W}_t} (s_i - \mathrm{Mean}(\mathcal{W}_t))^2}{|\mathcal{W}_t|}}$$

Standard deviation of the signal's strength

The standard deviation can be used instead of the variance. The interpretation of these two features is identical

$$\mathrm{Std}(\mathcal{W}_t) = \sqrt{\mathrm{Var}(\mathcal{W}_t)}$$

Median of the signal's strength

The median signal strenth over a window of measurements represents static characteristic changes in the received signal's strenth. It is more robust to noise than the mean.

It provides means to distinguish a standing person as well as her approximate location.

We define the ordered set of samples as

$$\mathcal{W}_{t,\mathrm{ord}} = \overline{s_1}, \ldots, \overline{s}_{|\mathcal{W}_t|} \ ; \ i < j \Rightarrow s_i \le s_j$$

From this, the median is derived as

$$\mathrm{Med}(\mathcal{W}_t) = s_{\lceil |\mathcal{W}_{t,\mathrm{ord}}|/2 \rceil}$$

Normalised spectral energy

The normalised spectral energy is a measure in the frequency domain of the received signal.

It has been used to capture periodic patterns such as walking, running or cycling.

$$\mathrm{E}_i = \sum_{k=1}^{n} \mathrm{P}_i(k)^2$$

Here, $\mathrm{P}_i(k)$ denotes the probability or dominance of a spectral band k:

$$\mathrm{P}_i(k) = \frac{\mathrm{FFT}_i(k)^2}{\sum_{j=1}^{n} \mathrm{FFT}_i(j)^2}$$

As usual, we calculate the k-th frequency component as

$$\mathrm{FFT}_i(k) = \sum_{t=(i-1)n+1}^{in} s(t) e^{-j\frac{2\pi}{N}kt}$$

Minimum and maximum signal strength

The minimum/ maximum signal strength over a window represents extremal signal peaks.

It can be utilised as an indicator for movement and other environmental changes

$$\mathrm{Min}(\mathcal{W}_t) = s_i \in \mathcal{W}_t \text{ with } \forall s_j \in \mathcal{W}_t : s_i \le s_j$$

$$\mathrm{Max}(\mathcal{W}_t) = s_i \in \mathcal{W}_t \text{ with } \forall s_j \in \mathcal{W}_t : s_i \ge s_j$$

Signal peaks within 10% of a maximum

Reflections at nearby or remote objects impact the signal strength at a receive antenna. When all peaks are of the similar magnitude, this is an indication that movement is farther away.

This feature can indicate near-far relations and activity of individuals.

$$h(s_i) = \begin{cases} 1 & \text{if } s_i \ge \max(s_1, \ldots, s_{|\mathcal{W}|}) \cdot 0.9 \\ 0 & \text{else} \end{cases}$$

$$\max_{0.9}(\mathcal{W}_t) = \sum_{s_i \in \mathcal{W}_t} h(s_i)$$

Fig. 4. Features utilised for the classification of activities. For space limitations, we omit the well known definitions of a signal's fast Fourier transformation and a signal's entropy. Equally, the definition of the third central moment and the difference between subsequent maxima are not listed here for their simplicity.

Table 1. Features and their significance after feature selection

Significance	Feature description
0.023	Maximum signal strength
0.010	Mean FFT
0.003	Normalised spectral energy
0.003	Mean signal strength
0.003	Median of the signal's strength
0.003	Difference between minimum and the maximum in one sample window
0.003	Minimum signal strength
0.002	Standard deviation of the signal's strength
0.002	Variance of the signal's strength
0.002	Signal peaks within 10% of a maximum
0.001	Third central moment
0.000	Entropy

For the case studies, we decided for a feature combination of *mean, variance, maximum* and *difference between maximum and minimum.*

4.2   Impact of the Sampling Frequency

Utilising RSSI from a system not covering a transmitter, one of our main concerns has been the sample rate. Since the receiver has no impact on the number of incoming packets, it has to rely on data connections made by other devices. From our experiments, we frequently captured about 50 to 70 packets per second on one channel (all APs and packet types). Considering only meaningful packets from a single AP, this figure easily dropped below 20 or even 10 on average. In addition, the stream of packets is fluctuating considerably. We might experience a second with only one or two packets followed by one with twice the average number of packets. Clearly, this fluctuation also affects the value calculated for the various features. In order to estimate the impact of a specific sample rate, we kept the window size constant and uniformly ignored or duplicated packets when a desired packet count was not met.

We distinguish between an empty office at ETH Zurich where the mobile phone is lying on a table, the same room with a person walking next to the table and a person holding the phone and handling it. Recordings have been taken over four days at different times of day. Each single activity is sampled for five minutes in a row. This was repeated on each day twice for all activities. Overall, about three hours of continuously sampled data has been produced and was employed for the study.

We utilised a Naive Bayes classifier with 100 sample points and a Loess window of 0.5, a classification tree in the implementation of the orange data mining tool with two or more instances at its leaves and a k-NN classifier with $k = 20$ (best results have been achieved with k between 10 and 20), and a 10-fold cross validation. Figure 5 depicts our results.

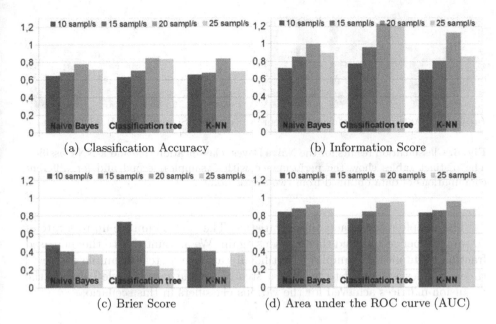

(a) Classification Accuracy

(b) Information Score

(c) Brier Score

(d) Area under the ROC curve (AUC)

Fig. 5. Classification results for the Naive Bayes, classification tree and k-NN classifier. The distinct tables show the performance with distinct sample rates.

The figure details the overall classification accuracy (CA) for all classifiers together with their information score (IS), Brier score and the area under the ROC[10] curve (AUC) as defined by [5,14]. The information score presents a measure of how well the classifier could learn a specific data set. The higher the value, the more often did the classifier predict the correct class. Brier score measures the mean squared difference between a predicted probability for an outcome and the actual ground truth. The AUC describes the probability that a classifier will rank a randomly chosen positive instance higher than a randomly chosen negative one.

Table 2. Confusion matrices for the Naive Bayes, classification tree and k-NN classifiers with a sample rate (RSSI information) of 20 samples per second

		Classification				Classification				Classification			
		activity	empty	holding	recall	activity	empty	holding	rec	activity	empty	holding	rec
Truth	activity	.714	.007	.279	.71	.879	.007	.114	.88	.829	.014	.157	.83
	empty	.007	.936	.057	.94	.029	.9	.071	.90	.021	.921	.057	.92
	holding	.286	.043	.671	.67	.186	.057	.757	.76	.207	.036	.757	.76
	precision	.709	.949	.667		.804	.933	.803		.784	.949	.779	

    (a) Naive Bayes classifier   (b) Classification tree   (c) k-NN classifier

---

[10] Receiver Operating Characteristic.

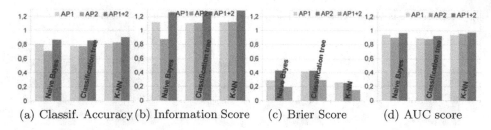

(a) Classif. Accuracy (b) Information Score   (c) Brier Score   (d) AUC score

Fig. 6. Classification results for the Naive Bayes, classification tree and k-NN classifier. The distinct tables show the performance with 5 samples/second and for different combinations of data obtained from two access points.

The sample rate impacts these statistics. The values improve up to a rate of 20 samples per second and then worsens again. We account this to the increased fraction of duplicated samples to artificially achieve a steady sample rate over time (samples we added to achieve a steady sample rate). Table 2 details the confusion matrices achieved for the various classifiers in this scenario.

4.3   Impact of the Distance to a Receiver

We also considered in the distance to the WiFi receiver of a mobile phone in which still a recognition is feasible. To this end, we conduct another case study in a lecture room of TU Braunschweig. In the study, the mobile phone is placed on top of a table, capturing packet information while a person is moving in varying distance to the device. We investigated the accuracy to distinguish between an empty environment, the environment with a person moving in 4 m distance and the environment with a person moving closer to the receiving mobile phone. Naturally, the classification accuracy deteriorates when the locations in which activity was performed are closer together (cf. Fig. 6). Table 3 shows for the k-NN classifier[11] that in this setting a person moving in 0.5 m distance can be well distinguished from the empty case and from a person moving in greater distance. While still in 4 m distance the signal received is distinguishable from an empty room, the accuracy is considerably lower.

Table 3. Confusion for activities in different distances to the phone (AP 1; k-NN)

		Classification 0.5m	4.0m	empty	recall		Classification 2.0m	4.0m	empty	recall		Classification 3.5m	4.0m	empty	recall
Truth	0.5m	**.981**	.019		.981	2.0m	**.872**	.115	.013	.872	3.5m	**.530**	.349	.121	.530
	4.0m	.026	**.768**	.206	.768	4.0m	.244	**.603**	.154	.603	4.0m	.403	**.396**	.201	.396
	empty	.013	.310	**.677**	.677	empty	.077	.205	**.718**	.718	empty	.154	.188	**.658**	.658
	precis.	.962	.702	.763		precis.	.731	.653	.812		precis	.488	.424	.671	

(a) Near and far   (b) Medium and far   (c) Greater distance

---

[11] For space constraints, we only depict results of the k-NN classifier. Results with other classifiers have been comparable.

Table 4. Utilising data from another access point in the same scenario

		Classification			
		0.5m	4.0m	empty	recall
Gr. truth	0.5m	**.940**	.034	.027	.940
	4.0m	.074	**.732**	.195	.732
	empty	.020	.174	**.805**	.805
	precision	.909	.779	.784	

(a) AP 2; k-NN classifier

		Classification			
		0.5m	4.0m	empty	recall
Gr. truth	0.5m	**1.0**			1.0
	4.0m	.027	**.846**	.128	.846
	empty	.007	.134	**.859**	.859
	precision	.968	.863	.871	

(b) AP 1+2; k-NN classifier

When the distance to the person moving is increased, naturally, the cases are more likely confused. However, note that in all cases the movement conducted in 4 m distance can be distinguished from the other two cases. Consequently, we conclude that there is a good potential to classify activities also in this distance so that for standard indoor environments a mobile phone can cover a typical room sufficiently.

In the case study described in Sect. 4.3, two dominant APs were present operating on the same frequency. Although the signal strength between both differed by about 10 dBm on average, the classification accuracy reached was comparable using packets from either AP (cf. Tables 3 and 4). However, by utilising the information observed from both APs, it is possible to further tweak the classification performance. We created features considering the data received from both APs simultaneously.

When the results are combined so that features are created from RSSI information from both APs, the accuracy can be further improved (cf. Fig. 6). Tables 4a and b depict the confusion matrices for the k-NN classifier in both cases.

5 Conclusion

We have presented our experiences with the recognition of activities from RSSI samples captured on a mobile phone. This is the first study of a passive RSSI-based AR system and the first to exploit the capabilities of an off-the-shelf mobile phone. In particular, we investigated the impact of the sampling rate, the distance of the observed passive subject and discussed the consideration of RSSI samples from multiple APs. In addition, we published and explained the tools developed in the scope of this study for the use in related research projects. We envision, that this research will open new possibilities for AR since mobile phones are very personal devices carried virtually everywhere and since, unlike with inertial sensors, RSSI-based AR is feasible also when the device is not carried on the body.

Acknowledgements. The authors would like to acknowledge funding by a fellowship within the Postdoc-Programme of the German Academic Exchange Service (DAAD).

References

1. Adib, F., Katabi, D.: See through walls with wi-fi! In: Proceedings of ACM SIG-COMM'13 (2013)
2. Hong, J., Ohtsuki, T.: Ambient intelligence sensing using array sensor: device-free radio based approach. In: Adjunct Proceedings of the 2013 ACM International Joint Conference on Pervasive and Ubiquitous Computing, UbiComp '13 (2013)
3. Ildis, O., Ofir, Y., Feinstein, R.: Wardriving from your pocket (2013). http://www.recon.cx/2013/slides/Recon2013-Omri%20Ildis%2c%20Yuval%20Ofir%20and%20Ruby%20Feinstein-Wardriving%20from%20your%20pocket.pdf
4. Kim, Y., Ling, H.: Human activity classification based on micro-doppler signatures using a support vector machine. IEEE Trans. Geosci. Remote Sens. **47**(5), 1328–1337 (2009)
5. Kononenko, I., Bratko, I.: Information-based evaluation criterion for classifier's performance. Mach. Learn. **6**(1), 67–80 (1991)
6. Patwari, N., Wilson, J., Ananthanarayanan, S., Kasera, S.K., Westenskow, D.R.: Monitoring breathing via signal strength in wireless networks. CoRR (2011) abs/1109.3898
7. Pu, Q., Gupta, S., Gollakota, S., Patel, S.: Whole-home gesture recognition using wireless signals. In: The 19th Annual International Conference on Mobile Computing and Networking (Mobicom'13) (2013)
8. Scholz, M., Riedel, T., Hock, M., Beigl, M.: Device-free and device-bound activity recognition using radio signal strength full paper. In: Proceedings of the 4th Augmented Human International Conference (2013)
9. Scholz, M., Sigg, S., Schmidtke, H.R., Beigl, M.: Challenges for device-free radio-based activity recognition. In: Proceedings of the 3rd workshop on Context Systems, Design, Evaluation and Optimisation (CoSDEO 2011), in Conjunction with MobiQuitous (2011)
10. Scholz, M., Sigg, S., Shihskova, D., von Zengen, G., Bagshik, G., Guenther, T., Beigl, M., Ji, Y.: Sensewaves: radiowaves for context recognition. In: Video Proceedings of the 9th International Conference on Pervasive Computing (Pervasive 2011) (2011)
11. Seifeldin, M., Saeed, A., Kosba, A., El-Keyi, A., Youssef, M.: Nuzzer: a large-scale device-free passive localization system for wireless environments. IEEE Trans. Mob. Comput. (TMC) **12**(7), 1321–1334 (2013)
12. Sigg, S., Scholz, M., Shi, S., Ji, Y., Beigl, M.: Rf-sensing of activities from non-cooperative subjects in device-free recognition systems using ambient and local signals. IEEE Trans. Mob. Comput. **13**(4), 907–920 (2013)
13. Sigg, S., Shi, S., Ji, Y.: Rf-based device-free recognition of simultaneously conducted activities. In: Adjunct Proceedings of the 2013 ACM International Joint Conference on Pervasive and Ubiquitous Computing, UbiComp '13 (2013)
14. Spackman, K.A.: Signal detection theory: valuable tools for evaluating inductive learning. In: 6th International Workshop on Machine Learning, pp. 160–163 (1989)
15. Xu, C., Firner, B., Moore, R.S., Zhang, Y., Trappe, W., Howard, R., An, N.: Scpl: indoor device-free multi-subject counting and localization using radio signal strength. In: The 12th ACM/IEEE Conference on Information Processing in Sensor Networks (ACM/IEEE IPSN) (2013)

AcTrak - Unobtrusive Activity Detection and Step Counting Using Smartphones

Vivek Chandel[✉], Anirban Dutta Choudhury, Avik Ghose,
and Chirabrata Bhaumik

TCS Innovation Lab Systems, Tata Consultancy Services, Kolkata 700156, India
{vivek.chandel,anirban.duttachoudhury,avik.ghose,c.bhaumik}@tcs.com

Abstract. In this paper we introduce "AcTrak", a system that provides training-free and orientation-and-placement-independent step-counting and activity recognition on commercial mobile phones, using only 3D accelerometer. The proposed solution uses "step-frequency" as a feature to classify various activities. In order to filter out noise generated due to normal handling of the phone, while the user is otherwise physically stationary, AcTrak is armed with a novel algorithm for step validation termed as Individual Peak Analysis (IPA). IPA uses peak-height and inter-peak interval as features. AcTrak provides realtime step count. It also classifies current activity, and tags each activity with the associated steps, resulting in a detailed analysis of activity recognition. Using our model, a step-count accuracy of 98.9 % is achieved. Further, an accuracy of 95 % is achieved when classifying stationary, walking and running/jogging. When brisk-walking is added to the activity set, still a reasonable level of accuracy is achieved. Since AcTrak is largely orientation and position agnostic, and requires no prior training, this makes our approach truly ubiquitous. Classification of step-based activity is done as walking, brisk-walking and running (includes jogging). So, after a session of workout, the subject can easily self-assess his/her accomplishment.

Keywords: Step counting · Activity detection · Unobtrusive sensing · Mobile sensing · Mobile computing · mHealth

1 Introduction

The sedentary nature of urban and semi-urban lifestyle coupled with easy access to basic resources like ample food has produced a new array of physical problems [15]. Hence, a controlled diet and ample physical activity become important aspects of health and wellness. It is important for subjects to monitor and assess their daily activities with respect to the benchmark recommended by medical practitioners or health/fitness experts. The recent boom in smartphone market has made it the most pervasive and ubiquitous sensing platform available with the masses. Hence if a method were to use smartphone sensors in a power and cost effective manner to provide activity monitoring, it would be of immense use. Professional pedometers and fitness gadgets provide activity monitoring and

© Institute for Computer Sciences, Social Informatics and Telecommunications Engineering 2014
I. Stojmenovic et al. (Eds.): MOBIQUITOUS 2013, LNICST 131, pp. 447–459, 2014.
DOI: 10.1007/978-3-319-11569-6_35

step-counting features. However, there are two major issues. Firstly, there is additional cost involved in buying and "wearing" the additional sensors. Secondly, most of these devices need to be "trained" for individual users to count steps and recognize activities. AcTrak attempts to solve the above issues by using smartphone sensor, namely the 3-axis accelerometer for step counting and activity recognition, using step-frequency and a novel IPA algorithm. Though Global Positioning System (GPS) can also be used to assess user activity, but as marked by Sun et al. [14], it cannot provide refined analysis of human movements. Additionally, GPS sensor drains a lot of power, and can only be used outdoors.

2   Previous Work

Human activity recognition using sensors has been a widely researched area. Accelerometers have become established sensors in this respect, although some researchers have also attacked the problem using machine vision [4,16]. Research has been carried out using wearable sensors [1,10]. These solutions give fine-tuned data for recognizing even static activities like sitting, standing and even different gestures, but poses obtrusion from wearing external device(s) that the subject may not be comfortable with. After accelerometers started becoming available in mobile devices, they were taken up for activity recognition [2,3,6,14,17]. Using accelerometer in mobile and other embedded devices as a pedometer has also been explored [3,7–9,11,13]. Marschollek et al. [9] compares various open and proprietary methods of step detection using a cell phone accelerometer. Some researches pose a constraint on orientation aspect of the device [3,6,12,17]. Sun et al. [14] has relaxed this requirement and has used resultant acceleration for detecting steps. However, it still requires exhaustive training for all possible orientations and device placement options. We observe that prior approaches in this direction have performed the step detection and activity classification by including measures which employ absolute amplitude profiles of the sensor data. These profiles change from person to person, from activity to activity or placement of mobile device with respect to body and hence require a training phase. Also prior arts have not taken into account the stationary noise periods occurring during device handling, which may be of large amplitudes comparable to that of the actual activities, and can result in false positives. These are two drawbacks that AcTrak tries to eliminate.

3   Methodology

The methodology used in AcTrak has been outlined in Fig. 1. Different stages of the method are discussed in the following subsections.

3.1   Data Preprocessing

The algorithm in our approach uses resultant acceleration for processing, thereby ensuring an orientation free usage of the mobile device [7,14]. Data from the

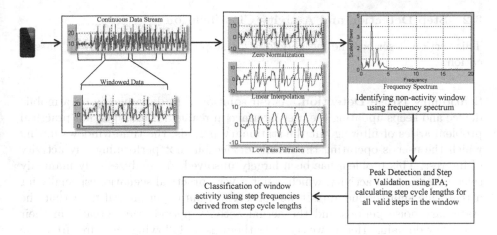

Fig. 1. AcTrak-Algorithm overview

3-axis accelerometer requires some pre-processing before using it for step detection in a discrete-time manner. A step-wise account of preprocessing process is described in the following sub-sections.

Windowing. At first, a window-based analysis is performed on the raw data stream coming from accelerometer. In this approach, a window interval of 2 s was chosen heuristically, which is short enough to provide a real time response to the user without missing a substantiate step information, and long enough in order to record inter-step temporal and frequency characteristics.

Zero Normalization. Next the data window is zero normalized eliminating the DC bias which is undesired in the frequency domain analysis, which is one of the subsequent steps.

Interpolation. Since the accelerometer data is captured at variable sampling rate due to the nature of software calls for sensor data acquisition [2], interpolation is used to make the signal in constant sampling rate, required for frequency domain analysis.

Low Pass Filtration. This step performs noise cancellation by filtering out the high frequency components (e.g. stray vibrations, internal sensor noises). We use an FIR low pass filter with a cutoff frequency of 4 Hz. Li et al. [7] uses a value of 3 Hz, but AcTrak uses a higher cutoff to also encompass faster step activities like running.

3.2 Step Detection and Activity Classification

This section describes the methodology for step detection and activity classification.

Stationary Noise Detection. As our solution runs dynamically on a mobile device and keeps updating the user interface in real time, an important practical problem arises of filtering out the stationary periods; the time-windows during which the user is operating the mobile device but not performing any activity of interest. This problem has been largely unsolved. [7] analyzes only manually selected periods of activity, which is not a very practical scenario, especially for a real time smartphone app. It was observed from experimental data that the stationary noise periods and the actual activity periods vary greatly in their frequency domains. Hence, we separate them using following measures from the Fast Fourier Transform (FFT) spectrum of the acceleration data window:

- *Dominant Amplitude* (A_d), the value of the largest Discrete Fourier Transform (DFT) coefficient
- *Dominant Frequency* (f_d), the frequency component exhibiting A_d
- *Peak Sharpness* (ps), the sum of squares of slopes for k DFT coefficients on either side of the highest peak in the frequency spectrum:

$$ps = \sum_{i=-k}^{k-1} \left(\frac{A(i) - A(i+1)}{A_d} \right)^2 \tag{1}$$

where $A(0)$ represents the largest DFT coefficient i.e. A_d.

The last measure differentiates distinct long and narrow peaks with substantial periodicity in the sensor data with otherwise short and wide peaks, which mostly represent noisy windows. Such wide peak spectrum have been observed when the mobile device experiences a jerk, e.g. while freely allowing the device to fall into the pocket. It was observed that except when the mobile device is hand-held, the order of the peak amplitudes of acceleration values pertaining to steps is well greater than $1.0\,\mathrm{m/s^2}$. This is evident because whenever the user places the device in the upper half of his body, the intensity of net acceleration is less than as compared to when the device is placed anywhere in the lower body, such as trouser pockets, where an additional component of the leg movement and free movement of the device in sometimes very loose pockets (like those in casual trousers) add up to give a higher resultant acceleration. Next, it was also found that in almost all of scenarios where the mobile device was placed with the lower body, the acceleration signals posed a different frequency spectrum, which contained, no more than, two major peaks, with an additional note that the amplitude of the second peak was no shorter that $\approx 80\,\%$ of the amplitude of the greater peak, as shown in Fig. 2(b).

In order to ensure the validity of the peaks we place limits on A_d followed by thresholds on ps and no. of peaks, P_n. This flow is shown in Fig. 3. A_l is a lower

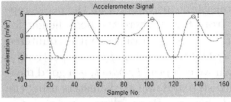

(a) Accelerometer Signal

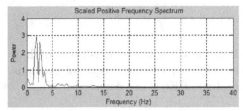

(b) Scaled Positive Frequency Spectrum

Fig. 2. Filtered acceleration signal and the related frequency spectrum

Fig. 3. Flow for deciding a stationary window

threshold limit on A_d and P_n is the number of peaks present with height at least 75 % of A_d. After a stationary window, activity and step update is given after processing two consecutive windows. Thereafter, updates are provided after each window.

Step Detection. The process of robust step-detection is important as the accuracy of both step count as well as activity classification depends largely on it. After a data window has been verified, as discussed above, to be non-stationary, the step detection algorithm is applied to that window. For identifying steps, we use a peak detection algorithm, with a constraint of minimum number of samples between two peaks. After identifying peaks, each peak is validated if it represents an actual step. Li et al. [7] uses Dynamic Time Warping (DTW) technique with some heuristics in order to validate the detected peaks as steps. As in Fig. 2(a), number of samples between consecutive steps are not uniform. Instead the number of samples for the whole step cycle shows the required periodicity. Naqvi et al. [11] tried to bring out a relationship between step frequency and threshold for the peak heights using the vertical axis signal from accelerometer. However their work poses an orientation constraint on the device.

We introduce IPA (Individual Peak Analysis), a novel and a robust method, in order to perform peak validation. Using information from the frequency spectrum of the data window, we get an estimate of the properties of valid peaks. For all the peaks, we observe two features, viz. peak height, i.e. the difference between peak crest ($pkHt$) and the least value until the previous valid peak (ppm), and the inter-peak intervals ($pDiff$). It was observed that the product of these two parameters in a window is a consistent measure for all the peaks representing valid steps. This is also evident from Fig. 4 where the peak height for peak 2 ($pkHt_2 + |ppm_{1,2}|$) and peak 3 ($pkHt_3 + |ppm_{2,3}|$) varies, but is countered with their corresponding peak differences ($pDiff_{1,2}$ and $pDiff_{1,2}$ respectively). Hence we derive that this new feature, which we call *peakProduct*, is a good measure for classifying accelerometer signal into step and non-step clusters using the frequency domain analysis. We define *peakProduct*, P_k as follows:

$$P_k = (pkHt_k - ppm_{k-1,k}) \times \frac{pDiff_{k-1,k}}{f_s} \tag{2}$$

where P_k denotes the product for k^{th} peak in the window and f_s is the sampling frequency. For $k = 1$, i.e., first peak of the window, last valid peak of previous window is taken into consideration. Parameters of Eq. 2 are depicted in Fig. 4.

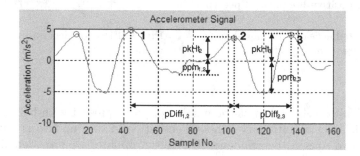

Fig. 4. Parameters for P_k

Since the values A_d and f_d represent the periodicity of steps, the cycles in the acceleration signal pertaining to valid steps are expected to exhibit similar values. The measure corresponding to P_k generated from the frequency spectrum of the window is $F_p = \frac{A_d}{f_d}$. After analyzing various windows of steps (≈ 5000) with the device placed at different positions, it was observed that for almost all the valid peaks, the product F_p behaved proportionally to the product P_k, as expected. Hence, the following criterion was selected for a peak to represent a valid step:

$$P_k \geq (\tau \times F_p) \tag{3}$$

Using regression we determined that a value of 1.3 for τ gave best validation results. We call the above peak validation method as IPA. This stage outputs a step cycle length vector, SCL, where SCL_i is the sample difference between i^{th} valid peak and $(i - 2)^{th}$ valid peak.

Case of Edge Peaks: As with all windowed analysis, there are peaks which are flat enough to make their presence at the edge of two consecutive windows (see Fig. 5). Such peaks would typically pass undetected by the peak detection algorithm used, producing a glitch in the overall step cycle length vector of the window. For solving this problem, AcTrak employs a smart technique whereby we mark the first sample of every window as a peak (if $amplitude > 0$), which is then further validated using IPA.

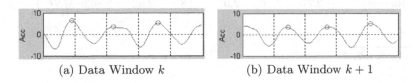

(a) Data Window k (b) Data Window $k+1$

Fig. 5. Two consecutive data windows with a flat undetected edge peak

Classification. As mentioned in Sect. 2, substantial research has been done in the field of activity classification using trained classifiers, which use various signal features as classification parameters, both amplitude and temporal. Classification results are fairly accurate [1,6,14] with these measures, but the success of the trained classifier depends on the similarity of situations of training phase and testing phase, which is not completely feasible practically especially in case of mobile devices which pose wide possibilities of placement options. In this paper, we have attempted to classify activities without using any training phase. Towards this end, we use only temporal measures of the activities, which take care of wide possibilities of amplitude characteristics of the sensor signals owing to different user positions and even different pocket profiles (jeans vs. casual trousers). We have chosen a subset of activities from existing classification researches, viz., walking, brisk walking and jogging/running, which can be differentiated on their temporal profiles alone, as a step towards a complete orientation and placement free unobtrusive method. We classify the mentioned activities using a windowed-analysis whereby we determine threshold step frequencies for the mentioned activities as f_{bw} and f_r.

To estimate these thresholds, we gathered data from five subjects of varied demographics (different from the test subjects used for gauging the classification performance in Sect. 4) and determined the mean step frequency for each activity as MSF_w, MSF_{bw} and MSF_r (Table 1). Thereafter we determined the boundary thresholds, f_{bw} as $\frac{MSF_w + MSF_{bw}}{2}$ ($= 1.85$) and f_r as $\frac{MSF_{bw} + MSF_r}{2}$ ($= 2.4$). Using SCL_i from step detection stage, we define four weight measures: w1, w2, w3 and w4 as shown in Fig. 6. The data window is then assigned as representing a particular activity as shown in Fig. 7. The four weights classify the activities on the basis of above calculated boundary thresholds, which can be defined with fair accuracy for a wide demography of persons. The key advantage of using only temporal features for classification is that it works seamlessly with any option of device placement.

Table 1. Step frequencies from test subjects

	Sub 1	Sub 2	Sub 3	Sub 4	Sub 5	Mean
Walking	1.78	1.72	1.81	1.7	1.755	1.753 (MSF_w)
Brisk walking	1.9	2.03	2.033	1.86	1.92	1.9486 (MSF_{bw})
Running	2.77	2.86	2.97	2.89	2.82	2.862 (MSF_r)

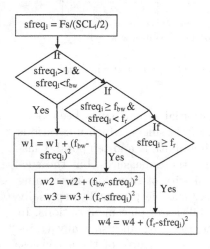

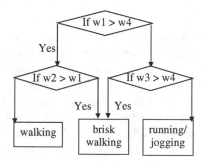

Fig. 6. Flow for assignment of activity weights

Fig. 7. Classification of activities on the basis of calculated activity weights

4   Experiments and Results

We produce results in a threefold manner, whereby first we show the effectiveness of the step-counting method and compare it with the established methods. Then we show the robustness of AcTrak in cancelling out stationary noise caused by normal operation of the mobile device and in the last phase, we illustrate the activity detection performance of AcTrak. The application was built on an iPhone with a sampling frequency of accelerometer as 80 Hz. For analyzing step count accuracy, four subjects were allowed to walk freely inside a typical office space, by keeping the phone in different orientations attached to different parts of the body as shown in Table 2. To compare with the step detection algorithm by Li et al. [7], five sets of accelerometer data was logged with an iPhone placed in the subject's trouser pocket. Results of AcTrak were obtained in real-time while the algorithm by Li et al. [7] (Peak Detector+Heuristics+DTW) was run offline. The results are shown in Table 3, where IPA outperforms the DTW in step validation. DTW was observed to deem invalid steps as valid in some very noisy situations in spite of applying proper heuristics, where IPA correctly eliminated invalid peaks.

AcTrak's error, as in Table 3, is also lower when compared to those of the open algorithms as analyzed by Marschollek et al. [9], where Wolf method yields least step detection error of 8.4 %, and also when compared to the energy algorithm by Schindhelm et al. [13], where the least error yielded is 3.6 %.

Next, the robustness of AcTrak in eliminating the random stationary noise is demonstrated. Two spells were performed whereby two different users operated on the mobile phone (games, texting etc.), randomly giving some jerks (placing on table, allowing the device to freely fall in the pocket etc.) The results were compared with the algorithm by Li et al. [7]. Results for the two spells, S1 and S2, are tabulated in Table 4. It can be seen that AcTrak efficiently avoids any wrong detection of steps in case of stationary noise and random operation of device, which is important from a practical perspective as already discussed in Sect. 3.2.

Table 2. AcTrak: step detection performance with various device placements

	Sub 1		Sub 2		Sub 3		Sub 4		
	A[a]	D[b]	A	D	A	D	A	D	Avg. Error %
Hand	90	76	84	83	96	91	85	70	9.9
Shirt's pocket	90	90	86	86	93	85	88	88	2.1
Trouser's front pocket	90	84	85	90	95	96	89	92	4.24
Trouser's rear pocket	92	90	85	83	95	91	90	81	4.68
Waist clip	89	96	85	84	94	91	87	83	4.2
Avg. error %	6.4		2.12		4.45		7.1		5.02

[a] Actual steps
[b] Detected steps

Table 3. AcTrak: step detection performance comparison

A	D: [7]	D: AcTrak	Error%: [7]	Error%: AcTrak
130	133	132	2.3	1.5
64	72	63	12.5	1.5
54	58	54	7.4	0.0
40	42	41	5.0	2.5
37	41	37	10.8	0.0
Avg. error %			7.6	1.1

Table 4. AcTrak: comparison of false detections in stationary noises

	Time	FD[c]: [7]	FD:AcTrak
S1	50 s	18	2
S2	40 s	16	0

[c] False step detections

Finally the results for activity detection are presented. Here, we used the HASC corpus 2011 data set [5] with individuals of varied demographics and using different devices for data logging. We performed classification for the activities stay, walk and jog, as available in the data set. We selected a set of 100 persons randomly to perform the classification and the resulting confusion matrix is presented in Table 5, where each entry represents the percentage of time classified under the head of a particular activity by AcTrak. Also the classification of [5] was preceded by a training phase including up to 80 individuals, where AcTrak doesn't use any training. Comparing with the classification accuracy as in [5], we achieve a better accuracy as shown in Table 5, even after aggregating the classification accuracy of Jog and Skip [5] to only Jog/Run(AcTrak) and Walk, Stairs Up and Stairs Down [5] to only Walk(AcTrak) in order to attempt a sensible and a fair comparison.

Table 5. AcTrak: comparison of activity classification accuracy with HASC corpus dataset [5] (all in % accuracy)

	Stay	Walk	Jog/Run	Accuracy [5]
Stay	**99.8**	0	0.2	**86.7**
Walk	2.1	**96.7**	1.2	**97.0**
Jog/Run	1.2	2.8	**96.2**	**82.3**

Table 6. Activity classification results (all in % error accumulated)

	Walk	Brisk walk	Run
Sub 1	0.00	0.00	0.00
Sub 2	17.19	19.57	0.00
Sub 3	3.33	4.55	15.00
Sub 4	7.02	17.95	0.00
Sub 5	0.00	25.71	8.33

In order to explore the accuracy of brisk walking using AcTrak, which was not possible in the previous comparison with [5] due to data availability limitation, we carried out an independent experiment using 5 volunteers. As like the previous case, since unsupervised and training free activity detection was performed it was very important to validate the algorithm against a variety of people spanning across demographics. As shown in Fig. 8, the same step-based activity may produce significantly different accelerometer signal for different subjects. In order to validate that the algorithm works well for most individuals, a set of five individuals were selected with varying demographies as illustrated in Table 7, and the volunteers were asked to perform the activities of interest, viz., walking, brisk-walking and running. Results collected over these subjects are depicted in Table 6, along with the percentage error accumulated for each activity.

The error was calculated against ground-truth data of step count annotated by the subjects themselves. Error percentage is given as:

$$Error\ Percentage = \frac{|Total\ Steps\ Detected - Steps\ Detected\ for\ Activity|}{Total\ Steps\ Detected} \times 100$$

As is clear from Table 6, the percentage error between walking and brisk walking is higher than between walking and running based activities. Also for a few subjects, brisk-walking and running came as overlapped activities. To point the above issue, individual step frequency during each activity for each subject were also recorded as presented in Table 8 where it can be seen that the step frequency for walking and brisk-walking for some individuals like subjects 3 and 4, are almost similar. Also for subject 2, brisk-walking and running step-frequencies are almost equal. Hence, the difference in frequency between walking and brisk walking is a fuzzy boundary that is open to human interpretation, whereas the activities of running/jogging can be easily differentiated from others. So, from Table 6 it is clear that an unconscious mix-up of activities had taken place during the experiment, leading to a marginally higher error. However, the purpose of AcTrak is served well, as it is built to correct similar errors often committed by people during workout sessions.

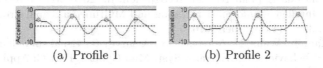

(a) Profile 1   (b) Profile 2

Fig. 8. Different acceleration signal profiles for brisk walking for two different subjects

Table 7. Demographics of different subjects

	Age	Height	Gender	Body	Weight
Sub 1	25–30	Short	Male	Slim	Light
Sub 2	25–30	Tall	Female	Fat	Heavy
Sub 3	35–40	Short	Male	Stout	Medium
Sub 4	25–30	Tall	Male	Stout	Heavy
Sub 5	40–45	Tall	Male	Slim	Medium

Table 8. Average step frequencies

	Walk (1.2–1.85)	Brisk walk (1.85–2.4)	Run (>2.4)
Sub 1	1.63	1.89	2.8
Sub 2	1.23	2.44	2.75
Sub 3	1.69	1.86	2.84
Sub 4	1.75	1.82	2.6
Sub 5	1.66	1.8	2.77

5   Conclusion and Future Work

In this work we have depicted AcTrak for unsupervised classification of common step-based activities on commercially available mobile devices. The method uses only temporal features, and hence is able to tolerate large variations in signal due to human imperfections, varied placement options and different activities. While competitive methods require extensive training, AcTrak requires none. For step detection, we use IPA to validate steps for multiple activities. Also we address the problem of false positives due to normal handling of the device.

As a future endeavor, we plan to include options for positioning the device at places like arm-bands, which is typical for workout sessions. This is a challenging problem, since multiple components from the arm movements needs to be captured in addition to vertical acceleration component of the overall body.

Also we plan to include detection of ascending and descending stairs. Though already addressed in existing literature, we aim at a completely unsupervised training-free method. Preliminary observations have shown that such classification is possible.

References

1. Bao, L., Intille, S.S.: Activity recognition from user-annotated acceleration data. In: Ferscha, A., Mattern, F. (eds.) PERVASIVE 2004. LNCS, vol. 3001, pp. 1–17. Springer, Heidelberg (2004)
2. Das, S., Green, L., Perez, B., Murphy, M., Perring, A.: Detecting user activities using the accelerometer on android smartphones (2010)
3. Derawi, M., Nickel, C., Bours, P., Busch, C.: Unobtrusive user-authentication on mobile phones using biometric gait recognition. In: 2010 Sixth International Conference on Intelligent Information Hiding and Multimedia Signal Processing (IIH-MSP), pp. 306–311, October 2010
4. Hu, W., Tan, T., Wang, L., Maybank, S.: A survey on visual surveillance of object motion and behaviors. IEEE Trans. Syst. Man Cybern. Part C: Appl. Rev. **34**(3), 334–352 (2004)
5. Kawaguchi, N.: Hasc corpus: large scale human activity corpus for the real-world activity understandings
6. Kwapisz, J.R., Weiss, G.M., Moore, S.A.: Activity recognition using cell phone accelerometers. ACM SIGKDD Explor. Newsl. **12**(2), 74–82 (2011)
7. Li, F., Zhao, C., Ding, G., Gong, J., Liu, C., Zhao, F.: A reliable and accurate indoor localization method using phone inertial sensors (2012)
8. Libby, R.: A simple method for reliable footstep detection in embedded sensor platforms (2009)
9. Marschollek, M., Goevercin, M., Wolf, K.-H., Song, B., Gietzelt, M., Haux, R., Steinhagen-Thiessen, E.: A performance comparison of accelerometry-based step detection algorithms on a large, non-laboratory sample of healthy and mobility-impaired persons. In: 30th Annual International Conference of the IEEE Engineering in Medicine and Biology Society, EMBS 2008, pp. 1319–1322. IEEE (2008)
10. Maurer, U., Smailagic, A., Siewiorek, D., Deisher, M.: Activity recognition and monitoring using multiple sensors on different body positions. In: International Workshop on Wearable and Implantable Body Sensor Networks, BSN 2006, pp. 4–116, April 2006
11. Naqvi, M.N.Z., Kumar, A., Chauhan, A., Sahni, K.: Step counting using smartphone-based accelerometer. Int. J. Comput. Sci. Eng. **4**(5), 675–681 (2012)
12. Parkka, J., Cluitmans, L., Ermes, M.: Personalization algorithm for real-time activity recognition using PDA, wireless motion bands, and binary decision tree. IEEE Trans. Inf. Technol. Biomed. **14**(5), 1211–1215 (2010)
13. Schindhelm, C.K.: Activity recognition and step detection with smartphones: towards terminal based indoor positioning system. In: 2012 IEEE 23rd International Symposium on Personal Indoor and Mobile Radio Communications (PIMRC), pp. 2454–2459. IEEE (2012)
14. Sun, L., Zhang, D., Li, B., Guo, B., Li, S.: Activity recognition on an accelerometer embedded mobile phone with varying positions and orientations. In: Yu, Z., Liscano, R., Chen, G., Zhang, D., Zhou, X. (eds.) UIC 2010. LNCS, vol. 6406, pp. 548–562. Springer, Heidelberg (2010)

15. Tremblay, M.S.T.M., Colley, R.C.C.R., Saunders, T.J.S.T., Healy, G.N.H.G., Owen, N.O.N.: Physiological and health implications of a sedentary lifestyle. Appl. Physiol. Nutr. Metab. **35**(6), 725–740 (2010)
16. Turaga, P., Chellappa, R., Subrahmanian, V.S., Udrea, O.: Machine recognition of human activities: a survey. IEEE Trans. Circ. Syst. Video Technol. **18**(11), 1473–1488 (2008)
17. Yang, J.: Toward physical activity diary: motion recognition using simple acceleration features with mobile phones. In: Proceedings of the 1st International Workshop on Interactive Multimedia for Consumer Electronics, pp. 1–10. ACM (2009)

Practical Image-Enhanced LBS
for AR Applications

Antonio J. Ruiz-Ruiz(✉), Pedro E. Lopez-de-Teruel, and Oscar Canovas

University of Murcia, Murcia, Spain
{antonioruiz,pedroe,ocanovas}@um.es

Abstract. We have designed a multisensor indoor LBS suitable for augmented reality applications which, mainly based on computer vision
techniques, provides precise estimations of both the 3D position and
rotation of the device. Our proposal makes use of state-of-the-art IMU
data processing techniques during the training phase in order to reliably
generate a 3D model of the targeted environment, thus solving typical
scalability issues related to visually repetitive structures in large indoor
scenarios. A very efficient camera resection technique will then be used
in the on-line phase, able to provide accurate 6 degrees of freedom estimations of the device position, with mean errors in the order of 5 cm and
response times below 250 ms.

Keywords: IMU · SIFT · Computer vision · LBS · Augmented reality

1 Introduction

Nowadays smartphones are equipped with many types of sensors, which is simpli-
fying the process of obtaining context information. Particularly, it is now possible
to obtain accurate location estimations using visual information provided by the
device camera. This is especially useful in augmented reality (AR) applications,
which seamlessly integrate the sensor and the display. However, image processing
is a time consuming task, which usually imposes the use of additional sensors to
limit the amount of required computation. The accuracy and performance of a
location based service (LBS) is closely related not only to the number of sensors
being used, but also to the quality of the context model they are based on. For
the last few years we have been publishing different approaches to address the
challenge of indoor precise localisation, using all the available sensors in order
to improve performance, accuracy and ease of deployment.

Our initial solution was a classical fingerprinting map based on 802.11 RSSIs
which also used SIFT (Scale Invariant Feature Transform) descriptors from
images obtained at different training points [18]. We found correspondences
between the images being acquired during the on-line phase and those obtained
during the training phase. Instead of examining the whole database of images we
constrained the space search to those acquired at places where the RSSIs signals

© Institute for Computer Sciences, Social Informatics and Telecommunications Engineering 2014
I. Stojmenovic et al. (Eds.): MOBIQUITOUS 2013, LNICST 131, pp. 460–473, 2014.
DOI: 10.1007/978-3-319-11569-6_36

were similar to the current ones. This solution was limited by the granularity of our sampling procedure, since we just returned the location estimation which provided more matchings with the current image.

We later extended the system to provide precise estimations of the position and rotation of the device with respect to some conveniently chosen world coordinate system [19]. Using visual Structure from Motion techniques (SfM) [10], we built off-line 3D reconstructions of the scenario from the correspondences among SIFT descriptors of training images extracted from recorded video sequences of the environment. The generation of those 3D models had to be supervised by a human operator to deal with repetitive structures (windows, doors, etc.) typically found in indoor scenarios, and which could affect the automatic modelling process, generating arbitrary layouts not matching the real scenario. Model accuracy was crucial for our posterior location estimation, based on a resection process and using the images captured by the devices during the on-line phase.

In this paper we present several key improvements in relation to these and other authors' works. First, we introduce the use of IMU (Inertial Measurement Units) to generate accurate 3D models in a mostly automatic and unsupervised manner. An operator carrying a tablet or smartphone walks around the indoor environment taking time indexed pictures that will be used to build the 3D model. Once the walk is finished, our training application uses the inertial sensor measurements to infer rough locations of the places from where each image was taken. The only input which is required is an approximate vectorial map of the scenario. Images are then automatically geo-tagged using the inferred pathway, and this approximate spatial information will be paramount to rule out comparisons between images taken from very different angles or distant positions, thus avoiding the aforementioned model generation failures due to visually similar structures.

Second, we have noticeably improved the resection process to determine the device pose. The new technique demands a fewer number of correct matchings to perform the camera resection, which speeds up the procedure and provides response times closer to the requirements imposed by AR applications. Moreover, since our 3D model is divided into different zones according to the characterisation of the 802.11 signals, we perform our matching process only against the 3D submodel where the RSSI signals from the surrounding antennas are similar to the current RSSI measurements. That is, RSSIs act as a filter for the involved image processing.

Third, we have performed an experimental analysis using different indoor locations and testing several configuration parameters to validate our proposal. We will show 3D models of large real indoor scenarios containing repetitive structures that were built using our image geo-tagging technique. We will also analyse the accuracy of our location estimations during the on-line phase using the new camera resectioning procedure. Finally, we will make use of an AR prototype in order to validate the location estimations and to demonstrate that our proposal is suitable for real-time applications.

2   Related Work

Many types of data and methods have been used to infer location. Though there are important contributions making use of a single sensor, better results can be obtained by integrating the information captured by multiple sensors. For example, [11,14] use WiFi signals and image recognition to estimate positions. However, these works are based on two-dimensional visual landmarks that must be placed in the scenario of interest, which involves the inclusion of obtrusive elements. One of our main objectives is to avoid special tagging or ad-hoc landmarks. In [1], a preliminary analysis of how image processing techniques like SIFT can be used to improve the accuracy in landmark-free LBSs is performed. SIFT features [13] provide a powerful mechanism to robustly match different images of a given scene, which is fundamental not only for visual recognition of objects or places [6], but also in the context of simultaneous localisation and three-dimensional scene reconstruction [20]. Alternatively, some other works on localisation have used other kind of features and associated local image descriptors instead of SIFT, such as SURF [15] or ASIFT [12].

On the other hand, there are also some works that try to track a device from a known initial position using dead-reckoning [2,5], where inertial sensor measurements are integrated over time. However, when dealing with noisy sensors, even small sensing errors are magnified by integration. This drawback can be addressed using map constraints and particle filtering [22]. In a recent work [17], authors present a proposal which is able to track users without any a priori knowledge about the user's initial location, stride-length or device placement. Though their paper is mainly focused on reducing the calibration effort required to build WiFi fingerprinting maps by means of crowdsourced data, some of their ideas have been inherited in our proposal. We will also make use of a particle filter augmented to estimate unknowns such as the stride length or the orientation. However, we will follow a different approach in order to estimate the orientation and the step detection. We start from a more constrained situation, since our operator will always behave in a known manner, and therefore we will be able to make some assumptions about the device placement and the human locomotion.

3   Building Accurate 3D Models Relying on Inertial Sensors

It is a well known fact that the accelerometers usually integrated in mobile devices are relatively noisy sensors. The great magnitude value of the always present gravity $(9.8\,\text{m/s}^2)$ with respect to interesting accelerations induced by user movements is indeed a problematic issue. Though, at least theoretically, the distance travelled could be calculated by integrating acceleration twice with respect to time, error accumulates rapidly after some seconds due to the presence of noise in readings.

To avoid this type of drifting we adopt the individual step count as the metric of walking distance, taking advantage of the fact that, when a person walks, their

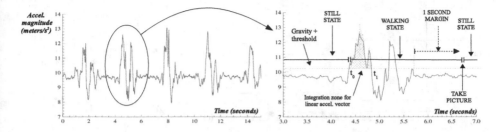

Fig. 1. Acceleration magnitude analysis.

feet periodically experiment a stationary stance phase of approximately 0.5 s in every step [5]. An intelligent integration scheme, that applies *zero velocity updates* (ZUPT) when detecting this stance phase, together with a carefully designed *Extended Kalman Filter* [21], is able to accurately estimate the position of a pedestrian for relatively long walks. However, this approach requires (*i*) better inertial sensors than those commonly found in typical mobile devices, and (*ii*) the sensor has to be mounted in the shoe of the operator, in order to take advantage of the ZUPT trick. In [17] the authors presented a proposal making use of the information from the compass, a particle filter, and an approximate vectorial map of the environment to correct the generated trajectories. But, once again, a basic requirement in that work is that users have to put their phones in the pocket or somewhere else where the periodic movement pattern is clearly noticeable.

Although none of these techniques are directly applicable in our case, since the operator must hold the tablet in their hands to take pictures of the environment, we somehow partially combine these two approaches in order to adapt them to our needs. Our training application suggests the kind of movements that the operator must perform while taking pictures of the environment in a way that (*i*) makes it easy to predict them, (*ii*) ensures that pictures are taken in the best imaging conditions, and (*iii*) simplifies the operator's job. Our application expects a movement pattern in which the operator stands still, takes a picture of the environment, moves to a nearby position (typically one meter away or so), and the process is repeated. These relative movements, though certainly noisy and suffering a considerable drift when integrated in the long term (see Fig. 2(a) for an example), will be the basis for a posterior particle filter that will fit these measurements to our scenario map, in a similar way to that performed in [17].

We analyse the magnitude $|\vec{a}|$ of the acceleration vector $\vec{a} = (a_x, a_y, a_z)$ in time, sampled at 50 Hz by the device and considering two main states of the operator: still and walking (see Fig. 1). The logic for changing from one to the other is: if the accelerometer signal exceeds the gravity $|\vec{g}| = 9.8\,\mathrm{m/s}^2$ by a predefined small threshold, we consider that the operator is walking. As there may be short periods of time where $|\vec{a}|$ falls below that threshold during movement, the application only gets back to the still state as long as $|\vec{a}|$ keeps under the threshold value for a period of at least one second. That instant the

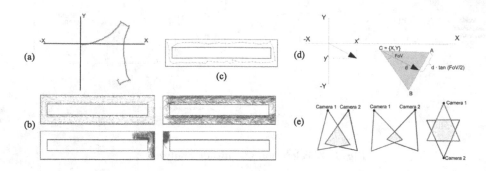

Fig. 2. (a) Raw input as obtained by the motion model. (b) Evolution of particles population as the operator moves, converging to a mostly monomodal state. (c) Corrected path estimation. (d) Approximate field of view covered by a camera. (e) Different examples of overlapping areas.

application automatically takes a picture, what helps in taking clear and sharp images since the mobile device is fairly still when the picture is taken.

Now we have to estimate the relative movement performed by the operator between two such instants. Double integration of linear acceleration to estimate displacement suffers from serious drifting issues, but the direction of movement is still acceptably estimated if the integration interval is short enough. Thus, we integrate only from the start of movement until the magnitude $\vec{a}$ falls under the threshold for the first time (instants t_0 and t_1 in Fig. 1). The output of this stage will be a unit norm direction vector $(\Delta x, \Delta y, \Delta z)$, leaving the stride length estimation to the subsequent particle filter:

$$\overrightarrow{\Delta x_{dev}} = (\Delta x, \Delta y, \Delta z) = \frac{\int_{t_0}^{t_1} (\vec{a} - \vec{g}) dt}{|\int_{t_0}^{t_1} (\vec{a} - \vec{g}) dt|} \tag{1}$$

However, since this vector refers to device coordinates, it still has to be corrected using an absolute rotation with respect to the world coordinates. Many mobile devices do in fact integrate compass, gravity and gyroscope readings to get a virtual sensor that provides a filtered output rotation $R_{dev \to wrl}$. Thus, our final estimation of the relative direction vector in world coordinates will be $\overrightarrow{\Delta x_{wrl}} = R_{dev \to wrl} \cdot \overrightarrow{\Delta x_{dev}}$.

To track the operator's movement we implemented a particle filter [21], which uses spatial restrictions of the a priori known indoor map to filter out long term drifting errors in the raw input trajectory. Figure 2(a–c) show the overall functioning of the particle filtering algorithm working in one of our scenarios (see also Sect. 5). A classical backward propagation indicates the final estimated path (Fig. 2(c)). It is worth noting that in the vectorial map modelling the 220 m² faculty hall we included a virtual rectangle in the center which, though non-existent in practice, models a zone avoided by the operator in their walks, and helps to get a faster convergence to a mostly monomodal state (Fig. 2(b)) while keeping a low sample size.

One of the most usual problems we found during the SfM process, which partly motivated our approach, is the existence of repetitive visual structures in different parts of the scenario (i.e. doors, windows, benches, etc.). That implies incorrect matches that, though being visually correct, are incorrect from a geographic point of view, and thus induce invalid 3D models. Our main goal in the training phase is to achieve an error-free 3D model, since it is essential for the accuracy of the posterior on-line resection process. Using the previously obtained rough estimations of the position and orientation of the training images to guide the 3D model reconstruction, we increase the robustness of the SfM process eliminating the need of a careful manual supervision which we had to perform in previous works [19] in order to fix false positive correspondences.

More precisely, the method we use to build the 3D model in a more unsupervised but reliable way is based on the generation of a pairwise candidate matching list. We determine which pairs of images must be compared to look for coincidences between them taking into account the position and orientation from which they were taken. As shown in Fig. 2(e), two images will be tried to match only if (i) the areas of the scenario that they cover are fairly well overlapped, and (ii) they have been taken with a difference in this angle below 50° (otherwise it would degrade the repeatability of features, as indicated in the original paper describing SIFT [13]). Additionally, greater angles differences between the optical axis of the cameras (180° in the last example) makes it impossible to expect finding good visual matching of the corresponding SIFT features.

To get the pairwise candidate matching list we first estimate the area covered by each camera. From the results obtained after executing the particle filter over the sensors data we were able to approximate the 2D location in the scenario $C = (X_i, Y_i)$ at which each image was taken during the training. We also obtained the rotation matrix R that gave us the approximate orientation of the smartphone at that moment. Moreover, considering that the typical camera pose when capturing the images keeps the imaging plane approximately vertical, the unit norm vector $(x', y') = (v_2, v_3)/|(v_2, v_3)|$, with $v = R^\top \cdot (0, 0, -1)\top$, gives us the approximate orientation of the optical axis projected on the floor. As detailed in Fig. 2(d), it is then possible to calculate the area covered by a camera estimating the points $A, B = (X, Y) + d \times ((x', y') \pm tan(FoV/2) \times (y', -x'))$, being d the maximum distance threshold beyond which we discard the obtained SIFT image features[1] and FoV the horizontal field of view of our camera. Finally, using the triangles generated for every camera position, we can compute their corresponding pairwise overlapping areas. These will provide us the list of matching candidate image pairs that will be used as input to the SfM process.

---

[1] Values for d in typical indoor scenarios are of a few meters (9 m in this work).

4   Camera Resection

Having described our improvements in the offline construction of the 3D model, in this section we focus on the optimization of the online phase, i.e., the estimation of the position of the device from a given set of matching 3D model points and 2D pixels in an input image. The *projection matrix* $P_{3\times4}$ defines the algebraic relationship $PX_i = x_i$ for every $X_i \leftrightarrow x_i$ correspondence when both the pixels $x_i = (x_i, y_i, 1)^\top$ and the 3D points $X_i = (X_i, Y_i, Z_i, 1)^\top$ are given in homogeneous coordinates [10]. Matrix P can be factorized as $K_{3\times3}R_{3\times3}[I| - C^\top]_{3\times4}$, where the relationship with the sought rotation R and 3D position C of the device in the 3D reference system is made explicit. This factorization depends also on K, the so-called camera *calibration matrix*. We focus on the simplest *precalibrated* case, in which the camera focal in pixels f is known in advance, $K = diag(f, f, 1)$, and $x_i = K^{-1}x_i^p$ is the way to obtain the working coordinates x_i from the original, image centered pixel coordinates x_i^p.

Camera resectioning consists on the estimation of R and C from potential matches $X_i \leftrightarrow x_i$. However, the SIFT matching process is always contaminated with a variable proportion ρ of *outliers*, i.e. wrong correspondences [13]. To filter them out, the robust RANSAC algorithm [4] selects random minimal subsets of the original correspondences set, from which it computes tentative locations of the device. In previous works [19] we used two classical approaches, namely the DLT algorithm [10] for the uncalibrated case (i.e., unknown K), and the Fiore algorithm [3] for the precalibrated case. These algorithms had the advantage of being based on simple linear algebra procedures, but unfortunately needed minimal subsets of 6 and 5 matchings, respectively. Since the RANSAC algorithm works iteratively by finding solutions from tentative random subsets of these minimal sizes until it eventually finds a subset free of outliers, the probability of finding a good subset diminishes exponentially with the size of such subsets. Thus, in this paper we propose to change the resection procedure by an *algebraic minimal solution* which only needs 3 correspondences. Though the algorithm gets slightly more complicated, as it is not linear any more, the advantages are far greater, because the theoretical probability of finding earlier a good minimal solution gets boosted, as we will also confirm experimentally in the next section. The general operation of the *P3P algorithm* (*pose from 3 points*) is summarized in Algorithm 1, though to implement the somewhat involved mathematical computations the reader is referred to [4].

Note that P3P first finds the depths (d_a, d_b, d_c) of the $X_{i=a,b,c}$ 3D points, i.e., their euclidean distance to camera center C, by solving a 4th degree polynomial. Thus, in fact it can produce up to 4 valid distinct solutions $(d_a(s_l), d_b(s_l), d_c(s_l))$, $l = 1 \ldots 4$. Once depths have been obtained, the estimation of the position C and rotation R of the device reduces to find the correct alignment of two triplets of 3D points, i.e. $(X_i, Y_i, Z_i) \leftrightarrow d_i \frac{(x_i, y_i, 1)}{\|(x_i, y_i, 1)\|_2}$ for $i = a, b, c$. If we first center both triplets on their respective means and then rescale them to a common average size, we are left with the simpler problem of estimating the unknown rotation between the two transformed sets of points. This is the well known *orthogonal Procrustes* problem, and the sought rotation is given by $R = V \cdot$

Algorithm 1. P3P algorithm

Require: Three 2D pixel $\leftrightarrow$ 3D model coordinates correspondences:
$$\{(x_a, y_a), (x_b, y_b), (x_c, y_c)\} \leftrightarrow \{(X_a, Y_a, Z_a), (X_b, Y_b, Z_b), (X_c, Y_c, Z_c)\}$$
(*) Compute five G_k ($k = 0 \ldots 4$) coefficients from (x_i, y_i) and (X_i, Y_i, Z_i), $i = a, b, c$. Solve the resulting 4th degree polynomial in variable s, $\sum_{k=0}^{4} G_k s^k = 0$ (up to 4 solutions).
    for all s_l, $l = 1 \ldots 4$, solution of polynomial **do**   (One possible resection for each s_l):
        (*) Obtain distances of 3D model points to camera center (depths $d_a(s_l), d_b(s_l), d_c(s_l)$).
        (**) Obtain $\mathtt{R}^j$ and C^j from depths d_a, d_b, d_c.
    end for
Ensure: Up to 4 different solutions for absolute orientation $\{\mathtt{R}^l, C^l\}$ of the device, $l = 1 \ldots 4$.

    (*) These steps involve a fair ammount of nonlinear computations, see [4] for details.

    (**) This step is performed using the *Procrustes algorithm* (explained in main text).

$diag(1, 1, Det(\mathtt{UV}^\top)) \cdot \mathtt{U}^\top$, where $\mathtt{U}_{3\times3}\mathtt{D}_{3\times3}\mathtt{V}_{3\times3}{}^\top$ is the Singular Value Decomposition (SVD) [8] of the matrix $\mathtt{YW}^\top$, being $\mathtt{W}_{3\times3}$ and $\mathtt{Y}_{3\times3}$ the matrices formed by stacking the corresponding transformed triplets of 3D points [9]. Once we have calculated the rotation matrix $\mathtt{R}$, it is very easy to obtain the translation vector C by undoing the previously performed centering and scaling of both set of 3D points.

Tentative solutions produced by successive executions of the P3P algorithm are then tested against the whole set of matches, measuring the *reprojection errors* ξ_i of $\mathtt{P}\mathbf{X}_i$ with respect to the corresponding $\mathbf{x}_i$. A given match $\mathbf{X}_i \leftrightarrow \mathbf{x}_i$ is considered an inlier if such ξ_i is below a given threshold ϵ. Once the number of inliers gets above the expected proportion $1 - \rho$, the RANSAC iteration stops, as we have found a valid solution confirmed by a sufficient number of matchings. If, on the contrary, the number of P3P attempts exceeds a given maximum without having found a valid solution, the resection is considered unsuccessful, as it can't return a reliable device position.

Once the set of inliers has been identified, the final pose is obtained by refining the P3P solution using all the available valid correspondences. Starting from the initial values of $\mathtt{R}$ and C, we use the nonlinear Gauss-Newton optimization algorithm [16] to iteratively minimize the sum of all *alignment errors* between the unit vectors $\frac{(x_i, y_i, 1)}{\|(x_i, y_i, 1)\|_2}$ and the corresponding $\frac{X_i - C}{\|X_i - C\|_2}$ for all valid correspondences i. This minimization is based on solving a linear equation whose coefficient matrix depends on the derivatives of the individual components of this cost with respect to the six parameters (α, β, γ) of $\mathtt{R}$ and (c_x, c_y, c_z) of C. A thorough mathematical derivation of this procedure falls out of the scope of this paper, but the resulting algorithm is included in Algorithm 2 for completeness (again, the reader is referred to [16] for further details on the Gauss-Newton technique). We can optionally make this procedure incremental by adding new correspondences according to the current $\{\tilde{R}, \tilde{C}\}$ until no more inliers are found.

Algorithm 2. Nonlinear Gauss-Newton refinement of R and C

Require: R, C and inlier set $\{\mathbf{X}_i = (X_i, Y_i, Z_i, 1) \leftrightarrow \mathbf{x}_i = (x_i, y_i, 1)\}_{i=1}^n$ estimated by P3P.

   Initial solution: Note that $\hat{\mathbf{x}}_i$ always contain input $\mathbf{x}_i$ rectified by current rotation $\tilde{R}$, $\forall i$:

$\tilde{C} = (\tilde{c}_x, \tilde{c}_y, \tilde{c}_z) \leftarrow C = (c_x, c_y, c_z);$ $R \leftarrow \tilde{R};$ $\hat{\mathbf{x}}_i = (\hat{x}_i, \hat{y}_i, 1) \leftarrow R^\top \mathbf{x}_i;$ $\forall i = 1..n;$

while not convergence of $\{\tilde{R}, \tilde{C}\}$ **and** $n_{iters} < max_{iters}$ **do**

   Jacobian computation: matrices J_i of partial derivatives of alignment error costs with respect to rotation and center increments $(\Delta\alpha, \Delta\beta, \Delta\gamma, \Delta c_x, \Delta c_y, \Delta c_z)$:

$\delta X_i \leftarrow X_i - \tilde{c}_x;$ $\delta Y_i \leftarrow Y_i - \tilde{c}_y;$ $\delta Z_i \leftarrow Z_i - \tilde{c}_z;$ $\forall i = 1..n$

$l_i \leftarrow \sqrt{\delta X_i^2 + \delta Y_i^2 + \delta Z_i^2};$ $l'_i \leftarrow \sqrt{\hat{x}_i^2 + \hat{y}_i^2 + 1};$ $\forall i = 1..n$

$$J_i \leftarrow \begin{bmatrix} \frac{\delta Y_i}{l_i} & \frac{\delta Z_i}{l_i} & 0 & \frac{-(\delta Y_i)^2 - (\delta Z_i)^2}{l_i^3} & \frac{(\delta X_i)(\delta Y_i)}{l_i^3} & \frac{(\delta X_i)(\delta Z_i)}{l_i^3} \\ \frac{-\delta X_i}{l_i} & 0 & \frac{\delta Z_i}{l_i} & \frac{(\delta X_i)(\delta Y_i)}{l_i^3} & \frac{-(\delta X_i)^2 - (\delta Z_i)^2}{l_i^3} & \frac{(\delta Y_i)(\delta Z_i)}{l_i^3} \\ 0 & \frac{-\delta X_i}{l_i} & \frac{-\delta Y_i}{l_i} & \frac{(\delta X_i)(\delta Z_i)}{l_i^3} & \frac{(\delta Y_i)(\delta Z_i)}{l_i^3} & \frac{-(\delta X_i)^2 - (\delta Y_i)^2}{l_i^3} \end{bmatrix} \quad \forall i = 1..n$$

   Current residuals: alignment errors for current solution:

$r_i \leftarrow (\delta X_i/l_i - \hat{x}_i/l'_i, \delta Y_i/l_i - \hat{y}_i/l'_i, \delta Z_i/l_i - 1/l'_i)^\top;$

   Solve Gauss-Newton step linear equation system: using all J_i jacobians and r_i residuals:

Stack J_i matrices and r_i vectors $\forall i$ to form matrix $J_{3n \times 6}$ and vector $r_{3n \times 1}$.

$(\Delta\alpha, \Delta\beta, \Delta\gamma, \Delta c_x, \Delta c_y, \Delta c_z) \leftarrow (J^\top J)^{-1} J^\top \cdot r;$

   Update solution: using obtained solution for rotation and center increments:

$$\tilde{R} \leftarrow \tilde{R} \begin{bmatrix} \cos(\Delta\alpha) & \sin(\Delta\alpha) & 0 \\ -\sin(\Delta\alpha) & \cos(\Delta\alpha) & 0 \\ 0 & 0 & 1 \end{bmatrix} \begin{bmatrix} \cos(\Delta\beta) & 0 & \sin(\Delta\beta) \\ 0 & 1 & 0 \\ -\sin(\Delta\beta) & 0 & \cos(\Delta\beta) \end{bmatrix} \begin{bmatrix} 1 & 0 & 0 \\ 0 & \cos(\Delta\gamma) & \sin(\Delta\gamma) \\ 0 & -\sin(\Delta\gamma) & \cos(\Delta\gamma) \end{bmatrix}$$

$\tilde{C} \leftarrow \tilde{C} + (\Delta c_x, \Delta c_y, \Delta c_z);$ $\hat{\mathbf{x}}_i = (\hat{x}_i, \hat{y}_i, 1) \leftarrow \tilde{R}^\top \mathbf{x}_i, \forall i = 1..n;$

end while

Ensure: Final polished solution $\{\tilde{R}, \tilde{C}\}$

---

5   Experimental Analysis

Experimental Environment: We conducted all our experiments in the ground floors of the Computer Science (scenario 1) and Veterinary Science (scenario 2) faculties in our campus, covering two areas of $220\,\mathrm{m}^2$ and $445\,\mathrm{m}^2$ respectively (Fig. 3(a–b)). During the training phase we used a custom sensor capture application running on a Samsung Galaxy Tab+ 7.0, to acquire all the relevant sensor data (WiFi, images, accelerometer, gravity, gyro and compass). RSSIs measurements were used to build a fingerprinting map, while images were postprocessed on an Intel Core i7 3.4 GHz server equipped with a Nvidia GeForce GTX580 GPU, using the SiftGPU library [23] to extract the SIFT features, as well as the VisualSfM software [24] in order to get the full 3D reconstructions from the matching SIFTs. The IMU and compass data were used as described in Sect. 3 in order to automatically guide these reconstructions. The same server acted also as the cloud in the posterior on-line phase, with the client mobile device sending

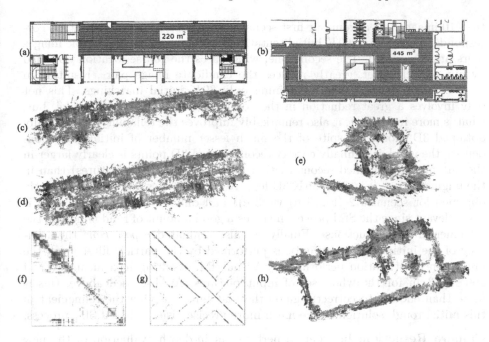

Fig. 3. (a–b) Ground floor plans of scenarios 1 and (2. c–e,h) 3D models obtained using both unguided and guided matching. (f–g) Unguided and guided matching matrices for scenario 1.

all its sensor readings to it in order to get its precise localisation. SiftGPU was used again for feature extraction in the client input image, while matching with features in the model was performed using an adapted version of the CUDA ENN (*Exhaustive Nearest Neighbour*) software [7]. It is key in our approach that this exhaustive search is performed only on a small subset of the whole set of features of the 3D model, using an initial coarse-grained localisation based on the RSSI and the available WiFi fingerprinting map [19]. Finally, all stages of the resection algorithm described in Sect. 4 were implemented using the QVision library [25].

3D Model Generation: Figs. 3(c,e) show two sample final results of the SfM process when the matching is not guided. It is clear that false positive matches caused by visually repetitive structures produce models that do not fit well with the corresponding scenarios. In previous versions of our system, these erroneous matchings –extremely frequent in indoor scenarios– had to be removed interactively by an operator in order to get fully correct reconstructions, in a cumbersome an tedious manual and incremental process. In contrast, when images were coarsely geotagged using the technique described in Sect. 3, we easily avoided those situations, since distant cameras were early discarded in the pairwise matching. This resulted in a smaller but also much more reliable set of matches. To illustrate this, Figs. 3(f–g) show two different *matching matrices* for the 510 images taken from our first scenario. The first, more dense matrix, corresponds to a total of 260 K initial tentative matchings when all possible images pairs are considered. The second one, which uses the coarse location obtained by our particle filter, greatly reduces the candidate image pairs, resulting in a much more sparse matrix containing only 30 K initial matchings. This not only involves a great reduction in the computing time of the 3D model, but, what is more important, it also remarkably improves the reliability of the finally obtained 3D model. In spite of the much lesser number of initial correspondences, the number of finally correct reconstructed 3D points is clearly larger in the automatically guided reconstruction (Fig. 3(d), 150 K 3D features) than in the unguided case (Fig. 3(c), 86 K 3D features). Similar results were consistently obtained for scenario 2 (Fig. 3(h) vs. 3(e)) and different executions –which is also relevant since the SfM process involves a good amount of randomness in the incremental reconstructions–. Finally, we also evaluated *a posteriori* the accuracy of the initial coarse estimations performed by the particle filter using the final refined estimation performed by VisualSfM, resulting in a mean error of 206 ± 113 cm for the whole set of input pictures. As discussed above, this is more than enough to correctly guide the matchings, leaving the refinement of this initial rough solution to the much more precise visually based SfM process.

Camera Resection: In order to perform an in-depth evaluation of the new camera resection technique presented in this paper, we have exhaustively tested the different configuration parameters mentioned in Sect. 4, in order to estimate their influence on the results. These parameters were (i) the reprojection error threshold ϵ that decides when a 2D$\leftrightarrow$3D correspondence is considered a tentative inlier, (ii) the minimum ratio of required inliers $1 - \rho$ over the total amount of correspondences used to validate a RANSAC triplet, and (iii) the mean residual $\sum_i \xi_i/N$ value obtained after resection that indicates the error in alignment for the final number N of inlier correspondences, which is a metric of the goodness of the obtained solution. Figures 4(a–b) illustrate the estimation error in *cm* that we have obtained using each set of parameters and running the process 50 times over a set of 30 640 $\times$ 480 images taken from different viewpoints in scenario 1. From these results we see that it is possible to obtain an average accuracy[2] down to 5 cm with a percentage of success of 97 % using the configuration $\epsilon = 0.01$, $1 - \rho = 0.3$, and $max(\sum_i \xi_i/N) = 0.002$. If we compare these results with those obtained in our previous work [19], where we obtained a mean error of 14.6 cm, we can confirm that we have notably improved the localisation accuracy. Furthermore, it is worth mentioning the reduction of the resection time, taking now less than 10 ms instead of 119 ms it took using the previous system (Fig. 4(c)). That time reduction allows to complete an entire cycle (from sensor data acquisition to 3D position estimation) in less than 250 ms, making the proposal ideal for applications requiring high accuracy and rapid response, like AR-based applications.

---

[2] The ground-truth considered to get these numbers was obtained using the 3D model of the scene, adding the test images and reestimating their reconstruction coordinates within it.

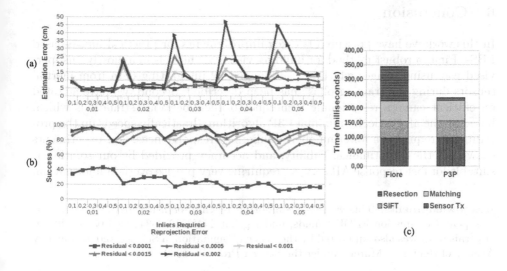

Fig. 4. (a–b) Resection error results and percentage of success after 1250 executions for each parameter set. (c) Performance comparison with previous proposal.

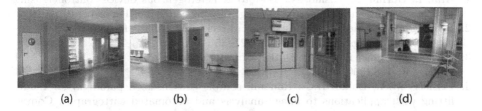

(a)   (b)   (c)   (d)

Fig. 5. AR results: (a–b) Scenario 1. (c–d) Scenario 2.

Augmented Reality Application: However, there is not best way to test our proposal than using it for AR purposes within a real scenario. We have developed an AR application for Android devices and have tested it in our two modelled scenarios. In Fig. 5 we can see how the AR perfectly matches to different sample input images, demonstrating the high accuracy reached by our resection process. We are aware that, though the response time of our resection service by the cloud is typically limited to less than 250 ms, this refreshment rate is still insufficient to fully cope with video input rates of mobile devices (25 fps = 40 ms in typical cameras). This problem can be alleviated using the gyroscope sensor to continuously detect small rotation changes of the device between successive resections, thus reducing the communication with the cloud.

6 Conclusion

In this work we have presented two key improvements for practical image-based LBSs. First, a robust method for building visual 3D models in a mostly unsupervised way using images which are geo-tagged by integrating data from inertial sensors during the training phase has been described. Second, we have adapted an efficient camera resectioning technique to infer location estimations which, based on the algebraically minimal P3P algorithm, drastically speeds up the procedure by requiring a fewer number of inliers correspondences. Our experiments show that the performance, liability, and accuracy provided by our solution is suitable for fast response AR services requiring very precise overlaid information.

Acknowledgments. This work was supported by the Spanish MINECO, as well as European Commission FEDER funds, under grant TIN2012-38341-C04-03. Additionally, this work was also supported by the Seneca Foundation, a Science and Technology Agency of Region of Murcia, under the Seneca Program 2009.

References

1. Arai, I., Horimi, S., Nishio, N.: Wi-foto 2: heterogeneous device controller using wi-fi positioning and template matching. In: Proceedings of Pervasive'10 (2010)
2. Beauregard, S., Haas, H.: Pedestrian dead reckoning: a basis for personal positioning. In: Proceedings of WPNC'06, pp. 27–35 (2006)
3. Fiore, P.D.: Efficient linear solution of exterior orientation. IEEE Trans. PAMI **23**(2), 140–148 (2001)
4. Fischler, M.A., Bolles, R.C.: Random sample consensus: a paradigm for model fitting with applications to image analysis and automated cartography. Comm. ACM **24**(6), 381–395 (1981)
5. Foxlin, E.: Pedestrian tracking with shoe-mounted inertial sensors. IEEE Comput. Graphics Appl. **25**(6), 38–46 (2005)
6. Fraundorfer, F., Wu, C., Frahm, J.M., Pollefeys, M.: Visual word based location recognition in 3D models using distance augmented weighting. In: Proceedings of 4th 3DPVT (2008)
7. Garcia, V., Debreuve, E., Barlaud, M.: Fast k-nearest neighbor search using GPU. In: IEEE Proceedings of CVPRW'08, pp. 1–6 (2008)
8. Golub, G., Van Loan, C.: Matrix Computations, 3rd edn. Johns Hopkins University Press, Baltimore (1996)
9. Gower, J.C., Dijksterhuis, G.B.: Procrustes Problems. Oxford University Press, Oxford (2004)
10. Hartley, R., Zisserman, A.: Multiple View Geometry in Computer Vision. Cambridge University Press, Cambridge (2003)
11. Hattori, K., et al.: Hybrid indoor location estimation system using image processing and WiFi strength. In: IEEE proceedings of WNIS 2009, pp. 406–411 (2009)
12. Li, X., Wang, J.: Image matching techniques for vision-based indoor navigation systems: performance analysis for 3D map based approach. In: IEEE Proceedings of the IPIN'12, pp. 1–8 (2012)
13. Lowe, D.: Distinctive image features from scale-invariant keypoints. IJCV **60**(2), 91–110 (2004)

14. Mulloni, A., Wagner, D., Barakonyi, I., Schmalstieg, D.: Indoor positioning and navigation with camera phones. IEEE Pervasive Comput. **8**(2), 22–31 (2009)
15. Murillo, A.C., Guerrero, J., Sagues, C.: SURF features for efficient robot localization with omnidirectional images. In: IEEE Proceedings of ICRA'07, pp. 3901–3907 (2007)
16. Nocedal, J., Wright, S.J.: Numerical Optimization. Springer, New York (1999)
17. Rai, A., Chintalapudi, K.K., Padmanabhan, V.N., Sen, R.: Zee: zero-effort crowdsourcing for indoor localization. IN: ACM Proceedings of MobiCom12, pp. 293–304 (2012)
18. Ruiz-Ruiz, A.J., Canovas, O., Rubio Muñoz, R.A., Lopez-de-Teruel Alcolea, P.E.: Using SIFT and WiFi signals to provide location-based services for smartphones. In: Puiatti, A., Gu, T. (eds.) MobiQuitous 2011. LNICST, vol. 104, pp. 37–48. Springer, Heidelberg (2012)
19. Ruiz-Ruiz, A.J., Lopez-de-Teruel, P.E., Canovas,O.: A multisensor LBS using SIFT-based 3D models. In: IEEE Proceedings of IPIN'12, pp. 1–10 (2012)
20. Se, S., Lowe, D., Little, J.: Vision based global localization and mapping for mobile robots. IEEE Trans. Robot. **21**(3), 364–375 (2005)
21. Thrun, S., Burgard, W., Fox, D.: Probabilistic Robotics. MIT Press, Cambridge (2005)
22. Woodman, O., Harle, R.: Pedestrian localisation for indoor environments. In: ACM Proceedings of Ubicomp'08, pp. 114–123 (2008)
23. Wu, C.: SiftGPU: a GPU implementation of scale invaraint feature transform (SIFT) (2012). http://cs.unc.edu/ccwu/siftgpu
24. Wu, C.: Towards Linear-time Incremental Structure from Motion. In: 3DV'13 (2013)
25. QVision Qt CV library, University of Murcia (2013). http://qvision.sourceforge.net

Appstrument - A Unified App Instrumentation and Automated Playback Framework for Testing Mobile Applications

Vikrant Nandakumar[✉], Vijay Ekambaram, and Vivek Sharma

IBM Research - India, Bangalore, India
{vikrant.nandakumar,vijaye12,vivek.irl}@in.ibm.com

Abstract. Mobile Test Automation is gaining significant importance for an app-tester because it helps to alleviate the voluminous effort and time associated in thoroughly testing an application. Challenges like diversity in mobile hardware, multiple operating systems, ever-increasing application complexity and high volume of test cases etc. reiterate the importance of exploiting automation techniques for mobile application testing. In order to exhaustively capture user actions during the record-phase, faithfully reproduce those actions during playback-phase and also to capture the relevant metrics while playing back, instrumentation of the *Application-under-test* (AUT) becomes an imperative process. However, the type and level of instrumentation is different and is very specific to the category of testing which has to be automated. This paper presents *Appstrument*, a unified framework for instrumenting mobile applications to make them ready for functional, performance and accessibility testing. This framework allows instrumenting the application to get it ready for either a single category of testing or a combination of two or more of these categories, with multiple optional features for each category. In addition to this, given a test script, the framework also supports automated playback of instrumented applications. *Appstrument* has been deployed and tested against some popular applications from *Google Play* (Android apps) and some IBM in-house iOS applications. Results indicate that this framework is able to successfully instrument a sizeable number of applications and effectively playback user-defined test cases automatically to collect relevant metrics/results corresponding to each category of testing.

Keywords: Mobile applications · Instrumentation · Android · iOS · Testing · Functional · Performance · Accessibility

1 Introduction

Testing mobile applications is an emerging research area that faces a variety of challenges due to increasing number of applications getting developed and a plethora of new devices being released into the market. These new devices have varied form factors, screen size, resolution, OS, hardware specification etc.

© Institute for Computer Sciences, Social Informatics and Telecommunications Engineering 2014
I. Stojmenovic et al. (Eds.): MOBIQUITOUS 2013, LNICST 131, pp. 474–486, 2014.
DOI: 10.1007/978-3-319-11569-6_37

which increases the difficulty to effectively test an application. Also, in comparison to conventional Desktop and Web applications, mobile applications have shorter release cycles (lesser time-to-market) and the update frequency is high, making it necessary for the tester to perform additional testing quite often. Due to these factors, testing a mobile application becomes a very expensive, laborious and time consuming process. IDC [1] predicts that smartphone shipments will reach 978 million in 2014. Hence, with the emerging smartphone market, there is a lot of emphasis on how applications perform on the actual devices. Of late, speed and performance have become the primary concern for consumers of mobile applications. This fact is emphasized in a recent Compuware survey which found that 4 out of 5 users expected an app to launch in 3 s or less. Considering these factors, its imperative to have an automated testing solution which would help save time, minimize human effort and ensure better quality and performance of mobile applications. In order to exhaustively capture user actions during the record-phase, faithfully reproduce those actions during playback-phase and also to capture the relevant metrics while playing back, instrumentation of the *Application-under-test* (AUT) becomes an imperative process. Instrumentation is the process of inserting few lines of code (hooks) in the original AUT to facilitate effective recording and automated replay of test cases.

In this paper, we present *Appstrument*, a unified app instrumentation and automated playback framework for testing mobile applications. *Appstrument* supports functional testing, performance testing and accessibility testing on Android and iOS applications. For each category of testing, this framework supports multiple features which can be used in isolation or in combination with a feature from a different category. Furthermore, the framework also supports automated playback of instrumented applications.

The rest of the paper is organized as follows. Section 2 talks about the motivation for this research work. The detailed architecture, design and implementation is discussed in Sect. 3. The framework evaluation and results are presented in Sect. 4. Section 5 throws light on a few other similar efforts in this domain, followed by Future work and Conclusion in Sect. 6.

2 Motivation

Mobile App instrumentation is primarily needed for getting complete control over an application during execution. Instrumentation is becoming necessary in automated mobile application testing due to the stringent nature of the mobile OS. Most of the existing solutions which bypass the app instrumentation requirement aren't straight forward and requires the device to be rooted/jail-broken [2]. Some of the testing solutions provided by the OSes like Android, suffer with the disadvantage of requiring the testers to code up the test case in a formal language like Java, VBScript etc. Furthermore, the current instrumentation and playback techniques used in testing mobile apps are very purpose-specific and limited to a particular type of testing. Lack of a unified consolidated framework to perform automated mobile application testing is the motivation behind this research work.

3   *Appstrument* Framework for Instrumentation and Playback

This section describes about the detailed design, architecture, implementation and working of the *Appstrument* framework.

3.1   System Architecture and Implementation

The overall architecture of the *Appstrument* framework is depicted in Fig. 1. It comprises of five different components

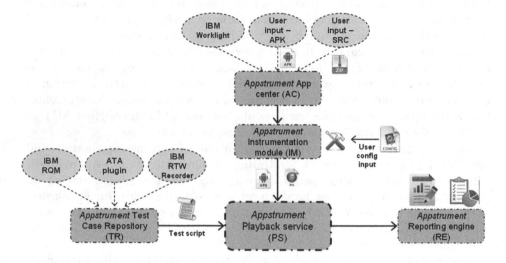

Fig. 1. *Appstrument* - Overall Architecture

1. ***Appstrument* Test Case Repository (TR)** is a collection of automated test scripts (list of test steps) which can be executed on the AUT by the playback service. TR is integrated with three different plugins viz. IBM `Rational Quality Manager` (RQM) [9], Automating Test Automation [3] and IBM `Rational Test Workbench` [10].
   (a) `IBM Rational Quality Manager` offers a collaborative environment for test planning, construction, and execution. It acts as a centralized repository for test cases and is integrated with a number of popular testing products available in the market. *Appstrument* TR has integration with RQM via an adapter through which it can fetch the test cases and push them to the Playback Service for execution on the AUT.
   (b) Automating Test Automation (ATA) [3] is a tool which addresses the problem of creating automated test scripts from manually written test cases. ATA integrates with the *Appstrument* TR and stores the tuple-based English-like Clearscript statements obtained by converting manual test cases.

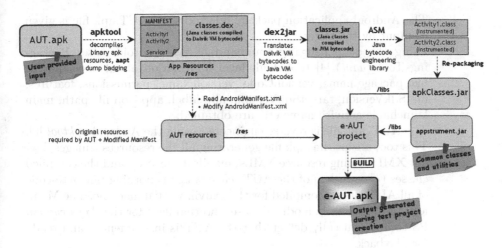

Fig. 2. Instrumentation in Android

(c) `IBM Rational Test Workbench` consists of a recorder engine which can capture the user-actions in the form of Clearscript statements. The tester can go with this option in situations when there are no manually written test cases available for the AUT.

2. *Appstrument* **App Center (AC)** contains the applications which are available for *Appstrument* Instrumentation Module (IM) for instrumentation.

   (a) `IBM Worklight` [11] is a comprehensive mobile application platform to build, run and manage mobile applications. The `IBM Worklight Application Center` [12] is an enterprise application store which allows the enterprise administrator to install, configure and administer a repository of mobile applications for use by individual employees and groups across the enterprise. *Appstrument* AC module has an in-built adapter to pull an application directly from the Worklight Application Center and pass it on to the *Appstrument* IM module.

   (b) *Appstrument* AC also provides an interface for the user to upload an APK file or the application source code in a zip file format. The need of an APK binary file is primarily for Android applications. However, in the case of iOS, there is a requirement for the application source code to be uploaded to the AC.

3. *Appstrument* **Instrumentation Module (IM)**

   (a) **Instrumentation in Android:** In the case of Android, the AUT is decompiled, reverse engineered and instrumented. The detailed instrumentation process in Android is described in Fig. 2. The following are the steps involved in the Android instrumentation process

- The Android application package referred to as AUT.apk file is given as input by the tester.
- Using the `dump badging` command of the Android Asset Packaging Tool (*aapt*) [4] tool, high level information about the .apk file like package name, versionCode, versionName, permissions, features, minSdkVersion, targetSdkVersion, app label, app icon file path, main launchable activity name etc. are obtained.
- The AUT .apk file is reverse engineered using the Android *apktool* [5]. This tool unzips the .apk file generating all the resources (images, layout XMLs, string resource XMLs, manifest file, etc.) and the compiled classes (*classes.dex*) of the AUT. *classes.dex* is nothing but byte-code of all AUT classes compiled for the Dalvik virtual machine. The Manifest XML is slightly modified to set internal flags for the *Appstrument* PS to automatically detect that the AUT is instrumented and ready for playback.
- In the next step, dex2jar [6] tool is used to decompile *classes.dex* to decode and understand the underlying Java classes. This tool translates the Dalvik VM byte-codes to the Java VM byte-codes. The resultant file is *classes.jar* which contains corresponding Java classes from *classes.dex*.
- The individual files from *classes.jar* is extracted by using the Java jar tool. From the Manifest file, the declared Activity information is obtained and using the ASM byte-code engineering library [7], the Java byte-code is loaded into the memory and altered in different ways.
- Once the bytecode is loaded, for each Activity class declared in the manifest, modifications are performed on the Android activity life cycle methods viz. *onCreate()*, *onStart()*, *onResume()*, *onPause()* and *onDestroy()*. These methods are modified to include an additional line towards the end of each method, which enables a call-out to *Appstrument* instrumenter class, thereby establishing control over the complete application during runtime.

(b) **Instrumentation in iOS:** In the case of an iOS application, there is a requirement for the AUT's source code to carry out the instrumentation process. The *Appstrument* library is linked with the AUT's source code and the AUT is built to get the instrumented AUT. However, in this process there is no modification of source code of the original AUT. We make use of the `Objective-C` *Method Swizzling* [8] concept to make the method in the AUT call an alternate implementation which is different from the original implementation. In the below example, since directly overriding the *sendEvent* method (called by UIApplication to dispatch events to views inside the window) would break the responder chain sequence, the `Objective-C` *Method Swizzling* concept is used to hook into our *Appstrument* adapter code on the iOS event bus using the original *sendEvent* method. Once the *sendEvent* method is swizzled, *Appstrument* gains access into the event bus at runtime and can push a new event during playback of the AUT.

```
<?xml version="1.0"?>
<Appstrument>
  - <FunctionalTesting>
      true
      <ImageCaptureAndMarkup>true</ImageCaptureAndMarkup>
      <VerificationPoints>true</VerificationPoints>
      <DynamicFind>true</DynamicFind>
  </FunctionalTesting>
  - <PerformanceTesting>
      false
      <ResourceMonitoring>false</ResourceMonitoring>
      <MethodLevelProfiling>false</MethodLevelProfiling>
      <EventProfiling>false</EventProfiling>
      <KernelAndUIthreadMapping>false</KernelAndUIthreadMapping>
  </PerformanceTesting>
  - <AccessibilityTesting>
      false
      <ImageCaptureAndMarkup>false</ImageCaptureAndMarkup>
      <AccessibilityAutoCorrection>false</AccessibilityAutoCorrection>
  </AccessibilityTesting>
</Appstrument>
```

Fig. 3. *Appstrument* config file

$$- \ (\text{void})\text{sendEvent} : (\text{UIEvent}*)\text{event};$$

(c) **Appstrument config file:** The *Appstrument* IM module takes a *App-strument config* file as input before it starts instrumenting the AUT. This *Appstrument config* file defines the different configuration parameters which have to be considered for generating the instrumented AUT. This file is in XML format and has a boolean flag *(true/false)* defined against each of the features for every category of testing. These features are optional for the user to choose and are in addition to (i) basic playback for Functional Testing, (ii) playback + resource monitoring for Performance Testing, (iii) playback + compliance check for Accessibility Testing. The details about the various features are explained in the following section. Figure 3 shows a sample *Appstrument config* file.

4. *Appstrument* **Playback Service (PS)**
The Playback Service is responsible for the execution of a test script on the AUT. PS picks up the test script from the Test case Repository (TR) and plays it back on the instrumented application from the Instrumentation Module (IM). The output of the playback is sent to the Reporting Engine (RE). Depending on the *Appstrument config* file provided to the IM module, certain features are enabled or disabled for each category of testing during playback. The details of features which are supported by the PS are as follows:

(a) **Features for Functional Testing**

   i. **Image Capture and Mark-up** - By enabling this feature during playback, the Playback Service will capture the snapshot of AUT's screen on which the action happens for a particular test step. Additionally, on the captured snapshot, the PS will draw a bounding box around the UI element which is associated with that test step to indicate to the tester where exactly in that screen the action has happened. For example, if a user clicks on the "Submit" button on a login page, then the snapshot of the login page with a bounding box around the "Submit" button is provided in the *Appstrument* Report.

ii. **Verification Points** - This is a feature by which the Playback Service can check if a particular UI element conforms with a tester-specified property like (i) verifying if a TextView contains the text as defined by the tester, (ii) location of the TextView on the screen etc. The verification point definitions are included as a part of the test script to be played back on a AUT.

iii. **Dynamic Find** - This feature helps the Playback Service to resolve dis-ambiguities in the test case to ensure a faithful playback on the AUT. For example, if the test step is *"Click on Submit button to the left of Reset Button"*, the Playback Service should be aware of other UI elements in close proximity to the *Submit* button. The details about these UI elements, referred as *associated element description*, are required to execute a test step with greater accuracy.

(b) **Features for Performance Testing**

i. **Resource Monitoring** - This default Performance Testing feature captures the various parameters like CPU Utilization, RAM Usage, Virtual Memory Usage, Network Traffic (incoming & outgoing) etc. *Appstrument* PS captures these parameters without any requirement for instrumentation of AUT.

ii. **Method-level profiling** - Enabling this feature would capture all the method level details with respect to the AUT. *Appstrument* logs messages during method start and exit to track these information.

iii. **Event profiling** - This feature captures all the system, user, UI events of the AUT occurring during playback to visualize the control and the data flow of the application.

iv. **Kernel and UI thread Mapping:** Having this feature enabled would help in capturing all the kernel thread activities (like Wifi service calls, Activity Manager, Window manager, etc.) and map these activities with respect to the AUT events to understand the performance bottlenecks.

(c) **Features for Accessibility Testing**

i. **Image Capture and Mark-up** - This feature is very similar to the Image Capture and Mark-up feature mentioned in Functional Testing. Unlike Functional Testing, the principal difference in accessibility testing is, instead of drawing a bounding box on the target UI element (for a single test step), the *accessibility non-compliant* UI element is highlighted to the tester in the playback report.

ii. **Accessibility Auto Correction** - Enabling this feature would not only identify the *accessibility non-compliant* UI element, but also try to perform an auto correction to make it compliant. For example, for an Android EditText widget, if the `android:hint` property is not set, this feature would employ the Dynamic Find (Functional testing feature) to identify a nearby associated label to fill in the property field thereby auto correcting the non-compliance error.

Appstrument Playback Mini Report: sample_test [7/22/13 12:57 PM]

Test:	sample_test [executed on 7/22/13 12:53 PM]
Categories to test:	Functional, Performance, Accessibility
Application:	IBM NUC Sensing App (version 4; created on 7/22/13 12:50 PM; executed on 7/22/13 12:53 PM)
Execution Status:	**Functional** – All steps passed **Performance** – Passed **Accessibility** - Failed. 1 or more elements failed the test
Device:	samsung GT-P3100 (Android; API level 15)

Fig. 4. *Appstrument* Playback Mini Report (Sample)

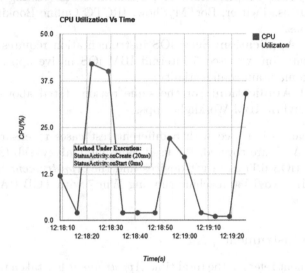

Fig. 5. *Appstrument* Performance Testing Report (Sample)

5. *Appstrument* Reporting Engine (RE)

Reporting Engine (RE) generates test reports for the test script executions on the AUT by the Playback Service. Depending upon the flags set in the *Appstrument config* file, reports are generated for various categories of testing along with the optional features under each category. RE generates two types of reports. Figure 4 shows an *Appstrument* Playback Mini Report which gives a summary of the test execution using the *Appstrument* framework. Figure 5 shows a detailed Performance Testing Report depicting the CPU utilization of the AUT with respect to time. Upon hovering over the graph, the method level details executed at that particular instance of time is also shown. Similarly, *Appstrument* RE generates detailed category-wise/feature-wise reports for a particular test script execution.

4   Evaluation

4.1   Testing Environment

In-order to show the impact of dynamic feature selection, we tested the *Appstrument* with the following categories of application:

- **Android-Native Application:** Apps considered for testing in this category are Calculator, S Planner, Quickoffice, IBM Sametime, Facebook and IBM sensing app.
- **Android-Hybrid Application:** Apps considered for testing in this category are RedBus, Twitter, BookMyShow, IRCTC Online Booking and IBM Worklight apps.
- **iOS-Native Application:** Since iOS instrumentation requires source-code for instrumentation, we used 5 internal IBM iOS native apps. (names not mentioned to maintain confidentiality)
- **iOS-Hybrid Application:** For the same reason stated above, we used 5 internal iOS hybrid IBM Worklight apps.

Each application is tested with 5 different test cases to ensure that most features of the AUT are covered. We used Samsung Galaxy Tab (Android 4.0) and iPhone 4S (iOS 6.1) as target devices and the *Appstrument* framework is deployed on a Lenovo T430 machine running Win 7 with 4 GB RAM and Intel Core i7 processor.

4.2   Time to Instrument

Time to Instrument refers to the total time *Appstrument* has taken to instrument the AUT. For evaluation purposes, we have instrumented all the applications mentioned in the Sect. 4.1. In Table 1, we have shown the time *Appstrument* has taken to instrument few popular Android applications for functional testing with all 3 features included. Instrumentation of the applications is a one-time process, as *Appstrument* saves the instrumented AUT in its repository for future testing purposes.

Table 1. Time to Instrument

AUT	Time to Instrument(ms)	Binary size(MB)
IBM SameTime	47280	1.13
Whatsapp	205237	10.4
Facebook	402860	13.7
Skype	246991	15.1
Flipboard	58499	2.3

4.3   Record and Playback

In order to evaluate *Appstrument* with respect to its playback capability, we tested each AUT (mentioned in the Sect. 4.1) with varying test-cases (both deterministic and non-deterministic). Non-Deterministic test-cases refer to the test-cases where the flow of execution and the interval time between test-steps varies with respect to the run-time inputs. *Appstrument* is able to playback all the test-cases with reduced overhead. Analysis with respect to the overhead is mentioned in the following sections.

4.4   Impact of Instrumentation on Functional Testing

Appstrument provides the various instrumented versions (as explained in Sect. 3.1) with respect to functional testing. A tester can choose the features required and the instrumentation overhead varies depending on these set of features.

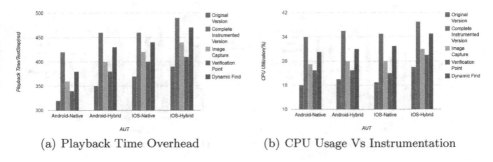

(a) Playback Time Overhead   (b) CPU Usage Vs Instrumentation

Fig. 6. Impact of instrumentation on functional testing

Figure 6(a) compares and analyzes the playback time of various instrumented versions. *X* axis represents the time taken for each test-step to execute during playback. From the graph, we observed the playback time of the various featured instrumented versions follow this order: {Complete instrumented version > Dynamic Find instrumented version > Image Capture instrumented version > Verification point instrumented version > Original Version} (Note: Original Version refers to the un-instrumented AUT). Interestingly, further analysis shows that the CPU utilization of these instrumented versions in Fig. 6(b) follows a similar pattern as the playback time. Since *Appstrument* allows specific configurations of the required features for functional testing, testers can reduce the instrumentation overhead based on their requirements. Table 2 shows the percentage of overhead reduced (with respect to the playback time) for various partially instrumented versions as compared to the complete instrumentation.

4.5   Impact of Instrumentation on Performance Testing

In Fig. 7(a), we compare various instrumented versions (as mentioned in Sect. 3.1) with respect to performance testing. Playback time of these instrumented versions varies with respect to the features selected. Table 3 shows the performance

Table 2. Functional testing-overhead reduction

AUT category	Image capture	Verification point	Dynamic find
Android-Native	14 %	19 %	10 %
Android-Hybrid	3 %	17 %	7 %
iOS-Native	9 %	13 %	4 %
iOS-Hybrid	10 %	16 %	4 %

overhead reduction obtained with respect to selective instrumentation as compared to complete instrumentation. For testers, there is a huge scope to reduce instrumentation overhead by choosing appropriate configurations based on their requirements.

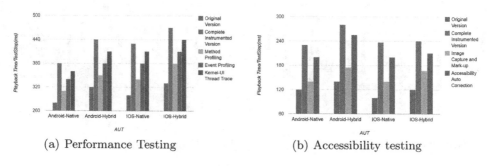

(a) Performance Testing   (b) Accessibility testing

Fig. 7. Impact of instrumentation on performance and accessibility testing

Table 3. Performance testing-overhead reduction

AUT category	Method profiling	Event profiling	Kernel-UI thread mapping
Android-Native	18 %	11 %	5 %
Android-Hybrid	20 %	14 %	7 %
iOS-Native	21 %	12 %	5 %
iOS-Hybrid	19 %	13 %	6 %

4.6   Impact of Instrumentation on Accessibility Testing

Figure 7(b) shows the analysis of the selective feature capability of *Appstrument* with respect to the Accessibility testing. Since features like Accessibility auto-correction and Image Capture and Mark-up (as mentioned in Sect. 3.1) incur more overhead as compared to the basic accessibility testing, the tester can choose these features as and when they are required. From Fig. 7(b), we also understand that the Accessibility auto-correction feature has a heavy overload on the AUT's performance as it nearly doubles the playback time of the complete test-case.

5   Related Work

A cursory examination of the literature in test automation for mobile applications clearly throws light on the significant attention devoted to the instrumentation techniques. Recent mobile testing publications like [14,16,18,19] clearly indicate the necessity for code instrumentation in mobile testing. Mobile automation testing products in the market like `TestStudio` from Telerik, `MonkeyTalk` from Gorilla Logic and `Jamo` from Jamo Solutions do instrumentation for mobile test automation. Recent papers in mobile performance testing like Energy Profiler [18] and AppInsight [14] instruments the AUT to capture all the performance related metrics with respect to the AUT. SIF [15] talks about creating abstractions for selective instrumentation and also recounts the advantages of selective instrumentation. Comparing *Appstrument* with these prior-arts, *Appstrument* provides a much detailed architecture for complete as well as selective instrumentation with respect to most common mobile testing categories like Functional, Performance and Accessibility testing.

6   Future Work and Conclusion

In this paper, we presented *Appstrument* - a unified framework for mobile application instrumentation and playback for automated testing. In future, we envision to include several other categories of testing like security testing, usability testing, localization testing etc. We have plans to expand on the features supported under each umbrella of testing. We intend to drastically improve our coverage with the diversity of applications and devices the framework currently supports. Efforts are on to come up with a solution to get rid of the source code requirement for iOS instrumentation. In sum, we foresee a better, powerful, efficient and versatile *Appstrument* framework in future which overcomes the various challenges associated with mobile test automation.

References

1. IDC Worldwide Smartphone 2012–2016 Forecast Update, June 2012
2. Gomez, L., et al.: RERAN: timing-and touch-sensitive record and replay for Android. In: ICSE '13 (2013)
3. Thummalapenta, S., et al.: Automating test automation. IBM Research report (2011)
4. Android, AAPT tool, July 2013. http://elinux.org/Android_aapt
5. Android, apktool, July 2013. https://code.google.com/p/android-apktool/
6. Dex2Jar tool, July 2013. http://code.google.com/p/dex2jar/
7. Bruneton, E.: ASM 4.0 - A Java bytecode engineering library, OW2 Consortium

8. Cocoa Dev, Method Swizzling, July 2013. http://cocoadev.com/MethodSwizzling
9. IBM Rational Quality Manager, July 2013. http://www-03.ibm.com/software/products/us/en/ratiqualmana/
10. IBM Rational Test Workbench, July 2013. http://www-03.ibm.com/software/products/us/en/rtw
11. IBM Worklight, July 2013. http://www-03.ibm.com/software/products/us/en/worklight/
12. Irvine, M., Maddocks, J.: Enabling Mobile Apps with IBM Worklight Application Center, IBM Redpaper, June 2013
13. Mahmud, J., Lau, T.: Lowering the barriers to website testing with CoTester. In: Proceedings of the 14th International Conference on Intelligent User Interfaces, pp. 169–178 (2010)
14. Ravindranath, L., Padhye, J., Agarwal, S., Mahajan, R., Obermiller, I., Shayandeh, S.: AppInsight: mobile app performance monitoring in the wild. In: Proceedings of the 10th USENIX Conference on Operating Systems Design and Implementation (OSDI'12), pp. 107–120 (2012)
15. Hao, S., Li, D., Halfond, W.G.J., Govindan, R.: SIF: a selective instrumentation framework for mobile applications. In: Proceeding of the 11th Annual International Conference on Mobile Systems, Applications, and Services (MobiSys '13), pp. 167–180 (2013)
16. Sama, M., Harty, J.: Using code instrumentation to enhance testing on J2ME: a lesson learned with JInjector. In: Proceedings of the 10th Workshop on Mobile Computing Systems and Applications (HotMobile '09) (2009)
17. Zhou, W., Zhang, X., Jiang, X.: AppInk: watermarking android apps for repackaging deterrence. In: Proceedings of the 8th ACM SIGSAC Symposium on Information, Computer and Communications Security (ASIA CCS '13), pp. 1–12 (2013)
18. Pathak, A., Hu, Y.C., Zhang, M.: Where is the energy spent inside my app?: fine grained energy accounting on smartphones with Eprof. In: Proceedings of the 7th ACM European Conference on Computer Systems (EuroSys '12), pp. 29–42 (2012)
19. Nath, S., Lin, F.X., Ravindranath, L., Padhye, J.: SmartAds: bringing contextual ads to mobile apps. In: Proceeding of the 11th Annual International Conference on Mobile Systems, Applications, and Aervices (MobiSys '13), pp. 111–124 (2013)

A Layered Secret Sharing Scheme for Automated Profile Sharing in OSN Groups

Guillaume Smith[1,2,3]([✉]), Roksana Boreli[1,2], and Mohamed Ali Kaafar[1,4]

[1] NICTA, Sydney, Australia
[2] University of New South Wales, Sydney, Australia
[3] ISAE - Université de Toulouse, Toulouse, France
[4] INRIA, Paris, France
guillaume.smith@nicta.com.au

Abstract. We propose a novel Layered secret sharing scheme and its application to Online Social Networks (OSNs). In current, commercially offered OSNs, access to users' profile information is managed by the service provider e.g. Facebook or Google+, based on the user defined privacy settings. A limited set of rules such as those governing the creation of groups of friends as defined by the user (e.g. circles, friend groups or lists) allow the users to define different levels of privacy, however they are arguably complex and rely on a trusted third party (the service provider) to ensure compliance. The proposed scheme enables automated profile sharing in OSN groups with fine grained privacy control, via a multi-secret sharing scheme comprising layered shares, created from user's profile attributes (multiple secrets), that are distributed to group members; with no reliance on a trusted third party. The scheme can be implemented via e.g. a browser plugin, enabling automation of all operations for OSN users. We study the security of the scheme against attacks aiming to acquire knowledge about user's profile. We also provide a theoretical analysis of the resulting level of protection for specific (privacy sensitive) attributes of the profile.

1 Introduction

Secret sharing schemes have been extensively used in a number of cryptographic and distributed computing applications [3]. Using secret sharing, a dealer shares a secret (any content, be it a numerical value, text string or a file) in a secure way, by creating a number of shares (cryptographic derivatives of the secret) and distributing them to a set of participants. A participant can access the secret by combining a specific number of shares, that has to be greater than the threshold.

In this paper, we consider the use of secret sharing to enable user-controlled and privacy preserving sharing of an Online Social Network (OSN) user's profile amongst groups of their direct connections (friends). In most commercially available OSNs, an OSN user currently stores their private data using the trusted OSN server. Access to their profile is managed by a policy, regulating which attributes (e.g. their location, date of birth, interests, etc.) may be obtained by

© Institute for Computer Sciences, Social Informatics and Telecommunications Engineering 2014
I. Stojmenovic et al. (Eds.): MOBIQUITOUS 2013, LNICST 131, pp. 487–499, 2014.
DOI: 10.1007/978-3-319-11569-6_38

their friends or other people. A number of challenges related to privacy in OSNs have been identified by researchers [10], including the reliance on the trusted third party (TTP) to manage the privacy control, the arguable complexity of how those controls are implemented in current OSNs and the limited flexibility of access controls (we note Google+ circles and Facebook lists are a step in the direction of improving the flexibility). This motivates our interest in using secret sharing to enable direct and fine grained user control of the accessibility of their private data.

We specifically consider the OSN user's requirements to share multiple profile attributes (secrets) with differing levels of security and privacy (i.e. thresholds), within groups of friends, without relying on a TTP. Additionally, an OSN user may not wish to disclose his level of desired privacy protection, and/or the difference in the number of attributes he is sharing with different friends (or groups of friends). The limitations of the currently proposed secret sharing schemes relate to both threshold flexibility and disclosure of scheme's parameters [12,20], which could be used to re-identify anonymous data [11].

We propose a novel Layered secret sharing scheme, that recursively embeds shares related to individual secrets in layers with increased protection, and encrypts each layer with a shares-based key. Each secret is then protected by a selected single secret-sharing scheme with its own threshold, and the number of secrets is hidden within the Layered scheme, which ensures that the thresholds remain unknown. The main contributions of this paper are as follows:

We **propose a new Layered secret sharing scheme** that enables flexible levels of security and privacy. We introduce **privacy-preserving automated profile sharing in OSN groups** as a possible use of our scheme. By generating Layered shares (comprising a selected set of attributes, corresponding to each group's privacy policy) and distributing a share to each member of the group, an OSN user automatically enforces the deployment of group's privacy policy and enables fine grained policy control within group's members, without relying on a TTP.

We **analyse the security of the scheme** for attacks that have a goal of illegitimately acquiring knowledge about users OSN profiles. Consequently, we show that no new Layered shares can be attained by any of the attacks that include a varying level of background knowledge. We provide an **analysis of the number of Layered shares** that an **attacker** who is at an arbitrary number of hops in the social graph from the node sharing his profile **may acquire**, which can be used to enable the profile owner to set the required level of protection offered to specific (privacy sensitive) attributes of the profile.

2   Background and Related Work

In a secret sharing scheme, a dealer securely shares a secret with a group of participants, by generating n shares using a cryptographic function. These are distributed to n participants; by aggregating shares, participants can gain access to the secret when the number of combined shares reaches the threshold t.

We note that the threshold needs to be distributed jointly with the shares. The most commonly used scheme, proposed by Shamir [14], is based on polynomial interpolation. It has the following properties:

Property S.1. *Shamir's scheme is information theoretically secure, that is, for a (t, n) scheme, knowledge of less than t shares does not provide any information about the remaining shares or the secret.*

Property S.2. *The secret is equivalent to a share, as it is a specific point on the curve defined by the polynomial used to both generate and decode shares.*

Shamir's scheme introduces a significant overhead as shares are of the same size as the secret [13]. Ramp schemes [19] have therefore been proposed to provide a trade-off between the size of the shares and the security of the scheme.

A generalized ramp scheme is defined by (t, L, n), where the parameter L relates to security, i.e. no information about the secret can be obtained if a participant has $x \leq (t - L)$ shares. In all ramp schemes, the size of the shares for a secret S, is $\frac{|S|}{L}$. [19] introduces the concepts of weak and strong ramp schemes. A strong ramp scheme with $L = t$ (used in our work) has the following properties:

Property R.1. *The ramp scheme is computationally secure, i.e. for a (t, n) scheme, possession of $x < t$ (less than t shares) does not provide any information about any remaining (unknown) shares and any part of the secret.*

Property R.2. *Knowledge of the secret in the ramp scheme enables reconstruction of all the related shares (coordinates used for shares computation are known).*

2.1   Sharing Multiple Secrets

A naive approach to share multiple secrets is to use, multiple times, a single secret sharing scheme. That may prove onerous in both terms of communication and computational overhead as each participant needs, for each shared secret, to receive and store a corresponding share [4]. Considering privacy, this approach will expose the number of shared secrets that is equal to the number of shares.

Multiple secret sharing schemes (e.g. [7,12,20]) have then been introduced with the objective of allowing one share per participant for all the secrets shared by a single user. From a profile sharing perspective, and more specifically when considering the different privacy levels a user may consider for each attribute, these schemes do not provide the desirable flexibility, as a profile's owner would not be allowed to parametrize the level of privacy for each secret (attribute).

A specific class of schemes consists of designs that allow a different threshold per secret (e.g. [7,17,18]). When used in profile sharing, each participant will have a priori knowledge about the number of shared secrets along with their corresponding thresholds, which doesn't fit the needs of users to not reveal how much of their personal information they are actually sharing.

2.2   Profile Sharing in OSNs

A possible approach to selective sharing of different information on popular OSNs, e.g. Facebook or Google+ is to define groups of friends (lists or circles) and set up a different privacy policy for each group. Alternatively, in order to prevent a central entity from accessing user data, [1] proposes an architecture where user data is encrypted and stored on an untrusted server. Other proposals e.g. *PeerSon*, [5], aim to distribute the online social network itself.

In practice, users may not be easily convinced to change from the well-established centralized OSNs only due to privacy concerns. References [8] and [2] e.g. specifically address user's privacy in the context of major OSNs, by providing browser-based plugins in order to enable user's control over their personal data.

Although there is user support for manually configured group based access control in OSNs, researchers have shown [6] that the majority of OSN users do not utilize this feature. Consequently automated algorithms for grouping friends (*e.g.* based on common interests, family relationship, etc.) have been studied e.g. in [21]. However, although the access control can be defined for groups (circles) of friends, all users in the same group share a common access policy. Our proposed Layered secret sharing scheme, as we will show, enables a finer grained access control policy that is based on the number of common friends, and automates the enforcement of this policy in each circle. This is implemented without having to rely on a trusted third party (i.e. the OSN operator).

3   Layered Secret Sharing Scheme

A dealer in our scheme generates Layered shares, which consist of a number of encrypted layers, each comprising (standard single secret sharing) shares related to a specific secret. Figure 1 shows the components of a Layered share.

The notations used in this paper are listed in Table 1. A dealer shares k secrets with n participants P_j $j = 1, ..., n$. The secrets S_i, $i = 1, ..., k$, have t_i corresponding thresholds. We assume these are ordered in terms of increasing magnitudes, with $(t_1 \leq t_2 \leq ... \leq t_k)$ and that the secret S_1 is the system secret,

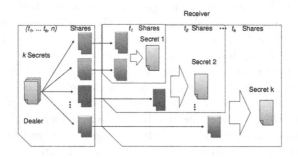

Fig. 1. Components in the Layered secret sharing scheme

Table 1. Notations used to describe the Layered secret sharing scheme

n	Number of Layered shares and participants
P_j	Participant j for $j = 1, ..., n$
k	Number of secrets shared (including the system secret)
S_i	Secret i, for $i = 1, ..., k$
$H(.)$	One-way hash function, publicly known
$[.]_K$	Symmetric encryption using the key K
$[.]^K$	Symmetric decryption using the key K
$[A\|\|B]$	Concatenation of content A and B
s^i_j	Share j related to the secret S_i
L^i_j	Layer i of the Layered share, containing the shares related to S_i to S_k
K_i	Key derived from the secret S_i
t_i	Threshold for the secret S_i
b_i	Number of additional shares needed to compute the key K_i

a random variable used for verification of Layered shares. For the use case of OSN profile sharing, S_2 is an OSN group's identifier.

Layered shares L^1_j, $j = 1, ..., n$, are generated according to steps outlined in Function *MakeLayered*. The secrets are included recursively within the Layered shares, starting from the secret with the highest threshold (S_k). At the $(k - i)^{th}$ step, to include the secret S_i in L^{i+1}_j for $j = 1, ..., n$, the dealer computes $n + b_i$ standard shares ($s^i_1, ..., s^i_{n+b_i}$) with a threshold t_i using the Function *MakeSingle*. *MakeSingle* utilizes either Shamir's scheme [14] or the ramp scheme from [19], with the choice depending on the size of S_i and the required security level.

b_i additional shares $s^i_{n+1}, \cdots, s^i_{n+b_i}$ are generated, then concatenated and hashed, using e.g. *SHA-2* to obtain the key K_i (ensuring the size of concatenation is at least the size of the encryption key, e.g. *AES* needs 128 or 256 bits keys).

Function MakeLayered($S_1, ..., S_k, t_1, ..., t_k$)

Initialization;
for $j \leftarrow 1$ **to** n **do**
   $L^{k+1}_j \leftarrow \varnothing$;
Generate n Layered shares by constructing k individual layers;
for $i \leftarrow k$ **to** 1 **do**
   MakeSingle produces $n + b_i$ (single secret sharing) shares according to the selected secret sharing mechanism
   $(s^i_1, ..., s^i_{n+b_i}) \leftarrow MakeSingle(S_i, t_i, scheme)$;
   $K_i \leftarrow H([s^i_{n+1}\|\| \cdots \|\|s^i_{n+b_i}])$;
   for $j \leftarrow 1$ **to** n **do**
      $L^i_j \leftarrow [t_i\|\|s^i_j\|\|[L^{i+1}_j]_{K_i}]$;

For $j = 1, ..., n$, each share s_j^i related to secret S_i is concatenated with the corresponding encrypted layer $[L_j^{i+1}]_{K_i}$: $L_j^i = [t_i||s_j^i||[L_j^{i+1}]_{K_i}]$. These steps are repeated until all secrets are included in the layers.

The n Layered shares are distributed by the dealer, with a single unique share and the share's index (j, L_j^1) sent to each participant over a secure channel. As in other secret sharing mechanisms, participants aggregate their shares to gain access to the secret(s) S_i, with the number of shares as per the threshold t_i.

To describe the decoding process by which a participant recovers one or more secrets, we assume that he has acquired x Layered shares, L_z^1 where $z = 1, ..., x$ (to simplify the notation, without loss of generality we assume that Layered shares are received in the order of their indexes). We also assume that the participant has previously decoded i secrets $S_1, ..., S_i$ with thresholds $t_1, ..., t_i$ and their corresponding keys $K_1, ..., K_i$, where i is defined by $t_i \le x - 1 < t_{i+1}$, using the previously received $x - 1$ Layered shares ($i = 0$ if no secrets have been decoded). Thus he has $x-1$ layers L_z^{i+1}, where $z = 1, ..., x-1$ and a Layered share L_x^1 that is yet to be processed. Function *DecodeLayered* describes the decoding process. In the first step, the "old" layers related to the previously decoded secrets need to, recursively, be removed and decrypted (using $K_1, ..., K_i$) from L_x^1. If $x == t_{i+1}$, function *DecodeSingle* can then be used to decode the secret S_{i+1} and also to compute as previously the key K_{i+1}. Finally the layers related to the secret S_{i+1} are removed from the x Layered shares and the following parts $[L_z^{i+2}]_{K_{i+1}}$ are decrypted, using the key K_{i+1}.

Function DecodeLayered(L_x^1)

Remove the layers related to the previously decoded secrets;
for $y \leftarrow 1$ **to** i **do**
  $[s_x^y||[L_x^{y+1}]_{K_y}] \leftarrow L_x^y$;
  $L_x^{y+1} \leftarrow [[L_x^{y+1}]_{K_y}]^{K_y}$;
Decode the secret S_{i+1} if there is a sufficient number of shares;
if $x == t_{i+1}$ **then**
  for $j \leftarrow 1$ **to** x **do**
    $[s_j^{i+1}||[L_j^{i+2}]_{K_{i+1}}] \leftarrow L_j^{i+1}$;
  DecodeSingle outputs the secret S_{i+1} and the shares $s_{n+1}^{i+1}, \cdots, s_{n+b_i}^{i+1}$;
  $(S_{i+1}, s_{n+1}^{i+1}, \cdots, s_{n+b_i}^{i+1}) \leftarrow$ DecodeSingle$(scheme, t_{i+1}, s_1^{i+1}, ..., s_x^{i+1})$;
  Generate the encryption key from the share s_{n+1}^{i+1};
  $K_{i+1} \leftarrow H([s_{n+1}^{i+1}||\cdots||s_{n+b_i}^{i+1}])$;
  Remove the layer related to S_{i+1} for all (available) Layered shares;
  for $j \leftarrow 1$ **to** x **do**
    $L_j^{i+2} \leftarrow [[L_j^{i+2}]_{K_{i+1}}]^{K_{i+1}}$;

3.1   Using Layered Shares for Profile Sharing in OSN Groups

To initialize the scheme, the dealer must first define circles of friends, C_i, and the attributes (secrets) he intends to share amongst the friends in each circle. He should also allocate friends to circles, either manually or using any of the proposed mechanisms, e.g. [21]. Then, for each circle and each shared attribute, the dealer should choose a privacy level for accessing the attribute (*i.e.* the threshold for each secret), that will, in our scheme, be equivalent to the number of common friends that a user in this circle needs to have with the profile owner. We acknowledge that this criteria may not be universally applicable to all OSN groups. However, we believe, as per [21], that the number of common friends represents a relevant and easy to understand metric for the OSN users.

The dealer then generates Layered shares (using *MakeLayered*) and distributes them to friends in a specific circle over a secure channel. Subsequently, each friend contacts their friends and collects the available Layered shares from the friends in common with the dealer (that also belong to the same circle). Any friend can then decode the accessible attributes according to the number of collected Layered shares, using *DecodeLayered*.

We envisage the profile sharing application to be implemented as a browser plugin, where all the operations related to the shares are automated and secure. We note that for the scheme to be operational, all participating OSN users need to have the plugin installed.

For new friend connection requests, the dealer first needs to select the appropriate circle for this new friend. Then, he needs to generate a new Layered share and index and send it over a secure channel to the new friend.

Finally, if a user wishes to remove a friend from a circle or change his circle, he has to renew all Layered shares for this circle, to ensure that his Layered share will not be usable in future exchanges. An alternative would be to use the proxy re-encryption approach from [9], that does not require share renewal.

4   Security Analysis for the OSN Application

4.1   Adversary Model

The threat scenario consists of adversaries that will attempt to access more information than what they may obtain legitimately i.e. from the Layered shares acquired either directly from the dealer or from the dealer's friend connections. This includes an honest but curious adversary who is an insider (a user) within the system and has access to a number of Layered shares, or a malicious user who obtains all information by monitoring communications of other nodes, by compromising nodes, *etc.*

4.2   Privacy of the Scheme

We assume the attacker has x Layered shares, $x \in [0, n]$. This will enable him access to corresponding secrets S_1 to S_i, decoded from those shares, with i

defined by the threshold $t_i \leq x < t_{i+1}$. The attacker also may have background knowledge of n_S, $n_S \in [0, k]$ secrets, their position in the layers and related thresholds. In the following, we consider the different scenarios related to the position of known secrets and the resulting gain by the attacker.

We consider the use of both Shamir's and the ramp scheme and utilize the properties of these schemes, defined in Sect. 2, in the security analysis.

The Attacker has Access only to Layered Shares: The privacy protection our scheme provides is equivalent to that of the underlying scheme, as defined by properties S.1 and R.1, respectively for Shamir's and the ramp scheme.

Attacker has Access to both Layered Shares and Background Knowledge: We first consider the cases when one of the following secrets, S_{i+1} or S_{i+2} is known, then generalise the analysis to the attacker having access to any number of secrets (not acquired from the available Layered shares).

The adversary knows secret S_{i+1} in addition to Layered shares: *For Shamir's scheme*, knowledge of the secret is equivalent to having access to an additional share related to S_{i+1} (see property S.2). If the new number of shares is below t_{i+1}, as per the property S.1, the attacker cannot progress further. If the threshold was reached, the attacker can recompute all related shares; consequently (from the additional shares), he can acquire the key K_{i+1} required to decrypt the next layer of shares within the available Layered shares.

For the ramp scheme, knowledge of the secret and the threshold t_{i+1}, as per property R.2, enables the attacker only to reconstruct the key K_{i+1} and access the next level of shares in the Layered scheme. Similarly to the case when Shamir's scheme is used, the attacker can, as the maximum gain, succeed in having access to x shares in the next layer of the Layered shares.

The adversary knows secret S_{i+2} together with Layered shares: Here, the adversary aims to access the unknown secret S_{i+1} and potentially further information about the remaining secrets.

For Shamir's scheme (re. S.2), there is no additional gain.

For the ramp scheme, (as per R.2) the attacker can reconstruct all the shares related to S_{i+2}. This would enable him access to K_{i+2} for decrypting the next level of shares in the Layered scheme, related to the secret S_{i+3}. But first the attacker needs to reconstruct the key K_{i+1} to be able to decode the Layered shares L_j^{i+1} and then the Layered shares L_j^{i+2} using the key K_{i+2}.

A plaintext attack, in which the adversary partially knows the decrypted text string, i.e. shares related to S_{i+2}, could be used to gain K_{i+1} (we note that, to the best of our knowledge, there has been as yet no successful plaintext attack on *AES*). Assuming this is successful, the attacker would obtain K_{i+1}, i.e. a cryptographic hash of b_{i+1} shares related to S_{i+1}. Assuming the attacker has sufficient computational resources to derive these shares from the one-way hash function, the resulting gain would be b_{i+1} additional shares related to S_{i+1}; if the threshold t_{i+1} is reached, the attacker will gain the additional secret S_{i+1}.

The adversary knows any number of subsequent secrets: For any case where the next layer of shares (in the Layered scheme) is protected by Shamir's scheme, and assuming the secret is known to the attacker, the maximum possible gain can be the availability of the key to decrypt the next layer. When the next layer is protected by the ramp scheme, the certain gain is the same key. When the second-next layer is based on Shamir's secret sharing, assuming a known secret, there is no possible gain; when it is based on the ramp scheme, again with a known secret, both the previous layer and the following layer may be decrypted. We note that no new Layered shares can be gained by the attacker with an arbitrary level of background information.

4.3   Analysis of Attacker's Access to Layered Shares

We now provide an analysis of the number of Layered shares that an adversary potentially may have access to, in the OSN scenario where a user is sharing his profile with direct friends.

We assume that an adversary is a node belonging to the social graph of the user and that he obtains information (shares) from his direct connections with a probability p_{j-1}, where $j > 1$ is the distance in hops between the attacker and the profile's owner. A node at a distance j from the owner is also referred as a j-degree friend. Second, we assume that the probability that an adversary will obtain shares decreases with the distance from the node sharing his profile and we only consider the path with the shortest distance as relevant in obtaining information (assuming that the probability to obtain shares on a longer path is negligible compared to the shortest path).

We assume that the direct friends of the owner follow the protocol and, although they may be tricked by the attacker, they would release only their own (single) Layered share, with a probability p_1. All other nodes (on the social graph of the profile owner) who have shares are adversaries. Therefore an attacker at a distance $j + 1$ will receive all available Layered shares from a j-degree friend of the owner ($j > 1$) with a probability p_j.

In the following analysis, we derive the probability that an attacker amongst the $j + 1$-degree friend with $j \geq 1$ will obtain x Layered shares, assuming the owner has n direct friends: $P_j(X = x \mid N = n)$. To this purpose, we consider two cases: we provide a detailed analysis for a close attacker, with $j = 1$ and we generalize the analysis for $j \geq 2$.

First, we consider an *attacker who is at a distance two from the profile owner*. Let $\mathscr{A}_1$ be the set of common friends of the attacker and the profile's owner of size A_1. The attacker will successfully acquire x Layered shares from $\mathscr{A}_1$ if he receives them from exactly x elements in $\mathscr{A}_1$ with a probability p_1, therefore:

$$P_1(X = x \mid N = n) = \sum_{a_1=x}^{n} P(A_1 = a_1 \mid N = n)\binom{a_1}{x}p_1^x(1 - p_1)^{a_1-x} \quad (1)$$

The distribution $P(A_1 = a_1 \mid N = n)$ can be computed for $a_1 \in [0, n]$ from the social graph of the selected OSN.

For the generic case of a *distant adversary* who is a $j + 1$-degree friend with $j \geq 2$, we assume that the nodes at a distance j for $j \geq 2$ receive independent sets of Layered shares (although any share can be in multiple sets), in line with the assumption that the further two nodes are from the profile's owner, the less chance they have to have common friends. Let A_j be the random variable describing the size of the intersection between the direct friends of the attacker and the j-degree friends of the profile's owner. We can then calculate:

$$P_j(X = x \mid N = n) = \sum_{a_j=0}^{\infty} P(X = x \mid N = n \wedge A_j = a_j) P(A_j = a_j \mid N = n)$$

(2)

where $P(A_j = a_j \mid N = n)$ can be computed from the OSN's social graph.

The probability that the attacker receives the Layered shares from k nodes amongst the A_j is equal to $\binom{a_j}{k} p_j^k (1 - p_j)^{a_j - k}$. Then the probability that one of the k nodes has x_y Layered shares for $y \in [1, k]$ is equal to $P_{j-1}(X = x_y \mid N = n)$. Finally we need to evaluate the probability that the size of the union of any k sets of size x_y amongst n of Layered shares is equal to x, denoted as $P(|U_1^k| = x \mid x_y)$. The derivation of this probability is included in our technical report[1]. We finally derive the probability that the attacker receives x Layered shares:

$$P(X = x \mid N = n \wedge A_j = a_j) = \sum_{k=1}^{a_j} \binom{a_j}{k} p_j^k (1 - p_j)^{a_j - k} \times$$

$$\sum_{y=1}^{k} \sum_{x_y=0}^{n} P(|U_1^k| = x \mid x_y) \prod_{z=1}^{k} P_{j-1}(X = x_z \mid N = n) \quad (3)$$

5   Implementation Considerations

To evaluate the practicality of our proposal, we need to ensure that the number of Layered shares that friends of an OSN user can obtain, is always greater than the minimum threshold required to protect against attacks. To obtain representative OSN parameters, we use the Facebook New Orleans dataset [16], comprising around 60,000 nodes, to derive the distributions required for calculating $P_j(X \geq x \mid N = n)$, as per Sect. 4.3. We choose three levels of resilience: such that less than, respectively, 1 %, 0.1 %, and 0.01 % of the adversaries at selected distances from the dealer are able to access data if corresponding thresholds t_{min}^j are chosen. We also choose two values for the probabilities p_j (5 % and 10 %) that a friend of the dealer will leak information to an adversary and for an adversary to forward all Layered shares to another adversary.

Figure 2 shows the calculated minimum thresholds for selected parameters. This figure also shows the average number of Layered shares that friends of a dealer will be able to acquire (the number of friends is varied between one and 100, the average number of Facebook friends [15]). We can observe that even with a high (10 %) leakage from dealer's friends and other adversaries, the number of available shares that the friends can acquire is greater than the minimum

---

[1] http://www.nicta.com.au/pub?id=7318

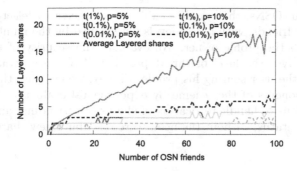

Fig. 2. Thresholds required to ensure a chosen level of protection against attackers at distance two from the dealer.

threshold required for the highest level of protection (99.99 %) against adversaries. We can also confirm the potential for having flexible privacy protection for shared attributes: an OSN user with 40 friends can have 5 different levels of protection, while the average Facebook user who has 100 friends may to have around 10 different levels of shared data protection.

We also compare the implementation complexity of Layered shares and the naive approach, i.e. when the same number of secrets is shared with a single secret sharing scheme. The comparison is based on the amount of time required to perform the generating and decoding of shares (Layered or single). We use the open source software: *ssss*[2] version 5, for secret sharing utilizing Shamir's scheme, *vdmfec*[3] for the ramp scheme and *openssl*[4] for symmetric encryption. We note that *vdmfec* implements a Reed-Solomon based weak ramp scheme, however we consider this sufficiently close in encoding/decoding complexity to a strong ramp scheme (considered in the rest of this work) for a rough estimate.

We consider an example use of the Layered scheme in Facebook, where an average user has around $n = 100$ friends. We assume that a user is sharing $k = 10$ attributes in a selected group (circle), with secret sharing thresholds ranging between 5 and 50 (with increments of 5).

Our results show that there is a very low overhead in the time taken to generate Layered shares (compared to generating single shares for the same secrets and thresholds) – up to 5 %.

6   Conclusion

We have proposed a new Layered multiple secret sharing scheme that fully preserves privacy of the data shared by the dealer, by protecting the number of secrets he is sharing and their thresholds. We consider the use of this scheme for

---

[2] http://point-at-infinity.org/ssss/
[3] http://freecode.com/projects/vdmfec
[4] http://www.openssl.org/

profile sharing in OSNs, that would enable direct access to selected attributes of the profile by friends, with access levels determined by the number of friends in common with the profile owner. We evaluate the security of the proposed scheme and analyse the level of threat posed by OSN users who are on the social graph of the user sharing his profile. Finally, we evaluate the complexity of critical components of the scheme by experimental evaluation. Future work includes extensions to handle revocation of shares (un-friending) and changes to the relationship status, without the need to re-distribute new shares.

References

1. Anderson, J., Diaz, C., Bonneau, J., Stajano, F.: Privacy-enabling social networking over untrusted networks. In: WOSN '09, pp. 1–6. ACM (2009)
2. Baden, R., Bender, A., Spring, N., Bhattacharjee, B., Starin, D.: Persona: an online social network with user-defined privacy. SIGCOMM 39(4), 135–146 (2009)
3. Beimel, A.: Secret-sharing schemes: a survey. In: Chee, Y.M., Guo, Z., Ling, S., Shao, F., Tang, Y., Wang, H., Xing, C. (eds.) IWCC 2011. LNCS, vol. 6639, pp. 11–46. Springer, Heidelberg (2011)
4. Blundo, C., Santis, A.D., Vaccaro, U.: Efficient sharing of many secrets. In: Enjalbert, P., Wagner, K.W., Finkel, A. (eds.) STACS 1993. LNCS, vol. 665. Springer, Heidelberg (1993)
5. Buchegger, S., Schiöberg, D., Vu, L.-H., Datta, A.: Peerson: P2p social networking: early experiences and insights. In: SNS '09, pp. 46–52. ACM (2009)
6. Cazabet, R., Leguistin, M., Amblard, F.: Automated community detection on social networks: useful? efficient? asking the users. In: ACM WI&C (2012)
7. Chan, C.-W., Chang, C.-C.: A scheme for threshold multi-secret sharing. Appl. Math. Comput. 166(1), 1–14 (2005)
8. Guha, S., Tang, K., Francis, P.: Noyb: privacy in online social networks. In: WOSN '08, pp. 49–54. ACM (2008)
9. Jahid, S., Mittal, P., Borisov, N.: Easier: encryption-based access control in social networks with efficient revocation. In: ASIACCS '11, pp. 411–415. ACM, New York (2011)
10. Liu, Y., Gummadi, K.P., Krishnamurthy, B., Mislove, A.: Analyzing Facebook privacy settings: user expectations vs. reality. In: 2011 ACM SIGCOMM Conference on Internet Measurement Conference, ACM IMC 2011 (2011)
11. Narayanan, A., Shmatikov, V.: Myths and fallacies of "personally identifiable information". Commun. ACM 53(6), 24–26 (2010)
12. Pang, L.-J., Wang, Y.-M.: A new (t, n) multi-secret sharing scheme based on shamir's secret sharing. Appl. Math. Comput. 167, 840–848 (2005)
13. Rabin, M.O.: Efficient dispersal of information for security, load balancing, and fault tolerance. J. ACM 36(2), 335–348 (1989)
14. Shamir, A.: How to share a secret. Commun. ACM 22(11), 612–613 (1979)
15. Ugander, J., Karrer, B., Backstrom, L., Marlow, C.: The anatomy of the Facebook social graph. CoRR, abs/1111.4503 (2011)
16. Viswanath, B., Mislove, A., Cha, M., Gummadi, K.P.: On the evolution of user interaction in Facebook. In: WOSN (2009)
17. Wang, F., Gu, L., Zheng, S., Yang, Y., Hu, Z.: A novel verifiable dynamic multi-policy secret sharing scheme. In: ICACT'10, pp. 1474–1479. IEEE Press (2010)

18. Waseda, A., Soshi, M.: Consideration for multi-threshold multi-secret sharing schemes. In: ISITA 2012, pp. 265–269, Oct 2012
19. Yamamoto, H.: Secret sharing system using (k, l, n) threshold scheme. Electron. Commun. Jpn. (Part I: Commun.) **69**(9), 46–54 (1986)
20. Yang, C.-C., Chang, T.-Y., Hwang, M.-S.: A (t, n) multi-secret sharing scheme. Appl. Math. Comput. **151**(2), 483–490 (2004)
21. Yildiz, H., Kruegel, C.: Detecting social cliques for automated privacy control in online social networks. In: IEEE International Conference on Pervasive Computing and Communications Workshops, pp. 353–359 (2012)

Distributed Key Certification Using Accumulators for Wireless Sensor Networks

Jun-Young Bae[1]([✉]), Claude Castelluccia[2], Cédric Lauradoux[2],
and Franck Rousseau[1]

[1] Grenoble Institute of Technology, Grenoble Informatics Laboratory – CNRS,
UMR 5217, 38402 Saint Martin D'Hères, France
{jun-young.bae,franck.rousseau}@imag.fr
[2] INRIA, 655 Avenue de L'Europe, 38334 St Ismier, France
{claude.castelluccia,cedric.lauradoux}@inria.fr

Abstract. In this work, we propose a key certification protocol for wireless sensor networks that allows nodes to autonomously exchange their public keys and verify their authenticity using one-way accumulators. We examine and compare different accumulator implementations for our protocol on the Sun SPOT platform. We observe that our protocol performs best with accumulators based on Elliptic Curve Cryptography (ECC): ECC-based accumulators have roughly the same speed as Secure Bloom filters, but they have a smaller memory footprint.

Keywords: Wireless sensor networks · One-way accumulators

1 Introduction

Wireless Sensor Networks (WSNs) are envisioned as a key part of what is now known as the *Internet of Things* (IoT). In a few years from now, large sensor networks, composed of myriads of inexpensive low-power and energy-constrained wireless nodes, will be commonplace. However, wireless communications are easy to eavesdrop and manipulate, thus more prone to serious attacks. Securing communications in wireless sensor network is, therefore, of utmost importance.

Two critical issues in WSNs are key distribution and certification. They are mandatory in order to establish confidentiality in the network. Over the last decade, symmetric cryptography was, by far, the most popular primitive used for key distribution and certification since asymmetric cryptography was considered to be computationally too heavy to handle for low-power sensor nodes (*e.g.* [7,9]). However, at the end of the last decade, Elliptic Curve Cryptography (ECC) started to be deployed on sensor nodes [15] which showed that asymmetric cryptography is feasible in WSNs.

If the cost of asymmetric cryptography is now no more an issue, there is still the problem of certifying the public keys of the nodes. We cannot simply preinstall the public key of the Certificate Authority (CA) and the digital certificates that guarantee the authenticity of the public keys of the nodes: any nodes that

© Institute for Computer Sciences, Social Informatics and Telecommunications Engineering 2014
I. Stojmenovic et al. (Eds.): MOBIQUITOUS 2013, LNICST 131, pp. 500–511, 2014.
DOI: 10.1007/978-3-319-11569-6_39

are certified by the same CA would potentially be able to communicate with each other, even if they are not supposed to be in the same network (*e.g.* your nodes would start communicating with your neighbor nodes, because they are produced and certified by the same manufacturer). A solution to this problem would be to allow the owner of the network to act as the CA and pre-install within each of the nodes the necessary cryptographic materials. However, this solution would not scale up for large number of nodes. Moreover, if the only way to install the cryptographic materials within the nodes is through the wireless medium, because they are located in places that are inaccessible (*e.g.* embedded inside walls), an attacker may initiate a Man-in-The-Middle (MiTM) attack and swap the public key and the certificates of the owner with its own. The contribution of this paper is to break through this problem by proposing a distributed key certification protocol based on *one-way accumulators* that is fully autonomous and does not require the use of CAs and certificates.

Accumulators are space/time efficient data structures that are used in order to verify if an element belongs to a predefined set. Several accumulator designs are available, ranging from RSA-based accumulators [2] to Secure Bloom filters [11]. We have studied and evaluated these different designs by implementing them on the Sun SPOT platform in order to determine which one is the most practical for our protocol in terms of processing speed, memory footprint, data transmission, and energy efficiency. We observe that our protocol has the best overall performance with ECC-based accumulators.

All the hypothesis used throughout this paper, for the nodes and the adversary, are defined in Sect. 2. The accumulators, as well as our protocol for distributed key certification, are described in Sect. 3. A brief security analysis of our protocol is available in Sect. 4. The performance evaluation and the impact of the choice of accumulators are discussed in Sect. 5. Previous work in the existing literature are reviewed in Sect. 6. Finally, Sect. 7 concludes our work and proposes future research directions.

2 Assumptions

In this work, we focus on securing large multi-hop networks that may be deployed alongside other unrelated networks. Wireless sensor nodes are low-power embedded devices. A gateway is used in order to collect data and/or relay traffic from the nodes that may be placed at any arbitrary position and may even be mobile. We need to be able to distinguish between different legitimate networks in order to prevent unwanted information leakage or unwillingly transiting external traffic (*i.e.* waste energy). We also need to prevent attackers from joining or tampering with the network.

2.1 Node Model

We assume that the nodes are *interface-less*: no physical interaction with the node is possible and the only way to communicate with them is through the wireless medium. This assumption is realistic considering the cases of *intelligent buildings* and *IoT*, in which nodes might be, for example, embedded inside walls. Manufacturers also tend to integrate various sensors into a single chip (System-on-Chip) so that they are easier to miniaturize, mass-produce, and deploy in a non-invasive way. We assume that these nodes are produced and distributed in batches by the manufacturer. This is a reasonable assumption, considering that manufacturers would probably not sell cheap, mass-produced nodes individually, and that at least a few nodes are needed in order to build a practical multi-hop WSN. We also consider that customizing nodes with specific cryptographic materials at production time is not much of a limitation. This process is already quite common for certain chip manufacturing, in which unique identifiers or calibration data are loaded after fabrication.

2.2 Attacker Model

Our solution is designed to deal with three particular threats: *Node injection*, *Node capture*, and *Denial-of-Service*.

Node injection – The adversary must not be able to inject its own node in the network.

Node capture – The adversary can gain full control of a node since we assume that the nodes are not *tamper-resistant*. This implies that all the node secrets are exposed to the adversary. In order to measure the resistance of a protocol, the number of communications that can be eavesdropped by the adversary after the capture of a node, is considered (see [8]). It does not include the communications of the compromised node.

Denial-of-Service (DoS) – The adversary may attempt to exhaust the resources of the nodes by sending bogus messages or requests. The protocol must protect all the computationally intensive operations: the adversary must not be able to trigger them easily.

We have considered that two attacks were outside the scope of this paper. A *Relay attack* is the most basic form of a MiTM attack. They can be used in order to mount more sophisticated attacks such as *Wormhole attacks* or DoS. Various solutions to this problem have been proposed [12,20]. In *Replication attacks*, the adversary injects nodes in the network that are copies of a legitimate node. Specific solutions to this problem exist [18].

3 Accumulator-Based Protocol

After reviewing the principles of different one-way accumulators, we describe how to choose and use them in order to verify keys in the context of sensors networks.

3.1 One-Way Accumulator

One-way accumulators are authenticated data structures similar to Bloom filters [3]. They were introduced by Benaloh and de Mare [2] under the name of

Accumulated Hashing. The purpose of an accumulator is to allow a user to decide whether an item belongs to a given set or not. This probabilistic data structure is known to be efficient in time and space at the cost of a probability of false positives.

Let us define two sets $\mathcal{A}$ and $\mathcal{B}$. $\mathcal{A}$ is the set of the accumulator and $\mathcal{B}$ is the set of the items to be accumulated. An accumulator for set $\mathcal{S} \subset \mathcal{B}$ of i items v_i is denoted $\mathbf{z}^i$. Accumulators are based on commutative functions.

Definition 1. *Function* $F : \mathcal{A} \times \mathcal{B} \rightarrow \mathcal{A}$ *is said to be commutative (or quasi-commutative [2]) if:* $F(F(a, b), c) = F(F(a, c), b), \forall a \in \mathcal{A}$ *and* $b, c \in \mathcal{B}$.

All accumulators implement the following components:

Key-Gen(s, K_{priv}, f) – Given security parameter s, master key K_{priv}, and key derivation algorithm f, it generates all the required key materials.

Build-Acc$(\mathbf{z}^0, v_1, \cdots, v_m)$ – From a commutative function, seed $\mathbf{z}^0 \in \mathcal{A}$ and m items $v_i \in \mathcal{B}$, value $\mathbf{z}^m$ is computed recursively:

$$\mathbf{z}^i = F(\mathbf{z}^{i-1}, v_i), \ i \text{ in } 1, \cdots, m.$$

Gen-Wit – Membership witness w_i is a value associated with each value v_i accumulated in $\mathbf{z}$. The witness is used during the verification of v_i.

Authenticate$(\mathbf{z}^m, v_i)$ – It decides whether item v_i belongs to accumulator $\mathbf{z}^m$. When a witness is needed, Authenticate verifies if the following equality is satisfied: $\mathbf{z}^m \overset{?}{=} F(w_i, v_i)$.

For simplicity, we use the notation $\mathbf{z}$ throughout the paper instead of $\mathbf{z}^i$.

3.2   Choosing an Accumulator

In this section, we present the available implementation choices for an accumulator based on asymmetric or symmetric cryptography.

Asymmetric Accumulators. In the original paper [2], Benaloh and de Mare suggested to use the modular exponentiation as a quasi-commutative function in order to create a one-way accumulator: $F(a, b) = a^b \bmod n$, with $a \in \mathcal{A}$ and $b \in \mathcal{B}$. For an appropriate choice of n, this function is one-way as long as the RSA assumption [19] holds. The Benaloh and de Mare accumulator works as follows:

Gen – This function generates all the values required by function F. Let us define $n = pq$ as the product of two safe primes p, q of approximately the same size. Further details on the security issues concerning the choice of n can be found in the original paper. We only review its main ideas in this section.

Build-Acc – Seed $\mathbf{z}^0$ is also needed in order to bootstrap the accumulator. Therefore, value $\mathbf{z}^i$ is computed recursively: $\mathbf{z}^i = F(\mathbf{z}^{i-1}, v_i)$.

Gen-Wit – With each value v_i belonging to accumulator $\mathbf{z}$, we associate *witness* denoted w_i. Witness w_i corresponding to item v_i is a *partial accumulator* that includes all the values in $\mathbf{z}$ except v_i.

Authenticate – Value v_i that belongs to $\mathbf{z}$ verifies the following equation:

$$F(w_i, v_i) = w_i^{v_i} \bmod n = \left(\mathbf{z}^0\right)^{\Pi_{j=1}^m v_j} \bmod n = \mathbf{z}.$$

Other quasi-commutative functions have been proposed [1,26]. The scalar-point product over elliptic curves is a natural choice. Let us denote a as a scalar and P, Q as two points of an elliptic curve such that: $Q = aP$. The Elliptic Curve Discrete Logarithmic Problem guarantees that it is computationally infeasible to deduce a from the knowledge of P and Q [13]. Therefore, Authenticate function for an ECC-based accumulator $\mathbf{z}$, item v_i, and witness w_i, is:

$$F(w_i, v_i) = v_i w_i = \left(\prod_{j=1}^m v_j\right) \mathbf{z}^0 = \mathbf{z}.$$

Symmetric Accumulators. A symmetric-key accumulator equivalent to the Benaloh and de Mare accumulators was proposed by Nyberg [17]. It is based on cryptographic hash functions and has a much simpler Authenticate function, because it does not require partial accumulators. The connection between Nyberg accumulators and Bloom filters was later made by Yum *et al.* [25] who also demonstrated that Bloom filters are better cryptographic accumulators than Nyberg accumulators in terms of the minimal false positive rate. In parallel and independently of the Nyberg's results, Goh proposed *Cryptographic/Secure Bloom filters* [11] with applications to private information retrieval in databases.

A symmetric accumulator is considered here as a ℓ-bit vector, $\mathbf{z} = (\mathbf{z}_1, \cdots, \mathbf{z}_\ell)$ with $\mathbf{z}_i \in \mathbb{F}_2$. The support of an ℓ-bit vector, denoted as $\mathrm{supp}(z)$, is the set of the non-zero coordinate indexes: $\mathrm{supp}(z) = \{i \in [1, \ell], z_i \neq 0\}$.

Build-Acc($\mathbf{z}^0, v_1, \cdots, v_m$) – The creation of the accumulator is done for m items (keys) using the following recursion: $\mathbf{z}^i = \mathbf{z}^{i-1} \vee g(v_i), i$ in $1, \cdots, m$ with $\vee$ the bitwise inclusive-or operator and g is a function from $\mathcal{B}$ to $\mathcal{A}$.

Authenticate($\mathbf{z}, v_i$) – We can observe from the previous equation that:

$$\mathrm{supp}(\mathbf{z}) = \mathrm{supp}(\mathbf{z}^{m-1}) \cup \mathrm{supp}(g(v_i)).$$

Therefore, item $v_i \in \mathcal{B}$ belongs to $\mathbf{z}$ if: $\mathrm{supp}(g(v_i)) \subset \mathrm{supp}(\mathbf{z})$.

For Bloom filters, Key-Gen function must generate k secrets keys, K_i from secret s. If H is a cryptographic hash function that can be keyed, function g is defined by:

$$\mathrm{supp}(g(v_i)) = \{H(K_i, v_i), \ i \in 1, \cdots, k\}.$$

The differences between Bloom filters and Secure Bloom filters are: (a) the use of HMAC-SHA-1 as a hash function and (b) the use of implementation trade-offs in order to reduce the number of computed hashes [14]. It is worth mentioning that many libraries use cryptographic hash functions for Bloom filters instead of universal hash functions.

False Positive Probability. Since accumulators are probabilistic data structures, they have to be carefully designed in order to control their false positive probability. Bari and Pfitzmann have shown how to reduce the false positive problem to the strong RSA assumption under certain conditions [1]. Benaloh and de Mare have shown that the false positive probability is negligible for $|n| \geq 1024$ bits. The same can be said about accumulators based on the 160-bit prime field ECC. For Bloom filters, the false positive probability p is shown to be: $\mathsf{p} = \left(1 - [1 - \frac{1}{\ell}]^{km}\right)^{k}$ [3].

3.3   Protocol

The protocol described in this paper is based on three functions: **initialization**, **ownership transfer**, and **node-to-node key verification**.

Initialization – The manufacturer assigns to each node N_i a pair of public/private keys denoted as (PK_{N_i}, SK_{N_i}). The public keys of all nodes PK_{N_i} belonging to the network are accumulated in **z**. In addition, the manufacturer generates a public/private key pair for the gateway and includes the public key of the gateway in accumulator **z** (*i.e.* the gateway is considered as any other node). The manufacturer stores **z** in every node. In addition, every node is set up with all the values needed for the accumulator including the witness w_i.

Ownership transfer – The final user of the network uses a gateway in order to manage and monitor the network. In order to transfer the ownership, the manufacturer provides the public/private key pair of the gateway to the final user. We assume that at a given time there is only one owner. The manufacturer needs to address two issues before transferring the ownership to the final user: (a) the gateway must be able to distinguish the nodes that belong to the network and (b) the nodes must recognize the public-key of the gateway. The first issue is solved by transferring **z** and all the necessary parameters from the manufacturer to the gateway. The gateway can then execute the Authenticate function just like any other node. The second problem is solved by including the public key of the gateway in **z**.

Node-to-node key verification – As shown in Fig. 1, the nodes exchange their public-keys PK_{N_i} with their corresponding witnesses w_i. They then execute the Verify function described in Algorithm 1. When a node determines that a public key belongs to the accumulator, it stores it as an entry in table T. The Lookup(T, PK_{N_i}) function verifies if the node has already verified the public key of node N_i. The Put(T, PK_{N_i}) function adds the public key of the node to the table. Once the nodes have mutually verified their public keys with Verify, they can establish a symmetric key through the Elliptic Curve Diffie-Hellman (ECDH) key agreement protocol [16].

4   Security Analysis

Our protocol inherits the major security properties of one-way accumulators: "one-way-ness" and resistance to forgery [1,2].

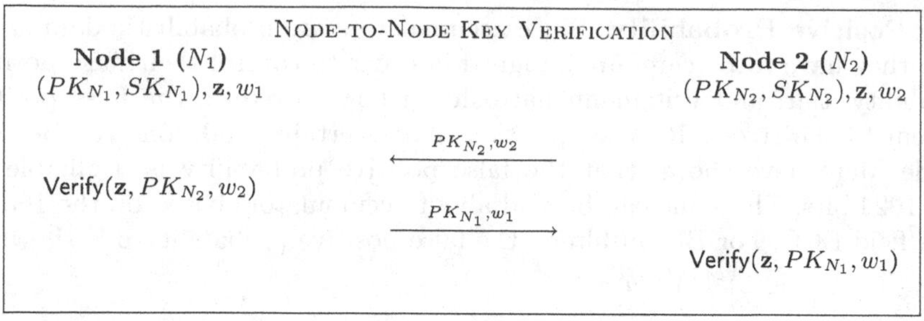

NODE-TO-NODE KEY VERIFICATION

Node 1 (N_1) Node 2 (N_2)
$(PK_{N_1}, SK_{N_1}), \mathbf{z}, w_1$ $(PK_{N_2}, SK_{N_2}), \mathbf{z}, w_2$

$$\xleftarrow{\quad PK_{N_2}, w_2 \quad}$$

Verify$(\mathbf{z}, PK_{N_2}, w_2)$

$$\xrightarrow{\quad PK_{N_1}, w_1 \quad}$$

Verify$(\mathbf{z}, PK_{N_1}, w_1)$

Fig. 1. Key certification protocol based on accumulators.

Algorithm 1. Verify$(\mathbf{z}, PK_{N_1}, w_1)$ function $(N_1$ by $N_2)$.
_____

if Lookup$(T, PK_{N_1}) = false$ **then**
   if Authenticate$(\mathbf{z}, PK_{N_1}, w_1) = true$ **then**
      Put(T, PK_{N_1})
   end if
else
   Do nothing (key already verified)
end if
_____

Node injection – The first attempt of the adversary might be to send its own public key and witness. In this case, the security of our protocol is reduced to the security of the accumulator.

Node capture – Due to the "one-way-ness" of accumulators, the capture of a node does not compromise the communications of other nodes: only the keys of the captured node are compromised.

Denial-of-Service (DoS) – The goal of the adversary is to make the nodes waste precious resources (*e.g.* energy). In order to achieve this goal, computationally expensive operations are triggered. We assume that the most expensive operation is ECDH and our protocol prevents an adversary to trigger useless ECDH computations. The lookup table T prevents the replay of correct messages that cause the exhaustion of node resources.

Please note that since the manufacturer produces each batch of nodes with distinct, pre-installed accumulators, the problem of "promiscuous" connections between certified nodes that should not belong to the same network, as well as the MiTM attack during the wireless pre-installation of cryptographic material that were mentioned in Sect. 1 become irrelevant.

5   Performance Evaluation

We have implemented the one-way accumulators of Benaloh and de Mare (we will call them RSA and ECC-based accumulators) and the Secure Bloom filter (hereafter simply referred to as Bloom filter) in Java ME[1] on Sun SPOTs[2]. Each Sun SPOT comes with a 180 MHz 32-bit ARM920T processor, 512 kB RAM, 4 MB Flash memory and a 3.7 V rechargeable 750 mAh lithium-ion battery. They have an integrated TI CC2420 radio chip operating in the 2.4 GHz band and compliant with IEEE 802.15.4. They also come with a readily available security API[3]. The elements accumulated in our implementation are 160-bit Elliptic Curve (EC) public keys using the $secp160r1$ curve domain parameters[4]. We have used the SHA-1 hashing algorithm[5] that generates 160-bit hash codes.

Once we have implemented all the different accumulators, we have measured the time that the various computations and transmissions within our protocol take in order to evaluate the total time required for a node-to-node key verification on Sun SPOTs. The entire node-to-node key verification between two Sun SPOTs (let us call them SPOT 1 and SPOT 2) using asymmetric accumulators (RSA-based and ECC-based accumulators), can be divided into four steps:

1. SPOT 1 sends its public key PK_1 and its witness w_1 to SPOT 2.
2. SPOT 2 executes Verify($\mathbf{z}, PK_1, w_1$).
3. SPOT 2 sends its public key PK_2 and its witness w_2 to SPOT 1.
4. SPOT 1 executes Verify($\mathbf{z}, PK_2, w_2$).

Node-to-node key verification using Bloom filters would only differ by the lack of witnesses in each step. We can see that step 3 to 4 is simply a repetition of step 1 to 2. Therefore, we have implemented step 1 and 2 to run between two SPOTs and we have then measured the duration of each step. Table 1 outlines the values of the parameters used for the different accumulator implementations. These values ensure an equivalent level of security for each implementation. Table 2a shows the results for each step with the implementations based on asymmetric accumulators and Bloom filters. For each measurement, one thousand 160-bit EC public keys have been accumulated. The time necessary for a node-to-node key verification between two SPOTs is obtained by multiplying the total time by two (e.g. $1.4 \times 2 = 2.8$ s for the key verification using Bloom filters).

The time that step 2 takes mostly consists of the execution time of the Authenticate function in Verify (see Sect. 3.3). We should also note that, although the time that step 2 takes when using Bloom filters is slightly less than when using ECC-based accumulators, it becomes equivalent or longer once p is set to 2^{-90} or less.

We have also estimated the energy consumption on the Sun SPOT based on the duration of each steps of the node-to-node key verification (cf. Table 2b). The most "energy-efficient" key verifications are the ones using Bloom filters and ECC-based accumulators. The extra energy that the key verification using ECC-based accumulators requires from step 1 to 3 compared with the one using

---

[1] http://www.oracle.com/technetwork/java/javame/

[2] http://www.sunspotworld.com/

[3] http://java.net/projects/spots-security

[4] http://www.secg.org/collateral/sec2_final.pdf

[5] http://www.ietf.org/rfc/rfc3174.txt

Table 1. Parameter values used in the accumulators.

Accumulator	Parameter	Value
RSA-based	Length of n	1024 bit
ECC-based	Curve domain parameters	$secp160r1$
Bloom	Value of p	2^{-80}

Table 2. Duration and energy consumption of node-to-node key verification.

(a) Duration of the first two steps in node-to-node key verification.

	Time (s)		
Step	RSA	ECC	Bloom
1	1.1	1.1	1.0
2	4.4	0.5	0.4
TOTAL	5.5	1.6	1.4

(b) Energy consumption during node-to-node key verification.

	Consumption (mAh)		
Step	RSA	ECC	Bloom
1	0.029	0.028	0.027
2	0.033	0.007	0.006
3	0.015	0.013	0.013
4	0.099	0.011	0.009
TOTAL	0.176	0.059	0.055

Bloom filters is due to the additional exchange of witnesses. However, the amount of energy consumed in step 4 of the key verification using Bloom filters would grow as the execution time of the Verify function increases due to a lower p.

Table 3a outlines the size of the public/private keys, accumulators and witnesses, used in node-to-node key verification. We can notice that much less memory is required in order to store asymmetric accumulators than Bloom filters. The advantage of using an ECC-based accumulator is apparent here, since it is only $(48 + 48)/14427 \approx 1/150$ of the size of a Bloom filter. Additionally, the

Table 3. Memory footprint of node-to-node key verification.

(a) Size of the variables used in node-to-node key verification.

	Size (bytes)		
Instance	RSA	ECC	Bloom
PK	1338	1338	1338
SK	1261	1261	1261
z	128	48	14427
w	128	48	N/A
TOTAL	2855	2695	17026

(b) Memory usage in node-to-node key verification.

	Usage (kB)		
Step	RSA	ECC	Bloom
1	79	78	78
2	0.0	0.0	0.0
3	53	43	36
4	3.1	3.6	1.6
TOTAL	135	125	116

size of Bloom filters rapidly increases as more elements are accumulated since they need to increase the number of bits per element in order to maintain their false positive probability [3]. Since the size of asymmetric accumulators is constant regardless of the number of accumulated elements, we can conclude that asymmetric accumulators have much better scalability in terms of accumulator size compared to Bloom filters. From the memory usage measurements shown in Table 3b, we can see that the two most "memory-efficient" key verifications are the ones using Bloom filters and ECC-based accumulators. However, the memory required in step 4 of the key verification using Bloom filters would increase if the number of accumulated keys increases or if p is set lower.

6 Related Work

Key establishment and distribution are critical problems in WSNs that have been deeply investigated by the community. Two schools are in competition on this topic: symmetric cryptography and asymmetric cryptography. Our work naturally belongs to the latter. Due to the lack of space, we will only briefly review the work based on asymmetric cryptography. We encourage the readers who are interested in further details on the work based on symmetric cryptography to consult [4,8] for a complete survey.

Asymmetric cryptography (more specifically, RSA-based cryptosystems) was, for a while, considered infeasible for sensor nodes. TinyPK [24] was the first attempt to implement a public-key infrastructure in WSNs. It uses the classical Diffie-Hellman (DH) protocol and a CA in order to certify the keys. The performance results were relatively modest and not promising for a practical application. Since then, TinyECC [15] and NanoECC [22] libraries proved the feasibility and the efficiency of ECC on sensor nodes. Low-cost hardware extensions have also been demonstrated [10,23]. The ECDH protocol has also been put into practice on WSNs. For example, Sun *et al.* used a "self-certified" ECDH protocol along with a polynomial-based weak authentication scheme in order to thwart DoS attacks initiated by bogus ECDH requests [21]. Our approach is the natural extension of these work: accumulators eliminate the need for CAs and certificates during key establishment.

7 Conclusion and Future Work

In this paper, we have proposed a key certification protocol that does not require CAs and certificates, in which nodes can autonomously verify the authenticity of the public keys they exchange using one-way accumulators. Our results show that the exchange and verification of public keys between two wireless sensor nodes can be performed within few seconds, while consuming little energy. Our analysis of the existing accumulators lets us conclude that ECC-based accumulators are best suited for our protocol since they perform as fast as Bloom filters while having a memory footprint that does not increase with the number of accumulated elements.

Our next immediate objective is to study how our protocol can be adapted for current WSN standards (802.15.4[6], RPL[7] etc.). Although many nodes produced nowadays are as powerful as Sun SPOTs (*e.g.* STM32W[8], albeit without a Java Virtual Machine), our protocol should also be tested on nodes with less processing power. Another issue that needs to be addressed is that our protocol cannot safely add and remove nodes from the network. Using dynamic accumulators [6] that allow you to add and remove elements may be a solution to this problem, but security flaws have been found in these designs [5].

Acknowledgement. This work was partially supported by the French National Research Agency projects ARESA2 and IRIS under contracts ANR-09-VERS-017 and ANR-11-INFR-016 respectively, and the European Commission FP7 project CALIPSO under contract 288879.

References

1. Barić, N., Pfitzmann, B.: Collision-free accumulators and fail-stop signature schemes without trees. In: Fumy, W. (ed.) EUROCRYPT 1997. LNCS, vol. 1233, pp. 480–494. Springer, Heidelberg (1997)
2. Benaloh, J.C., de Mare, M.: One-way accumulators: a decentralized alternative to digital signatures. In: Helleseth, T. (ed.) EUROCRYPT 1993. LNCS, vol. 765, pp. 274–285. Springer, Heidelberg (1994)
3. Bloom, B.H.: Space/time trade-offs in hash coding with allowable errors. Commun. ACM **13**, 422–426 (1970)
4. Buttyan, L., Hubaux, J.-P.: Security and Cooperation in Wireless Networks. Cambridge University Press, Cambridge (2007)
5. Camacho, P., Hevia, A.: On the impossibility of batch update for cryptographic accumulators. In: Abdalla, M., Barreto, P.S.L.M. (eds.) LATINCRYPT 2010. LNCS, vol. 6212, pp. 178–188. Springer, Heidelberg (2010)
6. Camenisch, J.L., Lysyanskaya, A.: Dynamic accumulators and application to efficient revocation of anonymous credentials. In: Yung, M. (ed.) CRYPTO 2002. LNCS, vol. 2442, p. 61. Springer, Heidelberg (2002)
7. Chan, H., Perrig, A.: PIKE: peer intermediaries for key establishment in sensor networks. In: INFOCOM, March 2005, pp. 524–535. IEEE (2005)
8. Chan, H., Perrig, A., Song, D.: Key distribution techniques for sensor networks. In: Raghavendra, C.S., Sivalingam, K.M., Znati, T. (eds.) Wireless Sensor Networks, pp. 277–303. Springer, New York (2004)
9. Eschenauer, L., Gligor, V.D.: A key-management scheme for distributed sensor networks. In: ACM Conference on Computer and Communications Security - CCS 2002, November 2002, pp. 41–47. ACM (2002)
10. Fan, J., Batina, L., Verbauwhede, I.: HECC goes embedded: an area-efficient implementation of HECC. In: Avanzi, R.M., Keliher, L., Sica, F. (eds.) SAC 2008. LNCS, vol. 5381, pp. 387–400. Springer, Heidelberg (2009)

---

[6] http://www.ieee802.org/15/pub/TG4.html
[7] http://www.ietf.org/rfc/rfc6550.txt
[8] http://www.st.com/web/en/catalog/mmc/FM141/SC1169/SS1581

11. Goh, E.-J.: Secure indexes. Cryptology ePrint Archive, Report 2003/216. http:// eprint.iacr.org/2003/216/ (2003)
12. Gollakota, S., Ahmed, N., Zeldovich, N., Katabi, D.: Secure In-Band wireless pairing. In: USENIX Security Symposium, August 2011
13. Hankerson, D., Menezes, A., Vanstone, S.: Guide to Elliptic Curve Cryptography. Springer, New York (2004)
14. Kirsch, A., Mitzenmacher, M.: Less hashing, same performance: building a better Bloom filter. Random Struct. Algorithms **33**(2), 187–218 (2008)
15. Liu, A., Ning, P.: TinyECC: a configurable library for elliptic curve cryptography in wireless sensor networks. In: International Conference on Information Processing in Sensor Networks - IPSN 2008, April 2008
16. NIST National Institute of Standards and Technology. Recommendation for Pair-Wise Key Establishment Schemes Using Discrete Logarithm Cryptography (Revised). NIST Special Publication 800-56A, March 2007
17. Nyberg, K.: Fast accumulated hashing. In: Gollmann, D. (ed.) FSE 1996. LNCS, vol. 1039, pp. 83–87. Springer, Heidelberg (1996)
18. Parno, B., Perrig, A., Gligor, V.D.: Distributed detection of node replication attacks in sensor networks. In IEEE Symposium on Security and Privacy - S&P 2005, May 2005
19. Rivest, R., Shamir, A., Adleman, L.: A method for obtaining digital signatures and public-key cryptosystems. Commun. ACM **21**, 120–126 (1978)
20. Singelée, D., Preneel, B.: Key establishment using secure distance bounding protocols. In: International Conference on Mobile and Ubiquitous Systems - MobiQuitous 2007, August 2007
21. Sun, K., Liu, A., Xu, R., Ning, P., Maughan, W.D.: Securing network access in wireless sensor networks. In: ACM Conference on Wireless Network Security - WISEC 2009, March 2009
22. Szczechowiak, P., Oliveira, L.B., Scott, M., Collier, M., Dahab, R.: NanoECC: testing the limits of elliptic curve cryptography in sensor networks. In: Verdone, R. (ed.) EWSN 2008. LNCS, vol. 4913, pp. 305–320. Springer, Heidelberg (2008)
23. Verbauwhede, I.: Low budget cryptography to enable wireless security. In: ACM Conference on Wireless Network Security, Invited talk, June 2011
24. Watro, R.J., Kong, D., fen Cuti, S., Gardiner, C., Lynn, C., Kruus, P.: TinyPK: securing sensor networks with public key technology. In: ACM Workshop on Security of Ad Hoc and Sensor Networks - SASN 2004, October 2004
25. Yum, D.H., Seo, J.W., Lee, P.J.: Generalized combinatoric accumulator. IEICE Trans. Inf. Syst. **E91.D**(5), 1489–1491 (2008)
26. Zachary, J.: A decentralized approach to secure management of nodes in distributed sensor networks. In: IEEE Military Communications Conference - MILCOM '03, October 2003

On Malware Leveraging the Android Accessibility Framework

Joshua Kraunelis[1]([⊠]), Yinjie Chen[1], Zhen Ling[2], Xinwen Fu[1], and Wei Zhao[3]

[1] Computer Science Department,
University of Massachusetts Lowell, Lowell, USA
{jkraunel,ychen1,xinwenfu}@cs.uml.edu
[2] Southeast University, Nanjing, China
zhen_ling@seu.edu.cn
[3] University of Macau, Macau, China
weizhao@umac.mo

Abstract. The number of Android malware has been increasing dramatically in recent years. Android malware can violate users' security, privacy and damage their economic situation. Study of new malware will allow us to better understand the threat and design effective anti-malware strategies. In this paper, we introduce a new type of malware exploiting Android's accessibility framework and describe a condition which allows malicious payloads to usurp control of the screen, steal user credentials and compromise user privacy and security. We implement a proof of concept malware to demonstrate such vulnerabilities and present experimental findings on the success rates of this attack. We show that 100 % of application launches can be detected using this malware, and 100 % of the time a malicious Activity can gain control of the screen. Our major contribution is two-fold. First, we are the first to discover the category of new Android malware manipulating Android's accessibility framework. Second, our study finds new types of attacks and complements the categorization of Android malware by Zhou and Jiang [21]. This prompts the community to re-think categorization of malware for categorizing existing attacks as well as predicting new attacks.

Keywords: Android · Malware · Attack

1 Introduction

The number of mobile malware samples has increased enormously over the past two years while mobile devices have become a ubiquitous tool in our daily life. In March 2013, Juniper Networks [8] reported their Mobile Threat Center had discovered over 276 thousand malware samples, a 614 % increase over 2012. With 92 % of mobile malware being Android malware, analyzing and categorizing these malware are important steps toward predicting new attacks.

In this paper, we explore a security and privacy risk hiding within the Android accessibility framework. The Android accessibility framework is developed to

© Institute for Computer Sciences, Social Informatics and Telecommunications Engineering 2014
I. Stojmenovic et al. (Eds.): MOBIQUITOUS 2013, LNICST 131, pp. 512–523, 2014.
DOI: 10.1007/978-3-319-11569-6_40

assist physically impaired users. Android developers can utilize accessibility applications programming interface (API) methods to provide customized accessibility services in their own applications. However, the accessibility service has access to critical sensitive information, including information about applications that are currently running and account information. Attackers could utilize such a vulnerability to conduct various types of attacks.

Our major contributions are summarized as follows:

- We are the first to identify malware leveraging Android's accessibility framework. The impact of this attack is severe, given that it can be used to activate various malicious payloads. For example, the payload can be various masquerade attacks, emulating Email, Facebook and other popular apps to steal user credentials and cause other damage. We test our proof-of-concept malware against multiple anti-malware applications and none are able to detect it.
- We identify a potential logic error in the way the Android user interface framework manages the order of application launches. When two applications are launched nearly simultaneously, both launch requests consider the first request to be processed as the next application to be launched, preventing the second launch from occurring. This can lead to a variety of attacks, such as denial of service and masquerade attacks, as we discuss in Sect. 3.3.
- Our study complements the categorization of Android malware by Zhou and Jiang [21], who present a systematic characterization of existing Android malware by their strategies of installation, activation, payload and permission use. We identify new events for activation and our attack shows that the payload can be other attacks, such as the masquerade attack demonstrated in this paper. This prompts the community to ask: are there better ways of classifying Android and other mobile malware? We hope this classification not only allows us a systematic and holistic study of existing malware, but also provides assistance to predict new attacks and design countermeasures.
- We also discuss possible countermeasures against the security risk from the Android accessibility framework.

The rest of the paper is organized as follows. Section 2 introduces Android accessibility service. Section 3 introduces our attack. We evaluate our proposed attack in Sect. 4, and discuss countermeasures in Sect. 5. Section 6 introduces other related work, and Sect. 7 concludes this paper.

2   Android Accessibility Service

An Android application must contain one or more of the following four components: Activity, Service, Broadcast Receiver, and Content Provider [5]. Activities represent tasks involving user interaction and can display drawable components, such as widgets, to the screen. The operating system ensures that only a single `Activity` for any application is displayed at once, i.e. only one application may be in the foreground at one time. Services are used for long running tasks that do not require a user interface. Unlike Activities, Services may run in the background and therefore multiple Services from different applications may run simultaneously. Broadcast Receivers receive messages, in the form of data constructs called Intents, from the Android system or user applications. An application must register for those Intents which it is interested in receiving. The registration of certain Intents may require permission to be granted by the user at install time. Content Providers enable data sharing between applications. The exploit presented in this paper will focus on Activities and Services.

The Android operating system contains an accessibility framework [1] for enhancing the experience of users who have visual or other impairments. Typical accessibility enhancements include enlargement and text-to-speech conversion of on-screen elements, high contrast color schemes, and haptic feedback. Android provides a Java API to its accessibility framework so that developers can integrate accessibility functionality into their applications. All drawable elements derive from a common ancestor, the View class, which contains built-in calls to Accessibility API methods. Thus, most user interface widgets in the Android framework make their accessibility information available by default, though developers are encouraged to provide additional information in the `android:contentDescription` XML layout attribute. Accessibility information such as the UI event type, class name of the object in which the event occurred or originated, and string value representing some associated data can be populated into an `AccessibilityEvent` object and dispatched to enabled `AccessibilityServices` via the appropriate method call [9]. There are twenty two `AccessibilityEvent` types.

Additionally, as of Android 1.6, developers may create custom accessibility services by extending the `AccessibilityService` class [2]. Descendants of `AccessibilityService` must override the onAccessibilityEvent method, which gets called each time an Accessibility Event occurs and is passed the populated `AccessibilityEvent` object. A custom `AccessibilityService` may then use the information contained in the `AccessibilityEvent` or optionally query the window content for the contextual data needed to perform its function. Naturally, the receipt of an event and its associated data and the ability to query window content present a security risk. For example, every time a user inputs text into an `EditText` widget, a custom `AccessibilityService` will receive an `AccessibilityEvent` with type `TYPE_VIEW_TEXT_CHANGED` that contains the text that the user input. To mitigate this risk, the Android system requires that `AccessibilityServices` be enabled manually by the user and displays a dialog window alerting the user to the risk.

3   Malware Exploiting Accessibility Service

In this section, we first give an overview of the malware that exploits the Android accessibility framework. We then address major challenges for such malware to work, including detection of the launch of a victim app and race condition between the victim app and malware.

3.1   Overview

We now introduce the novel malware's installation, activation, malicious payloads and permission uses.

Installation: The new Android malware can provide regular accessibility service as it claims and conduct attacks silently. Therefore, impaired users and users who prefer big font text may be interested in such malware and install it onto their phones. This installation strategy is *installation.others.3rdgroup* in [21], referring to apps that intentionally include malicious functionality. For brevity, we denote installation.others.3rdgroup as *trojan*, "a program made to appear benign that serves some malicious purpose" according to the taxonomy in [15], although this definition of trojan may be controversial.

Permission Uses: During installation, the malware requests the `BIND_ACCESSIBILITY_SERVICE` permission. After installation, users must enable the `AccessibilityService` in Android's Accessibility Settings menu. Since a legitimate accessibility service also requests such permission and requires enabling, users may not suspect the motivation of our malware. Of course, other permissions are required if the malicious payload requires them.

Activation: After the installation, our malware can derive a list of all installed applications in that phone. This can be achieved via many sources, such as the Package Manager. Based on which applications are installed, our malicious application could download various payloads and use them to launch different attacks. Each time a user launches an application from the home screen or the application drawer, our malicious accessibility service is activated, and a malicious payload which targets that application is also activated.

Here, we make one complement to the events which could be used by Android malware, introduced in [21]. As we introduced in Sect. 2, the `AccessibilityEvent` is one critical event, which carries sufficient information. There are twenty-two types of `AccessibilityEvent`, and these types of events can trigger various types of malicious payloads.

Malicious Payload: Since we know what applications are installed, we can use different malicious payloads to launch different attacks. For example, the default Email application source code is freely available from the Android Open Source Project [4]. In this case, our malicious payload could masquerade as the Email application. Therefore, when a user launches the Email application, a fake login window will display and prompt the user to input account name and password. Such account information is then collected and sent over an encrypted channel to a remote server.

To implement the masquerade attack in this example, we extract the `Account SetupBasics Activity` and its corresponding resources from the Email application, modify it, and package it into a fake application as a malicious payload. `AccountSetupBasics` is displayed when the Email application is launched and no previous email account has been setup. It was chosen because of its simple design, the popularity of the Email application, and having the fields required to demonstrate the attack. The `AccountSetupBasics` layout consists of two `EditText` widgets for username and password input, and two Buttons: one for activating the Manual Setup feature and the other for navigating to the next step in the setup process. The counterfeit `AccountSetupBasics` `Activity` included in our `AccessibilityService` application duplicates all of the graphical user interface elements of the victim `Activity`, but the email account setup functionality of the victim `Activity` has been removed. Though we have chosen to imitate the Email application's `AccountSetupBasics` `Activity` for this experiment, any `Activity` may be used in the attack. In this example, our `AccessibilityService` provides no additional accessibility features, but attackers could easily provide such features to increase the guile of this attack.

Therefore, we make one complement to the categorization of malicious payload in [21]. Android malware can perform blended attacks. The payload could contain a vector of payloads that perform different functions. *The payload itself can be other malware or attacks.* In the example above, our malware, a trojan app, contains a fake Email `Activity` that performs a masquerade attack.

For our trojan to work, there are two more details we have to address:

- How can the trojan detect the victim app launch? Although the malicious accessibility service is able to receive events related to `Activity` launch, it still needs to distinguish which app is generating these events so that it can launch the corresponding fake app and perform the masquerade attack.
- How can the trojan display itself to the user while the victim app is hidden in the background? When the user touches an app, this app will be launched. Which app, our trojan or the victim app, will be displayed? How can our trojan win the race condition?

We address these two issues below.

3.2   Detecting Application Launch

A crucial piece of our masquerade attack is the ability to detect the launch of a victim application. There is no public API to allow a user application to be notified when another application is launched. By registering to receive `AccessibilityEvent` callbacks in the application manifest, our custom `AccessibilityService` is guaranteed to be notified when an application is launched by the user. The notification comes in the form of an `Accessibility-Event` object that is delivered as an argument to our `AccessibilityService`'s `onAccessibilityEvent` method. The Launcher application, which is responsible for displaying icons and widgets on the home screen and maintaining the app drawer, populates the `AccessibilityEvent` when the Email application icon is clicked by the user.

From the information in the `AccessibilityEvent`, we can determine that the user clicked an icon in the Launcher, because the event type is `TYPE_VIEW_CLICKED` and the originating package name is com.android.launcher. We're able to identify which icon was clicked based on the Text field of the `Accessibility-Event`. In the case of attacking Email, the Text field is a single element list containing the string

"Email". Once the app launched by the user has been detected, the next step in the attack is to launch the malicious `Activity` instead of the user desired `Activity`. To do this, an Intent that specifies the malicious `Activity` to be launched is created and passed to the `startActivity` method of our `AccessibilityService`.

3.3   Racing to the Top

The launch of the malicious `Activity` from our `AccessibilityService` does not prevent the Launcher app from also calling `startActivity` to start the legitimate `Activity`. Both Activities are created and dispatched to the `Activity-Manager` to be displayed. As previously mentioned, only a single `Activity` may be displayed in the foreground at one time. This is a source of contention for our malicious `Activity`, which we want to be displayed instead of the victim `Activity` and without any suspicious screen flicker or transition animation that may alert the user to the presence of malware. Since the malicious `AccessibilityService` receives `AccessibilityEvent` and is able to detect launch of victim app, it has a chance to launch the malicious `Activity` before the victim `Activity` is launched.

There exists a source of contention for our malicious `Activity`. An attacker wants the malicious `Activity` to be displayed instead of the victim `Activity` without any suspicious screen flash, flicker, or transition animation that may alert the user to the presence of malware. To achieve this goal, the timing of launching malicious `Activity` should be carefully adjusted so that the malicious `Activity` is processed soon after the victim `Activity`. Therefore, the problem is how to derive an optimal delay for the malicious `Activity`. We present our analysis below.

We find that different delay of the malicious `Activity` produces four different statuses of the phone screen. Before introduce the four statuses, please note that when the malicious `Activity` is processed, a fake interface is created and displayed. Please also note that when the victim `Activity` is processed, a victim interface is created and displayed. Depending on the timing of processing each activity, there are four scenarios. (I) The malicious `Activity` is processed before the victim `Activity`. The fake interface will be displayed first, and then replaced by the victim interface. In this scenario, we can observe the victim interface showing up with a flash, and the status of phone screen is defined to be Ω_1. (II) The malicious `Activity` is processed before the victim `Activity`, but these two activities are processed nearly simultaneously. In this scenario, only the victim interface is displayed without a flash. The status of phone screen is defined to be Ω_2. (III) The malicious `Activity` is processed after the victim `Activity`, but these two activities are processed nearly simultaneously. In this scenario, only the fake interface is displayed without a flash. The status of phone screen is defined to be Ω_3. (IV) The malicious `Activity` is processed after the victim `Activity`. The victim interface will be displayed first, and then replaced by the fake interface. In this scenario, we can observe the fake interface showing up with a flash, and the status of phone screen is defined to be Ω_4. These statuses are listed in Table 1.

Table 1. List of phone screen statuses

	With flash	Without flash
Victim interface shows up	Ω_1	Ω_2
Fake interface shows up	Ω_4	Ω_3

It is obvious that an attacker will want the phone screen status to be Ω_3. Therefore, we need to derive an optimal delay time for the malicious `Activity`. However, for every victim app, the optimal delay time is different. To derive the optimal delay for a specific app, we can enumerate possible delay d to start the malicious `Activity` with delay d. The delay values producing the highest probability that status Ω_3 occur are the optimal ones.

Using the strategy above, we can derive an optimal delay for every victim app running on different phone models with different Android versions, and keep a record of these optimal delays in a remote server which provides all the malicious payloads we developed. When our malicious service tries to download a malicious payload from that server, the malicious service also sends a request to get an optimal delay to trigger that payload. Therefore, every time a victim app is launched, a fake interface is always shown without a flash.

4   Evaluation

To prove malware exploiting Android's accessibility framework is a new breed, we test our proof-of-concept implementation against four free Android mobile security applications from the Google Play Market: AVG AntiVirus, Norton Mobile Security, Lookout Mobile Security, and Trend Micro Mobile Security. None of the four detected any suspicious behavior or raised a flag during virus scanning while the `AccessibilityService` was enabled.

In the following, we provide the experimental results for detecting application launch and winning the race condition. The malicious `AccessibilityService` was tested on an Android emulator running Android 4.2, an HTC Nexus One running Android 2.3.6, and a Samsung Galaxy S2 running CyanogenMod 9.

4.1   Detecting Application Launch

In the Android versions we tested, application launch detection can be done for any application that defines a Launcher `Activity`. This is true because the objects that represent shortcut icons on the home screen and the app drawer are descendants of the `TextView` class, and do not override the behavior of the `onPopulateAccessibilityEvent` method. The `TextView`'s `onPopulateAccessibilityEvent` method adds the character string contained in its text field to the text list of character strings in the `AccessibilityEvent`. The `BubbleTextView` class used to represent shortcut icons will always store the title of the shortcut that is displayed in the home screen/app drawer in its text field. Therefore, the launch detection simply must match this title in order to detect application launch. Application shortcuts that belong to the hotseat, the horizontal space at the bottom of the default home screen that stays "docked" when navigating to alternate home screens, do not display a title but all shortcut icons in the application drawer do. Although the hotseat applications do not display a title, the `AccessibilityEvent` that is dispatched on click does contain the title, however this is not the case in CyanogenMod 9.

We tested the launch detection capability on the HTC Nexus One for the following six Android applications: Messaging, Email, LinkedIn, Facebook, Bank of America, and Browser. For each application, a shortcut icon was created on the home screen. The launch detection was successful for all six applications.

4.2 Winning Race Condition

During the launch detection testing, we noticed that the malicious `Activity` was not displayed instead of the victim `Activity` 100 % of the time, especially when the victim application was being launched for the first time since system boot. To test this, we performed two separate experiments. In the first experiment, we ensured the application we were launching was not running by pressing the *Force Stop* and *Clear Data* buttons under the corresponding *Settings -> Manage Applications -> All menu* for that application. These two operations effectively force the application to be reloaded from its initial state, as if the system had just booted. We then returned to the home screen, launched the application normally, and recorded which `Activity`, malicious or victim, was displayed. In the second experiment, we followed the same procedure, but instead of force stopping and clearing the data, we made sure that the victim application had previously been launched before relaunching from the home screen.

The two experiments were performed repeatedly for each of the aforementioned applications, and we observed the impact of the race condition discussed in Sect. 3.3. However, by setting the malicious `Activity` to sleep for specific time period before it is started, we can guarantee that the malicious `Activity` displays without a flash.

Now we evaluate our strategy of optimizing delay as discussed in Sect. 3.3. We choose Browser app and conduct two groups of tests on the HTC Nexus One running Android 2.3.6.

In the first group of tests, we test the Browser app with reloading. The procedure for our test is as follows. (I) We select a set of different delays, and choose each of these delays to launch our malicious `Activity`. (II) We press the *Force Stop* and *Clear Data* buttons under the corresponding *Settings -> Manage Applications -> All menu* for the Browser app. These two operations effectively force the application to be reloaded from its initial state when it is launched. (III) We launch the Browser app from home screen, and count the number of screen statuses we observe. (IV) For each delay, we repeat step (II) and (III) many times and calculate the rates of occurrences of those four statuses defined in Table 1. We present our experimental results in Table 2.

Table 2. Status with reloading

Delay (ms)	Ω_1	Ω_2	Ω_3	Ω_4
0	0 %	100 %	0 %	0 %
1–740	0 %	0 %	100 %	0 %
750	0 %	0 %	90 %	10 %
760	0 %	0 %	70 %	30 %
770	0 %	0 %	50 %	50 %
780	0 %	0 %	30 %	70 %
790	0 %	0 %	30 %	70 %
800	0 %	0 %	20 %	80 %
810	0 %	0 %	20 %	80 %
820	0 %	0 %	20 %	80 %
830	0 %	0 %	10 %	90 %
840	0 %	0 %	0 %	100 %

Table 3. Status without reloading

Delay (ms)	Ω_1	Ω_2	Ω_3	Ω_4
0	0 %	20 %	80 %	0 %
1–60	0 %	0 %	100 %	0 %
70	0 %	0 %	90 %	10 %
80	0 %	0 %	100 %	0 %
85	0 %	0 %	80 %	20 %
90	0 %	0 %	90 %	10 %
95	0 %	0 %	80 %	20 %
100	0 %	0 %	80 %	20 %
105	0 %	0 %	90 %	10 %
110	0 %	0 %	50 %	50 %
115	0 %	0 %	10 %	90 %
120	0 %	0 %	20 %	80 %
125	0 %	0 %	10 %	90 %
130	0 %	0 %	20 %	80 %
135–145	0 %	0 %	0 %	100 %

From Table 2, we make the following observations. (I) When delay is 0 ms, the victim interface shows up without a flash (Status Ω_2) 100 % of the time. (II) When delay increases from 1 ms to 740 ms, the fake interface shows up without a flash (Status Ω_3) 100 % of the time. (III) When delay increases from 750 ms to 840 ms, the rate of (Status Ω_3) decreases to 0 %, while the rate of fake interface showing up with a flash (Status Ω_4) increases to 100 %. Therefore, the optimal range of delay is between 1 ms and 740 ms.

In the second group of tests, we test the Browser app without reloading. The procedure for our test is as follows. (I) We set the delay of our malicious `Activity` to different values. (II) We launch the Browser app from the home screen, and record the status of the screen we observe. (III) For every setting of delay, we repeat step (II) a large amount of times, and calculate the rates of those four statuses defined in Table 1. We present our experimental results in Table 3.

From Table 3, we make the following observations. (I) When delay is 0 ms, 20 % of the time the victim interface shows up without a flash (Status Ω_2). 80 % of the time the fake interface shows up without a flash (Status Ω_3). (II) When delay increases from 1 ms to 60 ms, the fake interface shows up 100 % of the time without a flash. (III) When delay increases from 70 ms to 105 ms, the fake interface shows up 80 % to 90 % of the time without a flash, and the fake interface shows up 10 % to 20 % of the time with a flash (Status Ω_4). (IV) When delay increases from 110 ms to 145 ms, the probability of Status Ω_3 decreases to 0 %, while the probability of Status Ω_4 increases to 100 %. Therefore, we derive a range of optimal delay, which is between 1 ms and 60 ms.

In the first group of experiments, the range of optimal delay is between 1 ms and 740 ms. In the second group of experiments, the range of optimal delay is between 1 ms and 60 ms. Combining the experimental results from these two groups, the optimal delay for the malicious `Activity` is between 1 ms and 60 ms.

5   Discussion

The attacks mentioned above are not foolproof. There are certain safeguards built into Android devices to thwart a full device takeover by a malicious user. Recovery Mode is one such safeguard that allows the user to install a clean OS, wiping any malicious apps from the data partition in the process. An experienced user could use the Android Debug Bridge (ADB) to obtain a command shell into the device and launch applications from the command line *am* tool or even locate and uninstall the malicious applications. Applications launched from the *am* tool do not invoke the Launcher application, therefore our technique is unable to detect this.

As a countermeasure to the malicious `Activity` payload, the logic which reorders the `Activity` history stack and determines the next `Activity` to be displayed should be analyzed and corrected. The two main Android files containing said logic are frameworks/base/services/java/com/android/server/am/Activity ManagerService.java and frameworks/base/services/java/com/android/server/ am/ActivityStack.java. Ensuring that the next `Activity` to be displayed is indeed the `Activity` that was requested by `startActivity` could prevent the malicious `Activity` from being displayed instead of the legitimate `Activity`. However, this fix does not hinder launch detection and the attacker could simply delay the start of the malicious `Activity` for some short time, ensuring that the malicious `Activity` is displayed after all. The difference here is that there may be some obvious transition animation, if the developer of the legitimate app has not disabled it, from the legitimate `Activity` to the malicious `Activity`.

6   Related Work

In 2009, Schmidt *et al.* [19] made a survey of mobile malware and found that most malwares targets Symbian OS. Since Android OS was getting attention at that point and the authors investigated possibilities of malwares on Android, they explored "social engineering"-based Android malware, where the malicious functionality is hidden in a seemingly benign host app. Felt *et al.* [14] classify threats from third-party smartphone applications into *malware, grayware*, and *personal spyware*. Becher *et al.* [11] examine mechanisms securing sophisticated mobile devices in 2011. Threats were classified into four classes: *hardware centric, device independent, software centric*, and *user layer attacks* for the purpose of eavesdropping, availability attacks, privacy attacks and impersonation attacks. Existing security mechanisms are enumerated for various attacks.

Enck *et al.* [13] implemented *ded*, a Dalvik decompiler. *ded* transfers *.dex* file into Java source code. It was then used for analyzing security of 1,100 popular free Android applications. Zheng *et al.* [20] developed ADAM, an automated system for evaluating the detection of Android malware. ADAM uses repackaging and code obfuscation to generate different variants of a malware. Rastogi, Chen and Jiang [18] made similar effort to test state-of-the-art Android commercial mobile anti-malware products for detecting transformed malware. Such transformation techniques include polymorphism (where transformed code is still similar to the original code) and metamorphism (where transformed code is totally different from the original code, but with similar malware functionality). Zhou et al. [22] developed a system called DroidRanger, evaluating the health of Android markets, including the official Android Market, eoeMarket [6], alcatelclub [3], gfan [7], and mmoovv [10][1]. DroidRanger was able to find 211 malicious or infected apps out 204,040 apps from the five studied marketplaces, including two zero-day malware. Zhou and Jiang [21] made a one year effort and analyzed more than 1,200 malware samples, which covered a majority of state-of-the-art Android malware. Bugiel et al. [12] studied ways to defend against privilege-escalation attacks on Android. Such privilege-escalation attacks include confused deputy attacks and colluding attacks.

There are other survey works on mobile security and malware. Becher et al. [11] performs a comprehensive survey of mobile security from hardware to software. It is a comprehensive enumeration of existing wireless technologies and possible attacks against those technologies and devices. La Polla et al. [17] surveys mobile device security and complements the work in [11]. Peng et al. [16] performs a survey of malware on platforms such as Android, Windows Mobile and Symbian. The categorization of malware follows traditional jargons such as worms, viruses and trojans. They also survey malware propagation strategies. For our future work, we hope to have a system of categorization that systematically characterizes the underlying techniques of mobile malware.

7   Conclusion

This paper introduces a new type of malware that leverages Android's accessibility framework to activate its malicious payloads. The implementation of an example malicious application that uses the Accessibility APIs to masquerade as a legitimate application is detailed. Additionally, we describe how the emergence of this malware elicits the need for better malware categorization and characterization of malware. We describe results from the experiments we performed to quantify both the success of application launch detection and exploiting the logic error in the `ActivityStack` class. We show that, by adding a delay to the launch of the malicious `Activity`, we can guarantee 100 % that the malicious `Activity` will be displayed. We also discuss possible strategies to mitigate this type of malware.

---

[1] Link is no longer valid.

References

1. Accessibility. http://developer.android.com/guide/topics/ui/accessibility/index. html (2013)
2. Accessibility services. http://developer.android.com/guide/topics/ui/accessibility/ services.html (2013)
3. Alcatelclub. http://www.alcatelclub.com/ (2013)
4. Android open source project. http://source.android.com/ (2013)
5. Application fundamentals. http://developer.android.com/guide/components/ fundamentals.html (2013)
6. eoemarket. http://www.eoemarket.com/ (2013)
7. Gfan. http://www.gfan.com/ (2013)
8. Juniper networks third annual mobile threats report. http://www.juniper.net/us/ en/local/pdf/additional-resources/3rd-jnpr-mobile-threats-report-exec-summary. pdf (2013)
9. Making applications accessible. http://developer.android.com/guide/topics/ui/ accessibility/apps.html (2013)
10. Mmoovv. http://android.mmoovv.com/web/index.html (2013)
11. Becher, M., Freiling, F.C., Hoffmann, J., Holz, T., Uellenbeck, S., Wolf, C.: Mobile security catching up? revealing the nuts and bolts of the security of mobile devices. In: Proceedings of the 2011 IEEE Symposium on Security and Privacy, pp. 96–111 (2011)
12. Bugiel, S., Davi, L., Dmitrienko, A., Fischer, T., Sadeghi, A.-R., Shastry, B.: Towards taming privilege-escalation attacks on android. In: Proceedings of the 19th Network and Distributed System Security Symposium (NDSS) (2012)
13. Enck, W., Octeau, D., McDaniel, P., Chaudhuri, S.: A study of android application security. In: Proceedings of the 20th USENIX Conference on Security (2011)
14. Felt, A.P., Finifter, M., Chin, E., Hanna, S., Wagner, D.: A survey of mobile malware in the wild. In: Proceedings of the 1st ACM Workshop on Security and Privacy in Smartphones and Mobile Devices (SPSM) (2011)
15. Hunt, R., Hansman, S.: A taxonomy of network and computer attack methodologies. Comput. Netw. **24**(1) (2005). (Elsevier)
16. Peng, S., Yu, S., Yang, A.: Smartphone malware and its propagation modeling: a survey. IEEE Commun. Surv. Tutor. **PP**(99), 1–17 (2013)
17. Polla, M.L., Martinelli, F., Sgandurra, D.: A survey on security for mobile devices. IEEE Commun. Surv. Tutor. **15**(1), 446–471 (2013)
18. Rastogi, V., Chen, Y., Jiang, X.: Droidchameleon: evaluating android anti-malware against transformation attacks. Short Paper, Proceedings of the 8th ACM Symposium on Information, Computer and Communications Security (ASIACCS) (2013)
19. Schmidt, A.-D., Schmidt, H.-G., Batyuk, L., Clausen, J.H., Camtepe, S.A., Albayrak, S., Yildizli, C.: Smartphone malware evolution revisited: android next target? In: Proceedings of the 4th IEEE International Conference on Malicious and Unwanted Software (Malware 2009), pp. 1–7. IEEE (2009)
20. Zheng, M., Lee, P.P.C., Lui, J.C.S.: ADAM: an automatic and extensible platform to stress test android anti-virus systems. In: Flegel, U., Markatos, E., Robertson, W. (eds.) DIMVA 2012. LNCS, vol. 7591, pp. 82–101. Springer, Heidelberg (2013)
21. Zhou, Y., Jiang, X.: Dissecting android malware: characterization and evolution. In: Proceedings of IEEE Symposium on Security and Privacy (SP) (2012)
22. Zhou, Y., Wang, Z., Zhou, W., Jiang, X.: Hey, you, get off of my market: detecting malicious apps in official and alternative android markets. In: Proceedings of the 19th Network and Distributed System Security Symposium (NDSS) (2012)

Safe Reparametrization
of Component-Based WSNs

Wilfried Daniels[(✉)], Pedro Javier del Cid Garcia,
Wouter Joosen, and Danny Hughes

iMinds-DistriNet, KU Leuven, 3001 Heverlee, Belgium
{wilfried.daniels,pedrojavier.delcid,wouter.joosen,
danny.hughes}@cs.kuleuven.be

Abstract. Modern Wireless Sensor Networks are moving from singe-purpose custom built solutions towards multi-purpose application hosting platforms. These platforms support multiple concurrent applications managed by multiple actors. Reconfigurable component-models are a viable solution for supporting these scenarios by reducing management and development overhead while promoting software reuse. However, implicit parameter dependencies spanning component compositions make reconfiguration complex and error-prone. This paper proposes composition-safe reparametrization of components. This is accomplished by offering language annotations that allow component developers to make dependencies explicit and network protocols to resolve and enforce parameter constraints. Our approach greatly simplifies reparametrization while imposing minimal runtime overhead.

1 Introduction

Early WSNs supported single purpose applications with little or no runtime reconfiguration support. Typically, a single party built, owned and maintained the WSN. With the advent of shared sensing infrastructures, e.g. Smart Cities [7] and Smart Offices [10], WSNs are evolving to become more open and multi-purpose [9,13]. A single WSN infrastructure can host multiple applications at the same time that are managed by multiple actors.

Reconfigurable component models have proven to be a promising solution for managing the complexity of developing WSN applications [9]. Examples of runtime reconfigurable component systems include OpenCOM [5], RUNES [4], OSGi [12], REMORA [14] and LooCI [8]. These systems provide the capabilities required to manage component life-cycle, configuration, introspection, and assembly at runtime. An essential feature of component-based WSN infrastructures is component reuse, where one component can offer functionality to multiple application compositions. This way, both platform resources (i.e. Flash, RAM) and code are shared between applications.

Contemporary component-based systems have some drawbacks when sharing component instances. Configuration conflicts may arise due to resource competition and contention. While component binding dependencies are explicit in

© Institute for Computer Sciences, Social Informatics and Telecommunications Engineering 2014
I. Stojmenovic et al. (Eds.): MOBIQUITOUS 2013, LNICST 131, pp. 524–536, 2014.
DOI: 10.1007/978-3-319-11569-6_41

the form of interfaces and receptacles, implicit dependencies may arise in a software composition due to application level constraints which are enforced through the setting of configuration parameters. Consider a software composition that detects vehicle motion, using a composition of a magnetometer component and a motion detection component. The magnetometer component must sample at 2 Hz in order for the motion detection component to function properly. This required configuration generates an implicit *parameter* dependency between the magnetometer and motion detection components that is not expressible with state of the art component models.

Manually resolving these implicit dependencies is difficult and error-prone. In a multi-purpose WSN infrastructure where multiple actors reuse and reconfigure components, no single actor has an accurate understanding of all existing compositions and parameter dependencies. Existing compositions have to be introspected remotely, which incurs developer overhead and message passing overhead. Failure to resolve an implicit parameter dependency will cause disruption due to erroneous configurations of existing applications.

In this paper we present an approach that externalizes implicit distributed dependencies generated from component parametrization in distributed applications. This allows for automatic composition-safe reparametrization in multi-actor WSNs. Our solution has 3 elements: Firstly, we provide language constructs which can be used by component developers to make parameter constraints and dependencies explicit across component compositions. Secondly, a network protocol is presented which automatically resolves these dependencies when composing components at runtime and flags constrained parameters with the corresponding constraints. Lastly, we introduce a reparametrization algorithm which enforces constraints and enacts the necessary distributed reparametrization when setting constrained parameters, guaranteeing composition-safe reconfiguration.

Our evaluation shows that our approach reduces runtime reconfiguration effort and latency in scenarios where component sharing is necessary. It incurs very little development and runtime overhead that is quickly compensated for. Critically, we notice a significant decrease in network traffic when we compare our reparametrization algorithm to an automated back end graph walk to resolve parameter dependencies.

2 Motivation

One year ago our research group created a smart office environment that supports four applications. These applications are: facility management, workforce management, security and workplace safety, each of which is managed by a different stakeholder. For these applications, we have logged and analyzed reconfiguration effort and latency. Our analysis revealed the previously unknown problem of implicit dependencies between parametrized components in a composition. To further investigate, we conducted a series of experiments designed to better understand the impact that implicit dependencies have on reconfiguration effort and latency.

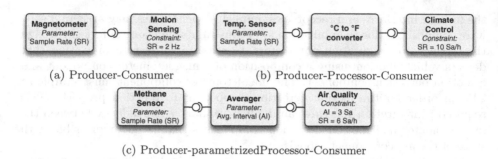

(a) Producer-Consumer   (b) Producer-Processor-Consumer

(c) Producer-parametrizedProcessor-Consumer

Fig. 1. Classes of compositions with implicit dependencies

Experiment Description. During the experiments, we tasked seven experienced component developers with a series of reconfiguration exercises to be
conducted on the smart office. In each exercise the component assembler had to
plan and enact an extension to one of the running applications. Throughout the
experiment we tracked reconfiguration effort, latency and disruption.

We assume there is no inter-stakeholder coordination of reconfiguration plans
and there is no up to date global view of the system. The assemblers all started
out having limited information in regards with the configuration and state of all
the running component instances and the applications.

The reconfiguration typically happens in 4 steps: (i) reading and understanding the required changes, (ii) identifying and remotely introspecting the components of interest to check if and how they are reusable, (iii) checking if the desired
reconfiguration adversely affects any of the running applications, (iv) creating
and executing a reconfiguration plan.

Results. Analysis revealed that implicit parameter dependencies arise every
time the consumer component has application requirements that constrain the
possible values used to configure the functionality implemented by the producer
component.

Classes of Component Compositions. We have identified three classes of
component compositions in our smart office environment where implicit dependencies are generated, see Fig. 1.

Figure 1a depicts a **Producer-Consumer** composition. This is the implementation of the scenario previously explained in the introduction, where a
Motion Sensing component requires a *Magnetometer* to sample at 2 Hz. In this
case, the *Motion Sensing* component has an implicit dependency with the sample interval of the *Magnetometer*. Therefore the application requirements reified
in the *Motion Sensing* component constrain the valid values for configuration
property in the *Magnetometer*.

Figure 1b exemplifies the **Producer-Processor-Consumer** composition,
where the implicit dependency is propagated from producer to consumer through

a data processing component without any configurable parameters, thus only relaying implicit dependencies. A *Temp. Sensor* component samples at 10 Sa/h, the reading's units are converted and consumed by a *Climate Control* actuator component.

In Fig. 1c, a **Producer-parametrizedProcessor-Consumer** composition is shown. The *Methane Sensor* component samples at a rate of 6 Sa/h, then an *Averager* component aggregates the data of 3 samples, which is consumed by an *Air Quality* component. *Averager* is a data processing component which has a configurable parameter that is constrained by the consumer, i.e. *Air Quality*. Both the *Methane Sensor* and *Averager* have implicit parameter dependencies with the consumer component because *Air Quality* has requirements on the temporal resolution of the readings. This constrains the valid parameter values for both *Averager* and *Methane Sensor*.

The software compositions classified above may be arbitrarily long, for instance having multiple Processors or parametrizedProcessors interconnected in a composition.

3   Background

In this section we discuss the requirements of our approach on component based middleware. We then enumerate the roles that a component can play during composition-safe reparametrization. Finally we provide a classification of constraint types.

3.1   Component Model Requirements

Our approach requires: (i) explicit interface and receptacle declarations, (ii) a unique identifier (*uid*) for each interface and receptacle type and (iii) reparametrization of running components. These requirements are met by all runtime reconfigurable components models, including: RUNES [4], REMORA [14], Open-COM [5] and LooCI [8].

3.2   Component Roles

Our analysis revealed three component roles, each of which must be considered when resolving distributed parametrization dependencies. We describe each of these roles, with reference to the example smart office compositions shown in Fig. 1.

1. **Constrained components:** These are components which produce events differently based upon their parametrization. A concrete example of such a component is the *Temp. Sensor* component shown in Fig. 1b. The Sampling Rate parameter (SR) influences how often temperature data is sensed and transmitted. which is constrained by the *Climate Control* component.

2. **Relaying components:** Relay components do not have constrained parameters, or constrain the parametrization of other components. They do however serve as a relay of parameter constraints along the chain of components in a composition. In Fig. 1b, the °C to °F converter is an example of a relaying component. It relays data between a constrained component *Temp. Sensor* and the constraining component *Climate Control.*

3. **Constraining components:** Constraining components consume data that is produced and processed by other components in the composition. Constraining components require a specific parametrization of components producing and processing the data. The *Climate Control* component shown in Fig. 1b is an example of a constraining component. It requires that the sampling rate of the *Temp. Sensor* component has a fixed value.

A component may play multiple roles at the same time. For example, the *Averager* component in Fig. 1c relays a parameter dependency from the *Methane Sensor* (Sampling Rate) and also has a constrained parameter (Averaging Interval). Both of these parameters are constrained by the *Air Quality* component.

3.3   Constraints

Constraining components impose two categories of parameter constraints: *Locking* and *Synchronizing*.

1. **Locking constraints** lock constrained parameters to a specific value or range. An example of this is the constraint imposed by the *Climate Control* component in Fig. 2a. This constraint locks the Sampling Rate parameter of *Temp. Sensor* to 10 Sa/h. Another possibility is constraining the range of acceptable parametrization, e.g. 8 to 14 Sa/h.

2. **Synchronizing constraints** require the synchronization of multiple parameters in the composition. This is illustrated in Fig. 2b, where the sampling rate of the 2 *Sensor* components has to be time synchronized in order for the *Comfort Level* component to aggregate the data and function properly.

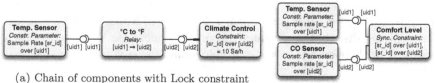

(a) Chain of components with Lock constraint

(b) Synchronize constraint

Fig. 2. Component roles and constraint types

4   Design

4.1   Language Annotations

In order to offer composition-safe reparametrization, component developers must specify parameter dependencies, relaying behaviour and constraints. To achieve this, we introduce a set of language annotations.

For *constrained components*, developers use the syntax shown in Listing 1 to identify constrained parameters. Constrained parameters are assigned an id, which is used by the constraint resolution protocol to reference the parameter. The component developer must specify both the id of the constrained parameter and the *uid* of associated the outgoing interface. Figure 2a shows an annotated version of the composition visualized in Fig. 1b. In this scenario, the *Temp. Sensor* component specifies `ConstrainedParameter(sr_id,uid1)` to define the constrained parameter.

For *relaying components*, developers must specify the *uid* of the incoming receptacle and the outgoing interface over which the dependencies have to be relayed. Listing 1 shows the syntax that is used by relaying components. For example, the $°C$ to $°F$ component in Fig. 2a specifies `DependencyRelay(uid1,uid2)`.

For *constraining components*, developers use the syntax shown in Listing 1. Constrained parameters are designated by their parameter id together with the *uid* of the incoming receptacle. The tuple formed by this pair of values uniquely specifies a constrained parameter. Lock constraints are specified by appending the parameter identifying tuple with the constraint itself, which is either a range or a single value. Synchronizing constraints are specified by providing a number of parameter-identifying tuples, the values of which must remain the same. The example lock constraint of the *Climate Control* component shown in Fig. 2a is expressed as follows `ParameterLock(sr_id,uid2,10Sa/h)`. The example synchronization constraint of the *Comfort Level* component shown in Fig. 2b is expressed as `ParameterSync({sr_id,uid1},{sr_id,uid2})`.

```
ConstrainedParameter(
        parameter-id,    //Reference to constr. parameter
        interface-uid);  //Outgoing interface uid

DependencyRelay(
        receptacle-uid,  //Incoming receptacle uid
        interface-uid);  //Outgoing interface uid

ParameterLock(
        parameter-id,    //Reference to constr. parameter
        receptacle-uid,  //Incoming receptacle uid
        constraint);     //Open/closed interval or value

ParameterSync(
        {parameter-id,   //Reference to constr. parameter
        receptacle-uid}, //Incoming receptacle uid
        {paramter-id,receptacle-uid}, ... );
```

Listing 1. Language annotations defining implicit parameter dependencies

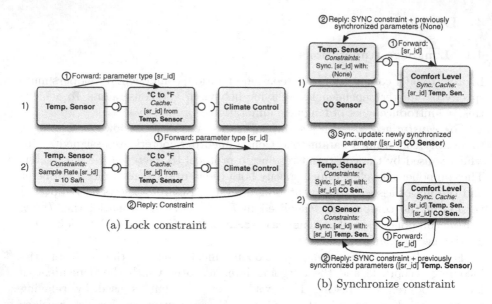

Fig. 3. Step-by-step constraint resolution of compositions from Fig. 2

4.2   Constraint Propagation Protocol

In this section, we introduce a network protocol that efficiently relays appropriate constraints from constraining components to constrained components. Bindings may be local, or may cross node boundaries, requiring the transmission of a radio message.

The constraint propagation protocol has two phases. In *phase one*, descriptions of constrained parameters are propagated along the chain of components as bindings are made. A caching mechanism is used at every component along the chain from the constrained component to the constraining component. Every time a new binding is made, the local cache of the component is checked for constrained parameters that should be forwarded. These cache entries are then forwarded along the chain as far as existing bindings allow. Passing constraint information along the component graph is required because components have no a priori knowledge of the application composition in which they will participate. In *phase two*, constraints are sent back directly to the constrained components.

The process of locking constraint propagation for the composition shown in Fig. 2a is shown in Fig. 3a. When the first binding is made, *Temp. Sensor* forwards its constrained parameter to the °C to °F component, which caches it. Next, when the last binding is made, °C to °F forwards this constrained parameter to *Climate Control*, which matches it with a lock constraint and sends this constraint back directly. A synchronizing constraint must be propagated to all synchronized components and thus the constraining components must store references to each synchronized parameter and its associated component. Figure 3b illustrates how synchronizing constraints are propagated when building the composition of Fig. 2b. When the first binding is made, *Temp. Sensor* forwards its constrained parameter to *Comfort Level*, where it is matched with a synchronization constraint. As there are currently no other synchronized parameters, none are sent back with the reply containing the synchronization constraint. When *CO Sensor* is bound, the same happens except this time a reference to sr_id on *Temp. Sensor* is sent back with the synchronization constraint to *CO Sensor*. Lastly, an update with a reference to sr_id on *CO Sensor* is sent to *Temp. Sensor*.

4.3 Constraint Enforcement Protocol

The constraint enforcement protocol ensures parameter constraints are maintained during reparametrization. This is accomplished by checking the constraints specified in the constraining component every time a parameter on a constrained component is set.

This requires 3 steps: (i) check all lock constraints on the parameter, and return a *Constraint not met* error message if one is broken, (ii) if no lock constraints are broken, tentatively store the new value for the parameter *(NPV)*, (iii) enforce all synchronization constraints by setting all synchronized parameters on remote components to *NPV*. This recursively triggers the same 3 step constraint check on the remote component. If any remote component returns a *Constraint not met* error message, the local change is rolled back and the same error is returned. If all parametrizations succeed, set the local parameter to *NPV* and return a *Success* message to the parametrizing entity.

5 Implementation and Evaluation

5.1 Implementation

A prototype was implemented on the LooCI [8] middleware. LooCI is a middleware for building distributed component based WSN applications. It complies with all of the requirements listed in Sect. 3. LooCI supports a number of platforms. We implemented our approach on the Contiki [6] based AVR Raven [1] port of LooCI. The Raven mote offers a 16 MHz Atmel MCU, 16 KB of RAM and 128 KB of flash memory. All of the functionality necessary was implemented using LooCI components, requiring no modifications to the middleware.

5.2 Evaluation

We evaluated the performance of our approach against the original version of LooCI in terms of both middleware overhead and commands issued. The performance was assessed in 3 specific scenarios inspired by our Smart Office deployment. The scenarios build on top of each other, and Fig. 4 shows the final complete distributed application composition. In every scenario, functionality is added by deploying new components and binding them to existing ones.

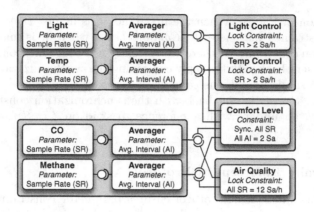

Fig. 4. Distributed component composition used in evaluation

In **scenario 1**, an automatic light/climate control system is deployed over 2 nodes. A first node collects the light and temperature readings and averages them. The controller components are deployed on a separate node and constrain the sensor sampling rates. **Scenario 2** expands upon the first scenario by introducing a node which samples and averages CO and Methane readings. All 4 sensor readings are aggregated in a *Comfort Level* component deployed on a separate node, which evaluates the level of comfort in an office. *Comfort Level* imposes a synchronization constraint on all sensors, together with a lock constraint on the averaging window of all averager components. In **scenario 3**, *Air Quality* is added, which uses the existing *CO* and *Methane* sensors. This component imposes additional constraints on the sampling rate of the sensors.

Component Size Overhead. Component sizes in reconfigurable component models are significant because they largely determine energy expenditure during deployment due to radio usage, and thus impact node lifetime. Our approach requires components to be annotated with metadata. The storage of this metadata incurs overhead on the size of the deployable components. On average, **scenario 1** incurs a component size overhead of 18.3 bytes, **scenario 2** incurs an extra 18.4 bytes and **scenario 3** incurs an extra 19 bytes. These overheads are insignificant when compared to an average unannotated component size of 790 bytes (worst case overhead of 2.4 %).

Static Middleware Overhead. Without any components deployed, LooCI still needs space in both flash and RAM memory in order to provide functionality. The additional components required to implement our approach increase this static overhead. We evaluate both Flash and RAM usage. Considering the 128 KB of flash and 16 KB of RAM available, our modified version uses respectively 5.3 % (65130 bytes vs. 58162 bytes) and 2 % (9351 bytes vs. 9030 bytes) more of the total flash and RAM than the original LooCI. In conclusion, the overhead imposed by our modifications is minimal.

Dynamic Middleware Overhead. The execution of components results in the dynamic allocation of RAM on top of the base consumption discussed in the previous subsection. Figure 5 shows a detailed breakdown of the average allocated memory per node. The allocations can be split in three categories: memory used by component instance bookkeeping, memory used for storing component bindings and dependency and constraint caches. Note that **scenario 2** and **scenario 3** have a higher average overhead then the first scenario in our prototype. This is due to the introduction of the synchronization constraint in the second scenario, which requires more cache space on each node. Taking into account the 16 KB RAM available, in the worst case (**scenario 2**) this means on average 0.83 % more RAM used on each node (213 bytes vs. 76.3 bytes).

Network Overhead. Another point of comparison is the overhead of messages sent over the network when reparametrizing and binding. When binding components dependencies are propagated, generating some message overhead. In case of **scenario 2** and **scenario 3**, we only count the messages sent when expanding the previous scenario. For **scenario 1**, we measured an increase from 6 to 12 messages, for **scenario 2** we increase from 10 to 62 and in **scenario 3** message overhead increases from 4 to 10.

It is clear that the modified version has more overhead due to the constraint propagation protocol, which runs at bind time. This is again most apparent in **scenario 2**, where a nontrivial amount of network traffic is generated keeping the synchronization caches consistent over all nodes. It is important to note that binding is less frequent than reparameterization, where the constraint enforcement protocol gives significant savings.

Table 1 gives an overview of the amount of messages sent when reparametrizing either one of the sampling rate parameters of the sensors, or the interval of one of the averagers. In the original version, the running component composition has to be remotely instrospected to ensure that all constraints are met. This generates significant network usage. A worst case example is the reparametrization

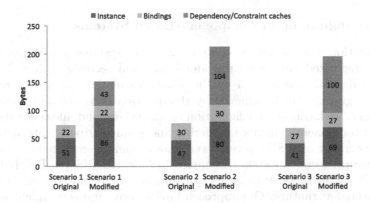

Fig. 5. Breakdown of the average dynamic RAM overhead for each scenario

Table 1. Number of messages and commands sent when reparametrizing

	Scenario 1		Scenario 2		Scenario 3	
	Messages	Commands	Messages	Commands	Messages	Commands
Sample Rate						
Original	8	8	31	31	32	32
Modified	1	1	4	1	4	1
Avg. Interval						
Original	4	4	6	6	6	6
Modified	1	1	1	1	1	1

of the sampling rate in scenario 3, where 28 extra messages have to be sent for each reparametrization. Our approach is thus a significant improvement.

Reparametrization Commands Issued. The advantages of our approach is also most apparent when comparing the amount of commands an actor has to issue and the associated network traffic generated during reparametrization. Table 1 shows this data for each scenario when reparametrizing the sampling rates and the averager intervals. Because the original version has no automatic constraint enforcement, the actor has to introspect the composition manually to ensure that all constraints are met and that the reparametrization is composition-safe. In all cases this generates significantly more commands and messages (on average 24 times more).

6   Related Work

In this section we provide an overview of the state of the art in two areas: reconfiguration approaches used in component-based systems and enhancing reconfiguration by leveraging metadata annotations.

6.1   Reconfiguration in Component-Based Systems

Reconfiguration approaches in component-based systems for WSNs can be broadly categorized into structural and behavioral reconfiguration [2]. Structural reconfiguration is defined by the ability to modify the structure of the component graph. This is achieved by the addition or removal of components and bindings. Behavioral reconfiguration on the other hand allows for the modification of component behavior by offering fine-grained adjustments at runtime.

In the context of WSNs, several well known component-based systems support structural reconfiguration. Examples include RUNES [4], REMORA [14] and LooCI [8]. In these systems, components can be deployed, configured and interconnected at runtime. Our approach builds upon, and is complementary to, these approaches by extending their capabilities through the externalization of implicit parameter dependencies.

Fine grained behavioral reconfiguration is commonly achieved by modifying component configuration parameters. Modifying component configuration parameters is commonly achieved by exposing a configuration interface, as in LooCI [8], RUNES [4] and REMORA [14]. To the best of our knowledge, no existing system checks parameter dependencies.

6.2 Metadata Annotation in Components

Using metadata to inform reconfiguration has been proposed in a variety of approaches. As in Meshkova et al. [11] who proposes a standardized metadata language for component-based WSNs aimed to enhance interoperability. An XML based language is used to describe component dependencies, interfaces, attributes etc. This metadata can be used in the backend for deployment decisions and runtime reconfiguration. Cervantes et al. [3] specify metadata in XML files called *Instance descriptors*, which are deployed along components. These are used to describe a context aware component model which dynamically adapts component compositions based on component availability.

Neither [11] nor [3] would actually run on resource constrained WSN nodes due to their processing and communication overheads. In order to overcome processing overheads they rely either on back end processing or a resource rich platform. Furthermore they are not concerned with energy expenditure, thus transmission overheads incurred in generating updated global view are suboptimal. Our metadata language refrains from using standardized markup languages and does not require updated global view to inform reparametrization. Thus it does not incur in high processing or transmission overheads.

7 Conclusion

In this paper we identified a new problem for distributed component-based systems: implicit parameter dependencies. These implicit distributed dependencies occur when parameters are constrained across component compositions and introduce complexity during reparametrization. We propose a solution which leverages annotated components to externalize and enforce these implicit constraints at runtime. We do this in a way which minimizes messaging over the network and with acceptable memory costs for a resource constrained platform. By resolving parameter constraints in the middleware, our approach greatly simplifies reparametrization by avoiding the need for extensive introspection to identify these implicit dependencies.

Acknowledgements. This research is partially supported by the Research Fund, KU Leuven and iMinds, and is conducted in the context of the COMACOD and ADDIS projects.

References

1. AVR RZ Raven Data Sheet. http://www.atmel.com/Images/doc8117.pdf (2013). Accessed 1 Aug 2013
2. Aksit, M., Choukair, Z.: Dynamic, adaptive and reconfigurable systems overview and prospective vision. In: International Conference on Distributed Computing Systems - Workshops (ICDCS '03), pp. 84–89. IEEE (2003)
3. Cervantes, H., Hall, R.S.: Automating service dependency management in a service-oriented component model. In: International Conference on Software Engineering (ICSE '04), pp. 614–623 (2004)
4. Costa, P., Coulson, G., Gold, R., Lad, M., Mascolo, C., Mottola, L., Picco, G.P., Sivaharan, T., Weerasinghe, N., Zachariadis, S.: The RUNES middleware for networked embedded systems and its application in a disaster management scenario. In: IEEE International Conference on Pervasive Computing and Communications (PerCom '07), pp. 69–78. IEEE (2007)
5. Coulson, G., Blair, G., Grace, P., Taiani, F., Joolia, A., Lee, K., Ueyama, J., Sivaharan, T.: A generic component model for building systems software. ACM Trans. Comput. Syst. **26**(1), 1–42 (2008)
6. Dunkels, A., Grönvall, B., Voigt, T.: Contiki - a lightweight and flexible operating system for tiny networked sensors. In: IEEE International Conference on Local Computer Networks (LCN '04), pp. 455–462. IEEE (Comput. Soc.) (2004)
7. Filipponi, L., Vitaletti, A., Landi, G., Memeo, V., Laura, G., Pucci, P.: Smart city: an event driven architecture for monitoring public spaces with heterogeneous sensors. In: Conference on Sensor Technologies and Applications (SENSORCOMM '10), July 2010, pp. 281–286. IEEE (2010)
8. Hughes, D., Thoelen, K., Maerien, J., Matthys, N., del Cid Garcia, P.J., Horré, W., Huygens, C., Michiels, S., Joosen, W.: LooCI: the Loosely-coupled Component Infrastructure. In: IEEE International Symposium on Network Computing and Applications (NCA '12) (2012)
9. Huygens, C., Hughes, D., Lagaisse, B., Joosen, W.: Streamlining development for networked embedded systems using multiple paradigms. IEEE Softw. **27**(5), 45–52 (2010)
10. Lau, S.-Y., Chang, T.-H., Hu, S.-Y., Huang, H.-J., Shyu, L.-D., Chiu, C.-M., Huang, P.: Sensor networks for everyday use: the BL-Live experience. In: IEEE International Conference on Sensor Networks, Ubiquitous, and Trustworthy Computing (SUTC '06), pp. 336–343. IEEE (2006)
11. Meshkova, E., Riihijarvi, J., Ansari, J., Rerkrai, K., Mahonen, P.: An extendible metadata specification for component-oriented networks with applications to WSN configuration and optimization. In: International Symposium on Personal, Indoor and Mobile Radio Communications (PIMRC '08), September 2008, pp. 1–6. IEEE (2008)
12. Rellermeyer, J.S., Alonso, G.: Concierge: a service platform for resource-constrained devices. ACM SIGOPS Oper. Syst. Rev. **41**(3), 245 (2007)
13. Rezgui, A., Eltoweissy, M.: Service-oriented sensor-actuator networks: promises, challenges, and the road ahead. Comput. Commun. **30**(13), 2627–2648 (2007)
14. Taherkordi, A., Loiret, F., Abdolrazaghi, A., Rouvoy, R., Le-Trung, Q., Eliassen, F.: Programming sensor networks using REMORA component model. In: Rajaraman, R., Moscibroda, T., Dunkels, A., Scaglione, A. (eds.) DCOSS 2010. LNCS, vol. 6131, pp. 45–62. Springer, Heidelberg (2010)

Toward Agent Based Inter-VM Traffic Authentication in a Cloud Environment

Benzidane Karim$^{(\boxtimes)}$, Saad Khoudali, and Abderrahim Sekkaki

Faculty of Sciences Ain Chock, University Hassan II, Casablanca, Morocco
k.benzidane@live.fr, {s.khoudali,a_sekkaki}@yahoo.fr

Abstract. Ubiquitous simply means being everywhere. The concept of Cloud Computing (CC) further strengthens the idea of Ubiquitous computing. On the other hand, one of the key enablers of CC is Virtualization. However, with the many advantages of virtualization comes certain limitations, especially related to security. Virtualization vulnerabilities and more specifically isolation, creates new targets for intrusion due to the complexity of access and difficulty in monitoring all interconnection points between systems, applications, and data sets. Hence, without strict control put in place within the Cloud, guests could violate and bypass security policies, intercept unauthorized client data, and initiate or become the target of security attacks. This article discusses the security and the visibility issues of inter-VM traffic, by proposing a solution for it within the Cloud context. The proposed approach provides Virtual Machines (VMs) authentication, communication integrity, and enforces trusted transactions, through security mechanisms, structures, policies, and various intrusion detection techniques.

Keywords: Ubiquitous computing · Cloud computing · Virtualization · Security · Intrusion detection

1 Introduction

Ubiquitous computing is considered as a big wave of computing after mainframe and CC, where many computers serve one person. CC is an enabler of ubiquitous computing, giving the user an interaction with its resources at anytime and from anywhere, informational retrieval, and multimodal interaction with the user and enhanced visualization capabilities. In effect, giving extremely new and futuristic abilities for users to look at and interact with at any time and from anywhere. Such ubiquity of cloud resources hold the promise of enabling new service models, where resources are seamlessly utilized at the time and location that are best suited to the needs of the current workload, while at the same time optimizing business objectives such as minimizing cost and maintaining service quality levels [1]. CC has generated interest from both industry and academia over these years. As an extension of Grid Computing and Distributed Computing, CC aims to provide users with flexible services in a transparent manner. Though Providing security in a distributed system requires more than user authentication with

© Institute for Computer Sciences, Social Informatics and Telecommunications Engineering 2014
I. Stojmenovic et al. (Eds.): MOBIQUITOUS 2013, LNICST 131, pp. 537–548, 2014.
DOI: 10.1007/978-3-319-11569-6_42

passwords or digital certificates and confidentiality in data transmission, the distributed model of CC makes it vulnerable and prone to sophisticated distributed and internal attacks. Since virtualization is the fundamental of the CC, offering higher machine efficiency due to increased utilization, energy savings, and the flexibility to build or destroy virtual machines (VMs) on demand to meet changing organizational needs, those advantages comes with some concerning security issues especially in the cloud context. In this research, we are focusing our work on inter-VM threats and VM hopping by proposing an authentication mechanism of each request communicating between VMs, and rejecting the non-compliant ones. Inter-VM threats occur when a hacker takes control of a VM and then gains access to the underlying hypervisor, allowing him to access and control all of the VMs on the system via VM hopping.

The remainder of the article is structured as follows: in the next section, we discuss some virtualization security issues in CC. The third section presents the core of our approach by explaining its components. In Sect. 4, we present the IP packet handling and processing by highlighting the use of the frame tag and the agents in a CC environment. The last section contains a summary and conclusions.

2   Background

One of the outstanding properties of virtualization is its ability to isolate co-resident Operating Systems (OSs) on the same physical platform. While isolation is an important property from a security perspective, co-resident virtual machines (VMs) often need to communicate and exchange a considerable amount of data. Multi-tenant infrastructures typically offer scaled performance and services based on shared resources, including databases, other applications, and OSs. For some organizations, this leaves them open to a variety of threats in a virtualized environment [2,3], these fall into a number of categories, centered mostly on the hypervisor: Hyperjacking, VM escape, VM hopping, VM migration, VM theft and inter-VM traffic.

Hyperjacking: is subverting the hypervisor or injecting a rogue hypervisor on top of the hardware layer. Since hypervisors run at the most privileged ring level on a processor, it would be hard or even impossible for any OS running on the hypervisor to detect it. In theory, a hacker with control of the hypervisor could control any virtual machine running on the physical server.

VM Hopping/Guest jumping: is the process of hopping from one VM to another VM using vulnerabilities in either the virtual infrastructure or a hypervisor. These attacks are often accomplished once an attacker has gained access to a low-value, thus less secure, VM on the same host, which is then used as a launch point for further attacks on the system. Because there are several VMs running on the same machine, there would be several victims of the VM hopping attack. An attacker can falsify the SaaS users data once he gains access to a targeted VM by VM hopping, endangering the confidentiality and integrity of SaaS. VM hopping is a considerable threat because several VMs can run on the same host making them all targets for the attacker.

VM mobility/migration: is enabling the moving or copying of VMs from one host to another over the network or by using portable storage devices without physically stealing or snatching a hard drive. It could lead to security problems such as spread of vulnerable configurations. The severity of the attack ranges from leaking sensitive information to completely compromising the OS. A man-in-the-middle can sniff sensitive data, manipulate services, and possibly even inject a rootkit. As IaaS lets users create computing platforms by importing a customized VM image into the infrastructure service. The impact on confidentiality, integrity, and availability via the VM mobility feature is quite large.

Inter-VM: In a traditional IT environment, network traffic can be monitored, inspected and filtered using a range of server security systems to try to detect malicious activity. But the problem with virtualized environments provides limited visibility to inter-VM traffic flows. This traffic is not visible to traditional network-based security protection devices, such as the network-based intrusion prevention systems (IPSs) located in network, and cannot be monitored in the normal way.

3   Our Approach

Virtualization is increasingly used in portions of the back-end of Infrastructure as a Service (IaaS), Platform as a Service (PaaS) and SaaS (Software as a Service) providers. The benefits of virtualization are well known, including multi-tenancy, better server utilization, and data center consolidation. Cloud Providers can achieve higher density, which translates to better margins and enterprises, can use virtualization to shrink capital expenditure on server hardware as well as increase operational efficiency. But as mentioned in the introduction, a malicious user has a huge hack domain since the inter-VM communication is blind to the security appliances on the LAN, giving him the possibility to take control of other VMs via a compromised one. Thereby, the focus of our work is about controlling this particular inter-VM traffic, analyzing it, and then preventing the non-compliant one.

Relating to other works especially in intrusion detection [4,5], we find that all of the measures that should be taken must be distributed since it is a Cloud environment [6], but the work done so far is about detecting and preventing a malicious traffic [7]. Our approach aims to control and analyze a particular traffic which is the inter-VM traffic by introducing a security structure characterize by a frame called frame tag added via an agent in the payload of the IP packet ensuring a high-level of integrity, so that the receiving VM's agent will detect, analyze and authenticate the incoming traffic then respond by accepting or rejecting this IP packet according to the compliance of the information on the frame tag. A compromised VM can be a jumping-off point in order to send requests to other VMs, for instance retrieving information in a malicious way

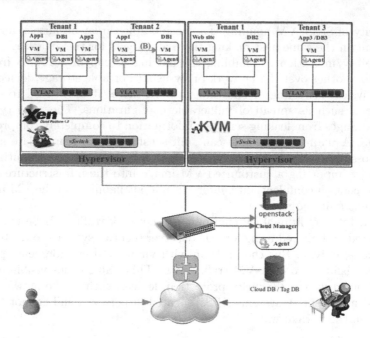

Fig. 1. A simple model for a Cloud Service Provider (Color figure online).

from a VM hosting a database, while in a legitimate scenario as depicted in Fig. 1, App1 hosted in a VM in tenant 1 sends a request to the DB1 hosted in another VM in order to get the requested information. Thereby, we are having two distinctive elements which are the tenant and the application. Hence, what we are trying to achieve with our approach is to authenticate each request communicating between VMs by encapsulating these two identifiers in the frame tag which will be an authentication factor for the IP packets by the sending VM' agent, then detected and analyzed by the receiving VM' agent and rejecting the non-compliant packets.

With this chapter, we provide a high level description of our proposed architecture, the frame tag, the security contract, policy management, how the agent works, and how they fit together. The goal of this description is to have a clear view of the overall approach, see how it fits into a Cloud environment, and to provide context for later chapter, describing a more detailed scenarios of packet handling and processing.

3.1 Frame Tag

Our approach is about identifying the application that sends the request (IP packet) to another machine in the same tenant. Hence, we propose a new structure of a frame called frame tag. The frame tag is generated between a pair of communicating agents, and it contains two fields: Tenant tag, and Application Tag.

The Tenant Tag Field: When a tenant is created an identity is assigned becoming the tenant tag and stored in a database. When a request is sent from a VM to another VM within the same tenant, the frame tag is generated and added by the agent in the payload of the IP packet and foreseeably the tenant tag, thereby ensuring the prevention of springboarding to another VM within another tenant, therefore adding a strong layer of tenant isolation.

The Application Tag Field: When an application is added and installed on a VM, the client has to certify the trustworthiness of this application by adding it via the console management, and then an ID is created to be the application tag and stored in a database. The use of the application tag in our approach, is that when App1 in Tenant1 sends a request to DB1 hosted in another machine within the same tenant and if the user did certify this application (App1) as a trustworthy one, the sending VM' agent will generate the frame tag in order to send this request by filling its fields with the right tenant tag and application tag.

3.2   Policy Management

In general, a Policy-based management (PM) is an administrative approach that is used to simplify the management of a given endeavor by establishing policies to deal with situations that are likely to occur [11].

In our case, the PM is the module responsible for handling outbound/inbound IP packets, in order to process them accordingly (such as processing the frame tag or the SC, inbound packets...). The output of the policy will be one of two actions -Discard, or Allow-. The protection afforded by the agents is defined by a database called the PM Database (PMD). This module will interact with the agent to update PMD and defines the processing of each outbound or inbound packet either needing a security service, and accepting, or dropping the packet.

IP packets are queued until being checked against the PM. If the policy indicates a packet needing to be dropped, then the inbound IP packet is expected to be discarded. When a packet is discarded, a reject policy is made so that the incoming packets from that host are dropped, because the host is considered compromised and a notification is made to the administrator. But if the policy indicates inbound/outbound inter-VM traffic, a special security processing is required. (Will be detailed in the next section)

3.3   Security Contract

The security and the integrity of the frame tag are critical. Hence, we introduced what we call a Security Contract (SC) (analogous to IPSec [8–10]). An SC is a uni-directional connection that affords security services to the frame tag carried by it. It is the establishment of a mutually agreed-upon security mechanisms and attributes (encryption algorithm, hash algorithms...) between two communicating VMs/agents to support a secure communication. To secure typical, bi-directional communication between two agents, a pair of SCs (one in each direction) is required. If two VMs, A and B, are communicating, then the host A will have an SC, SC-A, for processing its inbound packets. The host B will also create an SC, SC-B, for processing its inbound packets. Data sets associated with an SC are represented in the SC Database (SCD) and shared between agents. Once an SC is created, it is added to the SCD and identified by a Security Contract ID (SC-ID) defining its encryption algorithm (including key length), hash algorithms, lifetime, and the quick mode status (meaning no encryption is being performed).

Security Contract ID: Is a field on the SCD representing a unique value generated by the sender and used by a receiver to identify the SC from the SCD to which outbound packets should be bound.

Lifetime: Is a lifetime value of the SC to stay operational. The lifetime is divided into three fields in the SCD; key regeneration lifetime, busy session lifetime and idle session lifetime. Key regeneration lifetime is the key lifetime used in an SC. Whenever a key lifetime is reached, the SC is updated with the new regenerated key. Busy and idle session lifetimes are used to determine the lifetime of a session before the current used SC is expired and renegotiating another one.

During the negotiation of an SC, the VM sends three important fields; the SCI, the frame tag and a session token. The session token is a hash of the used SCI, frame tag and a time stamp. It is only valid till the session lifetime expires, and it is used as an inner tail on the payload in order to be authenticated during the communication.

In order to orchestrate those SCs and PM in a homogeneous way, each VM is embedded with an agent responsible for handling and processing them.

3.4   The Agent

The agents include similarities for minimal and lighter IDPS or firewall functionality, since it is an essential aspect of access control at the IP layer, they are also responsible of generating all the required fields and applying the PM. The agents behavior is depending on whether if they are receiving/analyzing or sending/generating a request. As IP packets flow into a VM, the agent doesn't perform a whole packet analysis, but only targets specific fields of the IP packets and responds by an automated acceptance or rejection according to the PM.

Every tenant in a Cloud environment has some critical machines and resources with a restricted access. For this purpose, the agent has an attribute within its PM called trust level and can take two distinct values; high and low, and it comes to the administrator to define the trust level of his machines/agents (for example a database with sensitive data can take a high trust level), this value will affect the behavior of the agent regarding the frame tag in terms of the inspection. There are two types of agents; master/manager and slave/regular agents. When an agent is freshly deployed it is assigned to a prior known master agent for management purposes. At the administrator side, the master agent plays the role of a front-end for the tenant in order to manage the deployed agents in terms of setting up their trust level, and to certify the trustworthiness of the applications running on the machines within the tenant, but also managing the SCs and the policies. Assigning the slave agents to their master agent means also having the right key pair in order to have encrypted and secured transactions between them, therefore preventing rogue requests to the master or having some VMs impersonating the master. The key pair could be changing periodically according to the administrators configuration. When a change of the key pair occurs the master agent sends a request to all his slave agents in order to update their keys.

As any intrusion detection and prevention system [12], the agent performs it analysis according to a set of rules in its PM, but in our case the agent has a self-generated rules defining what action should be taken regarding to its inbound IP packets. Besides the trust level component, the agent has another component called rules engine which is responsible for the self-generated rules based on the trust level value. The first task of the rules engine is to fetch the tenant tag and application tags, afterwards the rules engine checks the value of the trust level from the PMD in order to generate the proper rules set. When the trust level value is low, the generated rule will be is only about analyzing the tenant tag of the frame tag. On the other hand, if the trust level value is high this means that the generated rule is about analyzing both tenant tag and application tag of the frame tag (3).

In order to have a more accurate agent' behavior and targeted analysis, we introduced an inner header called a flag. The flag field is an indicator added by the sending agent at the beginning of the payload and it determines what action should be taken by the receiving agent depending on its value. The flag is a set of bits defining the type of data carried within the payload and can take several values: SC initiation flag, SC update flag, PM update flag, Data flag, Subscription flag, Rules and keys Update flag, and Trust level flag. The flag will be discussed more explicitly in later sections.

At the first run of a slave agent, it sends a request to its assigned master agent in order to retrieve its related tenant information. A tenant can contain several machines and accordingly several agents. Hence, a freshly deployed slave agent needs to recognize its neighboring agents within the same tenant, therefore comes the role of the flag field. When a slave agent is newly deployed, it sends a request to its master in order to subscribe its self and receive its tenant tag, applications tag and also information about its neighboring agents (IP address and trust level) and also populating the SCD with the SCs created so far. After this, the master agent sends specific frame tag with a particular flag called subscription flag to all the slave agents within the same tenant in order to have synchronization between the slave agents (the IP address and the trust level of the new slave agent). The trust level of a new slave agent is set by default to low but evidently it can be changed via the console management on the master agent by the admin if needed. When a change of a trust level occurs, the master agent sends a trigger to the designated slave agent in order to update its trust level. The request holds a particular value on the flag field called trust level update flag, so that the receiving agent will update its trust level and triggers an update of its rules set meaning a re-execution of the rules engine workflow. As for the rule update flag is triggered, when the admin at the console management adds an application as a trusted one, the master agent updates its database and sends a request with a rule update flag to all the agents within the same tenant in order to add the new application in their rules set and create a rule for it.

The implementation of distributed agents comes to relieve the pressure of hypervisor. Hence, we will have an improved resource management, and also no direct impact on the scalability and the performance factors, since that the agents are embedded in the VMs, and it comes to the Cloud manager to provision VMs on the fly with the needed resources. The role of the agents is to elevate the level of security in a Cloud environment by adding another layer of authentication via the frame tags. It acts like a light weight security appliance or an IDPS, more specifically like a Stack based IDPS, where the packets are examined as they go through the TCP/IP stack. The protection offered by this approach is based on requirements defined by the security policy established and maintained by an administrator.

Most OS kernels enable extensibility by exporting a standard generic link layer device interface. This allows us to make link-layer drivers a non-intrusive loadable kernel module. Thus, our approach should be designed to be deployed without patching to the guest OSes or the VMM sources. Also, the integrity of those agents is primal, hence operating wise, they are executed in a privileged system domain, (Ring 0 or Ring 1) so that the agents would be protected from being controlled by any malicious application running within the VM or a unauthorized users, and also in order to avoid any kind of impersonation.

This approach is an end-to-end security scheme designed to provide interoperable and high quality security for the inter-VM traffic. Generally, it is not affected by fragmentation, because the IP packets are fragmented after the agent' processing and the fragments are reassembled before the IP layer invokes the analysis process for further processing. On inbound processing, the agent will only get a reassembled packet from the IP layer. The set of security services offered includes integrity, data origin authentication, detection and rejection of none compliant packets. These services are provided at the IP layer, offering protection in a standard fashion for all protocols in the TCP/IP suite, and due to its transparency to applications, its implementation does not need to be configured separately for each application that uses TCP/IP.

4   IP Packet Handling and Processing

Relating to the model depicted in Fig. 1 that we are basing our work on, and after laying out the components of our approach, this section provides a working scenarios description of how our proposed approach works, to provide the security services noted above. The goal of this description is to be able to "picture" the overall process and architecture, see how it fits into a Cloud environment, and how the traffic is processed by the agents and how it is handled.

Most of the Cloud service providers have OS images and templates ready to use. According to our approach, the agents need to be already embedded in order to have a working scenario. When a client chooses an image or a template to run, the agent is in a larval mode meaning that it has to do specific tasks in order to be up and running. We should bear in mind that the OS images contain primary default encryption keys which will be used to initiate new agents for the communication with its master. Those primary encryption keys are updated and managed by the admin. At its first run, the agent knows only five things, its IP address, the IP address of its master, its trust level which is set by default to low, the key pair for the encrypted communication, and a default rule to accept incoming frame tags from its master. Thereby, the first thing that the agent does (Fig. 1, 1) is sending a request to its master agent in order to subscribe its self as a new slave agent in order to receive its tenant tag, the applications tags within the tenant, but also the IP addresses of its neighboring agents, and the shared SCD. Then, the new slave agent will start self-generating its rules set and change to listening mode. After this phase, comes the subscription phase of the new slave agent alongside the neighboring agents, this task is done by the master agent by sending the subscription flag having as data the IP address of the new slave agent. The receiving agents will have to begin at first, the analysis process by making sure that the incoming traffic is either from the master agent or another VM/agent within the same tenant (since that every slave agent knows its master and neighboring agents) in order to begin the packet inspection process by capturing the IP Packet and going directly to the first bits of the payload to check the inner header which is flag in order to know the nature of the request, which is for subscription purposes in this case.

The master also handles the management of the SCs. For instance, when the lifetime of the SC expires, it cannot be used anymore and another SC has to be renegotiated between the communicating VMs. In order to avoid the problem of breaking the communication when the SC expires, the agent warns its master that the SC is about to expire allowing it to notify the admin for a redefinition of this SC before a hard deletion. When the administrator updates the SC, the master sends the updated SC along with the SC update flag to all the agents of the same tenant in order to update the shared SCD. The same thing goes for a newly created SC.

The PM database is empty by default and only populated when a new policy entry is created, by sending a PM update flag from the master for the appropriate agent.

As aforementioned, the trust level at the first run of a slave agent is set by default to low, but when a change of this value occurs (Fig. 1, red) on the console management, the master agent sends a trust level update flag to the designated agent in order to change its trust level and accordingly its whole rules set, but also a subscription frame tag flag with the IP address and the new trust level of the selected slave agent to all its neighboring agents in order to update trust level value. The same thing happens when an application is added as a trusted one within the tenant (Fig. 1, yellow), the master agent sends a rule update flag

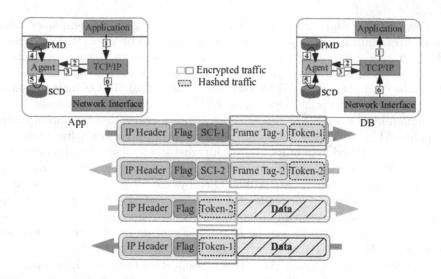

Fig. 2. The workflow of IP packet processing.

to all the slave agents in order to update their rules set by generating a rule for this application according to their trust level.

For a daily usage in a Cloud environment, a user can for example consult an application called App1 in tenant 2 (Fig. 1, blue), the incoming traffic from the user is considered an external traffic therefor the agent will not process it (according to its PM), but when the user tries for example to sign in by entering his login and password, evidently the App 1 will send a request to a database DB 1 in order to check the credentials. Let us consider the example network diagram shown in Fig. 2. For agent' processing (outbound and inbound), we will consider HTTP packets generated by App1 destined to DB 1 (both in tenant 2). First of all, the agent checks its PMD for a policy entry for this transaction. In our case, the policy on App1' VM mandates that packets destined to DB1' VM needs a security processing.

The basic outbound packet processing toward the DB1 occurs in the following sequence:

– App1 data is sent to the TCP/IP driver from the TCP/IP application.
– The TCP/IP driver sends an IP packet to the agent.
– The agent checks the packet for a policy match by looking up entries in the PMD.
– The agent checks the SCI by looking up on the SCD based on the policy entry, if there is not an appropriate SC, the agent chooses one randomly.
– The agent encapsulates the frame tag carrying the right credentials of the tenant tag of the tenant 2 and the application tag of App 1 (App 1 is a trusted application in tenant 2) within the SC initiation flag, the SCI and the token for the current communication session.
– Checksum recalculation.

- The IP packet is sent back to the TCP/IP driver.
- The TCP/IP driver sends the IP packet to the network interface.

Inbound processing is much simpler than outbound processing mainly because inner header construction is more complicated than header checking. The inbound packet processing from the App1 occurs in the following sequence:

- IP packets are sent from the network interface to the TCP/IP driver.
- The TCP/IP driver sends the IP packet to the agent.
- If the inbound packet contains an SC initiation flag.
- The agent extracts the SCI from the inner header.
- The agent then fetches the SC from the SCD using the sent SCI.
- If the SCD does not find the SC, an error is logged and the packet is dropped.
- If the SCD returns the SC entry, the agent decrypts the frame tag and the token.
- The agent authenticates the frame tag and stores the token for further communications.
- The agent sends that packet is sent to the TCP/IP driver.
- The TCP/IP driver performs IP packet processing as needed and sends the application data to the TCP/IP application.

After the initiation phase, the traffic between VMs is signed by the session token and instead of the SC initiation flag, the agent will send its requests with a data flag. Then the receiving end will have to decrypt and authenticate the token according to the negotiated SC. Hence, even if it is easy to make changes on the IP packet, it is very hard to change the payload to a desired value thanks to the randomness of the used SCIs (encryption methods, and hashing ...). Hence reducing the likelihood of payload tampering.

5   Conclusion

Cloud security is one of the buzz words in CC. Since virtualization is the fundamental of the CC, security and availability are critical for cloud environments because their massive amount of resources, simplifies several attacks to cloud services. In this paper, the focus of our work is about the visibility of the inter-VM traffic in a Cloud environment. Hence, we propose a new approach that gives an identity to this particular traffic, this identity is about the where and the who sends the request. Our approach relies on proposing a frame called frame tag that holds the proper credentials which are the tenant and the application that sends the IP packet, providing data origin authentication, and integrity, but also proposing an agent which is able to generate, capture and analyze this particular frame and respond to it by an automated acceptance or rejection, and also security mechanisms in order to ensure the integrity and security of this frame tag. The agent is the center-piece of our ongoing work. Therefore in our future work, we are trying to incorporate the autonomic computing characteristics on the agents functionality, in order to have not only a self-generating rule engine but also a self-optimized agent and have an analysis at wire speed to meet security and performance since that those are the two key elements for a good Cloud service, and also study the integration of Deep Packet Inspection and Deep Content Inspection to see which one is the best fit for an efficient inter-VM traffic inspection, but more importantly in order to keep the system informant is to log every suspicious move in a centralized server for a correlation purposes or even for a Security Information Event Management.

References

1. Van der Merwe, J., Ramakrishnan, K.K., Fairchild, M., Flavel, A., Houle, J., Lagar-Cavilla, H.A., Mulligan, J.: Towards a ubiquitous cloud computing infrastructure. In: 17th IEEE Workshop on Local and Metropolitan Area Networks (LANMAN), Long Branch, pp. 1–6 (2010)
2. 3 Ways to Secure Your Virtualized Data Center, 29 July 2010. http://www.serverwatch.com/trends/article.php/3895846/3-Ways-to-Secure-Your-Virtualized-Data-Center.htm
3. A comprehensive framework for securing virtualized data centers, HP, August 2010
4. Schulter, A., et al.: Intrusion detection for computational grids. In: 2nd International Conference New Technologies, Mobility, and Security. IEEE Press (2008)
5. Schulter, K.: Intrusion detection for grid and cloud computing. IEEE J. IT Prof. **12**, 38–43 (2010)
6. Gul, I., Hussain, M.: Distributed cloud intrusion detection model. Int. J. Adv. Sci. Technol. **34**, 71–82 (2011)
7. Mazzariello, C., Bifulco, R., Canonico, R.: Integrating a network IDS into an open source cloud computing environment. In: IEEE Sixth International Conference on Information Assurance and Security (2010)
8. Security Architecture for the Internet Protocol, RFC 4301
9. IP Authentication Header, RFC 4302
10. IP Encapsulating Security Payload (ESP), RFC 4303
11. Irani, F.N.H.A., Noruzi, M.R.: Looking on policy and social policy in the context of public administration and management. J. Public Adm. Gov. **1**(1), 106–114 (2011)
12. Scarfone, K., Mell, P.: Guide to Intrusion Detection and Prevention Systems (IDPS). Computer Security Resource Center (National Institute of Standards and Technology) (2007)

Adaptive Wireless Networks as an Example of Declarative Fractionated Systems

Jong-Seok Choi[2], Tim McCarthy[1], Minyoung Kim[1]([✉]), and Mark-Oliver Stehr[1]

[1] SRI International, Menlo Park, CA 94025, USA
{tim.mccarthy,minyoung.kim,markoliver.stehr}@sri.com
[2] Kyungpook National University, Daegu, Korea
choijongseok@knu.ac.kr

Abstract. Adaptive wireless networks can morph their topology and support information gathering and delivery activities to follow high-level goals that capture user interests. Using a case study of an adaptive network consisting of smart phones, robots, and UAVs, this paper extends a declarative approach to networked cyber-physical systems to incorporate quantitative aspects. This is done by distinguishing two levels of control. The temporal evolution of the macroscopic system state is controlled using a logical framework developed in earlier work while the microscopic state is controlled by an optimization algorithm or heuristic. This two-level declarative approach is built on top of a partially-ordered knowledge sharing model for loosely coupled distributed computing and is an example of a so-called fractionated system that can operate with any number of wireless nodes and quickly adapt to changes. Feasibility of the approach is demonstrated simulation and in a hybrid cyber-physical testbed consisting of robots, quadcopters, and Android devices.

Keywords: Cyber-physical systems · Distributed systems · Declarative control · Adaptive networks · MANETs · Swarms · Robots · UAVs

1 Introduction

Adaptive wireless networks are designed to morph in response to changing requirements and conditions. Such networks are becoming increasingly feasible with the emerging convergence of technologies in mobile networking, personal digital assistants (PDAs), smart phones, robotics, smart antennas, and sensors.

At the highest level of abstraction, an *adaptive wireless network* takes into account the user's information needs, adapts while sensing the environment, and tries to find a solution that best satisfies the user's requirements under the given constraints. Adaptive wireless networks are a special case of *networked cyber-physical systems* (NCPS). Robots are wireless nodes equipped with sensors and actuators that allow them to autonomously change location. PDAs carried by humans serve as user interfaces to the adaptive network. Different from traditional mobile ad hoc networks (MANETs), adaptive wireless networks are closer

© Institute for Computer Sciences, Social Informatics and Telecommunications Engineering 2014
I. Stojmenovic et al. (Eds.): MOBIQUITOUS 2013, LNICST 131, pp. 549–563, 2014.
DOI: 10.1007/978-3-319-11569-6_43

to content-based networks and solve a more general resource planning and optimization problem by utilizing the computational resources and sensor/actuator capabilities of each node, e.g., the capability to move, turn, take a picture, or sense a sound.

This paper generalizes a *declarative approach to distributed control* of NCPS [18] that distinguishes two levels of control: (1) distributed logic based on user-injected goals controls the system's evolving macroscopic state (e.g., the location of a swarm of UAVs or robots) and (2) an optimization algorithm drives the system's microscopic system (e.g., the formation of the swarm) in a direction that satisfies the specification of the macro-state that, in the most abstract approach, can be declaratively expressed as an objective function.

This paper focuses on a subclass of NCPS with distributed control called *heterogeneous fractionated systems*. Apart from their decentralized nature, they are characterized by the involvement of different types of nodes (PDAs, robots, and UAVs) that, if the same type, are interchangeable for the purposes of this application. One key implication of this model is the independence of the control algorithm from the number of nodes of each type available. Futhermore, both temporary or permanent failure/disconnections or rescaling of the system to adjust its resources can change the number of nodes at runtime. Reference [29] describes additional motivations for the fractionated approach to NCPS.

The unpredictability of the environment that immediately yields the traditional impossibility results for asynchronous systems dictates the use of a sufficiently weak, and hence (wirelessly) implementable, model for loosely-coupled distributed computing. This paper considers fractionated systems as a special case of the *partially ordered knowledge sharing* (POKS) model [17] which does not rely on any form of atomic transactions and only provides eventual consistency. In this declarative setting, *knowledge* refers to all information shared between the nodes, specifically observations (facts) and control actions (goals), as explained in [18] in more detail.

The primary contribution of this paper is the integration of qualitative and quantitative aspects in a unified declarative approach that widens the applicability of the distributed logical framework for NCPS [18]. A second contribution is the extension of the cyber-application software framework to support a hybrid testbed and new set of applications based on this generalized approach.

1.1   Motivating Scenario: Self-organizing Cyber-Physical Ensembles

An example of cyber-physical ensembles is a swarm of programmable ground robots and UAVs that perform a distributed surveillance mission — e.g., to achieve situation awareness during an emergency — by moving or flying to a suspicious location, collecting information, and returning to a base location in a formation that creates an effective sensing grid. This application also involves human-carried computing/communication devices such as smart phones that collect/report sensor data and inject users' interests into the system. Heterogeneous nodes have different capabilities: UAVs can fly and generate an encoded video stream with their front- and bottom-facing cameras. Additional computing

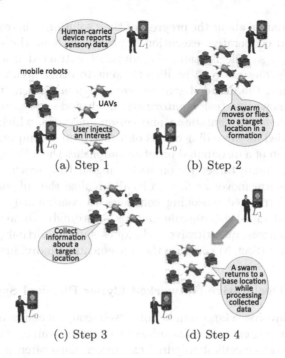

Fig. 1. A user's interest is injected into the network at a location L_0 around which the robots/UAVs are initially clustered randomly. A noise, recorded at a location L_1, triggers the distributed mission.

resources also enable UAVs to extract a snapshot from the encoded video and decode it into JPEG format. Robots can only move on the ground and decode the encoded snapshots from UAVs. The network is adaptive in the sense that it morphs in response to the users' needs.

Figure 1 exemplifies the scenario in which a hybrid swarm moves/flies to a location to investigate a noise reported by an Android phone. The swarm takes a snapshot of the area and returns to the base location. In this scenario, perturbations from the environment (e.g., wind), delayed/incomplete knowledge due to network disruption, and resource contention cause uncertainty. Real-world actions must compensate for temporary network disconnections or failures. These actions can only indirectly control parameters, such as a robot's position, that can be observed by sensors (e.g., GPS). Therefore, a swarm should dynamically configure itself, optimize its resources, and provide robust information dissemination services that adapt to the users' interest in a specific topic. This interest can induce cyber-physical control (e.g., robot positioning, UAV trajectory/formation modifications) and trigger additional sensing (e.g., snapshot of an area).

Goals (e.g., interests and controls) and facts (e.g., sensor readings and computational results) can arrive from the users and the environment at any time, and are opportunistically shared whenever connectivity exists. Programmable robots and UAVs compute their local solution based on local knowledge and exchange up-to-date information about the progress of their solution. These abilities enable a distributed and cooperative execution approach without the need for global coordination. In a sample mission, the snapshot extracted from the encoded video stream (*abstraction*) may be directly sent to other nodes if the network supports it. If not, the decoded stream (*computation*) is sent to other nodes in the form of knowledge (*communication*). Each node can potentially engage in many *abstractions*, *computations*, and *communications*, which are classes of operations regarded as three dimensions of a distributed computing cube.

The completion of a distributed proof accomplishes the mission. The solution assigns an approximate target region as a subgoal to a swarm's (*macro*-scale controls). The swarm moves or flies to locally realize the subgoal (*micro*-scale controls). The distributed reasoning continues to continuously recompute the local solutions and adjust *macro*-scale controls accordingly. To satisfy the subgoal of *micro*-scale controls, quantitative techniques such as virtual potential fields or artificial physics (Sect. 3) compute the movements of individual UAV/robots.

1.2 Towards Declarative Networked Cyber-Physical Systems

NCPS typically involves a large number of loosely-coupled components that must operate in challenging environments subject to few constraints. Traditional algorithms with problem-specific hardwired execution plans often poorly cover the state space's vast range of possible operating conditions. Declarative approaches rely on executable logical specifications operating on a higher level of abstraction to more directly define the behavior, thereby avoiding micro-management or over-specification of system behavior. Hence, these approaches potentially make the system more adaptive and resilient to changes of many kinds, such as failures, resource constraints, or changes in the number of nodes or the goals.

A *partially ordered knowledge sharing (POKS)* model based on opportunistic information exchange avoids hard constraints on connectivity which is typically wireless and unreliable. As in delay-/disruption-tolerant networks, a local cache partly compensates for the unreliability at each node. For this paper's model, the cache is called a *knowledge base* (KB). Furthermore, the application-dependent model uses a form of semantic networking to exploit the meaning of knowledge in terms of two partial orders referred to as *subsumption* and *replacement* orderings on knowledge units. The subsumption order $k \leq k'$ expresses that k' contains at least as much information as k: k can be discarded in the presence of k'. The replacement order $k \prec k'$ expresses that k is superseded by new information k', and the obsolete k is discarded. In this paper, the former order is used to concisely represent the logical structure (implication) of the current state, while the latter represents the passage of time without introducing logical inconsistencies.

The POKS model naturally expresses in-network computations by generating new knowledge as a function of knowledge received. A typical use of the replacement ordering defines it based on the creation time of the knowledge units, so that in-network transformations and computation can be applied to (unreliable) streams of knowledge, e.g., those generated by sensors.

In declarative networks it is useful to distinguish three classes of operations that can be performed at each node: abstractions, computations, and communications. Since the location at which the operations take place does not matter for the user who simply specifies the information needed in a declarative style, the system has the flexibility to map these operations to different nodes depending on resource availability and connectivity. Adaptive networks can, in addition, morph in response to the user's interest which is represented as a goal.

This paper entertains two approaches to representing and handling goals. Logic may qualitatively represent a goal that is satisfied through a deductive process. The logical framework for NCPS in [18] adopts this approach. It is based on a distributed proof-system defined on top of the POKS model that supports both forward and backward chaining in Horn clause theories. In this framework both facts and goals are uniformly represented as knowledge with suitable orderings and are directly used as an interface to cyber-physical devices (sensors and actuators, respectively).

Alternatively, an objective function may qualitatively represent a goal and measure its degree of satisfaction. This approach, which refers to the objective function as a *virtual potential*, is well known in the multi-agent system community. Related approaches such as artificial physics have been studied as well. Given an objective function, distributed optimization algorithm incrementally improve the satisfaction of the goal. As exemplified in [16], use of the POKS model supports a natural representation of distributed optimization algorithms using a subsumption ordering on the domain of the objective function that captures the degree of satisfaction.

2   Background — Cyber-Framework and Distributed Logic

To implement a distributed computing model based on POKS, the cyber-framework [17] provides a form of semantic networking with caching in a locally event-driven paradigm. The cyber-framework provides communication primitives that can shield applications from the complexities of dealing with dynamic topologies, delays/disruptions, and failures of all kinds. The cyber-framework also supports implementations with simulated and real environments including the network (e.g., wireless/wired) and cyber-physical devices (e.g., sensors, actuators). The knowledge dissemination component implements specific strategies (e.g., deterministic/probabilistic, unicast/broadcast) to propagate knowledge on top of the underlying network layer. The knowledge dissemination protocols make essential use of the POKS by replacing, and hence discarding, a unit of knowledge whenever a higher-ordered unit is received. Note that the kind of knowledge and its frequency of dissemination depends on the specific cyber-application and its objectives as reported in [7].

In the cyber-framework, knowledge is stored redundantly in local KBs that provide the *cyber-applications* with the abstraction of a distributed network cache. Each cyber-application runs on a *cyber-node* that is the smallest managed computational resource. Cyber-nodes can have attached *cyber-physical devices* (e.g., camera or motors) that observe or control the environment. Cyber-nodes form a hierarchy within a *cyber-engine* and a *cyber-host* that correspond to a specific process and a machine on which cyber-applications are running, respectively. By using the *cyber-API*, the interface provided by the cyber-framework, users can program set-up code that instantiates, composes, and configures cyber-node/engine/host and applications. A cyber-node provides services for posting events (local to the cyber-node) and knowledge (globally shared via dissemination) through the cyber-API — *postEvent* and *postKnowledge*, respectively. The API requires applications that define the local initialization and handling functions — *handleEvent* and *handleKnowledge*.

While the implementation of the cyber-framework provides an operational model for CPS, the declarative view of CPS enables users to describe the mission as a logical theory (e.g., Fig. 2). Distributed reasoning with asynchronous control has been implemented [18] on the cyber-framework with its underlying POKS model. Goals and facts are represented as knowledge that can be shared via POKS. At the level of an individual cyber-physical component, the logic provides a declarative interface for goal-oriented control and feedback through observations that are represented as logical facts. Inference and computation allow facts and goals to interact and form new facts or goals. The opportunity to exchange knowledge with other nodes should lead to cooperation, and the absence of such opportunities should lead to more autonomous behavior.

In this implementation of the logical framework in [18], each node is equipped with a knowledge manager (i.e., an implementation of the POKS model), a reasoner for declarative control, and attached devices. These devices may be considered sub-nodes that exhibit a declarative knowledge-based interface. New goals and facts can arrive at any time and be interleaved with the local inference processes. Two kinds of goals and facts exist: the *cyber-goals/cyber-facts* and *goals/facts* are the interface with the environment and the basis of inference, respectively. For example, the UAV generates both a cyber-fact of its current location that satisfies a corresponding cyber-goal and a fact/subgoal from forward or backward chaining. The demo scenario (Sect. 1.1) and its implementation (Sect. 4) experimented with a swarm of one to seven robots/UAVs in total and used two Android nodes. These nodes have fixed locations and serve as user access points to the cyber-physical system.

3   Integrating Logic with Quantitative Algorithms

Scalable control of NCPS with resource optimization requires highly decentralized and compositional approaches. Hence, this paper studies a new form of adaptive declarative networking for cyber-physical ensembles by integrating logical inference with quantitative algorithms. In a nutshell, declarative (i.e., logical) specifications serve as executable descriptions that guide the ensemble at the macro-scale, while evolving virtual potentials continuously perform micro-scale controls. Given a macroscopic goal that may have been obtained after decomposition of higher-level mission objectives, satisfaction of this subgoal requires

Forward Clauses:
$F1 : Noise(T, A) \Rightarrow Trigger(T, A).$
$F2 : Motion(T, A) \Rightarrow Trigger(T, A).$

Backward Clauses:
$B1 : Interest(T_I, I, E) \Leftarrow Result(T_I, T_T, 0, I), Deliver(T_I, T_T, 1, I, E).$
$B2 : Deliver(T_I, T_T, N_D, I, E) \Leftarrow Delivered(T_I, T_T, N_D, I, E).$
$B3 : Deliver(T_I, T_T, N_D, I, E) \Leftarrow Position(T_P, E, A), Position(T'_P, E', A'), E' \neq E,$
$\qquad MoveTo(T_I, T_T, N_D, 0, \infty, E', A), Deliver(T_I, T_T, N_D, I, E).$
$B4 : Result(T_I, T_T, N_D, I') \Leftarrow EncodedImage(T_I, T_T, N_D, I), I' = Decode(I).$
$B5 : EncodedImage(T_I, T_T, N_D, I) \Leftarrow Trigger(T_T, A), T_I \leq T_T,$
$\qquad MoveTo(T_I, T_T, N_D, 0, T_T + \Delta t_{sd}, E, A), TakeSnapshot(T_I, T_T, N_D, T_T + \Delta t_{sd}, A, I).$
$B6 : TakeSnapshot(T_I, T_T, N_D, D, A, I) \Leftarrow Snapshot(T_I, T_T, N_D, T_S, A, I), T_T \leq T_S, T_S \leq D.$
$B7 : MoveTo(T_I, T_T, N_D, D, E, A) \Leftarrow Position(T_P, E, A), T_P \leq D.$
$B8 : MoveTo(T_I, T_T, N_D, D, E, A) \Leftarrow Move(T_I, T_T, N_D, D, E, A).$

Replacement Ordering: (f denotes a fact, g, a goal and x denotes either)
$O1 : f : Position(t_P, e, \ldots) \prec f : Position(t'_P, e, \ldots)$ if $t_P < t'_P.$
$O2 : x : X(t_I, \ldots) \prec g : Interest(t'_I, \ldots)$ if $t_I < t'_I.$
$O3 : x : X(t_I, t_T, n_D, \ldots) \prec f : Result(t_I, t_T, n_D, \ldots)$ if $x : X \neq f : Result.$
$O4 : x : X(t_I, t_D, n_D, \ldots) \prec f : Deliver(t_I, t_D, n_D, \ldots)$ if $x : X \neq f : Deliver.$

Variables: T: time, D: snapshot deadline, A: area, E: ensemble, I: information, N: identifier
Constants: Δt_{sd}: relative snapshot deadline (max. delay from trigger event)

Fig. 2. Logical theory of the motivating scenario in Sect. 1.1 — The trigger condition is specified as forward clause $F1$. Backward clauses are evaluated only when a user or the reasoner injects a goal (or a new subgoal) that unifies with the conclusion of the clause. Orderings are specified to replace inferior facts/goals.

control of the micro-states of individual elements in the ensemble. In Fig. 2, forward and backward rules direct ensembles to accomplish a particular mission. Distributed algorithms optimize the formation objectives of these ensembles by moving or flying the UAVs/robots as a swarm to a specific location and generating appropriate facts (e.g., *Position*) to satisfy corresponding subgoals (e.g., *MoveTo*).

This paper describes a compositional declarative approach that expresses user objectives in a distributive logic and further decomposes them during translation into real-world actions or quantitative algorithms. Atomic goals are either built-in predicates/functions of the logic or actions directly realized by cyberphysical devices. Non-atomic logical goals for which a corresponding algorithm exists trigger the execution of that algorithm. If no such algorithm exists, the system attempts a distributed proof to simplify and solve the goal as far as possible, potentially injecting new subgoals during the proof's inference. Since each ensemble element may have different capabilities and a limited local view, the continuous evaluation of solutions with respect to the partial order preservers scalability in the context of loosely coupled systems. For example, facts are disseminated in the network to compensate for heterogeneity in the node capabilities and other limitations such as resource and sensor failures.

In Fig. 2, a user injects an *Interest* goal into the system. By processing conditions from left to right, the reasoner attempts to solve a *Result* goal. It fails at first because a corresponding *Result* fact representing a solution does not exist yet. The local reasoner feeds the new *Result* subgoal into the local KB. Some goals cannot be solved by means of the logical specification, but the local cyber-physical devices may handle the goal through real-world action: for example, by taking an image and adding it to the local KB. The *MoveTo* subgoal will generate a new *Position* fact when it is realized. The clause *B8* is of particular interest, since it initiates a change in the position of a swarm. In this unified approach, quantitative algorithms, e.g. potential-based optimization, realize the cyber-goal *Move*. As a result, a new *Position* cyber-fact will be generated if a swarm manages to move to the desired location within time constraints. Note that a goal can be matched with a fact anywhere in the network. The fully distributed reasoning process allows *Decode* to be solved at all ensemble elements, while *TakeSnapshot* can be only satisfied by ensemble elements with camera devices (UAVs in this scenario).

This work leverages the concept of a virtual potential [15] for micro-scale control of ensembles. Each ensemble element is driven by the desire to minimize its perception of, and hence its own contribution to, the virtual potential. In this scenario, the potential is designed to guide ensemble elements into position at a desired pair-wise distance in the formation. The potential also directs the elements to adapt when a new target location is selected as a macro-scale goal. The potential function declaratively captures the quality of a given swarm configuration as a weighted sum, $p = w_f p_f + w_l p_l$, where p_f and p_l are potentials corresponding to formation and desired location, respectively. As an example, the formation potential p_f should be minimized when a swarm creates a hexagonal lattice through the use of one of several possible distributed sensing grids as discussed in [28].

There are two ways to implement the potential-based approach. The most general approach, so far explored only in simulation, allows the user to specify a virtual potential function which is then solved by a generic distributed optimization algorithm. The alternative approach used in the experiments described here is based on the specification of the virtual potential indirectly through a force field, which is also known as *artificial physics* [28]. There are two kinds of forces, namely *formation forces* and *goal forces*, that define p_f and p_l in the above equation, respectively. Formation forces can be repulsive or attractive. Each ensemble element repels others closer than a desired distance R while attracting those further than R. Force balance must be maintained against p_f to map the goal force into p_l and keep the formation during movement to target location. Enforcement of an upper bound on the goal force (as explained in [28]) and tuning of the weights of composing potential achieves this balance.

4   Real World Deployment on Cyber-Physical Ensembles

The underlying cyber-framework was extended to support various abstractions and APIs for programming a heterogeneous testbed based on the Parrot AR.Drone 2.0 [22], iRobot Create [3] platforms, and various Android devices.

Heterogeneous Testbed: The AR.Drones and Creates were equipped with additional computing resources (Gumstix modules [12]) and sensors (GPS and

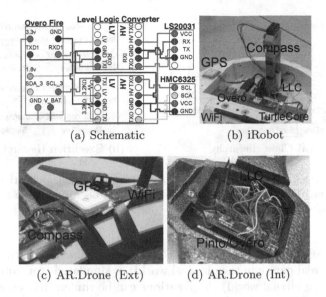

(a) Schematic (b) iRobot

(c) AR.Drone (Ext) (d) AR.Drone (Int)

Fig. 3. AR.Drones and Create robots were equipped with Gumstix Overo Fire [9] via a Pinto-TH [10] (AR.Drone) or TurtleCore [11] (Create) expansion board. Overo Fire is augmented with a GPS unit [20] via serial port and a digital compass [13] via I^2C. In between the sensors and the expansion board sit a pair of logic level converters [27].

digital compass) shown in Fig. 3 to increase their autonomy and improve capabilities such as localization in physical space. The Gumstix computer is also equipped with a WiFi antenna which provides communication via a peer-to-peer ad-hoc network. The testbed uses the Google Nexus S running CyanogenMod 7.2 with built-in digital compass, GPS, and camera as a standard Android device. As for the software side, the AR.Drones (firmware ver. 2.3.3) are controlled via WiFi, using a modified version of JavaDrone (ver. 1.3) [14] for sending commands and interpreting information from the drone's onboard sensors and video cameras. JavaDrone was modified to support video reception from the AR.Drone 2.0 by extracting video frames from the stream and passing them directly to the framework rather than attempting to decode them. This encoded frame data can be decoded later when it is deemed necessary, possibly on another device with more available computing resources. The Creates are controlled via a direct serial port connection from the Gumstix using the cyber-API which supports sending movement and audio commands.

Cyber-Framework Extension: Because it is written in Java, the cyber-framework runs directly on the ARM-based Gumstix module without modification. A variety of abstractions were implemented over the available devices to make writing applications easier and more consistent. To allow testing of the same code with both real and simulated scenarios, the cyber-framework supports two different device implementations for each device that share a common

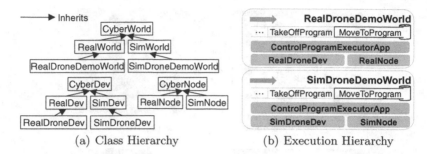

(a) Class Hierarchy   (b) Execution Hierarchy

Fig. 4. Class/Execution hierarchy enables the execution of same application code without modification. The Executor cyber-application controls a device via a sequence of ControlPrograms such as MoveToProgram.

interface as seen in Fig. 4. Each device is assigned a behavior which can be real (controlling a real device in the physical world) or simulated (controlling a simulated device in a virtual world). Applications can be run entirely on a simulated platform such as Stage [8] or Mason [4] without any code modification.

As a further abstraction over hardware devices, virtual Camera and Position devices that can be used independently of the underlying hardware (e.g., regardless of whether the hardware in use is a drone, robot, or phone) were implemented. The Camera device supports a single command that takes a snapshot of a given area. The Position device reports its location, and supports a variety of movement methods (e.g., waypoint-based or velocity-based).

For lower level programming of drone/robot actions, a *ControlProgram* interface allows users to write programs that will run periodically to send new commands to devices based on their current situation. These programs, which provide notification to their caller via events on completion, can be asynchronously launched and terminated at will. An example of such a program is the *MoveToProgram* which implements waypoint-based movement. The *Position* device uses *MoveToProgram* to implement the physical movement. *MoveToProgram* runs with device-specific frequency and at each invocation checks the current position of the device. It then issues direct movement commands to move closer to the desired destination. If the destination has been reached, *MoveToProgram* terminates.

Mission Deployment: To demonstrate the autonomous outdoor mission described in Sect. 1.1 and further elaborated in Fig. 2, GPS was used for localization without infrastructural support such as motion-tracking camera setups. To compensate for errors in GPS readings and facilitate simpler position and trajectory calculations, the testbed used differential GPS (10 Hz) [1] and a Cartesian ENU (East-North-Up) coordinate system [2]. For the AR.Drone, which lacks the capability to reliably stop at a fixed position and wait for its GPS readings to stabilize, a trajectory prediction filter was implemented to sit between the GPS sensor and the Drone API. This filter uses a least squares regression to fit movement to a polynomial curve to predict future positions.

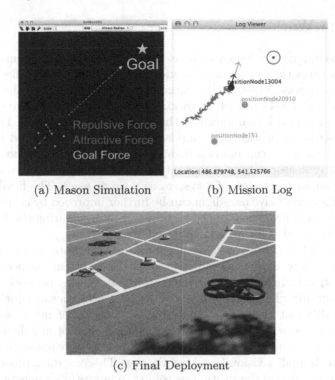

(a) Mason Simulation   (b) Mission Log

(c) Final Deployment

Fig. 5. Mission is tested on simulation and further fine-tuned towards real deployment. In the mission log, the robot is represented by a pointed black dot. The blue path represents the trajectory so far. The green arrow is a force acting on the robot. The bullseye is the swarm's goal, and grey dots represent the robot's belief about the positions of other robots.

Figure 5 shows the progress towards real world deployment. A swarm mission can be run entirely on a simulated platform to evaluate the algorithm's correctness and performance. In Fig. 5(a), a swarm of seven mobile nodes forms a hexagonal lattice maintained by artificial forces. The formation force dictates a 9 m distance between each pair of nodes, while the goal force attempts to push the entire swarm towards a target location. In Fig. 5(b), the same code is then deployed on a real device and the trajectory is recorded for further debugging and fine-tuning since the simulation lacks fidelity to accurately model the physical environment (e.g., movement delay, wind). The demo mission is deployed on two Android phones, three AD.Drones, and four Creates in a 70 × 35-m parking lot in Fig. 5(c). One Android phone generates a fact that represents an observation, e.g., a sensed noise, which triggers the distributed execution of a mission with the user's location as target area.

Once the swarm has reached at the target location, AR.Drones take encoded video frames via their front-facing camera, and extract an encoded frame. Creates then decode the frame and transmit it back to the phones.

5   Related Work

Declarative techniques are increasingly used in networking, in particular in data-centric sensor networks and recently in information-centric approaches for wired and wireless networks. NDlog [21], a variant of Datalog, refocuses the programming tasks on high-level issues of networking by providing a declarative language and dataflow framework that executes the compiled specifications. Declarative querying of sensor networks [32] composes services on the fly and in a goal-driven fashion using the concept of semantic streams. Meld [5] extends the ideas from declarative sensor networks to modular robots, i.e., ensembles of robots, by providing an abstract view of a system as a single asset. The flexibility and efficiency of the declarative paradigm can be further improved by correlating the logical and physical properties of the system and by integrating the logical and quantitative approaches for programming NCPS.

References [6,30] studied decentralized control of robotic or aerial swarms with a limited view of the system caused by intermittent connectivity and resource constraint. In particular, Swarmorph [24] utilizes network morphing to create a specific global structure of a heterogeneous swarm for collective responses to different tasks as a single entity. Swarms of micro aerial vehicles [19,23] have been studied as a newly emerging class of mobile sensor networks. However, in most cases the high-level goal is controlled by the base station with high-quality vision-based localization. This control approach requires infrastructure and makes the swarm less robust to failure/disconnections of specific elements, unlike the fully distributed and autonomous control of fractionated systems proposed here.

Most applications of virtual potential fields have considered single agents or localized unstructured ensembles. A notable exception is [26] which develops a compositional approach that results in a single potential function that coordinates a complex mission. A similar approach to aggregate motion control is inspired by flock behavior based on a distributed behavioral model [25] in which each simulated bird navigates according to its local perception of the dynamic environment, the laws of simulated physics, and a set of programmed behaviors. The computational field model [31] is based on concurrent objects in an open distributed environment guided by a metric space defined by mass, distance, gravitational force, repulsive force, and inertia of objects. Its communication model is based on object migration, an atomic primitive that is too strong for the kinds of environments targeted by this paper.

6   Conclusions and Future Directions

Generalizing earlier work, this paper investigates the use of virtual potential functions to extend a logical framework that combines qualitative and quantitative paradigms. After the general approach, which is based on a generic reasoning and optimization framework, was studied in simulation, the distributed logical framework was deployed for the first time on a newly developed hybrid NCPS testbed which consists of phones, robots, and drones. As a simplification, the approach describe here used an artificial-physics-based algorithm to implement the virtual potential instead of a generic distributed optimization algorithm. The deployment of the latter is in progress and has already been tested in simulations.

Adaptive wireless networks that can physically morph in response to mission requirements are an ideal application for the declarative approach proposed here because the distributed state space is too complex for traditional hardwired algorithmic solutions, especially in the absence of strong assumptions on the environment. The case study in this paper illustrates the basic idea by combining robots, drones, and phones, but there is potential for other applications with newly emerging technologies such as pico-satellite constellations, networked balloons, and networks of buoys. In addition to physical control over position and orientation, there are other dimensions of control associated with wireless technologies such as transmission power control and beam forming that could be investigated in future work. A core challenge of all these distributed control problems is that the coordination required to find acceptable solutions must rely on the same network that is continuously morphed and potentially disrupted by unforeseen events. Hence, a conceptual framework and tools to evaluate the stability and robustness of such fractionated systems constitute another important and challenging direction for future work.

Acknowledgments. We thank Walter Alvarez, Kyle Leveque, and Bryan Klofas at SRI International for their contributions to building the testbed. Support from National Science Foundation Grant 0932397 (A Logical Framework for Self-Optimizing Networked Cyber-Physical Systems) and Office of Naval Research Grant N00014-10-1-0365 (Principles and Foundations for Fractionated Networked Cyber-Physical Systems) is gratefully acknowledged. Any opinions, findings, and conclusions or recommendations expressed in this material are those of the authors and do not necessarily reflect the views of NSF or ONR.

References

1. Differential GPS. http://en.wikipedia.org/wiki/Differential_GPS
2. Geodetic Datum. http://en.wikipedia.org/wiki/Geodetic_system
3. iRobot Create. http://store.irobot.com/shop/index.jsp?categoryId=3311368
4. Mason multiagent simulation lib. http://cs.gmu.edu/eclab/projects/mason/
5. Ashley-Rollman, M.P., Goldstein, S.C., Lee, P., Mowry, T.C., Pillai, P.: Meld: a declarative approach to programming ensembles. In: IEEE International Conference on Intelligent Robots and Systems (2007)
6. Berman, S., Kumar, V., Nagpal, R.: Design of control policies for spatially inhomogeneous robot swarms with application to commercial pollination. In: ICRA, pp. 378–385. IEEE (2011)
7. Choi, J.-S., McCarthy, T., Yadav, M., Kim, M., Talcott, C., Gressier-Soudan, E.: Application patterns for cyber-physical systems. In: IEEE International Conference on Cyber-Physical Systems, Networks, and Applications, CPSNA'13 (2013)
8. Gerkey, B., Vaughan, R.T., Howard, A.: The player/stage project: tools for multi-robot and distributed sensor systems. In: 11th International Conference on Advanced Robotics (ICAR) (2003)

9. Gumstix. Overo Fire COM. https://www.gumstix.com/store/product_info.php? products_id=227
10. Gumstix. Pinto-TH. https://www.gumstix.com/store/product_info.php?products_id=239
11. Gumstix. TurtleCore. https://www.gumstix.com/store/product_info.php? products_id=280
12. Gumstix Inc. Gumstix. https://www.gumstix.com/
13. Honeywell Inc. HMC6352. http://magneticsensors.com/ magnetometers-compasses.php
14. JavaDrone. http://code.google.com/p/javadrone/
15. Khatib, O.: Real-time obstacle avoidance for manipulators and mobile robots. Int. J. Rob. Res. **5**, 90–98 (1986)
16. Kim, J., Kim, M., Stehr, M.-O., Oh, H., Ha, S.: A parallel and distributed meta-heuristic framework based on partially ordered knowledge sharing. J. Parallel Distrib. Comput. **72**(4), 564–578 (2012)
17. Kim, M., Stehr, M.-O., Kim, J., Ha, S.: An application framework for loosely coupled networked cyber-physical systems. In: IEEE/IFIP International Conference Embedded and Ubiquitous Computing, EUC'10, pp. 144–153 (2010)
18. Kim, M., Stehr, M.-O., Talcott, C.: A distributed logic for networked cyber-physical systems. Sci. Comput. Program. **78**, 2453–2467 (2013)
19. Kushleyev, A., Mellinger, D., Kumar, V.: Towards a swarm of agile micro quadrotors. In: Robotics: Science and Systems, July 2012
20. LOCOSYS Technology Inc. LS20031. http://www.locosystech.com/product.php? zln=en&id=20
21. Loo, B.T., Condie, T., Garofalakis, M., Gay, D.E., Hellerstein, J.M., Maniatis, P., Ramakrishnan, R., Roscoe, T., Stoica, I.: Declarative networking. Commun. ACM **52**(11), 87–95 (2009)
22. Parrot SA. AR. Drone 2.0. http://ardrone2.parrot.com/
23. Purohit, A., Sun, Z., Mokaya, F., Zhang, P.: Sensorfly: controlled-mobile sensing platform for indoor emergency response applications. In: International Conference on Information Processing in Sensor Networks (IPSN) (2011)
24. O'Grady, M.D.R., Christensen, A.L.: Swarmorph: multi-robot morphogenesis using directional self-assembly. IEEE Trans. Robot. **25**(3), 738–743 (2009)
25. Reynolds, C.W.: Flocks, herds and schools: a distributed behavioral model. In: 14th Annual Conference on Computer Graphics and Interactive Techniques, SIG-GRAPH '87, pp. 25–34 (1987)
26. Sentis, L., Mintz, M., Ayyagari, A., Battles, C., Ying, S., Khatib, O.: Large scale multi-robot coordination under network and geographical constraints. In: Proceedings of the IEEE International Symposium on Industrial, Electronics (2009)
27. Spark Fun Electronics. Logic Level Converter. https://www.sparkfun.com/ products/8745
28. Spears, W.M., Heil, R., Zarzhitsky, D.: Artificial physics for mobile robot formations. In: IEEE Internatioanl Conference on Systems, pp. 2287–2292 (2005)
29. Stehr, M.-O., Talcott, C., Rushby, J., Lincoln, P., Kim, M., Cheung, S., Poggio, A.: Fractionated software for networked cyber-physical systems: research directions and long-term vision. In: Agha, G., Danvy, O., Meseguer, J. (eds.) Formal Modeling: Actors, Open Systems, Biological Systems. LNCS, vol. 7000, pp. 110–143. Springer, Heidelberg (2011)
30. Swarmanoid Project. http://www.swarmanoid.org

31. Tokoro, M.: Computational field model: toward a new computing model/methodology for open distributed environment. In: Proceedings of the 2nd IEEE Workshop on Future Trends in Distributed Computing Systems (1990)
32. Whitehouse, K., Zhao, F., Liu, J.: Semantic streams: a framework for composable semantic interpretation of sensor data. In: Römer, K., Karl, H., Mattern, F. (eds.) EWSN 2006. LNCS, vol. 3868, pp. 5–20. Springer, Heidelberg (2006)

Elastic Ring Search for Ad Hoc Networks

Simon Shamoun[1]([✉]), David Sarne[1], and Steven Goldfeder[2]

[1] Bar Ilan University, Ramat Gan, Israel
srshamoun@yahoo.com
[2] Princeton University, Princeton, USA

Abstract. In highly dynamic mobile ad hoc networks, new paths
between nodes can become available in a short amount of time. We
show how to leverage this property in order to efficiently search for paths
between nodes using a technique we call elastic ring search, modeled after
the popular expanding ring search. In both techniques, a node searches
up to a certain number of hops, waits long enough to know if a path was
found, and searches again if no path was found. In elastic ring search,
the delays between search attempts are long enough for shorter paths to
become available, and therefore the optimal sequence of search extents
may increase and even decrease. In this paper, we provide a framework to
model this network behavior, define two heuristics for optimizing elastic ring search sequences, and show that elastic ring search can incur
significantly lower search costs than expanding ring search.

Keywords: MANET · Expanding ring search · Optimization

1 Introduction

An important function in ad hoc networks is the search for nodes, services, and
resources by forwarding requests from node to node. Using this function, nodes
can search for resources as the need and availability arises. The alternative, maintaining tables of all available resources, requires a significant amount of overhead
and may not even be possible given the dynamic changes that characterize ad
hoc networks. This is especially the case in mobile ad hoc networks due to node
movement and wireless connections.

Search functions feature most prominently in on demand routing protocols,
in which routes are established as needed [14]. Most on demand routing protocols
use broadcast flooding to establish routes, either a priori or when other search
attempts fail. In broadcast flooding, the search node broadcasts its query, which
is then rebroadcast by all nodes that receive the query from the source node or
any other node that subsequently broadcasts the query. The obvious drawback
of broadcast flooding is that all nodes that receive the query are required to
receive, process, and rebroadcast the query. This has a measurable cost to the
network, such as power and bandwidth consumption.

One way to ameliorate search costs is by using an expanding ring search
[4,6,8]. In expanding ring search (ERS), the search node assigns the query a time-
to-live (TTL) value, which limits the number of hops the query traverses along

© Institute for Computer Sciences, Social Informatics and Telecommunications Engineering 2014
I. Stojmenovic et al. (Eds.): MOBIQUITOUS 2013, LNICST 131, pp. 564–575, 2014.
DOI: 10.1007/978-3-319-11569-6_44

any path from the source, and consequently the cost of flooding. If, however, the number of hops to the target is greater than the TTL value, the search node must repeat the query with a larger TTL value, and repeatedly do so until the target is found. Only enough time is inserted between queries to ensure that no path was found. Although the total cost of this technique may sometimes be greater than the cost of full flooding, the expected cost is less when the sequence of TTL values is chosen correctly.

The optimal TTL sequence, the one that minimizes the expected cost of an expanding ring search, depends on the probability distribution of the number of hops to the target node. The searcher initially assumes that the distribution reflects some steady-state property of the network. With each query, the searcher updates its assumptions about the hop count probability distribution. Because the time between queries is very short, it is unlikely that new paths will become available at any time during the search, so the searcher assumes that only longer paths are available. Hence it uses *expanding* rings. However, if more time is inserted between queries, then there is a possibility that new paths, possibly shorter than the last TTL value used, will become available. In such a case, when a long time is inserted between queries, the searcher would update its assumptions about the hop count distribution differently. With enough time, these assumptions would return to the steady-state distribution.

In this paper, we introduce a search technique called Elastic Ring Search (ELRS) that leverages changes in the network topology to keep search costs low. ELRS is similar to ERS in that queries are assigned TTL values, but it differs in that enough time is sometimes inserted between queries to allow the probability distribution assumptions to return partially or completely to the steady-state. As such, it may be optimal to search up to increasing *and* decreasing ranges; hence, the rings are *elastic*. We specifically consider the following type of search: At equally spaced time intervals, the searcher issues a query with any TTL value or no query at all until the target is found or the search is terminated. ELRS can be succinctly described as a time-diffused TTL-based search with increasing and decreasing search rings. This is useful when the searcher does not need to immediately establish a connection with the target node, like when transferring files and data. To optimize its performance, one additional network property is needed—the rate at which the hop count probability distribution is assumed to return to the steady-state.

Our main contributions are the design of elastic ring search, the study of the aforementioned network properties, and the design of cost-efficient elastic ring search sequences. We specifically suggest a model for capturing the changes in the hop count probability distribution that is easily verified in simulations and simplifies the derivation of elastic ring search strategies. Our simulation results show that the average costs closely match the expected costs based on the model and analysis, implying that elastic ring search is practically beneficial. The outline of the remainder of the paper is as follows: We discuss related work in Sect. 2. We formally model the problem in Sect. 3, and analyze the problem and provide two heuristics to solve it in Sect. 4. In Sect. 5, we statistically analyze the steady-state properties, and we evaluate the cost of the two heuristics described in Sect. 4. Finally, we summarize our results in Sect. 6.

2   Related Work

Expanding ring search has been extensively analyzed in the literature [1,4–8]. Most analysis assumes that all nodes are distributed uniformly at random throughout the field [6–8]. The corresponding hop count probability and cost-per-hop for each TTL value are used to calculate the expected costs of various TTL sequences. Chang and Liu [4] show how to derive the optimal TTL sequence for an arbitrary cost function and hop count distribution when they are known *a priori*. They prove that the optimal randomized strategy when the probability distribution is not known has a tight worst-case approximation factor of e, and that this is the best approximation factor possible by any solution. Baryshnikov et al. [1], prove that the optimal deterministic strategy in this case is to double the TTL value each round and that it has a tight worst-case approximation factor of 4.

Blocking Expanding Ring Search (BERS) and its variations [11–13] are designed to reduce redundant transmissions of route requests incurred by expanding ring search. The searcher sends a route request only once, and sends a cancel message when it receives a route reply. Each node waits long enough to receive a cancel message before forwarding the request. Although BERS eliminates redundant transmissions, it does not necessarily incur lower expected costs than ERS because of the cancellation flood.

Hop count distributions and other steady-state properties of MANETS have been extensively studied. Yoon et al. [15] study the steady-state properties of the random waypoint mobility model. Bettstetter et al. [2,3] study the spatial node distribution under the random waypoint and random walk mobility models. Mukerjee and Avidor [10] analyze the hop count distribution when nodes are distributed uniformly at random, and Younes and Thomas [16] analyze the hop count distribution under the random waypoint model. However, none of these studies consider how these distributions change with new information, as we do in this paper.

3   Problem Model

In this section, we formally model the problem and define the probability model we use in this paper. Throughout the paper, we refer to the node conducting the search as the searcher or the source and the node being searched for as the target or destination. In the model and the analysis, we assume that all nodes in the network are connected.

Let $R = \{x_0 = 0, \ldots, x_m = x_{max}\}$, $x_i < x_{i+1}$ $\forall i$, be the set of m TTL values from which the searcher can choose. x_{max} is the TTL value required to reach all nodes in the network. Let $f(x)$ be the steady-state probability mass function (PMF) that characterizes the distance to the target, and $F(x)$ be the associated cumulative distribution function (CDF). The cost of flooding up to range x is denoted $C(x)$, which is typically a function of the number forwarding nodes. The analysis will sometimes refer to the normalized cost function $C'(x)$, which is defined as $C'(x) = C(x)/C(x_{max})$. The standard assumption in the literature is that these functions are known in advance [4,6–8].

A search strategy S is a sequence of n search ranges $[u_1, \ldots, u_n]$ chosen from the set R. The search is conducted in rounds, querying up to u_i in round i whenever $u_i > 0$ until the target is found. A non-decreasing strategy is a specific type of strategy in which the non-zero search ranges are non-decreasing. Formally stated, a search strategy $S = [u_1, \ldots]$ is non-decreasing if $\forall_i (u_i = 0 \vee \forall_{j<i} u_j \leq u_i)$. The time between consecutive rounds is fixed and long enough to send a packet to the furthest node and back [4,9], and even longer to allow the topology to change.

The probability that the distance to the target is x at the beginning of round i, before issuing a query up to u_i, depends on the search ranges used in the previous rounds. This is denoted $f(x|u_1, \ldots, u_{i-1})$. Likewise, the cumulative probability is denoted $F(x|u_1, \ldots, u_{i-1})$. The expected cost $J(S)$ of applying the search strategy $S = [u_1, \ldots, u_n]$ is therefore calculated as follows:

$$J(S) = C(u_1) + \sum_{i=2}^{n} \left(\prod_{j=1}^{i-1} (1 - F(u_j|u_1, \ldots, u_{j-1})) \right) C(u_i) \qquad (1)$$

The conditional probability function $f(x|u_1, \ldots, u_{i-1})$ is potentially different for every combination of values $u_1, \ldots, u_{i-1}$, since each failure to find the target reveals new information about its location. It is infeasible to define a separate function for each combination of values, since there is an exponential number of combinations. Instead, we define a generic model for the conditional probability. Not only does this make calculating the conditional probability feasible, it also makes it possible to derive efficient solutions. Because only non-decreasing strategies are addressed in this paper, we only describe how to calculate the conditional probability t time steps after the last non-zero search range r_1 was used.

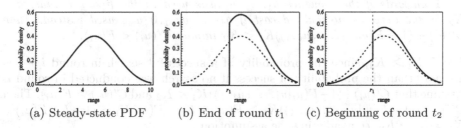

(a) Steady-state PDF   (b) End of round t_1 (c) Beginning of round t_2

Fig. 1. Changes in probability as elastic ring search progresses. The solid lines represent the beliefs at the time indicated by the caption, and the dashed lines indicate the steady-state distribution.

We begin with the following observation: In the instant after a search up to r_1 fails to find the target, the probability that the distance to the target, x, is less than or equal to x' is 0. Without any knowledge about the conditional probability for all remaining points, we assume that the probability that the distance to the target is $x > r_1$ is $\frac{1}{1-F(r_1)} f(x)$ (Fig. 1(b)). Let $g(x, r_1, t)$ be the probability that the distance to the target is $x \leq r_1$ t rounds after a search to r_1 fails to find the target, and let $G(x, r_1, t)$ be the cumulative function of $g(x, r_1, t)$. We will assume that $g(x, r_1, t)$ monotonically increases with t and that its value never exceeds $f(r_1)$. We also assume that the probability for all ranges $x \leq r_1$ is $g(x, r_1, t)$, regardless of any searches conducted in previous rounds. That is, knowledge of the probability for all distances $x \leq r_1$ is "reset" with a search to r_1. For all points $x > r_1$, we want to multiply $f(x)$ by some constant C such that $G(r_1, r_1, t) + C(1 - F(r_1)) = 1$, which gives us $C = \frac{1 - G(r_1, r_1, t)}{1 - F(r_1)}$ (Fig. 1(c)). We therefore have:

$$f(x|r_1, \underbrace{0, \ldots, 0}_{t-1}) = \begin{cases} g(x, r_1, t) & x \leq r_1 \\ \frac{1 - G(r_1, r_1, t)}{1 - F(r_1)} f(x) & x > r_1 \end{cases} \tag{2}$$

4   Analysis

Based on the how the distribution changes and the flooding costs, our goal is to find a sequence that minimizes (1), the expected cost of searching with an elastic ring search. We begin by establishing a necessary condition for a multi-round search to have a lower expected cost than full flooding. We then describe solutions for the best-case and worst-case scenarios, and finally provide two heuristics for the general case.

Theorem 1 establishes the intuitive notion that a search up to range x reduces the total cost only if the probability of success exceeds $C'(x)$. This extends a similar result in expanding ring search (Theorem 1 in [4]).

Theorem 1. *Given a search sequence $S = [u_1, \ldots, u_n]$ and any round $i < n$, let K_1 be the expected normalized cost of searching with $u_{i+1}, \ldots, u_n$ from round $i + 1$ onwards if the sequence $u_1, \ldots, u_i$ was used in the first i rounds, and K_2 be the expected normalized cost if $u_1, \ldots, u_{i-1}, 0$ was used instead. Then $C'(u_i) + (1 - F(u_i|u_1, \ldots, u_{i-1}))K_1 < K_2$ implies $C'(u_i) < F(u_i)$.*

Proof. $K_1 \geq K_2$, since the probability of a successful search in round $i + 1$ is no more than the probability of success if no search was conducted in round i. Assume that $C'(u_i) + (1 - F(u_i|u_1, \ldots, u_{i-1}))K_1 < K_2$ and $C'(u_i) \geq F(u_i)$. Then $C'(u_i) + (1 - F(u_i|u_1, \ldots, u_{i-1}))K_1 \geq F(u_i) + K_1 - F(u_i)K_1 = (1 - K_1)F(u_i) + K_1 > K_1 \geq K_2$, contradicting the assumption.

The following corollary establishes a necessary condition for a multi-round search to improve search costs.

Corollary 1. *If $C'(x) \geq F(x)$ for all x, then the optimal strategy is to flood the entire network in the first round.*

Ideally, the searcher can assume that $f(x_i|u_1, \ldots, u_{j-1}) = f(x_i)$, for all i, meaning that the probability of finding a node up to range x_i is unconditional. The next result establishes that the optimal strategy in this case when there is no time constraint on the search is an infinite sequence.

Theorem 2. *If the probability distribution is the same each round (i.e., $f(x|u_1, \ldots, u_i) = f(x)$, $\forall i$) and there is no constraint on the number of rounds, then the infinite sequence $[x, x, \ldots]$, for some x, is an optimal strategy.*

Proof. Let $V(S)$ be the expected cost of applying strategy S. Assume that the optimal strategy of least length is the finite sequence $S_1 = [u_1, \ldots, u_n]$. Let $S_1' = [u_2, \ldots, u_n]$. By definition, $V(S_1) < V(S_1')$. If the target is not found in round one, then the optimal strategy from round two onwards is $S_2 = [u_2, \ldots, u_n]$. Let $V'(S)$ be the cost of applying some strategy S after a search with u_1 failed to find the target in the first round. Let $S_2' = [u_1, \ldots, u_n]$, such that $V'(S_2) \leq V'(S_2')$. Since the probability distribution does not change, then the expected cost of applying any strategy in round two is unaffected by the search range used in round one. Therefore, $V(S_1) < V(S_1') = V'(S_2) \leq V'(S_2') = V(S_1)$, contradicting the assumption that S_1 is the optimal strategy. Rather, the optimal strategy is an infinite sequence S_{opt}. Since the searcher is faced with the same decision each round, the searcher can always choose the same search range. $\blacksquare$

According to this theorem, an optimal strategy under immediate convergence with no time constraints is to use the value of x each round that minimizes $\sum_{i=0}^{\infty}(1 - F(x))^i C(x) = \frac{C(x)}{F(x)}$ until the target is found. When the search is limited to n rounds, the optimal strategy can be derived by solving the following recursive formula for the optimal expected cost $V(n)$ of an n round strategy using backward induction on $1 \leq i \leq n$:

$$V(n) = C(x_{max}) \qquad V(i) = \min_{1 \leq j \leq m} \{C(x_j) + (1 - F(x_j))V(i + 1)\} \qquad (3)$$

The worst-case scenario is when there is no return to the steady-state, such as when the network is static. This is precisely the condition when expanding ring search is optimal. The optimal TTL sequence for expanding ring search can be derived in polynomial time by solving the following dynamic programming equations [4]:

$$V(x_m) = 0 \qquad V(x_i) = \min_{i+1 \leq j \leq m} \{C(x_j) + (1 - F(x_j|x_i))V(x_j)\} \qquad (4)$$

Here, $V(x_i)$ is the minimum expected cost-to-go, which is the cost of continuing the search, when a search using x_i fails to find the target. The first condition reflects the fact the search ends when searching up to x_m. The second condition reflects the fact that failing to find the target using x_i requires continuing the search with some TTL value $x_{j>i}$ that is larger than x_i. The cost-to-go in this case includes the cost $C(x_j)$ of searching up to x_j, plus the expected cost if the target is beyond x_j. This second value is the cost-to-go after searching with x_j multiplied by the probability $(1 - F(x_j|x_i))$ that the target is not within range x_j when it is already known that it is not within range x_i. The value of x_j that minimizes the cost-to-go for x_i is the one that is used to continue the search. $V(x_i)$ can be solved for backwards, for all $0 \leq i < m$. $V(x_0)$ reflects the expected cost of the optimal strategy. By recording the x_j chosen for each x_i, the optimal strategy can be extracted by following these links forwards from x_0.

It is not feasible to derive a similar solution for the general case because the cost-to-go at any round i depends on the entire subsequence $u_1 \ldots u_{i-1}$, which has an exponential number of combinations. Instead, we define two heuristics that use nondecreasing rings. The first heuristic is based on the optimal strategy for optimal conditions. The idea is to use the same TTL value at regular intervals until the last search round, at which time the entire network is flooded.

Heuristic 1. Choose the values of x and i, over all values of $x \in R$ and $i < n$, for which the strategy that uses x every i rounds has minimal cost.

Heuristic 1 takes advantage of node movement by not increasing the search extent, but does not guarantee a lower expected cost than expanding ring search. The second heuristic, the optimal nondecreasing ring search, is guaranteed to have an expected cost no greater than that of ERS. While this is still not necessarily the optimal elastic ring search, it can be solved for in $O(n^2 m^2)$ time and $O(nm)$ space using a dynamic programming formulation modeled after the formulation for expanding ring search.

Heuristic 2. Derive the optimal nondecreasing ring search with the following dynamic programming formulation, where $1 \leq \{j, k\} \leq m - 1$, $0 \leq i \leq n$, and $0 \leq s < n$.

$$V(n, j) = \infty \quad ; \quad V(i, m) = 0$$

$$V(s, k) = \min_{\substack{s < t \leq n \\ k \leq l \leq m}} \left\{ C(x_l) + (1 - F(x_l | x_k, \underbrace{0, \ldots, 0}_{t-s-1}))V(t, l) \right\} \tag{5}$$

In this formulation, $V(s, k)$ is the minimum expected cost-to-go when search range x_k is applied in round s, which is the expected remaining costs after round s. The cost of the optimal strategy is defined by $V(0, 0)$. In the derived strategy, the probability of success using search range x_l in round t is affected by the use of x_k in round s and only by x_k, as indicated by the expression $F(x_l | x_k, \underbrace{0, \ldots, 0}_{t-s-1}))$.

5   Evaluation

We set the cost function $C(x)$ to the number of nodes that would transmit a route request in a query up to range x in evaluating the two elastic ring search heuristics. For this purpose, it is only necessary to know the connectivity graph in each round of the search procedure. We used Java to simulate node movement, construct the connectivity graph at regular time steps, and construct the breadth-first search (BFS) tree of the connectivity graphs. The BFS tree is used to determine the cost-per-hop of a route request and the hop count to the destination. For each TTL value less than or equal to the depth of the tree, the cost-per-hop is the number of nodes at all depths up to but not including that TTL value. This is because the last nodes to receive the query do not retransmit it. For any TTL value larger than the depth of the tree, the cost-per-hop is the number of nodes in the tree. Note that this is not necessarily equal to all nodes in the network, since in practice, not all nodes are necessarily connected to the source. The hop count to the destination is its depth in the BFS tree. Throughout the discussion, we refer to the time steps as rounds. In an elastic ring search, each consecutive search round is conducted in consecutive rounds of movement. In an expanding ring search, all search rounds are conducted in the same movement round.

We simulated movement according to two settings, which we refer to as Scenario 1 and Scenario 2. In both settings, there are 250 nodes; the transmission range of each node is 100 m; the field size is 1200 × 1200 m; the source and destination are stationary throughout the simulation; and all other nodes move according to the random waypoint model with speeds randomly selected from the range 5 m/s to 8 m/s and a 2 s pause time between waypoints. The only differences between the settings are the (x, y) coordinates of the source and destination: In Scenario 1, their coordinates are $(200, 600)$ and $(200, 460)$, respectively, and in Scenario 2, their locations are $(200, 600)$ and $(200, 340)$, respectively. The time steps were set to 100 ms. The simulations ran for a total of 50 s (500 rounds).

Next we show how we determined the steady-state properties, and then we provide the results of our evaluation.

5.1   Steady-State Properties

The steady-state properties of the random waypoint model have been well studied [2,15], including the steady-state spatial node distribution [3] and hop count distribution [16]. Studies show that the nodes are concentrated in the center of the field in the steady-state node distribution, so the system is not immediately in the steady-state when nodes are initially assigned uniformly random locations. Our goal, therefore, is to establish when there is a steady-state to the hop count distribution and to derive the conditional probability distribution.

To demonstrate the existence of a steady-state, we used two statistical tests: the Kolmogorov-Smirnov test and the Wilcoxon Rank-sum test. Both are non-parametric tests, meaning they make no assumptions about the distribution of the data. They are used to test the null hypothesis that two sets of samples come from the identical distribution. That is, the data that we enter are samples drawn from larger distributions, and we are trying to determine whether the generating distributions are identical. The tests return a p-value, which is a number between 0 and 1 that answers the following question: if our null hypothesis was correct and these distributions are identical, what is the probability that we would draw samples that differ this greatly? Thus, a low p-value means that it would be very unlikely to obtain these two samples from one distribution. A high p-value is consistent with the assertion that the samples were drawn from identical distributions. A high p-value is not a proof that the distributions are identical, but rather it tells us that we cannot reject the null hypothesis that they are identical. A sufficiently low p-value, on the other hand, would serve as a basis for rejecting the null-hypothesis and concluding with relative certainty that the samples were not drawn from identical distributions.

We use these tests to show the progression of the p-values when comparing the distribution from each round to the steady-state distribution. We took the hop counts from rounds 3900–4000 over 1000 different simulations as representatives of the steady-state. We compared the samples at rounds $10, 20, \ldots$ from 500 simulations (unique to each round) to the steady-state using the two tests and checked if and by what round they attain and sustain consistently high p-values. Our results showed that after round 1000, the p-values are mostly over 0.3. It is noted that typically the assumption of having the two samples derived from the same distribution is rejected for $p = 0.05$. This leads us to believe that the system enters a steady-state after round 1000 in this case.

We derived the conditional probability function for Scenario 1 as follows. We recorded the hop count every round from round 1000 to round 1499 for 5,000 randomly initialized simulations. The hop counts were in the range $[2, 28]$, but the largest portion of samples were either 2 or 3. We then selected the data from the simulations for which the hop count was >3 in round 1000, which is the case when a search in round 1000 with a $TTL = 3$ would have failed to find the target. There were 632 such instances.

Figure 2 shows the number of samples equal to 2, 3, 4, and 5 hops each round. Each plot is close to a horizontal line, supporting the claim that the hop count distribution is in a steady-state. Figure 3 shows the number of samples equal to 2, 3, 4, or 5 hops each round in these instances. Here it is clear that the distribution converges back to the steady-state, in about 180 rounds, with the number of samples equal to 2 and 3 increasing each round and the number of samples equal to 4 and 5 decreasing.

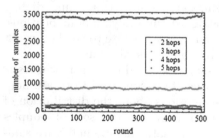   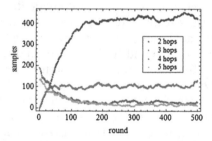

Fig. 2. Number of samples each round (Scenario 1)

Fig. 3. Number of samples each round when the hop count >3 in the first search round (Scenario 1)

We normalized the histogram of hop counts from this subset each round to 1, and then divided each bin by the corresponding bin in the normalized histogram of all samples. This gives us the coefficient by which $f(x)$, $x \in 2, 3$, would need to be multiplied at round $1000 + t$ to give us the conditional probability $g(x, 3, t)$ if the two histograms mentioned above were to correspond to $g(x, 3, t)$ and $f(x)$, respectively. We found the least-squares fit of each sequence of fractions to the function $\sum_{i=0}^{5} x^i$. Let $g'(t)$ be this function. We define $g(x, x', t) = g'(t)f(x)$ for all combinations of (x, x') in $g(x, x', t)$. Figure 4 shows the histogram of all

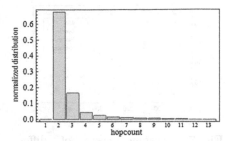

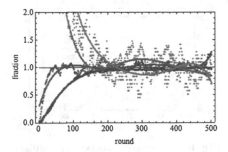

Fig. 4. Normalized histogram of hop count samples (Scenario 1)

Fig. 5. Functions fitted to fractional conditional distributions (Scenario 1)

samples normalized to 1. Figure 5 shows the sequence of fractions and the fitted curves that were used to define $g(x, x', t)$.

We followed the same procedure for Scenario 2. In this case, the range of hop counts in the distribution is $[3, 13]$, with most samples falling the range $[3, 7]$. We considered the conditional probability when the hop count was >4 and set $g(x, x', t)$ to the best fit of conditional probability of hop count 4 to the function $1 + \log t$. The time to converge in this case was longer than the previous case, about 300 rounds.

5.2   Results

For both Scenarios 1 and 2, we constructed the hop count distribution using samples from round 1000 from 500 simulations. We constructed the cost function in a similar manner, by counting the number of nodes at each level of the BFS tree in round 1000 over 500 simulations and taking the average. Using these distributions and cost functions, we derived the optimal expanding ring search, the expected cost of an infinite elastic ring search under optimal conditions, and the $50, 100, \ldots, 500$ round strategies using Heuristics 1 and 2. We simulated the use of these heuristics in 500 simulations for each sequence length, beginning from round 1000 in Scenario 1 and round 1500 in Scenario 2.

Figure 6 is a plot of the average cost of using expanding ring search, Heuristic 1, and Heuristic 2. Additionally, the expected cost under optimal conditions, according to Theorem 2, is included as a lower bound on expected costs. We can see from the figure that Heuristic 1 performs better than expanding ring search when it is allowed more than 50 rounds; Heuristic 2 always performs better than expanding ring search; Heuristic 2 performs slightly better than Heuristic 1; and both converge to the lower bound. Additionally, the average costs are very close to the expected costs (not shown), which shows that the estimation of $g(x, x', t)$ was adequate despite the fact that it did not account for all cases.

Figure 7 is a plot of the average costs of the different strategies. Here, Heuristics 1 and 2 are close in performance, but both are significantly better than expanding ring search, even when limited to 50 rounds. In this case, the potential difference between using expanding ring search and elastic ring search is significant. The average cost of expanding ring search is about 95, while the lower bound is about 55, which is about an additional 16 % reduction in costs

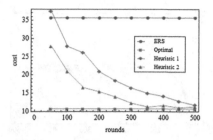
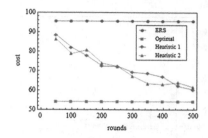

Fig. 6. Average costs of different search strategies in Scenario 1 (1 round = 100 ms)

Fig. 7. Average costs of different search strategies in Scenario 2 (1 round = 100 ms)

from full flooding. Both heuristics approach this lower bound when allowed 500 rounds.

6   Conclusion

As illustrated throughout the paper, when considering dynamic settings, the searcher can benefit substantially by deviating from the optimal expanding ring search to an elastic sequence. The frequent changes in the network topology are inherent in the problem definition, and the tolerance of delay characterizes several important applications (e.g., text messaging, emails, data collection). The new method takes advantage of the potential formation of new, potentially shorter, routes along time. In such cases, it is useful to delay search for some time (e.g., not to search in some of the rounds) as well as to search to reduced extents from time to time.

While the computational complexity of the dynamic programming approach presented in this paper for extracting the optimal ELRS sequence is substantial, efficient sequences can be extracted in polynomial time. Two such heuristics are given in this paper. The first repeats the same TTL value at regular intervals, while the second uses a non-decreasing sequence. These heuristics can be derived in polynomial run-time and their performance, as illustrated experimentally, converges to a lower bound on optimal costs. We believe that these solutions are ideal for ad-hoc networks that are inherently bounded by their power supply.

While this paper makes an important contribution to the research of expanding ring search in general by demonstrating the existence of a steady-state distribution, the use of such methods in practice requires the ability to learn the steady-state on the device. Therefore, an important area for future research is the parametric-based extraction of the steady-state distribution based, for example, on the number of nodes, and the broadcast capabilities of the devices being used. With this capability, each participant can generate the steady-state independently on their own device, or it can be generated when setting up the network. Another approach is to create a database of pre-generated steady-states and choose a best match according to the parameters above. As a data-driven algorithm, increasing the size of the database will increase the precision of the matches and thus increase the performance of ELRS using that data. With the constantly decreasing size and price of storage, it is certainly practical to store a very large database on the devices.

Acknowledgments. This work was supported in part by the Israeli Ministry of Industry and Trade under project RESCUE and ISF grant 1083/13.

References

1. Baryshnikov, Y.M., Coffman Jr, E.G., Jelenkovic, P.R., Momcilovic, P., Rubenstein, D.: Flood search under the california split rule. Oper. Res. Lett. **32**(3), 199–206 (2004)
2. Bettstetter, C., Hartenstein, H., Costa, X.P.: Stochastic properties of the random waypoint mobility model. Wireless Netw. **10**(5), 555–567 (2004)
3. Bettstetter, C., Resta, G., Santi, P.: The node distribution of the random waypoint mobility model for wireless ad hoc networks. IEEE Trans. Mob. Comput. **2**(3), 257–269 (2003)
4. Chang, N.B., Liu, M.: Revisiting the TTL-based controlled flooding search: optimality and randomization. In: Haas, Z.J., Das, S.R., Jain, R. (eds.) Proceedings of the 10th Annual International Conference on Mobile Computing and Networking (MobiCom '04), pp. 85–99. ACM, New York (2004)
5. Chang, N.B., Liu, M.: Controlled flooding search in a large network. IEEE/ACM Trans. Netw. **15**(2), 436–449 (2007)
6. Cheng, Z., Heinzelman, W.B.: Searching strategies for target discovery in wireless networks. Ad Hoc Netw. **5**(4), 413–428 (2007)
7. Deng, J., Zuyev, S.A.: On search sets of expanding ring search in wireless networks. Ad Hoc Netw. **6**(7), 1168–1181 (2008)
8. Hassan, J., Jha, S.K.: On the optimization trade-offs of expanding ring search. In: Sen, A., Das, N., Das, S.K., Sinha, B.P. (eds.) IWDC 2004. LNCS, vol. 3326, pp. 489–494. Springer, Heidelberg (2004)
9. Lee, S.-J., Belding-Royer, E.M., Perkins, C.E.: Scalability study of the ad hoc on-demand distance vector routing protocol. Int. J. Netw. Manag. **13**(2), 97–114 (2003)
10. Mukherjee, S., Avidor, D.: On the probability distribution of the minimal number of hops between any pair of nodes in a bounded wireless ad-hoc network subject to fading. In: IWWAN (2005)
11. Park, I., Pu, I.: Energy efficient expanding ring search. In: Asia International Conference on Modelling and Simulation, pp. 198–199. IEEE Computer Society (2007)
12. Pu, I., Shen, Y.: Enhanced blocking expanding ring search in mobile ad hoc networks. In: 2009 3rd International Conference on New Technologies, Mobility and Security (NTMS), 20–23 December 2009. pp. 1–5 (2009)
13. Pu, I., Shen, Y.: Analytical studies of energy-time efficiency of blocking expanding ring search. Math. Comput. Sci. **3**, 443–456 (2010)
14. Royer, E.M., Toh, C.-K.: A review of current routing protocols for ad hoc mobile wireless networks. IEEE Pers. Commun. **6**, 46–55 (1999)
15. Yoon, J., Liu, M., Noble, B.: Sound mobility models. In: Proceedings of the 9th Annual International Conference on Mobile computing and networking (MOBICOM '03), pp. 205–216. ACM, New York (2003)
16. Younes, O., Thomas, N.: Analysis of the expected number of hops in mobile ad hoc networks with random waypoint mobility. Electr. Notes Theor. Comput. Sci. **275**, 143–158 (2011)

Suitability of a Common ZigBee Radio Module for Interaction and ADL Detection

Jakob Neuhaeuser[✉], Tim C. Lueth, and Lorenzo T. D'Angelo

Institute of Micro Technology and Medical Device Technology,
Technische Universitaet Muenchen Garching, Garching, Germany
Jakob.neuhaeuser@tum.de

Abstract. In this contribution we analyze whether it is possible to use a ZigBee module to detect interactions. The detection is done using modules with adjustable communication range. From the data we want to draw conclusions about the activities of daily living (ADL). This is important to detect because small changes in behavior which might indicate the beginning of dementia or a mild cognitive impairment. We have already done promising experiments with a radio module. In this paper we analyze whether it is also possible to use a common ZigBee module. Therefore we compare it with the module we used already and then modify the antenna to shorten the range. Our findings show that it is possible to use the ZigBee module for interaction and ADL detection by adjustable range after modifications in the antenna circuit.

Keywords: Interaction · ADL · Radio module · Recognition zigbee

1 Introduction

As more and more people are getting older, it is increasingly important to detect illnesses like dementia at an early stage. Alzheimer dementia is usually a chronic illness characterized by a reduction in memory recall and mental performance and the implications this has for everyday activities (ADL) [1]. In order to measure the ADL objectively, we measure sADL (simple ADL) [2] through interactions between radio modules with scale able transmission range. In this paper we want to discuss whether it is possible to use a standard ZigBee module for our purpose and which modifications are necessary.

2 State of the Art

At the moment ADL are assessed through ADL scales like the Barthel Index [3], in order to determine the autonomy of a person. The data for the Index is collected by interviewing the patient about his or her ability to carry out daily routines. If possible the patient is interviewed, if not a relative or a nurse provides the data. The greatest disadvantage is the subjectivity which was proven amongst others by [4] and [5].

In research various projects are developing systems able to detect different ADLs automatically. In this article we want to focus on radio based systems. A lot of work

© Institute for Computer Sciences, Social Informatics and Telecommunications Engineering 2014
I. Stojmenovic et al. (Eds.): MOBIQUITOUS 2013, LNICST 131, pp. 576–587, 2014.
DOI: 10.1007/978-3-319-11569-6_45

was done on RFID-based systems. Here the advantage is that the transponders do not need their own energy source like a battery, because the energy is obtained from the RFID-Reader. Reference [6] for example, developed a glove and, later on, a wristband equipped with RFID readers [7]. The systems have a reading range of about 10 cm. UHF RFID, tags called WISPs, have a read range up to 10 m but have problems with orientation [8]. Another approach, which will be explained later on in detail, is to use a scalable transmission range of 0,5 m to 5 m to tag different objects. By wearing a recording device different interactions with objects can be monitored [9]. ZigBee was so far only used as a network system to collect Activities of Daily Living through different sensors like accelerometers and reed relay [10].

For our concept with different transmission ranges (see Sect. 3) it is important to use a radio module with a scalable transmission range. Therefore we took to a closer look at the systems available on the market (Table 1).

Table 1. Different radio modules with programmable transmission range (from datasheet)

Manufacturer	Model	Steps	min dBm	max dBm
Ingenieurbuero	RT868F4	4	−8	10
Laird Technologies	LT2510	4	8	17
IMST	iM201A	4	−18	0
IMST	iM871A	8	−8	13
amber-wireless	AMBZ420	16	−28	4,5
IMST	iM860A	16	−50	10
Atmel	**ATZB-24-A2**	**16**	**−17**	**3**
Nanotron	**NanoLOC**	**64**	**−36**	**0**

We did not find a lot of radio modules with scalable transmission ranges. Especially the ones which have different ranges are only adjustable in a few discrete steps, for example 4 or 8. The one we are using is adjustable in 64 steps (NanoLOC by Nanotron); the Zigbee module investigated in this paper has at least 16 (ATZB-24-A2 by Atmel).

3   Materials and Methods

The concept of our system is inspired by human communication [11]. When we talk, the volume of our voice is always chosen in such a way that the people one is talking to, but not all the people in the room, can hear. Reference [12] already applied this approach in robotics on infrared, to realize local communication between robots. Similar to this, we tag different objects and people who broadcast their own ID with different transmission ranges. In the first step we would like to give every object a specific transmission range (r_{sADL}), but later on, this can be dynamic, like the volume of our voice. Additionally, we define two different types of modules: the active-mote which sends out its ID and can receive and save other IDs and the passive-mote which can only send out its ID. With two active-motes (a, b) having different positions $p_{a/b}$ in a room, three different states can be concluded:

$$p_a \begin{pmatrix} x_a \\ y_a \\ z_a \end{pmatrix} ; p_b \begin{pmatrix} x_b \\ y_b \\ z_b \end{pmatrix} ; r_{sADL_a} > r_{sADL_b} \tag{1}$$

State 1: Both motes are outside the transmission range of each other:

$$|p_a - p_b| > r_{sADL_a} > r_{sADL_b} \tag{2}$$

State 2: Only one mote can "hear" the other:

$$r_{sADL_a} > |p_a - p_b| > r_{sADL_b} \tag{3}$$

State 3: Both motes can "hear" the other:

$$r_{sADL_a} > r_{sADL_b} > |p_a - p_b| \tag{4}$$

The event E_a is generated when the distance of both motes is smaller than the transmit range r_{sADLa}:

$$|p_a - p_b| < r_{sADL_a} \Rightarrow E_a \tag{5}$$

The event together with the duration is interpreted as a sADL (simple Activities of Daily Living [2]) and saved.

This concept was realized using a NanoLOC radio module [9] and evaluated in a day hospital [13]. Because of the module not being a mass product and also having a high power consumption of over 33 mA in RX mode, in this paper we want to evaluate whether the ZigBit Module from Atmel which needs only 19 mA in RX mode, is also suitable.

To check whether ZigBee with a scalable transmission range is applicable to detect sADL (simple Activities of Daily Living) a ZigBit module was implemented. The radio module ATZB-24-A2 from Atmel was chosen due to a transmission range scalable in 17 steps. The module consists of a microcontroller and a radio module with a double chip antenna (Fig. 1,1). Additionally we use a real-time-clock for time keeping (Fig. 1,2), as well as a flash-memory for data storage (Fig. 1,4) and an accelerometer (Fig. 1,3) as additional information source. The energy is stored in a 250 mAh li-po battery with charge controller (Fig. 1,5). As interface we chose a 30 pin connector (Fig. 1,6).

As it is intended for the modules being able to work within a ZigBee network, the program of the modules is based on Atmels ZigBit stack. The base mote, from which the data can be collected later on, is the coordinator that builds up the network. All other motes are children of the base. This is the reason why our network has the depth of one. The base can communicate directly with all other motes, when they are reachable. The active-motes can also communicate via peer2peer because they are

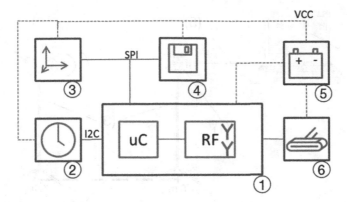

Fig. 1. Hardware setup: (1) ZigBit radiomodule with microcontroller and a double antenna/ Nanoloc moudle with microcotnroller (2) Real time clock (3) Accelerometer, (4) Flash memory, (5) Battery with chargecontrol, (6) Connector

implemented as router. The passive-mote can only send messages to the active-mote and is not able to receive messages from them as it is implemented as an end device. But the end device is still able to receive messages from the coordinator, which is not needed so far (see Fig. 2).

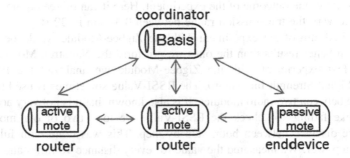

Fig. 2. Concept for using the system within the ZigBee-Standard

4   Validation

In the first step we evaluated our existing system with the Nanoloc-module. For that we took two of our modules called Eventlogger and enlarged the distance between both, step by step. To have less disruptions we mounted the modules on tripods. One module was sending out a message for 30 times and with the other module we checked how many of them were recognized (Fig. 3).

The results of the different transmission power compared to the distance are shown in Table 2. The green area is a recognition of over 90 % of the messages, yellow means less and red means none of the messages were received.

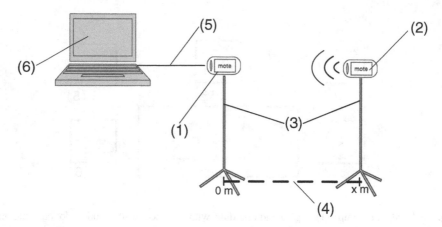

Fig. 3. Experiment for ranges of different transmission power steps of the Nanoloc-Module; sender-module (2) receiver-module (1), tripod (3) measured distance (4); interface cable and PC (5,6)

Although there are some gaps you find a tendency for a bigger transmission range with higher transmission power. The gaps are getting smaller when the system is tested in real environment. Therefore we mounted one module on the wall and the second one was worn by a test person. The procedure was the same as in the first experiment with the only difference that we took less transmission power values.

Table 3 shows the outcome of the experiment. Here it can be seen quite well that it is possible to vary the transmission range between 0.3–5 m in 29 steps.

The desired aim of the experiment with the Zigbee-Module would be to get the same or even better results than the ones we got form the Nanotron-Module.

In the first experiment with the Zigbee-Module we analyzed the RSSI-Value (Received Signal Strength Indication). The RSSI-Value sometimes is used to measure the distance between two radio modules. It is also known that it is not very accurate due to effects like fading. To check the RSSI-Value we took two of our modules and enlarged the distance between both, step by step. This was done with full and low transmission power. We measured the value for every distance 10 times and calculated the arithmetic average (Fig. 5).

As we saw problems in determining the distance based on the RSSI-value between 1,25 to 5 m another solution had to be found. In the next step the transmission range of the ZigBee Module was analyzed. As the module is intended to be used in homes and the range at the lowest transmission power is over 15 m, this does not meet our requirement of a transmission range between 0.5 and 5 m. Therefore we modified the antenna in order to reduce the transmission range. The receiving power of the receiver is influenced by the distance of transmitter and receiver, the power of the transmitter, the antenna gain of the transmitter and of the receiver. This is shown by Eq. 6:

$$P_R = P_T \left(\frac{\lambda}{4\pi d}\right)^\alpha G_R \, G_T \tag{6}$$

Table 2. Measured range of the module at different transmission power steps green: full reception (>90 %), yellow: reception in part, red: no reception (0 %)

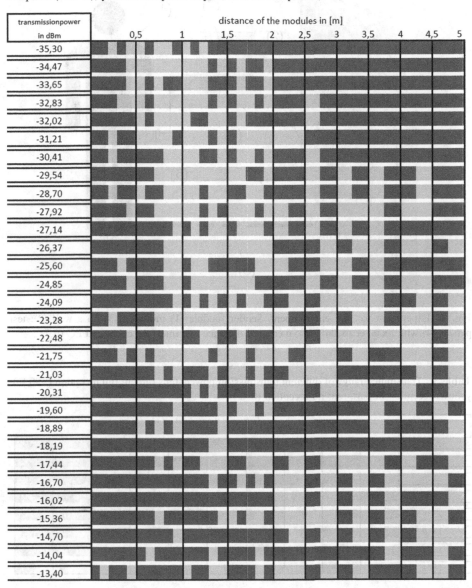

P_R *Power receiver,* P_T *Power transmission,* λ *wave length*
d distance, G_R/G_T *antenna gain receiver/transmitter*
α *materia and frequency dependent coeffcient*

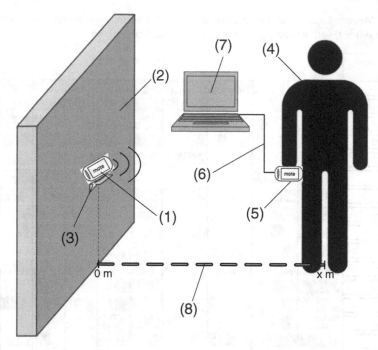

Fig. 4. Experiment for real environment. Sender module (1) mounted (3) on a wall (2); test person (4) with receiver module (5); measured distance (8); interface cable and PC (6,7)

Table 3. Transmitted range of different transmission power steps (green: full reception (>90 %), yellow: reception in part, red: no reception (0 %))

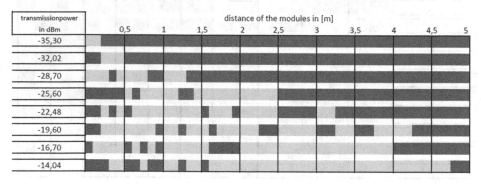

By reducing the power of the transmitter or the sensitivity of the receiver, the communication range can be reduced. Both effects are achieved by reducing the effectiveness of the antenna (Eq. 7).

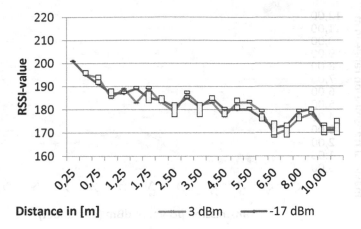

Fig. 5. RSSI-value over 10 values compared to the distance between the two modules

$$\eta = \frac{R_S}{R_S + R_V} \tag{7}$$

R_S radiation resistance, R_V ohmic resistance

Due to the effectiveness of the antenna being influenced by the resistance of the feed cable, it is possible to vary it by adding an additional resistor in the feed cable. Figure 4 shows the dependency of the maximal transmission range of different resistors (Fig. 6).

In the next step we modified both modules, as the receiving power is also modified by the resistance. The best suitable output for our requirements was achieved at 39 Ω (Fig. 7).

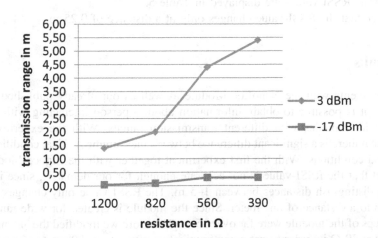

Fig. 6. Adding different resistances in the feed cable of the antenna to change its effectiveness, resulting in a reduction of transmission range

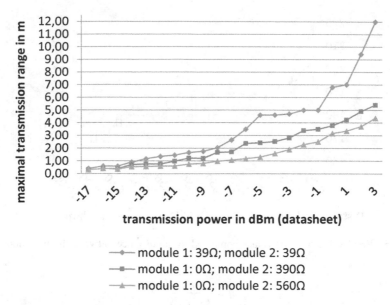

Fig. 7. Maximal transmission range for each adjustable transmission power (dBm out of the datasheet)

As we now had the correct range, the next step was to evaluate the reliability of the system using the 17 different transmission power settings. Therefore one module was set to transmit an ID as well as a consecutive number every 500 ms. The second module was set to receive the ID and to count how many IDs had to be sent in order to receive 10 messages. The distance between both modules was raised step by step. The outcome is shown in Table 4.

In our last experiment we checked once again the RSSI-value with the modified antenna. The RSSI values are displayed in Table 5.

We see that the RSSI-value changes only at a distance of 0.25 m.

5   Results

The experiments with the NanoLoc Module as well as our already published papers show that it is possible to obtain information about a person interacting with objects marked with modules with different transmission ranges. With the experiment we showed that there is a significant difference between measurements ideal conditions and nearly real conditions. With the first experiment together with the Zigbee Module we found out that the RSSI-value is not accurate enough for our demands, since it is not suited to distinguish distances between 1–5 m. The RSSI-value only changes significantly up to a distance of one meter. Since the module is created for wide ranges the power steps of the module were far over 15 m. Therefore we modified the antenna with a resistor at 39 Ω in order to get a communication range from 50 cm to some meters. The closer look at the reliability of the transmission range showed that there are also

Table 4. Reliability of the ZigBit-Module with a disturbed antenna (39 Ω) green: full reception (>90 %), yellow: reception in part, red: no reception (0 %)

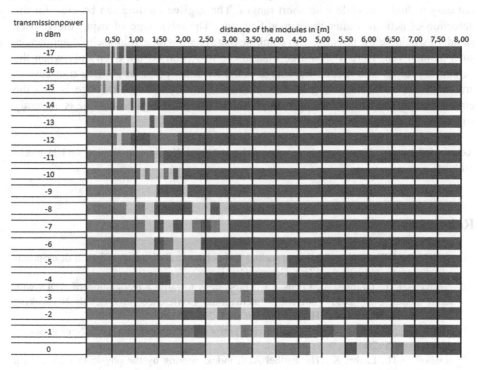

Table 5. RSSI-value over 10 measurements at different distances

Distance in m	0,25	0,5	0,75	1,0	1,25	1,5	1,75	2,0	2,25	2,5
RSSI-value over 10	171	166	165	165	165	165	165	165	165	165

distances where there is very stable communication followed by distances with an unstable communication. An interesting point in the last experiment is the RSSI-Value at small distances. At very near contact the RSSI-Value is still different, this could be used to detect close contact with a tagged object.

6   Conclusion

The experiments in this paper only consider communication in one alignment (all modules were oriented face to face). They show that it is possible to modify the antenna of a ZigBee module in order to get a transmission range from 50 cm to some meters.

This is the first step to be able to detect interactions for different reading ranges. The difficulty on the market is that only modules with wide ranges are available so it is not easy to find a module with short ranges. The ZigBee module can be used for the detection of activities after these modifications. The advantage of using the ZigBee standard would be the possibility to combine our system with e.g. household appliances such as the oven. Here it would be imaginable to switch on the oven only when the person is nearby. The second advantage is the modules price, as ZigBee transceivers are more and more becoming a mass product. One remaining challenge is that the circuit leads to the loss of the approval, therefore using the ZigBee module is currently still no valid alternative for our existing module.

Acknowledgments. The research is supported by Alfried Krupp von Bohlen und Halbach-Stiftung.

References

1. WHO: The ICD-10 classification of mental and behavioural disorders. Clinical descriptions and diagnostic guidelines. WHO, Geneva (1992)
2. Neuhaeuser, J., Czabke, A., Lueth, T.C.: First steps towards a recognition of ADLs with radio modules. In: 2011 13th IEEE International Conference on e-Health Networking Applications and Services (Healthcom), pp. 225–228 (2011)
3. Liu, K.P.Y., et al.: Activities of daily living performance in dementia. Acta Neurol. Scand. **116**(2), 91–95 (2007)
4. Ranhoff, A.H., Laake, K.: The barthel ADL index: scoring by the physician from patient interview is not reliable. Age Ageing **22**(3), 171–174 (1993)
5. Rubenstein, L.Z., Schairer, C., Wieland, G.D., Kane, R.: Systematic biases in functional status assessment of elderly adults: effects of different data sources. J. Gerontol. **39**(6), 686–691 (1984)
6. Philipose, M., et al.: Inferring activities from interactions with objects. IEEE Pervasive Comput. **3**(4), 50–57 (2004)
7. Wyatt, D., Philipose, M., Choudhury, T.: Unsupervised activity recognition using automatically mined common sense. In: Proceedings of the National Conference on Artificial Intelligence, vol. 20, pp. 21–27 (2005)
8. Buettner, M., Prasad, R., Philipose, M., Wetherall, D.: Recognizing daily activities with RFID-based sensors. In: Proceedings of the 11th International Conference on Ubiquitous Computing, pp. 51–60 (2009)
9. Czabke, A., Neuhauser, J., Lueth, T.C.: Recognition of interactions with objects based on radio modules. In: 2010 4th International Conference on Pervasive Computing Technologies for Healthcare (PervasiveHealth), pp. 1–8 (2010)
10. Diermaier, J., Neyder, K., Werner, F., Panek, P., Zagler, W.L.: Distributed accelerometers as a main component in detecting activities of daily living. In: Miesenberger, K., Klaus, J., Zagler, W.L., Karshmer, A.I. (eds.) ICCHP 2008. LNCS, vol. 5105, pp. 1042–1049. Springer, Heidelberg (2008)
11. D'Angelo, L.T., Czabke, A., Somlai, I., Niazmand, K., Lueth, T.C.: ART - a new concept for an activity recorder and transceiver. In: 2010 Annual International Conference of the IEEE Engineering in Medicine and Biology Society (EMBC), pp. 2132–2135 (2010)

12. Lueth, T.C., Grasman, R., Laengle, T., Wang, J.: Cooperation among distributed controlled robots by local interaction protocols. In: Invited paper at ISRAM Int'l. Symposium on Robotics and Manufacturing, Montpellier, France, vol. 6, pp. 405–410 (1996)
13. Neuhaeuser, J., Diehl-Schmid, J., Lueth, T.C.: Evaluation of a radio based ADL interaction recognition system in a day hospital for old age psychiatry with healthy probands. In: 2011 Annual International Conference of the IEEE Engineering in Medicine and Biology Society (EMBC) (2011)

The Need for QoE-driven Interference Management in Femtocell-Overlaid Cellular Networks

Dimitris Tsolkas[✉], Eirini Liotou, Nikos Passas,
and Lazaros Merakos

Department of Informatics and Telecommunications,
University of Athens, Athens, Greece
{dtsolkas, eliotou, passas, merakos}@di.uoa.gr

Abstract. Under the current requirements for mobile, ubiquitous and highly reliable communications, internet and mobile communication technologies have converged to an all-Internet Protocol (IP) packet network. This technological evolution is followed by a major change in the cellular networks' architecture, where the traditional wide-range cells (macrocells) coexist with indoor small-sized cells (femtocells). A key challenge for the evolved heterogeneous cellular networks is the mitigation of the generated interferences. In the literature, this problem has been thoroughly studied from the Quality of Service (QoS) point of view, while a study from the user's satisfaction perspective, described under the term "Quality of Experience (QoE)", has not received enough attention yet. In this paper, we study the QoE performance of VoIP calls in a femto-overlaid Long Term Evolution – Advanced (LTE-A) network and we examine how QoE can drive a power controlled interference management scheme.

Keywords: QoE · VoIP · Femtocells · LTE-A · E-model · Power control

1 Introduction

The International Telecommunication Union (ITU) has defined the fundamental requirements for the next generation (4G) telecommunication systems as described in International Mobile Telecommunications-Advanced (IMT-Advanced) [1]. Systems that fulfill the IMT-Advanced requirements promise an all packet-switched wireless network with data rates similar to those provided by wired communication networks, while all services are implemented over the Internet Protocol (IP). The first packet-based cellular system that is expected to deal with IMT-Advanced requirements is the Long Term Evolution - Advanced (LTE-A) [2]. LTE-A introduces a heterogeneous architecture where the conventional wide-range cells (macrocells) coexist with indoor small-sized cells, called femtocells [3].

Femtocells are low-power, small base stations connected to the operator's network via broadband lines, and they provide usually indoor coverage typically for a range of 10 m, for instance at the home or office. They are expected to be the most energy-efficient and cost-effective solution for improving the spatial spectrum utilization and

© Institute for Computer Sciences, Social Informatics and Telecommunications Engineering 2014
I. Stojmenovic et al. (Eds.): MOBIQUITOUS 2013, LNICST 131, pp. 588–601, 2014.
DOI: 10.1007/978-3-319-11569-6_46

for amplifying the indoor coverage, providing ubiquitous and seamless access to static or mobile end-users. More precisely, femtocells are an easy option to cover any communication gaps inside a certain area, caused either due to bad coverage (e.g., in the interior of a building) or due to low network capacity (e.g., in very crowded places). However, femtocell-overlaid networks define a highly interfered environment putting in priority the design of efficient Interference Management (IM) schemes [4].

The majority of IM approaches focus on guaranteeing the provided Quality of Service (QoS), promising mainly a high Signal to Interference plus Noise Ratio (SINR) at interfered (victim) users. However, a more attractive and suitable way to evaluate the quality of a provided service (especially for real-time services) is by measuring the end-users' satisfaction. Currently, the connection between network performance and end-users' satisfaction is not strictly defined. To give an example, the same throughput value may result to differently perceived data rates, giving in that way totally different impressions of the same provided service [5].

Recognizing the importance of quantifying the end-users' satisfaction, ITU has suggested the term Quality of Experience (QoE) as *"the overall acceptability of an application or service, as perceived subjectively by the end-user"* [6]. QoE is the most important factor for a user's decision on retaining a service or giving it up and this fact explains the emergence of shifting from QoS to QoE network management. Moreover, since interference is one of the key quality-deteriorating factors and has a direct impact on the users' perceived QoE, the design of QoE-driven IM mechanisms seems very appealing.

In this paper, we examine whether and in what extent the interferences in a femtocell-overlaid network are reflected as variations in the end-users' satisfaction. Firstly, we focus on Voice over IP (VoIP) services in an LTE-A network, and quantify the QoE deterioration of macrocell VoIP users due to the interference from femtocells. Sequentially, we examine the relation between the SINR and the perceived QoE at an interference-victim. Finally, we exploit these results to compare the basic Power Control (PC) IM scheme proposed by 3GPP [7] and a simple QoE-aware PC scheme, revealing the importance of involving QoE in the IM process.

The remainder of this paper is organized as follows. Section 2 presents the interference problem in the LTE-A heterogeneous networks. Afterwards, Sect. 3 describes the potential role of QoE in the interference management process, exploiting a quantitative relationship between the QoS and QoE terms. Section 4 summarizes the fundamental evaluation methods for VoIP quality and describes the adopted QoE estimation method. Finally, Sect. 5 provides the evaluation of the QoE values in the femto-overlaid LTE-A network, while Sect. 6 concludes the paper.

2 Interferences in the LTE-A Femtocell-Overlaid Network

2.1 Structure of the LTE-A Femtocell-Overlaid Network

The LTE-A system is divided into two basic subsystems (Fig. 1): the Evolved – Universal Mobile Telecommunications System (UMTS) Terrestrial Radio Access Network (E-UTRAN) and the Evolved Packet Core (EPC). This architecture has been adopted towards avoiding the hierarchical structures and providing increased scalability and efficiency. The EPC subsystem is a flat all-IP system designed to support high packet data rates and low latency in serving flows. The E-UTRAN subsystem implements the access network including large-sized base stations, called evolved NodeBs (eNBs), small-sized indoor base stations, called Home eNBs (HeNBs), and mobile terminals called User Equipments (UEs). In this paper, we refer to UEs served by the eNBs and HeNBs as Macrocell UEs (MUEs) and Femtocell UEs (FUEs) respectively.

Each (H)eNB has an IP address and is part of the all-IP network, while it is interconnected to other (H)eNBs through the X2 interface (Fig. 1). This interconnection allows collaboration among (H)eNBs in order to perform functions related to the resource, mobility and interference management. HeNBs are considered as low-power eNBs and realize the access network of the femtocells by spatially reusing the spectrum bands assigned to eNBs. HeNBs are closer to the end-users than the eNBs, improving in this way the indoor coverage, and thus users experience better channel conditions (higher QoE). However, HeNBs have the option to serve only a specific set of subscribed devices by adopting the so-called Closed Subscriber Group (CSG) mode, and they can be unpredictably switched on and off by the consumers, burdening in that way the received signals. Also, the spatial reuse of the spectrum amplifies the need for sophisticated interference management schemes, while the increased number of base stations with overlaying transmission ranges imposes the need for efficient control of the handovers. Under this heterogeneous environment, high quality services have to be delivered maximizing the end-user's experience. Since each type of service has different characteristics, requirements and restrictions, the end-user's experience strongly depends on the provided service. Nevertheless, real-time services, such as the VoIP, are the most suitable for QoE analysis, due to their high interaction with the end-user.

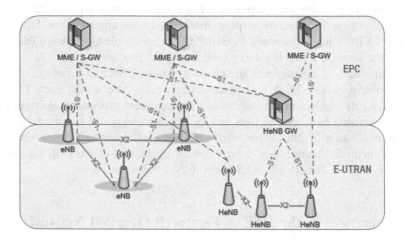

Fig. 1. LTE-A architecture

2.2 Interference Issues in the Femtocell-Overlaid LTE-A Network

We consider the network of Fig. 2, which represents a typical LTE-A heterogeneous network. We assume that macrocells and femtocells are synchronized, meaning that the uplink (UL) and downlink (DL) periods of both sub-networks have the exact same timing. In this kind of scenario, the parallel transmissions of eNBs and HeNBs during the DL, as well as of MUEs and FUEs during the UL may cause serious interference problems. To be more precise, during the UL, the MUEs may cause interference to the HeNBs, especially when MUEs are operating very close to a building where a HeNB is located. The same thing is valid during the DL, when transmitting HeNBs may also cause interference to closely located macro-receivers. In these two cases, the interference problem is locally present. However, the problem is much more severe during the DL regarding the eNB's transmissions, which may affect the femtocells' operation, since the eNB's signal is spread throughout the whole macrocell. As a consequence, such interference conditions are high likely to happen. The previously described interference scenario during the DL period is presented in Fig. 2.

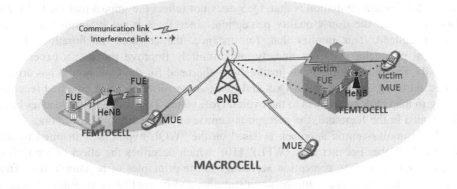

Fig. 2. Interference-scenario in the heterogeneous network under study (DL)

It is made clear that the DL period is very challenging in terms of interference, and mechanisms need to be deployed in order to avoid, reduce or manage it. One more reason that the DL is very challenging is that it concerns the perceived quality of communication from all the receiving mobile users, who may have various types of devices, may be communicating at different environments (open area, car, home, etc.), or may even have different expectations of the offered service. Even though UL interference problems may still be very severe, these are handled by the technologi-cally-advanced base stations and are not directly revealed to the users. Since the acceptability of a service, however, is determined by the end-users and not the oper-ators, we focus on DL IM, and we incorporate the user's perception in this process.

3 The Role of QoE in Interference Management

3.1 QoE and QoS Relationship

The "Quality of Service (QoS)" term was originally defined by ITU as *"the collective effect of service performance which determines the degree of satisfaction of a user of the service"* [8]. However, during the years, the study of QoS has lost this user-oriented approach and these days it is considered as just a subset of the more general QoE notion. Hence, QoS is no longer considered sufficient for the thorough characterization of a product or service as opposed to the most appealing QoE notion.

The reason to differentiate between QoS and QoE and to adopt QoE as the most suitable criterion for quality evaluation is twofold: First of all, QoS handles purely technical aspects regarding a service and does not incorporate any kind of human-related quality-affecting factors. This means that the same QoS level might not guarantee the same QoE level for two different users. Apart from the system's technical characteristics, other factors such as the context of use, the user-specific characteristics such as users' experiences and expectations, the delivered content and the pricing of a service make a significant impact on the finally perceived QoE as well [9]. The second reason for this differentiation is that, QoS does not reflect the impact that the technical factors have on the user's quality perception, since there is no straightforward connection defined. This implies that, for instance, the constant amelioration of one technical parameter does not linearly and infinitely improve the user's experience. Actually, this observation alone justifies why the need for the QoE notion has arisen. Based on this gap between the QoS and QoE, some formulas have emerged recently trying to map QoS parameters to the overall QoE value. Two different approaches have dominated in the literature: the perception-centric and the stimulus-centric one.

The stimulus-centric approach is based on the "WQL hypothesis" inspired by the so-called "Weber-Fechner Law (WFL)" [10], which describes the effect of a physical stimulus on the human perception according to the principles of psychophysics. This law claims that the relationship between stimulus and perception is logarithmic, which drives the conclusion that in order for a stimulus' change to be reliably detected by an observer, this has to differ from its original value by a constant fraction. From this law, the notion of "just noticeable differences" emerges, which describes the smallest detectable difference between two sequential levels of a particular stimulus.

Regarding the perception-centric QoS-QoE mapping, the so-called "IQX hypothesis" [11] has been proposed. According to this approach, the relationship between the QoE and one QoS degrading parameter is negative exponential and the change of QoE actually depends on the current level of QoE. The mapping curve between the QoE and the QoS disturbance consists of three clearly distinguishable regions, as shown in Fig. 3. The first one is the *constant optimal* region (Region 1 in Fig. 3), where the QoE is always excellent, regardless some initial impairments of one technical quality-affecting parameter. To be more precise, the QoE is not affected inside this region at all, either because some mechanisms inside the system provide some kind of tolerance to such impairments or simply because the human perception (e.g., vision or hearing) is not capable of distinguishing such changes. The second region of the QoS-QoE curve is characterized by *sinking* QoE in an exponential way (so that QoS disturbances are

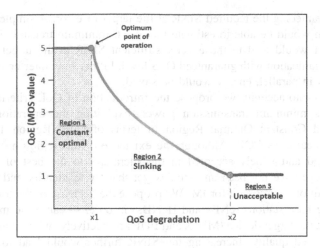

Fig. 3. The IQX hypothesis

more impactful when the QoE is higher), while the third and last region refers to *unacceptable* quality.

The clear discrimination among these three regions may be exploited by service providers not only for their own economic benefit but also for the common good. Regarding the providers' benefit perspective, since there can clearly be identified a region (Region 1) where the QoE is constantly excellent regardless some technical parameters' deterioration, the providers could deliberately deteriorate the performance of some technical parameters so that all users operate just on the turning point between Regions 1 and 2 (the point x_1 in Fig. 3, perhaps with some safety margin). This could be made possible by reducing resources such as spectrum resources or transmission power. As a result, all end-users will be pushed to operate on x_1 instead of any other "western" point of Region 1, since such a thing would not add to quality and also would consume resources for no reason. As a direct consequence, redundant resources could be released and saved to be provided to other users (for the common good) to who it would really make an impact on the perceived QoE (i.e., for users operating at Region 2 or 3, trying to "push" them towards Region 1's optimum point of operation).

3.2 QoE-aware Interference Management

As discussed in previous sections, the co-existence of femto- and macro-users operating on the same constrained resource pool causes interference problems in the network, while the study of the QoE could be beneficial for existing or future IM schemes.

The most common and direct way to mitigate the interferences is to adopt a PC-based IM scheme. However, an important trade-off is recognized when PC-based IM schemes are used; sufficient transmitted energy is required in order to ensure a specific QoS level at the receiver, but at the same time increasing the energy will cause higher interferences in the network and less battery life for the terminal. Consequently, the goal behind PC is to carefully limit the transmission power of the interference aggressor guaranteeing the required SINR at the target receiver. A simple yet efficient PC mechanism would be able to estimate the exact, minimum transmission power of the sender that would lead to the exactly sufficient SINR at the target receiver for faultless communication with guaranteed QoS level. In this way, interference would be smoothed, and in parallel, energy would be saved.

Taking this into account, we propose the introduction of QoE criteria to the estimation of this minimum transmission power, exploiting the operation inside the aforementioned Constant Optimal Region in terms of QoE (Region 1 in Fig. 3), abbreviated hereafter as COR. Although the existence of this region has been extensively discussed and widely accepted in the literature, to the best of the authors' knowledge, there have not been any studies yet that try to identify and measure the potential benefit of exploiting it for IM. We propose the decrease of the transmit power of all affecting base stations (eNBs and HeNBs) in order to cause the minimum sufficient SINR at the target device (MUEs and FUEs respectively) without any impact on the user perceived quality. Increasing the SINR further would lead to interference problems without any corresponding increase in the perceived quality, and thus, this is considered redundant and costly in terms of energy and resources.

The proposed QoE-aware scheme can be applied as an additional rule in any existing PC scheme. For instance, this rule may be applied on top of the PC scheme proposed by 3GPP [7]. The mathematic formula that describes this 3GPP-standardized scheme is as follows:

$$P_{Tx} = median(P_{eNB-HeNB} + PL_{HeNB-MUE}, P_{max}, P_{min}) \tag{1}$$

where P_{Tx} and $P_{eNB-HeNB}$ represent the transmit power of the HeNB (interference aggressor) and the measured received power from the eNB, respectively, while $PL_{HeNB-MUE}$ depicts the pathloss between the HeNB and the victim MUE. P_{max} and P_{min} parameters refer to predefined maximum and minimum transmit power settings, respectively, and depend on the device type.

Having defined the already standardized PC scheme, we present the proposed QoE-aware PC rule: *"If the estimated transmission power of the PC scheme is higher than the threshold power that leads to the lowest SINR in the constant optimal QoE region (i.e., optimum point of operation of Fig. 3), reduce this power up to its threshold value, using a safety margin".*

This leads to an enhanced formula that incorporates the proposed QoE-aware rule on top of the 3GPP PC scheme, as follows:

$$P'_{Tx} = max(P_{min}, P_{Tx(3GPP)} - \Delta P_{COR,opt}), \quad if \ \Delta P_{COR,opt} > 0 \tag{2}$$

where $\Delta P_{COR,opt}$ is the decrease in transmission power that moves the SINR from the SINR point that the $P_{Tx(3GPP)}$ defines, up to the "eastern" optimum point in the constant optimal region (COR). This formula will be applied only if the $P_{Tx(3GPP)}$ scheme provides a QoE score inside the constant optimal region, so that the $\Delta P_{COR,opt}$ is positive, and thus makes sense. The QoE score is measured using the Mean Opinion Score (MOS) scale, which is presented in the next section.

In the following, we provide the background for QoE estimation in VoIP services towards estimating the constant optimal QoE region and the gain of applying the proposed QoE-aware PC rule to a femtocell-overlaid LTE-A network.

4 QoE of the VoIP Service

4.1 Measuring the QoE of the VoIP Service

VoIP is one of the dominant services that will be provided by the LTE-A network. The VoIP requirements for the E-UTRAN sub-system are described in [12]. Practically, the VoIP service must be realized completely in packet switched (PS) domain and perform at least as efficiently (in terms of latency and bit rate) as the VoIP over Universal Mobile Telecommunications System (UMTS) in the circuit switched (CS) domain. Moreover, according to ITU, a VoIP user is considered to be in outage if less than 98 % of its VoIP packets have been delivered successfully to the user within a permissible delay bound of 50 ms, while the percentage of users in outage must be less than 2 % [13]. However, these bounds do not reflect the level of end-users' satisfaction. The end-users' satisfaction measured in QoE is a strongly subjective term and also one of the dominant factors for assessing a provided service. The most common measure of the QoE is the Mean Opinion Score (MOS) scale recommended in [14]. The MOS ranges from 1 to 5, with 5 representing the best quality, and is commonly produced by averaging the results of a subjective test, where end-users are called under a controlled environment to rate their experience with a provided service. However, this subjective methodology (use of questionnaires) is cost-demanding and practically inapplicable for real-time monitoring of the VoIP performance.

On the other hand, objective methods have been proposed to measure the speech quality. These methods can be classified into intrusive and non-intrusive methods. Intrusive methods, such as the Perceptual Speech Quality Measure (PSQM) and the PESQ (Perceptual Evaluation of Speech Quality), estimate the distortion of a reference signal that travels through a network by mapping the quality deterioration of the received signal to MOS values. However, the need for a reference signal is a drawback for using intrusive methods for QoE monitoring. To this end, non-intrusive methods have been defined such as the E-model and the ITU P.563 [15]. Since the ITU P.563 method has increased computational requirements, making it inappropriate for monitoring in real-time basis, we adopt the easier to be applied E-model described in the next section.

4.2 The E-model

The E-model has been proposed by the ITU-T for measuring objectively the MOS of voice communications by estimating the mouth-to-ear conversational quality as perceived by the user at the receive side, both as listener and talker [16]. It is a parametric model that takes into account a variety of transmission impairments producing the so-called Transmission Rating factor (R factor) scaling from 0 (worst) to 100 (best). Then a mathematic formula is used to translate this to MOS values. In the case of the baseline scenario where no network or equipment impairments exist, the R factor is given by:

$$R = R_0 = 94.2. \tag{3}$$

However, delays and signal impairments are involved in a practical scenario and hence the R factor is given by:

$$R = R_0 - I_s - I_d - I_{ef} + A \tag{4}$$

where:

I_s: the impairments that are generated during the voice traveling into the network,
I_d: the delays introduced from end-to-end signal traveling,
I_{ef}: the impairments introduced by the equipment and also due to randomly distributed packet losses,
A: allows for compensation of impairment factors when there are other advantages of access to the user (Advantage Factor). It describes the tolerance of a user due to a certain advantage that he/she enjoys, e.g., not paying for the service or being mobile. Typical value for cellular networks: $A = 10$.

Focusing on parameters which depend on the wireless part of the communication (transmissions between (H)eNB and UEs) it holds that [17]:

$$I_d = 0.024d + 0.11(d - 177.3)H(d - 177.3) \tag{5}$$

where:

$$H(x) = \begin{cases} 0, & x < 0 \\ 1, & x \geq 0 \end{cases} \tag{6}$$

and d is the average packet delivery delay. Also, assuming that the codec G.729a is used, the packet loss rate, referred here as p, affects the parameter I_{ef} as follows [17]:

$$I_{ef} = 11 + 40\ln(1 + 10p). \tag{7}$$

The R factor can be used as an assessment value; however, we transform it to MOS values to retrieve results comparable with results provided by subjective methods. The transformation formula is as follows:

$$MOS = \begin{cases} 1, & \text{if } R < 0, \\ 1 + 0.035R + R(R - 60)(100 - R) \cdot 7 \cdot 10^{-6}, & \text{if } 0 \leq R \leq 100, \\ 4.5, & \text{if } R > 100. \end{cases} \tag{8}$$

In the next section, we focus on the deterioration caused in parameters d and p in a femto-overlaid LTE-A network and on the resulting user perceived quality.

5 Simulation Model and Results

Towards quantifying the need for QoE-aware IM schemes, we first evaluate the impact of macrocell-femtocell coexistence on VoIP users' QoE. We assume an LTE-A network that consists of a target hexagonal macrocell with 6 neighboring cells and multiple femtocells inside the target cell area. Each femtocell is deployed with some probability inside a 10 m × 10 m apartment, while 25 apartments define a 50 m × 50 m square building block. Multiple building blocks are uniformly distributed inside the target cell area, while the femtocells reuse the licensed spectrum of the target macrocell, exacerbating the interference problem. For this scenario, we have expanded the open source system level simulator described in [18] to derive the QoS fluctuations, and used the E-model to translate them to MOS. The main simulation parameters are shown in Table 1:

Table 1. Simulation Parameters

Parameter	Value
Number of eNBs	7
Macrocell radius	500 m
eNBs TX power	43 dBm
Femtocell building block	3GPP based 5 × 5 building block
Apartment side	10 m
Number of HeNBs/building	Scalable
HeNBs TX power	20 dBm
HeNBs deployment	Co-channel
MUEs placement	Random (inside the macrocell area)
FUEs placement	Random (inside the apartments)
UEs in the system	Scalable
Traffic load per user	1 VoIP call
VoIP codec	G.729a
Duplex mode	FDD (focus on downlink)
Channel bandwidth/cell	10 MHz
Scheduling algorithm	Proportional fair
Flow duration	5 s
QoE model	E-model

At first, we examine the impact of femtocell deployment on the QoE performance of all types of end-users (MUEs and FUEs), assuming an increasing number of concurrent VoIP calls inside a target macrocell area. More specifically, 10 building blocks are uniformly distributed inside the target macrocell area, while each HeNB is located with 50 % probability into an apartment of a building block. We consider that the HeNBs operate in CSG mode and also that the 50 % of VoIP flows are originated indoors, while the rest of them outdoors. The results concerning the QoE of the users, represented using the MOS scale, are shown in Fig. 4.

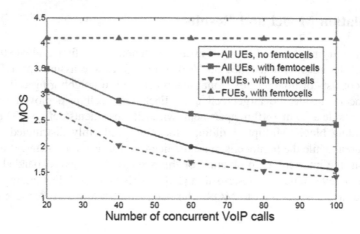

Fig. 4. Impact of the number of VoIP calls on QoE

As shown in this figure, on average, the femtocell proliferation improves the QoE experienced by VoIP users (the "All UEs, no femtocells" case has lower performance than the "All UEs, with femtocells" case). Nevertheless, this improvement is mainly caused due to the high QoE performance of VoIP calls served by femtocells, reaping femtocell benefits such as the proximity gain ("FUEs, with femtocells" case). Note that since each femtocell serves a low number of VoIP calls (practically 1 or 2) the increase on the total number of VoIP calls has negligible impact on FUEs' QoE, maintaining the high QoE performance. On the contrary, the QoE of MUEs seems to deteriorate due to the interference caused by the HeNBs ("MUEs, with femtocells" case). This observation validates the need for more investigation on how to mitigate the interferences caused to MUEs.

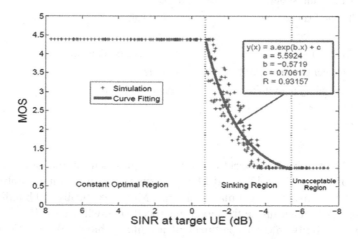

Fig. 5. Impact of SINR degradation on QoE

Moving one step further, in Fig. 5, we prove the existence of the constant optimal region discussed in Sect. 3 for any UE. To this end, we focus on a single building block and we monitor the performance of the VoIP call of a single user located close to a femtocell-overlaid building block, while the SINR at this user is constantly degraded. The reason of the SINR deterioration might be lower transmitted power from the serving base station or higher interferences imposed or even worse channel conditions, without any loss of generality. We depict the results in MOS (y axis) and SINR degradation (x axis) and perform curve fitting to define the function that best describes the simulated data. We observe that the IQX hypothesis is indeed validated, while there is a quite large COR available for exploitation. The optimum point of operation is identified for an SINR threshold value of around −0.8 dB for this scenario.

Having defined the constant optimal region for our scenario, we apply the proposed QoE-aware PC rule on top of the PC scheme proposed by the 3GPP, using the formulas of Sect. 3.2. In Fig. 6, we compare these two formulas depicting the resulting transmission power by each one of them, for constant and guaranteed QoE at FUEs. This means that all resulting plots have been derived ensuring the same maximum MOS value, both for the 3GPP scheme and for the QoE-aware PC scheme (blue & red curves in Fig. 6 respectively). As shown in this figure, the QoE-aware PC rule significantly reduces the required transmission power and thus the interference perceived by victim MUEs, maintaining in parallel the required high QoE level at the served FUEs.

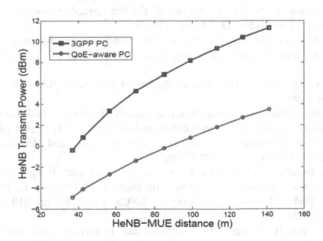

Fig. 6. Performance of QoE-enhanced 3GPP PC

6   Conclusions

In this paper, we focused on VoIP services in an LTE-A network, and quantified the QoE deterioration of macrocell users due to the interference from femtocells. Sequentially, we examined the relation between the QoE and the perceived SINR at an interference victim, defining the constant optimal region for the SINR. For all SINR values in this region the QoE is constant and in high level, making room for reducing the transmission power with no impact on the service perception of end-users. Finally, we exploited these results to compare the basic power control (PC) interference management (IM) scheme proposed by 3GPP and a simple QoE-aware PC scheme, revealing the importance of involving the QoE notion in the IM process.

Acknowledgments. This research has been co-financed by European Union (European Social Fund – ESF) and Greek national funds through the Operational Program "Education and Lifelong Learning" of the National Strategic Reference Framework (NSRF) – Research Funding Program: Heracleitus II and the CROSSFIRE (un-CoORdinated netwOrk StrategieS for enhanced inter-Ference, mobIlity, radio Resource, and Energy saving management in LTE-Advanced networks) MITN Marie Curie project.

References

1. ITU-R: Requirements related to technical performance for IMT-Advanced radio interface(s). Report M.2134 (2008)
2. 3GPP: Evolved Universal Terrestrial Radio Access (E-UTRA) and Evolved Universal Terrestrial Radio Access Network (E-UTRAN); Overall description; Stage 2. TS 36.300, version 10.7.0 (2012)
3. Andrews, J.G., Claussen, H., Dohler, M., Rangan, S., Reed, M.C.: Femtocells: past, present, and future. IEEE J. Sel. Areas Commun. **30**, 497–508 (2012)
4. Zahir, T., Arshad, K., Nakata, A., Moessner, K.: interference management in femtocells. IEEE Commun. Surv. Tutor. **15**, 293–311 (2013)
5. Singh, S., Andrews, J.G., de Veciana, G.: Interference shaping for improved quality of experience for real-time video streaming. IEEE J. Sel. Areas Commun. **30**, 1259–1269 (2012)
6. ITU-T: New Appendix I - Definition of Quality of Experience (QoE). Rec. P.10/G.100, Amendment 1 (2007)
7. 3GPP: Evolved Universal Terrestrial Radio Access (E-UTRA); FDD Home eNode B (HeNB) Radio Frequency (RF) requirements analysis. TR 36.921, version 10.0.0 (2011)
8. ITU-T: Terms and Definitions Related to Quality of Service and Network Performance Including Dependability. Rec. E.800 (2008)
9. Schatz, R., Hoßfeld, T., Janowski, L., Egger, S.: From packets to people: quality of experience as a new measurement challenge. In: Biersack, E., Callegari, C., Matijasevic, M. (eds.) Data Traffic Monitoring and Analysis. LNCS, vol. 7754, pp. 219–263. Springer, Heidelberg (2013)
10. Reichl, P., Tuffin, B., Schatz, R.: Logarithmic laws in service quality perception: where microeconomics meets psychophysics and quality of experience. Telecommun. Syst. **52**, 587–600 (2011)
11. Fiedler, M., Hossfeld, T., Tran-Gia, P.: A generic quantitative relationship between quality of experience and quality of service. IEEE Netw. **24**, 36–41 (2010)
12. 3GPP: Requirements for Evolved UTRA (E-UTRA) and Evolved UTRAN (E-UTRAN). TR 25.913, version 7.3.0 (2006)
13. ITU-R: Guidelines for Evaluation of Radio Interface Technologies for IMT-Advanced. Report M.2135 (2008)
14. ITU-T: Methods for Subjective Determination of Transmission Quality. Rec. P.800 (1996)
15. ITU-T: Single-ended method for objective speech quality assessment in narrow-band telephony applications. Rec. P.563 (2005)

16. ITU-T: The E-Model: A Computational Model for Use in Transmission Planning. Rec. G.107 (2012)
17. Cole, R.G., Rosenbluth, J.H.: Voice over IP performance monitoring. ACM SIGCOMM Comput. Commun. Rev. **31**, 9 (2001)
18. Piro, G., Grieco, L.A., Boggia, G., Capozzi, F., Camarda, P.: Simulating LTE cellular systems: an open-source framework. IEEE Trans. Veh. Technol. **60**, 498–513 (2011)

Modeling Guaranteed Delay of Virtualized Wireless Networks Using Network Calculus

Jia Liu[1], Lianming Zhang[1], and Kun Yang[2($\boxtimes$)]

[1] College of Physics and Information Science, Hunan Normal University,
Changsha, China
zlm@hunnu.edu.cn
[2] Network Convergence Laboratory, University of Essex, Colchester, UK
kunyang@essex.ac.uk

Abstract. Wireless network virtualization is an emerging technology that logically divides a wireless network element, such as a base station (BS), into multiple slices with each slice serving as a standalone virtual BS. In such a way, one physical mobile wireless network can be partitioned into multiple virtual networks each operating as an independent wireless network. Wireless virtual networks, as composed of these virtual BSs, need to provide quality of service (QoS) to mobile end user services. One such key QoS parameter is network delay, in particular upper bound delay. This paper presents a delay model for such a wireless virtual network. This delay model considers resources (in particular queues) of both physical nodes and virtual nodes and provides a realistic modelling of the delay behaviours of wireless virtual networks. Network calculus, which usually provides finer insight into a system, is utilized to fulfil the modelling task. The numerical results have shown the effectiveness of the proposed model. The model is useful for both off-line network planning and online network admission control.

Keywords: Wireless network virtualization · Delay modelling · Upper bound delay · Network calculus

1 Introduction

Wireless mobile network virtualization enables physical mobile network operators (PMNO) to partition their network resources into smaller slices and assign each slice to an individual virtual mobile network operator (VMNO) and then manages these virtual networks in a more dynamic and cost-effective fashion [1]. We name these virtualized individual networks as wireless virtual networks or WVNs. VMNOs pay the PMNO in a pay-as-you-use manner. Wireless network virtualization has its real-world bearing in mobile cellular networks. For instance, there are many mobile network operators such as Lebara in the UK that don't have their own physical network infrastructure such as base stations (BS), etc. They typically rent such physical network infrastructure from other MNOs that own the infrastructure. For example, Lebara rents Vodafone's networks to provide mobile services to its own end users. Such mobile users have a Lebara SIM card.

The purpose of virtual networks is to provide services to end users. Services of different traffic characteristics may run on the virtual networks. Therefore some kind of

© Institute for Computer Sciences, Social Informatics and Telecommunications Engineering 2014
I. Stojmenovic et al. (Eds.): MOBIQUITOUS 2013, LNICST 131, pp. 602–614, 2014.
DOI: 10.1007/978-3-319-11569-6_47

service differentiation shall be provided in the same way as it is provided in the physical networks. Before carrying out QoS control it is essential to understand behaviours of such virtual networks. Though there is much work on the modelling of physical wireless networks themselves, there is little work on virtual network modelling. Paper [2] presents some initial work on it but the considered network there is mesh networks. Furthermore, there is no closed-formed being deducted in terms of network delay. Nor does this model differentiate physical networks from virtual networks.

As in [1], our paper partitions a physical network node such as a base station into multiple slices. And this partitioning can be carried out in a dynamic manner using software, i.e., supporting software-defined radio networks. Each *slice* represents a virtual network node, e.g., a Lebara BS, as depicted in Fig. 1.

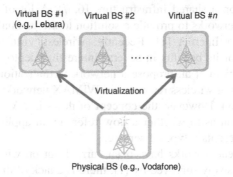

Fig. 1. Wireless network virtualization

As far as network modelling tools are concerned, the predominant ones are probability theory, queue theory. In this paper a new modelling tool called network calculus is utilized. Network calculus is a set of recent developments that enable the effective derivation of deterministic performance bounds in networking [3, 4]. Compared with some traditional statistic theories, network calculus has the merit that provides deep insights into performance analysis of deterministic bounds. Application areas for the network calculus cover a wide range of networking areas such as QoS control, resource allocation and scheduling, and buffer/delay dimensioning [3]. We have carried out some work on using network calculus on wireless sensor networks [5]. This paper extends this previous work into a new research area of network virtualization.

The technical aim of the paper is to propose a delay model for wireless virtual networks (WVNs). In comparison with the existing literature on similar work, this paper has the following major contributions: (1) to systematically analyse the roles in virtual wireless networks and to describe their relationships from a realistic network operation's perspective. The roles include physical networks, virtual networks, end users and service flows. These roles are to be expressed in the network calculus models. (2) To mathematically describe the above virtual wireless network system using network calculus. (3) To propose a QoS model of the virtual wireless network expressing network queue length and network delay in their upper bound terms and in a closed-form manner. The proposed model can help analyse delay guarantee on a per-flow granularity.

In the following sections, we first discuss existing research work on the modelling of virtual networks in Sect. 2. Section 3 presents the system model in terms of different roles including end users, flows, virtual networks (slices) and physical networks, based on which the problem to be addressed in the paper is further clarified. Section 4 models the above NC-formulated system in terms of queue length and delay. After presentation of the numerical results and performance analysis in Sect. 5, the paper is concluded in Sect. 6.

2   Related Work

Network virtualization has emerged as a flexible and efficient way to enable deploying customized services on a shared infrastructure [6, 7]. A lot of research works have developed on wired networks to provide a solution to the gradual ossification problem faced by the existing Internet [8]. Recently, wireless virtualization has attracted increasing attention for its benefits in several interesting deployment scenarios [1, 9, 10], etc. In [9], R. Kokku et al. propose a network virtualization substrate (NVS) for effective virtualization of wireless resources in WiMAX networks. The design provides flow-level virtualization. However, the concept of flows in NVS is not very clear [1]. There is no explanation as to whether a flow refers to an application service flow or packet flow or it represents a type of service.

Though many research works have been carried out on wireless network virtualization, as comprehensively surveyed by [1], there is a lack of the formal modelling of wireless virtual networks. System modelling can provide a useful means to study fundamental features of a system. This paper aims to fill this gap by providing a model of virtualized wireless networks. In particular the focus is given to one important feature of virtual networks, i.e., network delay.

There are various approaches to deal with delay-aware resource control in wireless networks. M. Tao et al. investigate the resource allocation problem in multiuser OFDM system with both delay-constrained and non-delay-constraint traffic [11]. However, the performance impact caused by the delay mechanism is not discussed. There is also an approach which is to convert average delay constraints into equivalent average rate constraints using the queuing theory [12, 13]. However, all these approaches are linked to a particular resource allocation or packet scheduling algorithm and thus are specific to the corresponding algorithms. In our paper, we aim to provide a more generic modelling of wireless virtual networks that is agnostic to resource allocation algorithms and agnostic to a specific network technology. Furthermore, a more expressive means of network modelling tool called network calculus is employed to fulfil the expected network modelling.

Some representative work that uses network calculus to conduct modelling of QoS parameters (in particular delay) is summarized as follows. Paper [14] has utilized network calculus to compute the delay of individual traffic flows in feed-forward networks under arbitrary multiplexing. The maximum end-to-end delay is calculated in [15], again for a feed-forward type of networks. An analytical framework is presented to analyse worst-case performance and to dimension resources of sensor networks [16]. The deterministic performance bound on end-to-end delay for self-similar traffic regulated by a fractal leaky bucket regulator is research into in [17] for ad hoc networks. On the basis of the notion of flows and micro-flows, Zhang et al. [5] propose, using arrival curves and service curves in the network calculus, a two-layer scheduling model for sensor nodes. This piece of work develops a guaranteed QoS model, including the upper bounds on buffer queue length/delay/effective bandwidth. This paper aims to use network calculus to provide a delay mode for wireless virtual networks.

3 System Model Description

3.1 Virtual Network and Virtual Queue

The network illustration of Fig. 1 is depicted in Fig. 2 with the concept of virtual queue. Each slice is allocated a virtual queue in its hosting physical network or network node. All these virtual queues share the data rate capacity of the physical network node, i.e., the physical BS, under the control of a scheduler. The scheduler will take into consideration the QoS requirements of the slices when carrying out resource scheduling. Each slice, as noted as $S1$, $S2$, ..., Sn respectively, represents a virtual BS.

The WVN system using virtual queues has the following merits, similar to the virtual buffer concept in [5].

(1) The model provides a minimum guaranteed service rate for every slice under constrained bandwidth. Namely, when a data flow passes through a physical BS it is guaranteed a minimum service rate as specified by its corresponding queue length and the scheduler.

(2) The queues and thus the network bandwidth of a physical BS are shared by all slices. And thus a better gain may be obtained by statistically multiplexing independent slices.

(3) The model simplifies performance analysis, making it suitable for more complex networks such as virtual networks where different roles co-exist.

3.2 Flow Types and Flow Control

Figure 2 illustrates the following two key roles in a network virtualization scenario: physical BS and virtual BS (i.e., slice). Each slice represents a VMN. Each slice has a slice ID. A slice is used by many end users. A user is physically represented by a mobile node in a network. A user may have multiple flows. For example, a user may use his/her smart phone to check emails via listening to an online music piece. Here emails and music pieces each represent a flow. The biggest differentiator amongst flow types is that they have different delay requirement. For instance, voice flow has more stringent delay requirement than non-real time emails. A flow represents a session and each flow has a flow ID. Each uplink packet has both a slice ID showing its belonging to which VMN and a flow ID identifying its service session within a user. The modelling of delay to be carried out in this paper is at a per-flow level.

Figure 3 depicts the relationship of these four key roles in WVNs: physical BS, virtual BS, users and flows. The packets from different users, as denoted as Ui in Fig. 3,

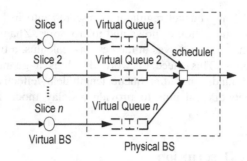

Fig. 2. Virtual network and virtual queue

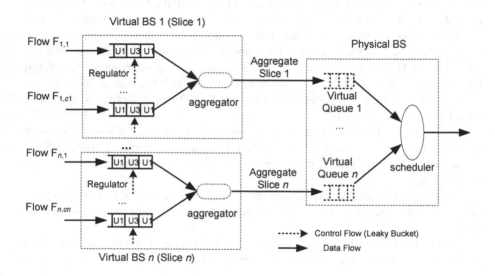

Fig. 3. Flows and slices

but of the same type (e.g., real-time), are put into the same queue in a slice. A leaky bucket source model is selected for each slice queue due to its simplicity and practical applicability. Therefore a leaky bucket regulator is applied to each slice queue to regulate the flows to enable non-rule flows to be controlled under certain conditions. A flow, regulated by the leaky bucket regulator, is indicated by envelope $\alpha(t)$ as shown in Eq. (1) [5],

$$\alpha(t) = r \cdot t + b, \qquad \forall t \geq 0, \tag{1}$$

where b is interpreted as the burst parameter, and r as the average arrival rate.

A flow in an interval $[t, t + \tau]$ is denoted by $A(t, t + \tau)$, and it has the following properties [5].

Property 1 (Additivity): $A(t_1, t_3) = A(t_1, t_2) + A(t_2, t_3), \forall t_3 > t_2 > t_1 > 0.$

Property 2 (Sub-additive Bound): $A(t, t + \tau) \leq \alpha(\tau), \forall t \geq 0, \forall \tau \geq 0.$

Property 3 (Independence): All micro-flows are independent.

4 Proposed Upper Bound Delay Model

In this section, we first describe the above WVN system using network calculus. And then the delay upper bound is deducted based on this WVN model. Before carrying out the above two tasks, some basics regarding network calculus is presented.

4.1 Preliminaries on Network Calculus

Network calculus is the results of the studies on traffic flow problems, min-plus algebra and max-plus algebra applied to qualitative or quantitative analysis for networks in recent years, and it belongs to tropical algebra and topical algebra [5]. Network calculus can be classified into two types: deterministic network calculus and statistical network calculus. The former, using arrival curves and service curves, is mainly used to obtain the exact solution of the bounds on network performance, such as queue length and queue delay, and so on. The latter, on the other hand, based on arrival curves and effective service curves, is used to obtain the stochastic or statistical bounds on the network performance. In this paper deterministic network calculus is utilized as our first step towards modelling WVN as a network calculus system. Some introductory material that is necessary to understand the network calculus modes in this paper is given below. For more information on network calculus please refer to [5, 6].

Theorem 1 (Queue Length and Queue Delay): Assume a slice passes through a physical BS, and the physical BS has an arrival curve $\alpha(t)$ and offers a service curve $\beta(t)$. The queue length Q and the queue delay D of the slice, passing through the physical BS, satisfy the following inequalities, respectively

$$Q \leq \sup_{t \geq 0} \{\alpha(t) - \beta(t)\}, \tag{2}$$

and

$$D \leq \inf_{t \geq 0} \{d \geq 0 : \alpha(t) \leq \beta(t + d)\}. \tag{3}$$

The proof of the theorem and more information about network calculus can be found in [5, 6].

4.2 System Description Using Network Calculus

In this sub-section, we model the WVN presented in Sect. 3 using network calculus. The process of the model is as follows. Firstly, a flow, entering a virtual BS, is regulated by a leaky bucket regulator as given in Eq. (1). Its arrival curve is denoted as $\alpha(t)$. The functions $\alpha(t)$ and $A(t, t + \tau)$ satisfy Property 2. Secondly, we assume the FCFS (first come, first served) strategy is adopted in a queue. This is reasonable as the packets in the same queue are of a same service type. But other more comprehensive queuing strategies may be applied here as well. Finally, the aggregated flows from a slice are scheduled in a way of a service curve $\beta(t)$. The service curve is further explained below.

From Properties 1 and 3, and Fig. 3, the aggregate slices $A_i(t, t + \tau)$ and flows $A_{i,k}(t, t + \tau)$, $k = 1, 2, \ldots, n$ satisfy

$$A_i(t, t + \tau) = \sum_{k=1}^{c_i} A_{i,k}(t, t + \tau), \quad \forall t, \tau > 0. \tag{4}$$

From Ref. [18], the equivalent envelope curve $\alpha_i(t)$ of the slices and the envelope curve $\alpha_{i,k}(t)$ $(k = 1, 2, \ldots, n)$ of the flows satisfy

$$\alpha_i(t) = \sum_{k=1}^{c_i} \alpha_{i,k}(t), \quad \forall t > 0. \tag{5}$$

The service curve $\beta_i(t)$ of Slice i is defined as

$$\beta_i(t) = \beta(t) - \sum_{k=1, k \neq i}^{n} \alpha_k(t - \theta_k), \quad \forall t > \theta \geq 0, \tag{6}$$

where $\beta(t)$ is interpreted as a service curve of physical BS, α_k as an arrival curve of the virtual queue k, and n as the number of the virtual queues(i.e., virtual networks) in the physical BS.

In order to simplify the calculation and without loss of generality, we assume the service curve $\beta(t)$ of the physical BS is a rate-latency function $\beta_{R,T}(t)$ given by

$$\beta(t) = \beta_{R,T}(t) = R \cdot (t - T), \quad \forall t > T > 0, \tag{7}$$

where R is interpreted as the service rate, T as the latency. Obviously for $R > 0$ and $0 \leq t \leq T$, we have $\beta_{R,T}(t) = 0$.

From Property 3, Eq. (5), the simple leaky bucket regulator Eq. (1), the envelope curve of the regulator is

$$\alpha_i(t) = \sum_{k=1}^{n} (b_{i,k} + r_{i,k}t). \tag{8}$$

From Eqs. (1) and (7), if $\sum_{i=1}^{n} r_i < R$, the parameter θ_i is optimized, and there is:

$$\theta_i = T + \frac{\sum_{k=1, k \neq i}^{n} b_k}{R}, i = 1, 2, \ldots, n.$$

Bringing θ_i into Eq. (6), and combining Eq. (5) with Eq. (8), there is:

$$\beta_i(t) = \left(R - \sum_{k=1, k \neq i}^{n} \sum_{j=1}^{c_j} r_{k,j} \right) \cdot \left(t - T - \frac{\sum_{k=1, k \neq i}^{n} \sum_{j=1}^{c_j} b_{k,j}}{R} \right). \tag{9}$$

Equation (9) shows that each slice entering the physical BS holds a certain service curve. And the service curve is not only decided by the total service curve of the physical BS scheduler, but also by the arrival curve of the slice.

4.3 The Proposed Delay Model

Now we present, using the network calculus, the guaranteed delay model.

Proposition 1 (Upper Bound on Queue Length): In an interval $[0, t]$, the upper bound on Q_i satisfies

$$Q_i = \sup_{t \geq 0} \left\{ \sum_{k=1}^{n} \left(b_{i,k} + r_{i,k}t \right) - \left(R - \sum_{k=1, k \neq i}^{n} \sum_{j=1}^{c_j} r_{k,j} \right) \cdot \left(t - T - \frac{\sum_{k=1, k \neq i}^{n} \sum_{j=1}^{c_j} b_{k,j}}{R} \right) \right\}. \tag{10}$$

Proof From Eq. (2), we have

$$Q_i \leq \sup_{t \geq 0} \{ \alpha_i(t) - \beta_i(t) \}. \tag{11}$$

Substituting Eqs. (8) and (9) into Eq. (11), there is

$$Q_i \leq \sup_{t \geq 0} \{ \alpha_i(t) - \beta_i(t) \}$$

$$= \sup_{t \geq 0} \left\{ \sum_{k=1}^{n} \left(b_{i,k} + r_{i,k}t \right) - \left(R - \sum_{k=1, k \neq i}^{n} \sum_{j=1}^{c_j} r_{k,j} \right) \cdot \left(t - T - \frac{\sum_{k=1, k \neq i}^{n} \sum_{j=1}^{c_j} b_{k,j}}{R} \right) \right\}.$$

Proposition 2 (Upper Bound on Queue Delay): In an interval $[0, t]$, the upper bound on D_i satisfies

$$D_i = T + \frac{\sum_{k=1}^{n} b_{i,k}}{R - \sum_{k=1, k \neq i}^{n} \sum_{j=1}^{c_j} r_{k,j}} + \frac{\sum_{k=1, k \neq i}^{n} \sum_{j=1}^{c_j} b_{k,j}}{R}. \tag{12}$$

Proof From Eq. (3), we obtain

$$D_i \leq \inf_{t \geq 0} \{ d \geq 0 : \alpha_i(t) \leq \beta_i(t + d) \}. \tag{13}$$

Substituting Eqs. (8) and (9) into Eq. (13), there is

$$
D_i \leq \inf_{t \geq 0} \left\{ d \geq 0 : \sum_{k=1}^{n} \left(b_{i,k} + r_{i,k} t \right) \leq \left(R - \sum_{k=1,k \neq i}^{n} \sum_{j=1}^{c_j} r_{k,j} \right) \cdot \left(t + d - T - \frac{\sum_{k=1,k \neq i}^{n} \sum_{j=1}^{c_j} b_{k,j}}{R} \right) \right\}
$$

$$
= \inf_{t \geq 0} \left\{ d \geq 0 : d \geq T + \frac{\sum_{k=1}^{n} \left(b_{i,k} + r_{i,k} t \right)}{R - \sum_{k=1,k \neq i}^{n} \sum_{j=1}^{c_j} r_{k,j}} - t + \frac{\sum_{k=1,k \neq i}^{n} \sum_{j=1}^{c_j} b_{k,j}}{R} \right\}.
$$

(14)

For $R \geq \sum_{k=1}^{n} \sum_{j=1}^{c_j} r_{k,j}$, from Eq. (14), we obtain

$$
D_i = T + \frac{\sum_{k=1}^{n} b_{i,k}}{R - \sum_{k=1,k \neq i}^{n} \sum_{j=1}^{c_j} r_{k,j}} + \frac{\sum_{k=1,k \neq i}^{n} \sum_{j=1}^{c_j} b_{k,j}}{R}.
$$

The leaky bucket regulators and aggregators don't increase the upper bounds on queue length/delay of a physical BS, and also don't increase the queue requirements of the physical BS.

5 Numerical Results and Analysis

5.1 Network/Flow Parameter Setup

The two-level model presented in Fig. 3 and Sect. 4 is used for all physical BSs. The service curves $\beta(t)$ of the physical BSs are given in Eq. (9), where R is the service rate and T as the latency of the service curves of the physical BSs. Three slices: Slice1, Slice2 and Slice3, marked as $A_1(t)$, $A_2(t)$ and $A_3(t)$ respectively, are used to showcase the evaluation results. It is assumed that Slice 1 $A_1(t)$ contains three flows: $A_{1,1}(t)$, $A_{1,2}(t)$, $A_{1,3}(t)$, Slice 2$A_2(t)$ contains two flows: $A_{2,1}(t)$ and $A_{2,2}(t)$, and Slice 3$A_3(t)$ contains one flow: $A_{3,1}(t)$. Here we assume that every flow is regulated by the leaky bucket regulator $\alpha(t)$ as shown in Eq. (8). The average arrival rate $r_{i,k}$ and the burst tolerance $b_{i,k}$ of the six flows are shown in Table 1. The arrival curves of the slices are given by Eq. (9). The unit of queue length Q is Mb. The units of delay D, the time t, and the latency T are ms and the unit of the service rate R is Mb/s except the units that are given.

In terms of evaluation methods, queue length and delay will be investigated against both flow arrival rate and physical BS's service rate. The impact of the traffic burstiness on the network performance is also looked into.

Table 1. Parameters of the three slices and their flows

Slices $A_i(t)$	Flows $A_{i,k}(t)$	Average arrival rate $r_{i,k}$(Kb/s)	Burst tolerance $b_{i,k}$(Kb)
$A_1(t)$	1	240	400
	2	320	360
	3	400	260
$A_2(t)$	1	450	420
	2	350	360
$A_3(t)$	1	700	550

5.2 Queue Length

Figure 4 shows the impact of the average arrival rate r on the queue length upper bounds. Queue length increases as the average arrival rate increases and this is applicable to all slices. Given a fixed service rate, more packets arriving naturally lead to an increased number of packets staying in the queues waiting to be transmitted and thus an increase queue length. As Slice 1 has more traffic to be transmitted – refer to Table 1, its queue length tends to be longer than the other two slices.

Figure 5 depicts the trend of queue lengths of different slices when the service rate R increases. In contrast to Fig. 4, the queue length decreases alongside the increase of service rate and this also applicable to all slices. This is intuitive as serving more packets means a fewer number of packets being buffered in the queues.

Figure 6 shows that the bursty nature of traffic also makes negative impact on network performance. As the level of burstiness increases, as indicated by the burst parameter b, the queue length increases significantly, even more significant than the impact caused by service rate (refer to Fig. 5). It also indicates that the influence of burstiness does not change too much across slices. There is only a small increase in queue length for heavy-load Slice 1 in comparison with Slice 3 which is less loaded.

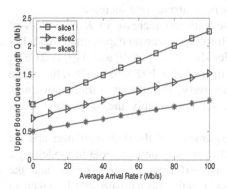

Fig. 4. Upper bound queue length vs. arrival rate ($T = 1$ ms, $R = 100$ Mb/s and $t = 25$ ms)

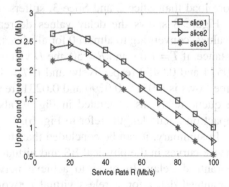

Fig. 5. Upper bound queue length vs. service rate ($T = 1$ ms and $t = 25$ ms)

In all these cases other parameters such as service rate R and latency T are fixed as indicated in the corresponding figure captions.

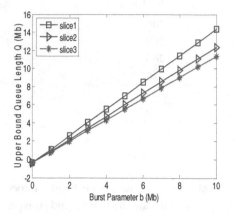

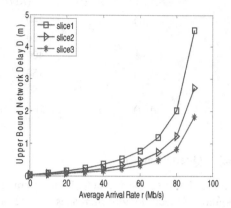

Fig. 6. Upper bound queue length vs. burst parameter ($T = 1$ ms, $R = 100$ Mb and $t = 5$ ms)

Fig. 7. Upper bound queue delay vs. average arrival rate ($T = 1$ ms, and $R = 100$ Mb)

5.3   Network Delay

Figures 7, 8 and 9 show the impact of the same set of variables (i.e., average arrival rate r, service rate R, and burst parameter b) on the upper bounds on queue delay D of a virtual slices. The behavior of network delay more or less follows the similar trend as queue length. It can be observed that the upper bound on D is smaller for larger service rate R.

Figure 7 plots the delay curves as a function of the average arrival rate r. It is obvious that the delay increases as more traffic comes into the system. The delay value starts slow and increases much more significantly as more traffic pours in and thus the network gets more loaded or even congested. This trend applies to all slices though the heavier the slice's load the more obvious the trend is. For instance, Slice 1, which has more load than Slice 2 and Slice 3, suffers more as arrival rate increases.

Figure 8 shows the delay values decrease with the increase of R regardless of T values, converging to almost 0 for all slices. It follows more an exponential trend. For instance, if $T = 1$ ms and $R = 50$, the D value for slices: $A_1(t)$, $A_2(t)$ and $A_3(t)$ is 0.0625, 0.0574 and 0.0452 respectively; and if $T = 1$ ms and $R = 100$ Mb, the D value of the three flows is 0.0315, 0.0290 and 0.0231, respectively. The impact of traffic burstiness on queue delay, as illustrated in Fig. 9, also follows roughly the same trend as its impact on queue length (refer to Fig. 6).

In summary, it can be concluded that the parameters of the flow regulators and the service curves in the physical BS and virtual BS play an important role in modelling a guaranteed delay. In order to achieve network performance improvement and the guaranteed delay for wireless virtual networks, certain mechanisms can be taken to reduce the upper bounds on (end-to-end) delay. These mechanisms may involve designing rational regulator parameters such the average arrival rate and the burst

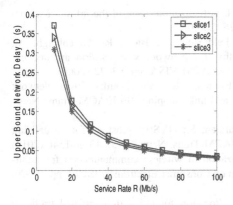

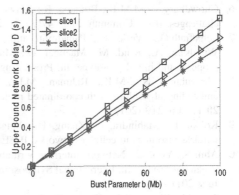

Fig. 8. Upper bound queue delay vs. service rate ($T = 1$ ms)

Fig. 9. Upper bound queue delay vs. burst parameter ($T = 1$ ms, and $R = 100$ Mb)

tolerance, and designing of rational scheduler parameters such as the service rate and the latency, of the wireless physical networks and wireless virtual networks.

6 Conclusions and Future Work

This paper has proposed a simple but realistic model for describing the upper bound delay of wireless virtual networks. Both service flows that represent service types and virtualized networks as presented by slices are considered in the model. In particular, a finer system modelling and performance analysis tool called network calculus has been adopted to describe the proposed model. Closed-formed formula for the upper bound delay has been deducted, which is useful for either offline wireless network planning or online virtual network admission control. Our immediate future work is to propose a scheduling algorithm based on the above QoS model. Another piece of future work is to extend the model to include other network parameters such as throughput.

References

1. Lu, X., Yang, K., Liu, Y., Zhou, D., Liu, S.: An elastic resource allocation algorithm enabling wireless network virtualization. Wiley Int. J. Wirel. Commun. Mobile Comput. (2012). doi:10.1002/wcm.2342
2. Matos, R., Marques, C., Sargento, S., et al.: Analytical modeling of context-based multi-virtual wireless mesh networks. Elsevier Int. J. Ad hoc Netw. **13**, 191–209 (2011)
3. Le Boudec, J.-Y., Thiran, P.: Network Calculus. Springer, London (2004)
4. Fidler, M.: A survey of deterministic and stochastic service curve models in the network calculus. IEEE Commun. Surv. Tutor. **12**(1), 59–86 (2010)
5. Zhang, L., Yu, J., Deng, X.: Modelling the guaranteed QoS for wireless sensor networks: a network calculus approach. EURASIP J. Wirel. Commun. Netw. **2011**, 82 (2011)

6. Chowdhury, N.M.M.K., Boutaba, R.: Network virtualization: state of the art and research challenges. IEEE Commun. Mag. **47**(7), 20–26 (2009)
7. Schaffrath,G., Werle, C., Papadimitriou,P., Feldmann, A., Bless, R., Greenhalgh, A., Wundsam, A., Kind, M., Maennel, O., Mathy, L.: Network virtualization architecture: proposal and initial prototype. In: Proceedings of ACM VISA, pp. 63–72 (2009)
8. Chowdhury, N.M.M.K., Rahman, M.R., Boutaba, R.: ViNEYard: virtual network embedding algorithms with coordinated node and link mapping. IEEE/ACM Trans. Netw. **20**(1), 206–219 (2012)
9. Kokku, R., Mahindra, R., Zhang, H., Rangarajan, S.: NVS: a substrate for virtualizing wireless resources in cellular networks. IEEE/ACM Trans. Netw. **20**(5), 1333–1346 (2012)
10. Ahn, S., Yoo, C., Network interface virtualization in wireless communication for multi-streaming service. In: International Symposium on Consumer Electronics (ISCE), pp. 67–70, June 2011
11. Tao, M., Liang, Y.C., Zhang, F.: Resource allocation for delay differentiated traffic in multiuser OFDM systems. IEEE Trans. Wirel. Commun. **7**(6), 2190–2201 (2008)
12. Hui, D.S.W., Lau, V.K.N., Wong, H.L.: Cross-layer design for OFDMA wireless systems with heterogeneous delay requirements. IEEE Trans. Wirel. Commun. **6**(8), 2872–2880 (2007)
13. Zarakovitis, C.C., Ni, Q., Skordoulis, D.E., Hadjinicolaou, M.G.: Power-efficient cross-layer design for OFDMA systems with heterogeneous QoS, imperfect CSI, and outage considerations. IEEE Trans. Veh. Technol. **61**(2), 781–798 (2012)
14. Schmitt, J.B., Zdarsky, F.A., Fidler,M.: Delay bounds under arbitrary multiplexing: when network calculus leaves you in the lurch. In: Proceedings of 27th IEEE International Conference on Computer Communications (INFOCOM'08), Phoenix, AZ, USA, April 2008
15. Bouillard, A., Jouhet, L., Thierry, E.: Tight performance bounds in the worst-case analysis of feed-forward networks. In: Proceedings of the 29th IEEE International Conference on Computer Communications (INFOCOM'10), San Diego, CA, USA, pp. 1316–1324, March 2010
16. Schmitt, J.B., Zdarsky, F.A., Thiele, L.: A comprehensive worst-case calculus for wireless sensor networks with in-network processing. In: Proceedings of the 28th IEEE International Real-Time Systems Symposium (RTSS'07), Tucson, AZ, USA, pp. 193–202, December 2007
17. Zhang, L.: Bounds on end-to-end delay jitter with self-similar input traffic in ad hoc wireless network. In: Proceedings of 2008 ISECS International Colloquium on Computing, Communication, Control, and Management (CCCM'08), Guangzhou, China, pp. 538–541, August 2008
18. Fidler, M., Sander, V.: A parameter based admission control for differentiated services networks. Comput. Netw. **44**(4), 463–479 (2004)

A Data Distribution Model for Large-Scale Context Aware Systems

Soumi Chattopadhyay[1], Ansuman Banerjee[1], and Nilanjan Banerjee[2][✉]

[1] Indian Statistical Institute, Kolkata, India
{mtc1203,ansuman}@isical.ac.in
[2] IBM Research - India, New Delhi, India
nilanjba@in.ibm.com

Abstract. Very large scale context aware systems are becoming a reality with the emerging paradigms such as machine-to-machine communications, crowdsensing, etc. Scalable data distribution is a critical requirement in such large scale systems for optimal usage of computing and communication resources. In this paper, we present a novel theoretical model for middleware design for such large-scale context aware systems that distributes only relevant data based on its *effective utility*. We also present extensive experimental results to validate the efficacy of our proposed model.

Keywords: Context-aware computing · Data distribution model

1 Introduction

We are witnessing an unprecedented instrumentation of our environment due to the rapid advancements in computing and networking technologies over the last decade. Large scale sensor network deployment, numerous devices connected over the Internet and the tremendous development and adoption of sensor enabled smartphones are enabling us to build context aware systems capturing physical contexts and interpret our personal objective world like never before. Context aware systems studied so far have been limited to small scale systems like smart homes, smart offices. Recent advances in cost, form and performance factors of computing and networking technologies are making the design and the deployment of very large scale, distributed context aware systems a reality. Machine-to-machine (M2M) or Internet of Things (IoT) is an emerging paradigm that is facilitating the development of such large scale distributed context aware systems. In M2M, powerful devices are connected to each other so that they can communicate among themselves to perform certain tasks. For example, efficient energy management is now possible with the large scale deployment of connected smart energy meters at home. Consider the following situation, where a large energy company provides a service to regulate the home temperature of its customers based on total energy load at the customer premises, the ambient temperature and the energy price. In order to provide such a service, the

© Institute for Computer Sciences, Social Informatics and Telecommunications Engineering 2014
I. Stojmenovic et al. (Eds.): MOBIQUITOUS 2013, LNICST 131, pp. 615–627, 2014.
DOI: 10.1007/978-3-319-11569-6_48

energy company collects the relevant data from various sources including the smart energy meters to derive a real-time context that determines whether to turn the air conditioners at the customer homes, on or off. Another contemporary phenomenon enabling large scale distributed context aware system is the rapid development and proliferation of smartphones equipped with sophisticated sensors. The new emerging paradigm of *crowdsensing* [1] leverages this truly pervasive, mobile sensor network of smartphones to provide a cheaper and more pervasive alternative for large scale sensor network based monitoring of physical environment. In crowdsensing, people with smartphones contribute data either voluntarily or driven by certain personal objectives or incentives. For example, in the absence of a dedicated sensor network, public authorities can monitor temperature, pollution level at a particular location by collecting the temperature and pollution data from volunteers who are carrying smartphones equipped with appropriate sensors and are present at that location.

The role of context data distribution in any such large scale distributed sensing network is very crucial to ensure the availability of the context data with the right quality, in the right place and at the right time i.e. with acceptable Quality of Context (QoC). Context data distribution consumes costly and scarce network bandwidth resource, making it a challenging task especially for very large scale distributed systems generating dynamic context data in huge volumes. Context data distribution is typically done by the context management middleware that transparently manages and routes huge volume of context data between the producers and the consumers, while ensuring the desired QoC. While different aspects of data distribution by context management middlewares have been explored in existing body of research works [2], the significant overhead of context data distribution for desired QoC that leads to system scalability and reliability issues have relatively been less explored.

In this paper, we address this particular problem of managing the overhead of context data distribution and propose a theoretical model for middleware design for large scale distributed context aware systems. Our approach stems from the observation that not all the data generated in a system is relevant for context computations and hence does not need to be distributed always, thereby saving network resources resulting in improved system resource utilization and efficiency. In our model, we propose a formal framework for the context management middleware that can identify the set of context data that is relevant to the currently defined context rules in the system for distribution, thereby reducing redundant context data dissemination. Simulation experiments show our proposed framework is capable of saving network resources significantly for very large scale systems.

Context data distribution, particularly in large-scale ubiquitous systems has been an important and fertile area of research work in the last decade or so. A comprehensive survey on the wide range of data distribution systems can be found in [2]. A number of proposals have been made to solve various issues with context data distribution in purely distributed context management systems [3] as well as in centralized context management systems [4]. The fundamental difference with this body of work on context data distribution and our proposed approach is that the prior works primarily used subscription matching in the context management middleware for efficient data dissemination, whereas our work proposes a novel approach of efficient data dissemination based on actual context data utility. In our proposed scheme, the producers disseminate only the context data that impacts the context consumed by the context-aware applications in the runtime.

2   A Motivating Example

We explain the motivation behind our work on a simple example of a monitoring system. Consider a scenario with 3 sensors, communicating with a central context management server. The first sensor records the water storage level along with the information on whether it is raining or not. The second sensor records the temperature and checks if it is favourable (in a certain range) and the third sensor measures a number of environmental parameters like CO2, chemicals, CO, hydrocarbons etc., to check if their values are within certain limits. The context management server implements the following context rules:

- *Context Rule 1:* Send a grain protection alert if any of the following holds:
    - It is raining and the water level > threshold (t_1) and the temperature is unfavourable.
    - If temperature is favourable, it is raining and water level > threshold (t_1).
    - The temperature is unfavourable and it is not raining and the water level < threshold (t_1).
    - The temperature is favourable, it is not raining and the water level < threshold (t_1).
- *Context Rule 2:* Send an air pollution alert if any of the following holds:
    - CO_2 measurement > threshold (t_4).
    - Chemical in the atmosphere > threshold (t_5).
    - Quantity of burning fossil fuels > threshold (t_6) and the emission of carbon monoxide, oxides of nitrogen, hydrocarbons and particulates > threshold (t_7).

The example presented here may appear to be non-intuitive and dry to the reader, but in reality, a general context system designer is equipped with very limited exposure to sophisticated logic and specification formalisms to be able to write context rules that are easily amenable to automated analysis. The example presented here is representative of the formal training (or lack of it) available to the designer. The context rules are usually expressed by domain experts (and not computer scientists/engineers/logicians) who model the system in natural language forms. We show here how a formal foundation can lead to remarkable efficiency in system performance as far as the transmission profile is concerned.

We now analyse the situation from the perspective of the sensors, which are entrusted with the responsibility of observing the parameters and communicating the values to the server, whenever there is a change in the value of the parameter. Values received from the sensor are used by the server to evaluate the two rules and accordingly decide the next course of action on the alert signals. We define a few Boolean variables in Table 1 to model some predicates on the sensor inputs. These predicates are used in the context rules. We also assume the sensors are able to evaluate the values of the predicates (in other words, the Boolean variables), before sending the update to the server. The sensors communicate the Boolean variables, and the server can act accordingly, since the predicate-to-Boolean map is available there as well. The communication is done using the Boolean variables, which takes fewer message bits, as opposed to transmitting the exact value of the observed sensor inputs. This could have equivalently done using some encoding scheme for the predicates directly. However, we use the Boolean encoding just for the sake of simplicity of illustration.

For the purpose of illustration, we consider random changes of the variables and depending on those changes we observe the number of transmissions. Table 2 contains a 0 or 1 depending on whether the value of the predicate (or equivalently the corresponding Boolean variable) is true or false. For example, if the water-level in the storage $>$ threshold (t_1) then the value of the Boolean variable $v_1 = 1$, otherwise $v_1 = 0$.

Table 1. Definition of the Boolean variables

v_1 : Water-level in the storage $>$ threshold (t_1)

v_2 : Raining or not

v_3 : The temperature lies between lower threshold (t_2) and upper threshold (t_3) value

v_4 : CO_2 measurement $>$ threshold (t_4)

v_5 : Chemical in the atmosphere $>$ threshold (t_5)

v_6 : Burning fossil fuels $>$ threshold (t_6)

v_7 : The emission of carbon monoxide, oxides of nitrogen, hydrocarbons and particulates $>$ threshold (t_7)

How Will Standard Transmission Methods Work? Consider a synchronous transmission scheme. In this case, each transmission involves the values of the variables, either periodically or aperiodically (when something new happens). In the case of a change-driven synchronous transmission scheme, whenever there is a change in the value of any sensor observed variable, a transmission message is triggered, with the message carrying the latest valuations of all the variables (irrespective of whether they have changed or not). Quite evidently, this is not quite an efficient dissemination scheme. For the purpose of illustration, we have considered in Table 2 a window of 10 instants, with each slot showing the valuation of each variable. In the synchronous scheme, a total of 70 (in each of the 10 slots, all the 7 variables are transmitted) transmissions are required. We now consider an asynchronous transmission scheme, i.e. transmission only occurs when there is a change and only the change is transmitted and not the entire snapshot. In this case, 57 transmissions are required as shown in Table 2.

Table 2. Random changes of variables with respect to time

Time Instant	v_1	v_2	v_3	v_4	v_5	v_6	v_7
1	1	0	0	1	0	0	1
2	0	1	1	1	1	1	0
3	1	0	0	1	0	0	1
4	0	1	1	1	1	1	0
5	1	0	0	1	0	0	1
6	0	1	1	0	1	1	0
7	1	0	0	1	1	0	1
8	0	1	1	0	1	1	1
9	1	0	0	0	0	1	1
10	0	1	1	0	1	1	1
Total changes	10	10	10	4	8	8	7

Table 3. Transmission of variables with respect to time in our method

Time Instant	v_1	v_2	v_3	$v_4 + v_5$	$v_6 \cdot v_7$
1	1	0	X	1	0
2	0	1	X	X	X
3	1	0	X	X	X
4	0	1	X	X	X
5	1	0	X	X	X
6	0	1	X	X	X
7	1	0	X	X	X
8	0	1	X	X	X
9	1	0	X	0	1
10	0	1	X	X	X
Total changes	10	10	0	2	2

Our Method at Work: If we analyse the context rules carefully, we can reduce the number of transmissions. If we observe context rule 1, we see that when it is raining and also the water level > threshold (t_1), the server sends the alert for protection of grain, irrespective of the temperature because in this case flood may occur. Again, if it is not raining and the water level < threshold (t_1), then also the server sends the alert without verifying whether the temperature is favourable or not because of the dryness in weather. Combining all the four cases, we can see the server does not need to know about the temperature for sending the protection alert. Hence, for rule 1, the sensor does not need to transmit the observations of temperature at all, since the server does not need to know about v_3 at all. Further, if we analyse the remaining two conditions [whether it is raining and whether the water level > threshold (t_1)], we see that the server sends an alert whenever both of them are true or both of them are false. So, the server changes its decision if any of them changes. Let us suppose, at a specific time instant, both of them are true. If one of them changes, the server has to change its decision. The same happens if both of them are false. Again, in the present instant, if one of them is true and the other is false and subsequently, if any of them changes, then either both of them become true or both of them become false. In this case as well, the server has to change its decision. So, knowing the values of both the variables v_1 and v_2 is *critical* to the server, since every change affects the server's decision. Our method can compute this critical set of variables in an efficient way.

If we observe the second rule, we see all the four variables are required to send the air pollution alert. However, as long as the CO_2 measurement > threshold (t_4), without knowing the status of the other three variables, the server can send the air pollution alert. The same happens if the chemical in the atmosphere > threshold (t_5). If the quantity of burning fossil fuels < threshold (t_6), the status of the emission of carbon monoxide, oxides of nitrogen, hydrocarbons and particulates does not affect the server's decision. However, if both the predicates are true at the same time instant, the server sends an air pollution alert irrespective of the status of the CO_2 measure and the chemical in the atmosphere. These observations lead to further reduction in the number of transmissions.

It is also possible to reduce the transmission by analysing the sensor's observations at the current snapshot. We can see that the 3rd sensor observes CO_2 measurement and Chemical in the atmosphere. If any of the predicates v_4 and v_5 is true, the server sends an air pollution alert. Hence, instead of sending the individual status of these predicates, the sensor can send true if either of them is true and false if none of them are true. The server does not need to know exactly which of the predicates is actually true. This saves message bits.

Based on the above observations, we define the *effective utility* of a sensor input, based on the relevance of transmission of the predicates appearing in the context rules. With our proposed optimizations, 24 transmissions are required. The transmissions are described in Table 3, where each cell entry denotes the value transmitted to the server (X indicates no transmission). In this work, we put forward a formal framework for reducing the number of update transmissions, thereby, contributing to the overall objective of sensor network design.

3   Detailed Methodology

We consider the following simple system setting in this work.

- A set of n distributed sensors, with no communication among themselves.
- Each sensor observes a set of environment parameters, in their sensing zone. The parameters can be of arbitrary data type. We further assume the sensing zones to be unique, in other words, no parameter is observed by more than one sensor. We assume this for simplicity of analysis.
- The sensors communicate with a central server S via message passing.
- The server S has a set of context-triggered actions.

At the server end, before the network is initialized, the server pre-processes the context rules using our method and communicates to the sensors, which observations are needed and at what instants. The overall objective of our scheme is to save the sensors from needless transmissions. Based on the values received from the sensors, the server evaluates the context-triggered actions and takes necessary steps. At the sensor end, the necessary set of predicates at the appropriate instants (as communicated to them by the server) are evaluated based on the observed values, and transmitted if needed. We illustrate our proposal in the following subsections. We begin with the definition of a data predicate.

Definition 1. Data Predicate: *A data predicate is an expression of the form* $< lexp > \bowtie < rexp >$, *where* $\bowtie \in \{=, \neq, <=, >=, <, >\}$, $< lexp >$ *and* $< rexp >$ *are data variables (e.g. temperature, humidity, CO_2 level etc.) or constants.* □

Given a valuation to its variables, a data predicate evaluates to *true* or *false*. Sensors transmit the Boolean values of relevant data predicates to the server.

Example 1. Consider a variable u which denotes the temperature of the system. A data predicate $\mathcal{P}$ is defined as: $\mathcal{P} : u < 20\,°C$. If the temperature is less than $20\,°C$ at any instant, $\mathcal{P}$ is evaluated as true, else it is false.   □

Definition 2. Context-Triggered Action: *A context action is an expression of the form Rule: Action, where Rule is a Boolean combination (using Boolean operators) of data predicates over data variables and Action is the resulting actuation performed by the server.* □

The intuitive semantics of a context-triggered action is as follows: the *Action* will be executed only if the variable values at the current snapshot makes the *Rule* evaluate to *true*. For the sake of simplicity, we assume that the rule base is free from contradiction, if not, a consistency check does the job.

Example 2. Following is an example context triggered action: Context Rule: Room temperature $> 20\,°C$ *and* AC is off. Action: Server turns on AC. □

3.1 Transmission Control Mechanism

We now explain the optimizations in message transmission proposed in this paper. We begin with a few definitions, which help us build the foundations of our analysis framework. We refer to the data predicates appearing in the context rules using Boolean variables with the obvious interpretation (the predicate-variable map in Table 1) as in Sect. 2. In the following discussion, we use the term variable to mean a Boolean variable, which stands for a Boolean-valued predicate defined over the sensor-observed variable (arbitrary type).

Definition 3. Co-factor: *The positive (negative) co-factor of a context rule C defined over a set of Boolean variables $V = \{v_1, v_2, \ldots v_n\}$ with respect to a variable $v_i \in V$ is obtained by substituting 1 (true) or 0 (false) in C.* □

The positive co-factor, denoted by C_{v_i} is obtained as $C_{v_i} = C(v_1, v_2, \ldots, v_i = 1, \ldots, v_n)$. Similarly, the negative co-factor, denoted as $C_{\bar{v}_i}$ is obtained as $C(v_1, v_2, \ldots, v_i = 0, \ldots, v_n)$. We now define the concept of decomposition of a context rule. This follows as a straightforward application of Shannon's expansion of Boolean functions [5]. The co-factors are independent of the variable v_i with respect to which they are computed.

Definition 4. Context Rule Decomposition: *The decomposition of a context rule C with respect to a variable $v \in V$ is obtained as: $C = v.C_v + \bar{v}.C_{\bar{v}}$, where C_v and $C_{\bar{v}}$ are respectively the positive and negative cofactors of C with respect to v.* □

Example 3. Consider a context rule $C = v_4 + v_5 + v_6.v_7$. The positive co-factor of C with respect to v_4 is $1 + v_5 + v_6.v_7 = 1$. The negative co-factor is $0 + v_5 + v_6.v_7 = v_5 + v_6.v_7$. The decomposition of C with respect to v_4 is $C = v_4.C_{v_4} + \bar{v}_4.C_{\bar{v}_4}$. $= v_4.1 + \bar{v}_4.(v_5 + v_6.v_7) = v_4 + v_5 + v_6.v_7$. □

Optimizations Based on Co-factors: We begin our proposal of reducing message transmissions with a simple observation in terms of co-factors. Consider, the current value of $v = 1$ for some variable $v \in \mathcal{V}$ and also consider for some context rule $\mathcal{C}$, $\mathcal{C}_v = f(v_{i_1}, \ldots, v_{i_l})$. In this case, to evaluate $\mathcal{C}$, the server does not need to know the status of the variables in $\mathcal{V} \setminus \{\{v_{i_1}, \ldots, v_{i_l}\} \bigcup \{v\}\}$ until v gets changed, where $\setminus$ is the set difference operation. So, the sensor does not transmit the status of those variables to the server accordingly. In the special case, when $\mathcal{C}_v$ or $\mathcal{C}_{\bar{v}}$ equals to a constant, i.e. 0 or 1, that means the change of the state of other variables are not reflected in $\mathcal{C}$ as long as the state of v remains same. So to evaluate $\mathcal{C}$, the server does not need the status of any other variable other than v until it changes. Hence, the sensor can keep on observing v, but transmit only when it changes. At the initialization stage, the server analyses the context rules and gathers the set of variables whose positive or negative co-factors evaluate to a constant. This information is passed on to the sensors, and the sensor precisely knows when to transmit the valuations of the other variables it observes. Depending on the current snapshot, the server informs the sensors which variables are required.

Example 4. Consider Context rule 2 in Sect. 2. We analyze the context rule in the following way: $\mathcal{C}(v_4, v_5, v_6, v_7) = v_4 + v_5 + v_6.v_7$, then positive co-factor of $\mathcal{C}$ w.r.t. v_4, $\mathcal{C}_{v_4} = 1 + v_5 + v_6.v_7 = 1$, negative co-factor of $\mathcal{C}$ w.r.t. v_4, $\mathcal{C}_{\bar{v}_4} = 0 + v_5 + v_6.v_7 = v_5 + v_6.v_7$. So, when $v_4 = 1$, the server does not require to know the status of v_5, v_6, v_7 until v_4 becomes 0. The same happens for v_5: as long as $v_5 = 1$, the server does not need any information about v_4, v_6, v_7. □

Context rule decomposition can be extended to multiple variables as well. The decomposition of a context rule $\mathcal{C}$ with respect to two variables $u, v \in \mathcal{V}$ is obtained as: $\mathcal{C} = uv.\mathcal{C}_{uv} + u\bar{v}\mathcal{C}_{u\bar{v}} + \bar{u}v.\mathcal{C}_{\bar{u}v} + \bar{u}\bar{v}\mathcal{C}_{\bar{u}\bar{v}}$, where, $\mathcal{C}_{uv}$, $\mathcal{C}_{u\bar{v}}$, $\mathcal{C}_{\bar{u}v}$, $\mathcal{C}_{\bar{u}\bar{v}}$ are Shannon co-factors with respect to multiple variables. The co-factors are obtained as follows: $\mathcal{C}_{uv}$ by substituting the value of $u = 1$ and $v = 1$ in $\mathcal{C}$, $\mathcal{C}_{u\bar{v}}$ by substituting the value of $u = 1$ and $v = 0$ in $\mathcal{C}$, $\mathcal{C}_{\bar{u}v}$ by substituting the value of $u = 0$ and $v = 1$ and $\mathcal{C}_{\bar{u}\bar{v}}$ by substituting the value of $u = 0$ and $v = 0$.

In certain cases, co-factor analysis involving multiple variables helps us reduce the transmission. But in this case, if we want to analyze the co-factors for a context rule defined over a set $\mathcal{V}$ of n variables, we have in all an exponential number (2^n) of combinations, considering all subsets of all cardinalities of $\mathcal{V}$. In our work, we restrict ourselves to two variable co-factor analysis. Again, instead of looking at all the variables in the variable set $\mathcal{V}$ for *multiple variable co-factor analysis*, we can even concentrate on a smaller set, containing the variables whose positive and negative co-factors are not constant.

Example 5. Consider context rule 2 in Example 1 and the current snapshot $v_4 = 0, v_5 = 0, v_6 = 1, v_7 = 1$. According to *single variable co-factor analysis*, the sensor needs to transmit the status of all the four variables, since none of the co-factors are constant. *Multiple variable co-factor analysis* reveals that $\mathcal{C}_{v_6 v_7} = v_4 + v_5 + 1.1 = 1$. So as long as v_6 and v_7 remain 1, the server does not need the information of v_4 and v_5. But if any of them changes, the server requires the information of v_4 and v_5. □

For each context rule, we first analyze single variable co-factor and create a decision table which contains two fields: the value of the variable and depending on that value of the variable which variables are not required to evaluate the context rule. This is followed by a two variable co-factor analysis using the variables whose positive and negative co-factors are not constant. If the set contains v number of variables, then we have $\binom{v}{2}$ many combinations, and for each combination, there exists four different values (corresponding to the four co-factors). The results of the two variables co-factor analysis is stored in the decision table in the same format.

Optimizations Based on Unateness Analysis: We define a few more concepts that further reduce the number of transmissions.

Definition 5. Unateness: *A context rule C is positive unate in v_i if changing the value of v_i from 0 to 1 keeps C constant or changes C from 0 to 1.*   □

$$C(v_1, v_2, \ldots, v_{(i-1)}, 1, v_{(i+1)}, \ldots, v_m) \geq C(v_1, v_2, \ldots, v_{(i-1)}, 0, v_{(i+1)}, \ldots, v_m).$$
Negative unateness is defined similarly.

The unateness criterion leads to an interesting observation. If for every v_i, C is either positive or negative unate in v_i, then C is said to be unate function otherwise C is called binate function. Suppose a context rule C is evaluated to 1 at some point of time according to the current snapshot. *Then the value of C does not change with the change of all those variables whose current value is 0 and in which C is positive unate.* In other words, these variables are not needed to be transmitted. As earlier, the server decides on these conditions in the pre-processing stage and informs the sensor about its transmission requirements.

Example 6. Consider one context rule $C = v_1.v_2.v_3.v_4 + v_5.v_6 + v_7$. Also consider the current snapshot ($v_1 = 1, v_2 = 1, v_3 = 1, v_4 = 1, v_5 = 0, v_6 = 0, v_7 = 0$), and according to this snapshot C evaluates to true. We can see that C is positive unate in $\{v_1, \ldots, v_7\}$. So as long as C remains 1, the change of all the variables whose current value is 0, i.e. $\{v_5, v_6, v_7\}$, does not affect the value of C. Accordingly the sensors are informed not to transmit these variables.

It is interesting to note that unate analysis takes care of the situation where co-factor analysis with respect to more than two variables are involved.

Optimizations Based on Effective Utility: Analyzing the criticality of a variable with respect to a context rule leads to further reductions. It is important to know which of the variables in the rule can actually influence the evaluation result of the rule. This is the effective utility of the variable with respect to the context rule. There may be some variables whose changes are not reflected in the context rule at all and there may be some variables for whom every change is crucial for the evaluation of the context rule. This is handled using *derivative analysis*.

Definition 6. Derivative: *The derivative of a context rule C with respect to a variable v_i is defined as the exclusive-or of the positive and negative co-factors of C with respect to the variable v_i, $\partial C / \partial v_i = C_{v_i} \oplus C_{\bar{v}_i}$.*   □

The intuitive idea is as follows. v_i can only change from 0 to 1 or 1 to 0. Consider the present value of v_i as 1, then $C = (1.C_{v_i} + 0.C_{\bar{v}_i}) = C_{v_i}$. When the value of v_i changes to 0, $C = (0.C_{v_i} + 1.C_{\bar{v}_i}) = C_{\bar{v}_i}$. C changes with change in v_i if the values of the positive and negative co-factors are different. This is expressed using $C_{v_i} \oplus C_{\bar{v}_i}$. Hence, $\partial C / \partial v_i$ denotes the change of the context rule C with respect to the variable v_i.

Analyzing the derivative leads us to interesting observations as below.

- $C_{v_i} \oplus C_{\bar{v}_i} = 0$, implies C is independent of v_i. This is because $C_{v_i} = C_{\bar{v}_i}$, hence C is not be affected with change in v_i. This means that the sensor does not need to send the status of v_i to the server at any time.
- $C_{v_i} \oplus C_{\bar{v}_i} = 1$, implies the variable v_i is *critical* to the server since every change in v_i is reflected in the context rule C. Hence, all updates to a critical variable have to be transmitted to the server.
- $C_{v_i} \oplus C_{\bar{v}_i} = g(v_1, v_2, \ldots, v_{i-1}, v_{i+1}, \ldots, v_m)$, implies g is free from v_i. In this case, the server requires to know the status of v_i at least once.

Example 7. Consider the first context rule in Sect. 2. We can analyze the context rule in the following way: $C(v_1, v_2, v_3) = v_1.v_2.\bar{v}_3 + v_1.v_2.v_3 + \bar{v}_1.\bar{v}_2.\bar{v}_3 + \bar{v}_1.\bar{v}_2.v_3$. The derivative of C w.r.t. v_3, $\partial C / \partial v_3 = C_{v_3} \oplus C_{\bar{v}_3} = 0$, Since no change of v_3 is reflected in C, the server does not require to know the status of v_3 at all. Consider the derivative of C with respect to v_1 and v_2, $\partial C / \partial v_1 = C_{v_1} \oplus C_{\bar{v}_1} = 1$; $\partial C / \partial v_2 = C_{v_2} \oplus C_{\bar{v}_2} = 1$, so all the changes of v_1 and v_2 are reflected in C. Therefore, the server requires to know every change of v_1, v_2.   □

Optimizations Based on Sensor's Data Analysis: The number of transmissions can be reduced further by analyzing the sensor's data in the current snapshot. Instead of sending the individual value of all variables, it can merge the value of some variables either by ANDing or by ORing, depending on the context. The variables sent by a sensor should have the following properties:

- The derivative of the variables with respect to some context rule must not be constant.
- Either all of them are part of a context rule or none of them are part of a context rule.
- One of the co-factors of each variables is constant.
  - If either of the co-factors of the variables is 1, then instead of sending their individual value sensor can send only one value by ORing them.
  - If either of the co-factors of the variables is 0, then instead of sending their individual value, sensor can send only one value by ANDing them.

Example 8. Consider the second context rule in the previous example. If a sensor needs to send the status of v_4 and v_5, then instead of sending their individual values, it is better to send the value of $v_4 + v_5$, because the context rule is true if any one of them is true and if both of them are false then the decision of the context rule depends on the value of v_6, v_7.   □

4   Putting Everything Together

We are given a set C of context rules over a set of Boolean predicates encoded as Boolean variables V. The server performs the following pre-processing steps.

- Step 1: The server performs derivative analysis. $V_1 = \{v \in V \text{ such that } \partial c/\partial v = 1, \exists c \in C\}$, $V_2 = \{v \in V \text{ such that } \partial c/\partial v = 0, \forall c \in C\}$; Based on the result, the server informs the sensors to stop monitoring the data variables corresponding to the data predicates belonging to V_2 and also to transmit all changes of the data predicates belonging to V_1.
- Step 2: Evaluates the positive and negative co-factors of all context rules with respect to each variable belonging to $(V \setminus V_2)$ in the cases where $\partial c/\partial v \neq 1$.
- Step 3: Analysis of the two variable co-factors for each context rule C using the set of variables such that C_v and $C_{\bar{v}}$ are not constant for all v in that variable set.
- Step 4: Sensor Data Analysis: (variables belonging to $V_3 = (V \setminus (V_1 \cup V_2)))$, the server can instruct the sensor which variables can be transmitted by ORing or ANDing. Let the new set be V_4, where some variables belonging to V_3 are combined into one. Though they are different data variables while observing, they are combined while transmitting.
- Step 5: For each context rule(C), find two sets of variables in which the context rule is positive and negative unate, such that $\forall v$ belong to that sets $\partial c/\partial v$ is not equal to constant.

The following are the execution time computations:

- Find the set of variables (V_c) to evaluate each context rule (C) depending on the current snapshot. Then the server informs the appropriate sensors to stop transmitting variables belonging to $V_3 \setminus (\cup_{c \in C} V_c)$.

5   Implementation and Results

We implemented the proposed framework in Java. We tested our method on two published context system descriptions (entries 5 and 12 of Table 4 corresponding to the descriptions in [6,7]) and random environments, where the number of variables, the context rules and the number of sensors and their observation sets were randomly generated. The results are shown in Table 4. We have compared our method with the asynchronous transmission scheme with respect to the number of transmissions. A graphical view of the comparative transmission numbers is shown in Table 5, showing the transmissions in usual case denoted by red line and the number of transmissions in our case denoted by the blue line, with increase in the number of variables (horizontal axis).

Table 4. Test-case statistics

No. of variables	No. of formulas	No. of sensors	Avg. observation of sensors	Tx in usual case	Tx in our case
3	1	1	3	24	14
4	3	2	2	26	21
6	1	2	3	52	29
6	9	2	3	51	30
6	1	1	6	49	9
8	8	3	3	65	35
9	5	3	3	62	34
10	15	3	3	80	27
12	19	4	3	100	20
15	10	7	2	131	46
16	3	8	2	120	23
16	5	3	5	129	35
19	5	5	4	134	40
26	29	12	2	213	68
26	140	13	2	206	159
33	15	10	3	251	79
37	19	12	3	296	81
38	48	20	2	301	104
39	11	20	2	303	84
51	8	16	3	408	79
58	29	6	9	458	123
60	44	8	8	489	117
74	40	20	4	566	209
90	68	24	4	728	289
100	138	38	3	836	341
109	80	33	3	887	366
182	48	4	50	1478	429
357	1022	2	150	2898	1972
624	143	11	57	4949	956
845	93	6	141	6727	959
858	22	6	143	6815	297
885	14	4	227	6961	187
1065	183	2	523	8495	1717
1070	148	15	72	8550	1689
1110	97	4	278	8888	1259
1119	64	19	59	8862	767
1358	116	17	80	10964	1614
1414	20	7	202	11385	284
1614	110	13	124	12856	1423
1670	136	14	120	13216	1537
1783	99	19	94	14256	1367

Table 5. Number of variables Vs Transmission of variables

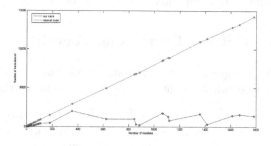

6   Conclusion

In this paper, we have proposed a new scheme for data dissemination in a large-scale context aware system. Experimental results show promising improvements in the number of transmissions. With context aware systems gaining widespread popularity in recent times, we believe our work will have interesting applications. We are currently working on generic data types and predicates and more complex context rules for more realistic applications of this work.

References

1. Ganti, R.K., Ye, F., Lei, H.: Mobile crowdsensing: current state and future challenges. IEEE Commun. Mag. **49**, 32–39 (2011)
2. Bellavista, P., Corradi, A., Fanelli, M., Foschini, L.: A survey of context data distribution for mobile ubiquitous systems. ACM Comput. Surv. **44**, 1–45 (2012)
3. Macedo, D.F., Santos, A.L.D., Nogueira, J.M.S., Pujolle, G.: A distributed information repository for autonomic context-aware MANETs. IEEE Trans. Netw. Serv. Manag. **6**, 45–55 (2009)
4. Li, F., Sanjin, S., Schahram, S.: COPAL: an adaptive approach to context provisioning. In: Proceedings of the IEEE 6th International Conference on Wireless and Mobile Computing, Networking, and Communications (WiMob10), pp. 286–293 (2010)
5. Hachtel, G.D., Somenzi, F.: Logic Synthesis and Verification Algorithms, 1st edn. Kluwer Academic Publishers, Norwell (2000)

6. Yao, W., et al.: Using ontology to support context awareness in healthcare. In: Proceedings of the 19th Workshop on Information Technologies and Systems (2009)
7. Wang, X.H., et al.: Ontology based context modeling and reasoning using OWL. In: Proceedings of the Second IEEE Annual Conference on Pervasive Computing and Communications Workshops, pp. 18–22 (2004)

EduBay: A Mobile-Based, Location-Aware Content Sharing Platform

Amit M. Mohan[1], Prasenjit Dey[2(✉)], and Nitendra Rajput[3]

[1] Department of Computer Science,
University of Illinois, Urbana-Champaign, IL, USA
muralim2@illinois.edu
[2] IBM Research India, G2, Manyata Tech Park,
Bangalore 560043, India
prasenjit.dey@in.ibm.com
[3] IBM Research India, 4 Block C, Institutional Area, Vasant Kunj,
New Delhi 110070, India
rnitendra@in.ibm.com

Abstract. Most natural sciences streams (zoology, botany, anthropology, agriculture etc.) require collecting a lot of artifacts from natural environments to understand their properties such as shape, size and appearance. Currently this is done through what are called "field trips" where students and researchers go to different places and collect/study specimens from that unique habitat. These field trips are mostly very notional since logistically and monetarily they are not very scalable. The interesting locations for field trips may also be quite far and remote from the current user location. We present in this work a location based content brokering platform EduBay where we bring together the *creators* of content (researchers, students or local people who get photographs, videos of the specimens; audio such as bird sounds etc.) and the *consumers* of the content (fellow students and researchers who need these artifacts for their studies). EduBay is built around the mobile platform since collecting audio, video, or photographs from natural surroundings can leverage the camera, microphone, and other sensors on the mobile device. The platform strongly leverages the location sensor on the mobile device to connect a content to its creation location since most of these interesting artifacts can sometimes be found only in some unique locations. The platform presents interesting location centric views to the creator as well as to the consumer for easy discoverability and searching of the content. The platform also provides a mechanism to validate new content or ascertain the value of a content using peer group crowdsourcing. To keep the creation and consumption of the content under balance, the platform keeps check on the creation and consumption behavior of each user and incentivizes them to create good content as much as they consume them.

Keywords: Mobile · Social · Brokering platform · Location based · Images · Audio · Video · Natural sciences · Crowdsourcing · Incentive mechanisms

1 Introduction

Most natural sciences streams (zoology, botany, anthropology, agriculture etc.) require collecting a lot of artifacts from natural environments to understand their shape, size,

© Institute for Computer Sciences, Social Informatics and Telecommunications Engineering 2014
I. Stojmenovic et al. (Eds.): MOBIQUITOUS 2013, LNICST 131, pp. 628–639, 2014.
DOI: 10.1007/978-3-319-11569-6_49

appearance, properties etc. Currently this is done through what are called "field trips" where students and researchers go to different places and collect/study specimens from that unique habitat. These field trips are mostly very notional since logistically and monetarily they are not very scalable. These interesting locations for field trips may also be quite far and remote from the current user location. We present in this work a location based content brokering platform EduBay where we bring together the *creators* of content and the *consumers* of the content. The *creators* of the content can be people who are fellow students or researchers from a location trying to help peer community and earn download credits (described later) for EduBay. It could also be people who are local residents for whom incentives could be in form of monetary benefits such as mobile credits, coupons etc. The content could be specimen photographs (flowers in bloom in a particular season, rare fern species), animal behavior video, audio of bird and animal sounds etc. The consumers of content would mostly be the peer community of students and researchers who are in need of the content. EduBay is built around the mobile platform since collecting audio, video, or photographs from natural surroundings can leverage the camera and microphone sensors on the mobile device. With the help of a mobile device the creator of the content can easily record a video, audio, or photograph of an artifact from the natural environment (without having to disturb or capture it) and upload it to the EduBay platform immediately from the content capture location. This provides a more hassle-free and seamless experience to the content creator who may not be very tech savvy. The platform also strongly leverages the location sensor on the mobile device to connect a content to its creation location since most of these interesting artifacts can sometimes be found only in some unique locations. For example reindeers are found only in the Nordic region or the birds of paradise are mostly found near Papua New Guinea. The platform presents interesting location centric views to the creator as well as to the consumer for easy discoverability and searching of the content.

The EduBay platform provides following unique features to the user:

(1) Seamless Content Creation: Tight integration of camera with the EduBay mobile application so that capture and upload of content to EduBay is seamless.
(2) Easy Discoverability and Search: Location centric views of content on the EduBay mobile application so that the consumer can easily browse through the map and find the content specific to a region.
(3) Request for Content: The consumer can put in a request for some content from a particular location and the creators from that location get notified of the request which they can help fulfill.
(4) Crowdsourced Verification: Not all uploaded content and its metadata may be of good quality. Users can express their vote for a content to verify how good/bad the content quality is.
(5) Fair Usage Policy: To ensure that users also create content as much as they consume them, we have a fair usage policy which allows consumption of content only if there is a reasonable instances of content creation by a user.

The EduBay platform has a creator and consumer application which enables the various functionalities for the roles different users are performing at different times. The content and the metadata are stored in a backend EduBay server consisting of an

Apache web server and a MySQL database. The EduBay mobile application is built on Android platform and the backend server programming is using PHP scripts.

The paper is organized as follows. We review some of the related work on content brokering platform (Sect. 2). We then describe the three components of the mobile client platform – content creation, content verification and content access (Sect. 3). The server piece of the EduBay platform is then described (Sect. 4) which presents the different databases and communication details between the client and the different servers. We conclude the paper with summary, discussions on the potential use cases and some technical next steps.

2   Related Work

The area of crowdsourcing for data collection and crowdsourced verification of the data has recently been a very active area of interest. The interest stems from the availability of more ubiquitous access to internet through mobile devices from which such data can be crowdsourced, and the ability to do small amount of computation during "dead time" while on the move.

Prominent among these are citizen science projects such as SETI Live [1] and Galaxy Zoo [2]. SETI Live provides a platform to harness the power of human computation for detecting interesting signals from outer space which may have help discover extra-terrestrial life beyond our planet. GalaxyZoo initiative helps classify different morphological aspects of galaxy images using the power of crowdsourcing which ultimately helps in the discovery of new galaxies.

There are also some new breed of mobile apps that are coming up which help in crowdsourcing environmental data from different locations through mobile devices. The data could be about the pressure, temperature, noise pollution etc. The mPING project [3] from National Oceanic and Atmospheric Administration helps collect precipitation data from citizens using a mobile application. The data is then presented on a map and further analysis can be done on severe data that are reported from a particular region. The pressureNET app [4] helps collect barometric pressure data from citizens which can then be used to predict very localized weather patterns. [5] uses a smartphone app to crowdsource noise pollution data from urban environments. These collected data can then be used for further modeling and prediction at a much higher level of granularity which are currently not possible with limited scale sensors that are deployed for collecting such data.

Using crowdsourcing to create content for mapping and their semantics has also gained interest. Sueda et al. [6] proposes a platform for crowdsourcing user generated content for knowing locations and addresses which may not be in the formal names of places on map by using geotagged Flickr images. Leveraging the mobile device's magnetometer and the accelerometer to crowdsource indoor map content of a building is discussed in [7]. The mCrowd [8] provides a platform to easily setup data collection experiments using mobile devices for different types of content.

The next breed of apps that are starting to appear and are most relevant to our work are the ones which help a peer community to collect data in natural sciences such as botany, zoology, ornithology, flora and fauna of a place, wildlife etc. [9] uses semantic web technology to organize the metadata and establish cause-effect relationship between different species. It uses a Firefox plugin to crowdsource peer community data and tag observation of species in different locations. This data can then be used to understand what species can cause an un-observed effect to other species in the environment. A very recent interesting initiative by Indian Institute of Science named Pakshi [10] uses a location based mobile app to crowdsource data of different bird species and then shows it as a visualization on the map for the peer community to understand the sightings of different species at different locations.

Our work goes a step further than Pakshi which is primarily a crowdsourced data collection and visualization mechanism. EduBay is a mobile centric location based social learning platform. It provides following functionalities:

- Crowdsourced specimen data from peer-community using mobile sensors
- Location based data creation and visualization
- Connect the content creators and consumers for on-demand content creation
- Crowdsourced verification mechanism of data on EduBay platform
- Fair usage policy mechanism for content creation and content consumption for incentivizing new data creation.

EduBay thus has a strong differentiation with respect to other platforms in terms of seamless integration of mobile device sensors for content creation, on-demand content creation for content that may be rare by connecting the creators and consumers (who need the content), crowdsourced verification mechanism to make sure the data is of good quality, and a fair usage policy mechanism to incentivize new content creation.

3 EduBay Client Applications

The EduBay platform consists of Android applications and a backend database server. In this section, we describe the features on the mobile client device. The user can create content in form of images, video and audio in the Android application and attach explicit meta-data along with the content. Some implicit metadata such as location (GPS), weather for the location, time of the year (date) etc. are captured automatically. The meta-data is stored in a MySQL database and the media (audio, video, ad images) is stored in a filestore, the pointer to which is stored in the database along with the meta-data. The application server is an Apache server. The architecture of the EduBay platform will be described in more detail in Sect. 4. We will now describe the different functionalities of EduBay that are delivered to the user through the Android application.

The Android application has two views:

- The Consumer Application: The EduBay Consumer app (will use app as short form for application hereon) delivers all the functionalities that are required by a user who is trying to get some content from EduBay. It provides functionalities such as search, browse, putting in a request etc. This part of the app will be described in more detail in Sect. 3.1.

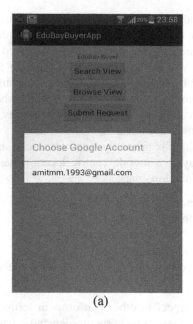

(a)   (b)

Fig. 1. Screenshots of the app showing (a) the app picking the email ID of the user from phone registry to track user operations; (b) search view to search with explicit meta-data.

- The Creator Application: The EduBay Creator app delivers all the functionalities that may be needed by a user trying to create some content for EduBay. It has tight integration with the mobile device camera to capture images, audio, video from the natural surroundings and immediately upload the content along with the metadata to the EduBay server. This part of the app will be described in more detail in Sect. 3.2.

When a user opens any of the views of the app, the app asks the user to confirm an email ID picked from the phone registry to attach an ID to the user. This is as shown in Fig. 1(a). This is useful in knowing which user created the content, verification of the content, and maintaining a fair usage policy for creation and consumption of content. These will be described in the following sections.

3.1 Consumer View

The consumer view of the app consists of three different functionalities. It allows the user to look for content in EduBay using explicit search or browse by location. If the user cannot find a content he/she is looking for, they can leave request for the content from a particular location on the EduBay platform. When creators from that particular location open their app they will see the request for content notification which they can fulfil. This is an unique location based feature of EduBay. When a user opens the consumer app, they see the following functionalities:

Search View: In this functionality, the user is presented with a form where they can fill-in the metadata details of the content they are looking for (if they know exactly the details of the content they are looking for) and search for the content. If they content is present in the EduBay platform, the user is presented with a link to download the content from the filestore. The user can click on those links and get the content on their mobile device. The view is as shown on Fig. 1(b).

Browse View: In this functionality, the user is presented with the content information present in the platform on a map. The user can quickly browse to a location where they think habitat of the content is and look for it. The user makes a "long-press" on the map location and all the content in vicinity of the location is fetched from EduBay. For example if someone is looking for a content about reindeer, they can directly browse to the Nordic region of the map and tap on that location and look for the content there. The view is as shown in Fig. 2(a). Once the content is found, the user can again tap on the information view markers and the content is downloaded on the device.

Request for Content: This is an unique feature of EduBay's location based services. If the user cannot find the content they are looking for, they can leave a request for other creators to get the content into the platform. The user can go to a location on the map from where they would like to get some content and "long-press" on the particular location. This opens up a meta-data form which the user can fill up and submit. Some of the meta-data such as the requester location, identity, etc. are prefilled. This content request with the metadata gets associated with the location and the users from that location can see it when they open the creator view of the app. They can choose to ignore or service the request. Once the request is fulfilled, the content goes to the main

(a)   (b)

Fig. 2. Screenshots of the app showing (a) the view to browse artefacts by location; (b) request for content by location that are not found on EduBay are notified to creators of that location.

EduBay database and gets deleted from the content-request database. This unique feature can be very useful for content on the long-tail for which not many creators may upload content into EduBay. The view is shown in Fig. 2(b).

3.2   Creator View

The creator view of the app provides all the functionalities that are required by a content creator. This includes seamless use of the camera to capture audio, video, images with the app and upload it immediately to the EduBay platform. It also allows to see content-request notifications for the current user location. The consumer app has following functionalities:

Create Content: When the user presses on this button, it opens the camera of the mobile device with which the user can capture image, video, or audio. Once the user has finished the capture the app shows the capture and asks for a confirmation whether the user would like to discard and re-capture or accept the current capture. Once accepted, the media is sent to the file store and a random number string for the file name and the location is returned to the app. The user is then presented with a form where they can fill up the content metadata. Implicit meta-data such as GPS location, and filestore media location, user identity (available from initial authentication as described above) are automatically filled. The user submits the form and the data is stored in the EduBay server. The app view is as shown in Fig. 3.

Service a Request for Content: In this functionality the user can see all the current request-for-content for the present creator location on a map as described in Sect. 3.1. The user can browse through the requests and if they would like to fulfil some request, they can tap on the marker which open up the camera and the user can follow the same steps as described in the content creation functionality above. The view is as shown in Fig. 4. Once the request is fulfilled, it is removed from request database and put in the main EduBay database, and the marker on the map disappears from the request notifications.

3.3   Crowdsourced Verification

The content that is created may not be always be of good quality. In EduBay platform we provide a way for the peer community to vote for the quality of the content. When a content is created, it is always available for viewing or download by the users from the Consumer View of the app. When users download a content, they are presented with a view of the content and its meta-data. The user has a way to vote "Like" and "Dislike" for the content. If a content receives more than 10 dislikes, the content is removed from the EduBay platform. In order to have a fair verification of the content, if a user tries to vote for his/her own uploaded content, the vote does not get counted. The identity of the user who is voting is established from the embedded identity of the user in the app which was given by the user when the app was first used, as was described earlier. A screenshot of the voting screen is as shown in Fig. 5.

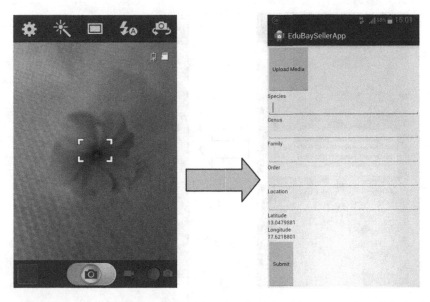

Fig. 3. Screenshots showing the process of capture of media and the entry of explicit meta-data to the media. Note that implicit meta-data such geo-location has been automatically filled once the media is captured.

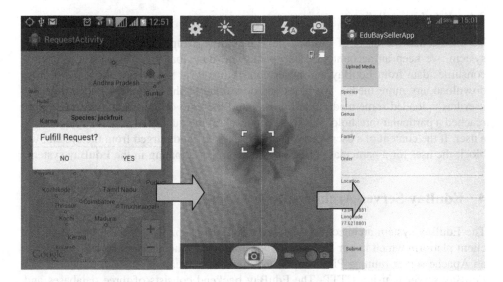

Fig. 4. Screenshots showing the process of fulfilling a content request. The content creator agrees to fulfil request from their current location which when accepted opens the camera and then bring up the form to attach explicit meta-data. As before implicit meta-data is automatically filled.

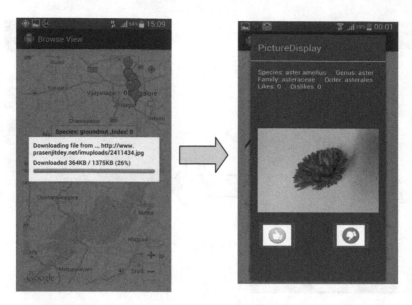

Fig. 5. Screenshots showing the crowdsourced verification process in EduBay. When the media is downloaded by a user they can "like" or "dislike" a content. A content with too many dislikes is purged from the system.

3.4 Fair Usage Policy

To ensure that the users of EduBay have incentive to upload good content into the system, we keep an account of each upload and download by a user. If a user only consumes data from EduBay and never contributes to it, we do not allow the user to download any more media. We block the download of the media until such time the user has uploaded some media into EduBay and the ratio of upload and download has reached a particular threshold. We also keep track of the quality of content uploaded by a user. If the content of a user is consistently "disliked" and purged from the system, we block the user for a particular period of time from participating in the EduBay system.

4   EduBay Server Architecture

The EduBay system architecture is as described in Fig. 6. The system consists of the client platform which in our case is an Android device. The backend EduBay Server is an Apache server running PHP scripts. All the communication between the client and EduBay server is using HTTP. The EduBay backend consists of three databases and one media store. All the databases are MySQL databases and the Media Store is a flat file server. The components are:

- *EduBay Meta-Data DB:* This is the main database which store all the media meta-data created by the user and also the implicit metadata such as location, time, user, media file location etc.

- *Content Request DB:* This stores the content-requests as described in Sect. 3.1. Once a request is fulfilled, the particular entry is removed from the database and transferred to the EduBay Meta-Data DB.
- *User Account DB:* This stores all the details about each user such as number of uploads and downloads, number of purged data due from the system due to dislikes etc.
- *Media Store:* This stores all the media files such as images, audio, video, or any other file. When file is uploaded into the Media Store, the original name is removed and a seven digit random number generated name is attached to it to avoid name clashes. This name is then passed to as reference in the main EduBay meta-data database.

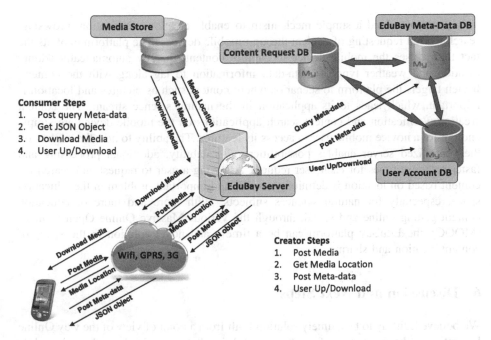

Fig. 6. The EduBay architecture where the creator and the consumer have different steps to follow for interacting with EduBay platform.

When a *creator* captures a media and wants to transfer it to EduBay, the Android application first transfers the media file to the Media Store and receives a seven digit random number generated name for the file and its location. The user then fills up the explicit meta-data form as described in Sect. 3.2. The implicit metadata such as location, media store location, time, user identity etc. gets automatically filled. The meta-data is then posted to EduBay server which is then transferred to the EduBay Meta-Data DB. The User Account DB also gets updated since the user has uploaded some content.

When a consumer wants to get some media from EduBay, the user goes to the search view or browse view of the EduBay Consumer Android App. When the user selects an artefact, meta-data of the artefact is posted to the EduBay server and the media location is queried from the EduBay Meta-Data DB. The Android App then uses the returned location of the Media Store and downloads the media from the Media Store. The User Account DB is also updated to reflect the download done by the user. If the user does not find some content in EduBay they can place a request for content as described in Sect. 3.1. These requests are stored in Content Request DB. When a request has been serviced by a creator, that request is removed from the content request database and the metadata and the media is transferred to the EduBay Meta-Data DB and Media Store respectively, just like any other created media content.

5   Conclusion

This paper presented a simple mechanism to enable creation, verification, browsing, searching and requesting of content through mobile devices. The platform exploits the fact that it uses the mobile device to capture content, thereby automatically adding location and weather type of meta-data information to tag along with the content. It then targets the platform to scenarios where content such as pictures and location is important, which leads to its application in the natural science stream. The content creation, verification and content search applications on the mobile device are simple enough for a novice mobile user to access its features. The ability to host the content on the centralized server enables possibilities of scalability, additional processing and faster response times for each user request. Allowing a user to request and search for content based on location is definitely a novel and important problem in the education space, especially for natural sciences subjects. With more and more of education content getting online and social, through the various Massive Online Open Courses (MOOC), the EduBay platform can be a timely and novel solution in the space of content creation and sharing.

6   Discussion and Next Steps

We believe EduBay to be a timely solution both from a point of view of the way Online Education is shaping up, and from the possibilities that now arise from the rich mobile devices. Recent work in online education has focused more on the content delivery [11, 12] than on content creation, whereas content creation has been identified as a real challenge in this space [13]. EduBay therefore can fit in as a strong platform to improve content creation in this changing space of education. It paves a new path for creating content through mobile devices – which have so far been restricted mostly for content consumption, especially in the education space.

Going forward, we plan to do pilots in two universities, which are geographically separated but have the same course curriculum, i.e. a university in Finland and India, on a course in natural science or agriculture department. By providing EduBay to students and teachers in this pilot, we hope to attract the usage of the system and determine its effectiveness in a real course. From a technical perspective, we plan to augment the data collected by deriving more meta-data from the content to enable richer search and browsing of this content. We would like to understand more in-depth how conflicts can be resolved and quality control can be done when content is created collaboratively. There are other multiple technical challenges in building such a system which we would like to study in our future work. These include higher level inferred metadata creation, multiple updates strategy, incremental update in metadata, schema evolution, etc. We also plan to extend EduBay for scenarios where it may not be restricted just to natural science subjects but also to collaboratively create any content that can be useful in the education context.

References

1. SETILive. http://www.setilive.org/
2. Galaxy Zoo. http://www.galaxyzoo.org/
3. mPING Project. http://www.nssl.noaa.gov/projects/ping/
4. pressureNET. http://www.cumulonimbus.ca/software/pressurenet/
5. Stevens, M., D'Hondt, E.: Crowdsourcing of pollution data using smartphones. In: UbiComp 2010, Copenhagen, Denmark, 26–29 Sep 2010 (2010)
6. Sueda, K., Miyaki, T., Rekimoto, J.: Social geoscape: visualizing an image of the city for mobile UI using user generated geo-tagged objects. In: Puiatti, A., Gu, T. (eds.) MobiQuitous 2011. LNICST, vol. 104, pp. 1–12. Springer, Heidelberg (2012)
7. Xuan, Y., Sengupta, R., Fallah, Y.: Crowd sourcing indoor maps with mobile sensors. In: Sénac, P., Ott, M., Seneviratne, A. (eds.) MobiQuitous 2010. LNICST, vol. 73, pp. 125–136. Springer, Heidelberg (2012)
8. Yan, T., Marzilli, M., Holmes, R., Ganesan, D., Corner, M.: mCrowd: a platform for mobile crowdsourcing. In: Proceedings of the 7th ACM Conference on Embedded Networked Sensor Systems, pp. 347–348. ACM (2009)
9. Sachs, J., Finin, T.: Social and semantic computing in support of citizen science. In: Proceedings of the 3rd Canadian Semantic Web Symposium, Vancouver Canada, Aug 2011, pp. 46–51 (2011)
10. Pakshi Project http://pakshi.co.in/
11. McGuire, C.J., Castle, S.R.: An analysis of student self-assessment of online, blended, and face-to-face learning environments. In: Implications for Sustainable Education Delivery International Education Studies 3.3 (2010)
12. Weller, M.: Delivering learning on the net: the why, what and how of online education. In: Open and Flexible Learning Series. Taylor & Francis, Boca Raton (2013)
13. Weld, D.S., Adar, E., Chilton, L., Hoffmann, R., Horvitz, E.: Personalized online education—a crowdsourcing challenge. In: Workshops at the Twenty-Sixth AAAI Conference on Artificial Intelligence (2012)

Enhancing Context-Aware Applications Accuracy with Position Discovery

Khaled Alanezi$^{(\boxtimes)}$ and Shivakant Mishra

Computer Science Department, University of Colorado,
Boulder, CO 80309-0430, USA
khaled.alanezi@colorado.edu, mishras@cs.colorado.edu

Abstract. Detecting user context with high accuracy using smartphone sensors is a difficult task. A key challenge is dealing with the impact of different smartphone positions on sensor values. Users carry their smartphones in different positions such as holding in their hand or keeping inside their pants or jacket pocket, and each of these smartphone positions affects various sensor values in different ways. This paper addresses the issue of poor accuracy in detecting user context due to varying smartphone positions. It describes the design and prototype development of a smartphone position discovery service that accurately detects a smartphone position, and then demonstrates that the accuracy of an existing context aware application is significantly enhanced when run in conjunction with this proposed smartphone position discovery service.

1 Introduction

Modern smartphones embody a large set of sensors that can be utilized to learn a wealth of information about a user's surrounding environment. Researchers view the availability of such sensors as an opportunity for developing context-aware applications that can provide services tailored for each user's context. Context-aware mobile computing is not a new research topic, for example, a survey paper [4] covering advances in this field was published more than a decade ago. Despite the concept being there for a while, a breakthrough for the number of context-aware applications offered in smartphones application markets (e.g., App Store for Apple iOS or Google Play for Android OS) is yet to happen. For the most part, the current context-aware applications do not meet users' high expectations from technology.

A key problem with current context aware applications is that they typically provide low level of accuracy, particularly when used in an environment different from what was conceived at the application development stage. A major reason leading to low accuracy is the wide variety of ways a user may carry his/her smartphone, henceforth referred to as *smartphone position*. Users carry their smartphones in different positions, e.g. in hand, in purse, in pants pocket, in shirt pocket, etc. Sometimes, their smartphones are in covered positions, in purse or pockets,

© Institute for Computer Sciences, Social Informatics and Telecommunications Engineering 2014
I. Stojmenovic et al. (Eds.): MOBIQUITOUS 2013, LNICST 131, pp. 640–652, 2014.
DOI: 10.1007/978-3-319-11569-6_50

while uncovered at other times, watching a video or talking on the phone. Sensor values of different sensors naturally vary based on smartphone position, which in turn impacts the accuracy of the context derived from these values.

The key idea explored in this paper is that the accuracy of context discovery can be significantly improved if the applications rely not only on the sensor values, but also on the knowledge of smartphone positions from which these values are collected. In particular, we propose a new classification methodology as a way to utilize smartphone position information to improve context discovery. During the training period, an application trains multiple classifiers, one for each smartphone position. During operational periods, the application first collects not only the sensor values but also learns the smartphone position using a generic smartphone position discovery service. Next, it chooses a position-specific classifier to discover the context.

We describe the design, implementation and evaluation of a generic smartphone position discovery service. This service utilizes sensor values collected from some carefully chosen sensors and detects smartphone position with a very high accuracy. We propose a two-stage classification method and demonstrate that the accuracy of an existing context-aware application is significantly improved when it is integrated with the proposed smartphone position discovery service following this two-stage classification methodology.

2   Related Work

We focus on studies aimed at providing generic solution for the smartphone position problem. The work in [9] anticipated the importance of body-position knowledge even before the popularity of sensor-equipped smartphones. Their analysis utilized wearable accelerometer sensor to differentiate between four body positions. Another early work [7], limited to on-table, in-hand, and inside-pocket positions, augmented smartphones with a 2D accelerometer and demonstrated an accuracy of 87 %. Some preliminary work to distinguish between the in-pocket and out-of-pocket body-positions is provided in [13] for a smartphone based on the microphone sensor. Good accuracy level of 80 % was achieved. However, this study is also limited considering the number of positions covered. A recent project [6] used accelerometer to detect nine body positions with an accuracy of 74.6 %. It identifies 60 relevant features for body position discovery. We believe that this result can be integrated with our work to increase the number of positions covered and enhance the overall accuracy of position discovery.

The work in [15] suggested the use of a rotation-based approach to recognize four body-positions. The presented solution is based on accelerometer and gyroscope. Achieved accuracy using SVM classification was 91.69 %. We achieve a comparable accuracy while covering a larger set of seven positions. The work in [3] targets body-position localization of wearable sensors used for health monitoring applications. Authors used SVM to achieve a localization accuracy of 87 % when distinguishing between 6 body-positions. The studied positions are typical for health sensors and are not applicable to smartphones. A completely different approach utilizing external multispectral material sensor is proposed in [8]. The solution is based on the idea that smartphone positions are typically correlated with surrounding material with specific features, which the sensor they used is able to detect. We defer from most of above solutions by covering a wide set of positions and by introducing the two-stage classification methodology for context-aware applications to utilize the smartphone position.

3   Position Discovery Service

3.1   Impact of Smartphone Position

Since context derivation starts from raw sensor data collected from smartphone sensors, it is important to understand the impact a smartphone position may have on the sensor values of different sensors. To understand this impact and identify the sensors that can be used to detect smartphone positions, we have conducted an extensive experimental study involving six popular smartphone sensors: accelerometer, microphone, gyroscope, magnetometer, GPS and light sensors. The details of this study are described in a technical report [1], and due to space limitation, we provide only a summary of this study here. The smartphone positions covered in this study and in our position discovery service design are shown in Fig. 1.

Fig. 1. Inspected positions from left to right, hand holding, talking on phone, watching a video, pants pocket, hip pocket, jacket pocket and on-table.

Table 1 summarizes the results for this study. All sensors, except for the GPS, are affected by the smartphone position. Sensor values of accelerometer, gyroscope and magnetometer are affected by the differences in vibrations at different smartphone positions. So, a context aware application that is based on these sensors values is likely to benefit from the knowledge of actual smartphone position. Light sensor is affected by the blocking of light. Therefore, context-aware applications using this sensor are likely to benefit from the knowledge of whether the phone is covered or uncovered. Finally, the microphone is affected by friction noise and an application utilizing this sensor will likely be interested of whether the phone is in the upper body position where friction is low or in the lower body position where friction is high. Also, this study has shown that a major factor affecting the sensor values besides the smartphone position is the physical context of the user. The sensor values of accelerometer, gyroscope, and magnetometer are affected by the vibrations in case of a walking user. However, these vibrations are missing in case of an idle user. As for running physical context, it can take various paces. A user might run very fast in one situation

Table 1. Summary of smartphone position impact study

Sensor	Affected	Cause	Required position
Accelerometer	Yes	Vibrations	Exact
Gyroscope	Yes	Vibrations	Exact
Microphone	Yes	Friction noise	Upper-body or lower-body
Light	Yes	Blocking of light	Covered or uncovered
Magnetometer	Yes	Vibrations	Exact
GPS	No	-	-

and run relatively slower in another. These different paces make it difficult to find any sensor data patterns from these three sensors that can be attributed to the position since these patterns will be overwhelmed by the effect of a running user. In addition, we looked at the popular position of on-table. Analogous to an idle user carrying a smartphone, the smartphone at this position will not experience any movement patterns. However, a distinguishing factor between the two situations is the orientation of the smartphone. A smartphone placed on a table will typically have the gravity component appearing in its z-axis.

3.2   Position Discovery Service: Design

Based on these observations, we have designed, implemented and evaluated a smartphone position discovery service that provides four types of information: (1) Is the user idle, walking or running? (2) Is the phone covered or uncovered? (3) Is the phone placed in upper body or lower body? (4) What is the actual smartphone position? This service is designed to be configurable, so that an application can choose to receive only one or two or all types of information.

The challenge in building this service is that it utilizes sensor data from specific sensors (e.g. accelerometer and gyroscope), whose values are dependent on the physical contexts of the user. It is possible that the data from a particular sensor under one smartphone position and user activity is indistinguishable from the data from the same sensor under a different smartphone position and user activity. We address this challenge by detecting user's physical context (idle, walking or running) and utilizing data from multiple sensors. The key idea is that different sensors are affected differently by various user contexts, and we exploit these differences to accurately detect smartphone positions.

To detect whether the smartphone is in covered or uncovered position, the service compares the online captured light intensity data with a predefined threshold. The situation is more complex when it comes to the other finer granularity information. For both the upper-body/lower-body and the exact smartphone position decisions, the service uses machine-learning libraries to compare knowledge obtained from online sensor data with knowledge from labeled training data prepared offline. This classification process involves data from accelerometer or gyroscope, or both sensors based on the preference of the serviced context-aware

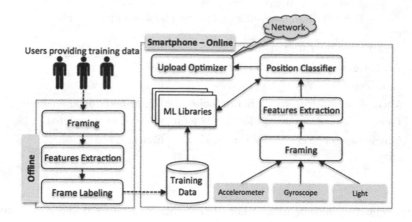

Fig. 2. Design for the smartphone position discovery service

application. Figure 2 illustrates this design. It is worth noting that the complete solution runs on the smartphone. The smartphone position service can be utilized locally by other applications running on the same smartphone or remotely by collaborative sensing applications running on other smartphones.

Offline Components: There are three offline components: Framing, Feature extraction and Frame labeling. The Framing component aims at capturing the repetitive patterns in the raw sensor data by dividing the data stream, from accelerometer and gyroscope, into five-second frames. Our choice of five-second frame size is based on analysis presented in [5] on the effect of frame size on step detection accuracy. Their analysis revealed that a frame size larger than three seconds is sufficient enough to provide good step detection accuracy and favored the five-second frame as it gives more accurate results.

The features extraction component calculates statistical features for each frame. Frame features must be chosen smartly to reveal the different patterns induced by each smartphone position. Our frame features are subset from the features presented in [10]. Based on our observations from smartphone position impact on sensor data [1], we have chosen the mean, variance, and standard deviation over 50 data points (10 data points per second) for each frame to capture the variations in accelerometer and gyroscope data. We have also included two other features related to each axis (average for each axis and average absolute difference of each axis) so as to capture the different orientations a smartphone can take for each position. This is because we noticed that each position has a common orientation that occurs quite frequently. Average of each axis captures the variation in the data due to body motion at the axis level. In addition, it reveals the nature of the orientation the smartphone is experiencing for each body position. Average absolute difference of each axis is the sum of the differences between each axis data point and the mean of that axis divided by the number of data points. We include the average absolute difference to enhance the solution accuracy in capturing the information revealed by axis data points.

A recent study [6] identified an extensive set of features for detecting smartphone positions. These features can be integrated to the position discovery service to expand covered set of positions and further enhance the accuracy. Finally, the frame labeling component labels each frame with the corresponding smartphone position before loading the data to the training database. The labeling process was done manually. We asked our users to capture the data for the different smartphone positions while walking and labeled resultant frame segments with the practiced smartphone position during the experiment. Each frame record carries two labels: upper-body/lower-body position and the exact smartphone position.

Online Components: There are seven online components: Training data, Machine learning libraries, Sensor values from accelerometer, gyroscope and/or light sensor, Framing, Feature extraction, Position classifier and Upload optimizer. The training data is the output from the offline components. Sensor data from ten users performing the same experiment for different smartphone positions was collected offline. After performing the (offline) framing and feature extraction processes, the resultant frame records constitute the knowledge database to be utilized for automatic discovery of smartphone position. Once ready, the training data is placed on the external memory card of the smartphone to be utilized by the smartphone position service.

We utilized Java language machine-learning libraries provided by the WEKA tool for Android [11]. The correctness of used classifiers was tested by performing a test experiment with the same training and test data on a desktop by normal WEKA and on Android device by WEKA for Android. Same results were obtained for the two experiments.

We chose three sensors (accelerometer, gyroscope and light sensor) for the service to operate on. Accelerometer is used for detecting physical context, accelerometer and/or gyroscope are used for detecting the actual phone position, and light sensor is used for detecting whether the phone is covered or uncovered. The use of two sensors for detecting actual phone position is subject to a tradeoff between energy consumption and smartphone position detection accuracy. The framing and features extraction components have the same functionalities as in the offline case. The only addition is the capture of average light intensity per frame, which is not required for training the classifier. The position classifier component receives the gathered online frame data and uses it in three ways. First, it compares the standard deviation of accelerometer magnitude with predefined thresholds to determine idle/walking/running contexts. Second, it consults the machine learning classifier to detect smartphone position information. Third, it compares the light intensity average of the frame with a predefined threshold to determine covered/uncovered position. In the case of idle or running contexts, the position service provides the latest smartphone position discovered under walking context along with a timestamp and leave it to the consuming context-aware application to use this cached smartphone position based on its accuracy preferences. Our goal here is to exploit the fact that, in some situations the user might change their physical context but maintain the same smartphone position.

Finally, the upload optimizer is utilized only in case the position is required to be relayed over the network as part of a collaborative sensing solution. We developed this component because we envision the smartphone position discovery service to be an important part of collaborative sensing applications. The upload optimizer logic is based on optimization techniques discussed in [14]. The optimizer implements three alternative techniques for upload optimization: (1) Upload whenever a position change occurs; (2) Upload when a position change persists for some period of time; and (3) Upload the position with the highest number of occurrences within a window of given size. While the first technique is simple and provides most accurate results, it is subject to noise due to momentary smartphone position changes. The second technique eliminates this noise and reports only more permanent position changes. Finally, the third technique is suitable when there are frequent smartphone position changes. This technique tries to report the most commonly occurring smartphone position.

Use Case Scenario: Assume a context-aware application that is interested in finding the exact position. Figure 3 demonstrates the flow of execution of the position discovery service to provide this information. In the beginning, the service uses the variance of the accelerometer for the captured window to detect the physical context. If the smartphone is idle, the service will detect if it is placed on table or any other position. In case the smartphone is idle and not on table, the exact position is difficult to provide and a cached recent value along with the activity is returned instead. Also, a running context means that position can't be detected and a cached value is returned. If the user is walking, the service will utilize the online features extracted from the accelerometer and gyroscope to provide the exact position.

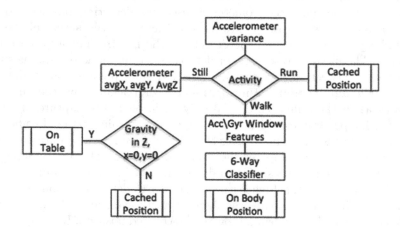

Fig. 3. Position service execution flow for a request for an exact position.

4   Implementation and Evaluation

We have implemented the proposed smartphone position discovery service on Samsung Galaxy Note device running Android version 4.0.3 (Ice Cream Sandwich). The device has a Dual-core 1.4 GHz ARM Cortex-A9 processor and 1 GB of RAM and is equipped with the accelerometer, gyroscope and light sensors required for the service. We collected data from ten different participants to train the smartphone position discovery classifier. Before conducting the experiment, an approval was obtained from the Institutional Review Board at the University of Colorado, Boulder. We asked each participant to carry the smartphone in the six smartphone positions. The experiment setup was kept as natural as possible. Participants were free to move at their own pace and place their smartphones at any orientation they liked. Next, we evaluate the accuracy of the service based on this collected training data.

Physical Contexts: To detect the physical context of a user, we calculate the standard deviation of the accelerometer magnitude and compare it to a predefined threshold. By observing the data we have chosen the threshold values of $0.5 \, \text{m/s}^2$ and $5 \, \text{m/s}^2$ to detect idle and running contexts respectively. These thresholds achieved near-perfect accuracy in our experiments.

Covered vs. Uncovered: We used a threshold of three luminous flux to detect a dimmed environment that results often from covered positions. This approach works well except for corner cases (e.g. complete absence of any light source in a room).

Upper-Body vs. Lower-Body: Smartphone positions covered in this research can be divided into two groups: upper-body group, including hand holding, talking on phone, watching a video, and jacket pocket; and lower-body group, including pants pocket and hip pocket. To detect the group that a smartphone is in, we trained the classifier with accelerometer data from 10 users and carried a 10-folds cross-validation test. The results of the classification process with different classifiers are shown in Table 2. The achieved accuracy using accelerometer is fairly high for the simple logistic regression and J48 classifiers. Therefore, we conclude that the accelerometer is the best candidate to perform this classification task and exclude gyroscope from our analysis.

Table 2. Upper-body vs. lower-body accuracy using accelerometer features

	Prediction accuracy (%)		
	Naive Bayes	Simple logistic regression	J48
Upper-body	89.2	91.2	92.8
Lower-body	77.2	90.5	83.9
Total accuracy	84.6	90.9	89.4

Exact Smartphone Position: Both accelerometer and gyroscope have shown sensitivity to smartphone positions. Our goal here is to compare between the two sensors. In the beginning, we conducted a test experiment with the six smartphone positions and collected the data for both the accelerometer and gyroscope. Then, to evaluate a single sensor, we kept the data for that sensor and deleted the data for the other sensor. By doing so, we ensure fair comparison since the three results we show next are basically for the same experiment, but, with different sensors included. Here we also used data from 10 users and performed a 10-folds cross-validation test. The classifiers employed are NB: Naive Bayes, MLP: Multilayer Perceptron, LR: logistic Regression, and J48. Table 3 illustrates the results of smartphone position classification using only accelerometer. We note that the J48 decision tree classifier achieves good accuracy of 88.5 % with the accelerometer as the only input. On the other hand, the Naive Bayes classifier had the lowest accuracy of 66.7 %. We also note that the source of confusion varies from one classifier to another for the same experiment. For example, in the multilayer perceptron experiment, the jacket-pocket position produced the lowest accuracy. On the other hand, with the Logistic Regression in use, the pants pocket position was the hardest position to classify.

Table 3. Accuracy using accelerometer

	Prediction accuracy (%)			
	NB	MLP	LR	J48
Handholding	75.9	83.8	94.5	97.8
Watching a video	91.8	93.2	96.0	97.0
Talking on phone	79.4	89.7	91.7	91.3
Pants pocket	65.4	67.9	58.0	78.2
Hip pocket	57.6	78.8	71.6	90.7
Jacket pocket	27.6	67.1	73.2	75.3
Total accuracy	66.7	80	80	88.5

Table 4. Accuracy using gyroscope

	Prediction accuracy (%)			
	NB	MLP	LR	J48
Handholding	72.2	78.4	85.4	63.6
Watching a video	64.7	81.8	84.8	84.2
Talking on phone	48.4	64.8	72.3	75.6
Pants pocket	60.6	82.0	75.5	55.2
Hip pocket	52.4	72.6	64.1	52.3
Jacket pocket	46.7	62.0	52.9	47.6
Total accuracy	57.6	74.0	72.7	62.9

Next, we evaluate the service when gyroscope is in use. Table 4 illustrates the results of smartphone position classification using only gyroscope. We note that all classifiers achieved lower total accuracy when compared to the use of accelerometer. This shows that the gyroscope is less sensitive to smartphone positions than accelerometer. Nevertheless, the accuracy achieved by the gyroscope is still at acceptable levels making the sensor worth considering for some cases. For example, some positions achieved accuracy level of above 80 % for some classifiers. However, the overall accuracy remains less than the values achieved when the accelerometer is in use.

Now, we consider the situation where we use both accelerometer and gyroscope to detect the smartphone position. Table 5 provides the position discovery results when features from both sensors are used in the classification. As expected, mostly all the classifiers achieved a gain in accuracy when compared to the previous two single-sensor configurations. We also note that three out of the four classifiers achieved very high accuracy levels (above 80 %). However, this improved accuracy comes at the cost of increased energy demands. When only accelerometer is employed the service drained 10 % from the battery in 10 h whereas, using both accelerometer and gyroscope drained more than 50 % within the same period of time. Finally, notice that none of the classifiers consistently produced best results in all three cases. However, the Naive Bayes classifiers always produced worst results due to its assumption of feature independence, which doesn't hold for our set of features.

Group Training vs. Custom Training: A smartphone is typically a personal device owned by a single user. Therefore the idea of each user (custom) training his/her position discovery classifier is worthwhile. We experimented with this idea, where a user trained his smartphone by performing the above-mentioned classifier training experiments. Next day, we collected sensor data from the same user and ran our smartphone position discovery service using the custom-trained classifier from the previous day. Table 6 shows the accuracy of smartphone position detection when both accelerometer and gyroscope data were used. We can see that the total accuracy for each classification algorithm has improved dramatically (compare the results with Table 5). One point to note is that the user wore similar clothing on both days in this experiment. We expect that the detection accuracy may be slightly lower for different style of clothing. One way to address this is to train the classifier with different clothing styles. The idea of training a classifier on smartphone by the user before application use has been used in [12]. However, the authors tried to keep the training period as minimum as possible as they believed that users might refrain from using applications requiring training beforehand. We share the same concern and believe that the position service can be installed with multiple users training data, which has shown acceptable accuracy levels, and the user is then given a choice for custom training.

Table 5. Accuracy using accelerometer and gyroscope

	Prediction accuracy (%)			
	NB	MLP	LR	J48
Handholding	76.6	86.4	98.9	92.6
Watching a video	92.4	91.3	98.0	95.8
Talking on phone	76.9	91.9	96.8	93.1
Pants pocket	73.2	85.8	78.8	75.9
Hip pocket	66.2	93.5	88.3	83.5
Jacket pocket	51.4	80.8	75.6	68.6
Total accuracy	73.0	88.6	89.3	84.9

Table 6. Accuracy using custom-training-data

	Prediction accuracy (%)			
	NB	MLP	LR	J48
Handholding	100	100	100	66.67
Watching a video	92.30	100	100	92.31
Talking on phone	100	100	100	100
Pants pocket	100	94.44	100	83.33
Hip Pocket	100	100	93.33	100
Jacket pocket	100	100	100	100
Total accuracy	98.71	99.07	98.88	90.38

On-Table Position: Due to its special nature, the on table position is handled separately. We directly use the window features of average x-axis, average y-axis, and average z-axis to detect this position. The z-axis value will be nearly equal to the gravity pull value of $9.8\,\mathrm{m/s^2}$ whereas the x-axis and y-axis will have the value of near zero. This approach detected this position with nearly perfect accuracy. However, we can think of rare situations that can confuse the approach such as placing the smartphone on a stand.

5   Two Stage Classification Method

Some context-aware applications are simply blocked by disadvantageous positions (e.g. camera-based application waiting for uncovered position). Other context-aware applications can operate in different smartphone positions, but with severe accuracy degradation when experiencing a smartphone position other than the one trained for. To address this issue, we propose a two-stages classification method. First, the offline training for the classifier is done with different smartphone positions to generate a separate classifier trained for each position. Second, with the presence of the smartphone position discovery service, the application first determines the current smartphone position and then chooses the classifier corresponding to that specific position during the classification process. To demonstrate the effectiveness of this approach, we have implemented a fall classification application that was proposed in [2]. This application detects the type of fall from four different fall categories namely forward trips, backward slips , left lateral falls, and right lateral falls. The output of this application can be used by experts in the field of elderly care to develop fall prevention mechanisms and to assist first responders in providing more customized emergency procedures. The experimental work in [2] placed the smartphone to the backside of a belt and users were asked to wear this belt and simulate the different categories of falls. First, we start on reflecting how severe the situation gets when arbitrary positions are introduced to the scene? We collected training and test data from arbitrary positions for the four types of falls and report classification accuracy in Table 7. The overall accuracy of this experiment is 72.22 %. Note that [2] reported an accuracy of 98.7 % when single position is used. Second, we collected multiple training files each corresponding to a smartphone position and containing the four types of falls. Afterwards, the user was asked to simulate the required four types of falls and the classifier was pointed to the training file corresponding to the smartphone position, *assuming the smartphone position is known in advance*. The confusion matrix of the second experiment is shown in Table 8. The results from these two experiments reflect a significant accuracy improvement from 72.22 % to 94.8 %.

Admittedly, the assumption of a complete knowledge of smartphone position is not a valid one. Therefore, we integrated the fall classification application with the online position discovery service and followed the above-mentioned two-stage classification method. Figure 4(a) and (b) show the "per-fall" and "overall" accuracies for this case. We also included the results from Tables 7 and 8 to make it easier to grasp the effect of introducing the smartphone position discovery service. Notice from Fig. 4(a) that the accuracies of trips and left lateral falls detection have been improved. For the other two types of falls, introducing

Table 7. Fall classification accuracy with arbitrary position.

		Prediction Accuracy (%)			
		Slips	Trips	Left	Right
Fall Type	Slips	**77.8**	0	0	22.2
	Trips	11.1	**88.9**	0	0
	Left	0	0	**33.3**	66.7
	Right	0	0	11.1	**88.9**

Table 8. Fall classification accuracy assuming known position.

		Prediction Accuracy (%)			
		Slips	Trips	Left	Right
Fall Type	Slips	**93.3**	0	6.7	0
	Trips	0	**100**	0	0
	Left	6.7	0	**93.3**	0
	Right	7.1	0	0	**92.2**

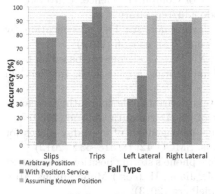

(a) Per-Fall Accuracy

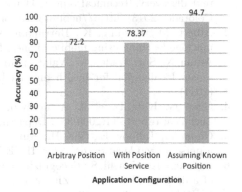

(b) Overall Accuracy

Fig. 4. Fall detection accuracy.

the position service to the scene didn't improve the results but didn't negatively impact them. Figure 4(b) reflects the overall accuracy improvement. The improvement in the case of "known-position" proves the fact that by introducing the position service, context-aware applications will achieve better results. We also saw an improvement for the case of with-the-position service. However, the improvement was not as significant as in the optimal situation. We noticed that our position service provided the correct position in most situations, but it was the fall classification that is difficult to achieve. We attribute this difficulty to arbitrary after fall behaviors such as standing immediately after fall or remaining stationary.

6   Conclusion

This paper presents a solution that runs solely on the smartphone to address the negative impact of different smartphone positions on context-aware applications accuracy. The proposed solution can act as a service provider to context-aware applications running on the same smartphone by providing them with smartphone position information. The service can answer the following four questions.

(1) Is the user idle, walking or running: (2) Is the smartphone covered or uncovered? (3) Is the smartphone attached to upper-body or lower-body? (4) What is the actual position of the smartphone? We evaluated the service by integrating it with an existing context-aware application for fall classification. Results show significant accuracy improvement proving the utility of the service.

References

1. Alanezi, K., Mishra, S.: Impact of smartphone position on sensor values and context discovery. Technical report, Department of Computer Science, University of Colorado (2013). http://ucblibraries.colorado.edu/repository
2. Albert, M., Kording, K., Herrmann, M., Jayaraman, A.: Fall classification by machine learning using mobile phones. PloS one 7(5), e36556 (2012)
3. Amini, N., Sarrafzadeh, M., Vahdatpour, A., Xu, W.: Accelerometer-based on-body sensor localization for health and medical monitoring applications. In: PerCom (2011)
4. Chen, G., Kotz, D., et al.: A survey of context-aware mobile computing research. Technical report, TR2000-381, Department of CS, Dartmouth College (2000)
5. Chon, Y., Talipov, E., Cha, H.: Autonomous management of everyday places for a personalized location provider. IEEE Trans. SMCC 42(4), 518–531 (2012)
6. Fujinami, K., Kouchi, S.: Recognizing a mobile phone's storing position as a context of a device and a user. In: Zheng, K., Li, M., Jiang, H. (eds.) MobiQuitous 2012. LNICST, vol. 120, pp. 76–88. Springer, Heidelberg (2013)
7. Gellersen, H.W., Schmidt, A., Beigl, M.: Multi-sensor context-awareness in mobile devices and smart artifacts. Mob. Netw. Appl. 7(5), 341–351 (2002)
8. Harrison, C., Hudson, S.E.: Lightweight material detection for placement-aware mobile computing. In: UIST (2008)
9. Kunze, K.S., Lukowicz, P., Junker, H., Tröster, G.: Where am i: recognizing on-body positions of wearable sensors. In: Strang, T., Linnhoff-Popien, C. (eds.) LoCA 2005. LNCS, vol. 3479, pp. 264–275. Springer, Heidelberg (2005)
10. Kwapisz, J.R., Weiss, G.M., Moore, S.A.: Activity recognition using cell phone accelerometers. ACM SIGKDD Explor. Newsl. 12(2), 74–82 (2011)
11. Marsan, R.J.: Weka for android. http://rjmarsan.com/research/wekaforandroid/
12. Miluzzo, E., Cornelius, C.T., Ramaswamy, A., Choudhury, T., Liu, Z., Campbell, A.T.: Darwin phones: the evolution of sensing and inference on mobile phones. In: MobiSys (2010)
13. Miluzzo, E., Papandrea, M., Lane, N.D., Lu, H., Campbell, A.T.: Pocket, bag, hand, etc.-automatically detecting phone context through discovery. In: PhoneSense (2010)
14. Musolesi, M., Piraccini, M., Fodor, K., Corradi, A., Campbell, A.T.: Supporting energy-efficient uploading strategies for continuous sensing applications on mobile phones. In: Floréen, P., Krüger, A., Spasojevic, M. (eds.) Pervasive 2010. LNCS, vol. 6030, pp. 355–372. Springer, Heidelberg (2010)
15. Shi, Y., Shi, Y., Liu, J.: A rotation based method for detecting on-body positions of mobile devices. In: UbiComp (2011)

How's My Driving? A Spatio-Semantic Analysis of Driving Behavior with Smartphone Sensors

Dipyaman Banerjee, Nilanjan Banerjee$^{(\boxtimes)}$,
Dipanjan Chakraborty, Aakash Iyer, and Sumit Mittal

IBM Research - India, New Delhi, India
{dipyaban,nilanjba,cdipanjan,aakiyer1,sumittal}@in.ibm.com

Abstract. Road accident is one of the major reasons for loss of human lives, especially in developing nations with poor road infrastructure and a driver needs to constantly negotiate with several adverse conditions to ensure safety. In this paper, we study several such adverse conditions that are relevant to safe driving and propose a novel method for identifying them as well as characterizing driving behavior for such conditions. Experimental results reveal that our proposed methodology is promising and more flexible than prior work in this area. In particular, our prediction results reveal that our methodology is an aggressive one where most of the bad driving behaviors are determined at the cost of a few instances of good behavior being falsely characterized as bad ones.

Keywords: Smartphone · Driving behavior · Analytics

1 Introduction

Road accident has been one of the banes of modern civilization, taking a significant toll on human lives. In U.S.A., motor vehicle crashes have claimed 4,544 teens between the ages of 16 and 19 in the year of 2005 alone[1]. While the rapid increase in the number of vehicles on the road has contributed to this scary statistics, negligent and rash driving has been the chief contributor. There have been many efforts to bring in some order to the traffic scenario by either monitoring and managing overall traffic or monitoring individual driving behavior. However, most of these solutions are primarily designed for developed countries with organized traffic infrastructure and practices. The solutions, consequently, are rendered ineffective for developing nations where the setting is much more chaotic. The problem becomes more complex in such a setting where it is not only the driver's fault that is responsible for an accident, but infrastructure, or rather the lack of it, and surrounding environment also play a significant role. The fact that India has the highest traffic accident rate worldwide, with 3,42,309 deaths reported in 2008 alone[2], is a testimony to that.

---

[1] WISQARS: www.cdc.gov/injury/wisqars.
[2] National Crime Records Bureau record: http://ncrb.nic.in/adsi2008/accidental-deaths-08.pdf.

© Institute for Computer Sciences, Social Informatics and Telecommunications Engineering 2014
I. Stojmenovic et al. (Eds.): MOBIQUITOUS 2013, LNICST 131, pp. 653–666, 2014.
DOI: 10.1007/978-3-319-11569-6_51

A large body of work on driving behavior analysis exploits data from In Vehicle Data Recorders (IVDR) [8, 10]. IVDRs are installed in the vehicles to provide information about speed, acceleration, manoeuvres, etc. The first application of IVDR was the event data recorder that was designed based on the "black box" used in aircrafts and primarily recorded crash information. Later, the event data recorders evolved to include specialized sensors integrated with vehicles to provide sophisticated information (e.g., vehicle steering wheel operation information) on the manoeuvring of a vehicle that could be used for driving behavior analysis. For example, the SmartCar testbed described in [8] recognizes driver maneuvers at a tactical level by recording the car's brake, gear, steering wheel angle, speed and acceleration throttle signals. Further, it maps these maneuvers to video signals that capture the contextual traffic, the driver's head and the driver's viewpoint. Such integrated IVDRs are not widely applicable across different types of vehicles. For instance, a solution based on steering wheel operation information would not be applicable to auto-rickshaws that ply in large numbers on Indian roads. To solve this problem, portable mobile units [6] were installed on vehicles to gather general information such as speed, acceleration, rotation, location, etc.

A significant body of work is emerging that uses smartphones of the drivers instead of the expensive, special-purpose mobile units. Paefgen et al. [9] evaluate a mobile application that assesses driving behavior based on in-vehicle acceleration measurements and gives corresponding feedback to drivers. Eren et al. [2] propose an approach to understand the driver behavior using smartphone sensors, more specifically, the accelerometer, gyroscope and the magnetometer. Using these sensors, they obtain position, speed, acceleration, deceleration and deflection angle sensory information and estimate commuting safety by statistically analyzing driver behavior. Johnson and Trivedi [3] propose a system that uses Dynamic Time Warping (DTW) and smartphone based sensor-fusion (accelerometer, gyroscope, magnetometer, GPS, video) to detect, recognize and record these actions without external processing. Use of smartphones to detect driving behavior has also been applied to motorcycles, where mobility and motion characteristics are different from that of a car. An example is [4], here the authors propose a system to comprehend a motorcycle's behavior using the acceleration and gyroscope sensors on the smartphone.

The IVDRs are either integrated or mounted on the vehicles and hence are not flexible enough to be applicable across a variety of vehicles. Mobile units, including smartphones, are loosely coupled with the vehicles and hence are free from this problem. However, none of the smartphone based solutions take ambient context (road conditions, traffic, etc.) into consideration while determining driving behavior. In this paper, we bridge this gap by first identifying parameters which define a *spatio-semantic ambient driving context* and propose a method for classifying driving behavior based on *segmentation* of a given trajectory along these parameters utilizing smartphone sensor data. Our specific contributions can be summarized as follows:

- A methodology for detecting *driving events* to characterize driving behavior and the *ambient context* from smartphone sensors, *accelerometer, gyroscope and GPS.*
- A methodology for classification of "good" and "bad" driving behavior given an ambient context.
- Performance evaluation of our methodology in characterizing driving behaviors against ground truths provided by expert observers.

2   Problem Description and Motivation

Driving is a skill that heavily depends on how the driver negotiates with the physical environment. We define *ambient context* as the factors in physical environments that become relevant to a driver. We classify ambient context into two categories:

1. Static Context: This includes context attributes whose value remains invariant for a substantial amount of time and across multiple trips. Examples of static context can be turns on the trajectory, road conditions such as potholes, bumps, etc.
2. Dynamic Context: This includes parameters which changes frequently with time and can vary across trips along the same route. This may include presence of other drivers, their driving behavior, temporary obstacles, etc.

Both static and dynamic context play an important role in determining drive quality. For example, a skilful driver would negotiate a sharp turn with a rough surface or a pothole on the road with more control than an unskilled or rash driver resulting in a safe and better experience for the people within the car and on the road. The type of context varies spatially and temporally. Figure 1a, b and c shows a few examples of static pathological ambient contexts, while Fig. 1d shows a pathological dynamic ambient context on a typical Indian road in New Delhi.

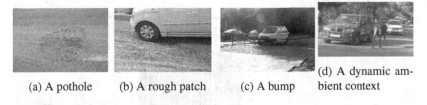

(a) A pothole   (b) A rough patch   (c) A bump   (d) A dynamic ambient context

Fig. 1. Examples of ambient context

While smartphone based static ambient context determination has been investigated in [7], dynamic contexts are far more difficult to measure and model compared to static contexts and require costlier set-ups like on-vehicle video cameras and data from other city-sensing infrastructure [11]. Due to logistics issues, we leave out dynamic ambient context determination from our study. As we shall see, there are significant challenges to construct a methodical solution towards determining rich drive profiles using static context itself.

Before we establish the critical role of ambient context in influencing driving behavior, let us define what we mean by *good* and *bad* driving behavior in the context of this work.

Definition 1. *Good driving behavior: – A "good" or "normal" behavior is where the driver negotiates an adverse condition such as a turn or a pothole, carefully, by driving with average speed profile for the adverse condition.*

Definition 2. *Bad driving behavior: – A "bad" or "rash" behavior is when the driver drives with higher-than-average speed profile for an adverse condition.*

We conducted an initial experiment to understand the impact of ambient context on driving behavior. We collected acceleration vectors of a car on two types of road surface while taking a turn: a smooth road and a road with a rough and bumpy surface. We requested the driver to drive in two states corresponding to *good* or *normal* behavior and *bad* or *rash* behavior on the same stretch of road (see Fig. 2a for the road stretch).

We implemented a prior method proposed by Eren et al. [2] to analyse driving behavior using smartphones. The method uses Dynamic Time Warping (DTW) to compare an unknown timeseries of drive data, with a few candidate classes. The assumption was, smaller the DTW distance, the better is the match between the test data and template. Figure 2b shows the results. DTW distances are plotted for each left turn, while being compared with a "good" left turn on a normal surface template in Fig. 2b. The actual labels are denoted by G and B representing good and bad driving respectively.

As can be clearly seen, the first 10 left turns have a very large DTW distance compared to the next 10 left turns. When compared against the true classifications, we observe some of the bad left turns actually have a better match to the

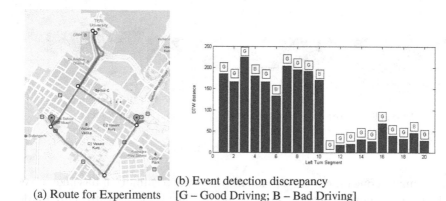

(b) Event detection discrepancy
(a) Route for Experiments   [G – Good Driving; B – Bad Driving]

Fig. 2. Demonstrating the relevance of ambient context

template than the good left turns, even though the template itself was for a good turn. Thus, ironically, on the rough surface, bad left turns matched better with a good left turn template than left turns which are truly good. This was caused by the inadvertent change in the speed profiles caused due to the roughness of the road surface. This highlights the need to consider 'context' when developing machine learning models for characterizing driving behavior, especially in chaotic driving conditions like those existing in India.

3   Solution Methodology

Determining driving context forms the basis of our work. As stated earlier, we only consider the static context attributes and determine how they are distributed along the driving trajectory. We observe that besides having the time-invariance property, static context attributes typically remain unchanged within a region in the trajectory e.g. rough patches, bumps, turns, etc. This allows us to divide the trajectory into segments (possibly overlapping) based on the attribute values. However, accuracy of such segmentation is critical as they represent context which directly impacts driving behavior. Table 1 lists the different static context attributes we consider in this work and some of the possible values they can have.

Table 1. Static contextual attributes

Road network	Straight, turns, roundabout, bends
Road neighborhood	School, traffic signal, market place, no label
Road surface condition	Smooth, bump, pothole

Road network information and road neighborhood information is available widely from Geographic Information Sources (GIS). Crowdsensed social media based data sources like OpenStreetMap[3] can augment the information quality available in GIS databases. However, there is no available large-scale data source that maintains road surface conditions. Hence, we try to estimate them using accelerometer readings from drive data across trips.

Figure 3 presents our solution methodology. Overall, our approach can be divided into three steps: (i) fusion of data from multiple information sources, including mobile GPS traces of the trip, to infer *spatio-semantically rich* sequence of segments, (ii) use accelerometer readings to augment the segments with road surface conditions like bumps, rough stretches, etc., and (iii) classify driving behavior in a given context. Next, we present the detail each of these steps.

---

[3] www.openstreetmap.org/

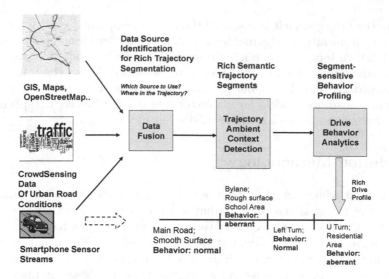

Fig. 3. Methodology for spatio-semantic analysis of driving behavior

3.1   Data Fusion

This step incrementally enriches the smartphone drive data to form a sequence of trajectory segments with corresponding static ambient context. Let T_i represent a trajectory of a single drive data from a trip i. $T_i = \{l_1^i, l_2^i, \cdots, l_n^i\}$ where l_j^i represent the jth GPS observation in the trajectory of trip i. We take T_i and use standard map-matching algorithms to recover the corresponding road network data from a GIS database. Next, we use spatial join algorithms to recover the semantic region tags around each road segment. Semantic regions represent geographical areas like residential, commercial, etc. Subsequently, for each road segment, we perform a k-nearest neighbor query to recover the nearby points of interests (PoI). This provides us with a list of GIS objects for every segment from which we can recover nearby location artifacts like schools, market places, etc. and use them to tag each GPS observation associated with that segment. For example, we can denote $s(l_m^i) = \{\text{straight road}, \text{school}\}$; $s(l_n^j) = \{\text{turn}, \text{market}\}$; where $s(l_m^i)$ and $s(l_n^i)$ represent semantic information associated with the GPS points l_m^i and l_n^i, respectively. We perform a simple change-point detection on all such semantically enriched GPS data points present in the trip and mark a change point wherever there is a difference of at least one tag between two subsequent GPS points, i.e. $s(l_m^i) \neq s(l_{m+1}^i)$. This yields a sequence of homogeneous segments consisting of invariant tags fused from GIS sources. Let us denote any k^{th} segment as sem^k. We define $sem^k = \{l_m^i, l_n^i, [tags^k]\}$ where l_m^i, l_n^i are the segment boundaries and $[tags^k]$ denotes the set of semantic tags associated with all the points present in the segment.

3.2   Accelerometer-Based Segment Data Enrichment

The semantically enriched trajectory was seeded from GPS observations. However, they are not sufficient to monitor fine-grained road surface conditions. Specially, the sampling frequency of GPS may vary across trips and make any velocity-driven approximation of road surface conditions inaccurate with respect to segment boundaries. The accelerometer being a low-power sensor, it is acceptable to sample it with high frequency. We use the accelerometer readings from the trip to recover road surface conditions like bumps, rough stretches and augment the trajectory with that information.

An accelerometer records acceleration along 3 mutually perpendicular axes – x, y, z. In a horizontal orientation, one axis points towards gravity **g** vector. The phone can be in different orientations in a car. Wearable computing literature [5] has studied before that the **g** can be estimated reasonably well from an unknown orientation. This enables conversion of the readings to a fixed reference orientation plane where one of the axes points towards **g**. We use this to first map the raw data to our reference orientation plane. Let us call $z = $ the axis pointing towards gravity; $y = $ axis pointing towards lateral movement of the car; $x = $ axis pointing towards the forward movement of the car.

In order to improve reliability of predicting road surface segments while accommodating personalized variations in driving, we have designed a novel (1) cross-trip majority-voting driven segmentation method of drive data and (2) subsequent use of an adaptive DBSCAN algorithm, to arrive at rich segments specifying road surface conditions. The segments derived from data fusion is augmented with these to arrive at the final rich segments based on which the driving behavior will be evaluated.

Cross-Trip Majority Voting. The **z** axis acceleration component can be used to estimate the vertical disturbances a car goes through while driving and therefore can be used to detect rough surfaces as they typically cause the car to jump abruptly. However, in order to build a reliable segmentation of the persistent road surface conditions, it is important to perform a time series consolidation of the readings across multiple trips on the same road network because (1) the segments may be of varying lengths; (2) usage related interjections can add unnecessary false positives; (3) mechanical properties of the car and its age can add false positives; (4) unknown temporary obstacles (rampant on New Delhi roads) can add unnecessary false positives. We next discuss our segmentation methodology in detail.

Let $ACC^i = [z_1^i, z_2^i, ..., z_n^i]$ be n z-axis acceleration readings of trip i. Given m trips across all users, we first time-synchronize ACC^i with corresponding available GPS readings T_i and localize them. Wherever GPS readings are sparse, we use velocity-based estimation to interpolate the GPS points corresponding to the ACC readings. Thereafter, we cluster T_i by applying a criteria based on the deviation of the corresponding z_x^i value from the mean of observations across that trip: $\mu \pm r\sigma$ (where r is a threshold, μ and σ are respectively the mean and s.d. of ACC_i). We applied this simple criteria because major parts of the trip are expected to be having relatively smooth road conditions and rough patches and obstacles are interspersed by stretches of smooth surface. Since we would only like to differentiate between the values observed on a smooth surface vs. a rough surface, this timeseries clustering criteria is sufficient, though it is trivial to extend this to include multiple clusters. Let us denote such a cluster in the time series for trip i as L_i^m where $L_i^m \subseteq T_i$, and m is the cluster type. For detecting only smooth and rough surfaces $m = 2$. Next, we aggregate readings from multiple trips to find clusters that are repeating across trips and approximately in the same location using the following voting rule:

A point $l_i^x \in T_i$ provides a vote to another point $l_j^y \in T_j$ for it to be part of cluster m iff
(1) $euclidean\_distance(l_x^i, l_y^j) \leq \tau$;
(2) $l_i^x \in L_i^m$ and $l_j^y \in L_j^m$.

In other words, if two points from two different trips are sufficiently close and belong to the same cluster type in their respective trips, they will cast one vote to each other. For any point l_i^j, we define $c_m(l_i^j)$ to denote the number of votes l_i^j has received for cluster m. After aggregating the readings in this manner across all available trips, we can use the following algorithm to determine the list of points that belong to each cluster by using a threshold on the number of votes (τ_{vote}) a point has received. In this process, we find the list of points for which the conditions are invariant across trips, while reducing the false positives and non-persistent condition generated noise per trip. Algorithm 1 formally presents the algorithm.

Input: List of all trip points L_{in}, List of cluster types C, voting threshold τ_{vote}.
Output: List of trip points L_{out} annotated with cluster types
$L_{out} \leftarrow \emptyset$;
foreach *point l_j^i in L_{in}* **do**
    if $max_{m \in ST} c_m(l_j^i) > \tau_{vote}$ **then**
        $L_{out} \leftarrow (l_j^i, m)$;
    end
end

Algorithm 1. Segment Type Determination Method Based On Cross-Trip Voting.

Adaptive DBSCAN. The cross-trip majority voting method produces a list of points and their corresponding cluster types where the cluster type represents the road surface condition. Let $l_1, c_1, l_2, c_2, \cdots, l_n, c_n$ be such n majority-voted points and corresponding surface types along a road network. Our objective is to group these points such that the resultant timeseries indicates the segments corresponding to the surface conditions along the network. We employ a variant of DBSCAN, recently proposed in [1] on the output of the majority voting step to do this. We first explain why DBSCAN is not suitable for our problem, followed by the elaboration of our algorithm, where we modify [1] to suite our requirements.

For a set of points L, DBSCAN defines the density of l_i, denoted as $N_r(l_i)$, as the number of points that are present in a radius r around l_i. l_i is called a *core point* if $N_r(l_i) \geq MinPts$, where $MinPts$ is a user-defined constant. All the points around l_i present in a radius r are called *directly density-reachable* from l_i. A position l_j is *density-reachable* from l_i if there is a reachability relationship $(l_*)_1, \ldots, (l_*)_l$, where $(l_*)_1 = l_i$ and $(l_*)_l = l_j$. Two positions l_i and l_j are *density-connected* if they are both density-reachable from a core point l_c. Let L^β be a set of points, where $l_i \sqsubset L^\beta$ is density-connected with $l_j \sqsubset L^\beta$ for all $i \neq j$. We can randomly select the unclustered points and cluster all density-reachable points into the same cluster. This way, we can divide L into k clusters, where $0 \leq k \leq |L|/MinPts$. From our perspective, however, DBSCAN does not consider the surface types associated with each point. Thus, it is possible that DBSCAN would find clusters that only group nearby GPS points, without being sensitive to whether they represent a road segment consisting of static surface conditions. Moreover, density variations of the GPS readings can adversely affect the clustering. To accommodate these drawbacks, we introduce a further constraint to the clustering process.

Definition 3. *Gravity Segment-reachable.* *Two tuples l_i, c_i and l_j, c_j are gravity segment-reachable if position l_i is density-reachable from l_j and $c_j = c_i$*

Definition 4. *Gravity Segment-connected.* *Two tuples l_i, c_i and l_j, c_j are gravity segment-connected if l_i and l_j are model density-reachable from a core tuple l_{core}, c_{core}.*

This adaptive DBSCAN process performs the partitioning of the majority-voted L, C sequence to create partitions that represent road surface segments. From each such segment, we recover $sem_k = l_m^k, l_n^k, c_{core}^k$. The output from this step is augmented with the semantic segments produced during data fusion. The segments produced here have overlaps with the segments produced before. We run the change point detection once more to split the overlaps into a sequence of non-overlapping segments. For e.g. a $sem^k = l_m^k, l_n^k, [school]$ would be split into

$l_m^k, l_i^k, [school, road_{smooth}],$
$l_i^k, l_j^k, [school, road_{bump}],$
$l_j^k, l_n^k, [school, road_{smooth}].$

3.3 Drive Profile Determination

Once we have created a rich segmentation of available trip data, our task is to measure driving behavior under the ambient conditions present in each segment. Let a trip $T_i = seg_1^i, seg_2^i, seg_3^i, \ldots, seg_N^i$ be N segments representing a road network $\mathcal{R}$. Let M=number of observed trips (across users) for road network $\mathcal{R}$. For a given seg_j^i, let $ACC_j^i[3]$ represent the vector of accelerometer readings in the jth segment of trip T_i. We capture this data and need to predict a driver's behavior in the segment. monitoring drive behavior [2] as collection of such fine-grained training data does not scale to practical settings. Our objective, on the other hand, is to use simple unsupervised clustering techniques to investigate whether it is possible to distinguish driving habits in each segment. For this purposent driving conditions. It is not realistic to use supervised approaches us, we attempt to distinguish drive habits over a certain ambient context into two classes : *normal* or *rash*. Given M trips and N segments on $\mathcal{R}$, we define a $M x N$ matrix $\mathcal{A} = \lfloor a_{ij} \rfloor, 0 \leq i,j \leq M, N$, where $a_{i,j} = ACC_j^i$.

Segment-Sensitive Driving Behavior Clustering. Feature sets play an important role towards clustering quality of the data. Intuitively, acceleration variations of the vehicle is an indicator for goodness of behavior. This variation can be captured using the $ACCx_j^i$ component of ACC_j^i. However, different ambient contexts call for different boundaries to differentiate between good and bad driving behavior. E.g. speed profile in residential areas is different from speed profiles on bigger roads. Similarly, the $ACCz_j^i$ components can be indicative of the road surface induced shocks, which can give an estimate of how the driver is maneuvering different surface conditions. $ACCy_j^i$ on the other hand, provides lateral acceleration profile in turns.

We apply clustering techniques to cluster the data along each segment $\mathcal{A}_{*j}$ across multiple trips. This allows us to compare the driving behavior within the same segment across multiple trips. We transform the data in each cell a_{ij} to a set of features first. Subsequently, we apply the well-known K-NN clustering algorithm to find k clusters. In our case, $k = 2$. The clustering in K-NN is dependent on the choice of the seed(s). Our idea is to identify *normal* and *rash* behavior. Unfortunately, without training data, it is impossible to determine the exact data characteristics of these classes. Hence, we make use of a domain knowledge that most drivers usually drive in a respectful way and hence represent *median* behavior. We choose two seeds – one that is nearest to $\zeta(ACC_j)$, and one that is outside $\zeta(ACC_j) \pm r\sigma$ band, where ζ is $median(A_j)$ and σ is the standard deviation. After the clustering process, we label the set around $\zeta(ACC_j)$ as *normal* and the other cluster as *aberrant*. Note that many feature transformations (time and frequency domain) are possible on $\mathcal{A}_{*j}$ before the clustering step. In the experiments section, we present results with respect to a few well-adopted time domain features, and report our results with respect to our clustering approach.

4   Experiments

We have used a 3-month old Hyundai Santro car and a Samsung Galaxy II smartphone equipped with GPS, accelerometer and gyroscope to record data for our experimental evaluations. A sensing stack was developed on the Android platform of the smartphone to record data from each sensor with custom sampling rates. We secured the phone in one of the chambers in the car dashboard so that the forward movement of the car is recorded by the x-axis and the vertical movement by the z-axis of the accelerometer data. Understanding usage-related induced noise and other such human-generated disturbance to the data stream is out of scope of this paper.

A full-fledged rich data collection across many users for our problem is quite costly. Apart from the users needing to volunteer with time and money (fuel), most importantly, in absence of 'ground truth', it is hard to validate results on drive behavior. Hence, all our evaluations are based on a volunteer-driven data collected over 10 trips on a road stretch in New Delhi, shown in Fig. 2a.

A single volunteer drove the car on the selected road segment in each of the trips. An expert driver in the passenger seat did an assessment of the drive quality (good or rash) for different segments and logged them as 'ground truth'. Note that according to the Definitions 1 and 2 given earlier, the ground truths should be determined using population based statistics, but in the absence of such statistics we have used subjective estimates of an expert driver as ground truths for this work. The accelerometer data was recorded with a sampling frequency of 30 Hz, while the GPS information was recorded every second. It took us approximately 10–15 min to record each trip. With this data, we focus on understanding: (1) Efficacy of our algorithms to identify ambient driving contexts (2) Performance of identifying drive behavior in those contexts[4]. Note that due to the nature of our methodology, there is no suitable reference algorithm to compare our results against. The most recent work [2] used dynamic time warping-based supervised classification. As described earlier, apart from conducting some initial experiments with this methodology and revealing its drawbacks, this methodology is unsuitable for our approach of developing an unsupervised learning methodology.

4.1 Ambient Context Determination

In our first experiment, we wish to understand the efficacy of identifying challenging ambient driving contexts. For this purpose, we have focused our experiments to a selection of ambient contexts involving turns and road surfaces to perform in-depth analysis of our methodology.

We determine two types of ambient contexts, $viz.$, turn contexts and road surface contexts. As mentioned, we employed GIS-based map-matching algorithm to the trajectory recorded by the GPS data for identifying the turns. Accelerometer based segment data enrichment and cross-trip majority voting approach described earlier were employed to identify segments in the trajectory of each trip that corresponds to the road surface conditions. We have reported the results for identifying bumps on our route (Fig. 2a). Three different values of τ_{vote} were used to demonstrate the efficacy of the cross-trip majority voting method. $\tau_{vote} = 0$ represents segments discovered from the union of all points across all trips which are labelled as 'rough'. Similarly, $\tau_{vote} = 1$ represents segments discovered from the points that are labelled as 'rough' by at least two trips and so on. Figure 4a shows the number (percentage) of bumps on the road that were discovered by our method. As we can observe, for $\tau_{vote} = 0$, initially, the number of segments discovered increases monotonically as we find new 'rough'

---

[4] In all our experiments we have used $r = 2.5$ for the clustering operation, both for segmentation as well as for driving behavior classification.

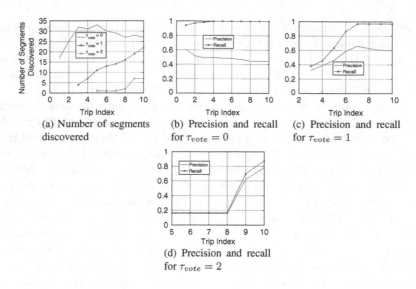

(a) Number of segments discovered

(b) Precision and recall for $\tau_{vote} = 0$

(c) Precision and recall for $\tau_{vote} = 1$

(d) Precision and recall for $\tau_{vote} = 2$

Fig. 4. Performance of ambient context discovery procedure

points on the trajectory as we include data from more trips, creating newer segments. However, increase in the number of segments also implies a corresponding decrease in the distance between two successive segment boundaries. Consequently, after a point, when the distance between two successive segments drops lower then the threshold of the adaptive DBSCAN algorithm, it automatically merges two successive segments resulting in a drop in the number of segments. This phenomenon can be observed from the plot shown for $\tau_{vote} = 0$. For higher values of τ_{vote}, increase in the number of segments is more sluggish as the probability for any point to acquire votes higher than τ_{vote} (and considered to be included in a segment) from same number of trips decreases with increasing τ_{vote}.

Figure 4b, c and d shows the accuracy of our segment discovery method which we compute by comparing against the ground truth. We observe that for all values of τ_{vote} the recall increases as more segments are discovered with increasing number of trips. The rate of increase becomes more sluggish for higher values of τ_{vote} as the segments are discovered slowly due to reason cited above. Observe that recall is highest for $\tau_{vote} = 0$ as it includes all points from all trips that are labelled as 'rough'. However, it also includes a large number of false positives which is reflected by the corresponding low precision value. For $\tau_{vote} = 1$, precision increases initially as we find more 'rough' points with increasing number of trips. However, as number of trip grows, after a point, it also starts including false positives resulting in a drop in its precision score. For $\tau_{vote} = 2$ we have a very low precision and recall at the beginning as it fails to find any segment for the reason stated above. However, due to the same reason it also includes minimum false positives as we increase the number of trips, resulting in a steady

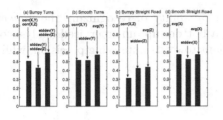 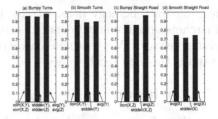

(a) Precision for segment based localized clustering   (b) Recall for segment based clustering

Fig. 5. Driving profile determination

Table 2. Features used in clustering for the four ambient contexts we have considered

Ambient context	Feature 1	Feature 2	Feature 3
Bumpy turn	corr(X,Y), corr(X,Z)	stddev(Y), stddev(Z)	avg(Y), avg(Z)
Smooth turns	corr(X,Y)	stddev(Y)	avg(Y)
Bumpy straight road	corr(X,Z)	stddev(Z)	avg(Z)
Smooth straight road	avg(X)	stddev(X)	avg(X)

increase in the precision score. We therefore select $\tau_{vote} = 2$ as our operating threshold for the adaptive DBSCAN algorithm.

4.2   Driving Characterization

Next, we performed experiments to identify driving behavior for an ambient context and validated our results with that of the ground truth collected using the expert driver. Here, we evaluate our proposed method of determining driving characteristics given an ambient context. We have considered 4 different ambient contexts - bumpy turn, smooth turn, bumpy straight road, smooth straight road - to characterize bad driving behavior for each ambient context. The characterization has been done following two approaches: (i) clustering localized segments (segment at a given location in the trajectory) across all the 10 trips and (ii) clustering all segments corresponding to a particular ambient context. Table 2, shows the features sets we chose for clustering different ambient contexts we have considered. The choice of these features are influenced by the accelerometer axes, which is expected to show maximum variation under a given context as discussed before in Sect. 3. Figure 5a and b shows the precision and recall values for identifying aberrant driving behaviors with our approach for the 4 ambient contexts. Although the precision is not notably high, ranging mostly between 50–60%, the recall values are much higher (80–90%) than the precision values implying that our method is an aggressive method where most of the aberrant driving behaviors are identified at the cost of a few normal driving behaviors being characterized as aberrant. However, unlike prior supervised learning methods presented earlier in the motivation section, which are dependent on limited training set data, our methodology demonstrates the capability of recognizing the impact of circumstantial ambient contexts using a bottom-up, unsupervised analysis of driving behavior. We continue to experiment towards improving precision, while retaining the high recall values.

5 Conclusion

Recently, a few research efforts have investigated supervised methodologies for driving behavior detection using smartphone sensors. However, we argue that in chaotic road settings, *ambient driving context* assumes importance in categorizing the driving behavior of an individual and it is hard to practically implement supervised data driven methodologies. In this paper, we present an information fusion-based methodology for determining ambient driving context using multiple data sources including smartphone sensors followed by the determination of driving behavior for a given ambient context. We focus on static ambient context and experiment with real data collected for a 'chaotic' road stretch in New Delhi. We report results demonstrating the feasibility and utility of our approach, while presenting insights on achievable quality for the determination of such fine-grained spatio-semantic driving behavior.

References

1. Cartier, S., et al.: Condense: managing data in community-driven mobile geosensor networks. In: SECON 2012, pp. 515–523. IEEE (2012)
2. Eren, H., et al.: Estimating driving behavior by a smartphone. In: Intelligent Vehicles Symposium (IV), 2012, pp. 234–239 (2012)
3. Johnson, D.A., Trivedi, M.M.: Driving style recognition using a smartphone as a sensor platform. In: Intelligent Transportation Systems (ITSC), pp. 1609–1615 (2011)
4. Kamimura, T., et al.: A system to comprehend a motorcycle's behavior using the acceleration and gyro sensors on a smartphone. In: Global Research and Education (2012)
5. Kunze, K., et al.: Which way am i facing: inferring horizontal device orientation from an accelerometer signal. In: ISWC 2009, pp 49–50 (2009)
6. Mitrovic, D.: Reliable method for driving events recognition. IEEE Trans. Intell. Transp. Syst. 6(2), 198–205 (2005)
7. Mohan, P., et al.: Nericell: rich monitoring of road and traffic conditions using mobile smartphones. In: SenSys 2008, pp. 323–336. ACM (2008)
8. Oliver, N., Pentland, A.P.: Graphical models for driver behavior recognition in a smartcar. In: Proceedings of the IEEE Intelligent Vehicles Symposium 2000 Cat No00TH8511, pp. 7–12 (2000)
9. Paefgen, J., et al.: Driving behavior analysis with smartphones: insights from a controlled field study. In: International Conference on Mobile and Ubiquitous Multimedia (2012)
10. Perez, A., et al.: Argos: an advanced in-vehicle data recorder on a massively sensorized vehicle for car driver behavior experimentation. IEEE Trans. Intell. Transp. Syst. 11(2), 463–473 (2010)
11. Qin, H., et al.: Heterogeneity-aware design for automatic detection of problematic road conditions. In: MASS 2011, pp. 252–261. IEEE (2011)

Impact of Contextual Factors
on Smartphone Applications Use

Artur H. Kronbauer[1,2(✉)] and Celso A.S. Santos[3]

[1] PMCC – IM – UFBA, Av. Adhemar de Barros, S/N, Salvador, Brazil
arturhk@gmail.com
[2] UNIFACS, R. Vieira Lopes N.2, Salvador, BA, Brazil
[3] DI – CT – UFES, Av. Fernando Ferrari S/N, CT VIII, Vitória, ES, Brazil
saibel@inf.ufes.br

Abstract. The development of methodologies and techniques to evaluate smartphones usability is an emerging topic in the scientific community and triggers discussions about which methodology is most appropriate. The lack of consensus is due to the inherent difficulty on capturing context data in the scenarios where the experiments take place and on relating them to the results found. This work aims to correlate potential usability problems in mobile applications with contextual factors that may occur during users' interactions on different devices, such as luminosity, device screen resolution, and the user's activity while interacting with the application. The methodology applied to carry out a field experiment take the following steps: identification of contextual factors that may influence users' interaction; use of the UXEProject infrastructure to support the automatic capture of applications' context data; implementation of long term experiments with real users using three different mobile applications over almost one year period. In this paper, we present and discuss the results obtained during this study.

Keywords: Usability evaluation · Experimentation · Logging · Context

1 Introduction

With the continuous advance of wireless networks and the great proliferation of smartphones, many applications are launched in the market every day. Nowadays, the requirements for the ubiquitous computing, which predicts software as part of people's daily life and available, transparently, at anytime, anywhere and from any device, have been increasingly explored to build these applications. This application's ubiquity is reached by automatically monitoring contextual information related to the use of these applications.

Collecting data from smartphone users' experiences and associating them to the context where the interactions occur is a great challenge for the Human-Computer Interaction (HCI) area. The situations change and the results from the tests are highly dependent on the context. As an example, a person that interacts with a mobile application sitting on his home sofa, will have different external interferences when compared to the same task done while walking on the street.

© Institute for Computer Sciences, Social Informatics and Telecommunications Engineering 2014
I. Stojmenovic et al. (Eds.): MOBIQUITOUS 2013, LNICST 131, pp. 667–679, 2014.
DOI: 10.1007/978-3-319-11569-6_52

In the literature, it is possible to find many authors who defend the necessity to relate the context influence on the users' interactions with these applications [1]. To conduct the studies with such a broad reach, it is necessary to use methodologies and techniques that carry out experiments that are able to collect data contextualized with the scenarios where the interactions take place [2]. This fact provokes a lot of discussion regarding the place where experiments are conducted (in the field or in the laboratory) [3], as well as the techniques which may be used to extract the best set of data that characterize the experiments [4]. This work was motivated by these discussions, having the following main contributions: (i) Comparison of the main approaches used to evaluate smartphone applications; (ii) Use the UXEproject infrastructure, as a new approach created with the potential to extract and relate quantitative, contextual and subjective data. (iii) Conduction of field experiments, relating contextual factors to usability metrics for smartphone applications.

The remainder of this paper is divided into six sections. Section 2 presents the state of the art concerning evaluations of smartphone usability, encompassing the investigation of the approaches used to carry out the usability experiments. Section 3 describes the UXEproject infrastructure adopted to facilitate the experiment presented in this work. Section 4 describes the methodology used for the execution of the experiment. Section 5 summarizes the presentation and discussion of the results obtained. Section 6 presents the conclusions and future prospects.

2 The State of the Art

The relationship between context and usability is an issue widely discussed by the scientific community which studies the influence of scenarios regarding the interaction with smartphones. The experiences show that humans usually interact with systems in unusual ways [5]. Thus, the insertion of users and real scenarios in the tests is essential to delineate the users' preferences and the consequent adaptation of products addressed to them [3].

Kawalek et al. [6] suggests evaluation methods which encompass different observation angles in the experiments, such as quantitative data (usability metrics), the subjective evaluation (users' feelings) and contextual data (e.g., environmental conditions and the devices' characteristics). The main problem is the lack of literature covering approaches that support these three requirements combined in a single experiment. Generally, only one or two of them are related.

Coursaris and Kim [7] carried out a systematic data survey, from 2000 to 2010, which allowed them to identify that 47 % of the works that evaluate mobile devices are done in the laboratory, 21 % in the field, 10 % used both scenarios and 22 % are conducted without the participation of users. A point to be observed is that many studies don't consider the mobile feature of such devices, applying traditional evaluation methods. Another fact which calls attention in the results presented is that 47 % of the studies evaluate individual and out of context tasks, 46 % are based on the technology used and only 14 % consider context data and the users' characteristics.

In order to identify the current reality of the usability investigations related to smartphones, this section presents a study encompassing works published from 2008 to

2012 that describe empirical experiments and investigate at least one of the following usability attributes: efficiency, effectiveness, satisfaction, learning, operability, accessibility, flexibility, usefulness and ease of use. The publication venues investigate were from the ACM, IEEE, Springer, and Google Scholar. Twenty-one works were selected, and they are listed in Table 1 along with the investigation techniques used. The results of this study are detailed as follows:

- The Table 1 summarizes the techniques used for data capture in usability experiments: 71.4 % used surveys 19 % logging, 14.2 % evaluators' direct observations, 14.2 % interviews with users, 19 % the think aloud technique and 28.5 % other less traditional techniques. The sum of percentages exceeds 100 % because 66.3 % of the experiments encompass more than one technique.

Table 1. Works (2008–2012) that investigate the usability of applications for smartphones.

Authors	Applied techniques
Burigat et al. (2008) [8]	Logging and surveys
Sodnik et al. (2008) [9]	Direct observation, interviews and logging
Fitchett and Cockburn (2009) [10]	Direct observation and interviews
Chin and Salomaa (2009) [11]	Logging on Web servers and surveys
Lai et al. (2009) [12]	On-line surveys and cognitive interviews
Ebner et al. (2009) [13]	Thinking Aloud and Survey
Hansen and Ghinea (2009) [14]	Survey
Bødker et al. (2009) [15]	Surveys, focus groups and individual interviews
Kim et al. (2010) [16]	Survey
Li and Yeh (2010) [17]	Survey
Maly et al. (2010) [18]	Logging, Thinking Aloud and direct observation
Grønli et al. (2010) [19]	Survey
Kang et al. (2011) [20]	Surveys and logging
Fetaji et al. (2011) [21]	MLUAT, Survey and Heuristic Evaluations
Hegarty and Wusteman (2011) [22]	Survey and Think Aloud
Grønli et al. (2011) [23]	Survey
Sparkes et al. (2012) [24]	Notes, Think Aloud and interview
Bradley et al. (2012) [25]	Surveys
Schaub et al. (2012) [26]	Logging and direct observation
Kirwan et al. (2012) [27]	Logging and on-line Survey
Spyridonis et al. (2012) [28]	Survey and Interview

- Concerning the amount of times each usability attribute was investigate, it's possible to conclude that Ease of use (100 %), Satisfaction (90.4 %), Effectiveness (76.1 %) and Efficiency (52.4 %) are the most investigated usability attributes.

- The number of participants was divided in three different ranges: 55 % of the experiments used from 5 to 24 participants, 20 % used from 25 and 44 participants and 25 % were carried out with over 44 users.
- Regarding the investigation scenario, 52.3 % of the experiments were conducted in laboratory, 33.3 % in the field, 9.5 % in both scenarios and 4.7 % with simulators.
- One of the main aspects to be highlighted is that only 3 experiments investigated contextual data, and were conducted in the laboratory, meeting the expectations and desires of a great number of researchers.
- The last issue to be pointed out is that none of the approaches captures the users' impressions concerning the application usability during their interactions, which could provide the correlation between the subjective data in the evaluations.

The main observation of the previous study was that in the experiments, surveys are used to collect data, which might complicate the correlation between different kinds of information in order to find out usability problems [29]. Furthermore, in most cases, contextual factors are not investigated, an issue posed by many researchers as a primary factor for advances in the usability evaluations area [1, 2, 7].

3   The *UXEProject* Infrastructure

The *UXEProject* infrastructure was built to give support to the usability evaluation based on the analysis of data captured directly from the devices. The formal model which originated the infrastructure can be found in full in [30]. It is conceptually divided in three units, which comprise: (1) mapping of tasks that will be investigated; (2) combination of traceability metrics which enables the capture of contextual data, usability statistics and subjective information regarding the experiences provided to users; and (3) the storage and evaluation of data captured during the experiments.

Using the *UXEProject*, the mapping of tasks is built through the capture of methods executed in the application that will be evaluated. The Evaluation Team is responsible for the choice and mapping of tasks, as well as the creation of data capture metrics. It is important to emphasize that it is not necessary to have programming experience to carry out these activities. The following subsections describe the tools used to encompass the predicted components in the three infrastructure units.

3.1   Mapping Unit

The first tool developed in the infrastructure encompasses the source code preparation to enable the mapping of tasks provided in the applications. This tool, named *Mapping Aspect Generator* (MAG), imports the source code from the application to be mapped and creates an Aspect that inserts the method *onUserInteraction*[1] in the classes that refer to the interaction layer. This process allows detecting the users' actions. In order

---

[1] Further details at http://developer.android.com/reference/android/app/Activity.html#onUser Interaction()

to have the application ready to be mapped, it is necessary to compile the application source code with the Aspect generated. After that, it is enough to embed the application in a smartphone to make the interactions.

So that the Evaluation Team maps the tasks, another tool, named Automatic Task Description (ATD), was developed. The ATD should be embedded in a device and executed simultaneously with the application that will be mapped. Thus, as the Evaluation Team interacts with the application, the methods executed are automatically captured to be used as steps for the conclusion of a task.

The ATD method consists of the use of a filter that identifies when there is a user interaction. The filter identifies which classes, methods and parameters of the application were used. This information is stored in a XML file, which will be sent to the server to be used in the creation of metrics.

3.2 Traceability Unit

The tool designed to allow the instrumentation of applications and to enable the data capture was named UXE Metrics Generation. This tool contains a library which has the structures of metrics to perform the measurements.

Initially, the tool has as input the XML file generated in the Mapping Unit. Then, the existing methods in the XML file are connected to the Metrics Library available in the tool, allowing the creation of Aspects responsible for the capture, transmission and persistence of data. At last, it is sufficient to compile the application's source code along with the Aspects generated and to embed the application in a device that will be utilized by a user.

To encompass the data collection, three types of metrics were defined. The usability and context metrics use the Logging technique [8, 9], and the subjective metrics use the Experience Sampling Method [31] technique.

In order that the data related to the experiments could be transmitted and stored on a database, a micro instance from the service known as Amazon EC2[2] was utilized.

3.3 Assessment Unit

To encompass the components defined in the Assessment Unit, the following processes were performed: (i) create and setup an FTP and a database (DB) server and make them available on the Internet; (ii) carry out the modeling of a DB and a Data Warehouse (DW) to store and enable the analysis of information captured during the experiments; (iii) create tools to detect the presence of new files in the FTP server, populate the DB and load the DW; and (iv) choose an OLAP tool to the data analysis.

The Database Management System selected to store the data was the MySql Community Server. In order to encompass the load of data on the DB, a tool named Data Load was developed. The steps executed by this tool are: detect the arrival of new files in the FTP server, extract the data and load them into the DB.

---

[2] Available at http://aws.amazon.com/ec2/

The last tool designed (ETL Maker) extracts, transforms and loads the data, transferring them from the DB to the DW. To make the data analysis easier, the OLAP tool Pentaho Analysis Services[3] was chosen.

4 Experiments Conducted

The experiment reported in this article was divided in six different phases (Table 2), based on the directives proposed in the DECIDE framework [32], which guided the specification of the steps during all phases of the experiment.

An important aspect of the experiment was to conduct exploratory research aiming to find applications that have attractive functionalities and with the possibility to be inserted in people's daily life. The applications considered include the following prerequisites: they must have been developed using the Java language and for the Android platform; their source code must be available and have explicit rights of use; they must have been built using good programming techniques, showing a good modularization of its functionalities, to allow the source code to be instrumented with AOP.

Three applications were selected for the experiments. The first application, named Mileage, aims to help the users to control their costs with fuel and other maintenance services of an automobile, such as oil change, brake pad change, among others. The second one was ^3 (Cubed), a music and video clips manager. On its main menu, it is possible to select songs or videos and play them. The last application, named Shuffle, schedules the activities that allow to link tasks to dates and times, besides permitting the association to projects and contexts. Figure 1 shows the three selected application interfaces and Table 3 details the tasks investigated in the usability experiments.

Another important aspect of the experiment was define the participants. The selection considered the profiles that were under analysis and their smartphones' features. Twenty-one users were selected, taking into consideration the age, educational grade, school background, occupation and purchasing power.

The relationship of the data used in the experiment was defined according to the capture strategies provided by the UXEProject infrastructure. Thus, the usability data was considered related to the mapped tasks, the users' profile, the smartphones' features and the contextual data obtained through sensors. The smartphones' screen features and the range of values considered to compose the interactions context were:

- Resolution (pixels): $\chi \leq 320 \times 240$ (low); $320 \times 240 < \chi \leq 320 \times 480$ (medium); $\chi > 320 \times 480$ (high)
- Size (inches): $\chi \leq 2.4$ (small); $2.4 < \chi \leq 3.5$ (medium); $\chi > 3.5$ (large)

So as to contextualize the environment where the interactions take place, the data are captured considering the degree of luminosity, the device position during the interactions and the speed in which the user moves. These context data are captured directly from the devices sensors and their reference values are the following:

- Luminosity (lux): $\chi \leq 100$ (low); $100 < \chi \leq 10000$ (medium); $\chi > 10000$ (high)

---

[3] Available at http://community.pentaho.com/

Table 2. Phases of experiment based on DECIDE framework.

(1) **D**etermine the goals	The major interest in the contextual factors which can interfere in the usability of the applications that will be analyzed
(2) **E**xplore the questions	Based on the objective to be reached, a set of questions was made to direct the experiments, and the data generation and analysis: − How does the luminosity of the interaction's scenario interfere in the performance of smartphone application users? − Which tasks are more affected by the position of the smartphone at the moment of the interactions? − How does the user's movement interfere in his interaction with the applications? − What is the difference in users' performance due to the smartphone setup? − What kind of context information can used to improve the usability analysis?
(3) **C**hoose the evaluation paradigm and techniques	The evaluation approach in this work should encompass some conditions, such as: the experiment has to be conducted in the field; without supervision; for a long period of time; data will be collected automatically; no restrictions concerning the number of users; no need to know how the applications were developed; potential to be applied to any application for the Android platform; no need to have the Evaluation Team to write the programming codes; possibility to analyze different kinds of data; possibility to specify the tasks to be analyzed In the face of the listed conditions, the *UXEProject* infrastructure was chosen, as it gives support to all requirements demanded
(4) **I**dentify the practical issues	In this phase, a great number of prerequisites were raised, among which it can be highlighted: (1) Selection of applications to be evaluated; (2) definition of the investigated tasks; (3) definition of the group of users to participate in the experiment; (4) definition of the data to be considered in the evaluation
(5) **D**ecide how to deal with ethical issues	A website was built for the conduction of the experiment. It brings explanations concerning the research and a term of use of the applications. In order that the user is enabled to download the applications, it is necessary that he explicit his agreement on participating in the experiment
(6) **E**valuate, Interpret, and present the data	Section 5 will present the results of the evaluations made during the experiment conduction. The data collection took place from 12/01/2011 to 11/30/2012

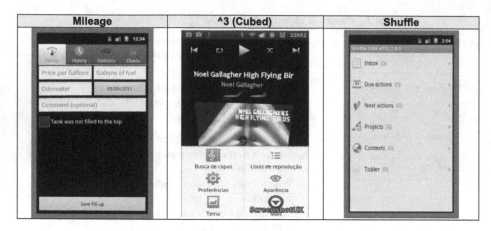

Fig. 1. The three selected mobile application interfaces.

Table 3. Tasks investigated in the experiments.

Application	Instrumented tasks	
Mileage	1. Register a vehicle	5. Add a new maintenance control
	2. Input data of a new fill-up	6. View the graph referring to the fuel price variation
	3. Setup a new data format	7. View the graph that refers to the traveled distance
	4. Modify the data in the history of fill-ups	8. Import stored data
^3 (Cubed)	1. Choose a song from a playlist	4. Choose a new presentation theme for the application
	2. Create a new playlist	
	3. Add a song to a playlist. Change the application's appearance	5. Open the Equalizer
Shuffle	1. Add an activity	6. Delete a context
	2. Delete activities from the inbox	7. Modify a project by choosing a context
	3. Modify an activity	
	4. Register a new project and choose an available context	8. Backup data
		9. Select the help option
	5. Register a new context	10. Create a scheduled activity

- Movement (m/s): $\chi < 0{,}2$ (stationary); $0{,}2 \leq \chi \leq 2{,}7$ (walking); $\chi > 2{,}7$ (motorized)
- Position: vertical; horizontal; mixed

5 Experimental Results

Initially, observed were the percentage values of tasks completed with errors in each application regarding the luminosity variation. The objective here is to identify the

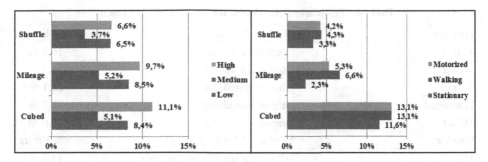

Fig. 2. Errors rate due to luminosity (left) and due to the movement speed (right)

possible influence of this contextual variable on the interactions. In order to conduct the analysis, the luminosity was isolated and related to the percentage of tasks completed with errors in each application, as presented in the left of the Fig. 2.

It was verified that, for all applications, the highest rates of errors in completed tasks occur when the luminosity is either too high or too low, that is, when the interaction scenario's conditions are not within the parameters considered standard, which proves the luminosity influence on users' performance.

The next evaluation refers to the speed in which users move when performing the interactions. The speed usually varies due to three possibilities: the user is either walking, or stationary, or in any kind of means of transportation. In Fig. 2, it is possible to identify in all applications that the actions performed with no movement show a lower error rate than the ones performed while moving.

The next analysis, detailed in Table 4, regards smartphone positions in the interactions. The aim here is to find usability problems in specific tasks related to the interaction position (vertical, horizontal or mixed). Only the tasks which had an error rate over 10 % related to the position of interaction are shown. This sort of information is useful for the applications developers, as in future versions of the applications, the interactions in positions of high error rate can be inhibited. Table 4 shows also that more than 50 % of the problems occur when the tasks are done in a mixed position, that is, they are started in a position and ended in another.

The following analysis verifies the existence of contextual variables interference related to smartphone characteristics, such as, screen resolution and size. In order to carry out this evaluation, the tasks executions were investigated considering the smartphones' characteristics. The data presented in left chart of the Fig. 3 allows identifying that the screen resolution influences significantly in the tasks execution speed, that is, the higher the resolution, the faster the tasks are concluded. We can observe, as for the application Cubed, once the resolution increases, in average 26.03 %, the task speed when compared to the low resolution. In the Mileage application, this difference is 19.66 % and, in the Shuffle, 17.17 %.

The same analysis made earlier was designed to verify the screen size influence on the users' interactions. In the right of Fig. 3 right, one can see that the screen size is another contextual variable which influences the performance of users. In the Cubed application, the average speed for the task execution decreases around 4.1 s when

Table 4. Error/failure rate due to the position of interaction

Position	Tasks – Mileage	% Errors
Vertical	Register a vehicle	16.7 %
Mixed	Register a vehicle	14.3 %
Vertical	Import stored data	21.1 %
Horizontal	Import stored data	18.2 %
Mixed	Import stored data	20.0 %
Position	Tasks – ^3 (Cubed)	% Errors
Mixed	Choose a song from a playlist	11.2 %
Mixed	Add a new song in/to a playlist	16.7 %
Vertical	Change the application's appearance	10.6 %
Horizontal	Choose a new theme	14.0 %
Position	Tasks – Shuffle	% Errors
Mixed	Add a new task	12.9 %
Mixed	Delete all activities	14.3 %
Vertical	Backup data	14.3 %
Mixed	Open the help option	20.0 %

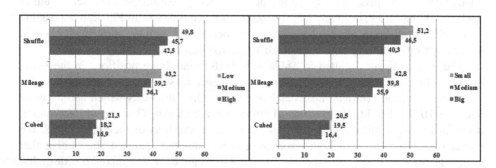

Fig. 3. Task execution time (in seconds) due to screen resolution (left) and size (right)

compared to the use of small screen smartphones. In the Mileage application, this difference is apparent around 6.9 s, and, in the Shuffle, the difference is 10.9 s.

A fact observed in the smartphones market is that, normally, the phones with smaller screen also have low resolution. Thus, the users' performance was observed considering the two variables simultaneously. The metrics used to measure the performance was the percentage of tasks completed with error. The Table 5(a) shows that the smaller the size and the lowest the resolution of the smartphones screen, more errors are found in the executed tasks. The difference between the extremes, that is, big screens with high resolution compared to small screens with low resolution, is 9.3 % of tasks executed with errors.

Table 5. Task error percentage considering (i) screen size and resolution variation and (ii) the purchasing power and screen resolution variation

screen size/resolution	Error(%)
high/big	4.8
high/medium	4.9
medium/big	6.7
medium/med	7.8
medium/small	9.7
low/medium	12.9
low/small	14.1

(a)

screen resolution/social class	Error(%)
high/high	5.2
low/high	12.3
high/medium	5.5
medium/medium	5.6
low/medium	9.6
medium/low	6.3
low/low	12.0

(b)

When analyzing the rate of tasks executed with errors along with the profile of participants, an intriguing fact was observed. The occurrence of errors in the low social class is greater than in the other classes. In order to search for an explanation for this result, the kind of device used in the experiment by these participants was investigated. The conclusion was that the rate of errors was not related to the users' purchasing power, but to the low resolution of the device's screen. As the majority of the people with low purchasing power used low resolution smartphones, an isolated analysis of the social class can lead to wrong conclusions. This latest analysis highlights one of the potentialities of the UXEProject infrastructure as it permits to associate different contextual factors in a single evaluation, decreasing thereby the possibility of wrong conclusions. In Table 5(b), it is observed that, regardless the purchasing power, the errors are more frequent when low resolution smartphones are used.

6 Conclusions and Future Works

From the Sect. 2 of this article, the conclusion is that the majority of experiments made to evaluate the usability of applications for smartphones use surveys to collect the data and there is no correlation between the contextual variables and the usability problems observed. This fact is contrary to expectations of many researchers in area.

The results obtained in the experiment showed that the UXEProject infrastructure is a good solution for the investigation of usability problems associated to different types of data, highlighting the data collection using the smartphones' sensors. With the experiments' results, it is observed that approximately 70 % of the interactions occur when users are stationary, having the device in a single position and with a normal environment luminosity. However, when these contextual factors change, the users make more mistakes and take longer to execute the tasks. This information suggest that the applications should, for example (i) make interactions impractical in positions which offer more probability of errors, forcing users to interact in an appropriate position; (ii) detect the external luminosity and try to balance the luminosity radiated by the device in order to guarantee a good visualization; and (iii) identify the user's movement and only enable the most usual functionalities, decreasing the visual pollution.

Another important observation concerns the smartphones' setup interference in the users' performance. Furthermore, it was proved that the correlation of different kinds of information are important for the conclusion of the results, as seen in the relationship between the errors rate and low purchasing power people. As a future work, it is intended to incorporate other sensors to the UXEProject, aiming to conduct new investigations involving different contextual factors.

References

1. Hansen, J.: An investigation of smartphone applications: exploring usability aspects related to wireless personal area networks, context-awareness, and remote information access. Dr' Thesis, Brunel University (2012)
2. Balagtas-Fernandez, F., Hussmann, H.: Evaluation of user-interfaces for mobile application development environments. In: Jacko, J.A. (ed.) HCI International 2009, Part I. LNCS, vol. 5610, pp. 204–213. Springer, Heidelberg (2009)
3. Jensen, K.L., Larsen, L.B: Evaluating the usefulness of mobile services based on captured usage data from longitudinal field trials. In: Proceedings of 4th International Conference on Mobile Technology, Application and Systems, pp. 675–682. ACM (2007)
4. Zhang, D., Adipat, B.: Challenges, methodologies, and issues in the usability testing of mobile applications. Int. J. HCI 18(3), 293–308 (2005)
5. Mallick, M.: Mobile and Wireless Design Essentials. Wiley, New York (2003)
6. Kawalek, J., Stark, A., Riebeck, M.: A new approach to analyze human-mobile computer interaction. J. Usability Stud. 3(2), 90–98 (2008)
7. Coursaris, C.K., Kim, D.J.: A meta-analytical review of empirical mobile usability studies. J. Usability Stud. 6(3), 117–171 (2011)
8. Burigat, S., Chittaro, L., Gabrielli, S.: Navigation techniques for small-screen devices: An evaluation on maps and web pages. Int. J. HC Stud. 66(2), 78–97 (2008)
9. Sodnik, J., et al.: A user study of auditory versus visual interfaces for use while driving. Int. J. HC Stud. 66(5), 318–332 (2008)
10. Fitchett, S., Cockburn, A.: Evaluating reading and analysis tasks on mobile devices: A case study of tilt and flick scrolling. In: 21st Annual Conference on Australian CHI, pp. 255–332 (2009)
11. Chin, A., Salomaa, J.P.: A user study of mobile web services and applications from the 2008 Beijing Olympics. In: 20th ACM Conference on Hypertext and Hypermedia, pp. 343–344 (2009)
12. Lai, J., et al.: Life360: Usability of mobile devices for time use surveys. In: American Association for Public Opinion Research Annual Conference, pp. 5582–5589 (2009)
13. Ebner, M., Stickel, C., Scerbakov, N., Holzinger, A.: A study on the compatibility of ubiquitous learning (u-Learning) systems at university level. In: Stephanidis, C. (ed.) UAHCI 2009, Part III. LNCS, vol. 5616, pp. 34–43. Springer, Heidelberg (2009)
14. Hansen, J., Ghinea, G.: Multi-platform bluetooth remote control. In: IEEE International Conference on for Internet Technology and Secured Transactions, pp. 1–2 (2009)
15. Bødker, M., et al.: Smart phones and their substitutes: task-medium fit and business models. In: 8th International Conference on Mobile Business, pp. 24–29. IEEE Computer Society (2009)
16. Kim, S., et al.: Mobile web 2.0 with multi-display buttons. Commun. ACM 53(1), 136–141 (2010)
17. Li, Y.M., Yeh, Y.S.: Increasing trust in mobile commerce through design aesthetics. Comput. Hum. Behav. 26(4), 673–684 (2010)
18. Maly, I., et al.: Interactive analytical tool for usability analysis of mobile indoor navigation application. In: The 3rd International Conference on Human System Interaction, pp. 259–266. IEEE (2010)

19. Grønli, T. et al.: Android, Java ME and windows mobile interplay: The case of a context-aware meeting room. In: 24th International Conference on Advanced Information Networking and Applications Workshops, pp. 920–925 (2010)
20. Kang, Y., et al.: Analysis of factors affecting the adoption of smartphones. In: ITMC, IEEE International, 919–925 (2011)
21. Fetaji, B., et al.: Assessing effectiveness in mobile learning by devising MLUAT methodology. Int. J. Comput. Commun. 5(3), 178–187 (2011)
22. Hegarty, R., Wusteman, J.: Evaluating EBSCOhost mobile. Libr. Hi Tech. 29(2), 320–333 (2011)
23. Grønli, T., et al.: Integrated Context-aware and cloud-based adaptive application home screens for android phones. In: 14th International Conference on HCI, pp. 427–435. Springer (2011)
24. Sparkes, J., et al.: A usability study of patients setting up a cardiac event loop recorder and blackberry gateway for remote monitoring at home. Off. J. Am. Telemed. Assoc. 18(6), 484–490 (2012)
25. Bradley, P.R., et al.: Smartphone application for transmission of ECG images in pre-hospital STEMI treatment. In: IEEE Systems and Information Engineering Design Symposium, pp. 118–123 (2012)
26. Schaub, F., et al.: Password entry usability and shoulder surfing susceptibility on different smartphone platforms. In: 11th International Conference on Mobile and Ubiquitous Multimedia (2012)
27. Kirwan, M., et al.: Using smartphone technology to monitor physical activity in the 10,000 Steps program: a matched case-control trial. J. Med. Internet Res. 14(2), e55 (2012)
28. Spyridonis, F., et al.: Evaluating the usability of a virtual reality-based android application in managing the pain experience of wheelchair users. In: 34th Annual International Conference of the IEEE EMBS - Engineering in Medicine and Biology Society, pp. 2460–2463 (2012)
29. Courage, C., Baxter, K.: Understanding Your User: A Practical Guide to User Requirements, Methods, Tools, and Techniques. Morgan Kaufmann Publishers, San Francisco (2005)
30. Kronbauer, A.H., et al.: Smartphone applications usability evaluation: A hybrid model and its implementation. In: 4th International Conference on Human-Centred Software Engineering, pp. 146–163 (2012)
31. Ickin, S., et al.: Factors influencing quality of experience of commonly used mobile applications. IEEE Commun. Mag. 50(4), 48–56 (2012)
32. Sharp, H., et al.: Interaction Design: Beyond Human-Computer Interaction, 2 edn. Wiley, New York (2007)

Short-Paper Session

A Highly Accurate Method for Managing Missing Reads in RFID Enabled Asset Tracking

Rengamathi Sankarkumar$^{(\boxtimes)}$, Damith Ranasinghe, and Thuraiappah Sathyan

Auto-ID Lab, The School of Computer Science, University of Adelaide,
Adelaide, Australia
{rengamathi.sankarkumar,damith.ranasinghe,
thuraiappah.sathyan}@adelaide.edu.au

Abstract. RFID based tracking systems have to overcome some significant challenges such as uncertainty to improve accuracy. We describe a highly accurate and scalable location tracking algorithm achieved by integrating an object compression technique with particle filtering.

Keywords: RFID · Tracking · Particle filter · Optimization · Supplychain

1 Introduction

Radio Frequency Identification (RFID) is a promising unique identification technology widely adopted for tracking applications such as the location of goods in supply chains where the motivation behind using RFID based tracking is to improve the visibility of objects travelling though a supply chain [1]. But, RFID technology cannot be directly utilized because to obtain an accurate location tracking system, first, we must overcome uncertainty in RFID based tracking networks [2]. Uncertainty in RFID data is mainly caused by missed reads, where tagged objects exist in a readable zone but the RFID readers fail to read the tags due to factors such as interference, noise, distance between the reader and the tag [4]. The missed reads make RFID data incomplete [2] and when such noisy data is used in tracking applications the location of objects can become ambiguous.

Recent research such as [3] applied smoothing techniques to clean individual tag streams and estimate tag counts in a given location. However, these techniques are not suitable to identify anomalies such as missed reads. In [2] authors used a time varying graph model to capture packaging level information (containment relationships) and the location of an object is estimated using data inferred from the graphical model. But, this technique can only be applied for objects having a containment relationship such as cases on a pallet.

In this paper, we present a technique that addresses location uncertainty caused by missed reads in an RFID enabled returnable asset tracking application [1]. We propose a highly accurate method for real time tracking capable of estimating the most likely location of assets under uncertainty (missed reads) based

© Institute for Computer Sciences, Social Informatics and Telecommunications Engineering 2014
I. Stojmenovic et al. (Eds.): MOBIQUITOUS 2013, LNICST 131, pp. 683–687, 2014.
DOI: 10.1007/978-3-319-11569-6_53

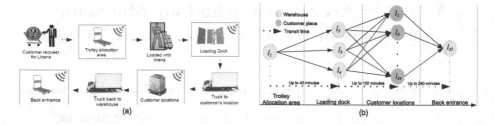

Fig. 1. (a) Business process (b) object flow model

on a sampling-based inference technique known as particle filters. Furthermore, we develop a real-time object compression technique by exploiting objects that travel together to optimize the tracking algorithm. Finally, we conduct extensive experiments and evaluate the performance of the proposed tracking algorithm. The rest of the paper is organized as follows Sect. 2 describes the problem we have considered; Sects. 3 and 4 explains the main contribution of the paper; and Sect. 5 concludes the paper.

2   Problem Statement

Before defining the problem, we define the notations used in this paper: (i) $L = \{l_p | p = 1, .., s\}$ denotes a set of locations where RFID tag reading capability is deployed; (ii) $T = \{t_i | i = 1, .., m\}$ gives a set of discrete time stamps; (iii) $O = \{o_j | j = 1, .., q\}$ is a set of tagged objects; and (iv) $transit = \{transit_{l_p} | p = 1, .., s\}$ denotes transit times between fixed locations. Then raw RFID reads from a reader can be represented by the schema $\{time(t_i), objectID(o_j), location(l_p)\}$.

Returnable asset management requirements are derived from a linen services company in South Australia. In this scenario, trolleys (objects) are the returnable assets which are attached with RFID tags to increase their visibility. The company's linen distribution scenario is depicted in Fig. 1, where RFID readers are installed in the trolley allocation area, loading docks, premises of customer locations and the back entrance of the company's warehouse. If there is a missed read in any of these locations then the location of the object is ambiguous. The particle filtering (PF) based tracking algorithm attempts to resolve this ambiguity by predicting the most likely location.

3   PF Based Tracking Algorithm with Object Compression

A particle filter can be applied to any non-linear recursive Bayesian filtering problem [4]. To define the problem of tracking, we consider the evolution of the state sequence from: (i) the **Motion Model** $x_t = f_t(x_{t-1}, v_{k-1})$, where f_t is a possible non-linear function, and v_{k-1} is i.i.d. process noise; and (ii) the **Measurement Model** $y_t = h_t(x_t, u_k)$, where h_t is a possible non-linear function,

---

Algorithm 1. *PF_based_tracking_with_object_compression*

Require: $raw\_reads^r = (T, O, L)$ where r = 1,2,... // (time, object ID, location) where
   $T = \{t_i | i = 1, .., m\}$, $O = \{o_j | j = 1, .., q\}$, $L = \{l_p | p = 1, .., 25\}$
Require: transit = $\{transit_k | k = 1, .., 25\}$, δt
1: $t \leftarrow r.t_1$ // get the initial time from raw_reads
2: **while** $\forall$ r $\in raw\_reads$ **do**
3:    **if** $r.t_i >= t$ **and** $r.t_i <= t + \delta t$ **then**
4:       **if** *new_object_found* **then**
5:          $object\_list.add(r.t_i, r.o_j, r.l_p, probability \leftarrow 1, new\_object \leftarrow true)$
6:       **else**
7:          $object\_list.update(r, probability, new\_object \leftarrow false)$
8:       **end if**
9:    **else**
10:       **while** $\forall o_j \in object\_list$ **do**
11:          $group\_object^n \leftarrow$ grouped objects by location for time window $[t$ and $t + \delta t]$
12:       **end while**
13:       **for** k = 1 **to** n **do**
14:          $hashtable.put(ID^k, group\_object^k)$
15:          $group \leftarrow (t, ID^k, location\ of\ k^{th} group\_object)$
16:          **if** $group\_object^k$ contains $new\_object(true)$ **then**
17:             initialize group
18:          **end if**
19:          predict, update, normalize and resample group
20:          $object^d \leftarrow hashtable.get(ID^k)$ //get back the compressed objects
21:          $object\_list.update(\forall d \in object, probability)$
22:       **end for**
23:       $t \leftarrow r.t_i$ // next t from r
24:    **end if**
25: **end while**
26: $current\_time \leftarrow$ current time from the system
27: **while** $not\_end\_of(object\_list)$ **do**
28:    $obj \leftarrow object\_list.get\_next$
29:    $max\_time \leftarrow obj.t_i + transit_{(obj.l_p)}$
30:    **if** $current\_time > max\_time$ **then**
31:       $pred\_loc \leftarrow$ the most likely location; $pred\_time \leftarrow obj.t_i + (transit_{(obj.l_p)})/2$
32:       $probability \leftarrow$ estimated probability of o_j
33:       $obj.t_i \leftarrow pred\_time, obj.l_p \leftarrow pred\_loc$
34:       $object\_list.update(obj)$
35:    **end if**
36: **end while**

---

and u_k is i.i.d. measurement noise. The PF consist of five steps: initialization, prediction, update, normalization and resampling [4].

The PF based tracking algorithm gives the most probable location l_p of the object o_j with N state particles, at every timestep t_i, as a probability distribution over l_p possible locations. The state space is defined along the x-axis. Every reader involved is represented as a sensor location along the x-axis.

The motion model is constructed with a transition matrix M. **Transition Matrix:** The transition probability is defined with a conditional probability, $p(L_{t_i}|L_{t_{i-1}})$ between locations L_{t_i} and $L_{t_{i-1}}$, where the current time step is t_i and previous time step is t_{i-1}. If L has p locations, then M can be represented by a $p \times p$ matrix. **Measurement Model:** The measurement model used to update particles is drawn from a Gaussian distribution, because it models the decreasing probability of a tag being read as tags moves further from a reader.

Even though PF can improve location tracking accuracy, it suffers from high computational cost when implemented in large scale tracking applications involving large number of objects. To overcome the computational cost, we optimize the particle filtering based tracking algorithm by compressing the object stream reported by readers. The real-time object compression technique exploits objects that travel together from one location to another (not containment relationships [3]). Our approach is based on compressing a group of trolleys (objects) that are travelling together within a time window to a single aggregated object as shown in Algorithm 1. This compression can be achieved in three steps: (i) create a dynamic time window δt and collect objects within that time window; (ii) group collected objects based on their location; and (iii) compress the group of trolleys to a single aggregated object. A hash table data structure is used to maintain a mapping between a grouped object and the trolleys contained within a group. A hash table also supports maintaining aggregation changes and disaggregation of trolleys from grouped objects. Then PF based tracking algorithm is applied to the aggregated object. The benefit of compressing the object stream is to minimize the need for using the PF based tracking algorithm for individual objects and to, consequently, achieve both greater scalability and accuracy.

In Algorithm 1, line 3–15 explains the object compression, resulting in one compressed trolley for each group. Line 16–24 explains the PF applied to the compressed trolley. Then, the location l_p with the highest probability is estimated as the most likely location. Line 27–36 checks for possible missed reads for objects currently being tracked by comparing the *current_time* with the *max_time* (t_i + *transit_time*).

4   Experiments and Results

We implemented the linen company's business process in Matlab (Fig. 1) and conducted extensive experiments to evaluate the performance of our tracking algorithm. In the simulation, the time duration from trolley allocation to its return to the back entrance is 2–6 h, read rate is defined as the probability that a tag is read successfully by a reader and the error rate is specified as the percentage of incorrect location predictions. The results reported were generated by averaging 10 repeated experimental runs using randomly generated trolley movement data.

Figure 2 concretely depicts that the object compression technique based PF outperforms the simple PF based tracking algorithm in terms of both accuracy and scalability. When the read rate is above 0.8, the error rate in object compression technique is below 5 %, which is a considerable improvement in accuracy

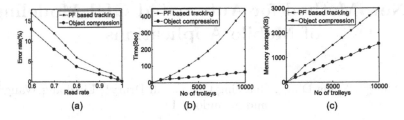

Fig. 2. Experimental results: (a) accuracy; (b) execution time; (c) memory usage

compared to PF based tracking algorithm. Figures 2(b) and (c) show the execution time and memory usage of the proposed algorithm, which clearly shows that the object compression technique significantly reduces the time taken and memory usage of the system.

5 Conclusion

In this paper, we presented an object location tracking algorithm that is robust under uncertainty and demonstrated its performance in an RFID enabled returnable asset management scenario. In practical deployments, the miss rate (1-read rate) is around 5 % and at this miss rate our system reduces the overall error rate to less than 2 % which is a significant improvement in performance. Comparing our algorithm with [2], where data compression is based on containment relationships, when read rate is 80 % and containment is 100 % their accuracy is around 94 % but with 0 % containment (similar to our scenario) the system accuracy falls to below 87 %. In contrast our tracking algorithm yields 96 % accuracy with a read rate of 80 % and outperforms the method in [2]. Furthermore, our technique can also be applied to contained objects, as in [2].

Acknowledgement. This work has been supported by ARC-Linkage grant LP100200114.

References

1. Wu, Y., Sheng, Q.Z., Ranasinghe, D., Yao, L.: PeerTrack: a platform for tracking and tracing objects in large-scale traceability networks. In: Proceedings of the 15th International Conference on EDBT, Berlin, Germany, pp. 586–589 (2012)
2. Nie, Y., Cocci, R., Cao, Z., Diao, Y., Shenoy, P.: Spire: efficient data inference and compression over RFID streams. IEEE TKDE **24**(1), 141–155 (2012)
3. Jeffery, S.R., Garofalakis, M., Franklin, M.: Adaptive cleaning for RFID data streams. In: Proceedings of the 32nd International Conference on VLDB Seol, Korea, pp. 163–174 (2006)
4. Yu, J., Ku, W.S., Sun, M.T., Lu, H.: An RFID and particle filter-based indoor spatial query evaluation system. In: Proceedings of the 16th International Conference on EDBT, pp. 263–274 (2013)

A New Method for Automated GUI Modeling
of Mobile Applications

Jing Xu[1(✉)], Xiang Ding[1], Guanling Chen[1], Jill Drury[1], Linzhang Wang[2],
and Xuandong Li[2]

[1] University of Massachusetts Lowell, Lowell, MA, USA
{jxu,xding,glchen,jdrury}@cs.uml.edu
[2] Nanjing University, Jiangsu, China
{lzwang,lxd}@nju.edu.cn

Abstract. It is often necessary to construct GUI models for automated
testing of event-driven GUI applications, so test cases can be generated
by traversing the GUI models systematically. It is, however, difficult to
apply traditional modeling techniques directly for mobile platforms as
common static models cannot reflect application behaviors under different contexts. To address these challenges, we propose a novel approach for automated GUI modeling of mobile applications and introduce
our unique definition of GUI state equivalence, which can reduce state
space and facilitate model merging. The proposed modeling method can
already discover subtle implementation issues. Real-world case studies
show that the proposed approach is effective for adaptive GUI modeling
on the Android platform.

Keywords: Automated modeling · Mobile applications · Android · Contextual behaviors

1 Introduction

Mobile apps are playing an increasingly important role in ubiquitous computing environments and cost-effective solutions are urgently needed to support the
testing of mobile apps. Mobile apps are a subset of the more general class of
event-driven Graphical User Interface (GUI) applications [1] and are often context aware [2]. Traditional GUI modeling techniques typically assume a static
model and fall short on context-aware apps that have dynamic behaviors and
are not just driven by GUI events.

In this paper, we present a new approach to automatically model GUIs for
mobile apps and we focus on the Android platform. We propose a *Coarse Grained
GUI Model* (CGGM) based on state machines. CGGM only uses the unique

This work is supported partly by the National Science Foundation under Grant No.
1016823 and 1040725. Any opinions, findings, and conclusions expressed in this work
are those of the authors.

© Institute for Computer Sciences, Social Informatics and Telecommunications Engineering 2014
I. Stojmenovic et al. (Eds.): MOBIQUITOUS 2013, LNICST 131, pp. 688–693, 2014.
DOI: 10.1007/978-3-319-11569-6_54

composition feature of a screen when identifying a GUI state. By not including a comprehensive set of properties of UI elements (thus called coarse grained), the GUI model is compact yet comprehensive; it also allows easy and meaningful aggregation of multiple models obtained through different runs, such as under different contextual situations.

2   Definition of Android Coarse-Grained GUI Model (CGGM)

To provide a cost-effective modeling solution for Android apps, the first major concern comes from the scaling issue of state machine models (the state explosion problem) [3]. To overcome that, we define the state of the GUI by emphasizing the group composition of GUI elements on the screen to identify a GUI state. The second concern is that most current GUI modeling techniques employ a static model. Therefore, they are unable to take into account context-based execution behaviors of GUIs. To tackle this problem, we perform multiple GUI rippings under different contexts. Taking advantage of our unique definition of GUI state equivalence, we can merge these models and obtain an adaptive model to include as many context-based execution behaviors as possible.

The level of model granularity is determined by how to define equivalence of two screen views. In previous research, the GUI state of a screen view (or a window for desktop apps) is usually defined as a set of triples $\{(w_i, p_j, v_k)\}$, where w_i is the widget in current window, p_j is the property of the widget and v_k is the value of the property and any change of any w_i, p_j or v_k would be considered to be a different state. In CGGM, each state represents a unique screen view that users interact with. We define the equivalence of two screen views in a way that if the composition of two screen views are the same, the two screen views are equivalent. To describe the composition of a screen view, we introduce the following definitions.

For Android app GUIs, *android:id* and *android:visibility* are two important properties of a View object on the screen. Android IDs are integer identities (IDs) associated with View objects and are used to find specific View objects within the hierarchy structure of a given GUI. If two GUI widgets on the screen share the same Android ID, they must also have similar behaviors. And we only deal with visible widgets that users could interact with.

Definition: A visible widget is a GUI widget that it is a View object, not a ViewGroup object, all its ancestors are visible and its visibility is set to VISIBLE.

Definition: Two widgets are *siblings* on a screen view if and only if they are both visible to users, of the same Android ID, of the same type (Android View type), and have the same structure of ancestors. Sibling widgets usually have common behaviors when interacting with users.

Definition: All siblings form a *group* on the screen view. The composition of a screen view is determined by widget groups. The most important property of a group is the homogeneity of widgets.

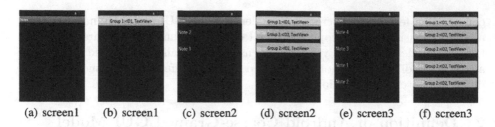

(a) screen1   (b) screen1   (c) screen2   (d) screen2   (e) screen3   (f) screen3

Fig. 1. Notepad screen views and their corresponding group composition

Definition: All sibling widgets in a group are of the same type, which is also the *type of the group*.

Definition: A *screen view* is composed by a set of *groups*.

Definition: The set of types of all groups on the screen describes the *pattern* of a screen view. As shown in Fig. 1(d), the pattern of screen view 1(c) is {TextView, TextView}.

Definition: If two groups from different screen views are in the same activity, of the same type and with the same Android ID for its elements, there is a *mapping* between these two groups.

As shown in Fig. 1(b), (d), (f), the first group of each screen view is a mapping to each other. They are actually the same widget on the screen but other parts of the screen view have changed.

Definition: Two *equivalent screen views* must be in the same activity, with the same number of groups, of the same pattern, and there is a one-to-one mapping for groups in the two screen views.

Definition: Two GUI states are equivalent if and only if the screen views they represent are equivalent.

3   Construction of Android Coarse-Grained GUI Model (CGGM)

Android mobile apps accept not only GUI events but also contextual events (such as network quality changes) [4]. To ensure the completeness of the model, we first get models by executing GUI ripping in different contexts, aiming at exploring varied execution behaviors caused by contextual changes. Then, models from different runs of GUI ripping are put together to examine inconsistent state transitions. Those inconsistencies can provide feedback to successive modeling process and are considered to be indicators of potential software deficiencies or context-based execution behaviors.

In each round, the GUI ripping process is driven by executing GUI events on widgets to invoke screen view changes or activity transitions. It would terminate normally when all scheduled GUI events are exercised according to the traversal algorithm. However, three break conditions can also stop the current ripping process: (1) another app is invoked from the AUT (Application Under Test), since our toolkit uses Robotium APIs that cannot get GUI structural data from a second app; (2) the app crashes due to certain *actions*; or (3) the screen view is stuck for more than 5 min.

Between each round, we manipulate application context before ripping and perform inconsistency examination between models. Inconsistent behaviors of the same or sibling widgets in different models can help find incorrect event logic or contextual application behaviors. The application and system status change during different runs of GUI ripping, which could help discover more hidden states. Most importantly, the CGGM enables a relatively high percentage of equivalent states in different models, which makes the model merging process feasible and also meaningful. By merging GUI models from different contexts, we can actually construct a dynamic model which is open to revision.

4   Case Studies

In this section, we show two examples of using the proposed method to model Android apps - Nihao and Ohmage. Nihao is a personalized intelligent app launcher which dynamically recommends apps the user is most likely to launch [5]. Ohmage is an participatory sensing platform which supports mobile phone-based data capture [6, 7]. Both apps are sensitive to contextual information such as location, app usage history, user's preference, and network conditions.

4.1   Nihao

For the main activity of Nihao, as shown in Fig. 2(a), 7 constant screen views that were not equivalent to each other were found during the process. One screen view was not captured and a final model consisting of 13 states is established, including 2 external states indicating a second app is invoked and 4 contextual states discovered by inconsistent state transitions under different contexts.

Nihao allows users to set the scope of apps and change ranking layout between Grid view and List view. Though the listed apps might change, the group composition of all the initial screen views are the same, thus they are all equivalent. As shown in Fig. 2, they all contain 10 groups in total where Group 1 ~ 7 are static, Group 8 is a textview, Group 9 are app icons and Group 10 are app names. Even if users choose a different view (grid or list), the CGGM model can still adapt to such a significant UI change, as shown in Fig. 2(b) and (c).

4.2   Ohmage

We modeled major components of Ohmage, as shown in Table 1. Components were modeled separately and could be reassembled to establish a model for the whole app. We stayed logged in while performing GUI ripping with the purpose of getting a re-visitable initial state.

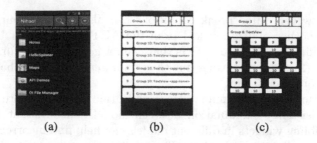

Fig. 2. Equivalent initial screen views of Nihao

Table 1. Inconsistent transitions in components

Components	States	Inconsistencies
Campaigns	23	6×2
Surveys	18	$2 \times 2 + 2 \times 3$
Response history	8	1×2
Upload queues	5	$1 \times 2 + 1 \times 3$
Help	3	0

As shown in Table 1, context-based transitions were counted for each component model. In the last column, $x \times y$ means that there are x places in the model that have y options of transitions depending on the context. Three types of sources have led to the varied transitions. First, the transition could be subject to updates of content presented. Such updates could be invoked by either actions triggered from GUIs or updates of sources on the ohmage server. Second, network conditions influenced execution behaviors. For example, if an "upload" event was triggered under a bad network condition, ohmage would present a dialogue with options "Retry Now, Retry Later, Delete" to deal with the situation. In good network conditions, such behaviors were hidden from GUIs. Finally, different exception handlers also resulted in various transitions.

5   Conclusions

The proposed method is proved to be an effective way to generate adaptive GUI models for Android mobile apps aware of contexts. The CGGM model could cover most of the functionalities of mobile apps and the results of model merging were also satisfying in terms of real context-based application behaviors discovered. The design of our ripping process, from the pure interaction perspective as of a real user's, could help find defective design of the layouts and support dynamically created UI elements.

References

1. Yang, W., Prasad, M.R., Xie, T.: A grey-box approach for automated GUI-model generation of mobile applications. In: Cortellessa, V., Varró, D. (eds.) FASE 2013 (ETAPS 2013). LNCS, vol. 7793, pp. 250–265. Springer, Heidelberg (2013)
2. Chen, G., Kotz, D.: A survey of context-aware mobile computing research. Dartmouth College, Technical report TR2000-381, November 2000. ftp://ftp.cs.dartmouth.edu/TR/TR2000-381.pdf
3. Graphical User Interface Testing Wiki Page. http://en.wikipedia.org/wiki/Graphical_user_interface_testing
4. Liu, Z., Gao, X., Long, X.: Adaptive random testing of mobile application. In: ICCET (2010)
5. Zhang, C., Ding, X., Chen, G., Huang, K., Ma, X., Yan, B.: Nihao: a predictive smartphone application launcher. In: Proceedings of MobiCase (2012)
6. Ramanathan, N., Alquaddoomi, F., Falaki, H., George, D., Hsieh, C., Jenkins, J., Ketcham, C., Longstaff, B., Ooms, J., Selsky, J., Tangmunarunkit, H., Estrin, D.: Ohmage: an open mobile system for activity and experience sampling. In: Proceedings of PervasiveHealth (2012)
7. Ohmage Homepage. http://ohmage.org/

Towards Augmenting Legacy Websites with Context-Awareness

Darren Carlson[1(✉)] and Lukas Ruge[2]

[1] Felicitous Computing Institute, National University of Singapore,
Singapore, Singapore
carlson@comp.nus.edu.sg
[2] Ambient Computing Group, University of Luebeck, Luebeck, Germany
ruge@itm.uni-luebeck.de

Abstract. Emerging context frameworks enable Websites to interact with the Internet of Things directly from the browser; however, Websites must be specifically designed to utilize such context framework support. As such, the majority of "legacy" Websites remains context-unaware. This paper presents an open approach for dynamically injecting context-awareness capabilities into legacy Websites on-demand, without requiring browser extensions, proxies or Website reengineering. Towards this end, we developed an extensible Bookmarklet framework that serves as a conduit between the user's browser and a server-side repository of enhancement plug-ins, which can used to dynamically augment any 3rd party Website with new content, adapted behavior and context framework support.

Keywords: Ubiquitous computing · Internet of things · Web of things

The rapid evolution of the Internet of Things (IoT) has outpaced the Web's ability to take advantage of the rich contextual information, smart devices and situated services that are now available in many everyday environments. However, emerging mobile context middleware, such as Ambient Dynamix [1], now enable Websites to interact with the IoT directly from the browser. Dynamix is a community-based approach for context-aware computing in which advanced sensing and acting capabilities are deployed *on-demand* to mobile devices as plug-ins. Dynamix runs as lightweight background service on the user's mobile device, leveraging the device itself as a sensing, processing and communications platform. Applications can request context support from a local Dynamix instance using simple application programming interfaces (APIs). Dynamix automatically discovers, downloads and installs the plug-ins needed for a given sensing or acting task. When the user changes environments, new or updated plug-ins can be deployed to the device at runtime, without the need to restart the application or framework.

Dynamix supports two principal app types: Android apps and Web apps. Android apps are defined as native applications that communicate with a local Dynamix service using the Android Interface Definition Language (AIDL). Web apps are hosted by native Web browsers, such a Google Chrome and Firefox. To support communication with browser-based Web apps, Dynamix exposes two local REST-based APIs using a customized Web server that is embedded within the Dynamix Service. Web apps communicate with

© Institute for Computer Sciences, Social Informatics and Telecommunications Engineering 2014
I. Stojmenovic et al. (Eds.): MOBIQUITOUS 2013, LNICST 131, pp. 694–698, 2014.
DOI: 10.1007/978-3-319-11569-6_55

Dynamix via Ajax, using two provided JavaScript support files that simplify service binding, API interactions, data serialization/deserialization, error handling and event processing (see [2]). An overview of the Dynamix architecture is shown in Fig. 1.

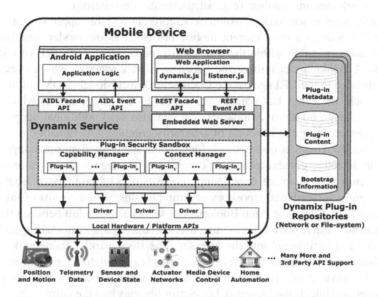

Fig. 1. Overview of the Dynamix architecture

As Websites must be specifically engineered to leverage Dynamix capabilities (e.g., they must reference and utilize the Dynamix JavaScript libraries), we investigated *augmented browsing* as a method of injecting Dynamix-based context support into 3rd party legacy Websites on-demand. Augmented browsing refers to the on-the-fly modification of web content for the purpose of customizing the browsing experience to the user. As modifications are performed outside of the origin server, Website reengineering is not required to introduce new functionality. Example augmentations include user interface (UI) changes (e.g., removing advertisements); adding supplemental information (e.g., keyword definitions); and providing new JavaScript libraries (e.g., jQuery). Common augmented browsing approaches include browser extensions, proxies, site-specific-browsers, and Bookmarklets. Of these, browser extensions are currently the most popular approach, as illustrated by the userscripts.org website, which hosts tens of thousands of augmentation scripts. Browser extensions are currently available for most desktop browsers; however, extension support is extremely limited on mobile devices at present.

Only a few projects have investigated *context-aware* Website augmentation. Most current approaches focus on page-specific context-aware adaptation, such as adding faceted browsing and novel data visualizations [3]; adding supplemental page information (e.g., providing pop-up annotations for scientific keywords) [4, 5]; customizing accessibility options to assist disabled users [6, 7]; and enabling website personalization based on sensor data provided by the browser (e.g., presenting nearby theaters showing movies mentioned in a blog post) [8]. Other approaches, such as the COIN

(COntext INjection) framework [9], automatically correlate a Web page's content with the mobile user's context – injecting context-sensitive cues that highlight relevant content (e.g., monuments passed, nearby buildings), and/or enrich page content with contextually relevant information (e.g., supplemental description).

Unlike browser extensions, *Bookmarklets* represent a viable approach for enabling augmented browsing on most current mobile browsers. Bookmarklets are JavaScript commands that are stored within the Uniform Resource Identifier (URI) of a standard bookmark. A Bookmarklet utilizes the `javascript:` scheme, which executes the scripts embedded in the URI against the Document Object Model (DOM) of the current page. As such, the script has unrestricted access to the target DOM, which it may inspect and change on-the-fly. Bookmarklets can also load additional scripts from a remote server, enabling the injection of arbitrarily complex functionality.

Using the Bookmarklet concept as a foundation, we created an open approach for dynamically injecting context-awareness capabilities into legacy Websites on-demand. Our approach, called Ambient Amp (Amp), consists of a browser-based Bookmarklet framework and a server-based repository of Amp plug-ins, which consist of JavaScripts and optional CSS styles. The Amp Bookmarklet serves as a conduit between the user's browser and the Amp repository, providing users access to page or domain specific Amp plug-ins that can be injected into the browser. The Bookmarklet framework provides plug-in discovery, installation and lifecycle services (e.g., initialization logic) along with an optional "canvas area" where each plug-in can display UI elements if needed. The Bookmarklet also injects the Dynamix JavaScript libraries into the current DOM, which enables Amp plug-ins to communicate with a local Dynamix instance. Amp augmented Websites can access the growing number of Dynamix plug-ins,[1] which provide access to rich context sensing (e.g., sleep state, heart-rate, activity recognition); home automation control (e.g., network light control); media device management (e.g., Universal Plug-and Play and AirPlay); and much more. The basic Amp workflow is shown in Fig. 2.

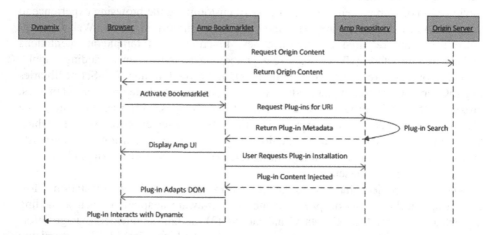

Fig. 2. The Basic Amp workflow

---

[1] http://ambientdynamix.org

The Amp Bookmarklet is installed into the user's browser using conventional methods (e.g., using Chrome's bookmark sync feature), where it can be activated through the bookmark menu or address bar. Once activated, the Amp Bookmarklet is displayed over the current Website as an unobtrusive menu tab, which remains in a fixed position on the right or left side of the browser window, as shown in Fig. 3. After rendering its UI, the Bookmarklet then contacts the remote Amp repository server using the address of the current page as a query term (see Fig. 2). The repository uses URI pattern matching to determine if any Amp plug-ins have been registered for the page or domain that the user is interacting with. URI-relevant plug-in metadata are returned to the Bookmarklet, where they are cached locally and shown to the user on request.

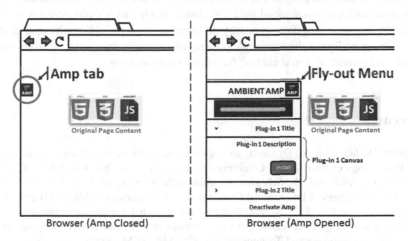

Fig. 3. The injected Amp tab (left) and Amp fly-out menu (right)

When the user taps the Amp tab, a fly-out menu opens to present the list of plug-ins that were discovered for the current page or domain. To maintain a low memory footprint, Amp plug-ins are not initially loaded; rather, only the title and description of each discovered plug-in are shown to the user, along with a button that can be used to install it. Tapping an "Install" button in the fly-out menu automatically loads the associated plug-in's JavaScript code and CSS styles into the browser. The Amp Bookmarklet monitors each plug-in's installation status and provides coordinated initialization once a plug-in's scripts and content are loaded. Initialization enables a plug-in to setup its internal state, display UI elements (if needed), bind to the local Dynamix framework, and activate its Web augmentation features. Once installed, an Amp plug-in can provide 3rd party Websites with new context-awareness features.

To our knowledge, Amp is the first Web augmentation framework to enable the injection of arbitrary context-awareness enhancements into any 3rd party Website (through Amp plug-ins); allow the installation of new (and updated) context sensing and actuation capabilities on-demand (through Dynamix); and support deployment into most current mobile browsers (through its Bookmarklet-based architecture). To validate our approach, we developed a fully operational prototype of the Amp Bookmarklet and repository, along with an example Amp plug-in called Stream to Screen (S2S), which dynamically augments the Flickr.com Website with the ability to stream photos to networked media devices discovered in the user's physical environment (to be described in an upcoming paper). Our initial experiments indicate that Amp can be rapidly injected into many 3rd party Websites and is interoperable with most Android-based mobile browsers, including Chrome, Firefox Mobile, Dolphin HD, and others.

We are focusing on several areas of future work. First, we are investigating secure methods of opening the Amp plug-in repository to external developers. By allowing 3rd party plug-in contributions, we aim to facilitate the emergence of a vibrant Amp developer community. We are also investigating the processing and memory overhead imposed by the Amp Bookmarklet on several commodity mobile devices. Finally, we are developing an Amp plug-in that uses multiple Dynamix plug-ins simultaneously to embed data from a popular social media Website into the user's physical environment, e.g., displaying newsfeed data on nearby ambient devices; providing physical alerts for site updates (e.g., light color changes); posting life-logging data gathered from external sensors; and providing voice control for various site features.

References

1. Carlson, D., Schrader, A.: Dynamix: an open plug-and-play context framework for android. In: Proceedings of International Conference on the Internet of Things (IoT2012) (2012)
2. Carlson, D., Altakrouri, B., Schrader, A.: AmbientWeb: bridging the web's cyber-physical gap. In: Proceedings of International Conference on the Internet of Things (IoT2012) (2012)
3. Huynh, D.F., Miller, R.C., Karger, D.R.: Enabling web browsers to augment web sites' filtering and sorting functionalities. In: Proceedings of 19th Annual ACM Symposium on User Interface Software and Technology, pp. 125–134. ACM (2006)
4. Chahinian, V., et al.: Proxiris, an augmented browsing tool for literature curation. In: Proceedings of 9th International Conference on Data Integration in the Life Sciences, Springer (2013)
5. Cruz, T., Nabuco, O.: Clinical eye: a tool for augmented browsing in the health domain. In: Proceedings of 2012 IEEE 21st International Workshop on Enabling Technologies: Infrastructure for Collaborative Enterprises (WETICE), pp. 432–437 (2012)
6. Bigham, J.P., Ladner, R.E.: Accessmonkey: a collaborative scripting framework for web users and developers. In: Proceedings of the 2007 International Cross-Disciplinary Conference on Web Accessibility (W4A), pp. 25–34. ACM (2007)
7. Mirri, S., Salomoni, P., Prandi, C.: Augment browsing and standard profiling for enhancing web accessibility. In: Proceedings of the International Cross-Disciplinary Conference on Web Accessibility, pp. 1–10. ACM (2011)
8. Ankolekar, A., Vrandečić, D.: Kalpana - enabling client-side web personalization. In: Proceedings of the Nineteenth ACM Conference on Hypertext and Hypermedia, pp. 21–26. ACM (2008)
9. Casteleyn, S., Woensel, W.V., Troyer, O.D.: Assisting mobile web users: client-side injection of context-sensitive cues into websites. In: Proceedings of the 12th International Conference on Information Integration and Web-Based Applications and Services, pp. 443–450. ACM (2010)

Improving Mobile Video Streaming with Mobility Prediction and Prefetching in Integrated Cellular-WiFi Networks

Vasilios A. Siris[(✉)], Maria Anagnostopoulou, and Dimitris Dimopoulos

Mobile Multimedia Laboratory, Department of Informatics,
Athens University of Economics and Business, Athens, Greece
vsiris@aueb.gr

Abstract. We present and evaluate a procedure that utilizes mobility and throughput prediction to prefetch video streaming data in integrated cellular and WiFi networks. The effective integration of such heterogeneous wireless technologies will be significant for supporting high performance and energy efficient video streaming in ubiquitous networking environments. Our evaluation is based on trace-driven simulation considering empirical measurements and shows how various system parameters influence the performance, in terms of the number of paused video frames and the energy consumption. The proposed approach has been implemented in an Android-based prototype.

1 Introduction

A major trend in mobile networks over the last few years is the exponential increase of powerful mobile devices, such as smartphones and tablets, with multiple heterogeneous wireless interfaces that include 3G/4G/LTE and WiFi. The proliferation of such devices has resulted in a skyrocketing growth of mobile traffic, which in 2012 grew 70 %, becoming nearly 12-times the global Internet traffic in 2000, and is expected to grow 13-fold from 2012 until 2017[1]. Moreover, mobile video traffic was 51 % of the total traffic by the end of 2012 and is expected to become two-thirds of the world's mobile data traffic by 2017. The increase of video traffic will further intensify the strain on cellular networks, hence reliable and efficient support for video traffic in future networks will be paramount.

The efficient, in terms of both network resource utilization and energy consumption, support for video streaming in future mobile environments with ubiquitous access will require integration of heterogeneous wireless technologies with complementary characteristics; this includes cellular networks with wide-area coverage and WiFi hotspots with high throughput and energy efficient data transfer. Moreover, the industry has already verified the significance of mobile data offloading: globally, 33 % of total mobile data traffic was offloaded onto WiFi networks or femtocells in 2012 (see Footnote 1).

---

[1] Source: Cisco Visual Networking Index: Global Mobile Data Traffic Forecast Update, 2012-2017, Feb. 6, 2013.

© Institute for Computer Sciences, Social Informatics and Telecommunications Engineering 2014
I. Stojmenovic et al. (Eds.): MOBIQUITOUS 2013, LNICST 131, pp. 699–704, 2014.
DOI: 10.1007/978-3-319-11569-6_56

Our goal is to quantify the improvements for mobile video streaming that can be achieved by exploiting mobility and throughput prediction to prefetch video data in local storage of WiFi hotspots, efficiently utilizing the resources of integrated cellular and WiFi networks. Although we consider mobile video data offloading to WiFi hotspots, our results and conclusions are potentially applicable to mobile video offloading to femto or small cell networks, where the backhaul throughput is smaller than the radio interface throughput. The work in this paper is different from our previous work in [11,13] that considers mobile data offloading for delay tolerant traffic, which requires transferring a file within a time threshold, and delay sensitive traffic, which requires minimizing the file transfer time; unlike these traffic types, video streaming requires a continuous transfer of video data to avoid degradation of user QoE (Quality of Experience), which thus requires a totally different prefetching procedure and evaluation.

2   Related Work

Prior work has demonstrated bandwidth predictability for cellular networks [15] and WiFi [8]. Bandwidth prediction for improving video streaming is investigated in [3], and for client-side pre-buffering to improve video streaming in [10]. Both [3,10] focus on cellular networks, while we consider integrated cellular-WiFi networks. Moreover, our goal is not to develop a new system for mobility and bandwidth prediction, but to evaluate mobility and throughput prediction to prefetch data in order to improve mobile video streaming.

Exploiting delay tolerance to increase mobile data offloading to WiFi is investigated in [1,6]. The work in [5] applies a user utility model for offloading traffic to WiFi, while [9,14] investigates usage of multiple heterogeneous wireless interfaces. Our work differs in that we focus on video streaming and exploit prefetching video data in local caches of WiFi hotpots along a vehicle's route.

The feasibility of using prediction together with prefetching is investigated in [2], which does not propose or evaluate specific prefetching algorithms. Prefetching for improving video file delivery in cellular femtocell networks is investigated in [4], and to reduce the peak load of mobile networks by offloading traffic to WiFi hotspots in [7]. Our work differs in that we consider prefetching in WiFi hotpspots along a vehicle's route to improve video streaming.

3   Mobility and Throughput Prediction for Prefetching

Mobility prediction can provide knowledge of how many WiFi hotspots a node (vehicle) will encounter, when they will be encountered, and for how long the node will be in each hotspot's range. In addition to this mobility information, we assume that information on the estimated throughput in the WiFi hotspots and the cellular network, at different positions along the vehicles's route, is also available; for the former, the information includes both the throughput for transferring data from a remote location, e.g., through an ADSL backhaul, and the throughput for transferring data from a local cache. Prefetching can provide gains when the throughput of transferring data from a local cache in the WiFi hotspot is higher than the throughput for transferring data from its original remote server location. This occurs when the backhaul link connecting the hotspot to the Internet has low capacity (e.g., in the case of an ADSL backhaul) or when it is congested; this is likely to become more common as the use of the IEEE 802.11n and 802.11ac standards increases.

The procedure to exploit mobility and throughput prediction for prefetching, Algorithm 1, defines the mobile's actions when it exits a WiFi hotspot, hence has only mobile access (Line 6), and when it enters a WiFi hotspot (Line 9). Mobility and throughput prediction allows the mobile to determine when it will encounter the next WiFi hotspot that has higher throughput than the cellular network's throughput. From the time to reach the next hotspot and the average video buffer playout rate, the mobile can estimate the position that the video stream is expected to reach (offset) when it arrives at the next WiFi hotspot (Line 7). The mobile instructs a local cache in the WiFi hotpot to cache the video stream starting from the estimated offset (Line 8).

Algorithm 1. Using mobility and throughput prediction to prefetch video data

```
 1: Variables:
 2:   R: average video buffer playout rate
 3:   T_next WiFi: average time until node enters range of next WiFi
 4:   Offset: estimated position in video stream when node enters next WiFi hotspot
 5: Algorithm:
 6: if  node exits WiFi hotspot  then
 7:     Offset ← R · T_next WiFi
 8:     Start caching video stream in next WiFi starting from Offset
 9: else if  node enters WiFi hotspot  then
10:     Transfer video data that has not been received up to Offset from original location
11:     Transfer video data from local cache
12:     Use remaining time in WiFi hotspot to transfer video data from original location
13: end if
```

When the node enters a WiFi hotspot, it might be missing some portion of the video stream up to the offset from which data was cached in the hotspot; this can occur if, due to time variations, the node reaches the WiFi hotspot earlier than the time it had initially estimated. In this case, the missing data needs to be transferred from the video's original remote location (Line 10), through the hotspot's backhaul link. Also, the amount of data cached in the WiFi hotspot can be smaller than the amount the node could download within the time it is in the hotspot's range. In this case, the node uses its remaining time in the WiFi hotspot to transfer data, as above, from the video's original location (Line 12).

4   Trace-Driven Evaluation

Our evaluation considers empirical measurements for the throughput of the cellular network and the SNR (Signal-to-Noise Ratio) of WiFi networks along a route between two locations in the center of Athens, Greece. Along the route we embed 2, 4, and 8 WiFi hotspots for different scenarios investigated. The details of the trace-driven simulation environment is presented in an extended version of this paper [12]. Moreover, here we present a small set of our evaluation results.

Number of video streams: Fig. 1(a) shows the number of paused frames as a function of the number of video streams, illustrating the high gains that can be achieved with prefetching: For 4 HD streams, prefetching achieves 48 % and 76 % fewer paused frames compared to when prefetching is not used (i.e., the WiFi network is used opportunistically), and when only the mobile (cellular) network is used. Moreover, prefetching can support 3 HD streams without paused frames, whereas WiFi without prefetching has 15 paused frames and using only the mobile network results in 60 paused frames.

Number of WiFi hotspots: Fig. 1(b) shows that the performance for the two mobile & WiFi schemes improves with more hotspots. Moreover, prefetching achieves more than 36 % fewer paused frames compared to when prefetching is not used.

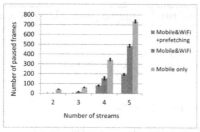

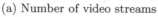

(a) Number of video streams

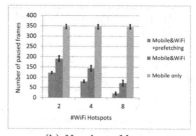

(b) Number of hotspots

Fig. 1. Paused frames for a different number of video streams and hotspots.

Throughput variability: Fig. 2(a) shows the influence of the variability of the mobile, WiFi, and ADSL backhaul throughput. A higher throughput variability increases the number of paused frames for all three schemes. Nevertheless, prefetching can achieve more than 45 % fewer paused frames compared to the mobile & WiFi scheme without prefetching, and more than 75 % fewer paused frames than when only the mobile network is used.

Energy consumption: Fig. 2(b) shows the energy consumption for a different number of video streams. Prefetching achieves lower energy consumption compared to the case where WiFi is used without prefetching, which in turn achieves lower energy consumption compared to the case where only the mobile network is used. The gains in terms of energy efficiency are comparatively lower than the gains of increased performance, in terms of a fewer number of paused frames, Fig. 1(a). This is due to the significantly higher power consumption per transferred data volume of the mobile network compared to WiFi.

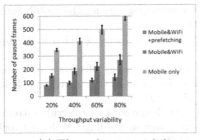

(a) Throughput variability

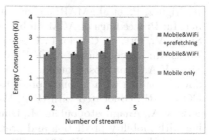

(b) Energy consumption

Fig. 2. Influence of throughput variability and energy consumption.

5   Conclusions and Future Work

We have presented and evaluated a procedure that exploits mobility and throughput prediction to prefetch video data in integrated mobile and WiFi networks, in order to improve mobile video streaming. The procedure can significantly reduce the number of paused frames (QoE), while being robust to time and throughput variability and achieve reduced energy consumption. The proposed approach has been implemented in an Android client for video playout that can stream video data from multiple servers.

Ongoing work includes evaluating the performance of our prototype implementation in a realistic setting. Also, future work includes adopting a standard protocol, based on MPEG-DASH (Dynamic Adaptive Streaming for HTTP), for communication between the mobile client and the video servers or caches.

References

1. Balasubramanian, A., Mahajan, R., Venkataramani, A.: Augmenting mobile 3G using WiFi. In: Proceedings of ACM MobiSys (2010)
2. Deshpande, P., Kashyap, A., Sung, C., Das, S.: Predictive methods for improved vehicular WiFi access. In: Proceedings of ACM MobiSys (2009)
3. Evensen, K., et al.: Mobile video streaming using location-based network prediction and transparent handover. In: Proceedingsof ACM NOSDAV (2011)
4. Golrezaei, N., et al.: FemtoCaching: wireless video content delivery through distributed caching helpers. In: Proceedings of IEEE Infocom (2012)
5. Hou, X., Deshpande, P., Das, S.R.: Moving bits from 3G to metro-scale WiFi for vehicular network access: an integrated transport layer solution. In: Proceedings of IEEE ICNP (2011)
6. Lee, K., Rhee, I., Lee, J., Chong, S., Yi, Y.: Mobile data offloading: how much can WiFi deliver? In: Proceedings of ACM CoNEXT (2010)
7. Malandrino, F., et al.: Proactive seeding for information cascades in cellular networks. In: Proceedings of IEEE Infocom (2012)
8. Nicholson, A.J., Noble, B.D.: BreadCrumbs: forecasting mobile connectivity. In: Proceedings of ACM Mobicom (2008)

9. Rodriguez, P., et al.: MAR: a commuter router infrastructure for the mobile internet. In: Proceedings of ACM MobiSys (2004)
10. Singh, V., Ott, J., Curcio, I.: Predictive buffering for streaming video in 3G networks. In: Proceedings of IEEE WoWMoM (2012)
11. Siris, V.A., Anagnostopoulou, M.: Performance and energy efficiency of mobile data offloading with mobility prediction and prefetching. In: Proceedings of IEEE CONWIRE, co-located with IEEE WoWMoM (2013)
12. Siris, V.A., Anagnostopoulou, M., Dimopoulos, D.: Improving mobile video streaming with mobility prediction and prefetching in integrated cellular-WiFi networks (extended version). arXiv:1310.6171 [cs.NI] (2013)
13. Siris, V.A., Kalyvas, D.: Enhancing mobile data offloading with mobility prediction and prefetching. In: Proceedings of ACM MOBICOM MobiArch Workshop (2012)
14. Tsao, C., Sivakumar, R.: On effectively exploiting multiple wireless interfaces in mobile hosts. In: Proceedings of ACM CoNEXT (2009)
15. Yao, J., Kahnere, S.S., Hassan, M.: An empirical study of bandwidth predictability in mobile computing. In: Proceedings of ACM WinTech (2008)

Integration and Evolution of Data Mining Models in Ubiquitous Health Telemonitoring Systems

Vladimer Kobayashi, Pierre Maret[✉], Fabrice Muhlenbach,
and Pierre-René Lhérisson

Laboratoire Hubert Curien, Université de Lyon, CNRS,
UMR 5516, 42000 Saint-Etienne, France
{Vladimer.Kobayashi,Pierre.Maret,Fabrice.Muhlenbach}@univ-st-etienne.fr

Abstract. Ubiquitous Health Telemonitoring Systems collect low level data with the aim to ameliorate the health condition of patients. Models from data mining are created to compute indicators regarding their status and activity (habits, abnormalities). Models can also help generate feedbacks and recommendations for patients as well as for remote formal and informal care givers. Essential features are that the models can be easily updated whenever new information is available and that data generated from the models can be readily accessible as well as sensed data. This paper addresses the challenge of conveniently incorporating in a Ubiquitous Health Telemonitoring System the creation, the use, and the updating of data mining models. We conducted first runs and generated results showing the feasibility as well as the effectiveness of the system.

Keywords: Ubiquitous systems · Telemonitoring · eHealth · Data mining models

1 Introduction

Healthcare provides a rich domain for the application of ubiquitous computing [3]. We used the term *Ubiquitous Health Telemonitoring System* (UHTS) to encapsulate the conglomeration of various technologies and techniques that facilitate human health monitoring at a distance. Technologies and techniques inconspicuously work together to give patients freedom in mobility, thereby maintaining their independent living. A quick survey of literature would reveal that a significant number of UHTSs have already been implemented. At their core, health telemonitoring systems are expected to accomplish two basic tasks, *i.e.* able to continuously collect data from patients wherever they are, and allow communication between patient and medical staff at a distance.

We can distinguish existing UHTSs as to how they handle and process the data they collect. It is worth noting that many systems only use, if they use at all, low level data processing techniques. Data sensed from patients are transmitted

© Institute for Computer Sciences, Social Informatics and Telecommunications Engineering 2014
I. Stojmenovic et al. (Eds.): MOBIQUITOUS 2013, LNICST 131, pp. 705–709, 2014.
DOI: 10.1007/978-3-319-11569-6_57

and screened and selected data are stored in static and centralized reposito-
ries and sporadically accessed by the concerned individuals. There are efforts to
incorporate higher level analytics to the stored data [4] but there is no straightforward solution as to how the results in the form of knowledge models (obtained
from applying higher level analytics such as data mining techniques) are integrated back to the system and how these knowledge models could be evolved
in the presence of new data. In retrospect existing systems lack an important
layer that is altogether able to develop, incorporate, and evolve models as well
as make the results accessible to various stakeholders in a manner that is relevant, timely, and unrestricted by location. Our belief is that any system that
collects data must also make use of the data to improve the operations of the
system and subsequently would lead to the amelioration of the condition of the
main target user. In the case of UHTS the main users are the patients to which
we aim to improve or maintain their health condition. The motivation is to
create models that can compute indicators regarding the status and activity of
patients. Moreover the indicators constitute different levels of information (from
detailed to coarse-grained) that will also be used either to generate automatic
suited feedbacks (to patients or to care givers). An essential feature is that the
models can be conveniently updated whenever new information or new scenarios are available. The challenge is for the entire process of creating, using, and
updating models should be efficiently incorporated in the ubiquitous telemonitoring system and, to generate information available to the right stakeholders.
In this paper we offered a solution to the challenge through the development of
an additional component that permitted the associated tasks.

2   Features of Ubiquitous Health Telemonitoring System

The primary users of a UHTS are the *patient* and the *medical practitioner*,
usually a physician. We can include more users as we add tasks and features in
the system. The features of UHTS are enumerated next.

1. Collection, Transmission, and Storing of health data from patient.
2. Communication between patient and physician.
3. Communication with other health stakeholders forming the patient social
   support groups.
4. Access privileges mechanism to the health data, under the control of the
   patient and with the advice of the doctor.

Additionally, we propose to consider these features:

5. Integration of models to generate higher level information from data.
6. Storing of the higher level information as health data.
7. Automatic recommendations and feedback to stakeholders (patient, etc.).

3 Requirements for Knowledge-Enriched Ubiquitous Health Telemonitoring System

Our implementation of UHTS has been reported recently in a paper explaining its different components [2]. The system is aptly called CHISel'd (Comprehensive Health Information System). We enhanced this system by supplying a component that accommodated models from data mining procedures. Moreover it has the capability to generate and store higher-level information inferred from sensed data. We call it the Knowledge Engine (KE) component. We named the improved system: Knowledge-Enriched Ubiquitous Health Telemonitoring System (**KE-UHTS**). Figure 1 shows the relationship among the different parts of a KE-UHTS.

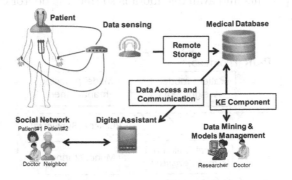

Fig. 1. The Knowledge-Enriched UHTS.

We identified four requirements of the Knowledge-Engine component:

1. Models from data mining could be easily added, modified, and deleted.
2. Possibility of patient-model customization within the platform.
3. Model-generated outputs (representing high level medical or activity information) are stored into the database.
4. Automatic recommendations and feedbacks are generated (through long-term use of the system) [1].

The intended users of the Knowledge-Engine component are the doctor and the researcher. The task of the researcher is to implement data mining algorithms and consequently to create the models. The role of the doctor is two-fold. The first role is to assist the researcher in the model creation process by providing domain expert knowledge and the second role is to validate the models. Also, the doctor is responsible for the assignment of feedbacks associated to the output of the models.

4   Implementation of the Knowledge Engine Component

Here we explain an implementation of KE Component with respect to CHISel'd. We started by making a choice regarding the tools we used to create the engine.

We selected the R software[1] to implement the data mining algorithms and we produced R scripts to store the created models. We picked the Java programming language to create an application that acted as the interface. The whole application is actually a combination of a Java interface (serving as the front-end) and the R software (serving as the back-end and doing all the model building and computational tasks). We call this application the P-JR (Program-Java-R) application (Fig. 2). What the doctor sees most of the time is the Java interface where majority of the activities such as model-patient assignment and process initiation/termination are effected. The Java interface also maintains a list of available patients and available models so that the doctor can easily make these associations.

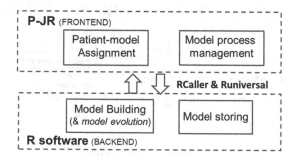

Fig. 2. The Knowledge-Engine showing the front-end and back-end programs.

In the P-JR application, when model running is activated it connects to the medical database to fetch the relevant raw data, when the data are collected the calculation commences, and finally the output from the model are written back to the database. In the database, we distinguished between raw data: the data collected directly from the patients; and context data: the data generated by the models. As for with raw data, the context data can also be accessed by stakeholders given the appropriate privileges.

We tested the KE component by creating test models and we have successfully completed the entire process. It starts by (a) entering the model (the doctor loads a R file and gives a description), then (b) the doctor assigns the model to a patient and activates the running of the model, next (c) each running of a model for a patient is a thread that can be stopped or killed, (d) the model reads raw data and generates output (context data) which is stored in the database, then (d) the data is made available for visualization on digital assistants, and (e) the

---

[1] http://www.r-project.org/

raw and context data is used to generate new models or to modify existing ones and the steps are repeated.

Medical raw data as well as context data in the database can be accessed by stakeholders from their digital assistant (android application on a mobile device) and depending on their access rights [2]. Through long-term use of the system we will be able to accumulate historical records regarding patient-model assignments and model-feedback associations. The gathered information will be used to improve the system to enable it to give automatic recommendations and oriented feedbacks.

5   Conclusion and Future Work

In this paper we have discussed and successfully demonstrated the development of a Knowledge Engine (KE) component that is crucial to any Ubiquitous Health Telemonitoring Systems (UHTS). The KE component is very well adapted for ubiquitous telemonitoring where raw data should be processed in real-time and high level information are computed and accessible on demand. The KE component is useful to implement the whole process, from model design to its integration and use into the system, i.e. the generation of context data. This is intended to help better monitor and support patients. Our approach makes it possible the dynamic inclusion of models created from data mining algorithms. We implemented the engine as a new component in an existing UHTS called CHISel'd which makes it a fully functional KE-UHTS. New data generated from the models is available in real-time and accessible from anywhere for instance on mobile devices. Also, new data is used to develop more models or to improve existing ones. Our next goal is to populate the model repository, conduct experiments to assess the over-all efficiency and reliability of the system, and to improve the operations in the interface.

References

1. Amatriain, X., Jaimes, A., Oliver, N., Pujol, J.: Data mining methods for recommender systems. In: Ricci, F., Rokach, L., Shapira, B., Kantor, P.B. (eds.) Recommender Systems Handbook, pp. 39–71. Springer, Berlin (2011)
2. De Coi, J.L., Delaunay, G., Albino, A.M., Muhlenbach, F., Maret, P., Lopez, G., Yamada, I.: The comprehensive health information system: a platform for privacy-aware and social health monitoring. In: Proceedings of IADIS e-Health 2012 (2012)
3. Kim, Y.B., Yoo, S., Kim, D.: Ubiquitous healthcare: technology and service. In: Ichalkaranje, N., Ichalkaranje, A., Jain, L.C. (eds.) Intelligent Paradigms for Assistive and Preventive Healthcare. Studies in Computational Intelligence, vol. 19, pp. 1–35. Springer, Berlin Heidelberg (2006)
4. Viswanathan, M., Yang, Y.K., Whangbo, T.K.: Data mining in ubiquitous healthcare. In: Funatsu, K. (ed.) New Fundamental Technologies in Data Mining, pp. 193–200. InTech, Rijeka (2011)

ITS-Light: Adaptive Lightweight Scheme to Resource Optimize Intelligent Transportation Tracking System (ITS) – Customizing CoAP for Opportunistic Optimization

Abhijan Bhattacharyya[✉], Soma Bandyopadhyay, and Arpan Pal

Innovation Lab, Tata Consultancy Services, Kolkata, India
{abhijan.bhattacharyya, soma.bandyopadhyay,
arpan.pal}@tcs.com

Abstract. In this paper we aim to reduce overall resource usage and improve throughput of an intelligent transportation tracking application. Primary improvements in terms of bandwidth and latency are achieved using CoAP (Constrained Application Protocol). We propose a novel approach to adapt CoAP's reliability mode for data transfer by inferring vehicle's motion-state from tracking information. Further, we make salient modifications in protocol to achieve even better optimization and improved throughput and scalability while using non-reliable data transfer mode of CoAP. Proposed scheme is analyzed based on results obtained both in real and emulated environments.

Keywords: M2M · Resource optimization · CoAP · Sensor gateway

1 Introduction and Motivation

We propose ITS-light as a light-weight solution for tracking vehicle, focusing on application layer optimizations. The key focus here is to accomplish reduction in communication cost, and improve performance in terms of latency while making the solution more scalable. The use-case specific resource optimization is performed here through imbibing situation awareness of CoAP [1]. It is to be noted that overall communication cost directly impacts energy requirement of devices which is critical for any battery operated sensor gateway like mobile phone.

In ITS vehicles update a backend server with vehicle tracking information (VTI) mainly comprising the tuple: <location, time-stamp, accelerometer-samples>. Existing ITS application uses HTTP at application layer which we replaced by CoAP.

Our previous work in [4] presents an extensive study on two promising lightweight protocols, CoAP and MQTT [8] and establishes CoAP as a better choice. In this paper we primarily propose a novel approach to dynamically adapt reliability mode of CoAP to optimize resource usage. Precisely, while making an update, reliable or non-reliable data transfer mode is chosen depending on inferred situation, i.e. motional-state of vehicle. Further we propose a unique variant of non-reliable mode with a reduced

© Institute for Computer Sciences, Social Informatics and Telecommunications Engineering 2014
I. Stojmenovic et al. (Eds.): MOBIQUITOUS 2013, LNICST 131, pp. 710–715, 2014.
DOI: 10.1007/978-3-319-11569-6_58

exchange to make overall ITS system even more lightweight when update-frequency of vehicle tracking information is high during fast movement of vehicle.

Our work draws inspiration from [5]. However, [5] deals with lower level of communication stack and proposes adaptation in terms of bit-rate, access point association, etc. using 'sensor hints'. It does not handle adaptation of application layer protocol characteristics for optimization of communication cost of sensors.

2 System Architecture

Figure 1(a, b) depict system architecture and functional components of proposed ITS respectively. Vehicles are equipped with Digi's ConnectPort-X5 M2 M gateway [2] having several sensors. Gateway accesses Internet using low bandwidth GPRS connection. Accelerometer data are collected over a configurable stipulated interval and VTI is periodically updated to back-end server by sensor-gateway.

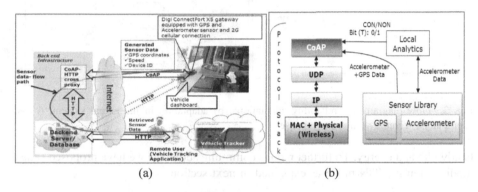

(a)   (b)

Fig. 1. (a) System Architecture. (b) Functional components of proposed adaptive ITS-light.

3 Adapting Data Transfer Mode Using Sensed Indication

CoAP supports two modes of reliability confirmable (CON), where the server replies back with an ACK to every request, and non-confirmable (NON) where the server does not reply with an ACK. Obviously, CON mode tries to ensure delivery through retransmissions unlike the NON mode. A flag (T) [1] in protocol header determines CON or NON mode, where T = 0 signifies CON and T = 1 signifies NON.

We propose to make the behavior of CoAP intelligent depending on motional-state of the vehicle inferred by local analytics at in-vehicle sensor-gateway. Figure 2(a) illustrates the logical flow to achieve this. The vehicle should update in CON mode when it moves slowly or is at rest. Thus ensuring best-effort data delivery since next update is due after a long time. On the other hand, NON mode is used when it is inferred that vehicle is moving fast. In this case, since update rate is very high, a stray loss in flight of data is soon to be compensated with the flights coming in quick succession. Here reliability is traded-off against opportunistic saving in consumed

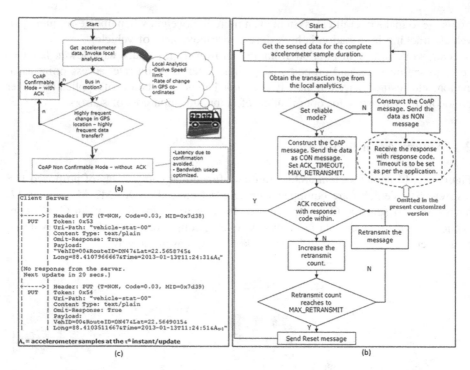

Fig. 2. Flow diagram: (a) reliability adaptation; (b) adaptation in the actual system. (c) An exemplary exchange with omit-response.

bandwidth and energy. To further reduce communication cost we have proposed salient modification in NON mode as explained in next section.

4   Application Specific Customization of CoAP

Although server does not respond back with an ACK in NON mode, still it responds back with a status code which is a zero payload message consisting of only 4 bytes of header, specifying "the result of the attempt to understand and satisfy the request" [1]. Therefore, even in NON mode, client has to wait for additional 4 bytes of response from server. So, for N numbers of NON updates there will be N*4 bytes of application layer responses where each response accumulates all headers from the underlying layers. N, over a period time, may be very large for large number of sensors with high rate of updates. These responses not only add to latency but add to overall load on network also. Even, from server side, catering huge number of update requests with status responses puts additional load. Thus addressing scalability issue.

When vehicle moves fast, status against every update with a fixed resource is deemed redundant. Optionally CoAP client may stop listening activity, thereby saving fair amount of energy. So, for further optimization, we have customized the protocol behavior by introducing an Omit-Response option which asks the server not to respond back and thus operates totally on a fire-and-forget basis (Fig. 2(b, c)).

5 Performance Measurement and Conclusion

Experimental Setup: Figure 3(a) depicts experimental setup inside a car. Laboratory arrangement [4] in (Fig. 3(b)) compares performance of modified NON mode against CON mode in terms of open-loop latency and bandwidth using a network emulator WANem [3], as real-field experiment does not allow control over communication channel. We have configured channel as 9.6 Kbps link with different packet losses (0 %, 10 %, 20 %).

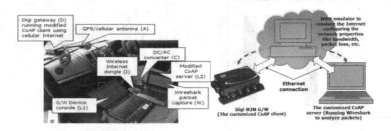

Fig. 3. Experiment set-up (a) on field (b) emulated environment.

Latency Measurement: Closed loop latency is measured by taking time difference between instants of sending information and reception of ACK at client end at in-vehicle gateway. The CON mode is essentially a closed-loop system while COAP-NON with Omit-Response is absolutely open-loop. For latter case open-loop latency is measured by taking time difference between transmit time from client and time at which message reached server (Fig. 4(a)). CON open-loop latency is still time difference between transmit time from client and time at which it 'finally' reaches server (Fig. 4(b)) with several retransmissions of same message in case message or ACK is lost or is delayed. Here time synchronization between backend server and CoAP-client is accomplished by using NTP [6].

Results, Analysis and Conclusion: Figure 5(a) shows average improvement in open-loop latency for proposed customized CoAP-NON over CoAP-CON in real field for varying vehicle speed. In case of former there is no duplicate transmission. Also it consumes less bandwidth (Fig. 5(b)) due to removal of return path and avoidance of duplicate and re-transmissions. Figure 5(c, d) establish advantage of trading-off

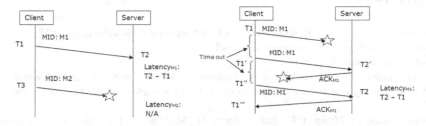

Fig. 4. Open-loop latency measurement (a) CoAP-NON with Omit-Response; (b) CoAP-CON

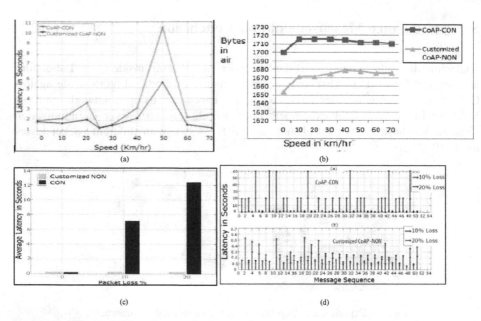

Fig. 5. For CoAP-CON and customized CoAP-NON. (a) open-loop-latency vs. vehicle speed, (b) total bytes transferred vs. vehicle speed (c) average latency vs. packet loss (d) a snapshot of latencies for continuous message instants for different packet losses

reliability against overall throughput. Here we have configured low bandwidth and lossy network using WANem. Figure 5(c), shows steady performance of customized NON mode despite lossy condition as transactions here are completely open-loop. Snapshot of consecutive instants of message exchange in Fig. 5(d) further strengthens this fact. Despite sporadic loss of data the overall rate of success and the achieved latency by the customized CoAP-NON shows noticeable improvement. Thus the proposed scheme promises to improve overall system performance, scalability, and should add value in terms of energy consumption as consumed numbers of bytes are directly proportional to energy requirement of the system.

Presently we are working on applying our proposed lightweight security scheme [7] to this solution for achieving an optimized secure solution.

References

1. Constrained Application Protocol (http://tools.ietf.org/html/draft-ietf-core-coap-18)
2. http://www.digi.com/pdf/dsconnectportx5.pdf
3. http://wanem.sourceforge.net/
4. Bandyopadhyay, S., Bhattacharyya, A.: Lightweight Internet protocols for Web enablement of sensors using constrained gateway devices. In: CPS workshop, ICNC, San Diego, USA (2013)
5. Ravindranath, L., Newport, C., Balakrishnan, H., Madden, S.: Improving wireless network performance using sensor hints. In: 8th USENIX Conference on NSDI11, CA, USA (2011)

6. Network Time Protocol Version. (http://tools.ietf.org/html/rfc5905)
7. Ukil, A., Bandyopadhyay, S., Bhattacharyya, A., Pal, A.: Lightweight security scheme for vehicle tracking system using CoAP. In: ASPI Workshop, UBICOMP, Zurich, Switzerland (2013)
8. http://mqtt.org/

MELON: A Persistent Message-Based Communication Paradigm for MANETs

Justin Collins[✉] and Rajive Bagrodia

University of California, Los Angeles, CA, USA
{collins,rajive}@cs.ucla.edu

Abstract. In this paper we introduce MELON, a new communication paradigm tailored to mobile ad hoc networks, based on novel interactions with a distributed shared message store. MELON provides remove-only, read-only, and private messages, as well as bulk message operations. The dynamic nature of MANETs is addressed with persistent messages, completely distributed message storage, and flexible communication patterns. We quantitatively compare a prototype implementation of MELON to existing paradigms to show its feasibility as the basis for new MANET applications. Experiments demonstrate 40 % better throughput on average than traditional paradigms, as well as 70 % faster local insertion and removal operations compared to an existing tuple space library.

1   Introduction

While smartphones are quickly becoming ubiquitous, most mobile applications continue to use a client-server model rather than communicating through mobile ad hoc networks (MANET). One reason may be the added challenges of developing a MANET application which must communicate with peers over unreliable shifting network topologies. While communicating over a single-hop wireless network (e.g., a WiFi access point or cellular tower) to a central server is simpler, MANETs are useful when communication is between nearby devices or when there is no network infrastructure, such as in disaster recovery situations or locations without cellular service.

To alleviate application development challenges posed by MANETs, several approaches to middleware and libraries have been proposed. The majority of these proposals are adapted forms of traditional distributed computing paradigms such as publish/subscribe, remote procedure calls, and tuple spaces, instead of MANET-focused paradigms [1].

In this paper, we introduce a new paradigm called MELON[1]. MELON overcomes frequent network disconnections in MANETs by providing message persistence in a distributed shared message store and can operate entirely on-demand, avoiding coupling between nodes. MELONs offer remove-only, read-only, and private messages, as well as bulk transfers. MELON also simplifies communication

---

[1] Message Exchange Language Over the Network.

© Institute for Computer Sciences, Social Informatics and Telecommunications Engineering 2014
I. Stojmenovic et al. (Eds.): MOBIQUITOUS 2013, LNICST 131, pp. 716–720, 2014.
DOI: 10.1007/978-3-319-11569-6_59

by returning messages in per host write order. We demonstrate that our proposed paradigm is practical by comparing performance of a prototype MELON implementation to canonical implementations of traditional paradigms in a MANET environment. Results show higher throughput with comparable latency.

2   MELON Design

Applications which are developed for MANETs must operate in an infrastructure-less, unreliable, and dynamic distributed environment. We consider disconnection handling, addressing and discovery, and flexible communication important features for MANET development.

The design of MELON is built around a distributed shared message store. Each device in the network may host any number of applications which access and contribute to the shared message store. Each application hosts a local message store which may be accessed by any local or remote application. Applications request messages (which may be local or remote) using message templates.

By communicating through a shared message store, the concept of connections between hosts is eliminated and thus disconnections are no longer an application layer concern. Hosts suddenly leaving the network do not disrupt an application and applications do not need to handle operations failing from intermittent network connectivity or physical wireless interference. The application is insulated from these issues by the semantics of the operations.

MELON also includes features uncommon to shared message stores to further simplify application development in MANETs. First, messages are returned in first-in first-out order per host. When a single host generates the majority of the messages, this removes the need to re-order messages in the application.

Secondly, MELON provides operations to only read messages which were not previously read by the same process. This enables an application to read all matching messages currently in the message store, then read only newly-added messages in subsequent operations, avoiding the multiple read problem [2].

Finally, MELON differentiates messages intended to persist and be read by many receivers from messages expected to be removed from the message store. For example, a news feed would have many readers but messages should not be removed. In contrast, in a job queue each job should be removed by exactly one worker. MELON supports both scenarios.

2.1   MELON Operations

Messages can be copied to the shared message store via a **store** or **write** operation. A **store** operation allows the message to later be removed. Messages saved with a **write** operation cannot be explicitly removed, only copied. Messages saved with a **store** may optionally be directed to a specific receiver. Only the addressee may access a directed message (Table 1).

Messages added via **store** may be retrieved by a **take** operation using a message template which specifies the content of the message to be returned.

Table 1. MELON operations

Operation	Return type	Action
store(*message, [address]*)	*null*	Store removable message
write(*message*)	*null*	Store read-only message
take(*template, [block = true]*)	*message* or *null*	Remove and return message
read(*template, [block = true]*)	*message* or *null*	Copy and return read-only message
take_all(*template, [block = true]*)	*array*	Bulk remove messages
read_all(*template, [block = true]*)	*array*	Bulk copy read-only messages

A **take** operation removes a message with matching content and returns it to the requesting process. A message may only be returned by a single **take** operation.

read operations also return a message matching a given template, but do not remove the original message. Any number of processes may read the same message, but repeated calls to **read** in the same process will never return the same message. Only messages stored with **write** may be returned by **read**.

MELON also includes the bulk operations **take_all** and **read_all** which mirror the basic operations, except all available matching messages will be returned. For **read_all**, only messages which were not previously returned by a **read** or **read_all** in the same process will be returned.

By default, all fetch operations will block the calling process until a matching message is available. MELON also provides non-blocking versions of these operations which return a null or empty value instead of blocking.

Due to the limited resources of most devices in a mobile network, storage space in MELON is explicitly bounded. Any message may be garbage collected prior to being removed by a **take** if capacity is reached.

Table 2. News server and reader

News Server	News Reader

`function report(category, headline) {`
`    write([category, headline])`
`}`
	`function fetch(category) {`
	`    return read_all([category, String])`
	`}`

Table 2 shows a sample application. One or more news servers generate news messages containing a news category and headline. The server uses **write** to disallow removal of news items. Any number of processes can consume the news as readers, using **read_all** to return all news items in a given category. Repeated calls to `fetch` will only return news items not already seen.

3 Quantitative Evaluation

To determine if MELON is a feasible solution for actual MANET applications, we chose to compare its performance to canonical implementations of

publish/subscribe, RPC, and tuple spaces. We evaluated applications with the
EXata network emulator [3] in order to run real applications and also have precisely repeatable environments with high fidelity network models. The scenario
distributed 50 nodes in a 150 m square grid moving with a random waypoint
mobility model. Signal propagation is limited to 50 m to match an indoor environment and force multihop routes, and the two-ray model is used for path loss.
802.11b WiFi is used with the AODV routing protocol.

Operation Speed. To establish a performance baseline, we measured the time
for the **write**, **read**, **store**, and **take** operations directly on a local message storage and compared the results to the LighTS [4] local tuple space implementation
used by LIME [5].

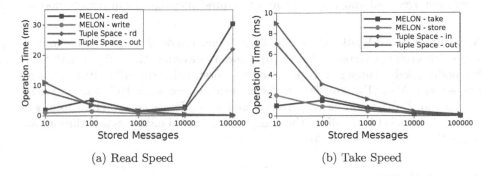

(a) Read Speed   (b) Take Speed

Fig. 1. Operation speeds

Since LighTS and MELON search messages linearly, non-destructive reads
are most affected by more stored messages. Removing messages is fast since the
matching message is always the first message in the store. All **take/in** operations
require less than 8 ms to execute on average. Storing messages is naturally faster
than removing for both implementations: storing a message takes less than 10 ms
on average, and usually less than 4 ms (Fig. 1).

Message Latency. Figure 2(a) shows the average latency between request and
receipt of a message. A single host writes out 1,000 messages with a 1 KB payload, and the other hosts read the messages concurrently. Tuple spaces and
MELON use the **rd/read** operations to retrieve the messages singularly. For
publish/subscribe, latency was measured as the time elapsed between receiving
sequential publications.

In these experiments, MELON and tuple spaces were the most affected by the
increase in node speed and packet loss, as well as having the highest latency when
nodes were at rest. MELON latency increased 29 % and tuple spaces increased
24 %. In contrast, RPC only increased 7 % and publish/subscribe actually had
the lowest latency at the highest node speed. Since publish/subscribe is push-
based and has very low overhead, it is able to take advantage of the increased

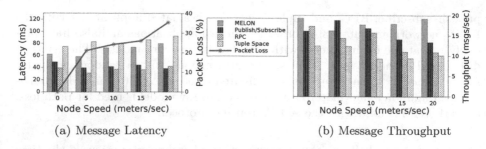

(a) Message Latency   (b) Message Throughput

Fig. 2. Communication performance

opportunities for transferring data. On the other hand, MELON and tuple spaces have high overhead and must repeatedly request messages from remote nodes.

Message Throughput. Throughput was measured on the receiver side in messages delivered per second. Figure 2(b) shows the average throughput with varying node speeds. Tuple spaces perform the worst, delivering 12.5–10.1 messages per second. MELON provides the best performance with 19.2–16.2 messages per second. Publish/subscribe performs well at moderate speeds (18.8 msgs/s at 5 m/s), but packet loss reduces the number of delivered messages and throughput drops 29 %–13.4 msgs/s at 20 m/s.

4   Conclusion

MELON is a new communication paradigm designed for MANET application and middleware development. It provides a unique combination of new features for interacting with a distributed shared message store, including separation of read-only messages and removable messages, private messages, bulk message operations, and tracking of read messages. In this paper we used real applications to compare MELON performance to existing communication paradigms and demonstrated acceptable performance in a MANET context.

References

1. Collins, J., Bagrodia, R.: Programming in mobile ad hoc networks. In: WICON '08: 4th International Conference on Wireless Internet, pp. 1–9. ICST (2008)
2. Rowstron, A., Wood, A.: Solving the linda multiple rd problem. In: Hankin, C., Ciancarini, P. (eds.) COORDINATION 1996. LNCS, vol. 1061, pp. 357–367. Springer, Heidelberg (1996)
3. Scalable Networks: Exata: an exact digital network replica for testing, training and operations of network-centric systems. Technical brief (2008)
4. Balzarotti, D., et al.: The lights tuple space framework and its customization for context-aware applications. Web Intell. Agent Syst. **5**(2), 215–231 (2007)
5. Murphy, A., et al.: Lime: a coordination middleware supporting mobility of hosts and agents. ACM Trans. Soft. Eng. Method. **15**(3), 279–328 (2006)

MVPTrack: Energy-Efficient Places and Motion States Tracking

Chunhui Zhang[1]([✉]), Ke Huang[1], Guanling Chen[1], and Linzhang Wang[2]

[1] Computer Science Department, University of Massachusetts Lowell,
1 University Avenue, Lowell, MA 01854, USA
{czhang,khuang,glchen}@cs.uml.edu
[2] Nanjing University, Nanjing, Jiangsu, China
lzwang@nju.edu.cn

Abstract. Contextual information such as a person's meaningful places (Different from a person's location (raw coordinates), place is an indoor or outdoor area where a person usually conducts some activity, in other words where it is meaningful to the person, such as home, office rooms, restaurants etc.) could provide intelligence to many smartphone apps. However, acquiring this context attribute is not straightforward and could easily drain the battery. In this paper, we propose M(Move)V(Vehicle)P(Place)Track, a continuous place and motion state tracking framework with a focus on improving the energy efficiency of place entrance detection through two techniques: (1) utilizing the mobility change not only for finding the sleeping opportunities for the high energy sensors, but also for providing hint for place entrance detection, (2) leveraging the place history for fast place entrance detection. We evaluated MVPTrack based on traces collected by five persons over two weeks. The evaluation results showed that MVPTrack used 58 % less energy than previous work and provided a much faster place entrance detection approach.

Keywords: Place sensing · Energy efficiency · Place awareness

1 Introduction

Continuous sensing of a person's daily visited places has been motivated by many use cases. For instance, *Nihao* [1], a place-aware smartphone app launcher that could dynamically arrange the app icons according to the user's current place since users tend to use different apps in different places. Another example is a *Smart Profile Switcher*. It could automatically change the smartphone profile according to the current places since phones are required to be muted for some place such as an office meeting room.

To support the place and motion-aware apps, we propose MVPTrack, a continuous place (detected based on WiFi fingerprint to offer room/floor level

This work is supported partly by the National Science Foundation under Grant No. 1040725 and No. 0917112.

© Institute for Computer Sciences, Social Informatics and Telecommunications Engineering 2014
I. Stojmenovic et al. (Eds.): MOBIQUITOUS 2013, LNICST 131, pp. 721–725, 2014.
DOI: 10.1007/978-3-319-11569-6_60

indoor place discriminability) and motion (based on accelerometer) state tracking framework with a focus on the energy efficiency. We evaluated our system based on traces collected by five persons over two weeks. The results showed that our framework used 58 % less energy than previous work [2] and provided a faster place entrance detection algorithm.

Previous WiFi fingerprint based place tracking solution [2] utilizes the accelerometer to find sleeping opportunities for the high energy sensors such as WiFi and GPS. But after a place exit was detected, the place sensors are kept on for entrance detection of next place which could potentially waste lots of energy if the transit between places took long time. Our contributions in this work is to (1) provide an energy efficient place entrance detection algorithm leveraging both mobility change and place history, (2) implement and evaluate the proposed work with detailed analysis about the characteristics of such a system.

The rest of this paper is organized as follows. In Sect. 2 we first discusses design of the system. Then, we show the system evaluation results in Sect. 3. Finally, Sect. 4 concludes with planned future work.

2   System Design

In this section we present the architecture of the MVPTrack framework, as shown in Fig. 1. The goal of this framework is to support *Place-aware* (focus of this paper) and *Motion-aware* applications robustly and in an energy efficient manner.

Motion Intensity Monitor (MIM) is a binary(Move or still) classifier continuously classifies the user's motion intensity (Eq. 2) with duty-cycling.

$$Acceleration = \sqrt{x^2 + y^2 + z^2} \tag{1}$$

$$Motion\ Intensity\ (MI) = Standard\ Deviation(Acceleration\ of\ samples) \tag{2}$$

we choose 1.2 as the threshold since it achieves the best place detection accuracy due to our experiment. When *MIM* captures the transition from mobile state to

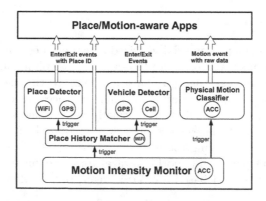

Fig. 1. Framework architecture

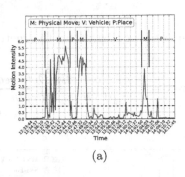

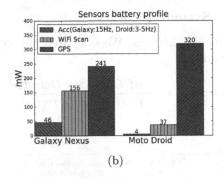

(a)   (b)

Fig. 2. (a) User motion intensity variation through a day (Smartphone is placed in the front pant pocket), (b) Sensors' battery profile for Galaxy Nexus and Motorola Droid

still and being still for a while (defined by a sliding window with window capacity C_m, the rationale is that people are tend to being still in a indoor place or in a vehicle), *Place history matcher (PHM)* is triggered. *PHM* tries to match the current WiFi fingerprint with the records stored in a place history table. This step is very powerful since it not only help avoid the unnecessary GPS readings used for vehicle detection comparing to the case without *PHM* but also shorten the place entrance detection time comparing to the time necessary to sense a stable radio environment in SensLoc. We choose Tanimoto Coefficient,

$$Similarity(v_1, v_2) = \frac{v_1 \cdot v_2}{||v_1||^2 + ||v_2||^2 - v_1 \cdot v_2} \tag{3}$$

as the metric of WiFi fingerprints similarity. If the similarity value is larger than a threshold δ_{fp}, an place enter event is fired immediately. Otherwise *Place Entrance Detector (PED)* is finally triggered. (We omit the discussion of *PED* since it shares the similar algorithm with SensLoc)

3 Evaluation

We evaluated the system against a dataset collected locally and compare the performance with SensLoc from three different perspectives, i.e. system accuracy, battery efficiency and detection delay.

3.1 Dataset

The dataset we collected contains the place/vehicle ground truth(enter/exit time and place name), a WiFi scanning trace and a GPS trace. We asked 5 testers to follow their daily routine for 2 weeks. This dataset is used to run both our algorithm and the algorithms we are comparing with. The recorded places includes home, office rooms, meeting rooms, school labs, library rooms, restaurants, shopping malls, supper markets, beaches, parks etc. The recorded vehicle includes cars, buses and subways.

3.2   System Accuracy

Evaluation Metrics. We evaluated the system accuracy based on the metrics defined in[2]:

$$Precision = \frac{\#\ of\ Correctly\ Detected}{\#\ of\ Total\ Detected}; Recall = \frac{\#\ of\ Correctly\ Detected}{\#\ of\ Ground\ Truth} \tag{4}$$

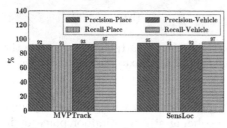
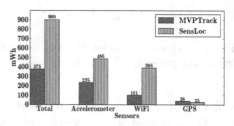

(a) Overall precision and recall for place/vehi-   (b) Daily average energy consumption for all
cle entrance/exit detection   testers

Fig. 3. Evaluation result

As the Fig. 3a suggests, for the places, our framework achieves 92 precision and 91 recall which maintains a comparable accuracy level with SensLoc.

3.3   Energy Efficiency

Sensor energy consumption estimation. We developed three battery profiling apps which only open one particular sensor and read it at the highest frequency. We ran the apps after the phone is fully charged until the battery is almost drained. Android system reports the percentage of the battery used by each app. Combining with the percentage value of how many battery consumed and the total battery capacity, we are able to estimate the power profile of an individual sensor. Figure 2b is generated through this method.

Figure 3b shows both the comparison of the overall energy consumption as well as the energy consumption of individual sensors. The accelerometer component of our system uses about half of the energy comparing to SensLoc since we use 25 % duty cycle while SensLoc uses 50 % which is not necessary. Our WiFi component uses one forth of the energy comparing to SensLoc due to our place entrance detection algorithm. Overall, our system use 58 % less energy than SensLoc which is a significant improvement.

3.4   Detection Delay

Besides the system accuracy and energy efficiency, the detection delay is also an importance metric for such a system since it reflects the real-timeness of the

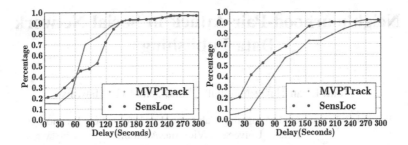

Fig. 4. Place and vehicle entrance detection delay. The left side is for the place and the right side is for the vehicle.

system. Figure 4 shows the CDF of both place and vehicle entrance detection delay. As we can see, about 65–70 % of the time, place entrance is detected between 60 seconds and 90 seconds which indicates that about 65–70 % of the total place visits were re-visits and they took the advantage of the *Place History Matcher* to effectively shorten the detection delay. Actually, after a longer period of time, a person's regularly visited places converge thus place history could constantly offer great real-timeness for the system.

4 Conclusion

In this paper, we propose a novel place entrance detection algorithm leveraging the user's mobility change and place history. The evaluation result shows it used 58 % less energy than previous work and provided a faster place entrance detection algorithm.

References

1. Zhang, C., Ding, X., Chen, G., Huang, K., Ma, X., Yan, B.: Nihao: a predictive smartphone application launcher. In: ser. MobiCASE'12 (2012)
2. Kim, D.H., Kim, Y., Estrin, D., Srivastava, M.B.: Sensloc: sensing everyday places and paths using less energy. In: ser. SenSys'10 (2010)

Neighbourhood-Pair Attack in Social Network Data Publishing

Mohd Izuan Hafez Ninggal$^{(\boxtimes)}$ and Jemal H. Abawajy

Parallel and Distributed Computing Lab School of Information Technology,
Deakin University, Victoria, Australia
{mninggal,jemal}@deakin.edu.au

Abstract. Vertex re-identification is one of the significant and challenging problems in social network. In this paper, we show a new type of vertex re-identification attack called neighbourhood-pair attack. This attack utilizes the neighbourhood topologies of two connected vertices. We show both theoretically and empirically that this attack is possible on anonymized social network and has higher re-identification rate than the existing structural attacks.

1 Introduction

Data publishing agencies, such as healthcare providers and public services, face fundamental challenges in how to release data to the public without violating the confidentiality of personal information. This problem has recently received considerable traction as more and more social network data has been released publicly to enable social network data analysis [1]. Currently, the privacy of individuals and the confidentiality of data in social network data publishing are protected through variety anonymization techniques. Some of these techniques include removing vertices labels such as the name or other personally identifiable information, the k-anonymity and l-diversity approaches for privacy [11] to conceal the identity of the individuals.

Privacy preservation in publishing social networks data is a challenging problem [2]. This is because a social network data has numerous types of structural information which could be manipulated by an adversary to re-identify individuals and breach their privacy. For example, the degree attack [3] manipulates the number of links of the targeted vertex. Similarly, the neighbourhood attack [2, 4] manipulates the link patterns among the direct neighbours of the targeted vertex in a social network.

In this paper, we present a new type of privacy attack called neighbourhood-pair attack in a social network. This attack utilizes the neighbourhood structure of a pair of connected vertices as the background knowledge of an adversary to query and re-identify targeted victims in a released social network data. Since neighbourhood pair structure consists of a large size of sub-graph, we identify a technique of how the structure of the neighbourhood-pair could be represented and show its practicality to facilitate the vertex re-identification.

The rest of the paper is structured as follows. In Sect. 2, the models used in the paper are discussed. The proposed attack and its analysis are discussed in Sect. 3 and 4 respectively. The conclusion is given in Sect. 5.

© Institute for Computer Sciences, Social Informatics and Telecommunications Engineering 2014
I. Stojmenovic et al. (Eds.): MOBIQUITOUS 2013, LNICST 131, pp. 726–731, 2014.
DOI: 10.1007/978-3-319-11569-6_61

2 Models

We model a social network data as a graph characterized as $G(V,E)$ where $V = \{v_1, v_2, \ldots, v_n\}$ is a set of n unlabeled vertices representing individuals in the social network. We represent the social links between individuals via unlabelled undirected edges $E \subseteq V \times V$. We assume that the data publisher releases useful social network data in a way that satisfies the data users need while at the same time preserving private information about the individuals in the data. To this end, we assume that the social network data graph $G(V,E)$ is sanitized into $\bar{G}(\bar{V}, \bar{E})$ before publishing using k-anonymization mechanism with $k = 2$.

An adversary $\mathcal{A}$ is interested in deriving private information such as the identity of an individual or an attribute value from $\bar{v} \in \bar{V}$. The outcome of structural attack depends on the background knowledge that an adversary $\mathcal{A}$ has. In [2, 5, 6], it is assumed that the adversary knows large set of structural information regarding the target vertex in a social network. In contrast, we assume that $\mathcal{A}$ knows the neighbourhood-pair information (shown in Fig. 1d) of $\bar{v} \in \bar{V}$ and $\bar{v} \in \bar{V}$ where $\bar{u}$ is an adjacent vertex of a vertex $\bar{v}$ such that $\bar{v} \neq \bar{u}$.

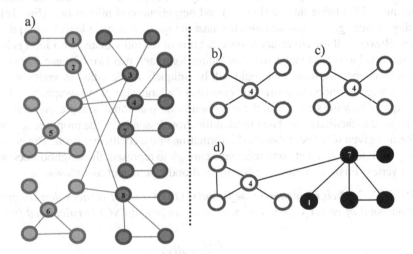

Fig. 1. An anonymized graph $\bar{G}(\bar{V}, \bar{E})$ (left) and structural knowledge (right).

3 Neighbourhood-Pair Attack

In this section, we present a new type of privacy attack called neighbourhood-pair attack in a social network. We will first define some background information needed to carry out the attack.

*DEFINITION 1 (**Structural Query**): Given a social network $G(V,E)$ and a target individual $t \in V$, a structural query q returns a set of vertices $\dot{v} \subset V$ based on the structural properties of $t \in V$.*

In the proposed neighbourhood-pair attack, an adversary $\mathcal{A}$ utilizes the neighbourhood structure of a pair of connected vertices as the background knowledge to reidentify targeted victims in an anonymised social network data. Specifically, let $t \in V$ and $u \in V$ be adjacent vertices in G such that $t \in V$ represents the target vertex where $t \neq u$. To utilise neighbourhood-pair information, the first step is to query the target vertex $t \in V$ by using the degree information. Assume the query returns a set of matching vertices $\boldsymbol{x} \subset V$. The smaller the cardinality of matching vertices (i.e., $\boldsymbol{x}$) is the higher the probability that the target victim $t \in V$ could be re-identified. To filter out $\boldsymbol{x}$ in order to find t, the adversary then compares the link structure among every neighbours of $\boldsymbol{x}$. By this, the adversary has manipulated the neighbourhood information for the query. We denote the set of matching vertices from the previous step as $\boldsymbol{y}$. Assume the return set $\boldsymbol{y} > 1$. The adversary then uses the neighbourhood information of u to find t in $\boldsymbol{y}$. The target victim could be definitely re-identified if and only if the cardinality of matching vertices is 1.

We now illustrate the neighbourhood-pair attack. Figure 1a is a sample of an anonymized social network graph. In fact, the social network graph is resistant to the degree attack [3] and the neighbourhood attack [2, 4]. By referring to Fig. 1a, assume the target victim is John who in the graph has been anonymized as vertex #4. When the adversary tries to query John using degree (Fig. 1b) and neighbourhood information (Fig. 1c), the matching vertices give ¼ probabilities because the query returns at least four equivalent vertices. However, if the adversary knows that one of the individuals, who John is linked to, is connected to other five persons (including John) and that two of these five persons are directly connected, then John could still be uniquely re-identified as vertex 4.

Since neighbourhood pair structure consists of a large size of sub-graph, we identify a technique of how the structure of the neighbourhood-pair could be represented and how it can be used to facilitate the vertex re-identification. Essentially, the proposed technique transforms a given set of neighborhood information into a coefficient form. The goal is to simplify the information yet comprehensive enough to represent the neighborhood set of a given vertex. First, we define the Neighbourhood Coefficient as follows:

*DEFINITION 2 (**Neighbourhood Coefficient**): Given a set of vertices that comprise a neighbourhood of vertex v, the neighbourhood coefficient (**NC**) is calculated by:*

$$NC = \frac{\gamma(v)}{\delta(v)} + d(v) \tag{1}$$

where $d(v)$ is the degree of vertex v; $\gamma(v) = \left\{ e_{ij} : v_i, v_j \in N, e_{ij} \in E \right\}$ is the existing links between the direct neighbours of v; $\delta(v)$ is the maximum number of links that could possibly exist between the direct neighbours of v and defined by $\frac{[|N| \cdot [|N|-1]]}{2}$.

For example, in the neighbourhood sub-graph in Fig. 1c, the vertex #4 has four neighbours and two of them are connected together. To transform this information into the NC, we first count the neighbours of vertex #4 which happens to be 4. Then we calculate the links that exist among the 4 neighbours of vertex #4. We find there is only 1 link connection that exists among the neighbours out of the maximum possible connections. We then calculate the maximum links that could possibly exist among these four neighbours by $\frac{[|4|.[|4|-1]]}{2} = 6$. The denominator is 2 because the graph considered here is undirected. Having that, the neighbourhood coefficient is $\frac{1}{6} + 4 = 4.167$. We include the degree information in the calculation because we want to differentiate between the fractions with common denominator. For instance, between $\frac{1}{3}$ and $\frac{2}{6}$. To use NC for query, all the vertices in the graph must be transformed into neighbourhood coefficient. Having the neighbourhood coefficient list, the adversary can then perform mapping using the particular neighbourhood-pair coefficient of the target victim that he already have in hand. The neighbourhood-pair is transcribed as:

$$NP = [NC_t, NC_u] \tag{2}$$

where NP is neighbourhood-pair, NC is the Neighbourhood Coefficient defined in (1), v is the targeted victim and u is one of the neighbours of v.

4 Performance Analysis

In this section, we analyses the performance of the proposed attack and compare it with the degree attack [3] and the neighbourhood attack [2, 4].

PROPOSITION 1: Neighbourhood-Pair attack has higher re-identification rate than degree and neighbourhood attack.

PROOF. Let v_j be a set of vertices, u_k be another set of vertices that are directly connected to v_j where $u_k \neq v_j$. Given $D(v_j)$ is the number of neighbours for vertex v_j called degree and $N(v_j)$ as the information about the links between u_k called neighbourhood. We denote $D(v_j) \subset N(v_j)$ as to show that the information about the neighbourhood does also include the information about the degree. Given $NP\{N(v_j), N(v_l)\}$ as the pair of neighbourhood for vertex v_j and v_l, then we denote $N(v_j) \subset NP[N(v_j), N(v_l)]$ to show that the neighbourhood-pair structure also does include neighbourhood information. Thus, we get $NP\{N(v_j), N(v_l)\} \supset N(v_j) \supset D(v_j)$ which means the neighbourhood-pair information has higher structural characteristic

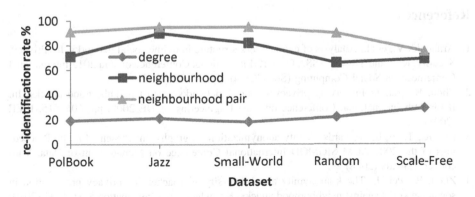

Fig. 2. The re-identification rate comparison graph

than the degree and neighbourhood information. Hence, using neighbourhood-pair to query target victim increases the chance of re-identification.   ■

The graph in Fig. 2 compares the re-identification rate among the three types of structural information over the five different datasets (i.e., **PolBooks**: a network of books sold by an online store where the edges between books represent the purchase frequency of the same buyers; **Jazz Musician Network**: a network of jazz musicians who collaborate in different bands. The vertices represent the band and edges represent the musicians in common; **Scale-Free**: a synthetic network with a power-law vertex degree distribution; **Random:** a synthetic random network where the vertices in this network are randomly connected based on probability p; and **Small-World:** a type of graph in which most vertices can be reached from every other vertex by a small number of hops).

The percentage represents the amount of vertex that is the dataset that are exposed to re-identification attack using the three types of graph structural information. The graph only covers unique matching vertices from the structural query that we performed. We ignore the vertices match that has 50 % probability. Therefore, this graph only shows the rate of vertices that definitely re-identified. The degree attack has set 20–30 % of the users to be definitely re-identified over all datasets that we tested. Even though this rate gives significant percentage in terms of the number of users who are in risk, the neighbourhood structural information gives more than double of the re-identification risk. Through all the datasets, more than 60 % of the users are definitely re-identified using neighbourhood information. However, it is evident that the re-identification rate using the neighbourhood-pair scored the highest in all five datasets.

5 Conclusion

In this paper, we identified a new type of attack called neighbourhood-pair attack to distinguish people in a dataset. We also proposed the neighbourhood coefficient to transform neighbourhood information into more simple form for query. We have shown theoretically and empirically that using the neighbourhood-pair structural information, the adversary has higher chances to successfully re-identify targeted victim.

References

1. Arnaboldi,V., et al.: Analysis of ego network structure in online social networks. In: Privacy, Security, Risk and Trust (PASSAT), 2012 International Conference on and 2012 International Confernece on Social Computing (SocialCom), pp. 31–40 (2012)
2. Zhou, B., Pei, J.: Preserving privacy in social networks against neighborhood attacks. In: IEEE 24th International Conference on Data Engineering, ICDE 2008, pp. 506–515. IEEE (2008)
3. Liu, K., Terzi, E.: Towards identity anonymization on graphs. In: Presented at the Proceedings of the 2008 ACM SIGMOD International Conference on Management of Data, Vancouver, Canada (2008)
4. Zhou, B., Pei, J.: The k-anonymity and l-diversity approaches for privacy preservation in social networks against neighborhood attacks. Knowledge and Information Syst. 1–31 (2010)

5. Zou, L., et al.: K-automorphism: A general framework for privacy preserving network publication. In: Proceedings of the VLDB Endowment, vol. 2, pp. 946–957 (2009)
6. Cheng, J., et al.: K-isomorphism: privacy preserving network publication against structural attacks. In: Proceedings of the 2010 ACM SIGMOD International Conference on Management of data, pp. 459–470 (2010)

On-demand Mobile Charger Scheduling
for Effective Coverage in Wireless Rechargeable
Sensor Networks

Lintong Jiang, Haipeng Dai, Xiaobing Wu[✉], and Guihai Chen

State Key Laboratory for Novel Software Technology, Nanjing University,
Nanjing 210023, Jiangsu, China
{jltong216,dhpphd2003}@gmail.com, {wuxb,gchen}@nju.edu.cn

Abstract. In this paper, we consider the problem of scheduling mobile chargers (MCs) in an on-demand way to maximize the covering utility (CU) in wireless rechargeable sensor networks (WRSNs), while nearly all previous related works assume the MCs move along predefined paths with perfect priori information. And the CU is defined to quantify the effectiveness of event monitoring. We propose three heuristics for this problem after proving its NP-Completeness. Finally we evaluate our solutions through extensive trace-driven simulations.

Keywords: On-demand charging · Event monitoring

1 Introduction

Many existing works [1–5] propose to use MCs to work in WRSNs with perfect priori information and predefined traveling path. On one hand, using MCs is much more energy efficient than deploying multiple static chargers. On the other hand, it is necessary to schedule the MCs to provide intensive charging power within a short distance.

In this paper, we consider the scenario where each MC responds the charging request in an on-demand way and recharges the requesting sensor via wireless to enable its continuous work.

The main contributions of this work are as follows.

– To the best of our knowledge, this is the first work considering the on-demand scheduling problem of MCs in WRSNs aiming to maximize the CU.
– We prove that the on-demand scheduling problem is NP-Complete and propose three algorithms by exploiting the spatial redundancy of WRSNs.
– We evaluate algorithms through extensive trace-driven simulations.

2 Related Work

The schemes proposed by [1–5] are based on the assumption of the availability of perfect priori knowledge. He *et al.* [6,7] consider the on-demand schedule of

© Institute for Computer Sciences, Social Informatics and Telecommunications Engineering 2014
I. Stojmenovic et al. (Eds.): MOBIQUITOUS 2013, LNICST 131, pp. 732–736, 2014.
DOI: 10.1007/978-3-319-11569-6_62

mobile elements in a different scenario, i.e., data collection applications. There is an online-like mobile charging schedules [13] targeting on prolonging the lifetime in WRSNs, but it is constrained by specific setting and thus not general. In this paper, we relax the constraint they set and focus on the goal of maximizing the CU rather than purely elongate the lifetime of network.

3   Problem Statement

Assume that m sensors $V = \{v_1, v_2, \ldots, v_m\}$ are randomly distributed in a 2D area along with n Point of Interests(PoI) $O = \{o_1, o_2, \ldots, o_n\}$. The sensing range of every sensor is r. The events at a PoI emerge one after another, and the arrival of events at PoIs is spatially and temporally independent. Different sensors may cover some PoIs in common due to spatial redundancy [8]. Let O_i represent the set of PoIs covered by sensor v_i. Furthermore, we assume that all sensors work can communicate directly with the sink. Multiple sinks [9] might be deployed [10] in the field for fear that the coverage of a single sink is limited. A sensor only reports its data (with size of b bits) to the nearest sink directly once it senses an event, but its request for recharging can be relayed by the sinks to the mobile charger since the sinks are out of energy concern and cover the whole field collectively. For convenience of exposition, we divide the sensors into two subsets, the set of active sensors V_a and the set of sensors requesting recharging V_r.

An MC maintains a requesting queue for the recharging requests and we assume an $M/G/1$ queue in Kendall's Notation. All the recharging requests will be recorded and those sensors that send these requests will be kept in the requesting queue by the MC. For any sensor i, we assume the received power $P_c^{(i)} = \eta_i \cdot P_{MC}$, which is far greater than its working power P_i, where η_i denotes the charging efficiency of sensor i and P_{MC} is the working power of MCs.

The recharging time mainly depends on P_{MC}, η_i, and total battery capacity, W, of the sensor, i.e. $t_c^{(i)} = \frac{W}{\eta_i \cdot P_{MC}}$. In addition, for sensor i, the service time $t_s^{(i)}$ consists of the traveling time $t_t^{(i)}$ and the charging time $t_c^{(i)}$. As for sensor i, its working power P_i depends on the rate of event generating f_i and the unit energy consumption e_i, i.e. $P_i = f_i \cdot e_i \cdot b$. Notably, we adopt the energy consumption model used in [11,12] to measure e_i. Hence, the average arrival rate (AAR) of the request λ can be estimated as $\lambda = \frac{\sum_{i=1}^{m} P_i}{(1-\alpha) \cdot W}$, where α denotes the recharging threshold factor. After finishing the service for the last request, the MC chooses the next target among the members in its requesting queue with its predefined rule and then moves for the target.

In order to define CU, we define *Global Effective Coverage* (GEC), the set of PoIs covered by actives sensors, at time t as $G(t) = \bigcup_{v_i \in V_a} O_i$ and *Global Coverage* (GC) as $M = \bigcup_{v_i \in V} O_i$. Intuitively, the **Covering Utility** (CU) denotes the ratio between above two as follow,

$$U(t) = |G(t)|/|M|. \tag{1}$$

We define *Incremental Effective Coverage* (IEC) as the set of PoIs that are going to be effectively covered. Formally, $I_j^{(i)} = \bigcup_{v_i \in V_a \cup \{j\}} O_i - \bigcup_{v_i \in V_a} O_i$ if sensor j is chosen before the MC makes its i-th selection.

Additionally, we assume a greedy strategy in order to maximize the overall CU. The MC tries to choose the next to-be-served sensor by updating the i-th *Piecewise Covering Utility* (PCU) with maximum of the average CU during the service time of the promising sensor j each time the MC finishes the last service.

$$U^{(i)} = \max_j \{ \frac{1}{t_s^{(j)}} \int_{t_{i-1}}^{t_{i-1}+t_s^{(j)}} U(t)dt \}. \tag{2}$$

To sum up, we formally formulate our problem as follows.

$$\textbf{Maximize} \quad \frac{1}{N} \sum_{i=1}^{N} U^{(i)}$$

$$\textbf{s.t.} \quad (1)(2),$$

where N denotes the number of the requests.

4   Theoretical Analysis and Solution

By similar analysis of [13], we can reduce the Geometric TSP problem to the problem and show its NP-completeness. Since it is NP-Complete, we resort to greedy algorithms. In the following parts, we will propose three greedy heuristics. Due to space limit, we just sketch these algorithms.

4.1   Maximal Next Coverage Utility First (MNCUF) Algorithm

MNCUF requires that the MC choose the current maximal IEC to serve. In other words, MC checks the requesting queue and chooses the sensor with maximum IEC currently as the next to-be-served sensor, which can be regarded as a specific instance for the strategy of maximizing PCU (2).

4.2   Maximal Average Coverage Utility First (MACUF) Algorithm

MACUF takes the trade-off between the travel time and IEC of every service into consideration and greedily selects the target with the following formulation.

$$U_j^{(i)} = \frac{|G(t_{i-1})| \cdot t_t^{(j)} + |G(t_{i-1}) + I_j^{(i)}|t_c^{(j)}}{t_s^{(j)} \cdot |M|} \tag{3}$$

where $U_j^{(i)}$ performs as the approximation candidate for PCU, which substitutes the right hand side of (2).

4.3   MACUF Algorithm with Multi-MCs

Suppose that there are n MCs in total, and they are numbered sequentially, $\{0, 1, \ldots, n-1\}$. Intuitively, although every MC receives and records the information of all the requests within the WRSNs, the i-th MC only serves the $(kn + i)$-th requests, where $k \in N$, with MACUF discipline.

5   Performance Evaluation

We utilize the same value setting of η, W and P_c as in our previous works [4]. In our scenario, the sensing field is a $100 \times 100\,\mathrm{m}^2$ square with 100 randomly distribute sensors, 300 PoIs and 10 sinks. Furthermore, we set the sensing range $r = 15\,\mathrm{m}$, the threshold factor $\alpha = 20\,\%$ and the message size is 2 Kbits, i.e., $b = 2000$. A total number of 100 requests are served during each simulation.

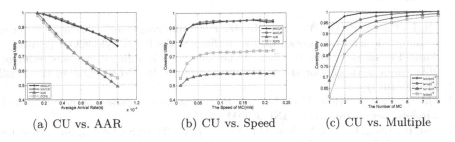

(a) CU vs. AAR   (b) CU vs. Speed   (c) CU vs. Multiple

Fig. 1. Performance comparisons from different perspectives

To the best of our knowledge, there are no existing works designed to maximize CU based on on-demand mobile charging in WRSNs. To exhibit the system performance of our algorithms, we tailor two on-demand mobile data collection disciplines, NJN [6] and FCFS [7], to adapt to the scenario we consider.

(1) *Evaluation of different rates of event generation:* we vary the rate of event generation, proportion to the Average Arrival Rate(AAR), and compare the CU of all four algorithms. In Fig. 1(a), the speed of MC v is set to $0.01\,\mathrm{m/s}$, which makes the traveling time essential. As can be seen, both of our algorithms outperform the existing ones in terms of CU.

(2) *Evaluation of different speeds of MC:* we continue to focus on the CU of all of the algorithms influenced by varied speed v. In this evaluation, $\lambda = 1 \times 10^{-4}$. Intuitively, with the speed increasing, the traveling overhead goes down, so as the response delay to the charging requests, which may lead to a higher CU. We plot the fact in the Fig. 1(b).

We deploy different numbers of MCs ($n = 1, 2, \ldots, 8$) in the sensing field and compare the CU with the varying AAR λ together. Figure 1(c) shows that the larger number of MCs we choose, the higher overall CU we obtain.

6   Conclusion

In this paper, we consider the on-demand mobile charger scheduling problem to maximize the CU of event monitoring in WRSNs. Due to the NP-completeness of this problem, we propose three heuristic algorithms. We evaluate the proposed algorithms through extensive trace-driven simulations.

Acknowledgment. This work is supported by 973 project under Grant No.2012CB316200, National Natural Science Foundation of China under Grant No. 61373130, No.61133006 and No.61021062, and National Undergraduate Innovation Program (G1210284052), and Research and Innovation Project for College Graduate Students of Jiangsu Province in 2012 under Grant No.CXZZ12 0056. This work is completed with the generous help from Qingyuan Jiang, Chenbin Ji and Gang He.

References

1. Fu, L., Cheng, P., Gu, Y., Chen, J., He, T.: Minimizing charging delay in wireless rechargeable sensor networks. In: Proceedings of the IEEE INFOCOM (2013)
2. Jiang, F., He, S., Cheng, P., Chen, J.: On optimal scheduling in wireless rechargeable sensor networks for stochastic event capture. In: Proceedings of the IEEE MASS (2011)
3. Shi, Y., Xie, L., Hou, Y.T., Sherali, H.D.: On renewable sensor networks with wireless energy transfer. In: INFOCOM (2011)
4. Dai, H., Jiang, L., Wu, X., Yau, D.K.Y., Chen, G., Tang, S.: Near optimal charging and scheduling scheme for stochastic event capture with rechargeable sensors. In: MASS (2013)
5. Dai, H., Wu, X., Xu, L., Chen, G., Lin, S.: Using minimum mobile chargers to keep large-scale wireless rechargeable sensor networks running forever. In: ICCCN (2013)
6. He, L., Yang, Z., Pan, J., Cai, L., Xu, J.: Evaluating service disciplines for mobile elements in wireless ad hoc sensor networks. In: Proceedings of the IEEE INFO-COM'12 (2012)
7. He, L., Yang, Z., Pan, J., Xu, J.: Evaluating on-demand data collection with mobile elements in wireless sensor networks. In: Proceedings of the IEEE VTC (2010)
8. Alfieri, A., Bianco, A., Brandimarte, P., Chiasserini, C.-F.: Exploiting sensor spatial redundancy to improve network lifetime. In: Proceedings of the IEEE Globe-Com'04 (2004)
9. Wu, X., Chen, G.: Dual-sink: using mobile and static sinks for lifetime improvement in wireless sensor networks. In: Proceedings of the IEEE ICCCN'07 (2007)
10. Zoltan, V., Rolland, V., Attila, V.: Deploying multiple sinks in multi-hop wireless sensor networks. In: Proceedings of the IEEE PERSER'07 (2007)
11. Cheng, B., Xu, Z., Chen, C., Guan, X.: Spatial correlated data collection in wireless sensor networks with multiple sinks. In: Computer Communications Workshops (INFOCOM WKSHPS) (2011)
12. Halgamuge, M.N., Zukerman, M., Ramamobanarao, K., Vu, H.L.: An estimation of sensor energy consumption. In: PIER (2009)
13. Marios, C., Nikoletseas, S., Raptis, T.P., Raptopoulos, C., Vasilakis, F.: Efficient energy management in wireless rechargeable sensor networks. In: MSWiM (2012)

Tailoring Activity Recognition to Provide Cues that Trigger Autobiographical Memory of Elderly People

Lorena Arcega, Jaime Font, and Carlos Cetina(⊠)

School of Computer Science, San Jorge University, Zaragoza, Spain
{larcega,jfont,ccetina}@usj.es

Abstract. About a 19 % of elderly population is associated with poor performance in assessments of memory; the phenomenon is known as Age-related Memory Impairment (AMI). Lifelogging technologies can contribute to compensate for memories deficits. However, no matter how functional technology is, older people will not use it if they perceive it as intrusive or embarrassing. This paper shows our work to tailor current activity recognition techniques (based on Emerging Patterns) to provide value for AMI people from RFID reading and GPS positioning. Evaluation shows (1) increases in the recall of autobiographical memories, (2) recognition issues, which require the supervision of the e-Memory Diary, and (3) evidences that this approach didn't suffer from the usual rejection showed to this technology by elderlies.

Keywords: RFID · Activity recognition · Age-related memory impairment

1 Introduction

About a 19 % of elderly population is associated with this decline in various memory abilities; the phenomenon is known as Age-related Memory Impairment (AMI) [8]. The use of external memory aids to help people to compensate for their memories deficits. The vision of lifelogging technologies [10] can significantly contribute to realize these external memory aids. Lifelogging technologies record multiple kinds of data as complete and automatically as possible for storing collections of heterogeneous digital objects that users generate or encounter. However, recent works have found that users with collections of thousands of digital photos never access the majority of them [11].

Furthermore, the particular domain of adoption of technology by elders is strictly dependent on a delicate acceptance process: no matter how functional

This work has been supported by *"Cátedra Ubiquitous"*, a joint research between *San Jorge University* and *Hiberus Tecnología*.

© Institute for Computer Sciences, Social Informatics and Telecommunications Engineering 2014
I. Stojmenovic et al. (Eds.): MOBIQUITOUS 2013, LNICST 131, pp. 737–742, 2014.
DOI: 10.1007/978-3-319-11569-6_63

technology is, older people will not use it, if they perceive it as intrusive, complex or embarrassing [7]. We believe that recent research efforts on activity recognition can play a key role to trigger autobiographical memory about past events. In order to be really accepted by elderlies, these techniques have to be shaped to meet the findings of recent literature about designing technology for elderlies [7].

This paper shows our efforts to tailor current activity recognition techniques to provide value for AMI persons. In particular, we tackle RFID reading and GPS positioning issues taking into account the 'look and feel' needs of elderlies. Then we apply Emerging Patterns as the activity recognition technique. To present the history of activities, we design an *e-Memory Diary*. Finally, to evaluate the improvement of autobiographical memory, we use a method similar to the one presented in [1]. The results of the evaluation show that our approach helps in improving the autobiographical recall. Furthermore, the behaviour of the participants suggests that this approach didn't suffer from the usual rejection showed to this technology by elderlies.

2   Related Work

Dobbins et al. [3] presents DigMem, a system for creating human digital memories (HDMs). The system creates HDMs that are composed of a variety of information. Various intelligent devices are used to gather data, whilst linked data is used to bring this information together. Their resulting set of interrelated data is presented, to the user, as a memory box of a temporal event. Lee and Dey [6] describe the design of a lifelogging system that captures photos, ambient audio, and location information. The system presents the selected cues for review in a way that maximizes the opportunities for the person with Episodic Memory Impairment to think deeply about these cues to trigger memory recollection on his own. The wearable devices and user interfaces of the above approaches do not address the acceptance process of elders adopting technology at home. On the other hand, our work provides evidences about the use of current activity recognition techniques to trigger users' memories and takes into account previous research efforts to achieve the acceptance of elderly adopting technology.

3   Our Sensing Platform: e-Memory Diary

To decide the sensing dimensions included in our approach we have taken into account the increasing popularity of smartphones and its capabilities. Modern smartphones incorporate many sensors that can be used to capture information and they can be also extended by wearable devices using connection capabilities.

For capture RFID tagged things that are touched by the users, we capture the digital object identifier and each one corresponds with a human-readable name. Despite the availability of RDIF-capable mobile devices, the identification process they provide disrupts the natural interaction between users and objects. Therefore, our sensing platform uses a RFID reader attached to a Bluetooth capable wrist-worn. In this way, users can just interact with an object in the

Fig. 1. Final prototype of our sensing platform (left). One of the users consulting de e-Memory Diary (right).

normal way. Therefore, the user feeds the approach whenever he touches a tagged thing, consciously or not. Finally we decide to encapsulate it as a watch because beyond the bare minimum of hardware and software the issue of look and feel needs to be addressed. The device should be perceived as cool not dorky or handicappy [5]. Figure 1 left shows the final watch.

For localization we use the GPS of the smartphone, we are aware of the limitations of GPS. We expect this issue to fade as sensors improve, but it is a significant concern for any deployment on currently available smartphone hardware. To improve location sensing, we can attach location information to those tags that we know will be static. RFID tags allow us to save additional information on it. So, we recorded static labels with their location. When our approach is used outside a familiar environment we obtain the geocoding with the Google API to find out the place and address where the user is. Google API enables us to get the points of interest (POIs) that the user has visited. This allows us to not only show geometric coordinates or an address, but show the name of the POI. Although we cannot overcome the sensor limitations entirely, we are designing the system to be as robust as possible to sensor errors.

In order to recognizing human activities from sensor readings we use Emerging Patterns (EP). An emerging pattern (EP) is a feature vector of each activity that describes significant changes between two classes of data [4]. Consider a dataset D that consists of several instances, each having a set of attributes and their corresponding values. To find these attributes *support* and *GrowthRate* are computed for every attribute. The support of an itemset X, is $count_D(X)/|D|$, where $count_D(X)$ is the number of instances in D containing X. The *Growth Rate* of an itemset X from D_1 to D_2 is 0 *if* $supp_1(X) = 0$ *and* $supp_2(X) = 0$, ∞ *if* $supp_1(X) = 0$ *and* $supp_2(X) > 0$, and $\frac{supp_2(X)}{supp_1(X)}$ *othrerwise*. EPs are itemsets with large growth rates from D_1 to D_2.

We have applied EPs in a similar way than in [4]. Each observation performed with our sensor platform contains an RFID tag, a timestamp, a human-readable location, accelerometer and gyro data. In order to apply EPs we have two different phases, the training phase and the activity recognition phase. In order to "train" the system, we need to select the activities set that we want to recognize and use them as raw data for the training phase. We have selected the activities

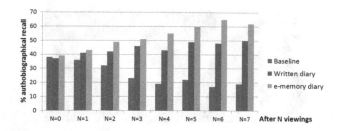

Fig. 2. Average recall of autobiographical events

described in the literature as commonly performed by elderlies [9]. We are aware that the technique applied for extracting the EP's and recognizing the activities can be improved, but we don't focus on this area and therefore we don't have any claim on this.

Finally, we design an interface that shows the information previously gathered while avoiding the rejection showed by elderly people to this kind of technology [7]. We have took into account the associative thinking of the human mind suggested in Memory Extender (Memex) [2]. In addition to that, in [10], Sellen et al. suggest moving away from an obsession with "capturing everything" to a more precise specification. Therefore, we focus on giving cues about past events of the user. We believe that these cues can trigger the associate thinking in order to enable user's recall autobiographical memories of the events performed.

Furthermore, the interface needs to map intuitively. Having that in mind we have designed our interface, the *e-Memory Diary*, to look like a traditional written diary, so elder people can feel comfortable as it looks like something that they already know. Figure 1 right shows an example of the use of the *e-Memory Diary*. It is structured like a written diary, the date is at the top followed by all the diary entries for that day. Each of the entries starts with the hour, and then the cue itself. We have three different kind of entries, activities, positions in readable format and the tagged objects touched that isn't part of any activity.

4   Case Study

The objective of the case study is to determine if the use of our approach, improves autobiographical memory recall in people that suffers from AMI. We have run the same experimentation with two different husbands and wives, following the same procedure than in [1]. The two couples were above 70 years old and one of the members of the couple has Age-related Memory Impairments (we will refer this member as AMI, and non-AMI for the other member).

As in [1], we evaluate three different conditions, an *e-Memory Diary* condition, a written diary condition (control) and a baseline condition (without using anything that might help her to remember). Figure 2 shows the results of the recall trials performed during the case study. It shows the average percentage result of the trials for both users, for all the three conditions evaluated. Figure 2 indicates that, as the number of *e-Memory Diary* and written diary viewings increased, there was an increase in the recall of autobiographical memories. By contrast the trend for the baseline condition is the opposite. It turns out that the improvement of the *e-Memory Diary* is greater than the written diary improvement.

In addition, the case study participants were concern about the customization possibilities of the *e-Memory Diary*. They argued that they wanted to add more details or even rewrite some of the entries in order to create a more personal diary. In fact, participants stated that they would prefer using the *e-Memory Diary* as a starting point rather than facing the challenge of writing out from the scratch the traditional diary every day. This behaviour suggests that the presented approach didn't suffer from the usual rejection showed to this technology by elderly people.

5   Conclusions

There are open topics regarding implications about privacy, security and the right of people to forget. However, we hope that our evaluation results and insights encourage researches to reach a trade-off between sensors bother and activity complexity that enables to bring more activity recognition techniques to the domain of memory aid technology for AMI population.

References

1. Berry, E., Kapur, N., Williams, L., Hodges, S., Watson, P., Smyth, G., Srinivasan, J., Smith, R., Wilson, B., Wood, K.: The use of a wearable camera, sensecam, as a pictorial diary to improve autobiographical memory in a patient with limbic encephalitis: a preliminary report. Neuropsychol. Rehabil. **17**(4–5), 582–601 (2007). Psychology Press
2. Bush, V., Wang, J.: As we may think. Atlantic Mon. **176**, 101–108 (1945)
3. Dobbins, C., Merabti, M., Fergus, P., Llewellyn-Jones, D.: Creating human digital memories for a richer recall of life experiences. In: ICNSC (2013)
4. Gu, T., Wu, Z., Tao, X., Pung, H., Lu, J.: epsicar: An emerging patterns based approach to sequential, interleaved and concurrent activity recognition. In: Pervasive Computing and Communications, 2009, PerCom 2009 (2009)
5. King, T.: Assistive Technology: Essential Human Factors. Allyn & Bacon Incorporated, Boston (1999)
6. Lee, M.L., Dey, A.K.: Lifelogging memory appliance for people with episodic memory impairment. In: Proceedings of the 10th International Conference on Ubiquitous Computing, UbiComp '08, New York, NY, USA, pp. 44–53. ACM (2008)
7. Leonardi, C., Mennecozzi, C., Not, E., Pianesi, F., Zancanaro, M., Gennai, F., Cristoforetti, A.: Knocking on elders' door: investigating the functional and emotional geography of their domestic space. In: CHI, NY, USA (2009)
8. Snyder, P.J., Nussbaum, P.D., Robins, D.L. (eds.): Age-related memory impairment. In: Clinical Neuropsychology: A Pocket Handbook for Assessment. American Psychological Association, Washington, DC (2006)

9. Katz, S., Ford, A.B., Moskowitz, R.W., Jackson, B.A., Jaffe, M.W.: Studies of illness in the aged: the index of ADL: a standardized measure of biological and psychosocial function. JAMA **185**(12), 914–919 (1963)
10. Sellen, A.J., Whittaker, S.: Beyond total capture: a constructive critique of lifelogging. Commun. ACM **53**(5), 70–77 (2010)
11. Whittaker, S., Bergman, O., Clough, P.: Easy on that trigger dad: a study of long term family photo retrieval. Pers. Ubiquit. Comput. **14**(1), 31–43 (2010)

Two-Way Communications Through Firewalls Using QLM Messaging

Sylvain Kubler[✉], Manik Madhikermi, Andrea Buda, and Kary Främling

School of Science, Aalto University, TUAS Building Otaniementie 17,
Espoo, Finland
{sylvain.kubler,manik.madhikermi,andrea.buda,kary.framling}@aalto.fi

Abstract. Nowadays, organizations make a point of protecting the confidentiality of their data and assets using firewalls, proxies and NATs, which goes against providing a high level of data usability and interoperability between distinct information systems, or "Things" in the so-called Internet of Things. Such security procedures often prevent two-way communications between nodes located on each side of the firewall. Quantum Lifecycle Management (QLM) messaging has been introduced as a messaging standard proposal that would fulfill the requirements for exchanging the kind of information required by an IoT. In this regard, the QLM piggy backing property proposed in that standard makes it possible to achieve two-way communication through a firewall. This property is introduced in this paper, along with the first proofs-of-concept.

Keywords: Internet of things · Quantum lifecycle management · Intelligent product · Network security · Piggy backing

1 Introduction

In the so-called *Internet of Things* (IoT) and *Cyber Physical Systems* (CPS), mobile users and objects will be able to dynamically discover and impromptu interact with heterogeneous computing, physical resources, as well as virtual data and environments [1]. Billions of devices are connected to the Internet and it is predicted that there will be 50–100 billions by 2020 [2]. This fascinating world brings with it new types of interactions among our daily-life objects and between organizations. However, despite the fact that the potential of IoT, CPS or similar concepts are widely recognized, there are still fundamental questions and issues that need to be addressed, for instance no proper agreement on a widely applicable, common standard for data exchange between organizations, whether in terms of data structure or data communication, has yet been reached. The QLM messaging standards are developed and proposed as a standard application-level interface that would fulfill the requirements for exchanging the kind of information required by an IoT, as presented in [3]. QLM messaging provides a wide range of interfaces and properties, among which a fundamental one relying on the "piggy backing" concept enables real-time communications

© Institute for Computer Sciences, Social Informatics and Telecommunications Engineering 2014
I. Stojmenovic et al. (Eds.): MOBIQUITOUS 2013, LNICST 131, pp. 743–747, 2014.
DOI: 10.1007/978-3-319-11569-6_64

and two-way communications with nodes located behind a firewall, proxy, or NAT (Network Address Translation). This is a crucial property of the messaging protocol to tackle the challenging conflict between *data security* and *data usability*; security making operations harder, when usability makes them easier [4]. Indeed, in certain situations, it might be needed to enable two-way communications through firewalls, for instance for real-time control and maintenance operations, or when products evolve in a mobile environment with intermittent connectivity that makes it difficult to provide the product with a permanent IP address. Accordingly, the objective of the paper is twofold: *(i)* to briefly introduce QLM messaging in Sect. 2, and *(ii)* to provide a technical proof-of-concept related to the QLM piggy backing property in Sect. 3.

2   QLM Messaging Interface

QLM messaging standards emerged out of the PROMISE EU FP6 project[1] in which the real-life industrial applications required the collection and management of product instance-level information for many domains. Information such as sensor readings, alarms, assembly, disassembly, shipping event, and other information related to the entire PLC needed to be exchanged between several organizations [5]. At the end of the PROMISE project, the work on these standards proposals was moved to the QLM workgroup of The Open Group[2]. QLM messaging consists of two standards proposals [3]: the QLM Messaging Interface (QLM-MI) and the QLM Data Format (QLM-DF).

In the QLM world, communication between the participants (e.g. products and backend systems) is done by passing messages between nodes using QLM-MI. The QLM "cloud" in Fig. 1 is intentionally drawn in the same way as for the Internet cloud. Where the Internet uses the HTTP protocol for transmitting HTML-coded information mainly intended for human users, QLM is used for conveying lifecycle-related information mainly intended for automated processing by information systems. In the same way as HTTP can be used for

Fig. 1. QLM "Cloud"

---

[1] http://www.promise-innovation.com
[2] http://www.opengroup.org/qlm/

transporting payloads also in other formats than HTML, QLM can be used for transporting payloads in nearly any format. XML might currently be the most common text-based payload format due to its flexibility that provides more opportunities for complex data structures, but others such as JSON, CSV can also be used. QLM-DF partly fulfills the same role in the IoT as HTML does for the Internet, meaning that QLM-DF is the content description model for things in the IoT. Information encoded using QLM-DF can be transported also by practically any information exchange protocol, such as Java Message Service (JMS), WSDL/SOAP, or ebXML Messaging Services. QLM-MI and QLM-DF are independent entities that reside in the Application layer of the OSI model, where QLM-MI is specified as the Communication level and QLM-DF is specified as the Format level. These two standards are presented in detail in [3,6].

QLM messaging has been defined to meet numerous IoT requirements listed in [3]. A defining characteristic of QLM messaging is that QLM nodes may act both as a "server" and as a "client", and therefore communicate directly with each other in a peer-to-peer manner. Typical examples of exchanged data are sensor readings, requests for historical data, *etc.* QLM defines four main operations: *(i)* Write, *(ii)* Immediate retrieval of information (Read), *(iii)* Subscription to an information (Read), and *(iv)* cancel (to cancel a subscription). A fundamental property[3] of QLM-MI is the piggy backing property that is crucial for real-time communications and to enable two-way communications through a firewall.

3   QLM Piggy Backing Model for Two-Way Communications

Data is precious nowadays, especially for companies whose product-related data is a valuable resource and should not be seen by other organizations. As a consequence, people take proactive measures to protect the security, confidentiality, and integrity of their data [7]. This inevitably leads to a challenging conflict between data *security* and *usability* [4]. For instance, it might be impossible to prevent uncontrolled situations (e.g., prevention of predictive maintenance), which can even become a conflict between *security* and *safety* [8]. It is therefore necessary to develop strategies to enable two-way communications through firewalls. A two-way communication with a remote host is a clear trend that evolved with the Web. For instance, HTML5 proposes a communication model using *WebSockets* that makes it possible to overcome firewalls and proxies. Similarly, the communication model for traversing firewalls in QLM consists in piggy backing (i.e., embedding) one or several new QLM requests with a QLM response. The main difference with existing models are that QLM does not necessary require an HTTP server to proceed to the exchange of information between two nodes, and a QLM message is self-contained[4] that enables useful information

---

[3] The reader could refer to [3] or [6] to obtain an exhaustive list of the QLM properties.
[4] The message contains all the necessary information to enable the recipient QLM node to appropriately handle the message (e.g., actions to be performed).

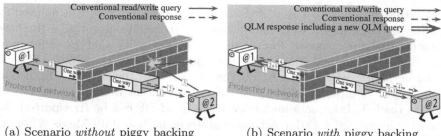

(a) Scenario *without* piggy backing   (b) Scenario *with* piggy backing

Fig. 2. Scenario using QLM responses *with* piggy backing

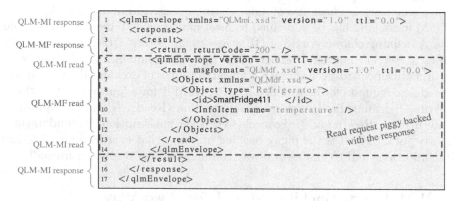

Fig. 3. QLM response used to piggy back the write request

for the recipient to be piggy backed with the QLM response, thus providing "standardized" two-way communications with remote hosts behind a firewall.

Figure 2 describes the model considered in the QLM piggy backing property. In this figure, a data communication between two nodes denoted respectively by @1 and @2 is performed, involving the presence of a firewall. This firewall does not permit @2 to reach @1 but does the opposite. This is illustrated in Fig. 2(a), in which a query has been sent successfully from @1 to @2 (see arrows "1" and "2" that respectively represent the QLM query and the response to acknowledge receipt of the request). Subsequently to this communication, @2 sends a new query to @1 (see arrow "3") that is stopped by the firewall. Figure 2(b) provides the same scenario but, this time, @2 piggy backs its own query(ies) with the response message (see arrow "2+3"). The query that is piggy backed with the response in our scenario is a read operation and its inclusion in the response message is shown in Fig. 3 (from rows 5 to 14). This figure highlights the QLM-MI and QLM-DF for both the response and the read operation. Regarding the read operation, it queries for the value of the InfoItem named **temperature** (see row 10) related to smart fridge of "id" **SmartFridge411** (see row 9; the smart fridge being node @1 in our case). @1 therefore receives these new request and is able to process it; in our case, it consists to send the requested value with a new

QLM response (see arrow "4" in Fig. 2(b)). This procedure (i.e., piggy backing new requests with a response) can thus continue for as long as nodes want to.

The piggy backing is also an essential property when products are located behind a NAT or when products evolve in a mobile environment with intermittent connectivity, which makes it difficult to provide the product with a permanent IP address. In such situations, the QLM piggy backing property enables to embed a new request in the QLM response message, regardless of the IP address of the node having performed the request.

4   Conclusion

This paper provides an overview of the QLM Messaging standards proposals that combine the main features of asynchronous, enterprise messaging protocols, with those of instant messaging protocols in a way that allows for peer-to-peer type communication. The main focus of the paper is the QLM "piggy backing" property that enables to switch from asynchronous messaging to instant messaging when one of the communicating systems is behind a firewall. A technical proof-of-concept is provided in this paper, which shows how important this functionality is in most real-life IoT applications. Existing protocols tend to be focused either on asynchronous or instant messaging, which limits their scope of IoT applications. The possibility of using only one protocol (QLM-MI) for all communication offers a clear advantage compared to the current state-of-the-art.

Official QLM-MI specifications will be made public by the QLM workgroup of The Open Group during 2013. However, several companies and academic organizations already use the newest QLM specifications.

References

1. Gershenfeld, N., Krikorian, R., Cohen, D.: The Internet of Things. Sci. Am. **291**(4), 76–81 (2004)
2. Perera, C., Zaslavsky, A., Christen, P., Georgakopoulos, D.: Context aware computing for the internet of things: a survey. IEEE Commun. Surv. Tutor. **99**, 1–41 (2013)
3. Framling, K., Maharjan, M.: Standardized communication between intelligent products for the IoT. In: 11th IFAC Workshop on Intelligent Manufacturing Systems. São Paulo (2013)
4. Chen, L.: Application perspectives for active safety system based on internet of vehicles. In: Proceedings of the FISITA 2012 World Automotive Congress. Beijing (2012)
5. Kiritsis, D., Bufardi, A., Xirouchakis, P.: Research issues on product lifecycle management and information tracking using smart embedded systems. Adv. Eng. Inform. **17**(3), 189–202 (2003)
6. Kubler, S., Madhikermi, M., Främling, K.: Deferred retrieval of IoT information using QLM messaging interface. In: 10th International Conference on Mobile Web Information Systems. Paphos (2013)
7. Bishop, M.: What is computer security? IEEE Secur. Priv. **1**(1), 67–69 (2003)
8. Li, M., Lou, W., Ren, K.: Data security and privacy in wireless body area networks. IEEE Wirel. Commun. **17**(1), 51–58 (2010)

Towards a Privacy Risk Assessment Methodology for Location-Based Systems

Jesús Friginal$^{(\boxtimes)}$, Jérémie Guiochet, and Marc-Olivier Killijian

LAAS-CNRS, 7 Avenue du Colonel Roche, 31400 Toulouse Cedex, France
{jesus.friginal,jeremie.guiochet,marco.killijian}@laas.fr

Abstract. Mobiquitous systems are gaining more and more weight in our daily lives. They are becoming a reality from our home and work to our leisure. The use of Location-Based Services (LBS) in these systems is increasingly demanded by users. Yet, while on one hand they enable people to be more "connected", on the other hand, they may expose people to serious privacy issues. The design and deployment of Privacy-Enhancing Technologies (PETs) for LBS has been widely addressed in the last years. However, strikingly, there is still a lack of methodologies to assess the risk that using LBS may have on users' privacy (even when PETs are considered). This paper presents the first steps towards a privacy risk assessment methodology to (i) identify (ii) analyse, and (iii) evaluate the potential privacy issues affecting mobiquitous systems.

Keywords: Privacy · Risk assessment · Location-based systems

1 Introduction

The vast deployment of myriads of sensors and the rapid growth in the number of mobile devices per person is providing enormous opportunities to create a new generation of innovative Location-Based Services (LBS) addressed to improve the welfare of our society. LBS are used in a variety of contexts, such as health, entertainment or work, like discovering the nearest cash machine, parking parcel, or getting personalised weather services.

Parallel to this revolution, numerous studies reveal potential privacy breaches in the use of these services given the sensitivity of the collected information, and how it is stored and exchanged [4]. From a privacy viewpoint, the main characteristic of LBS systems is that, apart from personal identity, users' location becomes a new essential asset to protect. A recent study from MIT [1] showed that 4 spatio-temporal points (approximate places and times), were enough to unequivocally identify 95 % people in a mobility database of 1.5 M users. The study shows that these constraints hold even when the resolution of the dataset is low. Therefore, even coarse or blurred information provides little anonymity. However, very few users are aware of the implications that a misuse of their location information may have on their privacy, and the potential consequences on their security and safety [2]. Tackling this issue becomes critical given the increasingly variety of attacks that may impact the privacy of users [4].

© Institute for Computer Sciences, Social Informatics and Telecommunications Engineering 2014
I. Stojmenovic et al. (Eds.): MOBIQUITOUS 2013, LNICST 131, pp. 748–753, 2014.
DOI: 10.1007/978-3-319-11569-6_65

By the time being, there is a range from simplistic on/off switches to sophisticated Privacy-Enhancing Technologies (PETs) using anonymisation techniques [8]. Today, few LBS offer such PETs, e.g., Google Latitude offers an on/off switch that allows to stick one's position to a freely definable location. Another set of techniques include location obfuscation, which slightly alter the location of the users in order to hide their real location while still being able to represent their position and receive services from their LBS provider. However, such efforts remain questionable in practice while suitable techniques to guarantee acceptable levels of risk remain unavailable. Consequently, the confident use of LBS requires not only the development of PETs, but also the definition of methodologies and techniques to assess and treat the privacy risk associated to LBS solutions. There exist many and various challenges in the deployment of LBS, but the need for identifying the risk related to the processing of personal data before determining the appropriate means to reduce them, is without doubt, one of the most important in the domain of LBS.

This short paper makes a step forward to explore the challenges that hinder the development of methodologies to assess the risk related to the lack of privacy of LBS. The rest of this paper is structured as follows. Section 2 shows the lack of techniques and guidelines to assess the privacy risk on LBS. Section 3 presents a privacy risk conceptual framework. Section 4 introduces our first approach towards privacy risk assess methodology for LBS. Finally, Sect. 5 closes the paper.

2   Privacy in Risk Standards

The concept of risk was first introduced in safety critical systems, but is now widely used in many domains, including information technology. Indeed, users, environment and organizations could be faced to the harm induced by the use of a new technology. The generic standard ISO/IEC-Guide73 defines the risk as the combination of the probability of an event and its consequence. This definition had to be adapted in the domain of security, where risk is defined as the "potential that a given threat will exploit vulnerabilities of an asset or group of assets and thereby cause harm to the organization" [6]. In this definition, the classic notion of *probability* of an event has been replaced by "potentiality" given the difficulty to estimate such a probability. The concept of *consequence* was also refined into "harm to the organization". The identification, analysis and

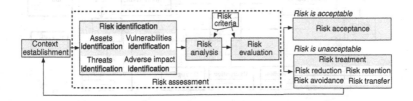

Fig. 1. Risk management process adapted from ISO 27005 [6].

evaluation of the risk, is defined in many standards and international directives as *risk assessment* within the risk management process, as Fig. 1 shows.

ISO standards such as [6] or regulatory documents produced by NIST [9], deal with security risk assessment and treatment. Unfortunately, there is no privacy ISO/IEC standard dedicated to privacy risk assessment. In order to protect user data, the European Commission unveiled in 2012 a draft [3] that will supersede the Data Protection Directive 95/46/EC. It is mainly about openness and obligations of organizations managing users personal data, and it does not include methods and techniques to analyse and assess the risks. A similar approach is presented in the USA Location Privacy Protection Act of 2012 (S.1233), in order to regulate the transmission and sharing of user location data. As in the European Directives, this bill specifies entities, data and its usage, but no analysis techniques are proposed, and much less in the domain of LBS.

3 Privacy Risk Conceptual Framework

This Section introduces the conceptual framework gathering the main notions relating to privacy risk. To illustrate these concepts, Fig. 2 shows the general meta-model concerning the entities and relations involved in the process. Our meta-model should not be seen as a closed proposal. Instead, it is a flexible abstraction interpreting privacy risk in a generic way for LBS.

As seen in Sect. 2, risk is generally defined as the combination of two factors: the potential occurrence of threats, and the consequences that such threats may cause on victims, also referred to as *adverse impact*. Analogously, the definition of risk could be easily adapted to the privacy domain by refining the concept of potential occurrence as *attacker capability*, which refers to the efforts and resources employed by the *threat source* to deploy *threat events* affecting a *privacy asset*. In the case of LBS, assets are mainly intangible. Among them, *identity* and *location* are the most important. For instance, the spatio-temporal data of an individual can be used to infer his movements and habits, to learn information about his centre of interests or even to detect a change from his usual behaviour. From these basic assets it is possible to obtain derived ones. It is to note that the asset value strongly depends on its precision. Fine-grained

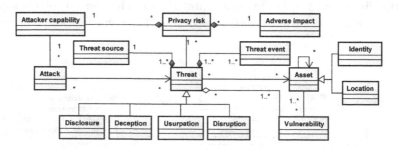

Fig. 2. General meta-model for privacy risk assessment

information concerning the who-where-when tuple is much more valuable than a coarse-grained one. For example, the value of knowing that a person, identified by the full name, will be at a place with a geo-temporal error of meters and seconds is higher than knowing that a person, only identified by the surname, will be potentially at a given city within an error window of two weeks.

In the domain of privacy, the notion of *threat* particularly refers to the *disclosure* of assets. In most of the cases, conversely to traditional security, threats are based on the potential correlation of partial informations (premises), assumed to be true, to derive more valuable information. To obtain such premises, attackers may appeal to the *usurpation* of identity, the *deception* of information or the *disruption* of services. A threat presents certain precision requirements. If such requirements are compatible with the precision provided by the asset, then the threat will be potentially feasible. For example, if a threat source requires knowing the exact current position of a user, and the only information available reveals only that the user is not at home, the threat will be hardly realisable. A threat, to be realisable, needs to exploit a *vulnerability* associated to the asset. Vulnerabilities refer to inherent weaknesses in the security procedures or internal controls concerning the asset. If there is a vulnerability without a corresponding threat, or a threat without a corresponding vulnerability, there is no risk. Next section exploits this meta-model for the privacy risk assessment.

4   Towards Privacy Risk Assessment for LBS

Thus Section presents a privacy risk assessment methodology following the framework of Fig. 1. The first step, risk identification involves the identification of risk sources, events, their causes and their potential consequences. The level of risk is then estimated in the risk analysis step. For this step, we will introduce metrics as risk criteria for the privacy risk analysis.

The goal of risk identification is to collect the information concerning the meta-model in Fig. 2 in a simple but structured way. First, it is necessary to identify the privacy assets. Among all the *Personal Identifiable Information*, learning the location of an individual is one of the greatest threat against his privacy. Essentially because starting with the location, many other private information can be derived [4]. Thus, once assets fixed, reasoning about the pertinent threats related to a particular asset is easier, for example inference attacks to disclose the POIs of an individual. Then, vulnerabilities will be defined as the lack of control mechanisms enabling the potential realisation of such threats on identified assets. Finally, the users of the methodology should qualitatively determine the adverse impact on the privacy of the asset. Such an intuitive technique will guide a more systematic identification of risks on the system.

The risk analysis stage aims at estimating the privacy risk. The first step towards this goal involves proposing mechanisms to quantitatively estimate the adverse impact and the attacker capability. Conversely to security, privacy presents a subjective component. Indeed, the adverse impact (AI) is a metric that depends on how a user perceives and interprets the importance of an asset [5]. The use of questionnaires can be very useful to estimate the adverse impact of a threatened asset. The estimation of the attacker capability (AC) is approached by most risk assessment standards and guidelines [6,9] through the assignation of a numeric value. While this approach is valid to provide a coarse-grained viewpoint of the threat, no detail about how threats are exploited is provided. To cover this lack, our methodology uses the concept of *attack tree*.

The risk evaluation stage is in charge of ranking privacy risks regarding specific criteria. Applying different criteria, such as the importance of the asset for the business, the reputation of users or the regulation fulfilment, may lead to different rankings. According to the selected criterion, risks, regardless if they were high, medium or low, will be characterised as acceptable, tolerable and non-acceptable following an As-Low-As-Reasonably-Practicable (ALARP) [7] strategy. The risks characterised as non-acceptable will be prioritised for their treatment. However, this stage is out the scope of this paper.

5   Conclusions

Privacy may be the greatest barrier to the long-term success of mobiquitous systems. However, despite many standards and approaches have been proposed to handle the problem of risk assessment, none, to the best of our knowledge has addressed the problem of managing the privacy risk for LBS. One of the major problems found in this paper concerns the identification of adequate information to carry out the risk assessment, as well as the way to process it.

Beyond this work, we are interested in studying the usefulness of our methodology to (i) guide the design PETs following a privacy-by-design approach, and (ii) compare and select (benchmark) the PETs that address the best the privacy requirements of mobiquitous systems.

Acknowledgements. This work is partially supported by the ANR French project AMORES (ANR-11-INSE-010) and the Intel Doctoral Student Honour Programme 2012.

References

1. de Montjoye, Y.-A., Hidalgo, C.A., Verleysen, M., Blondel, V.D.: Unique in the crowd: the privacy bounds of human mobility. Sci. Rep. **3**, 1–5 (2013)
2. Dobson, J., Fisher, P.: Geoslavery. IEEE Technol. Soc. Mag. **22**(1), 47–52 (2003)
3. European Commission. Proposal for a regulation of the european parliament and of the council on the protection of individuals (2012)
4. Gambs, S., Killijian, M.-O., del Prado Cortez, M.N.: Show me how you move and I will tell you who you are. Trans. Data Priv. **4**(2), 103–126 (2011)
5. Hong, J.I., Ng, J.D., Lederer, S., Landay, J.A.: Privacy risk models for designing privacy-sensitive ubiquitous computing systems. In: Proceedings of the 5th Conference on Designing Interactive Systems: Processes, Practices, Methods, and Techniques, pp. 91–100. ACM (2004)

6. ISO27005. Information technology - security techniques - information security risk management. International Standard Organisation (2008)
7. Melchers, R.E.: On the ALARP approach to risk management. Reliab. Eng. Syst. Saf. **71**(2), 201–208 (2001)
8. Mokbel, M.F., Chow, C.-Y., Aref, W.G.: The new casper: query processing for location services without compromising privacy. In: Proceedings of the 32nd International Conference on Very Large Data Bases, VLDB '06, VLDB Endowment, pp. 763–774 (2006)
9. NIST800-30. Information security, guide for conducting risk assessments. U.S. Department of Commerce, NIST) (2011)

Workshop

Mobility Models-Based Performance Evaluation of the History Based Prediction for Routing Protocol for Infrastructure-Less Opportunistic Networks

Sanjay K. Dhurandher[1], Deepak Kumar Sharma[2],
and Isaac Woungang[3(✉)]

[1] CAITFS, Division of Information Technology, NSIT,
University of Delhi, New Delhi, India
dhurandher@rediffmail.com
[2] Division of Computer Engineering, NSIT,
University of Delhi, New Delhi, India
dk.sharma1982@yahoo.com
[3] Department of Computer Science, Ryerson University,
Toronto, ON, Canada
iwoungan@scs.ryerson.ca

Abstract. In Opportunistic Networks (OppNets), the sender and receiver of a packet are not assumed to be connected with each other through an end-to-end continuous path. They exploit the contact opportunity that arises between the nodes due to their mobility to pass the messages from one place to another in the network. They do not rely on any pre-existing topology; rather they belong to a dynamic network topology. In this paper, the performance of our recently proposed History-Based Prediction for Routing protocol for infrastructure-less OppNets (so-called HBPR) is evaluated on two different mobility models – the Random Waypoint (RWP) and the Custom Human Mobility Model (CHMM). The HBPR protocol is evaluated against four performance metrics, namely, the number of messages delivered, the overhead ratio, the average hop count, and the average latency. Simulation results show a significant decline in the performance of HBPR for the RWP model compared to the CHMM model.

Keywords: OppNets · Opportunistic routing · Infrastructure-less protocol · Delay tolerant networks · The ONE (Opportunistic Network) simulator · Mobility models

1 Introduction

Opportunistic Networks [1] are considered as the sub-class of Delay Tolerant Networks (DTNs) [2]. They are the recent extensions of MANETs [3] that have become very popular among the researchers working in the area of wireless networking and mobile communication. In contrast to MANETs, nodes in OppNets are not aware about the network configuration and the route construction is not static but dynamic in nature due to the ever changing network topology. Due to the transient and un-connected nature of

© Institute for Computer Sciences, Social Informatics and Telecommunications Engineering 2014
I. Stojmenovic et al. (Eds.): MOBIQUITOUS 2013, LNICST 131, pp. 757–767, 2014.
DOI: 10.1007/978-3-319-11569-6_66

the nodes, routing and forwarding of messages becomes a challenging task in such type of networks. The source node or intermediate node can choose any node as next hop from a group of potential neighbors, which promises to take the message closer to the destination or to the destination node itself. Thus, traditional MANET routing protocols such as AODV [4], DSR [5] and internet routing protocols such as TCP/IP do not work in OppNet scenarios. However, their utility and potential for scalability make them a huge success. A few typical characteristics of OppNets are described as follows [6, 7]:

(a) *Highly mobile nodes:* The network nodes are highly mobile in nature making this type of network quite dynamic and ever-changing. These networks can originate from one node that acts as seed and dynamically adds neighboring nodes to the network as and when required.

(b) *Sparse connectivity:* Because of their high mobility it is likely that nodes that have recently met do not encounter each other for a long period of time and network partitions can occur. As such, the connectivity is sparse, intermittent and usually unpredictable.

(c) *Store-carry and forward method:* The routing and forwarding in OppNets is based on the store-carry and forward technique. The nodes can store messages with themselves until they find the destination or find a node that is a better carrier for the message than itself.

(d) *No end-to-end path:* OppNets can deliver messages even though there might be no knowledge of a previous path. The nodes do not have to worry about finding or creating an end-to-end connected path. They study and utilize other aspects such as, behavior and characteristics of nodes to deliver messages.

The routing protocols used by OppNets can be classified into two major categories: *Infrastructure-less protocols* and *Infrastructure-based protocols* [8]. The *Infrastructure-less protocols* make no previous assumptions regarding the nodes and the network topology. No infrastructure existence is assumed which can help in the forwarding of messages. On the other hand, the *Infrastructure-based Protocols* make use of some form of infrastructure to deliver the messages effectively; e.g. base stations and access points. The base stations can either guide other nodes or serve as intermediaries for storing the messages. Their presence helps in modeling a structure of the network, and thus effectively decreases the complexity of the message delivery.

The rest of the paper is organized as follows. Section 2 presents some related works. Section 3 describes the simulation setup. Section 4 is devoted to the simulation results, where we discuss and compare the performance of our recently proposed HBPR protocol [9] using two different mobility models. Finally, Sect. 5 concludes our work.

2   Related Work

In this section, a brief overview of the HBPR protocol [9] is provided, along with the a description of the Random Waypoint [10] and the Custom Human Mobility [9] Models.

2.1 HBPR Protocol

The History Based Prediction Routing (HBPR) protocol [9] predicts a node's future location based on the past information about its movement in the network. This prediction is then used for message passing in the network. The HBPR maintains two tables, namely the *Home Location* table and the *History* table. The *Home Location* table stores the location of a node which it visits more frequently. On the other hand, the *History* table is used to maintain a list of various locations visited by a node in the past. The next hop selection in HBPR is based on the calculation of a *Utility Metric*. This *Utility Metric* is obtained as a function of three parameters. The first parameter is the *Stability of node's movements*. For this parameter, a list of a node's average speeds over a period of time is maintained. Using this list, it can be observed whether the change in the average speeds is very large or nominal. A nominal change accounts for a stable node whereas a large change signifies an unstable movement. The second parameter is *Prediction of the direction of future movement using Markov Predictors*. For this parameter, Markov models [11] are used to predict the next location based on the past histories. A table is maintained with the frequencies of visits for every location for the given pattern of visits. This is then used to predict the next location. The third parameter is *the perpendicular distance of the neighboring nodes from the line of sight of source and destination (SD line)*. This metric is used to select those nodes which are closer to the *SD* line as they have to travel a lesser distance as compared to those which are away from it. The message is then forwarded to those nodes that have their *Utility Metric* value greater than the *Threshold (T)*. The HBPR protocol is described in-depth in [9].

2.2 Random Waypoint Model

In the Random Waypoint model [10], nodes in the network move randomly in any direction within the simulation area. It includes the pause time between any changes in the direction or speed of the nodes. A mobile node stays at a location for a certain period of time and then moves to the new destination by choosing a random speed from the maximum and minimum range already defined.

2.3 Custom Human Mobility Model

In OppNets, the movements of devices mimic the movements of the human subjects carrying them. It is very likely that nodes will have a predictable fashion in which they move and there are always a few places (*Home Location*) that they will visit more frequently than others. Thus, it can be assumed that devices display a Human Mobility pattern [12]. Keeping this in mind, the *Custom Human Mobility Model* [9] movement model is designed, with the aim to simulate the community relationships among the nodes. The nodes might travel to their *Home Location* more frequently as compared to other locations. The whole world size is divided into cells of 100 m × 100 m. The nodes are then grouped into six communities. Each community has a *Home Location* cell. At the start of the simulation, every node is present in its *Home Location*, which it disseminates through the network using its own *Home Location table*. The node travels to its *Home Location* with a probability p and to all other locations with probability $1 - p$.

3 Simulation Setup

The performance of HBPR protocol is evaluated using the ONE simulator [13]. The nodes are mobile and have been divided into six groups, where each group has 15 nodes. The first and third group nodes are of pedestrians with speed between 0.5 and 1.5 m/s. The second group is of cyclists with speed varying between 2.7 and 13.9 m/s. The fourth, fifth and sixth group nodes are cars with speeds varying in the range 7–10 m/s. The first, second and third groups have the same *Home Location* while the fourth, fifth and sixth groups have different *Home Locations*. The mobile nodes have a transmission range of 10 m and transmit at a speed of 2 Mbps. Each simulation is run for 43000 s. The total simulation area is taken to be 4500 m × 3400 m. A new message is generated at every 25–35 s and the message size varies from 500 KB to 1 MB. A constant bit-rate (CBR) traffic is generated between the nodes. The value of p is taken as 0.25 in this work.

The following settings and configurations have been used in our simulations:

(1) *Varying the number of nodes:* The total number of nodes in the simulation are varied as 90, 120, 150, 180, 210, 240, and 300. The number of nodes is kept fixed to 240 wherever it is not varied.

(2) *Varying the message Time-to-live (TTL):* The messages have their Time-to-live varied as 60, 90, 120, 150 & 180 s. The message TTL is kept fixed to150 s wherever it is not varied.

(3) *Varying the speed of nodes:* In order to evaluate the effect of node speed on the performance of HBPR, 3 sets of different speeds for different groups of nodes have been considered. In *Set 1,* the speed of nodes in group 1 and group 2 is fixed between 0.5 m/s and 1.5 m/s. Nodes in groups 4, 5 and 6 have their speed between 7 m/s and 10 m/s. Nodes in group 3 have their speed between 2.7 m/s and 13.9 m/s. In *Set 2*, the speed of nodes in groups 1 and 2 is fixed between 2.5 m/s and 4.5 m/s. Nodes in groups 4, 5 and 6 have their speed between 9 m/s and 12 m/s. Nodes in group 3 have their speed between 4.7 m/s and 19.9 m/s. In *Set 3*, the speed of nodes in groups 1 and 3 is fixed between 2.5 m/s and 4.5 m/s. Nodes in groups 4, 5 and 6 have speed between 7 m/s and 10 m/s. Nodes in group 2 have their speed between 2.7 m/s and 13.9 m/s. All nodes move according to their respective group speed wherever speed is not varied.

The considered performance metrics are:

(1) *Total number of messages delivered:* This is the count of the total number of messages successfully delivered to the destination node.

(2) *Average Hop Count:* This is the average of the number of intermediate nodes travelled by a message to reach the destination.

(3) *Overhead Ratio:* This is the average number of forwarded copies per message.

(4) *Average Latency:* This is the average of the difference between the message delivery time and message creation time.

4 Simulation Results

In this work, we have simulated the HBPR with only two mobility models namely the Random Waypoint (RWP) model and the Custom Human Mobility Model (CHMM). However, it can also be simulated on other mobility models such as Map Based Movement model [13], Shortest Path Map Based Movement model [13] etc. The results comparing the RWP model and the CHMM model are captured in Figs. 1, 2, 3, 4, 5, 6, 7, 8, 9, 10, 11 and 12. From these figures, it can be observed that the number of nodes, the message TTL, and the speed of nodes, do impact the performance of the HBPR routing protocol.

4.1 Performance of HBPR Under Varying Number of Nodes

In Fig. 1, it can be observed that when the number of nodes increases, the number of messages delivered also increases. The CHMM has more number of messages delivered compared to the RWP. Also, the rate of increment is more pronounced in case of CHMM. This is attributed to the fact that nodes in CHMM come to their home locations more frequently, and thus follow some pattern in their movement in the network. This is not the case with RWP. Figure 2 shows that the average hop count for a message remains comparable for both CHMM and RWP. In Fig. 3, the overhead ratio increases with the increase in the number of nodes. This is attributed to the fact that a node now has more number of potentially good neighbor nodes at its disposal that can forward or deliver the message towards the destination. However, the overhead ratio of HBPR remains much less for CHMM compared to RWP.

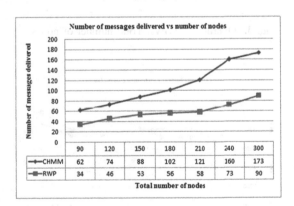

Fig. 1. Number of messages delivered vs. Total number of nodes.

In Fig. 4, it can be observed that the average latency for HBPR is lesser for RWP at smaller number of nodes and more pronounced at higher number of nodes as compared to the CHMM. This is justified by the fact that with the increase in number of nodes, there may be more nodes present in the network that have common home locations. This favors HBPR to deliver the messages to the destination in lesser time using CHMM.

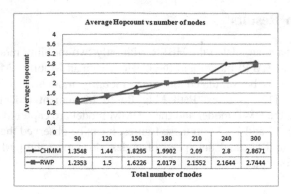

Fig. 2. Average hop count vs. Total number of nodes.

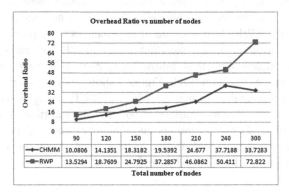

Fig. 3. Overhead ratio vs. Total number of nodes.

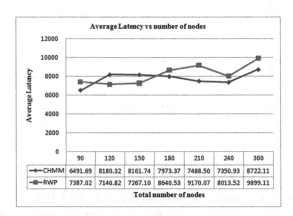

Fig. 4. Average latency vs. Total number of nodes.

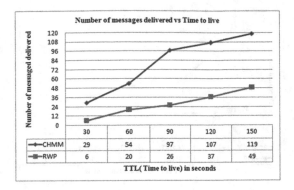

Fig. 5. Number of messages delivered vs. Time-to-live.

4.2 Performance of HBPR Under Varying Time-To-Live (TTL) Field Values

In Fig. 5, it can be observed that the number of messages delivered increases with the increase in the Time-to-live. This is attributed to the fact that with the increase in a message's TTL, a message can remain active in the network for a longer period of time, resulting in more messages getting delivered to the destination. The rate of increment and the total number of messages delivered is higher in CHMM as compared to RWP.

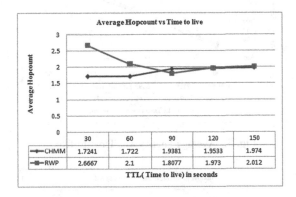

Fig. 6. Average hop count vs. Time-to-live.

In Fig. 6, it can be observed that the average hop count for a message is lesser for CHMM at smaller values of TTL. However, it remains comparable for both CHMM and RWP at higher values of TTL. In Fig. 7, it can be observed that the overhead ratio decreases with the increase in message TTL. This is attributed to the fact that with the increase in message TTL, the messages are given enough time to reach the destination and are not dropped on the way. This results in a limited number of copies of a particular message flowing in the network, and thus lowers the overhead ratio.

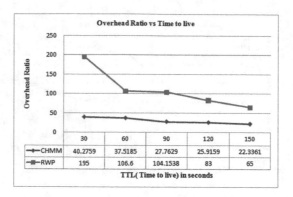

Fig. 7. Overhead ratio vs. Time-to-live.

In Fig. 8, it can be observed that the average latency for HBPR increases with the increase in message TTL. This is justified by the fact that with the increase in the value of TTL, a message will take more time for getting delivered. This may increase the overall value of the average latency/delay for all the messages in the network. However, it remains comparable for both CHMM and RWP.

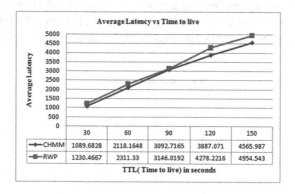

Fig. 8. Average latency vs. Time-to-live.

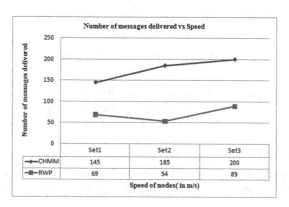

Fig. 9. Number of messages delivered vs. Speed of nodes.

4.3 Performance of HBPR Under Varying Node Speeds

In Fig. 9, it can be observed that the number of messages delivered is maximum for Set 3. This number is higher in case of CHMM as compared to RWP. Figure 10 shows that the average hop count for a message is higher for CHMM (compared to RWP) at all the three Speed Sets. Its value is lowest at Set 2 for both CHMM and RWP. From Fig. 11 (resp. Fig. 12), it can be observed that the overhead ratio (resp. the average latency) for HBPR is less in case of CHMM as compared to RWP in all the three Sets. These values are minimum for CHMM at Set 2 and for RWP at Set 3.

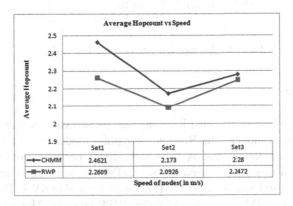

Fig. 10. Average hop count vs. Speed of nodes.

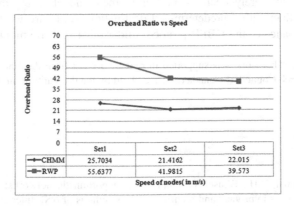

Fig. 11. Overhead ratio vs. Speed of nodes.

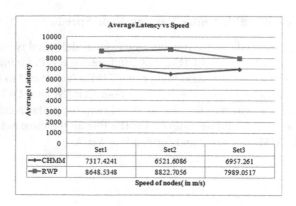

Fig. 12. Average latency vs. Speed of nodes.

5 Conclusion

In this work, the performance of HBPR is evaluated against various performance metrics using two movement models: the Random Waypoint model and the Custom Human Mobility model. Simulations results show that HBPR performs significantly well in terms of number of messages delivered when CHMM is used. The overhead ratio and average latency is also lesser in case of CHMM as compared to RWP. From these, it can be concluded that CHMM is best suited for the HBPR protocol. The use of CHMM can be attributed to the fact that HBPR is designed to perform best with human scenarios. It works on the existence of community such as structures and a recurring pattern. Hence, its performance will surely decrease in a movement model where the nodes move randomly rather than with a predetermined destination. As future work, we intend to study the performance of the HBPR protocol under other realistic mobility models.

Acknowledgment. This work was supported in part by a grant from the Natural Sciences and Engineering Research Council of Canada (NSERC) held by the third author, under Ref# RGPIN/293233-2011.

References

1. Lilien, L., Kamal, Z.H., Bhuse, V., Gupta, A.: Opportunistic networks: the concept and research challenges in privacy and security. In: Proceedings of NSF International Workshop on Research Challenges in Security and Privacy for Mobile and Wireless Networks (WSPWN 2006), Miami, pp. 134–147, March 2006
2. Fall, K.: A delay-tolerant network architecture for challenged internets. In: Proceedings of ACM SIGCOMM 2003, Karlsruhe, Germany, pp. 27–34, 25–29 August 2003
3. Toh, C.-K.: Ad Hoc Mobile Wireless Networks: Protocols and Systems. Prentice Hall PTR, Englewood Cliffs, ISBN: 0-13-007817-4 (2002)
4. Perkins, C.E., Belding-Royer, E.M., Das, S.: Ad hoc on demand distance vector (AODV) routing. IETF, RFC 3561, July 2003

5. Johnson, D., Maltz, D.: Dynamic source routing. In: Imielinski, T., Korth, H. (eds.) Mobile Computing, vol. 353, Chap. 5, pp. 153–181. Kluwer Academic Publishers, Dordrecht (1996)
6. Dhurandher, S.K., Sharma, D.K., Woungang, I., Chao, H.-C.: Performance evaluation of various routing protocols in opportunistic networks. In: Proceedings of IEEE GLOBECOM Workshop 2011, Houston, TX, USA, pp. 1067–1071, 5–9 December 2011
7. Huang, C.-M., Lan, K.-C., Tsai, C.-Z.: A survey of opportunistic networks. In: Proceedings of the 22nd International Conference on Advanced Information Networking and Applications Workshops (AINAW 2008), Okinawa, Japan, pp. 1672–1677, 25–28 March 2008
8. Pelusi, L., Passarella, A., Conti, M.: Opportunistic networking: data forwarding in disconnected mobile ad hoc networks. IEEE Commun. Mag. **44**(11), 134–141 (2006)
9. Dhurandher, S.K., Sharma, D.K., Woungang, I., Bhati, S.: HBPR: history based prediction for routing in infrastructure-less opportunistic networks. In: Proceedings of 27th IEEE International Conference on Advanced Information Networking and Applications (AINA-2013), Barcelona, Spain, pp. 931–936, 25–28 March 2013
10. Camp, T., Boleng, J., Davies, V.: A survey of mobility models for ad hoc network research. Wirel. Commun. Mob. Comput. (WCMC) (Special Issue on Mobile Ad Hoc Networking: Research, Trends and Applications) **2**(5), 483–502 (2002)
11. Ross, S.M.: Introduction to Probability Models. Academic Press, New York, ISBN-10: 0123756863 (1985)
12. Song, C., Qu, Z., Blumm, N., Barabasi, A.: Limits of predictability in human mobility. Science **327**(5968), 1018–1021 (2010). doi:10.1126/science.1177170
13. Keranen, A.: Opportunistic network environment simulator. Special Assignment Report, Helsinki University of Technology, Department of Communications and Networking, May 2008

LTE_FICC: A New Mechanism
for Provision of QoS and Congestion Control
in LTE/LTE-Advanced Networks

Fatima Furqan[(⊠)] and Doan B. Hoang[(⊠)]

INEXT Centre for Innovation in IT Services and Applications,
University of Technology, Sydney, Australia
Fatima.furqan@student.uts.edu.au,
dhoang@it.uts.edu.au

Abstract. In Long Term Evolution (LTE)/LTE-Advanced architecture, the basic schedulers allocate resources without taking congestion at the Evolved NodeB (eNodeB's) output buffer into account. This leads to buffer overflows and deterioration in overall Quality of Service (QoS). Congestion avoidance and fair bandwidth allocation is hardly considered in existing research for the LTE/LTE-Advanced uplink connections. This paper introduces a mechanism for LTE and LTE-Advanced, *LTE Fair Intelligent Congestion Control (LTE_FICC)*, to control congestion at an eNodeB. LTE_FICC jointly exists with the scheduler at the eNodeB to guarantee efficient traffic scheduling, in order to make the output buffer operate around a target operating point. LTE_FICC also overcomes the problem of unfair bandwidth allocation among the flows that share the same eNodeB interface. LTE_FICC is simple, robust and scalable, as it uses per queue rather than per flow accounting. To evaluate the effectiveness of the proposed algorithm, simulations were performed in Opnet using LTE module. The results demonstrated that LTE_FICC controls the eNodeB buffer effectively; prevents overflows; and ensures the QoS of flows in terms of fair bandwidth allocation, improved throughput and reduced queuing delay.

Keywords: Congestion control · QoS · Fairness · Throughput · Queuing delay · LTE · Opnet

1 Introduction

The 3rd Generation Partnership Project (3GPP) introduces the new architecture recognized as Evolved Packet System (EPS) in Rel. 8, as part of two parallel projects, System Architecture Evolution (SAE) and Long Term Evolution (LTE). SAE specifies the IP-based network core of the system called Evolved Packet Core (EPC). LTE defines the Radio Access Network (RAN) [1]. Motivated by the rising demands of advanced mobile services with higher data rates and stringent Quality of Service (QoS) requirements, 3GPP introduces LTE-Advanced in Rel.10. It supports data rate of 1 Gbps in downlink (DL) and 500 Mbps in uplink (UL) in scenarios of low mobility.

The 3GPP introduces LTE/LTE-Advanced with Orthogonal Frequency Division Multiplex (OFDM) based air interface. LTE supports scalable bandwidth up to

© Institute for Computer Sciences, Social Informatics and Telecommunications Engineering 2014
I. Stojmenovic et al. (Eds.): MOBIQUITOUS 2013, LNICST 131, pp. 768–781, 2014.
DOI: 10.1007/978-3-319-11569-6_67

20 MHz. LTE-Advanced supports bandwidth extension up to 100 MHz via Carrier Aggregation (CA). CA allows a mobile to transmit or receive on up to five Components Carriers (CCs), each of which can have maximum bandwidth of 20 MHz.

LTE/LTE-Advanced supports transmission in both Frequency Division Duplex (FDD) and Time Division Duplex (TDD) modes. In FDD mode, Frame structure type 1 is used. In frame structure type 1, each radio frame is 10 ms long and consists of 10 subframes of length 1 ms each. Each subframe consists of 2 slots of length 0.5 ms each. In time domain, each slot consists of either 6 or 7 OFDM symbols for long or short cyclic prefix (CP) respectively [2]. In frequency domain, each slot is described by a Resource Block (RB) and consists of 12 subcarriers each over 6 or 7 OFDM symbols.

To guarantee the service differentiation and provision of Quality of Service (QoS), LTE/LTE-Advanced employ the concept of bearer. A bearer identifies packet flows from one network element to another. Each bearer is associated with *QoS Class Identifier* (QCI) and *Allocation and Retention Priority* (ARP). QCI classifies the QoS class to which the bearer belongs and describes QoS parameters such as resource type, data rate, error rate and delay. ARP is an attribute of the bearer that indicates which bearer can be preempted by high priority bearers.

With respect to resource type, LTE/LTE-Advanced support *Guaranteed Bit Rate* (GBR) bearers and *Non Guaranteed Bit Rate* (non_GBR) bearers. In this paper, they are referred to as Classes of Bearers (CoBs). A GBR bearer is established or modified only on demand and reserves network resources corresponding the GBR value associated with it. A non_GBR bearer does not reserve network resources and may experiences congestion related packet losses [3]. Every QCI (GBR and Non-GBR) is associated with a priority level.

Scheduler plays a crucial role to ensure the provision of QoS requirements of the applications, which are defined in terms of bandwidth, delay and loss. LTE/LTE-Advanced eNodeB MAC sublayer schedules UL and DL transmissions and allocates RBs to the competing users. Scheduling is performed in every subframe. The basic schedulers like Round Robin (RR) and equal capacity sharing algorithm do not consider the QoS characteristics of the radio bearers. Additionally, none of these scheduling algorithms considers the queue length at an eNodeB. As a result, during congestion period when the core network is loaded, the queue at an eNodeB output buffer reaches its maximum and packets' loss starts. This leads to deterioration in the QoS experienced by existing connections.

The authors in [4] present CC scheme to provide fairness in heterogeneous radio access networks based on Radio Link control (RLC) packet discard. A congestion control (CC) mechanism is proposed in [5] that mitigates load in the network by removing the low priority bearers until the system load reaches to a predefined target value. The paper does not clearly discuss how the target load can be defined for a network. The authors in [6] propose a congestion control mechanism that protects an eNodeB output buffer from overflow by controlling the TCP advertisement window. RLC layer in an eNodeB monitors the buffer utilization and sets the congestion flag once it reaches to the threshold. So the proposed scheme violates the protocol layer design principles. The authors in [7] propose queue aware scheduling technique. The paper studies the performance of various queue aware scheduling schemes with an end-to-end congestion control scheme that controls the rate of elastic traffic and consequently affects the buffer status. The scheme is proposed for DL only. The end-to-end congestion scheme used in the paper involves the overhead of congestion field that is added in every packet.

The above mentioned schemes to perform load balancing are either based on thresholds or are applicable to a specific protocol, such as TCP only. They merely discuss the fair bandwidth allocation among flows of same CoB.

In this paper, we introduce an effective congestion control mechanism, namely LTE-Fair Intelligent Congestion Control (LTE_FICC). As discussed, the QoS framework of LTE-Advanced and LTE is the same. Therefore, the scheme is proposed for the uplink of both LTE and LTE-Advanced but is named as LTE_FICC for the sake of conciseness. LTE_FICC deals with both unfair bandwidth allocation and the congestion issues encountered in LTE/LTE-Advanced networks. It maintains the network traffic around a target operating point, hence avoids congestion and loss at the eNodeB output buffer. LTE_FICC uses a rate allocation scheme that takes degree of congestion at the eNodeB's output buffer into account. It estimates per queue fair share for all classes of bearers and sends the estimated rates as a feedback to the underlying scheduler at the eNodeB. LTE_FICC is simple because it employs a small number of parameters. It is effective in terms of operating with any basic underlying scheduling algorithm to minimize delay and to maintain high throughput.

The paper is organized as follows. Proposed scheme is presented in Sect. 2. Section 3 discusses the simulation setup and results. Finally, conclusion is given in Sect. 4.

2 Proposed Scheme

In this paper we introduce a new congestion control scheme namely LTE_Fair Intelligent Congestion Control (LTE_FICC) based on the basic principles of explicit feedback congestion control scheme namely Fair Intelligent Congestion Control (FICC) introduced in [8] for wired networks. FICC main idea is as follows.

1. FICC tries to maintain the queue length (Qlen) close to a target operating point (Q_0), so that the queue neither reaches to its capacity nor becomes empty and hence guarantees that the link is never idle unnecessarily.
2. In FICC, egress router uses Resource Discovery (RD) packets to probe available resources from routers inside the Diff-serve domain.
3. FICC adjusts the allowed class rate to minimize the variations in the buffer queue length.
4. FICC shares bandwidth equally among the connections of the same class. The left over bandwidth is shared fairly among connections that can take the additional share. To achieve this objective, when the network operates below a target point, FICC oversells the bandwidth to the connections in need.
5. FICC maintains information only per output queue, to make it more scalable.

```
FICC : At each router interface
If (receive RD (CCR,ER,DIR) = forward)
    If (Qlen > Q₀)
        If (ACR < MACR)
            MACR=MACR + β * (ACR-MACR)
    Else
            MACR=MACR + β * (ACR-MACR)
If (receive RD (CCR,ER,DIR) = backward)
    If (Qlen > Q₀)
```

$$f(Q) = \frac{(Buffer\_Size - Qlen)}{(Buffer\_Size - Q_0)}$$

```
    Else
```

$$f(Q) = \frac{(\alpha-1)*(Q_0 - Qlen)}{Q_0}$$

$$\text{(1)}$$

```
ER = Max (MinER, min(ER ,f(Q) * MACR)
```

The main aim of FICC is to calculate the explicit rate which reflects how much traffic could be handled by a transit router within the network. The calculated explicit rate is sent as a feed back to the source nodes. Mean explicit rate is defined as follows.

$$ER = MACR * f(Q) \tag{2}$$

Instead of fixed congestion thresholds which lead to unfairness in the network, FICC defines a target operating point (Q_0). To detect congestion, FICC employs an efficient function of queue size called "queue control function". The queue control function expresses the degree of network congestion that a router can tolerate.

f(Q) is a linear function as shown in Eq. (1). It is specified by three parameters namely α, Q_0 and Buffer_Size as shown in Eq. (1). Buffer_Size is the total size of the output buffer at the router. α can be considered as an oversell factor when the network is underutilized. The value of oversell factor determines how much traffic is encouraged to put inside the network and is higher than 1. f(Q) returns value between 0 to 1 for the queue length in the range of [Q_0, Buffer Size] and between 1 to α for the queue lengths in the range of [0, Q_0].

In FICC, router estimates the current traffic rate of all aggregates passing through it and allocates a fair share of the available bandwidth among its aggregates. For this purpose, FICC uses MACR (Mean Allowed Class Rate) and ACR (Allowed Class Rate). The MACR is an average of the current allowed rates of all aggregates [8]. The ACR is the rate at which the edge router admits a flow in the network.

As mentioned before, the QoS framework of LTE-Advanced and LTE is the same and LTE_FICC is the rate allocation scheme only, so LTE_FICC is proposed for both the networks. LTE_FICC is based on the basic idea of FICC in terms of buffer control. To make it effective for LTE/LTE-Advanced networks, new aspects have to be considered and hence LTE_FICC is distinct from FICC in following ways.

- The output queue status of an eNodeB depends on the output link capacity as well as on the capacity of the EPC. So a large queue length at an eNodeB buffer serves as an indication that the EPC is congested.

- FICC sends the explicit rate as a feedback to the source nodes of the end-to-end connection whereas LTE_FICC is employed as a separate module in an eNodeB. It estimates the expected rate for each CoB and passes it to the scheduler.
- LTE_FICC is flexible because it can operate with any underlying basic scheduler.
- LTE_FICC allocates resources fairly among flows of each CoB namely GBR and non_GBR.
- As the LTE/LTE-Advanced environment defines different types of bearers, so LTE_FICC takes different QoS requirements of each type of bearer into account.

2.1 Queue Control Function

LTE_FICC uses the same queue function as in FICC given in Eq. (1).

2.2 Expected Rate of Each Class of Bearer (ER_{CoB})

In order to keep the queue length around the target operating point, LTE_FICC estimates the current bandwidth allocated to connections of each CoB (GBR and non_GBR) and then calculates the expected rate (ER) for each CoB using the queue control function. To estimate the current bandwidth allocated to flows of each CoB, LTE_FICC similar to FICC, uses a variable named MACR but one for each CoB ($MACR_{CoB}$). We suggest two MACRs corresponding to two classes of bearers, namely $MACR_{GBR\_Total}$ and $MACR_{NonGBR}$.

$MACR_{GBR\_Total}$ maintains the mean value of the bandwidth allocated to all active connections of GBR bearers. It is obtained as the sum of $MACR_{GBR}$ and $MACR_{GBR\_Ad}$ and is estimated as follow.

$$MACR_{GBR\_Total} = MACR_{GBR} + MACR_{GBR\_Ad} \tag{3}$$

In Eq. (3) $MACR_{GBR}$ is the estimate of the bandwidth allocated to all GBR bearers to meet their respective GBR. $MACR_{GBR\_Ad}$ refers to the estimate of the additional bandwidth allocated to all GBR bearers, above their individual GBR, to meet their respective MBR. GBR bearers always obtain GBR even when the network is congested. Therefore, LTE_FICC operates only on $MACR_{GBR\_Ad}$, as it is the only part of resource allocation to GBR bearers that can be controlled by LTE_FICC. The resources allocated above the GBR will be referred to as GBR_Ad hereafter. $MACR_{non\_GBR}$ maintains the mean value of bandwidth allocated to all active connections of non_GBR bearers. In every sub frame, the scheduler at the eNodeB after allocating resources to flows, updates the values of $MACR_{GBR}$, $MACR_{GBR\_Ad}$ and $MACR_{nonGBR}$ as in Eq. (4).

if $Qlen > Q_0$

   if $\frac{ACR_{CoB}(t)}{Weight[QCI]} < MACR_{CoB}(t-1)$

$$MACR_{CoB}(t) = MACR_{CoB}(t-1) + \beta * \left(\frac{ACR_{CoB}}{Weight[QCI]} - MACR_{CoB}(t-1) \right) \tag{4}$$

else if $Qlen < Q_0$

$$MACR_{CoB}(t) = MACR_{CoB}(t-1) + \beta * \left(\frac{ACR_{CoB}}{Weight[QCI]} - MACR_{CoB}(t-1) \right)$$

In Eq. (4), β is an exponential average factor. $ACR_{CoB}(t)$ represents the actual bandwidth allocated to active connections in current subframe (t). $ACR_{CoB}(t)$ is estimated as follows.

$$ACR_{CoB}(t) = ER_{CoB}(t) * Weight[QCI] \tag{5}$$

Weight [QCI] is weight assigned by scheduler to each QCI based on its priority level in respective CoB and is further discussed in Sect. 3.4. For Example, in this paper QCI 1, 2, 3 and 4 from GBR CoB and QCI 6, 7, 8 and 9 from NonGBR CoB are assigned weights of 4, 3, 2 and 1 respectively. $ER_{CoB}(t)$ is the expected rate of each CoB and is estimated by LTE_FICC as in Eq. (6).

In Eq. (4), $MACR_{CoS}(t-1)$ and $MACR_{CoS}(t)$ reflects the mean of the allowed class rate of all active connections per class of service in previous and current frame respectively. When the network load exceeds the target operating point that is the Qlen is more than Q_0, LTE_FICC does not allow the $MACR_{CoB}(t)$ to increase further. Therefore, $MACR_{CoB}(t)$ does not track any value of current allocation ($ACR_{CoB}(t)$/ weight [QCI]) larger than current $MACR_{CoB}(t-1)$. The $MACR_{CoB}$ is regarded as an optimal mean allowed class rate if the network operates at the target operating point and the ER_{CoB} is set equal to it. While if the queue length is larger/smaller than the target operating point, the desired expected rate of each CoB is calculated as a function of f(Q) and corresponding $MACR_{CoB}$.

$$ER_{CoB}(t) = MACR_{CoB}(t-1) * f(Q) \tag{6}$$

2.3 Congestion Control Algorithm

LTE_FICC is executed only once in every subframe before the resources are allocated to connections by the scheduler.

The aim of LTE_FICC is to estimate the expected rate for each CoB that is non_GBR (ER_{non_GBR}) and GBR_Ad (ER_{GBR_Ad}) based on the current bandwidth allocated to the connections of each CoB that is $MACR_{CoB}$ and the queue control function f(Q).

2.3.1 Description of Algorithm

LTE_FICC sets the target operating point at a preset Buffer Utilization Ratio (BUR). It acquires the value of queue length from the router's output interface. It also obtains the estimates of $MACR_{CoB}(t-1)$ from the scheduler as shown in Fig. 1. LTE_FICC, estimates the degree of network congestion by calculating the f(Q).

When f(Q) is less than 1, indicating there is congestion in the network, LTE_FICC reduces the bandwidth allocated to all the non_GBR bearers. The step size of degradation is controlled by f(Q) as it provides an estimation of how much degradation is applied on this class of traffic. LTE_FICC then based on the degradation applied on

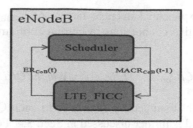

Fig. 1. LTE_FICC Module at eNodeB

non_GBR bearers, updates the estimates of Qlen, f(Q), MACR$_{non\_GBR}$ and the ER$_{non\_GBR}$. LTE_FICC keeps on reducing the ER$_{non\_GBR}$ until either the f(Q) is equal to or greater than 1 or ER$_{non\_GBR}$ reaches to minimum number of bits that must be allocated to a connection in UL (MIN_UL).

After degrading the connections of non_GBR, LTE_FICC again estimates congestion using f(Q), if f(Q) is again less than 1 indicating network is still operating above the target operating point, LTE_FICC reduces the additional bandwidth allocated above the GBR (GBR_Ad) to all the connections of the GBR CoB. LTE_FICC then based on the degradation applied on GBR bearers, updates the estimates of Qlen, f(Q), MACR$_{GBR\_Ad}$ and the ER$_{GBR\_Ad}$. LTE_FICC keeps on reducing the ER$_{GBR\_Ad}$ until either the f(Q) is equal to or greater than 1 or ER$_{GBR\_Ad}$ reaches to minimum number of bits that must be allocated to a bearer in UL (MIN_UL).

When f(Q) is greater than 1, indicating network is operating below its target level, LTE_FICC raises the additional bandwidth share above the GBR of all the GBR bearers. The step size for the share increase is still determined by f(Q) but at a different rate indicating how far the network is underutilized. LTE_FICC then based on the upgradation applied on GBR bearers, updates the estimates of Qlen, f(Q), MACR$_{GBR\_Ad}$ and the ER$_{GBR\_Ad}$. LTE_FICC keeps on increasing the ER$_{GBR\_Ad}$ until either the f(Q) is equal to or less than 1 or ER$_{GBR\_Ad}$ reaches to maximum number of bits (MAX_UL) that can be allocated to a bearer using Max_MCS and the maximum number of RBs in UL subframe (RB_UL_Subframe). Max_MCS is the maximum Modulation and Coding scheme (MCS) that can be supported by the LTE/LTE-Advanced networks for the UL.

After upgrading bandwidth allocated to flows of GBR bearers, LTE_FICC recalculates the f(Q) and if again f(Q) is greater than 1, indicating network is still operating below its target level, LTE_FICC raises the bandwidth share of all non_GBR bearers. LTE_FICC then based on the upgradation applied on non_GBR bearers, updates the estimates of Qlen, f(Q), MACR$_{non\_GBR}$ and the ER$_{non\_GBR}$. LTE_FICC keeps on increasing the ER$_{non\_GBR}$ until either the f(Q) is equal to or less than 1 or ER$_{non\_GBR}$ reaches to maximum number of bits (MAX_UL) that can be allocated to a bearer using Max_MCS and the RB_UL_Subframe.

```
Algorithm LTE-FICC:
  Initialization
              Q₀ = BufferSize * BUR
              MIN_UL  := 56
              MAX_UL  := Max_MCS * RB_UL_Subframe
1. Obtain Value of Current Qlen from BS output interface.
2. Obtain value of MACR_GBR_Ad and MACR_nonGBR from the scheduler.
3. Calculate f(Q) using Eq.(1).
4.
If f(Q) <1  /*Degradation Process*/
  For each CoB Non_GBR and GBR_Ad
      ER_CoB := MACR_CoB *f(Q)
      Do While ER_CoB > MIN_UL AND f(Q) < 1
          Qlen   := Qlen - RB_UL_Subframe *(MACR_CoB - ER_CoB)
          ACR_CoB := ER_CoB
          Recalculate f(Q) using Eq.(1).
          Update MACR_CoB using Eq.(4).
          ER_CoB := MACR_CoB *f(Q)
        End Do While
    End For
Else If f(Q > 1 /*Upgradation Process*/
  For each CoB GBR_Ad and Non_GBR
      ER_CoB := MACR_CoB *f(Q)
      Do While ER_CoB < MAX_UL AND f(Q) > 1
          Qlen := Qlen - RB_UL_Subframe *(MACR_CoB - ER_CoB)
          ACR_CoB := ER_CoB
          Recalculate f(Q) using Eq.(1).
          Update MACR_CoB using Eq.(4).
          ER_CoB := MACR_CoB *f(Q)
        End Do While
    End For
  End If
End If
Pass the estimated ER_GBR_Ad and ER_non_GBR to the Scheduler.
```

Once the expected rate of non_GBR and GBR_Ad is determined for the current subfarme, LTE_FICC passes the values of ER_{non_GBR} and ER_{GBR_Ad} to the scheduler as shown in Fig. 1.

2.4 Modified Round Robin (MRR)

The LTE module of opnet simulator [9] uses proportional fair scheduling to allocate resources to GBR connections to meet their respective GBR. It uses either equal capacity sharing algorithm or round robin algorithm to allocate resources to NonGBR, as well as to GBR connections above their respective GBR. In every subfarme, these basic scheduling algorithms always start scheduling from the highest priority QCI in a specific Class of bearer (CoB) (such as QCI 1 in GBR CoB and QCI 6 in NonGBR CoB) and keep on scheduling until all the queues at that priority level are empty. Consequently, these basic schedulers lead to unfair bandwidth allocation in the network. So we modified RR algorithm to ensure that connections at all priority levels are served.

The modified round robin algorithm always starts from the highest priority QCI in each CoB and in a RR manner scans to find a nonempty queue for scheduling. Once a queue is scheduled or there is no non empty queue at that level, the algorithm moves to next low priority QCI. The algorithm will continue to the next low priority levels and scan all queues from there too until a non empty queue is found. To maintain differentiation among different QCIs of a specific CoB, the modified round robin scheduling algorithm allocates resources to flows equals to ER_{CoB} X weight[QCI]. Once resources are determined then scheduler applies a binary search on the TB size table given in [10] for the value of ER_{CoB} X weight[QCI] and obtains the corresponding MCS and number of RBs to be allocated to the connection.

In this way, the modified round robin ensures that queues from all priority levels are scheduled. Also, it provides service differentiation according to the assigned weights.

3   Simulation Results

3.1   Simulation Setup

The overall goal of the simulation is to analyze the performance of the proposed algorithm to meet the QoS requirements of each class of bearer in terms of fairness, throughput and delay in a congested scenario. The simulations have been performed in system level simulator Optimized Network Engineering Tool (OPNET) release 17.1.A [9], using the LTE module. In the current simulation setup, User Equipments (UEs) are connected to an eNodeB that in turn is connected to the EPC. The EPC is connected to the server through the internet to reflect the actual deployment of the end-to-end network. The eNodeB operates in FDD mode and uses physical profile of 3 MHz bandwidth. The target point is set at 1/32 of the total buffer capacity of 3 Mbps. The link capacity between eNodeB and EPC is set at 1.3 Mbps to depict a high congestion scenario.

In the current simulation scenario, one cell is taken with a GBR UE and 7 nonGBR UEs. For the simulation the Max_MCS for all UEs is set at 15. The GBR_UE has two GBR bearers each with GBR of 64 kbps. The GBR UE transmits VOIP G.711 and 256 kbps H.263 video streams using GBR bearers with QCI-1 and QCI-4, respectively. Non_GBR UEs transmit VoIP G.711, 256 kbps H.263 video streams and 64 kbps web traffic using bearers with QCI-7, QCI-8 and QCI-9, respectively. The trace file for the 64 kbps and 256 kbps H.263 encoded Jurassic Park movie was obtained from the website in [11]. All connections start transmission at around 100 ms of the simulation and stop at end of simulation. The total simulation time is 500 s.

For the comparison a reference scenario is taken without the proposed LTE_FICC and without the modified round robin algorithm.

3.2   Queue Length (Qlen) and Traffic Dropped

Figure 2 shows Qlen at the eNodeB output buffer. Figure 2 confirms that if during the congestion periods, the scheduler allocates resources without taking the capacity of the output buffer at the eNodeB into account, a point will come when buffer overflows and the packets drop starts as shown in Fig. 3.

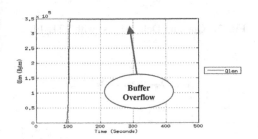

Fig. 2. Qlen (Bytes) at eNodeB without LTE_FICC

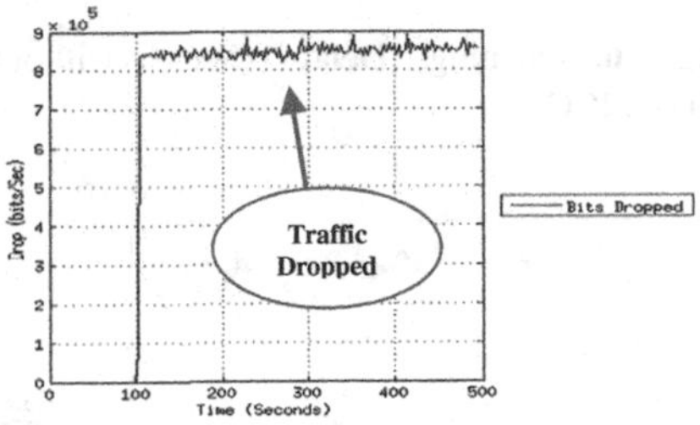

Fig. 3. Traffic dropped (bits/Sec) at eNodeB without LTE_FICC

Figure 4 shows the Qlen at the eNodeB output buffer with proposed LTE_FICC. With LTE_FICC, as soon as the Qlen reaches to Q_0, the LTE_FICC starts its operation and as designed maintains the Qlen close to the Q_0. Consequently, there is no loss at the eNodeB output interface as indicated by Fig. 5.

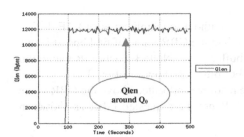

Fig. 4. Qlen (Bytes) at eNodeB with LTE_FICC

Fig. 5. Traffic dropped (bits/Sec) at eNodeB with LTE_FICC

3.3   Average Queuing Delay

Figures 6 and 7 show the queuing delay at the eNodeB output buffer. Initially, as there is less amount of data in the queue, so delay is less. As the transmission starts the amount of data in the queue increases and hence the delay increases. Figure 6 shows very high queuing delay which can be attributed to the fact that when LTE_FICC is not applied, the queue reaches to the maximum buffer capacity as shown in Fig. 2 and results in high delay. Figure 7 shows as LTE_FICC maintains queue length close the target point so the queuing delay is very low.

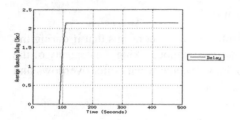

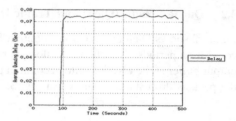

Fig. 6. Queuing Delay (Secs) without LTE_FICC

Fig. 7. Queuing Delay (Secs) with LTE_FICC

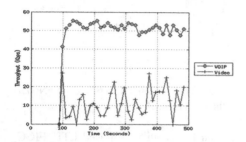

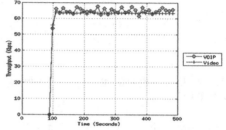

Fig. 8. Throughput (kbps) of GBR Bearers without LTE_FICC

Fig. 9. Throughput (kbps) of GBR Bearers with LTE_FICC

3.4   Throughput of GBR Bearers

Figure 8 shows the throughput of GBR bearers without the application of LTE_FICC. It shows that the GBR bearers are getting less than the GBR value of 64 kbps. It is due to the fact that when the queue length of the buffer at an eNodeB reaches its maximum capacity, it starts dropping the packets in FIFO order as shown in Fig. 3.

LTE_FICC upgrades or degrades only the resources allocated above the GBR value of GBR bearers. Therefore, flows of GBR CoB get the requested GBR as shown in Fig. 9.

3.5   Fair Resource Allocation

3.5.1   Fair Resource Allocation Among QCIs of Non_GBR CoB

Figure 10 shows the cumulative throughput for different QCIs of non_GBR CoB when equal capacity sharing algorithm or RR allocates resources. Figure 10 shows the throughput of web application with lowest priority QCI is almost zero as the two algorithms always start scheduling with highest priority QCI and serve it until all queues at that priority level are empty and results in unfairness to connections of low priority QCI.

Figure 11 shows modified round robin with LTE_FICC ensures that queues at all priority levels within the non_GBR CoB are served. To provide differentiation as the modified RR allocates resources according to the assigned weights of QCIs, so the throughput of each QCI is in the order of corresponding priority and hence proved

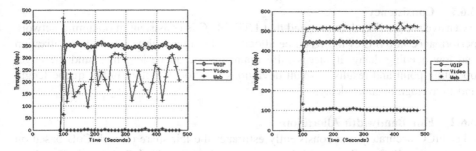

Fig. 10. Total Throughput (kbps) of Non-GBR bearers without LTE_FICC

Fig. 11. Total Throughput (kbps) of NonGBR bearers with LTE_FICC

fairness among QCIs of NonGBR CoB. The throughput of video traffic with QCI-9 is higher than throughput of voice traffic with QCI-8 because the video sources have more traffic to send waiting in queues and thus take the additional share when resources are available in network.

3.5.2 Fair Resource Allocation Among Flows of Same QCIs of Non_GBR CoB

Figure 12 shows that when scheduling is performed using equal capacity sharing algorithm then the network cannot provide fairness among flows of same QCIs. Figure 13 shows modified round robin with LTE_FICC provide fairness within QCI as flows at same priority level are getting same amount of resources.

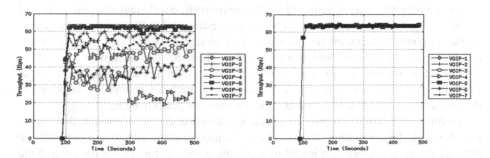

Fig. 12. Throughput (kbps) of NonGBR flows without LTE_FICC

Fig. 13. Throughput (kbps) of NonGBR flows with LTE_FICC

3.6 Discussion on Results

The current simulations do not include additional features of LTE-Advanced including the extended bandwidth of 100 MHz and the enhanced MIMO techniques. Further results shall be presented in future based on the enhanced attributes of LTE_Advanced.

3.6.1   Consistency

Extensive simulations demonstrated that LTE_FICC is consistent in obtaining network performance in terms of fair resource allocation, high throughput, high link utilization and low queuing delay. It successfully maintains the queue length around the target operating point and results in small deviations in eNodeB output buffer queue length and in average queuing delay.

3.6.2   Fair Bandwidth Allocation

LTE_FICC accurately and consistently estimates the fair share of each CoB based on its respective QoS attributes and the queue length at the eNodeB output buffer. Consequently, along with modified round robin, it ensures that the packets that already occupy the buffer represent fair share of the connections of different QCIs within each CoB.

3.6.3   Bounded Queue Length

The overselling feature of LTE_FICC allows the unconstrained connections to take up the resources that cannot be utilized by the constrained connections. This allows LTE_FICC to successfully maintain the queue length around the target operating point and ensures that the output link is always utilized.

4   Conclusion

A new congestion control algorithm LTE_FICC is proposed, for both LTE and LTE-Advanced networks, and is demonstrated to perform effectively and efficiently. Instead of using thresholds to reduce the network congestion, LTE_FICC employs a target operating point. It maintains the network traffic around the target point, hence avoids congestion and loss at the eNodeB output buffer. The paper presented only a partial set of simulation results due to space limits. In the current implementation the target operating point was set manually. The future work includes setting the target point dynamically, at a level that is suitable for the network performance.

In future, we aim to propose an effective admission control algorithm that works together with the congestion control scheme to minimize the end to end delay of the network connections. We also intend to apply the proposed congestion control and the admission control schemes on the different scenarios of Australian National Broadband Network (NBN).

References

1. Cox, C.: An introduction to LTE: LTE, LTE-Advanced, SAE, and 4G Mobile Communications. Wiley, London (2012)
2. 3GPP 36.211, Technical Specification Group Radio Access Network; Evolved Universal Terrestrial Radio Access (E-UTRA); Physical Channels and Modulation (Release 11)

3. 3GPP 23.203, Technical Specification Group Services and System Aspects; Policy and charging control architecture (Release 12)
4. Vulkan, C., Heder, B.: Congestion control in evolved HSPA systems. In: 2011 IEEE 73rd Vehicular Technology Conference (VTC Spring), pp. 1–6 (2011)
5. Kwan, R., et al.: On pre-emption and congestion control for LTE systems. In: 2010 IEEE 72nd Vehicular Technology Conference Fall (VTC 2010-Fall), pp. 1–5 (2010)
6. Qinlong, Q., et al.: Avoiding the evolved node B buffer overflow by using advertisement window control. In: 2011 11th International Symposium on Communications and Information Technologies (ISCIT), pp. 268–273 (2011)
7. Zolfaghari, A., Taheri, H.: Queue-aware scheduling and congestion control for LTE. In: 2012 18th IEEE International Conference on Networks (ICON), pp. 131–136 (2012)
8. Phan, H.T., Hoang, D.B.: FICC-DiffServ: A new QoS architecture supporting resources discovery, admission and congestion controls. In: Third International Conference on Information Technology and Applications (ICITA), pp. 710–715 (2005)
9. http://www.opnet.com (opnet modeler release 17.1.A)
10. 3GPP 36.213, Technical Specification Group Radio Access Network; Evolved Universal Terrestrial Radio Access (E-UTRA); Physical layer procedures, Release 11
11. H.263 Video Traces, 7 July 2013. http://www2.tkn.tuberlin.de/research/trace/ltvt.html

Virtual Wireless User: A Practical Design for Parallel MultiConnect Using WiFi Direct in Group Communication

Marat Zhanikeev[✉]

Computer Science and Systems Engineering, Kyushu Institute of Technology,
Kawazu 680-4, Iizuka-shi, Fukuoka-ken 820–8502, Japan
maratishe@gmail.com

Abstract. Several MultiConnect technologies are actively discussed in research today. MultiPath TCP (MPTCP) is capable of splitting one flow into subflows and balance the load across multiple access technologies. Multihoming is an older technology that makes it possible for network providers to balance load across multiple up- and down-links dynamically. Finally, Software Defined Networking (SDN) achieves the ultimate flexibility of connection and routing decisions. However, none of these technologies enable true (network or otherwise) resource-pooling in communications within arbitrary size user groups such as occur in meetings, class discussions, and ad-hoc communities in the wild. This paper proposes the concept of a Virtual Wireless User (VWU) which represents the entire group and appears as single user to an over-the-network service. Each group member is capable of MultiConnect using Wi-Fi Direct in parallel with any other connection method. Modeling based on real measurements shows that VWUs can achieve throughput in the order of tens of Mbps even if throughput of individual users is very low. The paper also formulates a formal optimization problem in relation to VWU.

Keywords: Virtual wireless user · Connectivity virtualization · Network access virtualization · MultiConnect · MultiPath · MultiHoming · Wi-Fi Direct · P2P Wi-Fi · Resource pooling · Group communication

1 Introduction

Many things are given the prefix *multiple* in networking today. First, there is the old yet currently active topic of *multihoming* [1]. RFC6182 recently defined MultiPath connectivity which can be implemented as MultiPath TCP (MPTCP) [3]. Dynamic connectivity can also be achieved using Software Defined Networking (SDN) [8]. All these methods share the following common features:

- there is one content (file, flow, etc.);
- there is one source (destination of an end-to-end path);

© Institute for Computer Sciences, Social Informatics and Telecommunications Engineering 2014
I. Stojmenovic et al. (Eds.): MOBIQUITOUS 2013, LNICST 131, pp. 782–793, 2014.
DOI: 10.1007/978-3-319-11569-6_68

– the one content is communicated between the user and the source via multiple parallel paths.

The main problem is that the above features are insufficient when describing a large set of applications. For example, traditional multipath technology cannot help communications within a group of users, where the new formulation is:

– the unit of content is its small piece (block, one file of many, etc.) [7];
– each unit of content can have at least two but potentially a large number of sources [12];
– there are multiple parallel paths as before, but paths are dynamically configured to connect to sources decided on the fly.

The new design (the one that fits the above new formulation) should have the following required components. Each user should have at least one of each *inter-* and *intra*-net connectivity – it is technically possible to work with one connectivity method but this would defeat the purpose. The *intranet* connection is expected to carry larger throughput than its *internet* counterpart. A *Virtual Wireless User* (VWU) is then defined as a virtual entity/application which pools all resources and performs load balancing between intra- and inter-nets. While traditional multipath technologies can double or at most triple throughput in practice, this paper shows that VWUs can theoretically feature arbitrarily large throughputs from the aggregate pools of singular connections.

There are several example applications which are done in groups of users. It can be a meeting of users gathered in a room, a class discussion, or an arbitrary size ad-hoc community gathering anytime anywhere. As long as resources within the group are controlled by a single application, the VWU can be created to represent the group before a Service Provider (SP).

Note that *MultiConnect* (propertly defined further on) does not explicitly require a connection-based transport protocol. For example, Delay Tolerant Networks (DTNs) can work with strict delay constraints [11] and can be used as the transport protocol within the *intranet*. In this case, content is exchanged in blocks or files [7].

Wi-Fi Direct is a recent technology [16] which makes it possible to create DTN-like intranets. It is also referred to as Wireless P2P [16]. Wi-Fi Direct pursues two objectives: (1) provide fast AP-less communication between two users, which is achieved by implementing lightweight APs inside users [16], and (2) facilitating ubiquity by minimizing overhead, for example, making it possible to have a continuous pairing with a printer [16]. While Wi-Fi Direct is like DTN in that the unit of exchange is a file, the specifications allow for a continuous operation which can support one-hop flows. Note that Wi-Fi Direct itself is not a MultiConnect technology where the latter needs an entire new application layer on top of the raw connectivity options provided by Wi-Fi Direct.

This paper makes the following contributions: (1) it is shown how Wi-Fi Direct can be used as a building block for a MultiConnect technology in group communications; (2) it is shown that Wi-Fi Direct is already fully implemented in practice today while multipath technologies are at early development stage; (3) results from real life measurements in combinations of 3G and WLAN with Wi-Fi Direct technologies are presented and analyzed; (4) MultiConnect of 3G and WLAN with Wi-Fi Direct is tested in practice and analyzed for throughput in parallel operation; (5) the Virtual Wireless User (VWU) is formulated and several models with VWU and an example optimization problem are presented.

2   Terminology and the Scope

Wi-Fi is difficult to type so it is shortened to *WiFi*. Traditional WiFi is *WLAN*. *3G* is the umbrella term for 3G, LTE and all other 3.xG cellular technologies.

Communication is classified into the two fundamental types of *connection-based* versus *hop-by-hop*, where the former can be represented by TCP and the latter by Delay Tolerant Networks (DTN) [10]. *Group communication* stands for an application in which members of a group communicate among each other. In this context, *intranets* connect all the users while *internets* connect each user to a Server Provider (SP) individually.

Multi-* technologies are classified into *multihoming, multipath* and *Multi-Connect*, where the last one is formulated for the first time in this paper (to the extent of this author's knowledge). MultiConnect is distinct from the other two technologies by having unique features (explained earlier), thus justifying the new term. Specifically, in this paper MultiConnect is defined as ability to use multiple access technologies in parallel. Note that this formulation is not sufficient for *multipath* which requires all access technologies to support end-to-end paths to the same destination. The *MultiConnect* has no such requirement.

Service Provider (SP), *Wireless User* (WU) and *Virtual Wireless User* (VWU) are the main three players in the scope of this paper. Remote players are Network Provider (NP or ISP), Content Provider (CP) and clouds.

3   Related Work

Multihoming is an old technology which has received renewed attention in view of high-throughput networking in CDNs [1]. By contrast, there are many multipath technologies considered in research today [2], ranging from I-WLAN and IFOM (3GPP) to MultiPath TCP (MPTCP), SCTP (RFC2960) and IMS method with its multipath RTP. MPTCP is leading in terms of implementation for which there is already a Linux kernel [4] tested in practice [3], but even MPTCP is much less widespread in devices today compared to WiFi Direct. MPTCP has been analyzed for performance as a resource pooling technology in environments with one source [6], while the *MultiConnect* technology presented in this paper uses multiple sources. MPTCP is still under active discussion in RFC6181, RFC6182, RFC6356, RFC6824, and RFC6897, where RFC6182 presents the fundamentals of the technology.

Network virtualization is not considered in existing research on multipath. Virtual networks are supposed to provide truly flexible routing and path establishment decisions – executed in software. Software Defined Networks (SDNs) with OpenvSwitch as the de-facto standard [8] are assumed to make routing decisions at the grain of individual packets. SDNs were shown to be slower than traditional networks, but slightly diminished performance is not a problem for end users [15]. ClickRouter [9] is a non-SDN way to make per-packet routing decisions and is very active in research today. SDN was tried in a multipath implementation at least once in [5] as part of a very crude implementation which installs Linux and then OpenvSwitch onto an originally Android smartphone.

Note that none of the above technologies consider resource pooling in groups. The resource pooling problem was originally proposed as part of distributed-rsync (dsync) [7]. The proposal is for group communication but does not use MultiConnect – instead, users have only one connection at a time.

In MultiConnect, congestion of wireless channels may pose a practical issue. Although channel congestion is out of scope of this paper, experiments in [13] show that one channel can be shared by many users with minimum effect on throughput up to a given point. Research in [13] can also serve as a reference into other research on this issue.

When content grain is a block of data or a file, DTN formulation is applicable [10]. RAPID is the most efficient DTN method today [11]. Under RAPID, latency-constrained delivery is possible. The method can be further improved when bandwidth is unreliable. Note that while DTN is a generic principle, group communications are not necessarily dynamic and unpredictable in practice. For example, people having a meeting in- or out-doors should not be difficult to work with. Such environments are perfect for WiFi Direct.

4   Practical Parallel Group MultiConnect

Figure 1 presents the taxonomy of practical MultiConnect reality today. The presentation is simple and shows two features: default technology in a pair and ability to use a technology in parallel with WiFi Direct. The simple message is that WiFi Direct can work with any common access technology including the LAN. Current support for WiFi Direct is limited in notebooks and desktops, but it is implemented by many smartphones and tablet computers.

Figure 2 shows the first abstraction leading to the main VWU formulation. The figure simply shows that users are connected to both intra- and inter-nets. We do not care about throughput for now. MultiConnect in this context is in that each user has at least two separate parallel connection methods. The design offers some side benefits as well. Even if some users have no internet connectivity, they can be supported by the intranet, where the latter are supposed to be faster by definition and thus facilitate situations when some users are supported by others in a group.

Figure 3 is the second abstraction, this time more about pooling of resources. WVU is positioned on the border between SP and users and is the single/only

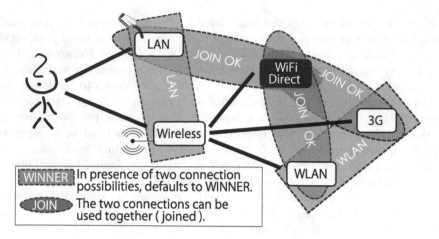

Fig. 1. Taxonomy of existing connectivity technology viewed in the practical aspect of *parallel usage*.

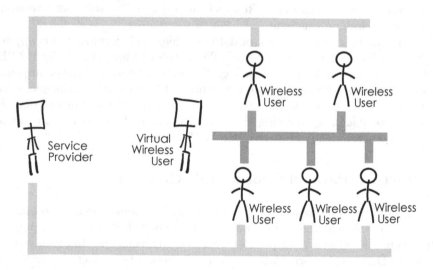

Fig. 2. Abstraction 1: Virtual Wireless User (VWU) made possible when members of a communication group support an *intranet* in parallel with each individual traditional *internet* connections.

contact person as far as SP is aware. Figure 3 also shows that throughput is important. SP-VWU throughput is the aggregate of internet connections of all users. VWU-WU aggregate throughput is the maximum throughput achieved by WiFi Direct inside the group, given the interference, etc.

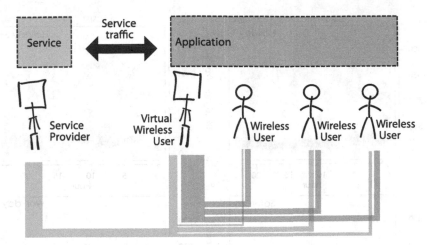

Fig. 3. Abstraction 2: A redesigned Abstraction 1 in such a way as to show that *service traffic* is exchanged only between the Virtual Wireless User (VWU) and Server Provider (SP) while VWU and the application it executes takes care of the communication within the *intranet*.

5 Measurements in Real Inter- and Intra-networks

This section presents real measurements for all technologies involved in the proposed MultiConnect as well as their parallel configurations. For 3G, day of week and time of day are important because ISP resources are contested by a large number of users, while WLANs merge into LANs for end-to-end traversal.

5.1 Internets: Real 3G Providers

The objective of this batch of measurements is to analyze 3G performance for several real providers. Three 3G providers (names omitted) were selected, where one provider limited throughput to 300 kbps under the contact, but the other two were supposed to provide full (best effort) capacity. The test ran continuously over the period of 3 months from mid-April 2013 with several tens of measurements collected every day. When presenting results, days are classified into Holiday 1 (Sunday), Holiday 3+ (longer holidays), Saturday, and Workday. Measurements were careful not to run over quota (2 Gb each month).

Each measurement result was obtained as follows. A 500 kb file was downloaded from a fixed server. Throughput is then measured by dividing 500 kb (x8 bits) by the download time in seconds.

Figure 4 shows measurement results. Lessons are obvious. The maximum achievable throughput is 1 Mbps but only occurs for one of three ISPs, while the other two feature very low throughput. There is great variation across hours of day and types of days.

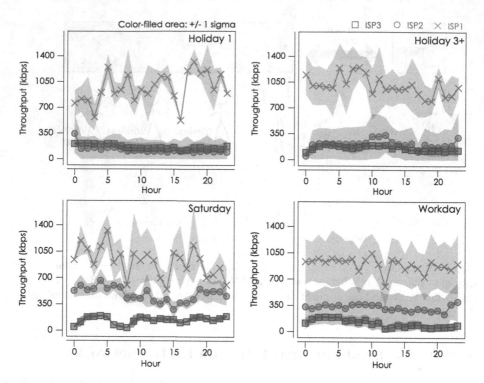

Fig. 4. Throughput performance for the three 3G ISPs split into the four kinds of days of the week. Color-filled areas are 1 sigma bands.

5.2   Intranets: WiFi Direct and Bluetooth

The objective of this batch of measurements is to compare the two available technologies in the intranet – WiFi Direct and Bluetooth 4.0. In a single measurement, 1, 5 or 10 files (max bulk size slightly above 1 Gb) are transferred between two smartphones. Distances of 1 m and 10 m are tested separately.

Figure 5 shows the results. WiFi Direct is clearly superior to Bluetooth, as much as 30 times better as shown in the second plot. However, distance has some effect on throughput and can cause up to 40 % decrease in throughput for extended sessions.

5.3   MultiConnect Performance

The objective of this batch of measurements is to cross WiFi direct with 3G or WLAN and test both in parallel, thus creating the first true *MultiConnect* in this paper. The same setup is used the same as in the previous case, only the sessions are parallel and end when the intranet connection completes.

Figure 6 has two features. WiFi Direct throughput is affected very little when used in parallel with a 3G connection while parallelization with WLAN can

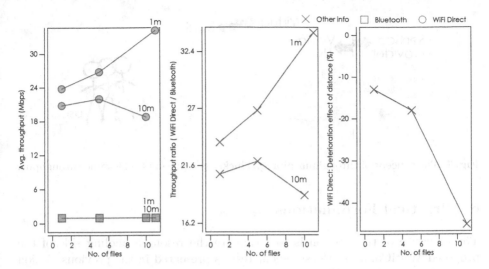

Fig. 5. Comparison of throughput in WiFi Direct versus Bluetooth 4.0 environments. Second and third plots present throughput ratio and the effect of throughput deterioration with distance in WiFi Direct.

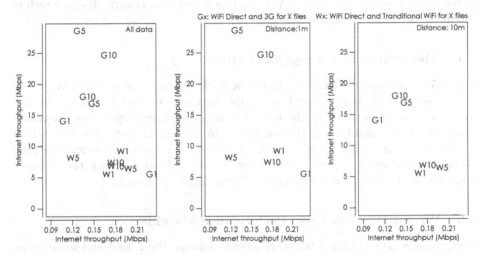

Fig. 6. Performance during MultiConnect where interference cannot be avoided. MultiConnect is compared in two configurations: *WiFi Direct with 3G* and *WiFi Direct with Traditional WiFi (WLAN).* W stands for WLAN and G for G3, both used together with WiFi Direct.

greatly diminish throughput. Also, there is a clear inverse relation between intra- and internet throughputs. It fact, the first feature might be a subset of the second since G3 throughput is lower in real networks.

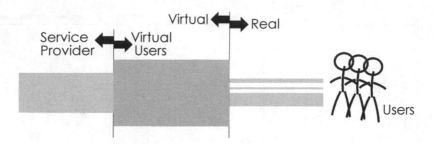

Fig. 7. The concept of throughput piping. Thickness represents achievable throughput.

6   Practical Formulations

The objective of this section is to formulate the resource pooling side of the proposed MultiConnect. Measurement results presented in the previous section are used for modeling. Finally, this section presents an example optimization problem based on the proposed design – a group sync with a cloud drive. Note that there can be numerous optimization formulations depending on a specific application. Also note that the VWU itself is based on a generic design which is intended to be application-independent.

6.1   Abstraction 3: Throughput Piping

Figure 7 is the final abstraction which now fully describes the role of VWU. The virtual section (middle) is used as a pipe between SP and Users. As before, intranet capacity is normally the largest in the pipe, even larger than the maximum achievable (end-to-end) throughput from SP. On the right side, the virtual section space is plugged with individual internet connections contributed by users. The objective is as was stated before – to balance between the intranet and internet traffic given the current leftover capacity in each.

6.2   Virtual Wireless User: Performance Margins

Performance model of the VWU is created as follows. First, best and worst cases are extracted from measurement data. For 3G, the data is grouped in hours of day. The other view is by the interference where higher intranet throughput inversely affects internet throughput and visa verse. Finally, the best and worst cases are analyzed relative to the throughput performance detected for WiFi Direct in measurement. This produces the single-user baseline, which is then expanded by multiplying by the number of users, up to 25, in order to emulate a range of groups from small to relatively large.

Figure 8 presents the results for the two views. The left side shows that the best case does not exceed WiFi Direct capacity even for 25 users. Note that the left side is based on real measurements without MultiConnect. The right side adds MultiConnect and shows that the best case stays below 25 % of

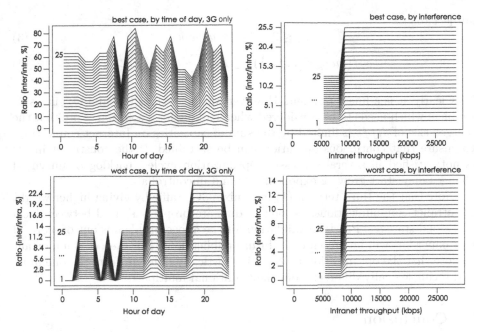

Fig. 8. Best and worst cases of performance projected for between 1 and 25 users inside the VWU.

WiFi Direct capacity even in the best case and under 15 % in the worst. The results support the *piping* model presented above and shows that WiFi Direct is difficult to overwhelm in realistic networking environments.

6.3 Virtual Wireless User: An Example Optimization Problem

Let us use U and C to denote *utilization* and *capacity*, respectively. $C_{network}$ would then denote *network capacity* and C_{cpu} CPU capacity (multi-core, etc.). $C_{i,inter}$ notation can be used to denote internet capacity of user i. L denotes *load* of a node – a generic metric describing processing overhead. The metric $diff$ can be used to denote sync diffs, measured in bytes or chunks of data to be updated. Finally, T denotes the time interval for one optimization cycle.

The optimization problem for a *group sync* based on a cloud drive (Google Drive, Dropbox, etc.) can then be written as:

$$minimize \quad w_1 \sum_{i \in group} diff_i + w_2 \sum_{i \in group} L_i + w_3 \sum_{i \in group} \frac{U_{i,network,sky}}{U_{i,network,floor}}, \quad (1)$$

where

$$L_i = U_{i,cpu} + U_{i,network} \quad \forall \quad i \in group, \quad (2)$$

subject to

$$L_i \leq 2 \quad \forall \quad i \in group, \tag{3}$$

$$sizeof(merge(\{diff_i\})) \leq T \sum_{i \in group} C_{i,out,network}. \tag{4}$$

Clearly, it is a linear problem. However, weight setting (w_1 and w_2) is a side problem which needs to be considered when looking for a solution. Note that the merged size of $diffs$ is limited by the sum of capacities on Internet connections to ensure that continuous operation can be sustained. If the constraint in (4) is not satisfied in several successive optimization cycles, backlog of unsynced changes may start growing exponentially and uncontrollably.

Note that the third term in (1) minimizes 3G traffic by giving higher weight to intranet communications, as long as diffs are property synced between local and cloud storages. Practical validation for the above problem is out of scope of this paper but will be presented in future publications. However, it is important to note that the optimization problem is drastically different from the one in [7] and technologically different from the traditional multipath.

7   Conclusion

This paper is the first to formulate both the *MultiConnect* design and propose a Virtual Wireless User which exploits MultiConnect – another new concept proposed in this paper – for resource pooling in group communications. Using WiFi Direct, each user can maintain traditional internet connections in parallel with intranet connections based on WiFi Direct. Since WiFi Direct is closer to the DTN communication paradigm, traditional multipath – where multiple paths are between the virtual wireless user (VWU) and remote service – is emulated using a given data grain, namely blocks of binary data, files, etc.

In this paper, real networking environments are measured and used to create realistic VWU models where the latter show that even groups up to 25 users each with its own 3G or traditional WiFi connection cannot overwhelm the intranet capacity provided by WiFi Direct.

VWU was also shown as a formal optimization problem independent of technologies in underlying connectivity. Using the formal problem, it is possible to create a VWU on top of any combination of connectivities and any organizational structure among users.

Future work will present implementation of the generic VWU application engine for smartphones and tablet devices. The two specific practical usecases that will be considered in future publications are the use of VWU for streaming in wireless networks and MultiConnect at the level of browsers where the latter have been shown recently in [14] to support multicore architectures and near-gigabit aggregate throughput.

References

1. Hau, T., Burghardt, D., Brenner, W.: Multihoming, content delivery networks, and the market for internet connectivity. Elsevier J. Telecommun. Policy **35**, 532–542 (2011)
2. Schmidt, P., Merz, R., Feldmann, A.: A first look at multi-access connectivity for mobile networking. In: ACM Workshop on Capacity Sharing (CSWS), pp. 9–14 (2012)
3. Chen, Y., Lim, Y., Gobbens, R., Nahum, E., Khalili, R., Towsley, D.: A measurement-based study of MultiPath TCP performance over wireless networks. In: ACM SIG-COMM Internet Measurement Conference (IMC) (2013)
4. MultiPath TCP: Linux Kernel Implementation. http://multipath-tcp.org. Accessed October 2013
5. Yap, K., Huang, T., Kobayashi, M., Yiakoumis, Y., McKeown, N., Katti, S., Parulkar, G.: Making use of all the networks around us: a case study in android. In: ACM SIGCOMM Workshop on Cellular Networks: Operations, Challenges, and Future Designs (CellNet), pp. 19–24 (2012)
6. Makela, A., Siikavirta, S., Manner, J.: Comparison of load-balancing approaches for multipath connectivity. Elsevier J. Comput. Netw. **56**, 2179–2195 (2012)
7. Pucha, H., Kaminsky, M., Andersen, D., Kozuch, M.: Adaptive file transfers for diverse environments. In: USENIX Annual Technical Conference, September 2013
8. OpenVSwitch project. http://openvswitch.org/. Accessed August 2008
9. Kohler, E., Morris, R., Chen, B., Jannotti, J., Kaashoek, M.: The click modular router. ACM Trans. Comput. Syst. (TOCS) **18**(3), 263–297 (2000)
10. Vasilakos, A., Zhang, Y., Spyropoulos, T.: Delay Tolerant Networks: Protocols and Applications. CRC Press, Boca Raton (2011)
11. Balasubramanian, A., Levine, B., Venkataramani, A.: DTN routing as a resource allocation problem. In: SIGCOMM, pp. 373–384, October 2007
12. Zhanikeev, M.: Multi-source stream aggregation in the cloud. In: Pathan, M., Sitaraman, R.K., Robinson, D. (eds.) Advanced Content Delivery and Streaming in the Cloud, Chap. 10. Wiley, New York (2013)
13. Zhanikeev, M.: Experiments on practical WLAN designs for digital classrooms. IEICE Commun. Express (ComEx) **2**(8), 352–358 (2013)
14. Zhanikeev, M.: Experiments with application throughput in a browser with full HTML5 support. IEICE Commun. Express **2**(5), 167–172 (2013)
15. Zhanikeev, M.: Experiences from measuring per-packet cost of software defined networking. IEICE Tech. Rep. Serv. Comput. (SC) **113**(86), 31–34 (2013)
16. Wi-Fi Peer-to-Peer: Best Practical Guide, Wi-Fi Alliance, December 2010

Small Cell Enhancement for LTE-Advanced Release 12 and Application of Higher Order Modulation

Qin Mu[✉], Liu Liu, Huiling Jiang, and Hidetoshi Kayama

DOCOMO Beijing Communications Laboratories Co., Ltd, Beijing, China
{mu,liul,jiang,kayama}@docomolabs-beijing.com.cn

Abstract. The mobile data traffic is expected to grow beyond 1000 times by 2020 compared with it in 2010. In order to support 1000 times of capacity increase, improving spectrum efficiency is one of the important approaches. Meanwhile, in Long Term Evolution (LTE)-Advanced, small cell and hotspot are important scenarios for future network deployment to increase the capacity from the network density domain. Under such environment, the probability of high Signal to Interference plus Noise Ratio (SINR) region becomes larger which brings the possibility of introducing higher order modulation, i.e., 256 Quadrature Amplitude Modulation (QAM) to improve the spectrum efficiency. In this paper, we will firstly introduce the ongoing small cell enhancement discussion in the 3rd Generation Partnership Project (3GPP). And then focus on the application of higher order modulation in small cell environment. Important design issues and possible solutions will be analyzed particularly in the higher order modulation discussion.

Keywords: Higher order modulation · Small cell · LTE-advanced release 12

1 Introduction

Long-term evolution (LTE) provides full IP packet-based radio access with low latency and adopts orthogonal frequency division multiple access (OFDMA) and single-carrier frequency division multiple access (SC-FDMA) in the downlink and uplink, respectively. The 3rd generation partnership project (3GPP) finalized the radio interface specifications for the next generation mobile system as LTE release 8 in 2008 [1,2]. In Japan, the commercial service of LTE was launched in December, 2010 under the new service brand of "Xi" (crossy) [3]. Meanwhile, in the 3GPP, there have been efforts targeting at establishing an enhanced LTE radio interface called LTE-Advanced (release 10 and beyond) [4,5] and the specification for LTE-Advanced release 11 is now freezed and the standardization for release 12 is started.

Mobile traffic data forecasts predict a tremendous growth in data traffic in the next several years and by some projections the traffic growth is expected to be

© Institute for Computer Sciences, Social Informatics and Telecommunications Engineering 2014
I. Stojmenovic et al. (Eds.): MOBIQUITOUS 2013, LNICST 131, pp. 794–805, 2014.
DOI: 10.1007/978-3-319-11569-6_69

1000 times of the data from the previous decade [6]. The primary drivers of this growth are the increased penetration of smartphone type handsets and various assorted mobile devices running a vast array of mobile applications, especially video applications. Furthermore, end-user expectations on achievable data rates are also continuously raised. Currently commercially available mobile networks typically offer end-user data rates up to in the order of a few Mbps. In the future, there will be demands for typical end-user data rates of several tens of Mbps, with hundreds of Mbps or even several Gbps of data rates demanded in specific scenarios.

Explosive overall mobile data traffic and rising expectations on achievable data rates on end-user side challenge the mobile network operators. To satisfy these future traffic-volume and end-user demands existing mobile networks need to evolve and be enhanced. Since obtaining new spectrum is quite cost-prohibitive as well as difficult due to various government regulations in different parts of the world, other ways are being looked into to achieve this demand. Most operators are increasingly drawn to the idea of network densification with small cells deployment to achieve the increasing traffic capacity [7]. Currently, there is a study item (SI) called "Small Cell enhancements for E-UTRA and EUTRAN" in progress to explore the potential of small cells in the 3GPP standards body [8].

The basic deployment of small cells that is being studied involves using an LTE base station that has much lower transmission power than a macro base station. Several different types of deployments are being considered such as small cells using the same or different carrier frequency as the macro base station, small cells deployed indoors or outdoors, small cells deployed in areas with or without overlapping macro cell coverage and so on. There are also some new techniques involved in the small cell enhancement discussion. For example, efficient small cell discovery for power saving and traffic offloading, small cell power on/off for the interference coordination and higher order modulation in small cell for improved spectral efficiency etc. In this paper, we focus on higher order modulation involved in the scenario where macro cell and small cell are deployed with separate carrier.

The rest of the paper are organized as follow. Firstly, more detailed descriptions about small cell enhancement are provided in Sect. 2. Secondly, we elaborates the higher order modulation in small cell including the motivation, design issues and comparison of possible solutions in Sect. 3. Finally, we conclude this paper in Sect. 4.

2   Small Cell Enhancement

2.1   Deployment Scenario Identified in 3GPP

3GPP decided in September 2012 to start a study on the scenarios and requirements of small cell enhancements. This study was completed successfully in December 2012 and the agreed deployment scenarios and relevant technical requirements are captured in a technical report [9]; these are briefly introduced hereinafter.

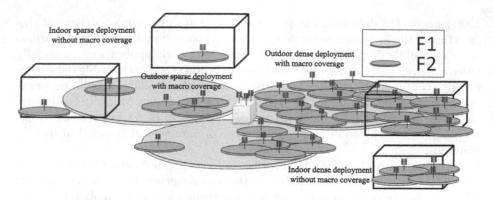

Fig. 1. Small cell deployment

Enhanced small cells can be deployed both with macro coverage and stand alone, both indoor and outdoor, and support both ideal and non-ideal back hauls. Enhanced small cells can also be deployed sparsely or densely. An illustration of possible deployment scenarios is shown in Fig. 1 [9].

2.1.1   With and Without Macro Coverage

Small cell enhancement should target the deployment scenario in which small cell nodes are deployed under the coverage of one or more than one overlaid macro-cell layer(s) in order to boost the capacity of already deployed cellular network. And it should also work without macro coverage, for example, in deep indoor situations.

2.1.2   Outdoor and Indoor

Small cell enhancement should target both outdoor and indoor small cell deployments. A key differentiator between indoor and outdoor scenarios is mobility support. In indoor scenarios, users normally stay stationary or move at very low speeds. In outdoor scenarios, operators may deploy small cell nodes to cover certain busy streets where relatively higher terminal speeds can be expected. 3GPP has decided to focus on low terminal speeds (up to 3 km/h) for indoor and medium terminal speeds (up to 30 km/h and potentially higher) for outdoor scenarios.

2.1.3   Backhaul

The backhaul, which generally means the link connecting the radio access network and core network, is another important aspect for small cell enhancement, especially when considering the potentially large number of small cell nodes to be deployed. 3GPP has decided both the ideal backhaul (i.e., very high throughput and very low latency backhaul such as dedicated point-to-point connection using optical fiber) and non-ideal backhaul (i.e., typical backhaul widely used in the market such as xDSL) should be studied.

2.1.4 Sparse and Dense

Small cell enhancement should consider sparse and dense small cell deployments. In some scenarios (e.g., hotspot indoor/outdoor places, etc.), single or a few small cell node(s) are sparsely deployed, e.g. to cover the hotspot(s). Meanwhile, in some scenarios (e.g., dense urban, large shopping mall, etc.), a lot of small cell nodes are densely deployed to support huge traffic over a relatively wide area covered by the small cell nodes. The coverage of the small cell layer is generally discontinuous between different hotspot areas. Each hotspot area can be covered by a group of small cells, i.e. a small cell cluster. For mobility/connectivity performance, both sparse and dense deployments should be considered with equal priority.

2.1.5 Synchronization

Both synchronized and un-synchronized scenarios should be considered between small cells as well as between small cells and macro cell(s). For specific operations e.g. interference coordination, carrier aggregation and inter-eNodeB coordinated multiple point transmission, small cell enhancement can benefit from synchronized deployments with respect to small cell search/measurements and interference/resource management. Therefore time synchronized deployments of small cell clusters are prioritized in the study and new means to achieve such synchronization shall be considered.

2.1.6 Spectrum

Small cell enhancement should address the deployment scenario in which different frequency bands are separately assigned to macro layer and small cell layer, respectively, where F1 and F2 in Fig. 1 correspond to different carriers in different frequency bands.

Small cell enhancement should be applicable to all existing and as well as future cellular bands, with special focus on higher frequency bands, e.g., the 3.5 GHz band, to enjoy the more available spectrum and wider bandwidth. Co-channel deployment scenarios between macro layer and small cell layer should be considered as well.

2.1.7 Traffic

In a small cell deployment, it is likely that the traffic will fluctuate greatly since the number of users per small cell node is typically not large due to the small coverage area. It is also likely that the user distribution is very non-uniform and fluctuates between the small cell nodes. It is also expected that the traffic could be highly asymmetrical, either downlink- or uplink-centric. Traffic load distribution in the time domain and spatial domain could be uniform or non-uniform.

2.1.8   Backward Compatibility

Backward compatibility, that is, the possibility for legacy user equipment (UE) to access a small-cell node/carrier, shall be guaranteed and the ability for legacy UE to benefit from small-cell enhancements can be considered.

2.2   New Techniques to Improve the Spectral Efficiency and Capacity in Small Cell

2.2.1   Small Cell Discovery

Different from in the homogeneous deployment, the UEs in small cell should always perform inter-frequency measurement in order to detect the surrounding small cells timely and make maximum use of them. Thus a well designed discovery signal and discovery mechanism will not only improve the power efficiency but also facilitate neighboring cell identification and synchronization.

2.2.2   Small Cell On/Off

The traffic in small cell fluctuates greatly in time domain and spatial domain. When there is no traffic, small cell should go "off" state quickly for more power saving. On the other hand, small cell should be activated timely when traffic arrives. In addition, when one cell experiences severe interference from neighboring cells, turning off some neighboring cells could mitigate interference and improve the overall performance. Hence manners to support prompt and flexible switch between small cell "on" state and small cell "off" state is quite beneficial for both power saving and interference reduction.

2.2.3   Higher Order Modulation

Sperate frequency for macro cell and small cell is the prioritized scenario. Due to the absence of strong interference from Macro cell high SINR performance is easily achieved which provides another chance to solve the explosive data problem from spectral efficiency dimension by introducing higher order modulation schemes. In 3GPP meeting discussion, many operators and vendors show their great interests [10–12]. In the following section, we will introduce this technique in details.

3   Higher Order Modulation in Small Cell

3.1   Motivation

The basic premise of 256 QAM introduction is that there should be some scenarios satisfy the usage SINR requirement. Figure 2 shows the spectral efficiency performance for various modulation schemes. The spectral efficiency is defined as $(1 - block\ error\ rate) \times modulation\ order \times coding\ rate$. The results are obtained by using piratical channel coding (Turbo coding) in AWGN scenario. From Fig. 2, it is observed that the switch point between 256 QAM and 64 QAM is around

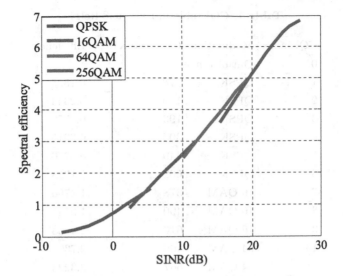

Fig. 2. Spectral efficiency

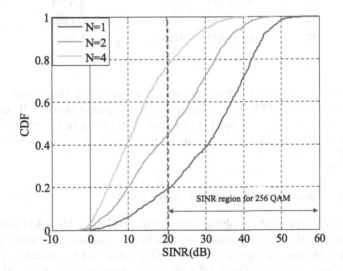

Fig. 3. SINR distribution

20 dB. Therefore, the precondition for 256 QAM introduction is there should be some small cell scenarios where some UEs could experience SINR larger than 20 dB.

In small cell deployment, the prioritized scenario is separate frequency for macro cell and small cell. As mentioned above, good SINR performance could be achieved due to the absence of strong interference from macro. Figure 3 shows the SINR geometry for different small cell density. In the figure, N denotes the

Table 1. CQI table in LTE Rel8-Rel11

CQI index	Modulation	Code rateX1024	Efficiency
0	Out of range		
1	QPSK	78	0.1523
2	QPSK	120	0.2344
3	QPSK	193	0.3770
4	QPSK	308	0.6016
5	QPSK	449	0.8770
6	QPSK	602	1.1758
7	16 QAM	378	1.4766
8	16 QAM	490	1.9141
9	16 QAM	616	2.4063
10	64 QAM	466	2.7305
11	64 QAM	567	3.3223
12	64 QAM	666	3.9023
13	64 QAM	772	4.5234
14	64 QAM	873	5.1152
15	64 QAM	948	5.5547

number of small cells per macro sector. It is observed that more than 20 % UEs could reach the SINR larger than 20 dB in sparse small cell deployment. Thus more than 20 % UEs could benefit from 256 QAM in the sparse small cell deployment. High cell throughput gain is expected from introducing 256 QAM in small cell.

3.2   Design Issues in Implement 256 QAM

In LTE release 8, quadrature phase shift keying (QPSK), 16 QAM and 64 QAM have been specified for data transmission. These modulation schemes are implemented in the channel quality indicator (CQI) table and modulation and coding scheme (MCS) table [13]. The CQI table is mainly used to assist the channel quality feedback from UEs to eNodeBs. The original CQI table includes 16 levels of different modulation and coding schemes, as shown in Table 1. UEs feed back the effective SINR by conveying the CQI index with 4 bits in uplink control indicator(UCI). The mapping from effective SINR to a corresponding CQI value is carried out such that a BLER lower than 0.1 is achieved by using corresponding modulation and coding rate. The MCS table is mainly used to inform the detailed modulation and coding schemes for physical downlink shared channel (PDSCH) or physical uplink shared channel (PUSCH) transmission. The original MCS table which is an extension of CQI table includes 32 levels of different modulation and coding schemes and 3 of them are reserved for future use. eNodeBs inform UEs of the detailed modulation and coding scheme in the table by conveying the corresponding MCS index with 5 bits in downlink control indicator (DCI).

In order to support 256 QAM in current LTE-Advanced system, the new entries of 256 QAM should be merged in the CQI table and MCS table. However, how to implement the new entries in these tables needs careful investigation by taking the performance gain, impact on the control signaling, specification effort etc. into consideration.

3.3   Possible Solutions

Based on whether to change the sizes of the tables and corresponding indicators, there are 2 potential alternatives to implement the 256 QAM in current network.

3.3.1   Alt.1 Extend the Tables and Corresponding Indicators

This alternative is a simple extension of the existing MCS/CQI tables. Contents based on 256 QAM can be attached at the end of the tables. This method guarantees the performance of UEs supporting 256 QAM since all the existing modulation levels can be reused. However, the changed table size will lead to the changed payload size of relevant indicator, e.g., DCI formats with larger MCS indication field and channel state reporting with larger CQI feedback bits should be defined. The increased payload sizes in general result in reduced robustness of the DCI and UCI. From the standardization aspect, additional specification effort is needed to specify the new DCI format and channel status reporting.

3.3.2   Alt.2 Keep the Same Table Size and Refine the Content

Keeping the same sizes of the tables has the advantage that the sizes of the relevant indicators are not affected. Hence, less specification effort is required due to no need to define new DCI format and channel status reporting. To keep less change on the interpretation of the new content in CQI/MCS table, a possible method is to remove some entries from the extended table in Alt.1 (extended table is formed by attaching new entries at the end of the existing tables). The entries contribute less cell throughput improvement will be removed. The removed entries could be the original content or the newly added content. It is noted that some MCS used in severe channel condition should be kept to maintain the basic service requirement. The detailed criteria for the remove is related to the spectral efficiency improvement brought by one entry and the possibility of the entry to be used. Both factors contribute to the cell throughput. For one entry other than entries used in severe channel condition, if it brings little improvement in the spectral efficiency or has little possibility to be used, it could be removed because of less improvement on the cell throughput. By this way, the cell throughput performance could be guaranteed to the largest extent.

Table 2. Simulation parameters

Deployment scenarios	Heterogeneous network with 3 small cells within one macro cell sector
Carrier configuration	Macro@ 2 GHz
	Small cell @3.5 GHz
System bandwidth	10 MHz
Channel model	ITU-UMa for Macro
	ITU-UMi for small cell
Number of UEs	10,20,30 UE (per macro sector)
DL transmission scheme	SU-MIMO with rank adaptation
UE speed	3 km/h
Tx power (Ptotal)	Macro:46 dBm
	Small cell: 30 dBm
Traffic model	Full buffer
Number of TX and RX antennas	For macro: 2×2
	For small cell: 2×2
Antenna configuration	CPA
UE receiver	MMSE
Feedback scheme	Rel-8 RI/CQI/PMI based on Rel-8 2Tx codebook
EVM	28 dB (4 %)

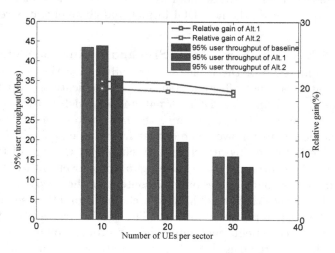

Fig. 4. 95 % user throughput performance

3.4 Performance Evaluation and Discussion

To compare the performance of these 2 alternatives. System level simulation is performed. The baseline for comparison is current LTE-Advanced performance

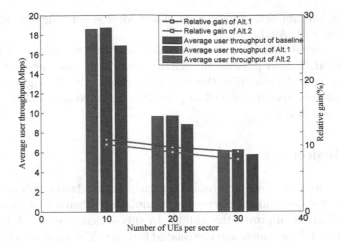

Fig. 5. Average user throughput performance

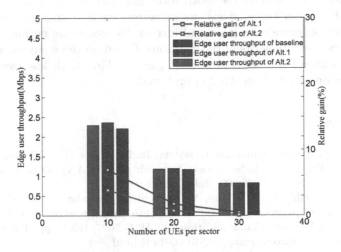

Fig. 6. Cell edge user throughput performance

with rank adaption. 95 % user throughput, average user throughput and 5 % user throughput will be evaluated. Furthermore, to model the RF impairment in realistic network, 4 % error vector magnitude (EVM) effect are assumed on the eNodeB side. Other detailed parameters are listed in Table 2.

According to the simulation results in Figs. 4, 5 and 6, we observe that both alternatives could achieve significant gain in 95 % UE throughput and average UE throughput. Small gain is obtained in 5 % user throughput. 5 % user through-put represents the cell edge user performance. For cell edge users, they have less chance of reaching high SINR to support 256 QAM. This is why the small gain is caused. Due to less entries supported in tables of Alt.2, it provides relative coarse channel condition information compared with Alt.1 as the same range of SINR is covered by less amount of indicators. Thus Alt.2 suffers slightly performance loss compared with Alt.1.

More supported indicators in Alt.1 yields slightly throughput gain. But on the other hand, it also pays more signaling overhead and specification effort for this little gain. Considering the tradeoff between the throughput gain and signaling overhead, specification effort pain. It is better to use Alt.2 to implement 256 QAM in small cell.

4   Conclusion

Small cell deployments are key tools to satisfy future traffic-volume and end-user service-level demands. Higher order modulation scheme based on small cell deployment further improves the ability. In this article, we first introduce the typical small cell deployment and the related features. Then focus on higher order modulation which is one of important technique for small cell enhancement. In the discussion, we elaborate the motivation and analyze the main design issues for 3GPP. Based on the analysis, we show our consideration on the possible solutions. Performance evaluation and further discussion are performed to analyze the merits and demerits of the solutions. Based on the analysis, we observe that Alt.2 achieves similar performance gain to Alt.1 with less overhead and standardization effort. Thus Alt.2 is preferred.

References

1. 3GPP LTE; Evolved Universal Terrestrial Radio Access (E-UTRA) and Evolved Universal Terrestrial Radio Access Network (E-UTRAN); Overall description; Stage 2, ser. TS, no. TS36.300, Rel-10 v10.8.0
2. Tanno, M., Kishiyama, Y., Miki, N., Higuchi, K., Sawahashi, M.,: Evolved utra-physical layer overview. In: 2007 IEEE 8th Workshop on Signal Processing Advances in Wireless Communications: SPAWC 2007, IEEE, pp. 1–8 (2007)
3. http://www.nttdocomo.com/pr/2010/001494.html
4. 3GPP, Evolved Universal Terrestrial Radio Access (E-UTRA); LTE physical layer; General description, ser.TS, December 2010, no. TS36.201, Rel-10 v10.0.0
5. Dahlman, E., Parkvall, S., Skold, J.: 4G: LTE/LTE-Advanced for Mobile Broadband. Academic Press, Boston (2011)
6. Aijaz, A., Aghvami, H., Amani, M.: A survey on mobile data offloading: technical and business perspectives, evolved utra-physical layer overview. IEEE Wirel. Commun. **202**, 104–112 (2013)
7. Nakamura, T., Nagata, S., Hai, T., Xiaodong, S.: Trends in small cell enhancements in LTE advanced. IEEE Commun. Mag. **512**, 98–105 (2013)
8. 3GPP, RP-122033: New Study Item Description: Small Cell enhancements for E-UTRA and E-UTRAN CHigher layer aspects, TSG-RAN, 58 meeting, June 2012
9. 3GPP, TR36.932 (V12.0.0), Scenarios and Requirements for Small Cell Enhancements for E-URTA and E-UTRAN, December 2012
10. 3GPP, R1–130136, ZTE, Consideration on high order modulation for small cell, RAN1 72 meeting, February 2013

11. 3GPP, R1–130341, Hitachi Ltd, Views on 256 QAM for small cell enhancement emph RAN1 72 meeting, February 2013
12. 3GPP, R1–130404, NTT DOCOMO, Enhanced Transmission Scheme for Small Cell Enhancement, emph RAN1 72 meeting, Febrary 2013
13. 3GPP, Evolved Universal Terrestrial Radio Access (E-UTRA); LTE physical layer; General description, ser.TS, December 2010, no. TS36.213, Rel-10 V9.2.0, June 2010

Author Index

Printed in the United States
By Bookmasters